INDEX TO

DISTRICT OF COLUMBIA LAND RECORDS

1792 - 1817

WESLEY E. PIPPENGER

HERITAGE BOOKS
2010

HERITAGE BOOKS
AN IMPRINT OF HERITAGE BOOKS, INC.

Books, CDs, and more—Worldwide

For our listing of thousands of titles see our website
at
www.HeritageBooks.com

Published 2010 by
HERITAGE BOOKS, INC.
Publishing Division
100 Railroad Ave. #104
Westminster, Maryland 21157

Copyright © 2010 Wesley E. Pippenger

All rights reserved. No part of this book may be reproduced or transmitted in any form or by any means, electronic or mechanical, including photocopying, recording or by any information storage and retrieval system without written permission from the author, except for the inclusion of brief quotations in a review.

International Standard Book Numbers
Paperbound: 978-0-7884-5249-9
Clothbound: 978-0-7884-8476-6

INTRODUCTION

Presented here are index entries for primary parties involved in items found in land record books, or deed books, of the District of Columbia, beginning in 1792. Covered are books A through AO39. These entries include a grantor, grantee, person(s) being bonded, person qualifying for military or public position, parties to civil suits, owner or property being surveyed, etc. Not included in this index are place names or other names buried within individual records.

The source citation for each entry includes book, old page, and new page. Two page numbers are provided because there are two series of land record books. The original, or "old" books, are in handwritten form and found at the National Archives, Record Group 351, Entry 112, on Pennsylvania Avenue in Washington, D.C.

About 1900 or so, typewritten copies of the original land record books were made—hence we have "new" books. These typewritten copies are located at the Office of Public Record, or D.C. Archives, on Naylor Court in Washington, D.C. The original, handwritten, books were used to compile this index because they are more reliable—the typewritten copies are widely known to contain many transcription and indexing errors. For example, it was common for the indexers of the typewritten copies to omit lists and/or declaration of slaves.

The first series of land record books begin with Book A, Parts 1 and 2, and proceeds through Book Z. This is followed by the series Book AA through AZ. After this, several series are found identified with initials of the recorder of deeds who created them (i.e. W.B., J.A.S., N.C.T., R.M.H., E.C.E., D., T.&R.), and ultimately begin in serial form with Deed Book 557.

Wesley E. Pippenger
Little Egypt
Tappahannock, Virginia

Index to District of Columbia Land Records, 1792-1817

Party	What	Party	Year	Liber	Old	New
A						
Abbot, Jane, w/o John, of G'tn.	Deed to	Olliver, Elizabeth	1808	U20	288	154
Abbot, Jane, w/o John et al	D. of T. to	English, David, cashier, of G'tn.	1817	AN38	352	259
Abbot, John	Deed fr	Templeman, John et al	1802	I9	013	016
Abbot, John	Deed fr	Stoddert, Benjamin et al	1802	I9	013	016
Abbott, Jane et al	Release fr	English, David, cashier	1817	AO39	394	267
Abbott, John	Release fr	Bank of Columbia	1802	I9		018
Abbott, John	B. of S. fr	Hagan, Monica	1809	W22	070	052
Abbott, John et al	Release fr	English, David, cashier	1817	AO39	394	267
Abbott, John, of G'tn.	Deed to	Goldsborough, Charles W.	1809	X23	079	059
Abbott, John, of G'tn.	B. of S. fr	Robertson, Thomas, of G'tn.	1812	AC28	147	109
Abert, Philip	Deed fr	Holmead, Anthony	1801	G7	257	351
Abert, Philip	Deed to	Sutton, Robert	1804	L11	155	154
Aborn, Henry	Deed fr	Fox, Joseph, Jr., Westm. Co. VA	1810	Y24	383	346
Aborn, Henry	Deed fr	Pratt, Henry et al	1812	AC28	470	334
Aborn, Henry	Deed to	Gardner, Esther	1812	AC28	220	164
Aborn, Henry	Deed to	Granger, Gideon, postmaster	1813	AE30	477	355
Aborn, Henry	D. of T. to	Aborn, Thomas, late of RI	1813	AE30	548	406
Aborn, Thomas, late of RI	D. of T. fr	Aborn, Henry	1813	AE30	548	406
Acken, William D.	Deed fr	Cocke, Buller	1816	AM37	448	322
Adam King & Co., of G'tn.	Deed fr	Chandler, Walter Story, of G'tn.	1805	N13	375	301
Adams, Alexander & R. West	Deed fr	O'Neale, Sarah, of Montg. Co.	1811	AC28	106	080
Adams, Billy, b. 5/15/87	Cert of Birth		1804	K10	330	341
Adams, George	B. of S. to	Costigan, Joseph	1811	AC28	044	033
Adams, George	B. of S. fr	Ensey, William	1815	AI34	148	169
Adams, George	B. of S. fr	Green, Simon	1816	AL36	170	170
Adams, George	Deed to	Clarke, Edward W.	1817	AO39	364	245
Adams, George	P. of Atty. fr	Macdaniel, Walter & Sarah Cannon	1817	AN38	503	364
Adams, George, constable	B. of S. to	Cross, Eli	1816	AM37	081	066
Adams, George, exr.	B. of S. to	Smith, Henry	1816	AL36	525	490
Adams, Henrietta, of Montg. Co.	B. of S. to	Ford, Edward, of G'tn.	1816	AL36	249	251
Adams, Henry	B. of S. to	Prout, William	1805	N13	400	318
Adams, Henry	Deed fr	Prout, William	1805	M12	117	111
Adams, Henry	Assign to	Cochran, Alexander, Jr.	1806	O14	178	116
Adams, Henry	B. of S. to	Hurly, Arnold	1809	W22	389	253
Adams, Henry	Agreement	Dodson, William (C), age 17	1817	AN38	271	198
Adams, Henry (C)	Certificate		1805	N13	279	231
Adams, Henry (C), of G'tn.	Convey fr	Lee, Thomas Sim, of Fredk. Co.	1813	AF31	122	082
Adams, Henry (C), of G'tn.	Deed fr	Moxley, Charles, of G'tn.	1816	AL36	220	225
Adams, Henry & Nicholas Franklin	Deed fr	Beall, George & Moses Liverpool	1810	Y24	301	274
Adams, Henry, of G'tn.	Deed fr	Lee, Thomas Sim, of Fredk. Co.	1815	AK35	252	200
Adams, Henry, ship carp., G'tn.	B. of S. to	Ratcliffe, Joseph, of G'tn.	1817	AO39	490	336
Adams, James	Slaves	From VA	1810	Y24	529	465
Adams, Joseph (C), age 27	Cert Free fr	Varnum, James M.	1814	AG32	116	087
Adams, Margaret	Deed to	Beall, Thomas & John M. Gantt	1793	A1-1	272	366
Adams, Margaret	Deed to	Higdon, Gustavus	1812	AD29	140	108
Adams, Margaret, of P.G. Co.	Lease fr	Armitage, Benjamin, New York NY	1804	L11	289	265
Adams, Margaret, of P.G. Co.	Deed to	Armitage, Benjamin, New York NY	1804	L11	287	263
Adams, Mary (C), body of	Order	To be at Heronimus' Tavern	1815	AI34	460	473
Adams, Samuel, of Fairfax Co. VA	Deed fr	Broadwater, Charles Lewis, of VA	1805	M12	361	373
Adams, Thomas	Deed fr	Reintzel, Anthony [Reintzell]	1808	T19	254	187
Adams, Thomas	D. of T. to	Parrott, Richard & John Mountz	1809	W22	001	001
Adams, Thomas, of G'tn.	Deed fr	Peter, John, of G'tn.	1809	V21	380	283
Adams, William	Assign to	Saintclere, George	1804	K10	326	335
Adams, William	Lease fr	Prout, William	1804	K10	325	333

Index to District of Columbia Land Records, 1792-1817

Party	What	Party	Year	Liber	Old	New
Adams, William	B. of S. fr	Dougherty, Patrick	1804	L11	394	349
Adams, William	Assign fr	Saintclere, George	1805	O14	074	046
Adams, William	Assign to	Booth, Jeremiah et al	1805	O14	077	047
Addington, Daniel et al	Assign fr	Poor, John	1810	X23	415	335
Addison, A. & Clement Smith	Receipt to	Calder, James	1813	AE30	342	255
Addison, Anthony	Agreement	Addison, Daniel Dulany	1797	B2B	675	445
Addison, Anthony	Deed to	Key, Philip Barton, of Annapolis	1800	E5	111	098
Addison, Anthony	Deed fr	Addison, John & Lucy	1800	E5	112	100
Addison, Anthony	Deed to	Murdock, John et al	1802	I9	277	452
Addison, Anthony	Deed to	Addison, Daniel Dulany	1807	R17	371	282
Addison, Anthony	B. of S. to	Smith, Clement	1808	T19	307	224
Addison, Anthony & Daniel D.	Partition	Hanson, Thomas H. & Wm. Baker	1797	B2B	676	446
Addison, Anthony et al	Deed to	Addison, Thomas G., of P.G. Co.	1811	AA26	024	019
Addison, Anthony, of P.G. Co.	Deed to	Addison, Daniel Dulany	1797	B2B	657	421
Addison, Anthony, of P.G. Co.	D. of T. to	Brent, William	1802	H8	593	559
Addison, Anthony, of P.G. Co.	Manumis to	[ ], James (Negro)	1806	P15	262	173
Addison, Anthony, of P.G. Co.	Deed to	Smith, Clement, of P.G. Co.	1808	T19	313	228
Addison, Anthony, of P.G. Co.	Deed to	Marbury, William	1808	T19	066	048
Addison, Anthony, of P.G. Co.	D. of T. to	Smith, Clement, of P.G. Co.	1810	Y24	487	430
Addison, Anthony, of P.G. Co.	Manumis to	[ ], Joe (C)	1812	AD29	141	110
Addison, Anthony, s/o Rev. Henry	Deed to	Young, Notley	1792	A1-1	171	244
Addison, Daniel Dulany	Deed fr	Addison, Anthony, of P.G. Co.	1797	B2B	657	421
Addison, Daniel Dulany	Agreement	Addison, Anthony	1797	B2B	675	445
Addison, Daniel Dulany	Deed fr	Addison, Anthony	1807	R17	371	282
Addison, Daniel Dulany, Annapolis	Deed to	Kirby, John Baptist et al	1808	T19	072	053
Addison, Daniel Dulany	Deed fr	Talburt, Lewis & John B. Kirby	1808	T19	083	060
Addison, Francis Key	B. of S. fr	Bayly, William	1817	AO39	197	145
Addison, George	Deed fr	Simmes, George, of P.G. Co.	1805	M12	154	150
Addison, Henry	Deed by	State of Maryland	1797	C3	095	078
Addison, John	Deed to	Murdock, John et al	1802	I9	279	456
Addison, John	Manumis to	[ ], Mary (Negro)	1802	G7		710
Addison, John	Manumis to	Hammond, Kitty (mulatto)	1805	M12	091	085
Addison, John	Deed to	Shaaff, John Thomas, Annapolis	1805	M12	297	299
Addison, John	Manumis to	Steele, Charles	1809	W22	167	117
Addison, John	Deed to	Shaaff, John Thomas, Annapolis	1809	X23	027	019
Addison, John	Manumis to	Pembroke, Jack (negro)	1810	Y24	013	11
Addison, John & Lucy	Deed to	Addison, Anthony	1800	E5	112	100
Addison, John, Jr. & Thomas G.	Deed to	Beall, Thomas & John M. Gantt	1793	A1-1	213	297
Addison, John Jr.	Deed to	Young, Notley, Sr.	1796	B2B	427	102
Addison, Lucy	Cert Free to	Cox, Ann (negro)	1810	Y24	215	198
Addison, Thomas G.	Manumis to	[ ], Esther (Negro)	1802	I9	580	941
Addison, Thomas G.	Deed to	[ ], Esther	1802	I9	580	941
Addison, Thomas G.	Manumis to	[ ], Yorrick (Negro)	1805	N13	405	322
Addison, Thomas G.	Manumis to	[ ], Fannie (Negro)	1805	O14	117	074
Addison, Thomas G.	Manumis to	Cupid, Harry (negro)	1807	R17	200	151
Addison, Thomas G.	Manumis to	Forrest, Joe	1807	T19	018	014
Addison, Thomas G.	Manumis to	Forrest, Dick (negro)	1808	T19	240	176
Addison, Thomas G., admr. of T.	B. of S. to	Miller, Peter	1809	W22	059	044
Addison, Thomas G.	B. of S. to	Blagden, George	1809	W22	073	054
Addison, Thomas G.	Release fr	Marbury, William	1809	W22	184	129
Addison, Thomas G., of P.G. Co.	Deed to	Shaaff, John Thomas, of A.A. Co.	1811	AA26	028	021
Addison, Thomas G., of P.G. Co.	Deed fr	Addison, Anthony & H.A. Callis	1811	AA26	024	019
Addison, Thomas G. et al	Mortgage fr	Cooledge, Samuel J.	1811	AA26	096	068
Addison, Thomas G., of P.G. Co.	Mortgage to	Hawkins, James, of P.G. Co.	1811	Z25	536	426
Addison, Thomas G., of P.G. Co.	Deed to	Kirby, Francis [Kerby]	1815	AH33	432	371

Index to District of Columbia Land Records, 1792-1817

Party	What	Party	Year	Liber	Old	New
Addison, Thomas Grafton	Manumis to	Beall, George	1801	G7		330
Addison, Thomas Grafton	Deed to	Densley, Hugh et al	1804	L11	215	202
Addison, Thomas Grafton et al	Mortgage fr	Densley, Hugh et al	1804	K10	144	155
Addison, Thomas Grafton, of P.G.	Deed to	Marbury, William	1804	K10	359	371
Addison, Thomas Grafton	Deed to	Evans, Philip	1806	O14	400	268
Addison, Thomas Grafton	Deed to	Shaaff, Thomas, M.D., Annapolis	1807	R17	149	115
Addison, Thomas Grafton	Deed to	Kirby, John B.	1808	T19	224	164
Addison, Thomas Grafton	Deed to	Moxley, Daniel	1809	V21	349	252
Addison, Walter D.	Deed to	Beall, Thomas & John M. Gantt	1793	A1-1	211	294
Addison, Walter D., of P.G. Co.	Manumis to	Bruce, James & Sarah	1805	N13	283	233
Addison, Walter D., Rev.	Deed fr	Threlkeld, John	1810	Y24	534	469
Addison, Walter D.	Manumis to	[ ], Kitty (negro)	1810	Z25	194	152
Addison, Walter D., Rev., of G'tn.	Deed fr	Threlkeld, John, of G'tn.	1814	AG32	306	224
Addison, Walter Dulaney, of G'tn.	Deed fr	King, George, of G'tn.	1816	AL36	147	147
Addison, Walter Dulany, of G'tn.	Deed to	Berry, Zachariah, of P.G. Co.	1810	Y24	411	370
Addison, Walter Dulany	Manumis to	Bush, Lucy, age 20, & dau. Patty	1813	AF31	118	080
Adlington, Daniel, insolvent	D. of T. to	Small, William, trustee	1811	Z25	447	352
Adlum, John	Deed fr	Heugh, John, of G'tn.	1817	AN38	189	137
Afflick, Thomas, heirs of	Deed to	Crookshank, Richard et al	1814	AG32	219	153
Afflick, Thomas, of Montg. Co.	Deed to	Williams, Thomas, of P.G. Co.	1796	B2B	426	100
Afflick, Thomas, of G'tn.	Deed fr	Furguson, Robert, of Charles Co.	1796	B2B	399	063
Afflick, Thomas, of Montg. Co.	Deed fr	Burnes, David, of P.G. Co.	1796	B2B	425	099
Afflick, Thomas, of G'tn.	Deed fr	Stewart, Adam, of Liverpool, Eng.	1797	B2B	653	417
Afflick, Thomas, of G'tn.	Deed to	Thompson, George, of G'tn.	1797	B2B	635	396
Aftley, Abraham (negro)	Manumis fr	Reintzel, Daniel	1806	O14	122	078
Aiken, John, insolvent	Deed to	Coyle, Thomas, trustee	1804	L11	196	187
Aiker, John	B. of S. to	Jordon, Hugh	1802	I9	306	503
Aikin, John, trustee	B. of S. fr	Dial, Annastatis, insolvent	1808	V21	139	101
Airs, Thomas	B. of S. to	Cooper, John & Richard D. Boyd	1809	X23	050	037
Aisburn, Jane, of G'tn. [Eastburn]	Deed to	Cloakey, Samuel, builder	1811	AB27	284	233
Aitken, John	Deed to	Hewit, James	1804	L11	153	153
Albrecht, Charles, of Phila. PA	Deed fr	Cist, Jacob, of Luzerne Co. PA	1814	AH33	269	234
Aldridge, James	B. of S. fr	Belt, Richard	1808	T19	375	268
Alexander, John	Deed fr	Stoddert, Benjamin et al	1801	G7	150	198
Alexander, John	Deed to	Haliday, Thomas	1806	O14	196	129
Alexander, John et al	Deed to	Jones, Charles	1807	T19	013	010
Alexander, Robert	Deed fr	Densley, Hugh	1802	I9	336	553
Alexander, Robert	Slaves	From Prince William Co. VA	1804	K10	241	
Alexander, Robert	Deed fr	Voss, Nicholas	1804	K10	239	247
Alexander, Robert	Deed fr	Williams, Jeremiah, of G'tn.	1805	M12	314	317
Alexander, Robert	Deed fr	Stoddert, Benjamin, of G'tn.	1805	N13	220	139
Alexander, Robert	Mortgage fr	Pearson, Lawson, bricklayer	1806	O14	205	135
Alexander, Robert	Slaves	From Prince William Co. VA	1806	P15	300	197
Alexander, Robert	B. of S. fr	Pearson, Lawson	1806	P15	307	202
Alexander, Robert	B. of S. fr	Ross, Samuel	1806	O14	242	159
Alexander, Robert	Mortgage to	Smallwood, Samuel N. et al	1807	S18	212	169
Alexander, Robert	Release to	Voss, Nicholas	1810	Z25	076	057
Alexander, Robert & Helen B.	Deed to	Costigan, Joseph	1809	X23	192	144
Alexander, Robert, Esq.	Deed fr	Brown, Robert, bricklayer	1808	T19	176	124
Alexander, Robert, Jr., P.W. Co.	Deed fr	Munroe, Thomas, Supt.	1802	I9	017	023
Alexander, Robert, New Orleans	Mortgage to	Cassin, Joseph & B.H. Latrobe	1809	X23	270	212
Alexander, Robert, New Orleans	Deed to	Pearson, Lawson	1811	AC28	103	077
Alexander, William Thornton et al	Deed to	Kennedy, John	1802	H8	589	554
Allen, Henry I.	D. of T. fr	Donaldson, Ronald	1814	AH33	141	134
Allen, Henry J.	Deed fr	Walker, Zachariah, trustee	1817	AN38	255	187

Index to District of Columbia Land Records, 1792-1817

Party	What	Party	Year	Liber	Old	New
Allen, Henry S.	Qualify	Lieutenant of Riflemen in Militia	1813	AF31	239	165
Allen, John, mer.	Deed fr	Bond, Joshua B. & Rebecca, PA	1811	AA26	169	116
Allen, Nathan et al	Manumis fr	Jackson, Joseph	1808	T19	374	267
Allen, Samuel	Deed fr	Balch, Stephen B.	1814	AG32	120	089
Allen, Samuel (C), of Montg. Co.	Lease to	Tolson, Alexander, of G'tn.	1816	AL36	481	453
Allen, Thomas	Deed fr	Law, John	1808	U20	357	195
Allen, Thomas	Qualify	Ensign in militia	1812	AD29	157	124
Allen, Thomas	Lease to	Maddox, William R.	1815	AK35	047	037
Allen, William, of G'tn.	Cert fr	Munroe, Thomas, Supt.	1816	AL36	413	396
Allison, Richard et al	Partition		1804	K10	306	312
Alt, Adam	Deed fr	Harbaugh, Leonard	1797	B2B	652	415
Ambush, Edward	Cert Free fr	Hanson, Thomas, of P.G. Co.	1807	T19	016	012
Ambush, James & John Stokes	B. of S. to	Cooper, John	1811	AB27	162	134
Ames, Benjamin	Deed to	McClan, Robert	1804	K10	221	230
Anacostia Bridge Company	Consent to	Greenleaf, James et al	1815	AH33	450	386
Anderson, Catharine	Deed fr	Roe, Cornelius McDermott	1807	S18	268	211
Anderson, Catherine	Deed to	Fowler, Samuel	1808	T19	403	284
Anderson, Catherine	Deed fr	Roe, Mary McDermott	1808	T19	325	237
Anderson, Catherine	Release fr	Fowler, Samuel	1812	AC28	261	191
Anderson, George	Deed fr	Doughty, William	1804	K10	224	232
Anderson, George et al	Deed to	Beall, Thomas & John M. Gantt	1793	A1-1	317	418
Anderson, George, of G'tn.	Deed fr	Garlick, Joseph	1792	A1-1	054	80
Anderson, George, of G'tn.	Deed to	Thompson, Jay, of G'tn.	1794	B2A	002	002
Anderson, Hannah	Marriage	Purk, Benjamin	1813	AF31	433	312
Anderson, James	Deed fr	Farrell, Zephaniah	1815	AI34	474	485
Anderson, John	B. of S. to	Coyle, Francis	1805	M12	140	135
Anderson, John B.	Deed to	Polock, Isaac	1802	I9	159	240
Anderson, John B.	Deed fr	Polock, Isaac	1802	I9	136	203
Anderson, Joseph	Cert Slaves	From TN	1816	AM37	437	313
Anderson, Juliana	Manumis to	Copper, Teney (negro)	1810	Y24	108	97
Anderson, Richard	Deed fr	Ross, Andrew, of G'tn.	1816	AK35	270	215
Anderson, Richard, of John, G'tn.	Agreement	Ross, Andrew, of G'tn.	1816	AM37	098	079
Anderson, Richard, of John, G'tn.	Deed to	Ross, Andrew, of G'tn.	1816	AM37	095	076
Anderson, Richard, of John, G'tn.	Deed to	Riggs, Elisha, of G'tn.	1816	AO39	014	011
Anderson, Samuel T., of NY	Manumis to	[ ], Nat (C)	1811	AB27	437	360
Andrews, Benjamin	B. of S. to	Lowry, Caesar	1805	N13	101	094
Andrews, Christopher	Deed to	Lear, Tobias	1815	AK35	232	183
Andrews, Christopher	Deed fr	Van Ness, John P. & Marcia	1815	AK35	244	193
Andrews, Christopher	Deed fr	Andrews, George	1815	AI34	094	107
Andrews, Christopher	D. of T. fr	Andrews, George	1816	AM37	351	254
Andrews, Christopher & Tim. P.	Deed to	Nourse, Joseph	1817	AN38	423	317
Andrews, Christopher et al	Deed fr	Dunlop, James	1817	AO39	550	378
Andrews, Christopher, s/o Geo.	Deed fr	Andrews, George & Elizabeth	1815	AK35	083	064
Andrews, Eliza et al	Deed fr	Dunlop, James	1817	AO39	550	378
Andrews, Elizabeth	Agreement	Andrews, George	1816	AM37	248	252
Andrews, George	Deed fr	Commissioners of Washington	1802	G7	517	658
Andrews, George	Deed fr	Commissioners of Washington	1802	G7	514	654
Andrews, George	Deed fr	Commissioners of Washington	1802	H8	118	115
Andrews, George	Lease fr	Lovell, William	1802	H8	281	266
Andrews, George	Deed fr	Shannon, Luke	1802	I9	560	907
Andrews, George	Qualify		1802	I9	477	785
Andrews, George	Deed fr	Lovell, William	1802	I9	057	078
Andrews, George	Deed to	Shoemaker, David	1804	L11	027	27
Andrews, George	Deed to	Smith, Clement	1805	M12	237	238
Andrews, George	B. of S. fr	White, Richard	1807	S18	014	013

Index to District of Columbia Land Records, 1792-1817

Party	What	Party	Year	Liber	Old	New
Andrews, George	Deed fr	Miller, William, of Phila. PA	1810	Y24	037	32
Andrews, George	Deed to	Clarke, Walter	1810	Y24	512	451
Andrews, George	Deed fr	Bassett, John & Betty Carter	1811	AA26	288	195
Andrews, George	Deed to	Andrews, Christopher	1815	AI34	094	107
Andrews, George	Deed fr	Van Ness, John P. & Marcia	1815	AK35	058	045
Andrews, George	Agreement	Andrews, Elizabeth	1816	AM37	248	252
Andrews, George	Deed fr	Laird, John, exr. of J. Carleton	1816	AM37	137	106
Andrews, George	Deed to	Andrews, Timothy P. & Elizabeth	1816	AM37	348	253
Andrews, George	Deed fr	Gales, Joseph, Jr.	1816	AO39	027	021
Andrews, George	D. of T. to	Andrews, Christopher	1816	AM37	351	254
Andrews, George	Agreement	Nourse, Joseph	1817	AN38	426	320
Andrews, George & N. King	Assign fr	Gillingham, George, of Phila. PA	1810	Z25	109	084
Andrews, George & Nicholas King	Deed fr	Lindo, Abraham	1810	Y24	366	331
Andrews, George & Elizabeth	Deed to	Andrews, Christopher, s/o Geo.	1815	AK35	083	064
Andrews, George & T. Webster	Deed fr	Heronimus, Pendleton	1816	AL36	046	046
Andrews, George, admrs. of	Deed to	Nourse, Joseph	1817	AN38	423	317
Andrews, George, as atty.	Assign fr	Hearn, John, s/o Wm., dec.	1816	AL36	146	146
Andrews, George, Capt.	Qualify	Captain in the Militia	1802	H8	525	485
Andrews, George, Cincinnati OH	Deed to	Bradley, Phineas & O.B. Brown	1813	AE30	120	092
Andrews, George et al	Deed to	Jones, Anthony	1802	H8	304	287
Andrews, George et al	Deed fr	Dunlop, James	1817	AO39	550	378
Andrews, George, trustee	Deed fr	Colvin, John B., insolvent	1810	Y24	033	29
Andrews, Jane et al	Deed fr	Dunlop, James	1817	AO39	550	378
Andrews, Richard	Cert fr	Commissioners of Washington	1801	G7	046	059
Andrews, Susanna et al	Deed fr	Dunlop, James	1817	AO39	550	378
Andrews, Timothy P.	Deed fr	Murdock, John, of G'tn.	1815	AK35	364	287
Andrews, Timothy P.	Deed fr	Dorsey, William H., of Montg. Co.	1815	AK35	361	285
Andrews, Timothy P.	Deed fr	Laird, John, exr. of J. Carleton	1816	AM37	383	276
Andrews, Timothy P. & Elizabeth	Deed fr	Andrews, George	1816	AM37	348	253
Andrews, Timothy P. et al	Deed fr	Dunlop, James	1817	AO39	550	378
Antrim, Parnell	B. of S. to	Linscott, Edward	1809	V21	214	151
Antrim, Parnell	Note to	Linscott, Edward	1809	V21	214	151
Appler, David	Deed fr	Appler, Jonathan	1817	AN38	420	315
Appler, David & Jonathan	Deed fr	McCleland, John	1811	Z25	313	245
Appler, David et al	Deed to	Thompson, Julia [Kaine]	1816	AL36	523	489
Appler, Jonathan	Assign fr	Bullus, John, of NY	1813	AF31	306	218
Appler, Jonathan	Assign fr	Bullus, John, of NY	1816	AL36	141	142
Appler, Jonathan	Deed to	Appler, David	1817	AN38	420	315
Appleton, Henry & John, Jr., of MA	Deed to	Appleton, John, mer., Salem MA	1801	G7	343	474
Appleton, Henry et al	Deed fr	Appleton, John, of Salem MA	1797	C3	225	189
Appleton, John, Jr. et al	Deed fr	Appleton, John, of Salem MA	1797	C3	225	189
Appleton, John, mer., Salem MA	Deed fr	Appleton, Henry & John, Jr., of MA	1801	G7	343	474
Appleton, John, of Salem MA	Deed fr	Johnson, Roger, of Frederick Co.	1797	B2B	685	461
Appleton, John, of Salem MA	Deed fr	Greenleaf, James, of Phila.	1797	B2B	696	478
Appleton, John, of Salem MA	Deed to	Appleton, Henry et al	1797	C3	225	189
Appleton, John, of Salem MA	Deed fr	Greenleaf, James, of Phila.	1797	B2B	640	402
Appleton, Nathaniel Walker	P. of Atty. fr	Greenleaf, James, New York NY	1794	B2A	080	103
Appleton, Nathaniel Walker	P. of Atty. fr	Greenleaf, James, New York NY	1794	B2A	077	100
Appleton, Nathaniel Walker	P. of Atty. fr	Greenleaf, James, New York NY	1794	B2A	081	105
Appleton, Nathaniel Walker	Deed fr	Johnson, Thomas, Frederick Co.	1794	B2A	057	070
Arderey, John, of G'tn.	Deed fr	Sherrard, Francis & Eleanor	1798	D4	065	055
Ardery, Alexander & William	Deed to	Way, Andrew, Jr. et al	1808	U20	256	137
Ardray, John, of G'tn.	Deed fr	Commissioners of Washington	1800	F6	007	005
Ardrey, Alexander et al	Deed to	Hellen, Walter	1806	Q16	115	074
Ardrey, Alexander William	Deed fr	Ardrey, John & Mary	1802	H8	329	308

Party	What	Party	Year	Liber	Old	New
Ardrey, John & Mary	Deed to	Ardrey, Alexander William	1802	H8	329	308
Ardrey, John et al	Deed to	Hellen, Walter	1806	Q16	115	074
Ardrey, Robert	Deed fr	Templeman, John & B. Stoddert	1813	AF31	007	005
Ardrey, William	Deed to	Hellen, Walter	1811	AB27	042	037
Ardrey, William	Deed to	Way, Andrew & George	1811	AC28	072	055
Ardrey, William et al	Deed to	Hellen, Walter	1806	Q16	115	074
Ardrey, Wm., s/o John, age 16	Apprentice to	King, Benjamin, blacksmith	1805	N13	307	249
Armat, Thomas & Elizabeth, of PA	Deed to	Nourse, Joseph	1799	D4	244	227
Armat, Thomas, of Phila.	Deed fr	Yates, John, of Balto.	1799	D4	242	224
Armat, Thomas, of Phila. PA	Deed to	Nourse, Joseph	1809	X23	178	132
Armistead, Robert	Slave	From VA	1805	N13	405	322
Armistead, Robert et al	Lease fr	Carleton, Joseph	1804	L11	267	246
Armistead, Robert et al	Deed to	Carleton, Joseph, of G'tn.	1805	M12	148	145
Armitage, Benjamin, attorney	Deed to	Cassin, James, of G'tn.	1815	AI34	305	338
Armitage, Benjamin, atty.	B. of S. to	Thornton, William	1815	AH33	420	362
Armitage, Benjamin, New York NY	Lease to	Adams, Margaret, of P.G. Co.	1804	L11	289	265
Armitage, Benjamin, New York NY	Deed fr	Adams, Margaret, of P.G. Co.	1804	L11	287	263
Armstrong, Andrew	Partition	Charlton, Ralph	1804	K10	177	186
Armstrong, Andrew	B. of S. to	Gatton, Azariah, of Alexa. Co.	1808	T19	079	057
Armstrong, Andrew et al	Deed fr	Stoddert, Benjamin	1802	I9	523	856
Armstrong, Andrew et al	Deed to	McKim, James	1807	R17	082	066
Armstrong, Andrew, shopkeeper	Mortgage to	Cherry, Robert, trader	1804	K10	141	153
Armstrong, James et al	Deed fr	McIntire, John	1802	I9	476	783
Armstrong, James et al	Deed fr	Kearney, John	1802	I9	474	780
Armstrong, James et al	Deed fr	Fallin, Edw. et al	1802	I9	406	673
Armstrong, James, of Balto. et al	Deed fr	Kearney, John	1801	G7	151	200
Armstrong, William	Deed fr	Polock, Jacob	1802	I9	363	601
Arnold, Aquilla K., of G'tn.	B. of S. fr	Arnold, Charles, of G'tn.	1817	AO39	182	135
Arnold, Charles, of G'tn.	B. of S. to	Arnold, Aquilla K., of G'tn.	1817	AO39	182	135
Arnot, John	Deed fr	Glover, Charles, trustee	1816	AL36	362	352
Arnot, John	Deed fr	Carr, Overton, trustee	1817	AO39	218	158
Arnott, John & Thomas Young	Deed fr	Sim, Patrick	1808	U20	114	065
Ash, James et al	Deed to	Underwood, Robert	1810	Y24	133	121
Ash, Phineas et al	Deed fr	Bailey, Daniel	1805	M12	063	059
Ash, Thomas, of PA et al	Deed fr	Bailey, Daniel, of PA	1807	S18	372	295
Ashley, John	Deed fr	Nicholson, John & Hannah	1797	B2B	692	471
Ashley, John	Deed fr	Nicholson, John & Hannah	1797	B2B	693	473
Ashley, John	Deed fr	Commissioners of Washington	1801	F6	202	131
Ashley, John	Deed fr	Commissioners of Washington	1801	G7	281	389
Ashley, John et al	D. of T. fr	Morris, Robert, of Phila. et al	1797	C3	204	172
Ashley, John et al	D. of T. fr	Morris, Robert, of Phila. et al	1797	C3	192	161
Ashley, John et al	Deed fr	Greenleaf, James, of Phila. et al	1797	C3	154	127
Ashley, John et al	Deed fr	Morris, Robert et al	1798	D4	030	025
Ashley, John et al	Deed fr	Morris, Robert, of Phila. et al	1798	C3	301	243
Ashley, John et al	Deed fr	Hanson, Alexander Contee	1798	C3	490	385
Ashley, John et al	Deed fr	Commissioners of Washington	1800	E5	372	353
Ashley, John et al	Deed fr	Commissioners of Washington	1800	E5	369	350
Ashley, John et al	Deed fr	Debbois, Lewis	1802	I9	261	423
Ashley, John et al	Deed fr	Dorsey, William H.	1802	I9	263	426
Ashley, John et al	Deed fr	Dorsey, William H. et al	1802	I9	568	920
Ashley, John et al	Deed to	Tingey, Thomas	1802	I9	213	336
Ashley, John et al	Deed fr	Tingey, Thomas	1802	I9	572	927
Ashley, John et al	Deed to	Underwood, Robert et al	1802	I9	217	342
Ashley, John et al	Deed to	Yeates, William	1802	H8	056	053
Ashley, John et al	P. of Atty. to	Greenleaf, James	1804	K10	101	107

Index to District of Columbia Land Records, 1792-1817

Party	What	Party	Year	Liber	Old	New
Ashley, John et al	Deed to	Sewall, Robert, of P.G. Co.	1805	N13	081	074
Ashley, John et al	P. of Atty. to	Greenleaf, James	1805	M12	377	388
Ashley, John et al	Deed to	May, Frederick	1805	N13	108	102
Ashley, John et al	Deed to	Elliott, Samuel, Jr.	1806	O14	362	242
Ashley, John et al	Deed to	Van Ness, John P.	1806	P15	105	065
Ashley, John et al	Deed to	Voss, Nicholas	1807	S18	025	021
Ashley, John et al	Deed to	Tilghman, William, of Phila. et al	1808	T19	086	061
Ashley, John et al	Quit to	Toole, Patrick	1809	X23	135	097
Ashley, John et al	Deed to	Cook, Orlando	1809	X23	245	190
Ashley, John et al	Deed to	Eliot, Samuel, Jr.	1809	W22	293	193
Ashley, John et al	Deed to	Griffin, Lancelot	1810	X23	319	256
Ashley, John et al	Deed fr	Munroe, Thomas, Supt.	1811	Z25	472	374
Ashley, John et al	Deed to	Varnum, James M.	1812	AC28	508	363
Ashley, John et al	Deed to	Jones, Walter, Jr.	1812	AC28	400	290
Ashley, John et al	Deed to	Latrobe, Benjamim H.	1812	AC28	445	318
Ashley, John et al	Deed to	Aborn, Henry	1812	AC28	470	334
Ashley, John et al	Deed to	Gales, Joseph, Jr.	1812	AE30	001	001
Ashley, John et al	Deed to	Heath, Nathaniel H.	1813	AE30	522	387
Ashley, John et al	Deed to	Van Ness, John P.	1813	AE30	485	360
Ashley, John et al	Deed to	Tuckfield, William H.P.	1813	AE30	230	184
Ashley, John et al	Deed to	Smallwood, Samuel N.	1813	AF31	032	022
Ashley, John et al	Deed to	Jones, Walter, Jr.	1813	AE30	328	246
Ashley, John et al	Deed fr	Miller, John, Jr. & Wm. Cranch	1814	AG32	330	240
Ashley, John et al	Deed to	McMurray, William	1814	AH33	171	159
Ashley, John et al	Deed to	Johnson, James W.	1814	AH33	004	004
Ashley, John et al	Deed to	Glover, Charles	1814	AH33	302	261
Ashley, John et al	Deed to	Wayne, Francis	1814	AH33	377	326
Ashley, John et al	Deed to	Van Ness, John P.	1814	AG32	313	229
Ashley, John et al	Deed to	Gales, Joseph, Jr.	1815	AK35	400	314
Ashley, John et al	Deed to	Walker, Zachariah	1815	AK35	404	317
Ashley, John et al	Deed to	Eliot, Samuel, Jr.	1816	AL36	171	171
Ashley, John et al	Deed to	Hoot, Samuel	1816	AL36	122	124
Ashley, John et al	Deed to	Brent, Robert	1816	AL36	538	502
Ashley, John, mer., of Phila.	Deed to	Travis, John, mer., of Phila.	1803	K10	085	91
Ashley, John, of Phila. et al	Deed to	Weightman, Roger C.	1811	AB27	228	186
Ashley, John, of Phila. et al	Deed to	Matthews, William, Rev.	1811	AB27	342	282
Ashley, John, of Phila. PA et al	Deed to	Weightman, Roger C.	1812	AD29	409	346
Ashley, John, of Phila. PA et al	Deed to	Weightman, Roger C.	1812	AD29	406	342
Ashley, John, of Phila. PA et al	Deed to	Weightman, Roger C.	1812	AD29	402	339
Ashley, John, trustee, et al	Deed to	Mara, Philip O.	1810	Z25	340	266
Ashley, Mary, wid/o T. Carpenter	Dower to	Brook, Samuel	1816	AM37	413	296
Ashly, John et al	B. of S. fr	Prout, William	1809	W22	380	247
Ashly, John et al	Deed to	Tingey, Thomas	1812	AC28	428	308
Ashton, Erasmus, of G'tn.	B. of S. to	Atkinson, Sarah Ann	1815	AK35	378	298
Ashton, John, of P.G. Co. et al	Deed fr	Threlkeld, John, of Montg. Co.	1796	B2B	500	197
Ashton, John, Rev. et al	Deed fr	Carroll, John, Rev. et al	1799	D4	283	265
Ashton, John, Rev. et al	Deed to	Walton, James et al	1799	D4	283	265
Astin, David, insolvent	Deed to	Johnson, Isaac, trustee	1805	N13	120	115
Astin, Nancy	Cert. Free fr	Jones, Mary	1814	AG32	365	264
Astley, Thomas, of Phila. et al	Deed fr	Travis, Elizabeth, admx. of John	1808	V21	102	077
Astley, Thomas, of Phila. et al	Deed to	Fox, Josiah	1808	V21	109	081
Athey, George, of G'tn.	Deed fr	King, Adam & Grace, of G'tn.	1810	Y24	299	295
Athey, George, of G'tn.	Deed to	Massey, Thomas, of G'tn.	1813	AF31	059	040
Athey, George, of G'tn.	Deed to	Beatty, Violetta, wid/o Dr. John	1816	AL36	475	448
Athey, Hezekiah, of G'tn.	Deed fr	Dorsey, William H., of G'tn.	1801	G7	399	533

Party	What	Party	Year	Liber	Old	New
Athey, Hezekiah, of G'tn.	Deed to	Connelly, John, of Montg. Co.	1805	O14	081	050
Athey, Walter F.	Deed fr	Smallwood, Leven	1802	I9	583	948
Athey, Walter F., of G'tn.	Deed to	Knowles, Henry, of G'tn.	1808	U20	012	007
Atkinson, Francis, mer., of NY	Deed fr	Lynch, Dominick et ux et al	1797	C3	032	26
Atkinson, John & Elizabeth, of NY	Deed to	Warder, Jeremiah, Jr. et al	1811	AB27	110	089
Atkinson, John, mer., of NY	Deed fr	Lynch, Dominick et ux et al	1797	C3	037	30
Atkinson, John, shoemaker	Deed fr	Beall, Thomas, of George, G'tn.	1792	A1-1	150	216
Atkinson, Sarah Ann	B. of S. fr	Ashton, Erasmus, of G'tn.	1815	AK35	378	298
Aubert, Henry	Deed to	McLaughlin, Charles	1802	I9	482	792
Aud, Ann & Mary Cecil	Deed to	Vanhorn, Archibald, of P.G. Co.	1816	AL36	262	263
Aurand, Christian et al	Deed fr	Hines, John	1812	AB27	543	443
Aurand, Daniel et al	Deed fr	Hines, John	1812	AB27	543	443
Aurand, David & Christianna	Deed fr	King, John, Sr.	1816	AL36	382	369
Aurand, David et al	Deed fr	Hines, John	1812	AB27	543	443
Aurand, John et al	Deed fr	Hines, John	1812	AB27	543	443
Austin, David, of G'tn.	Deed to	Murdock, John, of G'tn.	1802	I9	080	113
Avidh, J.B.	Cert fr	Munroe, Thomas, Supt.	1804	K10	230	238
Ayres, Thomas	Mortgage to	Somers, Nathan, of P.G. Co.	1809	V21	165	119

Index to District of Columbia Land Records, 1792-1817

Party	What	Party	Year	Liber	Old	New
B						
Bacchus, John	B. of S. to	Gray, Nathan	1817	AN38	272	199
Bacchus, John, of G'tn.	B. of S. to	Van Ness, John P.	1816	AL36	376	365
Bachman, Jacob	Deed fr	Skinner, Edward, in PA	1814	AH33	348	301
Bachtel, Isaac, of Bedford Co. PA	Deed fr	Rohrer, Frederick, s/o John	1792	A1-1	165	236
Bachtel, Isaac, Washington Co.	Deed to	Stoddert, Benjamin	1792	A1-1	166	238
Backer, Henry, of G'tn.	Deed fr	Stoddert, Benjamin, of G'tn. et al	1804	L11	389	346
Bacon, Benjamin	Deed fr	Commissioners of Washington	1798	D4	112	095
Bacon, Samuel	Deed fr	Sessford, John	1807	S18	040	033
Bacon, Samuel	Deed fr	McClelland, John	1807	S18	005	004
Bacon, Samuel	Deed fr	Moore, George	1808	U20	387	215
Bacon, Samuel	Deed to	Bestor, Harvey	1808	V21	071	056
Bacon, Samuel	Deed to	Sessford, John	1809	X23	116	082
Bacon, Samuel	Deed to	Moore, James	1809	V21	407	309
Bacon, Samuel	Deed fr	Moore, George	1815	AI34	020	021
Bacon, Samuel	Mortgage to	Queen, Nicholas L. et al	1815	AI34	193	221
Bacon, Samuel & George Moore	Assign fr	Thorpe, Thomas	1809	V21	419	329
Bacon, Samuel & George Moore	Deed fr	Whetcroft, William & Sarah et al	1812	AD29	523	441
Bacon, Samuel & George Moore	B. of S. to	Campbell, John	1815	AI34	510	515
Bacon, Samuel & Jos. Harbaugh	B. of S. fr	Shuck, Elizabeth	1816	AL36	246	249
Bailey, Daniel	Deed fr	Munroe, Thomas, Supt.	1802	I9	004	006
Bailey, Daniel	Deed fr	Munroe, Thomas, Supt.	1802	I9	003	004
Bailey, Daniel	Deed to	Pennock, Isaac et al	1805	M12	063	059
Bailey, Daniel, of PA	Deed to	Pennock, Isaac, of PA et al	1807	S18	372	295
Bailey, Jesse	Deed fr	Pierce, Isaac	1801	G7	459	595
Bailey, John	Cert fr	Commissioner of Public Buildings	1817	AO39	368	248
Bailey, Mary, wid/o Jesse	Deed fr	Lutz, John	1811	AB27	044	038
Bailey, Robert	B. of S. to	McGowan, John	1817	AO39	229	165
Bailey, Robert	D. of T. to	Ingle, John P.	1817	AO39	183	135
Bailey, Theodorus & Rebecca	Deed to	Thompson, Ezra et al	1802	G7	465	601
Bailey, Theodorus & Rebecca, NY	Deed to	Van Cortland, Philip, of NY	1804	M12	005	005
Bailey, Theodorus et al	Deed fr	Forrest, Uriah	1801	G7	079	102
Baily, Daniel	Deed fr	Chandler, Jacob	1805	M12	288	289
Baily, Daniel	Deed to	Spooner, William	1808	T19	109	078
Baily, Jesse	Agreement	Nourse, Joseph	1802	I9	457	754
Baily, Jesse & Mary	Deed to	Townsend, Henry	1801	G7	218	291
Baily, Jesse, of Montg. Co.	Deed to	Cloud, Abner, Jr., of Montg. Co.	1795	B2B	360	008
Baily, Jesse, of G'tn.	Deed fr	King, George, of G'tn.	1798	C3	341	274
Baily, John	Deed fr	Webster, Toppan	1814	AG32	198	138
Bain, Quintin	Deed fr	Forrest, Uriah	1801	G7	001	002
Bain, Quinton	Deed fr	Forrest, Uriah	1802	G7	525	668
Bain, Quinton, of G'tn.	Deed fr	Lowry, Ceasar, of G'tn.	1802	H8	222	212
Bain, Quinton, of G'tn.	Deed to	Payne, John, of Leesburg VA	1809	X23	102	074
Bain, Quinton [Bean]	Deed fr	Bussard, Daniel, of G'tn.	1804	L11	051	52
Bainbridge, Richard C.	B. of S. fr	Murrell, Bennett	1813	AE30	154	121
Baird, Andrew, carpenter, of G'tn.	Deed fr	Brookes, William, of G'tn.	1796	B2B	410	079
Baird, Margaret, wid.	Deed to	Miller, Peter, of Wash. Co. MD	1798	C3	429	337
Baird, Mary, of G'tn.	Deed fr	Thompson, George, of G'tn.	1810	Y24	368	332
Baise, David (negro)	Manumis fr	Stone, Mathew, of Charles Co.	1806	P15	266	175
Baker, Ann H.	Manumis to	[ ], Beck (C)	1812	AC28	351	254
Baker, Catharine	Deed fr	Cocking, William	1817	AO39	499	343
Baker, Corban, Jefferson Co. VA	Deed to	Kemp, Christian, of Frederick Co.	1810	X23	394	317
Baker, Elizabeth (yellow)	Deposition fr	Hamilton, Samuel	1807	R17	062	050
Baker, Henry	Lease fr	Dawes, Isaac	1802	I9	473	778
Baker, Henry	Lease to	Morgan, William	1811	AB27	050	042

Party	What	Party	Year	Liber	Old	New
Baker, Henry	Deed to	Baker, John & Edward Dawes	1812	AC28	284	206
Baker, Henry & Isaac Dawes	Deed fr	Hoye, John, of Allegany Co.	1814	AH33	003	003
Baker, Henry & John	Deed to	Gray, Nathaniel	1816	AL36	169	169
Baker, Henry et al	Deed fr	Gailor, Thomas	1802	I9	294	483
Baker, Henry et al	Deed to	Gassaway, Charles et al	1805	M12	147	143
Baker, Henry et al	Deed fr	Norris, Isaac, of G'tn.	1806	Q16	118	076
Baker, Henry, of G'tn.	Deed to	Baker, John, of G'tn.	1811	AB27	479	391
Baker, Henry, of G'tn.	Deed to	Baker, John, of G'tn.	1811	AB27	477	390
Baker, Jacob et al	D. of T. fr	Morris, Robert, of Phila. et al	1797	C3	192	161
Baker, Jacob et al	Deed fr	Greenleaf, James, of Phila. et al	1797	C3	154	127
Baker, Jacob et al	D. of T. fr	Morris, Robert, of Phila. et al	1797	C3	204	172
Baker, Jacob et al	Deed fr	Morris, Robert, of Phila. et al	1798	C3	301	243
Baker, Jacob et al	Deed fr	Morris, Robert et al	1798	D4	030	025
Baker, Jacob et al	Deed fr	Commissioners of Washington	1800	E5	372	353
Baker, Jacob et al	Deed fr	Commissioners of Washington	1801	G7	281	389
Baker, Jacob et al	Deed fr	Tingey, Thomas	1802	I9	572	927
Baker, Jacob et al	Deed fr	Dorsey, William H.	1802	I9	263	426
Baker, Jacob et al	Deed to	Tingey, Thomas	1802	I9	213	336
Baker, Jacob et al	Deed to	Underwood, Robert et al	1802	I9	217	342
Baker, Jacob et al	Deed fr	Dorsey, William H. et al	1802	I9	568	920
Baker, Jacob et al	Deed to	Yeates, William	1802	H8	056	053
Baker, Jacob et al	P. of Atty. to	Greenleaf, James	1804	K10	101	107
Baker, Jacob et al	Deed to	Sewall, Robert, of P.G. Co.	1805	N13	081	074
Baker, Jacob et al	P. of Atty. to	Greenleaf, James	1805	M12	377	388
Baker, Jacob et al	Deed to	May, Frederick	1805	N13	108	102
Baker, Jacob et al	Deed to	Van Ness, John P.	1806	P15	105	065
Baker, Jacob et al	Deed to	Elliott, Samuel, Jr.	1806	O14	362	242
Baker, Jacob et al	Deed to	Voss, Nicholas	1807	S18	025	021
Baker, Jacob et al	Deed to	Tilghman, William, of Phila. et al	1808	T19	086	061
Baker, Jacob et al	Deed to	Cook, Orlando	1809	X23	245	190
Baker, Jacob et al	B. of S. fr	Prout, William	1809	W22	380	247
Baker, Jacob et al	Quit to	Toole, Patrick	1809	X23	135	097
Baker, Jacob et al	Deed to	Griffin, Lancelot	1810	X23	319	256
Baker, Jacob et al	Deed fr	Munroe, Thomas, Supt.	1811	Z25	472	374
Baker, Jacob et al	Deed to	Varnum, James M.	1812	AC28	508	363
Baker, Jacob et al	Deed to	Aborn, Henry	1812	AC28	470	334
Baker, Jacob et al	Deed to	Jones, Walter, Jr.	1812	AC28	400	290
Baker, Jacob et al	Deed to	Tingey, Thomas	1812	AC28	428	308
Baker, Jacob et al	Deed to	Latrobe, Benjamim H.	1812	AC28	445	318
Baker, Jacob et al	Deed to	Gales, Joseph, Jr.	1812	AE30	001	001
Baker, Jacob et al	Deed to	Tuckfield, William H.P.	1813	AE30	230	184
Baker, Jacob et al	Deed to	Heath, Nathaniel H.	1813	AE30	522	387
Baker, Jacob et al	Deed to	Smallwood, Samuel N.	1813	AF31	032	022
Baker, Jacob et al	Deed to	Jones, Walter, Jr.	1813	AE30	328	246
Baker, Jacob et al	Deed to	Van Ness, John P.	1813	AE30	485	360
Baker, Jacob et al	Deed fr	Miller, John, Jr. & Wm. Cranch	1814	AG32	330	240
Baker, Jacob et al	Deed to	Van Ness, John P.	1814	AG32	313	229
Baker, Jacob et al	Deed to	McMurray, William	1814	AH33	171	159
Baker, Jacob et al	Deed to	Johnson, James W.	1814	AH33	004	004
Baker, Jacob et al	Deed to	Glover, Charles	1814	AH33	302	261
Baker, Jacob et al	Deed to	Wayne, Francis	1814	AH33	377	326
Baker, Jacob et al	Deed to	Gales, Joseph, Jr.	1815	AK35	400	314
Baker, Jacob et al	Deed to	Walker, Zachariah	1815	AK35	404	317
Baker, Jacob et al	Deed to	Hoot, Samuel	1816	AL36	122	124
Baker, Jacob et al	Deed to	Brent, Robert	1816	AL36	538	502

Index to District of Columbia Land Records, 1792-1817

Party	What	Party	Year	Liber	Old	New
Baker, Jacob et al	Deed to	Eliot, Samuel, Jr.	1816	AL36	171	171
Baker, Jacob, of Phila. PA, et al	Deed fr	Commissioners of Washington	1800	E5	369	350
Baker, Jacob, of Phila. PA	Deed fr	Commissioners of Washington	1801	F6	202	131
Baker, Jacob, of Phila. et al	Deed to	Matthews, William, Rev.	1811	AB27	342	282
Baker, Jacob, of Phila. et al	Deed to	Weightman, Roger C.	1811	AB27	228	186
Baker, Jacob, of Phila. PA et al	Deed to	Weightman, Roger C.	1812	AD29	402	339
Baker, Jacob, of Phila. PA et al	Deed to	Weightman, Roger C.	1812	AD29	406	
Baker, Jacob, of Phila. PA et al	Deed to	Weightman, Roger C.	1812	AD29	409	346
Baker, Jacob, trustee et al	Deed to	Eliot, Samuel, Jr.	1809	W22	293	193
Baker, Jacob, trustee, et al	Deed to	Mara, Philip O.	1810	Z25	340	266
Baker, John	B. of S. to	Mayer, Henry	1810	Y24	150	136
Baker, John	Deed fr	Dawes, Isaac, of Montg. Co.	1810	Y24	237	219
Baker, John	Deed fr	Mayer, Henry	1813	AE30	213	173
Baker, John & Edward Dawes	Deed fr	Baker, Henry	1812	AC28	284	206
Baker, John & Henry	Deed to	Gray, Nathaniel	1816	AL36	169	169
Baker, John & Edward Dawes	B. of S. fr	Chester, Samuel, of G'tn.	1817	AN38	546	397
Baker, John, exr. of John	Deed fr	Hoye, John et al	1806	O14	160	104
Baker, John, of G'tn.	Deed fr	Baker, Henry, of G'tn.	1811	AB27	479	391
Baker, John, of G'tn.	Deed fr	Baker, Henry, of G'tn.	1811	AB27	477	390
Baker, John, of G'tn.	Deed fr	Corporation of Georgetown	1813	AE30	214	173
Baker, John, of G'tn.	Lease fr	Burrows, John & Elizabeth	1817	AN38	488	352
Baker, John, of G'tn.	D. of T. to	Knowles, Henry, of G'tn.	1817	AO39	198	145
Baker, Michael, of Rockg. Co. VA	Mortgage fr	Eno, Edward, of G'tn.	1797	C3	187	158
Baker, Michael, of Rockg. Co. VA	Deed fr	Cunningham, John, of G'tn.	1797	C3	271	220
Baker, Murray (negro)	Manumis fr	Mackall, Leonard, of G'tn.	1809	X23	173	129
Baker, Nancy	Deed fr	Carr, Overton	1812	AC28	320	233
Baker, Nancy	Deed fr	Baker, Samuel H., of Pr. Wm. Co.	1812	AC28	319	232
Baker, Nancy H.	Deed fr	Baker, William, Jr.	1812	AC28	368	267
Baker, Nancy H.	Manumis to	Hicks, George (M)	1816	AK35	201	157
Baker, Nancy H.	Deed fr	Baker, William, admr. of Dr. Wm.	1816	AK35	201	157
Baker, Philip Thomas [William]	B. of S. to	Jefferson, Thomas	1808	V21	030	022
Baker, Philip Thomas	P. of Atty. fr	Baker, William	1808	V21	032	
Baker, Samuel	Agreement	Mills, Ephraim	1795	B2B	357	005
Baker, Samuel	Agreement	Gridly, Richard Jr.	1795	B2B	358	006
Baker, Samuel	Agreement	Simmons, James	1795	B2B	357	005
Baker, Samuel	Deed fr	Jarboe, Bennett	1802	H8	461	423
Baker, Samuel	Deed to	Kearney, John et al	1802	H8	324	304
Baker, Samuel	Deed to	Way, Andrew, Jr. et al	1802	H8	324	304
Baker, Samuel	Deed to	Gillis, Thomas H. et al	1802	H8	324	304
Baker, Samuel	Agreement	Creager, Michael	1804	L11	146	147
Baker, Samuel	Mortgage to	Evans, John	1805	M12	120	114
Baker, Samuel	Bond to	Toole, Patrick	1806	O14	313	208
Baker, Samuel	B. of S. to	Gatton, Azariah	1806	P15	280	185
Baker, Samuel	Deed to	Gatton, Azariah	1806	P15	281	185
Baker, Samuel	B. of S. to	Prout, William	1806	Q16	143	094
Baker, Samuel	B. of S. fr	Gatton, Azariah	1806	Q16	139	091
Baker, Samuel	Bond to	Toole, Patrick	1806	O14	315	209
Baker, Samuel	B. of S. to	Burrows, Edward	1807	R17	237	179
Baker, Samuel et al	Deed fr	Lyon, John	1802	I9	442	731
Baker, Samuel et al	Mortgage to	Gardner, John Frs., Charles Co.	1802	G7	501	639
Baker, Samuel et al	Deed to	Washington Building Company	1802	H8	321	302
Baker, Samuel et al	Deed to	Vint, John	1805	N13	185	165
Baker, Samuel et al	Manumis to	[ ], Nace (C), age 42	1813	AE30	229	183
Baker, Samuel H., of Pr. Wm. Co.	Deed to	Baker, Nancy	1812	AC28	319	232
Baker, Walter, Jefferson Co. VA	Deed to	Kemp, Christian, of Frederick Co.	1810	X23	394	317

Index to District of Columbia Land Records, 1792-1817

Party	What	Party	Year	Liber	Old	New
Baker, William	P. of Atty. to	Baker, Philip Thomas	1808	V21	032	
Baker, William, admr. of Dr. Wm.	Deed to	Baker, Nancy H.	1816	AK35	201	157
Baker, William, Jr.	Deed to	Baker, Nancy H.	1812	AC28	368	267
Baker, William, of P.G. Co. et al	Partition	Addison, Anthony & David	1797	B2B	676	446
Baker, William, of Balto. et al	Deed fr	Beck, Joseph, of Montg. Co.	1797	C3	236	196
Baker, William, of Balto. Co. et al	Deed to	Bussard, Daniel, of G'tn.	1812	AC28	182	138
Baker, Zachariah	Deed fr	King, George	1812	AC28	490½	349
Baker, Zachariah, of G'tn.	Agreement	Morgan, Nelly (negro)	1809	V21	300	218
Balch, Alfred	Deed to	Smith, William	1807	S18	327	256
Balch, Lewis P.W., of G'tn. et al	Deed to	Cooper, Isaac, of G'tn.	1812	AD29	041	029
Balch, Stephen B.	Deed to	McClary, Henry, Frederick Co.	1795	B2A	187	253
Balch, Stephen B., of Montg. Co.	Deed to	Weatherall, John, of Montg. Co.	1796	B2B	517	224
Balch, Stephen B., of G'tn.	Deed to	Hawker, Margaret, of G'tn.	1796	B2B	504	204
Balch, Stephen B., of G'tn.	Deed to	Weathoral, John, of G'tn.	1796	B2B	409	077
Balch, Stephen B.	Deed to	Steel, Matthew	1797	C3	246	203
Balch, Stephen B., of Montg. Co.	Deed to	Gamble, Thomas, of Montg. Co.	1797	C3	136	111
Balch, Stephen B., of G'tn.	Deed to	Knowles, Henry, of G'tn.	1798	D4	086	073
Balch, Stephen B.	Deed fr	Davidson, John	1801	G7	083	107
Balch, Stephen B., of G'tn.	Deed to	Lowry, Caesar, of G'tn.	1802	H8	500	460
Balch, Stephen B., of G'tn.	Deed fr	Davidson, John, of MD	1802	H8	479	440
Balch, Stephen B.	B. of S. to	Gloyd, George Holland	1804	K10	198	207
Balch, Stephen B.	Deed fr	Beatty, John M. et al	1805	M12	188	190
Balch, Stephen B., Rev.	Deed to	Travers, Elias Erl	1805	O14	036	022
Balch, Stephen B., of G'tn.	Deed to	Fields, William, of G'tn.	1806	P15	379	253
Balch, Stephen B.	Deed to	Swan, John	1807	R17	390	295
Balch, Stephen B., of G'tn.	Deed to	Fields, William, of G'tn.	1807	S18	100	081
Balch, Stephen B., Rev., of G'tn.	Deed to	Collins, John, of G'tn.	1807	R17	412	311
Balch, Stephen B., of G'tn.	Deed to	Bridges, John, of G'tn.	1807	R17	170	130
Balch, Stephen B., of G'tn.	Deed to	Coulter, Peter, of G'tn.	1809	V21	273	195
Balch, Stephen B., of G'tn.	Deed to	Patterson, Edgar, of G'tn.	1809	V21	211	149
Balch, Stephen B. & Eliza., of G'tn.	Deed to	Peter, John, of G'tn.	1809	W22	023	018
Balch, Stephen B., of G'tn.	Deed to	Quables, William, of G'tn.	1809	W22	062	046
Balch, Stephen B., of G'tn.	Deed fr	Bromley, Joseph & Mary	1810	Z25	298	233
Balch, Stephen B., of G'tn.	B. of S. to	Beall, Thomas B.	1811	AB27	345	286
Balch, Stephen B.	Deed to	Baltzer, George	1812	AC28	152	114
Balch, Stephen B., of G'tn.	Deed fr	Jennings, Thomas, Louisa Co. VA	1812	AD29	154	121
Balch, Stephen B.	Deed to	Riffel, George	1812	AD29	348	292
Balch, Stephen B., of G'tn.	Deed to	Hyde, Thomas, of G'tn.	1812	AD29	080	059
Balch, Stephen B.	Deed to	Barker, Murray	1812	AD29	189	153
Balch, Stephen B.	Deed to	Allen, Samuel	1814	AG32	120	089
Balch, Stephen B., Rev.	Deed to	Cox, John	1814	AH33	338	293
Balch, Stephen B., Rev.	Deed to	Kuhns, William	1815	AI34	034	040
Balch, Stephen B.	Deed fr	Forrest, Rebecca	1816	AL36	457	432
Balch, Stephen B.	Deed to	Coulter, Peter	1816	AL36	010	010
Balch, Stephen B.	Deed to	Ott, John	1817	AN38	511	370
Balch, Stephen B.	Deed to	Bussard, Daniel	1817	AN38	210	153
Balch, Stephen B., Rev.	Deed to	Thompson, Moses	1817	AN38	119	088
Balch, Stephen Bloomer, of G'tn.	Deed fr	Holmead, Anthony, of P.G. Co.	1796	B2B	402	067
Balch, Stephen Bloomer, of G'tn.	Deed to	Calder, James, of G'tn.	1801	G7	471	607
Balch, Stephen Bloomer, Rev. et al	Deed fr	Beatty, Charles	1802	H8	560	522
Balch, Stephen Bloomer, Rev. et al	Deed fr	Deakins, Francis	1802	H8	558	520
Balch, Stephen Bloomer, of G'tn.	Deed to	Calder, James, of G'tn.	1807	T19	005	004
Balding, William, of P.G. Co.	B. of S. to	Stettenius, Samuel	1810	Z25	105	081
Baldwin, Hadley & Abigail et al	Deed to	Townsend, Henry	1801	G7	218	291
Baldwin, Hadley et al	Deed to	Cokendafer, Leonard	1798	D4	099	083

Index to District of Columbia Land Records, 1792-1817

Party	What	Party	Year	Liber	Old	New
Baldwin, Hadley et al	Deed to	Townsend, Henry	1801	G7	216	288
Baley, Jesse & Mary et al	Deed to	Kogenderfer, Leonard	1799	D4	239	221
Baley, Jesse & Mary et al	Deed to	Holmead, John	1810	Y24	180	165
Ball, Erasmus	Slave	From VA	1805	M12	102	095
Ball, Henry W.	Slaves	From VA	1810	Z25	238	186
Ball, Henry W.	Mortgage to	Whann, David, of G'tn.	1811	AB27	187	154
Ball, Henry W.	Manumis to	Henry, William (negro) & wife	1811	Z25	172	136
Ball, Henry W.	Slaves	From VA	1811	Z25	420	330
Ball, Henry W.	Mortgage to	Ringgold, Tench	1811	AB27	053	045
Ball, Henry W.	Manumis to	Henry, William (C), & wife	1812	AD29	481	407
Ball, Henry W.	B. of S. to	Fisk, James, Barre VT	1813	AE30	224	180
Ball, Henry W.	B. of S. to	McCormick, Alexander	1815	AH33	380	329
Ball, James V.	Manumis to	[ ], Isaac (C), age 36	1817	AN38	393	292
Ball, Joseph & Sarah, of Phila. PA	Deed to	Meamy, John, mariner, of Phila.	1800	E5	343	330
Ball, Joseph & Sarah, of Phila. PA	Deed to	Meany, John, mariner, of Phila.	1800	E5	347	333
Ball, Joseph, of Phila.	Deed fr	Nicholson, John & Hannah, Phila.	1795	B2A	276	387
Ball, Joseph, of Phila. et al	Deed fr	Morris, Robert & Mary, of Phila.	1797	C3	007	5
Ball, Roger James	B. of S. to	Densley, Hugh	1801	G7	042	054
Ball, Thomas, of MD	B. of S. fr	Munroe, Jonathan	1802	H8	419	386
Balmain, Andrew	Deed to	Stone, Edward	1807	S18	402	321
Balmain, Nancy C., Fairfax Co. VA	Mortgage to	Stone, Ann, of G'tn.	1813	AE30	505	374
Baltimore, Hannah (C), age 25	Cert Free fr	Clarke, William	1813	AE30	152	119
Baltimore, Theresa [Trecy] (C)	Lease fr	Van Ness, John P. & Marcia	1817	AO39	264	189
Baltimore, Treacy	Lease fr	Cloakey, Samuel	1816	AK35	525	414
Baltrie, James	B. of S. fr	Baltrie, William, of G'tn.	1815	AK35	280	
Baltrie, William, of G'tn.	B. of S. to	Baltrie, James	1815	AK35	280	
Baltzel, John, of Frederick Town	Deed to	Gary, Everard, of G'tn.	1809	W22	352	228
Baltzell, George, Frederick Co.	Deed fr	Pierce, Thomas, of G'tn.	1804	L11	404	358
Baltzer, George	Deed fr	Balch, Stephen B.	1812	AC28	152	114
Baltzer, George	Deed to	Ott, John	1813	AE30	534	396
Baltzer, George, of G'tn.	D. of T. fr	Bogenrief, Valentine, of G'tn.	1812	AC28	230	171
Baltzer, George, of G'tn.	D. of T. to	Ott, John, of G'tn.	1813	AE30	532	394
Baltzer, Jacob	B. of S. fr	Gray, Nathaniel	1806	P15	050	030
Baltzer, Jacob, of G'tn.	Deed fr	Wilson, Levi G., of G'tn.	1814	AH33	100	092
Baltzer, Jacob, of G'tn.	Deed to	Cox, John, of G'tn.	1815	AK35	091	070
Baltzer, John	Plat		1802	H8	399	
Baltzer, John	Deed fr	Beall, Thomas B.	1802	I9	377	626
Baltzer, John	Deed fr	Beall, Thomas, of George	1802	H8	397	368
Baltzer, John	Deed fr	Deakins, Leonard M.	1807	S18	405	323
Baltzer, John, heirs of	Deed fr	Beatty, Charles A., of G'tn.	1813	AF31	421	303
Baltzer, John, Jr., of G'tn.	Deed fr	Fears, Thomas & Margaret	1798	D4	116	099
Baltzer, John, Jr., of G'tn.	Deed fr	Fears, Thomas & Margaret	1801	G7	373	506
Baltzer, John, Jr.	Deed fr	Fears, Margaret, w/o Thomas	1801	G7	054	070
Baltzer, John, Jr., of G'tn.	Deed fr	Templeman, John, of G'tn.	1804	L11	173	169
Baltzer, John, Jr.	Deed fr	Wayman, Charles et al	1804	L11	079	81
Baltzer, John, of Frederick Town	Deed to	Blodget, Samuel, Jr., of G'tn.	1793	A1-2	436	44
Baltzer, John, of G'tn.	Deed fr	Brent, Daniel Carrol, marshal	1805	N13	286	234
Baltzer, John, of G'tn.	Deed fr	Murdock, Addison, of G'tn.	1805	M12	375	386
Baltzer, Margaret, of G'tn.	Deed fr	Hyde, Thomas, of G'tn.	1811	AB27	155	129
Bancker, Charles N., of Phila. PA	D. of T. to	Guest, John, mer., of Phila. PA	1812	AC28	128	096
Bancker, Charles N., of Phila. PA	Deed to	Guest, John, of Phila. Co. PA	1812	AE30	019	015
Bane, Timothy et al	Deed fr	Roe, Cornelius McDermot	1801	G7	379	511
Bank of Columbia, President of	Deed fr	Beatty, Thomas J., of G'tn.	1796	B2B	414	084
Bank of Columbia, President of	Deed fr	Beatty, Thomas J., mer., of G'tn.	1796	B2B	415	086
Bank of Columbia, President of	Deed fr	Beatty, Charles, Col.	1799	D4	332	318

Party	What	Party	Year	Liber	Old	New
Bank of Columbia, President of	Deed fr	Beatty, Charles, Col.	1799	D4	332	318
Bank of Columbia, President of	Deed fr	Turner, Samuel, Jr.	1800	E5	181	171
Bank of Columbia	Mortgage fr	Beatty, Charles, Col.	1801	G7	164	218
Bank of Columbia	Mortgage fr	Thornton, William, Dr. et al	1801	G7	162	215
Bank of Columbia	Mortgage fr	Thornton, William, Dr.	1801	G7	161	213
Bank of Columbia	Deed fr	Stoddert, Benjamin	1801	G7	353	484
Bank of Columbia	Deed to	Chandler, Walter S.	1802	G7	519	660
Bank of Columbia	Release to	Gillis, Thomas	1802	H8	484	444
Bank of Columbia	Deed fr	Stoddert, Benjamin et al	1802	H8	386	358
Bank of Columbia	Deed fr	Templeman, John et al	1802	H8	386	358
Bank of Columbia	Release to	Stoddert, Benjamin	1802	H8	452	414
Bank of Columbia	Deed to	Turner, Samuel	1802	I9	342	563
Bank of Columbia	Deed fr	Smith, Clement	1802	I9	142	214
Bank of Columbia	Release to	Abbott, John	1802	I9		018
Bank of Columbia	Deed to	Hodnott, James	1802	I9	164	248
Bank of Columbia	Release to	Blodget, Samuel	1804	K10	409	424
Bank of Columbia	Deed to	Stoddert, Benjamin	1805	M12	334	338
Bank of Columbia	Deed fr	Lingan, James M., now of G'tn.	1807	R17	380	289
Bank of Columbia	Deed fr	Turner, Samuel, Jr.	1807	R17	145	112
Bank of Columbia	Deed fr	Templeman, John, of Allegany Co.	1807	S18	346	272
Bank of Columbia	Deed fr	Templeman, John	1807	S18	356	281
Bank of Columbia	Release to	Long, Frederick	1808	U20	298	159
Bank of Columbia	Release to	Reintzel, Anthony	1811	AB27	466	381
Bank of Columbia	Deed fr	Hoye, John, of G'tn.	1811	AB27	279	228
Bank of Columbia	Release to	Greer, James	1812	AC28	179	135
Bank of Columbia	Deed to	Corporation of Georgetown	1812	AC28	460	328
Bank of Columbia	Deed to	Dodge, Francis	1812	AC28	311	227
Bank of Columbia	Release to	Fletcher, Noah	1812	AD29	309	
Bank of Columbia	Release to	Heath, Nathaniel H.	1812	AD29	356	299
Bank of Columbia	Release to	Moore, James	1812	AD29	498	420
Bank of Columbia	Release to	Doughty, William	1812	AD29	394	332
Bank of Columbia	Release to	Heath, Nathaniel H.	1813	AF31	145	097
Bank of Columbia	Release to	Beatty, Charles, Col., heirs of	1814	AG32	106	080
Bank of Columbia	Release to	Smoot, Samuel	1814	AH33	260	227
Bank of Columbia	Deed fr	Lowndes, Francis & Jane, of G'tn.	1817	AN38	300	219
Bank of the United States	Deed fr	Willing, Thomas, of PA	1802	H8	214	204
Bank of the United States	Deed to	Willing, Thomas, of Phila. et al	1811	AA26	344	230
Bank of the Metropolis	Deed fr	Jackson, John G., fr. Harrison Co.	1814	AG32	295	215
Bank of United States	D. of T. fr	Lee, Richard Bland	1817	AN38	248	181
Bank of Washington	Deed fr	Carroll, Daniel, of *Duddington*	1810	Y24	394	356
Banker, Charles N., of Phila. PA	Release fr	Campbell, William, of Fredk. Co.	1811	AC28	016	012
Banker, Charles Nicole, of Phila.	Deed fr	Teackle, Littleton Dennis, Som	1808	T19	165	117
Banker, Charles Nicole, Phila. Co.	Deed fr	Teackle, Littleton Dennis, Som.	1808	T19	034	026
Banker, Charles Nicole, Phila. Co.	Deed fr	Teackle, Littleton Dennis, of MD	1810	Y24	396	358
Banks, John	B. of S. to	Skelly, Thomas	1802	I9	424	702
Banks, John	Convey to	Herty, Thomas	1807	S18	243	192
Banks, John, insolvent	B. of S. to	Porter, James A., trustee	1808	U20	183	102
Banks, John, trustee of	Deed fr	Templeman, John	1808	U20	315	168
Banning, Anthony	Deed to	Parrott, Richard	1810	Y24	281	257
Banning, Anthony, of Talbot Co.	Deed fr	Parrott, Richard, of Balto.	1798	C3	289	234
Baptist Church of Washington	Deed fr	Templeman, John, of G'tn.	1802	H8	509	468
Barber, Henny (C)	Manumis fr	Bradford, William (Y), of G'tn.	1814	AH33	283	246
Barber, Henry, of G'tn.	Deed to	Bradford, William, of G'tn.	1814	AH33	282	245
Barber, John	Release to	Farrel, Zepheniah	1802	H8	484	446
Barber, John	Deed to	Farrell, Zephaniah	1802	H8	485	446

Index to District of Columbia Land Records, 1792-1817

Party	What	Party	Year	Liber	Old	New
Barber, John, insolvent	Deed to	Harshman, Henry	1803	K10	075	81
Barber, John, trustee	Assign fr	Harshman, Henry, insolvent	1809	V21	420	321
Barber, Luke, exr. of G. Goldie	Deed fr	Young, Jacob, of Frederick Co.	1796	B2B	448	133
Barber, Luke W. et al	Deed fr	Beatty, Charles	1802	I9	255	412
Barber, Luke W. et al	Deed fr	Reintzel, Andrew	1802	I9	256	414
Barber, Luke White, St. Mary's Co.	Deed to	Worthington, William, Jr.	1815	AK35	279	219
Barber, Mary	Deed Gift fr	McPherson, Dorathy	1807	R17	359	273
Barclay, Ann	B. of S. fr	Barclay, George	1813	AE30	513	380
Barclay, George	B. of S. to	Barclay, Ann	1813	AE30	513	380
Barclay, James, of Phila. et al	Deed fr	Skyrin, John, of Frankford PA	1806	O14	012	009
Barclay, John D. & Mary Ann	Deed fr	Reinhart, Andrew	1813	AE30	188	150
Barclay, John D.	Deed fr	Brook, Samuel, trustee of J. Little	1815	AH33	392	339
Barclay, John D.	Deed to	Brook, Samuel	1815	AH33	394	340
Barclay, John D. & Mary Ann	Deed fr	Whann, William, of G'tn.	1816	AK35	530	419
Barclay, John Davidson, s/o Thos.	Deed fr	Davidson, Samuel, of G'tn.	1797	B2B	633	393
Barclay, John et al	Deed to	Beall, Thomas & John M. Gantt	1793	A1-1	276	371
Barclay, Mary Ann	Deed fr	Barclay, Thomas	1802	I9	324	533
Barclay, Susan, w/o Thos., of NY	Deed fr	Smith, Walter, of G'tn.	1816	AM37	102	082
Barclay, Thomas	Deed to	Morsell, James S.	1799	D4	279	262
Barclay, Thomas	Deed to	Barclay, Mary Ann	1802	I9	324	533
Barclay, Thomas, insolvent	Deed to	McCormick, Alexander, trustee	1804	K10	311	315
Barclay, Thomas, of Montg. Co.	Mortgage to	Hodgson, Nicholson & Co.	1796	B2B	582	327
Barclay, Thomas, of G'tn.	Deed to	Hodgson, John, of Balto.	1797	B2B	701	485
Barclay, Thomas, of G'tn.	Deed fr	Hoban, James	1797	B2B	697	479
Barker, John, a.k.a. Murdock	Deed to	Threlkeld, John	1815	AI34	495	502
Barker, John Addison [Murdock]	Deed to	Thruston, Buckner	1815	AI34	396	419
Barker, Murray	Deed fr	Balch, Stephen B.	1812	AD29	189	153
Barker, Murray	B. of S. fr	Magruder, Samuel B., Montg. Co.	1815	AH33	440	377
Barker, Murray, of G'tn.	D. of T. to	Hyde, Thomas, of G'tn.	1812	AD29	129	099
Barker, Murry	Manumis to	Barker, Sophia & children	1817	AO39	089	071
Barker, Murry, of G'tn.	B. of S. fr	Magruder, Samuel B.	1817	AO39	090	
Barker, Sophia & children	Manumis fr	Barker, Murry	1817	AO39	089	071
Barker, Thomas (C), of G'tn.	Deed fr	Suter, Alexander, of G'tn.	1813	AF31	119	080
Barklie, Alexander, of Ire.	Deed fr	Dunlap, Alexander, of NY	1816	AL36	140	141
Barksdale, William	Cert fr	Commissioners of Washington	1800	E5	250	244
Barksdale, William	Cert fr	Commissioners of Washington	1800	E5	250	243
Barlow, Joel	Deed fr	Holmead, Anthony	1809	W22	402	262
Barlow, Joel	Deed fr	Speake, Josias M. & Sarah	1809	W22	399	260
Barlow, Joel	Deed fr	Washington, William Augustine	1809	W22	404	263
Barlow, Joel	Deed fr	Thorpe, Thomas	1810	Z25	095	071
Barlow, Joel	Deed fr	Bussard, Daniel, of G'tn.	1810	Z25	098	075
Barlow, Joel	B. of S. to	Wheaton, Joseph	1811	AB27	351	291
Barlow, Joel et al	Deed fr	Carroll, Daniel, of *Duddington*	1810	Y24	394	356
Barnes, Henry	B. of S. to	Barnes, Matthew	1805	M12	397	411
Barnes, Jesse	B. of S. to	Barnes, William H.	1816	AL36	456	431
Barnes, John	Manumis to	[ ], Peggy (C) and children	1811	AB27	072	061
Barnes, John & Catharine	B. of S. to	Duncanson, John et al	1813	AF31	471	342
Barnes, John & Catharine Connell	Deed to	Blake, James H.	1814	AG32	425	308
Barnes, John, clerk Charles Co.	Cert Free to	Thomas, Clement	1816	AL36	424	405
Barnes, John, of G'tn.	Lease fr	Dick, Margaret, of G'tn.	1810	Z25	151	119
Barnes, John, of G'tn.	Deed fr	Brown, William	1816	AM37	217	160
Barnes, John, of G'tn.	Deed to	Boyle, John	1817	AN38	291	213
Barnes, John, plt.	Suit	Brown, William, def.	1816	AM37	217	160
Barnes, John, trustee of	Deed to	Wayman, Charles, of G'tn.	1805	M12	256	258
Barnes, Matthew	B. of S. fr	Barnes, Henry	1805	M12	397	411

Party	What	Party	Year	Liber	Old	New
Barnes, Nancy (C)	Cert Free fr	Forrest, James, of St. Mary's Co.	1815	AK35	042	033
Barnes, Phebe (C), age 25	Manumis fr	Harkness, Samuel	1812	AD29	285	234
Barnes, Reason	B. of S. to	McCutchin, Thomas, of G'tn.	1809	W22	370	239
Barnes, William H.	B. of S. fr	Barnes, Jesse	1816	AL36	456	431
Barnet, Thomas & Margaret	P. of Atty. to	Wingert, Charles	1814	AH33	107	100
Barney, John H., of Balto.	B. of S. fr	Waterman, Thomas	1801	G7	437	573
Barney, John H., of G'tn.	Deed fr	Polock, Isaac, of G'tn.	1802	H8	522	482
Barney, John H.	B. of S. fr	Willson, Sarah	1802	H8	201	193
Barney, John H., of G'tn.	Deed to	Barney, Joshua	1805	M12	320	324
Barney, John H.	Discharge to	McDaniel, James (mulatto)	1805	M12	319	322
Barney, John H., insolvent	Deed to	Corcoran, Thomas, trustee	1807	R17	050	040
Barney, Joshua et al	Deed fr	Barney, John H., of G'tn.	1805	M12	320	324
Barrett, John	B. of S. to	Newman, Thomas, of P.G. Co.	1813	AF31	483	353
Barrie, Gaspard, of New Orleans	Deed fr	Willock, William, of Norfolk	1817	AN38	174	126
Barron, James	Deed fr	Stewart, John	1817	AO39	443	304
Barron, Walter	Deed fr	Berry, Hezekiah	1806	P15	122	078
Barron, Walter	Assign fr	Berry, Hezekiah	1806	P15	102½	063
Barron, Walter	B. of S. fr	Berry, Hezekiah	1806	P15	111	069
Barron, Walter	Deed fr	Threlkeld, John	1813	AE30	443	329
Barron, Walter et al	Deed fr	Weatherall, John	1799	D4	426	398
Barron, Walter et al	B. of S. fr	Caffrey, Daniel	1802	H8	508	467
Barron, Walter, of St. Mary's Co.	D. of T. to	King, Charles	1813	AF31	373	268
Barron, William H.	Cert Slaves	From Prince William Co. VA	1817	AO39	067	055
Barry, Garret	Deed fr	Scott, Michael, now of Balto.	1805	N13	222	190
Barry, Garrett	Deed to	Law, Thomas	1806	P15	036	022
Barry, Garrett	Deed fr	Law, Thomas	1806	P15	034	021
Barry, Garrett	Deed to	Barry, James D.	1807	R17	244	184
Barry, James	Cert fr	Commissioners of Washington	1796	B2B	451	137
Barry, James	Cert fr	Commissioners of Washington	1796	B2A	339	478
Barry, James	Cert fr	Commissioners of Washington	1796	B2B	451	137
Barry, James	Deed fr	Forrest, Uriah & Samuel Hanson	1801	G7	003	004
Barry, James	Agreement	Barry, Redmond & Garrett	1801	G7	203	271
Barry, James	Deed to	Ross, Charles & John Simpson	1801	G7	145	191
Barry, James	Deed fr	Commissioners of Washington	1801	G7	468	604
Barry, James	Deed fr	Fitzhugh, William, s/o William	1801	G7	288	399
Barry, James	Deed to	Barry, Redmond & Garrett	1801	F6	193	124
Barry, James	Deed fr	Carroll, Daniel, of *Duddington*	1801	G7	233	311
Barry, James	Deed fr	Hoxton, Stanislaus, of MD	1802	G7	537	682
Barry, James	Deed fr	O'Brien, James	1802	H8	235	224
Barry, James	Deed fr	Carroll, Margaret, of Balto. et al	1802	H8	599	566
Barry, James	Deed fr	Stewart, William, of G'tn.	1802	H8	232	221
Barry, James	Deed to	O'Brien, James	1802	H8	346	323
Barry, James	Deed fr	May, Frederick, Dr.	1802	H8	445	409
Barry, James	Deed to	Booth, John & Jeremiah	1802	H8	590	556
Barry, James	Deed to	Perry, James, of Trinidad	1802	I9	032	042
Barry, James	Deed fr	Smith, Robert & Samuel, Balto.	1804	K10	256	262
Barry, James	Deed fr	Morsell, James Sewall, trustee	1804	K10	214	224
Barry, James	Deed fr	Coles, John, of New London CN	1804	K10	169	179
Barry, James	Deed fr	Brent, Robert, guardian	1806	O14	288	191
Barry, James	Deed fr	Young, Notley, heirs of	1806	O14	284	188
Barry, James	Receipt fr	Hoxton, Stanislaus, of P.G. Co.	1806	O14	186	121
Barry, James	Cert fr	Munroe, Thomas, Supt.	1806	O14	382	255
Barry, James	Deed fr	Munroe, Thomas	1806	O14	383	255
Barry, James	Deed fr	Hoxton, Stanislaus, of P.G. Co.	1806	O14	183	120
Barry, James	Deed to	Johnson, Joseph et al	1806	Q16	310	237

Index to District of Columbia Land Records, 1792-1817

Party	What	Party	Year	Liber	Old	New
Barry, James	Indemnify fr	Law, Thomas	1806	Q16	302	230
Barry, James	Mortgage to	Wheat, Joseph	1807	Q16	351	270
Barry, James & Johanna, of NY	Deed to	May, Frederick	1807	S18	320	251
Barry, James D.	Deed fr	Law, Thomas	1802	I9	441	729
Barry, James D.	Deed fr	Greenleaf, James	1804	L11	349	316
Barry, James D.	Deed fr	Barry, Garrett	1807	R17	244	184
Barry, James D. et al	Lease fr	Law, Thomas	1808	T19	093	066
Barry, James D.	Deed to	Olliver, John, of Balto.	1809	W22	091	128
Barry, James D.	Deed fr	Ross, Charles, of Phila. et al	1809	W22	087	064
Barry, James D.	Mortgage to	Carroll, Daniel, of *Duddington*	1810	Y24	404	364
Barry, James D.	Release fr	Oliver, John, of Balto.	1811	AB27	475	388
Barry, James D.	Deed fr	Law, Thomas & Edmund	1811	AB27	355	294
Barry, James D. & S. Pleasonton	Deed fr	Bowie, Washington	1816	AL36	484	456
Barry, James David	Deed fr	Law, Thomas	1804	L11	344	312
Barry, James David	Deed to	May, Frederick et al	1804	L11	346	313
Barry, James et al	Deed fr	Fitzhugh, William, s/o William	1799	D4	250	234
Barry, James et al	Deed to	Harrison, William, of Balto.	1800	E5	335	323
Barry, James, for *St. Elisabeth*	Cert Surv	Fenwick, George	1806	O14	187	122
Barry, James, heirs	Deed fr	Forrest, Uriah & Samuel Hanson	1801	G7	002	003
Barry, James, mer., of Balto.	Cert fr	Commissioners of Washington	1797	B2B	469	161
Barry, James, mer., of Balto.	Deed fr	Smith, Robert, attorney, of Balto.	1799	D4	171	152
Barry, James, mer.	Deed fr	Crawford, Nathaniel, Gent.	1800	F6	055	034
Barry, James, of Balto.	Deed fr	Young, Notley	1795	B2A	203	278
Barry, James, of Balto.	Deed to	Simpson, John, of Phila.	1796	B2B	491	185
Barry, James, of Balto.	Deed fr	Carroll, Daniel, of *Duddington*	1796	B2B	490	183
Barry, James, of Balto.	Deed fr	Scott, Gustavus, of G'tn.	1796	B2B	489	182
Barry, James, of Balto.	Deed fr	Law, Thomas	1796	E5		224
Barry, James, of Balto.	Deed to	Harrison, William, of Balto.	1796	B2B	492	186
Barry, James, of Balto.	Cert fr	Commissioners of Washington	1796	B2B	454	141
Barry, James, of Balto.	Deed fr	Carroll, Daniel, of *Duddington*	1797	C3	096	79
Barry, James, of Balto.	Deed fr	Carroll, Daniel, of *Duddington*	1797	C3	229	191
Barry, James, of Balto.	Deed fr	Law, Thomas	1798	C3	278	225
Barry, James, of Balto.	Deed fr	Patton, James, mer., of Alexa.	1798	C3	448	352
Barry, James, of Balto.	Cert fr	Commissioners of Washington	1799	D4	387	369
Barry, James, of Balto.	Cert fr	Commissioners of Washington	1799	D4	386	369
Barry, James, of Balto.	Deed fr	Commissioners of Washington	1799	E5	044	034
Barry, James, of Balto.	Deed fr	Commissioners of Washington	1799	E5	039	029
Barry, James, of Balto.	Deed fr	Patton, James, of Alexa.	1799	E5	043	033
Barry, James, of Balto.	Deed fr	Commissioners of Washington	1799	E5	041	031
Barry, James, of Balto.	Deed fr	Johnson, Thomas, Frederick Co.	1800	E5	200	193
Barry, James, of Balto.	Deed to	Ross, Charles & John Simpson	1800	E5	187	178
Barry, James, of NY	Deed fr	Ford, Lewis	1806	Q16	077	049
Barry, James [Bury]	Lease fr	May, Frederick	1812	AB27	516	422
Barry, John, of Montg. Co.	Deed fr	Parrott, Richard, of Balto.	1798	C3	293	237
Barry, Nathan	Cert fr	Commissioners of Washington	1796	B2A	339	478
Barry, Redmond & Garrett	Agreement	Barry, James	1801	G7	203	271
Barry, Redmond & Garrett	Deed fr	Barry, James	1801	F6	193	124
Barry, Redmond & Garrett	Deed fr	Law, Thomas	1801	G7	140	184
Barry, Richard	Deed fr	Thornton, William	1813	AE30	289	220
Barry, Richard	Deed to	Pairo, Thomas W.	1813	AE30	343	256
Barry, Richard	Deed fr	Pairo, Thomas W.	1813	AE30	287	219
Barry, Robert, of Balto.	Deed fr	Brent, Daniel Carroll, marshal	1805	M12	055	052
Barry, Thomas Johnson, of G'tn.	Deed to	Carr, Overton	1799	D4	390	371
Barry,Garett P.	B. of S. fr	Hays, Laurence	1804	L11	020	19
Bartleman, William, of Alexa.	Deed fr	Fallon, Edward & John Kearney	1804	K10	125	135

Party	What	Party	Year	Liber	Old	New
Barwin, Thomas	Deed to	Peter, David, of G'tn.	1807	R17	194	147
Bassett, John & Betty Carter	Deed to	Andrews, George	1811	AA26	288	195
Bassett, John & Betty Carter	Deed to	Grammar, Frederick, of Annapolis	1811	Z25	375	294
Bassett, John, Hanover Co. VA	Deed to	Nourse, Joseph	1817	AN38	425	318
Bassett, John, of VA	Deed fr	Van Ness, John P. & Marcia	1808	U20	190	105
Bastian, Charles	Manumis to	[ ], Will (Negro)	1805	N13	084	077
Bastian, Charles, insolvent	Deed to	McClan, Robert	1804	K10	200	208
Bastian, Charles, trustee	B. of S. fr	Norris, William, insolvent	1805	M12	405	429
Bates, David	Lease fr	Young, Thomas	1809	W22	074	055
Bates, David	Deed fr	Slater, Charles, of Wmsn. Co. TN	1812	AD29	048	035
Bates, David	D. of T. fr	Cooper, John	1813	AE30	211	171
Bates, David	Deed fr	Corporation of Washington	1815	AK35	142	110
Bates, David	D. of T. fr	Hamilton, Letty H.	1815	AK35	098	076
Bates, David	Deed fr	Corporation of Washington	1815	AK35	135	104
Bates, David	Deed fr	Corporation of Washington	1815	AK35	137	106
Bates, David	Deed fr	Corporation of Washington	1815	AK35	140	108
Bates, David	Deed fr	Corporation of Washington	1815	AK35	147	113
Bates, David	Deed fr	Corporation of Washington	1815	AK35	144	111
Bates, David	Deed fr	Corporation of Washington	1815	AK35	156	120
Bates, David	Deed fr	Corporation of Washington	1815	AK35	161	124
Bates, David, constable	Deed to	Young, Thomas	1808	U20	405	226
Bates, David, constable	Deed to	Stephenson, James S. et al	1811	AA26	084	060
Bath Houses to be erected	Bond	Shuck, Frederick, of Alexa. Co.	1813	AE30	436	322
Baum & Pritchard	Deed fr	Hesler, Joseph	1802	I9	547	889
Baum, John C. et al	Deed fr	Gilpin, Bernard, of Montg. Co.	1807	R17	376	286
Baum, John C., of G'tn.	Deed fr	Deakins, Francis, exors. et al	1809	V21	201	142
Baum, John C.	Qualify	Ensign of a light infantry	1812	AD29	216	177
Baum, John C., of G'tn.	D. of T. to	Cookendaffer, Thomas	1817	AN38	463	334
Bausman, Benjamin et al	Deed fr	Link, Adam & Jane, Jefferson Co.	1811	AB27	128	105
Bausman, Benjamin, of Balto.	Deed to	Thompson, John C., of G'tn.	1813	AF31	124	084
Bayard, John Hodge & Rebecca	Deed to	Dorsey, Joshua, of Frederick Co.	1799	E5	069	056
Bayard, John Hodge & Rebecca	Deed to	Beatty, Charles, Sr.	1800	E5	115	102
Bayard, William et al	Release to	Nourse, Joseph	1813	AF31	011	008
Bayer, Michael & Peter Engle	Deed fr	Beall, Thomas & John M. Gantt	1792	A1-1	086	126
Bayley, Jesse	Deed fr	Beatty, Charles, heirs of	1806	Q16	163	108
Bayley, Jesse	Deed to	Pierce, Isaac	1808	T19	287	210
Bayley, Mary	Deed fr	Renner, Daniel & Daniel Bussard	1812	AD29	175	140
Bayley, Mary, of G'tn.	Deed to	Renner, Daniel, of G'tn.	1812	AD29	147	115
Bayley, Mountjoy & Elizabeth et al	Deed to	Beatty, Charles, Sr.	1800	E5	115	102
Bayley, Robert, s/o William	Deed to	Ott, John, Dr., of G'tn.	1808	T19	172	123
Bayley, William	Deed to	Magruder, George, of G'tn.	1798	D4	146	128
Bayley, William et al	Deed to	Tillotson, Thomas, of NY	1795	B2A	255	356
Bayley, William, Jr., of Balto.	Deed to	Ott, John, Dr., of G'tn.	1808	T19	173	122
Bayley, William, Sr.	Deed to	Ott, John, Dr.	1808	T19	170	170
Bayly, Daniel	Deed fr	Carroll, Daniel, of *Duddington*	1804	K10	294	296
Bayly, Daniel	Deed fr	Frank, George	1804	K10	158	169
Bayly, Jesse et al	Deed fr	Upperman, Henry, of G'tn.	1801	G7	030	038
Bayly, Jesse, of G'tn.	Deed fr	Threlkeld, John, of G'tn.	1794	B2A	145	192
Bayly, Mountejoy & Elizabeth et al	Deed to	Dorsey, Joshua, of Frederick Co.	1799	E5	069	056
Bayly, Mountjoy	P. of Atty. to	Warring, Marsham	1801	G7		314
Bayly, Mountjoy	Lease fr	Munroe, Thomas, Supt.	1813	AF31	192	130
Bayly, Mountjoy	Lease to	Dobbins, David	1813	AF31	194	131
Bayly, Mountjoy	Assign to	Law, John	1813	AF31	201	136
Bayly, Mountjoy	Lease to	Tuckfield, William H.P.	1813	AF31	197	133
Bayly, Mountjoy	D. of T. to	Carr, Overton	1817	AO39	255	184

Index to District of Columbia Land Records, 1792-1817

Party	What	Party	Year	Liber	Old	New
Bayly, Mountjoy, Gen., Frederick	Deed to	Lingan, James McCubbin, G'tn.	1801	G7	234	313
Bayly, Mountjoy, of Frederick Co.	Deed fr	Dorsey, Joshua, of Frederick Co.	1800	E5	282	276
Bayly, Mountjoy, of NY	Deed fr	Shoemaker, Charles, of MD	1802	I9	071	100
Bayly, William	Deed to	Stoddert, Benjamin, of G'tn.	1794	B2A	099	129
Bayly, William	Deed to	Lingan, James M., of G'tn.	1795	B2A	192	261
Bayly, William	Deed to	Weems, John, Dr., of G'tn.	1795	B2A	256	358
Bayly, William	Deed to	Beatty, Thomas J., of G'tn.	1795	B2A	191	259
Bayly, William	Deed fr	Standage, Eleazer	1795	B2A	266	372
Bayly, William	Deed to	Threlkeld, John	1795	B2A	177	239
Bayly, William	Deed fr	Standage, Eleazer	1796	B2B	421	094
Bayly, William	Deed to	Combs, Joseph	1799	D4	297	280
Bayly, William	Cert fr	Commissioners of Washington	1799	D4	300	284
Bayly, William	Deed to	Stras, George F., of VA	1799	D4	339	326
Bayly, William	Deed to	Beatty, Charles	1800	E5	283	277
Bayly, William	Deed to	Reintzel, Andrew, of Fairfax Co.	1800	E5		139
Bayly, William	Deed fr	Lingan, James Macubbin, of G'tn.	1800	E5	079	066
Bayly, William	Deed to	Young, Notley & Clement Hill	1800	E5	315	305
Bayly, William	Deed to	Digges, George, trustees of	1800	E5	315	305
Bayly, William	Deed fr	Lowndes, Francis & Charles	1800	E5	237	230
Bayly, William	Deed to	Mackall, Walter, of Calvert Co.	1800	F6	002	002
Bayly, William	Discharge		1802	I9	401	666
Bayly, William	B. of S. to	Addison, Francis Key	1817	AO39	197	145
Bayly, William, def.	Suit	Kirby, John Baptist & Francis, plt.	1810	Z25	023	019
Bayly, William et al	Deed to	Tillotson, Thomas, of NY	1794	B2A	094	123
Bayly, William et al	Deed to	Templeton, John	1794	B2A	097	127
Bayly, William et al	Deed fr	Duncanson, William Mayne et al	1797	C3	103	84
Bayly, William et al	Deed to	Marbury, William	1802	H8	362	337
Bayly, William, of P.G. Co.	Deed fr	Coombs, Joseph, of P.G. Co.	1795	B2B	356	003
Bayly, William, of P.G. Co.	Lease to	Beatty, Thomas J., of G'tn.	1796	B2B	609	363
Bayly, William, of P.G. Co.	Deed to	Threlkeld, John, of Mont. Co.	1796	B2B	382	038
Bayly, William, of P.G. Co.	Deed to	Lynch, Dominick & Comfort Sands	1796	B2B	384	040
Bayly, William, of P.G. Co.	Deed fr	Stoddert, Benjamin, of G'tn.	1798	C3	515	405
Bayly, William, of P.G. Co.	Deed fr	French, George, of Montg. Co.	1798	C3	389	309
Bayly, William, of P.G. Co.	Deed to	Kirby, John Baptist & Francis	1810	Z25	020	016
Bayne, Elsworth, of P.G. Co.	B. of S. to	Guss, Charles	1807	R17	353	269
Bayne, Horatio & Elizabeth	Deed to	Gray, Catharine, infant d/o Wm.	1815	AI34	310	343
Bayne, Horatio et al	Bond to	United States	1809	X23	316	253
Beal, Samuel, of G'tn.	Lease to	Mackall, Leonard, of G'tn.	1811	AA26	303	205
Beale, George	Deed fr	Law, Thomas	1813	AF31	003	002
Beale, George, mer.	Deed fr	Maltby, Sarah, now of Phila.	1814	AG32	388	282
Beale, Samuel, of G'tn.	Deed fr	Jones, Charles, of Montg. Co.	1812	AC28	299	218
Beale, Thomas K.	Mortgage to	Orr, Benjamin G. et al	1802	I9	145	219
Beale, Thomas K.	Deed to	Van Ness, John P.	1802	I9	327	539
Beale, Thomas K.	Deed to	Blount, George	1802	I9	426	706
Beale, Thomas K.	Deed fr	Roberts, Owen	1802	H8	051	048
Beale, William D.	Lease to	Glasco, John	1802	I9	220	348
Beall, Acquila et al	Deed to	Beall, Lewis	1803	K10	089	95
Beall, Alexander, of Frederick Co.	Deed to	Hazel, Jeremiah	1804	K10	237	245
Beall, Alexander Robert, of GA	Deed to	Beall, Samuel, of Montg. Co.	1810	X23	372	299
Beall, Alfred, Uriah & Elizabeth	Deed fr	Law, Thomas	1812	AD29	337	281
Beall, Ann (M)	Cert Free fr	Duncastle, Sally	1813	AE30	157	124
Beall, Aquila	B. of S. fr	Brice, Ann	1802	I9	291	477
Beall, Aquila, of P.G. Co.	Manumis to	[ ], Sall (negro)	1806	Q16	305	232
Beall, Aquila, of Montg. Co.	Manumis to	[ ], Charity (C) and others	1814	AH33	077	069
Beall, Basil B.	B. of S. to	Chandler, Walter S.	1807	R17	054	043

Index to District of Columbia Land Records, 1792-1817

Party	What	Party	Year	Liber	Old	New
Beall, Basil D.	B. of S. to	Magruder, George B.	1807	R17	087	069
Beall, Basil D.	B. of S. to	Richardson, David K.	1807	R17	287	219
Beall, Basil M., Montg. Co. et al	Deed to	Reinhart, Andrew	1805	O14	088	055
Beall, Basil M., of Montg. Co.	Deed to	Beall, James, s/o James	1813	AE30	439	325
Beall, Benjamin	B. of S. to	Matten, Ann	1814	AH33	177	163
Beall, Benjamin (C), age 32	Cert Free fr	Beall, Washington	1814	AH33	003	003
Beall, Betsey (C)	Manumis fr	Wadsworth, Elizabeth	1814	AH33	001	001
Beall, Betsey (M)	Cert Free fr	Duncastle, Sally	1813	AE30	157	124
Beall, Brooke, heirs of	Agreement	Beall, Brooke, heirs of	1802	I9	439	726
Beall, Daniel & Ann, of Montg. Co.	Deed to	Smith, Samuel Harrison	1808	T19	184	131
Beall, Elijah	Deed fr	Davidson, John, of Annapolis	1799	D4	399	378
Beall, Elijah	Deed to	Reintzel, Anthony	1802	I9	446	737
Beall, Elijah et al	Deed fr	Long, John, of G'tn.	1799	D4	209	192
Beall, Elijah, of Montg. Co.	Deed fr	Dorsey, William H., of Montg. Co.	1798	C3	359	288
Beall, Elijah, of Loudoun Co. VA	Deed to	Long, John, of G'tn.	1808	T19	148	104
Beall, Ely	Deed fr	Beall, Thomas, of George	1801	G7	393	526
Beall, Ely & Octavia, Fred. Co. VA	Deed to	Littler, Nathan, Frederick Co. VA	1806	P15	015	009
Beall, George	Deed to	Stoddert, Benjamin, of G'tn.	1793	A1-1	180	255
Beall, George	Manumis fr	Addison, Thomas Grafton	1801	G7		330
Beall, George	Manumis to	[ ], Cloe (negro) and 4 children	1807	R17	352	268
Beall, George	Manumis to	Hill, Lethy (mulatto)	1807	S18	180	146
Beall, George	Slaves	From VA	1810	X23	359	287
Beall, George	Deed fr	Laird, John, exr. of J. Carleton	1814	AG32	046	037
Beall, George	Manumis to	Beall, James	1816	AK35	363	286
Beall, George & Moses Liverpool	Deed to	Adams, Henry & Nicholas Franklin	1810	Y24	301	274
Beall, George & Moses Liverpoole	Deed fr	Chandler, Jacob	1810	Y24	068	061
Beall, George & Moses Liverpool	Deed to	Franklin, Nicholas	1814	AG32	165	118
Beall, George, s/o Col. George	Deed to	Beall, Thomas	1792	A1-1	117	171
Beall, George, Sr.	Deed fr	Beall, Thomas, of George	1794	B2A	013	014
Beall, George, Sr.	Deed fr	Beall, Patrick Sim, of P.G. Co.	1805	N13	113	108
Beall, Gustavus	D. of T. to	English, David	1817	AN38	345	254
Beall, Gustavus, of G'tn.	Deed fr	Boarman, Eleanor, wid., of G'tn.	1816	AL36	212	219
Beall, Gustavus, of G'tn.	Convey fr	Milligan, Joseph, of G'tn.	1817	AN38	344	253
Beall, Hezekiah, Berkeley Co. VA	Deed fr	Beall, Thomas Brooke, of G'tn.	1798	C3	378	301
Beall, Hezekiah, Jefferson Co. VA	Deed to	Brooke, Thomas A.	1806	P15	119	076
Beall, Hezekiah, Jefferson Co. VA	Mortgage fr	Peter, John, mer., of G'tn.	1809	W22	276	184
Beall, Hezekiah, Jefferson Co. VA	Deed fr	Fleet, Henry, of G'tn.	1809	W22	367	237
Beall, Hezekiah, Jefferson Co. VA	Deed to	Peter, John, mer., of G'tn.	1809	W22	327	212
Beall, Hezekiah, of Montg. Co.	Deed to	Brown, Robert, of P.G. Co.	1798	C3	472	372
Beall, Hezekiah, of Loudoun Co.	B. of S. to	Fleet, Henry, of G'tn.	1812	AD29	474	401
Beall, James	Deed fr	Ward, William	1802	I9	380	631
Beall, James	Manumis fr	Beall, George	1816	AK35	363	286
Beall, James, s/o James	Deed fr	Stoddart, Benjamin et al	1793	A1-1	319	421
Beall, James, s/o James	Deed to	Beall, Thomas & John M. Gantt	1793	A1-1	321	422
Beall, James, s/o James	Deed fr	Beall, Basil M., of Montg. Co.	1813	AE30	439	325
Beall, John	Deed to	Beall, Thomas & John M. Gantt	1793	A1-1	381	488
Beall, John	Deed fr	Stoddert, Benjamin & W. Deakins	1793	A1-1	378	485
Beall, John, of G'tn.	Deed to	Gibbs, Nicholas, of G'tn.	1793	A1-1	193	272
Beall, Joshua	Deed to	Greenfield, Walter T., of P.G. Co.	1811	Z25	123	096
Beall, Joshua	Deed fr	Greenfield, Walter T., of P.G. Co.	1811	Z25	126	098
Beall, Lewis	Deed fr	Beall, Upton et al	1803	K10	089	95
Beall, Lloyd et all	Deed fr	Holmead, Anthony	1800	E5	238	232
Beall, Margery, Frederick Co. VA	Deed to	Stewart, William, of G'tn.	1808	T19	080	057
Beall, Nancy et al	Deed to	Smith, Clement	1811	Z25	478	379
Beall, Ninian	Deed to	Burns, Benjamin	1812	AC28	181	136

Party	What	Party	Year	Liber	Old	New
Beall, Ninian & Benjamin Burns	Deed fr	Bickley, Robert S., of Phila. PA	1810	Y24	264	243
Beall, Ninian & George Crandell	Deed fr	Sutton, Robert, of PA	1810	Y24	303	276
Beall, Ninian & Benjamin Burnes	Deed fr	Bickley, Robert S., of Phila. PA	1812	AD29	031	022
Beall, Patrick	Deed to	Dunlop, James, of G'tn.	1792	A1-1	112	163
Beall, Patrick	Deed to	Beall, Thomas	1792	A1-1	116	170
Beall, Patrick, of P.G. Co.	Deed to	Stoddert, Benjamin, Montg. Co.	1797	B2B	656	419
Beall, Patrick Sim, of P.G. Co.	Deed to	Beall, George, Sr.	1805	N13	113	108
Beall, Robert Lemar	Deed to	Laird, John, of G'tn.	1794	B2A	139	183
Beall, Samuel, of G'tn.	Deed fr	Owings, Christopher, of G'tn.	1805	N13	385	308
Beall, Samuel, of G'tn.	Deed fr	Dodge, Allen & Francis, of G'tn.	1809	V21	236	168
Beall, Samuel, of G'tn.	Deed to	Webster, Toppan	1809	V21	347	251
Beall, Samuel, of Montg. Co.	Deed fr	Beall, Alexander Robert, of GA	1810	X23	372	299
Beall, Samuel, of G'tn.	Lease to	Kile, Alexander, of G'tn.	1811	AB27	132	109
Beall, Samuel, of G'tn.	Deed fr	Jones, Charles C., of Montg. Co.	1815	AK35	037	029
Beall, Samuel, of G'tn.	Lease to	Harris, Joseph (C)	1815	AI34	525	529
Beall, Samuel, of Montg. Co.	B. of S. to	Wilmington, John, of G'tn.	1816	AL36	309	305
Beall, Thomas	Deed fr	Beall, Patrick	1792	A1-1	116	170
Beall, Thomas	Deed fr	Beall, George, s/o Col. George	1792	A1-1	117	171
Beall, Thomas	Deed to	McAlister, Richard	1793	A1-1	359	
Beall, Thomas	P. of Atty. fr	Shellman, John, Sr., Fredk. Co.	1793	A1-2	409	18
Beall, Thomas	Deed to	Jenkins, Thomas	1802	I9	290	476
Beall, Thomas	Deed to	McCleary, Henry	1802	I9	513	840
Beall, Thomas	Deed to	Waters, William	1802	I9	522	853
Beall, Thomas	Deed to	Calder, James	1802	I9	522	855
Beall, Thomas	Deed to	Evans, William et al	1802	I9	196	305
Beall, Thomas	Deed to	Kurtz, Christian	1802	I9	521	852
Beall, Thomas	Deed to	Ritchie, Abner	1802	I9	512	839
Beall, Thomas	Deed to	McCleary, Henry	1802	I9	542	884
Beall, Thomas	Deed to	Hedges, Nicholas	1802	I9	292	479
Beall, Thomas	Deed fr	Trundle, Horatio, of G'tn.	1816	AL36	416	399
Beall, Thomas & John M. Gantt	Deed fr	Brogden, William et al	1792	A1-1	052	77
Beall, Thomas & John M. Gantt	Deed fr	Young, Notley & George Digges	1792	A1-1	042	63
Beall, Thomas & John M. Gantt	Deed fr	Mantz, John, of Frederick Co.	1792	A1-1	070	103
Beall, Thomas & John M. Gantt	Deed fr	Doll, Conrad, of Frederick Co.	1792	A1-1	084	123
Beall, Thomas & John M. Gantt	Deed fr	Markell, William, s/o Conrad	1792	A1-1	163	234
Beall, Thomas & John M. Gantt	Deed fr	Lingenfelter, Ann, wid/o John	1792	A1-1	088	129
Beall, Thomas & John M. Gantt	Deed fr	Beard, Margaret et al	1792	A1-1	110	160
Beall, Thomas & John M. Gantt	Deed fr	Craik, James & Richard Conway	1792	A1-1	057	85
Beall, Thomas & John M. Gantt	Deed fr	Myer, Henry & Frederick Reahl	1792	A1-1	090	131
Beall, Thomas & John M. Gantt	Deed fr	Byer, Jacob	1792	A1-1	072	106
Beall, Thomas & John M. Gantt	Deed fr	Miller, Samuel, of Frederick Co.	1792	A1-1	098	143
Beall, Thomas & John M. Gantt	Deed fr	Holmead, Anthony	1792	A1-1	007	12
Beall, Thomas & John M. Gantt	Deed fr	Lingan, James McCubbin	1792	A1-1	022	34
Beall, Thomas & John M. Gantt	Deed fr	Boarman, Raphael	1792	A1-1	064	94
Beall, Thomas & John M. Gantt	Deed fr	Beatty, Thomas, of Frederick Co.	1792	A1-1	100	146
Beall, Thomas & John M. Gantt	Deed fr	Schell, Charles, of Frederick Co.	1792	A1-1	135	196
Beall, Thomas & John M. Gantt	Deed fr	Shellman, John, St., Frederick Co.	1792	A1-1	096	140
Beall, Thomas & John M. Gantt	Deed fr	Davidson, Samuel	1792	A1-1	027	41
Beall, Thomas & John M. Gantt	Deed fr	Johnson, James & Roger	1792	A1-1	047	71
Beall, Thomas & John M. Gantt	Deed fr	Slater, Jonathan	1792	A1-1	032	48
Beall, Thomas & John M. Gantt	Deed fr	Koontz, Henry, Andrew Low et al	1792	A1-1	102	148
Beall, Thomas & John M. Gantt	Deed fr	Magruder, John Read, merchant	1792	A1-1	119	173
Beall, Thomas & John M. Gantt	Deed fr	McCleery, Henry, of Frederick Co.	1792	A1-1	139	202
Beall, Thomas & John M. Gantt	Deed fr	Hooe, Robert Townsend, Alexa.	1792	A1-1	055	81
Beall, Thomas & John M. Gantt	Deed fr	Walker, George	1792	A1-1	017	27

Party	What	Party	Year	Liber	Old	New
Beall, Thomas & John M. Gantt	Deed fr	Carroll, Daniel	1792	A1-1	012	19
Beall, Thomas & John M. Gantt	Deed fr	Johnson, Thomas & Daniel Carroll	1792	A1-1	044	66
Beall, Thomas & John M. Gantt	Deed fr	Porter, Samuel & James Steret	1792	A1-1	141	205
Beall, Thomas & John M. Gantt	Deed fr	Pierce, James	1792	A1-1	035	52
Beall, Thomas & John M. Gantt	Deed fr	Beatty, Charles, Sr.	1792	A1-1	128	186
Beall, Thomas & John M. Gantt	Deed fr	Brent, George, of Stafford Co. VA	1792	A1-1	037	56
Beall, Thomas & John M. Gantt	Deed fr	Smith, Amos, of Frederick Co.	1792	A1-1	080	117
Beall, Thomas & John M. Gantt	Deed fr	Beatty, Charles	1792	A1-1	025	38
Beall, Thomas & John M. Gantt	Deed fr	Bayer, Michael & Peter Engle	1792	A1-1	086	126
Beall, Thomas & John M. Gantt	Deed fr	Stoddert, Benjamin	1792	A1-1	005	8
Beall, Thomas & John M. Gantt	Deed fr	Walter, Henry, of Frederick Co.	1792	A1-1	082	120
Beall, Thomas & John M. Gantt	Deed fr	Murdock, George	1792	A1-1	133	193
Beall, Thomas & John M. Gantt	Deed fr	Young, William	1792	A1-1	003	5
Beall, Thomas & John M. Gantt	Deed fr	Young, Abraham	1792	A1-1	029	45
Beall, Thomas & John M. Gantt	Deed fr	Price, John & Michael Stooker	1792	A1-1	106	154
Beall, Thomas & John M. Gantt	Deed fr	Woodard, Clement	1792	A1-1	015	23
Beall, Thomas & John M. Gantt	Deed fr	Ott, Adam, of Washington Co.	1792	A1-1	131	190
Beall, Thomas & John M. Gantt	Deed fr	Rench, John, of Washington Co.	1792	A1-1	137	199
Beall, Thomas & John M. Gantt	Deed fr	Raymer, Michael & Joseph Doll	1792	A1-1	076	112
Beall, Thomas & John M. Gantt	Deed fr	Davison, Elias	1792	A1-1	110	160
Beall, Thomas & John M. Gantt	Deed fr	Beall, William Murdock	1792	A1-1	159	227
Beall, Thomas & John M. Gantt	D. of T. fr	Morton, Thomas	1792	A1-1	046	68
Beall, Thomas & John M. Gantt	Deed fr	Young, Notley	1792	A1-1	010	16
Beall, Thomas & John M. Gantt	Deed fr	Jacques, Denton	1792	A1-1	144	207
Beall, Thomas & John M. Gantt	Deed fr	Kolb, Michael, Jr.	1792	A1-1	074	109
Beall, Thomas & John M. Gantt	Deed fr	Cramphin, Thomas	1792	A1-1	049	73
Beall, Thomas & John M. Gantt	Deed fr	Thomas, Philip	1792	A1-1	147	212
Beall, Thomas & John M. Gantt	Deed fr	Strever, Joachim, Frederick Co.	1792	A1-1	094	137
Beall, Thomas & John M. Gantt	Deed fr	Peter, Robert	1792	A1-1	020	30
Beall, Thomas & John M. Gantt	Deed fr	Neale, James, s/o Bernard	1792	A1-1	059	88
Beall, Thomas & John M. Gantt	Deed fr	Grahame, Richard, Calvert Co.	1792	A1-1	061	90
Beall, Thomas & John M. Gantt	Deed fr	Thomas, Philip et al	1792	A1-1	108	157
Beall, Thomas & John M. Gantt	Deed fr	Shover, Barbara, wid/o Simon	1792	A1-1	104	152
Beall, Thomas & John M. Gantt	Deed fr	Stewart, Charles & Jas. McCulloch	1793	A1-1	348	453
Beall, Thomas & John M. Gantt	Deed fr	Warring, Henry, devisee of Bazil	1793	A1-1	374	481
Beall, Thomas & John M. Gantt	Deed fr	Coolidge, Samuel Judson	1793	A1-1	307	406
Beall, Thomas & John M. Gantt	Deed fr	Hill, Henry	1793	A1-1	354	460
Beall, Thomas & John M. Gantt	Deed fr	Brookes, John Smith	1793	A1-1	305	404
Beall, Thomas & John M. Gantt	Deed fr	Anderson, George et al	1793	A1-1	317	418
Beall, Thomas & John M. Gantt	Deed fr	Warring, Marsham et al	1793	A1-1	371	478
Beall, Thomas & John M. Gantt	Deed fr	Hemsley, William & Sarah	1793	A1-1	251	342
Beall, Thomas & John M. Gantt	Deed fr	Klinger, Henry	1793	A1-1	369	476
Beall, Thomas & John M. Gantt	Deed fr	Davidson, Samuel	1793	A1-1	358	464
Beall, Thomas & John M. Gantt	Deed fr	Lee, Thomas Sim & Mary	1793	A1-1	259	351
Beall, Thomas & John M. Gantt	Deed fr	Richmond, Christopher, in Phila.	1793	A1-1	279	374
Beall, Thomas & John M. Gantt	Deed fr	Hill, Henry, of Phila. PA	1793	A1-1	289	386
Beall, Thomas & John M. Gantt	Deed fr	Ridenhour, David	1793	A1-1	323	425
Beall, Thomas & John M. Gantt	Deed fr	Mantz, Frs., Peter, David, Isaac	1793	A1-1	256	348
Beall, Thomas & John M. Gantt	Deed fr	Tilghman, Peregrine	1793	A1-1	206	288
Beall, Thomas & John M. Gantt	Deed fr	Matthews, Daniel, of VA	1793	A1-1	261	354
Beall, Thomas & John M. Gantt	Deed fr	Fowler, Jubb, of Anne Arundel Co.	1793	A1-1	233	321
Beall, Thomas & John M. Gantt	Deed fr	Stuart, Charles	1793	A1-1	247	337
Beall, Thomas & John M. Gantt	Deed fr	Manavill, Patrick & Mary	1793	A1-1	361	468
Beall, Thomas & John M. Gantt	Deed fr	Schnebley, Henry	1793	A1-1	364	471
Beall, Thomas & John M. Gantt	Deed fr	Ham, Peter	1793	A1-1	237	326

Index to District of Columbia Land Records, 1792-1817   23

Party	What	Party	Year	Liber	Old	New
Beall, Thomas & John M. Gantt	Deed fr	Scyle, John, of G'tn.	1793	A1-1	315	415
Beall, Thomas & John M. Gantt	Deed fr	Clagett, Hezekiah	1793	A1-1	249	339
Beall, Thomas & John M. Gantt	Deed fr	Beall, John	1793	A1-1	381	488
Beall, Thomas & John M. Gantt	Deed fr	Johns, Lingan, Deakins et al	1793	A1-1	227	314
Beall, Thomas & John M. Gantt	Deed fr	Brice, John, of Annapolis	1793	A1-1	346	451
Beall, Thomas & John M. Gantt	Deed fr	Ferrell, James	1793	A1-1	333	437
Beall, Thomas & John M. Gantt	Deed fr	Wolgamoth, John	1793	A1-1	366	473
Beall, Thomas & John M. Gantt	Deed fr	Magrath, William	1793	A1-1	313	412
Beall, Thomas & John M. Gantt	Deed fr	Beall, James, s/o James	1793	A1-1	321	422
Beall, Thomas & John M. Gantt	Deed fr	Tilghman, James, of Q.A. Co.	1793	A1-1	282	377
Beall, Thomas & John M. Gantt	Deed fr	Addison, John, Jr. & Thomas G.	1793	A1-1	213	297
Beall, Thomas & John M. Gantt	Deed fr	Flick, Andrew, of Orange Co. VA	1793	A1-1	296	393
Beall, Thomas & John M. Gantt	Deed fr	Dulany, Walter	1793	A1-1	217	303
Beall, Thomas & John M. Gantt	Deed fr	Beanes, William	1793	A1-1	300	399
Beall, Thomas & John M. Gantt	Deed fr	Hall, Benjamin & Elizabeth C.	1793	A1-1	267	360
Beall, Thomas & John M. Gantt	Deed fr	Medtart, Jacob, of Frederick	1793	A1-1	231	318
Beall, Thomas & John M. Gantt	Deed fr	Crawford, David & Nathaniel	1793	A1-1	298	396
Beall, Thomas & John M. Gantt	Deed fr	Mackie, Ebenezer et al	1793	A1-1	292	389
Beall, Thomas & John M. Gantt	Deed fr	Addison, Walter D.	1793	A1-1	211	294
Beall, Thomas & John M. Gantt	Deed fr	Carroll, Charles, of *Carrollton*	1793	A1-1	215	300
Beall, Thomas & John M. Gantt	Deed fr	Earle, James, of Kent Co.	1793	A1-1	287	383
Beall, Thomas & John M. Gantt	Deed fr	Hairy, David, exr. of Martin	1793	A1-1	351	456
Beall, Thomas & John M. Gantt	Deed fr	Hepburn, Samuel	1793	A1-1	329	432
Beall, Thomas & John M. Gantt	Deed fr	Ross, David, Horatio & Archibald	1793	A1-1	254	345
Beall, Thomas & John M. Gantt	Deed fr	Johnson, Thomas & Ph. Thomas	1793	A1-1	389	496
Beall, Thomas & John M. Gantt	Deed fr	Adams, Margaret	1793	A1-1	272	366
Beall, Thomas & John M. Gantt	Deed fr	Williams, Thomas Owen	1793	A1-1	327	429
Beall, Thomas & John M. Gantt	Deed fr	Dick, Mason & Thomas	1793	A1-1	309	408
Beall, Thomas & John M. Gantt	Deed fr	Steuart, John	1793	A1-1	204	285
Beall, Thomas & John M. Gantt	Deed fr	Golden, Samuel, s/o Frederick	1793	A1-1	383	490
Beall, Thomas & John M. Gantt	Deed fr	Scott, Upton	1793	A1-1	208	291
Beall, Thomas & John M. Gantt	Deed fr	Milliken, Mark	1793	A1-1	187	265
Beall, Thomas & John M. Gantt	Deed fr	Buchanan, Thomas	1793	A1-1	302	401
Beall, Thomas & John M. Gantt	Deed fr	Leeke, Ann	1793	A1-1	331	434
Beall, Thomas & John M. Gantt	Deed fr	Garlick, Joseph	1793	A1-1	336	439
Beall, Thomas & John M. Gantt	Deed fr	Calvert, Elizabeth	1793	A1-1	220	306
Beall, Thomas & John M. Gantt	Deed fr	Barclay, Petit, Poland	1793	A1-1	276	371
Beall, Thomas & John M. Gantt	Deed fr	Davidson, John, of Annapolis	1793	A1-1	224	311
Beall, Thomas & John M. Gantt	Deed fr	Campbell, Francis et al	1793	A1-1	274	369
Beall, Thomas & John M. Gantt	Deed fr	Tilghman, Richard, of Q.A. Co.	1793	A1-1	270	363
Beall, Thomas & John M. Gantt	Deed fr	Hollyday, James, of Q.A. Co.	1793	A1-1	284	380
Beall, Thomas & John M. Gantt	Deed fr	Fitzhugh, William	1793	A1-2	443	52
Beall, Thomas & John M. Gantt	Deed fr	Casey, John	1793	A1-2	406	15
Beall, Thomas & John M. Gantt	Deed fr	King, William	1793	A1-2	433	42
Beall, Thomas & John M. Gantt	Deed fr	Jenifer, Daniel, Jr., devisee of D.	1793	A1-2	409	18
Beall, Thomas & John M. Gantt	Deed fr	Worman, Henry, of Frederick Co.	1793	A1-2	440	49
Beall, Thomas & John M. Gantt	Deed fr	Hoffman, Jacob, of Balto.	1793	A1-2	421	30
Beall, Thomas & John M. Gantt	Deed fr	Bowie, Fielder et al	1793	A1-2	392	1
Beall, Thomas & John M. Gantt	Deed fr	Zeller, Jacob	1793	A1-2	413	22
Beall, Thomas & John M. Gantt	Deed fr	Warring, Basil	1793	A1-2	429	37
Beall, Thomas & John M. Gantt	Deed fr	Chiswell, Joseph N.	1793	A1-2	426	34
Beall, Thomas & John M. Gantt	Deed fr	Tilley, John	1793	A1-2	401	9
Beall, Thomas & John M. Gantt	Deed fr	Peter, Robert	1793	A1-2	395	3
Beall, Thomas & John M. Gantt	Deed fr	McDade, John & Milley of Balto.	1794	A1-2	479	84
Beall, Thomas & John M. Gantt	Deed to	Commissioners of Washington	1797	B2B	615	372

Index to District of Columbia Land Records, 1792-1817

Party	What	Party	Year	Liber	Old	New
Beall, Thomas & Elijah, of G'tn.	Deed to	McCleery, Henry, of Frederick	1801	G7	088	114
Beall, Thomas B., of G'tn.	Deed to	Craig, Robert, of G'tn.	1797	C3	147	120
Beall, Thomas B., of George, G'tn.	Deed to	Thompson, John, Capt., G'tn.	1800	E5	268	262
Beall, Thomas B., s/o George	Deed fr	Brooke, Samuel	1802	G7	505	645
Beall, Thomas B., of George	Deed to	Fields, William	1802	H8	035	033
Beall, Thomas B., of G'tn.	Deed to	Scott, William	1802	H8	003	003
Beall, Thomas B.	Deed fr	Beall, Thomas, of George	1802	H8	274	260
Beall, Thomas B.	Deed to	Parrott, Richard	1802	I9	356	588
Beall, Thomas B.	Deed to	Baltzer, John	1802	I9	377	626
Beall, Thomas B.	Deed fr	Speake, Josias M.	1802	I9	304	500
Beall, Thomas B.	Deed to	Corcoran, James	1802	I9	467	769
Beall, Thomas B.	Deed fr	Thompson, John	1802	I9	162	245
Beall, Thomas B. et al	Deed to	Hofman, Richard	1802	I9	374	620
Beall, Thomas B.	Deed to	Riggs, George W.	1802	I9	315	518
Beall, Thomas B.	Deed to	Duby, John	1802	I9	352	581
Beall, Thomas B., of G'tn.	Deed to	Fields, William, of G'tn.	1804	K10	174	183
Beall, Thomas B., trustee	Deed to	Wilson, Zadock, of Montg. Co.	1804	K10	352	365
Beall, Thomas B., of G'tn.	Deed to	Dixon, Thomas, of G'tn.	1804	K10	199	207
Beall, Thomas B., of G'tn.	Deed to	Renner, Daniel & Daniel Bussard	1804	K10	107	114
Beall, Thomas B., of G'tn.	Deed to	Fields, William, of G'tn.	1805	M12	383	395
Beall, Thomas B., trustee	Deed to	Thompson, George	1805	N13	262	218
Beall, Thomas B., trustee	Deed to	Patterson, Benjamin	1805	O14	142	092
Beall, Thomas B.	Deed to	Smith, William	1805	M12	215	217
Beall, Thomas B., of G'tn.	Deed to	Waters, William, of Fairfax Co. VA	1806	O14	342	228
Beall, Thomas B.	Deed to	McDaniel, James	1807	R17	298	227
Beall, Thomas B.	Deed to	McDaniel, Leonard	1807	R17	299	228
Beall, Thomas B.	Deed to	Wineberger, George	1808	T19	286	209
Beall, Thomas B.	Deed to	Ober, Robert	1808	T19	161	113
Beall, Thomas B.	Deed to	Fields, William	1808	T19	129	092
Beall, Thomas B., of G'tn.	Deed to	Morris, Nathaniel, of G'tn.	1808	U20	130	074
Beall, Thomas B.	Deed to	Fields, William	1808	U20	159	090
Beall, Thomas B., of G'tn.	Deed to	Huber, Andrew, of G'tn.	1808	V21	041	031
Beall, Thomas B., Capt.	Deed fr	Beall, Thomas, of Erasmus	1808	V21	008	006
Beall, Thomas B., of G'tn.	Deed fr	Morsell, James S., of G'tn. et al	1809	W22	083	061
Beall, Thomas B.	Deed to	Lipscomb, John, of G'tn.	1809	X23	167	123
Beall, Thomas B., of G'tn.	Mortgage fr	Peter, John, mer., of G'tn.	1809	W22	279	186
Beall, Thomas B., of G'tn.	Deed to	Lanham, Elisha, of G'tn.	1810	Y24	253	233
Beall, Thomas B., of G'tn.	Deed to	Dixon, Thomas, of G'tn.	1810	Y24	060	053
Beall, Thomas B., of G'tn.	Deed to	Fields, William, of G'tn.	1810	Z25	335	261
Beall, Thomas B., of G'tn.	Deed to	Gaines, Richard, of G'tn.	1810	Y24	044	038
Beall, Thomas B.	Deed fr	Maxwell, George	1811	AB27	431	355
Beall, Thomas B.	Deed to	Walker, Nathan, of MD	1811	AC28	004	003
Beall, Thomas B., of G'tn.	Deed to	Davis, James, of MD	1811	Z25	542	431
Beall, Thomas B.	B. of S. fr	Balch, Stephen B., of G'tn.	1811	AB27	345	286
Beall, Thomas B., of G'tn.	Lease to	Trundle, Horatio, of G'tn.	1813	AF31	315	225
Beall, Thomas B., of G'tn.	Deed to	McCutchen, Thomas, of G'tn.	1813	AF31	384	276
Beall, Thomas B., of G'tn.	Deed fr	Gaines, Richard, of Cincinnati OH	1813	AE30	309	232
Beall, Thomas B., of G'tn.	Lease to	Lanham, Elisha, of G'tn.	1814	AG32	396	288
Beall, Thomas B. et al	Deed to	Bussard, Daniel	1815	AH33	397	343
Beall, Thomas B., of G'tn.	Deed to	Lanham, Elisha, of G'tn.	1816	AM37	158	121
Beall, Thomas B. & C.A. Burnett	D. of T. fr	Davis, Richard, of G'tn.	1816	AM37	421	302
Beall, Thomas B., of G'tn.	B. of S. to	Morsell, James S.	1816	AL36	432	412
Beall, Thomas Brooke	Deed fr	Beall, Thomas, of George	1794	B2A	015	016
Beall, Thomas Brooke	Deed to	Greenfield, Gabriel	1795	B2A	179	242
Beall, Thomas Brooke, of G'tn.	Deed to	Peter, Robert, of G'tn.	1796	B2B	547	272

Index to District of Columbia Land Records, 1792-1817

Party	What	Party	Year	Liber	Old	New
Beall, Thomas Brooke, Montg. Co.	Deed to	Morris, Randal, of Montg. Co.	1797	C3	190	160
Beall, Thomas Brooke, of G'tn.	Deed to	Beall, Hezekiah, Berkeley Co. VA	1798	C3	378	301
Beall, Thomas Brooke, of G'tn.	Deed to	Beck, Joseph, of G'tn.	1798	C3	409	324
Beall, Thomas Brooke, of G'tn.	Deed fr	Beall, Thomas, of George, G'tn.	1802	G7	571	720
Beall, Thomas Brooke, Capt.	Deed to	Wilson, John, of MD	1805	O14	005	005
Beall, Thomas Brooke	Deed to	Wilson, Isaac & Levey G.	1806	O14	291	193
Beall, Thomas Brooke	Deed fr	Beall, Thomas, of George	1806	Q16	166	110
Beall, Thomas Brooke, of G'tn.	Deed to	Smith, Anthony, of P.G. Co.	1807	S18	324	254
Beall, Thomas Brooke	Deed to	Doyle, John B., of Phila. PA	1807	R17	335	255
Beall, Thomas Brooke	Deed to	Wilson, Lancelot, of Henry	1808	T19	391	277
Beall, Thomas Brooke, exr. of G.	Manumis to	Fleet, Rachel (negro)	1808	U20	225	121
Beall, Thomas Brooke, of G'tn.	Lease to	McCutchen, Thomas	1812	AD29	235	195
Beall, Thomas Brooke	Deed fr	Davidson, Lewis Grant	1814	AG32	398	290
Beall, Thomas Brooke	B. of S. to	Morsell, James S.	1815	AI34	032	037
Beall, Thomas Brooke, of G'tn.	Deed fr	Davis, Richard, of G'tn.	1815	AI34	040	047
Beall, Thomas et al	Deed fr	Wishair, Appetonia, wid/o George	1792	A1-1	092	134
Beall, Thomas et al	Deed fr	Fisher, Margaret, wid/o Adam	1792	A1-1	078	115
Beall, Thomas et al	Deed to	Beatty, Thomas Johnson	1793	A1-1	185	262
Beall, Thomas et al	Deed to	Beatty, Thomas, Jr.	1793	A1-1	181	257
Beall, Thomas et al	Deed fr	Reintzel, Anthony, of G'tn.	1793	A1-1	183	259
Beall, Thomas et al	Deed fr	Hanson, Alexander Contee	1797	C3	095	78
Beall, Thomas et al	Deed to	Lee, Thomas Sim, of G'tn.	1799	D4	190	173
Beall, Thomas et al	Deed fr	Beatty, John M. et al	1805	N13	011	012
Beall, Thomas K.	Mortgage to	Willis, John	1802	I9		188
Beall, Thomas K.	Assign to	Cooper, Isaac	1803	K10	080	86
Beall, Thomas M. & John M. Gantt	Deed fr	Henderson, Richard	1793	A1-1	202	282
Beall, Thomas, of George, G'tn.	Deed to	Atkinson, John, shoemaker	1792	A1-1	150	216
Beall, Thomas, of George et al	Deed fr	Burnes, David	1792	A1-1	002	1
Beall, Thomas, of George, G'tn.	Deed to	Man, George, of Annapolis	1793	A1-1	265	358
Beall, Thomas, of George	Deed to	Man, George, of Annapolis	1793	A1-2	445	54
Beall, Thomas, of George, of G'tn.	Deed to	Gregg, Joshua, of G'tn.	1793	A1-2	457	66
Beall, Thomas, of George, of G'tn.	Deed to	Connelly, Thomas, of G'tn.	1793	A1-2	452	60
Beall, Thomas, of George	Deed to	Laird, John	1793	A1-1	311	411
Beall, Thomas, of George, of G'tn.	Deed to	Hedges, Nicholas, of G'tn.	1794	A1-2	471	77
Beall, Thomas, of George	Deed fr	Stoddert, Benjamin	1794	A1-2	491	94
Beall, Thomas, of George	Deed to	Davis, Charles	1794	A1-2	487	90
Beall, Thomas, of George	Deed to	Dorsey, William H.	1794	A1-2	485	88
Beall, Thomas, of George	Deed to	Brookes, Henry	1794	B2A	158	208
Beall, Thomas, of George	Deed to	Davidson, Craik & Dorsey	1794	B2A	054	067
Beall, Thomas, of George	Deed to	Beall, George, Sr.	1794	B2A	013	014
Beall, Thomas, of G'tn.	Deed to	Craigg, Robert, of G'tn.	1794	B2A	112	149
Beall, Thomas, of George	Deed to	Davidson, Samuel	1794	B2A	053	065
Beall, Thomas, of George	Deed to	Upperman, Henry	1794	B2A	154	203
Beall, Thomas, of George	Deed to	Orme, Lucy	1794	B2A	043	051
Beall, Thomas, of George	Deed to	Stoddert, Benjamin	1794	B2A	059	074
Beall, Thomas, of George	Deed to	Beall, Thomas Brooke	1794	B2A	015	016
Beall, Thomas, of George	Deed to	Lowndes, Francis	1794	B2A	019	019
Beall, Thomas, of George	Deed fr	Stoddert, Peter, Lee, Beatty et al	1795	B2A	166	222
Beall, Thomas, of George et al	Lease to	Bowman, Peter	1795	B2A	353	499
Beall, Thomas, of George	Deed to	Williams, Samuel, cooper	1795	B2A	206	283
Beall, Thomas, of George	Deed to	Weems, John, Dr.	1795	B2A	258	360
Beall, Thomas, of George	Deed to	Williams, Elisha O.	1795	B2A	205	281
Beall, Thomas, of George, G'tn.	Deed to	King, William, of G'tn.	1795	B2A	201	275
Beall, Thomas, of George.	Deed to	Reintzel, Daniel	1795	B2B	363	012
Beall, Thomas, of George	Deed to	Kurtz, Christian	1795	B2B	359	007

Party	What	Party	Year	Liber	Old	New
Beall, Thomas, of George	Deed to	Magruder, William B.	1795	B2B	355	002
Beall, Thomas, of George, G'tn.	Deed to	Lucas, Henry, of G'tn.	1795	B2B	354	001
Beall, Thomas, of George	Deed to	Casanave, Peter, of Montg. Co.	1796	B2B	509	213
Beall, Thomas, of George, of G'tn.	Deed to	White, Andrew, of G'tn.	1796	B2B	566	303
Beall, Thomas, of George et al	Lease to	Middleton, Joseph et al	1796	B2B	508	211
Beall, Thomas, of George	Deed to	Reintzel, Daniel	1796	B2B	522	233
Beall, Thomas, of George	Deed to	Lingan, Nicholas	1796	B2B	441	122
Beall, Thomas, of George	Deed to	Casanave, Peter, of Montg. Co.	1796	B2B	510	214
Beall, Thomas, of George	Deed to	Casanave, Peter, of Montg. Co.	1796	B2B	511	216
Beall, Thomas, of George, of G'tn.	Deed to	Lee, Thomas Sim, of G'tn.	1796	B2B	607	360
Beall, Thomas, of George	Deed to	Davidson, Samuel, of Montg. Co.	1797	C3	055	45
Beall, Thomas, of Samuel	Deed to	Forrest, Uriah, of Montg. Co.	1797	C3	062	50
Beall, Thomas, of George, farmer	Deed to	Deakins, Leonard, of P.G. Co.	1797	B2B	644	405
Beall, Thomas, of Samuel	Deed to	Dunlop, James, of Montg. Co.	1797	C3	119	97
Beall, Thomas, of George	Deed to	Beatty, Charles	1798	C3	432	339
Beall, Thomas, of George	Deed fr	Stoddert, Benjamin	1798	C3	450	353
Beall, Thomas, of George, of G'tn.	Deed to	Lee, Thomas Sim, of G'tn.	1798	C3	423	333
Beall, Thomas, of George	Deed to	Plater, Thomas	1798	C3	436	342
Beall, Thomas, of George	Deed to	Slater, Thomas	1798	C3	466	367
Beall, Thomas, of George, of G'tn.	Deed to	Magruder, Patrick, of G'tn.	1798	C3	443	348
Beall, Thomas, of George	Deed to	Threlkeld, Sarah	1798	C3	477	376
Beall, Thomas, of George, farmer	Deed to	Craik, William, Gent.	1798	D4	067	057
Beall, Thomas, of Samuel et al	Deed to	O'Reilly, Henry	1799	D4	290	273
Beall, Thomas, of George, of G'tn.	Deed to	Turner, Samuel, Jr., of G'tn.	1800	E5	192	184
Beall, Thomas, of George	Deed to	Dorsey, William H.	1800	E5	401	374
Beall, Thomas, of George, of G'tn.	Deed to	Mackall, Walter, of Calvert Co.	1800	E5	128	116
Beall, Thomas, of George, of G'tn.	Deed to	Lingan, James Maccubbin, of G'tn.	1800	F6	001	001
Beall, Thomas, of George	Deed fr	Dorsey, William Hammond	1800	E5	276	270
Beall, Thomas, of George	Deed to	Dorsey, William H.	1800	E5	165	154
Beall, Thomas, of George	Deed to	Dorsey, William Hammond	1801	G7	250	339
Beall, Thomas, of George et al	Deed to	Nourse, Joseph	1801	G7	073	095
Beall, Thomas, of George	Deed to	Lingan, Nicholas	1801	F6	157	098
Beall, Thomas, of George et al	Deed fr	Pearce, Isaac	1801	G7	143	189
Beall, Thomas, of George	Deed to	Beall, Ely	1801	G7	393	526
Beall, Thomas, of George	Deed to	Nourse, Joseph	1801	G7	116	148
Beall, Thomas, of George et al	Lease to	Corcoran, Thomas	1801	G7	175	233
Beall, Thomas, of George	Deed to	Peter, Robert	1801	G7	302	421
Beall, Thomas, of George	Deed to	Rigdon, Thomas	1801	G7	255	347
Beall, Thomas, of George et al	Deed to	Nourse, Joseph	1801	G7	372	504
Beall, Thomas, of George	Plat		1802	H8	399	
Beall, Thomas, of George	Deed to	Gant, John Mackall	1802	H8	327	306
Beall, Thomas, of George	Deed to	Baltzer, John	1802	H8	397	368
Beall, Thomas, of George	Deed to	Beall, Thomas B.	1802	H8	274	260
Beall, Thomas, of George	Deed to	Lingan, James Maccubbin	1802	H8	319	300
Beall, Thomas, of George, G'tn.	Deed to	Beall, Thomas Brooke, of G'tn.	1802	G7	571	720
Beall, Thomas, of George	Deed to	Plater, John Rousby	1802	H8	320	301
Beall, Thomas, of George	Deed to	White, James, of Montg. Co.	1803	K10	065	70
Beall, Thomas, of George	Deed to	Parrott, Richard	1804	L11	052	53
Beall, Thomas, of George, G'tn.	Deed to	Gantt, John M., of P.G. Co.	1804	L11	142	143
Beall, Thomas, of George	Deed to	Smith, William, joiner	1804	L11	353	319
Beall, Thomas, of George, G'tn.	Deed to	Gantt, John M., of P.G. Co.	1804	L11	143	144
Beall, Thomas, of George	Deed to	Davidson, Samuel	1804	L11	055	56
Beall, Thomas, of George, G'tn.	Deed to	Luffborough, Nathan, of G'tn.	1804	M12	010	011
Beall, Thomas, of George	Deed to	Dorsey, William H.	1804	M12	042	041
Beall, Thomas, of George	Deed to	Upperman, Henry, Jr.	1805	M12	400	413

Index to District of Columbia Land Records, 1792-1817   27

Party	What	Party	Year	Liber	Old	New
Beall, Thomas, of George	Deed to	Shorter, John & John Shorter (C)	1805	M12	164	162
Beall, Thomas, of George	Deed to	Lee, Thomas Sim	1805	M12	061	057
Beall, Thomas, of George	Exchange	Wilson, Lancelot	1805	M12	359	367
Beall, Thomas, of George	Deed to	Williams, Harriet, w/o Capt. Elisha	1805	M12	398	411
Beall, Thomas, of George	B. of S. fr	Wilson, Lancelot	1805	M12	359	367
Beall, Thomas, of George	B. of S. fr	Wilson, Lancelot	1805	M12	092	085
Beall, Thomas, of George	Deed to	Love, Sarah	1805	M12	374	384
Beall, Thomas, of George et al	Deed to	Morgan, William	1805	N13	299	243
Beall, Thomas, of George	Deed fr	Peter, John, admr. of John	1805	N13	231	196
Beall, Thomas, of George, G'tn.	Deed to	Lee, Thomas Sim, of G'tn.	1805	N13	378	303
Beall, Thomas, of George	Deed to	Mackall, Christianna, w/o Benj.	1805	O14	083	051
Beall, Thomas, of George	Deed to	Wirt, John, joiner	1806	O14	240	156
Beall, Thomas, of George, of G'tn.	Deed to	Cox, John, mer., of G'tn.	1806	P15	276	182
Beall, Thomas, of George	Deed to	Beatty, John M. & Charles A.	1806	P15	025	015
Beall, Thomas, of George, of G'tn.	Deed fr	Riggs, Elisha	1806	P15	369	246
Beall, Thomas, of George, trustee	Deed to	Williams, Elisha W., mer.	1806	P15	337	223
Beall, Thomas, of George, of G'tn.	Deed to	Dyer, Henry O.	1806	P15	340	224
Beall, Thomas, of George	Deed to	Beall, Thomas Brooke	1806	Q16	166	110
Beall, Thomas, of George	Deed to	Bloice, Jonathan	1806	Q16	330	253
Beall, Thomas, of George	Deed to	Fleet, Henry, black man	1807	S18	038	032
Beall, Thomas, of George	Deed fr	Calder, James	1807	S18	383	305
Beall, Thomas, of George	Deed to	Calder, James	1807	T19	006	005
Beall, Thomas, of George	Deed to	Smith, William, joiner	1807	Q16	338	259
Beall, Thomas, of George et al	Deed to	Threlkeld, John	1807	R17	073	059
Beall, Thomas, of George	Agreement	Rowles, Joseph E., for mill dam	1808	T19	178	126
Beall, Thomas, of George	Deed to	Magruder, George	1808	T19	133	094
Beall, Thomas, of George	Deed to	Rowles, Joseph E.	1808	U20	376	207
Beall, Thomas, of George	Deed to	Heath, Nathaniel H.	1808	U20	382	211
Beall, Thomas, of Erasmus	Deed to	Beall, Thomas B., Capt.	1808	V21	008	006
Beall, Thomas, of George	Deed to	Bussard, Daniel	1808	V21	131	096
Beall, Thomas, of George	Deed to	Eliason, Ebenezer	1809	V21	295	214
Beall, Thomas, of George, of G'tn.	Deed to	Magruder, George, of G'tn.	1809	V21	159	114
Beall, Thomas, of George	Deed to	Magruder, Middleton B. et al	1809	W22	396	258
Beall, Thomas, of George	Deed to	Riggs, George Washington	1809	W22	363	235
Beall, Thomas, of George	Deed to	English, David	1809	W22	340	220
Beall, Thomas, of George, of G'tn.	Deed to	Nourse, Joseph, of G'tn.	1809	W22	239	162
Beall, Thomas, of George	Deed to	Deakins, Leonard M. & John Hoye	1809	W22	140	099
Beall, Thomas, of George, of G'tn.	Deed to	Beall, Thomas B., of G'tn.	1809	W22	083	061
Beall, Thomas, of George	Deed to	Tenny, Isaac & Robert Ober	1809	X23	089	066
Beall, Thomas, of George	Deed to	Crommett, Mary Ann, of G'tn.	1809	X23	271	213
Beall, Thomas, of George	Deed to	Smith, Andrew	1810	Y24	217	199
Beall, Thomas, of George	Deed to	Nourse, Charles J.	1810	Y24	214	196
Beall, Thomas, of George	Deed fr	Parrott, Richard	1810	Y24	188	173
Beall, Thomas, of George	Deed to	Heath, Nathaniel	1810	Z25	084	064
Beall, Thomas, of George	Deed to	Hedges, Nicholas	1810	Y24	468	414
Beall, Thomas, of Geo. et al	Deed to	Beverly, Robert	1811	AA26	036	028
Beall, Thomas, of Geo.	Deed to	Peter, George	1811	AB27	361	300
Beall, Thomas, of Geo.	Deed to	Nourse, Joseph	1811	AB27	204	167
Beall, Thomas, of Geo.	Deed to	Dixon, James	1811	AB27	294	241
Beall, Thomas, of Geo.	Deed to	English, David	1811	AB27	295	242
Beall, Thomas, of Geo.	Plat	Mill Street	1811	AB27	206	
Beall, Thomas, of Geo.	Deed to	Peter, John	1811	AC28	043	032
Beall, Thomas, of George et al	Deed to	Smith, Clement	1811	Z25	478	379
Beall, Thomas, of Geo., of G'tn.	Deed to	Dodge, Francis, of G'tn.	1812	AD29	484	409
Beall, Thomas, of Geo.	Deed to	Davidson, Lewis Grant	1812	AD29	370	312

Index to District of Columbia Land Records, 1792-1817

Party	What	Party	Year	Liber	Old	New
Beall, Thomas, of Geo.	Deed to	French, Charles	1812	AC28	483	344
Beall, Thomas, of Geo.	Deed to	Foxall, Henry	1812	AC28	419	301
Beall, Thomas, of Geo., of G'tn.	Deed to	Peckham, Caleb, of G'tn.	1813	AE30	386	285
Beall, Thomas, of Geo.	Deed to	Parrott, Richard	1813	AE30	085	065
Beall, Thomas, of Geo., of G'tn.	Deed to	Riggs, Romulus, of G'tn.	1814	AH33	500	429
Beall, Thomas, of Geo.	Deed to	Wingard, Abraham	1814	AH33	085	077
Beall, Thomas, of Geo.	Deed to	Shepperd, Lodowick	1814	AH33	044	040
Beall, Thomas, of Geo., of G'tn.	Deed to	Dodge, Francis, of G'tn.	1815	AK35	429	336
Beall, Thomas, of Geo., of G'tn.	Deed to	English, David	1816	AL36	516	483
Beall, Thomas, of Geo., of G'tn.	Deed to	Reinagle, Anna	1816	AL36	096	097
Beall, Thomas, pf George	Deed to	Corporation of Georgetown	1798	D4	145	127
Beall, Thomas, Sr., of George	Deed to	Brookes, William H.	1804	K10	137	149
Beall, Upton & Lewis	Deed to	Williams, Elisha O. et al	1802	I9	576	933
Beall, Upton et al	Deed to	Beall, Lewis	1803	K10	089	95
Beall, Upton, of Montg. Co.	Manumis to	[ ], Yarrow (negro)	1807	R17	264	201
Beall, Upton, of Montg. Co.	D. of T. fr	Williams, Harriet	1810	X23	365	293
Beall, Warring	B. of S. to	Kedglie, Ann	1817	AN38	391	290
Beall, Washington	Cert Free to	Beall, Benjamin (C), age 32	1814	AH33	003	003
Beall, William D.	Certificate	Brigade Major, Inspector of Militia	1805	M12	132	127
Beall, William D.	B. of S. to	Nicholls, William S., of G'tn.	1809	V21	353	255
Beall, William D.	Deed to	Beatty, Charles A., Dr.	1809	W22	272	182
Beall, William Dent, bookkeeper	Convey to	Smith, Clement	1807	S18	366	287
Beall, William M., Jr., of Fredk. Co.	Deed fr	Simpson, John, of G'tn.	1814	AG32	289	210
Beall, William Murdock	Deed fr	Brandenburgher, Christopher	1792	A1-1	161	230
Beall, William Murdock, farmer	Deed fr	Engles, Peter, of Frederick Co.	1792	A1-1	125	183
Beall, William Murdock	Deed to	Beall, Thomas & John M. Gantt	1792	A1-1	159	227
Beall, William Murdock	Deed fr	Stoddert, Benjamin & W. Deakins	1793	A1-1	379	486
Beall, William Murdock, Frdk. Co.	Deed fr	Turner, Thomas, of G'tn.	1800	E5	246	239
Beall, William Murdock, Jr.	Deed fr	Crown, Samuel T.	1812	AD29	158	124
Beall, William T. & Eleanor	Deed to	Van Horn, Archibald & Elizabeth A.	1806	P15	240	160
Beall, Zachariah & Samuel	Deed to	Key, Philip Barton, of Annapolis	1797	B2B	627	386
Beall, Zebedee et al	Deed to	Beall, James, s/o James	1813	AE30	439	325
Bealle, Thomas K.	Lease fr	Lovell, William	1802	I9	503	825
Bean, Arey Minty	Deed fr	Law, Thomas	1816	AL36	501	470
Bean, Colmore	Qualify	Ensign in first legion of militia	1812	AD29	397	335
Bean, George	B. of S. fr	McCormick, Benson L.	1806	O14	162	106
Bean, John	B. of S. fr	Bean, Richard	1808	U20	378	208
Bean, John	B. of S. fr	Bean, Richard	1813	AE30	132	103
Bean, John	Deed fr	Bean, Richard	1813	AE30	131	102
Bean, John	Deed fr	Farrell, Zephaniah	1814	AH33	075	067
Bean, John	Deed fr	Kirby, John B.	1816	AL36	086	087
Bean, Mary	B. of S. fr	Bean, Timothy, her father	1812	AD29	012	009
Bean, Richard	B. of S. to	Bean, John	1808	U20	378	209
Bean, Richard	Deed to	Bean, John	1813	AE30	131	102
Bean, Richard	B. of S. to	Bean, John	1813	AE30	132	103
Bean, Samuel	B. of S. to	Forrest, Alexander	1811	AB27	409	337
Bean, Timothy	B. of S. to	Bean, Mary, his daughter	1812	AD29	012	009
Beanes, William	Deed fr	Beall, Thomas & John M. Gantt	1793	A1-1	300	399
Beans, Colmore	Manumis to	[ ], Flora (C), d/o Monica	1811	AB27	163	135
Beans, Colmore	Manumis to	[ ], Anna (C)	1815	AG32	347	251
Beans, Colmore	Manumis to	[ ], Scipio	1815	AG32	457	330
Beans, William B.	Receipt	[ ], Polly (negro)	1806	P15	381	254
Bearcroft, William, of G'tn.	Deed fr	Craik, William, of Alexa., exr. of	1809	V21	243	173
Beard, Lewis	Certificate	Justice of Peace, Rowan Co. NC	1809	V21	318	233
Beard, Margaret et al	Deed fr	Beall, Thomas & John M. Gantt	1792	A1-1	110	160

Index to District of Columbia Land Records, 1792-1817

Party	What	Party	Year	Liber	Old	New
Beatth, Charles, heirs of	Deed to	Stoddert, Benjamin	1806	P15	094	058
Beatty & Hawkins Addition to G.T.	List		1798	K10	001	
Beatty & Hawkins Addition to G.T.	Description		1798	K10	008	
Beatty, Charles	Deed to	Beall, Thomas & John M. Gantt	1792	A1-1	025	38
Beatty, Charles	Deed fr	Beall, Thomas, of George	1798	C3	432	339
Beatty, Charles	Deed to	Nourse, Joseph, of Phila.	1799	D4	184	165
Beatty, Charles	Deed fr	Hanson, Alexander Contee	1799	D4	234	216
Beatty, Charles	Deed fr	Graff, John, s/o Michael, of PA	1799	D4	384	367
Beatty, Charles	Deed to	Brookes, William	1800	E5	170	159
Beatty, Charles	Deed to	Reintzel, Andrew, of Fairfax Co.	1800	E5	085	072
Beatty, Charles	Deed fr	Bayly, William	1800	E5	283	277
Beatty, Charles	Deed to	Clements, Elizabeth, of G'tn.	1801	G7	352	483
Beatty, Charles	Deed fr	Clark, James & Elizabeth, of PA	1801	G7	137	181
Beatty, Charles	Deed to	Nourse, Joseph	1802	G7	567	716
Beatty, Charles	Deed to	Offutt, Ozias	1802	H8	072	067
Beatty, Charles	Deed to	Upperman, Henry	1802	H8	113	109
Beatty, Charles	Deed to	Ritchie, Abner	1802	H8	442	406
Beatty, Charles	Lease to	Renner, Daniel et al	1802	H8	191	183
Beatty, Charles	Deed to	Balch, Stephen Bloomer, Rev. et al	1802	H8	560	522
Beatty, Charles	Deed to	Edwards, John	1802	H8	591	557
Beatty, Charles	Lease to	Bussard, Daniel et al	1802	H8	191	183
Beatty, Charles	Deed to	Corcoran, Thomas	1802	H8	562	525
Beatty, Charles	Lease to	Walker, George	1802	H8	413	382
Beatty, Charles	Deed to	Presbyterian Congregation of G'tn.	1802	H8	562	525
Beatty, Charles	Deed to	Rowles, Joseph E. et al	1802	I9	255	412
Beatty, Charles	Deed to	Ritchie, Abner	1802	I9	512	838
Beatty, Charles	Lease to	Brome, George	1802	I9	436	722
Beatty, Charles	Deed to	Upperman, George	1802	I9	244	393
Beatty, Charles	Lease to	Ritchie, Abner	1802	I9	046	062
Beatty, Charles	Deed to	Beatty, Thomas J.	1802	I9	485	797
Beatty, Charles	Deed to	Wingard, Abraham	1802	I9	161	243
Beatty, Charles	Deed to	Walker, George	1802	I9	242	388
Beatty, Charles	Deed to	Schnider, Abraham	1802	I9	030	040
Beatty, Charles	Deed to	Bohrer, Abraham	1802	I9	514	842
Beatty, Charles	Deed to	Bolser, John, Jr.	1802	I9	077	109
Beatty, Charles	Lease to	Neale, Richard S.	1802	I9	435	719
Beatty, Charles	Deed to	Mason, John T.	1802	I9	519	849
Beatty, Charles	Deed fr	Feburier, Nicholas, an insolvent	1804	K10	176	185
Beatty, Charles	Lease to	Edwards, John	1804	L11	102	104
Beatty, Charles	Lease to	Beatty, Thomas, Jr., Frederick Co.	1804	K10	110	118
Beatty, Charles	Lease to	Miller, George	1804	K10	398	413
Beatty, Charles	Deed fr	Offutt, Ozias, Dr., of Montg. Co.	1807	R17	341	260
Beatty, Charles & Wm. Clark, deft.	Suit	Davidson, John, plt.		K10	007	
Beatty, Charles A., of G'tn.	Mortgage fr	Williams, Stuart, of P.G. Co.	1797	C3	053	44
Beatty, Charles A. et al	Deed to	McClann, Robert, of G'tn.	1805	M12	363	371
Beatty, Charles A. et al	Deed fr	Davidson, John, of Annapolis	1805	M12	044	043
Beatty, Charles A. et al	Deed to	Kemp, Henry	1805	M12	179	179
Beatty, Charles A. et al	Deed to	Chappel, John	1805	M12	369	379
Beatty, Charles A. et al	Lease to	McGrath, Thomas	1805	M12	165	164
Beatty, Charles A. et al	Deed to	Reintzel, John, Dr.	1805	M12	384	396
Beatty, Charles A. et al	Deed to	Balch, Stephen B.	1805	M12	188	190
Beatty, Charles A. et al	Deed to	Patterson, Edgar	1805	N13	249	208
Beatty, Charles A. et al	Deed to	Beall, Thomas et al	1805	N13	011	012
Beatty, Charles A.	Deed fr	Beatty, Thomas J., now of NC	1805	N13	148	138
Beatty, Charles A.	Deed fr	Beatty, John M.	1805	N13	258	216

Index to District of Columbia Land Records, 1792-1817

Party	What	Party	Year	Liber	Old	New
Beatty, Charles A.	Deed to	Beatty, John M.	1805	N13	257	214
Beatty, Charles A., of G'tn.	Deed to	Magruder, George B., of G'tn.	1805	N13	178	160
Beatty, Charles A. et al	Deed to	Lutz, John	1806	Q16	016	010
Beatty, Charles A., Dr.	Deed to	Davies, Benjamin	1806	P15	082	050
Beatty, Charles A.	Deed to	Beatty, John M.	1807	R17	348	265
Beatty, Charles A. & John M.	Deed fr	Ritchie, Abner	1807	Q16	342	262
Beatty, Charles A., Dr.	Deed fr	Beall, William D.	1809	W22	272	182
Beatty, Charles A., Dr.	Deed fr	Beatth, John M., Dr.	1810	X23	399	321
Beatty, Charles A., Dr.	Deed to	Lutz, John	1810	Y24	496	437
Beatty, Charles A., Dr.	Deed to	Lutz, John	1810	Z25	270	212
Beatty, Charles A., Dr.	Deed to	Beatty, John M., Dr.	1810	X23	401	323
Beatty, Charles A., Dr.	Deed to	Pearce, Isaac	1810	X23	364	292
Beatty, Charles A., Dr.	Deed fr	Marbury, William	1811	AA26	077	055
Beatty, Charles A., Dr.	Deed to	Magruder, Eliza Lidia Mary, d/o N.	1811	AA26	185	126
Beatty, Charles A., Dr.	Deed to	Morgan, William, mer.	1811	AB27	052	044
Beatty, Charles A., Dr., of G'tn.	Deed to	Renner, Daniel, of G'tn.	1811	AB27	063	054
Beatty, Charles A., Dr.	Deed to	Belt, Joseph Sprigg	1811	Z25	406	319
Beatty, Charles A., Dr.	Deed to	Bohrer, George, Gent.	1811	Z25	128	100
Beatty, Charles A., Dr.	Deed to	Bradley, Abraham, Esq.	1811	Z25	517	411
Beatty, Charles A., Dr.	Deed to	Robey, Theophilus et al	1811	Z25	384	302
Beatty, Charles A., Dr. et al	Deed to	Marbury, William	1811	Z25	377	296
Beatty, Charles A., Dr.	Deed to	Ober, Robert, mer.	1812	AD29	226	181
Beatty, Charles A., Dr.	Deed to	Wiley, David	1812	AD29	165	131
Beatty, Charles A.	Deed to	Gannon, James	1812	AD29	089	067
Beatty, Charles A.	Deed to	Stone, Edward	1813	AF31	510	373
Beatty, Charles A.	Deed to	Burbeck, Henry, Col.	1813	AF31	501	364
Beatty, Charles A., Dr.	Deed fr	Crommitt, Mary Ann	1813	AE30	514	381
Beatty, Charles A., of G'tn.	Deed to	Baltzer, John, heirs of	1813	AF31	421	303
Beatty, Charles A.	Deed to	Moore, James	1814	AG32	207	144
Beatty, Charles A., Dr.	Deed to	Calder, James	1814	AG32	059	046
Beatty, Charles A., Dr., of G'tn.	Deed fr	English, David, of G'tn.	1814	AG32	031	025
Beatty, Charles A.	Deed fr	Eliason, Ebenezer	1814	AH33	096	089
Beatty, Charles A.	Deed to	Garey, Everard	1814	AH33	029	026
Beatty, Charles A.	Deed to	Collins, Elizabeth, w/o Hezekiah	1814	AH33	334	289
Beatty, Charles A., Dr.	Deed to	Wetzell, Frederick	1815	AH33	510	438
Beatty, Charles A., Dr., of G'tn.	Deed to	Bohrer, Jacob	1815	AI34	251	284
Beatty, Charles A.	Deed fr	Chandler, Walter Story	1816	AL36	137	138
Beatty, Charles A.	Deed to	Kennedy, James	1816	AL36	019	020
Beatty, Charles A., of G'tn.	Deed to	Ritter, Peter	1816	AL36	210	217
Beatty, Charles A.	Deed to	Brackenridge, John & P. Bradley	1816	AM37	092	074
Beatty, Charles A., of G'tn.	Deed fr	Whann, William, of G'tn.	1816	AL36	136	136
Beatty, Charles A., Dr., of G'tn.	D. of T. to	Ott, John	1817	AN38	525	380
Beatty, Charles A.	Deed to	Pierce, Isaac	1817	AN38	116	086
Beatty, Charles A.	Deed to	Whann, William et al	1817	AO39	294	210
Beatty, Charles Affordby, of G'tn.	P. of Atty. fr	Beatty, Thomas J., in NC	1805	L11	410	365
Beatty, Charles, Col.	Deed to	Bank of Columbia, President of	1799	D4	332	318
Beatty, Charles, Col.	Deed to	Scott, Gustavus	1800	E5	224	217
Beatty, Charles, Col.	Mortgage to	Bank of Columbia	1801	G7	164	218
Beatty, Charles, Col.	Deed to	McCleery, Henry	1804	K10	266	272
Beatty, Charles, Col., heirs of	Release fr	Bank of Columbia	1814	AG32	106	080
Beatty, Charles et al	Deed to	Casanave, Peter	1795	B2A	238	331
Beatty, Charles et al	Deed to	Casanave, Peter	1795	B2A	238	331
Beatty, Charles et al	Deed to	Beall, Thomas, of George	1795	B2A	166	222
Beatty, Charles et al	Decree for	Deakins, William et al	1797	C3	015	12
Beatty, Charles, heirs of	Deed to	Ritchie, Abner, of G'tn.	1805	N13	077	070

Index to District of Columbia Land Records, 1792-1817   31

Party	What	Party	Year	Liber	Old	New
Beatty, Charles, heirs of	Deed to	Wingard, Abraham	1805	N13	285	234
Beatty, Charles, heirs of	Deed to	Gloyd, Jonathan	1805	N13	180	161
Beatty, Charles, heirs of	Deed to	Hyde, Thomas	1805	N13	102	095
Beatty, Charles, heirs of	Deed to	Hyde, Thomas	1805	N13	103	097
Beatty, Charles, heirs of	Deed to	Holmead, John	1805	N13	055	051
Beatty, Charles, heirs of	D. of T. to	Holmead, John	1805	N13	053	049
Beatty, Charles, heirs of	Deed to	Kennedy, James	1805	O14	032	020
Beatty, Charles, heirs of	Deed to	Lutz, John	1806	O14	296	196
Beatty, Charles, heirs of	Deed to	Whann, William	1806	O14	312	207
Beatty, Charles, heirs of	Deed to	Upperman, Henry, Jr.	1806	O14	278	184
Beatty, Charles, heirs of	Deed to	Dixon, Thomas	1806	O14	318	211
Beatty, Charles, heirs of	Deed to	Stewart, William	1806	O14	274	181
Beatty, Charles, heirs of	Deed to	Corcoran, Thomas	1806	O14	193	127
Beatty, Charles, heirs of	Deed to	Hedges, Nicholas	1806	O14	199	130
Beatty, Charles, heirs of	Deed to	Davies, Benjamin	1806	O14	252	166
Beatty, Charles, heirs of	Deed to	Brookes, Joseph	1806	O14	251	165
Beatty, Charles, heirs of	Deed to	Garey, Everard, of G'tn.	1806	O14	283	187
Beatty, Charles, heirs of	Deed to	Hoye, John et al	1806	O14	334	222
Beatty, Charles, heirs of	Deed to	Crown, Samuel T.	1806	O14	201	132
Beatty, Charles, heirs of	Deed to	McClan, Robert	1806	O14	236	155
Beatty, Charles, heirs of	Deed to	Ott, John, Dr.	1806	O14	180	118
Beatty, Charles, heirs of	Deed to	Williamson, David, of Balto.	1806	O14	230	151
Beatty, Charles, heirs of	Deed to	Magruder, Ninian, Dr.	1806	P15	199	133
Beatty, Charles, heirs of	Deed to	Gray, Nathan	1806	P15	359	238
Beatty, Charles, heirs of	Deed to	Turner, Samuel Jr.	1806	P15	021	013
Beatty, Charles, heirs of	Deed to	King, George	1806	P15	289	191
Beatty, Charles, heirs of	Deed to	Craig, George	1806	P15	039	023
Beatty, Charles, heirs of	Deed to	Johns, Richard	1806	P15	068	051
Beatty, Charles, heirs of	Deed to	Hutchins, Samuel	1806	P15	084	051
Beatty, Charles, heirs of	Deed to	Bussard, Daniel	1806	P15	092	057
Beatty, Charles, heirs of	Deed to	King, Adam	1806	P15	096	059
Beatty, Charles, heirs of	Deed to	Thomson, George	1806	P15	326	216
Beatty, Charles, heirs of	Deed to	Browning, Joseph	1806	P15	299	196
Beatty, Charles, heirs of	Deed to	Fox, Bartleson	1806	P15	330	218
Beatty, Charles, heirs of	Deed to	Kennedy, James	1806	P15	361	240
Beatty, Charles, heirs of	Deed to	Duffey, Bryan	1806	P15	155	101
Beatty, Charles, heirs of	Deed to	King, James C.	1806	P15	102	062
Beatty, Charles, heirs of	Deed to	Bayley, Jesse	1806	Q16	163	108
Beatty, Charles, heirs of	Deed to	Ritchie, Abner	1806	Q16	254	175
Beatty, Charles, heirs of	Deed to	Reintzel, Anthony et al	1807	Q16	383	294
Beatty, Charles, heirs of	Deed to	Renner, Daniel & Daniel Bussard	1807	R17	404	305
Beatty, Charles, heirs of	Deed to	Keifer, Henry [Kefer]	1807	R17	260	197
Beatty, Charles, heirs of	Deed to	Kemp, Henry	1807	R17	218	163
Beatty, Charles, heirs of	Deed to	Williams, Thomas O.	1807	S18	158	129
Beatty, Charles, heirs of	Deed to	McClan, Elizabeth	1807	Q16	341	261
Beatty, Charles, heirs of	Deed to	Hedges, Nicholas	1808	U20	184	102
Beatty, Charles, heirs of	Deed to	Nevitt, Joseph & T. Robey	1808	T19	393	279
Beatty, Charles, heirs of	Deed to	Williams, Elisha W.	1809	X23	234	181
Beatty, Charles, heirs of	Release fr	Whann, William	1814	AG32	106	080
Beatty, Charles, of G'tn.	Deed fr	McLain, John & Joseph, of NC	1793	A1-2	397	6
Beatty, Charles, of G'tn.	Deed fr	McClain, George et al	1794	A1-2	494	97
Beatty, Charles, of G'tn.	Lease to	Jones, John, of G'tn.	1794	A1-2	476	81
Beatty, Charles, of Montg. Co.	Deed to	Prout, William, of Montg. Co.	1795	B2A	280	392
Beatty, Charles, of G'tn.	Deed to	O'Reily, Henry, of G'tn.	1795	B2A	231	321
Beatty, Charles, of G'tn.	Deed to	Beatty, Thomas J., of G'tn.	1795	B2A	349	493

Index to District of Columbia Land Records, 1792-1817

Party	What	Party	Year	Liber	Old	New
Beatty, Charles, of G'tn.	Deed to	Lingan, Nicholas, merchant	1795	B2A	173	233
Beatty, Charles, of G'tn.	Deed to	Deakins, William Jr., mer., G'tn.	1796	B2B	548	274
Beatty, Charles, of Montg. Co.	Deed to	Chiswell, Joseph Newton	1796	B2B	515	222
Beatty, Charles, of Montg. Co.	Deed to	Borer, Peter, of Montg. Co.	1796	B2B	392	052
Beatty, Charles, of G'tn.	Deed fr	Gammon, James, of Montg. Co.	1796	B2B	423	096
Beatty, Charles, of G'tn.	Deed fr	King, Charles & Mary	1797	C3	134	109
Beatty, Charles, of G'tn.	Deed to	Long, John, hatter, of G'tn.	1797	C3	110	99
Beatty, Charles, of Montg. Co.	Deed fr	Middagh, John, s/o John	1797	C3	126	103
Beatty, Charles, of Montg. Co.	Deed to	King, George, of Montg. Co.	1797	C3	138	112
Beatty, Charles, of Montg. Co.	Deed to	King, George, of Montg. Co.	1797	C3	139	114
Beatty, Charles, of G'tn.	Deed to	Retrie, William, of G'tn.	1797	C3	112	92
Beatty, Charles, of G'tn.	Deed fr	Eastburn, Robinson & Jesse	1797	B2B	686	462
Beatty, Charles, of G'tn.	Deed to	Beatty, Thomas Johnson, of G'tn.	1798	C3	338	272
Beatty, Charles, of G'tn.	Deed fr	Beatty, Thomas Johnson, of G'tn.	1798	D4	006	005
Beatty, Charles, of G'tn.	Deed to	Beatty, Thomas Johnson, of G'tn.	1798	D4	078	066
Beatty, Charles, of G'tn.	Deed to	Weyenberger, George	1800	E5	157	146
Beatty, Charles, of G'tn.	Deed to	Waters, William, of G'tn.	1802	I9	069	097
Beatty, Charles, of Frederick Co.	N. of S.	Hawkins, George Fraser	1803	K10	006	6
Beatty, Charles, of G'tn.	Deed to	Worthington, Charles	1803	K10	062	67
Beatty, Charles, of G'tn. et al	Deed to	Templeman, John, of G'tn.	1804	L11	185	178
Beatty, Charles, of G'tn.	Deed to	Gitzendanner, Christian, of G'tn.	1804	K10	271	276
Beatty, Charles, Sr.	Deed to	Beall, Thomas & John M. Gantt	1792	A1-1	128	186
Beatty, Charles, Sr. et al	Deed to	Dorsey, William Hammond	1795	B2A	237	330
Beatty, Charles, Sr., of G'tn.	Deed fr	Lee, Thomas Sim et al	1795	B2A	242	336
Beatty, Charles, Sr. et al	Deed to	Warring, Marsham, of G'tn.	1795	B2A	252	351
Beatty, Charles, Sr.	Deed fr	Beatty, Thomas, Jr.	1795	B2A	198	271
Beatty, Charles, Sr.	Deed fr	Edelen, Rebecca et al	1800	E5	115	102
Beatty, Elie et al	Deed to	Hedges, Nicholas	1807	T19	011	009
Beatty, George A., Dr., of G'tn.	Deed to	Calder, James, of G'tn.	1813	AE30	346	259
Beatty, John M. et al	Deed to	McClann, Robert	1805	M12	363	371
Beatty, John M. et al	Deed to	Chappel, John	1805	M12	369	379
Beatty, John M. et al	Deed to	Kemp, Henry	1805	M12	179	179
Beatty, John M. et al	Lease to	McGrath, Thomas	1805	M12	165	164
Beatty, John M. et al	Deed to	Reintzel, John, Dr.	1805	M12	384	396
Beatty, John M. et al	Deed to	Balch, Stephen B.	1805	M12	188	190
Beatty, John M. et al	Deed fr	Davidson, John, of Annapolis	1805	M12	044	043
Beatty, John M. et al	Deed to	Patterson, Edgar	1805	N13	249	208
Beatty, John M.	Deed fr	Beatty, Charles A.	1805	N13	257	214
Beatty, John M. & Charles A.	Deed fr	Threlkeld, John, Gent.	1805	N13	302	245
Beatty, John M. et al	Deed to	Beall, Thomas et al	1805	N13	011	012
Beatty, John M.	Deed to	Beatty, Charles A.	1805	N13	258	216
Beatty, John M. & Charles A.	Deed to	Corporation of Georgetown	1805	O14	001	001
Beatty, John M. & Charels A.	Release to	Gaither, Henry, Col.	1806	O14	203	134
Beatty, John M. & Charles A.	Deed to	Meddert, Jacob	1806	O14	346	231
Beatty, John M. & Charles A.	Deed fr	Davidson, John, Gen., Annapolis	1806	O14	280	185
Beatty, John M. & Charles A.	Deed to	Nourse, Joseph	1806	O14	353	236
Beatty, John M. & Charles A.	Deed to	King, George	1806	P15	288	190
Beatty, John M. & Charles A.	Deed fr	Beall, Thomas, of George	1806	P15	025	015
Beatty, John M. & Charles A.	Deed to	Doughty, William, Capt.	1806	P15	100	062
Beatty, John M.	Deed fr	Davidson, John, of Annapolis	1806	Q16	190	128
Beatty, John M. & Charles A.	Deed to	Nourse, Michael	1806	Q16	192	129
Beatty, John M.	Deed to	Nourse, Michael	1806	Q16	189	127
Beatty, John M. & Charles A.	Deed fr	Magruder, George	1807	Q16	385	296
Beatty, John M. & Charles A.	Deed to	Clarke, Robert	1807	Q16	365	280
Beatty, John M. & Charles A.	Deed to	Kennedy, James	1807	Q16	391	300

Index to District of Columbia Land Records, 1792-1817

Party	What	Party	Year	Liber	Old	New
Beatty, John M. & Charles A.	Deed fr	King, James C.	1807	R17	277	211
Beatty, John M. & Charles A.	Deed fr	Offutt, Ozias, Dr., admr. of	1807	R17	337	257
Beatty, John M.	Deed fr	Beatty, Charles A.	1807	R17	348	265
Beatty, John M. & Charles A.	Deed to	Corporation of Georgetown	1807	R17	339	258
Beatty, John M. & Charles A.	Deed to	Stewart, David, of G'tn.	1807	S18	023	020
Beatty, John M. & Charles A.	Deed fr	Corporation of Georgetown	1807	S18	387	308
Beatty, John M. & Charles A.	Deed to	Corcoran, Thomas	1807	S18	068	057
Beatty, John M. & Charles A.	Deed to	Waters, William, of G'tn.	1808	T19	044	033
Beatty, John M. & Charles A.	Deed to	Tenny, Isaac & Robert Ober	1808	U20	090	050
Beatty, John M. & Charles A.	Deed to	Whann, William & George King	1808	U20	300	160
Beatty, John M. & Charles A.	Deed to	Parrott, Richard	1808	U20	018	011
Beatty, John M. & Charles A.	Deed to	Bussard, Daniel, Jr.	1809	W22	345	223
Beatty, John M. & Charles A.	Deed to	Reintzel, Anthony	1809	W22	361	234
Beatty, John M. & Charles A.	Deed to	Peerce, Isaac	1809	W22	410	266
Beatty, John M., Dr.	Deed to	Mitchell, Mary, wid/o Capt. John	1810	Y24	054	048
Beatty, John M., Dr.	Deed fr	Beatty, Charles A., Dr.	1810	X23	401	323
Beatty, John M., Dr.	Deed to	Beatty, Charles A., Dr.	1810	X23	399	321
Beatty, Thomas	Deed fr	Middagh, John Gaither et al	1798	C3	416	328
Beatty, Thomas	Deed fr	Carey, William, of G'tn.	1799	D4	235	217
Beatty, Thomas	Deed to	Ritchie, Abner	1802	H8	131	128
Beatty, Thomas	Deed to	Ritchie, Abner	1802	H8	130	126
Beatty, Thomas & Henry O'Reily	Deed fr	Downes, Henry & Winefred	1793	A1-1	175	249
Beatty, Thomas J., of G'tn.	Cert fr	Commissioners of Washington	1792	B2A	288	402
Beatty, Thomas J., of G'tn.	Deed to	Ochenbrod, William	1793	A1-1	197	277
Beatty, Thomas J., of G'tn.	Deed fr	Bayly, William	1795	B2A	191	259
Beatty, Thomas J.	Deed fr	Jenkins, Thomas, of Charles Co.	1795	B2A	196	267
Beatty, Thomas J., of G'tn.	Deed fr	Beatty, Charles, of G'tn.	1795	B2A	349	493
Beatty, Thomas J.	Deed fr	Lingan, James McCubbin, G'tn.	1795	B2A	194	263
Beatty, Thomas J., of G'tn.	Deed to	Magruder, Edward, Mont. Co.	1795	B2B	373	026
Beatty, Thomas J.	Deed fr	Reintzel, Anthony, of G'tn.	1796	B2B	486	178
Beatty, Thomas J., of G'tn.	Lease fr	Bayly, William, of P.G. Co.	1796	B2B	609	363
Beatty, Thomas J., of G'tn.	Deed to	Bank of Columbia, President of	1796	B2B	414	084
Beatty, Thomas J., of G'tn.	Deed to	Cramphin, Thomas, of Montg. Co.	1796	B2B	487	179
Beatty, Thomas J., mer., of G'tn.	Deed to	Bank of Columbia, President of	1796	B2B	415	086
Beatty, Thomas J.	Transfer to	Purcell, Pierce	1796	B2B	452	138
Beatty, Thomas J.	Transfer to	Purcell, Pierce	1796	B2B	451	138
Beatty, Thomas J.	Deed to	Stoddert, Benjamin	1802	I9	485	798
Beatty, Thomas J.	Deed fr	Beatty, Charles	1802	I9	484	797
Beatty, Thomas J.	Deed fr	Wayman, Charles	1802	I9	574	931
Beatty, Thomas J., in NC	P. of Atty. to	Beatty, Charles Affordby, of G'tn.	1805	L11	410	365
Beatty, Thomas J. et al	Deed to	McClann, Robert, of G'tn.	1805	M12	363	371
Beatty, Thomas J. et al	Deed fr	Davidson, John, of Annapolis	1805	M12	044	043
Beatty, Thomas J. et al	Lease to	McGrath, Thomas	1805	M12	165	164
Beatty, Thomas J. et al	Deed to	Chappel, John	1805	M12	369	379
Beatty, Thomas J. et al	Deed to	Kemp, Henry	1805	M12	179	179
Beatty, Thomas J.	Deed to	Reintzel, John, Dr.	1805	M12	384	396
Beatty, Thomas J. et al	Deed to	Balch, Stephen B.	1805	M12	188	190
Beatty, Thomas J. et al	Deed to	Beall, Thomas et al	1805	N13	011	012
Beatty, Thomas J., now of NC	Deed to	Beatty, Charles A.	1805	N13	148	138
Beatty, Thomas Johnson	Deed fr	Deakins, William et al	1793	A1-1	185	262
Beatty, Thomas Johnson, of G'tn.	Deed to	King, Adam, merchant, of G'tn.	1795	B2A	267	374
Beatty, Thomas Johnson	Deed fr	Wallach, Charles et al	1795	B2A	350	495
Beatty, Thomas Johnson, of G'tn.	Deed fr	Beatty, Charles, of G'tn.	1798	C3	338	272
Beatty, Thomas Johnson	Deed to	Forrest, Uriah	1798	C3	508	399
Beatty, Thomas Johnson, of G'tn.	Deed to	King, George, of G'tn.	1798	D4	073	061

Party	What	Party	Year	Liber	Old	New
Beatty, Thomas Johnson, of G'tn.	Deed to	Beatty, Charles, of G'tn.	1798	D4	006	005
Beatty, Thomas Johnson, of G'tn.	Deed fr	Beatty, Charles, of G'tn.	1798	D4	078	066
Beatty, Thomas, Jr.	Deed fr	Deakins, William et al	1793	A1-1	181	257
Beatty, Thomas, Jr., of G'tn.	Deed fr	Fenwick, James, of St. Mary's Co.	1794	B2A	101	132
Beatty, Thomas, Jr.	Deed fr	Crawford, David	1794	B2A	102	134
Beatty, Thomas, Jr., of G'tn.	Deed to	Lingan, Nicholas, of G'tn.	1795	B2A	202	276
Beatty, Thomas, Jr.	Deed to	Beatty, Charles, Sr.	1795	B2A	198	271
Beatty, Thomas, Jr., of G'tn.	Deed to	Schultz, Henry, of G'tn.	1796	B2B	589	337
Beatty, Thomas, Jr.	Cede to	Corporation of Georgetown	1797	B2B	619	376
Beatty, Thomas, Jr., Frederick Co.	Deed to	French, George	1798	D4	162	143
Beatty, Thomas, Jr., Frederick Co.	Lease fr	Beatty, Charles	1804	K10	110	118
Beatty, Thomas, Jr.	Deed fr	Magruder, George, collector, G'tn.	1807	S18	239	189
Beatty, Thomas, Jr., trustee et al	Deed fr	Melvin, James, of G'tn.	1808	T19	206	148
Beatty, Thomas, Jr., of G'tn.	Deed to	Mayer, Henry, of G'tn.	1813	AE30	126	098
Beatty, Thomas, Jr.	Assign to	Craig, Henrietta, admx. of Robert	1814	AH33	022	020
Beatty, Thomas, Jr.	B. of S. to	Craig, Henrietta, admx. of Robert	1814	AH33	020	018
Beatty, Thomas, Jr.	B. of S. to	Mayer, Henry	1814	AH33	020	018
Beatty, Thomas, Jr. et al	Deed to	Bussard, Daniel	1815	AH33	397	343
Beatty, Thomas, of G'tn.	Cert fr	Commissioners of Washington	1792	B2A	288	403
Beatty, Thomas, of Frederick Co.	Deed to	Beall, Thomas & John M. Gantt	1792	A1-1	100	146
Beatty, Thomas, of Frederick Co.	Deed fr	Davidson, John, of Annapolis	1800	F6	045	028
Beatty, Thomas, of MD	Deed to	Ritchie, Abner, of G'tn.	1802	H8	601	568
Beatty, Thomas, of MD	Deed to	Gosler, John	1810	Y24	382	345
Beatty, Thomas, Sr.	Deed to	Holtzman, George	1811	AB27	446	367
Beatty, Threlkeld & Deakins Addn.	Plats		1803	K10	047	
Beatty, Violetta, wid/o Dr. John	Deed fr	Athey, George, of G'tn.	1816	AL36	475	448
Beatty, Violletta, wid/o Dr. John	Deed to	Ott, John	1816	AL36	418	400
Beatty, William, exrs. of	Deed to	Hedges, Nicholas	1807	T19	011	009
Beatty, William, Frederick Co. et al	Deed to	Ritchie, Abner	1801	G7	205	274
Beatty, William, of Frederick Co.	Deed to	Thomas, Philip	1792	A1-1	067	99
Beaven, Leonard, of Charles Co.	B. of S. to	Knoblock, John	1811	AA26	084	060
Beck, Dorcas	Manumis to	[ ], Maria (C)	1814	AH33	092	084
Beck, James, of P.G. Co.	B. of S. fr	Beck, Samuel Waters	1811	Z25	538	428
Beck, John, of G'tn.	Deed to	Walker, Nathan, of G'tn.	1796	B2B	447	131
Beck, Joseph et al	Deed fr	Beck, Richard, of G'tn.	1805	M12	123	117
Beck, Joseph, of Montg. Co.	Deed to	Baker, William, of Balto. et al	1797	C3	236	196
Beck, Joseph, of G'tn.	Deed fr	Beall, Thomas Brooke, of G'tn.	1798	C3	409	324
Beck, Joseph, of G'tn.	Deed to	Beck, Richard, of G'tn.	1800	F6		025
Beck, Joseph, of G'tn. et al	Deed to	Beck, Richard, mer.	1806	Q16	264	184
Beck, Rezin, of P.G. Co.	Deed fr	Reintzel, Anthony, of G'tn.	1805	M12	156	152
Beck, Rezin, of G'tn.	Deed fr	Beck, Richard, of G'tn.	1806	Q16	054	035
Beck, Richard	Deed fr	Morris, Randa.	1802	I9	273	446
Beck, Richard & John Eliason	B. of S. fr	*Browning & Renshaw*	1806	Q16	147	097
Beck, Richard et al	Deed fr	Holmead, Anthony	1800	E5	238	232
Beck, Richard et al	Deed fr	Eliason, Ebenezer & Ann	1809	V21	290	210
Beck, Richard, mer., of G'tn.	Deed to	Tingey, Thomas, Capt. U.S.N.	1805	M12	313	316
Beck, Richard, mer.	Deed fr	Beck, Joseph, of G'tn. et al	1806	Q16	264	184
Beck, Richard, of G'tn.	Deed fr	Beck, Joseph, of G'tn.	1800	F6		025
Beck, Richard, of G'tn.	Deed fr	Sanford, Hector, of G'tn.	1805	N13	227	193
Beck, Richard, of G'tn.	Deed fr	Tingey, Thomas	1805	M12	196	197
Beck, Richard, of G'tn.	Deed to	Beck, Joseph et al	1805	M12	123	117
Beck, Richard, of G'tn.	Deed fr	Morsell, James Sewall, of G'tn.	1806	P15	032	019
Beck, Richard, of G'tn.	Deed to	Beck, Rezin, of G'tn.	1806	Q16	054	035
Beck, Richard, of G'tn.	Mortgage to	Foxhall, Henry, of G'tn.	1810	Y24	192	177
Beck, Richard, oif G'tn.	Deed fr	Tingey, Thomas, Capt.	1807	S18	375	297

Index to District of Columbia Land Records, 1792-1817   35

Party	What	Party	Year	Liber	Old	New
Beck, Samuel Waters, insolvent	B. of S. to	Brewer, Joseph	1811	AA26	107	074
Beck, Samuel Waters	B. of S. to	Beck, James, of P.G. Co.	1811	Z25	538	428
Beckwith, Charles & Cassandra	Deed to	Mitchell, John, of Montg. Co.	1813	AF31	270	189
Beckwith, Charles, of Montg. Co.	Deed to	Templeman, John, of G'tn.	1796	B2B	424	097
Becraft, Benjamin	Deed to	Laird, John, of G'tn.	1801	G7	171	228
Becraft, William, of G'tn.	Deed fr	Dorsey, William H., of Montg. Co.	1815	AI34	205	234
Becraft, William, of G'tn.	Deed fr	Dorsey, William H., of Montg. Co.	1816	AO39	050	042
Beeding, Mary	B. of S. to	Lake, George	1817	AO39	171	127
Belknap, Stephen, trustee	Deed fr	Mills, Peter	1813	AF31	235	162
Bell, Charles	Deed fr	Porterfield, John, of Berkeley Co.	1815	AI34	074	084
Bell, George	Deed to	Brown, Peter	1812	AC28	447	319
Bell, George (mulatto)	Deed fr	May, Frederick	1805	M12	306	308
Bell, George (mulatto)	Deed fr	May, Frederick	1806	P15	003	002
Bell, James	Deed to	Woolls, George	1802	I9	252	406
Bell, John Briggs	B. of S. fr	Carleton, Joseph, of G'tn.	1807	S18	208	166
Bell, Samuel	Deed fr	Jackson, Agnes, trustee	1807	S18	406	325
Bell, William et al	Deed to	Underwood, Robert	1810	Y24	133	121
Belle, Benjamin (C)	B. of S. to	Porter, James A.	1811	AB27	069	058
Bellzor, Elizabeth, Frederick Co.	Deed fr	Kingla, Joseph	1804	K10	321	328
Belt, Ann, of G'tn.	Deed to	Chesley, Ann, of G'tn.	1804	L11	043	43
Belt, Benjamin	D. of T. to	Glover, Charles	1817	AN38	403	301
Belt, Benjamin M. et al	B. of S. fr	Edelen, Ignatius	1812	AD29	019	014
Belt, Benjamin M.	Deed fr	Van Ness, John P. & Marcia	1813	AF31	382	275
Belt, Benjamin M. et al	Mortgage fr	Bacon, Samuel	1815	AI34	193	221
Belt, Benjamin M.	Convey to	Knoblock, John	1815	AK35	094	073
Belt, Benjamin M.	Deed fr	Moore, George	1815	AK35	458	359
Belt, Benjamin M.	Deed to	Moore, George	1815	AI34	523	527
Belt, Benjamin M.	Deed fr	Corporation of Washington	1816	AK35	492	387
Belt, Benjamin M.	Convey fr	Brown, Stewart, of Balto.	1816	AM37	353	256
Belt, Benjamin M.	Deed to	Smith, Richard, of G'tn.	1816	AM37	207	153
Belt, Hiram	D. of T. to	Hellen, Walter	1810	X23	370	297
Belt, James	Deed fr	Lanham, Elisha, of G'tn.	1816	AM37	474	342
Belt, John	Deed fr	French, William, of Henry Co. VA	1793	A1-2	437	46
Belt, Joseph S.	Lease to	Orme, Thomas	1794	B2A	031	035
Belt, Joseph S.	B. of S. to	Scott, Leonard (C), of Annapolis	1801	G7	338	468
Belt, Joseph Sprigg	Deed to	Reintzel, Anthony	1793	A1-1	179	254
Belt, Joseph Sprigg	B. of S. fr	Orme, John	1810	Y24	317	289
Belt, Joseph Sprigg	Deed fr	Beatty, Charles A., Dr.	1811	Z25	406	319
Belt, Joseph Sprigg	Deed to	Bohrer, George	1813	AF31	326	233
Belt, Joseph Sprigg	Deed to	Grayson, William, Dr.	1813	AF31	037	026
Belt, Joseph Sprigg	Deed fr	Nevitt, Joseph	1813	AF31	237	163
Belt, Joseph Sprigg	Deed to	Hutton, John	1813	AF31	433	312
Belt, Richard	B. of S. to	Aldridge, James	1808	T19	375	268
Belt, Richard W., insolvent	B. of S. to	Hughes, Thomas, trustee	1808	V21	135	099
Belt, William S., Jr. et al	Deed fr	Gooding, John, of Balto.	1810	Y24	151	137
Bennett, Charles, of Alexa. et al	Deed to	Dunlap, John	1805	M12	370	380
Bennett, Charles, of Alexa.	B. of S. fr	Tilley, Robert	1807	R17	198	150
Bennett, Fenwick, of P.G. Co.	Deed fr	Burnes, David, of P.G. Co.	1797	C3	105	86
Bennett, James	Deed fr	Lenox, Peter	1811	Z25	412	324
Bennett, James	Mortgage fr	Varden, Charles	1816	AL36	249	252
Benson, Eden, of G'tn.	Deed fr	Deakins, Leonard M. et al	1807	S18	060	050
Benson, Edin	Deed fr	Ford, William [Foard]	1806	Q16	068	043
Benson, Edin	B. of S. fr	Foard, William	1806	Q16	053	034
Benson, Edin, of G'tn.	Deed fr	Dorsey, William H., of G'tn.	1806	Q16	051	033
Benson, John	Deed fr	Turner, Thomas	1802	I9	455	750

Index to District of Columbia Land Records, 1792-1817

Party	What	Party	Year	Liber	Old	New
Benson, John	B. of S. fr	Burch, Jane	1805	M12	176	175
Bentley, Caleb & Henrietta T.	Deed fr	Canby, Samuel T.W. & Sarah	1809	X23	091	067
Bentley, John H., of Balto. MD	Deed to	Butler, Silas & Timothy Winn	1813	AE30	161	128
Bentley, John Hunter, of Balto.	Assign fr	Wood, William	1810	X23	377	303
Bentley, Joseph	Deed fr	Brown, Robert	1801	G7	123	158
Bentley, Joseph	B. of S. fr	Kremer, John	1802	H8	199	191
Bentley, Joseph	Deed to	Flaut, Christian	1805	M12	078	072
Bentley, Joseph	Lease fr	Downes, George	1805	N13	306	323
Bentley, Joseph	B. of S. to	Speake, Samuel	1806	P15	225	155
Bentley, Joseph	Deed to	Moore, George	1806	P15	258	170
Bentley, Joseph, insolvent	Deed to	Dougherty, James, trustee	1806	P15	329	218
Bently, Joseph	Deed to	Gillies, Thomas H.	1804	L11	363	327
Bently, Joseph	Lease fr	Downes, George	1805	N13	406	323
Berkley, George	B. of S. to	Cross, William	1801	G7	272	375
Bernabeu, John B., of Balto.	Deed fr	Covachick, Joseph, mer., of NY	1800	E5	269	263
Bernard, John	Deed fr	Davidson, John	1802	I9	495	813
Berron, Jerome	B. of S. to	Sparrow, William	1817	AN38	455	328
Berry, Ester E., of Montg. Co.	Assign fr	Bussard, Daniel	1816	AL36	259	260
Berry, Hezekiah	Deed to	Barron, Walter	1806	P15	122	078
Berry, Hezekiah	Assign to	Barron, Walter	1806	P15	102½	063
Berry, Hezekiah	B. of S. to	Barron, Walter	1806	P15	111	069
Berry, Hezekiah	Deed to	Hogan, Thady, trustee	1808	V21	136	099
Berry, Hezekiah et al	Deed fr	Weatherall, John	1799	D4	426	398
Berry, John W., of Balto. Co. MD	Deed fr	Williams, Elisha W., of G'tn.	1812	AC28	135	101
Berry, John Wilkes, of Montg. Co.	Deed fr	Parrott, Richard, of Balto.	1798	C3	418	330
Berry, Richard	B. of S. to	Thompson, John C.	1812	AD29	444a	374
Berry, Richard	B. of S. to	Thompson, John C.	1813	AE30	208	169
Berry, William, of P.G. Co.	Deed fr	Wheeler, Leonard T.	1807	R17	322	245
Berry, William Warman & Lucy	Deed fr	Magruder, Charles	1793	A1-1	194	274
Berry, Zachariah, of MD	Deed fr	Stoddert, Benjamin, of G'tn.	1802	H8	469	430
Berry, Zachariah, of P.G. Co.	Deed fr	Addison, Walter Dulany, of G'tn.	1810	Y24	411	370
Berry, Zachariah, of P.G. Co.	Mortgage fr	Williams, Elisha W., of G'tn.	1812	AB27	551	450
Bestor, Harvey	Deed fr	Bacon, Samuel	1808	V21	071	056
Bestor, Harvey	Deed to	Bradley, Phineas	1811	Z25	552	439
Bestor, Harvey	Qualify	Lieutenant in militia	1812	AD29	171	137
Bestor, Harvey	B. of S. fr	Gray, Stephen W.	1814	AH33	375	324
Bestor, Harvey	Deed fr	Edwards, Horace H.	1815	AK35	435	341
Bestor, Harvey	Deed fr	Varden, Charles	1816	AL36	333	326
Bestor, Harvey	D. of T. to	Huddleston, Joseph	1816	AL36	518	485
Bestor, Harvey & H.H. Edwards	D. of T. to	Fletcher, Noah & J. Huddleston	1812	AD29	277	229
Bestor, Harvey & H.H. Edwards	Deed fr	Huddleston, Joseph	1812	AD29	300	246
Bestor, Harvey & H.H. Edwards	Deed fr	Fletcher, Noah & J. Huddleston	1815	AK35	438	343
Betterton, Benjamin	B. of S. to	Cochrane, Alexander	1804	K10	264	270
Betterton, Benjamin, insolvent	B. of S. to	McNantz, Charles, trustee	1810	Y24	516	454
Betz, Frederick	Assign fr	Frethy, Edward	1801	G7	301	419
Betz, Frederick	Deed to	Betz, George	1802	I9	325	535
Betz, Frederick, insolvent	B. of S. to	Munroe, Jonathan, trustee	1805	M12	402	416
Betz, George	Deed fr	Betz, Frederick	1802	I9	325	535
Betz, George, of Balto.	Lease to	Thorp, John, of Balto. Co.	1804	K10	204	213
Bevan, Mathew L., of Phila. PA	Mortgage fr	Cherry, Robert	1806	O14	332	221
Bevan, Mathew L., of Phila. PA	Deed fr	Cherry, Robert	1807	S18	379	301
Bevan, Mathew L.	Convey fr	Chandler, Walter S.	1807	S18	377	299
Bevan, Matthew L., of Phila. PA	Deed fr	Chandler, Walter Story	1813	AE30	520	385
Beverley, James B.	Slave	From VA	1816	AL36	104	105
Beverley, Robert	Slave	From VA	1806	Q16	331	254

Index to District of Columbia Land Records, 1792-1817

Party	What	Party	Year	Liber	Old	New
Beverly, Maria	B. of S. to	Beverly, Robert	1811	AA26	087	061
Beverly, Maria	Manumis to	Samuel, Griffen (C)	1812	AC28	305	222
Beverly, Maria, rel/o Robert	B. of S. to	Beverly, Robert	1812	AC28	477	338
Beverly, Munford, Culpeper Co.	Assign to	Ross, James, Fredericksburg VA	1806	O14	108	068
Beverly, Robert	Slaves	From VA	1805	N13	279	230
Beverly, Robert	Slave	From VA	1807	R17	306	233
Beverly, Robert	Slave		1809	W22	064	048
Beverly, Robert	Deed fr	Beall, Thomas, of Geo. et al	1811	AA26	036	028
Beverly, Robert	Deed to	Clarke, George	1811	AB27	056	047
Beverly, Robert	B. of S. fr	Beverly, Maria	1811	AA26	087	061
Beverly, Robert	Slave	From *Blandfield*, Essex Co. VA	1812	AC28	355	258
Beverly, Robert	B. of S. fr	Beverly, Maria, rel/o Robert	1812	AC28	477	338
Beverly, Robert	Deed fr	Lee, John, of G'tn.	1815	AI34	163	187
Beverly, Robert, of *Blandfield*, VA	Deed fr	Dorsey, William Hammond	1805	M12	267	268
Beverly, Robert, of *Blandfield*, VA	Mortgage to	Dorsey, William Hammond	1805	N13	044	043
Beverly, Robert, of G'tn.	Release fr	Van Ness, John P.	1809	W22	060	045
Bias, Samuel (C), age 24y 5m	Cert Slave	Richards, G.	1817	AN38	017	014
Bickley, John	Agreement	Simmons, James	1795	B2B	372	024
Bickley, John, bricklayer	Agreement	Morris, Robert & John Nicholson	1796	B2B	584	330
Bickley, John, bricklayer	Agreement	Nicholson, John, of Phila.	1796	B2B	584	330
Bickley, Robert S., of Phila. PA	Cert fr	Munroe, Thomas, Supt.	1804	L11	408	363
Bickley, Robert S., of Phila. PA	Deed fr	Blodget, Samuel, Jr. et al	1805	L11	410	364
Bickley, Robert S.	P. of Atty. fr	Pratt, Henry & George Budd	1806	Q16	178	119
Bickley, Robert S.	Deed fr	Brent, Daniel Carroll, trustee et al	1807	R17	026	022
Bickley, Robert S., of Phila. PA	Deed to	Brent, Daniel Carroll	1807	R17	398	301
Bickley, Robert S., of Phila. PA	Deed to	Hickey, James	1810	Y24	256	235
Bickley, Robert S., of Phila. PA	Deed to	Burns, Benjamin & Ninian Beall	1810	Y24	264	243
Bickley, Robert S., of Phila. PA	P. of Atty. to	Boyd, Washington	1810	Y24	008	006
Bickley, Robert S., Phila. PA et al	Deed to	United States	1810	Y24	267	245
Bickley, Robert S., of Phila. PA	Deed to	Burnes, Benjamin & Ninian Beall	1812	AD29	031	022
Bickley, Robert S., of Phila. PA	Deed to	Brent, Daniel C., of Stafford Co.	1812	AD29	029	020
Bickley, Robert S., Holmsburg PA	Deed to	Dunlop, James	1813	AE30	404	298
Bickley, Robert S., Holmsberg PA	Deed to	Dougherty, James	1813	AF31	240	166
Bickley, Robert S., agent for	Agreement	Scallan, James	1816	AL36	500	469
Bickley, Robert S., Bucks Co. PA	Deed to	Gilliss, Thomas H. et al	1817	AN38	564	411
Bickley, Robert S., Bucks Co. PA	Deed to	Glover, Charles	1817	AN38	333	243
Biddle, Charles et al	R. of M. to	Magruder, William B.	1794	B2A	039	045
Biddle, Clement, of Phila., assigns.	Deed to	Beall, Thomas & John M. Gantt	1793	A1-1	276	371
Bigham, Hugh	Deed fr	Polock, Isaac	1802	H8	153	148
Bigham, Hugh, of Adams Co. PA	Deed to	Thorpe, Thomas	1806	O14	390	260
Billing, Joseph	B. of S. to	Ingle, Henry	1807	R17	126	098
Billis, Thomas H. et al	Deed fr	Baker, Samuel	1802	H8	324	304
Billmyer, Thomas	Deed to	Moore, James	1816	AM37	308	225
Billmyer, Thomas	Deed fr	Van Ness, John P. & Marcia	1816	AL36	241	245
Billmyer, Thomas	Deed to	Ellis, John	1817	AN38	542	394
Billmyer, Thomas [Billinger]	Release fr	Moore, James	1817	AN38	540	392
Binney, Hor. et al	Release to	Nourse, Joseph	1813	AF31	011	008
Biot, John	Lease fr	Carleton, Joseph, of G'tn.	1805	O14	153	099
Biot, John	B. of S. fr	Elliot, Rufus	1807	S18	147	121
Birch, Samuel Lewis & Jesse	Deed to	Jenkins, Thomas, of Frs., P.G. Co.	1807	S18	279	219
Bird, Alice	Deed to	Logan, George W.	1812	AD29	534	451
Bird, Alice	Deed to	Southerland, Thomas J.	1815	AI34	443	459
Bird, Alice	Cert Slaves	From VA to MD on 22 JUL 1816	1816	AM37	173	131
Bird, Alice, late Dermott	Deed fr	Brent, Daniel Carroll, marshal	1809	W22	142	101
Bird, Thomas & Alice et al, def.	Suit	Suttle, Henry, plt.	1810	X23	390	314

Party	What	Party	Year	Liber	Old	New
Bird, Thomas & Alice	Deed to	Ward, William	1811	AA26	319	215
Bird, Thomas & Alice	Mortgage to	Clarke, Francis	1811	AB27	404	332
Birth, James	Deed to	Lenox, Peter	1807	R17	269	205
Birth, James	Deed fr	Lenox, Peter	1807	R17	036	030
Birth, James & John Shaw	Deed fr	Ott, John	1807	R17	058	046
Birth, James & John Shaw	Deed fr	Hewitt, John, assignee U. Forrest	1807	S18	333	261
Birth, James & John Shaw	Deed fr	King, Josias Wilson & John Kilty	1809	W22	052	039
Birth, James et al	Deed fr	Cooke, Thomas	1802	H8	038	036
Bishop, Charles, of Balto. MD	B. of S. fr	Staley, Jacob, of G'tn.	1812	AE30	004	003
Bitourzy, Germain B., Rev. et al	Deed fr	Neale, Francis I., Rev., of G'tn.	1814	AG32	025	020
Bitourzy, Germain B., Rev. et al	Deed fr	Neale, Leonard, Rev.	1814	AG32	029	022
Bixby, Nathaniel P., of G'tn.	B. of S. to	Russel, Frederick A., of G'tn.	1817	AO39	205	150
Bixby, Nathaniel P., of G'tn.	D. of T. to	Davis, Richard & Thos. C. Wright	1817	AO39	144	109
Black, Samuel	B. of S. to	Wortz, Lucy	1814	AG32	097	073
Black, Stephen B., of G'tn.	Deed fr	Walker, Nathan, of G'tn.	1797	B2B	632	392
Blagden, George	Deed fr	Burnes, David	1794	B2A	023	025
Blagden, George	Deed to	Deakins, Francis	1798	D4	167	148
Blagden, George	Deed fr	Commissioners of Washington	1799	D4	327	312
Blagden, George	Deed fr	Carroll, Daniel, of *Duddington*	1801	G7	072	093
Blagden, George	Deed fr	Commissioners of Washington	1802	H8	064	060
Blagden, George	Deed fr	Hurdle, Thomas	1806	P15	374	249
Blagden, George	Deed fr	Dorsey, William H., of G'tn.	1807	R17	141	109
Blagden, George	Deed fr	Carroll, Daniel, of *Duddington*	1808	U20	194	107
Blagden, George	B. of S. fr	Clements, Martha	1809	X23	047	035
Blagden, George	B. of S. fr	Addison, Thomas G.	1809	W22	073	054
Blagden, George	Deed fr	Munroe, Thomas, Supt.	1810	Y24	476	421
Blagden, George	Mortgage fr	Cranch, William	1810	Y24	461	409
Blagden, George	Deed to	Sweeny, George	1810	Y24	532	467
Blagden, George	Deed fr	Carroll, Daniel, of *Duddington*	1811	AA26	068	050
Blagden, George	Deed fr	Thornton, William	1811	AA26	054	042
Blagden, George	D. of T. fr	Charles, Richard	1811	AA26	242	165
Blagden, George	Release to	Cranch, William	1816	AL36	150	150
Blagden, George & Robert Brent	D. of T. fr	Huddleston, Joseph, stonecutter	1810	Y24	242	223
Blagden, George et al	Deed fr	Brent, Daniel	1804	M12	027	027
Blagden, George et al	Release to	Brent, Daniel & William et al	1806	P15	062	037
Blagden, George et al	Deed fr	Carroll, Daniel, of *Duddington*	1811	AA26	249	169
Blagden, George, exr. of J. Emery	Deed to	Cook, Orlando	1811	Z25	465	368
Blagden, George, exr. of J. Emery	Deed to	Frank, George	1813	AF31	022	015
Blagden, George, mason	P. of Atty. fr	Swinton, Archibald, in Scot.	1808	U20	312	166
Blagden, George, trustee et al	Cert fr	Munroe, Thomas, Supt.	1813	AE30	350	262
Blagdon, George	Deed fr	Thornton, William	1802	H8	529	489
Blagg, John	Deed fr	Walker, George	1802	I9	233	371
Blagge, John, of NY et al	Deed fr	Walker, George	1802	G7	446	582
Blaire, John A., insolvent	Deed to	Jones, Charles, trustee	1805	N13	319	257
Blake, Betty H., w/o Dr. James H.	Letter to	Heigh, James	1807	S18	265	208
Blake, James H., of G'tn.	Deed fr	Brookes, Henry	1795	B2B	374	027
Blake, James H., Dr., of G'tn.	Deed to	Blake, Joseph, Capt., Calvert Co.	1799	D4	295	279
Blake, James H., Dr.	B. of S. fr	Lovejoy, John N., of G'tn.	1802	H8	437	401
Blake, James H., Dr.	Deed fr	Heigh, James, of Balto Co.	1807	S18	265	208
Blake, James H., Dr. & Betty H.	Deed to	Eliason, John	1808	T19	242	178
Blake, James H. et al	Deed fr	Jackson, John G., fr. Harrison Co.	1814	AG32	295	215
Blake, James H.	Deed fr	Ratcliffe, Richard, chan. comr.	1814	AG32	436	315
Blake, James H.	Deed fr	Barnes, John & Catharine Connell	1814	AG32	425	308
Blake, James H., mayor of Wash.	Deed to	Glover, Charles	1815	AI34	111	127
Blake, James H., mayor of Wash.	Deed to	Lenox, Peter	1815	AI34	106	121

Index to District of Columbia Land Records, 1792-1817

Party	What	Party	Year	Liber	Old	New
Blake, James H., mayor or Wash.	Deed to	Way, Andrew & George	1815	AI34	108	123
Blake, James H.	Deed fr	Buchanan, Thomas, of MD	1816	AL36	108	109
Blake, James H., Dr.	Deed fr	Shorter, Thomas	1816	AL36	157	158
Blake, James H.	Cert Free to	Hopewell, Dinah, oif Calvert Co.	1816	AM37	347	252
Blake, James H., Dr.	Deed fr	King, Samuel, of Newport RI	1816	AM37	314	229
Blake, James H.	Deed fr	Laird, John, exr. of J. Carleton	1816	AM37	526	390
Blake, James H.	Deed fr	Talbot, George W., of NY	1816	AM37	317	231
Blake, James H.	Deed to	McCormick, James et al	1816	AO39	003	002
Blake, James H.	Deed to	McCormick, James	1816	AO39	006	005
Blake, James H.	Cert Free to	Butler, Susan	1817	AO39	195	143
Blake, James H.	Deed fr	Slater, Sarah, wid/o David, P.G.	1817	AO39	468	321
Blake, James H.	Deed fr	Queen, Nicholas L.	1817	AO39	436	298
Blake, James H. et al	Deed fr	Bickley, Robert S., Bucks Co. PA	1817	AN38	564	411
Blake, James Heigh et al	Deed to	Clark, Francis	1810	Y24	374	338
Blake, James Heighe, Dr., G'tn.	D. of T. to	Heighe, James, Calvert Co.	1796	B2B	549	276
Blake, James Heighe, of G'tn.	Mortgage fr	Egan, Thomas Henry, Calvert Co.	1796	B2B	552	280
Blake, James Heighe, Dr., of G'tn.	Deed fr	Egan, Thomas Henry, Calvert Co.	1797	B2B	628	388
Blake, James Heighe, Dr., G'tn.	Deed to	Heighe, James, Capt., Calvert Co.	1799	D4	291	275
Blake, James Heighe et al	Deed to	Donohoo, Patrick	1810	Y24	062	055
Blake, James Heighe et al	Deed to	Scholfield, Joseph L.	1810	Y24	073	065
Blake, John, of Charleston SC	Deed fr	Burrows, Wm. B., Wm. et al	1804	L11	120	122
Blake, Joseph, Capt., Calvert Co.	Deed fr	Blake, James H., Dr., of G'tn.	1799	D4	295	279
Blake, Thomas H.	Qualify	Lieutenant, First Legion of Militia	1812	AC28	480	341
Blakeney, Abel & Mary, of Alexa.	Deed to	Smith, William, Loudoun Co. VA	1807	Q16	366	281
Blakeney, Abel, of Alexa.	B. of S. fr	Smith, William & Sarah, of Alexa.	1802	G7		697
Blakeney, Abel, of Alexa.	Deed to	Smith, William, of Loudoun Co. VA	1807	S18	385	307
Blanchard, William	Assign fr	Cochran, David	1816	AL36	004	004
Blanchard, William	Cert fr	Munroe, Thomas, Supt.	1817	AN38	016	013
Blanchard, William	Deed to	Glover, Charles	1817	AN38	185	134
Bland, Delilah	B. of S. fr	Walker, Sarah, her mother	1810	Z25	157	124
Bland, Edward	Agreement	Grantt, George	1811	Z25	388	305
Bland, Edward	Mortgage to	Cox, George & John Minitree	1813	AF31	514	376
Bland, Edward	B. of S. to	Walker, Zachariah	1814	AH33	060	054
Bland, Edward & George Grant	Deed fr	Dunlap, James, of G'tn.	1807	R17	103	080
Blane, William	L. of Atty. to	Law, Thomas	1802	H8	426	392
Blane, William, of Eng.	P. of Atty. to	Law, Thomas	1807	S18	236	
Blodget, Benjamin, of Boston MA	Cert fr	Commissioners of Washington	1792	B2A	295	414
Blodget, George	Suit	Munroe, Thomas	1804	L11	116	119
Blodget, R., wid/o Samuel	Assign to	Patterson, James	1817	AN38		049
Blodget, Samuel	Deed fr	Brent, Robert	1795	B2A	217	301
Blodget, Samuel	Deed to	Scott, Gustavus	1795	B2A	262	366
Blodget, Samuel	P. of Atty. to	Reintzel, Daniel or Jno. Stickney	1796	B2B	524	235
Blodget, Samuel	Deed to	Lowndes, Francis	1802	H8	012	011
Blodget, Samuel	Deed fr	Brent, Robert	1802	H8	013	012
Blodget, Samuel	Deed to	Ketland, Thomas	1802	I9	184	283
Blodget, Samuel	Lease to	Fennell, Edward	1804	K10	317	323
Blodget, Samuel	Lease to	Carpenter, Thomas	1804	L11	082	84
Blodget, Samuel	Lease to	Keef, William	1804	K10	274	279
Blodget, Samuel	Release fr	Bank of Columbia	1804	K10	409	424
Blodget, Samuel	Deed to	Stoddert, Benjamin	1811	AB27	022	021
Blodget, Samuel et al	Mortgage to	Bank of Columbia	1801	G7	162	215
Blodget, Samuel, Jr., Boston MA	Cert fr	Commissioners of Washington	1792	B2A	294	412
Blodget, Samuel, Jr., Boston MA	Cert fr	Commissioners of Washington	1792	B2A	295	414
Blodget, Samuel, Jr., of G'tn.	Deed fr	Baltzer, John, of Frederick Town	1793	A1-2	436	44
Blodget, Samuel, Jr., of Boston	Deed fr	Burnes, David	1794	B2A	075	097

Index to District of Columbia Land Records, 1792-1817

Party	What	Party	Year	Liber	Old	New
Blodget, Samuel, Jr.	Deed to	Peter, Thomas et al	1794	B2A	009	010
Blodget, Samuel, Jr.	Deed fr	Burnes, David	1794	B2A	074	096
Blodget, Samuel, Jr.	Deed to	Johnson, Thomas, Jr. et al	1794	B2A	009	010
Blodget, Samuel, Jr., of Phila. PA	Deed fr	Polock, Isaac, of G'tn.	1797	C3	077	64
Blodget, Samuel, Jr., of Phila. PA	Deed to	Smith, Samuel, of Balto.	1799	D4	424	396
Blodget, Samuel, Jr., of Phila. PA	Deed to	Tudor, William, of Boston	1800	F6	079	049
Blodget, Samuel, Jr.	Deed to	Smith, William M.	1802	I9	179	274
Blodget, Samuel, Jr. et al	Deed to	Bickley, Robert S., of Phila.	1805	L11	410	364
Blodget, Samuel, mer., of Phila.	Deed to	Euen, Thomas M.	1800	E5	272	266
Blodget, Samuel, now of Phila. PA	Deed to	Forrest, Uriah et al	1795	B2A	265	371
Blodget, Samuel, of Boston MA	Deed fr	Fendall, Philip Richard, Alexa.	1792	A1-1	130	189
Blodget, Samuel, of Phila.	Deed fr	Burnes, David	1794	B2A	017	018
Blodget, Samuel, of Phila.	Deed to	Frethey, Edward	1801	G7	299	416
Blodget, Samuel, of Phila.	Deed to	Commissioners of Washington	1801	G7	016	020
Blodget, Samuel, of Phila.	Deed to	Daugherty, James	1801	G7	316	442
Blodget, Samuel, of Phila.	Deed to	Caldwell, Elias B.	1801	G7	293	407
Blodgett, Samuel	Deed fr	Etting, Solomon, of Balto.	1801	G7	222	296
Blodgett, Samuel et al	Deed to	Lindsey, Adam	1801	G7	269	371
Blodgett, Samuel et al	Deed to	Lindsey, Adam	1801	G7	267	367
Blodgett, Samuel, Jr.	Deed fr	Commissioners of Washington	1801	G7	261	357
Blodgett, Samuel, of Phila. PA	Deed to	Templeton, John, of G'tn.	1801	G7	220	295
Blodgett, Samuel, of Phila. PA	Deed to	United States Insurance Company	1801	G7	097	125
Bloice, Jonathan	Deed fr	Beall, Thomas, of George	1806	Q16	330	253
Bloor, John	Deed to	Young, Thomas	1802	I9	447	739
Bloor, John	Cert fr	Munroe, Thomas, Supr.	1802	I9	200	313
Bloor, John	Deed to	Wilson, John A.	1806	P15	283	186
Blount, George	Deed fr	Beale, Thomas K.	1802	I9	426	706
Blount, George	Deed to	Dorsey, William H.	1802	I9	580	940
Blount, George	Deed fr	Dorsey, William H.	1802	I9	287	469
Blount, George	Deed fr	Dorsey, William H.	1802	I9	535	874
Blount, George	Mortgage to	Kramer, Henry	1804	K10	277	281
Blount, George	Assign to	Laurie, James, Rev.	1809	V21	228	162
Blount, George, insolvent	Deed to	Reed, William F., trustee	1809	X23	205	155
Blount, George, sadler	Assign to	More, James	1803	K10	068	74
Blout, George, trustee	Deed fr	Duffee, Mary, insolvent	1804	L11	272	250
Bloxham, James, of Alexa.	Deed fr	Peyton, T.W., of Alexa.	1817	AO39	149	112
Blunt, George	B. of S. to	Duffy, Mary	1809	W22	047	035
Boarman, Charles	Deed fr	Fenwick, Charles	1802	H8	134	131
Boarman, Charles		Certificate of Slaves	1802	H8	008	008
Boarman, Charles	Deed fr	Threlkeld, John	1813	AF31	466	338
Boarman, Charles, of G'tn.	Cert Free to	[ ], Samuel, shoemaker	1814	AG32	457	330
Boarman, Eleanor, wid., of G'tn.	Deed to	Beall, Gustavus, of G'tn.	1816	AL36	212	219
Boarman, Gerrard S.		Certificate of Slaves	1802	I9		095
Boarman, Raphael	Deed to	Beall, Thomas & John M. Gantt	1792	A1-1	064	94
Boarman, Raphael W.	Deed fr	Hedges, Nicholas	1815	AK35	062	048
Boarman, Richard B.A.	Slaves		1808	T19	295	216
Boarman, Richard B.A.	Deed fr	Bussard, John R., of Montg. Co.	1810	Z25	017	013
Boarman, Richard B.A., of G'tn.	Deed fr	Reintzel, John, of G'tn.	1810	Z25	016	012
Bodge, John, Allegany Co. et al	Assign to	Herty, Thomas	1805	N13	079	072
Bogenreiff, Margaret, of G'tn.	Deed fr	Reintzel, Anthony, of G'tn.	1811	Z25	418	329
Bogenreiff, Margaret, of G'tn.	Deed to	Bogenreiff, Valentine, of G'tn.	1815	AK35	319	254
Bogenreiff, Valentine, of G'tn.	Deed fr	Reintzel, Anthony, of G'tn.	1811	Z25	417	327
Bogenreiff, Valentine, of G'tn.	Deed fr	Gantt, Thomas T., of G'tn.	1815	AI34	002	003
Bogenreiff, Valentine, of G'tn.	Deed fr	Bogenreiff, Margaret, of G'tn.	1815	AK35	319	254
Bogenrief, Valentine, of G'tn.	D. of T. to	Baltzer, George, of G'tn.	1812	AC28	230	171

Index to District of Columbia Land Records, 1792-1817

Party	What	Party	Year	Liber	Old	New
Bogenrieff, Margaret	Deed fr	Reintzell, Anthony	1810	Y24	018	015
Bogenrieff, Margaret, of G'tn.	Deed to	Reintzel, Anthony, of G'tn.	1810	Z25	237	185
Bogenrieff, Valentine, of G'tn.	D. of T. to	Smith, Walter, of G'tn.	1815	AK35	320	255
Bogenriff, Margaret et al	Deed to	Reintzel, Anthony	1809	W22	364	236
Bohrer, Abraham	Deed fr	Beatty, Charles	1802	I9	514	842
Bohrer, George	Deed fr	Reintzel, Anthony, Gent. et al	1807	S18	134	109
Bohrer, George	Deed to	Ott, John, Dr., Gent.	1807	S18	136	111
Bohrer, George	Deed fr	Belt, Joseph Sprigg	1813	AF31	326	233
Bohrer, George, Gent.	Deed fr	Beatty, Charles A., Dr.	1811	Z25	128	100
Bohrer, George, of G'tn.	Deed fr	Gebhart, John, of Frederick Co.	1812	AD29	145	113
Bohrer, George, of G'tn.	Deed to	Miller, Jacob, of P.G. Co.	1813	AF31	355	253
Bohrer, George, of G'tn.	Deed fr	Bussard, Daniel, of G'tn.	1813	AF31	328	234
Bohrer, George, of G'tn.	Deed to	McDaniel, John	1815	AK35	471	370
Bohrer, George, of G'tn.	Lease to	Putnam, Ernestus, of G'tn.	1816	AL36	070	071
Bohrer, George, Sr.	Deed to	Reintzel, Anthony, Gent.	1807	S18	135	110
Bohrer, Jacob	Deed to	Brooke, Samuel	1809	V21	164	118
Bohrer, Jacob	Deed fr	Thomas, Gustavus, trustee of	1809	V21	162	117
Bohrer, Jacob	Deed fr	Williams, Elisha W., of G'tn.	1811	AC28	077	058
Bohrer, Jacob	Deed fr	Moore, Alexander	1814	AH33	320	276
Bohrer, Jacob	Deed fr	Beatty, Charles A., Dr., of G'tn.	1815	AI34	251	284
Bohrer, Jacob	Deed to	Mackall, Benjamin F.	1816	AO39	041	034
Bohrer, Jacob	Deed to	Mackall, Benjamin F.	1816	AO39	043	036
Bohrer, Jacob, of G'tn.	Deed fr	Boyle, David & Jane, Pr. Wm. Co.	1810	Y24	502	442
Bohrer, Jacob, of G'tn.	Deed to	Georgetown Lancaster School	1812	AD29	107	082
Bohrer, Jacob, of G'tn.	Deed to	Mayer, Henry	1814	AG32	167	119
Bohrer, Jacob, of G'tn.	Deed fr	Lanham, Elisha, of G'tn.	1815	AK35	215	169
Bohrer, Jacob, of G'tn.	Deed to	Mayer, Henry	1816	AL36	183	182
Bohrer, Mary	Deed fr	Wingerd, Abraham	1801	G7	201	268
Bohrer, Mary	Deed to	Gary, Everard	1802	I9	212	333
Bohrer, Mary M.	Deed to	Colclazier, Thomas	1814	AG32	280	200
Bohrer, Mary, wid., of G'tn.	Deed to	Kalklazer, Thomas, blacksmith	1803	K10	061	66
Boice, John	Deed fr	Chandler, Jacob	1802	I9	133	199
Bolser, John, Jr.	Deed fr	Beatty, Charles	1802	I9	077	109
Bomford, George, Col.	Deed fr	Simmons, William	1816	AM37	243	178
Bomford, George, Col.	Deed fr	Simmons, William	1816	AM37	246	180
Bomford, George, Col.	Deed fr	Simmons, William	1816	AM37	244	179
Bomford, George, Col.	B. of S. fr	Thornton, Jane et al	1817	AO39	105	082
Bond, James	Manumis fr	Caldwell, Timothy	1809	V21	230	168
Bond, Joshua B., of Phila. PA	Deed fr	Lee, Henry, of Westm. Co. VA	1801	G7	001	001
Bond, Joshua B., of Phila. et al	Deed fr	Fitzhugh, Philip	1801	G7	237	318
Bond, Joshua B. & Rebecca, PA	Deed to	Allen, John, mer.	1811	AA26	169	116
Bond, Nathan, of Boston MA	Cert fr	Commissioners of Washington	1792	B2A	295	413
Bond, Nathan, of Boston MA	Cert fr	Commissioners of Washington	1792	B2A	294	411
Bond, Nathan, of Boston MA	Cert fr	Commissioners of Washington	1792	B2A	296	415
Bond, Nathan, of Boston MA	Cert fr	Commissioners of Washington	1792	B2A	296	416
Bond, Nathan, of Boston MA	Cert fr	Commissioners of Washington	1796	B2A	337	475
Bond, Nathan, of Boston MA	Cert fr	Commissioners of Washington	1796	B2A	337	475
Bond, Nathan, of Boston MA	Cert fr	Commissioners of Washington	1796	B2A	337	474
Bond, Nathan, of Boston MA	Cert fr	Commissioners of Washington	1796	B2A	338	476
Bond, Nathan, of Portland MA	Deed to	Perkins, Joseph & Isaac	1801	G7	289	401
Bond, Nathaniel, of Portland MA	Deed to	Perkins, Joseph & Isaac	1801	F6	234	154
Bond, Phineas, of Phila. et al	D. of T. fr	Travis, Elizabeth, admx. of John	1808	V21	102	077
Bond, Phineas, of Phila. et al	Deed to	Fox, Josiah	1808	V21	109	081
Bond, Samuel & Richard D. Boyd	Deed fr	Picknall, Richard Henry	1809	X23	045	033
Bond, Samuel & Barney Parsons	Deed to	Mahony, Barney, of P.G. Co.	1812	AC28	501	357

Index to District of Columbia Land Records, 1792-1817

Party	What	Party	Year	Liber	Old	New
Bond, William	Deed fr	Crookshanks, John, of G'tn.	1797	B2B	634	394
Bond, William	B. of S. fr	Macpherson, Samuel	1802	I9	005	007
Bond, William	Manumis to	Queen, Milley	1802	H8	343	319
Bontz, Henry & Philip Rohr	Deed fr	Ritchie, Abner, sheriff	1800	E5	379	358
Bontz, Henry et al	Deed fr	Ritchie, Abner, sheriff	1800	E5	379	358
Boogher, Frederick, Frederick Co.	Deed to	Deakins, Francis	1800	E5	354	339
Boone, Arnold, of G'tn.	Deed to	Cox, John, of G'tn.	1815	AK35	089	068
Boone, Arnold, of G'tn.	Deed to	Dodge, Francis, of G'tn.	1815	AI34	181	207
Boone, Artnold, of G'tn.	Lease fr	Reintzel, Anthony, of G'tn.	1811	AB27	470	384
Boone, Edward, of G'tn.	Deed fr	Threlkeld, John, of Montg. Co.	1797	C3	175	147
Boone, Edward, of Charles Co.	Deed to	Middleton, Ignatius, of Charles Co.	1799	D4	195	178
Boone, Francis	B. of S. fr	Boone, Joseph	1801	G7	232	311
Boone, Ignatius	B. of S. to	Prout, William	1805	N13	115	110
Boone, Ignatius	Deed to	Law, John	1813	AE30	344	257
Boone, Ignatius, of Nicholas	Deed fr	Threlkeld, John	1800	E5	138	126
Boone, Ignatius, of Nicholas	Deed to	Middleton, Ignatius, Charles Co.	1800	E5	201	194
Boone, John	Manumis to	[ ], Terry (C)	1811	AA26	094	066
Boone, Joseph	B. of S. to	Boone, Francis	1801	G7	232	311
Boone, Joseph, of P.G. Co.	Cert fr	Commissioners of Washington	1797	B2B	475	167
Boone, Joseph, sheriff	Release to	Spalding, John et al	1799	E5	053	042
Bootes, Samuel	B. of S. to	Moore, James et al	1805	N13	383	307
Bootes, Samuel, innkeeper, G'tn.	B. of S. to	Patterson, Benjamin, of G'tn.	1806	O14	248	163
Booth, Edward	B. of S. fr	Club, Thomas	1805	N13	280	231
Booth, Elizabeth & S. Smallwood	D. of T. to	Caldwell, Elias B.	1816	AM37	229	168
Booth, Elizabeth et al	D. of T. to	Caldwell, Elias B.	1817	AN38	396	296
Booth, Jeremiah	Slaves	From King George Co. VA	1804	K10	330	
Booth, Jeremiah	Slaves	From King George Co. VA	1806	Q16	298	227
Booth, Jeremiah, Boyd's Hole VA	Deed fr	Barry, James	1802	H8	590	556
Booth, Jeremiah et al	Deed fr	Barry, James	1806	Q16	310	237
Booth, John, of Boyd's Hole VA	Deed fr	Barry, James	1802	H8	590	556
Booth, Mordecai	Contract to	Smallwood, Samuel N.	1815	AI34	173	198
Boothe, Benjamin	B. of S. fr	Wetherall, Charles	1817	AO39	151	114
Boothe, Edward	B. of S. fr	Howe, Alban	1812	AD29	360	303
Boothe, Edward	B. of S. to	Johnson, Joseph	1813	AF31	060	041
Boothe, George	B. of S. to	Scott, Henry	1817	AN38	162	118
Boothe, Jer. at al	Assign fr	Winsatt, Margaret	1805	O14	079	049
Boothe, Jeremiah	Slaves	From King George Co. VA	1805	M12	410	426
Boothe, Jeremiah	Slaves	From King George Co. VA	1806	P15	005	003
Boothe, Jeremiah et al	Assign fr	Adams, William	1805	O14	077	047
Borer, Peter, of G'tn.	Assign fr	Jones, John, of G'tn.	1794	B2A	164	218
Borer, Peter, of Montg. Co.	Deed fr	Beatty, Charles, Montgomery Co.	1796	B2B	392	052
Borrows, Joseph	Deed fr	Murdock, John, of G'tn.	1811	Z25	437	343
Borrows, Joseph	Deed fr	Dorsey, William H., of Balto.	1811	Z25	438	345
Borrows, Joseph	Deed to	Lewis, Samuel, Jr.	1812	AD29	136	195
Borrows, Joseph	Deed fr	Dorsey, William H., of Balto. MD	1812	AD29	297	244
Borrows, Joseph	Deed to	Cooper, William	1812	AD29	064	046
Borrows, Joseph	Deed to	Crawford, William	1812	AD29	227	187
Borrows, Joseph	Release to	Lewis, Samuel, Jr.	1816	AM37	471	340
Boswell, Benjamin	B. of S. to	Criger, Mary	1802	H8	343	320
Boswell, Benjamin & Mary	Deed to	Morsell, James Sewall, of G'tn.	1810	Y24	056	049
Boswell, Clement	Deed fr	Collard, George	1801	F6	175	110
Boswell, George, of P.G. Co.	B. of S. fr	Boswell, William	1807	R17	033	027
Boswell, Rhody, of Charles Co.	B. of S. to	Harriden, Nathaniel	1814	AG32	326	238
Boswell, Sarah (dau.)	Deed fr	Boswell, William	1802	H8	456	419
Boswell, William	Deed to	Boswell, Sarah (dau.)	1802	H8	456	419

Index to District of Columbia Land Records, 1792-1817

Party	What	Party	Year	Liber	Old	New
Boswell, William	Slaves	From MD	1806	Q16	094	060
Boswell, William	B. of S. to	Boswell, George, of P.G. Co.	1807	R17	033	027
Botelar, Alexander H.	Manumis to	[ ], Nathaniel (C)	1816	AL36	012	013
Boteler, Edward L., of P.G. Co.	Deed fr	Carleton, George, bricklayer, P.G.	1809	W22	394	256
Botner, Elias, of Alexa. Co.	Deed to	Miller, John S. & John Lutz	1811	AB27	359	297
Boucher, John Thomas	Deed fr	White, James & Nathan Lanham	1794	B2A	011	012
Boucher, John Thomas, P.G. Co.	Deed to	Lee, Thomas Sim, of G'tn.	1796	B2B	526	239
Boucher, John Thomas, P.G. Co.	Deed to	Murry, William, Dr., of G'tn.	1796	B2B	397	060
Boucher, John Thomas, P.G. Co.	Deed fr	Deakins, William Jr., of G'tn.	1796	B2B	441	123
Boucher, John Thomas, P.G. Co.	Release fr	Deakins, William Jr., of G'tn.	1796	B2B	554	283
Boucher, John Thomas, P.G. Co.	Deed to	Cramphin, Thomas, of Montg. Co.	1796	B2B	555	284
Boucher, John Thomas	Deed fr	White, James, Sr.	1796	B2B	516	223
Boucher, John Thomas	Deed to	Dorsey, William Hammond	1799	E5	090	
Boudinot, Elias et al	Release to	Nourse, Joseph	1813	AF31	011	008
Bourne, Sylvanus, of Boston MA	Deed to	Groeneveldt, Gilles et al	1796	B2B	496	192
Bowe, Kitty (M)	Cert. Free fr	McKee, Samuel, Garrad Co. KY	1815	AH33	451	387
Bowen, John	Lease fr	Prout, William	1810	Y24	145	132
Bowen, Thomas	Deed fr	May, Frederick	1805	M12	305	307
Bowen, Thomas	Deed fr	May, Frederick	1808	T19	057	042
Bowhay, William	Deed fr	Boyd, Washington	1810	Y24	092	082
Bowie, Fielder et al	Deed to	Beall, Thomas & John M. Gantt	1793	A1-2	392	1
Bowie, John, of Montg. Co.	Lease to	Morgan, William, of G'tn.	1816	AL36	533	498
Bowie, John, of Montg. Co.	Deed fr	Morgan, William, of G'tn.	1816	AL36	536	500
Bowie, Robert, of P.G. Co.	B. of S. to	Clarke, Walter	1816	AL36	545	508
Bowie, Thomas Contee, P.G. Co.	Deed fr	Deakins, William Jr., of G'tn.	1797	C3	243	201
Bowie, Walter, of P.G. Co. et al	Manumis to	[ ], Kate (C)	1815	AI34	004	004
Bowie, Washington	Deed fr	Johns, Aqula, of P.G. Co.	1808	U20	391	217
Bowie, Washington	Deed fr	Corporation of Georgetown	1808	U20	394	319
Bowie, Washington	Deed fr	Loundes, Francis	1809	W22	411	267
Bowie, Washington	Deed fr	Peter, Thomas, exr. of Robert	1812	AC28	325	237
Bowie, Washington	Mortgage fr	Stewart, David, trustee of Wm.	1812	AD29	509	430
Bowie, Washington	Indenture fr	Hedges, William Ritchie, s/o Nich.	1812	AD29	223	183
Bowie, Washington	Deed fr	Shaw, John & Thomas Corcoran	1813	AF31	437	314
Bowie, Washington	Release to	Nourse, Joseph	1813	AE30	397	292
Bowie, Washington	B. of S. fr	Reintzel, Valentine, of G'tn.	1813	AE30	546	405
Bowie, Washington	Deed fr	Georgetown, Major, Aldermen etc.	1814	AG32	179	127
Bowie, Washington	Deed to	Barry, James D. & S. Pleasonton	1816	AL36	484	456
Bowie, Washington	Deed fr	Key, Francis D.	1816	AL36	281	280
Bowie, Washington	Deed fr	Key, Francis D.	1816	AL36	482	455
Bowie, Washington	Deed fr	Richards, George	1817	AO39	058	048
Bowie, Washington & Margaret	Deed to	Mayor & Council of Georgetown	1807	R17	232	179
Bowie, Washington & John Kurtz	Deed fr	Smith, Andrew, of G'tn.	1812	AD29	542	457
Bowie, Washington & Margaret C.	Deed to	Peter, Sarah, wid/o David, of G'tn.	1814	AH33	353	305
Bowie, Washington & Margaret C.	Deed to	Brookes, Joseph, of G'tn.	1815	AH33	509	437
Bowie, Washington & John Kurtz	Deed to	Smith, Andrew	1815	AI34	402	425
Bowie, Washington, assignees of	Deed to	King, Adam	1804	L11	073	75
Bowie, Washington, assignees of	Deed to	Baltzer, John, Jr.	1804	L11	079	81
Bowie, Washington, assignees of	Deed to	King, George	1804	L11	075	77
Bowie, Washington, assignees of	Deed to	Dorsey, William H.	1804	L11	071	73
Bowie, Washington, bankrupt	Deed to	Nourse, Joseph	1804	K10	183	192
Bowie, Washington, bankrupt	Deed to	Smith, Walter et al	1804	K10	247	254
Bowie, Washington et al	Deed fr	Heugh, John, of G'tn., trustee	1815	AI34	091	104
Bowie, Washington, Gent.	Deed fr	Waters, William, Gent.	1810	Y24	101	092
Bowie, Washington, mer., of G'tn.	Deed to	Smith, Walter & Clement	1800	E5	144	133
Bowie, Washington, mer.	Deed fr	Upperman, Henry, Jr.	1810	Y24	102	093

Party	What	Party	Year	Liber	Old	New
Bowie, Washington, of G'tn.	Deed fr	Magruder, William B., of Balto.	1800	E5	136	124
Bowie, Washington, of G'tn.	Deed fr	Magruder, William B., of Balto.	1800	E5	133	121
Bowie, Washington, of G'tn.	Deed fr	Dorsey, William H., of G'tn.	1807	S18	046	038
Bowie, Washington, of G'tn.	Deed fr	Williams, Elisha, of G'tn.	1810	Y24	100	091
Bowie, Washington, of G'tn.	D. of T. fr	Reintzel, Valentine, of G'tn.	1810	Z25	121	094
Bowie, Washington, of G'tn. et al	Mortgage fr	Turner, Samuel, Jr., of G'tn.	1811	Z25	514	408
Bowie, Washington, of G'tn.	Deed to	King, Charles, of G'tn.	1812	AD29	367	309
Bowie, Washington, of G'tn.	Deed fr	Nourse, Joseph, of G'tn.	1812	AC28	117	088
Bowie, Washington, of G'tn.	Deed to	Goszler, John, of G'tn.	1812	AD29	465	391
Bowie, Washington, of G'tn.	Deed fr	Pickerell, John, of G'tn.	1814	AG32	142	102
Bowie, Washington, of G'tn.	Deed fr	Williams, Elisha, of G'tn.	1814	AG32	024	019
Bowie, Washington, of G'tn.	Deed fr	Eliason, John, of G'tn.	1814	AH33	349	302
Bowie, Washington, of G'tn.	Deed to	Lee, William, of G'tn.	1815	AH33	550	471
Bowie, Washington, of G'tn.	Deed fr	Scott, Sabret, of G'tn.	1816	AL36	283	281
Bowie, Washington, of G'tn.	Deed fr	Magruder, James A., of G'tn.	1816	AM37	233	171
Bowie, Washington, of G'tn.	Deed to	Porter, David, Com.	1816	AL36	166	167
Bowie, Washington, of G'tn.	Deed fr	Fitzhugh, Samuel, of G'tn.	1817	AO39	369	248
Bowie, Washington, of G'tn.	Deed to	Jones, Raphael, of G'tn.	1817	AN38	092	070
Bowling, Robert, of Alexa.	Lease fr	Latrobe, Benjamin Henry	1814	AG32	033	026
Bowman, John B., of G'tn.	Deed fr	Lucas, Henry, of G'tn.	1795	B2A	250	349
Bowman, John B. et al	Lease fr	Huter, Conrad, of G'tn.	1796	B2B	602	353
Bowman, Peter	Lease fr	Deakins, William et al	1795	B2A	353	499
Bowman, Peter, of G'tn.	Mortgage to	Henderson, John	1796	B2B	442	124
Boyd, Abraham	P. of Atty. fr	Wells, Nathan	1800	E5	162	151
Boyd, Ann et al	Deed fr	Scott, George, exr. of George	1795	B2B	368	020
Boyd, Ann et al	Deed to	Greenleaf, James, New York NY	1796	B2B	445	128
Boyd, George	B. of S. to	Scott, Isabella	1811	AB27	500	409
Boyd, John	B. of S. fr	Boyd, William	1808	U20	402	224
Boyd, Richard D. & Samuel Bond	Deed fr	Picknall, Richard Henry	1809	X23	045	033
Boyd, Richard D.	B. of S. fr	Picknall, Richard H.	1809	X23	159	117
Boyd, Richard D. & John Cooper	B. of S. fr	Airs, Thomas	1809	X23	050	037
Boyd, Richard D.	B. of S. to	Thomas, George N.	1810	Z25	137	108
Boyd, Richard D., insolvent	Deed to	Thomas, George N., trustee	1810	Z25	168	133
Boyd, Richard D.	B. of S. to	McCormick, Alexander	1810	Y24	511	449
Boyd, Washington	B. of S. fr	Pencock, Robert Ware, attorney	1804	K10	142	154
Boyd, Washington	Manumis to	[ ], Jacob (Negro)	1804	K10	143	155
Boyd, Washington	Deed fr	McClan, Robert	1809	V21	267	191
Boyd, Washington	Deed fr	Hanson, Washington	1809	V21	258	185
Boyd, Washington	Deed fr	Caldwell, Elias, trustee	1809	V21	168	121
Boyd, Washington	Deed to	Bowhay, William	1810	Y24	092	082
Boyd, Washington	Deed fr	Munroe, Thomas, Supt.	1810	Y24	332	301
Boyd, Washington	P. of Atty. fr	Bickley, Robert S., of Phila. PA	1810	Y24	008	006
Boyd, Washington	Deed fr	Washington Building Company	1812	AC28	498	356
Boyd, Washington	B. of S. fr	Stephenson, Clotworthy	1812	AC28	383	279
Boyd, Washington	Deed to	Caldwell, Elias B.	1812	AC28	173	130
Boyd, Washington	Cert fr	Brumley, Joseph, collector 1st W.	1813	AE30	321	241
Boyd, Washington	Cert fr	Brumley, Joseph, collector 1st W.	1813	AE30	320	240
Boyd, Washington	D. of T. fr	Burford, John A.	1813	AE30	475	353
Boyd, Washington	Cert fr	Brumley, Joseph, collector 1st W.	1813	AE30	319	239
Boyd, Washington	Cert fr	Brumley, Joseph, collector 1st W.	1813	AE30	319	239
Boyd, Washington	Deed to	Gardner, Esther	1813	AF31	292	208
Boyd, Washington	B. of S. fr	Hewitt, James	1814	AG32	402	293
Boyd, Washington	B. of S. fr	Vallet, Peter	1814	AH33	356	308
Boyd, Washington	Deed fr	Minifee, Charles & James Ewell	1814	AG32	173	123
Boyd, Washington	Deed to	Wilson, John A.	1815	AI34	218	249

Index to District of Columbia Land Records, 1792-1817

Party	What	Party	Year	Liber	Old	New
Boyd, Washington	Deed fr	Washington Building Company	1815	AI34	156	179
Boyd, Washington	Deed to	Hewitt, William	1815	AH33	478	408
Boyd, Washington	B. of S. fr	Minor, Daniel	1816	AL36	068	069
Boyd, Washington	Deed to	Worthington, William	1816	AM37	024	019
Boyd, Washington	Mortgage fr	Whetcroft, Henry	1816	AK35	484	380
Boyd, Washington & C. Glover	Deed fr	Moriarty, Ambrose	1814	AG32	162	116
Boyd, Washington, agent	Agreement	Scallan, James	1816	AL36	500	469
Boyd, Washington, collector	Deed to	Johnson, Joseph	1805	M12	258	260
Boyd, Washington, collector	Deed to	Varden, Ezra	1805	N13	196	172
Boyd, Washington, collector	Deed to	Marshall, Barbara	1805	N13	006	006
Boyd, Washington, collector	Deed to	Holmead, John	1805	O14	008	007
Boyd, Washington, collector	Deed to	Varden, Charles	1806	P15	116	074
Boyd, Washington, collector	Deed to	King, Robert	1806	P15	200	134
Boyd, Washington, collector	Deed to	Connell, Catharine	1811	AB27	181	149
Boyd, Washington, collector	Deed to	Templeman, George, Allegany Co.	1815	AI34	335	367
Boyd, Washington, coroner	Bond to	United States	1802	I9	116	170
Boyd, Washington et al	Deed fr	Johnson, Catherine	1801	G7	385	517
Boyd, Washington et al	Deed fr	Munroe, Thomas, Supt.	1802	I9	374	621
Boyd, Washington et al	Deed fr	Parsons, Joseph B.	1807	R17	123	095
Boyd, Washington et al	Deed to	Parsons, Joseph Baker	1808	T19	023	018
Boyd, Washington et al	Manumis to	[ ], Hanson (negro)	1808	T19	126	089
Boyd, Washington et al	Suit ads	Potomac Company	1812	AG32	258	183
Boyd, Washington, marshal	Deed to	Tippett, Cartwright	1808	U20	353	192
Boyd, Washington, marshal	Deed to	McCormick, James	1808	U20	346	187
Boyd, Washington, marshal	Deed to	Cozens, William R.	1808	U20	349	189
Boyd, Washington, marshal	Deed to	Hagner, Peter	1808	V21	067	053
Boyd, Washington, marshal	Deed to	Bussard, Daniel, of G'tn.	1809	X23	147	106
Boyd, Washington, marshal	Deed to	Goszler, John, of G'tn.	1809	W22	325	211
Boyd, Washington, marshal	Deed to	O'Neale, William	1809	W22	343	221
Boyd, Washington, marshal	Deed to	Moore, James	1811	AA26	312	211
Boyd, Washington, marshal	Deed to	Costigan, Joseph	1811	AB27	285	234
Boyd, Washington, marshal	Deed to	Van Ness, John P.	1811	AB27	154	127
Boyd, Washington, marshal	Deed to	Bridges, John, of G'tn.	1811	AB27	399	329
Boyd, Washington, marshal	Deed to	Cozens, William R.	1811	AC28	087	066
Boyd, Washington, marshal	Deed to	Goszler, John, of G'tn.	1812	AD29	466	394
Boyd, Washington, marshal	Deed to	Wharton, Frankliln	1812	AC28	503	359
Boyd, Washington, marshal	Deed to	Webster, Toppan	1812	AC28	340	246
Boyd, Washington, marshal	Deed to	Parsons, William	1813	AE30	415	306
Boyd, Washington, marshal	Deed to	Hamilton, Christiana	1814	AG32	392	286
Boyd, Washington, marshal	Deed to	Fenwick, Thomas	1814	AG32	253	180
Boyd, Washington, marshal	Deed to	Murdock, John	1814	AG32	440	318
Boyd, Washington, marshal	Deed to	Coombe, Griffith	1814	AH33	078	070
Boyd, Washington, marshal	Deed to	Cocke, Buller	1815	AK35	086	066
Boyd, Washington, marshal	Deed to	Peltz, John	1815	AK35	397	313
Boyd, Washington, marshal	Deed to	Holland, Edward	1816	AL36	477	450
Boyd, Washington, marshal	Deed to	Caldwell, Elias B.	1816	AL36	371	360
Boyd, Washington, marshal	Deed to	Sexton, Francis, of NY	1816	AL36	443	421
Boyd, Washington, marshal	Deed to	Neale, Francis, Rev., of G'tn.	1816	AL36	279	278
Boyd, Washington, marshal	Deed to	Cannon, Sarah	1816	AM37	335	243
Boyd, Washington, marshal	Deed to	Ewell, Thomas, Dr.	1816	AM37	310	226
Boyd, Washington, marshal	Deed to	Edwards, Lewis	1816	AO39	016	013
Boyd, Washington, marshal	Deed to	Jones, Richard, of G'tn.	1817	AO39	211	154
Boyd, Washington, marshal	Deed to	Van Ness, John P.	1817	AN38	070	055
Boyd, William	B. of S. to	Boyd, John	1808	U20	402	224
Boyer, Augustin, by his attorney	Deed to	Finlay, Oliver P., of Alexa.	1809	V21	390	294

Index to District of Columbia Land Records, 1792-1817

Party	What	Party	Year	Liber	Old	New
Boyer, Augustin, of Tioga Co. NY	B. of S. to	Boyer, Richard M., of G'tn.	1809	V21	390	293
Boyer, Augustine & Richard M.	Deed fr	Stoddert, Benjamin, of G'tn.	1801	G7	284	394
Boyer, Richard M., of G'tn.	B. of S. fr	Boyer, Augustin, of Tioga Co. NY	1809	V21	390	293
Boyer, Richard M.	Deed fr	Dawes, Isaac	1810	Z25	065	049
Boyer, Richard Montgomery, G'tn.	Deed to	Finlay, Oliver P., of Alexa.	1809	V21	390	294
Boyer, Richard Montgomery, G'tn.	D. of T. to	Jones, Benjamin & Horatio, G'tn.	1811	AA26	240	164
Boyert, P.C.F.	Assign to	Long, Robert	1811	AC28	048	036
Boyert, P.C.F.	B. of S. to	Long, Robert & James Johnston	1811	AC28	046	035
Boyle, David & Jane, Pr. Wm. Co.	Deed to	Bohrer, Jacob, of G'tn.	1810	Y24	502	442
Boyle, David, of Pr. Wm. Co. VA	Deed fr	Huie, Hellen Grant, of Pr. Wm. Co.	1809	V21	375	278
Boyle, Eghtane M.	Mortgage to	Sandford, George	1808	V21	126	083
Boyle, John	Deed fr	Eliot, Samuel, Jr.	1816	AL36	388	375
Boyle, John	Deed fr	Barnes, John, of G'tn.	1817	AN38	291	213
Brackenridge, John	Deed fr	Commissioners of Washington	1801	F6	189	121
Brackenridge, John	Deed to	Bradley, Phineas	1801	G7	483	620
Brackenridge, John	Deed fr	Commissioners of Washington	1801	F6	186	119
Brackenridge, John	Deed to	McDonald, Archibald	1811	AB27	131	108
Brackenridge, John	Mortgage fr	French, George	1813	AE30	406	499
Brackenridge, John	Deed to	French, George	1813	AE30	392	289
Brackenridge, John	Manumis to	Herbert, Polly (C), age 20	1816	AM37	223	164
Brackenridge, John & Eleanor	Deed to	Macdaniel, Ezekiel	1814	AG32	231	164
Brackenridge, John & P. Bradley	Deed fr	Beatty, Charles A.	1816	AM37	092	074
Brackenridge, John, of Montg. Co.	B. of S. fr	Wood, Hezekiah	1810	Y24	078	069
Braden, Elizabeth, of G'tn.	Deed fr	Thompson, James	1813	AE30	515	382
Braden, Elizabeth [Braiden]	Deed fr	Thompson, James	1812	AC28	369	258
Bradey, Nathaniel	Deed to	Law, John	1808	U20	355	193
Bradford, William (Y), of G'tn.	Manumis to	Barber, Henny (C)	1814	AH33	283	246
Bradford, William, of G'tn.	Deed fr	Barber, Henny, of G'tn.	1814	AH33	282	245
Bradley, Abraham, Esq.	Deed fr	Beatty, Charles A., Dr.	1811	Z25	517	411
Bradley, Abraham, Jr.	Deed fr	Commissioners of Washington	1801	G7	434	569
Bradley, Abraham, Jr.	Deed fr	King, Josias W. & Letitia et al	1811	AC28	069	052
Bradley, Abraham, Jr.	Deed fr	Bradley, Phineas, trustee	1811	Z25	548	436
Bradley, Abraham, Jr.	Deed to	Bradley, Phineas	1811	Z25	550	437
Bradley, Abraham, Jr.	D. of T. fr	Hewitt, James	1811	AA26	396	263
Bradley, Abraham, Jr.	Release to	Hewitt, James	1813	AF31	209	141
Bradley, Abraham, Jr., Montg. Co.	Deed fr	Key, Philip B. & Jos. W. Clagett	1815	AH33	401	346
Bradley, Arthur	Cert Free fr	Washington, William A.	1810	Y24	143	130
Bradley, Francis	Deed fr	McDougall, Duncan Stewart et ux	1801	G7	070	091
Bradley, Phineas	Deed fr	Brackenridge, John	1801	G7	483	620
Bradley, Phineas	Deed to	Gilliss, Thomas H. et al	1801	G7	368	500
Bradley, Phineas	Deed fr	Dove, Joseph	1801	G7	134	176
Bradley, Phineas	Deed fr	Brown, Robert	1802	I9	246	397
Bradley, Phineas	Deed fr	Davis, Charles B.	1809	X23	249	194
Bradley, Phineas	Deed to	Lambert, Morris, of G'tn.	1809	X23	284	225
Bradley, Phineas	Deed fr	Dixon, James, Duplin Co. NC et al	1810	X23	339	272
Bradley, Phineas	Deed fr	Bestor, Harvey	1811	Z25	552	439
Bradley, Phineas	Deed fr	Bradley, Abraham, Jr.	1811	Z25	550	437
Bradley, Phineas	Deed to	McDaniel, Ezekiel	1811	Z25	527	419
Bradley, Phineas	Deed to	Hewitt, James	1811	AA26	389	259
Bradley, Phineas	Deed to	Davis, Charles B.	1812	AD29	171	137
Bradley, Phineas	Deed to	Brown, Obadiah B.	1812	AD29	263	217
Bradley, Phineas	Deed to	Burrows, Joseph	1812	AC28	317	230
Bradley, Phineas	Release to	McLean, Cornelius	1814	AH33	358	310
Bradley, Phineas	D. of T. fr	McLean, Cornelius	1814	AH33	180	166
Bradley, Phineas	Deed to	Tate, Andrew	1814	AG32	283	203

Party	What	Party	Year	Liber	Old	New
Bradley, Phineas	D. of T. fr	McLean, Cornelius	1815	AI34	412	435
Bradley, Phineas	Deed to	Varnum, James M.	1815	AI34	492	500
Bradley, Phineas	Deed fr	Varnum, James M.	1815	AI34	496	503
Bradley, Phineas	Deed fr	Whetcroft, William, heirs of	1815	AI34	076	085
Bradley, Phineas	Deed to	District of Columbia	1815	AH33	543	465
Bradley, Phineas	B. of S. to	Threlkeld, John	1817	AO39	254	183
Bradley, Phineas	B. of S. fr	Worthan, Charles, carpenter	1817	AN38	213	155
Bradley, Phineas & O.B. Brown	Deed fr	Andrews, George, Cincinnati OH	1813	AE30	120	092
Bradley, Phineas & John Davis	Deed fr	Holland, Edward	1817	AO39	225	163
Bradley, Phineas et al	Deed fr	Thorpe, Thomas	1804	L11	365	329
Bradley, Phineas et al	Deed to	Thorpe, Thomas	1808	U20	410	229
Bradley, Phineas et al	Deed fr	Beatty, Charles A.	1816	AM37	092	074
Bradley, Phineas et al	Deed to	Elliott, Samuel, Jr.	1816	AM37	194	145
Bradley, Phineas, trustee	Deed to	Farrell, Zephaniah	1811	AB27	075	063
Bradley, Phineas, trustee	Deed to	Bradley, Abraham, Jr.	1811	Z25	548	436
Bradley, William A. & T. Hughes	Deed fr	Munroe, Thomas & Frances	1815	AI34	250	283
Bradley, William A.	Deed to	Hughes, Thomas	1816	AK35	498	392
Bradley, William A.	Deed fr	Van Ness, John P. & Marcia	1816	AL36	119	120
Bradley, William A. & T. Hughes	Manumis to	[ ], Minty (C)	1816	AM37	076	062
Bradley, William A. & S. Eliot, Jr.	Deed fr	Whetcroft, Henry & Sarah	1816	AM37	410	294
Bradley, William Alfred	Deed fr	Hebb, William, of P.G. Co.	1816	AL36	117	118
Brady, Francis	Deed fr	Walls, George, of P.G. Co.	1812	AC28	180	136
Brady, Francis	Lease fr	Brady, Nathaniel	1812	AC28	378	275
Brady, Joshua	Manumis to	Lyles, Isaac (negro)	1807	R17	038	031
Brady, Michael	Deed fr	Polock, Isaac	1802	I9	303	497
Brady, Michael	Deed fr	Moore, Nicholas	1808	V21	036	026
Brady, Michael	Deed fr	Moore, Nicholas	1808	V21	127	093
Brady, Nathaniel	Lease fr	Prout, William	1806	Q16	237	163
Brady, Nathaniel	Deed fr	Brown, Thomas	1807	S18	398	317
Brady, Nathaniel	Deed fr	Brashears, John W.	1807	S18	237	188
Brady, Nathaniel	Deed fr	Law, John, by P. of Atty.	1807	S18	396	315
Brady, Nathaniel	Deed to	Brashears, John W.	1807	S18	205	164
Brady, Nathaniel	Deed to	Franklin, Nicholas	1808	U20	123	070
Brady, Nathaniel	Lease fr	Little, Israel	1808	T19	210	152
Brady, Nathaniel	Deed fr	Taylor, John & Margaret	1811	AB27	070	059
Brady, Nathaniel	Assign fr	Little, Israel	1811	AB27	065	056
Brady, Nathaniel	Release to	Brashears, John W.	1812	AD29	290	238
Brady, Nathaniel	Lease to	Brady, Francis	1812	AC28	378	275
Brady, Nathaniel	Mortgage to	Watterston, George	1812	AD29	352	295
Brady, Nathaniel	Deed fr	Davis, Ahasuerus, of Charles Co.	1814	AH33	064	057
Brady, Nathaniel, trustee	Deed fr	Prout, William	1813	AF31	184	124
Braiden, Elizabeth	D. of T. to	Mountz, John	1813	AE30	541	401
Brakenridge, John	Deed fr	Brooke, Samuel	1802	I9	507	831
Brakenridge, John, clerk, P.G. Co.	Deed fr	White, James, Sr., of P.G. Co.	1798	C3	343	276
Bramlett, Lensford M. & Sarah et al	Deed to	Orr, Benjamin Grayson	1817	AN38	198	144
Brandenburgher, Christopher	Deed to	Beall, William Murdock	1792	A1-1	161	230
Brandt, Christopher & Rosannah	Deed to	Conrad, Frederick, of VA	1800	E5	217	211
Brangle, Lawrence	Deed fr	McCleery, Henry	1806	P15	306	201
Brannan, John	Partition	Hunt, William	1817	AO39	460	316
Brannan, John et al	Deed to	Ingle, John P. & Eleazar Lindsley	1817	AO39	206	150
Brannon, John & William Hunt	Deed fr	Gordon, Elisha & Elizabeth, Phila.	1815	AK35	101	078
Brashear, A.D. & G.I.	Deed fr	Brashear, Nathaniel	1802	I9	490	805
Brashear, Ann et al	Deed fr	Reintzel, Andrew, now of G'tn.	1800	E5	251	244
Brashear, Belt & Anne, Fredk. Co.	Deed to	Cook, John, of Frederick Co.	1805	N13	354	285
Brashear, Nathaniel	Deed to	Brashear, A.D. & G.I.	1802	I9	490	805

Party	What	Party	Year	Liber	Old	New
Brashears, Jeremiah	B. of S. to	Soper, Alexander, of P.G. Co.	1811	AA26	089	063
Brashears, John D., insolvent	Deed to	Crawford, Jacob, trustee	1805	O14	073	044
Brashears, John M.	Deed fr	Bryan, Wilson	1805	N13	274	228
Brashears, John W.	Deed to	Brady, Nathaniel	1807	S18	237	188
Brashears, John W.	Deed fr	Brady, Nathaniel	1807	S18	205	164
Brashears, John W.	Manumis to	[ ], Treacy (negro)	1807	R17	351	267
Brashears, John W.	Deed to	Poston, Bartholomew	1809	W22	186	130
Brashears, John W.	Release fr	Brady, Nathaniel	1812	AD29	290	238
Brashears, John W.	Convey fr	Laird, John, exr. of Jos. Carleton	1812	AD29	468	395
Brashears, John W.	Deed fr	Laird, John, exr. of J. Carleton	1813	AF31	369	264
Brashears, John W. et al	B. of S. fr	Parry, Stephen	1814	AG32	305	222
Brashears, Nathaniel	B. of S. to	Cherry, Robert	1802	I9	015	020
Brashears, Nathaniel	Deed fr	Prout, William	1808	U20	068	038
Brashears, Nathaniel	Lease fr	Prout, William	1815	AH33	389	337
Brashears, Nathaniel	Deed to	Herbert, James	1815	AI34	416	437
Brashears, Richard B.	Deed to	Pairo, Thomas W.	1815	AH33	480	410
Brashears, Trueman, of Alexa.	Deed fr	Steuart, William, of G'tn.	1811	Z25	385	303
Brashears, Trueman, of Alexa.	Deed fr	Stuart, David, of G'tn.	1812	AB27	529	432
Brashears, Trueman, of Alexa. Co.	Deed fr	Morsell, James S., of G'tn.	1812	AB27	531	433
Brashears, Trueman, of Alexa.	D. of T. to	Taylor, Robert I., of Alexa.	1812	AB27	533	433
Bratt, Watta Bragg & Anna et al	Deed to	King, James Carrol	1805	M12	307	309
Brauer, Frederick	B. of S. fr	Keller, Frederick, of G'tn.	1816	AL36	420	401
Breck, Samuel	Mortgage fr	Templeman, John, of G'tn.	1806	P15	001	001
Breckenridge, James, Gen., of VA	Deed fr	Patison, Mary, of Dorchester Co.	1816	AL36	377	366
Breckenridge, John & P. Bradley	Deed to	Elliott, Samuel, Jr.	1816	AM37	194	145
Breckenridge, John, Rev. et al	D. of T fr	Van Ness, John P. & Marcia	1817	AN38	252	185
Breckenridge, Nelly, w/o John	Deed fr	White, James, Jr., of Montg. Co.	1813	AF31	413	298
Brengle, Laurence, Frederick Co.	Deed fr	Schnertzel, George, Sr., Fredk.	1804	K10	181	189
Brengle, Laurence, Frederick Co.	Deed fr	Davidson, John, of Annapolis	1804	K10	364	378
Brengle, Laurence, Frederick Co.	Deed fr	Cross, Lewis & Mary, of VA	1804	K10	383	397
Brengle, Lawrence, Frederick Co.	Deed fr	Dern, Frederick & Elizabeth	1804	K10	322	330
Brengle, Lawrence, Frederick Co.	Deed fr	Buckius, John, Jr. & William	1804	K10	295	297
Brengle, Lawrence, Frederick Co.	Deed fr	Buckius, John, Sr., Frederick Co.	1804	L11	164	162
Brengle, Lawrence, Frederick Co.	Deed fr	Hobbs, William C. & Christiana	1805	M12	142	138
Brengle, Lawrence, Frederick Co.	Deed fr	Ramsberg, Jacob, exr. V. Steckle	1805	N13	372	299
Brengle, Lawrence, Frederick Co.	Deed to	McCleery, Henry, Frederick Co.	1806	P15	303	199
Brengle, Lawrence, Frederick Co.	Deed to	Holtzman, Jacob, of G'tn.	1808	U20	336	181
Brengle, Lawrence [Bringle]	Deed fr	Schnertzel, George	1802	I9	589	954
Brengle, Lawrence [Bringle]	Deed fr	Carberry, Henry & Susanna	1802	I9	590	955
Brensinger, Christian, of Balto.	Deed to	Myer, John Jeremiah [Myers]	1813	AF31	136	091
Brent, Adelaide, d/o Daniel C.	Deed Gift fr	Brent, Daniel Carroll	1805	M12	232	234
Brent, Daniel	Deed fr	Munroe, Thomas, Supr.	1802	I9	258	416
Brent, Daniel	Slave		1804	K10	211	
Brent, Daniel	Slave	From VA	1805	M12	161	158
Brent, Daniel	Deed fr	Van Ness, John P. & Marcia	1805	M12	350	356
Brent, Daniel	Deed fr	Pleasonton, Stephen	1806	Q16	020	013
Brent, Daniel	Deed fr	Digges, William Dudley, P.G. Co.	1815	AK35	067	052
Brent, Daniel	Manumis to	[ ], Mary (C)	1816	AK35	255	202
Brent, Daniel	Deed fr	Eliot, Samuel, Jr.	1817	AO39	323	230
Brent, Daniel	Deed fr	Eliot, Samuel, Jr.	1817	AN38	049	040
Brent, Daniel & William et al	Release fr	Van Ness, John P. et al	1806	P15	062	037
Brent, Daniel & William	Deed fr	Clerklee, James, of Charles Co.	1816	AM37	260	191
Brent, Daniel C.	Deed to	Child, Henry	1802	I9	346	571
Brent, Daniel C.	Qualify		1802	I9	463	764
Brent, Daniel C.	Deed to	Van Ness, John P.	1802	I9	545	887

Index to District of Columbia Land Records, 1792-1817

Party	What	Party	Year	Liber	Old	New
Brent, Daniel C.	Deed to	Stewart, William	1802	I9	552	896
Brent, Daniel C.	Deed to	Johns, Aquila	1802	I9	343	566
Brent, Daniel C.	Slave		1806	Q16	314	240
Brent, Daniel C., of Stafford Co.	Deed fr	Bickley, Robert S., of Phila. PA	1812	AD29	029	020
Brent, Daniel C.	Cert. to	McNantz, Charles	1812	AC28	239	177
Brent, Daniel Carroll, marshal	Deed to	Queen, Joseph	1801	G7	370	502
Brent, Daniel Carroll, marshal	Deed to	May, Frederick	1802	H8	446	410
Brent, Daniel Carroll, marshal	Deed to	Threlkeld, John, of G'tn.	1804	K10	319	326
Brent, Daniel Carroll, marshal	Deed to	McLaughlin, Charles, of G'tn.	1804	L11	260	
Brent, Daniel Carroll, marshal	Deed to	Moore, George	1804	L11	368	331
Brent, Daniel Carroll, marshal	Deed to	Ott, John, of G'tn.	1804	L11	057	58
Brent, Daniel Carroll, marshal	Deed to	Cranch, William	1804	L11	156	155
Brent, Daniel Carroll, marshal	Deed to	Thornton, William	1804	L11	358	323
Brent, Daniel Carroll, marshal	Deed to	Dawes, Isaac, of G'tn.	1804	L11	180	174
Brent, Daniel Carroll, marshal	Deed to	Mitchell, John, of G'tn.	1804	L11	281	258
Brent, Daniel Carroll	Deed Gift to	Brent, William, s/o Daniel C.	1805	M12	230	232
Brent, Daniel Carroll	Deed Gift to	Brent, Adelaide, d/o Daniel C.	1805	M12	232	234
Brent, Daniel Carroll, marshal	Deed to	McCreery, William, of Balto.	1805	M12	229	230
Brent, Daniel Carroll, marshal	Deed to	Barry, Robert, of Balto.	1805	M12	055	052
Brent, Daniel Carroll	Deed to	Duvall, Gabriel	1805	M12	284	285
Brent, Daniel Carroll	Deed Gift to	Brent, Eleanor C., d/o Daniel C.	1805	M12	231	233
Brent, Daniel Carroll, marshal	Deed to	Simmes, George, of P.G. Co.	1805	M12	152	148
Brent, Daniel Carroll, marshal	Deed to	Johnston, James	1805	N13	252	211
Brent, Daniel Carroll, marshal	Deed to	Taylor, James N., of Phila. et al	1805	O14	140	091
Brent, Daniel Carroll, marshal	Deed to	Underwood, Robert	1805	O14	138	090
Brent, Daniel Carroll, marshal	Deed to	Baltzer, John, of G'tn.	1805	N13	286	234
Brent, Daniel Carroll, marshal	Deed to	Cochran, Alexander	1805	O14	106	066
Brent, Daniel Carroll, marshal	Deed to	Brent, Robert	1806	P15	333	220
Brent, Daniel Carroll, marshal	Deed to	Bullus, John	1806	Q16	135	088
Brent, Daniel Carroll, trustee et al	Deed to	Varden, Ezra	1807	Q16	404	311
Brent, Daniel Carroll, trustee et al	Deed to	Bickley, Robert S., of Phila. PA	1807	R17	026	022
Brent, Daniel Carroll, trustee et al	Deed to	Mathers, James	1807	R17	022	019
Brent, Daniel Carroll	Deed fr	Bickley, Robert S., of Phila. PA	1807	R17	398	301
Brent, Daniel Carroll, trustee et al	Deed to	Lindsay, Adam	1807	R17	251	190
Brent, Daniel Carroll, trustee et al	Deed to	Varden, Charles H.	1807	R17	016	014
Brent, Daniel Carroll, trustee et al	Deed to	Lenox, Peter	1807	R17	271	206
Brent, Daniel Carroll, marshal	Deed to	Van Ness, John P.	1807	S18	030	025
Brent, Daniel Carroll, trustee et al	Deed to	Howe, Robert F., of G'tn.	1807	S18	001	001
Brent, Daniel Carroll	Deed to	Law, Thomas	1807	S18	007	006
Brent, Daniel Carroll, trustee et al	Deed to	Thornton, William	1807	S18	094	076
Brent, Daniel Carroll, marshal	Deed to	Dixon, Thomas	1808	T19	323	235
Brent, Daniel Carroll, marshal	Deed to	Peter, John, of G'tn.	1808	U20	007	004
Brent, Daniel Carroll, marshal	Deed to	Renner, Daniel, of G'tn.	1808	U20	028	017
Brent, Daniel Carroll, marshal	Deed to	Kirby, John B.	1808	T19	268	197
Brent, Daniel Carroll, marshal	Deed to	Bird, Alice, late Dermott	1809	W22	142	101
Brent, Daniel Carroll, marshal	Deed to	Cranch, William	1809	W22	128	091
Brent, Daniel Carroll, marshal	Deed to	Thompson, Jonah, of Alexa. et al	1813	AF31	261	182
Brent, Daniel et al	Convey fr	Gillis, Thomas H. et al	1804	L11	104	108
Brent, Daniel et al	Deed to	Van Ness, John P. et al	1804	M12	027	027
Brent, Daniel et al	Deed fr	Law, Thomas	1805	N13	260	217
Brent, Daniel et al	Deed fr	Dorsey, William H., of Balto.	1809	X23	239	186
Brent, Daniel et al	Deed fr	Tingey, Thomas	1810	Y24	406	366
Brent, Daniel et al	Deed to	Boyd, Washington	1812	AC28	498	356
Brent, Daniel, of Stafford Co. VA	Deed fr	Carroll, Elizabeth	1799	D4	318	302
Brent, Daniel, trustee	Convey to	Davis, John	1816	AM37	292	214

Index to District of Columbia Land Records, 1792-1817

Party	What	Party	Year	Liber	Old	New
Brent, Eleanor & Robert Young	Deed fr	Young, Notley, heirs of	1802	H8	499	458
Brent, Eleanor & Robert Y.	Deed to	McNantz, Charles	1812	AC28	229	170
Brent, Eleanor C., d/o Daniel C.	Deed Gift fr	Brent, Daniel Carroll	1805	M12	231	233
Brent, Eleanor et al	Deed to	Giberson, William	1810	Y24	446	396
Brent, Elizabeth, w/o Daniel	Deed fr	Heath, Nathaniel H.	1815	AI34	333	366
Brent, George, of Stafford Co. VA	Deed to	Beall, Thomas & John M. Gantt	1792	A1-1	037	56
Brent, J.G. & Robert	Deed to	Sim, Patrick Jr.	1802	I9	417	691
Brent, Robert	Deed fr	Young, Notley	1795	B2A	228	317
Brent, Robert	Deed to	Blodget, Samuel	1795	B2A	217	301
Brent, Robert	Deed fr	Commissioners of Washington	1798	D4	119	102
Brent, Robert	Deed fr	Carroll, Elizabeth	1799	D4	317	301
Brent, Robert	Cert fr	Commissioners of Washington	1800	F6	111	069
Brent, Robert	Deed to	Blodget, Samuel	1802	H8	013	012
Brent, Robert	Deed to	McCleary, Henry	1802	H8	352	328
Brent, Robert	Deed fr	Cranch, William	1804	L11	218	205
Brent, Robert	Deed fr	Brent, Daniel Carroll, marshal	1806	P15	333	220
Brent, Robert	Deed fr	Law, Thomas	1807	S18	228	181
Brent, Robert	Deed to	Clarke, Francis	1807	R17	392	297
Brent, Robert	Deed fr	Young, Nicholas	1809	X23	196	148
Brent, Robert	Cert Free to	Smith, William (mulatto)	1809	W22	227	
Brent, Robert	Cert Free to	Shorter, Charles	1809	W22	126	090
Brent, Robert	Release to	Cranch, William	1810	Z25	352	275
Brent, Robert	Deed fr	Brent, William	1810	Z25	255	199
Brent, Robert	Cert Free to	Jackson, Joseph, children of	1811	AB27	396	326
Brent, Robert	Cert Free to	Fletcher, Elender et al	1811	AB27	395	325
Brent, Robert	Cert Free to	Jones, William et al	1811	AB27	395	325
Brent, Robert	Cert Free to	Frazer, Patk. & Cath., children of	1811	AB27	396	326
Brent, Robert	Cert Free to	Shorter, Mary, grandchildren of	1811	AB27	395	325
Brent, Robert	Deed fr	Dorsey, William H., of Montg. Co.	1814	AH33	081	072
Brent, Robert	Deed fr	Murdock, John, of G'tn.	1814	AH33	079	071
Brent, Robert	Deed fr	Fenwick, Thomas & Eleanor	1814	AG32	213	149
Brent, Robert	Deed fr	Corporation of Washington	1815	AI34	191	219
Brent, Robert	Deed fr	Corporation of Washington	1815	AI34	187	215
Brent, Robert	Deed fr	Corporation of Washington	1815	AI34	189	217
Brent, Robert	Deed fr	Pratt, Henry et al	1816	AL36	538	502
Brent, Robert	D. of T. fr	Mulloy, John	1816	AL36	087	089
Brent, Robert	Deed fr	King, Josias W. & Catharine	1817	AN38	550	400
Brent, Robert	Deed fr	Edmonston, James N., constable	1817	AN38	381	283
Brent, Robert	Bond fr	Whetcroft, Catharine	1817	AN38	550	400
Brent, Robert	Convey to	Brent, Robert Young	1817	AO39	396	269
Brent, Robert & Samuel Hamilton	Convey to	Van Ness, John P.	1806	P15	271	178
Brent, Robert & George Blagden	D. of T. fr	Huddleston, Joseph, stonecutter	1810	Y24	242	223
Brent, Robert & Tench Ringgold	Agreement	French, Daniel	1811	AB27	379	314
Brent, Robert & Thomas Fenwick	B. of S. fr	Coombe, Griffith	1812	AC28	309	225
Brent, Robert & Rev. John Carroll	Deed to	Wilson, Zadock	1817	AO39	483	335
Brent, Robert et al	Deed fr	Lee, Thomas S.	1802	I9	261	422
Brent, Robert et al	Deed fr	Webb, Thomas	1802	I9	190	295
Brent, Robert et al	Deed to	Casanave, Ann et al	1802	I9	022	029
Brent, Robert et al	Deed fr	O'Brien, William	1805	M12	095	088
Brent, Robert et al	Division	Young, Notley, exrs. of	1808	T19	318	232
Brent, Robert et al	Partition		1809	V21	240	171
Brent, Robert et al	Deed fr	Casanave, Ann	1817	AO39	079	064
Brent, Robert, exr. of N. Young	Receipt to	Docker, Gilbert	1805	N13	219	188
Brent, Robert, guardian	Deed to	Barry, James	1806	O14	288	191
Brent, Robert, Sr.	Deed fr	Carroll, Elizabeth, of Montg. Co.	1817	AN38	428	321

Index to District of Columbia Land Records, 1792-1817

Party	What	Party	Year	Liber	Old	New
Brent, Robert, trustee	Deed to	Wilson, Zadock	1817	AO39	488	
Brent, Robert Young	Deed fr	Thompson, Henry, of Balto.	1816	AL36	026	027
Brent, Robert Young	Convey fr	Brent, Robert	1817	AO39	396	269
Brent, Robert Young et al	Deed fr	Casanave, Ann	1817	AO39	079	064
Brent, William	Deed fr	Commissioners of Washington	1800	E5	119	106
Brent, William	P. of Atty. fr	Law, Thomas	1802	H8	423	390
Brent, William	D. of T. fr	Addison, Anthony, of MD	1802	H8	593	559
Brent, William	D. of T. fr	Law, Thomas	1802	H8	420	387
Brent, William	Qualify		1802	I9	464	764
Brent, William	Deed fr	Munroe, Thomas, Supt.	1802	I9	257	415
Brent, William	Deed to	Murdock, John et al	1802	I9	279	455
Brent, William	Slaves	From VA	1805	M12	175	175
Brent, William	D. of T. fr	King, Nicholas	1805	O14	114	072
Brent, William	Deed fr	Willmans, Frederick, Berks Co.	1806	P15	124	079
Brent, William	D. of T. fr	O'Reily, Henry, of G'tn.	1806	O14	167	109
Brent, William	Release to	King, Nicholas	1807	Q16	357	274
Brent, William	Deed to	Hoye, John & L.M. Deakins	1808	T19	408	287
Brent, William	Deed fr	Law, John	1808	U20	234	126
Brent, William	Agreement	Hoban, James	1808	V21	045	034
Brent, William	Deed fr	Huddlestone, Joseph	1808	V21	024	018
Brent, William	Deed fr	Law, John	1808	T19	339	246
Brent, William	Cert fr	Munroe, Thomas, Supt.	1809	X23	063	048
Brent, William	D. of T. fr	Roe, Bernard McDermott	1809	W22	389	253
Brent, William	Deed fr	Carroll, Daniel, of *Duddington*	1810	Y24	402	362
Brent, William	D. of T. fr	Purcell, Pierce	1810	Y24	052	046
Brent, William	Deed fr	Clerklee, James	1810	Y24	136	124
Brent, William	Deed to	White, Levi	1810	Z25	253	198
Brent, William	Deed to	Brent, Robert	1810	Z25	255	199
Brent, William	Deed to	Carroll, Daniel, of *Duddington*	1810	Y24	400	361
Brent, William	D. of T. fr	Huddleston, Joseph	1811	AC28	045	034
Brent, William	Mortgage to	Clerklee, James, of Charles Co.	1812	AD29	546	460
Brent, William	D. of T. fr	Forrest, Joseph & Edmund Law	1812	AD29	239	198
Brent, William	Deed fr	Clerklee, James, of Charles Co.	1812	AD29	244	202
Brent, William	Mortgage fr	Thruston, Buckner	1813	AF31	474	344
Brent, William	Deed fr	Ewell, Thomas	1813	AE30	264	204
Brent, William	D. of T. fr	Whelan, Nicholas	1813	AF31	062	043
Brent, William	D. of T. fr	McLeod, John	1815	AH33	426	367
Brent, William	Deed to	Mulloy, John	1815	AK35	341	270
Brent, William	Deed to	McNemara, Mary	1816	AL36	498	468
Brent, William	Release fr	Clerklee, James, of Charles Co.	1816	AM37	257	189
Brent, William	Deed to	Callan, Nicholas	1816	AL36	421	403
Brent, William	B. of S. fr	Spalding, Richard	1817	AN38	383	285
Brent, William & James Hoban	Deed fr	Dent, Charles	1808	T19	241	177
Brent, William & Thomas Sim Lee	Deed to	Hoye, John & Leonard M. Deakins	1809	V21	416	318
Brent, William & James Hoban	Deed to	Mackey, William, of G'tn.	1809	X23	099	072
Brent, William & Philip B. Key	Deed to	Young, Moses	1814	AG32	217	152
Brent, William & Philip B. Key	Deed to	Glover, Charles	1814	AG32	215	150
Brent, William & John Davidson	D. of T. fr	Whelan, Nicholas	1814	AG32	169	120
Brent, William & Daniel	Deed fr	Clerklee, James, of Charles Co.	1816	AM37	260	191
Brent, William & Thomas Law	Release to	Forrest, Joseph & Edmund Law	1816	AL36	106	107
Brent, William & Francis S. Key	Deed fr	Williams, Elie, of G'tn.	1817	AN38	205	149
Brent, William C., of MD	Deed fr	Neale, William, of MD	1802	H8	432	398
Brent, William et al	Deed fr	Johnson, Catherine	1801	G7	385	517
Brent, William et al	Deed fr	Woodward, Augustus B.	1804	L11	244	225
Brent, William et al	Deed fr	Tingey, Thomas	1810	Y24	406	366

Party	What	Party	Year	Liber	Old	New
Brent, William et al	Deed to	Boyd, Washington	1812	AC28	498	356
Brent, William et al	Deed fr	Jackson, John G., fr. Harrison Co.	1814	AG32	295	215
Brent, William et al	B. of S. fr	Willis, Perrin	1816	AM37	366	265
Brent, William, s/o Daniel C.	Deed Gift fr	Brent, Daniel Carroll	1805	M12	230	232
Brent, William, trustee	Deed to	Patterson, Edgar	1808	V21	045	034
Brent, William, trustee	Release to	Clerklee, James	1812	AD29	242	200
Brent, William, trustee	Deed to	Lewis, Joseph Saunders, of PA	1816	AM37	224	165
Breshears, Nathaniel et al	Deed fr	Willson, James	1802	H8	495	455
Breshears, Richard B.	Deed fr	Jarboe, Bennett	1802	H8	481	442
Brevitt, John & H. Hardisty, Balto.	Deed fr	Etting, Solomon, of Balto. Co.	1816	AL36	059	060
Brevitt, John, of Balto.	Deed fr	Elzey, Arnold	1817	AO39	292	208
Brewer, Joseph	Receipt to	Pearce, G.	1809	W22	184	128
Brewer, Joseph	B. of S. fr	Beck, Samuel Waters, insolvent	1811	AA26	107	074
Brewer, Joseph, of G'tn.	Deed fr	Brooke, Samuel, of PA	1814	AG32	362	262
Briarwood, Giles (C) & wife Henny	Manumis fr	Ross, Richard	1814	AH33	221	195
Brice, Ann	B. of S. to	Beall, Aquila	1802	I9	291	477
Brice, John, of Annapolis	Deed to	Beall, Thomas & John M. Gantt	1793	A1-1	346	451
Brice, Thomas P.	Deed fr	Prout, William	1808	U20	271	144
Brickley, John	Deed fr	Greenleaf, James, of Phila.	1798	C3	354	284
Bridge, John, of G'tn.	Release fr	Cocking, William	1815	AI34	258	291
Bridge, John, of G'tn.	D. of T. to	Ott, John	1815	AI34	259	292
Bridges, John	B. of S. fr	Turner, Nancy	1802	I9	201	315
Bridges, John	B. of S. fr	Turner, Nanny	1802	I9	001	001
Bridges, John	Deed fr	Fowler, Thomas	1802	I9	533	871
Bridges, John	B. of S. fr	Willson, Sarah	1804	K10	243	251
Bridges, John	B. of S. to	Herty, Thomas	1807	R17	323	245
Bridges, John	Deed to	Cocking, William	1811	AB27	145	122
Bridges, John	Lease fr	Cocking, William	1814	AH33	284	247
Bridges, John et al	B. of S. fr	Finigan, Rosannah	1816	AM37	145	112
Bridges, John, of G'tn.	Deed fr	Turner, Nanny	1802	H8	313	295
Bridges, John, of G'tn.	Bond fr	Slimmer, Christian & Ann	1804	K10	288	290
Bridges, John, of G'tn.	Mortgage to	Lufborough, Nathan, of G'tn.	1804	K10	245	252
Bridges, John, of G'tn.	Deed fr	King, Ezekiel	1805	N13	193	170
Bridges, John, of G'tn.	Deed fr	Cochran, Alexander	1805	N13	039	039
Bridges, John, of G'tn.	Deed to	Donovan, John, of Hancock Town	1807	S18	336	264
Bridges, John, of G'tn.	Deed fr	Balch, Stephen B., of G'tn.	1807	R17	170	130
Bridges, John, of G'tn.	Deed fr	Walker, Elijah, of G'tn.	1811	AB27	149	124
Bridges, John, of G'tn.	Deed fr	Boyd, Washington, marshal	1811	AB27	399	329
Bridges, John, of G'tn.	Deed fr	Burriss, John & Elizabeth, of G'tn.	1813	AF31	295	210
Briggs, Isaac et al	Cert fr	Munroe, Thomas, Supr.	1808	T19	349	252
Brightwell, John L., of P.G. Co.	B. of S. fr	Thomas, George Naylor	1809	V21	325	240
Briscoe, Edward, of Charles Co.	Deed fr	Harkness, Samuel	1814	AG32	093	070
Briscoe, Richard I.	Qualify	Justice of the Peace	1814	AG32	029	022
Briscoe, Richard S.	Qualify	Lieutenant in Militia	1808	V21	056	045
Briscoe, Richard S.	Cert free to	Thomas, Ann (M), & children	1813	AF31	230	158
Briscoe, Richard Sothoron	Deed fr	Worthington, William	1810	Y24	189	174
Brison, Sarah	B. of S. fr	Kealey, Daniel	1809	V21	285	205
Bristed, Richard, trustee	D. of T. fr	O'Connell, John, insolvent	1811	Z25	526	417
Broadback, Jacob	Deed fr	Edmonston, Brooke	1814	AH33	118	111
Broadwater, Charles Lewis, of VA	Deed to	Adams, Samuel, Fairfax Co. VA	1805	M12	361	370
Broadwell, James, of G'tn.	B. of S. fr	Wilson, Isaac, of G'tn.	1814	AH33	230	201
Broadwell, James, of G'tn.	Lease fr	Peter, Thomas, of G'tn.	1816	AL36	486	457
Broadwell, John	Bond to	Frethy, Edward et al	1804	K10	286	289
Brodbeck, Jacob	Deed fr	Edmonston, Franklin	1815	AI34	329	362
Brodbeck, Jacob	Deed fr	Edmonston, Cassandra, of MD	1815	AI34	330	363

Index to District of Columbia Land Records, 1792-1817

Party	What	Party	Year	Liber	Old	New
Brodbeck, Jacob	Deed fr	Jones, Thomas D., of MD	1817	AN38	030	024
Brodeau, Ann	Deed fr	Commissioners of Washington	1802	H8	450	413
Brodeau, Ann	Deed fr	Munroe, Thomas, Supt.	1802	I9	136	205
Brodeau, Ann	Deed to	Peter, David et al	1805	M12	337	342
Brodeau, Ann	Deed fr	Thornton, William	1805	N13	104	098
Brodeau, Ann	Release to	Van Ness, John P.	1810	Y24	325	295
Brodeau, Ann	Release to	McDonald, Alexander	1811	AB27	177	146
Brodeau, Ann	Deed to	Tayloe, John, Col.	1815	AK35	100	077
Brodess, Edward	B. of S. to	Doyle, Anne S.	1806	P15	176	117
Brodhag, Charles F., of G'tn.	Deed to	Smith, Clement, of G'tn.	1805	M12	077	071
Brogden, William et al	Deed to	Beall, Thomas & John M. Gantt	1792	A1-1	052	77
Brome, George	Deed fr	Beatty, Charles	1802	I9	436	722
Bromley, Joseph & Mary	Deed to	Balch, Stephen B., of G'tn.	1810	Z25	298	233
Bromley, Mary & Thomas Peter	B. of S. to	Hawkins, Matilda	1812	AC28	159	118
Bromley, Mary & Thomas Peter	Manumis to	[ ], Matilda (C)	1812	AC28	159	118
Bromley, Thomas Peter & Mary	Deed to	Craven, John et al	1811	AA26	280	190
Bronaugh, Jeremiah H.	Deed fr	Brooke, Thomas A.	1810	Z25	221	173
Bronaugh, John W.	Slaves	From VA	1807	T19	019	015
Bronaugh, John W.	Slave	From *Cedar Grove* VA	1808	U20	324	174
Bronaugh, John W.	Slave	From VA	1808	T19	317	231
Bronaugh, John W.	Slave		1809	X23	039	028
Bronaugh, John W.	Slaves	From VA	1811	AA26	242	165
Bronaugh, John W.	Deed fr	Threlkeld, John	1816	AM37	020	016
Bronaugh, John W.	Deed fr	Grayson, William	1816	AM37	017	014
Bronaugh, John W., of G'tn.	Deed fr	Grayson, William & wife, of G'tn.	1816	AM37	019	015
Bronaugh, John W.	Cert Slave	From VA	1817	AO39	152	114
Bronaugh, John W.	Cert Slave	[ ], Ham (C), age 12	1817	AN38	396	295
Bronaugh, William J.	Manumis to	[ ], Richard (C)	1817	AN38	172	125
Brook, Joseph	Deed fr	Renner, Daniel	1812	AE30	009	007
Brook, Roger et al	Deed fr	Shoemaker, Jonathan	1808	T19	114	081
Brook, Samuel	Deed fr	Barclay, John D.	1815	AH33	394	340
Brook, Samuel	Dower fr	Ashley, Mary, wid/o T. Carpenter	1816	AM37	413	296
Brook, Samuel	Deed fr	Ryan, Henry & Mary	1816	AM37	214	158
Brook, Samuel, trustee of J. Little	Deed to	Barclay, John D.	1815	AH33	392	339
Brook, William H., of G'tn.	Deed to	Shipley, Ellenor, w/o Rezin	1815	AH33	435	373
Brooke, Gerard et al	Cert fr	Munroe, Thomas, Supr.	1808	T19	349	252
Brooke, Henry, of P.G. Co.	Deed to	Maxwell, George	1809	V21	370	273
Brooke, Henry, s/o Nicholas, P.G.	Deed fr	Wade, Robert P.	1805	M12	355	363
Brooke, James B.	Mortgage fr	Lyles, Thomas C.	1814	AH33	136	129
Brooke, Joseph, of G'tn.	Deed to	Renner, Daniel, of G'tn.	1810	Z25	335	262
Brooke, Samuel	Deed to	Beall, Thomas B., s/o George	1802	G7	505	645
Brooke, Samuel	Deed fr	Gilpin, Bernard	1802	H8	224	213
Brooke, Samuel	Deed to	Brakenridge, John	1802	I9	507	831
Brooke, Samuel	Deed fr	Bohrer, Jacob	1809	V21	164	118
Brooke, Samuel	Deed fr	Kurtz, George, of Phila. et al	1811	AB27	264	216
Brooke, Samuel	Deed fr	Finley, Oliver P., of Alexa.	1812	AD29	020	015
Brooke, Samuel	Deed fr	Gilpin, Bernard, of Montg. Co.	1813	AF31	273	192
Brooke, Samuel, Gent.	Deed fr	Thomas, Gustavus, free black	1807	R17	034	028
Brooke, Samuel, of Montg. Co.	Deed fr	Craik, William, Montg. Co. et al	1797	C3	151	124
Brooke, Samuel, of Montg. Co.	Deed to	Thornbrough, Joseph, of PA	1804	K10	355	367
Brooke, Samuel, of Montg. Co.	Deed to	Thomson, George, of G'tn.	1806	P15	193	129
Brooke, Samuel, of PA	Deed to	Brewer, Joseph, of G'tn.	1814	AG32	362	262
Brooke, Samuel, trustee	Deed to	Starke, Belfield	1802	G7	509	649
Brooke, Samuel, trustee	Deed to	Bohrer, Jacob	1809	V21	162	117
Brooke, Thomas A.	Deed to	Glasco, John et al	1802	I9	584	946

Index to District of Columbia Land Records, 1792-1817

Party	What	Party	Year	Liber	Old	New
Brooke, Thomas A.	Deed fr	Beall, Hezekiah, Jefferson Co. VA	1806	P15	119	076
Brooke, Thomas A.	Deed to	Bronaugh, Jeremiah H.	1810	Z25	221	173
Brooke, Thomas A., of G'tn.	Deed fr	Nourse, Joseph, of G'tn.	1811	AA26	196	134
Brooke, Thomas A., of Montg. Co.	B. of S. to	Newman, Francis	1812	AC28	308	224
Brooke, Thomas A., of Montg. Co.	Deed to	United States [George Bumford]	1815	AK35	003	002
Brooke, Thomas A., Montg. Co.	Deed to	Smith, John Kilty, of G'tn.	1817	AO39	139	106
Brooke, William H., of G'tn.	Deed to	Mayn, Adam, of G'tn.	1814	AH33	072	064
Brookes, Henry	Deed fr	Beall, Thomas, of George	1794	B2A	158	208
Brookes, Henry	Deed to	Blake, James H., of G'tn.	1795	B2B	374	027
Brookes, Henry, guard. et al	Deed to	Law, Thomas Sim	1801	G7	341	472
Brookes, John Smith	Deed to	Beall, Thomas & John M. Gantt	1793	A1-1	305	404
Brookes, Joseph	Deed to	Orme, Nathan	1802	I9	260	420
Brookes, Joseph	Deed to	King, George	1802	I9	268	435
Brookes, Joseph	Deed to	King, George	1802	I9	269	438
Brookes, Joseph	Deed to	Brooks, William H.	1802	G7	565	713
Brookes, Joseph	Deed fr	Offutt, Ozias, Dr.	1806	O14	249	164
Brookes, Joseph	Deed fr	Beatty, Charles, heirs of	1806	O14	251	165
Brookes, Joseph	Deed to	King, George	1808	U20	010	006
Brookes, Joseph	Deed to	Clarke, William	1808	V21	023	017
Brookes, Joseph	Deed to	Whann, William	1808	T19	337	245
Brookes, Joseph	Deed fr	King, George	1808	U20	374	205
Brookes, Joseph	Deed fr	Chandler, Walter Story & Margaret	1809	X23	259	203
Brookes, Joseph	Deed fr	Bussard, Daniel, of G'tn.	1816	AL36	376	365
Brookes, Joseph	Deed to	Gantt, Thomas T.	1816	AM37	248	182
Brookes, Joseph	Deed fr	Whann, William	1817	AO39	142	107
Brookes, Joseph	Deed fr	Threlkeld, John	1817	AN38	461	332
Brookes, Joseph, of G'tn.	Deed fr	Dorsey, William H., of G'tn.	1802	G7	563	712
Brookes, Joseph, of G'tn.	Deed to	Bussard, Daniel, of G'tn.	1809	X23	252	196
Brookes, Joseph, of G'tn.	Deed fr	Thompson, George, of G'tn.	1809	V21	313	229
Brookes, Joseph, of G'tn.	Quit to	Murdock, John et al	1809	V21	312	228
Brookes, Joseph, of G'tn.	Deed to	Mudd, Thomas J., of G'tn.	1810	Y24	278	254
Brookes, Joseph, of G'tn.	Deed fr	King, Adam, of G'tn.	1810	Y24	530	465
Brookes, Joseph, of G'tn.	Deed fr	Robertson, William, of G'tn.	1811	AB27	417	344
Brookes, Joseph, of G'tn.	Deed fr	Moore, Alexander, of G'tn.	1811	AB27	415	342
Brookes, Joseph, of G'tn.	Deed to	Moore, Alexander, of G'tn.	1811	AB27	486	398
Brookes, Joseph, of G'tn.	Deed to	Moore, Alexander, of G'tn.	1811	AB27	074	062
Brookes, Joseph, of G'tn.	Deed to	Pickrell, John, of G'tn.	1811	AB27	341	281
Brookes, Joseph, of G'tn.	Deed fr	Bowie, Washington & Margaret C.	1815	AH33	509	437
Brookes, Joseph, of G'tn.	Deed fr	Whann, William, of G'tn.	1815	AK35	113	087
Brookes, Joseph, of G'tn.	Lease fr	Whann, William, of G'tn.	1815	AK35	442	347
Brookes, Joseph, of G'tn.	Deed fr	Henderson, Sarah, of G'tn.	1815	AK35	116	089
Brookes, Joseph, of G'tn.	Deed fr	Smith, Clement, of G'tn.	1815	AK35	119	092
Brookes, Joseph, of G'tn.	Deed fr	Whann, William, of G'tn.	1815	AK35	111	086
Brookes, Joseph, of G'tn.	Lease fr	Corcoran, Thomas, of G'tn.	1815	AK35	117	091
Brookes, Joseph, of G'tn.	Assign to	Cox, John, of G'tn.	1816	AM37	460	331
Brookes, Joseph, of G'tn.	Deed to	McKelden, Andrew, of G'tn.	1816	AM37	148	114
Brookes, Joseph, of G'tn.	Deed fr	Cox, John, Col., of G'tn.	1816	AM37	057	047
Brookes, Joseph, of G'tn.	Assign to	King, Charles, of G'tn.	1816	AM37	192	143
Brookes, Joseph, of G'tn.	Deed to	Gantt, Thomas T.	1816	AL36	032	034
Brookes, Joseph, of G'tn.	Deed to	Clement, Smith, of G'tn.	1817	AO39	135	102
Brookes, Joseph, of G'tn.	Deed to	Pickrell, John, of G'tn.	1817	AO39	152	114
Brookes, Joseph, of G'tn.	Lease fr	Corcoran, Thomas, of G'tn.	1817	AN38	458	330
Brookes, Walter	Deed fr	Deakins, William Jr.	1794	B2A	155	204
Brookes, Walter, of Montg. Co.	Deed to	Hosack, John, of Montg. Co.	1796	B2B	417	088
Brookes, Walter, of Montg. Co.	Deed to	Marbury, William	1814	AG32	322	235

Index to District of Columbia Land Records, 1792-1817

Party	What	Party	Year	Liber	Old	New
Brookes, William	Deed fr	Beatty, Charles	1800	E5	170	159
Brookes, William H., of G'tn.	Deed fr	Davidson, John	1802	H8	437	402
Brookes, William H.	Deed fr	Beall, Thomas, Sr., of George	1804	K10	137	149
Brookes, William H., of G'tn.	Deed to	Massey, Thomas, of G'tn.	1804	K10	117	126
Brookes, William H., of G'tn.	Deed fr	King, James Carroll, mer., G'tn.	1804	K10	138	150
Brookes, William H., of G'tn.	Deed to	Murdock, John, of G'tn.	1805	M12	053	050
Brookes, William H., of G'tn.	Deed fr	Bussard, Daniel, of G'tn.	1810	Y24	531	466
Brookes, William Henry, of G'tn.	Deed to	Wineberger, Jacob, of G'tn.	1810	X23	287	228
Brookes, William, of G'tn.	Deed to	Baird, Andrew, carpenter, of G'tn.	1796	B2B	410	079
Brooks, Charles	Manumis to	[ ], Nancy (C), his wife, children	1812	AD29	100	074
Brooks, Charles	B. of S. fr	Edelen, Edward E., of P.G. Co.	1812	AD29	100	074
Brooks, Charles	Lease fr	Law, Thomas	1816	AM37	505	370
Brooks, Joseph	Deed fr	Brooks, William H.	1801	F6	192	123
Brooks, Joseph	B. of S. to	Mitchell, Thomas L.	1801	G7	007	009
Brooks, Joseph	Lease to	Moore, Alexander	1810	Z25	180	142
Brooks, Joseph	Deed to	Whann, David	1812	AD29	098	074
Brooks, Joseph	Deed to	Whann, David	1812	AD29	191	155
Brooks, Joseph	Lease fr	Hoye, John, of Allegany Co.	1815	AI34	072	081
Brooks, Joseph	Deed fr	Bussard, Daniel	1816	AL36	528	493
Brooks, Joseph et al	Suit ads	Potomac Company	1812	AG32	258	183
Brooks, Joseph, of G'tn.	Deed to	King, George, of G'tn.	1804	L11	220	206
Brooks, Joseph, of G'tn.	Deed fr	King, George, of G'tn.	1804	L11	300	275
Brooks, Joseph, of G'tn.	Deed to	Robinson, William, of G'tn.	1810	Z25	178	141
Brooks, Joseph, of G'tn.	Deed to	Cox, John	1813	AF31	389	281
Brooks, Joseph, of G'tn.	Deed to	Smith, Clement, of G'tn.	1813	AE30	389	287
Brooks, Joseph, of G'tn.	Deed to	Cox, John, of G'tn.	1814	AH33	009	008
Brooks, Joseph, of G'tn.	Lease fr	Whann, William	1815	AI34	070	079
Brooks, Joseph, of G'tn.	Lease fr	Whann, William	1815	AI34	068	077
Brooks, Joseph, of G'tn.	Lease fr	Whann, William	1815	AI34	066	075
Brooks, Joseph, of G'tn.	Deed fr	Mackall, Benjamin F., of G'tn.	1816	AL36	529	495
Brooks, Thomas A.	Lease to	Glasco, John	1802	I9	220	348
Brooks, William & Margaret	D. of T. to	Jones, John	1806	O14	268	177
Brooks, William et al	Lease fr	Carleton, Joseph, of G'tn.	1804	L11	273	251
Brooks, William H.	Deed fr	Davis, Charles	1794	B2A	104	137
Brooks, William H.	Deed to	Brooks, Joseph	1801	F6	192	123
Brooks, William H.	Deed to	Massey, Thomas	1802	H8	312	293
Brooks, William H.	Deed fr	Brookes, Joseph	1802	G7	565	713
Brooks, William H. [Brookes]	Deed fr	Hazel, Jeremiah	1804	K10	324	332
Brooks, William H., of G'tn.	Deed to	Hazel, Jeremiah, of G'tn.	1804	K10	234	243
Brooks, William H., of G'tn.	Deed to	Newton, Ignatius, of G'tn.	1805	N13	229	195
Brooks, William H.	Deed fr	Smallwood, Horatio	1816	AM37	458	330
Brooks, William H.	Deed to	Magruder, George B.	1817	AN38	261	191
Broome, George G.	B. of S. to	Newton, Ignatius	1806	O14	164	107
Broome, George [Brome]	Assign to	Williamson, David	1809	W22	044	033
Brother, Eleanor, exrx. Henry	Deed to	Brother, Henry, s/o Henry	1794	B2A	020	022
Brother, Henry, of Frederick Co.	Deed to	McCleery, Henry	1794	B2A	021	023
Brother, Henry, s/o Henry	Deed fr	Brother, Eleanor, exrx. of Henry	1794	B2A	020	022
Brown, Amos et al	Deed fr	Prout, William	1802	H8	217	207
Brown, Amos, of Balto.	Deed to	Fuller, Oliver, of Balto.	1805	M12	018	018
Brown, Amy, age 48	Manumis fr	Pyfer, Henry, of G'tn.	1813	AF31	140	094
Brown, Blanch	B. of S. to	Hessey, Caleb	1809	W22	206	142
Brown, Dolly	Deed to	Doughlass, Robert H., Fairfax Co.	1815	AK35	131	101
Brown, Dolly	B. of S. to	Douglass, Robert H., Fairfax Co.	1816	AL36	344	335
Brown, Dolly	B. of S. fr	Douglass, Robert H., Fairfax Co.	1816	AL36	366	356
Brown, Dolly	B. of S. fr	Douglass, Robert H., Fairfax Co.	1816	AL36	367	357

Party	What	Party	Year	Liber	Old	New
Brown, Dolly	B. of S. fr	Douglass, Robert H., Fairfax Co.	1816	AL36	366	355
Brown, Dolly (C), w/o Peter	Manumis fr	Douglass, Robert H.	1815	Al34	429	448
Brown, Elizabeth	Deed fr	Foyles, Thomas & Thomas Young	1813	AE30	167	132
Brown, Frederick	Deed fr	Rawlins, John	1815	AK35	038	030
Brown, George G.	B. of S. to	Newton, Ignatius	1805	O14	044	027
Brown, George, insolvent	Deed to	Peacock, Robert Ware, trustee	1804	L11	197	188
Brown, George Washington	B. of S. to	Spalding, Enoch	1811	AA26	316	213
Brown, Gustavus A., of Alexa.	Deed to	Grayson, William	1815	AK35	420	329
Brown, Henry	B. of S. fr	Pickrell, Richard H.	1809	X23	034	024
Brown, James, of Q.A. Co.	Cert fr	Commissioners of Washington	1799	B2B	483	176
Brown, James, of Q.A. Co.	Deed to	Brown, Joel	1800	E5	206	199
Brown, Jesse	Lease fr	Prout, William	1802	I9	450	743
Brown, Joel	Deed to	Hodgeson, Joseph	1798	C3	514	403
Brown, Joel	Agreement	Forrest, Uriah	1799	D4	397	377
Brown, Joel	Agreement	Forrest, Uriah	1799	D4	397	377
Brown, Joel	Deed to	Johnson, William A., B'burgh.	1800	E5	207	200
Brown, Joel	Deed fr	Brown, James, of Q. Anne's Co.	1800	E5	206	199
Brown, Joel	Deed fr	Johnston, William, of B'burgh.	1800	E5	215	209
Brown, Joel	Agreement	Sprogell, John Lodwick	1801	G7	065	084
Brown, Joel	Agreement	Sprogell, Thomas Y.	1801	G7	065	084
Brown, Joel	Convey fr	Sprogell, Thomas Yorke	1801	G7	064	083
Brown, Joel	Convey fr	Sprogell, John Lodwick	1801	G7	064	083
Brown, Joel	Deed fr	Hewitt, John, assignee	1802	I9	054	074
Brown, Joel	Deed fr	Forrest, Uriah, assignee of	1802	I9	054	074
Brown, Joel	Qualify	Captain of First Legion of Militia	1802	H8	520	480
Brown, Joel	Deed fr	Forrest, Uriah	1804	K10	333	344
Brown, Joel	Deed fr	O'Neale, William & Rhoda	1804	K10	254	261
Brown, Joel	Deed to	Jameson, Walter, of Charles Co.	1805	O14	127	082
Brown, Joel	Deed fr	Keagy, Abraham, of MD	1812	AD29	439	368
Brown, Joel	Deed to	Thompson, James	1815	AH33	522	447
Brown, Joel & John Pickrell, G'tn.	Deed fr	Stout, Jacob, of G'tn.	1816	AM37	470	339
Brown, Joel et al	Deed fr	Lingan, James McCubbin, of G'tn.	1797	C3	018	14
Brown, Joel et al	Deed fr	Eliason, Ebenezer & Ann	1809	V21	290	210
Brown, Joel et al	D. of T. fr	Foxall, Henry	1816	AL36	357	348
Brown, Joel, of G'tn.	Lease fr	Chew, Cassandra, of G'tn.	1804	K10	282	285
Brown, Joel, of G'tn.	Deed fr	Stoddert, Benjamin, of G'tn.	1804	L11	305	280
Brown, Joel, of G'tn.	Deed fr	French, Arianna, of G'tn.	1805	N13	062	057
Brown, Joel, of G'tn.	Deed fr	Lane, Samuel & Rachel, of G'tn.	1810	X23	362	290
Brown, Joel, of G'tn.	D. of T. to	Smith, Clement, of G'tn.	1813	AF31	085	058
Brown, Joel, of G'tn.	Manumis to	[ ], Henny (C)	1813	AF31	217	148
Brown, Joel, of G'tn.	Deed fr	Lufborough, Nathan	1813	AF31	082	056
Brown, Joel, of G'tn.	Deed to	Worthington, William	1815	AK35	276	219
Brown, Joel, of G'tn.	Mortgage fr	Davis, Gideon	1816	AM37	446	320
Brown, Joel, of G'tn.	Lease fr	Smith, Clement, of G'tn.	1817	AN38	018	015
Brown, Joel, of G'tn.	Release to	Davis, Gideon	1817	AO39	259	187
Brown, Joel, trustee et al	Deed fr	Morgan, William, of G'tn.	1814	AH33	010	009
Brown, John	B. of S. to	Dowers, John	1801	G7	279	385
Brown, John	Mortgage to	Nowlan, Edward, of Phila.	1801	G7	262	359
Brown, John, of Balto.	Mortgage fr	Dove, Joseph & Benjamin Owens	1808	V21	063	050
Brown, Joseph G.	B. of S. to	Brown, Keith	1814	AH33	152	144
Brown, Keith	B. of S. fr	Brown, Joseph G.	1814	AH33	152	144
Brown, Mary Ann et al	Deed fr	Chandler, Walter Story	1813	AE30	190	152
Brown, Mathew	Cert fr	Commissioners of Washington	1801	G7	276	380
Brown, Mathew	B. of S. fr	Drummond, Hugh	1806	Q16	304	232
Brown, Mathew	Mortgage to	Wickem, James, of Phila. PA	1809	V21	149	109

Index to District of Columbia Land Records, 1792-1817

Party	What	Party	Year	Liber	Old	New
Brown, Mathew, of Balto.	Deed fr	Law, Thomas	1801	G7	277	383
Brown, Matthew	B. of S. fr	Markland, John, of Charles Co.	1808	U20	044	025
Brown, Matthew	B. of S. to	Wickam, James, of Phila. PA	1809	W22	413	268
Brown, Matthew, children of et al	Deed fr	Chandler, Walter Story	1813	AE30	190	152
Brown, Matthew, of Balto.	Deed fr	Law, Thomas	1799	D4	407	384
Brown, Matthew, printer, of Balto.	Deed fr	Maddox, Notley	1799	D4	342	330
Brown, Monica (C)	Manumis fr	Ringgold, Tench	1813	AF31	305	217
Brown, Nelly, d/o William	B. of S. fr	Brown, William	1811	AB27	077	064
Brown, O.B.	Slave	From Hertford NC	1808	U20	376	206
Brown, Obadiah B.	Slave		1810	Y24	319	291
Brown, Obadiah B. & Geo. Moore	D. of T. fr	Huddleston, Joseph	1812	AC28	204	154
Brown, Obadiah B.	Deed fr	Bradley, Phineas	1812	AD29	263	217
Brown, Obadiah B.	B. of S. fr	Moore, Elizabeth	1813	AF31	232	160
Brown, Obadiah B.	D. of T. fr	Polk, Charles P.	1813	AF31	154	104
Brown, Obadiah B., Rev. et al	D. of T. fr	Van Ness, John P. & Marcia	1817	AN38	252	185
Brown, Obadiah Bruen	Deed fr	Tate, Andrew	1816	AL36	514	482
Brown, Obadian B. & Ph. Bradley	Deed fr	Andrews, George, Cincinnati OH	1813	AE30	120	092
Brown, Obediah B. & E. Reynolds	D. of T. fr	Van Ness, John P.	1816	AM37	175	132
Brown, Peter	Deed fr	Bell, George	1812	AC28	447	319
Brown, Richard et al	Deed fr	Chandler, Walter Story	1813	AE30	190	152
Brown, Robert	Deed fr	Burnes, David	1797	C3	052	42
Brown, Robert	Deed to	Hardesty, Samuel, Jr.	1798	D4	109	092
Brown, Robert	Deed fr	Burnes, David	1798	D4	013	011
Brown, Robert	Deed fr	Commissioners of Washington	1800	F6	007	047
Brown, Robert	Deed to	Lambert, Morris	1801	G7	061	078
Brown, Robert	Deed to	Bentley, Joseph	1801	G7	123	158
Brown, Robert	Deed to	Hoban, James	1801	G7	417	552
Brown, Robert	Deed to	Bradley, Phineas	1802	I9	246	397
Brown, Robert	Deed fr	Thecker, James	1802	I9	443	732
Brown, Robert	Deed to	Smallwood, Samuel N.	1802	I9	329	542
Brown, Robert	Deed to	Cist, Jacob	1802	I9	340	560
Brown, Robert	Lease fr	Prout, William	1802	I9	183	281
Brown, Robert	B. of S. to	McCormick, Alexander	1804	K10	331	341
Brown, Robert	Deed to	Hazel, Jeremiah	1805	M12	128	123
Brown, Robert	Deed fr	Carroll, Daniel, of *Duddington*	1806	P15	208	139
Brown, Robert	Deed to	Cocking, William	1807	R17	342	261
Brown, Robert	Deed to	Wright, Matthew	1808	T19	377	269
Brown, Robert	Deed fr	Dunlop, James & Joseph Carleton	1809	X23	055	041
Brown, Robert	B. of S. to	Wright, Matthew	1809	X23	062	046
Brown, Robert	Deed fr	Chandler, Walter Story	1809	X23	070	053
Brown, Robert	Deed fr	Heron, William	1810	X23	379	304
Brown, Robert	Deed to	Cassidy, Nicholas	1813	AF31	508	371
Brown, Robert	Deed to	King, Ezekiel	1813	AF31	548	406
Brown, Robert	Deed to	Cloakey, Samuel	1814	AG32	062	048
Brown, Robert	Deed to	Cassiday, Nicholas	1814	AG32	287	208
Brown, Robert	Deed fr	Chandler, Walter Story	1816	AM37	279	204
Brown, Robert & Elizabeth	B. of S. to	St. Cleare, Reason	1812	AC28	380	277
Brown, Robert, bricklayer	Deed fr	Hoban, James	1805	M12	216	218
Brown, Robert, bricklayer	Deed to	Alexander, Robert, Esq.	1808	T19	176	124
Brown, Robert, carpenter N. yard	Release fr	Smallwood, Samuel N.	1805	N13	312	253
Brown, Robert et al	Deed to	Beall, Thomas et al	1793	A1-1	292	389
Brown, Robert et al	Deed fr	Jones, Anthony	1802	H8	304	287
Brown, Robert et al	Deed to	Gannon, James, of G'tn.	1804	M12	012	013
Brown, Robert, house joiner	Deed to	Threlkeld, John	1801	G7	334	465
Brown, Robert, of P.G. Co.	Deed fr	Beall, Hezekiah, of Montg. Co.	1798	C3	472	372

Party	What	Party	Year	Liber	Old	New
Brown, Samuel	Relinquish to	Jones, Arthur, of Phila.	1797	B2B	621	379
Brown, Samuel	Sale fr	McDonough, William	1805	O14	123	
Brown, Samuel	B. of S. to	Mechlin, Joseph	1805	N13	181	162
Brown, Samuel, Dr., now of KY	Deed fr	Dermott, James Reed	1801	F6	135	083
Brown, Samuel, Dr., Lexington KY	Deed to	Campbell, Robert, bookseller, PA	1801	F6	139	085
Brown, Samuel, of Lexington KY	P. of Atty. to	King, Nicholas	1801	F6		088
Brown, Sarah	B. of S. fr	Brown, William	1806	P15	318	210
Brown, Stewart	Deed fr	Polock, Isaac	1802	H8	021	020
Brown, Stewart	Deed to	Davidson, Alexander	1802	H8	132	129
Brown, Stewart, mer., of Balto.	Deed fr	Carroll, Daniel, of *Duddington*	1801	F6	229	150
Brown, Stewart, of Balto.	Convey to	Belt, Benjamin M.	1816	AM37	353	256
Brown, Thomas	Lease fr	Prout, William	1806	P15	267	176
Brown, Thomas	Deed to	Brady, Nathaniel	1807	S18	398	317
Brown, Valentine et al	Deed fr	Chandler, Walter Story	1813	AE30	190	152
Brown, William	Deed fr	Pearson, Lawson & Joseph Dove	1801	G7	128	167
Brown, William	B. of S. to	Brown, Sarah	1806	P15	318	210
Brown, William	B. of S. to	Brown, Nelly, d/o William	1811	AB27	077	064
Brown, William	Deed to	Barnes, John, of G'tn.	1816	AM37	217	160
Brown, William, def.	Suit	Barnes, John, plt.	1816	AM37	217	160
Browning & Renshaw, of G'tn.	B. of S. fr	Hurdle, Leonard	1805	M12	184	185
Browning & Renshaw	B. of S. to	Eliason, John & Richard Beck	1806	Q16	147	097
Browning, Joseph	Deed fr	Beatty, Charles, heirs of	1806	P15	299	196
Browning, Joseph	Deed to	Love, Charles	1806	Q16	072	045
Browning, Joseph, of G'tn. et al	B. of S. to	Cochrane, Alexander	1807	S18	296	232
Bruce, Harriot, of G'tn. et al	Deed to	Brumly, Mary	1804	L11	323	296
Bruce, Jacob	Manumis fr	Goldsborough, John M.	1813	AF31	003	002
Bruce, James & Sarah	Manumis fr	Addison, Walter D., of P.G. Co.	1805	N13	283	233
Bruff, Thomas	Deed fr	Thompson, John	1803	K10	076	82
Bruff, Thomas	Deed to	King, William, cabinet maker, G'tn.	1805	M12	296	297
Brumley, Joseph, collector	Deed to	Middleton, Elizabeth	1811	AA26	257	175
Brumley, Joseph, collector 1st W.	Cert to	Boyd, Washington	1813	AE30	319	239
Brumley, Joseph, collector 1st W.	Cert to	Boyd, Washington	1813	AE30	321	241
Brumley, Joseph, collector 1st W.	Cert to	Boyd, Washington	1813	AE30	319	239
Brumley, Joseph, collector 1st W.	Cert to	Boyd, Washington	1813	AE30	320	240
Brumley, Joseph, collector	Deed to	McIntire, Samuel	1813	AF31	422	304
Brumley, Joseph, collector	Deed to	McKim, James	1814	AG32	293	213
Brumley, Joseph, collector	Assign to	Nourse, Joseph	1816	AI34	451	464
Brumley, Mary & Thomas Peter	Manumis to	[ ], Maria (C)	1816	AL36	127	128
Brumly, Mary	Deed fr	Bruce, Harriet et al	1804	L11	323	296
Brumly, Mary et al	Deed to	Clarke, William	1808	U20	250	133
Brundige, James	D. of T. fr	Ober, Robert, of G'tn.	1814	AG32	270	191
Brundige, James, of Balto.	Deed to	Kennedy, James, of G'tn.	1816	AL36	021	022
Bruner, Jacob & Eleanor	Deed to	Lipscomb, John, of G'tn.	1817	AN38	082	064
Bruner, Stephen & Barbara	Deed to	Lenox, Peter, of P.G. Co.	1796	B2B	569	307
Brunner, John & Adam Mayne	Assign fr	Hoot, Samuel	1812	AC28	338	245
Brunner, John, of Henry	Assign fr	McGrath, Thomas	1811	AA26	355	237
Brunner, John, of Henry, of G'tn.	Assign to	Mayer, Henry	1815	AI34	503	509
Brush, John C.	Mortgage to	Grammar, Gotlieb C.	1814	AH33	149	141
Brush, John C.	Deed to	Underwood, John	1816	AM37	132	103
Bryan, Benjamin	Deed fr	Law, Thomas	1801	G7	091	117
Bryan, Benjamin	B. of S. to	Bryan, Wilson	1801	G7	180	241
Bryan, Benjamin	Deed fr	Graham, James	1804	L11	148	149
Bryan, Benjamin	Deed fr	Prout, William	1807	R17	176	135
Bryan, Benjamin	Deed fr	Prout, William	1807	R17	007	007
Bryan, Benjamin	Deed to	McKim, James & Thomas Herty	1807	R17	010	009

Party	What	Party	Year	Liber	Old	New
Bryan, Benjamin	Deed to	McKim, James & Thomas Herty	1807	R17	179	137
Bryan, Benjamin	Assign to	McKim, James & Thomas Herty	1808	T19	050	038
Bryan, Benjamin	Deed to	Vint, John	1808	U20	086	048
Bryan, Benjamin	Lease fr	Prout, William	1808	T19	380	271
Bryan, Benjamin	B. of S. fr	Selby, Henry	1808	T19	097	069
Bryan, Benjamin	B. of S. to	Prout, William	1809	X23	049	036
Bryan, Benjamin	Assign to	Cocking, William	1811	AB27	084	070
Bryan, Benjamin & Mary	Deed to	Roberts, John et al	1801	G7	092	118
Bryan, Benjamin, trustee	Deed fr	Russ, Samuel, insolvent	1810	Y24	182	167
Bryan, Betsey (M)	Deposition fr	Shanks, Elizabeth, G'tn.	1817	AN38	221	161
Bryan, James D.	Deed to	Casteel, Edmund	1816	AO39	046	038
Bryan, Maria Henrietta, of Phila.	Deed fr	Davidson, Lewis Grant	1815	AK35	055	042
Bryan, Mary Ann	Deed Gift fr	Bryan, Thomas	1815	AI34	517	521
Bryan, Thomas	Lease fr	Prout, William	1806	P15	353	234
Bryan, Thomas	B. of S. fr	Gibson, Gerrard	1808	U20	009	006
Bryan, Thomas	Deed Gift to	Bryan, Mary Ann	1815	AI34	517	521
Bryan, Wilson	B. of S. fr	Bryan, Benjamin	1801	G7	180	241
Bryan, Wilson	Cert fr	Commissioners of Washington	1801	G7	110	140
Bryan, Wilson	Deed fr	Farrell, Zephaniah	1805	N13	270	224
Bryan, Wilson	Deed to	Brashears, John M.	1805	N13	274	228
Bryan, Wilson	B. of S. fr	Little, Israel	1806	O14	352	235
Bryden, James	Mortgage to	Bryden, William	1802	I9	192	299
Bryden, James, of Balto.	Deed fr	Walker, George, Gent.	1801	G7	285	395
Bryden, James, of Balto.	Deed fr	Carr, Overton	1802	G7	566	715
Bryden, William	Mortgage fr	Bryden, James	1802	I9	192	299
Bryson, Sarah	Deed fr	Kealey, Daniel	1816	AM37	009	007
Bryson, Sarah	Deed fr	Prout, William	1816	AM37	011	009
Bryson, Sarah	Deed fr	Prout, William	1816	AM37	013	010
Bryson, Sarah	Deed to	Kealy, Daniel	1816	AO39	033	027
Buchanan, James A. et al	Deed fr	Gilliss, Thomas H.	1802	I9	517	846
Buchanan, Loveday	Deed to	Pairo, Thomas William	1805	M12	299	301
Buchanan, Loveday et al	Deed to	French, Ariana	1804	L11	396	351
Buchanan, Thomas	Deed to	Beall, Thomas & John M. Gantt	1793	A1-1	302	401
Buchanan, Thomas	Deed fr	Dorsey, William H., of Balto. Co.	1813	AF31	188	127
Buchanan, Thomas, Charles Co.	Deed to	Greenleaf, James, New York NY	1794	B2A	120	161
Buchanan, Thomas, of MD	Deed to	Dupuy, William	1815	AI34	142	162
Buchanan, Thomas, of MD	Deed to	Gilliss, Thomas H.	1815	AI34	468	480
Buchanan, Thomas, of MD	Deed to	Blake, James H.	1816	AL36	108	109
Buchannan, Thomas	Deed fr	Dorsey, William H., of Balto. Co.	1814	AG32	077	058
Buchannan, Thomas	Deed fr	Murdock, John, of G'tn.	1815	AI34	037	043
Buckius, John, Jr., Frederick Co.	Deed to	Brengle, Lawrence, Frederick Co.	1804	K10	295	297
Buckius, John, Sr., Frederick Co.	Deed to	Brengle, Lawrence, Frederick Co.	1804	L11	164	162
Buckius, William, Frederick Co.	Deed to	Brengle, Lawrence, Frederick Co.	1804	K10	295	297
Budd, George & Henry Pratt	P. of Atty. to	Bickley, Robert S.	1806	Q16	178	119
Buddicomb, James, Capt.	Confiscation	State of Maryland	1805	M12	392	
Buford, Daniel, of G'tn.	Deed fr	King, James C., lumber merchant	1801	G7	280	387
Bulger, Margaret, of P.G. Co.	Deed fr	Weatherall, John, of Montg. Co.	1796	B2B	561	294
Bullett, Thomas James, Talbot Co.	Deed to	Huie, Helen Grant, Pr. Wm. Co.	1806	P15	323	213
Bullock, George, of Charles Co.	B. of S. to	Carbery, Thomas	1806	Q16	195	132
Bullock, Richard	B. of S. to	Watterston, David	1810	Z25	366	287
Bullus, John	Deed fr	Munroe, Thomas, Supt.	1802	I9	060	082
Bullus, John	Deed fr	Crandell, Thomas & Sarah, Alexa.	1805	N13	295	240
Bullus, John	Deed fr	Perkins, Benjamin	1806	Q16	141	092
Bullus, John	Deed fr	Brent, Daniel Carroll, marshal	1806	Q16	135	088
Bullus, John	Deed to	Stoddert, Benjamin	1807	R17	330	251

Party	What	Party	Year	Liber	Old	New
Bullus, John	Deed to	Wharton, Franklin	1807	S18	251	198
Bullus, John, Dr.	Deed to	Gillaspie, George, of Phila. et al	1804	L11	066	68
Bullus, John et al	Deed fr	Wadsworth, Charles, Hartford CN	1804	L11	326	298
Bullus, John et al	Deed fr	Wadsworth, Charles, in Norfolk VA	1804	L11	327	299
Bullus, John, M.D.	Deed fr	Lingan, James Maccubbin, G'tn.	1802	H8	309	292
Bullus, John, M.D.	Deed to	Perkins, Benjamin, carpenter	1806	Q16	074	047
Bullus, John, of NY	Release fr	Van Ness, John P. & Marcia	1810	Z25	001	001
Bullus, John, of NY	Assign to	Appler, Jonathan	1813	AF31	306	218
Bullus, John, of NY	Assign to	Appler, Jonathan	1816	AL36	141	142
Bumford, George [United States]	Deed fr	Brooke, Thomas A., of Montg. Co.	1815	AK35	003	002
Bunch, June	Deed to	Frost, John T.	1804	K10	318	325
Bundy, Thomas (yellow)	Cert of Birth		1804	K10	316	323
Bunnel, Eliab & Wm. B. Robertson	Deed fr	Magruder, Ninian, Dr., of G'tn.	1817	AN38	027	022
Bunnel, Eliab et al	Deed to	Smith, Clement, of G'tn.	1817	AN38	025	021
Bunnell, Eliab & W.B. Robertson	Lease fr	Smith, Clement	1814	AH33	156	147
Bunnell, Eliab & W.B. Robertson	D. of T. fr	Smith, Clement	1814	AH33	157	148
Bunnell, Eliab & W.B. Robertson	Lease fr	Magruder, Ninian, Dr., of G'tn.	1816	AL36	084	086
Bunnell, Eliab, of G'tn. et al	Lease fr	Pickrell, John, of G'tn.	1817	AO39	154	116
Bunnell, Elial et al	Lease fr	Dodge, Francis	1813	AF31	552	409
Bunnell, Elial, of G'tn. et al	Deed to	Dodge, Francis, of G'tn.	1815	AI34	543	548
Bunnell, Elias & W.B. Robertson	B. of S. fr	Weeden, Henry, of G'tn.	1813	AF31	172	116
Buntin, Aaron	Deed fr	Wigfield, Anne	1805	N13	255	213
Buntin, Aaron	Deed fr	Wigfield, Ann	1806	P15	342	226
Buntin, Aaron	Deed fr	Wigfield, Elizabeth	1806	P15	347	230
Buntin, Aaron, of Balto. Co.	Deed to	Farrell, Zephaniah	1807	S18	156	127
Bunyie, Robert	Lease fr	Prout, William	1804	L11	306	281
Bunyie, William	Lease fr	Prout, William	1801	G7	483	622
Bunyie, William	Deed to	Catalano, Salvadora, U.S.N.	1809	X23	064	048
Bunyie, William	Deed to	Catalano, Salvadora, U.S.N.	1809	X23	060	045
Burbeck, Henry, Col.	Deed fr	Beatty, Charles A.	1813	AF31	501	364
Burbeck, Henry, New London CN	Deed to	Shepperd, Lodowick, of G'tn.	1814	AH33	046	041
Burch, Benjamin	Qualify		1802	I9	447	738
Burch, Benjamin	B. of S. to	Carroll, Daniel, of *Duddington*	1805	M12	266	267
Burch, Benjamin	D. of T. to	Elliott, Samuel, Jr.	1815	AI34	530	534
Burch, Benjamin, insolvent	Deed to	Cochrane, Alexander, Jr., trustee	1806	Q16	084	053
Burch, Benjamin, trustee	Deed fr	Gregory, Nathaniel, insolvent	1810	X23	411	332
Burch, Catherine, d/o Jane	Deed fr	Burch, Jane	1805	M12	342	348
Burch, Henry	Assign to	Moore, George	1811	AA26	049	038
Burch, Henry	Deed fr	Hughes, Thomas	1812	AC28	165	122
Burch, Henry	Deed to	Moore, George	1812	AC28	167	124
Burch, Jane	B. of S. to	Laville, Nancy, only d/o Daniel	1804	K10	406	420
Burch, Jane	B. of S. to	Maran, Jesse	1805	M12	343	348
Burch, Jane	Deed to	Burch, Catherine, d/o Jane	1805	M12	342	348
Burch, Jane	B. of S. to	Benson, John	1805	M12	176	175
Burch, Jane, insolvent	B. of S. to	Kenner, James, trustee	1805	N13	156	145
Burch, John Henry, s/o Theo. Y.	B. of S. fr	Burch, Theophilus Y.	1810	Y24	274	251
Burch, Joseph Newton et al	Deed to	Marbury, William	1811	Z25	377	296
Burch, Keziah	Slave		1806	P15	288	190
Burch, Remigius	Lease fr	Van Ness, John P. & Marcia	1816	AM37	379	273
Burch, Samuel	D. of T. fr	Gregory, Nathaniel	1809	V21	400	303
Burch, Samuel	D. of T. fr	McLean, Cornelius	1811	AC28	097	073
Burch, Samuel	Assign fr	Leiper, George R., of P.G. Co.	1811	AB27	270	221
Burch, Samuel	Release to	McLean, Cornelius	1812	AD29	417	351
Burch, Samuel	D. of T. fr	Miller, George	1812	AE30	053	050
Burch, Samuel	Deed to	Dunn, Thomas	1815	AI34	109	125

Index to District of Columbia Land Records, 1792-1817

Party	What	Party	Year	Liber	Old	New
Burch, Samuel	Deed fr	Crowley, Edward	1816	AL36	205	212
Burch, Samuel	Deed to	Stinger, Frederick	1816	AM37	340	247
Burch, Samuel	D. of T. to	Wilson, Henry M.	1816	AL36	543	506
Burch, Samuel	Deed fr	Eliot, Samuel, Jr.	1817	AN38	186	135
Burch, Samuel	Deed to	Felins, Jacob	1817	AN38	011	009
Burch, Samuel	Deed to	Wilson, Offa, of P.G. Co.	1817	AN38	416	311
Burch, Samuel	D. of T. fr	Tims, Henry	1817	AN38	226	165
Burch, Susan	B. of S. fr	Lee, Mary	1811	AA26	328	220
Burch, Susan	Cert fr	Munroe, Thomas, Supt.	1811	AA26	045	035
Burch, Theophilus Y.	B. of S. to	Burch, John Henry, s/o Theo. Y.	1810	Y24	274	251
Burchan, John, of New York NY	Deed to	Poor, John	1815	AK35	246	195
Burd, Edward et al	Deed fr	Burd, Edward Shippen, Phila. PA	1809	V21	365	268
Burd, Edward et al	Partition	Young, Moses	1810	X23	216	165
Burd, Edward et al	Deed fr	Howell, Benjamin B.	1812	AD29	518	437
Burd, Edward et al	Deed fr	Waln, Robert, Jr., of Phila., mer.	1815	AK35	152	118
Burd, Edward Shippen, Phila. PA	D. of T. to	Morris, Thomas et al	1809	V21	365	268
Burd, Edward Shippen et al	Deed fr	Waln, Robert, Jr., of Phila., mer.	1815	AK35	152	118
Burd, Shippen Edward et al	Deed fr	Howell, Benjamin B.	1812	AD29	518	437
Burden, Henry R.	Deed fr	Estep, Alexander & Barbara	1817	AO39	496	340
Burden, Henry R.	Transfer fr	Solomon, Lewis	1817	AO39	458	
Burden, Henry R.	Deed to	Estep, Alexander	1817	AO39	459	315
Burdine, Reuben	Deed fr	Welch, Valentine & Mary Ann	1817	AO39	383	259
Burdine, William	B. of S. to	Murray, Thomas	1815	AH33	463	396
Burford, Henry	Lease fr	Lovell, William	1802	H8	161	155
Burford, Henry	Assign to	Underwood, Robert	1802	I9	563	912
Burford, Henry	Deed to	Willis, John	1802	H8	167	161
Burford, Henry	B. of S. to	Densley, Hugh	1803	K10	067	72
Burford, Henry	Deed to	Rutherford, William	1804	L11	216	203
Burford, Henry	Deed fr	Corporation of Washington	1815	AK35	173	134
Burford, Henry	Deed fr	Corporation of Washington	1815	AK35	179	139
Burford, Henry	Deed fr	Corporation of Washington	1815	AK35	176	137
Burford, Henry	Deed fr	Corporation of Washington	1815	AK35	159	122
Burford, Henry	Deed fr	Corporation of Washington	1815	AK35	164	126
Burford, Henry	Deed fr	Corporation of Washington	1815	AK35	166	127
Burford, Henry	Deed fr	Corporation of Washington	1815	AK35	167a	129
Burford, Henry	Deed fr	Corporation of Washington	1815	AK35	170	131
Burford, Henry	Deed fr	Laird, John, exr. of J. Carleton	1816	AM37	439	315
Burford, John A.	Deed to	Lindsey, Adam	1804	L11	194	186
Burford, John A.	Deed fr	Hall, John	1804	K10	341	352
Burford, John A.	Deed fr	Templeton, John, of G'tn.	1804	K10	339	351
Burford, John A. & Hannah, Alexa.	Deed to	Crandell, Thomas, of Alexa.	1805	N13	290	236
Burford, John A. et al	Assign fr	Poor, John	1810	X23	415	335
Burford, John A.	Mortgage to	Farrell, Zephaniah	1812	AD29	478	405
Burford, John A.	D. of T. to	Boyd, Washington	1813	AE30	475	353
Burford, John A.	D. of T. to	Love, John	1813	AF31	050	034
Burford, John A.	B. of S. to	Glover, Charles	1814	AG32	377	273
Burgess, Samuel	Deed fr	Glover, Charles, trustee	1812	AC28	372	271
Burgess, Samuel	Deed to	Vinson, Charles	1813	AE30	083	063
Burgess, Samuel	Qualify	Ensign 1st regiment	1813	AE30	472	351
Burke, John	Deed fr	Love, Sarah	1816	AL36	105	106
Burnes, Ann	Deed fr	Dorsey, William H.	1802	H8	159	153
Burnes, Ann	Deed to	Mason, John, of G'tn.	1802	H8	082	076
Burnes, Ann	Release to	Laird, John, of G'tn.	1802	G7	512	652
Burnes, Ann, wid/o David	Deed to	Lansdale, Thomas, of P.G. Co.	1802	I9	006	008
Burnes, Ann, wid.	Deed to	Dorsey, William H.	1802	I9	008	010

Index to District of Columbia Land Records, 1792-1817

Party	What	Party	Year	Liber	Old	New
Burnes, Anne	Release to	Polock, Isaac	1802	H8	141	137
Burnes, Benjamin & Ninian Beall	Deed fr	Bickley, Robert S., of Phila. PA	1812	AD29	031	022
Burnes, David	Deed to	Beall, Thomas, s/o George et al	1792	A1-1	002	1
Burnes, David	Deed to	Dermott, James Ree	1794	B2A	004	005
Burnes, David	Deed to	Blodget, Samuel, of Phila.	1794	B2A	017	018
Burnes, David	Deed to	Pratt, John Wilkes et al	1794	B2A	006	006
Burnes, David	Deed to	Johnson, Thomas Jr.	1794	B2A	026	029
Burnes, David	Deed to	Blodget, Samuel, Jr.	1794	B2A	074	096
Burnes, David	Deed to	Magruder, John Smith et al	1794	B2A	006	006
Burnes, David	Deed to	Blodget, Samuel, Jr., of Boston	1794	B2A	075	097
Burnes, David	Deed to	Fenwick, Bennett	1794	B2A	061	077
Burnes, David	Deed to	Blagden, George	1794	B2A	023	025
Burnes, David	Deed to	Johnson, John	1795	B2A	189	256
Burnes, David	Deed to	Johnson, Thomas Jr.	1795	B2A	188	254
Burnes, David	Assign to	Roe, Owen McDermot	1795	B2A	248	347
Burnes, David	Deed fr	Lingan, James Maccubbin	1796	B2B	580	325
Burnes, David	Deed to	Dowling, Michael	1796	B2B	394	055
Burnes, David	Deed to	Caffrey, Anthony, Rev.	1797	B2B	636	397
Burnes, David	Deed to	Brown, Robert	1797	C3	052	42
Burnes, David	Deed to	Wilson, Alexander	1797	C3	051	41
Burnes, David	Deed fr	Stephenson, Clotworthy	1798	D4	015	012
Burnes, David	Deed to	Munroe, Thomas	1798	D4	063	053
Burnes, David	Deed to	Roe, Owen McDermott	1798	C3	498	491
Burnes, David	Deed to	Grammar, Frederick, of Annapolis	1798	D4	153	135
Burnes, David	Deed to	Brown, Robert	1798	D4	013	011
Burnes, David	Deed fr	Purcell, Pierce	1799	D4	311	295
Burnes, David	Deed to	Rutherford, Andrew et al	1799	D4	174	155
Burnes, David, Gent.	Deed to	Mackay, William, merchant, PA	1795	B2A	254	354
Burnes, David, of P.G. Co.	Cert fr	Commissioners of Washington	1792	B2A	286	400
Burnes, David, of P.G. Co.	Cert fr	Commissioners of Washington	1792	B2A	287	402
Burnes, David, of P.G. Co.	Deed to	Polock, Isaac, mer., of GA	1796	B2B	507	210
Burnes, David, of P.G. Co.	Deed to	Afflick, Thomas, of Montg. Co.	1796	B2B	425	099
Burnes, David, of P.G. Co.	Deed to	Lynch, Dominick & Comfort Sands	1796	B2B	489	181
Burnes, David, of P.G. Co.	Deed to	Martin, Maria & Eleonora	1796	B2B	530	245
Burnes, David, of P.G. Co.	Deed to	Crookshanks, John, of Montg. Co.	1796	B2B	439	119
Burnes, David, of P.G. Co.	Deed to	Philips, Isaac et al	1797	C3	079	65
Burnes, David, of P.G. Co.	Deed to	Fenwick, Burnett, of P.G. Co.	1797	C3	105	86
Burnes, David, of P.G. Co.	Deed to	Hellen, Walter, of G'tn.	1797	C3	100	82
Burnes, David, of P.G. Co.	Deed to	Stephenson, Clotworthy, P.G. Co.	1798	C3	501	394
Burnes, George	Deed fr	Dermot, James R.	1803	K10	078	84
Burnes, George	Deed fr	Hurley, Daniel et al	1805	N13	075	068
Burnes, George	Mortgage fr	Johnson, James	1811	AC28	022	017
Burnes, George, trustee	B. of S. fr	Meyer, Philip, insolvent	1805	M12	068	063
Burnes, George, trustee	B. of S. fr	Burnes, John, insolvent	1805	M12	406	420
Burnes, John et al	Deed fr	King, Nicholas	1805	M12	093	086
Burnes, John, insolvent	B. of S. to	Burnes, George, trustee	1805	M12	406	420
Burnes, Marcia, by her guard.	Deed to	Polock, Isaac	1802	H8	147	143
Burnes, Marcia, by her guard.	Deed to	Laird, John	1802	G7	509	650
Burnes, Marcia, guard. of	Deed to	Dorsey, William H., assignee of	1802	I9	007	009
Burnes, Marcia, guard. of	Deed to	Dorsey, William H.	1802	I9	009	011
Burnes, Thomas	B. of S. to	Pearce, Thomas W.	1806	O14	277	183
Burnes, William	B. of S. to	Coombe, Griffith	1806	O14	262½	173
Burness, Ann	Deed to	Dorsey, William Hammond	1805	M12	268	269
Burneston, Isaac, Balto. Co. et al	Deed to	Bussard, Daniel, of G'tn.	1812	AC28	182	138
Burneston, Isaac, of Balto. et al	Deed fr	Beck, Joseph, of Montg. Co.	1797	C3	236	196

Index to District of Columbia Land Records, 1792-1817

Party	What	Party	Year	Liber	Old	New
Burnet, Charles A. et al	Mortgage fr	Rigdon, Thomas	1802	H8	009	008
Burnett, Charles A.	Deed to	Reintzell, Daniel et al	1806	Q16	320	245
Burnett, Charles A., of G'tn.	Deed fr	Chandler, Walter S.	1811	AB27	207	169
Burnett, Charles A., of G'tn.	Deed to	Corcoran, Thomas, of G'tn.	1813	AE30	479	356
Burnett, Charles A., of G'tn.	Deed fr	Williams, Thomas Owen, of P.G.	1814	AG32	411	299
Burnett, Charles A., of G'tn.	Deed fr	Corcoran, Thomas, of G'tn.	1814	AH33	372	322
Burnett, Charles A. & T.B. Beall	D. of T. fr	Davis, Richard, of G'tn.	1816	AM37	421	302
Burnett, Charles et al	Deed fr	Threlkeld, John, coroner	1799	D4	351	338
Burnett, Elizabeth	B. of S. fr	Davis, Sarah	1806	P15	046	028
Burns, Benjamin	Deed fr	Beall, Ninian	1812	AC28	181	137
Burns, Benjamin & Ninian Beall	Deed fr	Bickley, Robert S., of Phila. PA	1810	Y24	264	243
Burns, George	B. of S. fr	Johnston, James	1812	AB27	527	430
Burns, George	Deed fr	Hancock, James & Elizabeth	1815	AH33	471	402
Burns, George	Deed fr	Hancock, James & Elizabeth	1815	AH33	469	400
Burns, George & John C. Dickson	Mortgage fr	Hickey, James	1811	AB27	233	190
Burns, William, trustee	Deed fr	Mandell, Daniel, insolvent	1810	Y24	463	410
Burrell, John, s/o Alexander	Deed to	Wootton, Richard, planter	1793	A1-2	439	47
Burriss, John & Elizabeth, of G'tn.	Deed to	Bridges, John, of G'tn.	1813	AF31	295	210
Burroughs, Edward	Slaves		1802	H8	123	119
Burrows, Edward	Cert fr	Commissioners of Washington	1797	B2B	462	153
Burrows, Edward	Deed fr	Greenleaf, James, of Phila.	1797	C3	269	219
Burrows, Edward	Agreement	May, Frederick et al	1799	E5	050	040
Burrows, Edward	Agreement	Eliot, Samuel, Jr. et al	1799	E5	050	040
Burrows, Edward	Agreement	Spaulding, John et al	1799	E5	050	040
Burrows, Edward	Deed fr	Densley, Hugh et al	1805	N13	250	209
Burrows, Edward	Deed fr	Masters, John	1807	S18	137	112
Burrows, Edward	B. of S. fr	Baker, Samuel	1807	R17	237	179
Burrows, Edward	Deed fr	Johns, Aquila, of P.G. Co.	1807	S18	141	115
Burrows, Edward & John Spalding	Release to	May, Frederick & Samuel Eliot, Jr.	1803	K10	066	71
Burrows, Edward et al	B. of S. fr	Wade, Robert P.	1808	V21	092	071
Burrows, Edward, of P.G. Co.	Cert fr	Commissioners of Washington	1793	B2A	314	442
Burrows, John & Elizabeth	Lease to	Baker, John, of G'tn.	1817	AN38	488	352
Burrows, John, insolvent	B. of S. to	Collard, George, trustee	1808	T19	202	145
Burrows, John, of G'tn.	Assign fr	Grant, William V. & N. Warner	1817	AO39	137	104
Burrows, John, of G'tn.	B. of S. fr	Hoover, Peter, of G'tn.	1817	AO39	248	179
Burrows, Joseph	Deed fr	Commissioners of Washington	1801	G7	138	182
Burrows, Joseph	Deed fr	Munroe, Thomas, Supt.	1802	H8	538	498
Burrows, Joseph	Deed to	Geyer, Daniel	1802	I9	534	873
Burrows, Joseph	Deed fr	Gaines, Richard	1811	AA26	201	138
Burrows, Joseph	D. of T. fr	Lewis, Samuel, Jr.	1812	AD29	214	175
Burrows, Joseph	Deed fr	Bradley, Phineas	1812	AC28	317	230
Burrows, William E.	Release to	Loring, Israel	1802	H8	508	467
Burrows, William et al	Deed to	Blake, John, of Charleston SC	1804	L11	120	122
Burrows, William et al	Deed fr	Thompson, James	1804	L11	308	283
Burrows, William W.	Deed fr	Loring, Isaac	1801	G7	199	266
Burrows, William W.	Deed fr	Thompson, James	1802	I9	432	715
Burrows, William Ward et al	Deed to	Blake, John, of Charleston SC	1804	L11	120	122
Burrows, William Ward et al	Deed fr	Thompson, James	1804	L11	308	283
Bury, James	Assign fr	Smith, Dennis	1812	AB27	520	425
Bury, James	Deed fr	May, Frederick	1814	AH33	139	132
Bury, James [Barry]	Lease fr	May, Frederick	1812	AB27	516	422
Busey, Charles	Deed to	Powell, Nicholas	1802	I9	230	366
Busey, Samuel	B. of S. to	Newton, John S.	1810	Y24	324	294
Bush, Lucy, age 20, & dau. Patty	Manumis fr	Addison, Walter Dulany	1813	AF31	118	080
Bushby, Mary	Deed fr	Laird, John, exr. of J. Carleton	1814	AG32	244	174

Party	What	Party	Year	Liber	Old	New
Bushby, William	Agreement	Gardner, Peter	1801	G7	080	104
Bushell, William, of Phila. PA	Deed fr	Carroll, Daniel, of *Duddington*	1800	E5	208	202
Bussard, Daniel	Deed fr	Renner, Daniel	1802	H8	046	043
Bussard, Daniel	Deed fr	Ransburgh, John D.	1802	I9	554	898
Bussard, Daniel	Deed fr	King, James C.	1802	I9	239	384
Bussard, Daniel	Deed fr	Renner, Daniel	1802	H8	044	042
Bussard, Daniel	Deed fr	Lee, Mary, wid/o Henry Butler	1805	N13	396	316
Bussard, Daniel	B. of S. fr	Newton, Ignatius, of G'tn.	1805	O14	043	026
Bussard, Daniel	Deed fr	Threlkeld, John	1805	O14	027	017
Bussard, Daniel	Deed fr	Sutton, Robert	1805	N13	390	311
Bussard, Daniel	Deed fr	Parkinson, Edward, of MD	1806	Q16	090	058
Bussard, Daniel	Deed fr	Beatty, Charles, heirs of	1806	P15	092	057
Bussard, Daniel	Deed fr	Beall, Thomas, of George	1808	V21	131	096
Bussard, Daniel	Deed fr	French, John B. et ux	1808	V21	080	062
Bussard, Daniel	Deed fr	Davidson, Ann Maria, late of A.	1809	W22	347	224
Bussard, Daniel	Deed fr	Hedges, Nicholas et ux	1809	X23	288	229
Bussard, Daniel	Release to	Guy, Everard	1809	W22	354	229
Bussard, Daniel	Deed fr	Corcoran, Thomas	1810	Y24	504	444
Bussard, Daniel	Deed fr	Magruder, Ninian, Dr.	1810	Y24	501	441
Bussard, Daniel	Deed to	Davidson, John	1810	Z25	093	068
Bussard, Daniel	Deed fr	Dunback, Elizabeth, of G'tn.	1810	X23	385	310
Bussard, Daniel	Deed to	Hughes, Thomas	1812	AC28	114	086
Bussard, Daniel	Deed fr	Presbyterian Congregation, G'tn.	1812	AC28	185	140
Bussard, Daniel	B. of S. fr	Parburt, George [Parvert]	1812	AD29	035	025
Bussard, Daniel	Deed fr	Glover, Charles	1812	AD29	504	425
Bussard, Daniel	Deed fr	Wineberger, Jacob, of G'tn.	1812	AD29	522	440
Bussard, Daniel	Deed fr	Presbyterian Congregation of G'tn.	1812	AD29	521	439
Bussard, Daniel	Deed fr	Threlkeld, John	1812	AD29	149	117
Bussard, Daniel	Deed to	Mudd, Thomas J.	1813	AE30	462	344
Bussard, Daniel	Agreement	Holtzman, Jacob, heirs of	1815	AI34	026	030
Bussard, Daniel	Assign fr	Jones, Benjamin W.	1815	AH33	396	342
Bussard, Daniel	Deed fr	Renner, Daniel et al	1815	AH33	397	343
Bussard, Daniel	Deed to	Lewis, Henry	1816	AK35	533	421
Bussard, Daniel	Assign to	Berry, Ester E., of Montg. Co.	1816	AL36	259	260
Bussard, Daniel	Deed to	Brooks, Joseph	1816	AL36	528	493
Bussard, Daniel	Qualify	Justice of the Peace	1816	AL36	148	149
Bussard, Daniel	Deed fr	Corcoran, Thomas, of G'tn.	1816	AL36	303	300
Bussard, Daniel	Deed to	Morton, William	1816	AL36	062	063
Bussard, Daniel	Deed to	Holtzman, George	1816	AM37	428	307
Bussard, Daniel	Deed fr	Balch, Stephen B.	1817	AN38	210	153
Bussard, Daniel	Deed to	Smallwood, Horatio	1817	AO39	091	072
Bussard, Daniel	Deed fr	Bussard, Philip, of VA	1817	AN38	214	156
Bussard, Daniel & Daniel Renner	Deed fr	Beall, Thomas B., of G'tn.	1804	K10	107	114
Bussard, Daniel & Daniel Renner	Deed to	Bussard, John R.	1804	K10	108	115
Bussard, Daniel & Daniel Renner	Deed fr	Deakins, Francis, of G'tn.	1804	K10	103	110
Bussard, Daniel & Daniel Renner	Deed fr	Beatty, Charles, heirs of	1807	R17	404	305
Bussard, Daniel & Daniel Renner	Release fr	Reeder, Benjamin & Eleanor	1807	R17	401	303
Bussard, Daniel & Daniel Renner	Deed fr	King, George, of G'tn.	1808	U20	132	075
Bussard, Daniel & Daniel Rener	Deed fr	Peter, John	1809	V21	383	286
Bussard, Daniel & Daniel Renner	Deed fr	McClann, Robert, of G'tn.	1809	X23	292	232
Bussard, Daniel & Daniel Renner	Deed fr	Wright, Thomas C.	1809	X23	256	200
Bussard, Daniel & Daniel Renner	Deed to	Hoye, John	1809	X23	210	159
Bussard, Daniel & Daniel Renner	Release to	King, Adam, of G'tn.	1809	X23	283	224
Bussard, Daniel & Daniel Renner	Deed fr	Mountz, Jacob, collector, G'tn.	1809	X23	289	230
Bussard, Daniel & Daniel Renner	Deed fr	Maffitt, Samuel, of G'tn.	1809	X23	256	200

Index to District of Columbia Land Records, 1792-1817

Party	What	Party	Year	Liber	Old	New
Bussard, Daniel & Daniel Renner	Deed fr	Heise, Christian	1810	Z25	155	122
Bussard, Daniel & Daniel Renner	Release to	Smith, Walter	1810	Y24	202	186
Bussard, Daniel & Thomas Thorpe	Deed to	Davidson, John	1810	Z25	090	068
Bussard, Daniel & Daniel Renner	Deed to	Bayley, Mary	1812	AD29	175	140
Bussard, Daniel et al	Lease fr	Beatty, Charles	1802	H8	191	183
Bussard, Daniel et al	Deed fr	Nicholls, Samuel	1802	I9	551	895
Bussard, Daniel et al	B. of S. fr	Fowler, Benjamin	1804	L11	054	55
Bussard, Daniel et al	Deed fr	Easterday, Daniel	1806	P15	308	203
Bussard, Daniel et al	Deed fr	Magruder, George, collector, G'tn.	1807	S18	203	163
Bussard, Daniel et al	Suit ads	Potomac Company	1812	AG32	258	183
Bussard, Daniel, Gent., of G'tn.	Deed fr	King, Adam, of G'tn.	1809	X23	148	107
Bussard, Daniel, Jr.	Deed fr	Beatty, John M. & Charles A.	1809	W22	345	223
Bussard, Daniel, of G'tn.	Deed fr	Stoddert, Benjamin, of G'tn.	1804	K10	106	113
Bussard, Daniel, of G'tn.	Deed fr	Gary, Everard, of G'tn.	1804	K10	104	111
Bussard, Daniel, of G'tn.	Deed to	Stewart, John, of Frederick Co.	1804	L11	147	148
Bussard, Daniel, of G'tn.	Deed to	Bain, Quinton	1804	L11	051	52
Bussard, Daniel, of G'tn.	Deed fr	Reinhart, Andrew	1805	N13	131	125
Bussard, Daniel, of G'tn.	Deed fr	Davidson, John, of Annapolis	1805	N13	391	312
Bussard, Daniel, of G'tn.	Deed fr	Smallwood, Leavan, of G'tn.	1805	N13	394	314
Bussard, Daniel, of G'tn.	Deed fr	Thorpe, Thomas	1805	M12	134	129
Bussard, Daniel, of G'tn.	Deed fr	Devilbiss, George, exr. of John	1805	M12	136	132
Bussard, Daniel, of G'tn. et al	Deed fr	Easterday, Daniel, of G'tn.	1806	P15	399	268
Bussard, Daniel, of G'tn. et al	Deed fr	Reeder, Benjamin, of Morgantown	1807	R17	224	168
Bussard, Daniel, of G'tn.	Deed fr	King, James C., of G'tn.	1808	U20	153	087
Bussard, Daniel, of G'tn.	Deed fr	Brookes, Joseph, of G'tn.	1809	X23	252	196
Bussard, Daniel, of G'tn.	Deed fr	Boyd, Washington, marshal	1809	X23	147	106
Bussard, Daniel, of G'tn.	Deed to	Lorman, William, of Balto. et al	1810	X23	327	261
Bussard, Daniel, of G'tn.	Deed to	Brookes, William H., of G'tn.	1810	Y24	531	466
Bussard, Daniel, of G'tn.	Deed to	Magruder, Ninian, Dr., of G'tn.	1810	Y24	356	322
Bussard, Daniel, of G'tn., trustee	Deed to	Daws, Isaac, of G'tn.	1810	Y24	082	074
Bussard, Daniel, of G'tn.	Deed fr	Renner, Daniel, of G'tn.	1810	Z25	337	264
Bussard, Daniel, of G'tn.	Deed to	Barlow, Joel	1810	Z25	098	075
Bussard, Daniel, of G'tn.	Deed to	Norris, Stephen, of G'tn.	1812	AC28	282	205
Bussard, Daniel, of G'tn.	Deed to	Renner, Daniel	1812	AC28	382	278
Bussard, Daniel, of G'tn.	Deed fr	Baker, William & Isaac Burneston	1812	AC28	182	138
Bussard, Daniel, of G'tn.	B. of S. fr	Etter, Joseph, of G'tn.	1812	AC28	374	272
Bussard, Daniel, of G'tn.	Deed fr	Shaw, Polly, of G'tn.	1812	AD29	148	116
Bussard, Daniel, of G'tn.	Deed to	Smith, Clement, of G'tn.	1812	AD29	034	024
Bussard, Daniel, of G'tn.	Deed to	Holtzman, Jacob, of G'tn.	1812	AE30	008	007
Bussard, Daniel, of G'tn.	Deed fr	Renner, Daniel, of G'tn.	1813	AF31	308	220
Bussard, Daniel, of G'tn.	Deed to	Bohrer, George, of G'tn.	1813	AF31	328	234
Bussard, Daniel, of G'tn.	Deed to	Peltz, John	1813	AE30	472	351
Bussard, Daniel, of G'tn.	Deed fr	Murdock, John, of G'tn.	1813	AF31	134	090
Bussard, Daniel, of G'tn.	Deed to	Renner, Daniel, of G'tn.	1814	AG32	196	137
Bussard, Daniel, of G'tn.	Deed to	Glover, Charles	1815	AH33	477	407
Bussard, Daniel, of G'tn.	Deed fr	Mountz, Jacob, of G'tn., collector	1815	AI34	053	060
Bussard, Daniel, of G'tn.	Deed to	Magruder, Ninian, of G'tn.	1815	AI34	044	050
Bussard, Daniel, of G'tn.	Deed fr	Murdock, John, of G'tn.	1815	AI34	025	029
Bussard, Daniel, of G'tn.	Deed to	Smith, Clement, of G'tn.	1815	AK35	108	083
Bussard, Daniel, of G'tn.	B. of S. fr	Moran, Jesse	1815	AK35	066	051
Bussard, Daniel, of G'tn.	Deed to	Smith, Clement, of G'tn.	1815	AK35	109	084
Bussard, Daniel, of G'tn.	Deed to	Brookes, Joseph	1816	AL36	376	364
Bussard, Daniel, of G'tn.	Deed fr	Willett, Burgess, of Montg. Co.	1816	AM37	426	305
Bussard, Daniel, of G'tn.	Deed to	Smith, Richard	1816	AL36	176	176
Bussard, Daniel, of G'tn.	D. of T. to	English, David, cashier, of G'tn.	1817	AN38	348	256

Index to District of Columbia Land Records, 1792-1817

Party	What	Party	Year	Liber	Old	New
Bussard, Daniel, of G'tn.	Deed to	Whann, William, of G'tn.	1817	AN38	195	141
Bussard, John R.	Deed to	Ransburg, John D.	1801	G7		076
Bussard, John R.	Deed to	King, James C., of G'tn.	1801	G7	225	300
Bussard, John R.	Deed fr	Renner, Daniel & Daniel Bussard	1804	K10	108	115
Bussard, John R., of P.G. Co.	Deed fr	Lee, Mary, late wid/o H. Butler	1809	W22	225	153
Bussard, John R., of P.G. Co.	Deed fr	Butler, Edward M., of KY	1809	X23	238	184
Bussard, John R., of Montg. Co.	Deed to	Boarman, Richard B.A.	1810	Z25	017	013
Bussard, John R.	Deed to	Hilleary, Lewis	1813	AE30	165	131
Bussard, Philip et al	Lease fr	Schultze, Henry	1816	AK35	502	396
Bussard, Philip, of VA	Deed to	Bussard, Daniel	1817	AN38	214	156
Busserd, John R., of Frederick Co.	Deed fr	Forrest, Uriah	1800	E5	243	237
Busti, Paul, mer., of PA	Deed fr	Harrison, George et al	1802	I9	119	174
Busy, Samuel, of Montg. Co.	Deed fr	French, Charles & Mariamne	1814	AH33	228	200
Butler, Abraham	Cert Free fr	Parker, Eleanor P.	1817	AO39	319	227
Butler, Betsy	Cert Free fr	Proctor, Sarah (C)	1812	AD29	553	553
Butler, Bill	Cert Free fr	McWilliams, Alex	1809	W22	349	226
Butler, Charles	Deed fr	Gilpin, Bernard	1802	H8	125	121
Butler, Chloe	Cert Free to	Young, Ann (C), age 26	1813	AE30	549	408
Butler, David (C)	Cert Free fr	Hewes, Archibald	1812	AD29	174	139
Butler, Edward M.	B. of S. to	Wilson, John A.	1805	O14	152	099
Butler, Edward M., of KY	Deed to	Bussard, John R., of P.G. Co.	1809	X23	238	184
Butler, Edward Mann	Deed to	Holmead, John	1805	O14	003	004
Butler, Edward, of P.G. Co.	Deed fr	Butler, Thomas, of G'tn.	1807	R17	246	186
Butler, George	Cert Free		1810	Z25	063	047
Butler, Henny	Cert Free		1807	S18	038	032
Butler, Henny (mulatto)	Manumis fr	Butler, Toby	1804	L11	302	277
Butler, Henry (C)	Manumis fr	Staley, Jacob, of G'tn.	1815	AI34	371	399
Butler, Hetty	Manumis fr	Doyle, Eliza, of G'tn.	1816	AK35	483	379
Butler, Hetty, of G'tn.	B. of S. fr	Doyle, Eliza, of G'tn.	1816	AK35	482	378
Butler, Ignatius	Petition	Hill, Henry	1807	R17	140	109
Butler, John	Deed fr	Forrest, Uriah et al	1802	H8	265	251
Butler, John	Deed fr	Hanson, Samuel, of Samuel et al	1802	H8	265	251
Butler, Joseph, s/o Mary	Indenture to	Newton, Ignatius, of G'tn.	1811	AB27	418	345
Butler, Liucender S. (C), age 12	Cert Slave fr	Gustine, J.T. et al	1814	AH33	203	184
Butler, Mann	Deed to	Neale, Francis, Rev.	1805	O14	041	025
Butler, Mann, s/o Henry et al	Deed fr	Bussard, Daniel	1805	N13	396	316
Butler, Mary (C)	Cert Free fr	Shorter, Jenny (C)	1817	AO39	063	052
Butler, Mary, d/o Robert	Manumis fr	Butler, Butler	1810	Y24	405	365
Butler, Philice	Manumis fr	Selby, Philip Butler	1806	Q16	069	043
Butler, Philis (negro)	Manumis fr	Selby, Philip	1808	U20	137	078
Butler, Robert	Deed fr	Holmead, John	1807	R17	168	128
Butler, Robert	Manumis to	Butler, Mary, d/o Robert	1810	Y24	405	365
Butler, Robert, of G'tn.	D. of T. to	King, Charles, of G'tn.	1810	Y24	517	454
Butler, Silas	Deed fr	Powell, Cuthbert & George Taylor	1810	Y24	326	296
Butler, Silas	Deed fr	Glover, Charles	1812	AD29	159	126
Butler, Silas	Deed fr	Forrest, Joseph, trustee	1813	AF31	068	047
Butler, Silas	R. Dower fr	Wadsworth, Elizabeth, rel/o Chas.	1814	AH33	119	112
Butler, Silas & Timothy Winn	Deed fr	Bentley, John H., of Balto. MD	1813	AE30	161	128
Butler, Silas & Timothy Winn	Deed fr	Yeaton, William, of Alexa.	1813	AF31	103	070
Butler, Silas & Timothy Winn	Deed fr	Wadsworth, Elizabeth	1814	AH33	120	113
Butler, Susan	Cert Free fr	Blake, James H.	1817	AO39	195	143
Butler, Thomas	Deed fr	Gilpin, Bernard	1802	H8	228	217
Butler, Thomas, of G'tn.	Deed to	Curran, John, of G'tn.	1807	R17	005	005
Butler, Thomas, of G'tn.	Deed to	Butler, Edward, of P.G. Co.	1807	R17	246	186
Butler, Toby	Manumis to	Butler, Henny (mulatto)	1804	L11	302	277

Party	What	Party	Year	Liber	Old	New
Butter, Mary (C)	Cert Free to	Datcher, Francis, s/o Reb. Cole	1816	AM37	022	018
Byer, Jacob	Deed to	Beall, Thomas & John M. Gantt	1792	A1-1	072	106
Byus, Stanley	Qualify		1802	I9	551	894
Byus, Stanley	B. of S. to	Gillis, Thomas H.	1806	O14	071	043

Party	What	Party	Year	Liber	Old	New
C						
Caffray, Anthony, Rev.	Cert fr	Commissioners of Washington	1798	B2B	478	172
Caffray, Anthony, Rev.	Cert fr	Commissioners of Washington	1798	B2B	479	172
Caffray, Anthony, Rev.	Deed to	Carroll, John, Rt. Rev.	1804	L11	182	176
Caffray, Millicent	Slaves	From MD	1806	Q16	127	083
Caffrey, Anthony, Rev.	Deed fr	Burnes, David	1797	B2B	636	397
Caffrey, Daniel	B. of S. to	Barron, Walter et al	1802	H8	508	467
Caffrey, Daniel	B. of S. to	Healy, Patrick et al	1802	H8	508	467
Caffrey, Daniel	Manumis to	[ ], Esther, and her son William	1812	AD29	428	360
Caffry, Anthony, Rev., Dublin, Ire.	Deed to	Hoban, James	1811	AA26	351	235
Caffry, Daniel	Assign to	Matthews, William, Rev.	1814	AG32	317	232
Caldenbaugh, Andrew, of G'tn.	Deed to	Davidson, John, of Annapolis	1801	G7	141	186
Calder, James	Deed fr	Balch, Stephen B.	1801	G7	471	507
Calder, James	Deed fr	Beall, Thomas	1802	I9	522	853
Calder, James	D. of T. to	Smith, Walter et al	1806	O14	303	201
Calder, James	Mortgage to	Smith, Walter	1806	O14	300	199
Calder, James	Deed to	Beall, Thomas, of George	1807	S18	383	305
Calder, James	Deed fr	Beall, Thomas, of George	1807	T19	006	005
Calder, James	B. of S. fr	Thomas, John, 3rd	1810	Y24	032	028
Calder, James	Receipt fr	Smith, Clement & A. Addison	1813	AE30	342	255
Calder, James	Deed fr	Beatty, Charles A., Dr.	1814	AG32	059	046
Calder, James et al	Deed fr	Evans, Samuel et al	1798	D4	099	083
Calder, James et al	Deed fr	Pierce, Isaac et al	1799	D4	239	221
Calder, James, of G'tn.	Deed fr	Commissioners of Washington	1800	E5	235	228
Calder, James, of G'tn.	Deed fr	Commissioners of Washington	1800	E5	285	280
Calder, James, of G'tn.	Deed fr	Commissioners of Washington	1800	E5	285	279
Calder, James, of G'tn.	Deed fr	Balch, Stephen Bloomer, of G'tn.	1801	G7	471	607
Calder, James, of G'tn.	Deed fr	Commissioners of Washington	1802	G7	538	685
Calder, James, of G'tn.	Deed fr	Balch, Stephen Bloomer, of G'tn.	1807	T19	005	004
Calder, James, of G'tn.	Deed fr	Mitchell, John, of G'tn.	1808	U20	053	030
Calder, James, of G'tn.	Deed to	Carberry, Henry, of G'tn.	1809	X23	243	189
Calder, James, of G'tn.	Deed fr	Kokenderfer, Leonard, of G'tn.	1809	W22	251	169
Calder, James, of G'tn.	Deed to	Kokenderfer, Leonard, of G'tn.	1809	X23	268	211
Calder, James, of G'tn.	Deed to	Varden, Charles et al	1811	AA26	104	073
Calder, James, of G'tn.	Deed fr	Beatty, George A., Dr., of G'tn.	1813	AE30	346	259
Calder, James, of G'tn.	Deed to	Milligan, Joseph, of G'tn.	1813	AF31	026	018
Calder, James, of G'tn.	Deed fr	Fletchall, Thomas, of Montg. Co.	1813	AE30	077	058
Calder, James, of G'tn.	Convey to	Lear, Tobias	1815	AK35	455	357
Calder, James [Colder]	Deed fr	Davidson, Lewis Grant	1815	AK35	013	010
Calder, William	Deed fr	Key, Philip B. & Jos. W. Clagett	1814	AH33	204	185
Calder, William, of G'tn.	Deed fr	Gaines, Richard, Hamilton Co. OH	1813	AE30	340	254
Calder, William, of G'tn.	Deed to	Lanham, Elisha, of G'tn.	1816	AL36	392	378
Caldwell, David, of PA	Deed fr	Munroe, Thomas, Supt.	1802	H8	493	453
Caldwell, E.B., for M. Scott	B. of S. to	Shorter, Moses	1806	Q16	293	223
Caldwell, Elias B. et al	Bond to	United States	1801	G7	347	478
Caldwell, Elias B.	Deed fr	Blodget, Samuel, of Phila.	1801	G7	293	407
Caldwell, Elias B. et al	Deed fr	Blodgett, Samuel, of Phila.	1801	G7	097	125
Caldwell, Elias B.	Deed fr	Fowler, John, of KY	1802	H8	188	180
Caldwell, Elias B.	Deed fr	Wayman, Charles	1802	I9	344	568
Caldwell, Elias B. et al	Deed to	Smith, Walter et al	1804	K10	247	254
Caldwell, Elias B., of G'tn. et al	Deed to	Washington, William A.	1804	K10	252	259
Caldwell, Elias B., of G'tn.	Deed to	Gunnell, Henry, of Fairfax Co. VA	1804	L11	029	28
Caldwell, Elias B., trustee	Deed fr	Haywood, Thomas, insolvent	1804	L11	082	84
Caldwell, Elias B., trustee	Deed fr	Munroe, Thomas, Supt.	1804	L11	291	267
Caldwell, Elias B., trustee	Deed to	Patterson, Edgar	1806	P15	402	270

Index to District of Columbia Land Records, 1792-1817

Party	What	Party	Year	Liber	Old	New
Caldwell, Elias B.	Deed to	Stoddert, Benjamin, of G'tn.	1806	P15	392	262
Caldwell, Elias B., trustee	Deed to	Simmons, William	1806	P15	317	209
Caldwell, Elias B. et al	Deed to	Smith, Walter, of G'tn.	1806	O14	245	161
Caldwell, Elias B. et al	Deed to	Corcoran, Thomas	1806	P15	171	113
Caldwell, Elias B.	B. of S. fr	Templeman, John	1808	U20	232	125
Caldwell, Elias B.	Cert fr	Munroe, Thomas, Supt.	1808	V21	055	044
Caldwell, Elias B., exr.	Deed to	Parrott, Richard	1809	V21	251	179
Caldwell, Elias B.	Cert fr	Munroe, Thomas, Supt.	1809	V21	389	293
Caldwell, Elias B.	Deed fr	Carroll, Daniel & Ann, *Duddington*	1809	V21	392	296
Caldwell, Elias B. & Eli Williams	D. of T. fr	Wilkinson, James, insolvent	1811	AC28	056	043
Caldwell, Elias B. & Eli Williams	Deed fr	Wilkinson, James, insolvent	1811	AC28	057	044
Caldwell, Elias B.	Deed fr	Wheaton, Joseph	1811	AB27	487	399
Caldwell, Elias B.	Deed fr	Boyd, Washington	1812	AC28	173	130
Caldwell, Elias B.	Qualify	Captain of cavalry in militia	1812	AD29	179	144
Caldwell, Elias B.	Deed to	Campbell, Levin H.	1812	AC28	176	133
Caldwell, Elias B., trustee et al	Cert fr	Munroe, Thomas, Supt.	1813	AE30	350	262
Caldwell, Elias B.	Deed fr	Corporation of Washington	1815	AI34	233	264
Caldwell, Elias B.	Deed fr	Gales, Joseph, Jr. & Sarah J.M.	1816	AK35	519	409
Caldwell, Elias B.	Deed fr	Key, Francis S.	1816	AK35	521	411
Caldwell, Elias B.	Deed fr	Boyd, Washington, marshal	1816	AL36	371	360
Caldwell, Elias B.	D. of T. fr	McLeod, John	1816	AL36	384	371
Caldwell, Elias B.	Mortgage fr	Stewart, Richard	1816	AL36	271	270
Caldwell, Elias B. & John Coyle	Deed to	Wilson, John A.	1816	AL36	399	384
Caldwell, Elias B.	D. of T. fr	Smallwood, Sam. & Eliz. Boothe	1816	AM37	229	168
Caldwell, Elias B.	Deed fr	Zantzinger, William P.	1816	AM37	235	173
Caldwell, Elias B.	D. of T. fr	Latrobe, Benjamin H. & Marh E.	1816	AO39	021	017
Caldwell, Elias B.	Deed to	Zantzinger, William P.	1817	AN38	134	098
Caldwell, Elias B.	D. of T. fr	Smallwood, S.N. & Eliz. Booth	1817	AN38	396	296
Caldwell, Elias, trustee	Deed to	Boyd, Washington	1809	V21	168	121
Caldwell, Mary et al	Deed fr	Caldwell, Timothy	1802	I9	570	923
Caldwell, Timothy	Deed to	Lingan, James Maccubbin	1802	H8	572	536
Caldwell, Timothy	Deed to	Caldwell, Mary et al	1802	I9	570	923
Caldwell, Timothy	Deed to	McGowan, John	1802	I9	571	925
Caldwell, Timothy	Deed fr	Sprogell, Thomas Y.	1802	H8	183	175
Caldwell, Timothy	Deed fr	Templeman, John, of G'tn.	1804	L11	129	131
Caldwell, Timothy	Deed fr	Gilliss, Thomas H.	1805	O14	045	027
Caldwell, Timothy	Deed fr	Lingan, James Macubbin, G'tn.	1805	M12	396	409
Caldwell, Timothy	Deed to	McCleland, John	1805	M12	407	422
Caldwell, Timothy	Deed to	Glascow, John	1806	P15	159	105
Caldwell, Timothy	Deed fr	Templeman, John, Allegany Co.	1806	P15	161	106
Caldwell, Timothy	Deed to	Worthington, William, the younger	1806	O14	260	171
Caldwell, Timothy	Deed to	Granger, Gideon	1808	T19	259	191
Caldwell, Timothy	Deed fr	McGowan, John et al	1808	T19	269	198
Caldwell, Timothy	B. of S. to	Templeman, John, Allegany Co.	1808	U20	127	072
Caldwell, Timothy	Deed to	Moore, George	1808	U20	097	054
Caldwell, Timothy	Deed to	Granger, Gideon	1808	T19	278	204
Caldwell, Timothy	Manumis to	Bond, James	1809	V21	230	164
Caldwell, Timothy, now of Phila.	Deed fr	Granger, Gideon & Mindwell P.	1812	AE30	015	012
Caldwell, Timothy, of Phila. PA	Deed fr	Forrest, Uriah	1800	E5	365	347
Caldwell, Timothy, of Phila. PA	D. of T. to	McCormick, Alexander et al	1812	AE30	017	014
Caldwell, Timothy, of Phila. PA	Mortgage to	Moore, John, brickmaker, of Phila.	1813	AF31	245	170
Caldwell, Timothy, of Phila. PA	Release fr	McCormick, Alex. & Wm. O'Neale	1813	AF31	243	168
Caldwell, Timothy, of Phila. PA	Deed fr	Gardner, William P.	1814	AH33	278	242
Callahan, John	Deed fr	Wayman, Charles	1802	I9	167	254
Callan, Nicholas	B. of S. fr	McNemara, Roger & Mary	1809	X23	035	026

Index to District of Columbia Land Records, 1792-1817

Party	What	Party	Year	Liber	Old	New
Callan, Nicholas	B. of S. to	Roe, Sarah McDermott et al	1810	Y24	524	461
Callan, Nicholas	Deed fr	Brent, William	1816	AL36	421	403
Callan, Nicholas, trustee	Assign fr	Kent, Luke, insolvent	1811	AC28	050	038
Callan, Patrick	Deed fr	Venable, Joseph	1814	AF31	522	384
Callen, Henry	B. of S. to	Maguire, Hugh & N. Callen	1808	U20	072	040
Callen, Nicholas et al	B. of S. fr	Callen, Henry	1808	U20	072	040
Callen, Partrick	B. of S. fr	Cooper, John	1815	AK35	056	044
Callis, Henry A. et al	Deed to	Addison, Thomas G., of P.G. Co.	1811	AA26	024	019
Calvert, Ann & William Thornton	Deed to	Pairo, Thomas W.	1809	X23	187	140
Calvert, Edward H., of P.G. Co.	B. of S. to	Minifie, Charles	1805	N13	107	101
Calvert, Elizabeth	Deed to	Beall, Thomas & John M. Gantt	1793	A1-1	220	306
Calvert, George, of P.G. Co.	Deed fr	Sim, Thomas	1816	AL36	238	243
Calvert, George, P.G. Co. et al	Deed fr	Law, Thomas & Eliza Park	1804	L11	127	129
Calvert, George, P.G. Co. et al	Deed fr	Law, Thomas	1804	L11	114	117
Calvert, George, P.G. Co. et al	Agreement	Law, Thomas	1804	L11	125	127
Calvert, Joseph	Deed fr	Thornton, William	1802	H8	511	470
Calvert, Joseph, admx. of	Deed to	Pairo, Thomas W.	1809	X23	187	140
Camillier, Vincent	B. of S. fr	Myers, John	1815	AK35	374	295
Cammack, William	Deed fr	Wheeler, Luke & John Cowper	1812	AC28	154	115
Campbell, Alexander, s/o William	Deed to	Willett, Burgess, of Montg. Co.	1816	AM37	135	105
Campbell, Arthur	Deed fr	McKee, James	1811	AB27	256	209
Campbell, Arthur	B. of S. to	Campbell, Thomas	1811	AB27	062	053
Campbell, Arthur	Deed to	Wharton, Franklin	1812	AD29	317	260
Campbell, Fanny	Manumis fr	Cranch, William	1813	AE30	188	150
Campbell, Francis et al	Deed to	Beall, Thomas & John M. Gantt	1793	A1-1	274	369
Campbell, Hugh G., U.S.N.	Deed fr	Commissioners of Washington	1800	F6	050	031
Campbell, James	Deed fr	Wheeler, Luke & John Cowper	1814	AG32	127	093
Campbell, John	B. of S. fr	Queen, Nicholas L.	1814	AH33	092	085
Campbell, John	Deed fr	Randall, John, of Annapolis	1815	AI34	038	044
Campbell, John	Deed fr	King, Josias W. & Mary	1815	AI34	508	513
Campbell, John	Deed fr	McClelland, John	1815	AI34	506	511
Campbell, John	Deed to	McClelland, John	1815	AI34	382	408
Campbell, John	B. of S. fr	Bacon, Samuel & George Moore	1815	AI34	510	515
Campbell, John	Deed to	Lenox, Peter	1815	AK35	449	352
Campbell, John	Deed fr	Laird, John, exr. of J. Carleton	1816	AM37	401	288
Campbell, John	Deed fr	Randall, John, of Annapolis	1816	AK35	531	419
Campbell, John, agent	Deed fr	McCormick, Alexander	1817	AN38	208	152
Campbell, John, exors. of	Deed to	Beall, Thomas & John M. Gantt	1793	A1-1	274	369
Campbell, Levin H.	Deed fr	Caldwell, Elias B.	1812	AC28	176	133
Campbell, Mary, of G'tn.	B. of S. fr	Martell, William, of G'tn.	1816	AM37	456	329
Campbell, Peter	Deed C.	State of Maryland	1799	D4	398	377
Campbell, Peter	Deed C.	State of Maryland	1799	D4	253	237
Campbell, Robert, bookseller, PA	Deed fr	Brown, Samuel, Dr., Lexington KY	1801	F6	139	085
Campbell, Thomas	B. of S. fr	Campbell, Arthur	1811	AB27	062	053
Campbell, William	Cert fr	Commissioners of Washington	1797	B2B	474	167
Campbell, William	Transfer fr	Forrest, Uriah	1797	B2B	474	167
Campbell, William	Deed to	Marbury, William	1801	G7	015	
Campbell, William	Deed fr	Wayman, Charles	1802	I9	197	307
Campbell, William	Deed fr	Glover, Charles	1814	AH33	053	047
Campbell, William, Frederick Co.	Deed fr	Stoddert, Benjamin, of G'tn.	1797	C3	132	107
Campbell, William, Frederick Co.	Deed to	Reintzel, Anthony, of G'tn.	1801	F6	163	101
Campbell, William, Frederick Co.	Deed to	Marbury, William, of G'tn.	1801	G7	015	018
Campbell, William, Frederick Co.	Deed fr	King, George	1806	Q16	156	103
Campbell, William, Frederick Co.	Deed to	Teakle, Littleton Dennis, Som. Co.	1806	P15	227	151
Campbell, William, Frederick Co.	Mortgage fr	Teackle, Littleton Dennis, Som.	1806	Q16	207	140

Index to District of Columbia Land Records, 1792-1817

Party	What	Party	Year	Liber	Old	New
Campbell, William, of Annapolis	Deed fr	Henderson, Richard	1792	A1-1	168	240
Campbell, William, of Annapolis	Mortgage fr	Davidson, William, of Annapolis	1796	B2B	545	269
Campbell, William, of A.A. Co.	Deed fr	Stoddert, Benjamin, of G'tn.	1797	B2B	684	458
Campbell, William, of Fredk. Co.	Release to	Banker, Charles N., of Phila. PA	1811	AC28	016	012
Campbell, William, of Fredk. Co.	Release to	King, George, of G'tn.	1815	AK35	021	016
Campbell, William, of Fredk. Co.	Deed fr	Key, Francis S.	1815	AH33	473	404
Campbell, Willliam et al	Deed fr	Duncanson, William Mayne et al	1797	C3	103	84
Cana, Frederick	Deed fr	Hall, John	1805	O14	094	058
Cana, Frederick	Deed to	Hall, John	1810	X23	361	289
Cana, Frederick	Deed fr	McGowan, John	1815	AK35	207	162
Canby, Israel T., of KY	Manumis to	[ ], Henrietta (M) & child Maria	1815	AH33	558	478
Canby, William et al	Deed to	Bentley, Caleb & Henrietta T.	1809	X23	091	067
Cannon, Abial	Deed to	McDonald, Walter	1817	AN38	270	197
Cannon, Charles	Deed to	Joy, Henry B.	1815	AI34	414	436
Cannon, John	B. of S. fr	Joy, Barton	1802	I9	489	804
Cannon, John	Deed fr	Stoddert, Benjamin	1802	I9	224	355
Cannon, John	Lease to	Cassin, Joseph	1806	P15	078	047
Cannon, John	Deed to	Costigan, Joseph	1806	P15	098	060
Cannon, John	Release to	Cannon, Sarah	1815	AI34	036	042
Cannon, John & Richard Spalding	Mortgage fr	Masters, Ezekiel	1812	AD29	313	257
Cannon, Sarah	Release fr	Cannon, John	1815	AI34	036	042
Cannon, Sarah	Deed fr	Boyd, Washington, marshal	1816	AM37	335	243
Cannon, Sarah	Deed fr	Moody, John & Betsey	1817	AN38	163	119
Carberry, Henry & Susanna	Deed to	Brengle, Lawrence	1802	I9	590	955
Carberry, Henry, of G'tn.	Deed fr	Calder, James, of G'tn.	1809	X23	243	189
Carberry, Thomas & James	Deed fr	Neale, William, Jr., St. Mary's Co.	1816	AL36	434	413
Carbery, Thomas	B. of S. fr	Bullock, George, of Charles Co.	1806	Q16	195	132
Carcand, David, of Calvert Co.	Deed fr	Stoddert, Benjamin & U. Forrest	1792	A1-1	121	176
Carcand, David, of Calvert Co.	Bond to	King, Adam & George	1804	K10	118	127
Carcand, David, of Calvert Co.	Lease to	King, George, of G'tn.	1813	AF31	484	353
Carey, Edward & Ann	Deed to	Townsend, Henry	1801	G7	218	291
Carey, William, of G'tn.	Deed to	Beatty, Thomas Jr.	1799	D4	235	217
Carico, James & Mary	Deed to	Holmead, John	1815	AK35	426	334
Carleton, George, bricklayer	Deed fr	Smith, William, joiner	1804	M12	009	009
Carleton, George, bricklayer, P.G.	Deed to	Boteler, Edward L., of P.G. Co.	1809	W22	394	256
Carleton, Joseph	Deed to	Williams, Benjamin	1802	I9	271	441
Carleton, Joseph	Deed fr	Williams, Benjamin	1802	I9	270	439
Carleton, Joseph	Lease to	Armstead, Robert et al	1804	L11	267	246
Carleton, Joseph	Assign fr	Dunlop, James	1812	AD29	276	227
Carleton, Joseph	Division	Dunlap, James	1816	AL36	345	336
Carleton, Joseph & James Dunlop	Deed to	Brown, Robert	1809	X23	055	041
Carleton, Joseph et al	Cert fr	Commissioners of Washington	1797	B2B	459	149
Carleton, Joseph et al	Deed fr	Moyers, John	1801	G7	242	325
Carleton, Joseph et al	Deed fr	Commissioners of Washington	1802	H8	453	416
Carleton, Joseph et al	Deed fr	Munroe, Thomas et al	1802	I9	229	364
Carleton, Joseph et al	Deed fr	Tousard, Lewis	1802	H8	138	134
Carleton, Joseph, exr. of	Convey to	Brashears, John W.	1812	AD29	468	395
Carleton, Joseph, of G'tn.	Deed to	Wicoff, Isaac, of Phila. PA	1792	A1-1	114	167
Carleton, Joseph, of G'tn.	Deed to	Wicoff, Isaac, of Phila. PA	1792	A1-1	115	169
Carleton, Joseph, of G'tn.	Deed fr	Swearingan, Thomas, Sr.	1794	A1-2	497	100
Carleton, Joseph, of G'tn.	Deed fr	King, William, of G'tn.	1795	B2A	219	303
Carleton, Joseph, of G'tn.	Deed to	Nowland, John	1804	L11	205	194
Carleton, Joseph, of G'tn.	Deed to	Perkins, Jeremiah	1804	L11	275	253
Carleton, Joseph, of G'tn.	Deed to	Smith, William	1804	L11	207	196
Carleton, Joseph, of G'tn.	Lease to	Brooks, William et al	1804	L11	273	251

Party	What	Party	Year	Liber	Old	New
Carleton, Joseph, of G'tn.	Lease to	Crawley, Timothy et al	1804	L11	282	259
Carleton, Joseph, of G'tn.	Deed to	Hunter, Thomas	1805	M12	222	223
Carleton, Joseph, of G'tn.	Lease to	Biot, John	1805	O14	153	099
Carleton, Joseph, of G'tn.	Deed fr	Armstead, Robert et al	1805	M12	148	145
Carleton, Joseph, of G'tn.	Deed to	Lake, George	1805	M12	219	221
Carleton, Joseph, of G'tn.	Lease to	Summers, Thomas	1806	P15	072	044
Carleton, Joseph, of G'tn.	Deed to	Picknall, Richard Henry	1807	Q16	345	264
Carleton, Joseph, of G'tn.	B. of S. to	Bell, John Briggs	1807	S18	208	166
Carleton, Joseph, of G'tn.	Deed to	Lake, George	1808	U20	238	128
Carleton, Joseph, of G'tn. et al	Deed to	Wright, Matthew	1809	W22	301	208
Carleton, Joseph, of G'tn.	Deed to	Stanton, Patrick	1809	W22	169	119
Carleton, Joseph, of G'tn.	Deed to	Crowley, Timothy	1809	V21	386	290
Carleton, Joseph, of G'tn.	Lease to	Crowley, John	1809	V21	384	288
Carleton, Joseph, of G'tn.	Release fr	Summers, Thomas	1813	AE30	158	124
Carlin, Wesley, insolvent	Deed to	Fox, Bartleson, trustee	1815	AI34	001	001
Carlisle, Henry, of G'tn.	Deed to	Carlton, Joseph, of G'tn.	1793	A1-2	399	7
Carlon, James	Deed fr	Stoddert, Benjamin et al	1804	K10	344	355
Carlon, James	Mortgage to	Stoddert, Benjamin et al	1804	K10	370	384
Carlon, James	Deed to	Carlon, John	1804	K10	345	357
Carlon, John	Deed fr	Carlon, James	1804	K10	345	357
Carlton, Joseph & James Dunlap	Deed fr	Hanson, Samuel, of Samuel	1807	R17	136	106
Carlton, Joseph et al	Oblig. fr	Morris, Robert et al	1802	H8	100	091
Carlton, Joseph et al	Lease fr	Parsons, Bernard	1806	O14	370	246
Carlton, Joseph et al	Deed fr	Hanson, Samuel, of Samuel	1807	R17	128	101
Carlton, Joseph, of G'tn.	Deed fr	Jones, Benjamin White, sheriff	1792	A1-1	051	76
Carlton, Joseph, of G'tn.	Deed fr	Carlisle, Henry, of G'tn.	1793	A1-2	399	7
Carmical, Alexander et al, of G'tn.	Deed to	Wehrly, David, of G'tn.	1811	AB27	252	205
Carmical, Alexander, of G'tn.	Deed fr	Wehrly, David, of G'tn. [Wherly]	1811	AB27	058	050
Carmical, Alexander, of G'tn.	Deed fr	Healy, Joseph & Nancy, of Balto.	1811	AB27	059	051
Carmichael, Alexander et al	Deed fr	Polock, Isaac	1798	D4	003	002
Carmichael, Alexander, of G'tn.	Deed fr	Reintzel, Anthony, of G'tn.	1802	G7	487	624
Carmichael, Alexander, of G'tn.	Deed to	Smith, Edward Lowe, of G'tn.	1807	R17	261	199
Carmichael, Alexander, of G'tn.	Deed to	Cavanagh, Peter, of Balto.	1816	AL36	154	154
Carmichaell, Alexander, of G'tn.	Deed fr	Reintzel, Anthony, of G'tn.	1807	R17	202	153
Carmick, Daniel, Capt., of PA	Deed fr	Stoddert, Benjamin, of G'tn.	1801	G7	333	463
Carpenter, Thoams, Jr., trustee	Deed fr	Carpenter, Thomas, Sr., insolvent	1811	AA26	267	181
Carpenter, Thomas	Mortgage to	Cox, John, merchant	1801	G7	306	427
Carpenter, Thomas	Deed fr	Deakins, Francis, of G'tn.	1802	H8	270	256
Carpenter, Thomas	Deed fr	Forrest, Uriah	1802	H8	119	115
Carpenter, Thomas	Release fr	Cox, John	1802	I9	059	081
Carpenter, Thomas	Deed fr	Willson, Richard	1802	I9	232	370
Carpenter, Thomas	Mortgage to	Fricke, Augustus	1802	I9	487	801
Carpenter, Thomas	Plat	Square west of 492	1802	I9		082
Carpenter, Thomas	Plat	Square 463	1802	I9		082
Carpenter, Thomas	Lease fr	Blodget, Samuel	1804	L11	082	83
Carpenter, Thomas	B. of S. to	Reily, Sarah, of Phila. PA	1805	N13	138	131
Carpenter, Thomas	Mortgage to	Huddlestone, Joseph	1806	O14	165	107
Carpenter, Thomas, Jr., insolvent	Deed to	Varden, Ezra	1812	AC28	396	288
Carpenter, Thomas, Sr., insolvent	Deed to	Carpenter, Thomas, Jr., trustee	1811	AA26	267	181
Carpenter, Thomas, taylor	Deed to	Fricke, Augustus, mer., of Phila.	1804	L11	222	207
Carpenter, Thomas, trustee	Deed fr	Deterly, John, insolvent	1805	N13	124	119
Carpenter, Thomas, trustee	Deed fr	Densley, Hugh, insolvent	1805	N13	306	248
Carpenter, Thomas, trustee	Deed to	Clark, Francis	1811	AB27	401	331
Carr, Overton	Deed to	Walker, George	1798	D4	090	076
Carr, Overton	Deed fr	Walker, George	1798	D4	091	077

Index to District of Columbia Land Records, 1792-1817   73

Party	What	Party	Year	Liber	Old	New
Carr, Overton	Assign Mort.	Lyles, William	1799	E5	154	
Carr, Overton	Deed fr	Beatty, Thomas Johnson, of G'tn.	1799	D4	390	371
Carr, Overton	Deed to	Sprigg, William O., of G'tn.	1801	G7	204	272
Carr, Overton	Deed to	Walker, George	1801	F6	173	109
Carr, Overton	Deed to	Bryden, James, of Balto.	1802	G7	566	715
Carr, Overton	Deed fr	Walker, George	1802	H8	439	404
Carr, Overton	Release to	Walker, George	1802	G7	559	708
Carr, Overton	Cert free to	Lewis, Nelly (M), age 22	1812	AD29	302	248
Carr, Overton	Deed to	Baker, Nancy	1812	AC28	320	233
Carr, Overton	Cert Free to	Rollins, Bob (C), age 35	1813	AF31	240	166
Carr, Overton	Manumis to	[ ], Letty (C), & dau. Patsey	1813	AF31	158	106
Carr, Overton	Deed fr	Glover, Charles & Jas. Davidson	1815	AI34	347	378
Carr, Overton	Deed to	Henley, Robert, U.S.N.	1815	AI34	398	422
Carr, Overton	Mortgage fr	Cooper, George	1816	AM37	454	327
Carr, Overton	Deed to	Lenox, Peter	1817	AN38	263	192
Carr, Overton	Deed to	Jones, Walter	1817	AN38	303	222
Carr, Overton	Deed to	Jones, Walter	1817	AN38	310	227
Carr, Overton	Deed to	Law, John	1817	AN38	354	260
Carr, Overton	Deed to	Cheshire, Archibald	1817	AO39	160	120
Carr, Overton	D. of T. fr	Bayly, Mountjoy	1817	AO39	255	184
Carr, Overton et al	Mortgage fr	Densley, Hugh et al	1804	K10	144	156
Carr, Overton, exrs. of	Manumis to	[ ], Bobadil (C)	1812	AD29	131	101
Carr, Overton, of P.G. Co.	Deed fr	Walker, George, of Phila.	1797	C3	171	144
Carr, Overton, trustee	Deed to	Way, Andrew, Jr.	1817	AN38	321	235
Carr, Overton, trustee	Deed to	Sprigg, Benjamin	1817	AN38	155	113
Carr, Overton, trustee	Deed to	Dougherty, Thomas	1817	AO39	542	373
Carr, Overton, trustee	Deed to	Eliot, Samuel, Jr.	1817	AO39	522	360
Carr, Overton, trustee	Deed to	Arnot, John	1817	AO39	218	158
Carr, Overton, trustee	Deed to	Eliot, Samuel, Jr. [Elliott]	1817	AO39	533	367
Carr, Samuel, Albemarle Co. VA	Manumis to	[ ], Malinda (negro)	1809	V21	301	219
Carrere, John	Assign to	Neale, Leonard, Rev.	1808	T19	328	239
Carrico, James & Mary	Deed fr	Holmead, John	1815	AK35	337	267
Carrol, Patrick	Marriage C.	Corcoran, Susanna	1810	X23	343	275
Carroll, Airy (mulatto)	Manumis fr	Speake, Josias M.	1810	Z25	133	104
Carroll, Charles et al	Deed fr	Patterson, Edgar, of G'tn.	1811	AC28	093	070
Carroll, Charles, of *Carrollton*	Deed to	Beall, Thomas & John M. Gantt	1793	A1-1	215	300
Carroll, Charles, of *Bellevue*	D. of T. to	Davidson, James	1813	AF31	018	013
Carroll, Charles, of *Bellevue*	Deed fr	Nourse, Joseph	1813	AF31	013	010
Carroll, Charles, of Belle Vue NY	Deed fr	Davidson, James	1816	AL36	337	329
Carroll, Charles, trustees of	Deed to	Davidson, Samuel	1793	A1-1	356	463
Carroll, Charles, trustees of	Deed to	Carroll, Henry Hill, of Balto. Co.	1793	A1-1	353	459
Carroll, Charles, trustees of	Deed to	Hall, Benjamin, of Q.A. Co.	1795	B2B	366	017
Carroll, Daniel	Com. to	Gantt, John M.	1792	A1-1	001	1
Carroll, Daniel	Deed to	Fenwick, George, of G'tn.	1802	H8	555	517
Carroll, Daniel	Lease to	Minchin, John	1802	I9	166	253
Carroll, Daniel	Deed to	Crown, William	1802	I9	565	916
Carroll, Daniel	Deed to	Law, Thomas & Edmund Law	1811	AA26	153	106
Carroll, Daniel & Thomas Johnson	Deed to	Beall, Thomas & John M. Gantt	1792	A1-1	044	66
Carroll, Daniel & Henry Hill	Deed fr	Commissioners of Washington	1801	G7	067	087
Carroll, Daniel & Ann, *Duddington*	Deed to	Caldwell, Elias B.	1809	V21	392	296
Carroll, Daniel Carrool	Division	Law, Thomas	1807	S18	011	009
Carroll, Daniel et al	Deed to	Davidson, Samuel	1793	A1-1	356	463
Carroll, Daniel et al	Deed to	Hill, Henry, Jr.	1793	A1-1	360	466
Carroll, Daniel et al	Deed to	Carroll, Henry Hill, of Balto. Co.	1793	A1-1	353	459
Carroll, Daniel et al	Deed to	Greenleaf, James	1794	B2A	044	052

Party	What	Party	Year	Liber	Old	New
Carroll, Daniel et al	Deed fr	Greenleaf, James	1794	B2A	137	181
Carroll, Daniel et al	Agreement	Greenleaf, James	1794	B2A	070	090
Carroll, Daniel et al	Cert to	Young, Notley	1794	B2A	109	145
Carroll, Daniel et al	Cert to	Greenleaf, James	1794	B2A	108	143
Carroll, Daniel et al	P. of Atty. to	Greenleaf, James, New York NY	1794	B2A	110	146
Carroll, Daniel et al	Cert to	Greenleaf, James, for 500 lots	1794	B2A	047	056
Carroll, Daniel et al	Assign to	United States for Seat of Gov.[1]	1794	B2A	121	162
Carroll, Daniel, of *Duddington*	Deed to	Beall, Thomas & John M. Gantt	1792	A1-1	012	19
Carroll, Daniel, of *Duddington*	Cert fr	Commissioners of Washington	1793	B2A	308	433
Carroll, Daniel, of *Duddington*	Cert fr	Commissioners of Washington	1793	B2A	310	436
Carroll, Daniel, of *Duddington*	Cert fr	Commissioners of Washington	1793	B2A	309	434
Carroll, Daniel, of *Duddington*	Cert fr	Commissioners of Washington	1793	B2A	310	435
Carroll, Daniel, of *Duddington*	Cert fr	Commissioners of Washington	1793	B2A	310	434
Carroll, Daniel, of *Duddington*	Cert fr	Commissioners of Washington	1793	B2A	311	437
Carroll, Daniel, of *Duddington*	Deed to	Dermot, James Reed	1795	B2A	249	347
Carroll, Daniel, of *Duddington*	Deed fr	Magruder, John Read, P.G. Co.	1795	B2B	372	024
Carroll, Daniel, of *Duddington*	Deed to	Barry, James, of Balto.	1796	B2B	490	183
Carroll, Daniel, of *Duddington*	Exchange	Collard, George	1796	B2B	513	219
Carroll, Daniel, of *Duddington*	Cert fr	Commissioners of Washington	1797	B2B	461	151
Carroll, Daniel, of *Duddington* et al	Mortgage fr	Piercy, James	1797	B2B	690	468
Carroll, Daniel, of *Duddington*	Deed to	Barry, James, of Balto.	1797	C3	096	79
Carroll, Daniel, of *Duddington*	Deed fr	Law, Thomas	1797	C3	256	210
Carroll, Daniel, of *Duddington*	Deed to	Barry, James, of Balto.	1797	C3	229	191
Carroll, Daniel, of *Duddington*	Deed fr	Dermott, James R.	1797	C3	254	208
Carroll, Daniel, of *Duddington*	Deed to	Deblois, Lewis	1798	C3	316	255
Carroll, Daniel, of *Duddington*	Deed to	Washington, George, Gen.	1798	D4	121	104
Carroll, Daniel, of *Duddington*	Deed to	Sewall, Robert	1799	D4	359	346
Carroll, Daniel, of *Duddington*	Deed to	Dermott, James R.	1800	E5	191	182
Carroll, Daniel, of *Duddington*	Deed to	Langley, Edward	1800	E5	210	204
Carroll, Daniel, of *Duddington*	Deed to	Bushell, William, of Phila.	1800	E5	208	202
Carroll, Daniel, of *Duddington*	Deed fr	Commissioners of Washington	1800	E5	124	112
Carroll, Daniel, of *Duddington*	Deed to	Dalton, Katharine	1801	G7	430	565
Carroll, Daniel, of *Duddington*	Deed to	Carroll, John, Rev., of Balto.	1801	G7		462
Carroll, Daniel, of *Duddington*	Deed to	Brown, Stewart, mer., of Balto.	1801	F6	229	150
Carroll, Daniel, of *Duddington*	Deed to	Blagdin, George	1801	G7	072	093
Carroll, Daniel, of *Duddington*	Deed to	Law, Thomas	1801	G7	087	112
Carroll, Daniel, of *Duddington*	Deed to	Barry, James	1801	G7	233	311
Carroll, Daniel, of *Duddington*	Deed fr	Commissioners of Washington	1801	G7	053	068
Carroll, Daniel, of *Duddington*	Deed fr	Commissioners of Washington	1801	G7	051	066
Carroll, Daniel, of *Duddington*	Deed to	Jones, Thomas	1802	G7	573	722
Carroll, Daniel, of *Duddington*	Deed to	Ingle, Henry	1802	H8	396	366
Carroll, Daniel, of *Duddington*	Deed to	Lovell, William	1802	H8	568	531
Carroll, Daniel, of *Duddington*	Deed fr	Commissioners of Washington	1802	H8	331	310
Carroll, Daniel, of *Duddington*	Deed to	McCarthy, John	1802	H8	567	529
Carroll, Daniel, of *Duddington*	Deed to	McCarthy, John	1802	H8	563	526
Carroll, Daniel, of *Duddington*	Deed to	Fenwick, Mary	1802	H8	549	510
Carroll, Daniel, of *Duddington*	Deed fr	Hepburn, Daniel	1802	I9	048	065
Carroll, Daniel, of *Duddington*	Deed to	Bayly, Daniel	1804	K10	294	296
Carroll, Daniel, of *Duddington*	Deed fr	Munroe, Thomas, Supt.	1804	K10	335	346
Carroll, Daniel, of *Duddington*	D. of P.	Carroll, Sarah, w/o Henry H.	1805	M12	353	359
Carroll, Daniel, of *Duddington*	Deed to	Ingraham, Alexander	1805	M12	382	393
Carroll, Daniel, of *Duddington*	Deed to	Martin, James	1805	M12	380	391

[1]For lots in Carrollsburgh and Hamburgh.

Index to District of Columbia Land Records, 1792-1817

Party	What	Party	Year	Liber	Old	New
Carroll, Daniel, of *Duddington*	B. of S. fr	Burch, Benjamin	1805	M12	266	267
Carroll, Daniel, of *Duddington*	Deed to	Tippit, Cartwright	1806	P15	397	266
Carroll, Daniel, of *Duddington*	Deed to	Queen, Nicholas L.	1806	P15	377	252
Carroll, Daniel, of *Duddington*	Deed to	Brown, Robert	1806	P15	208	139
Carroll, Daniel, of *Duddington*	Deed to	Miller, Peter	1806	P15	167	111
Carroll, Daniel, of *Duddington*	B. of S. fr	King, Richard	1806	P15	114	072
Carroll, Daniel, of *Duddington*	Deed to	Emack, William	1807	R17	291	222
Carroll, Daniel, of *Duddington*	Deed to	McMahon, Robert	1807	R17	304	232
Carroll, Daniel, of *Duddington*	Deed fr	Law, Thomas	1807	R17	227	170
Carroll, Daniel, of *Duddington*	Deed to	Dixon, John C.	1807	R17	219	165
Carroll, Daniel, of *Duddington*	Deed to	Mayor & Council of Washington	1807	R17	228	228
Carroll, Daniel, of *Duddington*	Deed to	Blagden, George	1808	U20	194	107
Carroll, Daniel, of *Duddington*	Deed to	Varden, Joseph	1809	X23	029	020
Carroll, Daniel, of *Duddington*	Cert fr	Munroe, Thomas, Supt.	1809	V21	388	292
Carroll, Daniel, of *Duddington*	Deed to	Ingle, Henry	1809	W22	267	178
Carroll, Daniel, of *Duddington*	Deed to	Bank of Washington	1810	Y24	394	356
Carroll, Daniel, of *Duddington* et al	D. of T. fr	Hickey, James	1810	Y24	258	238
Carroll, Daniel, of *Duddington*	Deed fr	Brent, William	1810	Y24	400	361
Carroll, Daniel, of *Duddington*	Deed to	Brent, William	1810	Y24	402	362
Carroll, Daniel, of *Duddington*	Mortgage fr	Barry, James D.	1810	Y24	404	364
Carroll, Daniel, of *Duddington*	Deed to	Ringold, Tench et al	1810	Z25	083	063
Carroll, Daniel, of *Duddington*	Deed to	Coombe, Griffith	1811	AA26	251	171
Carroll, Daniel, of *Duddington*	Deed to	Docker, Gilbert	1811	AA26	254	172
Carroll, Daniel, of *Duddington*	Deed to	Coombe, Griffith et al	1811	AA26	249	169
Carroll, Daniel, of *Duddington*	Deed to	Blagden, George	1811	AA26	068	050
Carroll, Daniel, of *Duddington*	Deed to	Smallwood, Samuel N.	1811	AA26	058	044
Carroll, Daniel, of *Duddington*	Deed to	Minchin, John	1811	AA26	265	180
Carroll, Daniel, of *Duddington*	Deed to	Digges, William Dudley	1811	AB27	444	365
Carroll, Daniel, of *Duddington*	Deed fr	Munroe, Thomas, Supt.	1811	AC28	071	054
Carroll, Daniel, of *Duddington*	Deed fr	Law, Thomas & Edmund Law	1811	AC28	067	051
Carroll, Daniel, of *Duddington*	Deed fr	Smallwood, Samuel N.	1811	AC28	065	050
Carroll, Daniel, of *Duddington* et al	Deed fr	Patterson, Edgar, of G'tn.	1811	AC28	093	070
Carroll, Daniel, of *Duddington*	Deed to	Sanford, George	1812	AD29	211	173
Carroll, Daniel, of *Duddington* et ux	Deed to	Thruston, Buckner	1812	AD29	004	003
Carroll, Daniel, of *Duddington*	Cert. fr	Munroe, Thomas, Supt.	1812	AD29	010	007
Carroll, Daniel, of *Duddington*	Lease to	Pic, Francis	1812	AD29	163	129
Carroll, Daniel, of *Duddington*	Deed to	Miller, Peter	1813	AE30	282	216
Carroll, Daniel, of *Duddington*	Deed to	Thruston, Buckner	1813	AF31	435	313
Carroll, Daniel, of *Duddington*	Deed to	Emack, William	1814	AF31	519	380
Carroll, Daniel, of *Duddington*	Deed to	Stevens, Samuel	1814	AG32	378	275
Carroll, Daniel, of *Duddington*	Deed to	Cook, Stephen	1815	AI34	384	410
Carroll, Daniel, of *Duddington*	Deed to	Mattingly, Edward	1815	AI34	182	209
Carroll, Daniel, of *Duddington*	Deed fr	Nicholls, Henry, of Balto.	1815	AK35	413	324
Carroll, Daniel, of *Duddington*	Deed to	Smallwood, Samuel N.	1815	AI34	513	518
Carroll, Daniel, of *Duddington*	Deed fr	Walker, Zachariah, trustee	1816	AL36	028	029
Carroll, Daniel, of *Duddington*	Cert fr	Munroe, Thomas, Supt.	1816	AL36	303	299
Carroll, Daniel, of *Duddington*	Deed to	Coombe, Griffith	1816	AL36	272	272
Carroll, Daniel, of *Duddington* et al	Deed to	Smallwood, Samuel N.	1816	AL36	161	161
Carroll, Daniel, of *Duddington*	Deed fr	Munroe, Thomas, Supt.	1816	AM37	417	299
Carroll, Daniel, of *Duddington*	Lease to	McNeal, James	1816	AM37	181	136
Carroll, Daniel, of *Duddington*	Lease to	McCaffrey, William	1816	AO39	024	019
Carroll, Daniel, of *Duddington*	Deed to	Downs, Hillidey	1817	AO39	202	148
Carroll, Daniel, of *Duddington*	Deed to	Cross, Elie	1817	AO39	365	246
Carroll, Daniel, of *Duddington*	Deed to	Dickson, John C.	1817	AO39	375	253
Carroll, Daniel, of *Duddington*	Deed to	Smallwood, Samuel N.	1817	AO39	326	232

Index to District of Columbia Land Records, 1792-1817

Party	What	Party	Year	Liber	Old	New
Carroll, Daniel, of *Duddington*	Deed to	Munroe, Thomas	1817	AN38	384	285
Carroll, Daniel, P.G. Co. et al	Deed to	Hall, Benjamin, of Q.A. Co.	1795	B2B	366	017
Carroll, Daniel, trustee of	Deed to	Wilson, Zadock	1817	AO39	488	
Carroll, Elizabeth	Deed fr	Young, Notley & Mary Carroll	1799	D4	317	301
Carroll, Elizabeth	Deed to	Brent, Daniel, of Stafford Co. VA	1799	D4	318	302
Carroll, Elizabeth	Deed to	Brent, Robert	1799	D4	317	301
Carroll, Elizabeth	Manumis to	[ ], Nan (negro)	1808	V21	112	083
Carroll, Elizabeth	Manumis to	Landrick, William (negro)	1810	Y24	334	302
Carroll, Elizabeth, of Montg. Co.	Deed to	Brent, Robert, Sr.	1817	AN38	428	321
Carroll, Henry	Cert fr	Commissioners of Washington	1795	B2A	333	467
Carroll, Henry H., of Balto. Co.	Deed fr	Commissioners of Washington	1801	G7	049	062
Carroll, Henry Hill, of Balto. Co.	Deed fr	Carroll, Daniel et al	1793	A1-1	353	459
Carroll, Henry Hill & Daniel	Deed fr	Commissioners of Washington	1801	G7	067	087
Carroll, James	B. of S. fr	Green, James	1806	O14	213	141
Carroll, John, Dr., Rev. et al	Deed to	Wilson, Zadock	1817	AO39	483	332
Carroll, John, Most Rev. et al	Deed fr	Neale, Leonard, Rev.	1814	AG32	029	023
Carroll, John, of Balto. et al	Deed fr	Threlkeld, John, of Montg. Co.	1796	B2B	500	197
Carroll, John, Rev. et al	Deed to	Walton, James, Rev. et al	1799	D4	286	268
Carroll, John, Rev. et al	Deed to	Walton, James, Rev. et al	1799	D4	283	265
Carroll, John, Rev., of Balto.	Deed fr	Carroll, Daniel, of *Duddington*	1801	G7		462
Carroll, John, Rev.	Deed to	Simms, Patrick, Jr.	1802	I9	417	691
Carroll, John, Rev. et al	Deed fr	Neale, Francis I., Rev., of G'tn.	1814	AG32	025	020
Carroll, John, Rt. Rev.	Deed fr	Caffray, Anthony, Rev.	1804	L11	182	176
Carroll, John, Rt. Rev.	Deed fr	Casanave, Ann	1808	T19	319	233
Carroll, Margaret, of Balto. et al	Deed to	Barry, James	1802	H8	599	566
Carroll, Mary et al	Deed fr	Purcell, Pierce	1809	X23	160	118
Carroll, Patrick & Susanna, G'tn.	Deed to	Lee, John, of G'tn.	1813	AF31	428	308
Carroll, Patrick & Susanna	Deed to	Fenwick, Francis	1814	AH33	345	299
Carroll, Patrick, of G'tn.	Deed fr	Deakins, Leonard M. et al	1807	R17	258	196
Carroll, Patrick, of G'tn.	Deed to	Lee, John, of G'tn.	1813	AF31	426	306
Carroll, Patrick, taylor, of G'tn.	Deed fr	Threlkeld, John, of G'tn.	1798	C3	463	364
Carroll, Richard	Deed to	Mackall, Leonard	1815	AI34	404	427
Carroll, Sarah, w/o Henry H.	D. of P.	Carroll, Daniel, of *Duddington*	1805	M12	353	359
Carroll, William B.	Deed to	Digges, William Dudley	1815	AH33	444	381
Carroll, William Brent, s/o Daniel	Deed fr	Digges, William Dudley, P.G. Co.	1815	AH33	443	380
Carrollsburgh	Deed	Erecting a Town called	1793	A1-1	353	459
Carrollsburgh	Deed	Erecting a Town called	1793	A1-1	360	466
Carrollsburgh	Deed	Erecting a Town called	1793	A1-1	356	463
Carruthers, John & David, Balto.	Deed fr	Hosack, John, of G'tn.	1796	B2B	567	305
Carson, George, of Alexa.	Deed fr	Smith, William	1816	AL36	439	417
Carson, Thomas	B. of S. fr	Johnston, James	1812	AD29	508	429
Carter, Charles, of *Shirley*	Deed fr	Commissioners of Washington	1800	E5	083	070
Carter, Frances Ann	Marriage	Law, John	1815	AK35	260	207
Carter, Jacob, of G'tn.	Deed fr	Gary, Everard, of G'tn.	1812	AC28	478	339
Carter, James B., of G'tn. et al	B. of S. to	Crawford, William & John Hoye	1812	AD29	161	127
Carter, James B.	Slaves	From Virginia	1814	AG32	045	035
Carter, John	Deed fr	Johnston, Tunis, of VA	1802	H8	127	123
Carter, John M., of G'tn. et al	B. of S. to	Crawford, William & John Hoye	1812	AD29	161	127
Carter, John M., of G'tn.	Deed fr	Lee, Thomas S., of Fredk. Co.	1815	AI34	064	072
Carter, Stacy	Cert Free fr	Parrott, Richard	1807	S18	066	055
Cartwright, Elizabeth	B. of S. to	Feales, William	1802	H8	036	034
Carver, Jonathan, d. 1/21/1780	Death		1817	AN38		337
Casanave, Ann	Lease to	McCue, Owen	1808	V21	032	024
Casanave, Ann	Deed to	Carroll, John, Rt. Rev.	1808	T19	319	233
Casanave, Ann	Manumis to	Shorter, Nancy (negro)	1808	U20	393	219

Index to District of Columbia Land Records, 1792-1817

Party	What	Party	Year	Liber	Old	New
Casanave, Ann	Deed to	Cheshire, Archibald	1814	AG32	035	027
Casanave, Ann	Deed to	Wightt, John M.	1815	AI34	015	016
Casanave, Ann	Deed to	Brent, Robert et al	1817	AO39	079	064
Casanave, Peter	Deed fr	Smith, Ignatius	1794	B2A	092	120
Casanave, Peter	Deed to	Dorsey, William Hammond	1794	B2A	072	093
Casanave, Peter	Deed fr	White, James, Sr.	1795	B2A	230	323
Casanave, Peter	Deed fr	Beatty, Charles et al	1795	B2A	238	331
Casanave, Peter	Cert fr	Commissioners of Washington	1796	B2A	335	472
Casanave, Peter et al	Deed to	Beatty, Charles, Sr., of G'tn.	1795	B2A	242	336
Casanave, Peter et al	Deed fr	Warring, Marsham	1795	B2A	253	353
Casanave, Peter et al	Deed fr	Dorsey, William H.	1795	B2A	235	327
Casanave, Peter, mer., of G'tn.	Deed fr	Chase, Samuel, of Balto.	1794	B2A	091	118
Casanave, Peter, of G'tn.	Cert fr	Commissioners of Washington	1792	B2A	283	395
Casanave, Peter, of G'tn.	Deed to	King, William, of G'tn.	1794	B2A	062	079
Casanave, Peter, of Montg. Co.	Deed fr	Wootton, Turner, P.G. Co., planter	1795	B2B	367	018
Casanave, Peter, of Montg. Co.	Deed fr	Beall, Thomas, of George	1796	B2B	511	216
Casanave, Peter, of Montg. Co.	Deed to	Forrest, Uriah, of Montg. Co.	1796	B2B	530	246
Casanave, Peter, of G'tn.	Deed fr	Stoddert, Benjamin, of G'tn.	1796	B2B	519	228
Casanave, Peter, of Montg. Co.	Deed fr	Beall, Thomas, of George	1796	B2B	510	214
Casanave, Peter, of G'tn.	Deed to	Dorsey, William H., of G'tn.	1796	B2B	527	240
Casanave, Peter, of Montg. Co.	Deed fr	Beall, Thomas, of George	1796	B2B	509	213
Casanave, Peter, trustee for	Deed to	Thornbrough, Joseph, of PA	1804	K10	355	367
Casey, Casey	Slave	From VA	1808	U20	175	098
Casey, John	Deed to	Beall, Thomas & John M. Gantt	1793	A1-2	406	15
Casey, John, of GA	Deed to	Washington, Thomas Lund, P.G.	1805	M12	403	417
Cassiday, Nicholas	Deed fr	Brown, Robert	1814	AG32	287	208
Cassidy, Nicholas	Deed fr	Brown, Robert	1813	AF31	508	371
Cassin, James	Deed fr	Costigan, Joseph	1808	U20	060	034
Cassin, James	Assign to	Wharton, Franklin	1809	X23	149	108
Cassin, James	Qualify	Captain of 1st brigade of militia	1813	AE30	394	290
Cassin, James & Tabitha et al	Deed to	Holmead, John	1814	AH33	286	249
Cassin, James, of G'tn.	Deed fr	Armitage, Benjamin, attorney	1815	AI34	305	339
Cassin, James, of G'tn.	D. of T. to	Deakins, Leonard M., of P.G. Co.	1815	AI34	339	372
Cassin, James, of G'tn.	D. of T. to	Magruder, George	1816	AK35	494	389
Cassin, James, of G'tn.	D. of T. to	Harrison, Gustavus, of G'tn.	1816	AK35	496	390
Cassin, Joseph	Lease fr	Cannon, John	1806	P15	078	047
Cassin, Joseph	B. of S. fr	Mullany, Michael	1808	T19	311	227
Cassin, Joseph	Deed fr	McClain, Thomas	1808	U20	161	091
Cassin, Joseph	Lease fr	Prout, William	1809	V21	219	156
Cassin, Joseph	B. of S. to	Prout, William	1809	V21	223	158
Cassin, Joseph	Deed fr	Prout, William	1809	V21	225	160
Cassin, Joseph	Deed fr	McCormick, Alexander	1809	W22	130	093
Cassin, Joseph	Certificate	Captain in 1st Legion of Militia	1809	X23	007	004
Cassin, Joseph	Cert. Free to	Hews, William & Milly	1812	AC28	166	124
Cassin, Joseph	D. of T. to	McCormick, Alexander	1813	AE30	253	198
Cassin, Joseph	P. of Atty. fr	Slater, Henry, of TN et al	1817	AN38	200	146
Cassin, Joseph	Slave Births	Liverpool, Moses, b. 25 JAN 1801	1817	AN38	502	363
Cassin, Joseph & B.H. Latrobe	Mortgage fr	Alexander, Robert, New Orleans	1809	X23	270	212
Cassin, Joseph & J. Davis, of Abel	B. of S. fr	King, Benjamin	1813	AE30	276	212
Cassin, Tabitha Marbury, w/o Jas.	Deed fr	Deakins, Leonard M., of P.G. Co.	1814	AH33	256	223
Casteel, Edmond [Cassseel]	B. of S. fr	Leach, Asel, of Charles Co.	1817	AN38	180	131
Casteel, Edmund	Deed fr	Wigfield, Robert & Mary	1810	Z25	214	168
Casteel, Edmund	Assign fr	Ensey, William	1816	AO39	045	037
Casteel, Edmund	Deed fr	Bryan, James D.	1816	AO39	046	038
Casteel, Edmund & Mary	Deed to	Hilton, Samuel	1812	AD29	006	004

Index to District of Columbia Land Records, 1792-1817

Party	What	Party	Year	Liber	Old	New
Casteele, Edmund & Mary	Deed to	Griswold, Chester, Otsego Co. NY	1810	Z25	043	032
Catalano, Salvadora	Deed fr	Prout, William	1809	X23	086	064
Catalano, Salvadora	Deed fr	Sardo, Michael	1812	AC28	303	221
Catalano, Salvadora, U.S.N.	Deed fr	Bunyie, William	1809	X23	060	045
Catalano, Salvadora, U.S.N.	Deed fr	Bunyie, William	1809	X23	064	
Catolina, Salvadora	Deed to	Sardo, Michael	1812	AB27	226	183
Caton, James, of Balto.	Deed fr	Ray, James	1799	D4	313	296
Caton, John	Deed fr	Dorsey, William H., of G'tn.	1807	R17	212	159
Caton, John	Deed fr	May, Frederick	1809	X23	169	125
Caton, John, of Balto.	B. of S. to	Fennell, Edward	1809	W22	392	255
Caton, William, late of Alexa.	D. of T. to	Law, Edmund	1809	X23	272	215
Caton, William, of Alexa.	Deed to	Gadsby, John, of Balto.	1810	X23	332	265
Caucand, David, of Calvert Co.	Deed fr	Stoddert, Benjamin	1801	G7	241	323
Causin, Gerard	B. of S. to	Clarke, Robert, of G'tn.	1810	Y24	307	279
Causin, Gerrard N., St. Mary's Co.	Deed to	Felius, Jacob	1814	AG32	206	144
Cavanagh, Peter, of Balto.	Deed fr	Carmichael, Alexander, of G'tn.	1816	AL36	154	154
Cazenave, Ann et al	Deed fr	Young, Benjamin et al	1802	I9	022	029
Cecil, Mary & Ann Aud [Cissell]	Deed to	Vanhorn, Archibald, of P.G. Co.	1816	AL36	262	263
Cessford, John [Sessford]	Lease fr	Roe, C. McD.	1802	I9	223	353
Chalmers, John, Jr.	Lease fr	Prout, William	1817	AN38	399	297
Chalmers, John, Jr.	D. of T. to	Eliot, Samuel, Jr.	1817	AN38	400	299
Chalmers, John, Sr. & Jr.	Mortgage to	Weems, William	1812	AC28	449	321
Chambers, Maxwell	Certificate	Justice of Peace, Rowan Co. NC	1809	V21	318	233
Chambers, Sarah, by F. Foushee	Slaves	From VA	1806	O14	163	106
Chambers, Sarah, by F. Foushee	Slaves	From VA	1806	P15	196	131
Champlin, John T. et al	Deed fr	Polock, Isaac	1802	H8	011	010
Champlin, Thomas, of Montg. Co.	Deed fr	Beatty, Thomas J., of G'tn.	1796	B2B	487	179
Chandler, Jacob	Deed fr	Tuckfield, William H.P.	1802	I9	183	280
Chandler, Jacob	Deed fr	Munroe, Thomas, Supt.	1802	I9	131	196
Chandler, Jacob	Deed to	Ingram, Alexander	1802	I9	134	200
Chandler, Jacob	Deed to	Boice, John	1802	I9	133	199
Chandler, Jacob	Deed to	Baily, Daniel	1805	M12	288	289
Chandler, Jacob	Deed to	Davis, Ahasuerus et al	1806	P15	018	011
Chandler, Jacob	Deed to	Spooner, William	1809	X23	084	062
Chandler, Jacob	Deed to	Liverpoole, Moses & George Beall	1810	Y24	068	061
Chandler, Salter S.	Manumis to	[ ], Henny (negro)	1807	S18	091	074
Chandler, Walter	Deed fr	Loring, Israel	1802	I9	417	691
Chandler, Walter S.	Deed fr	Davidson, Samuel, of G'tn.	1796	B2B		070
Chandler, Walter S., of G'tn.	Deed fr	Reid, James, of G'tn.	1796	B2B	438	117
Chandler, Walter S., of G'tn.	Deed fr	Deakins, William Jr., of G'tn.	1797	C3	072	59
Chandler, Walter S.	Deed fr	Commissioners of Washington	1799	D4	224	207
Chandler, Walter S., of Balto.	Deed to	Commissioners of Washington	1800	E5	122	110
Chandler, Walter S., of G'tn.	Deed fr	Commissioners of Washington	1800	E5	121	109
Chandler, Walter S., of G'tn.	Deed fr	Commissioners of Washington	1800	E5	126	114
Chandler, Walter S.	Deed fr	Bank of Columbia	1802	G7	519	660
Chandler, Walter S., of G'tn.	Deed fr	Thornton, William	1802	G7	521	663
Chandler, Walter S.	Deed to	Cramphin, Thomas	1802	H8	170	164
Chandler, Walter S.	Manumis to	[ ], Nick (Negro)	1802	H8	074	068
Chandler, Walter S., of G'tn.	Deed fr	Weems, John, physician, of G'tn.	1802	H8	286	270
Chandler, Walter S.	Deed fr	Commissioners of Washington	1802	H8	298	282
Chandler, Walter S.	Deed fr	Commissioners of Washington	1802	H8	296	280
Chandler, Walter S.	Deed fr	Reintzel, Anthony	1802	I9	200	313
Chandler, Walter S.	Deed fr	Forrest, Uriah	1802	I9	444	733
Chandler, Walter S.	Qualify		1802	I9	464	764
Chandler, Walter S.	Deed fr	Templeman, John	1802	I9	418	707

Index to District of Columbia Land Records, 1792-1817

79

Party	What	Party	Year	Liber	Old	New
Chandler, Walter S., of G'tn.	Mortgage fr	Loring, Israel	1802	I9	049	066
Chandler, Walter S. et al	Deed fr	Beatty, Charles, of G'tn.	1803	K10	062	67
Chandler, Walter S. & P.B. Key	Deed fr	West, Stephen et al	1804	K10	112	120
Chandler, Walter S.	Deed fr	Voss, Nicholas	1804	L11	095	97
Chandler, Walter S., of G'tn.	Deed to	Owen, Isaac, of G'tn.	1805	M12	254	255
Chandler, Walter S.	Agreement	Davis, Thomas, ship carpenter	1806	Q16	013	008
Chandler, Walter S.	Deed fr	Stoddert, Benjamin	1807	Q16	392	301
Chandler, Walter S., of G'tn.	Deed to	Picknal, John	1807	Q16	343	263
Chandler, Walter S.	B. of S. fr	Beall, Basil B.	1807	R17	054	043
Chandler, Walter S.	Convey to	Bevan, Mathew L.	1807	S18	377	299
Chandler, Walter S., of G'tn.	Deed to	Pickerell, John	1808	T19	063	046
Chandler, Walter S.	Deed to	Rose, Robert	1809	X23	168	124
Chandler, Walter S.	Certificate	Justice of the Peace	1810	Y24	286	262
Chandler, Walter S.	Deed to	Williams, Elisha W., of G'tn.	1811	AB27	035	031
Chandler, Walter S.	Deed to	Burnett, Charles A., of G'tn.	1811	AB27	207	169
Chandler, Walter S.	Deed to	Morsell, James S.	1811	AB27	397	327
Chandler, Walter S.	Deed to	Wright, Matthew	1811	AB27	373	309
Chandler, Walter S.	Deed fr	Morsell, James S., trustee, of G'tn.	1812	AD29	075	055
Chandler, Walter S.	Deed fr	Mursell, James S., trustee, of G'tn.	1812	AD29	074	053
Chandler, Walter S. & Margaret	Deed to	Turner, Thomas, of G'tn.	1815	AK35	205	160
Chandler, Walter S.	Deed to	Ott, John	1816	AM37	130	101
Chandler, Walter Story	Deed fr	Wilkins, William, of Annapolis	1795	B2A	184	249
Chandler, Walter Story, of G'tn.	Deed fr	Ogle, Benjamin, Frederick Town	1795	B2A	185	251
Chandler, Walter Story	Deed to	Stewart, Walter, of Phila. PA	1795	B2A	197	269
Chandler, Walter Story et al	Deed fr	Peter, Robert	1795	B2A	199	273
Chandler, Walter Story, of G'tn.	Deed fr	Hite, Isaac, of Frederick Co. VA	1797	B2B	637	398
Chandler, Walter Story, of G'tn.	Deed to	Deakins, William Jr., of G'tn.	1797	C3	258	211
Chandler, Walter Story	Deed fr	Stone, John Hoskins, of Balto.	1800	E5	391	367
Chandler, Walter Story	Deed fr	Lear, Tobias, of Fairfax Co. VA	1800	E5	386	363
Chandler, Walter Story, of G'tn.	Deed to	Rogers, William	1801	G7	156	207
Chandler, Walter Story	Deed to	Doughty, William	1801	G7	414	548
Chandler, Walter Story	Deed fr	Orme, Thomas	1801	G7	107	137
Chandler, Walter Story, of G'tn.	Deed to	Weems, John, Dr., of G'tn.	1801	G7	261	358
Chandler, Walter Story	Deed fr	Hanson, Samuel, of Hanson et al	1802	I9	050	068
Chandler, Walter Story	Deed fr	Forrest, Uriah et al	1802	I9	050	068
Chandler, Walter Story	Deed fr	Forrest, Uriah	1802	G7	524	667
Chandler, Walter Story	P. of Atty. fr	Rogers, William	1802	H8	063	059
Chandler, Walter Story	Deed to	Van Ness, John P.	1803	K10	073	79
Chandler, Walter Story	Deed to	Travers, Nicholas	1804	K10	389	404
Chandler, Walter Story, of G'tn.	Deed to	Weems, John, of G'tn.	1804	L11	007	7
Chandler, Walter Story	Deed fr	Key, Philip Barton	1804	L11	096	99
Chandler, Walter Story, of G'tn.	Deed fr	Craik, William, of Fairfax Co. VA	1805	N13	064	058
Chandler, Walter Story, of G'tn.	Deed to	King, George & Adam	1805	N13	375	301
Chandler, Walter Story, of G'tn.	Deed to	Stoddert, Benjamin, of G'tn.	1805	M12	304	305
Chandler, Walter Story, of G'tn.	Deed to	Voss, Nicholas	1805	M12	057	054
Chandler, Walter Story, of G'tn.	Deed to	Plater, Thomas, of Montg. Co.	1806	P15	052	031
Chandler, Walter Story	Deed to	Farrell, Zepheniah	1806	P15	177	118
Chandler, Walter Story	Deed fr	Plater, Thomas, of Montg. Co.	1806	P15	278	183
Chandler, Walter Story	Deed fr	Cherry, Walter	1806	P15	286	188
Chandler, Walter Story	Deed to	Pravotte, Peter	1807	S18	314	246
Chandler, Walter Story, of G'tn.	Deed to	Harrison, Richard, of G'tn.	1807	Q16	399	307
Chandler, Walter Story, G'tn. et al	Deed to	Oden, Benjamin, of P.G. Co.	1807	R17	408	308
Chandler, Walter Story	Deed fr	Rogers, William, of New Orleans	1808	V21	027	020
Chandler, Walter Story	Deed to	Gannon, James	1808	V21	054	043
Chandler, Walter Story	Deed to	Cochrane, Alexander, Jr.	1808	T19	166	118

Index to District of Columbia Land Records, 1792-1817

Party	What	Party	Year	Liber	Old	New
Chandler, Walter Story	Deed to	McCauley, George	1808	U20	385	213
Chandler, Walter Story	Deed to	Gantt, Edward, ship carpenter	1809	V21	145	106
Chandler, Walter Story	Deed fr	Rogers, Thomas, of Balto.	1809	V21	261	186
Chandler, Walter Story	Deed to	Whalan, Nicholas	1809	W22	107	077
Chandler, Walter Story	Deed to	Stephenson, James S.	1809	X23	301	240
Chandler, Walter Story & Margaret	Deed to	Brookes, Joseph	1809	X23	259	203
Chandler, Walter Story	Deed to	Young, Thomas & Samuel	1809	X23	152	110
Chandler, Walter Story	Deed to	Brown, Robert	1809	X23	070	053
Chandler, Walter Story	Deed fr	Rogers, Daniel, of Balto. Co.	1810	Y24	071	063
Chandler, Walter Story	Deed fr	Key, Philip Barton, of Montg. Co.	1810	Y24	227	209
Chandler, Walter Story	Deed to	deKrafft, Charles	1810	Y24	196	180
Chandler, Walter Story	Deed to	Harrison, Richard	1810	Y24	440	392
Chandler, Walter Story & Margaret	Deed to	Pickrell, John	1810	Y24	011	010
Chandler, Walter Story	Deed to	Key, Philip B., of Montg. Co.	1810	Y24	385	348
Chandler, Walter Story	Deed fr	Plater, John Rousby & Elizabeth	1810	Y24	231	213
Chandler, Walter Story	Deed to	Gannon, James	1810	Y24	070	062
Chandler, Walter Story	Deed fr	Plater, John Rousby, St. Mary's	1810	Y24	229	211
Chandler, Walter Story	Deed to	Davis, Thomas	1811	Z25	533	423
Chandler, Walter Story	Deed to	Weems, John et al	1812	AD29	500	422
Chandler, Walter Story	Deed to	Wilson, Joseph	1812	AE30	047	036
Chandler, Walter Story	Deed to	Cheshire, Archibald	1812	AD29	548	461
Chandler, Walter Story	Deed to	Minitree, John	1813	AE30	193	154
Chandler, Walter Story	Deed to	Bevan, Matthew L., of Phila. PA	1813	AE30	520	385
Chandler, Walter Story	Deed to	McCauley, George	1813	AE30	503	373
Chandler, Walter Story	Deed to	Tuckfield, William H.P.	1813	AF31	545	404
Chandler, Walter Story	Deed to	Brown, Richard et al	1813	AE30	190	152
Chandler, Walter Story	Deed to	Beatty, Charles A.	1816	AL36	137	138
Chandler, Walter Story	Deed to	Rush, Richard, of PA	1816	AM37	377	272
Chandler, Walter Story	Deed to	Ott, John	1816	AM37	133	104
Chandler, Walter Story	Deed to	Brown, Robert	1816	AM37	279	204
Chaney, Samuel	B. of S. to	Harrington, Absolem	1808	T19	369	264
Chapline, Joseph	Deed fr	Chapline, William Williams	1798	D4	125	107
Chapline, Joseph	Deed to	Wingard, Abraham, of G'tn.	1812	AD29	218	179
Chapline, William Williams	Deed to	Chapline, Joseph	1798	D4	125	107
Chapman, Henry H. et al	Deed to	Snowden, Thomas	1802	I9	381	632
Chapman, Henry H., Charles Co.	Mortgage fr	Davidson, Samuel, Jr., of Balto.	1805	N13	329	265
Chapman, Henry H., Charles Co.	Release to	Davidson, Samuel	1816	AL36	071	073
Chapman, Henry H., Annapolis	Deed to	Cutts, Richard	1817	AO39	238	172
Chapman, Mary, w/o Henry H.	Deed fr	Davidson, Samuel	1810	Y24	342	310
Chapman, William, of G'tn.	Sale to	Payne, Nathan, of Fayette Co. KY	1805	M12	295	
Chapman, Winifred	Deed fr	Peck, Joseph	1808	U20	181	100
Chappel, John	Deed fr	Beatty, John M. et al	1805	M12	369	379
Charles, Richard	Deed fr	Ingram, Alexander & Mary	1805	O14	025	016
Charles, Richard	Deed fr	Prout, William	1808	T19	199	142
Charles, Richard	D. of T. to	Blagden, George	1811	AA26	242	165
Charles, Richard	Deed fr	Prout, William	1817	AN38	149	109
Charles, Richard	Deed to	Stamp, Francis	1817	AN38	150	110
Charleton, Armstrong	Deed fr	Dillon, Robert	1806	P15	400	269
Charlton, Ralph	Deed to	Peter, David et al	1804	L11	378	338
Charlton, Ralph	Deed fr	Peter, David, trustee	1804	L11	347	315
Charlton, Ralph	Deed to	Wright, Matthew	1804	L11	355	321
Charlton, Ralph	Partition	Armstrong, Andrew	1804	K10	177	186
Charlton, Ralph	Release fr	Wright, Mathew	1806	P15	079	048
Charlton, Ralph	Deed fr	Corporation of Washington	1815	AK35	440	345
Charlton, Ralph et al	Deed fr	Stoddert, Benjamin	1802	I9	523	856

Index to District of Columbia Land Records, 1792-1817

Party	What	Party	Year	Liber	Old	New
Chase, Samuel	Naturalize	Smith, Andrew	1795	B2A	281	394
Chase, Samuel, of Balto.	Deed to	Casanave, Peter, mer., of G'tn.	1794	B2A	091	118
Chatelin, Anne, late Pic, of G'tn.	Deed to	Holmead, John	1815	AI34	280	316
Cheeseman, Eleanor	Cert Free fr	Parrott, Richard	1807	S18	066	055
Cheney, Jesse	B. of S. fr	Mincher, William	1805	M12	292	293
Cherry, Robert	B. of S. fr	Brashears, Nathaniel	1802	I9	015	020
Cherry, Robert	Deed fr	Simm, Patrick, Jr.	1802	I9	438	725
Cherry, Robert	Mortgage to	Bevan, Mathew L., of Phila. PA	1806	O14	332	221
Cherry, Robert	Deed to	Chandler, Walter Story	1806	P15	286	188
Cherry, Robert	Deed to	Bevan, Mathew L., of Phila. PA	1807	S18	379	301
Cherry, Robert	Deed to	Smallwood, Samuel N.	1810	X23	393	316
Cherry, Robert, mortgagee et al	Deed to	McKim, James	1807	R17	082	066
Cherry, Robert, trader	Mortgage fr	Armstrong, Andrew, shop keeper	1804	K10	141	153
Cheshire, Archibald	Deed fr	Chandler, Walter Story	1812	AD29	548	461
Cheshire, Archibald	Plat		1812	AD29	550	
Cheshire, Archibald	Deed fr	Casanave, Ann	1814	AG32	035	027
Cheshire, Archibald	Deed fr	Wright, John M.	1817	AO39	159	119
Cheshire, Archibald	Deed fr	Carr, Overton	1817	AO39	160	120
Chesley, Ann, of G'tn.	Deed fr	Belt, Ann, of G'tn.	1804	L11	043	43
Chesley, Ann, of G'tn.	Deed to	Whann, Adam, of Elkton MD	1807	S18	199	159
Chesley, Anne, of G'tn.	Deed fr	Magruder, William B. et al	1804	L11	372	333
Chester, Samuel	B. of S. to	Lovely, John V.	1811	AA26	183	124
Chester, Samuel	B. of S. to	Laurence, John	1817	AO39	096	076
Chester, Samuel, of G'tn.	B. of S. to	Baker, John & Edward Dawes	1817	AN38	546	397
Cheston, Isabella, of Balto. MD	Deed to	Elliott, Richard	1813	AE30	368	273
Chew, Cassandra et al	Deed to	Clarke, William	1808	U20	250	133
Chew, Cassandra, of G'tn.	Lease to	Brown, Joel, of G'tn.	1804	K10	282	285
Chiene, Margaret, of Phila. PA	Mortgage fr	Dempsie, Elizabeth, wid.	1810	Y24	088	079
Chiene, Margaret, of Phila.	Release to	Dempsie, Elizabeth	1812	AB27	547	447
Child, Henry	Deed fr	Brent, Daniel C.	1802	I9	346	571
Child, Henry H.	Deed to	Thompson, Henry	1802	I9	347	573
Childs, Henry	Deed fr	Polock, Isaac et al	1802	H8	020	019
Chilton, Thomas	Slaves	From Loudoun Co. VA	1806	P15	135	088
Chisholm, Elizabeth	Manumis to	Clarke, Ann (C)	1814	AH33	084	076
Chisman, Jesse	Cert Free fr	Dawson, Thomas	1808	U20	169	095
Chiswell, Joseph N.	Deed fr	Stoddert, Benj. & Wm. Deakins	1793	A1-2	424	33
Chiswell, Joseph N.	Deed to	Beall, Thomas & John M. Gantt	1793	A1-2	426	34
Chiswell, Joseph Newton	Deed fr	Beatty, Charles, of Montg. Co.	1796	B2B	515	222
Christian, John	Deed fr	Law, Thomas	1802	H8	190	182
Chub, Robert	Manumis to	[ ], Priscilla (negro)	1806	P15	285	188
Church, Lewis	B. of S. to	Mattingley, Edward	1817	AO39	071	058
Cissell, Mary & Ann Aud [Cecil]	Deed to	Vanhorn, Archibald, of P.G. Co.	1816	AL36	262	263
Cist, Charles, of Phila. PA	Deed fr	Middleton, Joseph	1801	G7	223	298
Cist, Charles, of Phila. PA	Deed to	Haga, Godfrey, of Phila. PA	1805	N13	009	010
Cist, Jacob	Deed fr	Commissioners of Washington	1801	G7	196	262
Cist, Jacob	Deed fr	Brown, Robert	1802	I9	340	560
Cist, Jacob	Deed to	Way, Andrew, Jr. et al	1808	T19	070	051
Cist, Jacob et al	Deed fr	Munroe, Thomas, Supt.	1807	R17	315	239
Cist, Jacob, of Luzerne Co. PA	Deed to	Albrecht, Charles, of Phila. PA	1814	AH33	269	234
Cist, Jacob, of PA	Deed to	Dixon, Thomas, of G'tn.	1817	AO39	506	348
Clagett, Darius	Release fr	Marbury, William	1815	AK35	477	374
Clagett, Darius	Convey fr	Getty, Robert, of G'tn.	1815	AK35	473	371
Clagett, Darius, of G'tn.	Mortgage to	Getty, Robert, of G'tn.	1816	AM37	437	314
Clagett, Hezekiah	Deed to	Beall, Thomas & John M. Gantt	1793	A1-1	249	339
Clagett, James	Bond fr	United States	1801	G7	012	

Party	What	Party	Year	Liber	Old	New
Clagett, James	Deed to	Hoye, John et al	1807	R17	055	044
Clagett, James et al	Bond to	United States	1801	G7	012	015
Clagett, James et al	Mortgage fr	Harbaugh, Leonard	1804	L11	247	228
Clagett, Jane	Deed to	Robertson, Samuel	1815	AI34	063	071
Clagett, Jane, of G'tn.	Deed fr	Murdock, Addison	1807	S18	393	313
Clagett, Joseph W., of P.G. et al	Deed fr	Diggs, William, of Montg. Co.	1805	N13	143	135
Clagett, Joseph W. & P.B. Key	Deed to	Calder, William	1814	AH33	204	185
Clagett, Joseph W., P.G. Co. et al	Deed to	Bradley, Abraham, Jr., Montg. Co.	1815	AH33	401	346
Clagett, Joseph White, P.G. Co.	Deed to	Stone, Edward, of G'tn.	1815	AK35	288	230
Clagett, Richard & Martha et al	Deed to	Luffborough, Nathan	1801	G7	282	391
Clagett, Thomas John, Rev.	Deed fr	Roberts, Owen	1801	G7	126	163
Clagett, Thomas John, Rt. Rev.	Deed to	Williams, Thomas Owen, P.G. Co.	1805	N13	100	092
Clagett, Walter	Deed fr	Deakins, William Jr., of G'tn.	1796	B2B	434	112
Clagett, William, of G'tn.	Deed fr	Patterson, Edgar, of G'tn.	1814	AG32	050	039
Clagett, William W.	Deed fr	Suter, Alexander	1814	AH33	293	254
Claggett, Hezekiah, of Balto. Co.	B. of S. fr	Lowe, Barbara	1813	AE30	367	272
Claggett, James, of Montg. Co.	B. of S. fr	Claggett, Jane	1811	Z25	397	312
Claggett, Jane	B. of S. to	Claggett, James, of Montg. Co.	1811	Z25	397	312
Claggett, Joseph W., of P.G. Co.	Deed fr	Key, Philip Barton, of Montg. Co.	1815	AH33	272	237
Claggett, Walter	Deed fr	Green, Charles D.	1801	F6	181	115
Claggett, Walter, reps. of	Bond to	Riggs, Romulus & Wm. S. Nicholls	1813	AF31	072	049
Claggett, Walter, reps. of	Award to	Riggs, Romulus & Wm. S. Nicholls	1813	AF31	073	050
Claggett, William, of G'tn.	Deed to	Magruder, Ninian, of G'tn.	1814	AG32	274	194
Clancy, Patrick & John	Deed fr	Dorsey, William H., of G'tn.	1807	R17	211	158
Clare, Benjamin, of G'tn.	Deed to	Fennell, Edward	1807	R17	238	179
Clare, Benjamin, trustee	Assign fr	Harris, John, insolvent	1808	V21	134	098
Clare, Mary	Deed fr	Holmead, John	1811	AB27	123	101
Clark, Burton	Deed C.	State of Maryland	1799	D4	398	377
Clark, Elizabeth et al	Deed fr	McConnell, John	1813	AE30	326	244
Clark, Francis	Deed fr	Cochrane, Alexander, Sr. et al	1810	Y24	374	338
Clark, Francis	D. of T. to	Ott, John, of G'tn.	1811	AA26	172	118
Clark, Francis	Deed fr	Carpenter, Thomas, trustee	1811	AB27	401	331
Clark, Francis	Deed fr	Hoban, James	1811	AA26	207	142
Clark, Francis, children & heirs of	Deed fr	McConnell, John	1813	AE30	326	244
Clark, Isaac	Deed fr	Morton, William, trustee	1817	AO39	448	307
Clark, James & Elizabeth, of PA	Deed to	Beatty, Charles	1801	G7	137	181
Clark, Jane et al	Deed fr	McConnell, John	1813	AE30	326	244
Clark, Jane, now Meigs et al	D. of T. to	Meigs, Josiah & J. Forsyth	1815	AK35	421	330
Clark, John et al	Deed fr	McConnell, John	1813	AE30	326	244
Clark, Joseph, of G'tn.	B. of S. fr	Gardner, John, of G'tn.	1804	K10	216	226
Clark, Lettetia et al	Deed fr	McConnell, John	1813	AE30	326	244
Clark, Robert, of G'tn.	Deed fr	Dillehay, Thomas L. & Mary, MD	1817	AO39	511	351
Clark, Samuel, of G'tn.	Deed fr	Polock, Abigail, of Montg. Co.	1805	M12	085	079
Clark, Satterlee	Deed fr	Peter, George, of G'tn.	1816	AL36	454	429
Clark, Thomas et al	Deed fr	Peter, Robert	1795	B2A	199	273
Clark, William	B. of S. fr	Forrest, Joseph	1808	T19	219	161
Clark, Wm. & Charles Beatty, deft.	Suit	Davidson, John, plt.		K10	007	
Clarke, Abram	Convey fr	Washington Building Company	1813	AE30	430	318
Clarke, Abram	B. of S. to	Knoblock, John	1813	AF31	311	222
Clarke, Alban	Deed fr	Smallwood, Horatio & Charlotte	1814	AG32	327	238
Clarke, Alban	Deed fr	Clarke, Edward	1815	AI34	532	536
Clarke, Alban	Deed to	Clarke, Edward	1815	AI34	535	539
Clarke, Alban	Deed to	Clarke, Edward	1815	AI34	534	538
Clarke, Alban	Deed fr	Mauro, Philip & Elizabeth	1815	AI34	514	519
Clarke, Alban	Deed fr	Law, John	1816	AL36	091	092

Index to District of Columbia Land Records, 1792-1817

Party	What	Party	Year	Liber	Old	New
Clarke, Alben	Deed to	Grayson, William	1815	AK35	418	327
Clarke, Albin	Deed to	King, Charles & Hezekiah Langley	1816	AM37	090	072
Clarke, Ann (C)	Manumis fr	Chisholm, Elizabeth	1814	AH33	084	076
Clarke, Bailey E.	Deed fr	Coombs, Joseph	1799	D4	301	285
Clarke, Bailey Erles, of P.G. Co.	Deed fr	Prout, William	1804	M12	028	029
Clarke, Edward	Deed fr	Clarke, Robert	1815	AI34	420	441
Clarke, Edward	Deed fr	Clarke, Alban	1815	AI34	535	539
Clarke, Edward	Deed to	Clarke, Alban	1815	AI34	532	536
Clarke, Edward	Deed fr	Clarke, Alban	1815	AI34	534	538
Clarke, Edward	Deed to	Lewis, Henry	1816	AM37	030	025
Clarke, Edward, of G'tn.	Deed to	Traverse, Nicholas, of G'tn.	1816	AM37	442	317
Clarke, Edward W.	Deed fr	Adams, George	1817	AO39	364	245
Clarke, Eliza	B. of S. fr	Jenkins, Francis	1814	AG32	146	105
Clarke, Eliza & John McGowan	Assign to	Sutherland, Thomas Janey	1814	AH33	316	273
Clarke, Elizabeth & J. McGowan	Deed to	Patterson, James	1813	AF31	376	270
Clarke, Elizabeth & S. Holtzman	B. of S. fr	Hubbard, Dyer	1814	AG32	263	187
Clarke, Frances et al	Deed fr	McConnell, John	1813	AE30	326	244
Clarke, Francis	Deed to	Munroe, Thomas	1806	P15	190	127
Clarke, Francis	Deed fr	Brent, Robert	1807	R17	392	297
Clarke, Francis	Mortgage to	Young, Moses	1810	Y24	421	378
Clarke, Francis	Deed fr	Dant, James, of KY	1810	Y24	377	341
Clarke, Francis	Mortgage fr	Bird, Thomas & Alice	1811	AB27	404	332
Clarke, Francis & John M'Connell	Release fr	Van Ness, John P.	1811	AC28	002	002
Clarke, Francis, admrs. of	Deed to	Patterson, James	1813	AF31	376	270
Clarke, Francis et al	Deed to	Donohoo, Patrick	1810	Y24	062	055
Clarke, Francis et al	Deed to	Scholfield, Joseph L.	1810	Y24	073	065
Clarke, George	Deed fr	Beverly, Robert	1811	AB27	056	047
Clarke, George	Deed fr	Smith, Walter, of G'tn.	1816	AM37	283	208
Clarke, George & Michael Nourse	D. of T. fr	Webster, Toppan	1817	AO39	310	
Clarke, Horatio D.	B. of S. fr	Price, Handley	1817	AO39	279	199
Clarke, Horatio D.	B. of S. fr	Price, Handley	1817	AO39	277	198
Clarke, Isaac	Deed fr	Glover, Charles	1815	AH33	497	426
Clarke, Isaac	D. of T. to	Ott, David	1815	AH33	498	427
Clarke, Isaac, of Alexa.	Deed to	Clarke, Walter	1817	AO39	450	308
Clarke, James	Lease fr	Maddox, Notley	1801	G7	115	146
Clarke, John	Agreement	Lovell, William	1802	I9	168	256
Clarke, Joseph	Lease fr	Lanham, Elisha	1802	I9	427	707
Clarke, Joseph	Assign to	Wright, Thomas C., of G'tn.	1804	L11	312	286
Clarke, Joseph	Deed fr	Lanham, Elisha, of G'tn.	1811	Z25	448	353
Clarke, Joseph	Deed to	Worthington, William	1812	AC28	110	083
Clarke, Joseph & Robert	B. of S. fr	Orme, Nathan	1808	T19	370	264
Clarke, Joseph S.	Qualify	Militia officer	1812	AD29	174	140
Clarke, Joseph S.	Manumis to	[ ], Joe (C), age 38	1812	AE30	005	004
Clarke, Joseph S.	Deed fr	Young, Richard & Mahlon Roach	1816	AL36	256	258
Clarke, Joseph S.	Deed fr	Glover, Charles	1816	AL36	252	254
Clarke, Joseph S.	Deed fr	Van Ness, John P. & Marcia	1816	AM37	035	028
Clarke, Lawson & Fielder Parker	B. of S. to	Howe, Ignatius	1811	AB27	497	406
Clarke, Robert	Deed fr	Threlkeld, John	1800	E5	302	295
Clarke, Robert	Lease fr	Lanham, Elisha	1801	G7	274	378
Clarke, Robert	B. of S. fr	Clarke, William	1802	H8	202	193
Clarke, Robert	Deed fr	Simms, Edward	1802	I9	354	584
Clarke, Robert	Assign fr	Kaldenbach, Andrew	1806	P15	089	054
Clarke, Robert	Deed fr	Beatty, John M. & Charles A.	1807	Q16	365	264
Clarke, Robert	Deed fr	Collins, John	1808	T19	350	252
Clarke, Robert	B. of S. fr	Speake, Edward	1809	V21	352	254

Party	What	Party	Year	Liber	Old	New
Clarke, Robert	Deed fr	Dawes, Isaac	1810	Y24	305	278
Clarke, Robert	Deed fr	Ritchie, Abner	1810	Y24	304	277
Clarke, Robert	Deed fr	Prout, William	1810	Y24	156	142
Clarke, Robert	Deed to	Neale, Francis, Rev.	1811	AC28	089	068
Clarke, Robert	Deed fr	Pierce, Ignatius	1812	AC28	404	293
Clarke, Robert	Deed fr	Dunlop, James	1812	AD29	068	049
Clarke, Robert	Deed to	Dougherty, James & Mary	1813	AF31	517	379
Clarke, Robert	Deed to	Clarke, Edward	1815	AI34	420	441
Clarke, Robert & Ignatius Pearce	Deed fr	King, George	1810	Y24	109	099
Clarke, Robert, Jr.	B. of S. fr	Clarke, William	1802	H8	123	120
Clarke, Robert, of G'tn.	Deed fr	Deakins, Francis, of G'tn.	1804	K10	218	227
Clarke, Robert, of G'tn.	B. of S. fr	Causin, Gerard	1810	Y24	307	279
Clarke, Robert, of G'tn.	Deed to	Cox, John, Col., of G'tn.	1816	AM37	463	333
Clarke, Robert, of G'tn.	Deed fr	White, John B. & Lucy	1817	AN38	244	179
Clarke, Robert, painter	Deed fr	Van Ness, John P. & Marcia	1811	AB27	484	396
Clarke, Samuel	Manumis to	[ ], Polly (C)	1812	AD29	085	063
Clarke, Satterlee	Deed fr	Davidson, Lewis Grant	1816	AM37	450	323
Clarke, Walter	Deed fr	Andrews, George	1810	Y24	512	451
Clarke, Walter	Convey fr	Herty, Thomas	1814	AG32	308	225
Clarke, Walter	B. of S. fr	Bowie, Robert, of P.G. Co.	1816	AL36	545	508
Clarke, Walter	Deed fr	Clarke, Isaac, of Alexa.	1817	AO39	450	308
Clarke, Walter & Joseph	Assign fr	Kaldenbach, Andrew	1806	O14	221	146
Clarke, Walter & Joseph	Deed fr	Dorsey, William H., of Balto.	1810	Y24	435	388
Clarke, Walter, painter	Deed fr	Van Ness, John P. & Marcia	1811	AB27	191	157
Clarke, William	B. of S. to	Clarke, Robert	1802	H8	202	193
Clarke, William	B. of S. to	Clarke, Robert, Jr.	1802	H8	123	120
Clarke, William	Deed fr	Wehrly	1806	Q16	033	021
Clarke, William	Deed fr	Chew, Cassandra & Mary Brumly	1808	U20	250	133
Clarke, William	Deed fr	Brookes, Joseph	1808	V21	023	017
Clarke, William	Lease fr	Thompson, James	1811	AA26	022	017
Clarke, William	Deed fr	Thompson, James	1812	AC28	370	269
Clarke, William	Cert Free to	Baltimore, Hannah (C), age 25	1813	AE30	152	119
Clarke, William	Deed fr	Thompson, James	1813	AF31	342	244
Clarke, William & Robert	B. of S. to	King, Benjamin	1805	M12	239	240
Clarke, William, of G'tn.	Deed to	Mudd, Thomas J., of G'tn.	1809	V21	323	238
Clarke, Wlliam	Deed to	Mackall, Benjamin F.	1810	Y24	216	198
Clask, Robert	Deed fr	Deakins, Francis, of G'tn.	1802	H8	581	545
Claxton, Thomas	B. of S. fr	Duvall, Delilah & Sarah, P.G. Co.	1809	W22	265	178
Claxton, Thomas	Deed fr	Law, Thomas	1816	AL36	305	301
Clayton, Rachel, Newc. Co. DE	B. of S. to	West, John, Newcastle Co. DE	1809	V21	307	224
Claytor, John & John Randall, Jr.	B. of S. to	Hagner, Peter	1814	AG32	422	306
Clements, Edward	B. of S. to	Ekton, Offa	1811	Z25	346	270
Clements, Elizabeth et al	Deed Gift fr	Clements, Susanna, of G'tn.	1810	Y24	510	449
Clements, Elizabeth, of G'tn.	Deed fr	Beatty, Charles	1801	G7	352	483
Clements, Francis H. et al	Deed Gift fr	Clements, Susanna, of G'tn.	1810	Y24	510	449
Clements, John et al	Deed Gift fr	Clements, Susanna, of G'tn.	1810	Y24	510	449
Clements, Joseph, of G'tn.	Deed to	Clements, Rebecca, of G'tn.	1811	AB27	194	159
Clements, Joseph, of G'tn.	Deed to	Norris, Daniel & Catherine, of MD	1812	AD29	288	237
Clements, Martha	B. of S. to	Blagden, George	1809	X23	047	035
Clements, Martha et al	Deed Gift fr	Clements, Susanna, of G'tn.	1810	Y24	510	449
Clements, Mary A.H. et al	Deed Gift fr	Clements, Susanna, of G'tn.	1810	Y24	510	449
Clements, Rebecca	Deed fr	Fenwick, Francis	1815	AK35	392	308
Clements, Rebecca, of G'tn.	Deed fr	Clements, Joseph, of G'tn.	1811	AB27	194	159
Clements, Richard Alford, s/o O.	Deposition	Left Ear Bitten Off by Horse	1813	AG32	006	005
Clements, Robert S. et al	Deed Gift fr	Clements, Susanna, of G'tn.	1810	Y24	510	449

Index to District of Columbia Land Records, 1792-1817

Party	What	Party	Year	Liber	Old	New
Clements, Susanna, of G'tn.	Deed Gift to	Clements, Robert S. et al	1810	Y24	510	449
Clements, Thomas, of Montg. Co.	Lease fr	Williamson, David, of Balto. Co.	1815	AK35	128	099
Clements, Thomas, of G'tn.	Deed to	Smallwood, Horatio, of G'tn.	1816	AM37	483	351
Clements, William H. et al	Deed Gift fr	Clements, Susanna, of G'tn.	1810	Y24	510	449
Clephan, Lewis	Deed fr	Stoddert, Benjamin	1802	I9	296	485
Clephan, Lewis	Deed fr	McDonald, Andrew	1802	I9	379	629
Clephan, Lewis	Deed to	Sutton, Robert	1804	L11	041	40
Clephan, Lewis	Mortgage fr	Vint, John	1805	N13	352	283
Clephan, Lewis	Release to	McDonald, Andrew, of G'tn.	1805	O14	145	094
Clephan, Lewis	B. of S. to	Vint, John	1805	N13	321	259
Clephan, Lewis	Deed fr	Murdock, John, of G'tn.	1807	R17	206	155
Clephan, Lewis	D. of T. fr	McDonald, Andrew & Catherine	1808	T19	395	280
Clephan, Lewis	Deed fr	Shoemaker, David	1809	X23	001	001
Clephan, Lewis	Deed fr	Hay, Robert	1809	X23	174	129
Clephan, Lewis	Deed to	Van Ness, John P.	1812	AD29	452	380
Clephan, Lewis	Deed to	Miller, Jacob	1812	AD29	001	001
Clephan, Lewis	Deed to	Doolen, Bernard	1813	AE30	060	045
Clephan, Lewis & A. McDonald	Deed to	Wright, Matthew	1812	AC28	150	112
Clephan, Lewis & A. McDonald	Deed to	Wright, Matthew	1812	AD29	275	227
Clephan, Lewis, of Montg. Co.	Deed fr	Crookshanks, John, of Montg. Co.	1797	C3	019	15
Clephan, Lewis, printer	Deed fr	Commissioners of Washington	1800	E5	104	091
Clephan, Lewis [Clephane]	B. of S. to	O'Brien, William	1806	P15	081	049
Clerklee, James	Deed to	Brent, William	1810	Y24	136	124
Clerklee, James	Release fr	Brent, William, trustee	1812	AD29	242	200
Clerklee, James	Deed to	Forrest, Alexander	1812	AD29	248	205
Clerklee, James & Margaret R.	Deed to	Threlkeld, John	1810	Y24	538	472
Clerklee, James, of P.G. Co.	Deed fr	Slater, David & Sarah	1808	T19	330	240
Clerklee, James, of Charles Co.	Deed to	Brent, William	1812	AD29	244	202
Clerklee, James, of Charles Co.	Mortgage fr	Brent, William	1812	AD29	546	460
Clerklee, James, of Charles Co.	Release to	Brent, William	1816	AM37	257	189
Clerklee, James, of Charles Co.	Deed to	Brent, Daniel & William	1816	AM37	260	191
Clerklee, James, of Charles Co.	Deed to	McDonald, John G.	1816	AM37	253	186
Clinger, Henry, joiner	Deed fr	Spiker, Benjamin	1793	A1-1	342	446
Clinger, Henry, joiner	Deed fr	Spiker, Henry, joiner	1793	A1-1	339	443
Cliver, George	B. of S. fr	Downs, George	1806	P15	127	082
Cliver, George & Samuel Cloakey	B. of S. fr	Edelin, Ignatius	1812	AC28	486	346
Cloakey, Samuel	Deed to	Willson, Robert	1802	I9	018	025
Cloakey, Samuel	Deed fr	Hay, Robert	1808	V21	053	041
Cloakey, Samuel	Deed fr	Van Ness, John P. & Maria	1811	AB27	305	251
Cloakey, Samuel	Deed fr	Van Ness, John P. & Maria	1811	AB27	307	252
Cloakey, Samuel	Deed fr	Van Ness, John P. & Marcia	1811	AB27	312	257
Cloakey, Samuel	Mortgage fr	Peltz, John	1811	AA26	270	184
Cloakey, Samuel	Mortgage fr	Speake, Samuel	1812	AD29	094	071
Cloakey, Samuel	Release to	Speake, Samuel	1813	AF31	512	374
Cloakey, Samuel	Deed fr	Kirk, John	1813	AE30	419	309
Cloakey, Samuel	Deed fr	Brown, Robert	1814	AG32	062	048
Cloakey, Samuel	Lease to	Baltimore, Treacy	1816	AK35	525	414
Cloakey, Samuel & George Cliver	B. of S. fr	Edelin, Ignatius	1812	AC28	486	346
Cloakey, Samuel, builder	Mortgage to	Van Ness, John P.	1811	AB27	143	119
Cloakey, Samuel, builder	Deed fr	Eastburn, Jane, of G'tn. [Aisburn]	1811	AB27	284	233
Cloakey, Samuel, carpenter et al	Deed fr	Van Ness, John P. & Marcia	1808	V21	051	040
Clockey, Samuel	Deed to	McMinn, Thomas	1801	G7	148	195
Clokey, Samuel	Deed fr	Commissioners of Washington	1800	E5	328	316
Clokey, Samuel	Deed to	Wilson, Robert	1800	E5	331	319
Clokey, Samuel	Deed fr	Commissioners of Washington	1800	E5	329	318

Index to District of Columbia Land Records, 1792-1817

Party	What	Party	Year	Liber	Old	New
Clokey, Samuel	Deed to	Weightman, Roger C.	1813	AE30	348	260
Cloud, Abner & Susanna	Deed to	Townsend, Henry	1801	G7	218	291
Cloud, Abner et al	Deed to	Kogenderfer, Leonard et al	1799	D4	239	221
Cloud, Abner et al	Deed to	Holmead, John	1810	Y24	180	165
Cloud, Abner, Jr., of Montg. Co.	Deed fr	Baily, Jesse, Montgomery Co.	1795	B2B	360	008
Cloud, Abner, of Montg. Co.	Lease to	Main, Thomas, of Montg. Co.	1797	C3	248	204
Cloud, Abner, of Montg. Co.	Deed to	Main, Thomas, of Montg. Co.	1797	C3	148	122
Cloud, Amos & Samuel Paxton	Deed to	Way, Nicholas, of Wilmington DE	1793	A1-2	403	12
Cloud, Amos et al	Deed to	Way, Nicholas, physic, of DE	1793	A1-2	405	14
Cloud, Amos, heirs of	Deed to	Townsend, Henry	1801	G7	218	291
Cloud, Joseph & Eliza et al	Deed to	Townsend, Henry	1801	G7	216	288
Cloud, Joseph & Eliza, Phila. PA	Deed to	Gary, Everard, of G'tn.	1805	N13	164	151
Cloud, Joseph et al	Deed to	Cokendafer, Leonard	1798	D4	099	083
Club, Thomas	B. of S. to	Booth, Edward	1805	N13	280	231
Clubb, Druey Ann	B. of S. fr	Saunders, Joseph	1812	AD29	311	255
Clyver, George & George Moore	Mortgage fr	Gannon, James	1810	Y24	235	217
Coates, James et al	Deed fr	Sentorius, Mary Ann	1802	I9	578	937
Coates, Samuel et al	Deed fr	Burd, Edward Shippen, Phila. PA	1809	V21	365	268
Coates, Samuel et al	Partition	Young, Moses	1810	X23	216	165
Coates, Samuel et al	Release to	Nourse, Joseph	1813	AF31	011	008
Cochran, Alexander	B. of S. to	Law, Thomas	1802	G7	508	647
Cochran, Alexander	Deed to	Bridges, John, of G'tn.	1805	N13	039	039
Cochran, Alexander	Deed fr	Brent, Daniel Carroll, marshal	1805	O14	106	066
Cochran, Alexander & Robert	B. of S. fr	McCormick, Michael	1806	P15	223	149
Cochran, Alexander, going to Ire.	Deed to	Dye, Reuben	1812	AC28	354	256
Cochran, Alexander, Jr.	B. of S. fr	Harshman, Henry	1804	L11	245	227
Cochran, Alexander, Jr.	Agreement	Wigfield, Robert	1805	N13	034	036
Cochran, Alexander, Jr.	Mortgage fr	Harshman, Henry	1805	M12	098	091
Cochran, Alexander, Jr.	Deed fr	Tidgen, Henry	1806	P15	070	043
Cochran, Alexander, Jr.	Deed to	Kirby, John Baptist	1806	P15	179	119
Cochran, Alexander, Jr.	Deed to	Cocke, Buller	1808	T19	352	254
Cochran, Alexander, Jr., to Ire.	P. of Atty. to	Smith, Hugh, of Alexa.	1809	V21	403	306
Cochran, David	Assign to	Blanchard, William	1816	AL36	004	004
Cochran, David, mer.	Assign fr	Cochran, William, mer., of Balto.	1815	AH33	494	423
Cochran, Eleanor	Deed fr	Threlkeld, John	1816	AM37	171	130
Cochran, William & David, Balto.	Assign fr	Cochrane, Alexander	1810	Y24	098	088
Cochran, William, mer., of Balto.	Assign to	Cochran, David, mer.	1815	AH33	494	423
Cochrane, Alexander	B. of S. fr	Betterton, Benjamin	1804	K10	264	270
Cochrane, Alexander	B. of S. fr	Hurdle, Thomas	1807	S18	296	231
Cochrane, Alexander	B. of S. fr	Browning, Joseph, of G'tn. et al	1807	S18	296	232
Cochrane, Alexander	B. of S. fr	Sutherland, George	1808	T19	103	073
Cochrane, Alexander	Deed fr	McLean, Cornelius	1809	X23	261	204
Cochrane, Alexander	Assign to	Cochran, William & David, Balto.	1810	Y24	098	088
Cochrane, Alexander	D. of T. fr	Washington, Lund, of G'tn.	1811	AB27	447	367
Cochrane, Alexander & Eleanor	Deed to	McLeod, John	1810	Z25	023	018
Cochrane, Alexander, Jr., trustee	Deed fr	Burch, Benjamin, insolvent	1806	Q16	084	053
Cochrane, Alexander, Jr.	Deed fr	Standage, Eleazer & Mary	1807	S18	176	143
Cochrane, Alexander, Jr.	Deed to	Parker, Fielder	1807	S18	411	318
Cochrane, Alexander, Jr.	Deed fr	Tuckfield, William H.P.	1808	T19	137	097
Cochrane, Alexander, Jr. et al	Deed fr	Law, Thomas	1808	T19	139	099
Cochrane, Alexander, Jr.	Deed fr	Chandler, Walter Story	1808	T19	166	118
Cochrane, Alexander, Jr., by atty.	Deed to	Farrell, Zephaniah	1809	X23	037	027
Cochrane, Alexander, Sr. et al	Deed to	Scholfield, Joseph L.	1810	Y24	073	065
Cochrane, Alexander, Sr. et al	Deed to	Donohoo, Patrick	1810	Y24	062	055
Cochrane, Alexander, Sr. et al	Deed to	Clark, Francis	1810	Y24	374	338

Index to District of Columbia Land Records, 1792-1817

Party	What	Party	Year	Liber	Old	New
Cochrane, Alexr. & Eleanor, def.	Suit	McLeod, John, plt.	1810	Z25	023	018
Cochrane, David et al	Deed fr	Munroe, Thomas, Supt.	1813	AE30	426	314
Cochrane, William et al	Deed fr	Munroe, Thomas, Supt.	1813	AE30	426	314
Cocke, Buller	Slaves	From Norfolk VA	1804	L11	171	
Cocke, Buller	Slaves	From Isle of Wight Co. VA	1805	N13	098	090
Cocke, Buller	Deed fr	Cochran, Alexander, Jr.	1808	T19	352	254
Cocke, Buller	Deed fr	Law, Thomas	1810	X23	413	334
Cocke, Buller	P. of Atty. fr	Cowper, William & Ann P.P.	1811	AB27	321	264
Cocke, Buller	Deed fr	May, Frederick	1812	AD29	482	407
Cocke, Buller	Deed fr	Law, Edmund, trustee of Thomas	1812	AC28	302	220
Cocke, Buller	Mortgage fr	Wertz, Henry, Jr.	1813	AF31	224	154
Cocke, Buller	Deed fr	Ewell, Thomas	1813	AF31	167	112
Cocke, Buller	Deed fr	Davidson, James & Rich. Forrest	1814	AG32	143	103
Cocke, Buller	Deed to	McCauley, George	1814	AH33	116	108
Cocke, Buller	Deed fr	Boyd, Washington, marshal	1815	AK35	086	066
Cocke, Buller	Deed fr	Corporation of Washington	1815	AK35	261	207
Cocke, Buller	Deed to	Acken, William D.	1816	AM37	448	322
Cocke, Buller & Eliza	Deed to	Sinclair, Arthur, Lt., U.S.N.	1811	AB27	452	371
Cocke, Buller & Edmund Law	Deed to	Prout, William	1815	AK35	218	171
Cocke, Buller, atty. for Cowper	Deed to	Sanford, Daniel, of Norfolk VA	1811	AB27	319	263
Cocke, Butler	Deed fr	Tingey, Thomas	1806	Q16	064	040
Cocke, Butler	Slave	From Norfolk VA	1807	S18	014	012
Cocker, William	B. of S. fr	Wheeler, Edward	1811	AA26	223	153
Cocking, William	Deed fr	Morgan, William, of G'tn.	1807	R17	068	055
Cocking, William	Deed fr	Brown, Robert	1807	R17	342	251
Cocking, William	Deed fr	Vint, John	1808	T19	025	020
Cocking, William	Deed fr	Francis, William, of Phila. PA	1808	V21	078	061
Cocking, William	Deed fr	Wright, Thomas C.	1811	AA26	227	155
Cocking, William	Deed fr	Wright, Thomas C.	1811	AA26	224	154
Cocking, William	Deed fr	Wright, Thomas C.	1811	AA26	230	158
Cocking, William	Deed fr	Bridges, John	1811	AB27	145	122
Cocking, William	Assign fr	Bryan, Benjamin	1811	AB27	084	070
Cocking, William	Deed to	Hebb, William, of P.G. Co.	1812	AE30	033	025
Cocking, William	Deed to	Nicholls, William S., of G'tn. et al	1812	AD29	498	420
Cocking, William	Deed to	Hebb, William, of P.G. Co.	1812	AE30	045	034
Cocking, William	Assign to	Young, Samuel W., Loudoun Co.	1813	AF31	360	257
Cocking, William	Lease to	Young, Samuel W., Loudoun Co.	1813	AF31	362	259
Cocking, William	Deed fr	Hogan, Thady	1814	AG32	366	265
Cocking, William	Deed fr	Prout, William	1814	AG32	160	115
Cocking, William	Lease to	Bridges, John	1814	AH33	284	247
Cocking, William	Release to	Bridge, John, of G'tn.	1815	AI34	258	291
Cocking, William	Deed to	King, Robert	1815	AH33	507	435
Cocking, William	Deed to	Riggs, Romulus, of G'tn.	1815	AH33	481	411
Cocking, William	Deed to	Steiner, Henry M.	1816	AL36	521	487
Cocking, William	Deed fr	Wright, Thomas C.	1816	AL36	139	139
Cocking, William	Deed fr	Van Ness, John P. & Marcia	1817	AN38	492	355
Cocking, William	Deed to	Baker, Catharine	1817	AO39	499	343
Cocking, William, of G'tn.	Deed fr	Wright, Thomas C., of G'tn.	1808	V21	073	058
Cockrill, Jeremiah	Deed Gift to	Thornton, Jane	1810	Y24	547	480
Coeper, John & Luke Wheeler	D. of T. to	Wilson, Alexander	1817	AN38	062	049
Coghlan, William	Deed to	Dawes, Isaac	1802	G7	585	734
Coghlan, William	Deed fr	Johnson, William Andrew	1802	G7	582	731
Coghlan, William, of P.G. Co.	Deed to	Hoban, James	1797	C3	135	110
Coglan, Wm., of Charleston SC	Transfer to	Hoban, James	1798	B2B	476	169
Cokendafer, Leonard et al	Deed fr	Evans, Samuel et al	1798	D4	099	083

Party	What	Party	Year	Liber	Old	New
Colclazer, Jacob, of G'tn.	Lease fr	Peter, Thomas, of G'tn.	1816	AM37	072	058
Colclazer, Thomas, of G'tn.	D. of T. to	Smith, Clement, of G'tn.	1814	AG32	264	188
Colclazer, Thomas, of G'tn.	B. of S. to	King, Charles	1816	AL36	434	413
Colclazier, Thomas	Deed fr	Bohrer, Mary M.	1814	AG32	280	200
Colder, James [Calder]	Deed fr	Davidson, Lewis Grant	1815	AK35	013	010
Cole, Bennet	Deed fr	Lacey, Benjamin, of G'tn.	1806	P15	328	216
Cole, Bennett	Deed to	Mitchell, James & Eleanor	1802	I9	429	711
Cole, Bennett	Deed fr	McFarland, Henry	1802	I9	373	618
Cole, Jane, wid/o Bennet	B. of S. to	Gittings, William	1806	Q16	262	182
Cole, Samuel, of Balto. MD	Deed fr	Moscrop, Henry, of MD	1802	H8	308	290
Cole, William, Balto. et al	Deed to	Chesley, Anne, of G'tn.	1804	L11	372	333
Coleman, Alley et al	B. of S. fr	Coleman, Michael	1805	N13	004	004
Coleman, John	B. of S. fr	Coleman, Michael, bootmaker	1805	N13	004	004
Coleman, Joseph, of Alexa.	Deed to	French, George, of G'tn.	1794	B2A	105	138
Coleman, Joseph, of Alexa.	Deed to	French, George, of G'tn.	1798	C3	403	319
Coleman, Mary Ann et al	B. of S. fr	Coleman, Michael, bootmaker	1805	N13	004	004
Coleman, Michael, bootmaker	B. of S. to	Coleman, William et al	1805	N13	004	004
Coles, John	Cert fr	Commissioners of Washington	1795	B2A	331	464
Coles, John	Deed fr	Deakins, Francis	1802	I9	141	212
Coles, John	Agreement	Threlkeld, John, of G'tn.	1806	O14	218	144
Coles, John	Agreement	Hoye, John [Hoy]	1807	S18	124	101
Coles, John	Deed to	Davidson, John	1809	V21	215	153
Coles, John et al	Deed fr	Dalton, Tristram & Tobias Lear	1799	E5	061	049
Coles, John, now of G'tn.	Deed to	Hellen, Walter	1807	S18	125	103
Coles, John, now of G'tn.	Deed fr	Threlkeld, John, of G'tn.	1807	S18	173	141
Coles, John, of CN et al	Deed fr	Dalton, Tristram et al	1798	D4	148	131
Coles, John, of New London CN	Deed to	Berry, James	1804	K10	169	179
Coles, John, of Balto.	Deed fr	Deakins, Francis, exors. of	1806	O14	214	141
Coles, John, of Balto.	Deed fr	Deakins, Leonard M., of G'tn. et al	1807	S18	120	098
Coles, John, of New London CN	Deed to	Emack, William	1807	S18	185	150
Coles, John, of New London CN	Deed to	Cooke, William, of Balto.	1808	U20	041	024
Coles, John, of New London CN	Deed fr	Cooke, William, of Balto. Co.	1810	Y24	387	350
Coles, John, of New London CN	Deed to	Crawford, William, of G'tn.	1811	AB27	405	334
Coles, [John], of Phila. PA	Cert fr	Commissioners of Washington	1793	B2A	304	426
Collard, George	Exchange	Carroll, Daniel, of *Duddington*	1796	B2B	513	219
Collard, George	Deed fr	Commissioners of Washington	1800	E5	106	093
Collard, George	Deed to	Collard, Samuel, of Fairfax Co.	1801	F6	176	111
Collard, George	Deed to	Kirby, Francis	1801	F6	178	113
Collard, George	Deed to	Boswell, Clement	1801	F6	175	110
Collard, George	Deed to	[blank], Henry	1802	I9	500	820
Collard, George	Cert fr	Munroe, Thomas, Supt.	1804	L11	332	303
Collard, George	Cert fr	Munroe, Thomas, Supt.	1804	L11	331	302
Collard, George	Deed fr	Prout, William	1808	U20	342	185
Collard, George	Deed fr	Wigfield, James J. & G.S. Davis	1810	Y24	131	119
Collard, George	Assign to	Young, James	1811	AA26	237	162
Collard, George et al	Deed fr	Holmead, Anthony	1800	E5	238	232
Collard, George, trustee	B. of S. fr	Burrows, John, insolvent	1808	T19	202	145
Collard, George, trustee	Deed fr	Lee, Peter, insolvent	1810	Y24	025	021
Collard, George, trustee	Deed to	Wharton, Franklin	1813	AE30	334	250
Collard, Samuel & Rachel, of VA	Deed to	Kerby, Francis, of P.G. Co.	1813	AE30	399	294
Collard, Samuel, of Fairfax Co.	Deed fr	Collard, George	1801	F6	176	111
Collet, Ann, of Paterson NJ	Assign to	Coote, Thomas & David Ott	1817	AO39	305	217
Collins, Andrew, s/o John	Gift Deed fr	Collins, John, of G'tn.	1817	AN38	561	409
Collins, Ann	Cert Free		1810	Z25	236	185
Collins, Elizabeth, w/o Hezekiah	Deed fr	Beatty, Charles A.	1814	AH33	334	289

Index to District of Columbia Land Records, 1792-1817

Party	What	Party	Year	Liber	Old	New
Collins, Henrietta et al	Deed Gift fr	Collins, Zachariah	1814	AG32	064	049
Collins, Hezekiah	Deed fr	Threlkeld, John	1804	L11	151	151
Collins, Hezekiah	Deed fr	Threlkeld, John	1807	R17	400	302
Collins, Hezekiah	Deed fr	Magruder, Ninian, Dr.	1809	X23	295	235
Collins, James	B. of S. fr	Collins, John	1804	L11	062	63
Collins, John	B. of S. to	Collins, James	1804	L11	062	63
Collins, John	B. of S. to	Gray, Thomas et al	1805	M12	177	177
Collins, John	Deed to	Clarke, Robert	1808	T19	350	240
Collins, John, of G'tn.	Deed fr	Balch, Stephen B., Rev., of G'tn.	1807	R17	412	311
Collins, John, of G'tn.	Gift Deed to	Collins, Andrew, s/o John	1817	AN38	561	409
Collins, Joshua et al	B. of S. fr	Collins, John	1805	M12	177	177
Collins, Leonard et al	Deed Gift fr	Collins, Zachariah	1814	AG32	064	049
Collins, Susannah & Ann Proctor	Cert Free to	Wiseman, Thomas S. (M), age 23	1817	AO39	092	073
Collins, Susannah et al	Deed Gift fr	Collins, Zachariah	1814	AG32	064	049
Collins, William A.	Deed fr	Peter, George & Sarah et al	1816	AL36	491	462
Collins, William [Collings]	Cert Free to	Grimes, Ann, sevant	1814	AG32	054	042
Collins, Zachariah	Deed Gift to	Collins, Leonard et al	1814	AG32	064	049
Coltman, William	Deed fr	Commissioners of Washington	1800	E5	288	281
Coltman, William	Deed fr	Commissioners of Washington	1800	E5		282
Coltman, William	Deed to	Morin, Lewis	1806	Q16	047	030
Coltman, William	Deed to	Lear, Benjamin L.	1816	AM37	479	347
Columbia Turnpike Company	Deed fr	Fenwick, Thomas & Eleanor	1812	AC28	263	192
Columbia Turnpike Roads	Deed fr	Ewell, Thomas	1813	AE30	337	252
Colvin, John B., insolvent	Deed to	Andrews, George, trustee	1810	Y24	033	029
Colvin, John B.	B. of S. to	Holcomb, John	1812	AC28	394	286
Combe, Griffith	Deed fr	Law, Thomas	1802	H8	175	168
Combs, Joseph	Deed to	Bayly, William	1799	D4	297	280
Commercial Co. of Washington	B. of S. fr	Forrest, Joseph et al	1808	U20	037	021
Commissioner of Public Buildings	Cert to	Talbott, Charles	1817	AO39	464	319
Commissioner of Public Buildings	Cert to	Bailey, John	1817	AO39	368	248
Commissioner of Public Buildings	Cert to	Graham, John	1817	AO39	335	239
Commissioners (multiple)	Cert to	Deakins, Wm., Jr. & U. Forrest	1797	B2B	473	166
Commissioners (multiple)	Cert to	Duncanson, William M.	1797	B2B	465	157
Commissioners (multiple)	Cert to	Law, Thomas	1797	B2B	469	162
Commissioners (multiple)	Cert to	Dunlop, James & Joseph Carleton	1797	B2B	459	149
Commissioners (S1, L multiple)	Cert to	Peter, Robert	1797	B2B	461	150
Commissioners (S1, L12)	Cert to	Konig, Heinrich, of G'tn.	1793	B2A	307	430
Commissioners (S1, L12)	Cert to	Cook, Thomas & Jos. E. Rowles	1796	B2B	453	141
Commissioners (S1, L13)	Cert to	Harbaugh, Leonard	1796	B2B	456	145
Commissioners (S1, L13)	Cert to	Cook, Thomas	1796	B2B	456	145
Commissioners (S1, L8, 10)	Cert to	Harbaugh, Leonard	1796	B2B	456	145
Commissioners (S1, L9)	Cert to	Harbough, Leonard	1798	B2B	482	175
Commissioners (S10, L1, 3)	Deed to	Hoban, James	1798	C3	319	257
Commissioners (S101, L18)	Cert to	Forrest, Uriah, of Montg. Co.	1797	B2B	476	169
Commissioners (S101, L18)	Cert to	Campbell, William	1797	B2B	474	167
Commissioners (S101, L7, 19)	Cert to	Pierce, Thomas	1795	B2A	332	465
Commissioners (S102, L2)	Cert to	Ross, Richard, of Bladensburgh	1793	B2A	313	441
Commissioners (S102, L2)	Cert to	Ross, Richard	1796	B2B	455	144
Commissioners (S105, L14)	Cert to	Stiner, Jacob, Jr.	1795	B2A	333	468
Commissioners (S105, L3)	Cert to	Harrison, Richard, of Phila.	1797	B2B	463	155
Commissioners (S105, L4)	Cert to	Lear, Tobias, of Portsmouth NH	1792	B2A	284	398
Commissioners (S105, L4)	Cert to	Lear, Tobias	1795	B2A	330	463
Commissioners (S105, L7, 8)	Cert to	Sluby, Nicholas	1795	B2A	331	464
Commissioners (S1054, L2)	Cert to	Boone, Joseph, of P.G. Co.	1797	B2B	475	167
Commissioners (S107, L4)	Cert to	Gilchrist, James, of Phila.	1792	B2A	285	398

Index to District of Columbia Land Records, 1792-1817

Party	What	Party	Year	Liber	Old	New
Commissioners (S119, L13)	Cert to	May, Frederick & Samuel Eliot, Jr.	1798	B2B	477	170
Commissioners (S122, L5)	Cert to	Maniville, Mary, w/o Patrick	1794	B2A	324	455
Commissioners (S122, L7)	Cert to	French, William et al	1793	B2A	322	452
Commissioners (S124, L4)	Cert to	Klinger, Henry	1793	B2A	316½	446
Commissioners (S126, L22, 23)	Cert to	Welsh, Jacob, of Lunenburg MA	1792	B2A	284	397
Commissioners (S126, L28)	Cert to	Casanave, Peter, of G'tn.	1792	B2A	283	395
Commissioners (S126, L29)	Cert to	Shippen, Thomas Lee, of Phila.	1791	B2A	283	396
Commissioners (S126, L29)	Cert to	Shippen, Thomas Lee, of Phila.	1791	B2A	283	396
Commissioners (S126, L31)	Cert to	Carroll, Henry	1795	B2A	333	467
Commissioners (S127, L28, 29)	Cert to	Lee, Thomas Sim	1795	B2A	330	463
Commissioners (S143, L10)	Cert to	Gridley, Richard	1797	B2B	462	152
Commissioners (S15, L1-3)	Cert to	Johnson, Thomas	1796	B2B	453	139
Commissioners (S15, L13-16)	Cert to	Johnson, Thomas	1796	B2B	452	139
Commissioners (S16, L15, 16)	Cert to	Hellen, Walter	1795	B2A	331	465
Commissioners (S16, L17)	Cert to	Hoban, James & Peirce Purcell	1792	B2A	290	406
Commissioners (S16, L22, 23)	Cert to	Ober, Richard	1795	B2A	329	461
Commissioners (S16, L22)	Cert to	Ober, Richard, of G'tn.	1792	B2A	291	407
Commissioners (S16, L23)	Cert to	Ober, Richard, of G'tn.	1792	B2A	290	406
Commissioners (S168, L21)	Cert to	Forrest, Uriah	1797	B2B	472	164
Commissioners (S169, L19, 20)	Cert to	Gadsden, Philip	1796	B2B	454	142
Commissioners (S169, L21)	Cert to	Brown, James, of Q.A. Co.	1799	B2B	483	176
Commissioners (S170, L15, 16)	Cert to	Peter, Robert	1797	B2B	461	150
Commissioners (S170, L7, 8)	Cert to	Scott, Gustavus	1796	B2B	457	145
Commissioners (S171, L east of)	Deed to	Queen of Portugal	1798	C3	474	374
Commissioners (S172, L1)	Cert to	Weems, John, Dr., of G'tn.	1793	B2A	309	434
Commissioners (S172, L1)	Deed to	Crawford, David	1798	C3	509	400
Commissioners (S200, L1)	Cert to	Blodget, Samuel, Boston MA	1792	B2A	295	414
Commissioners (S200, L10)	Cert to	Stuart, Walter, of Phila. PA	1793	B2A	301	422
Commissioners (S200, L11)	Cert to	Stuart, Walter, of Phila. PA	1793	B2A	302	424
Commissioners (S200, L16)	Cert to	Purcell, Peirce & James Hoban	1792	B2A	299	420
Commissioners (S200, L17)	Cert to	Purcell, Peirce & James Hoban	1792	B2A	299	419
Commissioners (S200, L2)	Cert to	Templeman, John, of Boston MA	1792	B2A	293	410
Commissioners (S200, L3)	Cert to	Ketland, [Thomas], of Phila. PA	1792	B2A	296	415
Commissioners (S200, L3)	Cert to	Ketland, Thomas	1798	B2B	480	173
Commissioners (S200, L8)	Cert to	Stuart, Walter, of Phila. PA	1793	B2A	303	425
Commissioners (S200, L9)	Cert to	Stuart, Walter, of Phila. PA	1793	B2A	302	424
Commissioners (S21, L1)	Cert to	Washington, George, Esq.	1798	B2B	482	175
Commissioners (S21, L4)	Cert to	Washington, George, Esq.	1798	B2B	481	175
Commissioners (S218, L1)	Deed to	Emery, John	1804	L11	118	121
Commissioners (S218, L22)	Deed to	Emery, John	1804	L11	117	120
Commissioners (S221, whole)	Cert to	Davidson, Samuel	1793	B2A	306	429
Commissioners (S221, whole)	Cert to	Davidson, Samuel	1794	B2A	323	453
Commissioners (S222, L10)	Deed to	Sutton, Robert	1798	C3	482	380
Commissioners (S224, L1)	Cert to	Beatty, Thomas J., of G'tn.	1792	B2A	288	403
Commissioners (S224, L1)	Cert to	Purcell, Pierce	1796	B2B	452	138
Commissioners (S224, L12)	Cert to	Washington, William Augustine	1792	B2A	287	401
Commissioners (S224, L12)	Cert to	Gouges, Arnauld	1795	B2A	334	468
Commissioners (S224, L12)	Cert to	Washington, William A.	1795	B2A	334	468
Commissioners (S224, L13)	Cert to	Washington, William Augustine	1792	B2A	287	401
Commissioners (S224, L13)	Cert to	Washington, William A.	1795	B2A	334	469
Commissioners (S224, L13)	Cert to	Gouges, Arnauld	1795	B2A	334	469
Commissioners (S224, L16)	Cert to	Beatty, Thoams J., of G'tn.	1792	B2A	288	402
Commissioners (S224, L16)	Cert to	Purcell, Pierce	1796	B2B	452	138
Commissioners (S224, L4)	Cert to	Hoban, James & Peirce Purcell	1792	B2A	288	403
Commissioners (S224, L5)	Cert to	Hoban, James	1798	B2B	476	169

Party	What	Party	Year	Liber	Old	New
Commissioners (S224, L8)	Cert to	Burnes, David, of P.G. Co.	1792	B2A	286	400
Commissioners (S224, L9)	Cert to	Burnes, David, of P.G. Co.	1792	B2A	287	402
Commissioners (S224, whole)	Deed to	Jackson, John G.	1810	X23	352	282
Commissioners (S225, L1)	Cert to	Stuart, Walter, of Phila. PA	1793	B2A	302	423
Commissioners (S225, L10)	Cert to	Roe, Patrick McDermot, of G'tn.	1792	B2A	298	417
Commissioners (S225, L11)	Cert to	Metcalf, Thomas, of Phila. PA	1792	B2A	293	410
Commissioners (S225, L11)	Cert to	Metcalf, Thomas	1796	B2B	452	140
Commissioners (S225, L16)	Cert to	Stuart, Walter, of Phila. PA	1793	B2A	303	426
Commissioners (S225, L2)	Cert to	Stewart, Walter, of Phila. PA	1793	B2A	300	421
Commissioners (S225, L3)	Cert to	Stuart, Walter, of Phila. PA	1793	B2A	303	425
Commissioners (S225, L4, 5)	Deed to	Hoban, James	1798	C3	484	381
Commissioners (S225, L4)	Cert to	Moore, Thomas L., of Phila. PA	1793	B2A	301	422
Commissioners (S225, L5)	Cert to	Moore, Thomas L., of Phila. PA	1793	B2A	301	423
Commissioners (S225, L6)	Cert to	Gilman, Peter, of Boston MA	1792	B2A	294	413
Commissioners (S225, L7)	Cert to	Blodget, Samuel, Jr., Boston MA	1792	B2A	294	412
Commissioners (S225, L8)	Cert to	Blodget, Benjamin, of Boston MA	1792	B2A	295	414
Commissioners (S228, L6)	Cert to	Philips, Nathaniel, of Phila. PA	1793	B2A	304	427
Commissioners (S228, L6)	Deed to	Hay, Robert	1798	C3	493	387
Commissioners (S252, L21)	Deed to	Hay, Robert	1798	C3	494	389
Commissioners (S253, L1)	Deed to	Sherrard, Francis	1798	C3	464	365
Commissioners (S253, L6)	Cert to	Roe, Cornelius McDermot, of G'tn.	1792	B2A	292	409
Commissioners (S253, L7)	Cert to	Templeman, John, of Boston MA	1792	B2A	297	417
Commissioners (S253, L7)	Cert to	Templeman, John	1795	B2A	335	471
Commissioners (S253, L8)	Cert to	Templeman, John, of Boston MA	1792	B2A	297	417
Commissioners (S253, L9)	Cert to	Templeman, John, of Boston MA	1792	B2A	297	416
Commissioners (S254, L1)	Cert to	Roe, Cornelius McDermot, of G'tn.	1792	B2A	292	409
Commissioners (S254, L10)	Cert to	Stephenson, Clotworthy	1796	B2B	457	147
Commissioners (S254, L11)	Cert to	Williamson, Colin, of G'tn.	1792	B2A	289	405
Commissioners (S254, L11)	Cert to	Williamson, Collin	1796	B2A	339	477
Commissioners (S254, L2)	Cert to	Davidson, Samuel	1793	B2A	306	429
Commissioners (S254, L2)	Cert to	Davidson, Samuel	1794	B2A	323	453
Commissioners (S254, L5)	Cert to	Harbaugh, Leonard	1796	B2B	456	144
Commissioners (S254, L7)	Cert to	Van Horne, Gabriel P., of P.G. Co.	1792	B2A	289	404
Commissioners (S259, L9)	Cert to	Gridley, Richard	1797	B2B	474	166
Commissioners (S288, L14)	Cert to	May, Frederick & Samuel Eliot, Jr.	1798	B2B	477	171
Commissioners (S289, L1)	Cert to	Edwards, Henry	1797	B2B	458	148
Commissioners (S289, L13)	Cert to	Davidson, Samuel	1793	B2A	306	429
Commissioners (S290, L11)	Cert to	Richmond, Christopher	1795	B2A	334	470
Commissioners (S290, L12)	Cert to	Edwards, Henry	1793	B2A	307	431
Commissioners (S290, L12)	Cert to	Richmond, Christopher	1796	B2A	337	473
Commissioners (S290, L12)	Cert to	Edwards, Henry	1796	B2A	337	473
Commissioners (S290, L13)	Cert to	Ketland, [Thomas], of Phila. PA	1792	B2A	293	411
Commissioners (S290, L13)	Cert to	Jones, Charles	1793	B2A	307	431
Commissioners (S290, L13)	Cert to	Sweeny, George & Sarah	1797	B2B	459	148
Commissioners (S320, L7)	Deed to	Hellriggle, Christian L.	1798	C3	503	395
Commissioners (S323, L8)	Cert to	Roe, Cornelius McDermot, of G'tn.	1792	B2A	291	408
Commissioners (S323, L9)	Cert to	Roe, Cornelius McDermot, of G'tn.	1792	B2A	292	408
Commissioners (S33, L5, 6)*	Cert to	Thornton, William, Dr.	1797	B2B	475	168
Commissioners (S346, L1, 7-8)	Deed to	Lenox, Peter	1798	C3	471	371
Commissioners (S347, L2)	Deed to	Lenox, Peter	1798	C3	471	371
Commissioners (S351N, L2)	Cert to	May, Frederick & Samuel Eliot, Jr.	1798	B2B	477	170
Commissioners (S376, L5, 6)	Cert to	Caffray, Anthony, Rev.	1798	B2B	478	172
Commissioners (S376, L7)	Cert to	Caffray, Anthony, Rev.	1798	B2B	479	172
Commissioners (S377, L1)	Cert to	Crocker, John	1797	B2B	464	155
Commissioners (S4, L1)	Cert to	Ober, Richard, of G'tn.	1792	B2A	291	407

Index to District of Columbia Land Records, 1792-1817

Party	What	Party	Year	Liber	Old	New
Commissioners (S4, L1)	Cert to	Ober, Richard	1795	B2A	329	461
Commissioners (S4, L2)	Cert to	Lee, Richard Bland, of VA	1792	B2A	289	405
Commissioners (S4, L2)	Cert to	Scott, Sabret	1797	B2B	468	161
Commissioners (S406, L4)	Cert to	Estave, Andrew	1796	B2A	335	471
Commissioners (S406, L4)	Cert to	Deakins, William Jr., of G'tn.	1796	B2A	335	471
Commissioners (S406, L5, 6)	Cert to	Deakins, William Jr.	1796	B2A	338	476
Commissioners (S407, L12, 13)	Cert to	Philips, Grout & West	1797	B2B	464	155
Commissioners (S408, L1)	Cert to	Bond, Nathan, of Boston MA	1792	B2A	294	411
Commissioners (S408, L1)	Cert to	Bond, Nathan, of Boston MA	1796	B2A	337	475
Commissioners (S408, L2)	Cert to	Bond, Nathan, of Boston MA	1792	B2A	296	416
Commissioners (S408, L2)	Cert to	Bond, Nathan, of Boston MA	1796	B2A	338	476
Commissioners (S431, L12)	Cert to	Kid, Robert, of Phila. PA	1793	B2A	312	439
Commissioners (S431, L7, 8)	Cert to	Dermot, James R.	1796	B2A	336	472
Commissioners (S431, L7)	Cert to	Dermot, James R.	1793	B2A	313	440
Commissioners (S431, L8)	Cert to	Dermot, James R.	1793	B2A	312	439
Commissioners (S456, L17, 18)	Cert to	Morris, Robert & John Nicholson	1796	B2B	452	140
Commissioners (S457, L18)	Cert to	Jamieson, Andrew & Jas. Maitland	1796	B2B	455	142
Commissioners (S457, L18)	Cert to	Maitland, James	1796	B2B	455	143
Commissioners (S488, L2, 3)	Cert to	Matthews, William Penrose, Balto.	1798	B2B	478	171
Commissioners (S489, L1)	Cert to	Purcell, Peirce & James Hoban	1792	B2A	299	419
Commissioners (S489, L13)	Cert to	Davidson, Samuel	1794	B2A	323	453
Commissioners (S489, L2)	Cert to	Hoban, James & Peirce Purcell	1792	B2A	298	418
Commissioners (S5, L11, 17)	Cert to	Crawford, David	1797	B2B	473	165
Commissioners (S5, L11)	Cert to	Contee, Richard A.	1797	B2B	463	154
Commissioners (S5, L11)	Cert to	Smith, V. & Suter, et al.	1797	B2B	463	154
Commissioners (S5, L12)	Cert to	Warley, George	1794	B2A		457
Commissioners (S5, L18)	Cert to	Stephenson, Clotworthy	1796	B2B	458	147
Commissioners (S5, L8)	Cert to	Ober, Richard, of G'tn.	1792	B2A	289	404
Commissioners (S5, L8)	Cert to	Ober, Richard	1795	B2A	329	461
Commissioners (S532, L1)	Cert to	Burrows, Edward, of P.G. Co.	1793	B2A	314	442
Commissioners (S532, L1)	Cert to	Burrows, Edward	1797	B2B	462	153
Commissioners (S533, L5)	Cert to	Bond, Nathan, of Boston MA	1792	B2A	296	415
Commissioners (S533, L5)	Cert to	Bond, Nathan, of Boston MA	1796	B2A	337	474
Commissioners (S533, L6)	Cert to	Bond, Nathan, of Boston MA	1792	B2A	295	413
Commissioners (S533, L6)	Cert to	Bond, Nathan, of Boston MA	1796	B2A	337	475
Commissioners (S57, L4)	Cert to	Warring, Marsham, of G'tn.	1793	B2A	313	441
Commissioners (S598, L10)	Cert to	United States	1794	B2A	327	459
Commissioners (S598, L4)	Cert to	United States	1794	B2A	327	459
Commissioners (S598, L8)	Cert to	United States	1794	B2A	329	461
Commissioners (S599, L6)	Cert to	United States	1794	B2A	326	457
Commissioners (S603, L1-3, 14)	Cert to	United States	1794	B2A	328	460
Commissioners (S604, L3)	Cert to	United States	1794	B2A	327	458
Commissioners (S606, L2)	Cert to	Washington, William A.	1793	B2A	318	447
Commissioners (S607, L7)	Cert to	Washington, William A.	1793	B2A	315	443
Commissioners (S608, L4)	Cert to	Coolidge, Samuel J.	1794	B2A	325	456
Commissioners (S609, L9)	Cert to	Washington, William A.	1793	B2A	319	449
Commissioners (S610, L13)	Cert to	United States	1794	B2A	328	460
Commissioners (S611, L15)	Cert to	United States	1794	B2A	329	461
Commissioners (S634, L2, 3)	Cert to	Gadsden, Philip	1796	B2B	454	142
Commissioners (S651, L1)	Cert to	Coolidge, Samuel J.	1794	B2A	325	456
Commissioners (S653, L10)	Cert to	Augustine, William	1793	B2A	315	442
Commissioners (S653, L19)	Cert to	United States	1794	B2A	328	460
Commissioners (S655, L2)	Cert to	Hooe, Robert T.	1793	B2A	322	453
Commissioners (S656, L9)	Cert to	United States	1794	B2A	328	460
Commissioners (S660, L6)	Cert to	United States	1794	B2A	329	461

Index to District of Columbia Land Records, 1792-1817

Party	What	Party	Year	Liber	Old	New
Commissioners (S662, L1)	Cert to	Barry, James	1796	B2A	339	478
Commissioners (S662, L6)	Cert to	United States	1794	B2A	327	459
Commissioners (S663, L7)	Cert to	Washington, William A.	1793	B2A	320	450
Commissioners (S664, L3)	Cert to	Washington, William A.	1793	B2A	319	449
Commissioners (S664, L4)	Cert to	Lear, Tobias & Co.	1793	B2A	308	432
Commissioners (S664, L5)	Cert to	Lear, Tobias & Co.	1793	B2A	308	432
Commissioners (S664, L6)	Cert to	United States	1794	B2A	328	460
Commissioners (S665, L multiple)	Cert to	Carroll, Daniel, of *Duddington*	1797	B2B	461	151
Commissioners (S665, L16)	Cert to	Carroll, Daniel	1793	B2A	310	435
Commissioners (S665, L17)	Cert to	Carroll, Daniel, of *Duddington*	1793	B2A	310	434
Commissioners (S665, L18)	Cert to	Carroll, Daniel, of *Duddington*	1793	B2A	310	436
Commissioners (S665, L22)	Cert to	Carroll, Daniel, of *Duddington*	1793	B2A	308	433
Commissioners (S666, L1)	Cert to	United States	1794	B2A	328	460
Commissioners (S667, L11)	Cert to	United States	1794	B2A	327	458
Commissioners (S667, L12-14)	Cert to	Washington, George, Pres.	1793	B2A	311	437
Commissioners (S667, L15)	Cert to	Carroll, Daniel	1793	B2A	309	434
Commissioners (S667, L5, 12-14)	Cert to	Washington, George, Esq.	1798	B2B	481	174
Commissioners (S667, L5)	Cert to	Washington, George, Pres.	1793	B2A	310	436
Commissioners (S690, portion)	Cert to	Law, Thomas	1796	B2A	336	473
Commissioners (S693, half)	Cert to	Law, Thomas	1796	B2A	336	473
Commissioners (S699, portion)	Cert to	Law, Thomas	1796	B2A	336	473
Commissioners (S703, L2)	Cert to	United States	1794	B2A	327	459
Commissioners (S704, L8)	Cert to	Washington, William A.	1793	B2A	317½	446
Commissioners (S705, L2)	Cert to	Dermott, James R.	1797	B2B	468	160
Commissioners (S707, L2)	Cert to	Decloise, Lewis	1798	B2B	479	173
Commissioners (S708, L10, 11)	Cert to	Barry, James, mer., of Balto.	1797	B2B	469	161
Commissioners (S708, L4, 5)	Cert to	Barry, James, mer., of Balto.	1797	B2B	469	161
Commissioners (S708, L4)	Cert to	Barry, James	1796	B2B	451	137
Commissioners (S708, L5, 8)	Cert to	Barry, James	1796	B2A	339	478
Commissioners (S725, L1)	Cert to	Carroll, Daniel, of *Duddington*	1793	B2A	311	437
Commissioners (S725, L2)	Cert to	Dermot, James R., of G'tn.	1793	B2A	312	439
Commissioners (S725, L3)	Cert to	Casanave, Peter	1796	B2A	335	472
Commissioners (S725, L3)	Cert to	Dermott, James R.	1796	B2A	335	472
Commissioners (S725, L7)	Cert to	Dulany, Benjamin, of VA	1793	B2A	311	438
Commissioners (S728, L14, 15)	Cert to	Nicholls, Henry	1795	B2A	332	466
Commissioners (S728, L14)	Cert to	Nicholls, Henry, of Balto.	1793	B2A	300	420
Commissioners (S728, L15)	Cert to	Nicholls, Henry, of Balto.	1793	B2A	300	421
Commissioners (S728, L16)	Cert to	Washington, Lund	1797	B2B	467	160
Commissioners (S728, L5)	Cert to	Nicklin, Philip, of Phila. PA	1793	B2A	304	427
Commissioners (S729, L10)	Cert to	Watson, James, of NY	1793	B2A		429
Commissioners (S729, L18)	Cert to	Watson, James, of NY	1793	B2A	305	428
Commissioners (S729, L22)	Cert to	Crammond, James, of Phila. PA	1793	B2A	305	428
Commissioners (S729, L22)	Cert to	Crammond, James	1795	B2A	332	467
Commissioners (S729, L23)	Cert to	Coles, [John], of Phila. PA	1793	B2A	304	426
Commissioners (S729, L23)	Cert to	Coles, John	1795	B2A	331	464
Commissioners (S729, L27)	Cert to	Robertson, Alexander	1796	B2A	338	477
Commissioners (S729, L8, 9, 26)	Cert to	Hoban, James	1797	B2B	462	152
Commissioners (S732, portion)	Cert to	Law, Thomas	1796	B2A	336	473
Commissioners (S74, L5, 12-13)	Cert to	Polock, Isaac	1804	K10	382	396
Commissioners (S74, L6, 9-10)	Cert to	Polock, Isaac	1804	K10	382	396
Commissioners (S740, whole)	Cert to	Law, Thomas	1796	B2A	336	473
Commissioners (S741, whole)	Cert to	Law, Thomas	1796	B2A	336	473
Commissioners (S743, portion)	Cert to	Law, Thomas	1796	B2A	336	473
Commissioners (S744, whole)	Cert to	Law, Thomas	1796	B2A	336	473
Commissioners (S75, L13-14)	Deed to	Hodgson, Joseph	1798	C3	331	267

Party	What	Party	Year	Liber	Old	New
Commissioners (S770, portion)	Cert to	Law, Thomas	1796	B2A	336	473
Commissioners (S771, L2, 3)	Cert to	Barry, James, of Balto.	1796	B2B	454	141
Commissioners (S78, L1, 30)	Cert to	O'Neale, William	1797	B2B	465	157
Commissioners (S78, L10)	Cert to	O'Neale, William	1797	B2B	467	159
Commissioners (S78, L19, 20)	Cert to	Gilchrist, James, of Phila.	1792	B2A	285	298
Commissioners (S78, L2)	Cert to	O'Neale, William	1795	B2A	334	469
Commissioners (S78, L3)	Cert to	Hodgson, Joseph	1795	B2A	330	462
Commissioners (S78, L9, 10)	Cert to	Welsh, Jacob, of Lunenburg MA	1792	B2A	286	400
Commissioners (S78, L9)	Cert to	O'Neale, William	1797	B2B	467	159
Commissioners (S79, L10)	Cert to	Welch, Jacob, of Lunenburg MA	1792	B2A	285	399
Commissioners (S79, L3)	Cert to	Porter, Samuel & James Sterrett	1793	B2A	316	444
Commissioners (S79, L5)	Cert to	Davidson, John	1795	B2A	334	470
Commissioners (S79, L7, 19)	Cert to	Peirce, Thomas, of Smithfield VA	1792	B2A	285	399
Commissioners (S8, L1-7, 17-18)	Deed to	Templeman, John	1798	C3	287	232
Commissioners (S80, L6)	Cert to	Klinger, Henry	1793	B2A	317	445
Commissioners (S802, L4-6)	Cert to	Law, Thomas	1797	B2B	472	165
Commissioners (S802, L7)	Cert to	Dermott, James Reed	1796	B2B	457	146
Commissioners (S81, L14)	Cert to	French, William et al	1793	B2A	321	451
Commissioners (S83, L1)	Cert to	Schnebely, Henry, Dr.	1797	B2B	461	151
Commissioners (S9, L3)	Cert to	Lear, Tobias, of Phila. PA	1793	B2A	306	430
Commissioners (S9, L3)	Cert to	Lear, Tobias	1797	B2B	464	156
Commissioners (SE667, L4-6)	Cert to	Washington, George, Esq.	1798	B2B	481	174
Commissioners (SE98, L10)	Cert to	Cunningham, Cornelius	1798	B2B	480	173
Commissioners of Turnpike Road	Certificate		1811	AB27	193	159
Commissioners of Washington	Cert to	United States	1794	B2A	329	461
Commissioners of Washington	Cert to	United States	1794	B2A	328	460
Commissioners of Washington	Cert to	Young, Notley	1794	B2A	109	145
Commissioners of Washington	Cert to	Greenleaf, James, New York NY	1794	B2A	143	188
Commissioners of Washington	Assign to	United States	1794	B2A	121	162
Commissioners of Washington	Deed fr	Greenleaf, James, New York NY	1795	B2A	229	318
Commissioners of Washington	Cert to	Morris, Wash. R. & Jas. Greenleaf	1796	B2A	336	473
Commissioners of Washington	Cert to	Barry, James	1796	B2B	451	137
Commissioners of Washington	Request fr	Washington, George, Pres.	1796	B2B	588	336
Commissioners of Washington	Agreement	Greenleaf, James & Robert Morris	1796	B2B	541	263
Commissioners of Washington	Agreement	Morris, Robert & James Greenleaf	1796	B2B	544	267
Commissioners of Washington	Request fr	Washington, George, Pres.	1796	B2B	588	336
Commissioners of Washington	Agreement	Greenleaf, James & Robert Morris	1796	B2B	544	267
Commissioners of Washington	Agreement	Greenleaf, James	1796	B2B	540	261
Commissioners of Washington	Agreement	Greenleaf, James	1796	B2B	544	267
Commissioners of Washington	Deed fr	Morris, Robert, of Phila.	1796	B2B	419	091
Commissioners of Washington	Agreement	Young, Notley	1797	B2B	463	153
Commissioners of Washington	Deed fr	Beall, Thomas & John M. Gantt	1797	B2B	616	372
Commissioners of Washington	Cert to	Burrows, Edward	1797	B2B	462	153
Commissioners of Washington	Order	United States, to survey streets	1798	C3	320	259
Commissioners of Washington	Deed to	Polock, Isaac	1798	D4	097	082
Commissioners of Washington	Deed to	Bacon, Benjamin	1798	D4	112	095
Commissioners of Washington	Deed to	Forrest, Uriah et al	1798	D4	137	119
Commissioners of Washington	Deed to	Forrest, Uriah et al	1798	D4	135	118
Commissioners of Washington	Deed to	Brent, Robert	1798	D4	119	102
Commissioners of Washington	Cert to	Robertson, Alexander, stonecutter	1799	D4	379	363
Commissioners of Washington	Deed to	Thompson, Hugh, of Balto.	1799	D4	227	210
Commissioners of Washington	Deed to	Sprigg, Margaret	1799	D4	421	394
Commissioners of Washington	Deed to	Blagden, George	1799	D4	327	312
Commissioners of Washington	Deed to	Truxton, Thomas	1799	D4	412	388
Commissioners of Washington	Deed to	Dalton, Tristram	1799	D4	319	303

Index to District of Columbia Land Records, 1792-1817

Party	What	Party	Year	Liber	Old	New
Commissioners of Washington	Cert to	Bayly, William	1799	D4	300	284
Commissioners of Washington	Deed to	Walker, George	1799	D4	254	238
Commissioners of Washington	Deed to	Jackson, Jonathan	1799	D4	231	213
Commissioners of Washington	Deed to	Chandler, Walter S.	1799	D4	224	207
Commissioners of Washington	Cert to	Forrest, Uriah	1799	D4	361	347
Commissioners of Washington	Deed to	Pratt, Carey, of Winchester VA	1799	D4	185	167
Commissioners of Washington	Deed to	Lingan, James M., of G'tn.	1799	D4	392	373
Commissioners of Washington	Deed to	Sewall, Robert	1799	D4	252	236
Commissioners of Washington	Deed to	McHenry, James, Sec., of Phila.	1799	D4	352	340
Commissioners of Washington	Deed to	Mercer, John, of Fredericksburg	1799	D4	415	391
Commissioners of Washington	Agreement	Moore, James, butcher, of G'tn.	1799	D4	335	322
Commissioners of Washington	Deed to	Whann, William	1799	D4	277	260
Commissioners of Washington	Deed to	Truxton, Thomas	1799	D4	411	388
Commissioners of Washington	Deed to	Mercer, John Francis	1799	D4	412	389
Commissioners of Washington	Deed to	Fenwick, Bennett	1799	D4	403	382
Commissioners of Washington	Cert to	Barry, James, of Balto.	1799	D4	387	369
Commissioners of Washington	Deed to	Mercer, John Francis	1799	D4	418	393
Commissioners of Washington	Cert to	Langley, Edward	1799	D4	386	368
Commissioners of Washington	Cert to	Barry, James, of Balto.	1799	D4	386	369
Commissioners of Washington	Deed to	Van Maunierck, Anthony, of PA	1799	D4	330	316
Commissioners of Washington	Deed to	Elliott, Richard	1799	D4	337	324
Commissioners of Washington	Deed to	Cunningham, Cornelius	1799	D4	324	309
Commissioners of Washington	Deed to	Dermott, James Reed	1799	D4	260	245
Commissioners of Washington	Deed to	Cook, Charles	1799	D4	262	247
Commissioners of Washington	Deed to	Nourse, Joseph, of Phila.	1799	D4	302	286
Commissioners of Washington	Deed to	Plowden, Edward, St. Mary's Co.	1799	D4	340	327
Commissioners of Washington	Cert to	Kirk, Milesius Thomas	1799	D4	362	348
Commissioners of Washington	Deed to	Roe, Edward McDermott	1799	D4	381	365
Commissioners of Washington	Deed to	Eliot, Samuel	1799	D4	222	205
Commissioners of Washington	Deed to	Harrison, Richard, of Phila.	1799	D4	246	229
Commissioners of Washington	Deed to	Dermott, John James	1799	D4	258	243
Commissioners of Washington	Deed to	Davidson, William et al	1799	D4	226	208
Commissioners of Washington	Deed to	Kerr, Alexander, of Alexa.	1799	E5	055	044
Commissioners of Washington	Deed to	Barry, James, of Balto.	1799	E5	039	029
Commissioners of Washington	Deed to	Kearney, John	1799	E5	037	027
Commissioners of Washington	Deed to	Barry, James, of Balto.	1799	E5	041	031
Commissioners of Washington	Deed to	Barry, James, of Balto.	1799	E5	044	034
Commissioners of Washington	Deed to	Lewis, Lawrence, of VA	1799	E5	046	036
Commissioners of Washington	Deed to	Willson, Samuel	1800	E5	226	220
Commissioners of Washington	Deed to	Chandler, Walter S. et al	1800	E5	131	119
Commissioners of Washington	Deed to	Peter, Robert, of G'tn.	1800	E5	198	190
Commissioners of Washington	Deed to	Crookshank, John et al	1800	E5	131	119
Commissioners of Washington	Deed to	Chandler, Walter S., of G'tn.	1800	E5	126	114
Commissioners of Washington	Deed to	Brent, William	1800	E5	119	106
Commissioners of Washington	Deed to	Carroll, Carroll, of *Duddington*	1800	E5	124	112
Commissioners of Washington	Deed to	Chandler, Walter S., of G'tn.	1800	E5	121	109
Commissioners of Washington	Deed to	Clokey, Samuel	1800	E5	329	318
Commissioners of Washington	Deed to	Carter, Charles, of *Shirley*	1800	E5	083	070
Commissioners of Washington	Deed to	Swann, John, of Balto.	1800	E5	397	372
Commissioners of Washington	Deed to	Nicklin, Philip et al	1800	E5	116	104
Commissioners of Washington	Deed to	Corcoran, Thomas	1800	E5	103	091
Commissioners of Washington	Deed to	Mickle, John, of Balto.	1800	E5	221	214
Commissioners of Washington	Deed fr	Pollard, Robert et al	1800	E5	154	143
Commissioners of Washington	Deed to	Calder, James, of G'tn.	1800	E5	235	228
Commissioners of Washington	Deed fr	Johnson, Charles et al	1800	E5	154	143

Index to District of Columbia Land Records, 1792-1817

Party	What	Party	Year	Liber	Old	New
Commissioners of Washington	Deed to	English, David et al	1800	E5	139	128
Commissioners of Washington	Deed to	Smallwood, Samuel N.	1800	E5	143	132
Commissioners of Washington	Deed fr	Pickell, George et al	1800	E5	154	143
Commissioners of Washington	Deed fr	United States	1800	E5	149	137
Commissioners of Washington	Deed to	Coltman, William	1800	E5	288	281
Commissioners of Washington	Deed to	Hoban, James	1800	E5	383	361
Commissioners of Washington	Deed to	Middleton, Joseph	1800	E5	189	180
Commissioners of Washington	Cert to	Movin, Lewis	1800	E5	337	324
Commissioners of Washington	Cert to	Deblois, Lewis	1800	E5		356
Commissioners of Washington	Surveys	United States	1800	E5	406	379
Commissioners of Washington	Agreement	Piercy, James	1800	E5	192	183
Commissioners of Washington	Deed to	Collard, George	1800	E5	106	093
Commissioners of Washington	Cert to	Powell, Cuthbert	1800	E5		158
Commissioners of Washington	Order	Survey streets in B. & H. Addtn.	1800	E5		379
Commissioners of Washington	Deed to	Middleton, James	1800	E5	108	095
Commissioners of Washington	Deed to	Coltman, William	1800	E5		282
Commissioners of Washington	Deed to	Hoban, James	1800	E5	161	150
Commissioners of Washington	Deed to	Veitch, William	1800	E5	109	097
Commissioners of Washington	Cert to	Kearney, James	1800	E5	381	359
Commissioners of Washington	Deed to	McNantz, Charles	1800	E5	223	216
Commissioners of Washington	Cert to	Barksdale, William	1800	E5	250	244
Commissioners of Washington	Cert to	Kearney, John	1800	E5	403	376
Commissioners of Washington	Cert to	Barksdale, William	1800	E5	250	243
Commissioners of Washington	Cert to	Deblois, Lewis	1800	E5	357	341
Commissioners of Washington	Deed to	Frost, Amariah	1800	E5	190	181
Commissioners of Washington	Deed to	Pratt, Henry et al	1800	E5	372	353
Commissioners of Washington	Deed to	Corcoran, Thomas, of G'tn.	1800	E5	301	293
Commissioners of Washington	Deed to	Clokey, Samuel	1800	E5	328	316
Commissioners of Washington	Deed fr	Chandler, Walter S., of Balto.	1800	E5	122	110
Commissioners of Washington	Deed to	Clephan, Lewis, printer	1800	E5	104	091
Commissioners of Washington	Deed to	Pratt, Henry et al	1800	E5	369	350
Commissioners of Washington	Deed to	Green, Charles D. et al	1800	E5	139	128
Commissioners of Washington	Cert to	Deakins, Francis	1800	E5	162	151
Commissioners of Washington	Deed to	Key, Philip Barton, of Annapolis	1800	E5	322	312
Commissioners of Washington	Deed to	Griffith, Robert Eaglefield et al	1800	E5	117	104
Commissioners of Washington	Deed to	Calder, James, of G'tn.	1800	E5	285	280
Commissioners of Washington	Deed to	Lavely, Catherine, of Balto.	1800	E5	340	327
Commissioners of Washington	Deed to	Calder, James, of G'tn.	1800	E5	285	279
Commissioners of Washington	Deed to	Wilson, John C., of Princess Ann	1800	F6	066	041
Commissioners of Washington	Deed to	Thompson, James	1800	F6	071	044
Commissioners of Washington	Deed to	Campbell, Hugh G., U.S.N.	1800	F6	050	031
Commissioners of Washington	Cert to	Lynn, Adam	1800	F6	014	010
Commissioners of Washington	Deed to	Smallwood, Samuel N.	1800	F6	081	050
Commissioners of Washington	Deed to	Traverse, Nicholas & Elias E.	1800	F6	110	068
Commissioners of Washington	Cert to	Smith, Samuel, of Balto.	1800	F6	089	054
Commissioners of Washington	Deed to	Snyder, Jacob	1800	F6	047	030
Commissioners of Washington	Deed to	Thompson, James	1800	F6	068	042
Commissioners of Washington	Deed to	Forrest, Uriah	1800	F6	004	004
Commissioners of Washington	Deed to	Ardray, John, of G'tn.	1800	F6	007	005
Commissioners of Washington	Deed to	Brown, Robert	1800	F6	077	047
Commissioners of Washington	Deed to	Densley, Hugh	1800	F6	096	059
Commissioners of Washington	Cert to	Gilchrist, James	1800	F6	065	040
Commissioners of Washington	Deed to	Wadsworth, Charles	1800	F6	030	019
Commissioners of Washington	Deed to	May, John, of Boston MA	1800	F6	036	023
Commissioners of Washington	Deed to	Gaither, Henry, Col., U.S.A.	1800	F6	075	046

Party	What	Party	Year	Liber	Old	New
Commissioners of Washington	Deed to	Densley, Hugh	1800	F6	094	058
Commissioners of Washington	Cert to	Kerr, Alexander	1800	F6		025
Commissioners of Washington	Cert to	Gaither, Henry	1800	F6	049	031
Commissioners of Washington	Deed to	Etting, Hetty, of Balto.	1801	F6	128	079
Commissioners of Washington	Deed to	Brackenridge, John	1801	F6	189	121
Commissioners of Washington	Deed to	Rutter, Thomas, of Balto.	1801	F6	125	078
Commissioners of Washington	Deed to	Flaut, Christian	1801	F6	178	114
Commissioners of Washington	Deed to	Brackenridge, John	1801	F6	186	119
Commissioners of Washington	Deed to	Elzey, Arnold	1801	F6	151	093
Commissioners of Washington	Deed to	Ehrenzella, George, of Phila.	1801	F6	236	156
Commissioners of Washington	Deed to	Etting, Reuben, of Balto.	1801	F6	122	076
Commissioners of Washington	Deed to	Ford, James	1801	F6	213	138
Commissioners of Washington	Deed to	Ehrenzeller, George, of Phila.	1801	F6	234	155
Commissioners of Washington	Deed to	Etting, Solomon, of Balto.	1801	F6	118	073
Commissioners of Washington	Cert to	Brent, Robert	1801	F6	111	069
Commissioners of Washington	Deed to	Pratt, Henry et al	1801	F6	202	131
Commissioners of Washington	Deed to	Elzey, Arnold	1801	F6	145	089
Commissioners of Washington	Cert to	O'Reilly, Henry	1801	F6	134	083
Commissioners of Washington	Deed to	Stoddert, Benjamin	1801	F6	226	147
Commissioners of Washington	Deed to	Wand, Thomas	1801	G7	473	609
Commissioners of Washington	Deed to	Stoddert, Benjamin, of G'tn.	1801	G7	405	539
Commissioners of Washington	Deed to	Baker, Jacob et al	1801	G7	281	389
Commissioners of Washington	Deed to	Stoddert, Benjamin, of G'tn.	1801	G7	310	433
Commissioners of Washington	Deed to	Wayman, Charles, of G'tn.	1801	G7	258	353
Commissioners of Washington	Deed to	Stoddert, Benjamin, of G'tn.	1801	G7	407	541
Commissioners of Washington	Deed to	Lovell, William	1801	G7	404	537
Commissioners of Washington	Cert to	Thompson, George et al	1801	G7	453	589
Commissioners of Washington	Deed to	Templeman, John, of G'tn.	1801	G7	313	437
Commissioners of Washington	Deed to	McCleery, William, of Balto.	1801	G7	090	116
Commissioners of Washington	Deed to	Stoddert, Benjamin, of G'tn.	1801	G7	312	435
Commissioners of Washington	Cert to	Roe, Bernard McDermot	1801	G7	433	569
Commissioners of Washington	Deed to	Ashley, John et al	1801	G7	281	389
Commissioners of Washington	Deed to	Miller, John, Jr. et al	1801	G7	281	389
Commissioners of Washington	Cert to	Brown, Mathew	1801	G7	276	380
Commissioners of Washington	Deed to	Barry, James	1801	G7	468	604
Commissioners of Washington	Deed to	Blodgett, Samuel, Jr.	1801	G7	261	357
Commissioners of Washington	Deed to	Etting, Shinah, of Balto.	1801	F6	131	081
Commissioners of Washington	Deed to	Stoddert, Benjamin	1801	G7	181	242
Commissioners of Washington	Deed to	Carroll, Henry Hill & Daniel	1801	G7	067	087
Commissioners of Washington	Deed to	King, Robert Sr. & Jr.	1801	G7	044	056
Commissioners of Washington	Deed to	Stoddert, Benjamin	1801	G7	190	254
Commissioners of Washington	Deed to	Corcoran, Thomas, of G'tn.	1801	G7	036	046
Commissioners of Washington	Cert to	Andrews, Richard	1801	G7	046	059
Commissioners of Washington	Cert to	[too mutilated to copy]	1801	G7	150c	
Commissioners of Washington	Deed to	Dove, Joseph	1801	G7	102	131
Commissioners of Washington	Deed to	Carroll, Daniel & Henry Hill	1801	G7	067	087
Commissioners of Washington	Deed to	Lawrence, Clement, of Phila.	1801	G7	033	042
Commissioners of Washington	Deed to	McNantz, Charles	1801	G7	050	064
Commissioners of Washington	Deed to	May, Frederick, Dr.	1801	G7	019	025
Commissioners of Washington	Deed to	Carroll, Daniel, of *Duddington*	1801	G7	051	066
Commissioners of Washington	Deed to	Walker, George	1801	G7	247	333
Commissioners of Washington	Deed to	Lovell, William	1801	G7		539
Commissioners of Washington	Deed to	Williamson, David, of Balto.	1801	G7	149	197
Commissioners of Washington	Deed to	Lenox, Peter	1801	G7	136	179
Commissioners of Washington	Deed to	Voss, Nicholas	1801	G7	082	106

Index to District of Columbia Land Records, 1792-1817

Party	What	Party	Year	Liber	Old	New
Commissioners of Washington	Deed to	Roberts, Owen	1801	G7	127	165
Commissioners of Washington	Deed fr	Blodget, Samuel, of Phila.	1801	G7	016	020
Commissioners of Washington	Deed to	Forrest, Uriah	1801	G7	046	059
Commissioners of Washington	Deed to	Carroll, Henry H., of Balto. Co.	1801	G7	049	062
Commissioners of Washington	Deed to	Stoddert, Benjamin	1801	G7	182	244
Commissioners of Washington	Deed to	Ford, James	1801	G7	135	178
Commissioners of Washington	Cert to	Bryan, Wilson	1801	G7	110	140
Commissioners of Washington	Deed to	Prout, William	1801	G7	253	343
Commissioners of Washington	Deed to	Francis, Thomas W. et al	1801	G7	281	389
Commissioners of Washington	Deed to	Cist, Jacob	1801	G7	196	262
Commissioners of Washington	Cert to	Etting, Solomon	1801	G7	178	237
Commissioners of Washington	Deed to	Winder, Levin, Somerset Co. MD	1801	G7	317	444
Commissioners of Washington	Cert to	Crookshank, John et al	1801	G7	453	589
Commissioners of Washington	Deed to	Bradley, Abraham, Jr.	1801	G7	434	569
Commissioners of Washington	Deed to	Joy, Absalom	1801	G7		010
Commissioners of Washington	Deed to	United States	1801	G7	157	208
Commissioners of Washington	Deed to	Johnson, Thomas, Frederick Co.	1801	G7	071	093
Commissioners of Washington	Cert to	Dermott, James R.	1801	G7	245	331
Commissioners of Washington	Deed to	Johnson, Thomas, Frederick Co.	1801	G7	071	092
Commissioners of Washington	Cert to	Duane, William	1801	G7	197	264
Commissioners of Washington	Deed to	Carroll, Daniel, of *Duddington*	1801	G7	053	068
Commissioners of Washington	Deed to	Stoddert, Benjamin	1801	G7	184	246
Commissioners of Washington	Deed to	Handley, John	1801	G7	032	040
Commissioners of Washington	Deed to	Minifie, Charles	1801	G7	045	057
Commissioners of Washington	Deed to	Burrows, Joseph	1801	G7	138	182
Commissioners of Washington	Deed to	Stoddert, Benjamin	1801	G7	187	250
Commissioners of Washington	Deed to	Rathie, John B., of Loudoun Co.	1801	G7	474	611
Commissioners of Washington	Deed to	Lovell, William	1801	G7		538
Commissioners of Washington	Deed to	Stretch, Joseph	1801	G7	034	044
Commissioners, of Washington	Cert to	Karrick, Joseph & Joshua Percival	1801	G7	185	248
Commissioners of Washington	Deed to	Lovell, William	1801	G7		010
Commissioners of Washington	Deed to	Stoddert, Benjamin	1801	G7	455	591
Commissioners of Washington	Deed to	Renner, Daniel	1801	G7	160	211
Commissioners of Washington	Deed to	Robertson, Alexander	1801	G7	130	170
Commissioners of Washington	Deed to	Shoemaker, Rachel, w/o David	1801	G7	476	613
Commissioners of Washington	Deed to	Pratt, Henry et al	1801	G7	281	389
Commissioners of Washington	Deed to	Andrews, George	1802	G7	514	654
Commissioners of Washington	Deed to	Templeman, John, of G'tn.	1802	G7	494	632
Commissioners of Washington	Deed to	Murdock, John	1802	G7	540	686
Commissioners of Washington	Deed to	Andrews, George	1802	G7	517	658
Commissioners of Washington	Deed to	Hoban, James	1802	G7	577	726
Commissioners of Washington	Deed to	Templeman, John, of G'tn.	1802	G7	492	630
Commissioners of Washington	Deed to	Prout, William	1802	G7	575	724
Commissioners of Washington	Deed to	Templeman, John, of G'tn.	1802	G7	490	628
Commissioners of Washington	Deed to	Calder, James, of G'tn.	1802	G7	538	685
Commissioners of Washington	Deed to	Murdock, John, of G'tn	1802	G7	542	689
Commissioners of Washington	Deed to	Hines, John	1802	H8	209	200
Commissioners of Washington	Deed to	Jarboe, Barnett	1802	H8	036	035
Commissioners of Washington	Deed to	Templeman, John	1802	H8	178	170
Commissioners of Washington	Deed to	Stoddert, Benjamin	1802	H8	087	080
Commissioners of Washington	Deed to	May, John, of MA	1802	H8	273	259
Commissioners of Washington	Deed to	Stoddert, Benjamin	1802	H8	226	215
Commissioners of Washington	Deed to	Purcell, Pierce	1802	H8	089	082
Commissioners of Washington	Deed to	Blagden, George	1802	H8	064	060
Commissioners of Washington	Deed to	Andrews, George	1802	H8	118	115

Index to District of Columbia Land Records, 1792-1817

Party	What	Party	Year	Liber	Old	New
Commissioners of Washington	Cert to	Herty, Thomas	1802	H8	201	192
Commissioners of Washington	Deed to	Stoddert, Benjamin	1802	H8	084	077
Commissioners of Washington	Deed to	Dunlop, James et al	1802	H8	453	416
Commissioners of Washington	Deed to	Harbaugh, Leonard	1802	H8	276	262
Commissioners of Washington	Deed to	Roberts, Owen	1802	H8	127	124
Commissioners of Washington	Cert to	Nourse, Michael	1802	H8	105	102
Commissioners of Washington	Deed to	Chandler, Walter S.	1802	H8	298	282
Commissioners of Washington	Deed to	Farrell, Zephaniah	1802	H8	116	113
Commissioners of Washington	Deed to	Brodeau, Ann	1802	H8	450	413
Commissioners of Washington	Deed to	Walker, George	1802	H8	444	408
Commissioners of Washington	Deed to	McHenry, James	1802	H8	066	061
Commissioners of Washington	Deed to	Carleton, Joseph et al	1802	H8	453	416
Commissioners of Washington	Deed to	Carroll, Daniel, of Duddington	1802	H8	331	310
Commissioners of Washington	Cert to	Walker, David	1802	H8	124	121
Commissioners of Washington	Deed to	Thompson, William	1802	H8	355	331
Commissioners of Washington	Deed to	Chandler, Walter S.	1802	H8	296	280
Commissioners of Washington	Deed to	Stoddert, Benjamin	1802	H8	060	056
Commissioners of Washington	Deed to	Sullivan, Murto, of VA	1802	I9	063	087
Commissioners of Washington	Cert to	St. Clare, George	1802	I9	071	099
Commissioners of Washington	Assign to	Ross, Richard	1809	W22	248	167
Compton, Henry T.	Mortgage to	Swann, William T., of P.G. Co.	1810	Y24	494	435
Compton, Henry T.	D. of T. to	Swann, William T., of P.G. Co.	1810	Y24	492	434
Coningham, Cornelius	B. of S. to	Waring, Martham, of G'tn.	1801	G7	438	574
Coningham, Cornelius	Deed fr	Munroe, Thomas	1802	G7	591	740
Coningham, Cornelius	Assign to	Munroe, Thomas	1803	K10	079	85
Coningham, Cornelius	B. of S. to	Munroe, Thomas	1804	L11	061	62
Coningham, Cornelius	B. of S. to	Munroe, Thomas	1805	O14	089	055
Coningham, Cornelius	B. of S. to	Davis, Mary	1807	Q16	369	283
Coningham, Cornelius	B. of S. to	Duvall, Gabriel	1809	W22	342	221
Coningham, Cornelius	Deed to	Duvall, Gabriel	1810	Y24	171	156
Conkling, Augustine	Exchange	Turner, Nanny	1802	I9	001	001
Conley, Charles	B. of S. to	Van Ness, John P.	1817	AN38	101	076
Connell, Catharine	Deed fr	Boyd, Washington, collector	1811	AB27	181	149
Connell, Catharine	Deed to	Moore, James	1813	AE30	375	277
Connell, Catharine et al	Assign fr	McCue, Owen	1808	V21	089	078
Connell, Catherine	Deed to	Law, John	1812	AC28	294	214
Connell, Catherine	Assign to	Wight, John M. & George Moore	1812	AD29	024	017
Connell, Catherine, of Hampton	Deed to	Emmerson, John, of Norfolk	1817	AO39	232	168
Connelly, John, Jr., of G'tn.	Deed to	McPherson, Henry, of G'tn.	1814	AH33	340	294
Connelly, John, of Montg. Co.	Deed fr	Athey, Hezekiah, of G'tn.	1805	O14	081	050
Connelly, John, of G'tn.	Deed fr	Dorsey, William H., of G'tn.	1807	R17	286	218
Connelly, John, of G'tn.	Mortgage to	Davis, Henry, of G'tn.	1814	AH33	196	179
Connelly, Patrick & John, of G'tn.	Deed fr	Dorsey, William H., of G'tn.	1807	R17	283	216
Connelly, Patrick, of G'tn.	Deed fr	McDono, William	1804	L11	227	211
Connelly, Patrick, of G'tn.	Deed fr	Dorsey, William H., of G'tn.	1807	R17	284	217
Connelly, Thomas, of G'tn.	Deed fr	Beall, Thomas, of George, of G'tn.	1793	A1-2	452	60
Connely, John, of G'tn.	Deed to	Moxley, Charles, of G'tn.	1813	AF31	521	383
Conner, Thomas, late of P.G. Co.	Slaves	From Prince George's Co. MD	1808	T19	055	039
Conner, William	B. of S. to	Spunogle, Margaret	1807	S18	175	142
Connolly, Michael & Elizabeth et al	Deed to	Wehrly, Jonathan, of Balto. Co.	1811	AB27	248	202
Connor, Jeremiah, insolvent	B. of S. to	Kenner, James, trustee	1805	M12	405	420
Connor, Martin, of Montg. Co.	Deed fr	Crowley, Thomas	1806	P15	238	158
Connor, Martin, of Montg. Co.	Assign fr	Crowley, Thomas	1806	P15	235	157
Connor, Thomas et al	B. of S. fr	Wade, Robert P.	1808	V21	092	071
Connor, William, insolvent	B. of S. to	Coombs, John, trustee	1808	T19	385	274

Index to District of Columbia Land Records, 1792-1817

Party	What	Party	Year	Liber	Old	New
Conrad, Frederick	D. of T. to	King, Adam	1801	G7	155	205
Conrad, Frederick	Cert		1802	I9	299	491
Conrad, Frederick, of VA	Deed fr	Brandt, Christopher & Rosannah	1800	E5	217	211
Constitution of the Wash. Assoc.			1801	G7	208	278
Contee, Benjamin	Partition		1812	AD29	433	363
Contee, Benjamin & Sarah R.	Deed to	Lee, James Clerk et al	1809	V21	361	264
Contee, Dorah (negro)	Deed fr	Slye, Thomas G., of G'tn.	1804	L11	213	200
Contee, Mariah	Cert Free fr	Slye, Thomas G.	1815	AI34	331	364
Contee, Mariah	Cert Free fr	Slye, Thomas G.	1816	AK35	259	205
Contee, P.A.L.	P. of Atty. to	Smoot, Alexander	1813	AG32	005	004
Contee, Richard	Assign to	Suter, John, of G'tn.	1797	B2B	463	154
Contee, Richard A.	Transfer to	Craurford, David	1797	B2B	473	165
Contee, Thomas	Deed to	Slater, Sarah	1802	I9	308	507
Contee, Thomas	Deed fr	Slater, David	1802	I9	272	442
Conway, Richard & James Craik	Deed to	Beall, Thomas & John M. Gantt	1792	A1-1	057	85
Coocke, Buller	Deed fr	Duddell, James	1808	U20	169	095
Cook, Charles	Deed fr	Polock, Isaac	1798	D4	045	038
Cook, Charles	Deed fr	Commissioners of Washington	1799	D4	262	247
Cook, Charles	Deed to	Peter, Robert	1801	G7	432	567
Cook, Charles	Deed to	Orme, Nathan, of G'tn.	1801	G7	254	345
Cook, James	Deed fr	Feburier, Nicholas	1798	C3	370	295
Cook, James et al	Deed fr	Dulany, Matthew	1797	B2B	626	385
Cook, John	B. of S. fr	Cook, Stephen	1809	X23	048	035
Cook, John, now of Frederick Co.	Deed to	Dunlap, John	1805	N13	265	221
Cook, John, of New Market et al	Deed fr	Reintzel, Andrew, now of G'tn.	1800	E5	251	244
Cook, John, of Frederick Co.	Deed fr	Brashear, Belt & Anne, Fredk. Co.	1805	N13	354	285
Cook, John, of Montg. Co.	Deed to	Dunlap, Alexander, of NY	1805	N13	357	288
Cook, Mary	Deed fr	Walker, James	1817	AN38	336	246
Cook, Orlando	B. of S. fr	Jones, Charles	1805	N13	090	082
Cook, Orlando	Agreement	Jones, Charles	1806	O14	297	197
Cook, Orlando	Qualify	Light Infantry	1808	U20	041	024
Cook, Orlando	Deed fr	Pratt, Henry et al	1809	X23	245	190
Cook, Orlando	Deed fr	Blagden, George, exr. of J. Emery	1811	Z25	465	368
Cook, Orlando	Deed fr	Huddleston, Joseph	1811	Z25	475	376
Cook, Orlando	Deed to	Huddleston, Joseph	1811	Z25	469	372
Cook, Orlando & Anne	Mortgage to	Entwisle, Isaac, of Alexa.	1813	AE30	511	378
Cook, Orlando et al	Agreement	Law, Thomas	1798	D4	155	137
Cook, Orlando et al	Lease fr	Law, Edmund, atty. of Thomas	1811	Z25	462	366
Cook, Orlando, stone cutter	D. of T. to	Greenleaf, James, of Phila. PA	1809	W22	384	249
Cook, Stephen	B. of S. to	Cook, John	1809	X23	048	035
Cook, Stephen	Deed fr	Carroll, Daniel, of *Duddington*	1815	AI34	384	410
Cook, Thomas	Transfer fr	Harbaugh, Leonard	1796	B2B	456	145
Cook, Thomas	Cert to	Barry, James, of Balto.	1796	B2B	454	141
Cook, Thomas	Cert Slave	From Frederick Co. MD	1815	AI34	147	169
Cook, Thomas & Jos. E. Rowles	Cert fr	Commissioners of Washington	1796	B2B	453	141
Cook, Thomas et al	Deed to	Schnively, Henry	1800	E5	175	165
Cook, Thomas et al	Deed to	Livers, Anthony	1801	G7	463	599
Cook, Thomas, exr. of W. Hellen	Cert Slave	From Calvert Co. MD	1817	AN38	483	349
Cook, Thomas, exr. W. Hellen	Cert Slaves	From MD	1817	AO39	175	130
Cook, Thomas, merchant, et al	Deed to	Schneily, Henry, merchant	1800	E5	152	141
Cook, Thomas, of Frederick Co.	Deed to	Rowles, Joseph Evan	1804	M12	030	031
Cook, Thomas, of Frederick Co.	Deed to	Dunlap, John, of G'tn.	1805	M12	245	246
Cook, Thomas, of Frederick Town	Deed to	Riddle, Joseph	1805	M12	201	203
Cook, Thomas, of Frederick Co.	Deed fr	Rowles, Joseph Evan	1805	M12	247	249
Cooke, David	Lease fr	Law, Thomas	1812	AC28	199	152

Index to District of Columbia Land Records, 1792-1817

Party	What	Party	Year	Liber	Old	New
Cooke, George & T. Woodward	D. of T. to	Corcoran, Thomas, of G'tn.	1815	AH33	490	419
Cooke, George & T. Woodward	Deed fr	Morgan, William, of G'tn.	1815	AK35	415	325
Cooke, George & Th. Woodward	Deed to	Yerby, John, of G'tn.	1816	AL36	200	208
Cooke, George & Th. Woodward	Deed to	Foxall, Henry, of G'tn.	1816	AL36	131	132
Cooke, George & Th. Woodward	D. of T. to	Corcoran, Thomas, of G'tn.	1816	AL36	077	079
Cooke, George, of G'tn. et al	Deed to	Yerby, John, of G'tn.	1815	AI34	079	090
Cooke, George, of G'tn.	Deed to	Corcoran, Thomas, of G'tn.	1816	AM37	160	122
Cooke, George, of G'tn.	Deed fr	Woodward, Thomas, of G'tn.	1816	AL36	495	466
Cooke, Joseph, of Phila. PA	Deed fr	Dermott, James Reed	1797	B2B	700	484
Cooke, Joseph, of Phila. PA	Mortgage to	Dermott, James R.	1797	C3	001	1
Cooke, Thomas	Deed to	Shaw, John et al	1802	H8	038	036
Cooke, Thomas, Frederick Co.	D. of T. fr	Prout, William	1808	T19	168	119
Cooke, William, of Balto.	Deed fr	Coles, John, of New London CN	1808	U20	041	024
Cooke, William, of Balto. Co.	Deed to	Coles, John, of New London CN	1810	Y24	387	350
Cooke, William, of Balto.	Deed to	Ritchie, Abner	1810	Y24	310	282
Cookendaffer, Thomas	D. of T. fr	Baum, John C., of G'tn.	1817	AN38	463	334
Cookendorfer, Leonard	Lease to	Cookendorfer, Thomas	1816	AL36	410	393
Cookendorfer, Thomas	Lease fr	Cookendorfer, Leonard	1816	AL36	410	393
Cookindaffer, Leonard	Deed fr	Davidson, John	1801	G7	027	034
Cooledge, Samuel J.	Mortgage to	Marshall, Richard et al	1811	AA26	096	068
Cooledge, Samuel Judson	Deed to	Rozer, Henry	1794	B2A	144	191
Coolidge, Charles & Hetty, of MA	Manumis to	Harper, Ann (C)	1816	AM37	039	033
Coolidge, Margaret, of P.G. Co.	B. of S. to	O'Neall, William	1808	V21	060	048
Coolidge, Samuel	Cert fr	Commissioners of Washington	1794	B2A	325	456
Coolidge, Samuel J.	Deed to	Darnall, Robert	1794	A1-2	493	96
Coolidge, Samuel J., of P.G. Co.	Deed fr	Hoban, James	1809	W22	335	217
Coolidge, Samuel J.	Receipt to	Munroe, Thomas	1809	V21	318	234
Coolidge, Samuel J.	B. of S. to	Young, Moses	1811	AB27	117	096
Coolidge, Samuel Judson	Deed to	Beall, Thomas & John M. Gantt	1793	A1-1	307	406
Coombe, Benjamin	Deed to	Lingan, James Maccubbin	1802	H8	579	543
Coombe, Benjamin	Deed to	Rawn, David, of G'tn.	1804	K10	231	239
Coombe, Benjamin, Kent Co. DE	Deed fr	Forrest, Uriah	1801	G7	023	029
Coombe, Benjamin, of Smyrna DE	Deed to	Waters, William	1811	AB27	352	291
Coombe, Griffith	B. of S. fr	Burnes, William	1806	O14	262½	173
Coombe, Griffith	Mortgage to	Smith, Samuel H.	1807	R17	039	032
Coombe, Griffith	Mortgage fr	Kilty, John & Josias Wilson King	1809	W22	208	208
Coombe, Griffith	Deed to	Ingle, Henry	1809	V21	142	105
Coombe, Griffith	Certificate	Commissioner of Turnpike Road	1810	Y24	293	268
Coombe, Griffith	Deed fr	May, Frederick	1810	Z25	242	189
Coombe, Griffith	D. of T. fr	Peltz, John	1810	X23	337	269
Coombe, Griffith	Release fr	Smith, Samuel H.	1811	AB27	289	237
Coombe, Griffith	Deed fr	Carroll, Daniel, of *Duddington*	1811	AA26	251	171
Coombe, Griffith	Mortgage fr	Cooper, John	1811	AB27	301	248
Coombe, Griffith	B. of S. to	Brent, Robert & Thomas Fenwick	1812	AC28	309	225
Coombe, Griffith	Deed fr	Boyd, Washington, marshal	1814	AH33	078	070
Coombe, Griffith	Deed fr	Hamilton, Christiana	1814	AG32	394	287
Coombe, Griffith	B. of S. to	Dobbyn, John	1815	AI34	377	404
Coombe, Griffith	B. of S. fr	Taylor, John, late of Charles Co.	1815	AI34	377	404
Coombe, Griffith	Deed fr	Johnson, George	1815	AH33	417	359
Coombe, Griffith	Cert Free to	Tilman, Nice (C)	1815	AI34	388	413
Coombe, Griffith	Deed fr	Key, Francis S.	1816	AK35	505	398
Coombe, Griffith	Deed to	Law, Thomas	1816	AL36	274	273
Coombe, Griffith	Deed fr	Carroll, Daniel, of *Duddington*	1816	AL36	272	272
Coombe, Griffith	Deed fr	Wharton, Franklin	1816	AL36	411	394
Coombe, Griffith	Deed fr	Law, Thomas	1816	AL36	275	275

Index to District of Columbia Land Records, 1792-1817

Party	What	Party	Year	Liber	Old	New
Coombe, Griffith	Deed to	Sanford, George	1816	AL36	288	286
Coombe, Griffith	Mortgage fr	King, Benjamin, of Balto.	1816	AM37	444	319
Coombe, Griffith & Joseph Forrest	Road Order	Alexanders Island to boundary	1814	AH33	095	088
Coombe, Griffith & Thomas Law	Agreement	Young, James	1816	AL36	278	277
Coombe, Griffith et al	Lease fr	Law, Thomas	1808	T19	093	066
Coombe, Griffith et al	Deed fr	Carroll, Daniel, of *Duddington*	1811	AA26	249	169
Coombe, Griffith, mer., Phila. PA	Manumis to	[ ], Nice (negro)	1806	P15	389	260
Coombs, John	B. of S. to	Jones, Charles	1809	W22	320	208
Coombs, John, trustee	B. of S. fr	Connor, William, insolvent	1808	T19	385	274
Coombs, Joseph	Deed to	Clarke, Bailey E.	1799	D4	301	285
Coombs, Joseph, of P.G. Co.	Deed to	Bayly, William, of P.G. Co.	1795	B2B	356	003
Coomes, Joseph	Deed fr	Downes, Mary, spinster	1794	B2A	041	048
Cooms, Sarah, of Charles Co.	Deed to	Renner, Daniel	1816	AM37	199	148
Cooper, Betsey et al	Convey fr	Cooper, John & Catherine	1808	U20	055	031
Cooper, Caty et al	Convey fr	Cooper, John & Catherine	1808	U20	055	031
Cooper, Charlotte et al	Convey fr	Cooper, John & Catherine	1808	U20	055	031
Cooper, Ereri et al	Convey fr	Cooper, John & Catherine	1808	U20	055	031
Cooper, George	Mortgage to	Harbaugh, Joseph	1813	AF31	550	408
Cooper, George	Mortgage to	Carr, Overton	1816	AM37	454	327
Cooper, George	Release fr	Harbaugh, Joseph	1816	AL36	494	464
Cooper, George	Manumis to	[ ], Jerry (C)	1817	AO39	174	129
Cooper, Isaac	Assign fr	Beall, Thomas K.	1803	K10	080	86
Cooper, Isaac, of G'tn.	Deed fr	Balch, Lewis P.W., of G'tn. et al	1812	AD29	041	029
Cooper, John	B. of S. to	Middleton, Electus et al	1807	S18	047	039
Cooper, John	B. of S. to	Kain, Patrick	1808	T19	131	093
Cooper, John	B. of S. to	Scholfield, Joseph et al	1810	X23	409	330
Cooper, John	Mortgage to	Coombe, Griffith	1811	AB27	301	248
Cooper, John	B. of S. fr	Stokes, John & James Ambush	1811	AB27	162	134
Cooper, John	D. of T. to	Bates, David	1813	AE30	211	171
Cooper, John	B. of S. to	Callen, Partrick	1815	AK35	056	044
Cooper, John & Catherine	Convey to	Cooper, Charlotte et al	1808	U20	055	031
Cooper, John & Richard D. Boyd	B. of S. fr	Airs, Thomas	1809	X23	050	037
Cooper, John & Luke Wheeler	Deed to	Willock, William	1812	AC28	422	304
Cooper, Lavinia	Cert Free to	Turner, Celia (C), age 23	1813	AE30	225	181
Cooper, Loyed John et al	Convey fr	Cooper, John & Catherine	1808	U20	055	031
Cooper, Mary or Lowry	Deed fr	Threlkeld, John	1810	Z25	244	191
Cooper, Molly (C)	Cert Free to	Shorter, Anna (C)	1811	AB27	095	078
Cooper, Nancy et al	Convey fr	Cooper, John & Catherine	1808	U20	055	031
Cooper, Polly et al	Convey fr	Cooper, John & Catherine	1808	U20	055	031
Cooper, Robert	Deed fr	Laird, John, exr. of J. Carleton	1813	AF31	537	397
Cooper, Stephen	Slave		1816	AL36	171	171
Cooper, Suseana et al	Convey fr	Cooper, John & Catherine	1808	U20	055	031
Cooper, William	Deed fr	Wright, Thomas C.	1812	AD29	179	144
Cooper, William	Deed fr	Borrows, Joseph	1812	AD29	064	046
Cooper, William	Deed fr	King, Robert	1813	AF31	300	213
Cooper, William	Deed fr	Moore, George	1815	AI34	325	357
Cooper, William	Release fr	Queen, Nicholas Lewis	1815	AH33	516	443
Cooper, William	Deed fr	Law, Thomas	1815	AH33	514	441
Coote, Thomas & David Ott	Assign fr	Collet, Ann, of Paterson NJ	1817	AO39	305	217
Coote, Thomas & David Ott	Convey fr	Law, Thomas	1817	AO39	303	216
Cope, Israel & Jasper, of Balto.	Deed fr	Templeman, John, of G'tn.	1805	O14	149	097
Cope, Israel & Jasper, of Balto.	Deed fr	Templeman, John, of G'tn.	1809	V21	249	177
Cope, Israel, of Balto.	Deed fr	Lingan, James M., of Montg. Co.	1809	X23	051	038
Cope, Jasper, mer., of Balto.	Deed fr	Harvy, Peter, coachmaker, Phila.	1807	S18	142	116
Cope, Jasper, of Balto.	Deed to	Davis, Shadrach	1808	T19	263	194

Index to District of Columbia Land Records, 1792-1817

Party	What	Party	Year	Liber	Old	New
Cope, Jasper, of Phila. PA	Deed fr	Dorsey, William H., of Balto.	1810	X23	388	312
Cope, Jasper, of Phila. PA	Deed fr	Murdock, John	1810	X23	387	311
Copp, Andrew & Elizabeth	Deed to	Ridenhour, David	1793	A1-1	344	448
Copper, Teney (negro)	Manumis fr	Anderson, Juliana	1810	Y24	108	097
Coppersmith, Henry, of G'tn.	Convey fr	McLann, Robert, Cumb. Co. PA	1816	AL36	403	387
Coppersmith, John et al	Deed fr	Smith, Lewis, of G'tn.	1817	AN38	500	361
Coppersmith, Lewis F. et al	Deed fr	Smith, Lewis, of G'tn.	1817	AN38	500	361
Coppersmith, Magdalena et al	Deed fr	Smith, Lewis, of G'tn.	1817	AN38	500	361
Coppersmith, Mary Ann et al	Deed fr	Smith, Lewis, of G'tn.	1817	AN38	500	361
Corcoran, Alexander, Jr.	Assign fr	Adams, Henry	1806	O14	178	116
Corcoran, James	Qualify	Captain of infantry	1813	AE30	531	393
Corcoran, James, of G'tn.	Deed fr	Stone, Edward	1814	AG32	375	272
Corcoran, Susanna	Marriage C.	Carrol, Patrick	1810	X23	343	275
Corcoran, Thomas	Deed fr	Commissioners of Washington	1800	E5	103	091
Corcoran, Thomas	Lease fr	Beal, Thomas, of George et al	1801	G7	175	233
Corcoran, Thomas	Deed to	Weems, John, physician	1802	H8	283	268
Corcoran, Thomas	Deed fr	Wayman, Charles, of G'tn.	1802	H8	195	186
Corcoran, Thomas	Deed fr	Deakins, Francis	1802	H8	002	002
Corcoran, Thomas	Deed fr	Davidson, John	1802	H8	196	188
Corcoran, Thomas	Qualify	Justice of the Peace	1802	H8	199	190
Corcoran, Thomas	Deed fr	Beall, Thomas B.	1802	I9	467	769
Corcoran, Thomas	Deed fr	Jackson, Jonathan, trustees of	1805	O14	134	086
Corcoran, Thomas	Deed fr	Beatty, Charles, heirs of	1806	O14	193	127
Corcoran, Thomas	Deed fr	Caldwell, Elias B. et al	1806	P15	171	113
Corcoran, Thomas	Deed fr	Beatty, John M. & Charles A.	1807	S18	068	057
Corcoran, Thomas	Bond to	Corporation of Georgetown	1808	T19	258	190
Corcoran, Thomas	Cert Free to	McDaniel, John	1809	V21	379	282
Corcoran, Thomas	Cert Free to	McDaniel, William	1809	V21	379	282
Corcoran, Thomas	Deed to	Bussard, Daniel	1810	Y24	504	444
Corcoran, Thomas	Deed fr	Heath, Nathaniel H.	1811	Z25	507	402
Corcoran, Thomas	Qualify	Justice of the Peace	1812	AD29	463	390
Corcoran, Thomas	Deed to	Hartman, Charles	1817	AO39	213	155
Corcoran, Thomas & Thos. Hyde	Release to	Livers, Anthony	1812	AD29	080	059
Corcoran, Thomas & John Shaw	Deed to	Bowie, Washington	1813	AF31	437	314
Corcoran, Thomas, Esq.	Deed fr	Parrott, Richard	1810	Y24	522	459
Corcoran, Thomas et al	Mortgage fr	Livers, Anthony, of G'tn.	1801	G7	466	603
Corcoran, Thomas et al	Deed fr	Mitchell, John, of G'tn.	1806	P15	144	093
Corcoran, Thomas et al	Deed fr	Green, Charles D., Somerset Co.	1808	T19	203	145
Corcoran, Thomas, of G'tn.	Deed fr	Orme, Thomas, of G'tn.	1800	E5	244	238
Corcoran, Thomas, of G'tn.	Deed fr	Mountz, John, of G'tn.	1800	E5	271	264
Corcoran, Thomas, of G'tn.	Deed fr	Commissioners of Washington	1800	E5	301	293
Corcoran, Thomas, of G'tn.	Deed to	Ramsey, John, of Phila.	1801	F6	240	160
Corcoran, Thomas, of G'tn.	Manumis to	[ ] Peter (Negro)	1801	G7	326	457
Corcoran, Thomas, of G'tn.	Deed fr	Davidson, John, of Annapolis	1801	G7	436	571
Corcoran, Thomas, of G'tn.	Deed fr	Commissioners of Washington	1801	G7	036	046
Corcoran, Thomas, of G'tn.	Deed fr	Ramsey, John, by his attorney	1801	F6	238	158
Corcoran, Thomas, of G'tn.	Deed fr	McIntire, Samuel	1802	H8	244	232
Corcoran, Thomas, of G'tn.	Deed fr	Scott, William A. & Anne, P.G. Co.	1805	O14	131	084
Corcoran, Thomas, of G'tn.	Deed fr	Davidson, John, of Annapolis	1805	O14	133	086
Corcoran, Thomas, of G'tn.	Deed fr	Murdock, Addison	1807	R17	324	247
Corcoran, Thomas, of G'tn.	Deed fr	Jones, John G., of G'tn.	1808	U20	065	037
Corcoran, Thomas, of G'tn.	Deed fr	Mountz, Jacob, collector, of G'tn.	1810	Y24	523	460
Corcoran, Thomas, of G'tn.	Release to	Snowden, Richard P. et al	1810	Y24	263	242
Corcoran, Thomas, of G'tn.	Deed fr	Mountz, Jacob, collector, of G'tn.	1810	X23	325	260
Corcoran, Thomas, of G'tn.	Deed fr	Morsell, James S., of G'tn.	1811	Z25	530	421

Party	What	Party	Year	Liber	Old	New
Corcoran, Thomas, of G'tn.	Deed to	Hand, Ann	1812	AD29	461	388
Corcoran, Thomas, of G'tn.	Deed to	Lenox, Peter	1812	AE30	050	037
Corcoran, Thomas, of G'tn.	Deed fr	Lenox, Peter	1812	AD29	472	399
Corcoran, Thomas, of G'tn.	Deed fr	Lee, Thomas Sim, of Fredk. Co.	1813	AF31	318	227
Corcoran, Thomas, of G'tn.	Deed fr	Duffy, Bryan, of G'tn.	1813	AF31	065	045
Corcoran, Thomas, of G'tn.	D. of T. fr	Duffy, Bryan, of G'tn.	1813	AE30	249	191
Corcoran, Thomas, of G'tn.	Deed fr	Burnett, Charles A., of G'tn.	1813	AE30	479	356
Corcoran, Thomas, of G'tn.	D. of T. fr	Reintzel, Daniel, of G'tn.	1814	AG32	040	032
Corcoran, Thomas, of G'tn.	Deed fr	Georgetown, Mayor & Aldermen	1814	AG32	371	269
Corcoran, Thomas, of G'tn.	Deed fr	Lee, Thomas S., of Fredk. Co.	1814	AG32	373	271
Corcoran, Thomas, of G'tn.	Deed to	Williams, John S., of G'tn.	1814	AG32	346	250
Corcoran, Thomas, of G'tn.	Deed to	Burnett, Charles A., of G'tn.	1814	AH33	372	322
Corcoran, Thomas, of G'tn.	Deed fr	Hyde, Thomas, of G'tn.	1814	AH33	280	244
Corcoran, Thomas, of G'tn.	Deed to	Miller, William, of G'tn.	1815	AI34	235	267
Corcoran, Thomas, of G'tn.	D. of T. fr	Cooke, George & T. Woodward	1815	AH33	490	419
Corcoran, Thomas, of G'tn.	Lease to	Brookes, Joseph, of G'tn.	1815	AK35	117	091
Corcoran, Thomas, of G'tn.	Deed fr	Fleet, Henry, of G'tn.	1815	AI34	082	093
Corcoran, Thomas, of G'tn.	D. of T. fr	Woodward, Thomas & G. Cooke	1816	AL36	077	079
Corcoran, Thomas, of G'tn.	Deed to	Bussard, Daniel	1816	AL36	303	300
Corcoran, Thomas, of G'tn.	Deed to	Owens, Issac, of G'tn.	1816	AL36	174	175
Corcoran, Thomas, of G'tn.	Deed fr	Cooke, George, of G'tn.	1816	AM37	160	122
Corcoran, Thomas, of G'tn.	Lease to	Brookes, Joseph, of G'tn.	1817	AN38	458	330
Corcoran, Thomas, trustee	Deed fr	Barney, John H., insolvent	1807	R17	050	040
Corless, Matthias, grocer, Phila.	Deed fr	Van Mannierck, Anthony, Phila.	1801	G7	348	479
Corless, Matthias, grocer, Phila.	Deed fr	Van Mannierck, Anthony, Phila.	1801	G7	350	481
Corly, James, insolvent	Deed to	Dolan, Bernard, trustee	1811	AA26	166	114
Corning, Zephorah	B. of S. fr	Prime, William	1806	O14	350	234
Corning, Zephorah	Assign fr	Prime, William	1806	O14	349	233
Corporation & Mayor Washington	Cert fr	Munroe, Thomas, Supt.	1807	S18	013	012
Corporation for the Poor, Presby.	Mortgage fr	Nicholson, John, of Phila.	1795	B2A	278	390
Corporation of Georgetown	Cede fr	Peter, Robert	1797	B2B	619	377
Corporation of Georgetown	Cede fr	Reintzel, Anthony	1797	B2B	619	377
Corporation of Georgetown	Deed fr	Beall, Thomas, s/o George	1798	D4	145	127
Corporation of Georgetown			1799	E5	406	
Corporation of Georgetown	Deed fr	Mitchell, John, of G'tn.	1802	I9	130	194
Corporation of Georgetown	Deed fr	King, Adam, of G'tn.	1802	I9	129	192
Corporation of Georgetown	Deed fr	Magruder, George B. et al	1805	N13	091	083
Corporation of Georgetown	Bond fr	Williams, Elisha O. et al	1805	N13	094	086
Corporation of Georgetown	Deed fr	Mason, John, of *Mason's Island*	1805	O14	051	030
Corporation of Georgetown	Deed fr	Beatty, John M. & Charles A.	1805	O14	001	001
Corporation of Georgetown	Bond fr	Magruder, George B.	1806	O14	394	263
Corporation of Georgetown	Deed fr	Murdock, Addison	1806	P15	146	095
Corporation of Georgetown	Bond fr	Mackall, Leonard	1806	O14	392	262
Corporation of Georgetown	Deed fr	Beatty, John M. & Charles A.	1807	R17	339	258
Corporation of Georgetown	Deed to	Beatty, John M. & Charles A.	1807	S18	387	308
Corporation of Georgetown	Bond fr	Magruder, George B.	1808	T19	262	193
Corporation of Georgetown	Deed to	Bowie, Washington	1808	U20	394	219
Corporation of Georgetown	Bond fr	Mackall, Leonard et al	1808	T19	258	190
Corporation of Georgetown	Bond fr	Magruder, George B., inspector	1809	V21	399	302
Corporation of Georgetown	Deed to	Eliason, Ebenezer, of G'tn. et al	1810	Z25	328	256
Corporation of Georgetown	Deed fr	Peter, Thomas et al	1811	AB27	135	112
Corporation of Georgetown	Deed fr	Dorsey, William H., of Balto. Co.	1812	AD29	266	220
Corporation of Georgetown	Deed fr	Bank of Columbia	1812	AC28	460	328
Corporation of Georgetown	Lease to	Thompson, Josias, of G'tn. et al	1813	AE30	408	301
Corporation of Georgetown	Deed to	Baker, John, of G'tn.	1813	AE30	214	173

Party	What	Party	Year	Liber	Old	New
Corporation of Georgetown	Deed to	Bowie, Washington	1814	AG32	179	127
Corporation of Georgetown	Deed to	Corcoran, Thomas, of G'tn.	1814	AG32	371	269
Corporation of Georgetown	Receipt to	Dodge, Allen & Francis	1816	AK35	485	381
Corporation of Georgetown	Assign fr	Eveleth, John, inventor & patentee	1817	AN38	004	004
Corporation of Washington	Bond fr	Lowe, Michael, inspector	1809	W22	079	059
Corporation of Washington	Deed to	Glover, Charles	1815	AI34	120	137
Corporation of Washington	Deed to	Glover, Charles	1815	AI34	118	135
Corporation of Washington	Deed to	Glover, Charles	1815	AI34	116	133
Corporation of Washington	Deed to	Lenox, Peter	1815	AI34	106	121
Corporation of Washington	Deed to	Glover, Charles	1815	AI34	111	127
Corporation of Washington	Deed to	Glover, Charles	1815	AI34	113	129
Corporation of Washington	Deed to	Glover, Charles	1815	AI34	115	131
Corporation of Washington	Deed to	Glover, Charles	1815	AI34	122	140
Corporation of Washington	Deed to	Emack, William	1815	AI34	169	194
Corporation of Washington	Deed to	Caldwell, Elias B.	1815	AI34	233	264
Corporation of Washington	Deed to	Lindsay, Adam	1815	AI34	208	237
Corporation of Washington	Deed to	Hoye, John, of G'tn.	1815	AI34	226	257
Corporation of Washington	Deed to	O'Neale, William	1815	AI34	266	300
Corporation of Washington	Deed to	O'Neale, William	1815	AI34	268	302
Corporation of Washington	Deed to	O'Neale, William	1815	AI34	269	304
Corporation of Washington	Deed to	O'Neale, William	1815	AI34	271	306
Corporation of Washington	Deed to	O'Neale, William	1815	AI34	273	308
Corporation of Washington	Deed to	O'Neale, William	1815	AI34	275	310
Corporation of Washington	Deed to	Lindsay, Adam	1815	AI34	206	235
Corporation of Washington	Deed to	Emack, William	1815	AI34	167	192
Corporation of Washington	Deed to	Joncherez, Alexander L., of G'tn.	1815	AI34	292	237
Corporation of Washington	Deed to	Joncherez, Alexander L., of G'tn.	1815	AI34	296	330
Corporation of Washington	Deed to	Joncherez, Alexander L., of G'tn.	1815	AI34	298	332
Corporation of Washington	Deed to	Hoye, John, of G'tn.	1815	AI34	224	255
Corporation of Washington	Deed to	Joncherez, Alexander L., of G'tn.	1815	AI34	303	336
Corporation of Washington	Deed to	Emack, William	1815	AI34	166	190
Corporation of Washington	Deed to	Joncherez, Alexander L., of G'tn.	1815	AI34	305	339
Corporation of Washington	Deed to	Joncherez, Alexander L., of G'tn.	1815	AI34	307	341
Corporation of Washington	Deed to	Joncherez, Alexander L., of G'tn.	1815	AI34	311	344
Corporation of Washington	Deed to	Joncherez, Alexander L., of G'tn.	1815	AI34	313	346
Corporation of Washington	Deed to	Joncherez, Alexander L., of G'tn.	1815	AI34	315	348
Corporation of Washington	Deed to	Joncherez, Alexander L., of G'tn.	1815	AI34	317	350
Corporation of Washington	Deed to	Joncherez, Alexander L., of G'tn.	1815	AI34	319	352
Corporation of Washington	Deed to	Joncherez, Alexander L., of G'tn.	1815	AI34	321	354
Corporation of Washington	Deed to	Shoemaker, David	1815	AI34	228	259
Corporation of Washington	Deed to	Hoye, John, of G'tn.	1815	AI34	222	253
Corporation of Washington	Deed to	Glover, Charles	1815	AI34	123	142
Corporation of Washington	Deed to	Young, Moses	1815	AI34	161	185
Corporation of Washington	Deed to	Taylor, Thomas & Josias	1815	AI34	354	385
Corporation of Washington	Deed to	Taylor, Thomas & Josias	1815	AI34	356	387
Corporation of Washington	Deed to	Taylor, Thomas	1815	AI34	359	389
Corporation of Washington	Deed to	Taylor, Thomas	1815	AI34	361	391
Corporation of Washington	Deed to	Hoye, John, of G'tn.	1815	AI34	220	251
Corporation of Washington	Deed to	Lindsay, Adam	1815	AI34	210	239
Corporation of Washington	Deed to	Lindsay, Adam	1815	AI34	201	230
Corporation of Washington	Deed to	Lindsay, Adam	1815	AI34	215	245
Corporation of Washington	Deed to	Lindsay, Adam	1815	AI34	213	243
Corporation of Washington	Deed to	Lindsay, Adam	1815	AI34	203	232
Corporation of Washington	Deed to	Simmons, William	1815	AI34	389	414
Corporation of Washington	Deed to	Simmons, William	1815	AI34	391	416

Party	What	Party	Year	Liber	Old	New
Corporation of Washington	Deed to	Brent, Robert	1815	AI34	191	219
Corporation of Washington	Deed to	Brent, Robert	1815	AI34	189	217
Corporation of Washington	Deed to	Brent, Robert	1815	AI34	187	215
Corporation of Washington	Deed to	Queen, Nicholas L.	1815	AI34	536	541
Corporation of Washington	Deed to	Lowry, Mary	1815	AI34	417	439
Corporation of Washington	Deed to	Lindsay, Adam	1815	AI34	211	241
Corporation of Washington	Deed to	Joncherez, Alexander L., of G'tn.	1815	AI34	300	334
Corporation of Washington	Deed to	Emack, William	1815	AI34	171	196
Corporation of Washington	Deed to	Glover, Charles	1815	AI34	134	154
Corporation of Washington	Deed to	Scholfield, Andrew, of Alexa.	1815	AI34	498	505
Corporation of Washington	Deed to	Scholfield, Andrew, of Alexa.	1815	AI34	500	507
Corporation of Washington	Deed to	Glover, Charles	1815	AI34	132	152
Corporation of Washington	Deed to	Hagner, Peter	1815	AI34	125	144
Corporation of Washington	Deed to	Joncherez, Alexander L., of G'tn.	1815	AI34	290	325
Corporation of Washington	Deed to	Burford, Henry	1815	AK35	179	139
Corporation of Washington	Deed to	Burford, Henry	1815	AK35	176	137
Corporation of Washington	Deed to	Burford, Henry	1815	AK35	173	134
Corporation of Washington	Deed to	Burford, Henry	1815	AK35	170	131
Corporation of Washington	Deed to	Burford, Henry	1815	AK35	167a	129
Corporation of Washington	Deed to	Burford, Henry	1815	AK35	166	127
Corporation of Washington	Deed to	Burford, Henry	1815	AK35	164	126
Corporation of Washington	Deed to	Bates, David	1815	AK35	161	124
Corporation of Washington	Deed to	Edwards, Horace H.	1815	AK35	469	368
Corporation of Washington	Deed to	Edwards, Horace H.	1815	AK35	466	366
Corporation of Washington	Deed to	Edwards, Horace H.	1815	AK35	464	364
Corporation of Washington	Deed to	Burford, Henry	1815	AK35	159	122
Corporation of Washington	Deed to	Bates, David	1815	AK35	144	111
Corporation of Washington	Deed to	Purcell, Pierce	1815	AK35	453	355
Corporation of Washington	Deed to	Bates, David	1815	AK35	140	108
Corporation of Washington	Deed to	Charlton, Ralph	1815	AK35	440	345
Corporation of Washington	Deed to	Bates, David	1815	AK35	137	106
Corporation of Washington	Deed to	Edwards, Horace H.	1815	AK35	433	339
Corporation of Washington	Deed to	Bates, David	1815	AK35	135	104
Corporation of Washington	Deed to	Bates, David	1815	AK35	147	113
Corporation of Washington	Deed to	Farrell, Zephaniah	1815	AK35	035	027
Corporation of Washington	Deed to	Farrell, Zephaniah	1815	AK35	032	025
Corporation of Washington	Deed to	Farrell, Zephaniah	1815	AK35	030	023
Corporation of Washington	Deed to	Farrell, Zephaniah	1815	AK35	027	021
Corporation of Washington	Deed to	Bates, David	1815	AK35	142	110
Corporation of Washington	Deed to	Orr, John	1815	AK35	338	268
Corporation of Washington	Deed to	Farrell, Zephaniah	1815	AK35	024	019
Corporation of Washington	Deed to	Whann, William, of G'tn.	1815	AK35	240	190
Corporation of Washington	Deed to	Davidson, John	1815	AK35	296	236
Corporation of Washington	Deed to	Davidson, John	1815	AK35	293	234
Corporation of Washington	Deed to	Farrell, Zephaniah	1815	AK35	022	017
Corporation of Washington	Deed to	Davidson, John	1815	AK35	285	228
Corporation of Washington	Deed to	Whann, William, of G'tn.	1815	AK35	242	191
Corporation of Washington	Deed to	Kerr, Alexander	1815	AK35	268	213
Corporation of Washington	Deed to	Kerr, Alexander	1815	AK35	265	211
Corporation of Washington	Deed to	Kerr, Alexander	1815	AK35	263	209
Corporation of Washington	Deed to	Cocke, Buller	1815	AK35	261	207
Corporation of Washington	Deed to	Glover, Charles	1815	AK35	011	009
Corporation of Washington	Deed to	Glover, Charles	1815	AK35	009	007
Corporation of Washington	Deed to	Bates, David	1815	AK35	156	120
Corporation of Washington	Deed to	Glover, Charles	1815	AK35	006	005

Index to District of Columbia Land Records, 1792-1817

Party	What	Party	Year	Liber	Old	New
Corporation of Washington	Deed to	Belt, Benjamin M.	1816	AK35	492	387
Corporation of Washington	Deed to	Scholfield, Issachar	1816	AL36	234	239
Corporation of Washington	Deed to	Patterson, Edgar, of G'tn.	1816	AL36	074	075
Corporation of Washington	Deed to	Goulding, John	1816	AL36	268	268
Corporation of Washington	Deed to	Goulding, John	1816	AL36	266	266
Corporation of Washington	Deed to	Scholfield, Issachar	1816	AL36	232	237
Corporation of Washington	Deed to	McCormick, James	1816	AM37	527	391
Corporation of Washington	Deed to	McCormick, James	1816	AM37	524	388
Corporation of Washington	Deed to	Thompson, Joseph	1816	AM37	201	149
Corporation of Washington	Deed to	McCormick, James	1816	AM37	519	383
Corporation of Washington	Deed to	Lewis, Samuel, Jr.	1816	AM37	493	359
Corporation of Washington	Deed to	McCormick, James	1816	AM37	510	375
Corporation of Washington	Deed to	McCormick, James	1816	AM37	517	381
Corporation of Washington	Deed to	McCormick, James	1816	AM37	512	377
Corporation of Washington	Deed to	McCormick, James	1816	AM37	514	379
Corporation of Washington	Deed to	McCormick, James	1816	AM37	522	386
Corporation of Washington	Deed to	McCormick, James	1816	AO39	003	003
Corporation of Washington	Deed to	McCormick, James	1816	AO39	001	001
Corporation of Washington	Deed to	McCormick, James	1816	AO39	006	005
Corporation of Washington	Deed to	Scholfield, Mahlon, of Alexa.	1817	AN38	486	350
Costen, George (negro)	Manumis fr	Law, Thomas	1807	R17	289	221
Costen, Margaret et al	Manumis fr	Law, Thomas	1807	R17	288	220
Costigan, Joseph	Lease fr	Voss, Nicholas	1801	G7	440	576
Costigan, Joseph	Deed fr	Voss, Nicholas	1802	I9	317	521
Costigan, Joseph	D. of T. fr	Hall, John	1805	N13	085	078
Costigan, Joseph	Deed fr	Cannon, John	1806	P15	098	060
Costigan, Joseph	Deed fr	Peter, David, trustee	1806	Q16	017	011
Costigan, Joseph	Deed to	Cassin, James	1808	U20	060	034
Costigan, Joseph	Deed fr	Kerr, Alexander	1808	U20	118	067
Costigan, Joseph	Deed fr	Alexander, Robert	1809	X23	192	144
Costigan, Joseph	Deed fr	Boyd, Washington, marshal	1811	AB27	285	234
Costigan, Joseph	B. of S. fr	Adams, George	1811	AC28	044	033
Costigan, Joseph	B. of S. fr	Hoxton, Stanislaus, of P.G. Co.	1811	Z25	555	441
Costigan, Joseph	Deed to	O'Brian, John	1811	AB27	214	174
Costigan, Joseph	Deed to	Wharton, Franklin	1812	AC28	506	362
Costin, Delphy et al	Manumis fr	Law, Thomas	1807	R17	409	309
Costine, William	B. of S. fr	Holmes, Joseph	1805	O14	028	018
Cotterill, Thomas, mer., of NY	Deed to	Ward, Matthias, bookseller, of NY	1810	Y24	250	230
Cotterill, Thomas, mer., of NY	Deed fr	Taylor, James, of Southwark	1810	Y24	247	228
Cottman, William	Convey to	Lear, Benjamin L.	1815	AK35	457	358
Coulter, Peter	Deed to	Crouse, Henry	1809	V21	271	194
Coulter, Peter	D. of T. to	Hollingshead, John	1810	Y24	469	416
Coulter, Peter	Release fr	Johns, Susanna, of G'tn.	1812	AC28	503	358
Coulter, Peter	Deed fr	Balch, Stephen B.	1816	AL36	010	010
Coulter, Peter	Deed to	Sheele, Augustus Daniel	1817	AN38	536	389
Coulter, Peter, of G'tn.	Deed fr	Balch, Stephen B., of G'tn.	1809	V21	273	195
Coulter, Peter, of G'tn.	Mortgage to	Johns, Susanna, of G'tn.	1809	V21	314	230
Courts, John, heirs of, def.	Suit	French, George, plt.	1815	AK35	018	014
Courts, John, of Charles Co.	Deed fr	Craik, William, planter	1799	E5	063	051
Covachiche, Joseph	P. of Atty. fr	Lynch, Dominick & Comfort Sands	1796	B2B	450	136
Covachiche, Joseph, in G'tn.	P. of Atty. to	Deakins, William Jr., of G'tn.	1796	B2B	608	362
Covachick, Joseph, mer., of NY	Deed fr	Lynch, Dominick et ux et al	1797	C3	021	17
Covachick, Joseph, mer., of NY	Deed to	Bernabeu, John B., of Balto.	1800	E5	269	263
Covachick, Joseph, of NY, in G'tn.	P. of Atty. to	Deakins, William Jr., of G'tn.	1797	C3	046	36
Cowper, John & Luke Wheeler	Deed to	Granberry, John	1812	AD29	531	448

Index to District of Columbia Land Records, 1792-1817

Party	What	Party	Year	Liber	Old	New
Cowper, John & Luke Wheeler	Deed to	Myers, Moses	1812	AD29	527	444
Cowper, John & Luke Wheeler	Deed to	Cammack, William	1812	AC28	154	115
Cowper, John & Luke Wheeler	Deed to	Campbell, James	1814	AG32	127	093
Cowper, John & Luke Wheeler, VA	Deed to	Thorburn, James	1817	AN38	140	103
Cowper, John & Luke Wheeler, VA	Deed to	Herron, Walter	1817	AN38	136	100
Cowper, John et al	Schedule to	Lockerman, John	1817	AN38	143	105
Cowper, John, of Norfolk VA et al	Deed fr	Stoddert, Benjamin	1801	G7	410	544
Cowper, John, of Norfolk et al	Deed to	Wright, Stephen	1814	AG32	459	332
Cowper, William	Deed fr	Craven, Tunis	1802	I9	151	227
Cowper, William & Ann P.P.	P. of Atty. to	Cocke, Buller	1811	AB27	321	264
Cowper, William, I. of W. Co. VA	Deed to	Sanford, Daniel, of Norfolk VA	1811	AB27	319	263
Cox, Ann (negro	Cert Free fr	Addison, Lucy	1810	Y24	215	198
Cox, George	Deed fr	Prout, William	1807	S18	195	156
Cox, George	Deed fr	Prout, William	1814	AH33	276	241
Cox, George & John Minitree	Mortgage fr	Bland, Edward	1813	AF31	514	376
Cox, George & John Minitree	Release to	Walker, Zachariah	1815	AI34	155	178
Cox, James S., of Phila. et al	Deed fr	Bank of the United States	1811	AA26	344	230
Cox, James S., of Phila. et al	Deed to	Lenox, David	1811	AA26	333	223
Cox, John	B. of S. fr	Threlkeld, John	1801	G7		
Cox, John	B. of S. fr	Threlkeld, John	1801	G7	153	203
Cox, John	Deed fr	Templeman, John	1802	H8	174	167
Cox, John	Release to	Carpenter, Thomas	1802	I9	059	081
Cox, John	Qualify		1802	I9	466	767
Cox, John	Assign fr	Jones, Edward	1802	G7	522	665
Cox, John	Deed fr	Gantt, Edward, Dr.	1804	L11	018	18
Cox, John	Qualify	Captain of Cavalry, 1st MIlitia	1806	P15	143	093
Cox, John	Deed fr	Presbyterian Congregation of G'tn.	1811	AB27	392	323
Cox, John	Deed fr	Pickrell, John	1813	AF31	391	282
Cox, John	Deed fr	Brooks, Joseph, of G'tn.	1813	AF31	389	281
Cox, John	Deed fr	King, Charles	1813	AF31	387	279
Cox, John	Indenture fr	Gray, William (C), as servant	1813	AF31	394	285
Cox, John	Deed fr	Balch, Stephen B., Rev.	1814	AH33	338	293
Cox, John	Release fr	English, David et al	1816	AL36	199	206
Cox, John & Walter Smith, of G'tn.	Deed to	Melvin, James	1810	X23	162	119
Cox, John, Col., of G'tn.	Deed fr	Holtzman, George, of G'tn.	1816	AL36	527	492
Cox, John, Col., of G'tn.	Deed fr	Clarke, Robert, of G'tn.	1816	AM37	463	333
Cox, John, Col., of G'tn.	Deed to	Brookes, Joseph, of G'tn.	1816	AM37	057	047
Cox, John et al	D. of T. fr	Calder, James	1806	O14	303	201
Cox, John et al	Deed fr	Murdock, Addison	1806	Q16	057	036
Cox, John et al	D. of T. fr	Melvin, James	1806	O14	307	203
Cox, John et al	Suit ads	Potomac Company	1812	AG32	258	183
Cox, John, mer., of G'tn.	Deed fr	Murdock, Addison	1806	P15	274	180
Cox, John, mer., of G'tn.	Deed fr	Beall, Thomas, of George, of G'tn.	1806	P15	276	182
Cox, John, merchant	Mortgage fr	Carpenter, Thomas	1801	G7	306	427
Cox, John, merchant	B. of S. fr	Love, Charles	1804	L11	017	17
Cox, John, of G'tn.	Lease fr	Smith, James, of Frederick Co.	1800	E5	178	169
Cox, John, of G'tn.	Deed fr	Templeman, John, of G'tn.	1802	H8	368	342
Cox, John, of G'tn.	Deed to	Cox, Thomas Campbell, of SC	1804	K10	171	181
Cox, John, of G'tn.	Deed fr	Munroe, Thomas, Supt.	1805	M12	360	368
Cox, John, of G'tn.	Assign fr	White, Levi	1805	M12	248	250
Cox, John, of G'tn.	Assign to	Wharton, Franklin	1810	Y24	034	030
Cox, John, of G'tn.	Deed fr	Mickle, John, of Balto.	1811	AB27	389	321
Cox, John, of G'tn.	Deed fr	Morris, Randal, of G'tn.	1811	AA26	035	027
Cox, John, of G'tn.	Deed fr	Mickle, John, of Balto.	1812	AC28	216	162
Cox, John, of G'tn.	Deed fr	Holmead, John	1812	AC28	116	087

Party	What	Party	Year	Liber	Old	New
Cox, John, of G'tn.	Deed to	Matthews, William, Rev.	1813	AE30	345	258
Cox, John, of G'tn.	Deed to	Smith, Sophia, of G'tn.	1814	AG32	053	041
Cox, John, of G'tn.	Deed fr	Brooks, Joseph, of G'tn.	1814	AH33	009	008
Cox, John, of G'tn.	Deed to	Mackall, Benjamin F., of G'tn.	1814	AG32	016	012
Cox, John, of G'tn.	Deed fr	Smith, Walter, of G'tn.	1815	AI34	018	019
Cox, John, of G'tn.	Deed to	Munroe, Thomas	1815	AI34	230	261
Cox, John, of G'tn.	Deed to	Smith, Walter, of G'tn.	1815	AI34	029	033
Cox, John, of G'tn.	D. of T. fr	McKenney, William, of G'tn.	1815	AK35	301	240
Cox, John, of G'tn.	Deed fr	Boone, Arnold, of G'tn.	1815	AK35	089	068
Cox, John, of G'tn.	Deed fr	Waring, Henry, of Montg. Co.	1815	AK35	090	069
Cox, John, of G'tn.	Deed fr	Riley, Mary, of Montg. Co.	1815	AK35	092	071
Cox, John, of G'tn.	Deed fr	Baltzer, Jacob, of G'tn.	1815	AK35	091	070
Cox, John, of G'tn.	Deed fr	Pickrell, John, of G'tn.	1816	AL36	101	102
Cox, John, of G'tn.	Deed fr	Washington, George C., of MD	1816	AL36	202	210
Cox, John, of G'tn.	Deed fr	Davis, John P., of G'tn.	1816	AL36	203	211
Cox, John, of G'tn.	Assign fr	Brookes, Joseph, of G'tn.	1816	AM37	460	331
Cox, John, of G'tn.	Deed to	Duvall, William N.	1816	AK35	528	417
Cox, Josiah	B. of S. to	Weiskopff & Keller	1809	W22	414	269
Cox, Josias	B. of S. to	Johnston, James	1811	Z25	435	342
Cox, Josias	Deed to	Tweedy, David, trustee	1813	AF31	065	044
Cox, Thomas Cambell, of SC	Deed to	Way, Andrew & George	1813	AE30	480	357
Cox, Thomas Campbell, of SC	Deed fr	Cox, John, of G'tn.	1804	K10	171	181
Cox, Walter	P. of Atty. fr	Ware, Gustavus M., of Lynchburg	1811	AB27	409	337
Cox, Zachariah	Deed to	Gardner, James	1802	I9	506	829
Coxon, Jesse W.	Deed fr	Walker, Zachariah	1813	AF31	272	191
Coyle, Andrew	D. of T. to	Glover, Charles	1814	AH33	267	233
Coyle, Andrew	Deed fr	Whetcroft, Henry & Sarah	1814	AH33	142	135
Coyle, Andrew	B. of S. fr	Martin, Honore, of Rockville MD	1815	AI34	491	499
Coyle, Andrew	Release fr	Glover, Charles	1815	AI34	490	497
Coyle, Andrew	D. of T. to	Elliot, Samuel, Jr.	1816	AL36	181	180
Coyle, Andrew et al	Deed fr	Fairfax, Ferdinando	1817	AO39	275	197
Coyle, Francis	B. of S. fr	Anderson, John	1805	M12	140	135
Coyle, Francis	Deed fr	Fletcher, William, of P.G. Co.	1817	AO39	419	285
Coyle, John	Assign fr	Schroeder, Henry, of Balto.	1810	Z25	161	128
Coyle, John & Elias B. Caldwell	Deed to	Wilson, John A.	1816	AL36	399	384
Coyle, John, trustee et al	Cert fr	Munroe, Thomas, Supt.	1813	AE30	350	262
Coyle, Thomas	Lease fr	Dermott, Alice	1808	T19	308	225
Coyle, Thomas, trustee	Deed fr	Aiken, John, insolvent	1804	L11	196	187
Cozens, William R.	Deed fr	Forrest, Uriah et al	1802	I9	581	942
Cozens, William R.	Deed fr	Forrest, Uriah et al	1802	I9	583	944
Cozens, William R.	Deed to	Templeman, John	1802	I9	371	615
Cozens, William R.	Deed fr	Boyd, Washington, marshal	1808	U20	349	189
Cozens, William R.	Deed fr	Lanham, Elisha	1810	Y24	166	152
Cozens, William R.	Deed fr	Boyd, Washington, marshal	1811	AC28	087	066
Cozens, William R.	Deed fr	Wright, Thomas C., of G'tn.	1813	AF31	410	295
Cozens, William R.	Deed fr	Eliason, Ebenezer	1814	AG32	405	296
Cozens, William R.	Deed to	Maus, John H.	1815	AH33	483	413
Cozenstrom, R.	Deed fr	Hewitt, John, trustee et al	1806	O14	227	149
Crabb, John	Deed fr	Laird, John, of G'tn.	1813	AE30	117	090
Crabb, John	Plat	G and 6½ streets	1816	AM37		093
Crabb, John	Deed fr	McLeod, John	1816	AM37	116	091
Crafen, Tunis, by trustee	Deed to	Thomas, John Valentine	1815	AK35	214	168
Craig, Ann, late Glover et al	Deed fr	Craig, Robert, of G'tn.	1800	F6		036
Craig, George	Deed fr	Beatty, Charles, heirs of	1806	P15	039	023
Craig, George, of G'tn.	Deed fr	Dorsey, William H., of G'tn.	1807	R17	186	142

Index to District of Columbia Land Records, 1792-1817

Party	What	Party	Year	Liber	Old	New
Craig, George, of G'tn.	Deed to	Fahy, Mark, of G'tn.	1811	AA26	324	218
Craig, Henrietta, admx. of Robert	B. of S. fr	Beatty, Thomas, Jr.	1814	AH33	020	018
Craig, Henrietta, admx. of Robert	Assign fr	Beatty, Thomas, Jr.	1814	AH33	022	020
Craig, Henrietta, of G'tn., wid/o R.	Deed to	Wilson, John A.	1815	AI34	083	095
Craig, James & William Miller	Deed fr	Wagner, Jacob, of G'tn.	1813	AF31	203	137
Craig, John, estate of	Deed to	Barry, James	1804	K10	214	224
Craig, John et al	Deed fr	Simson, John, of PA et al	1802	H8	120	117
Craig, John et al	Deed fr	Ross, Charles et al	1802	H8	120	117
Craig, John et al	Deed fr	Ross, Charles et al	1806	P15	230	153
Craig, John, of Phila.	Deed fr	Stoddert, Benjamin	1804	L11	321	294
Craig, Robert	Deed fr	Polock, Isaac	1798	D4	147	129
Craig, Robert	Deed fr	Jackson, Samuel, of G'tn.	1799	D4	220	203
Craig, Robert	Cert fr	Munroe, Thomas, Supt.	1802	I9	068	095
Craig, Robert	Lease fr	Presbyterian Congregation, G'tn.	1812	AC28	186	142
Craig, Robert	Mortgage fr	Weaden, Henry	1812	AD29	362	304
Craig, Robert et al	Lease fr	Reintzel, Anthony	1811	Z25	490	389
Craig, Robert et al	Deed to	Joncherez, Alexander L.	1812	AD29	383	323
Craig, Robert, of G'tn.	Deed fr	Beall, Thomas B., of G'tn.	1797	C3	147	120
Craig, Robert, of G'tn.	Deed to	Craig, Ann, late Glover et al	1800	F6		036
Craig, Robert, of G'tn.	Deed fr	Lingan, Nicholas, of G'tn.	1802	H8	410	379
Craig, Robert, of G'tn.	Deed to	Hodges, Thomas C., of G'tn.	1802	I9	014	019
Craig, Robert, of G'tn.	Deed fr	Ratrie, William, of G'tn.	1804	K10	337	348
Craig, Robert, of G'tn.	Mortgage fr	Edwards, John, of G'tn.	1805	O14	112	070
Craig, Robert, of G'tn. et al	B. of S. fr	Bootes, Samuel	1805	N13	383	307
Craig, Robert, of G'tn.	B. of S. fr	Jones, Edward, of G'tn.	1809	X23	025	017
Craig, Samuel, of Alexa.	Deed fr	King, William, of G'tn.	1795	B2A	347	490
Craigg, George, of G'tn.	Deed fr	Craigg, Robert, of G'tn.	1794	B2A	113	150
Craigg, Robert, of G'tn.	Deed to	Craigg, George, of G'tn.	1794	B2A	113	150
Craigg, Robert, of G'tn.	Deed fr	Beall, Thomas, of G'tn.	1794	B2A	112	149
Craik, James & Richard Conway	Deed to	Beall, Thomas & John M. Gantt	1792	A1-1	057	85
Craik, William et al	Deed fr	Johns, Richard	1794	B2A	052	063
Craik, William et al	Deed fr	Thomas, Samuel 3rd	1794	B2A	051	062
Craik, William et al	Deed fr	Beall, Thomas, s/o George	1794	B2A	054	067
Craik, William, exor. of	Deed to	French, George, of G'tn.	1812	AD29	338	282
Craik, William, Gent.	Deed fr	Beall, Thomas, of George, farmer	1798	D4	067	057
Craik, William, Montg. Co. et al	Deed to	Brooke, Samuel, of Montg. Co.	1797	C3	151	124
Craik, William, of Montg. Co. et al	Deed fr	Davidson, Samuel, of Montg. Co.	1797	C3	152	125
Craik, William, of Fairfax Co. VA	Deed fr	Deakins, Leonard M., G'tn. et al	1805	M12	393	406
Craik, William, of Fairfax Co. VA	Deed to	Chandler, William Story, of G'tn.	1805	N13	064	058
Craik, William, of Alexa., exr. of	Deed to	Bearcroft, William	1809	V21	243	173
Craik, William, planter	Deed to	Courts, John, of Charles Co.	1799	E5	063	051
Crammond, James	Cert fr	Commissioners of Washington	1795	B2A	332	467
Crammond, James, of Phila. PA	Cert to	Watson, James	1793	B2A	305	428
Cramphin, Thomas	Deed to	Beall, Thomas & John M. Gantt	1792	A1-1	049	73
Cramphin, Thomas	Cert fr	Magruder, John Reed, Jr.	1797	B2B	643	405
Cramphin, Thomas	Deed fr	Chandler, Walter S.	1802	H8	170	164
Cramphin, Thomas, of G'tn.	Deed fr	Deakins, William Jr., of G'tn.	1793	A1-2	459	67
Cramphin, Thomas, of Montg. Co.	Deed fr	Boucher, John Thomas, P.G. Co.	1796	B2B	555	284
Cramphin, Thomas, of Montg. Co.	Deed to	McMurray, Joseph & William	1806	Q16	245	169
Cramphin, Thomas, of Montg. Co.	Deed to	Harding, Edward, of Montg. Co.	1807	Q16	373	286
Cramphin, Watkins, of DE	Deed to	Holmead, John	1813	AE30	167	133
Cranch, William	P. of Atty. fr	Morris, Robert	1796	B2B	390	049
Cranch, William	P. of Atty. fr	Morris, Robert, of Phila. PA	1797	B2B	663	428
Cranch, William	P. of Atty. fr	Greenleaf, James, of Phila.	1797	C3	251	206
Cranch, William	Discharge	Kirkland, George W.	1801	G7	548	

Index to District of Columbia Land Records, 1792-1817

Party	What	Party	Year	Liber	Old	New
Cranch, William	Cert to	Taney, Francis Lewis	1801	G7	337	468
Cranch, William	Deed to	Brent, Robert	1804	L11	218	205
Cranch, William	Deed fr	Brent, Daniel Carroll, marshal	1804	L11	156	155
Cranch, William	Manumis to	[ ], Sarah (negress)	1806	Q16	096	062
Cranch, William	B. of S. fr	Kirby, John B.	1806	O14	337	224
Cranch, William	Deed fr	Greenleaf, James, of Phila. PA	1806	Q16	229	157
Cranch, William	Deed fr	May, Frederick	1808	T19	098	069
Cranch, William	Deed fr	Greenleaf, James, of Phila. PA	1808	T19	060	044
Cranch, William	Mortgage fr	Shanks, Michael	1809	W22	031	024
Cranch, William	Deed fr	Brent, Daniel Carroll, marshal	1809	W22	128	091
Cranch, William	Deed to	Eliot, Samuel, Jr. & Wm. Thornton	1810	Z25	200	157
Cranch, William	Release fr	Brent, Robert	1810	Z25	352	275
Cranch, William	Deed fr	Somerville, David, stone cutter	1810	Y24	417	375
Cranch, William	Mortgage to	Blagden, George	1810	Y24	461	409
Cranch, William	Release to	Greenleaf, James, of PA	1811	AB27	159	132
Cranch, William	Release to	May, Frederick	1811	AB27	493	403
Cranch, William	Manumis to	Campbell, Fanny	1813	AE30	188	150
Cranch, William	Deed fr	Johnson, Jane, of Fredericksburg	1813	AE30	187	149
Cranch, William	Release fr	Blagden, George	1816	AL36	150	150
Cranch, William	Deed to	Gales, Joseph, Jr.	1816	AL36	151	151
Cranch, William & J. Milller, Jr.	Deed to	Pratt, Henry et al	1814	AG32	330	240
Cranch, William et al	P. of Atty. R	Nicholson, John	1796	B2B	591	340
Cranch, William et al	Deed fr	Ray, James, mer.	1797	C3	176	149
Cranch, William et al	Deed to	Ward, Joshua, of VA	1804	L11	175	170
Cranch, William et al	D. of T. fr	Thornton, William	1810	Z25	198	156
Cranch, William et al	Deed fr	Carroll, Daniel, of *Duddington*	1810	Y24	394	356
Cranch, William, Gent.	B. of S. fr	Prentiss, William, merchant	1796	B2B	532	248
Cranch, William, judge	P. of Atty. to	Greenleaf, James, of Phila.	1804	K10	375	389
Cranch, William, late of MA	P. of Atty. fr	Greenleaf, James, New York NY	1795	B2A	233	324
Cranch, William, trustee et al	Deed to	May, Frederick	1805	N13	108	102
Cranch, William, trustee et al	Quit to	Eliot, Samuel, Jr.	1809	W22	293	197
Crandell, George & Ninian Beall	Deed fr	Sutton, Robert, of PA	1810	Y24	303	276
Crandell, Thomas & Sarah, Alexa.	Deed to	Bullus, John	1805	N13	295	240
Crandell, Thomas, of Alexa.	Deed fr	Burford, John A. & Hannah, Alexa.	1805	N13	290	236
Crauford, David	Transfer fr	Contee, Richard A.	1797	B2B	473	165
Craven, Elijah et al	Deed fr	Bromley, Thomas Peter & Mary	1811	AA26	280	190
Craven, John	Deed fr	Templeman, John	1802	I9	204	320
Craven, John	Deed fr	Polk, Charles P.	1802	I9	533	871
Craven, John	Deed fr	Templeman, John	1805	M12	251	252
Craven, John	D. of T. to	English, David, cashier	1815	AK35	051	040
Craven, John	Deed to	Munroe, Thomas	1816	AL36	350	340
Craven, John et al	Deed fr	Sutton, Robert & Catharine	1809	V21	178	123
Craven, John et al	Deed fr	Bromley, Thomas Peter & Mary	1811	AA26	280	190
Craven, Nancy et al	Deed fr	Bromley, Thomas Peter & Mary	1811	AA26	280	190
Craven, Tunis	Deed to	Cowper, William	1802	I9	151	227
Craven, Tunis	Deed fr	Munroe, Thomas, Supt.	1802	I9	128	190
Craven, Tunis	Deed to	Marsteller, Philip G., of Alexa.	1808	U20	106	059
Craven, Tunis	Convey to	Tingey, Thomas	1808	U20	267	142
Craven, Tunis	Slave	From VA	1808	T19	384	273
Craven, Tunis, trustee of	Deed to	Winn, Timothy	1813	AF31	067	046
Craven, Tunis, trustee of	Deed to	Butler, Silas	1813	AF31	068	047
Craven, Tunis, trustee of	Deed to	Harrison, John	1813	AE30	333	249
Craver, Jacob	Deed fr	Stockwell, Mark	1804	K10	395	409
Craver, Philip	B. of S. to	Prout, William	1812	AD29	123	094
Crawford, David	Deed to	Beatty, Thomas, Jr.	1794	B2A	102	134

Party	What	Party	Year	Liber	Old	New
Crawford, David	Deed fr	Commissioners of Washington	1798	C3	509	400
Crawford, David	Mortgage fr	Walker, George	1800	E5	073	060
Crawford, David & Nathaniel	Deed to	Beall, Thomas & John M. Gantt	1793	A1-1	298	396
Crawford, David et al	Deed to	Walker, George	1802	H8	338	316
Crawford, David, of MD, exrs. of	Deed to	Walker, George	1802	H8	338	316
Crawford, David [Crauford]	Cert fr	Commissioners of Washington	1797	B2B	473	165
Crawford, Jacob	B. of S. to	Crawford, James	1802	I9	437	724
Crawford, Jacob, trustee	Deed fr	Lewis, Elizabeth, insolvent	1804	L11	179	173
Crawford, Jacob, trustee	Deed fr	Brashears, John D., insolvent	1805	O14	073	044
Crawford, James	B. of S. fr	Crawford, Jacob	1802	I9	437	724
Crawford, James	B. of S. to	Crawford, Thomas Jefferson	1807	S18	408	326
Crawford, James et al	Deed fr	Ross, Charles et al	1806	P15	230	153
Crawford, James, Jr., of Phila. PA	Deed to	Moylan, Jasper, of Phila. PA	1808	T19	354	255
Crawford, James, younger, Phila.	Deed fr	Fitzsimons, Thomas, Phila. et al	1804	L11	131	133
Crawford, James, younger, Phila.	Deed fr	Fitzsimons, Thomas, Phila. et al	1804	L11	135	137
Crawford, James, younger, Phila.	Deed fr	Fitzsimons, Thomas, Phila. et al	1807	R17	062	050
Crawford, Nathaniel et al	Deed to	Walker, George	1802	H8	338	316
Crawford, Nathaniel, Gent.	Deed fr	Barry, James, merchant	1800	F6	055	034
Crawford, Thomas Jefferson	B. of S. fr	Crawford, James	1807	S18	408	326
Crawford, William	B. of S. fr	Heisler, Joseph, of G'tn.	1809	W22	105	076
Crawford, William	Apprentice	[ ], Kitty (negro)	1809	W22	105	076
Crawford, William	Deed fr	Borrows, Joseph	1812	AD29	227	187
Crawford, William	B. of S. fr	Husler, Joseph	1812	AD29	008	006
Crawford, William	Deed fr	Peter, George	1813	AF31	151	102
Crawford, William	Deed fr	Duane, William, of Phila. PA	1815	AI34	136	156
Crawford, William	Release fr	Weightman, Roger C.	1815	AI34	138	159
Crawford, William & John Hoye	B. of S. fr	Carter, John M., of G'tn. et al	1812	AD29	161	127
Crawford, William, heirs of	Deed fr	Thornbrough, Joseph, of PA	1817	AO39	370	249
Crawford, William, of G'tn.	Deed fr	Riggs, George W., of G'tn.	1810	Y24	026	022
Crawford, William, of G'tn. et al	Deed fr	Bussard, Daniel, of G'tn.	1810	X23	327	261
Crawford, William, of G'tn.	Deed fr	Coles, John, of New London CN	1811	AB27	405	334
Crawford, William, of G'tn.	Deed fr	Lee, Thomas S., of G'tn.	1811	AB27	098	080
Crawford, William, of G'tn.	Mortgage fr	Lufborough, Nathan	1812	AD29	344	288
Crawford, William, of G'tn.	Deed fr	Gaines, Richard, of Cincinnati OH	1813	AF31	149	100
Crawford, William, of G'tn.	Release to	Lufborough, Nathan	1813	AE30	489	363
Crawford, William, of G'tn.	Deed fr	Smith, Walter, of G'tn.	1814	AH33	059	052
Crawford, William, of G'tn.	Deed fr	Patterson, Edgar, of G'tn.	1814	AH33	082	074
Crawford, William, of G'tn.	Deed fr	Lee, Thomas Sim, of *Needwood*	1814	AH33	330	285
Crawford, William, of G'tn.	Deed fr	Riggs, George W., of Balto.	1814	AH33	328	283
Crawford, William, of G'tn.	Deed fr	Magruder, Middleton B. et al	1815	AI34	141	161
Crawford, William, of G'tn.	Deed to	Ross, Richard, of Montg. Co.	1816	AM37	290	212
Crawford, William, of G'tn.	Deed to	Lorman, William, of Balto.	1816	AM37	286	209
Crawford, William, of G'tn.	Deed to	Lorman, William, of Balto.	1816	AM37	288	211
Crawley, Timothy et al	Lease fr	Carleton, Joseph	1804	L11	282	259
Craycroft, Charles Electius	D. Gift fr	Edelin, Susannah, grandmother	1813	AF31	256	178
Craycroft, Mary Ann	D. Gift fr	Edelin, Susannah, her mother	1813	AF31	255	177
Craycroft, Thomas	Lease fr	Parker, Fielder	1812	AC28	172	129
Craycroft, Thomas	Assign to	Koontz, Frederick	1816	AL36	437	416
Creager, John & Elizabeth	Deed to	Holtzman, George	1810	X23	349	280
Creager, John, now of G'tn.	Deed fr	Davidson, Anna Maria, of G'tn.	1810	X23	373	299
Creager, Laurence, of G'tn.	Deed to	Morsell, James Sewall, of G'tn.	1810	Y24	056	049
Creager, Mary, wid/o Laurence	Deed to	Morsell, James Sewall, of G'tn.	1810	Y24	056	049
Creager, Michael	Agreement	Baker, Samuel	1804	L11	146	147
Creager, Michael	Deed to	Ratrie, William, Jr.	1816	AM37	197	146
Creager, Michael, Alexa., et al	Deed to	Scholfield, Issachar & Mahlon	1799	D4	289	271

Party	What	Party	Year	Liber	Old	New
Creditors of Henop & Co.	Memo fr	Henop, Philip	1802	I9	002	003
Creiger, Michael	Deed fr	Doughty, William, of G'tn.	1804	L11	058	59
Criddle, Jonathan	Deed fr	O'Conner, Dannis	1812	AD29	056	040
Criddle, Jonathan	Deed fr	Hurley, William	1816	AL36	058	059
Criger, Mary	B. of S. fr	Boswell, Benjamin	1802	H8	343	320
Criger, Mary	B. of S. fr	Boswell, Benjamin	1802	H8	343	320
Crocken, James, of G'tn.	B. of S. to	Tanner, Mary Ann, of G'tn.	1817	AN38	538	391
Crocker, John	Cert fr	Commissioners of Washington	1797	B2B	464	155
Crocker, John	Transfer fr	Morris, Robert & James Greenleaf	1797	B2B	464	155
Crocker, John, of Martinsburgh	Deed to	Dixon, John, of Martinsburgh VA	1799	D4	230	212
Crocker, John, physician	Agreement	Law, Thomas	1796	B2B	418	090
Crocker, John, physician	Mortgage to	Law, Thomas	1797	B2B	630	390
Crocket, Elizabeth	B. of S. to	Shorter, John	1817	AO39	107	083
Crockett, Betsey (M)	Cert Free fr	Hewitt, William, register	1815	AI34	218	249
Crockett, Betty (C)	Cert. Free fr	Rapine, Daniel	1811	AC28	055	042
Crommelin, Robert Daniel et al	Deed fr	Greenleaf, James	1794	B2A	065	083
Crommelin, Robert Daniel et al	Deed to	Greenleaf, James, New York NY	1796	B2B	493	188
Crommett, Mary Ann, of G'tn.	Deed fr	Beall, Thomas, of George	1809	X23	271	213
Crommitt, Mary Ann	Deed to	Beatty, Charles A., Dr.	1813	AE30	514	381
Cromwell, Jesse	B. of S. fr	Fish, Francis, of Fairfax Co. VA	1810	Y24	010	009
Cromwell, Jesse, of Montg. Co.	Deed fr	Ober, Robert	1814	AF31	503	366
Crook, Bernard	Deed fr	Lenox, Peter	1798	C3	298	241
Crook, Bernard & Agnes	Deed to	Smith, William, of Alexa.	1800	E5	280	274
Crook, Bernard et al	Deed fr	Morton, Thomas, of Montg. Co.	1796	B2B	559	290
Crookshank, Ann et al	Deed fr	Jones, Walter, Jr., trustee	1814	AG32	219	153
Crookshank, John	Deed fr	Craig, Robert, of G'tn.	1800	F6		036
Crookshank, John	Deed fr	Snyder, Jacob	1800	F6	053	033
Crookshank, John	Cert fr	Commissioners of Washington	1801	G7	453	589
Crookshank, John	Deed fr	Fenwick, George	1802	I9	124	184
Crookshank, John	Deed fr	Threlkeld, John	1802	I9	579	938
Crookshank, John et al	Deed fr	Commissioners of Washington	1800	E5	131	119
Crookshank, John et al	Deed fr	Jones, Walter, Jr., trustee	1814	AG32	219	153
Crookshank, John, of G'tn.	B. of S. fr	Ragan, John	1802	G7	488	625
Crookshank, Richard et al	Deed fr	Jones, Walter, Jr., trustee	1814	AG32	219	153
Crookshanks, John, of Montg. Co.	Deed fr	Burnes, David, of P.G. Co.	1796	B2B	439	119
Crookshanks, John, of G'tn.	Deed to	Bond, William	1797	B2B	634	394
Crookshanks, John, of Montg Co.	Deed to	Clephan, Lewis, of Montg. Co.	1797	C3	019	15
Crosdale, George, of Balto. et al	Deed fr	Stoddert, Benjamin	1806	P15	393	263
Cross, Eli	B. of S. fr	Adams, George, constable	1816	AM37	081	066
Cross, Elie	B. of S. fr	Stokes, John	1816	AL36	122	123
Cross, Elie	Deed fr	Carroll, Daniel, of *Duddington*	1817	AO39	365	246
Cross, Lewis & Mary, of VA	Deed to	Brengle, Laurence, Frederick Co.	1804	K10	383	397
Cross, Middleton	B. of S. fr	Cross, William	1802	H8	237	226
Cross, Rachel & Eli	Manumis to	[ ], Sall (C)	1812	AB27	283	232
Cross, William	B. of S. fr	Berkley, George	1801	G7	272	375
Cross, William	B. of S. to	Cross, Middleton	1802	H8	237	226
Cross, William	B. of S. to	Johnston, Margery	1802	H8	268	254
Cross, William	B. of S. to	Prout, William	1808	U20	372	204
Crossfield, Ichiel	B. of S. to	Patterson, Edgar, of G'tn.	1813	AF31	164	111
Crossfield, Jeheel	B. of S. to	Triplett, Sarah	1808	V21	019	014
Crossfield, Jehiel, insolvent	Assign to	Whetcroft, Henry, trustee	1809	V21	379	282
Crouse, Henry	Deed fr	Coulter, Peter	1809	V21	271	194
Crow, John et al	Release fr	Thornton, William	1805	M12	207	208
Crow, John, of G'tn. et al	Release to	Peacock, Robert Ware et al	1805	M12	209	210
Crow, John, of G'tn. et al	Deed fr	Davidson, John	1805	M12	203	205

Party	What	Party	Year	Liber	Old	New
Crow, John, of Frederick Co. VA	Deed to	Wright, Thomas C.	1806	P15	301	198
Crowley, Bartholomew	B. of S. fr	Crowley, Mark	1804	K10	180	189
Crowley, Bartholomew	B. of S. to	Ledan, Nicholas, his son-in-law	1812	AD29	132	102
Crowley, Edward	Deed to	Burch, Samuel	1816	AL36	205	212
Crowley, John	Lease fr	Carleton, Joseph, of G'tn.	1809	V21	384	288
Crowley, Mark	B. of S. to	Crowley, Bartholomew	1804	K10	180	189
Crowley, Thomas	Assign to	Connor, Martin, of Montg. Co.	1806	P15	235	157
Crowley, Thomas	Deed to	Connor, Martin, of Montg. Co.	1806	P15	238	158
Crowley, Thomas	B. of S. to	Wheaton, Nicholas	1807	Q16	340	261
Crowley, Thomas	B. of S. to	Whelan, Nicholas	1808	T19	316	231
Crowley, Thomas & Edward	Agreement	Wheelan, Nicholas	1807	S18	081	067
Crowloy, Timothy	Deed fr	Carleton, Joseph, of G'tn.	1809	V21	386	290
Crown, Mary Ann, heirs of Truman	Convey to	Smith, Walter	1815	AK35	277	221
Crown, Samuel T.	Deed fr	Beatty, Charles, heirs of	1806	O14	201	132
Crown, Samuel T.	Deed to	Rodes, George	1807	S18	382	304
Crown, Samuel T.	Deed fr	Ritchie, Abner	1808	V21	050	039
Crown, Samuel T.	Deed to	Ott, John, Dr.	1810	Z25	138	109
Crown, Samuel T.	Deed to	Beall, William Murdock, Jr.	1812	AD29	158	124
Crown, Trueman	Convey fr	Lingan, James M.	1814	AH33	235	205
Crown, William	Deed fr	Carroll, Daniel	1802	I9	565	916
Crown, William	Deed to	Simpson, Tobias	1817	AN38	224	164
Crusey, Betsey (C), age 33	Cert Free fr	Stewart, Catherine	1813	AF31	230	158
Culp, John M., Sr., of Frederick	Deed to	Culp, Michael, Jr., of Frederick	1793	A1-1	177	252
Culp, Michael, Jr. [Kolb]	Deed to	Beall, Thomas & John M. Gantt	1792	A1-1	074	109
Culp, Michael, Jr. [Kolb]	Deed to	Hellen, Walter, of G'tn.	1793	A1-2	416	25
Culp, Michael, Jr., of Frederick	Deed fr	Culp, John M., Sr., of Frederick	1793	A1-1	177	252
Cumberland, William	Assign to	Evans, Thomas, of Balto.	1805	N13	326	264
Cummings, Mary	Deed fr	Johnson, Thomas, of Fredk. Co.	1817	AN38	028	023
Cummins, John	Deed fr	Ireland, Elizabeth & John Staines	1806	Q16	259	180
Cummins, John	Deed fr	Duckworth, George	1808	T19	047	035
Cunningham, Cornelius	Cert fr	Commissioners of Washington	1798	B2B	480	173
Cunningham, Cornelius	Deed fr	Commissioners of Washington	1799	D4	324	309
Cunningham, Cornelius	Deed to	Munroe, Thomas	1800	E5	159	148
Cunningham, Cornelius	Lease fr	Law, John	1808	V21	061	048
Cunningham, John	Receipt fr	[ ] Katy (Negro)	1801	G7		122
Cunningham, John, Calvert Co.	Deed fr	Dawes, Isaac, tanner, of G'tn.	1796	B2B	449	134
Cunningham, John, of G'tn.	Deed to	Baker, Michael, of Rockg. Co. VA	1797	C3	271	220
Cupid, Betzy and child	Cert Free fr	Stoddert, Benjamin	1807	S18	185	150
Cupid, Harry (negro)	Manumis fr	Addison, Thomas G.	1807	R17	200	151
Curran, Eleanor, of G'tn.	D. of T. to	Thompson, John & B. Owens	1812	AD29	253	209
Curran, John	Deed fr	Laird, John, exr. of J. Carleton	1814	AG32	076	057
Curran, John, of G'tn.	Deed fr	Butler, Thomas, of G'tn.	1807	R17	005	005
Curran, Morgan	Deed fr	Young, Moses	1814	AG32	108	081
Curran, William, of G'tn.	Deed fr	Eastburn, Joseph, Adams Co. KY	1799	D4	429	400
Curran, William, of G'tn.	Deed fr	Eastburn, Isaac Washington, G'tn.	1799	D4	357	344
Currie, James	Deed fr	Stras, George Fredk. & Martha	1807	Q16	215	145
Currill, James	Deed fr	McMullin, Archibald	1811	AA26	307	207
Curtis, Eliza (M), age 16	Cert. Free fr	Varnum, James M.	1815	AH33	558	477
Curtis, Henry, of St. Mary's Co.	Cert Free		1806	P15	083	051
Custis, Elizabeth Parke, of VA	Deed fr	Law, Thomas	1796	E5		224
Cutter, Nathaniel, of NH	Deed fr	Munroe, Thomas, Supt.	1802	I9	053	073
Cutter, Nathaniel, Portsmouth NH	Deed to	Parry, Edward, Portsmouth NH	1806	P15	384	256
Cutts, Ann, w/o Hon. Richard	Deed fr	Munroe, Thomas, Supt.	1805	M12	051	049
Cutts, Richard	Deed fr	Doughty, William	1817	AO39	237	171
Cutts, Richard	Cert fr	Munroe, Thomas, Supt.	1817	AO39	242	174

Party	What	Party	Year	Liber	Old	New
Cutts, Richard	Deed fr	Chapman, Henry H. et al	1817	AO39	238	172
Cutts, Richard	Cert fr	Munroe, Thomas, Supt.	1817	AO39	241	174

Index to District of Columbia Land Records, 1792-1817

Party	What	Party	Year	Liber	Old	New
D						
Dair, Shadrack	Deed fr	Glover, Charles, trustee	1814	AH33	132	126
Dale, James, of Balto., heirs of	Convey to	Dougherty, Daniel, of Alexa.	1815	AI34	199	228
Dale, Richard, mer., of Phila. PA	Deed fr	Read, William & Ann, of Phila. PA	1812	AC28	439	315
Dalton, Katharine	Deed fr	Deblois, Lewis	1799	D4	401	380
Dalton, Katharine	Deed fr	Deblois, Lewis	1800	E5	377	356
Dalton, Katharine	Deed to	Deblois, Lewis	1800	E5	358	341
Dalton, Katharine	Deed fr	Carroll, Daniel, of *Duddington*	1801	G7	430	565
Dalton, Katharine	Deed fr	Deblois, Lewis	1801	G7	428	563
Dalton, Katherine	Deed fr	Deblois, Lewis	1799	E5	072	059
Dalton, Tristam et al	Deed fr	Lear, Tobias, of G'tn.	1794	B2A	152	201
Dalton, Tristam, of G'tn.	Deed fr	King, William & William Prout	1796	B2B	407	074
Dalton, Tristam, of G'tn.	Deed fr	Prout, William	1796	B2B	408	076
Dalton, Tristam, of G'tn.	Deed fr	King, William & William Prout	1796	B2B	405	072
Dalton, Tristram	Deed to	Deblois, Lewis	1797	C3	089	73
Dalton, Tristram	Deed fr	Commissioners of Washington	1799	D4	319	303
Dalton, Tristram	Deed to	Peter, Robert, of G'tn.	1799	D4	309	293
Dalton, Tristram	P. of Atty. fr	Lear, Tobias, of Fairfax Co.	1800	E5		154
Dalton, Tristram	Deed to	Deblois, Lewis	1800	E5	142	130
Dalton, Tristram	Deed to	Hellen, Walter	1802	H8	016	015
Dalton, Tristram & Tobias Lear	Deed to	Griffith, Robert Eaglefield et al	1799	E5	061	049
Dalton, Tristram & Tobias Lear	Deed to	Coles, John et al	1799	E5	061	049
Dalton, Tristram & Tobias Lear	Deed to	Hobson, Jonathan et al	1799	E5	061	049
Dalton, Tristram et al	Deed fr	Holmead, Anthony	1795	B2A	226	314
Dalton, Tristram et al	Deed to	Deakins, William, Jr., of G'tn.	1797	C3	221	186
Dalton, Tristram et al	Deed fr	Greenleaf, James	1798	D4	055	046
Dalton, Tristram et al	Deed to	Hobson, Jonathan et al	1798	D4	148	131
Dalton, Tristram et al	Deed to	Deakins, William, Jr., of G'tn.	1798	D4	062	052
Dalton, Tristram et al	Deed fr	Peter, Robert, of G'tn.	1799	D4	321	305
Dalton, Tristram et al	Deed to	Deakins, William, Jr.	1800	E5	163	152
Dalton, Tristram et al	Deed to	Kennedy, John	1802	H8	589	554
Dalton, Tristram et al	Deed to	Kennedy, John	1802	H8	589	554
Dalton, Tristram, mer.	Deed to	Deblois, Lewis	1797	C3	090	74
Dalton, Tristram, mer.	Deed fr	Lear, Tobias, mer.	1798	C3	317	256
Dalton, Tristram, of P.G. Co. et al	Deed to	Deakins, William, Jr., of G'tn.	1797	C3	223	187
Dalton, Tristram, of G'tn. et al	Deed to	Deakins, William, Jr., of G'tn.	1797	C3	218	183
Dalton, White et al	Deed to	Kennedy, John	1802	H8	589	554
Dangerfield, M.H.	Cert Free to	Shorter, Catharine & children	1808	U20	361	197
Dant, James	Deed fr	Greenleaf, James, of Phila.	1798	C3	336	271
Dant, James	Agreement	Speake, Samuel	1810	Y24	108	098
Dant, James, late of KY	B. of S. to	Fenwick, Mary Ann	1801	G7	011	014
Dant, James, of KY	Deed to	Clarke, Francis	1810	Y24	377	341
Dant, Thomas	Deed fr	Riffle, George [Riffel]	1816	AL36	160	160
Dant, Thomas	Deed fr	Magruder, Ninian, Dr., of G'tn.	1816	AK35	370	291
Dant, Thomas, of G'tn.	Deed to	Magruder, Ninian	1816	AL36	017	018
Dant, Thomas, of G'tn.	Deed to	Davis, John P., of G'tn.	1816	AM37	016	012
Dant, Thomas [Dantt]	Deed fr	Riffle, George	1814	AG32	154	110
Dantt, Thomas	Deed to	Davis, Richard	1814	AG32	303	221
Darnall, John	Deed fr	Lovering, William	1800	E5	393	368
Darnall, John	Deed fr	Maddox, Notley, sheriff	1800	E5	279	273
Darnall, John	Deed fr	Maddox, Notldy	1800	E5	279	273
Darnall, John	Deed fr	Turner, Thomas, of G'tn.	1800	E5	291	285
Darnall, John	Deed to	Maddox, Notley	1801	G7	297	412
Darnall, Robert	Deed fr	Coolidge, Samuel J.	1794	A1-2	493	96
Darne, Simon	D. of T. fr	Scott, Allen	1815	AI34	146	167

Index to District of Columbia Land Records, 1792-1817　　　　　　　　　　　　　　　117

Party	What	Party	Year	Liber	Old	New
Darnes, William, Montg. Co. et al	Deed to	Peter, John, of G'tn.	1817	AO39	245	177
Dasheill, Lucretia & Warren	B. of S. fr	Dasheill, Sarah	1801	G7	174	232
Dasheill, Sarah	B. of S. to	Dasheill, Lucretia & Warren	1801	G7	174	232
Dashiell, George	B. of S. to	Martin, Honore	1811	AA26	002	002
Dashiell, George, of G'tn.	B. of S. to	Milligan, Joseph, of G'tn.	1811	AB27	356	295
Dashiell, Thomas B.	B. of S. fr	Willson, Sarah	1809	W22	211	145
Datcher, Francis, s/o Reb. Cole	Cert Free fr	Butter, Mary (C)	1816	AM37	022	018
Daugherty, Barney, of Balto.	Deed to	Deblois, Lewis, of Alexa.	1810	Z25	352	276
Daugherty, James	Deed fr	Blodget, Samuel, of Phila.	1801	G7	316	442
Daugherty, Joseph	Cert fr	Munroe, Thomas, Supt.	1805	M12	270	271
Daugherty, Joseph	Manumis to	Tanner, Lethe (yellow)	1810	Y24	370	335
Daugherty, Joseph	B. of S. fr	Pratt, Rachel, of P.G. Co.	1810	Y24	369	334
Daugherty, Joseph	Deed fr	McClelland, John	1814	AH33	122	115
Daugherty, Joseph & Mary	Mortgage to	McClelland, John	1810	X23	333	266
Daugherty, Vincent	B. of S. to	Moore, James et al	1811	Z25	556	442
David, Thomas & George Peter	Deed to	Peter, John, of G'tn.	1810	Z25	038	028
Davidson, Alexander	Deed fr	Brown, Stewart	1802	H8	132	129
Davidson, Ann Marcia, of G'tn.	Deed to	Randall, John, of Annapolis	1809	X23	042	031
Davidson, Ann Maria, exrx. John	Deed to	Ritchie, Abner	1807	S18	278	217
Davidson, Ann Maria, late of A.	Deed to	Magruder, Ninian, of G'tn.	1809	W22	357	231
Davidson, Ann Maria, late of A.	Deed to	Bussard, Daniel	1809	W22	347	224
Davidson, Ann Maria, of G'tn.	Deed to	Williams, Benjamin, of G'tn.	1809	X23	203	153
Davidson, Ann Maria, of G'tn.	Deed to	O'Neale, Henry	1809	X23	200	152
Davidson, Ann Maria, of G'tn.	Deed to	Kennedy, James, of G'tn.	1809	X23	176	131
Davidson, Ann Maria, of G'tn.	Deed to	Key, Francis Scott, of G'tn.	1810	X23	375	301
Davidson, Ann Maria, wid.	Deed to	Ritchie, Abner	1810	Y24	308	380
Davidson, Ann Maria, exrx.	Deed to	Wright, Thomas C., of G'tn.	1810	Z25	304	238
Davidson, Ann Maria, exrx.	Deed to	Magruder, Ninian, physic, of G'tn.	1810	Z25	307	240
Davidson, Ann Maria, wid/o John	Release to	Lutz, John	1810	Z25	269	211
Davidson, Ann Maria, exrx.	Deed fr	Grammar, Frederick, of Annapolis	1810	Z25	319	249
Davidson, Ann Maria, exrx.	Release fr	Whetcroft, Burton, of Annapolis	1810	Z25	321	251
Davidson, Ann Maria, exrx.	Release fr	Marbury, William	1810	Z25	324	253
Davidson, Ann Maria, of Annapolis	Deed to	Marbury, William, of G'tn.	1811	Z25	372	292
Davidson, Ann Maria, of Annapolis	Deed to	Smith, Clement	1811	Z25	481	382
Davidson, Anna Maria, of G'tn.	Deed to	Whann, Adam, of G'tn.	1809	X23	317	254
Davidson, Anna Maria, of G'tn.	Deed to	Creager, John, now of G'tn.	1810	X23	373	299
Davidson, Anna Maria, Annapolis	Deed fr	Marbury, William, trustee	1811	AB27	219	178
Davidson, Elias et al	Deed to	Beall, Thomas & John M. Gantt	1792	A1-1	110	160
Davidson, Henry	Manumis fr	Olliver, Thomas	1808	V21	070	055
Davidson, Henry, in N. Britain	Deed fr	Davidson, Samuel	1793	A1-2	454	62
Davidson, James	Deed to	Bernard, John	1802	I9	495	813
Davidson, James	Deed fr	Munroe, Thomas, Supt.	1809	W22	274	178
Davidson, James	Deed fr	Kilty, John & Josias Wilson King	1810	Y24	296	271
Davidson, James	Mortgage fr	Deblois, Lewis, of Alexa.	1810	Y24	293	268
Davidson, James	Deed fr	Patterson, Edgar, of G'tn.	1810	Z25	250	196
Davidson, James	Release to	Patterson, Edgar, of G'tn.	1811	AC28	091	069
Davidson, James	Deed fr	Nourse, Joseph	1811	AA26	209	143
Davidson, James	Deed fr	Prout, William & wife Sarah	1811	AC28	038	028
Davidson, James	Deed to	Lewis, Joseph S., of Phila. PA	1813	AF31	479	349
Davidson, James	Deed fr	Forrest, Richard & Charles Glover	1813	AF31	476	346
Davidson, James	D. of T. fr	Carroll, Charles, of *Bellevue*	1813	AF31	018	013
Davidson, James	Deed to	Nourse, Joseph	1813	AF31	012	010
Davidson, James	Deed to	Carroll, Charles, of Belle Vue NY	1816	AL36	337	329
Davidson, James & R. Forrest	Deed to	Davidson, John	1813	AF31	539	399
Davidson, James & Rich. Forrest	Deed to	Cocke, Buller	1814	AG32	143	103

Index to District of Columbia Land Records, 1792-1817

Party	What	Party	Year	Liber	Old	New
Davidson, James & C. Glover	Deed to	Carr, Overton	1815	AI34	347	378
Davidson, James & Rich. Forrest	Deed to	Lewis, Joseph S., of Phila. PA	1815	AI34	345	377
Davidson, James et al	Release to	Nourse, Joseph	1813	AF31	011	008
Davidson, James, Jr., trustee	Deed fr	Wilson, Samuel	1805	M12	080	074
Davidson, James, Jr.	Deed fr	Perkins, Benjamin	1807	R17	248	187
Davidson, James, Jr.	Deed to	Van Ness, John P.	1808	U20	103	058
Davidson, James, Jr.	Mortgage fr	Kilty, John & Josias Wilson King	1809	W22	215	157
Davidson, James, Jr.	Deed fr	Deblois, Lewis	1812	AD29	202	164
Davidson, James, Jr.	Deed to	Granger, Gideon	1813	AF31	481	351
Davidson, James, of Q.A. Co.	Deed fr	Richmond, William, trustee	1800	E5	203	196
Davidson, John	Deed to	Gannon, James, of G'tn.	1798	C3	506	398
Davidson, John	Deed to	McCleary, Henry, of Frederick Co.	1798	D4	050	042
Davidson, John	Deed to	Rogers, Wm., Thos., Marg. & Dan.	1800	E5	077	064
Davidson, John	Deed to	Cookindaffer, Leonard	1801	G7	027	034
Davidson, John	Deed to	Holmead, Anthony et al	1801	G7	142	187
Davidson, John	Deed to	Prout, William	1801	G7	154	204
Davidson, John	Deed to	Peacock, Robert Ware, attorney	1801	G7	105	134
Davidson, John	Deed to	Balch, Stephen B.	1801	G7	083	107
Davidson, John	Deed to	Krouz, Theodorus	1801	G7	142	187
Davidson, John	Deed to	Corcoran, Thomas	1802	H8	196	188
Davidson, John	Deed to	Kaldenback, Andrew, of G'tn.	1802	H8	378	351
Davidson, John	Deed to	Brookes, William H., of G'tn.	1802	H8	437	402
Davidson, John	Deed to	Upperman, George	1802	I9	450	743
Davidson, John	Deed to	Smith, Walter	1802	I9	172	263
Davidson, John	Lease to	Stevenson, Clotworthy	1802	I9	459	758
Davidson, John	Deed to	Maynard, Thomas	1802	I9	289	474
Davidson, John	Deed fr	Munroe, Thomas et al	1802	I9	364	604
Davidson, John	Deed to	Orme, Thomas	1802	I9	203	317
Davidson, John	Deed to	Deakins, Francis	1802	I9	468	771
Davidson, John	Deed fr	Murdock, John	1802	I9	575	932
Davidson, John	Deed to	Deakins, Francis	1802	I9	350	578
Davidson, John	Deed to	Ogle, Benjamin	1802	I9	254	411
Davidson, John	Deed fr	Davidson, Samuel	1804	L11	328	300
Davidson, John	Deed fr	Stoddert, Benjamin et al	1804	L11	062	64
Davidson, John	Deed fr	Peacock, Robert Ware	1804	L11	014	14
Davidson, John	Cert fr	Munroe, Thomas, Supt.	1804	K10	316	322
Davidson, John	Assign fr	Stephenson, Clotworthy	1804	K10	279	283
Davidson, John	Deed to	O'Hara, James, of Pittsburgh PA	1805	M12	181	182
Davidson, John	Deed to	Beatty, John M. et al	1805	M12	044	043
Davidson, John	B. of S. fr	Sprogell, Thomas Y.	1805	M12	274	274
Davidson, John	Deed to	Crow, John, of G'tn. et al	1805	M12	203	205
Davidson, John	Deed to	Wayman, Charles	1805	M12	255	256
Davidson, John	Mortgage fr	Rhodes, William	1806	O14	211	139
Davidson, John	B. of S. fr	Nicholls, Robert H.	1806	O14	209	138
Davidson, John	B. of S. fr	Gillis, John H.	1807	Q16	398	306
Davidson, John	Deed fr	Gillis, Thomas H.	1807	Q16	388	298
Davidson, John	Deed to	McLean, Cornelius	1807	S18	282	221
Davidson, John	Deed to	McClelland, John	1808	V21	065	052
Davidson, John	Deed fr	Kilty, John & Josias Wilson King	1809	X23	017	011
Davidson, John	Deed fr	Coles, John	1809	V21	215	153
Davidson, John	D. of T. fr	Washington, Lund & Susanna	1809	V21	319	234
Davidson, John	Assign fr	Thorpe, Thomas	1810	X23	189	142
Davidson, John	Deed to	McLean, Cornelius	1810	Y24	094	085
Davidson, John	Deed fr	Richmond, Eliz., of Durham, Eng.	1810	Y24	218	201
Davidson, John	Deed fr	Richmond, Christopher, of Eng.	1810	Y24	221	204

Index to District of Columbia Land Records, 1792-1817

Party	What	Party	Year	Liber	Old	New
Davidson, John	Deed fr	Thorpe, Thomas & Daniel Bussard	1810	Z25	090	068
Davidson, John	Deed fr	Bussard, Daniel	1810	Z25	093	071
Davidson, John	Deed fr	Hagner, Peter	1811	AB27	504	412
Davidson, John	Deed to	Hagner, Peter	1811	AB27	495	405
Davidson, John	Deed to	Grammer, Gotlieb Christopher	1812	AD29	234	193
Davidson, John	Deed to	McLean, Cornelius	1813	AF31	396	286
Davidson, John	Deed fr	Davidson, Jas. & Rich. Forrest	1813	AF31	539	399
Davidson, John	Deed to	Forrest, Joseph	1813	AE30	280	215
Davidson, John	Deed to	Lewis, Joseph S., of Phila. PA	1813	AF31	538	398
Davidson, John	Deed to	McLean, Cornelius	1815	AI34	240	272
Davidson, John	Deed fr	Corporation of Washington	1815	AK35	296	236
Davidson, John	Deed to	Fletcher, William, now of MD	1815	AK35	390	307
Davidson, John	Deed fr	Corporation of Washington	1815	AK35	293	234
Davidson, John	Deed fr	Corporation of Washington	1815	AK35	285	228
Davidson, John	B. of S. fr	Greeves, Catharine, of Alexa.	1816	AK35	478	375
Davidson, John	Manumis to	Smallwood, George	1816	AK35	480	376
Davidson, John & William Brent	D. of T. fr	Whelan, Nicholas	1814	AG32	169	120
Davidson, John, Capt.	B. of S. fr	Rhodes, William	1805	M12	158	156
Davidson, John et al	Deed fr	Gillis, Thomas Handy	1804	L11	262	241
Davidson, John et al	Deed fr	Carroll, Daniel, of *Duddington*	1810	Y24	394	356
Davidson, John, Gen., Annapolis	Deed to	Beatty, John M. and Charles A.	1806	O14	280	185
Davidson, John, Gen., exrx. of	Deed to	Meddert, Jacob	1807	S18	241	190
Davidson, John, Gen., exrx. of	Deed to	Ritchie, Abner	1810	Y24	308	380
Davidson, John, Gen., exrx. of	Deed to	Ritchie, Abner	1810	Z25	267	210
Davidson, John, Gen., exrx. of	Deed to	Smith, Clement	1810	Z25	285	224
Davidson, John, of Annapolis	Deed fr	Davidson, Samuel, of G'tn.	1792	A1-1	040	61
Davidson, John, of Annapolis	Deed to	Beall, Thomas & John M. Gantt	1793	A1-1	224	311
Davidson, John, of Annapolis	Deed to	Dunlap, John, of G'tn.	1794	B2A	076	098
Davidson, John, of Annapolis	Deed to	King, George, of G'tn.	1794	B2A	160	211
Davidson, John, of Annapolis	Deed to	Doyle, Alexander, of G'tn.	1794	B2A	090	116
Davidson, John, of Annapolis	Deed fr	Dorsey, William H.	1795	B2A	183	247
Davidson, John, of Annapolis	Deed to	Ragon, Daniel, of G'tn.	1795	B2A	165	220
Davidson, John, of Annapolis	Deed to	Dulany, Matthew, of G'tn.	1795	B2A	343	484
Davidson, John, of Annapolis	Deed to	Threlkeld, John, *Knaves Disapp.*	1795	B2A	178	240
Davidson, John, of Annapolis	Deed to	Magruder, Nathaniel, carpenter	1795	B2A	182	245
Davidson, John, of Annapolis	Deed to	Rigdon, Thomas, of G'tn.	1795	B2B	365	016
Davidson, John, of Annapolis	Deed to	O'Reilly, Johnson Michael	1797	B2B	658	422
Davidson, John, of Annapolis	Deed to	James, James, of G'tn.	1797	C3	117	96
Davidson, John, of Annapolis	Deed to	Kaldenbauch, Andrew, of G'tn.	1798	C3	407	323
Davidson, John, of Annapolis	Deed to	Reintzel, Alexander	1798	C3	469	369
Davidson, John, of Annapolis	Deed to	Ritchie, Abner	1798	C3	452	356
Davidson, John, of Annapolis	Deed to	Sands, Mary, of G'tn.	1798	C3	323	260
Davidson, John, of Annapolis	Deed to	Dunlap, John, of G'tn.	1798	C3	320	259
Davidson, John, of Annapolis	Deed to	Orme, Thomas, of Montg. Co.	1798	C3	438	344
Davidson, John, of Annapolis	Deed to	Williams, Thomas O.	1799	D4	308	292
Davidson, John, of Annapolis	Deed to	Hedges, Nicholas	1799	D4	367	353
Davidson, John, of Annapolis	Deed to	Reily, Hugh	1799	D4	189	171
Davidson, John, of Annapolis	Deed to	Ritchie, William, of Frederick Co.	1799	D4	326	311
Davidson, John, of Annapolis	Deed to	Beall, Elizabeth	1799	D4	399	378
Davidson, John, of Annapolis	Deed to	Smith, Mary	1799	D4	363	350
Davidson, John, of Annapolis	Deed fr	Wootton, Richard	1799	D4	315	299
Davidson, John, of Annapolis	Deed to	Doll, Joseph, of Frederick Co.	1799	E5	049	039
Davidson, John, of Annapolis	Deed to	Doll, Conrad, of Frederick Co.	1799	E5	048	037
Davidson, John, of Annapolis	Deed to	Schultze, Henry, of G'tn.	1800	E5	333	321
Davidson, John, of Annapolis	Deed to	Kemp, Ludwick, of Frederick Co.	1800	E5	290	283

Index to District of Columbia Land Records, 1792-1817

Party	What	Party	Year	Liber	Old	New
Davidson, John, of Annapolis	Deed to	Beatty, Thomas, of Frederick Co.	1800	F6	045	028
Davidson, John, of Annapolis	Deed to	Thompson, George	1800	E5	375	354
Davidson, John, of Annapolis	Deed to	Link, Adam, of Frederick Co.	1800	E5	267	261
Davidson, John, of Annapolis	Deed to	Caldenbaugh, Andrew, of G'tn.	1801	G7	141	186
Davidson, John, of Annapolis	Deed to	Corcoran, Thomas, of G'tn.	1801	G7	436	571
Davidson, John, of Annapolis	Deed to	Ritchie, Abner	1802	G7	551	699
Davidson, John, of MD	Deed to	Ritchie, Abner, of G'tn.	1802	H8	470	432
Davidson, John, of MD	Deed to	Hines, John, of G'tn.	1802	H8	497	457
Davidson, John, of MD	Deed to	Kaldenbach, Andrew, of G'tn.	1802	H8	474	435
Davidson, John, of MD	Deed to	Kaldenbach, Andrew, of G'tn.	1802	H8	475	436
Davidson, John, of MD	Deed to	Balch, Stephen B., of G'tn.	1802	H8	479	440
Davidson, John, of MD	Deed to	Grammar, Frederick, of MD	1802	H8	477	438
Davidson, John, of Annapolis	Deed to	Whetcroft, Burton et al	1804	L11	089	91
Davidson, John, of Annapolis	Deed to	Brengle, Laurence, Frederick Co.	1804	K10	364	378
Davidson, John, of Annapolis	Deed to	Whetcroft, Burton et al	1804	K10	219	228
Davidson, John, of Annapolis	Deed to	Corcoran, Thomas, of G'tn.	1805	O14	133	086
Davidson, John, of Annapolis	Deed to	Beatty, Thomas J. et al	1805	M12	044	043
Davidson, John, of Annapolis	Deed to	Bussard, Daniel, of G'tn.	1805	N13	391	318
Davidson, John, of Annapolis	Deed to	Beatty, John M.	1806	Q16	190	128
Davidson, John, of Annapolis	Deed to	Stoner, Stephen & Henry	1807	Q16	379	291
Davidson, John, plt.	Suit	Beatty, Charles & Wm. Clark, deft.		K10	007	
Davidson, John, plt.	Suit	Gordon, John, def.	1797	C3	107	87
Davidson, Justina, d/o Duncan	Deed fr	Davidson, Samuel	1793	A1-2	456	64
Davidson, Lewis G.	Deed to	Macdaniel, Ezekiel	1817	AN38	164	120
Davidson, Lewis Grant	Deed fr	Beall, Thomas, of Geo.	1812	AD29	370	312
Davidson, Lewis Grant	Deed to	Beall, Thomas Brooke	1814	AG32	398	290
Davidson, Lewis Grant, of G'tn.	Deed to	French, George, of G'tn.	1814	AH33	183	168
Davidson, Lewis Grant	Deed fr	Robertson, Thomas	1814	AH33	012	011
Davidson, Lewis Grant, of G'tn.	Deed to	Whetcroft, Burton	1814	AH33	128	122
Davidson, Lewis Grant	Deed to	Suter, Alexander	1814	AH33	351	304
Davidson, Lewis Grant	Deed fr	Robertson, Thomas & Daniel Kurtz	1815	AK35	043	033
Davidson, Lewis Grant	Deed to	Calder, James [Colder]	1815	AK35	013	010
Davidson, Lewis Grant	Deed to	Bryan, Maria Henrietta, of Phila.	1815	AK35	055	042
Davidson, Lewis Grant	Deed to	Smith, Richard	1815	AK35	018	014
Davidson, Lewis Grant	Deed to	Walker, George	1815	AH33	518	444
Davidson, Lewis Grant	Deed to	Rush, Richard, of PA	1816	AM37	374	270
Davidson, Lewis Grant	Deed to	Rush, Richard, of PA	1816	AM37	369	266
Davidson, Lewis Grant	Deed to	Clarke, Satterlee	1816	AM37	450	323
Davidson, Lewis Grant et al	Deed to	Cutts, Richard	1817	AO39	238	172
Davidson, Lewis Grant	Deed to	Rush, Richard, of PA	1817	AO39	481	330
Davidson, Margaret & M. et al	Deed fr	Commissioners of Washington	1799	D4	226	208
Davidson, Samuel	Deed to	Beall, Thomas & John M. Gantt	1792	A1-1	027	41
Davidson, Samuel	Deed fr	Rozer, Henry et al	1793	A1-1	356	463
Davidson, Samuel	Deed to	Beall, Thomas & John M. Gantt	1793	A1-1	356	464
Davidson, Samuel	Deed to	Davidson, Henry, in N. Britain	1793	A1-2	454	62
Davidson, Samuel	Deed to	Davidson, Justina, d/o Duncan	1793	A1-2	456	64
Davidson, Samuel	Deed to	Davidson, Sarah, d/o Duncan	1793	A1-2	455	63
Davidson, Samuel	Cert fr	Commissioners of Washington	1793	B2A	306	429
Davidson, Samuel	Deed fr	Beall, Thomas, of George	1794	B2A	053	065
Davidson, Samuel	Cert fr	Commissioners of Washington	1794	B2A	323	453
Davidson, Samuel	Deed fr	White, James, Sr. & James, Jr.	1794	B2A	114	151
Davidson, Samuel	Deed fr	White, James, Sr. & James, Jr.	1794	B2A	147	194
Davidson, Samuel	Deed fr	Jones, John Courts, Charles Co.	1796	B2B	521	231
Davidson, Samuel	Deed to	Chandler, Walter S.	1796	B2B		070
Davidson, Samuel	Deed fr	Harbaugh, Leonard	1796	B2B	612	367

Index to District of Columbia Land Records, 1792-1817   121

Party	What	Party	Year	Liber	Old	New
Davidson, Samuel	Deed to	Gantt, John Mackall, of G'tn.	1797	C3	130	106
Davidson, Samuel	Deed to	Lingan, James M.	1797	B2B	614	370
Davidson, Samuel	Deed fr	Stoddert, Benjamin et al	1797	B2B	613	369
Davidson, Samuel	Deed to	Edmonston, Ninian & Alexander	1798	C3	439	345
Davidson, Samuel	Deed to	King, Nicholas	1798	C3	434	341
Davidson, Samuel	Deed to	Peerce, William, s/o Edw., Balto.	1799	D4	266	250
Davidson, Samuel	Deed to	Pigott, Edward, of Phila.	1801	F6	206	133
Davidson, Samuel	Deed to	Shaaff, Arthur, of Annapolis	1801	G7	076	099
Davidson, Samuel	Deed to	Lovering, Charles Fox, s/o Wm.	1801	G7	364	496
Davidson, Samuel	Deed to	Gantt, John Mackall	1801	G7	075	098
Davidson, Samuel	Deed to	Robertson, Henry, s/o Wm.	1801	G7	153	201
Davidson, Samuel	Lease to	Gardiner, John	1801	G7	383	515
Davidson, Samuel	Deed to	Eno, Richard	1801	G7	100	128
Davidson, Samuel	Deed fr	Suter, John	1802	I9	590	956
Davidson, Samuel	Deed to	Magruder, Middleton B. et al	1802	I9	453	748
Davidson, Samuel	Deed to	Suter, John	1802	H8	026	025
Davidson, Samuel	Deed fr	Beall, Thomas, of George	1804	L11	055	56
Davidson, Samuel	Deed to	Davidson, John	1804	L11	328	300
Davidson, Samuel	Deed to	King, Samuel Davidson, s/o N.	1807	R17	110	086
Davidson, Samuel	Deed to	Smith, Samuel Harrison	1807	R17	383	291
Davidson, Samuel	Deed to	King, Samuel Davidson, s/o N.	1809	X23	267	209
Davidson, Samuel	B. of S. fr	Thornton, William	1809	X23	182	136
Davidson, Samuel	Deed to	King, Susan, d/o Nicholas	1809	X23	262	206
Davidson, Samuel	Deed to	King, Mary Gaunt, d/o Nicholas	1809	X23	264	207
Davidson, Samuel	Deed to	King, Robert Fielder, s/o Nicholas	1809	X23	265	208
Davidson, Samuel	Deed to	Chapman, Mary, w/o Henry H.	1810	Y24	342	319
Davidson, Samuel	Release fr	Chapman, Henry H., Charles Co.	1816	AL36	071	073
Davidson, Samuel, Esq., of G'tn.	Deed to	Magan, Michael Joseph	1800	E5	363	345
Davidson, Samuel et al	Deed fr	Thomas, Samuel 3rd	1794	B2A	051	062
Davidson, Samuel et al	Deed fr	Johns, Richard	1794	B2A	052	063
Davidson, Samuel et al	Deed fr	Beall, Thomas, s/o George	1794	B2A	054	067
Davidson, Samuel et al	Deed fr	Commissioners of Washington	1799	D4	226	208
Davidson, Samuel, Jr., of Balto.	Mortgage to	Chapman, Henry Henley	1805	N13	329	265
Davidson, Samuel, of G'tn.	Deed to	Davidson, John, of Annapolis	1792	A1-1	040	61
Davidson, Samuel, of G'tn.	Deed fr	Pierce, James	1792	A1-1	039	58
Davidson, Samuel, of G'tn.	Deed fr	Walker, George	1793	A1-1	176	251
Davidson, Samuel, of G'tn.	Deed to	Chandler, Walter S.	1796	B2B		070
Davidson, Samuel, of G'tn.	Deed to	Barclay, John Davidson, s/o Thos.	1797	B2B	633	393
Davidson, Samuel, of Montg. Co.	Deed to	Brooke, Samuel, of Montg. Co.	1797	C3	151	124
Davidson, Samuel, of Montg. Co.	Deed to	Craik, William, of Montg. Co. et al	1797	C3	152	125
Davidson, Samuel, of Montg. Co.	Deed to	Parrott, Richard, of Montg. Co.	1797	C3	093	77
Davidson, Samuel, of Montg. Co.	Deed fr	Beall, Thomas, of George	1797	C3	055	45
Davidson, Samuel, of G'tn.	Deed to	Polock, Isaac, of Savannah GA	1797	B2B	645	407
Davidson, Samuel, of G'tn.	Deed to	Suter, John & Richard his son	1806	Q16	243	167
Davidson, Samuel, of Balto.	P. of Atty. to	King, Nicholas	1811	AB27	444	364
Davidson, Samuel, of Balto. MD	Agreement	McDonald, Alexander	1812	AD29	169	135
Davidson, Samuel, of Balto.	Deed to	McDonald, Alexander	1816	AL36	510	478
Davidson, Samuel, of Balto.	Deed to	McClelland, John	1816	AO39	018	014
Davidson, Sarah, d/o Duncan	Deed fr	Davidson, Samuel	1793	A1-2	455	63
Davidson, William	Deed fr	Nourse, Charles J., of G'tn.	1811	AA26	179	122
Davidson, William et al	Deed fr	Commissioners of Washington	1799	D4	226	208
Davidson, William, of Annapolis	Mortgage to	Campbell, William, of Annapolis	1796	B2B	545	269
Davidson, William, of Phila. PA	Deed fr	Blodget, Samuel, mer., of Phila.	1800	E5	272	266
Davies, Benjamin	Deed fr	Beatty, Charles, heirs of	1806	O14	252	166
Davies, Benjamin	Deed fr	Beatty, Charles A., Dr.	1806	P15	082	050

Party	What	Party	Year	Liber	Old	New
Davis, Ahasuerus, of Charles Co.	Deed fr	Chandler, Jacob	1806	P15	018	011
Davis, Ahasuerus, of Charles Co.	Deed to	Brady, Nathaniel	1814	AH33	064	057
Davis, Ann	B. of S. fr	Vernon, William W.	1809	V21	328	242
Davis, Benjamin	Deed to	Wright, Thomas C.	1809	X23	237	184
Davis, Benjamin	B. of S. fr	Smith, Richard, of G'tn.	1815	AH33	439	377
Davis, Briscoe, of G'tn.	D. of T. to	Davis, Richard, of G'tn.	1816	AL36	184	183
Davis, Briscoe, of G'tn.	B. of S. to	Robb, John N.	1816	AL36	195	202
Davis, Charles	Deed to	Brooks, William H.	1794	B2A	104	137
Davis, Charles	Deed fr	Beall, Thomas, of George	1794	A1-2	487	90
Davis, Charles B., Sr. et al	Deed to	Whann, William, of Montg. Co.	1796	B2B	551	279
Davis, Charles B., Jr. et al	Deed to	Whann, William, of Montg. Co.	1796	B2B	551	279
Davis, Charles B.	Deed fr	English, David & Sarah (Threlkeld)	1805	M12	088	082
Davis, Charles B.	Deed to	Bradley, Phineas	1809	X23	249	194
Davis, Charles B.	Deed fr	Bradley, Phineas	1812	AD29	171	137
Davis, Charles B., of G'tn.	Deed to	English, David, of G'tn.	1816	AM37	358	259
Davis, Charles B., of G'tn.	Deed fr	Maul, John P.	1816	AM37	232	170
Davis, Charles B., of G'tn. et al	Deed to	Lipscomb, William C., of G'tn.	1817	AN38	085	066
Davis, Charles Beckwith	Deed fr	Dowens, George	1804	L11	270	248
Davis, Charles, of Montg. Co.	Deed to	King, Adam, of Montg. Co.	1796	B2B	385	043
Davis, Edward	Deed fr	Owens, Barrak, of G'tn.	1816	AL36	247	250
Davis, Edward et al	Lease fr	Peter, David, heirs of	1816	AM37	402	289
Davis, Edward, of G'tn.	Deed fr	Reintzel, Daniel, of G'tn.	1811	AB27	096	079
Davis, Edward, of G'tn.	Assign to	Mackall, Leonard	1815	AI34	323	356
Davis, Francis	B. of S. to	Mead, Simon	1812	AD29	471	398
Davis, Francis	B. of S. to	Wharton, Zephaniah	1816	AL36	007	007
Davis, George & Ann	Deed to	Wigfield, Sarah	1814	AG32	210	147
Davis, George L., trustee	Deed fr	McNemara, Roger	1810	X23	380	306
Davis, George S.	Deed fr	Wigfield, James J.	1808	U20	030	018
Davis, George S.	Deed to	Minifie, Charles	1809	V21	189	134
Davis, George S.	B. of S. to	Wigfield, Sarah	1810	Y24	337	306
Davis, George S. et al	Deed to	Collard, George	1810	Y24	131	119
Davis, George S., trustee	D. of T. fr	Wigfield, James, insolvent	1810	Y24	544	478
Davis, George S. & Ann	Deed to	Law, John	1811	AA26	150	104
Davis, George S. & Ann	Deed to	Talbert, Lewin & Osborn Warner	1811	AA26	001	001
Davis, George S.	B. of S. to	Wigfield, Sarah	1813	AF31	335	239
Davis, George Smith & Ann	Deed to	Wigfield, Sarah	1810	Y24	336	305
Davis, Gideon	Mortgage to	Brown, Joel, of G'tn.	1816	AM37	446	320
Davis, Gideon	Release fr	Brown, Joel, of G'tn.	1817	AO39	259	187
Davis, Heney (C)	Marriage	Oliver, Thomas (C), 12 FEB 1807	1808	V21	070	055
Davis, Henry, of G'tn.	Mortgage fr	Connelly, John, of G'tn.	1814	AH33	196	179
Davis, Isaac, f/o Enos R.	Cert Free to	Johnson, Abraham (C)	1813	AE30	509	377
Davis, James, of MD	Deed fr	Beall, Thomas B., of G'tn.	1811	Z25	542	431
Davis, John	Agreement	Tingey, Thomas	1813	AF31	507	370
Davis, John	Convey fr	Washington Building Company	1816	AM37	292	214
Davis, John	B. of S. to	Weightman, Roger C.	1817	AO39	125	096
Davis, John	Mortgage fr	Peltz, John	1817	AN38	170	124
Davis, John & Phineas Bradley	Deed fr	Holland, Edward	1817	AO39	225	163
Davis, John, of Abel	Deed fr	King, Benjamin	1806	Q16	029	019
Davis, John, of Abel	B. of S. fr	Smallwood, Samuel N., exr.	1809	X23	302	242
Davis, John, of Able	B. of S. fr	Hughes, Theophilus	1811	AB27	195	161
Davis, John, of Abel	Assign fr	Mason, Edward	1813	AF31	472	342
Davis, John, of Abel & J. Cassin	B. of S. fr	King, Benjamin	1813	AE30	276	212
Davis, John, of Abel et al	Mortgage fr	Spalding, John	1814	AG32	403	294
Davis, John, of Abel et al	Mortgage fr	Minitree, John	1814	AH33	035	031
Davis, John, of Abel	Release to	Minitree, John, of G'tn.	1815	AK35	255	203

Index to District of Columbia Land Records, 1792-1817

Party	What	Party	Year	Liber	Old	New
Davis, John P., of G'tn.	Deed fr	Weeden, Henry, of G'tn.	1814	AH33	174	162
Davis, John P.	Deed fr	Magruder, Ninian, of G'tn.	1816	AL36	100	100
Davis, John P., of G'tn.	Deed fr	Kelly, John, of G'tn.	1816	AL36	423	404
Davis, John P., of G'tn.	Deed to	Cox, John, of G'tn.	1816	AL36	203	211
Davis, John P., of G'tn.	Deed fr	Dant, Thomas, of G'tn.	1816	AM37	016	012
Davis, John P.	Deed fr	Knoblock, John	1817	AO39	465	319
Davis, Jonas, of G'tn.	Deed fr	Lanham, Elisha, of G'tn.	1810	Y24	224	206
Davis, Kitty (C), age 35	Manumis fr	Varnum, James M.	1816	AM37	119	094
Davis, Margaret, of Charles Co.	Deed fr	Chandler, Jacob	1806	P15	018	011
Davis, Mary	B. of S. fr	Coningham, Cornelius	1807	Q16	369	283
Davis, Otho H., of G'tn.	B. of S. to	Stewart, William	1808	U20	404	226
Davis, Philip B.	B. of S. to	Eddington, James	1811	Z25	396	311
Davis, Richard	Deed fr	Dantt, Thomas	1814	AG32	303	221
Davis, Richard	Deed fr	Reintzel, Valentine	1815	AI34	057	065
Davis, Richard & Thos. C. Wright	D. of T. fr	Bixby, Nathaniel P., of G'tn.	1817	AO39	144	109
Davis, Richard, of G'tn.	Deed to	Beall, Thomas Brooke, of G'tn.	1815	AI34	040	047
Davis, Richard, of G'tn.	D. of T. to	Burnett, Charles A. & T.B. Beall	1816	AM37	421	302
Davis, Richard, of G'tn.	D. of T. fr	Davis, Briscoe, of G'tn.	1816	AL36	184	183
Davis, Sarah	B. of S. to	Burnett, Elizabeth	1806	P15	046	028
Davis, Sarah & John	B. of S. fr	Walker, Sarah	1810	Z25	239	187
Davis, Shadrach	Deed fr	Tingey, Thomas	1807	R17	052	042
Davis, Shadrach	Deed to	Tingey, Thomas, Capt.	1807	R17	265	202
Davis, Shadrach	Deed fr	Cope, Jasper, of Balto.	1808	T19	263	194
Davis, Shadrach	Deed fr	Tuckfield, William H.P.	1814	AG32	086	065
Davis, Shadrack	Apprentice fr	Myer, John, s/o John, age 15	1805	N13	305	247
Davis, Shadrack & Thos. Holyday	Mortgage fr	McLeod, John	1812	AD29	205	167
Davis, Shadrick	Release fr	Tingey, Thomas	1810	Z25	203	160
Davis, Shadrick	Qualify	Lieutent in 2nd regiment	1813	AE30	389	287
Davis, Shadrick & Thos. Holliday	Release to	McLeod, John	1813	AF31	105	071
Davis, Thomas	Deed fr	Chandler, Walter Story	1811	Z25	533	423
Davis, Thomas, insolvent	Deed to	Speake, Samuel, trustee	1805	N13	004	004
Davis, Thomas M. & Sarah	Deed to	House, David	1808	U20	255	136
Davis, Thomas, of G'tn.	Deed fr	Stoddert, Benjamin, of G'tn.	1804	M12	033	034
Davis, Thomas, of G'tn.	Deed to	Shaw, Lemuel, of G'tn.	1805	M12	185	186
Davis, Thomas, ship carpenter	Agreement	Chandler, Walter S.	1806	Q16	013	008
Davis, Thomas, ship carpenter	Deed to	Winn, Timothy, purser in Navy	1813	AF31	405	293
Davison, John, of Annapolis	Deed to	King, George, of G'tn.	1794	B2A	159	210
Daw, William & Susannah et al	Deed to	Lovell, William, of Balto.	1811	Z25	467	370
Dawe, William & Susannah et al	Mortgage to	Lovell, William, Sr., of Balto.	1814	AH33	112	104
Dawes, Abraham, of Fauquier Co.	P. of Atty. to	Ragan, Edward, of G'tn.	1816	AL36	464	438
Dawes, Edward & John Baker	Deed fr	Baker, Henry	1812	AC28	284	206
Dawes, Edward & John Baker	B. of S. fr	Chester, Samuel, of G'tn.	1817	AN38	546	397
Dawes, Edward et al	Convey to	Redman, James, of G'tn.	1816	AL36	463	437
Dawes, Edward, of G'tn.	Deed fr	Middleton, Ignatius, of Charles Co.	1815	AK35	394	310
Dawes, Henry et al	Convey to	Redman, James, of G'tn.	1816	AL36	463	437
Dawes, Isaac	Deed fr	Threlkeld, John	1794	B2A	037	042
Dawes, Isaac	Deed fr	Coghlan, William	1802	G7	585	734
Dawes, Isaac	Lease to	Baker, Henry	1802	I9	473	778
Dawes, Isaac	Deed fr	Deakins, Leonard M. et al	1805	M12	187	188
Dawes, Isaac	Deed to	Miles, Henry, of St. Mary's Co.	1808	U20	146	083
Dawes, Isaac	Deed to	Miles, Henry, of St. Mary's Co.	1808	U20	151	086
Dawes, Isaac	Deed fr	Miles, Henry, of St. Mary's Co.	1808	U20	148	085
Dawes, Isaac	Deed to	Boyer, Richard M.	1810	Z25	065	049
Dawes, Isaac	Deed fr	Hedges, Nicholas, guardian	1810	Z25	068	051
Dawes, Isaac	Deed to	Clarke, Robert	1810	Y24	305	278

Index to District of Columbia Land Records, 1792-1817

Party	What	Party	Year	Liber	Old	New
Dawes, Isaac	Deed fr	Wilson, Henry	1811	AA26	147	102
Dawes, Isaac & Henry Baker	Deed fr	Hoye, John, of Allegany Co.	1814	AH33	003	003
Dawes, Isaac et al	Deed fr	Gailor, Thomas	1802	I9	294	483
Dawes, Isaac et al	Deed to	Gassaway, Charles	1805	M12	147	143
Dawes, Isaac et al	Deed to	Deakins, Francis et al	1805	M12	147	143
Dawes, Isaac et al	Deed fr	Norris, Isaac, of G'tn.	1806	Q16	118	076
Dawes, Isaac et al	Convey to	Redman, James, of G'tn.	1816	AL36	463	437
Dawes, Isaac, farmer, Montg. Co.	Deed fr	Williams, Robert, blacksmith, G'tn.	1811	AA26	277	188
Dawes, Isaac, farmer, Montg. Co.	Deed to	Williams, Robert, blacksmith, G'tn.	1811	AA26	286	194
Dawes, Isaac, of G'tn.	Deed fr	Brent, Daniel Carroll, marshal	1804	L11	180	174
Dawes, Isaac, of Montg. Co.	Deed to	Baker, John	1810	Y24	237	219
Dawes, Isaac, tanner, of G'tn.	Mortgage to	Templeman, John, mer., of G'tn.	1794	B2A	038	044
Dawes, Isaac, tanner, of G'tn.	Deed to	Cunningham, John, Calvert Co.	1796	B2B	449	134
Dawes, Mordecai, of Harford Co.	Convey to	Redman, James, of G'tn.	1816	AL36	463	437
Dawes, Mordecai, of Harford Co.	P. of Atty. to	Ragan, Edward, of G'tn.	1816	AL36	466	439
Daws, Isaac, of G'tn.	Deed fr	Deakins, Francis, of G'tn. et al	1804	L11	390	347
Daws, Isaac, of G'tn.	Deed fr	Bussard, Daniel, of G'tn., trustee	1810	Y24	082	074
Dawson, John	Manumis to	Lee, Maria (M)	1812	AC28	130	098
Dawson, Joshua	Deed fr	Gilliss, Thomas H.	1813	AF31	107	072
Dawson, Thomas	Slave	From Fairfax Co. VA	1805	M12	055	052
Dawson, Thomas	Cert Free to	Chisman, Jesse	1808	U20	169	095
Dawson, William & Eleanor, Eng.	Deed to	Threlkeld, John, of G'tn.	1816	AM37	169	128
Dawson, William, Wakefield, Eng.	Deed to	Threlkeld, John	1812	AD29	448	377
Day, Edward, of Balto. Co.	Deed to	Dougherty, Daniel, of Alexa.	1815	AI34	200	229
De Arce, Don Manual et al	Deed to	Prout, William	1817	AO39	474	325
Deakins, Ann Orme et al	Deed to	Holmead, John	1814	AH33	286	249
Deakins, Ann Orme, of G'tn.	Deed fr	Deakins, Leonard M., of P.G. Co.	1814	AH33	256	223
Deakins, Francis	Deed to	McClary, Henry, of Frederick Co.	1792	A1-1	123	180
Deakins, Francis	Deed to	Lingan, James Maccubbin	1798	C3	485	382
Deakins, Francis	Deed fr	Blagden, George	1798	D4	167	148
Deakins, Francis	Deed fr	Dermott, James Reed	1798	D4	089	075
Deakins, Francis	Deed to	Threlkeld, John et al	1798	D4	088	074
Deakins, Francis	Agreement	Duncanson, William M.	1798	C3	451	355
Deakins, Francis	Mortgage to	Peyton, Valentine	1800	E5		177
Deakins, Francis	Deed to	Forrest, Uriah	1800	E5	385	362
Deakins, Francis	Cert fr	Commissioners of Washington	1800	E5	162	151
Deakins, Francis	Deed fr	Boogher, Frederick, Frederick Co.	1800	E5	354	339
Deakins, Francis	Deed fr	Dermott, James Reed	1800	E5	185	176
Deakins, Francis	Deed fr	Loundes, Francis & Charles	1800	E5	351	336
Deakins, Francis	Deed to	Mason, John	1800	E5	261	255
Deakins, Francis	Deed fr	Plater, John Rowlsby, of G'tn.	1800	E5	353	337
Deakins, Francis	Deed fr	Wayman, John	1800	E5	146	135
Deakins, Francis	Deed to	Worthington, William, Jr.	1800	F6	109	067
Deakins, Francis	Deed fr	Marbury, William	1802	H8	111	107
Deakins, Francis	Deed to	Doyle, Elizabeth	1802	H8	062	058
Deakins, Francis	Deed to	Balch, Stephen Bloomer, Rev. et al	1802	H8	558	520
Deakins, Francis	Deed to	Threlkeld, John et al	1802	H8	361	336
Deakins, Francis	Deed to	Tayloe, John	1802	H8	068	063
Deakins, Francis	Deed to	Corcoran, Thomas	1802	H8	002	002
Deakins, Francis	Deed to	Forrest, Uriah	1802	H8	272	258
Deakins, Francis	Deed to	Kerr, Alexander	1802	H8	272	257
Deakins, Francis	Deed to	Presbyterian Congregation of G'tn.	1802	H8	558	520
Deakins, Francis	Deed to	Stewart, William	1802	I9	267	433
Deakins, Francis	Deed to	Smith, Walter	1802	I9	173	264
Deakins, Francis	Deed fr	Maddox, Notley	1802	I9	140	211

Index to District of Columbia Land Records, 1792-1817

Party	What	Party	Year	Liber	Old	New
Deakins, Francis	Deed to	Coles, John	1802	I9	141	212
Deakins, Francis	Deed fr	Davidson, John	1802	I9	468	771
Deakins, Francis	Deed fr	Davidson, John	1802	I9	350	578
Deakins, Francis	Deed to	Templeman, John	1802	I9	264	428
Deakins, Francis	Deed to	Threlkeld, John	1804	L11	295	271
Deakins, Francis	Deed to	Threlkeld, John	1804	L11	293	269
Deakins, Francis, devisee of Wm.	Deed fr	Stoddert, Benjamin, of G'tn.	1801	G7		283
Deakins, Francis, devisee of Wm.	Deed fr	Stoddert, Benjamin, of G'tn.	1801	G7	214	285
Deakins, Francis, devisee of Wm.	Assign to	Tayloe, John	1801	G7	409	543
Deakins, Francis et al	Deed to	Plater, John R.	1798	D4	104	088
Deakins, Francis et al	Deed fr	Commissioners of Washington	1798	D4	137	119
Deakins, Francis et al	Deed fr	Commissioners of Washington	1798	D4	135	118
Deakins, Francis et al	Deed fr	Plater, John Rowsby, of G'tn.	1799	D4	194	177
Deakins, Francis et al	Deed to	Lenthall, John	1800	E5	308	299
Deakins, Francis et al	Deed to	Plater, John Rowsby, of G'tn.	1800	E5	325	315
Deakins, Francis et al	Deed to	Templeman, John & B. Stoddert	1801	G7	113	144
Deakins, Francis et al	Deed to	McCoy, Robert	1801	G7	224	299
Deakins, Francis et al	Deed fr	Holmead, Anthony	1801	G7	227	303
Deakins, Francis et al	Deed to	Thomas, Evan	1801	F6	168	105
Deakins, Francis et al	Deed to	Stoddert, Benjamin	1802	I9	248	400
Deakins, Francis et al	R. of S.	Mayor of Georgetown	1803	K10	031	31
Deakins, Francis et al	Deed to	Yarro, Acquilla	1803	K10	071	77
Deakins, Francis et al	Mortgage fr	Harbaugh, Leonard	1804	L11	247	228
Deakins, Francis et al	Deed fr	Johns, Richard	1805	M12	069	064
Deakins, Francis et al	Deed fr	Dawes, Isaac et al	1805	M12	147	143
Deakins, Francis, exors. of	Deed to	Coles, John, of Balto.	1806	O14	214	141
Deakins, Francis, exors. et al	Deed to	Baum, John C., of G'th.	1809	V21	201	142
Deakins, Francis, exors. of	Deed to	Lucas, Bennett	1809	V21	247	176
Deakins, Francis, exrs. of	Deed to	Forrest, Benjamin S.	1813	AF31	491	358
Deakins, Francis, of Montg. Co.	Deed to	Threlkeld, John, of Montg. Co.	1796	B2B	486	177
Deakins, Francis, of G'tn.	Deed fr	Peter, Robert, of G'tn.	1798	C3	505	396
Deakins, Francis, of G'tn.	Deed to	Lyles, William, of P.G. Co.	1798	C3	406	321
Deakins, Francis, of G'tn.	Deed to	Johnson, Joshua, late of London	1799	D4	213	197
Deakins, Francis, of G'tn.	Deed to	Walker, George, butcher, G'tn.	1800	E5	249	242
Deakins, Francis, of G'tn.	Deed to	[ ], Yarrow (Negro)	1800	E5	080	067
Deakins, Francis, of G'tn.	Deed fr	Templeman, John, of G'tn.	1801	F6	115	071
Deakins, Francis, of G'tn.	Deed to	Ross, William, of G'tn.	1801	G7	029	035
Deakins, Francis, of G'tn.	Agreement	Tillotson, Thomas, of NY	1801	G7	120	154
Deakins, Francis, of G'tn.	Deed to	Forrest, Uriah	1801	G7	078	101
Deakins, Francis, of G'tn.	Deed to	Foxall, Henry, of Phila.	1801	F6	148	091
Deakins, Francis, of G'tn.	Deed fr	Threlkeld, John, of G'tn.	1802	G7	589	738
Deakins, Francis, of William, Jr.	Deed to	Neale, Francis, Rev.	1802	H8	463	425
Deakins, Francis, of G'tn.	Deed to	Carpenter, Thomas	1802	H8	270	256
Deakins, Francis, of G'tn.	Deed to	Clark, Robert	1802	H8	581	545
Deakins, Francis, of G'tn.	Deed to	Threlkeld, John, of G'tn.	1802	G7	590	739
Deakins, Francis, of G'tn.	Deed to	Clarke, Robert, of G'tn.	1804	K10	218	227
Deakins, Francis, of G'tn. et al	Deed to	Barry, James	1804	K10	169	179
Deakins, Francis, of G'tn. et al	Deed to	Daws, Isaac, of G'tn.	1804	L11	390	347
Deakins, Francis, of G'tn. et al	Deed to	Backer, Henry, of G'tn.	1804	L11	389	346
Deakins, Francis, of G'tn.	Deed to	Renner, Daniel & Daniel Bussard	1804	K10	103	110
Deakins, Jane et al	Deed to	Deakins, Francis	1802	H8	361	336
Deakins, Leonard M., of G'tn. et al	Deed to	Frush, William, of G'tn.	1807	R17	231	173
Deakins, Leonard et al	Deed to	Foxall, Henry	1805	O14	117	075
Deakins, Leonard et al	Deed to	Hyde, Thomas	1805	O14	120	077
Deakins, Leonard M., G'tn. et al	Deed to	Craik, William, of Fairfax Co. VA	1805	M12	393	406

Party	What	Party	Year	Liber	Old	New
Deakins, Leonard M. et al	Deed to	Dawes, Isaac	1805	M12	187	188
Deakins, Leonard M. et al	Deed to	Nourse, Joseph, of G'tn.	1806	O14	357	238
Deakins, Leonard M. et al	Deed to	Baker, John, exr. of John	1806	O14	160	104
Deakins, Leonard M., of G'tn. et al	Deed to	Laird, John, of G'tn.	1806	Q16	294	223
Deakins, Leonard M. et al	Deed fr	Beatty, Charles, heirs of	1806	O14	334	222
Deakins, Leonard M., of G'tn. et al	Deed to	Lehault, Louis Joseph et al	1807	R17	378	287
Deakins, Leonard M. et al	Deed to	Carroll, Patrick, of G'tn.	1807	R17	258	196
Deakins, Leonard M. et al	Deed fr	Clagett, James	1807	R17	055	044
Deakins, Leonard M. et al	Deed to	Benson, Eden, of G'tn.	1807	S18	060	050
Deakins, Leonard M. et al	Deed to	Lucas, Bennet, of G'tn.	1807	S18	062	051
Deakins, Leonard M.	Deed to	Baltzer, John	1807	S18	405	323
Deakins, Leonard M., of G'tn. et al	Deed to	Coles, John, of Balto.	1807	S18	120	098
Deakins, Leonard M. et al	Deed to	King, James C.	1807	S18	087	071
Deakins, Leonard M., of G'tn. et al	Deed to	Wright, Thomas C., of G'tn.	1807	S18	316	248
Deakins, Leonard M. & John Hoye	Deed fr	White, James, of Montg. Co.	1807	S18	271	213
Deakins, Leonard M., of G'tn. et al	Deed fr	Brent, William	1808	T19	408	287
Deakins, Leonard M. & John Hoye	Deed to	King, Enoch	1808	U20	293	156
Deakins, Leonard M. et al	Deed to	Lucas, Bennett	1809	V21	247	176
Deakins, Leonard M. & John Hoye	Deed fr	Lee, Thomas Sim & William Brent	1809	V21	416	318
Deakins, Leonard M. & John Hoye	Deed to	Robey, Theophilus & Jos. Nevitt	1809	W22	263	176
Deakins, Leonard M. & John Hoye	Deed to	Threlkeld, John	1809	W22	085	063
Deakins, Leonard M. & John Hoye	Deed fr	Threlkeld, John	1809	W22	132	094
Deakins, Leonard M. & John Hoye	Deed to	Robertson, Thomas	1809	W22	026	020
Deakins, Leonard M. & John Hoye	Deed fr	Beall, Thomas, of George	1809	W22	140	099
Deakins, Leonard M. & John Hoye	Deed to	Riggs, George W., of G'tn.	1809	W22	193	135
Deakins, Leonard M., of G'tn.	Deed fr	Robertson, Thomas, of G'tn.	1809	W22	078	058
Deakins, Leonard M. & John Hoye	Deed fr	Muir, John, of Annapolis et al	1809	W22	009	007
Deakins, Leonard M. & John Hoye	Deed to	Williams, Elisha W.	1809	X23	206	156
Deakins, Leonard M. & John Hoye	Deed to	Foxall, Henry	1809	X23	194	146
Deakins, Leonard M. & John Hoye	Deed to	Ober, Robert, of G'tn.	1809	X23	007	005
Deakins, Leonard M. & John Hoye	Deed fr	Marbury, William, of G'tn.	1810	Y24	128	116
Deakins, Leonard M. & John Hoye	Deed to	Livers, Ignatius	1812	AD29	398	335
Deakins, Leonard M. & John Hoye	Deed to	Robertson, Thomas, of G'tn.	1812	AD29	441	370
Deakins, Leonard M. & John Hoye	Deed to	Hines, John, of G'tn.	1813	AE30	220	177
Deakins, Leonard M., of P.G. Co.	Deed to	Lee, Thomas S., of Fredk. Co.	1813	AF31	446	321
Deakins, Leonard M., of P.G. Co.	Deed fr	Lee, Thomas S., of Fredk. Co.	1813	AF31	442	318
Deakins, Leonard M., of P.G. Co.	Deed fr	Lee, Thomas S., of Fredk. Co.	1813	AF31	443	319
Deakins, Leonard M. & John Hoye	Deed to	Patterson, Edgar, of G'tn.	1813	AF31	215	146
Deakins, Leonard M., of P.G. Co.	Deed fr	Lee, Thomas S., of Fredk. Co.	1813	AF31	444	319
Deakins, Leonard M., of P.G. Co.	Deed to	Forrest, Benjamin S.	1813	AF31	491	358
Deakins, Leonard M.	Plat	Washington St. & Virginia Ave.	1813	AF31	466	
Deakins, Leonard M.	Certificate	List of 101 lots, Washington St.	1813	AF31	448	322
Deakins, Leonard M., of P.G. Co.	Deed to	Cassin, Tabitha Marbury, w/o Jas.	1814	AH33	256	223
Deakins, Leonard M. & John Hoye	Deed to	Thompson, Jonah, of Alexa. et al	1814	AH33	038	034
Deakins, Leonard M., of P.G. Co.	Deed to	Dodge, Francis, of G'tn.	1815	AI34	180	206
Deakins, Leonard M., of P.G. Co.	D. of T. fr	Cassin, James, of G'tn.	1815	AI34	339	372
Deakins, Leonard M. & John Hoye	D. of T. to	Morsell, James S. & Wm. Whann	1815	AK35	347	274
Deakins, Leonard M. & John Hoye	Deed to	Whann, William & J.S. Morsell	1815	AK35	343	271
Deakins, Leonard M., P.G. Co.	Deed to	Threlkeld, John	1817	AN38	295	215
Deakins, Leonard M. et al	Decree	Threlkeld, John	1817	AN38	295	215
Deakins, Leonard, of P.G. Co.	Deed fr	Beall, Thomas, of George, farmer	1797	B2B	644	405
Deakins, Nancy et al	Deed to	Smith, Clement	1811	Z25	478	379
Deakins, Tabitha et al	Deed to	Smith, Clement	1811	Z25	478	379
Deakins, Tobitha et al	Deed fr	Deakins, Francis	1798	D4	088	074
Deakins, William & Benj. Stoddert	Deed fr	Funk, Jacob, of KY	1793	A1-1	192	271

Index to District of Columbia Land Records, 1792-1817

Party	What	Party	Year	Liber	Old	New
Deakins, William & Jane et al	Decree agt	Beatty, Charles et al	1797	C3	015	12
Deakins, William et al	Deed to	Templeman, John, of G'tn.	1794	B2A	063	080
Deakins, William, Jr.	Deed fr	Shellman, John, of Frederick Co.	1792	A1-1	149	215
Deakins, William, Jr., of G'tn.	Deed fr	Kemp, Henry, of Frederick Co.	1792	A1-1	122	179
Deakins, William, Jr.	Deed fr	Heirshman, Matthias	1792	A1-1	162	232
Deakins, William, Jr., of G'tn.	Deed fr	Rogers, Matthew, of New York NY	1792	A1-1	154	221
Deakins, William, Jr., of G'tn.	Deed fr	Zimmerman, Michael, Fredk. Co.	1792	A1-1	124	181
Deakins, William, Jr. et al	Deed to	Beall, John	1793	A1-1	378	485
Deakins, William, Jr. et al	Deed fr	Reintzel, Anthony, of G'tn.	1793	A1-1	183	259
Deakins, William, Jr. et al	Deed to	Hairy, David, exr. of Martin	1793	A1-1	338	442
Deakins, William, Jr. et al	Deed to	Beatty, Thomas Johnson	1793	A1-1	185	262
Deakins, William, Jr. et al	Deed to	Beatty, Thomas, Jr.	1793	A1-1	181	257
Deakins, William, Jr. et al	Deed to	Williams, Thomas Owen	1793	A1-1	325	428
Deakins, William, Jr. et al	Deed to	Peter, Robert, assignee of Wells	1793	A1-1	386	493
Deakins, William, Jr. et al	Deed to	Beall, Thomas & John M. Gantt	1793	A1-1	227	314
Deakins, William, Jr. et al	Deed fr	Funk, Jacob, of Jefferson Co. KY	1793	A1-1	189	268
Deakins, William, Jr., of G'tn.	Deed fr	Funk, Henry, of Washington Co.	1793	A1-1	198	278
Deakins, William, Jr. et al	Deed to	Beall, William M.	1793	A1-1	379	486
Deakins, William, Jr. et al	Deed to	Beall, James, s/o James	1793	A1-1	319	421
Deakins, William, Jr. et al	Deed to	Thomas, Philip, of Frederick Co.	1793	A1-1	387	494
Deakins, William, Jr. et al	Deed to	Flick, Andrew, of Orange Co. VA	1793	A1-1	294	392
Deakins, William, Jr. et al	Deed to	French, William & John Marr	1793	A1-2	432	40
Deakins, William, Jr. et al	Deed to	King, William	1793	A1-2	419	28
Deakins, William, Jr., of G'tn.	Deed to	Cramphin, Thomas, of G'tn.	1793	A1-2	459	67
Deakins, William, Jr., of G'tn.	Deed to	Mayor of Georgetown	1793	A1-2	461	69
Deakins, William, Jr. et al	Deed to	Chiswell, Joseph N.	1793	A1-2	424	33
Deakins, William, Jr. et al	Deed to	Beall, Thomas & John M. Gantt	1793	A1-2	392	1
Deakins, William, Jr.	Deed to	Threlkeld, Elizabeth, w/o John	1794	B2A	050	060
Deakins, William, Jr.	Deed to	Brookes, Walter	1794	B2A	155	204
Deakins, William, Jr., of G'tn.	Deed to	Stoddert, Benjamin, of G'tn.	1794	B2A	096	125
Deakins, William, Jr. et al	Deed to	Greenleaf, James, New York NY	1794	B2A	083	108
Deakins, William, Jr. et al	Deed to	Kershner, Marlin	1794	B2A	162	214
Deakins, William, Jr., of G'tn.	Deed to	Templeman, John, of G'tn.	1794	B2A	064	082
Deakins, William, Jr. et al	Deed to	Thomas, Evan	1794	B2A	093	121
Deakins, William, Jr.	Deed to	Threlkeld, John	1794	B2A	049	058
Deakins, William, Jr., of G'tn.	Deed to	Greenleaf, James, New York NY	1794	B2A	085	110
Deakins, William, Jr.	Deed to	Peirce, Isaac	1794	B2A	156	206
Deakins, William, Jr. et al	Deed to	Tillotson, Thomas, of NY	1794	B2A	094	123
Deakins, William, Jr. et al	Deed to	Templeman, John	1794	B2A	097	127
Deakins, William, Jr., of G'tn.	Deed to	Forrest, Uriah	1795	B2A	209	288
Deakins, William, Jr. et al	Deed fr	Dorsey, William H.	1795	B2A	235	327
Deakins, William, Jr. et al	Deed to	Beatty, Charles, Sr., of G'tn.	1795	B2A	242	336
Deakins, William, Jr. et al	Lease to	Bowman, Peter	1795	B2A	353	499
Deakins, William, Jr. et al	Cert fr	Magruder, John R.	1795	B2A	171	229
Deakins, William, Jr. et al	Deed fr	Warring, Marsham	1795	B2A	253	353
Deakins, William, Jr., of G'tn.	Deed fr	Harry, David, of Washington Co.	1795	B2A	204	280
Deakins, William, Jr. et al	Deed to	Casanave, Peter	1795	B2A	238	331
Deakins, William, Jr., of G'tn.	Deed to	Stoddert, Benjamin, of G'tn.	1795	B2A	264	369
Deakins, William, Jr.	Receipt fr	Roe, Owen McDermot	1795	B2A	281	394
Deakins, William, Jr. et al	Cert fr	Magruder, John R.	1795	B2A	171	230
Deakins, William, Jr. et al	Deed to	Beall, Thomas, of George	1795	B2A	166	222
Deakins, William, Jr. et al	Deed to	Warring, Marsham, of G'tn.	1795	B2A	252	351
Deakins, William, Jr. et al	Deed to	Tillotson, Thomas, of NY	1795	B2A	255	356
Deakins, William, Jr. et al	Deed to	Dorsey, William Hammond	1795	B2A	237	330
Deakins, William, Jr., of G'tn.	Deed to	Orme, Thomas	1795	B2A	210	289

Index to District of Columbia Land Records, 1792-1817

Party	What	Party	Year	Liber	Old	New
Deakins, William, Jr., of G'tn.	Deed fr	Klinger, Henry, Washington Co.	1795	B2A	212	293
Deakins, William, Jr.	Cert fr	Commissioners of Washington	1796	B2A	338	476
Deakins, William, Jr., of G'tn.	Cert fr	Commissioners of Washington	1796	B2A	335	471
Deakins, William, Jr., of G'tn.	Deed to	Morris, Robert & John Nicholson	1796	B2B	604	356
Deakins, William, Jr. et al	Lease to	Middleton, Joseph et al	1796	B2B	508	211
Deakins, William, Jr., of G'tn.	P. of Atty. fr	Covochicke, Joseph, of NY	1796	B2B	608	362
Deakins, William, Jr., of G'tn.	Deed to	Boucher, John Thomas, P.G. Co.	1796	B2B	441	123
Deakins, William, Jr. et al	Receipt fr	Holston, George M.	1796	B2B	382	038
Deakins, William, Jr., mer., G'tn.	Deed fr	Beatty, Charles, of G'tn.	1796	B2B	548	274
Deakins, William, Jr., of G'tn.	Deed to	Clagett, Walter	1796	B2B	434	112
Deakins, William, Jr. et al	Deed fr	Morris, Robert & John Nicholson	1796	B2B	566	302
Deakins, William, Jr., of G'tn.	Release to	Boucher, John Thomas, P.G. Co.	1796	B2B	554	283
Deakins, William, Jr.	Deed fr	Hardy, George & Priscilla	1796	B2B	391	051
Deakins, William, Jr., of G'tn.	Deed fr	Wykoff, Isaac, of Phila.	1796	B2B	556	287
Deakins, William, Jr., Montg. Co.	Deed to	Taney, Francis Lewis, Montg. Co.	1796	B2B	514	220
Deakins, William, Jr., of G'tn.	Deed fr	Jenkins, Mary, of P.G. Co.	1796	B2B	396	059
Deakins, William, Jr., of G'tn.	Deed fr	Greenleaf, James, of Phila.	1797	B2B	615	371
Deakins, William, Jr. et al	Deed to	Mailey, Jacob, of Phila. PA	1797	B2B	667	434
Deakins, William, Jr.	Deed fr	Morris, Robert, of Phila.	1797	B2B	676	447
Deakins, William, Jr. & U. Forrest	Cert fr	Commissioners of Washington	1797	B2B	473	166
Deakins, William, Jr.	Deed fr	Morris, Robert, of Phila.	1797	B2B	680	453
Deakins, William, Jr., of G'tn.	Deed to	Templeman, John, of G'tn.	1797	C3	235	195
Deakins, William, Jr., of G'tn.	Deed to	Chandler, Walter S., of G'tn.	1797	C3	072	59
Deakins, William, Jr., of G'tn.	P. of Atty. fr	Covachick, Joseph, of NY, in G'tn.	1797	C3	046	36
Deakins, William, Jr., of G'tn.	Deed fr	Dalton, Tristram, of P.G. Co. et al	1797	C3	223	187
Deakins, William, Jr.	Deed fr	King, Adam & Grace	1797	C3	262	214
Deakins, William, Jr., of G'tn.	Deed fr	Chandler, Walter Story, of G'tn.	1797	C3	258	211
Deakins, William, Jr., of G'tn.	Deed to	Bowie, Thomas Contee, P.G. Co.	1797	C3	243	201
Deakins, William, Jr. et al	Deed fr	Duncanson, William M.	1797	C3	125	102
Deakins, William, Jr. et al	Deed to	Thomson, William, of Montg. Co.	1797	C3	098	81
Deakins, William, Jr. et al	Deed fr	Hanson, Alexander Contee	1797	C3	095	78
Deakins, William, Jr.	Deed fr	Threlkeld, John, of Montg. Co.	1797	C3	260	213
Deakins, William, Jr., of G'tn.	Deed fr	Greenleaf, James, of Phila.	1797	C3	169	141
Deakins, William, Jr., of G'tn.	Deed fr	Dalton, Tristram et al	1797	C3	221	186
Deakins, William, Jr., of G'tn.	Deed fr	Dalton, Tristram, of G'tn. et al	1797	C3	218	183
Deakins, William, Jr.	Agreement	Duncanson, William M.	1798	C3	451	355
Deakins, William, Jr., of G'tn.	D. of T. fr	Polock, Isaac	1798	C3	395	314
Deakins, William, Jr., of G'tn.	Deed fr	Dalton, Tristram & T. Lear	1798	D4	062	052
Deakins, William, Jr. et al	R. of D. fr	Morris, Mary et al	1798	C3	364	292
Deakins, William, Jr. et al	Deed fr	Morris, Robert, of Phila. et al	1798	C3	362	292
Deakins, William, Jr.	Deed fr	Polock, Isaac	1800	E5	396	371
Deakins, William, Jr.	Deed to	Thomson, George	1800	E5	255	249
Deakins, William, Jr., of G'tn.	Deed to	Mason, John	1800	E5	260	253
Deakins, William, Jr.	Deed fr	Dalton, Tristram & Tobias Lear	1800	E5	163	152
Deakins, William, Jr.	Deed to	Mason, John	1800	E5	257	251
Deakins, William, of G'tn.	Deed fr	Reintzel, Valentine, of G'tn.	1793	A1-1	376	483
Deakins, William, of G'tn.	Deed fr	Thompson, Jay, of Fayette Co. PA	1796	B2B	358	006
Deakins, Wm., Jr. & U. Forrest	Transfer fr	Morris, Robert & James Greenleaf	1797	B2B	473	166
Dean, Charles, of G'tn.	Deed fr	Mackey, William, of G'tn.	1816	AL36	415	397
Dearborn, Henry	Manumis to	Lewis, Lucy (negro)	1806	O14	116	074
Dearborn, Henry	Manumis to	Frazier, Patrick (negro)	1808	U20	126	072
Dearborn, Henry, Gen.	Cert fr	Munroe, Thomas, Supt.	1804	L11	037	36
Dearborn, Henry, of Boston	Deed to	Munroe, Thomas	1817	AO39	423	288
Deas, William, of Phila. PA	Deed to	Dorsey, William H., of G'tn.	1804	K10	163	174
deBlock, Francis, of Balto.	Deed fr	Johnson, Thomas, Frederick Co.	1800	F6	104	064

Party	What	Party	Year	Liber	Old	New
DeBlock, Lucy, wid/o Francis	Deed to	Deluis, Frederick, of Bremen	1807	Q16	210	142
Deblois, Lewis	Deed fr	Dalton, Tristram	1797	C3	089	73
Deblois, Lewis	Deed fr	Dalton, Tristram, mer.	1797	C3	090	74
Deblois, Lewis	Deed fr	Carroll, David, of *Duddington*	1798	C3	316	255
Deblois, Lewis	Deed to	Prout, William	1798	D4	103	087
Deblois, Lewis	Deed to	Dalton, Katharine	1799	D4	401	380
Deblois, Lewis	Deed fr	Prout, William	1799	D4	343	331
Deblois, Lewis	Deed to	Dalton, Katherine	1799	E5	072	059
Deblois, Lewis	Deed to	Prout, William	1799	D4	198	181
Deblois, Lewis	Deed fr	Forrest, Uriah	1800	E5	359	342
Deblois, Lewis	Deed fr	Dalton, Katharine	1800	E5	358	341
Deblois, Lewis	Cert fr	Commissioners of Washington	1800	E5		356
Deblois, Lewis	Cert fr	Commissioners of Washington	1800	E5	359	341
Deblois, Lewis	Deed to	Dalton, Katharine	1800	E5	377	356
Deblois, Lewis	Deed fr	Dalton, Tristram	1800	E5	142	130
Deblois, Lewis	Deed to	Dalton, Katharine	1801	G7	428	563
Deblois, Lewis	Deed to	Ashley, John	1802	I9	261	423
Deblois, Lewis	B. of S. fr	Russell, Joseph	1810	Z25	141	112
Deblois, Lewis	B. of S. fr	White, Levi	1811	AB27	191	156
Deblois, Lewis	Deed to	Davidson, James, Jr.	1812	AD29	202	164
Deblois, Lewis & R. Weightman	B. of S. fr	Van Zandt, Nicholas B.	1810	Z25	002	002
Deblois, Lewis, of Alexa.	Mortgage to	Davidson, James	1810	Y24	293	268
Deblois, Lewis, of Alexa.	Deed fr	Daugherty, Barney, of Balto.	1810	Z25	352	276
Deblois, Louis	Mortgage to	Tingey, Thomas	1802	I9	217	340
DeBlois, Lewis et al	P. of Atty. R.	Nicholson, John	1796	B2B		340
Debow, Solomon	D. of T. fr	Ritchie, Abner	1809	W22	113	082
Debow, Solomon, Caswell Co. NC	Deed fr	Goszler, John, of G'tn.	1809	W22	393	256
Debow, Solomon, now of VA	Deed to	Robertson, Samuel	1815	AI34	459	472
Debow, Solomon, of NC	Deed to	Goszler, John, of G'tn.	1809	W22	373	242
DeCloise, Lewis	Cert fr	Commissioners of Washington	1798	B2B	479	173
DeCow, Rachel	Manumis to	Ross, Nancy (negro) & child	1811	Z25	187	147
Deery, Patrick	Deed fr	Roe, Cornelius McDermott	1802	H8	521	480
Deery, Patrick	Deed fr	Roe, Cornelius McDermott	1807	S18	044	036
Degge, Robert T.	Slaves	From VA	1810	Y24	073	065
Degge, William	Slaves	From Lancaster Co. VA	1810	Y24	073	065
Deiry, Patrick	Deed fr	Roe, Cornelius McDermott	1806	O14	191	125
deKrafft, Charles	Deed fr	Chandler, Walter Story	1810	Y24	196	180
deKrafft, Edward B.	Mortgage to	McClelland, John, trustee	1813	AE30	234	187
deKrafft, Edward B.	Release fr	McClellan, John et al	1813	AF31	532	393
deKrafft, Edward B.	Release fr	Moore, George et al	1813	AF31	280	198
DeKrafft, Charles	Deed to	Glover, Charles	1815	AH33	548	469
DeKrafft, Edward	Deed fr	Edwards, Horace H., of CN	1817	AO39	096	076
deKraft, Edward B.	Deed fr	Ryan, Henry & Mary	1812	AE30	010	008
Delaney, George	Deed to	Ward, William	1816	AL36	050	051
Delany, Matthew	Deed to	Gitzendanner, Christian	1804	L11	145	146
Delius, Everhard	Deed fr	Johnson, Joshua, of G'tn.	1799	D4	217	200
Delphy, Richard	B. of S. to	Thiker, James	1802	G7	526	669
Delphy, Richard	Assign to	Dolan, Bernard	1802	G7	526	670
Delphy, Richard	Lease fr	Prout, William	1806	P15	250	165
Delphy, Richard	B. of S. fr	Woods, David	1808	U20	025	015
Delphy, Richard	Deed to	McKim, James	1810	Y24	084	075
Delphy, Richard	B. of S. to	Prout, William	1814	AG32	290	211
Deluis, Frederick, of Bremem	Deed fr	Shultze, John Earnest Christian	1807	Q16	210	142
Dempsey, John	Lease fr	Prout, William	1801	G7	176	235
Dempsey, John	Lease to	Tool, Philip	1801	G7	481	618

Party	What	Party	Year	Liber	Old	New
Dempsey, John	Deed to	Shaw, Ann	1802	I9	527	861
Dempsey, John	Deed fr	May, Frederick	1803	K10	059	64
Dempsie, Elizabeth	P. of Atty. to	Smallwood, Samuel N.	1810	X23	392	316
Dempsie, Elizabeth	Release fr	Chiene, Margaret, of Phila.	1812	AB27	547	447
Dempsie, Elizabeth, of Phila. PA	Marriage to	Smallwood, Samuel N.	1815	AI34	173	198
Dempsie, Elizabeth, wid.	Mortgage to	Chiene, Margaret, of Phila. PA	1810	Y24	088	079
Dempsie, John	Deed fr	Shaw, Alexander, of Balto. MD	1802	I9	114	167
Dempsie, John	Deed fr	Middleton, James	1805	N13	089	080
Dempsie, John & Elizabeth	Manumis to	[ ], Frambo (negro)	1809	W22	338	219
Dempsie, John et al	Deed fr	Alexander, Robert	1807	S18	212	169
Dempsie, John, gardener	Deed fr	Munroe, Thomas, Supt.	1802	I9	048	065
Dempsie, John, Gent.	Deed to	May, Frederick, physician	1801	G7	022	027
Dempsie, John, Gent.	Deed fr	May, Frederick, physician	1801	G7	020	026
Dempsie, John, Gent.	Release to	May, Frederick, physician	1807	S18	016	014
Dempsie, Lavinia, alias Cooper	Cert Free fr	Lucas, Ignatius	1813	AE30	190	152
Denison, Robert, Jr., of Phila. PA	Deed fr	Polock, Isaac	1798	C3	392	311
Denison, Robert, Jr., of Phila. PA	Deed to	Polock, David	1801	G7	210	281
Denison, Robert, Jr., of Phila. PA	P. of Atty. to	Munroe, Thomas	1801	G7	207	277
Denison, Robert, Jr., of Phila. PA	Deed fr	Polock, David	1801	G7	062	080
Denmore, Richard et al	Deed to	Wright, Thomas C.	1807	Q16	358	275
Dennis, John & Samuel Wilson	Deed fr	Stoddert, Benjamin et al	1801	G7	117	150
Dennis, John et al	Deed fr	Lingan, John McCubbin	1801	G7	118	152
Dennison, Robert, Jr., of Phila. PA	Deed fr	Polock, Isaac	1799	D4	205	188
Densley, Hugh	Deed fr	Commissioners of Washington	1800	F6	094	058
Densley, Hugh	Deed fr	Commissioners of Washington	1800	F6	096	059
Densley, Hugh	Deed to	Thompson, James	1801	G7	453	590
Densley, Hugh	Deed fr	Ball, Roger James	1801	G7	042	054
Densley, Hugh	Deed to	Herty, Thomas	1801	G7	480	617
Densley, Hugh	Deed to	Morsell, James Sewell, of G'tn.	1802	G7	554	702
Densley, Hugh	Deed fr	Hurley, Daniel	1802	H8	585	551
Densley, Hugh	Mortgage fr	Peacock, Robert Ware	1802	H8	255	242
Densley, Hugh	Deed to	Alexander, Robert	1802	I9	336	553
Densley, Hugh	Deed to	Hurley, Daniel	1802	I9	036	048
Densley, Hugh	Deed to	Hurley, Daniel	1802	I9	035	046
Densley, Hugh	B. of S. fr	Burford, Henry	1803	K10	067	72
Densley, Hugh	Deed to	Lovering, William	1804	L11	099	101
Densley, Hugh	Mortgage to	Webb, Thomas, of Montg. Co.	1805	M12	104	097
Densley, Hugh	B. of S. to	Evans, Robert	1805	M12	122	116
Densley, Hugh	Deed fr	Webb, Thomas, of Montg. Co.	1817	AO39	232	167
Densley, Hugh et al	Deed to	Washington Building Company	1802	H8	321	302
Densley, Hugh et al	Mortgage to	Gardner, John Frs., Charles Co.	1802	G7	501	639
Densley, Hugh et al	Mortgage to	Addison, Thomas Grafton et al	1804	K10	144	156
Densley, Hugh et al	Deed fr	Addison, Thomas Grafton	1804	L11	215	202
Densley, Hugh et al	Deed to	Burnes, George	1805	N13	075	068
Densley, Hugh et al	Deed to	Burrows, Edward	1805	N13	250	209
Densley, Hugh et al	Assign to	Herty, Thomas	1805	N13	079	072
Densley, Hugh et al	Deed to	Kirby, John Baptist	1805	M12	317	320
Densley, Hugh, insolvent	Deed to	Carpenter, Thomas, trustee	1805	N13	306	248
Densly, Hugh	B. of S. to	Knight, James, Jr. & Eleanor	1804	L11	258	238
Densly, Hugh	Deed fr	Knight, James	1804	L11	184	177
Dent, Charles	Deed fr	Dorsey, William H.	1802	I9	164	249
Dent, Charles	Deed to	Hoban, James & William Brent	1808	T19	241	177
Dent, George Washington, of GA	Deed to	Ritchie, Abner	1811	AB27	167	138
Dent, Lewis W., of Charles Co.	Deed to	Ritchie, Abner	1811	AB27	173	142
Dent, Patrick, of P.G. Co.	Deed to	Ritchie, Abner	1811	AB27	175	144

Index to District of Columbia Land Records, 1792-1817 131

Party	What	Party	Year	Liber	Old	New
Dent, William, Sr.	Cert Free to	Swann, Mary	1810	Z25	114	089
Dermot, James R., of G'tn.	Cert fr	Commissioners of Washington	1793	B2A	312	439
Dermot, James R.	Cert fr	Commissioners of Washington	1793	B2A	313	440
Dermot, James R.	Cert fr	Commissioners of Washington	1793	B2A	312	439
Dermot, James R.	Cert fr	Commissioners of Washington	1796	B2A	336	472
Dermot, James R.	Cert fr	Commissioners of Washington	1796	B2A	335	472
Dermot, James R.	Deed to	Burnes, George	1803	K10	078	84
Dermot, James Reed	Deed fr	Carroll, Daniel, of *Duddington*	1795	B2A	249	347
Dermot, James Reed	Deed fr	Morris, Robert & John Nicholson	1796	B2B	560	293
Dermott, Alice	Slave	From VA	1807	R17	053	043
Dermott, Alice	Lease to	Coyle, Thomas	1808	T19	308	225
Dermott, Alice, now Bird	Deed fr	Brent, Daniel Carroll, marshal	1809	W22	142	101
Dermott, Alice, of Stafford VA	Deed fr	Harrison, Robert	1806	P15	312	206
Dermott, James R.	Deed to	Carroll, Daniel, of *Duddington*	1797	C3	254	208
Dermott, James R.	Mortgage fr	Cooke, Joseph	1797	C3	001	1
Dermott, James R.	Deed fr	Fitzhugh, William, s/o William	1799	D4	250	234
Dermott, James R.	Deed to	Washington, Lund	1799	D4	233	215
Dermott, James R.	Deed fr	Washington, Lund, of Colchester	1800	E5	149	138
Dermott, James R.	Deed fr	Carroll, Daniel, of *Duddington*	1800	E5	191	182
Dermott, James R.	Cert fr	Commissioners of Washington	1801	G7	245	331
Dermott, James R.	Deed to	Harrison, John	1802	H8	266	252
Dermott, James R.	Deed to	Tanner, Pierce L., of Alexa.	1802	H8	574	537
Dermott, James R.	Deed to	Suttle, Henry, of G'tn.	1810	X23	391	314
Dermott, James Reed	Deed fr	Burnes, David	1794	B2A	004	005
Dermott, James Reed	Transfer fr	Morris, Robert & James Greenleaf	1796	B2B	457	146
Dermott, James Reed	Deed to	McCormick, Alexander	1796	B2B	576	319
Dermott, James Reed	Cert fr	Commissioners of Washington	1796	B2B	457	146
Dermott, James Reed	Transfer to	Washington, Lund	1797	B2B	467	160
Dermott, James Reed	Cert fr	Commissioners of Washington	1797	B2B	468	160
Dermott, James Reed	Deed to	Jones, Arthur, of Phila.	1797	B2B	620	378
Dermott, James Reed	Deed to	Cooke, Joseph, of Phila.	1797	B2B	700	484
Dermott, James Reed	Deed fr	Scott, Gustavus et al	1797	B2B	672	440
Dermott, James Reed	Deed to	Deakins, Francis	1798	D4	089	075
Dermott, James Reed	Deed fr	Commissioners of Washington	1799	D4	260	245
Dermott, James Reed et al	Deed to	Harrison, William, of Balto.	1800	E5	335	323
Dermott, James Reed	Deed to	Minor, John, of Fredericksburg	1800	E5	253	247
Dermott, James Reed	Deed to	Deakins, Francis	1800	E5	185	176
Dermott, James Reed	Deed to	Brown, Samuel, Dr., now of KY	1801	F6	135	083
Dermott, John James	Deed fr	Commissioners of Washington	1799	D4	258	243
Dern, Frederick & Elizabeth	Deed to	Brentle, Lawrence, Frederick Co.	1804	K10	322	330
Derr, John & Catharine et al	Deed to	Stoner, Stephen, of Frederick Co.	1810	Z25	182	144
Deterly, Elizabeth	Deed fr	Deterly, John	1802	H8	139	135
Deterly, John	Lease fr	Templeman, John	1801	G7	345	476
Deterly, John	Deed to	Deterly, Elizabeth	1802	H8	139	135
Deterly, John, insolvent	Deed to	Carpenter, Thomas, trustee	1805	N13	124	119
Deveney, Daniel, of G'tn.	D. of T. to	Nicholls, William S., of G'tn.	1817	AO39	340	243
Devilbiss, George, exr. of John	Deed to	Bussard, Daniel, of G'tn.	1805	M12	136	132
Dial, Anastasia	Deed fr	Roby, Theophilus	1802	H8	015	014
Dial, Anna Statia, of G'tn.	Deed fr	Gary, Ann, wid/o Everard of G'tn.	1815	Al34	073	082
Dial, Annastasia et al	Deed fr	Moore, Nicholas et al	1804	K10	310	314
Dial, Annastatia	Deed to	Moore, Nicholas	1804	K10	393	408
Dial, Annastatia	Release fr	Kaldenbaugh, Andrew	1804	K10	197	205
Dial, Annastatia	Deed to	Gary, Everard	1806	Q16	197	133
Dial, Annastatia	B. of S. to	Gary, Everard	1806	P15	319	211
Dial, Annastatia, insolvent	B. of S. to	Aikin, John, trustee	1808	V21	139	101

Index to District of Columbia Land Records, 1792-1817

Party	What	Party	Year	Liber	Old	New
Dick, Elizabeth	Manumis to	[ ], Hannah (C)	1812	AB27	503	411
Dick, Elizabeth	Manumis to	[ ], Margery (C)	1812	AB27	503	411
Dick, James, exors. of	Deed to	Beall, Thomas & John M. Gantt	1793	A1-1	348	453
Dick, Margaret	Deed to	Moore, James	1815	AI34	051	058
Dick, Margaret et al	Deed fr	Stewart, William & Helen	1809	X23	277	219
Dick, Margaret et al	Deed to	Corporation of Georgetown	1811	AB27	135	112
Dick, Margaret, of G'tn.	Lease to	Barnes, John, of G'tn.	1810	Z25	151	119
Dick, Margaret, of G'tn.	Lease to	Lanham, Elisha, of G'tn.	1810	Z25	076	057
Dick, Mason & Thomas	Deed to	Beall, Thomas & John M. Gantt	1793	A1-1	309	408
Dick, Thomas	Deed fr	Hanson, Alexander Contee	1798	D4	017	015
Dick, Thomas	Deed to	Laird, John	1798	D4	016	014
Dickinson, Philemon	Deed fr	Morris, Robert et al	1798	D4	034	028
Dickson, John C.	Cert Free to	Shorter, Nelly	1810	Z25	368	288
Dickson, John C. & George Burns	Mortgage fr	Hickey, James	1811	AB27	233	189
Dickson, John C.	Deed fr	Carroll, Daniel, of *Duddington*	1817	AO39	375	253
Diel, Ann Stacy	Deed to	Wiley, Abel	1802	H8	290	274
Digge, Robert F., of Alexa. Co.	Manumis to	[ ], George (C)	1814	AG32	043	034
Digges, Catherine	Deed fr	Digges, William Dudley	1812	AC28	392	285
Digges, Catherine	Manumis to	Jackson, Nancy (C), and Maria	1812	AD29	441	370
Digges, Edward	Manumis to	Gray, William (C), age 24	1813	AF31	393	284
Digges, George & Notley Young	Deed to	Beall, Thomas & John M. Gantt	1792	A1-1	042	63
Digges, George, trustees of	Deed fr	Bayly, William	1800	E5	315	305
Digges, Susannah	Cert free to	Smith, Thomas (M)	1812	AD29	211	173
Digges, William	Slaves	From Lancaster Co. VA	1812	AC28	284	206
Digges, William	B. of S. to	Whips, Reuben	1817	AO39	306	218
Digges, William Dudley	Deed fr	Carroll, Daniel, of *Duddington*	1811	AB27	444	364
Digges, William Dudley	Deed to	Digges, Catherine	1812	AC28	392	285
Digges, William Dudley	Deed fr	Carroll, William B.	1815	AH33	444	381
Digges, William Dudley, P.G. Co.	Deed to	Carroll, William Brent, s/o Daniel	1815	AH33	443	380
Digges, William Dudley, P.G. Co.	Deed to	Brent, Daniel	1815	AK35	067	052
Diggs, William, of Montg. Co.	Deed to	Key, Philip Barton et al	1805	N13	143	135
Dillehay, Thomas L. & Mary, MD	Deed to	Clark, Robert, of G'tn.	1817	AO39	511	351
Dillon, Robert	Deed to	Charleton, Armstrong	1806	P15	400	269
Dillon, Robert, insolvent	Deed to	Jones, Charles, trustee	1805	N13	155	144
Dinmore, Bridget	Deed fr	Wright, Thomas C., of G'tn.	1814	AH33	244	212
Dinmore, Bridget	Deed to	Wright, Thomas C., of G'tn.	1817	AN38	539	392
Dinmore, Richard	Deed fr	Hanson, Samuel, of Samuel et al	1801	G7	287	398
Dinmore, Richard	B. of S. to	Wright, Thomas C.	1808	U20	187	104
Dinmore, Richard	Deed fr	Glover, Charles	1811	AA26	032	024
Dinmore, Richard, of Alexa.	Deed fr	Lyon, James, printer	1804	L11	191	183
District of Columbia	Deed fr	Casanave, Ann et al	1815	AH33	543	465
Ditty, Roger, of A.A. Co.	Deed fr	Magruder, Nathaniel	1796	B2B	590	339
Dixon, Elizabeth	B. of S. fr	Johnson, Thomas	1811	AA26	199	135
Dixon, James	Deed fr	Beall, Thomas, of Geo.	1811	AB27	294	241
Dixon, James	Deed fr	English, David, of G'tn.	1816	AL36	237	241
Dixon, James, Duplin Co. NC et al	Deed to	Bradley, Phineas	1810	X23	339	272
Dixon, James, of G'tn.	Deed fr	Dixon, Thomas, of G'tn.	1807	S18	183	148
Dixon, James, of G'tn.	Deed to	Gibson, Richard, of G'tn.	1814	AG32	338	244
Dixon, John C.	B. of S. fr	Sandhagan, Frederick	1807	R17	316	240
Dixon, John C.	Deed fr	Carroll, Daniel, of *Duddington*	1807	R17	219	165
Dixon, John C.	B. of S. fr	Vallett, Peter	1807	R17	275	209
Dixon, John C.	B. of S. fr	Irwin, Charles	1807	R17	347	264
Dixon, John, of Martinsburgh VA	Deed fr	Crocker, John, of Martinsburgh	1799	D4	230	212
Dixon, Thomas	Deed fr	Beatty, Charles, heirs of	1806	O14	318	211
Dixon, Thomas	Deed fr	Brent, Daniel Carroll, marshal	1808	T19	323	235

Index to District of Columbia Land Records, 1792-1817

Party	What	Party	Year	Liber	Old	New
Dixon, Thomas	Deed fr	Renner, Daniel	1814	AH33	301	260
Dixon, Thomas	Deed to	Renner, Daniel	1814	AH33	262	229
Dixon, Thomas	Deed to	English, David, cashier	1815	AI34	406	428
Dixon, Thomas, of G'tn.	Deed fr	English, David & wife Sarah, G'tn.	1802	I9	118	173
Dixon, Thomas, of G'tn.	Deed fr	Beall, Thomas B., of G'tn.	1804	K10	199	207
Dixon, Thomas, of G'tn.	Deed fr	Fields, William, of G'tn.	1805	M12	389	401
Dixon, Thomas, of G'tn.	Deed to	Dixon, James, of G'tn.	1807	S18	183	148
Dixon, Thomas, of G'tn.	Deed to	Williams, Elisha W., of G'tn.	1809	W22	162	113
Dixon, Thomas, of G'tn.	Deed fr	Beall, Thomas B., of G'tn.	1810	Y24	060	053
Dixon, Thomas, of G'tn.	Deed to	Pickerill, John, of G'tn.	1810	Y24	176	161
Dixon, Thomas, of G'tn.	Lease to	Robertson, Joseph, of G'tn.	1811	AB27	134	111
Dixon, Thomas, of G'tn.	Deed fr	Pickerell, John, of G'tn.	1812	AC28	240	177
Dixon, Thomas, of G'tn.	Deed to	English, David	1816	AL36	057	057
Dixon, Thomas, of G'tn.	Deed fr	Cist, Jacob, of PA	1817	AO39	506	348
Dobbin, David	Deed fr	Hedges, Hanson	1812	AD29	286	235
Dobbins, David	Agreement	Duby, John	1803	K10	083	90
Dobbins, David	Deed fr	Walker, Zachariah	1813	AE30	500	370
Dobbins, David	Lease Fr	Bayly, Mountjoy	1813	AF31	194	131
Dobby, John	Deed fr	Ewell, Thomas	1813	AE30	491	364
Dobbybn, John	Deed fr	Heard, James B.	1808	U20	096	053
Dobbyn, John	Mortgage to	Ewell, Thomas, of G'tn.	1813	AF31	074	051
Dobbyn, John	Deed fr	Ewell, Thomas & Elizabeth	1813	AE30	273	210
Dobbyn, John	B. of S. fr	Coombe, Griffith	1815	AI34	377	404
Dobbyns, Samuel & Ann, of NC	Deed to	Beatty, Charles, of G'tn.	1794	A1-2	494	97
Docker, Gilbert	Receipt fr	Brent, Robert, exr. of N. Young	1805	N13	219	188
Docker, Gilbert	Deed fr	Carroll, Daniel, of *Duddington*	1811	AA26	254	172
Docker, Gilbert	Deed fr	Law, Thomas	1812	AD29	038	027
Dodge, Allen & Francis	Agreement	Kennedy, Matthew	1805	N13	182	163
Dodge, Allen & Francis	Deed fr	Holmead, Anthony	1806	P15	271	179
Dodge, Allen & Francis, of G'tn.	Deed fr	Oden, Benjamin, of P.G. Co.	1807	R17	406	307
Dodge, Allen & Francis, of G'tn.	Deed fr	Thorpe, Thomas	1808	T19	371	265
Dodge, Allen & Francis	Release to	Wilson, John, of Henry	1808	V21	001	001
Dodge, Allen & Francis, of G'tn.	Deed to	Beall, Samuel, of G'tn.	1809	V21	236	168
Dodge, Allen & Francis	Receipt fr	Corporation of Georgetown	1816	AK35	485	381
Dodge, Allen, Newbury Port MA	Deed fr	King, George, of G'tn.	1805	N13	173	157
Dodge, Allen, Newbury Port MA	Deed to	Hollingshead, John et al	1810	Z25	049	036
Dodge, Allen, Newbury Port MA	Lease to	Elliott, Richard	1813	AF31	468	339
Dodge, Francis	Deed fr	Bank of Columbia	1812	AC28	311	227
Dodge, Francis	Lease to	Bunnell, Elial et al	1813	AF31	552	409
Dodge, Francis	Manumis to	Turner, Elleck (C), age 43	1813	AE30	550	408
Dodge, Francis	Deed fr	Kennedy, James	1813	AF31	551	409
Dodge, Francis, Newbury Port MA	Deed fr	Holmead, Anthony	1806	P15	271	179
Dodge, Francis, of G'tn.	B. of S. fr	Kennedy, Mathew, of G'tn.	1805	N13	177	159
Dodge, Francis, of G'tn. et al	Deed fr	King, George, of G'tn.	1805	N13	173	157
Dodge, Francis, of G'tn.	Deed fr	Reintzel, Daniel, of G'tn.	1809	W22	231	157
Dodge, Francis, of G'tn. et al	Deed to	Hollingshead, John et al	1810	Z25	049	036
Dodge, Francis, of G'tn.	Deed fr	Lingan, Nicholas, of G'tn.	1811	Z25	393	308
Dodge, Francis, of G'tn.	B. of S. fr	Ellis, Philip	1811	AA26	042	032
Dodge, Francis, of G'tn.	Deed fr	Reintzel, Anthony, of G'tn.	1811	AB27	467	383
Dodge, Francis, of G'tn.	Deed fr	Beall, Thomas, of Geo., of G'tn.	1812	AD29	484	409
Dodge, Francis, of G'tn. et al	Lease to	Elliott, Richard	1813	AF31	468	339
Dodge, Francis, of G'tn.	Deed fr	Deakins, Leonard M., of P.G. Co.	1815	AI34	180	206
Dodge, Francis, of G'tn.	Deed fr	Boone, Arnold, of G'tn.	1815	AI34	181	207
Dodge, Francis, of G'tn.	Deed fr	Smith, Andrew, of Richmond	1815	AK35	430	338
Dodge, Francis, of G'tn.	Deed fr	Beall, Thomas, of Geo., of G'tn.	1815	AK35	429	336

Party	What	Party	Year	Liber	Old	New
Dodge, Francis, of G'tn.	Deed fr	Bunnell, Elial, of G'tn. et al	1815	AI34	543	548
Dodge, Francis, of G'tn.	Deed fr	Lancaster, Stephen, of G'tn.	1816	AL36	393	379
Dodge, Francis, of G'tn.	Deed fr	Lanham, Elisha, of G'tn.	1816	AL36	395	381
Dodge, Francis, of G'tn.	Deed to	Lancaster, Stephen, of G'tn.	1816	AL36	396	382
Dodge, Francis, of G'tn.	Deed to	Murdock, John	1817	AO39	320	228
Dodson, Ann	Cert Free fr	Hutchinson, Samuel, heirs of	1817	AO39	247	178
Dodson, William (C), age 17	Agreement	Adams, Henry	1817	AN38	271	198
Dolan, Bernard	Assign fr	Delphy, Richard	1802	G7	526	670
Dolan, Bernard, trustee	B. of S. fr	Theker, James, insolvent	1808	U20	117	067
Dolan, Bernard, trustee	Deed fr	Corly, James, insolvent	1811	AA26	166	114
Dole, Conrad	Deed fr	Ritchie, Abner	1804	K10	268	274
Dole, Conrad	Deed to	Ritchie, Abner	1804	K10	267	273
Dole, Conrad, of Frederick Co.	Deed fr	Hoof, John, of Rocking. Co., heirs	1804	K10	363	376
Dole, Conrad [Doll]	Deed fr	Hoof, John, heirs, Augusta Co. VA	1804	K10	360	373
Doll, Conrad	Deed to	Ott, John	1809	W22	265	177
Doll, Conrad, of Frederick Co.	Deed to	Beall, Thomas & John M. Gantt	1792	A1-1	084	123
Doll, Conrad, of Frederick Co.	Deed fr	Davidson, John, of Annapolis	1799	E5	048	037
Doll, Conrad, of Frederick Town	Deed to	Doll, George, s/o Conrad	1805	M12	194	195
Doll, Conrad, of Frederick Co.	Deed fr	Doll, Joseph, of Frederick Co.	1808	T19	293	214
Doll, Conrad [Dole]	Deed fr	Hoof, John, heirs, Augusta Co. VA	1804	K10	360	373
Doll, George, s/o Conrad	Deed fr	Doll, Conrad, of Frederick Town	1805	M12	194	195
Doll, Jacob	Deed to	McClan, Robert	1795	B2A	271	379
Doll, James	Deed fr	Polock, Isaac	1802	I9	205	321
Doll, Joseph et al	Deed to	Beall, Thomas & John M. Gantt	1792	A1-1	076	112
Doll, Joseph, of Frederick Co.	Deed fr	Davidson, John, of Annapolis	1799	E5	049	039
Doll, Joseph, of Frederick Co.	Deed to	Doll, Conrad, of Frederick Co.	1808	T19	293	214
Doll, Margaret, d/o Conrad	Deed to	Stickell, Solomon, her son-in-law	1815	AI34	031	036
Donahoe, Patrick	Deed fr	Dorsey, William H., of G'tn.	1807	R17	050	041
Donahoe, Patrick	Deed fr	Dorsey, William H., of G'tn.	1807	R17	093	073
Donaldson, John, late Alexa. Co.	Cert Slaves	From Alexa. Co. VA	1817	AN38	544	395
Donaldson, Ronald	Lease fr	Kerr, Alexander	1813	AE30	225	181
Donaldson, Ronald	Qualify	Lieutenant of Infantry	1814	AH33	332	287
Donaldson, Ronald	D. of T. to	Allen, Henry I.	1814	AH33	141	134
Donaldson, Thomas, of G'tn.	B. of S. to	Hyde, Thomas, of G'tn.	1817	AN38	531	386
Doncastle, Elizabeth, Sr.	Deed to	Doncastle, Elizabeth, the younger	1792	A1-1	167	239
Doncastle, Elizabeth, the younger	Deed fr	Doncastle, Elizabeth, Sr.	1792	A1-1	167	239
Donnahue, Morgan	Deed fr	Van Ness, John P. et ux	1806	Q16	025	016
Donnelly, Simon, of Balto.	Deed fr	Kirk, Milesius Thomas, of G'tn.	1801	F6	195	126
Donohew, Patrick	B. of S. fr	Fleharty, Peter	1802	H8	383	356
Donohoe, James	Deed fr	O'Connor, Lawrence, of NY	1807	S18	168	136
Donohoe, John, s/o Patrick	B. of S. fr	Donohoe, Patrick	1815	AH33	457	391
Donohoe, Patrick	B. of S. to	Donohoe, John, s/o Patrick	1815	AH33	457	391
Donohoo, Patrick	Deed fr	Patterson, Edgar et al	1810	Y24	062	055
Donoughoo, Bridget et al	Deed fr	Donoughoo, Patrick	1814	AH33	001	001
Donoughoo, John et al	Deed fr	Donoughoo, Patrick	1814	AH33	001	001
Donoughoo, Margaret et al	Deed fr	Donoughoo, Patrick	1814	AH33	001	001
Donoughoo, Mary et al	Deed fr	Donoughoo, Patrick	1814	AH33	001	001
Donoughoo, Patrick	Deed to	Donoughoo, John et al	1814	AH33	001	001
Donoughoo, Sarah et al	Deed fr	Donoughoo, Patrick	1814	AH33	001	001
Donovan, John, of Hancock Town	Deed fr	Bridges, John, of G'tn.	1807	S18	336	264
Doolen, Bernard	Deed fr	Clephan, Lewis	1813	AE30	060	045
Dooling, Michael	Deed to	Miller, George	1807	R17	365	278
Dooly, Barney et al	Deed fr	O'Brien, William	1805	M12	095	088
Dorman, Samuel C.	B. of S. to	Staley, Jacob, of G'tn.	1812	AD29	090	068
Dorsey, Andrew	Manumis fr	Gilman, Nicholas, of Exeter NH	1810	X23	253	197

Party	What	Party	Year	Liber	Old	New
Dorsey, Clement	Deed fr	Dorsey, William H.	1802	H8	039	038
Dorsey, Edward	Manumis to	[ ], Amelia (C)	1817	AN38	381	282
Dorsey, Joshua	P. of Atty. to	Warring, Marsham	1801	G7		317
Dorsey, Joshua, of Frederick Co.	Deed fr	Edelen, Rebecca et al	1799	E5	069	056
Dorsey, Joshua, of Frederick Co.	Deed to	Bayly, Mountjoy, of Frederick Co.	1800	E5	282	276
Dorsey, Joshua, of Frederick	Deed to	Lingan, James McCubbin	1801	G7	235	315
Dorsey, Rosetta	R. Dower to	Edelin, Ignatius	1809	V21	322	237
Dorsey, Walter, attorney, of Balto.	Deed to	Dorsey, William Hammond	1801	G7	273	376
Dorsey, Walter, of St. Mary's Co.	Deed fr	Dorsey, William H.	1794	B2A	100	131
Dorsey, William H.	Deed to	Robertson, William	1794	A1-2	483	87
Dorsey, William H.	Deed fr	Beall, Thomas, of George	1794	A1-2	485	88
Dorsey, William H.	Deed to	Dorsey, Walter, of St. Mary's Co.	1794	B2A	100	131
Dorsey, William H.	Deed to	Davidson, John, of Annapolis	1795	B2A	183	247
Dorsey, William H.	Deed to	Williams, Elisha O.	1795	B2A	195	265
Dorsey, William H.	Deed to	Lee, Thomas S. et al	1795	B2A	235	327
Dorsey, William H., of G'tn.	Deed fr	Casanave, Peter, of G'tn.	1796	B2B	527	240
Dorsey, William H., of G'tn.	P. of Atty. fr	Lynch, Dominick & Comfort Sands	1796	B2B	523	234
Dorsey, William H., of G'tn.	P. of Atty. fr	Oden, Benjamin	1796	B2B	558	289
Dorsey, William H., of Montg. Co.	Deed to	Wright, John, of Montg. Co.	1797	C3	230	192
Dorsey, William H., of Montg. Co.	Deed to	Craik, William, of Montg. Co. et al	1797	C3	152	125
Dorsey, William H.	Cede to	Corporation of Georgetown	1797	B2B	619	376
Dorsey, William H., of Montg. Co.	Deed to	Beall, Elijah, of Montg. Co.	1798	C3	359	288
Dorsey, William H.	Deed fr	Maddox, Notley, sheriff	1799	D4	298	281
Dorsey, William H.	Agreement	Kid, Robert, of Phila.	1800	E5	243	236
Dorsey, William H.	Deed fr	Beall, Thomas, of George	1800	E5	401	374
Dorsey, William H.	Deed fr	Beall, Thomas, of George	1800	E5	165	154
Dorsey, William H.	Deed to	Lewis, Kendall M., Sussex Co. DE	1801	G7	094	121
Dorsey, William H., of G'tn.	Deed to	Riggs, George W., of G'tn.	1801	G7	206	275
Dorsey, William H.	Deed to	Walker, George, Jr.	1801	G7	230	308
Dorsey, William H., of G'tn.	Deed to	Duane, William, of Phila.	1801	G7	388	521
Dorsey, William H., of G'tn.	Deed to	Athey, Hezekiah, of G'tn.	1801	G7	399	533
Dorsey, William H., of G'tn.	Deed to	Brookes, Joseph, of G'tn.	1802	G7	563	712
Dorsey, William H.	Deed to	Dorsey, Clement	1802	H8	039	038
Dorsey, William H.	Deed to	Burnes, Anne	1802	H8	159	153
Dorsey, William H.	Deed to	Woodward, William	1802	H8	157	151
Dorsey, William H. et al	Deed fr	Munroe, Thomas et al	1802	I9	364	604
Dorsey, William H.	Deed fr	Burnes, Ann, wid.	1802	I9	008	010
Dorsey, William H.	Deed fr	Oakley, John, guard.	1802	I9	009	011
Dorsey, William H. et al	Deed to	Pratt, Henry et al	1802	I9	568	920
Dorsey, William H.	Deed fr	Blount, George	1802	I9	580	940
Dorsey, William H.	Deed to	Foxton, William	1802	I9	272	444
Dorsey, William H.	Deed to	Pratt, Henry et al	1802	I9	263	426
Dorsey, William H., assignee of	Deed fr	Burnes, Marcia, guard. of	1802	I9	007	009
Dorsey, William H.	Deed to	Woodward, William	1802	I9	335	552
Dorsey, William H.	Lease to	Joncherez, A.C.	1802	I9	312	514
Dorsey, William H.	Deed to	Hayne, Matthias	1802	I9	165	250
Dorsey, William H.	Deed to	Goszler, Henry	1802	I9	403	669
Dorsey, William H.	Deed to	Smallwood, Leven	1802	I9	586	950
Dorsey, William H.	Deed fr	Burnes, Marcia, guard. of	1802	I9	009	011
Dorsey, William H.	Deed to	Shaw, John et al	1802	I9	373	619
Dorsey, William H.	Lease to	McLean, Cornelius	1802	I9	240	386
Dorsey, William H.	Lease to	Mundy, Peter	1802	I9	468	772
Dorsey, William H.	Deed to	Tiethy, Edw.	1802	I9	186	287
Dorsey, William H.	Lease to	Blount, George	1802	I9	287	469
Dorsey, William H.	Lease to	Herty, Thomas	1802	I9	311	512

Party	What	Party	Year	Liber	Old	New
Dorsey, William H.	Deed to	Frethy, Edward	1802	I9	282	461
Dorsey, William H.	Lease to	Blount, George	1802	I9	535	874
Dorsey, William H.	Lease to	Woodward, William	1802	I9	481	790
Dorsey, William H.	Deed to	Dent, Charles	1802	I9	164	249
Dorsey, William H.	Deed to	Taylor, John	1802	I9	195	303
Dorsey, William H.	Deed to	Morgan, William	1804	K10	358	370
Dorsey, William H.	Deed fr	Beall, Thomas, of George	1804	M12	042	041
Dorsey, William H., of G'tn.	Deed fr	Deas, William, of Phila.	1804	K10	163	174
Dorsey, William H., of G'tn.	Deed to	Tayloe, John	1804	K10	263	269
Dorsey, William H., of G'tn.	Deed to	Magruder, Ninian, of G'tn.	1805	M12	408	423
Dorsey, William H.	Deed to	Nevitt, William	1805	M12	074	068
Dorsey, William H., of G'tn.	Deed to	Reintzel, Anthony, of G'tn.	1805	M12	114	107
Dorsey, William H.	Deed to	West, Joseph D.	1805	M12	112	105
Dorsey, William H., of G'tn.	Deed to	Kid, Robert, of Phila. PA	1805	N13	398	317
Dorsey, William H.	Mortgage fr	Parrott, Richard	1805	N13	074	067
Dorsey, William H., of G'tn.	Deed to	Wheaton, Joseph	1805	N13	112	107
Dorsey, William H., of G'tn.	Mortgage to	Van Ness, John P.	1805	N13	042	041
Dorsey, William H., of G'tn.	Deed to	Keyne, Matthias	1805	O14	035	021
Dorsey, William H., of G'tn.	Deed fr	Tayloe, John	1806	P15	362	241
Dorsey, William H.	Deed to	Wagner, Jacob	1806	Q16	045	029
Dorsey, William H., of G'tn.	Deed to	Travers, Elias	1806	Q16	256	177
Dorsey, William H., of G'tn.	Deed to	Benson, Edin, of G'tn.	1806	Q16	051	033
Dorsey, William H., of G'tn.	Deed to	Tayloe, John, of G'tn.	1806	Q16	129	084
Dorsey, William H., of G'tn.	Deed to	Harvey, Samuel, of Phila. PA	1806	Q16	305	233
Dorsey, William H.	Deed fr	Jackson, Jonathan, trustees of	1806	P15	064	039
Dorsey, William H., of G'tn.	Deed to	Lingan, Nicholas, of G'tn.	1807	Q16	333	256
Dorsey, William H., of G'tn.	Deed to	King, Charles, of G'tn.	1807	R17	280	213
Dorsey, William H., of G'tn.	Deed to	Connelly, Patrick, of G'tn.	1807	R17	284	217
Dorsey, William H., of G'tn.	Deed to	Whelan, Thomas	1807	R17	331	252
Dorsey, William H., of G'tn.	Deed to	Connelly, Patrick & John, of G'tn.	1807	R17	283	216
Dorsey, William H., of G'tn.	Deed to	Donahoe, Patrick	1807	R17	050	041
Dorsey, William H., of G'tn.	Deed to	Murdock, John, of G'tn.	1807	R17	414	313
Dorsey, William H., of G'tn.	Deed to	Connelly, John, of G'tn.	1807	R17	286	218
Dorsey, William H., of G'tn.	Deed to	Blagden, George	1807	R17	141	109
Dorsey, William H., of G'tn.	Deed fr	King, William, Jr., of G'tn.	1807	R17	060	048
Dorsey, William H.	Deed to	Parrott, Richard	1807	R17	135	104
Dorsey, William H., of G'tn.	Deed to	Donahoe, Patrick	1807	R17	093	073
Dorsey, William H., of G'tn.	Deed to	Craig, George, of G'tn.	1807	R17	186	142
Dorsey, William H., of G'tn.	Deed to	Caton, John	1807	R17	212	159
Dorsey, William H., of G'tn.	Deed to	Martin, Honore, of Montg. Co.	1807	R17	080	064
Dorsey, William H., of G'tn.	Deed to	Clancy, Patrick & John	1807	R17	211	158
Dorsey, William H., of G'tn.	Deed to	King, George, of G'tn.	1807	R17	281	215
Dorsey, William H., of G'tn.	Deed to	Wheelan, Nicholas	1807	R17	056	045
Dorsey, William H., of G'tn.	Deed to	Forrest, Richard	1807	S18	067	055
Dorsey, William H., of G'tn.	Deed to	Holmes, William, of Montg. Co.	1807	S18	082	067
Dorsey, William H., of G'tn.	Deed to	O'Connor, Lawrence, Montg. Co.	1807	S18	077	063
Dorsey, William H., of G'tn.	Deed to	Bowie, Washington, of G'tn.	1807	S18	046	038
Dorsey, William H., of Balto.	Deed to	King, William, Jr., of G'tn.	1808	T19	386	275
Dorsey, William H., of Balto. Co.	Deed to	Edelin, Ignatius	1808	U20	109	062
Dorsey, William H., of Balto.	Deed to	Foxton, William	1808	U20	134	077
Dorsey, William H., of Balto.	Deed to	Lenox, Peter	1808	U20	367	200
Dorsey, William H., of Balto.	Deed to	Parrott, Richard	1808	T19	232	170
Dorsey, William H., of Balto.	Deed to	Stewart, William	1809	W22	376	244
Dorsey, William H., of Balto.	Deed to	Brent, Daniel et al	1809	X23	239	186
Dorsey, William H., of Balto.	Deed to	Huddleston, Joseph	1809	W22	122	087

Index to District of Columbia Land Records, 1792-1817   137

Party	What	Party	Year	Liber	Old	New
Dorsey, William H., of Balto.	Deed to	Cope, Jasper, of Phila. PA	1810	X23	388	312
Dorsey, William H., of Balto.	Deed to	Huddlestone, Joseph	1810	Y24	448	398
Dorsey, William H., of Balto.	Deed to	Jones, Charles	1810	Y24	442	393
Dorsey, William H., of Balto.	Deed to	Hagner, Peter	1810	Y24	426	381
Dorsey, William H., of Balto.	Deed to	Clarke, Walter & Joseph	1810	Y24	435	388
Dorsey, William H., of Balto.	Deed to	Hogan, Thady	1810	Y24	429	384
Dorsey, William H., of Balto.	Deed to	Travers, Nicholas, of G'tn.	1810	Z25	246	193
Dorsey, William H., of Balto. Co.	Release fr	Tayloe, John	1810	Z25	014	011
Dorsey, William H., of Balto. Co.	Deed to	Moore, James	1810	Z25	072	054
Dorsey, William H., of Balto.	Deed to	Lewis, Kendall M., Sussex Co. DE	1810	Z25	207	163
Dorsey, William H., of Balto.	Deed to	Magruder, Ninian, Dr., of G'tn.	1811	AA26	013	010
Dorsey, William H., of Balto.	Deed to	Underwood, Robert	1811	AA26	309	208
Dorsey, William H., of Balto.	Deed to	Reintzel, Valentine, of G'tn.	1811	AA26	377	250
Dorsey, William H., of Balto.	Deed to	McClelland, John	1811	AA26	003	002
Dorsey, William H., of Balto.	Deed to	Hereford, John	1811	AA26	190	129
Dorsey, William H., of Balto. Co.	Deed to	Nevitt, William, of G'tn.	1811	AB27	281	230
Dorsey, William H., of Balto. Co.	Deed to	Mauro, Philip & Conradt Schwartz	1811	AB27	223	181
Dorsey, William H., of Balto.	Deed to	Travers, Sidney	1811	AC28	051	039
Dorsey, William H., of Balto.	Deed to	Borrows, Joseph	1811	Z25	438	345
Dorsey, William H., of Balto.	Deed to	Murdock, John, of G'tn.	1811	Z25	407	320
Dorsey, William H., of Balto.	Deed to	Laurie, James, Rev.	1811	Z25	450	355
Dorsey, William H., of Balto. Co.	Deed to	King, Vincent, of G'tn.	1812	AC28	268	196
Dorsey, William H., of Balto. Co.	Deed to	Corporation of Georgetown	1812	AD29	266	220
Dorsey, William H., of Balto. MD	Deed to	Borrows, Joseph	1812	AD29	297	244
Dorsey, William H., of Balto. Co.	Deed to	Heath, Nathaniel H.	1812	AD29	355	298
Dorsey, William H., of Balto. Co.	Deed to	Fletcher, Noah	1812	AD29	305	250
Dorsey, William H., of Balto. Co.	Deed to	Moore, James	1812	AD29	495	418
Dorsey, William H., of Balto. Co.	Deed to	Doughty, William, of G'tn.	1812	AD29	392	331
Dorsey, William H., of Balto. Co.	Deed to	Mauro, Philip & Conrad Schwartz	1812	AC28	258	189
Dorsey, William H., of Balto.	Deed to	Marbury, William, of G'tn.	1813	AF31	346	246
Dorsey, William H., of Balto. Co.	Deed to	Shuck, Frederick	1813	AF31	053	036
Dorsey, William H., of Balto.	Deed to	Gilliss, Thomas H.	1813	AF31	110	074
Dorsey, William H., of Balto. Co.	Deed to	Buchanan, Thomas	1813	AF31	188	127
Dorsey, William H., of Balto.	Deed to	Heath, Nathaniel H.	1813	AF31	142	095
Dorsey, William H., of Balto. Co.	Deed to	Buchannan, Thomas	1814	AG32	077	058
Dorsey, William H., of Montg. Co.	Deed to	Way, Andrew & George	1814	AG32	234	167
Dorsey, William H., of Montg. Co.	Deed to	Foxall, Henry, of G'tn.	1814	AH33	186	170
Dorsey, William H., of Montg. Co.	Deed to	Smoot, Samuel, of G'tn.	1814	AH33	259	226
Dorsey, William H., of Montg. Co.	Deed to	French, George, of G'tn.	1814	AH33	200	182
Dorsey, William H., of Montg. Co.	Deed to	Brent, Robert	1814	AH33	081	072
Dorsey, William H., of Montg. Co.	Deed to	Gillis, Thomas H.	1814	AH33	239	208
Dorsey, William H., of Montg. Co.	Deed to	Gilliss, Thomas H.	1815	AI34	471	482
Dorsey, William H., of Montg. Co.	Deed to	King, Charles	1815	AI34	327	359
Dorsey, William H., of Montg. Co.	Deed to	McLean, Cornelius [Maclean]	1815	AI34	239	271
Dorsey, William H., of Montg. Co.	Deed to	Smith, Clement & John Pickrell	1815	AK35	106	082
Dorsey, William H., of Montg. Co.	Deed fr	Murdock, John, of G'tn.	1815	AK35	452	354
Dorsey, William H., of Montg. Co.	Deed to	Andrews, Timothy P.	1815	AK35	361	285
Dorsey, William H., of Montg. Co.	Deed to	Wilson, John A.	1815	AK35	182	141
Dorsey, William H., of Montg. Co.	Deed to	Becraft, William, of G'tn.	1815	AI34	205	234
Dorsey, William H., of Montg. Co.	Deed to	Fitzhugh, Samuel, of G'tn.	1816	AK35	518	408
Dorsey, William H., of Montg. Co.	Deed to	Williams, John S., of G'tn.	1816	AL36	314	310
Dorsey, William H., of Montg. Co.	Deed to	Moxley, Charles, of G'tn.	1816	AL36	216	223
Dorsey, William H., of Montg. Co.	Deed to	Smith, Clement & John Pickrell	1816	AL36	470	443
Dorsey, William H., of Montg. Co.	Deed to	Smoot, Samuel, of G'tn.	1816	AM37	166	126
Dorsey, William H., of Montg. Co.	Deed to	Becraft, William, of G'tn.	1816	AO39	050	042

Party	What	Party	Year	Liber	Old	New
Dorsey, William H., of Montg. Co.	Deed to	Randall, Daniel	1817	AO39	069	057
Dorsey, William H., of Montg. Co.	Deed to	McGrath, Thomas	1817	AO39	388	262
Dorsey, William H., of Montg. Co.	Deed to	Ott, David	1817	AO39	061	051
Dorsey, William Hammond et al	Deed fr	Johns, Richard	1794	B2A	052	063
Dorsey, William Hammond et al	Deed fr	Thomas, Samuel 3rd	1794	B2A	051	062
Dorsey, William Hammond et al	Deed fr	Beall, Thomas, s/o George	1794	B2A	054	067
Dorsey, William Hammond	Deed fr	Cassanave, Peter	1794	B2A	072	093
Dorsey, William Hammond	Deed fr	Gilmer, Stewart & Moncreiff	1795	B2A	208	286
Dorsey, William Hammond	Deed fr	Beatty, Charles et al	1795	B2A	237	330
Dorsey, William Hammond et al	Deed to	Brooke, Samuel, of Montg. Co.	1797	C3	151	124
Dorsey, William Hammond	Deed fr	O'Neale, Lawrence, of Montg. Co.	1798	C3	332	268
Dorsey, William Hammond et al	Deed fr	Maddox, Notley	1798	D4	060	050
Dorsey, William Hammond et al	Deed fr	Maddox, Notley	1800	E5	090	077
Dorsey, William Hammond	Deed to	Beall, Thomas, of George	1800	E5	276	270
Dorsey, William Hammond, G'tn.	Deed to	McCutchin, John, of G'tn.	1801	G7	336	466
Dorsey, William Hammond	Deed fr	Dorsey, Walter, attorney, of Balto.	1801	G7	273	376
Dorsey, William Hammond, Esq.	Deed to	Williams, Jeremiah, mechant	1801	G7	424	559
Dorsey, William Hammond	Deed fr	Beall, Thomas, of George	1801	G7	250	339
Dorsey, William Hammond	Deed to	McDonald, Andrew	1802	H8	399	370
Dorsey, William Hammond et al	Deed fr	Gillis, Thomas Handy	1804	L11	262	241
Dorsey, William Hammond	Deed to	Gillaspie, George, of Phila. et al	1804	L11	064	66
Dorsey, William Hammond	Mortgage fr	Beverly, Robert, of *Blandfield*, VA	1805	N13	044	043
Dorsey, William Hammond, G'tn.	Deed fr	Van Ness, John P. & Marcia	1805	N13	242	204
Dorsey, William Hammond	Deed to	Smith, Walter	1805	N13	268	223
Dorsey, William Hammond	Deed fr	Burnes, Ann	1805	M12	268	269
Dorsey, William Hammond	Deed to	Beverly, Robert, of *Blandfield*, VA	1805	M12	267	268
Dorsey, William Hammond, G'tn.	Deed fr	Wagner, Jacob	1806	Q16	331	254
Dorsey, William Hammond et al	Deed to	Threlkeld, John	1807	R17	073	059
Dorsey, William Hammond, Balto.	Release fr	Van Ness, John P.	1810	Z25	281	221
Dorsey, William Hammond, Balto.	Deed to	King, William, Jr., of G'tn.	1811	AB27	137	114
Dorsey, William Y.	Deed to	Wayman, Charles, of G'tn. et al	1804	L11	071	73
Dorsey, Wliam H., of Balto. MD	Deed to	Edwards, Horace Hampden	1812	AD29	294	242
Dougherty, Barney	Deed fr	Prout, William	1806	O14	323	214
Dougherty, Daniel, of Alexa.	Convey fr	Dale, James, of Balto., heirs of	1815	AI34	199	228
Dougherty, Daniel, of Alexa.	Deed fr	Day, Edward, of Balto. Co.	1815	AI34	200	229
Dougherty, Eleanor	B. of S. fr	Daugherty, Vincent	1811	Z25	556	442
Dougherty, James	Deed fr	Bickley, Robert S., Holmsberg PA	1813	AF31	240	166
Dougherty, James & Mary	Deed fr	Clarke, Robert	1813	AF31	517	379
Dougherty, James, trustee	Deed fr	Bentley, Joseph, insolvent	1806	P15	329	218
Dougherty, James, trustee	D. of T. fr	West, John	1810	Y24	139	126
Dougherty, Patrick	B. of S. to	Adams, William	1804	L11	394	349
Dougherty, Patrick	B. of S. to	Howard, Peter	1805	O14	151	098
Dougherty, Thomas	Deed fr	Carr, Overton, trustee	1817	AO39	542	373
Doughlass, Robert H., Fairfax Co.	Deed fr	Brown, Dolly	1815	AK35	131	101
Doughty, William	Deed fr	Ellis, Robert	1801	G7	413	547
Doughty, William	Deed fr	Chandler, Walter Story	1801	G7	414	548
Doughty, William	Deed fr	Munroe, Thomas, Supt.	1802	H8	550	512
Doughty, William	Deed fr	Sprogell, Thomas Y.	1802	H8	096	087
Doughty, William	Deed to	Sprogell, Thomas Y.	1802	H8	172	165
Doughty, William	Deed fr	Moore, James	1802	H8	251	238
Doughty, William	Assign to	Moore, James	1802	H8	248	236
Doughty, William	Deed fr	Munroe, Thomas, Supt.	1802	H8	552	513
Doughty, William	Qualify		1802	I9	464	765
Doughty, William	Deed to	Anderson, George	1804	K10	224	232
Doughty, William	B. of S. to	Myers, John	1810	Y24	474	419

Index to District of Columbia Land Records, 1792-1817   139

Party	What	Party	Year	Liber	Old	New
Doughty, William	Release fr	Bank of Columbia	1812	AD29	394	332
Doughty, William	D. of T. to	Morgan, William	1813	AF31	078	054
Doughty, William	Deed to	Fitzhugh, Samuel, of G'tn.	1815	AI34	186	213
Doughty, William	Release fr	Morgan, William, of G'tn.	1815	AI34	184	211
Doughty, William	Deed to	Cutts, Richard	1817	AO39	237	171
Doughty, William, Capt.	Deed fr	Beatty, John M. & Charles A.	1806	P15	100	062
Doughty, William et al	Deed fr	Eliason, Ebenezer & Ann	1809	V21	290	210
Doughty, William et al	D. of T. fr	Foxall, Henry	1816	AL36	357	348
Doughty, William, of G'tn.	Deed to	Creiger, Michael	1804	L11	058	59
Doughty, William, of G'tn.	Deed to	Neale, Leonard, Rt. Rev.	1805	N13	366	295
Doughty, William, of G'tn.	Deed to	Love, Charles, of G'tn.	1806	P15	137	089
Doughty, William, of G'tn.	Deed to	Suter, Alexander, of G'tn.	1811	Z25	505	401
Doughty, William, of G'tn.	Deed fr	Dorsey, William H., of Balto. Co.	1812	AD29	392	331
Doughty, William, of G'tn.	Deed fr	Murdock, John, of G'tn.	1812	AD29	391	229
Doughty, William, trustee et al	Deed fr	Morgan, William, of G'tn.	1814	AH33	010	009
Douglas, Edward, of G'tn.	Deed fr	Weatheral, John, of G'tn.	1799	E5	057	047
Douglas, James, of P.G. Co.	B. of S. fr	Douglas, John	1806	P15	253	167
Douglas, John	B. of S. to	Douglas, James, of P.G. Co.	1806	P15	253	167
Douglas, John (negro)	Manumis fr	Stelle, Pontius D.	1809	W22	174	122
Douglas, John et al	Mortgage fr	Minitree, John	1814	AH33	035	031
Douglas, Robert		Confiscation Deed, 50 acres	1798	C3	490	385
Douglass, John	Deed fr	Law, Thomas	1807	R17	001	001
Douglass, Robert H.	Manumis to	Brown, Dolly (C), w/o Peter	1815	AI34	429	448
Douglass, Robert H., Fairfax Co.	B. of S. to	Brown, Dolly	1816	AL36	366	356
Douglass, Robert H., Fairfax Co.	B. of S. to	Brown, Dolly	1816	AL36	366	355
Douglass, Robert H., Fairfax Co.	B. of S. to	Brown, Dolly	1816	AL36	367	357
Douglass, Robert H., Fairfax Co.	B. of S. fr	Brown, Dolly	1816	AL36	344	335
Dove, Joseph	Deed fr	Holmead, Anthony, of Montg. Co.	1797	C3	050	40
Dove, Joseph	Deed to	Bradley, Phineas	1801	G7	134	176
Dove, Joseph	Deed fr	Commissioners of Washington	1801	G7	102	131
Dove, Joseph	Deed fr	Tolmie, Robert, of G'tn.	1801	G7	103	132
Dove, Joseph	Lease fr	Jones, John G.	1802	I9	314	516
Dove, Joseph	Deed to	Goddart, John B., of MD	1806	Q16	092	059
Dove, Joseph	B. of S. fr	Warner, Osborn	1810	Z25	371	291
Dove, Joseph	B. of S. to	Moore, James, Sr. & G. Kleiber	1815	AH33	488	418
Dove, Joseph & Lawson Pearson	Deed to	Brown, William	1801	G7	128	167
Dove, Joseph & Benjamin Owens	Mortgage to	Brown, John, of Balto.	1808	V21	063	050
Dove, Marmaduke	Deed to	King, Benjamin, trustee	1811	AC28	031	023
Dowens, George	Deed fr	Middleton, Joseph	1800	E5	263	256
Dowens, George	Deed to	Davis, Charles Beckwith	1804	L11	270	248
Dowers, John	B. of S. fr	Brown, John	1801	G7	279	385
Dowling, Michael	Deed fr	Burnes, David	1796	B2B	394	055
Dowling, Michael	Deed to	Thorpe, Thomas	1802	I9	348	574
Dowling, Michael	Lease to	Tharpe, Thomas	1802	I9	112	163
Downes, George	Deed fr	Glover, Charles	1804	L11	286	262
Downes, George	Lease to	Bently, Joseph	1805	N13	406	323
Downes, George	B. of S. fr	Nally, John	1805	M12	088	081
Downes, George, Loudoun Co. VA	Deed to	Moore, George	1806	Q16	151	099
Downes, Henry & Winefred et al	Deed to	Beatty, Thomas & Henry O'Reily	1793	A1-1	175	249
Downes, Mary, of Montg. Co.	B. of S. to	Hurdle, Thomas	1806	P15	352	233
Downes, Mary, spinster	Deed to	Coomes, Joseph	1794	B2A	041	048
Downs, George	Slave	From Loudoun Co. VA	1804	L11	269	
Downs, George	B. of S. to	Oliver, George	1806	P15	127	082
Downs, Hillidey	Deed fr	Carroll, Daniel, of *Duddington*	1817	AO39	202	148
Dowrey, James	Cert Free to	Prout, Anna (M), age 17	1813	AF31	242	168

Party	What	Party	Year	Liber	Old	New
Dowry, Hercules (C), under 45	Manumis fr	Thompson, Semus, yellow	1813	AE30	430	317
Dowson, Joseph, an insolvent	Deed to	Peacock, Robert Ware	1803	K10	096	102
Doyle, Alexander, of G'tn.	Deed fr	Davidson, John, of Annapolis	1794	B2A	090	116
Doyle, Anne S.	B. of S. fr	Brodess, Edward	1806	P15	176	117
Doyle, Eliza, of G'tn.	Manumis to	Butler, Hetty	1816	AK35	483	379
Doyle, Eliza, of G'tn.	B. of S. to	Butler, Hetty, of G'tn.	1816	AK35	482	378
Doyle, Elizabeth	Deed fr	Deakins, Francis	1802	H8	062	058
Doyle, Elizabeth	B. of S. fr	King, George, of G'tn.	1802	I9		192
Doyle, Elizabeth, of G'tn.	Deed to	Hazle, Jeremiah	1802	G7	532	676
Doyle, Elizabeth, wid/o Alexander	Deed to	King, Adam, of G'tn.	1797	C3	084	69
Doyle, Elizabeth, wid/o Alexander	Deed to	King, George, of G'tn.	1797	C3	129	105
Doyle, John B., of Phila. PA	Deed fr	Beall, Thomas Brooke	1807	R17	335	255
Drane, Anthony, of P.G. Co.	B. of S. to	Drane, David, of P.G. Co.	1806	O14	159	103
Drane, David	B. of S. to	Lenmon, Isiah	1809	V21	155	112
Drane, David, of P.G. Co.	B. of S. fr	Drane, Anthony, of P.G. Co.	1806	O14	159	103
Drane, James Haddock & Mary	Deed fr	White, James, of Montg. Co.	1813	AF31	502	365
Drane, Thomas	Slaves	From Montgomery Co. MD	1816	AL36	242	246
Drane, Washington	Deed fr	Given, Thomas	1817	AO39	100	078
Drane, Washington	Deed to	Jones, Walter	1817	AO39	103	080
Druet, James	Agreement	Maul, John P.	1817	AO39	120	092
Drummond, Hugh	B. of S. to	Brown, Mathew	1806	Q16	304	232
Drummond, John	Lease fr	Prout, William	1806	Q16	148	097
Drummond, John	B. of S. to	Prout, William	1809	X23	087	065
Duane, William	Deed fr	Commissioners of Washington	1801	G7	197	264
Duane, William, of Phila. PA	Deed fr	Dorsey, William H., of G'tn.	1801	G7	388	521
Duane, William, of Phila. PA	Deed fr	Woodward, William & Anne	1804	K10	300	303
Duane, William, of Phila.	Mortgage to	Weightman, Roger Chew	1812	AB27	521	425
Duane, William, of Phila. PA	Deed to	Crawford, William	1815	AI34	136	156
Duby, John	Deed fr	Beall, Thomas B.	1802	I9	352	581
Duby, John	Agreement	Dobbins, David	1803	K10	083	90
Duckworth, George	Deed fr	Smallwood, Samuel N.	1802	I9	528	863
Duckworth, George	Deed fr	Stoddert, Benjamin, of G'tn.	1802	G7	562	711
Duckworth, George	Deed to	Cummins, John	1808	T19	047	035
Duddell, James	Deed to	Coocke, Buller	1808	U20	169	095
Duer, James, of Snow Hill	Deed fr	Peter, Robert	1802	H8	109	105
Duffee, Mary, insolvent	Deed to	Blount, George, trustee	1804	L11	272	250
Duffey, Bryan	Deed fr	Beatty, Charles, heirs of	1806	P15	155	101
Duffey, Bryan, of G'tn.	Deed fr	Renner, Daniel, of G'tn.	1811	AC28	042	032
Duffy, Bryan	Deed fr	Threlkeld, John & Elizabeth	1807	S18	113	093
Duffy, Bryan	Deed to	Renner, Daniel	1810	X23	386	311
Duffy, Bryan, of G'tn.	Lease fr	Thomson, William, of G'tn.	1809	W22	147	104
Duffy, Bryan, of G'tn.	Deed to	Corcoran, Thomas, of G'tn.	1813	AF31	065	045
Duffy, Bryan, of G'tn.	D. of T. to	Corcoran, Thomas, of G'tn.	1813	AE30	249	196
Duffy, Mary	B. of S. fr	Blunt, George	1809	W22	047	035
Duguid, William et al	Assign fr	Ober, Richard	1795	B2A	329	461
Duguid, William, mer., of Balto.	Deed to	Somerville, James, mer., Balto.	1801	F6	208	134
Dulaney, Matthew, of G'tn.	Deed fr	Linn, Philip, of Frederick Co.	1804	K10	179	188
Dulaney, Walter	Deed to	Beall, Thomas & John M. Gantt	1793	A1-1	217	303
Dulany, Anne	B. of S. to	Pic, Mary A.	1809	W22	166	116
Dulany, Benjamin, of VA	Cert fr	Commissioners of Washington	1793	B2A	311	438
Dulany, Benjamin, of Alexa.	Cert fr	Munroe, Thomas, Supt.	1806	Q16	145	095
Dulany, Daniel	Manumis to	[ ], Baxter (C)	1816	AK35	356	281
Dulany, Eliza	Slaves	From VA	1806	Q16	313	239
Dulany, Elizabeth, of Alexa.	Deed to	Dulany, James H. & Bladen	1816	AM37	143	110
Dulany, James H. & Bladen	Deed fr	Dulany, Elizabeth, of Alexa.	1816	AM37	143	110

Index to District of Columbia Land Records, 1792-1817

Party	What	Party	Year	Liber	Old	New
Dulany, Matthew	Deed to	Mason, Gantt & Cook	1797	B2B	626	385
Dulany, Matthew, of G'tn.	Deed fr	Davidson, John, of Annapolis	1795	B2A	343	484
Dulany, Matthew, of G'tn.	Deed fr	Murphy, William, of G'tn.	1795	B2A	225	312
Dulany, Michael	Deed fr	Threlkeld, John	1802	I9	581	941
Dulany, Michael	Deed to	Ott, John	1815	Al34	154	176
Dulany, Walter, of MD	Deed fr	Hanson, Alexander Contee	1802	H8	553	515
Duley, Hezekiah, of Calvert Co.	Deed to	Smith, Samuel Harrison	1808	T19	192	137
Duley, John, of Mason Co. KY	Deed to	Smith, Samuel Harrison	1810	Y24	183	168
Duley, Jonathan & Catharine	Deed to	Smith, Samuel Harrison	1808	T19	182	129
Duley, Joseph Ford & Rebecca	Deed to	Smith, Samuel Harrison	1807	S18	293	229
Duley, William & Ann, Montg. Co.	Deed to	Smith, Samuel Harrison	1808	T19	190	135
Duley, William, of Montg. Co.	Deed fr	Wells, Nathan & Sophia, of KY	1805	N13	309	250
Duly, Jonathan & Wm., Montg.	Bond to	Smith, Samuel Harrison	1804	K10	404	419
Duly, Zadock & Susanna, of KY	Deed to	Smith, Samuel Harrison	1808	T19	178	127
Dunback, Elizabeth, of G'tn.	Deed to	Bussard, Daniel	1810	X23	385	310
Dunback, Elizabeth [Dunbough]	Deed to	Landes, Abraham	1813	AF31	028	020
Duncanson, John et al	B. of S. fr	Barnes, John & Catharine	1813	AF31	471	342
Duncanson, William M.	Deed fr	Greenleaf, James, New York, NY	1795	B2A	273	382
Duncanson, William M. et al	Deed fr	Morris, Robert & John Nicholson	1796	B2B	566	302
Duncanson, William M.	Cert fr	Commissioners of Washington	1797	B2B	465	157
Duncanson, William M. et al	R. of D. fr	Morris, Mary et al	1798	C3	364	292
Duncanson, William M. et al	Deed fr	Morris, Robert, of Phila. et al	1798	C3	362	289
Duncanson, William M., heirs of	B. of S. fr	Barnes, John & Catharine	1813	AF31	471	342
Duncanson, William Mayne	Mortgage fr	Morris, Robert, of Phila. et al	1796	B2B	411	081
Duncanson, William Mayne	Debt to	Morris, Robert, of Phila.	1796	B2B	390	049
Duncanson, William Mayne	Deed to	Robertson, John Starkes, of NY	1797	B2B	613	368
Duncanson, William Mayne	Mortgage fr	Nicholson, John, of Phila. PA	1797	C3	011	8
Duncanson, William Mayne	Deed to	Deakins, William, Jr. et al	1797	C3	125	102
Duncanson, William Mayne	Deed fr	Morris, Robert & Mary et al	1797	C3	238	197
Duncanson, William Mayne et al	Deed to	Campbell, William et al	1797	C3	103	84
Duncanson, William Mayne	Deed to	Ray, James, of Lamberton NJ	1797	C3	068	56
Duncanson, William Mayne	Deed fr	Robertson, John Stearkes, of NY	1800	E5	241	234
Duncanson, William Mayne	D. of T. to	Templeman, John	1801	G7	338	469
Duncanson, William Mayne	B. of S. to	Templeman, John	1802	G7	499	637
Duncastle, Sally	Cert Free to	Beall, Ann (M)	1813	AE30	157	124
Duncastle, Sally	Cert Free to	Beall, Betsey (M)	1813	AE30	157	124
Duncastle, Sarah, of G'tn.	Deed to	Gannon, James, of G'tn.	1810	Y24	456	405
Dunlap, Alexander	Manumis to	[ ], Richard (negro)	1805	N13	394	314
Dunlap, Alexander, of NY	Deed fr	Cook, John, of Montg. Co.	1805	N13	357	288
Dunlap, Alexander, of NY	Deed to	Barklie, Alexander, of Ire.	1816	AL36	140	141
Dunlap, Elizabeth	Deed fr	Peter, Robert	1801	G7	461	598
Dunlap, Henry	Deed to	McCormick, Alexander	1802	I9	086	123
Dunlap, Henry	Deed fr	Prout, William	1802	I9	086	121
Dunlap, Henry	Deed to	Peacock, Robert Ware	1804	K10	262	268
Dunlap, Henry	Deed to	Patterson, Edgar	1813	AE30	081	061
Dunlap, Henry, insolvent	B. of S. to	Thompson, John, trustee	1805	M12	107	100
Dunlap, James	Lease to	Hunter, Thomas	1806	O14	376	250
Dunlap, James	Lease to	McCoy, Jesse	1806	O14	373	248
Dunlap, James	Division	Carleton, Joseph	1816	AL36	345	336
Dunlap, James & Joseph Carlton	Deed fr	Hanson, Samuel, of Samuel	1807	R17	136	105
Dunlap, James & John Laird	Deed fr	Hanson, Samuel, of Samuel	1816	AL36	324	318
Dunlap, James et al	Deed fr	Tousard, Lewis	1802	H8	138	134
Dunlap, James et al	Oblig. fr	Morris, Robert et al	1802	H8	100	091
Dunlap, James et al	Lease to	Parsons, Bernard	1806	O14	370	246
Dunlap, James et al	Deed fr	Hanson, Samuel, of Samuel	1807	R17	128	100

Party	What	Party	Year	Liber	Old	New
Dunlap, James, of G'tn.	Deed to	Bland, Edward & George Grant	1807	R17	103	080
Dunlap, James, of G'tn. et al	Deed to	Wright, Matthew	1809	W22	301	197
Dunlap, John	Deed fr	Plater, Thomas	1793	A1-2	418	26
Dunlap, John	Deed fr	Cook, John, now of Frederick Co.	1805	N13	265	221
Dunlap, John	Deed fr	Riddle, Joseph, of Alexa. et al	1805	M12	370	380
Dunlap, John, of G'tn.	Deed fr	Davidson, John, of Annapolis	1794	B2A	076	098
Dunlap, John, of G'tn.	Deed fr	O'Reily, Henry, of G'tn.	1795	B2A	239	333
Dunlap, John, of G'tn.	Deed fr	Davidson, John, of Annapolis	1798	C3	320	259
Dunlap, John, of G'tn.	Deed fr	Cook, Thomas, of Frederick Co.	1805	M12	245	246
Dunlop, Elizabeth et al	Deed fr	Stewart, William & Helen	1809	X23	277	219
Dunlop, James	Deed fr	King, George & Margaret	1798	C3	356	286
Dunlop, James	Deed fr	McCoy, Jesse	1809	W22	315	205
Dunlop, James	Assign to	Carleton, Joseph	1812	AD29	276	227
Dunlop, James	Deed to	Clarke, Robert	1812	AD29	068	049
Dunlop, James	Deed fr	Bickley, Robert S., Holmsburg PA	1813	AE30	404	298
Dunlop, James	Deed to	Andrews, Christopher et al	1817	AO39	550	378
Dunlop, James & Joseph Carleton	Deed to	Brown, Robert	1809	X23	055	041
Dunlop, James et al	Cert fr	Commissioners of Washington	1797	B2B	459	149
Dunlop, James et al	Deed to	Moyers, John	1801	G7	242	325
Dunlop, James et al	Deed fr	Commissioners of Washington	1802	H8	453	416
Dunlop, James et al	Deed fr	Munroe, Thomas, Supt.	1802	I9	229	364
Dunlop, James, Jr.	D. of T. fr	Johnson, George	1817	AN38	108	081
Dunlop, James, of G'tn.	Deed fr	Beall, Patrick	1792	A1-1	112	163
Dunlop, James, of Montg. Co.	Deed fr	Beall, Thomas, of Samuel	1797	C3	119	97
Dunlop, James, of G'tn.	Deed fr	Morris, Robert, of Phila.	1797	B2B	674	444
Dunlop, James, of G'tn.	Deed to	Matthews, William, Rev.	1814	AG32	311	227
Dunn, James C., of G'tn.	D. of T. to	Kurtz, Daniel, of G'tn.	1817	AN38	411	308
Dunn, James C., of G'tn.	Deed fr	Reintzel, Valentine, of G'tn.	1817	AN38	410	306
Dunn, Thomas	B. of S. fr	Easterday, Daniel	1810	Y24	526	463
Dunn, Thomas	Deed fr	Burch, Samuel	1815	AI34	109	125
Duprey, William	Deed fr	Munroe, Thomas, Supt.	1802	I9	111	162
Dupuy, William	Deed fr	Buchanan, Thomas, of MD	1815	AI34	142	164
Durety, William	Deed to	Phillips, John	1802	I9	411	681
Durity, Francis	B. of S. fr	Phillips, John	1805	N13	124	120
Durity, William, trustee	Convey fr	Hurdle, Thomas, insolvent	1804	L11	279	257
Durr, John, Jr.	Lease fr	Van Ness, John P. & Marcia	1817	AO39	243	175
Durr, John, Jr.	Lease fr	Van Ness, John P. & Marcia	1817	AO39	261	175
Dutton, John	Qualify	Ensign in first legion of militia	1812	AD29	438	368
Dutton, Notley, Charles Co. et al	Manumis to	Ingraham, John	1817	AN38	299	218
Duval, William	Deed fr	Gitzandanner, Christian	1805	M12	211	212
Duvall, Delilah & Sarah, P.G. Co.	B. of S. to	Claxton, Thomas	1809	W22	265	177
Duvall, Edmund B.	B. of S. fr	Duvall, Sarah, of P.G. Co.	1808	U20	101	057
Duvall, Edward Washington	Qualify	Ensign in 1st Legion Militia	1810	Z25	111	086
Duvall, G.	Cert Free to	Shorter, Henny (yellow)	1808	T19	205	148
Duvall, Gabriel	B. of S. fr	Duvall, William, of G'tn.	1805	M12	283	284
Duvall, Gabriel	Deed fr	Brent, Daniel Carroll	1805	M12	284	285
Duvall, Gabriel	Deed fr	Smoot, Alexander S.	1805	M12	282	283
Duvall, Gabriel	Deed to	Nourse, Joseph, of G'tn.	1805	M12	286	287
Duvall, Gabriel	Deed fr	Woodward, Augustus B., of MI	1806	Q16	240	166
Duvall, Gabriel	B. of S. fr	Coningham, Cornelius	1809	W22	342	221
Duvall, Gabriel	Deed fr	Kilty, John & Josias W. King	1809	V21	409	311
Duvall, Gabriel	Deed fr	Coningham, Cornelius	1810	Y24	171	156
Duvall, Gabriel	Release to	Smoot, Alexander S.	1811	AB27	045	039
Duvall, Gabriel	Mortgage fr	Duvall, William, of G'tn.	1813	AE30	284	217
Duvall, Gabriel	Deed to	Woodward, Augustus B., of MI	1813	AE30	414	305

Party	What	Party	Year	Liber	Old	New
Duvall, Gabriel et al	Deed fr	Jackson, John G., fr. Harrison Co.	1814	AG32	295	215
Duvall, Samuel, of G'tn.	Deed to	Renner, Daniel, of G'tn.	1810	X23	410	331
Duvall, Sarah, of P.G. Co.	B. of S. to	Duvall, Edmund B.	1808	U20	101	057
Duvall, William, innkeeper, of G'tn.	Deed fr	Threlkeld, John, of G'tn.	1813	AE30	128	099
Duvall, William N., of G'tn.	Deed fr	Wirt, John, of G'tn.	1812	AC28	131	099
Duvall, William N., of G'tn.	Deed to	Morton, William, of G'tn.	1816	AL36	040	041
Duvall, William N.	Deed fr	Cox, John, of G'tn.	1816	AK35	528	417
Duvall, William, of G'tn.	Deed fr	Gitzandanner, Christian, of G'tn.	1805	M12	209	211
Duvall, William, of G'tn.	B. of S. to	Duvall, Gabriel	1805	M12	283	284
Duvall, William, of G'tn.	Mortgage to	Duvall, Gabriel	1813	AE30	284	217
Dye, Reuben	Deed fr	Cochran, Alexander, going to Ire.	1812	AC28	354	256
Dye, Reuben, of Fairfax Co. VA	Deed fr	McLeod, John	1813	AE30	495	367
Dye, Reuben, of Fairfax Co.	Deed fr	Smith, Hugh, of Alexa.	1814	AH33	361	313
Dyer, Elizabeth, of Montg. Co. et al	Convey to	Redman, James, of G'tn.	1816	AL36	463	437
Dyer, Fielder Allison & Elizabeth	Deed fr	Dyer, William	1805	M12	373	383
Dyer, Henry O.	B. of S. fr	Wayman, Henry	1806	O14	156	102
Dyer, Henry O., mer., of G'tn.	Deed fr	Murdock, Addison, Gent.	1806	P15	345	229
Dyer, Henry O.	Deed fr	Beall, Thomas, of George, of G'tn.	1806	P15	340	224
Dyer, Henry O., mer., of G'tn.	B. of S. to	Smith, Rachael (mulatto)	1806	Q16	060	036
Dyer, Henry O., of G'tn.	Deed to	Gooding, John, of Balto.	1809	X23	022	015
Dyer, John	Deed fr	Wigfield, James	1806	P15	292	192
Dyer, John, seaman	Deed to	Wigfield, James	1806	P15	293	193
Dyer, William	Deed to	Dyer, Fielder Allison & Elizabeth	1805	M12	373	383

Index to District of Columbia Land Records, 1792-1817

Party	What	Party	Year	Liber	Old	New
E						
Eaglesfield, Robert et al	Deed fr	Dalton, Tristram et al	1798	D4	148	131
Eakin, James et al	B. of S. to	Ford, John	1805	N13	017	018
Earle, James, of Kent Co.	Deed to	Beall, Thomas & John M. Gantt	1793	A1-1	287	383
Earle, James, of Talbot Co.	Release fr	Hollyday, James, Q. Anne's Co.	1799	D4	182	163
Easenbeck, William	Cert fr	Munroe, Thomas, Supt.	1808	U20	052	029
Eastburn, Isaac Washington, G'tn.	Deed to	Curran, William, of G'tn.	1799	D4	357	344
Eastburn, Isaac Washington, G'tn.	Deed to	Norris, Isaac, of G'tn.	1799	D4	409	386
Eastburn, James, mer., of NY	Deed fr	Ward, Matthias, of NY	1812	AC28	364	264
Eastburn, Jane	Deed fr	Lyon, John	1804	L11	203	192
Eastburn, Jane, of G'tn.	Deed fr	Magruder, George, collector, G'tn.	1804	K10	402	416
Eastburn, Jane, of G'tn.	Deed to	Ritter, Peter, of G'tn.	1810	Y24	481	425
Eastburn, Jane, of G'tn. [Aisburn]	Deed to	Cloakey, Samuel, builder	1811	AB27	284	233
Eastburn, Jane, wid/o Benjamin	Deed fr	Eastburn, Robinson, Frederick Co.	1796	B2B	538	258
Eastburn, Jessey, s/o Benjamin	Deed fr	Eastburn, Robinson, s/o Benjamin	1797	B2B	623	382
Eastburn, Joseph, Adams Co. KY	Deed to	Curran, William, of G'tn.	1799	D4	429	400
Eastburn, Joseph, Mont. Co.	Deed fr	Eastburn, Robinson, Frederick Co.	1795	B2B	363	013
Eastburn, Robinson & Jesse	Deed to	Beatty, Charles, of G'tn.	1797	B2B	686	462
Eastburn, Robinson, Frederick Co.	Deed to	Eastburn, Joseph, Mont. Co.	1795	B2B	363	013
Eastburn, Robinson, Frederick Co.	Deed to	Eastburn, Jane, wid/o Benjamin	1796	B2B	538	258
Eastburn, Robinson, Frederick Co.	Deed to	Eastburn, Washington	1798	D4	038	031
Eastburn, Robinson, Frederick Co.	Deed to	Richardson, John, of NY	1803	K10	099	106
Eastburn, Robinson, s/o Benjamin	Deed to	Eastburn, Jessey, s/o Benjamin	1797	B2B	623	382
Eastburn, Sarah, w/o Robinson	R. of D. to	Richardson, John	1804	K10	350	362
Eastburn, Washington	Deed fr	Eastburn, Robinson, Frederick Co.	1798	D4	038	031
Easterday, Daniel	Deed to	Renner, Daniel et al	1806	P15	308	203
Easterday, Daniel	B. of S. to	Dunn, Thomas	1810	Y24	526	463
Easterday, Daniel, of G'tn.	Deed to	Renner, Daniel, of G'tn. et al	1806	P15	399	268
Easton, David	Deed to	Hewitt, Thomas	1806	P15	371	247
Easton, David, insolvent	Deed to	Huty, Thomas	1806	P15	395	265
Eaton, John	B. of S. to	Eaton, Washington	1806	Q16	239	165
Eaton, Washington	B. of S. fr	Eaton, John	1806	Q16	239	165
Edd, John, of G'tn.	B. of S. fr	Poston, Fielder B., of G'tn.	1817	AO39	177	132
Eddington, James	B. of S. fr	Davis, Philip B.	1811	Z25	396	311
Edelen, Edward	B. of S. fr	Thornton, William	1805	M12	355	362
Edelen, Edward E., of P.G. Co.	B. of S. to	Brooks, Charles	1812	AD29	100	075
Edelen, Ignatius	Deed to	Queen, Nicholas L.	1811	AB27	510	417
Edelen, Ignatius	B. of S. to	Moore, George et al	1812	AD29	019	014
Edelen, Rebecca et al	Deed to	Dorsey, Joshua, of Frederick Co.	1799	E5	069	056
Edelen, Rebecca et al	Deed to	Beatty, Charles, Sr.	1800	E5	115	102
Edelin, Electus, of P.G. Co.	Deed fr	Prout, William	1805	M12	075	069
Edelin, Ignatius	Deed fr	Dorsey, William H., of Balto. Co.	1808	U20	109	062
Edelin, Ignatius	Deed to	Palmer, Jesse C.	1808	T19	136	095
Edelin, Ignatius	Deed to	Palmer, Jesse C.	1808	T19	134	095
Edelin, Ignatius	R. Dower fr	Dorsey, Rosetta	1809	V21	322	237
Edelin, Ignatius	B. of S. to	Cliver, George & Samuel Cloakey	1812	AC28	486	346
Edelin, Ignatius et al	Deed to	Meade, Simon	1808	U20	112	063
Edelin, Susannah	D. Gift to	Craycroft, Mary Ann, her dau.	1813	AF31	255	177
Edelin, Susannah	D. Gift to	Craycroft, Charles Electius	1813	AF31	256	178
Edmondson, Susanna et al	Deed to	Kaegy, Abraham, of DE	1805	M12	157	154
Edmondston, Edward	D. of T. fr	Farrand, William	1811	AC28	049	037
Edmondston, Enoch	Slaves	List	1814	AG32	244	174
Edmonson, James N.	Assign fr	Hillard, Thomas	1817	AO39	057	047
Edmonson, James N.	Release fr	Van Ness, John P. & Marcia	1817	AO39	191	141
Edmonston, Alexander, Montg. Co.	Deed fr	Davidson, Samuel	1798	C3	439	345

Party	What	Party	Year	Liber	Old	New
Edmonston, Brooke	Deed fr	Edmonston, Ninian, of P.G. Co.	1812	AC28	190	144
Edmonston, Brooke	Lease fr	Majors, John	1813	AF31	324	231
Edmonston, Brooke	Deed to	Broadback, Jacob	1814	AH33	118	111
Edmonston, Cassandra, of MD	Deed to	Brodbeck, Jacob	1815	AI34	330	363
Edmonston, Edward	Qualify	Captain Grenadiers 1st regiment	1813	AE30	472	351
Edmonston, Edward	Qualify	Captain of Grenadiers	1813	AE30	403	297
Edmonston, Edward, constable	Bond to	United States	1810	X23	346	277
Edmonston, Enoch, of Montg. Co.	Deed fr	Moore, George & Verlinda	1815	AK35	216	170
Edmonston, Franklin	Deed to	Brodbeck, Jacob	1815	AI34	329	362
Edmonston, James N., constable	Deed to	Brent, Robert	1817	AN38	381	283
Edmonston, Ninian, of P.G. Co.	Deed to	Edmonston, Brooke	1812	AC28	190	144
Edmonston, Ninian, P.G. Co. et al	Deed fr	Davidson, Samuel	1798	C3	439	345
Edmonston, Thomas	Deed fr	Mayne, Adam	1817	AN38	552	402
Edwards, Henry	Cert fr	Commissioners of Washington	1793	B2A	307	431
Edwards, Henry	Transfer to	Johnson, Thomas, Jr.	1796	B2A	337	473
Edwards, Henry	Cert fr	Commissioners of Washington	1796	B2A	337	473
Edwards, Henry	Transfer fr	Morris, Robert & James Greenleaf	1797	B2B	458	148
Edwards, Henry	Cert fr	Commissioners of Washington	1797	B2B	458	148
Edwards, Horace H.	Release to	Way, Andrew & George	1810	Y24	160	146
Edwards, Horace H. & H. Bestor	D. of T. to	Fletcher, Noah & J. Huddleston	1812	AD29	277	229
Edwards, Horace H. & H. Bestor	Deed fr	Huddleston, Joseph	1812	AD29	300	246
Edwards, Horace H.	Qualify	Ensign in militia	1812	AD29	171	137
Edwards, Horace H. & H. Bestor	Deed fr	Fletcher, Noah & J. Huddleston	1815	AK35	438	343
Edwards, Horace H.	Deed to	Macdaniel, Ezekiel	1815	AK35	462	363
Edwards, Horace H.	Deed fr	Corporation of Washington	1815	AK35	466	366
Edwards, Horace H.	Deed to	Bestor, Harvey	1815	AK35	435	341
Edwards, Horace H.	Deed fr	Corporation of WAshington	1815	AK35	433	339
Edwards, Horace H.	Deed fr	Corporation of Washington	1815	AK35	469	368
Edwards, Horace H.	Deed fr	Corporation of Washington	1815	AK35	464	364
Edwards, Horace H., of CN	Deed to	DeKrafft, Edward	1817	AO39	096	076
Edwards, Horace Hampden et al	Deed fr	Munroe, Thomas, Supt.	1807	R17	315	239
Edwards, Horace Hampden et al	Deed fr	Ardery, Alexander & William	1808	U20	256	137
Edwards, Horace Hampden	Deed fr	Stinger, Solomon	1808	U20	243	130
Edwards, Horace Hampden et al	Cert fr	Munroe, Thomas, Supt.	1808	U20	345	187
Edwards, Horace Hampden et al	Deed fr	Cist, Jacob	1808	T19	070	051
Edwards, Horace Hampden	Deed to	Way, Andrew & George	1809	V21	402	305
Edwards, Horace Hampden	Deed fr	Dorsey, William H., of Balto. MD	1812	AD29	294	242
Edwards, John	Deed fr	Beatty, Charles	1802	H8	591	557
Edwards, John	Lease fr	Beatty, Charles	1804	L11	102	104
Edwards, John, of G'tn.	Mortgage to	Craig, Robert, of G'tn.	1805	O14	112	070
Edwards, John, of G'tn.	Deed to	Williamson, David, of Balto.	1807	S18	188	152
Edwards, John, trustee	Deed fr	Galer, Thomas, insolvent	1804	L11	094	97
Edwards, Lewis	Deed fr	Boyd, Washington, marshal	1816	AO39	016	013
Edwards, Lewis	Deed fr	Morsell, James S., trustee	1817	AN38	008	007
Egan, Thomas Henry, Calvert Co.	Deed fr	Johnson, Rinaldo, of P.G. Co.	1796	B2B	548	273
Egan, Thomas Henry, Calvert Co.	Mortgage to	Blake, James Heighe, of G'tn.	1796	B2B	552	280
Egan, Thomas Henry, Calvert Co.	Deed to	Blake, James Heighe, Dr., of G'tn.	1797	B2B	628	388
Ehrenzella, George, of Phila. PA	Deed fr	Commissioners of Washington	1801	F6	236	156
Ehrenzeller, George & Henrietta	Deed to	Vaughan, John, mer., of Phila. PA	1810	Y24	354	320
Ehrenzeller, George & Henrietta	Deed to	Vaughan, John, mer., of Phila. PA	1810	Y24	351	318
Ehrenzeller, George, of Phila. PA	Deed fr	Commissioners of Washington	1801	F6	234	155
Ekton, Offa	B. of S. fr	Clements, Edward	1811	Z25	346	270
Elford, John	Deed to	McClann, Andrew	1806	P15	336	222
Eliason, Ebenezer	B. of S. to	Igan, Ephraim	1801	G7	170	227
Eliason, Ebenezer	Deed fr	Forrest, Uriah	1801	G7	026	033

Party	What	Party	Year	Liber	Old	New
Eliason, Ebenezer	Deed fr	Taylor, William	1802	I9	458	755
Eliason, Ebenezer	Mortgage fr	Loring, Israel	1802	I9	193	301
Eliason, Ebenezer	Deed to	McDonald, Alexander	1807	S18	275	215
Eliason, Ebenezer	Deed fr	Whann, William	1807	S18	367	293
Eliason, Ebenezer	B. of S. fr	Mattingly, Thomas	1808	T19	151	106
Eliason, Ebenezer	Deed fr	Beall, Thomas, of George	1809	V21	295	214
Eliason, Ebenezer	Deed to	McPherson, John	1814	AH33	087	079
Eliason, Ebenezer	Deed to	Beatty, Charles A.	1814	AH33	096	089
Eliason, Ebenezer	Deed to	Cozens, William R.	1814	AG32	405	296
Eliason, Ebenezer	Mortgage to	Lyon, John	1815	AI34	095	108
Eliason, Ebenezer & Ann	Deed to	Parrott, Richard et al	1809	V21	290	210
Eliason, Ebenezer & B. Hersey	Deed to	Foxall, Henry, of G'tn.	1814	AH33	192	175
Eliason, Ebenezer et al	Deed fr	Parrott, Richard, of G'tn.	1814	AG32	380	276
Eliason, Ebenezer, late of G'tn.	Deed fr	McDonald, Alexander, of G'tn.	1807	S18	370	293
Eliason, Ebenezer, of G'tn.	Mortgage to	Foxall, Henry, of G'tn.	1809	W22	004	004
Eliason, Ebenezer, of G'tn. et al	Deed fr	Corporation of Georgetown	1810	Z25	328	256
Eliason, Ebenezer, of G'tn. et al	Lease to	Foxall, Henry, of G'tn.	1810	Z25	332	259
Eliason, John	Deed fr	Blake, James H., Dr. & Betty H.	1808	T19	242	178
Eliason, John	B. of S. to	Laird, John	1814	AH33	129	123
Eliason, John & Richard Beck	B. of S. fr	*Browning & Renshaw*	1806	Q16	147	097
Eliason, John et al	Deed fr	Eliason, Ebenezer & Ann	1809	V21	290	210
Eliason, John et al	D. of T. fr	Foxall, Henry	1816	AL36	357	348
Eliason, John, of G'tn.	D. of T. fr	Ratcliffe, Joseph, of G'tn.	1811	AA26	294	199
Eliason, John, of G'tn.	D. of T. fr	Ratcliffe, Joseph, of G'tn.	1811	AA26	291	197
Eliason, John, of G'tn.	Deed to	Bowie, Washington, of G'tn.	1814	AH33	349	302
Eliason, John, trustee et al	Deed fr	Morgan, William, of G'tn.	1814	AH33	010	009
Eliot, Samuel	Deed fr	Commissioners of Washington	1799	D4	222	205
Eliot, Samuel	Assign to	May, Frederick	1802	I9	457	755
Eliot, Samuel & Frederick May	Deed fr	Spalding, John, of Piscataway MD	1803	K10	066	71
Eliot, Samuel, Jr. et al	Cert fr	Commissioners of Washington	1798	B2B	477	170
Eliot, Samuel, Jr. et al	Cert fr	Commissioners of Washington	1798	B2B	477	170
Eliot, Samuel, Jr. et al	Cert fr	Commissioners of Washington	1798	B2B	477	171
Eliot, Samuel, Jr. et al	Agreement	Burrows, Edward	1799	E5	050	040
Eliot, Samuel, Jr. et al	Deed fr	Barry, James David	1804	L11	346	313
Eliot, Samuel, Jr.	Deed to	May, Frederick	1805	N13	150	140
Eliot, Samuel, Jr.	Deed to	May, Frederick	1805	N13	152	142
Eliot, Samuel, Jr.	Deed fr	Greenleaf, James, of Phila. PA	1806	Q16	232	159
Eliot, Samuel, Jr. & Frederick May	Deed to	Jones, Rachael	1806	Q16	145	095
Eliot, Samuel, Jr.	Deed fr	Law, Thomas	1808	S18	330	259
Eliot, Samuel, Jr. et al	Deed to	Fletcher, Betsey	1808	U20	128	073
Eliot, Samuel, Jr.	Quit fr	Pratt, Henry, trustee et al	1809	W22	293	193
Eliot, Samuel, Jr. & Wm. Thornton	Deed fr	Cranch, William	1810	Z25	200	157
Eliot, Samuel, Jr.	B. of S. fr	Washington, Lund & Susanna	1811	AB27	288	236
Eliot, Samuel, Jr.	D. of T. fr	Wheaton, Joseph	1812	AC28	160	120
Eliot, Samuel, Jr.	Deed to	Fairfax, Ferdinando, Jefferson Co.	1812	AB27	544	444
Eliot, Samuel, Jr.	D. of T. fr	Hickey, James	1813	AF31	218	149
Eliot, Samuel, Jr.	D. of T. fr	Heath, Nathaniel H.	1813	AE30	276	213
Eliot, Samuel, Jr.	D. of T. fr	Middleton, James	1814	AH33	254	220
Eliot, Samuel, Jr.	D. of T. fr	Riley, William	1815	AK35	365	288
Eliot, Samuel, Jr.	Deed to	Boyle, John	1816	AL36	388	375
Eliot, Samuel, Jr. & W.A. Bradley	Deed fr	Whetcroft, Henry & Sarah	1816	AM37	410	294
Eliot, Samuel, Jr. & wife Mary	Deed to	Simpson, Josias	1816	AM37	371	268
Eliot, Samuel, Jr.	Deed fr	Gales, Joseph, Jr. & Sarah J.M.	1816	AL36	156	156
Eliot, Samuel, Jr.	D. of T. fr	Chalmers, John, Jr.	1817	AN38	400	299
Eliot, Samuel, Jr.	Assign fr	Miller, John, Jr., of Phila.	1817	AN38	418	313

Party	What	Party	Year	Liber	Old	New
Eliot, Samuel, Jr.	Deed to	Machen, Lewis H.	1817	AN38	013	011
Eliot, Samuel, Jr.	Deed to	Brent, Daniel	1817	AN38	049	040
Eliot, Samuel, Jr.	Deed to	Burch, Samuel	1817	AN38	186	135
Eliot, Samuel, Jr.	Deed fr	Minor, Lucy L., exrx. of John	1817	AN38	558	406
Eliot, Samuel, Jr.	Deed to	Orr, Benjamin Grayson	1817	AO39	073	060
Eliot, Samuel, Jr.	Deed to	Weightman, Roger Chew	1817	AO39	168	125
Eliot, Samuel, Jr.	D. of T. fr	Orr, Benjamin Grayson	1817	AO39	400	272
Eliot, Samuel, Jr.	Deed to	Hill, Henry V.	1817	AO39	082	066
Eliot, Samuel, Jr. [Elliott]	Deed fr	Carr, Overton, trustee	1817	AO39	533	367
Eliot, Samuel, Jr.	Deed fr	Carr, Overton, trustee	1817	AO39	522	360
Eliot, Samuel, Jr.	Deed to	Brent, Daniel	1817	AO39	323	230
Ellicott, William	B. of S. to	Watterston, George	1814	AG32	123	091
Elliot, Samuel	Agreement	Jones, Rachel	1802	I9	282	461
Elliot, Samuel et al	Deed to	Patterson, James	1802	H8	260	247
Elliot, Samuel, Jr. et al	Deed to	Wade, Anne	1802	H8	504	464
Elliot, Samuel, Jr.	Deed fr	Pratt, Henry et al	1806	O14	362	242
Elliot, Samuel, Jr.	Deed fr	Kid, Robert, of Phila. PA	1806	O14	360	240
Elliot, Samuel, Jr.	Deed to	May, Frederick	1808	T19	366	262
Elliot, Samuel, Jr. et al	D. of T. fr	Thornton, William	1810	Z25	198	156
Elliot, Samuel, Jr.	Deed fr	Pratt, Henry et al	1816	AL36	171	171
Elliot, Samuel, Jr.	D. of T. fr	Coyle, Andrew	1816	AL36	181	180
Elliott, Barnard, of Charleston SC	Deed fr	Walker, George	1801	F6	198	128
Elliott, Lynde, of G'tn.	Deed fr	Laird, John, exr. of J. Carleton	1813	AF31	030	021
Elliott, Richard	Deed fr	Commissioners of Washington	1799	D4	337	324
Elliott, Richard	Deed fr	Templeman, John, of G'tn.	1801	G7	101	129
Elliott, Richard	B. of S. fr	Elliott, Rufus	1811	AC28	085	065
Elliott, Richard	Deed fr	Peter, George	1812	AD29	045	032
Elliott, Richard	Cert. fr	Munroe, Thomas, Supt.	1812	AD29	044	032
Elliott, Richard	D. of T. to	English, David, of G'tn.	1813	AF31	554	411
Elliott, Richard	Deed fr	Cheston, Isabella, of Balto. MD	1813	AE30	368	273
Elliott, Richard	Lease fr	Dodge, Allen & Francis	1813	AF31	468	339
Elliott, Richard & Lynde	Deed fr	Farrell, Zephaniah	1810	Y24	206	189
Elliott, Robert	Lease fr	May, Frederick	1812	AD29	176	141
Elliott, Robert	Release to	May, Frederick	1815	AI34	014	015
Elliott, Rufus	B. of S. to	Biot, John	1807	S18	147	121
Elliott, Rufus	B. of S. to	Elliott, Richard	1811	AC28	085	065
Elliott, Samuel, Jr.	Agreement	Fenwick, Bennett	1795	B2B	382	037
Elliott, Samuel, Jr.	Release to	Kidd, Robert, of PA	1802	I9	059	081
Elliott, Samuel, Jr.	Deed fr	Wheaton, Joseph	1812	AC28	210	158
Elliott, Samuel, Jr.	D. of T. fr	Burch, Benjamin	1815	AI34	530	534
Elliott, Samuel, Jr.	Deed to	Walker, Joseph	1815	AI34	456	469
Elliott, Samuel, Jr. [Eliot]	Deed fr	Heath, Nathaniel H.	1815	AI34	458	470
Elliott, Samuel, Jr.	Release to	Heath, Nathaniel H.	1815	AI34	332	365
Elliott, Samuel, Jr.	Deed fr	Breckenridge, John & P. Bradley	1816	AM37	194	145
Elliott, Samuel, Jr.	Deed to	Way, George	1816	AL36	048	048
Elliott, Samuel, Jr. [Eliot]	Deed fr	Carr, Overton, trustee	1817	AO39	533	367
Ellis, John	Deed fr	Billmyer, Thomas	1817	AN38	542	394
Ellis, Philip	B. of S. to	Dodge, Francis, of G'tn.	1811	AA26	042	032
Ellis, Robert	Bond fr	Kearney, John	1801	G7	321	451
Ellis, Robert	Mortgage to	Taylor, James N. & Henry Toland	1801	G7	390	523
Ellis, Robert	Deed fr	Kearney, John	1801	G7	396	530
Ellis, Robert	Mortgage fr	Kearney, John	1801	G7	319	447
Ellis, Robert	Deed to	Doughty, William	1801	G7	413	547
Ellis, Robert	Deed fr	Nourse, Joseph, of G'tn.	1802	I9	092	133
Ellis, Robert	Deed to	Peacock, Robert W.	1802	I9	579	939

Party	What	Party	Year	Liber	Old	New
Ellis, Robert	B. of S. to	Oddlin, Eleanor	1802	I9	456	752
Ellis, Robert	Deed to	Smallwood, Samuel N.	1802	I9	529	865
Ellis, Samuel B.	Qualify	Lieutanent, First Legion of Militia	1812	AC28	480	341
Ellis, Samuel B.	Lease fr	Hebron, Abigail, of Petersburg	1817	AO39	454	312
Ellsworth, George, trustee	B. of S. fr	Finnicum, Benjamin, involvent	1808	V21	049	037
Elsey, Arnold	Deed fr	Leatherbury, John & Sarah	1807	S18	288	225
Elzen, Arnold	Deed fr	Stevens, John, of MD	1806	Q16	022	014
Elzey, Arhold	Manumis to	[ ], Nanny (negress), two children	1806	Q16	175	116
Elzey, Arnold	Deed fr	Commissioners of Washington	1801	F6	145	089
Elzey, Arnold	Deed fr	Commissioners of Washington	1801	F6	151	093
Elzey, Arnold	Deed to	Jones, John, of MD	1802	H8	528	487
Elzey, Arnold	Deed fr	Stevens, John, of Worcester Co.	1805	N13	333	269
Elzey, Arnold	Manumis to	[ ], Jenny (negress), and son	1806	Q16	174	115
Elzey, Arnold	Manumis to	[ ], Fender (negro)	1807	S18	128	104
Elzey, Arnold	B. of S. to	Young, Moses	1813	AF31	528	389
Elzey, Arnold	Deed to	Brevitt, John, of Balto.	1817	AO39	292	208
Emack, William	Deed fr	Carroll, Daniel, of *Duddington*	1807	R17	291	222
Emack, William	Deed fr	Coles, John, of New London CN	1807	S18	185	150
Emack, William	Deed fr	Carroll, Daniel, of *Duddington*	1814	AF31	519	380
Emack, William	Deed fr	Corporation of Washington	1815	AI34	169	194
Emack, William	Deed fr	Corporation of Washington	1815	AI34	167	192
Emack, William	Deed fr	Corporation of Washington	1815	AI34	166	190
Emack, William	Deed fr	Corporation of Washington	1815	AI34	171	196
Emery, John	Deed fr	Commissioners of Washington	1804	L11	118	121
Emery, John	Deed fr	Commissioners of Washington	1804	L11	117	120
Emery, John et al	Deed fr	Piercy, James, sugar refiner	1800	E5	197	189
Emess, Barton	Deed to	Thompson, George	1802	H8	354	329
Emmerson, John, of Norfolk	Deed fr	Connell, Catherine, of Hampton	1817	AO39	232	168
Engle, John P. [Ingle]	D. of T. fr	Bailey, Robert	1817	AO39	183	135
Engle, Peter & Michael Bayer	Deed to	Beall, Thomas & John M. Gantt	1792	A1-1	086	126
Engles, Peter, of Frederick Co.	Deed to	Beall, William Murdock, farmer	1792	A1-1	125	183
English, David	Deed to	Melvin, James	1802	I9	150	226
English, David	Mortgage fr	Melvin, James	1802	I9	233	373
English, David	Deed fr	Beall, Thomas, of George	1809	W22	340	220
English, David	Deed fr	Beall, Thomas, of Geo.	1811	AB27	295	242
English, David	Deed fr	Green, Charles D., of NJ	1812	AC28	193	147
English, David	Deed fr	Presbyterian Congregation, G'tn.	1812	AC28	196	149
English, David	Deed fr	Presbyterian Congregation, G'tn.	1812	AC28	197	150
English, David	Deed fr	Suter, Alexander	1815	AH33	409	353
English, David	Deed fr	Beall, Thomas, of Geo., of G'tn.	1816	AL36	516	483
English, David	Deed fr	Dixon, Thomas, of G'tn.	1816	AL36	057	057
English, David	D. of T. fr	Suter, Alexander	1816	AL36	052	053
English, David	Deed fr	Suter, Alexander	1816	AM37	179	135
English, David	D. of T. fr	Beall, Gustavus	1817	AN38	345	254
English, David & wife Sarah, G'tn.	Deed to	Dixon, Thomas, of G'tn.	1802	I9	118	173
English, David & Sarah (Threlkeld)	Deed to	Davis, Charles B.	1805	M12	088	082
English, David, cashier	Deed fr	Nourse, Joseph	1814	AG32	223	156
English, David, cashier	D. of T. fr	Landes, Abraham	1815	AH33	407	351
English, David, cashier	D. of T. fr	Craven, John	1815	AK35	051	040
English, David, cashier Union B.	Deed fr	Dixon, Thomas	1815	AI34	406	428
English, David, cashier	Release to	Nourse, Joseph	1816	AL36	243	247
English, David, cashier	D. of T. fr	Lancaster, Stephen	1816	AM37	360	261
English, David, cashier, of G'tn.	D. of T. fr	Kengla, Lewis, of G'tn.	1817	AN38	342	251
English, David, cashier, of G'tn.	D. of T. fr	Abbot, Jane & Elizabeth Oliver	1817	AN38	352	259
English, David, cashier	Release to	Abbott, John et al	1817	AO39	394	267

Index to District of Columbia Land Records, 1792-1817

Party	What	Party	Year	Liber	Old	New
English, David, cashier, of G'tn.	D. of T. fr	Bussard, Daniel, of G'tn.	1817	AN38	348	256
English, David et al	Deed fr	Commissioners of Washington	1800	E5	139	128
English, David et al	Deed to	Claggett, Walter	1801	F6	181	115
English, David et al	Release to	Cox, John	1816	AL36	199	206
English, David, of G'tn.	Deed to	Reintzel, Anthony, of G'tn.	1811	AB27	302	249
English, David, of G'tn.	Deed to	Gains, Richard, of G'tn.	1811	Z25	165	130
English, David, of G'tn.	Deed to	Pickerill, John, of G'tn.	1811	Z25	519	412
English, David, of G'tn.	Mortgage fr	Reintzel, Anthony, of G'tn.	1811	AA26	039	030
English, David, of G'tn.	Deed to	Webster, Toppan	1812	AD29	115	088
English, David, of G'tn.	Deed fr	Peter, John, of G'tn.	1812	AD29	414	349
English, David, of G'tn.	D. of T. fr	Elliott, Richard	1813	AF31	554	411
English, David, of G'tn.	Deed fr	Marbury, Wm. & John Peter, G'tn.	1813	AF31	279	197
English, David, of G'tn.	Assign fr	Wright, Thomas C., of G'tn.	1814	AG32	429	311
English, David, of G'tn.	Deed to	Beatty, Charles A., Dr., of G'tn.	1814	AG32	031	025
English, David, of G'tn.	Deed fr	McChesney, William, of G'tn.	1814	AH33	224	198
English, David, of G'tn.	D. of T. fr	Wright, Thomas C., of G'tn.	1814	AG32	433	313
English, David, of G'tn.	Deed to	Reintzel, Valentine	1815	AI34	055	063
English, David, of G'tn.	D. of T. to	Foxall, Henry	1816	AL36	351	342
English, David, of G'tn.	Deed to	Dixon, James	1816	AL36	237	241
English, David, of G'tn.	Deed fr	Renner, Daniel, of G'tn.	1816	AL36	054	055
English, David, of G'tn.	Deed fr	Davis, Charles B., of G'tn.	1816	AM37	358	259
English, David, of G'tn.	Deed fr	Johnson, Joshua, of Fredk. Co.	1817	AO39	337	240
English, David, printer, et al	Deed fr	Lyles, William	1799	E5	059	048
English, David, printer, et al	Mortgage to	Lyles, William	1800	E5	184	175
English, David, printer, et al	Mortgage to	Lyles, William	1801	G7	188	252
English, Joseph, insolvent	B. of S. to	Parrott, Richard, trustee	1805	M12	106	099
English, Robert, of Winchester	Mortgage fr	Peacock, Robert Ware	1802	H8	506	466
Ennis, Ezekial, of Shen. Co. VA	Deed fr	Woodward, Francis, Shen. Co. VA	1804	K10	331	342
Ennis, Polly	Cert Free fr	Herty, Thomas, notary	1809	W22	373	241
Eno, Edward, butcher	Assign to	Miller, Peter	1806	Q16	257	178
Eno, Edward, of G'tn.	Deed fr	Lingan, James M., of G'tn.	1797	C3	185	156
Eno, Edward, of G'tn.	Mortgage to	Baker, Michael, of Rockg. Co. VA	1797	C3	187	158
Eno, Richard	Deed fr	Davidson, Samuel	1801	G7	100	128
Eno, Richard	Deed to	Wright, Thomas C.	1810	Y24	371	336
Ensey, William	B. of S. to	Adams, George	1815	AI34	148	169
Ensey, William	Assign to	Casteel, Edmund	1816	AO39	045	037
Ensey, William	Deed fr	Prout, William	1816	AL36	110	112
Ensey, William	B. of S. to	Jenkins, John	1817	AO39	230	167
Entwisle, Isaac, of Alexa.	Mortgage fr	Cook, Orlando & Anne	1813	AE30	511	378
Erskine, Elizabeth	Deed fr	Mayne, Adam	1817	AN38	203	147
Esenbeck, William	Cert fr	Munroe, Thomas, Supt.	1805	M12	146	143
Esenbeck, William	Mortgage to	Grammar, Gottlieb Christopher	1814	AH33	124	118
Esenbeck, William	Deed to	Mayor, Henry	1815	AK35	073	057
Estave, Andrew	Cert fr	Commissioners of Washington	1796	B2A	335	471
Estep, Alexander	Qualify	Militia officer	1812	AD29	361	304
Estep, Alexander	B. of S. to	Grammer, G.C. & Geo. Kleiber	1815	AI34	369	398
Estep, Alexander	Deed fr	Burden, Henry R.	1817	AO39	459	315
Estep, Alexander & Barbara et al	Release to	deKrafft, Edward B.	1813	AF31	280	198
Estep, Alexander & Barbara	Deed to	Burden, Henry R.	1817	AO39	496	340
Estep, Joseph	B. of S. fr	Selby, Philip B.	1811	Z25	404	317
Estep, Joseph	Deed to	Selby, Henry Estep et al	1814	AG32	349	253
Estep, Joseph	B. of S. to	Foyle, Thomas	1814	AH33	319	275
Esterday, Daniel	B. of S. to	Ritchie, Abner	1804	K10	183	191
Eton, John	Deed to	Magruder, George	1807	R17	293	223
Etter, Joseph	B. of S. fr	Walter, Thomas R.	1817	AN38	290	212

Party	What	Party	Year	Liber	Old	New
Etter, Joseph, of G'tn.	B. of S. to	Bussard, Daniel, of G'tn.	1812	AC28	374	272
Etting, Hetty, of Balto.	Deed fr	Commissioners of Washington	1801	F6	128	079
Etting, Reuben, of Balto.	Deed fr	Commissioners of Washington	1801	F6	122	076
Etting, Shinah, of Balto.	Deed fr	Commissioners of Washington	1801	F6	131	081
Etting, Solomon	Cert fr	Commissioners of Washington	1801	G7	178	237
Etting, Solomon	Deed to	Hughes, Christopher	1802	I9	431	713
Etting, Solomon	Deed to	Spear, Joseph	1802	I9	245	394
Etting, Solomon	Deed to	Peter, David et al	1805	M12	329	333
Etting, Solomon, of Balto.	Deed fr	Commissioners of Washington	1801	F6	118	073
Etting, Solomon, of Balto.	Deed to	Blodgett, Samuel	1801	G7	022	296
Etting, Solomon, of Balto. Co.	Lease to	McElwee, John, mer., of Balto.	1804	L11	033	32
Etting, Solomon, of Balto. MD	Deed to	McElwee, Rebecca, wid/o John	1812	AD29	086	064
Etting, Solomon, of Balto. Co.	Deed to	Brevitt, John & Henry Hardisty	1816	AL36	059	060
Euen, Thomas M., of Phila. PA	Deed fr	Blodget, Samuel, mer., of Phila.	1800	E5	272	266
Evans, Charles	B. of S. to	Wilson, John	1802	G7	513	654
Evans, Charles	B. of S. to	Martin, Honore, of Montg. Co.	1804	L11	285	261
Evans, Charles	Deed to	Wilson, John	1804	L11	141	142
Evans, Evan	Deed fr	Stoddert, Benjamin	1802	H8	025	023
Evans, Evan	Deed fr	Munroe, Thomas, Supt.	1802	I9	028	037
Evans, Evan	Deed fr	Stoddert, Benjamin	1802	I9	288	471
Evans, Evan	Deed to	Rinehart, Andrew	1802	I9	494	811
Evans, Evan	Deed to	Evans, Evan, Jr., New Castle DE	1810	X23	335	268
Evans, Evan	Mortgage fr	Watson, James	1811	AB27	388	320
Evans, Evan, insolvent	Deed to	McClan, Robert, trustee	1804	L11	139	
Evans, Evan, Jr., New Castle DE	Deed fr	Evans, Evan	1810	X23	335	268
Evans, Evan, of N.C. Co. DE	Deed fr	Scholfield, Issachar & Mahlon	1797	B2B	666	433
Evans, Jesse, Jr.	B. of S. to	Evans, Mary, exrx. of Philip	1817	AO39	374	252
Evans, John	Mortgage fr	Baker, Samuel	1805	M12	120	114
Evans, John	Assign to	Evans, Robert	1809	W22	057	043
Evans, John et al	Deed fr	Lyon, John	1802	I9	442	731
Evans, John et al	Deed to	Vint, John	1805	N13	185	165
Evans, John, of G'tn.	Mortgage to	Wilson, John A.	1805	N13	318	256
Evans, Lucy	B. of S. fr	Evans, Philip	1813	AF31	220	150
Evans, Lucy (C), of G'tn.	Deed fr	Hurley, John, of Montg. Co. MD	1812	AD29	546	460
Evans, Mary, exrx. of Philip	B. of S. fr	Evans, Jesse, Jr.	1817	AO39	374	252
Evans, Philip	Deed fr	Addison, Thomas Grafton	1806	O14	400	268
Evans, Philip	B. of S. fr	Moore, John O.	1810	Y24	163	148
Evans, Philip	B. of S. to	Evans, Lucy	1813	AF31	220	150
Evans, Philip	Deed fr	Prout, William	1815	AH33	452	387
Evans, Philip	Deed fr	Prout, William	1815	AH33	453	389
Evans, Robert	B. of S. fr	Densley, Hugh	1805	M12	122	116
Evans, Robert	Assign fr	Evans, John	1809	W22	057	043
Evans, Samuel & Hannah et al	Deed to	Townsend, Henry	1801	G7	216	288
Evans, Samuel & Hannah, of PA	Deed to	Gary, Everard, of G'tn.	1805	N13	161	149
Evans, Samuel et al	Deed to	Cokendafer, Leonard & J. Calder	1798	D4	099	083
Evans, Thomas B., removed	Slaves		1801	G7		533
Evans, Thomas, of Balto.	Assign fr	Cumberland, William	1805	N13	326	264
Evans, William et al	Deed fr	Beall, Thomas	1802	I9	196	305
Eveleth, John, inventor & patentee	Assign to	Corporation of Georgetown	1817	AN38	004	004
Ewell, James	B. of S. to	Magruder, Patrick	1811	AB27	412	340
Ewell, James	B. of S. to	Weems, Mason L.	1814	AH33	025	023
Ewell, James	Deed fr	Hearn, Isaac, of A.A. Co.	1817	AN38	041	033
Ewell, James & Charles Minifee	Deed to	Boyd, Washington	1814	AG32	173	123
Ewell, James, Dr. et al	Mortgage fr	Minifie, Charles	1811	AA26	273	185
Ewell, Thomas	Slaves	From VA	1806	A16	303	230

Party	What	Party	Year	Liber	Old	New
Ewell, Thomas	Deed fr	Law, Thomas & Edmund	1812	AE30	006	005
Ewell, Thomas	Deed to	Columbia Turnpike Roads	1813	AE30	337	252
Ewell, Thomas	Deed fr	Guest, John & wife, of Phila. PA	1813	AE30	244	193
Ewell, Thomas	Deed to	Brent, William	1813	AE30	264	204
Ewell, Thomas	Deed to	Scholfield, Issachar, of P.G. Co.	1813	AE30	527	390
Ewell, Thomas	Mortgage fr	Scholfield, Joseph L. & Isachar	1813	AE30	260	202
Ewell, Thomas	Deed to	Dobbyn, John	1813	AE30	491	364
Ewell, Thomas	Mortgage fr	Scholfield, Issachar, of P.G. Co.	1813	AF31	076	052
Ewell, Thomas	Deed to	Cocke, Buller	1813	AF31	167	112
Ewell, Thomas	Mortgage fr	Wertz, Henry, Jr.	1813	AF31	179	120
Ewell, Thomas	Deed fr	Scholfield, Joseph L. & Isachar	1814	AH33	368	319
Ewell, Thomas	Mortgage to	Ott, David	1814	AH33	134	127
Ewell, Thomas	Deed fr	Scholfield, Joseph L. & I.	1814	AG32	202	141
Ewell, Thomas	Deed fr	Scholfield, Isachar	1814	AH33	366	317
Ewell, Thomas	Release to	Scholfield, Joseph L. & Issachar	1815	AI34	353	384
Ewell, Thomas	Deed to	Middleton, Smallwood C.	1815	AK35	126	097
Ewell, Thomas	Mortgage fr	Gales, Joseph, Jr.	1816	AM37	167	127
Ewell, Thomas	Deed to	Ott, David	1817	AN38	453	326
Ewell, Thomas & Elizabeth	Deed to	Scholfield, Joseph L. et al	1813	AE30	256	200
Ewell, Thomas & Elizabeth	Deed to	Forrest, Alexander	1813	AE30	271	209
Ewell, Thomas & Elizabeth	Deed to	Dobbyn, John	1813	AE30	273	210
Ewell, Thomas, Dr.	Manumis to	[ ], Fanny (C), age 40	1813	AE30	240	190
Ewell, Thomas, Dr.	Deed fr	Boyd, Washington, marshal	1816	AM37	310	226
Ewell, Thomas, of G'tn.	Mortgage fr	Dobbyn, John	1813	AF31	074	051
Ewell, Thomas, of G'tn.	D. of T. to	Ott, John, of G'tn.	1815	AK35	298	238
Ewell, Thomas, of G'tn.	D. of T. to	Ott, John, of G'tn.	1817	AN38	104	078
Ewing, Thomas, exrs. of	Deed to	Barry, James	1804	K10	256	262

Party	What	Party	Year	Liber	Old	New
F						
Fagan, Daniel	Agreement	Zantzinger, William P.	1817	AN38	504	364
Fahey, Mark, of G'tn.	D. of T. to	Mountz, John, of G'tn.	1813	AF31	340	242
Fahey, Mark, of G'tn.	Deed to	Reintzel, Valentine, of G'tn.	1814	AH33	337	292
Fahy, Mark, of G'tn.	Deed fr	Craig, George, of G'tn.	1811	AA26	324	218
Fairfax, Ferdinand	Cert Free to	[ ], Sephania	1816	AL36	509	478
Fairfax, Ferdinand, Berkeley Co.	Deed fr	Young, Samuel Wade, of VA	1801	G7	108	139
Fairfax, Ferdinand, Berkeley Co.	Deed fr	Jenners, Abiel & Deborah	1802	G7	557	706
Fairfax, Ferdinand, Berkeley Co.	Deed fr	Young, Alexander	1802	G7	556	704
Fairfax, Ferdinando	Deed to	Coyle, Andrew et al	1817	AO39	275	197
Fairfax, Ferdinando et ux, of VA	Deed to	Wormley, James, of Britain	1802	I9	033	043
Fairfax, Ferdinando, Jefferson Co.	Deed fr	Eliot, Samuel, Jr.	1812	AB27	544	444
Fairfax, Ferdinando, of VA	Deed fr	Polock, Isaac	1802	I9	081	115
Fairfax, Ferdinando, of VA	Deed fr	Polock, Isaac	1802	I9	027	036
Fairfax, Fernando, Berkeley Co.	Deed fr	Lee, Henry & Anne, Westm. Co.	1799	E5	067	055
Fairfax, Sarah, wid., in Eng.	Ltr. of Atty.	Fairfax, Thomas, s/o Bryan	1811	AA26	282	191
Fairfax, Thomas, s/o Bryan	Ltr. of Atty.	Fairfax, Sarah, wid., in Eng.	1811	AA26	282	191
Fallon, Edw.	Deed fr	Kearney, John	1802	I9	404	671
Fallon, Edw.	Deed fr	Kearney, John	1802	I9	404	670
Fallon, Edw.	Deed fr	Kearney, John	1802	I9	405	672
Fallon, Edw. et al	Deed to	McIntrie, John et al	1802	I9	406	673
Fallon, Edward & John Kearney	Deed to	Morris, Benjamin W. et al	1804	K10	114	123
Fallon, Edward & John Kearney	Deed to	Taylor, James N. & Henry Toland	1804	K10	139	151
Fallon, Edward & John Kearney	Deed to	Bartleman, William, of Alexa.	1804	K10	125	135
Fallon, Edward & Mary Anne	Deed to	Morrow, John, of Balto. MD	1813	AE30	417	307
Fallon, Mary Ann	Deed fr	Kennedy, John	1802	I9	471	775
Farr, Abraham, of Alexa.	Deed fr	Lingan, James M., of G'tn.	1799	D4	263	248
Farrand, William	D. of T. to	Edmonston, Edward	1811	AC28	049	037
Farrant, Thomas	Manumis to	Floyd, Ann	1816	AK35	408	320
Farrell, Patrick	Deed fr	Prout, William	1807	S18	308	241
Farrell, Zephaniah	Deed fr	Barber, John	1802	H8	485	446
Farrell, Zephaniah	Deed fr	Commissioners of Washington	1802	H8	116	113
Farrell, Zephaniah	Deed fr	Bryan, Wilson	1805	N13	270	224
Farrell, Zephaniah	Deed fr	Chandler, Walter Story	1806	P15	177	118
Farrell, Zephaniah	Deed fr	Buntin, Aaron, of Balto. Co.	1807	S18	156	127
Farrell, Zephaniah	Deed fr	Standage, Eleazor & Mary	1809	W22	019	014
Farrell, Zephaniah	Deed fr	Smith, Hugh, of Alexa.	1809	X23	037	027
Farrell, Zephaniah	Deed fr	Kilty, John & Josias Wilson King	1809	V21	339	243
Farrell, Zephaniah	Deed to	Elliott, Richard & Lynde	1810	Y24	206	189
Farrell, Zephaniah	Deed to	Kerby, John Baptist	1811	Z25	442	348
Farrell, Zephaniah	Deed fr	Bradley, Phineas, trustee	1811	AB27	075	063
Farrell, Zephaniah	Deed to	Greenleaf, James, of Phila.	1812	AB27	198	162
Farrell, Zephaniah	Mortgage fr	Burford, John A.	1812	AD29	478	405
Farrell, Zephaniah	Deed fr	Laird, John, of G'tn.	1813	AF31	322	230
Farrell, Zephaniah	Transfer fr	Minifee, Charles	1813	AE30	469	349
Farrell, Zephaniah	Deed to	Bean, John	1814	AH33	075	067
Farrell, Zephaniah	Deed to	Anderson, James	1815	AI34	474	485
Farrell, Zephaniah	Deed fr	Corporation of Washington	1815	AK35	024	019
Farrell, Zephaniah	Deed fr	Corporation of Washington	1815	AK35	027	021
Farrell, Zephaniah	Deed fr	Corporation of Washington	1815	AK35	030	023
Farrell, Zephaniah	Deed fr	Corporation of Washington	1815	AK35	022	017
Farrell, Zephaniah	Deed fr	Corporation of Washington	1815	AK35	032	025
Farrell, Zephaniah	Deed fr	Corporation of Washington	1815	AK35	035	027
Farrell, Zephaniah	Lease to	Gilliam, Thomas	1817	AN38	093	071
Farrell, Zephaniah et al	Mortgage fr	Minifie, Charles	1811	AA26	273	185

Party	What	Party	Year	Liber	Old	New
Farrington, Lewis, Somerset Co.	Deed fr	Prout, William	1808	T19	104	074
Faulkner, James, Berkeley Co.	Deed to	Portersfield, John, Berkeley Co.	1808	T19	124	087
Fauntleroy, Moore, Richm. Co. VA	Will		1804	L11	187	179
Fauntleroy, Moore, Richm. Co. VA	Will		1806	Q16	130	084
Faw, Abraham, of Montg. Co.	Deed to	Orme, Thomas, Montgomery Co.	1795	B2A	212	292
Feales, William	B. of S. fr	Cartwright, Elizabeth	1802	H8	036	034
Fears, Margaret, w/o Thomas	Deed to	Baltzer, John, Jr.	1801	G7	054	070
Fears, Thomas & Margaret	Deed to	Baltzer, John, Jr., of G'tn.	1798	D4	116	099
Fears, Thomas & Margaret	Deed to	Baltzer, John, Jr., of G'tn.	1801	G7	373	506
Feburier, Nicholas	Deed to	Cook, James	1798	C3	370	296
Feburier, Nicholas	Deed fr	Forrest, Uriah, of Montg. Co.	1798	C3	368	294
Feburier, Nicholas	Deed to	Pic, Francis et al	1802	I9	252	407
Feburier, Nicholas et al	B. of S. to	Mitchell, John	1804	K10	246	253
Feburier, Nicholas, insolvent	Deed to	Beatty, Charles	1804	K10	176	185
Feburier, Nicholas, insolvent	Deed to	Peter, Robert, trustee	1805	N13	233	198
Felins, Jacob	Deed fr	Burch, Samuel	1817	AN38	011	009
Felius, Jacob	Deed fr	Causin, Gerrard N., St. Mary's Co.	1814	AG32	206	144
Feltwell, William, Jr., of Hays, Eng.	Deed to	Simmons, William	1805	N13	349	281
Feltwell, William, of Hayes, Eng.	Deed fr	Hellen, Walter	1804	L11	399	354
Fendall, Philip Richard, of Alexa.	Deed to	Blodget, Samuel, of Boston MA	1792	A1-1	130	189
Fendall, Philip Richard, of Alexa.	Deed to	Wayman, Charles, of G'tn.	1805	M12	256	258
Fennell, Edward	Lease fr	Blodget, Samuel	1804	K10	317	323
Fennell, Edward	Deed fr	Clare, Benjamin, of G'tn.	1807	R17	238	179
Fennell, Edward	B. of S. fr	Caton, John, of Balto.	1809	W22	392	255
Fenwick, Bennett	Deed fr	Burnes, David	1794	B2A	061	077
Fenwick, Bennett	Agreement	Elliott, Samuel, Jr.	1795	B2B	382	037
Fenwick, Bennett	Deed fr	Commissioners of Washington	1799	D4	403	382
Fenwick, Bennett, of P.G. Co.	Deed to	Fenwick, Richard, St. Mary's Co.	1798	C3	413	327
Fenwick, Francis	Deed fr	Carroll, Patrick & Susanna	1814	AH33	345	299
Fenwick, Francis	Deed to	Clements, Rebecca	1815	AK35	392	308
Fenwick, Francis & Eleanor	Deed fr	Sewall, Clement et al	1809	V21	303	221
Fenwick, Francis, of G'tn.	D. of T. to	Murdock, John, of G'tn.	1816	AL36	459	433
Fenwick, George	Deed fr	Threlkeld, John	1794	B2A	007	008
Fenwick, George	Deed fr	Threlkeld, John	1800	E5	127	115
Fenwick, George	Deed to	Crookshank, John	1802	I9	124	184
Fenwick, George	Deed to	Boarman, Charles	1802	H8	134	131
Fenwick, George	Deed fr	Threlkeld, John	1803	K10	055	59
Fenwick, George	Cert Surv	Barry, James, for *St. Elisabeth*	1806	O14	187	112
Fenwick, George	Deed fr	King, James Carrol	1808	U20	138	079
Fenwick, George & Margaret	Deed to	McIntosh, Thomas	1810	Y24	313	284
Fenwick, George, of Montg. Co.	Deed fr	Threlkeld, John, of Montg. Co.	1796	B2B	501	199
Fenwick, George, of G'tn.	Deed to	Potts, William	1802	H8	407	376
Fenwick, George, of G'tn.	Deed fr	Carroll, Daniel	1802	H8	555	517
Fenwick, Helena	Manumis to	Gibson, Joshua (C)	1813	AF31	098	066
Fenwick, James, of St. Mary's Co.	Deed to	Beatty, Thomas, Jr., of G'tn.	1794	B2A	101	132
Fenwick, James, of MD	Deed fr	Young, Nicholas, of MD	1806	Q16	086	055
Fenwick, Mary	Deed fr	Carroll, Daniel, of Duddington	1802	H8	549	510
Fenwick, Mary Ann, of G'tn.	Deed fr	Munroe, Thomas	1801	G7	427	562
Fenwick, Mary Ann	Deed fr	Dant, James, late of KY	1801	G7	011	014
Fenwick, Mary Ann	Deed fr	Munroe, Thomas	1802	G7	420	662
Fenwick, Mary Ann, wid.	Mortgage fr	Jackson, John G., of VA	1810	Y24	171	157
Fenwick, Mary Ann	Deed to	Jackson, John G., Harrison Co. VA	1810	X23	350	281
Fenwick, Richard	B. of S. to	Hyde, Thomas	1801	G7	365	497
Fenwick, Richard	B. of S. fr	Hyde, Thomas	1805	N13	008	009
Fenwick, Richard	B. of S. to	Lenox, Peter	1805	N13	008	009

Party	What	Party	Year	Liber	Old	New
Fenwick, Richard	B. of S. to	Shaw, James	1807	S18	001	001
Fenwick, Richard	B. of S. to	Tunnicliff, William	1807	R17	360	274
Fenwick, Richard	Manumis to	[ ], Peter [Big Peter] (negro)	1808	U20	322	172
Fenwick, Richard	Manumis to	[ ], Mordecai (negro)	1808	U20	323	173
Fenwick, Richard	B. of S. to	Neale, Leonard, Rev.	1808	T19	327	238
Fenwick, Richard	B. of S. to	Wilson, John A.	1809	V21	396	300
Fenwick, Richard	B. of S. to	Villard, Andrew J.	1809	X23	119	085
Fenwick, Richard	Release fr	Villard, Andrew J.	1810	Z25	203	159
Fenwick, Richard, St. Mary's Co.	Deed fr	Fenwick, Bennett, of P.G. Co.	1798	C3	413	327
Fenwick, Thomas	Deed fr	Boyd, Washington, marshal	1814	AG32	253	180
Fenwick, Thomas & Eleanor	Deed to	Columbia Turnpike Company	1812	AC28	263	192
Fenwick, Thomas & Robert Brent	B. of S. fr	Coombe, Griffith	1812	AC28	309	225
Fenwick, Thomas & Eleanor	Deed to	Brent, Robert	1814	AG32	213	149
Feres, Chloe	Slave		1810	X23	355	
Ferguson, Charlotte & children	Manumis fr	Johns, Susannah & Richard	1815	AI34	079	089
Ferguson, David	P. of Atty. fr	Ferguson, William, Ontario Co. NY	1804	L11	322	295
Ferguson, David, Ontario Co. NY	Deed fr	Wirt, Henry, of Ontario Co. NY	1805	N13	336	270
Ferguson, David, Ontario Co. NY	Deed fr	Ferguson, William, Ontario Co. NY	1805	N13	340	274
Ferguson, David, Ontario Co. NY	Deed to	Thompson, William	1806	O14	067	040
Ferguson, David, Ontario Co. NY	Deed fr	Weatherall, John, of G'tn.	1806	Q16	252	174
Ferguson, David, Ontario Co. NY	B. of S. fr	Weatherall, John, of G'tn.	1806	P15	381	255
Ferguson, David, Ontario Co. NY	Deed to	Owens, Isaac, of G'tn.	1807	R17	344	262
Ferguson, Eliz., Ontario Co. NY	P. of Atty. to	Ferguson, David	1804	L11	322	295
Ferguson, James	Receipt fr	Lanham, Asa	1804	L11	411	366
Ferguson, James	B. of S. to	Read, Thomas, of Montg. Co.	1805	N13	404	321
Ferguson, James	Deed fr	Lanham, Aza, of Wilkes Co. GA	1807	R17	106	082
Ferguson, James	Deed to	Worthington, Charles	1807	R17	111	087
Ferguson, John	Qualify		1802	I9	466	768
Ferguson, William, of P.G. Co.	Deed to	Thompson, John, of G'tn.	1798	C3	441	346
Ferguson, William, Onatrio Co. NY	Deed to	Ferguson, David, Ontario Co. NY	1805	N13	340	274
Ferguson, William, Ontario Co. NY	P. of Atty. to	Ferguson, David	1804	L11	322	295
Ferrell, James	Deed to	Beall, Thomas & John M. Gantt	1793	A1-1	333	437
Fields, William	Deed fr	Beall, Thomas B., of George	1802	H8	035	033
Fields, William	Deed fr	Van Ness, John P. & Marcia	1804	L11	069	70
Fields, William	Deed to	Hedges, Nicholas	1806	P15	375	250
Fields, William	Bond to	McCutchin, James	1807	R17	012	011
Fields, William	Deed fr	Beall, Thomas B.	1808	T19	129	092
Fields, William	Deed fr	Beall, Thomas B.	1808	U20	159	090
Fields, William	B. of S. fr	Hurdle, Ann, of G'tn.	1810	Y24	157	144
Fields, William	B. of S. fr	Graves, Benjamin	1810	Y24	364	329
Fields, William	Deed to	Wilson, John A.	1817	AN38	181	131
Fields, William, of G'tn.	Deed fr	Beall, Thomas B., of G'tn.	1804	K10	174	183
Fields, William, of G'tn.	Deed fr	Beall, Thomas B., of G'tn.	1805	M12	383	395
Fields, William, of G'tn.	Deed to	Dixon, Thomas, of G'tn.	1805	M12	389	401
Fields, William, of G'tn.	Assign fr	Mahone, John, of G'tn.	1805	M12	192	194
Fields, William, of G'tn.	Deed fr	Balch, Stephen B., of G'tn.	1806	P15	379	253
Fields, William, of G'tn.	Deed fr	Balch, Stephen B., of G'tn.	1807	S18	100	081
Fields, William, of G'tn.	Deed to	Thompson, John et al	1808	U20	227	122
Fields, William, of G'tn.	D. of T. to	Thompson, John, of G'tn.	1809	X23	128	092
Fields, William, of G'tn.	Release fr	Thompson, John, of G'tn.	1810	Z25	310	243
Fields, William, of G'tn.	Deed to	Thompson, John, of G'tn.	1810	Z25	300	235
Fields, William, of G'tn.	Deed fr	Beall, Thomas B., of G'tn.	1810	Z25	335	261
Fields, William, of G'tn.	Deed to	Lipscomb, John, of G'tn.	1812	AC28	140	105
Fields, William, of G'tn.	Mortgage fr	Reed, Osten, of G'tn.	1812	AD29	003	002
Fields, William, of G'tn.	D. of T. to	Thompson, James	1812	AD29	252	208

Index to District of Columbia Land Records, 1792-1817

Party	What	Party	Year	Liber	Old	New
Fields, William, of G'tn.	Deed to	Thompson, James, Col.	1814	AH33	245	213
Fields, William, of G'tn.	Deed to	Morris, George, of G'tn.	1815	AI34	425	445
Fielius, Jacob	Deed fr	Mauro, Philip, of Balto.	1815	AI34	060	068
Finagen, Rosanna	B. of S. to	Thompson, George, of G'tn.	1809	V21	311	227
Finigan, Rosanna	B. of S. to	Waters, Benjamin	1805	M12	099	092
Finigan, Rosannah	B. of S. to	Bridges, John et al	1816	AM37	145	112
Finlay, Oliver P., of Alexa.	Deed fr	Boyer, Richard Montgomery, G'tn.	1809	V21	390	294
Finley, Oliver P., of Alexa.	Deed to	Brooke, Samuel	1812	AD29	020	015
Finnicum, Benjamin	B. of S. to	McDonald, Andrew	1808	T19	344	248
Finnicum, Benjamin, insolvent	B. of S. to	Ellsworth, George, trustee	1808	V21	049	037
Finnicum, Benjamin, of G'tn.	B. of S. to	McDonald, Andrew	1808	T19	342	248
First Presbyterian Congregation	Cert fr	Munroe, Thomas, Supt.	1813	AE30	350	262
Fish, Francis, of Fairfax Co. VA	B. of S. to	Cromwell, Jesse	1810	Y24	010	009
Fisher, James	Deed fr	Gadsden, Philip	1806	P15	043	026
Fisher, James C. et al	Release to	Nourse, Joseph	1813	AF31	011	008
Fisher, James, Charleston SC	Release to	Gadsden, James, Charleston SC	1817	AN38	292	214
Fisher, John, s/o Adam	Deed to	Beall, Thomas & John M. Gantt	1792	A1-1	078	115
Fisher, Margaret, wid/o Adam	Deed to	Beall, Thomas & John M. Gantt	1792	A1-1	078	115
Fisk, James, Barre VT	B. of S. fr	Ball, Henry W.	1813	AE30	224	180
Fisk, James, of Barre VT	Manumis to	[ ], Phillis (C)	1813	AF31	490	357
Fitzgerald, Thomas	Deed fr	King, Nicholas, late of Charles Co.	1804	L11	171	167
Fitzgerald, William	Cert fr	Munroe, Thomas, Supt.	1804	L11	094	96
Fitzgerald, William	Assign to	Wightt, John M. & George Moore	1812	AC28	512	366
Fitzgerald, William	B. of S. to	Hearn, John	1813	AE30	413	304
Fitzgerrald, William	Deed fr	Quinn, Edward	1810	Y24	143	130
Fitzhugh, Charlotte	Slaves		1806	Q16	015	010
Fitzhugh, Philip	Deed fr	Vermonnet, John	1798	C3	365	292
Fitzhugh, Philip	Deed fr	Jackson, Samuel, of G'tn.	1800	F6	085	052
Fitzhugh, Philip	Deed fr	Forrest, Uriah	1801	G7	048	061
Fitzhugh, Philip	Deed to	Thornton, William	1801	G7	243	327
Fitzhugh, Philip	Deed to	Bond, Joshua B., of Phila. et al	1801	G7	237	318
Fitzhugh, Philip	Receipt fr	Moscrop, Henry	1802	I9	088	125
Fitzhugh, Philip et al	Agreement	Schofield, J. & M.	1799	D4	241	224
Fitzhugh, Philip, of MD	Deed fr	Villard, Andrew Joseph	1802	I9	084	120
Fitzhugh, Philip, of P.G. Co.	Deed to	Villard, Joseph	1807	R17	395	299
Fitzhugh, R.H.	Slaves	From Fairfax Co. VA	1817	AN38	366	270
Fitzhugh, Samuel	Lease fr	Melvin, James	1813	AF31	282	199
Fitzhugh, Samuel	Deed fr	King, Vincent	1815	AH33	400	345
Fitzhugh, Samuel	Deed to	King, William	1815	AK35	427	335
Fitzhugh, Samuel	D. of T. to	Key, Philip Barton	1815	AI34	480	489
Fitzhugh, Samuel	D. of T. to	Ridgley, William G.	1817	AN38	328	240
Fitzhugh, Samuel, of G'tn.	Mortgage fr	White, Levi	1811	AA26	393	261
Fitzhugh, Samuel, of G'tn.	Deed fr	Doughty, William	1815	AI34	186	213
Fitzhugh, Samuel, of G'tn.	Deed fr	Murdock, John, of G'tn.	1816	AK35	517	407
Fitzhugh, Samuel, of G'tn.	Deed fr	Dorsey, William H., of Montg. Co.	1816	AK35	518	408
Fitzhugh, Samuel, of G'tn.	Deed to	Smith, Clement, of G'tn.	1816	AL36	473	446
Fitzhugh, Samuel, of G'tn.	Deed fr	Johnson, Thomas, of Fredk. Co.	1816	AM37	436	313
Fitzhugh, Samuel, of G'tn.	Deed to	Bowie, Washington, of G'tn.	1817	AO39	369	248
Fitzhugh, Samuel, of G'tn.	Deed to	Hayman, William	1817	AN38	409	409
Fitzhugh, William	Deed to	Beall, Thomas & John M. Gantt	1793	A1-2	443	52
Fitzhugh, William, s/o William	Deed to	Barry, James et al	1799	D4	250	234
Fitzhugh, William, s/o William	Deed to	Barry, James	1801	G7	288	399
Fitzpatrick, Nicholas	B. of S. to	O'Brien, James, of Balto.	1815	AH33	560	479
Fitzsimmons, Thomas, Phila. et al	Deed to	Hansenclever, Mary, wid., Phila.	1810	X23	305	244
FitzSimmons, Thomas et al	Deed to	Ludlow, Daniel, of NY	1807	Q16	217	148

Index to District of Columbia Land Records, 1792-1817

Party	What	Party	Year	Liber	Old	New
Fitzsimons, Thomas, Phila. et al	Deed to	Crawford, James, younger, Phila.	1804	L11	135	137
Fitzsimons, Thomas, Phila. et al	Deed to	Crawford, James, younger, Phila.	1804	L11	131	133
Fitzsimons, Thomas, Phila. et al	Deed to	Read, William, mer., of Phila.	1805	M12	125	119
Fitzsimons, Thomas, Phila. et al	Deed to	Poleske, Charles G., Phila. et al	1805	N13	021	023
Fitzsimons, Thomas, Phila. et al	Deed to	Crawford, James, younger, Phila.	1807	R17	062	050
Fitzsimons, Thomas, Phila. et al	Deed to	Read, William, mer., of Phila. PA	1809	V21	276	198
FitzSimons, Thomas, Phila. et al	Deed to	Leamy, John, mer.	1808	T19	153	108
Flaherty, James	Deed to	King, William, of G'tn.	1795	B2B	365	015
Flaut, Christian	Deed fr	Commissioners of Washington	1801	F6	179	114
Flaut, Christian	Deed fr	Bentley, Joseph	1805	M12	078	072
Flaut, Christian	Deed to	Jones, Charles	1807	S18	200	160
Flaut, Christian	Deed fr	Snyder, Jacob, of VA	1807	S18	190	154
Flaut, Christian & Hannah	Deed to	Somerville, David	1807	S18	256	202
Flaut, Joseph	B. of S. fr	Sanders, Thomas	1809	X23	105	076
Flaut, Joseph	B. of S. to	Sanders, Catherine	1809	X23	133	095
Flaut, Joseph, insolvent	Deed to	Hughes, Thomas, trustee	1806	P15	316	208
Flecher, Noah & James Varnum	Release to	Hildreth, Ezekiel	1817	AO39	498	342
Fleet, Ann Warren (C), d/o Henry	Manumis fr	Fleet, Henry (C), of G'tn.	1816	AL36	425	406
Fleet, Henry	Manumis to	[ ], James	1804	K10	243	250
Fleet, Henry	Manumis to	[ ], Betsey	1804	K10	243	250
Fleet, Henry	Manumis to	[ ], Nan	1804	K10	243	250
Fleet, Henry	Manumis to	[ ], Patience	1804	K10	243	250
Fleet, Henry	Manumis to	[ ], Maria (negro)	1809	V21	177	127
Fleet, Henry	Assign to	Kile, Alexander	1812	AD29	180	145
Fleet, Henry (C), of G'tn.	Manumis to	Fleet, Ann Warren (C), d/o	1816	AL36	425	406
Fleet, Henry, black man	Deed fr	Beall, Thomas, of George	1807	S18	038	032
Fleet, Henry, of G'tn.	Lease fr	Heater, Conrad, of G'tn.	1804	L11	021	20
Fleet, Henry, of G'tn.	Deed to	Beall, Hezekiah, Jefferson Co. VA	1809	W22	367	237
Fleet, Henry, of G'tn.	Lease fr	Nourse, Michael	1810	Z25	045	034
Fleet, Henry, of G'tn.	B. of S. fr	Beall, Hezekiah, of Loudoun Co.	1812	AD29	474	401
Fleet, Henry, of G'tn.	Deed to	Kile, Alexander, of G'tn.	1812	AB27	541	441
Fleet, Henry, of G'tn.	Deed to	Corcoran, Thomas, of G'tn.	1815	AI34	082	093
Fleet, Henry, of G'tn.	Deed fr	Smith, Richard, of G'tn.	1815	AH33	524	449
Fleet, Henry, of G'tn.	Deed to	Kile, Alexander, of G'tn.	1815	AH33	526	451
Fleharty, Peter	B. of S. to	Donohew, Patrick	1802	H8	383	356
Fletchall, Thomas, Jr., of SC	Deed to	Fletchall, Thomas, of Montg. Co.	1806	O14	173	113
Fletchall, Thomas, of Montg. Co.	Deed fr	Fletchall, Thomas, Jr., of SC	1806	O14	173	113
Fletchall, Thomas, of Montg. Co.	Deed to	Calder, James, of G'tn.	1813	AE30	077	058
Fletcher, Betsey	Agreement	May, Frederick	1802	I9	282	460
Fletcher, Betsey	Deed fr	May, Frederick & Samuel Eliot, Jr.	1808	U20	128	073
Fletcher, Charles, s/o Michael & E.	Cert Free fr	Brent, Robert	1811	AB27	395	326
Fletcher, Elender, d/o Michael & E.	Cert Free fr	Brent, Robert	1811	AB27	395	326
Fletcher, Elizabeth, d/o M. & E.	Cert Free fr	Brent, Robert	1811	AB27	395	326
Fletcher, Mary	Cert Free fr	French, John B.	1810	Z25	132	104
Fletcher, Michael	Manumis fr	Smith, Robert	1811	AB27	516	422
Fletcher, Michael, s/o M. & E.	Cert Free fr	Brent, Robert	1811	AB27	395	326
Fletcher, Noah	Deed fr	Murdock, John, of G'tn.	1812	AD29	303	249
Fletcher, Noah	Deed fr	Dorsey, William H., of Balto. Co.	1812	AD29	305	250
Fletcher, Noah	Release fr	Bank of Columbia	1812	AD29	309	
Fletcher, Noah	Deed fr	Kerr, Alexander	1814	AG32	442	320
Fletcher, Noah	D. of T. to	Varnum, James M.	1816	AL36	001	001
Fletcher, Noah	Deed fr	Laird, John, exr. of J. Carleton	1816	AM37	427	306
Fletcher, Noah & J. Huddleston	D. of T. fr	Edwards, Horace H. & H. Bestor	1812	AD29	277	229
Fletcher, Noah & J. Huddleston	Deed to	Edwards, Horace H. & H. Bestor	1815	AK35	438	343
Fletcher, Noah & J.M. Varnum	Deed fr	Hildreth, Ezekiel	1816	AL36	003	003

Index to District of Columbia Land Records, 1792-1817 157

Party	What	Party	Year	Liber	Old	New
Fletcher, William	Assign fr	Peacock, Robert	1801	G7	243	328
Fletcher, William	Deed fr	Munroe, Thomas	1802	I9	153	230
Fletcher, William	Deed fr	Roe, Cornelius McDermott	1804	K10	208	218
Fletcher, William	Convey fr	Tuckfield, William H.	1804	K10	207	216
Fletcher, William	Assign fr	McLaughlin, James	1804	K10	205	215
Fletcher, William	B. of S. fr	McCloskey, William, of P.G. Co.	1805	N13	205	178
Fletcher, William et al	Deed fr	Munroe, Thomas, Supt.	1802	I9	151	229
Fletcher, William, now of MD	Deed to	Wannell, Thomas	1815	AK35	385	303
Fletcher, William, now of MD	Deed fr	Davidson, John	1815	AK35	390	307
Fletcher, William, of P.G. Co.	Deed to	Coyle, Francis	1817	AO39	419	285
Flett, Rachel (negro)	Manumis fr	Beall, Thomas Brooke, exr. of G.	1808	U20	225	121
Flick, Andrew, of Orange Co. VA	Deed fr	Stoddert, Benjamin & W. Deakins	1793	A1-1	294	392
Flick, Andrew, of Orange Co. VA	Deed to	Beall, Thomas & John M. Gantt	1793	A1-1	296	393
Floyd, Ann	Manumis fr	Farrant, Thomas	1816	AK35	408	320
Floyd, William & Edw. H. Nicholls	Deed fr	Munroe, Thomas, Supt.	1816	AM37	115	091
Floyd, William & Edw. H. Nicoll	Deed fr	Ringgold, Tench	1816	AM37	025	020
Foard, William	B. of S. to	Benson, Edin	1806	Q16	053	034
Ford, Athanasius [Lewis]	B. of S. to	Watterstone, David	1815	AI34	516	521
Ford, Edward	B. of S. to	Spalding, Bernard	1811	AA26	034	026
Ford, Edward	Release fr	Spalding, Bernard	1812	AD29	124	095
Ford, Edward, of G'tn.	B. of S. fr	Adams, Henrietta, of Montg. Co.	1816	AL36	249	251
Ford, James	Deed fr	Commissioners of Washington	1801	G7	135	178
Ford, James	Deed fr	Commissioners of Washington	1801	F6	213	138
Ford, John	B. of S. fr	Eakin, James et al	1805	N13	017	018
Ford, Joseph, St. Mary's Co. et al	Deed fr	Prout, William	1802	I9	016	022
Ford, Lewis	Qualify	Deputy Clerk County Court	1802	H8	545	506
Ford, Lewis	Deed to	Barry, James, of NY	1806	Q16	077	049
Ford, Lewis	Deed to	Fricke, Augustus, of Phila. PA	1807	S18	063	053
Ford, Lewis & Toppan Webster	Deed fr	Lovell, William, of Balto.	1807	R17	075	061
Ford, Lewis & Toppan Webster	Deed fr	Lovering, William, of Balto.	1809	W22	101	073
Ford, Lewis et al	B. of S. to	Ford, John	1805	N13	017	018
Ford, Lewis, of St. Mary's Co.	Deed to	Wadsworth, Charles, Alexa. Co.	1809	V21	298	216
Ford, Lewis, of St. Mary's Co.	D. of T. to	Webster, Toppan	1809	W22	219	150
Ford, Mahlon et al	Partition		1804	K10	306	310
Ford, Sarah	Deed fr	Hollenback, William	1814	AG32	184	130
Ford, William [Foard]	Deed to	Benson, Edin	1806	Q16	068	043
Forde, Standish et al	Deed to	Meany, John, mariner, of Phila.	1800	E5	347	333
Forde, Standish, mer., et al	Deed to	Meamy, John, mariner, of Phila.	1800	E5	343	330
Forde, Standish, of Phila. et al	Deed fr	Morris, Robert & Mary, of Phila.	1797	C3	007	5
Forrest, Alexander	Deed fr	Prout, William	1804	L11	177	172
Forrest, Alexander	Deed fr	Prout, William	1810	Y24	185	170
Forrest, Alexander	Deed fr	Prout, William	1810	Y24	186	171
Forrest, Alexander	B. of S. fr	Bean, Samuel	1811	AB27	409	337
Forrest, Alexander	Assign fr	Johnston, James	1811	AB27	406	335
Forrest, Alexander	Deed fr	Clerklee, James	1812	AD29	248	205
Forrest, Alexander	D. of T. fr	McWilliams, Alexander	1813	AE30	057	043
Forrest, Alexander	Deed fr	Ewell, Thomas & Elizabeth	1813	AE30	271	209
Forrest, Benjamin S.	Deed fr	Harbaugh, Leonard et al, exrs.	1813	AF31	491	358
Forrest, Benjamin S.	Deed to	Hoye, John, of Allegany Co.	1814	AH33	016	014
Forrest, Dick (negro)	Manumis fr	Addison, Thomas G.	1808	T19	240	176
Forrest, Henry	Deed to	Joncherez, Alexander L.	1811	AB27	441	362
Forrest, James, of St. Mary's Co.	Cert Free to	Barnes, Nancy (C)	1815	AK35	042	033
Forrest, Joe	Manumis fr	Addison, Thomas G.	1807	T19	018	014
Forrest, John B.	Deed fr	St. Clair, George	1816	AM37	491	358
Forrest, John B.	Deed fr	Prout, William	1816	AM37	066	054

Party	What	Party	Year	Liber	Old	New
Forrest, Joseph		Certificate of Slaves	1802	H8	497	456
Forrest, Joseph	Deed fr	Gantt, Edward	1805	N13	282	232
Forrest, Joseph	Deed fr	MacCreery, William, of Balto.	1808	T19	212	154
Forrest, Joseph	B. of S. to	Clark, William	1808	T19	219	161
Forrest, Joseph	Deed fr	Magruder, George, collector, G'tn.	1809	W22	092	067
Forrest, Joseph	Certificate	Commissioner of Turnpike Road	1810	Y24	292	267
Forrest, Joseph	Qualify	Justice of the Peace	1810	Z25	249	195
Forrest, Joseph	Deed fr	Hodnett, James	1811	AB27	348	288
Forrest, Joseph	Deed fr	Davidson, John	1813	AE30	280	215
Forrest, Joseph	Deed to	Smith, Clement, of G'tn.	1814	AG32	051	040
Forrest, Joseph	Deed fr	Laird, John, of G'tn.	1814	AH33	019	017
Forrest, Joseph	B. of S. fr	Ramsey, Andrew & Catherine	1816	AL36	059	060
Forrest, Joseph	Deed fr	Hoye, John, of Allegany Co.	1816	AL36	064	065
Forrest, Joseph	Deed fr	Stockwell, Sarah, of Ire.	1816	AM37	062	050
Forrest, Joseph	Deed fr	Stockwell, John	1816	AM37	063	052
Forrest, Joseph	Convey to	Goldsborough, Howe, of MD	1816	AL36	342	333
Forrest, Joseph	Agreement	Hoot, Samuel	1817	AN38	010	008
Forrest, Joseph	Deed fr	Lufborough, Nathan	1817	AO39	446	306
Forrest, Joseph & Edmund Law	Deed fr	Hellen, Walter	1811	AB27	213	173
Forrest, Joseph & Edmund Law	D. of T. to	Brent, William	1812	AD29	239	198
Forrest, Joseph & Griffith Coombe	Road Order	Alexanders Island to boundary	1814	AH33	095	
Forrest, Joseph & Edmund Law	Deed to	Wharton, Franklin	1816	AL36	107	1-9
Forrest, Joseph & Edmund Law	Release fr	Law, Thomas & William Brent	1816	AL36	106	107
Forrest, Joseph, agent	Deed to	Hagner, Peter	1810	Y24	202	185
Forrest, Joseph et al	B. of S. to	Commercial Co. of Washington	1808	U20	037	021
Forrest, Joseph et al	Deed fr	Munroe, Thomas, Supt.	1811	AA26	259	176
Forrest, Joseph et al	Suit ads	Potomac Company	1812	AG32	258	183
Forrest, Joseph, of G'tn.	Deed to	King, Adam, of G'tn.	1796	B2B	606	359
Forrest, Joseph, trustee	Convey to	Steuart, William	1808	U20	247	132
Forrest, Joseph, trustee	Deed to	Butler, Silas	1813	AF31	068	047
Forrest, Joseph, trustee	Deed to	Harrison, John	1813	AE30	333	249
Forrest, Joseph, trustee	Deed to	Winn, Timothy	1813	AF31	067	046
Forrest, Joseph, trustee	Deed to	Thomas, John Valentine	1815	AK35	214	168
Forrest, Joseph, trustee	Deed to	Hilton, Samuel	1817	AO39	115	089
Forrest, Julius	Deed fr	Thornton, William	1816	AM37	468	337
Forrest, Rebecca	Deed to	Turner, Thomas & Samuel	1810	Y24	203	187
Forrest, Rebecca	Deed to	Balch, Stephen B.	1816	AL36	457	432
Forrest, Richard	Deed to	Morsell, James S.	1799	D4	255	240
Forrest, Richard	Manumis to	[ ], Harry (Negro)	1802	H8	276	261
Forrest, Richard	Deed fr	Dorsey, William H., of G'tn.	1807	S18	067	055
Forrest, Richard & Chas. Glover	Deed to	Parrott, Richard, of G'tn.	1813	AF31	378	272
Forrest, Richard & Charles Glover	Deed to	Davidson, James	1813	AF31	476	346
Forrest, Richard & Chas. Glover	Deed to	Young, Moses	1813	AF31	380	273
Forrest, Richard & Jas. Davidson	Deed to	Davidson, John	1813	AF31	539	399
Forrest, Richard & J. Davidson	Deed to	Cocke, Buller	1814	AG32	143	103
Forrest, Richard & Charles Glover	Deed to	Tayloe, John	1815	AK35	120	093
Forrest, Richard & Jas. Davidson	Deed to	Lewis, Joseph S., of Phila. PA	1815	AI34	345	377
Forrest, Richard et al	B. of S. to	Commercial Co. of Washington	1808	U20	037	021
Forrest, Richard et al	Suit ads	Potomac Company	1812	AG32	258	183
Forrest, Uriah	Deed fr	Turner, Catherine & John Hawker	1792	A1-1	169	242
Forrest, Uriah	Deed to	Worthington, Charles, Dr., of G'tn.	1793	A1-2	447	55
Forrest, Uriah	Deed fr	French, George, of G'tn.	1794	B2A	001	001
Forrest, Uriah	Deed fr	Pierce, Isaac	1794	B2A	027	030
Forrest, Uriah	Deed fr	James, James	1794	A1-2	501	
Forrest, Uriah	Deed fr	Pierce, Isaac	1795	B2A	190	257

Party	What	Party	Year	Liber	Old	New
Forrest, Uriah	Deed fr	Deakins, William, Jr., of G'tn.	1795	B2A	209	288
Forrest, Uriah	Transfer to	Campbell, William	1797	B2B	474	167
Forrest, Uriah	Cert fr	Commissioners of Washington	1797	B2B	472	164
Forrest, Uriah	Deed fr	Polock, Isaac, of G'tn.	1797	C3	088	072
Forrest, Uriah	Transfer fr	Morris, Robert & James Greenleaf	1797	B2B	472	164
Forrest, Uriah	Deed fr	Morris, Robert, of Phila. et al	1798	C3	517	406
Forrest, Uriah	Deed fr	Beatty, Thomas Johnson	1798	C3	508	399
Forrest, Uriah	Deed to	Polock, Isaac	1798	C3	385	306
Forrest, Uriah	Agreement	Brown, Joel	1799	D4	397	377
Forrest, Uriah	Cert fr	Commissioners of Washington	1799	D4	361	347
Forrest, Uriah	Deed fr	Scott, Gustavus	1799	D4	388	370
Forrest, Uriah	Deed to	Scott, Gustavus	1799	D4	369	354
Forrest, Uriah	Deed to	Scott, Gustavus	1799	D4	371	356
Forrest, Uriah	Deed to	Scott, Gustavus	1799	D4	373	358
Forrest, Uriah	Deed to	Swann, John, Esq., of Balto.	1800	E5	400	374
Forrest, Uriah	Deed to	Caldwell, Timothy, of Phila.	1800	E5	365	347
Forrest, Uriah	Deed to	Mechlin, Joseph, late of Phila.	1800	E5	367	349
Forrest, Uriah	Deed to	Magruder, Ninian, Dr., of G'tn.	1800	E5	303	295
Forrest, Uriah	Deed to	State of Maryland	1800	E5	305	298
Forrest, Uriah	Deed to	Deblois, Lewis	1800	E5	359	342
Forrest, Uriah	Deed fr	Scott, Gustavus	1800	E5	200	192
Forrest, Uriah	Deed to	Busserd, John R., of Frederick Co.	1800	E5	243	237
Forrest, Uriah	Deed fr	Deakins, Francis	1800	E5	385	362
Forrest, Uriah	Deed fr	Commissioners of Washington	1800	F6	004	004
Forrest, Uriah	Deed to	Holmes, Hugh, of Winchester VA	1801	F6	243	163
Forrest, Uriah	Deed fr	Commissioners of Washington	1801	G7	047	059
Forrest, Uriah	Deed to	Hedrick, John	1801	G7	248	334
Forrest, Uriah	Deed to	Bailey, Theodorus et al	1801	G7	079	102
Forrest, Uriah	Deed to	Ham, Peter	1801	G7	131	171
Forrest, Uriah	Deed fr	Ham, Peter	1801	G7	308	430
Forrest, Uriah	Deed to	Van Cortlandt, Philip, of NY	1801	G7	079	102
Forrest, Uriah	Deed to	Harkness, Samuel	1801	G7	024	031
Forrest, Uriah	Deed fr	Plater, John Rousby	1801	G7	082	106
Forrest, Uriah	Deed to	Coombe, Benjamin, Kent Co. DE	1801	G7	023	029
Forrest, Uriah	Relinquish to	Stoddert, Benjamin	1801	G7	265	364
Forrest, Uriah	Deed to	Lingan, James M.	1801	G7	290	403
Forrest, Uriah	Deed to	Eliason, Ebenezer	1801	G7	026	033
Forrest, Uriah	Deed fr	Ham, Peter	1801	G7	132	173
Forrest, Uriah	Deed to	Bain, Quintin	1801	G7	001	002
Forrest, Uriah	Deed to	Fitzhugh, Philip	1801	G7	048	061
Forrest, Uriah	Deed to	Templeman, John	1801	G7	111	141
Forrest, Uriah	Deed fr	Deakins, Francis, of G'tn.	1801	G7	078	101
Forrest, Uriah	Deed to	Reintzel, Daniel	1802	G7	523	666
Forrest, Uriah	Deed to	Bain, Quinton	1802	G7	525	668
Forrest, Uriah	Deed to	Chandler, Walter Story	1802	G7	524	667
Forrest, Uriah	Deed fr	Templeman, John et al	1802	G7	529	674
Forrest, Uriah	Deed to	Plater, John R.	1802	H8	288	272
Forrest, Uriah	B. of S. to	Key, Philip Barton	1802	H8	256	243
Forrest, Uriah	Deed to	Carpenter, Thomas	1802	H8	119	115
Forrest, Uriah	Mortgage to	Plater, John R.	1802	H8	292	276
Forrest, Uriah	Deed to	Rinehart, Andrew	1802	H8	542	503
Forrest, Uriah	Deed fr	Deakins, Francis	1802	H8	272	258
Forrest, Uriah	Discharge	Bankruptcy	1802	H8	537	497
Forrest, Uriah	Deed to	Key, Philip B.	1802	H8	291	275
Forrest, Uriah	Deed to	Chandler, Walter S.	1802	I9	444	733

Party	What	Party	Year	Liber	Old	New
Forrest, Uriah	Deed to	Tousard, Louis	1802	I9	558	904
Forrest, Uriah	Deed to	Lingan, James M.	1802	I9	075	106
Forrest, Uriah	Deed to	Lowndes, Charles et al	1802	I9	075	106
Forrest, Uriah	Deed to	Plater, John R.	1802	I9	075	106
Forrest, Uriah	Deed to	Davidson, James	1802	I9	363	602
Forrest, Uriah	Deed to	Nourse, Joseph	1804	K10	313	319
Forrest, Uriah	Deed to	Brown, Joel	1804	K10	333	344
Forrest, Uriah	Deed to	Pearce, Isaac	1804	K10	315	321
Forrest, Uriah	Deed fr	Stoddert, Benjamin	1805	N13	001	001
Forrest, Uriah	B. of S. to	Templeman, John	1810	Y24	114	104
Forrest, Uriah & Benj. Stoddert	Deed fr	Pearce, Catherine, rel/o Benj. N.	1792	A1-1	063	93
Forrest, Uriah & Benj. Stoddert	Deed fr	Lower, Christian et al	1792	A1-1	151	217
Forrest, Uriah & Benj. Stoddert	Deed to	Carcand, David, of Calvert Co.	1792	A1-1	121	176
Forrest, Uriah & Wm. Deakins, Jr.	Cert fr	Commissioners of Washington	1797	B2B	473	166
Forrest, Uriah & Samuel Hanson	Deed to	Tingey, Thomas	1800	F6	092	056
Forrest, Uriah & Samuel Hanson	Deed to	Stoddert, Benjamin	1801	G7	330	461
Forrest, Uriah & Samuel Hanson	Deed to	Barry, James, heirs	1801	G7	002	003
Forrest, Uriah & Samuel Hanson	Deed to	Barry, James	1801	G7	003	004
Forrest, Uriah, assignee of	Deed to	Brown, Joel	1802	I9	054	074
Forrest, Uriah et al	Deed to	Beall, Thomas & John M. Gantt	1793	A1-1	227	314
Forrest, Uriah et al	Deed to	Greenleaf, James, New York NY	1794	B2A	086	111
Forrest, Uriah et al	Deed to	Beall, Thomas, of George	1795	B2A	166	222
Forrest, Uriah et al	Deed fr	Blodget, Samuel, now of Phila.	1795	B2A	265	371
Forrest, Uriah et al	Deed to	Scott, Gustavus	1795	B2A	263	367
Forrest, Uriah et al	Deed to	Stone, John H.	1795	B2A	172	230
Forrest, Uriah et al	Deed fr	Morris, Robert & John Nicholson	1796	B2B	566	302
Forrest, Uriah et al	Deed to	Davidson, Samuel	1797	B2B	613	369
Forrest, Uriah et al	R. of D. fr	Morris, Mary et al	1798	C3	364	292
Forrest, Uriah et al	Deed fr	Morris, Robert, of Phila. et al	1798	C3	362	289
Forrest, Uriah et al	Deed fr	Commissioners of Washington	1798	D4	137	119
Forrest, Uriah et al	Deed to	Plater, John Rowsly, of G'tn.	1798	D4	104	088
Forrest, Uriah et al	Deed fr	Commissioners of Washington	1798	D4	135	118
Forrest, Uriah et al	Deed to	Waters, Jonathan	1799	D4	236	219
Forrest, Uriah et al	Deed fr	Plater, John Rowsby, of G'tn.	1799	D4	194	177
Forrest, Uriah et al	Deed to	Plater, John Rowsby, of G'tn.	1800	E5	325	315
Forrest, Uriah et al	Deed to	Wilson, John Custis, Somerset Co.	1801	G7	119	153
Forrest, Uriah et al	Deed to	Wilson, Samuel & John Dennis	1801	G7	117	150
Forrest, Uriah et al	Deed to	Templeman, John & B. Stoddert	1801	G7	113	144
Forrest, Uriah et al	Deed to	McCoy, Robert	1801	G7	224	299
Forrest, Uriah et al	Bond to	United States	1801	G7	347	478
Forrest, Uriah et al	Deed to	Templeman, John	1801	G7	038	049
Forrest, Uriah et al	Deed to	Law, Thomas	1801	G7	014	017
Forrest, Uriah et al	Deed to	Prout, William	1802	G7	576	725
Forrest, Uriah et al	Deed to	Butler, John	1802	H8	265	251
Forrest, Uriah et al	Deed to	Yeaton, William	1802	H8	204	195
Forrest, Uriah et al	Deed to	Kerr, Alexander	1802	H8	348	324
Forrest, Uriah et al	Deed to	Cozens, William R.	1802	I9	581	942
Forrest, Uriah et al	Deed to	Cozens, William R.	1802	I9	583	944
Forrest, Uriah et al	Deed to	Stoddert, Benjamin	1802	I9	248	400
Forrest, Uriah et al	Deed to	Tousard, Louis	1802	I9	558	905
Forrest, Uriah et al	Deed to	Lanham, Elisha	1802	I9	361	598
Forrest, Uriah et al	Deed to	Chandler, Walter Story	1802	I9	050	068
Forrest, Uriah et al	Deed to	Parrott, Richard	1804	K10	369	382
Forrest, Uriah et al	Deed to	Thornton, William	1804	K10	116	125
Forrest, Uriah et al	Deed to	Parrott, Richard	1805	N13	218	187

Index to District of Columbia Land Records, 1792-1817

Party	What	Party	Year	Liber	Old	New
Forrest, Uriah, of G'tn.	Deed fr	Morris, Robert & John Nicholson	1796	B2B	577	320
Forrest, Uriah, of Montg. Co.	Deed fr	Casanave, Peter, of Montg. Co.	1796	B2B	530	246
Forrest, Uriah, of Montg. Co.	Deed to	Polock, Isaac	1797	B2B	647	410
Forrest, Uriah, of Montg. Co.	Cert fr	Commissioners of Washington	1797	B2B	476	169
Forrest, Uriah, of Montg. Co.	Deed to	Garey, Everard, of Montg. Co.	1797	B2B	625	384
Forrest, Uriah, of G'tn. et al	Deed fr	Duncanson, William Mayne	1797	C3	125	102
Forrest, Uriah, of Montg. Co.	Deed to	Polock, Isaac	1797	C3	123	101
Forrest, Uriah, of Montg. Co.	Deed fr	Beall, Thomas, of Samuel	1797	C3	062	50
Forrest, Uriah, of Montg. Co.	Deed fr	Stoddert, Benjamin, of G'tn.	1798	C3	379	303
Forrest, Uriah, of Montg. Co.	Deed fr	Stoddert, Benjamin, of G'tn.	1798	C3	453	357
Forrest, Uriah, of Montg. Co.	Deed fr	Stoddert, Benjamin, of G'tn.	1798	C3	458	360
Forrest, Uriah, of Montg. Co.	Deed to	Reintzel, Daniel, of G'tn.	1798	C3	386	308
Forrest, Uriah, of Montg. Co.	Deed to	Feburier, Nicholas	1798	C3	368	294
Forsyth, John & Josiah Meigs	D. of T. fr	Meigs, Samuel William et al	1815	AK35	421	330
Foster, John, of Alexa.	Deed fr	Polock, Isaac	1800	E5	169	159
Foster, John, of Alexa.	Deed to	Skyrin, of Phila.	1804	L11	055	55
Foster, Mahlon	B. of S. to	Foster, Sarah	1808	V21	070	056
Foster, Sarah	B. of S. fr	Foster, Mahlon	1808	V21	070	056
Fouke, George & Elizabeth	Deed to	Mayn, Adam, s/o John, of G'tn.	1812	AD29	152	119
Fowler, Ann	B. of S. fr	Fowler, William	1817	AO39	514	353
Fowler, Anne, wid/o Elijah	Deed to	Simms, Edward, of Charles Co.	1801	G7	256	349
Fowler, Benjamin	B. of S. to	Renner, Daniel et al	1804	L11	054	55
Fowler, Elisha	Deed to	Fowler, Thomas	1805	M12	253	254
Fowler, Elisha	B. of S. to	Thompson, Rachael, his dau.	1816	AL36	343	334
Fowler, John, of KY	Deed to	Caldwell, Elias B.	1802	H8	188	180
Fowler, Joseph	Deed fr	Prout, William	1816	AM37	001	001
Fowler, Jubb, of A.A. Co.	Deed to	Beall, Thomas & John M. Gantt	1793	A1-1	233	321
Fowler, Samuel	Deed fr	Anderson, Catherine	1808	T19	403	284
Fowler, Samuel	Deed fr	Prout, William	1809	V21	289	209
Fowler, Samuel	Release to	Anderson, Catherine	1812	AC28	261	191
Fowler, Samuel	D. of T. fr	Jarrad, George	1813	AE30	509	377
Fowler, Samuel	D. of T. fr	Jarrad, George	1815	AK35	049	038
Fowler, Thomas	Deed to	Bridges, John	1802	I9	533	871
Fowler, Thomas	Deed fr	Fowler, Elisha	1805	M12	253	254
Fowler, Thomas, insolvent	Deed to	Sheppard, Walter, trustee	1804	L11	343	312
Fowler, William	B. of S. to	Fowler, Ann	1817	AO39	514	353
Fox, Bartleson	Deed fr	Beatty, Charles, heirs of	1806	P15	330	218
Fox, Bartleson	Deed fr	Holmead, John	1811	Z25	445	350
Fox, Bartleson, of G'tn.	Deed fr	Scott, Sabret, of G'tn.	1804	K10	229	237
Fox, Bartleson, of G'tn.	B. of S. to	Lefevre, Lewis, of G'tn.	1807	Q16	224	152
Fox, Bartleson, trustee	Deed fr	Carlin, Wesley, insolvent	1815	AI34	001	001
Fox, Edward, auctioneer, et al	Deed to	Pratt, Henry et al	1797	C3	154	127
Fox, Edward et al	B. in C. fr	Pratt, Henry et al	1799	E5	003	003
Fox, George et al	Release to	Nourse, Joseph	1813	AF31	011	008
Fox, Joseph, Jr.	Deed fr	Polock, Isaac	1802	I9	410	680
Fox, Joseph, Jr., Westm. Co. VA	Deed to	Aborn, Henry	1810	Y24	383	346
Fox, Josiah	Deed fr	Astley, Thomas & Phineas Bond	1808	V21	109	081
Fox, Josiah	Manumis to	[ ], Edwin (negro)	1809	X23	279	221
Fox, Josiah	Manumis to	[ ], Betty (negro)	1809	X23	280	222
Fox, Josiah	Manumis to	[ ], William (negro)	1809	X23	281	222
Fox, Josiah	D. of T. to	Morgan, William, of G'tn.	1813	AE30	323	243
Foxall, Henry	Deed fr	Stoddert, Benjamin	1800	F6	090	055
Foxall, Henry	Deed fr	Scott, Sabret	1802	I9	471	776
Foxall, Henry	Deed fr	Lingan, James M.	1804	L11	005	6
Foxall, Henry	Manumis to	[ ], Henrietta (Negro)	1805	M12	144	140

Index to District of Columbia Land Records, 1792-1817

Party	What	Party	Year	Liber	Old	New
Foxall, Henry	Manumis to	[ ], Phillis (Negro)	1805	M12	377	387
Foxall, Henry	Deed fr	Threlkeld, John	1805	N13	037	038
Foxall, Henry	Deed fr	Deakins, Leonard et al	1805	O14	117	075
Foxall, Henry	Deed fr	Watson, John	1806	Q16	184	124
Foxall, Henry	Deed fr	Glascow, John	1807	S18	197	158
Foxall, Henry	Deed fr	Threlkeld, John	1808	V21	069	054
Foxall, Henry	Deed fr	Walls, James, Frederick Co. VA	1809	V21	281	202
Foxall, Henry	Deed fr	Deakins, Leonard M. & John Hoye	1809	X23	194	146
Foxall, Henry	Deed fr	Lingan, James M., of Montg. Co.	1810	Y24	195	179
Foxall, Henry	Deed fr	Shaw, Lemuel	1811	AA26	221	151
Foxall, Henry	Deed fr	Ober, Robert, of G'tn.	1811	AA26	215	147
Foxall, Henry	Deed fr	Jones, John G.	1811	AB27	108	088
Foxall, Henry	Manumis to	[ ], Jenny (C) and children	1811	AB27	116	095
Foxall, Henry	Manumis to	[ ], Lotty (C)	1811	AB27	115	094
Foxall, Henry	Deed fr	Morgan, William	1811	AC28	062	047
Foxall, Henry	Deed to	Parrott, Richard	1812	AC28	407	295
Foxall, Henry	Deed fr	Stoddert, Benjamin, Bladensburg	1812	AC28	418	302
Foxall, Henry	Mortgage fr	Parrott, Richard	1812	AC28	411	298
Foxall, Henry	Deed fr	Beall, Thomas, of Geo.	1812	AC28	419	303
Foxall, Henry	Deed fr	Owens, Isaac	1812	AC28	413	299
Foxall, Henry	Deed fr	Parrott, Richard	1812	AC28	416	301
Foxall, Henry	Deed fr	Parrott, Richard & Jno. Mountz, Jr.	1812	AD29	143	111
Foxall, Henry	Mortgage fr	Parrott, Richard	1814	AH33	188	172
Foxall, Henry	Deed fr	Walker, David	1815	AH33	535	458
Foxall, Henry	Manumis to	[ ], Rachael (C)	1816	AL36	356	347
Foxall, Henry	D. of T. to	Owens, Isaac et al	1816	AL36	357	348
Foxall, Henry	Manumis to	[ ], Frederick (C)	1816	AL36	354	344
Foxall, Henry	Manumis to	Shorter, Martha (C)	1816	AL36	353	344
Foxall, Henry	Manumis to	Shorter, Ann (C)	1816	AL36	355	345
Foxall, Henry	D. of T. fr	English, David, of G'tn.	1816	AL36	351	342
Foxall, Henry	Manumis to	[ ], Frederick (C)	1816	AL36	355	345
Foxall, Henry	Deed to	Mason, John, Gen.	1816	AM37	239	175
Foxall, Henry	Deed fr	Tillotson, Thomas & Margaret, NY	1817	AN38	075	059
Foxall, Henry et al	Deed fr	Eliason, Ebenezer & Ann	1809	V21	290	210
Foxall, Henry, of Phila. PA	Deed fr	Deakins, Francis, of G'tn.	1801	F6	148	091
Foxall, Henry, of G'tn.	Deed fr	Templeman, John, of G'tn.	1804	L11	009	9
Foxall, Henry, of Alexa.	Deed fr	Moscrop, Henry	1805	N13	135	129
Foxall, Henry, of G'tn.	Deed fr	King, James C., of G'tn.	1808	T19	222	162
Foxall, Henry, of G'tn.	Mortgage fr	Eliason, Ebenezer, of G'tn.	1809	W22	004	004
Foxall, Henry, of G'tn.	B. of S. to	Ott, John, of G'tn.	1810	X23	406	328
Foxall, Henry, of G'tn.	Lease fr	Eliason, Ebenezer, of G'tn. et al	1810	Z25	332	259
Foxall, Henry, of G'tn.	Deed fr	Magruder, Ninian, of G'tn.	1811	AA26	079	056
Foxall, Henry, of G'tn.	Release to	Glasco, John	1812	AD29	459	387
Foxall, Henry, of G'tn.	Deed fr	Magruder, Ninian, of G'tn.	1813	AE30	138	107
Foxall, Henry, of G'tn.	Deed fr	Parrott, Richard, of G'tn.	1813	AE30	143	111
Foxall, Henry, of G'tn.	Mortgage fr	Webster, Toppan	1813	AE30	139	108
Foxall, Henry, of G'tn.	Deed fr	Jones, John G.	1813	AE30	141	110
Foxall, Henry, of G'tn.	Deed fr	Smith, Clement, of G'tn.	1813	AE30	144	112
Foxall, Henry, of G'tn.	Deed fr	Patterson, Edgar, of G'tn.	1814	AG32	036	028
Foxall, Henry, of G'tn.	Deed fr	Eliason, Ebenezer & B. Hersey	1814	AH33	192	175
Foxall, Henry, of G'tn.	Deed fr	Dorsey, William H., of Montg. Co.	1814	AH33	186	170
Foxall, Henry, of G'tn.	Deed fr	Lee, Thomas Sim, of *Needwood*	1814	AH33	190	173
Foxall, Henry, of G'tn.	Deed fr	Patterson, Edgar, of G'tn.	1814	AG32	037	030
Foxall, Henry, of G'tn.	Deed fr	Smith, Walter, trustee of J. Lingan	1815	AH33	532	455
Foxall, Henry, of G'tn.	Deed fr	Kile, Alexander, of G'tn.	1815	AH33	528	452

Index to District of Columbia Land Records, 1792-1817 163

Party	What	Party	Year	Liber	Old	New
Foxall, Henry, of G'tn.	Release to	Watson, John, of Balto.	1815	AH33	551	472
Foxall, Henry, of G'tn.	Deed fr	Smith, Walter, trustee of J. Lingan	1815	AH33	529	453
Foxall, Henry, of G'tn.	Deed fr	Lambert, Moris, of G'tn.	1815	AH33	534	457
Foxall, Henry, of G'tn.	Deed to	Linkins, James, of G'tn.	1816	AL36	292	290
Foxall, Henry, of G'tn.	Deed fr	Woodward, Thomas & G. Cooke	1816	AL36	131	132
Foxall, Henry, of G'tn.	Deed to	Smith, Walter, agent	1816	AM37	204	151
Foxall, Henry, plt.	Suit	Tillotson, Thomas & Margaret, def.	1816	AN38	073	057
Foxall, Henry, trustee et al	Deed fr	Morgan, William, of G'tn.	1814	AH33	010	009
Foxhall, Henry, of G'tnl.	Mortgage fr	Beck, Richard, of G'tn.	1810	Y24	192	177
Foxon, William, trustee	B. of S. fr	Ricks, Joseph, insolvent	1808	T19	218	159
Foxton, William	Deed fr	Dorsey, William H.	1802	I9	272	444
Foxton, William	Deed fr	Dorsey, William H., of Balto.	1808	U20	134	077
Foyales, Thomas et al	Deed fr	Wigfield, Matthew	1808	U20	208	113
Foyle, Thomas	Deed to	Vint, John	1804	L11	380	339
Foyle, Thomas	B. of S. fr	Estep, Joseph	1814	AH33	319	275
Foyles, Thomas & Thomas Young	Deed to	Brown, Elizabeth	1813	AE30	167	132
Foyles, Thomas & Thomas Young	Deed to	Greenleaf, James, Allen Town PA	1814	AH33	299	259
Foyles, Thomas & J. Middleton	Deed fr	Mayhue, Clement & Mary	1816	AM37	099	079
Franc, Lewis, of Balto. MD	Release fr	Villard, Andrew Joseph	1812	AD29	173	138
Franc, Lewis [Frank]	D. of T. to	Villard, Andrew J.	1811	AA26	260	177
Francis, Thomas W. et al	D. of T. fr	Morris, Robert, of Phila. et al	1797	C3	192	161
Francis, Thomas W. et al	D. of T. fr	Morris, Robert, of Phila. et al	1797	C3	204	172
Francis, Thomas W. et al	Deed fr	Morris, Robert et al	1798	D4	030	025
Francis, Thomas W. et al	Deed fr	Hanson, Alexander Contee	1798	C3	490	385
Francis, Thomas W. et al	Deed fr	Commissioners of Washington	1800	E5	372	353
Francis, Thomas W. et al	Deed fr	Commissioners of Washington	1800	E5	369	350
Francis, Thomas W. et al	Deed fr	Commissioners of Washington	1801	F6	202	131
Francis, Thomas W. et al	Deed fr	Commissioners of Washington	1801	G7	281	389
Francis, Thomas W. et al	Deed to	Law, Thomas	1802	H8	351	327
Francis, Thomas W. et al	Deed to	Yeates, William	1802	H8	056	053
Francis, Thomas W. et al	Deed fr	Dorsey, William H. et al	1802	I9	568	920
Francis, Thomas W. et al	Deed to	Underwood, Robert et al	1802	I9	217	342
Francis, Thomas W. et al	Deed fr	Dorsey, William H.	1802	I9	263	426
Francis, Thomas W. et al	Deed fr	Tingey, Thomas	1802	I9	572	927
Francis, Thomas W. et al	Deed to	Tingey, Thomas	1802	I9	213	336
Francis, Thomas W. et al	Deed to	Van Ness, John P.	1806	P15	105	065
Francis, Thomas W. et al	Deed to	Voss, Nicholas	1807	S18	025	021
Francis, Thomas W. et al	Deed to	Tilghman, William, of Phila. et al	1808	T19	086	061
Francis, Thomas W. et al	Deed to	Cook, Orlando	1809	X23	245	190
Francis, Thomas W. et al	Deed fr	Munroe, Thomas, Supt.	1811	Z25	472	374
Francis, Thomas Willing et al	Deed fr	Greenleaf, James, of Phila. et al	1797	C3	154	127
Francis, Thomas Willing et al	Deed fr	Morris, Robert, of Phila. et al	1798	C3	301	243
Francis, Thomas Willing et al	P. of Atty. to	Greenleaf, James	1804	K10	101	107
Francis, Thomas Willing et al	Deed to	May, Frederick	1805	N13	108	102
Francis, Thomas Willing et al	Deed to	Sewall, Robert, of P.G. Co.	1805	N13	081	074
Francis, Thomas Willing et al	Deed to	Elliott, Samuel, Jr.	1806	O14	362	242
Francis, Thomas Willing et al	B. of S. fr	Prout, William	1809	W22	380	247
Francis, Thomas Willing et al	Quit to	Toole, Patrick	1809	X23	135	097
Francis, Thomas Willing et al	Deed to	Eliot, Samuel, Jr.	1809	W22	293	219
Francis, Thomas Willing et al	Deed to	Griffin, Lancelot	1810	X23	319	256
Francis, Thomas Willing, et al	Deed to	Mara, Philip O.	1810	Z25	340	266
Francis, Thomas Willing et al	Deed to	Matthews, William, Rev.	1811	AB27	342	282
Francis, Thomas Willing et al	Deed to	Weightman, Roger C.	1811	AB27	228	186
Francis, Thomas Willing et al	Deed to	Aborn, Henry	1812	AC28	470	334
Francis, Thomas Willing et al	Deed to	Varnum, James M.	1812	AC28	508	363

Party	What	Party	Year	Liber	Old	New
Francis, Thomas Willing et al	Deed to	Latrobe, Benjamim H.	1812	AC28	445	318
Francis, Thomas Willing et al	Deed to	Tingey, Thomas	1812	AC28	428	308
Francis, Thomas Willing et al	Deed to	Jones, Walter, Jr.	1812	AC28	400	290
Francis, Thomas Willing et al	Deed to	Weightman, Roger C.	1812	AD29	406	342
Francis, Thomas Willing et al	Deed to	Weightman, Roger C.	1812	AD29	409	346
Francis, Thomas Willing et al	Deed to	Weightman, Roger C.	1812	AD29	402	339
Francis, Thomas Willing et al	Deed to	Gales, Joseph, Jr.	1812	AE30	001	001
Francis, Thomas Willing et al	Deed to	Tuckfield, William H.P.	1813	AE30	230	184
Francis, Thomas Willing et al	Deed to	Van Ness, John P.	1813	AE30	485	360
Francis, Thomas Willing et al	Deed to	Smallwood, Samuel N.	1813	AF31	032	022
Francis, Thomas Willing et al	Deed to	Jones, Walter, Jr.	1813	AE30	328	246
Francis, Thomas Willing et al	Deed to	Heath, Nathaniel H.	1813	AE30	522	387
Francis, Thomas Willing et al	Deed fr	Miller, John, Jr. & Wm. Cranch	1814	AG32	330	240
Francis, Thomas Willing et al	Deed to	Van Ness, John P.	1814	AG32	313	229
Francis, Thomas Willing et al	Deed to	Glover, Charles	1814	AH33	302	261
Francis, Thomas Willing et al	Deed to	McMurray, William	1814	AH33	171	159
Francis, Thomas Willing et al	Deed to	Wayne, Francis	1814	AH33	377	326
Francis, Thomas Willing et al	Deed to	Johnson, James W.	1814	AH33	004	004
Francis, William, of Phila. PA	Deed fr	Lenthall, John	1808	V21	075	059
Francis, William, of Phila. PA	Deed to	Cocking, William	1808	V21	078	061
Frank, George	Deed to	Green, James	1802	H8	140	137
Frank, George	Deed to	Bayly, Daniel	1804	K10	158	169
Frank, George	Deed fr	Blagden, George, exr. of J. Emery	1813	AF31	022	015
Frank, George	Deed to	Franzoni, Gusseppe	1813	AF31	024	017
Frank, John	Qualify	Ensign in militia	1812	AD29	171	137
Frank, Lewis	Deed fr	Hendley, Richard	1814	AF31	496	363
Frank, Lewis & Mary Ann	Deed to	Villard, Andrew Joseph	1817	AO39	281	200
Frank, Lewis [Frank]	Deed fr	Villard, Andrew Joseph	1811	AC28	005	004
Franklin, George, c/o Nicholas	Cert. Free fr	Gilman, Jacob	1814	AG32	303	220
Franklin, James, c/o Nicholas	Cert. Free fr	Gilman, Jacob	1814	AG32	303	220
Franklin, Jane, c/o Nicholas	Cert. Free fr	Gilman, Jacob	1814	AG32	303	220
Franklin, John, c/o Nicholas	Cert. Free fr	Gilman, Jacob	1814	AG32	303	220
Franklin, Nicholas	Deed fr	Brady, Nathaniel	1808	U20	123	070
Franklin, Nicholas	Deed fr	Liverpool, Moses & George Beall	1814	AG32	165	118
Franklin, Nicholas & Henry Adams	Deed fr	Liverpool, Moses & George Beall	1810	Y24	301	274
Franklin, Phillis, c/o Nicholas	Cert. Free fr	Gilman, Jacob	1814	AG32	303	220
Franklin, Robert, c/o Nicholas	Cert. Free fr	Gilman, Jacob	1814	AG32	303	220
Franklin, Susan, c/o Nicholas	Cert. Free fr	Gilman, Jacob	1814	AG32	303	220
Franks, Mary	Lease fr	Maddox, Notley, of P.G. Co.	1816	AM37	067	055
Franzoni, Gusseppe	Deed fr	Frank, George	1813	AF31	024	017
Frazer, Calline, d/o Patk. & Cath.	Cert Free fr	Brent, Robert	1811	AB27	396	326
Frazer, James, s/o Patk. & Cath.	Cert Free fr	Brent, Robert	1811	AB27	396	326
Frazer, Margaret, d/o Patk. & Cath.	Cert Free fr	Brent, Robert	1811	AB27	396	326
Frazer, Mary, d/o Patk. & Cath.	Cert Free fr	Brent, Robert	1811	AB27	396	326
Frazer, Richard	Qualify		1802	I9	171	261
Frazer, Richard	Slaves	From King William Co. VA	1804	K10	242	
Frazier, Patrick	Lease fr	Shoemaker, David	1810	Y24	527	463
Frazier, Patrick (negro)	Manumis fr	Dearborn, Henry	1808	U20	126	072
Frazier, Richard	Assign fr	Knight, James	1802	H8	374	348
Frazier, William & Mary et al	Deed to	Reintzel, Anthony	1809	W22	364	237
Free, John	Deed fr	Wigfield, James & Ann	1808	U20	157	089
Free, John	Deed to	Free, John, Jr.	1809	X23	103	075
Free, John	Deed fr	Mayhue, James	1811	AB27	114	093
Free, John, Jr.	Deed fr	Free, John	1809	X23	103	075
Free, John, sadler	Deed to	Greenleaf, James, of Phila.	1812	AB27	201	165

Index to District of Columbia Land Records, 1792-1817

Party	What	Party	Year	Liber	Old	New
Free, John, shoemaker	Deed fr	Lanham, Asa, h/o Notley	1804	K10	157	168
Free, Sarah & her son John, Jr.	Deed fr	Standage, Eleazer	1811	AB27	106	087
Freeman, Constant	Slaves	From Norfolk VA	1816	AL36	431	411
Freeman, Constant	Mortgage to	Smith, Edmund & E.H. Nicholl	1816	AM37	280	206
Freeman, Constant	Deed fr	Smith, Edmund & Edw. H. Nicoll	1816	AM37	354	256
Freeman, John & John Shorter	B. of S. fr	Johnson, Thomas	1816	AM37	334	243
French, Anne et al	D. Gift fr	French, John B., Sr.	1813	AF31	235	163
French, Ariana	Deed fr	Munroe, Thomas, Supt.	1804	L11	158	157
French, Ariana	Deed fr	Holmead, John, Anthony & S.	1804	L11	401	356
French, Ariana, exrx. of George	Deed to	Weems, John, Dr., of G'tn.	1806	P15	237	157
French, Ariana, exrx. of George	Deed to	West, Joseph	1806	P15	156	102
French, Arianna	Deed fr	Holmead, Anthony	1799	D4	199	182
French, Arianna	Deed fr	Holmead, John, Anthony & S.	1804	L11	396	351
French, Arianna, dev/o George	Deed to	King, George & Adam	1804	K10	290	291
French, Arianna, devisee of Geo.	Deed to	French, George, of G'tn.	1806	Q16	202	136
French, Arianna et al	Deed to	Greenleaf, James	1796	B2B	445	128
French, Arianna, of G'tn.	Deed to	Brown, Joel, of G'tn.	1805	N13	062	057
French, Arianna, wid/o Geo. et al	Deed to	Jones, Charles C., of Montg. Co.	1810	Z25	086	065
French, Bernard	Deed fr	Gross, Jacob	1802	H8	108	105
French, Bernard	Transfer fr	Gross, Jacob	1802	H8	107	104
French, Charles	Deed fr	Beall, Thomas, of Geo.	1812	AC28	483	344
French, Charles	Deed fr	French, George et al	1813	AF31	249	173
French, Charles & Mariamne	Release to	Lufborough, Nathan	1812	AD29	050	036
French, Charles & Mariamne	Deed to	Busy, Samuel, of Montg. Co.	1814	AH33	228	200
French, Charles et al	Deed to	Wetzel, Frederick	1812	AD29	017	012
French, Charles et al	Deed to	Risener, Henry	1812	AD29	445	374
French, Charles et al	Deed to	French, Robert	1813	AF31	250	174
French, Charles et al	Deed to	French, George	1813	AF31	247	171
French, Charles et al	Deed to	Weems, Elizabeth	1813	AF31	253	176
French, Daniel	Agreement	Brent, Robert & Tench Ringgold	1811	AB27	379	314
French, Elizabeth et al	D. Gift fr	French, John B., Sr.	1813	AF31	235	163
French, George	Deed fr	Graham, William, of Balto.	1794	B2A	142	186
French, George	Deed fr	Walker, Nathan	1798	D4	020	017
French, George	Deed to	Weatherall, John	1798	D4	168	149
French, George	Deed fr	Polock, Isaac	1798	D4	160	141
French, George	Deed fr	Beatty, Thomas, Jr., Frederick Co.	1798	D4	162	143
French, George	Deed fr	Brackenridge, John	1813	AE30	392	289
French, George	Deed fr	Weems, Elizabeth et al	1813	AF31	247	171
French, George	Mortgage to	Brackenridge, John	1813	AE30	406	299
French, George	Deed to	Smith, Richard, of G'tn.	1815	AK35	016	013
French, George	D. of T. to	Smith, Clement, of G'tn.	1817	AN38	023	019
French, George, children of	Deed to	Jones, Charles C., of Montg. Co.	1810	Z25	086	065
French, George et al	Deed fr	Scott, George, exr. of George	1795	B2B	368	020
French, George et al	Deed to	Greenleaf, James, New York NY	1796	B2B	445	128
French, George et al	Deed to	French, Robert	1813	AF31	250	174
French, George et al	Deed to	French, Charles	1813	AF31	249	173
French, George et al	Deed fr	Weems, Elizabeth, of G'tn., exrx.	1813	AE30	390	288
French, George et al	Deed to	Weems, Elizabeth	1813	AF31	253	176
French, George, heirs of	Deed to	French, George	1813	AF31	247	171
French, George, of G'tn.	Deed to	Forrest, Uriah	1794	B2A	001	001
French, George, of G'tn.	Deed fr	Coleman, Joseph, of Alexa.	1794	B2A	105	138
French, George, of G'tn.	Deed fr	Sterret, James & Samuel Porter	1795	B2B	371	022
French, George, of G'tn.	Deed fr	Porter, Samuel & Jas. Sterrett	1795	B2B	371	022
French, George, of G'tn.	Deed fr	Raymer, Michael, Frederick Town	1796	B2B	395	058
French, George, of Montg. Co.	Deed fr	Low, Andrew, of Frederick Co.	1796	B2B	394	056

Party	What	Party	Year	Liber	Old	New
French, George, of G'tn.	Deed to	McClan, Robert, of G'tn.	1796	B2B	528	242
French, George, of G'tn.	Deed fr	Coleman, Joseph, of Alexa.	1798	C3	403	319
French, George, of Montg. Co.	D. of T. fr	King, William, of P.G. Co.	1798	C3	478	377
French, George, of G'tn.	Deed to	Lee, Henry, Gen., of VA	1798	D4	166	147
French, George, of Montg. Co.	Deed to	Bayly, William, of P.G. Co.	1798	C3	389	309
French, George, of G'tn.	Deed to	Mason, John, merchant	1799	D4	181	162
French, George, of G'tn.	Deed fr	French, Arianna, devisee of Geo.	1806	Q16	202	135
French, George, of G'tn.	Deed fr	Lee, Edmund Jennings, of Alexa.	1812	AD29	338	282
French, George, of G'tn., heirs of	Deed to	Key, Philip B., of Montg. Co.	1813	AE30	507	375
French, George, of G'tn.	Deed to	Lanham, Elisha, of G'tn.	1813	AE30	111	085
French, George, of G'tn.	Deed fr	Dorsey, William H., of Montg. Co.	1814	AH33	200	182
French, George, of G'tn.	Deed fr	Davidson, Lewis Grant, of G'tn.	1814	AH33	183	168
French, George, of G'tn.	Deed to	Lanham, Elisha, of G'tn.	1814	AH33	243	211
French, George, of G'tn.	Deed to	Smith, Richard, of G'tn.	1814	AH33	199	181
French, George, of G'tn.	Deed to	Smith, Richard, of G'tn.	1814	AH33	292	253
French, George, plt.	Suit	Courts, John, heirs of, def.	1815	AK35	018	014
French, James	B. of S. to	Russ, Samuel	1804	K10	329	339
French, John B.	Deed fr	Sanders, Thomas	1806	Q16	113	073
French, John B.	Deed to	Bussard, Daniel	1808	V21	080	062
French, John B.	Cert Free to	Fletcher, Mary	1810	Z25	132	104
French, John B., Jr. et al	D. Gift fr	French, John B., Sr.	1813	AF31	235	163
French, John B., Sr.	D. Gift to	French, John B., Jr. et al	1813	AF31	235	163
French, Mariamne C. et al	Deed to	Risener, Henry	1812	AD29	445	374
French, Mariamne C. et al	Deed to	Wetzel, Frederick	1812	AD29	017	012
French, Mariamne C. & John Peter	Deed to	Wetzel, Frederick	1817	AN38	280	205
French, Robert	Deed fr	Weems, Elizabeth et al	1813	AF31	250	174
French, Robert et al	Deed to	French, George	1813	AF31	247	171
French, Robert et al	Deed to	Weems, Elizabeth	1813	AF31	253	176
French, Robert et al	Deed to	French, Charles	1813	AF31	249	173
French, Robert et al	Deed fr	Weems, Elizabeth, of G'tn., exrx.	1813	AE30	390	288
French, Robert, of G'tn.	D. of T. to	Ott, John, of G'tn.	1815	AI34	261	294
French, Samuel	B. of S. to	Kearnes, Francis, of G'tn.	1801	G7	173	231
French, William et al	Cert fr	Commissioners of Washington	1793	B2A	322	452
French, William et al	Cert fr	Commissioners of Washington	1793	B2A	321	451
French, William, of Henry Co. VA	Deed to	Belt, John	1793	A1-2	437	46
French, William, of Henry Co. VA	Deed fr	Watson, John, of Henry Co. VA	1793	A1-2	431	39
French, William, of Henry Co. VA	Deed fr	Stoddert, Benj. & Wm. Deakins	1793	A1-2	432	40
Fresh, William, of G'tn.	Deed fr	Holmead, Anthony	1809	W22	378	245
Fresh, William, of G'tn.	Deed fr	Hoye, John, of G'tn.	1813	AF31	412	297
Fresh, William, of G'tn.	Deed to	Suter, Alexander, of G'tn.	1814	AG32	201	140
Fresh, William, of G'tn.	Deed fr	Glover, Charles, trustee	1814	AG32	021	016
Frethey, Edward	Deed fr	Blodget, Samuel, of Phila.	1801	G7	299	416
Frethy, Edward	Deed fr	Dorsey, William H.	1802	I9	282	461
Frethy, Edward et al	Bond fr	Broadwell, James	1804	K10	286	289
Frethy, Edward, of OH	Assign to	Varden, Ezra	1807	R17	132	102
Fricke, Augustus	Mortgage fr	Carpenter, Thomas	1802	I9	487	801
Fricke, Augustus, mer., of Phila.	Deed fr	Carpenter, Thomas, taylor	1804	L11	222	207
Fricke, Augustus, of Phila. PA	Deed fr	Ford, Lewis	1807	S18	063	053
Frickfield, William H.	Deed fr	Munroe, Thomas, Supt.	1802	I9	132	198
Friend, James	Deed to	Sinclair, George	1804	M12	034	035
Friend, James	Deed fr	Prout, William	1815	AK35	396	311
Friend, James, baker	Deed fr	Tingey, Thomas, Gent.	1804	L11	039	39
Friese, Philipo R.I., of Balto. MD	Deed fr	Moscrop, Henry, of MD	1802	H8	514	472
Frost, Amariah	Deed to	Ladd, John G., of Alexa.	1800	E5	312	304
Frost, Amariah	Deed fr	Commissioners of Washington	1800	E5	190	181

Party	What	Party	Year	Liber	Old	New
Frost, Amariah	Mortgage to	Jones, Thomas	1801	G7	394	528
Frost, Amariah	B. of S. to	O'Neale, William	1802	H8	027	026
Frost, Amariah & Esther	Deed to	Ladd, John Gardiner, of Alexa.	1800	E5	309	300
Frost, John T.	B. of S. fr	Sims, Henry	1802	H8	382	355
Frost, John T.	B. of S. fr	Tuckfield, William H.P.	1802	I9	489	803
Frost, John T.	Deed fr	Bunch, Jane	1804	K10	318	325
Frost, John T.	B. of S. to	Miller, Peter	1806	Q16	070	044
Frost, John T., trustee	B. of S. fr	Richmond, Braddock	1811	AB27	304	250
Frost, John T.	B. of S. to	McCormick, Alexander	1812	AC28	306	223
Frost, John Thomas, insolvent	B. of S. to	Kenner, James, trustee	1805	M12	406	421
Frthey, Edw.	Assign to	Betz, Frederick	1801	G7	301	419
Frush, William, of G'tn.	Deed fr	Deakins, Leonard & John Hoye	1807	R17	231	173
Fry, Godfrey	B. of S. fr	Koontz, Jacob	1806	O14	352	235
Fry, James	Lease fr	Prout, William	1802	G7	546	693
Fry, James	Lease fr	Prout, William	1803	K10	094	100
Fry, James	Deed fr	Ratcliffe, William	1806	P15	263	174
Fry, James	Deed to	Radcliff, William	1806	Q16	224	153
Fry, James Thomas et al	Deed fr	Carleton, Joseph, of G'tn.	1804	L11	282	259
Fry, John, assignees of	Deed to	Waln, Robert, Jr., of Phila., mer.	1815	AK35	150	115
Fry, John, Jr., of Phila. PA	Deed fr	Walker, George	1797	B2B	694	475
Fry, Thomas	Mortgage to	Naylor, John L. & William Moore	1811	AC28	041	030
Fry, Thomas	Cert Free to	Rounds, Kitty	1814	AF31	517	379
Fry, Thomas	Cert Free to	Williams, Treasy	1814	AF31	517	379
Fry, Thomas, insolvent	Deed to	Heard, James B., trustee	1806	P15	349	231
Fuller, Oliver et al	Deed fr	Prout, William	1802	H8	217	207
Fuller, Oliver, of Balto.	Deed fr	Brown, Amos, of Balto.	1805	M12	018	018
Funk, Henry	Deed fr	Funk, Henry, Sr., heirs of	1792	A1-1	126	184
Funk, Henry, of Washington Co.	Deed to	Deakins, William, Jr., of G'tn.	1793	A1-1	198	278
Funk, Henry, Sr., heirs of	Deed to	Funk, Henry, Jr.	1792	A1-1	126	184
Funk, Jacob, of KY	Deed to	Stoddert, Benjamin & W. Deakins	1793	A1-1	192	271
Funk, Jacob, of Jefferson Co. KY	Deed to	Stoddert, Benjamin & W. Deakins	1793	A1-1	189	268
Funk, Jacob, of P.G. Co., yeoman	Deed to	Stricker, George, of Frederick Co.	1811	Z25	425	333
Funk, Jacob, yeoman	Deed to	Kurtz, Frederick, of Frederick Co.	1793	A1-1	186	263
Furguson, William, of P.G. Co.	Deed to	Laird, John, of G'tn.	1804	K10	328	337
Furgusson, Robert, of Charles Co.	Deed to	Afflick, Thomas, of G'tn.	1796	B2B	399	063

Party	What	Party	Year	Liber	Old	New
G						
Gaddes, Samuel	Deed Gift fr	Gaddes, William	1806	O14	328	218
Gaddes, William	Deed Gift to	Gaddes, Samuel	1806	O14	328	218
Gadsby, John, of Balto.	Deed fr	Caton, William, of Alexa.	1810	X23	332	265
Gadsden, James, Charleston SC	Deed to	Law, Edmund	1817	AN38	297	217
Gadsden, James, Charleston SC	Release fr	Fisher, James, Charleston SC	1817	AN38	292	214
Gadsden, Philip	Cert fr	Commissioners of Washington	1796	B2B	454	142
Gadsden, Philip	Deed to	Fisher, James	1806	P15	043	026
Gailor, Thomas	Deed to	Dawes, Isaac et al	1802	I9	294	483
Gailor, Thomas, of G'tn.	Mortgage to	Wingard, Abraham, of G'tn.	1804	K10	124	134
Gaines, Richard	Assign fr	Manning, Charles	1804	K10	305	309
Gaines, Richard	Deed fr	Lanham, Elisha et al	1805	N13	202	176
Gaines, Richard	Deed to	Jones, Raphael	1805	N13	215	186
Gaines, Richard	Deed fr	Pickerill, Benjamin & Alethe	1809	V21	357	260
Gaines, Richard	Deed to	Burrows, Joseph	1811	AA26	201	138
Gaines, Richard	Manumis to	[ ], Harry (C)	1813	AE30	171	136
Gaines, Richard, Hamilton Co. OH	Deed to	Trundle, Horatio, of G'tn.	1813	AF31	317	226
Gaines, Richard, Hamilton Co. OH	Deed to	Calder, William, of G'tn.	1813	AE30	340	254
Gaines, Richard, Hamilton Co. OH	Deed fr	Mountz, John, of G'tn.	1813	AE30	317	238
Gaines, Richard, of G'tn.	Deed fr	Lanham, Elisha, of G'tn.	1808	T19	030	023
Gaines, Richard, of G'tn.	Deed fr	Lanham, Elisha, of G'tn.	1810	Y24	096	087
Gaines, Richard, of G'tn.	Deed to	Lanham, Elisha, of G'tn.	1810	Y24	254	234
Gaines, Richard, of G'tn.	Deed fr	Beall, Thomas B., of G'tn.	1810	Y24	044	038
Gaines, Richard, of G'tn.	D. of T. to	Mountz, John, Jr., of G'tn.	1811	AA26	298	201
Gaines, Richard, of Cincinnati OH	Deed to	Crawford, William, of G'tn.	1813	AF31	149	100
Gaines, Richard, of Cincinnati OH	Deed to	Patterson, Edgar, of G'tn.	1813	AF31	332	237
Gaines, Richard, of Cincinnati OH	Deed to	Beall, Thomas B., of G'tn.	1813	AE30	309	232
Gaines, Richard, of Cincinnati OH	Deed to	Webster, Toppan	1813	AE30	543	402
Gains, Richard, of G'tn.	Deed fr	Lanham, Elisha, of G'tn.	1809	W22	071	053
Gains, Richard, of G'tn.	Deed fr	Lanham, Elisha, of G'tn.	1810	Y24	279	255
Gains, Richard, of G'tn.	Lease fr	Peter, David, of G'tn.	1810	Y24	093	083
Gains, Richard, of G'tn.	Deed fr	English, David, of G'tn.	1811	Z25	165	130
Gaither, Benjamin & Daniel	Deed to	Ross, Andrew & S. Pleasonton	1814	AH33	336	290
Gaither, Benjamin & Henry, MD	Deed to	Vinson, Charles	1817	AO39	113	088
Gaither, Benjamin & Daniel, MD	Deed to	King, Robert	1817	AO39	176	130
Gaither, Henry	Cert fr	Commissioners of Washington	1800	F6	049	031
Gaither, Henry	Deed fr	Lee, Thomas S.	1802	I9	360	596
Gaither, Henry	Release fr	Munroe, Thomas, Supr.	1812	AD29	258	213
Gaither, Henry, Col., U.S.A.	Deed fr	Commissioners of Washington	1800	F6	075	046
Gaither, Henry, Col.	Release fr	Beatty, John M. & Charles A.	1806	O14	203	134
Gaither, Henry, Col.	Deed fr	Snyder, Abraham	1806	O14	202	133
Gaither, Henry, of Montg. Co.	Deed to	Jones, Charles Courts, Montg. Co.	1810	Y24	115	105
Gale, Joseph T. (C)	Affidavit	Prouse, Peregrine	1804	K10	187	
Galer, Thomas, insolvent	Deed to	Edwards, John, trustee	1804	L11	094	97
Gales, Joseph	Cert. fr	Munroe, Thomas, Supt.	1812	AC28	514	367
Gales, Joseph & Sarah J.M.	Deed to	Jones, Walter	1815	AI34	422	442
Gales, Joseph, Jr.	Deed fr	Pratt, Henry et al	1812	AE30	001	001
Gales, Joseph, Jr. et al	Deed fr	Wilson, William	1813	AE30	194	156
Gales, Joseph, Jr.	Deed fr	Pratt, Henry et al	1815	AK35	400	314
Gales, Joseph, Jr. & Sarah J.M.	Deed to	Caldwell, Elias B.	1816	AK35	519	409
Gales, Joseph, Jr.	Deed fr	Cranch, William	1816	AL36	151	151
Gales, Joseph, Jr. & Sarah J.M.	Deed to	Eliot, Samuel, Jr.	1816	AL36	156	156
Gales, Joseph, Jr.	B. of S. fr	Young, Richard	1816	AM37	496	363
Gales, Joseph, Jr.	Lease fr	Van Ness, John P.	1816	AM37	388	279
Gales, Joseph, Jr.	Lease fr	Van Ness, John P.	1816	AM37	385	277

Index to District of Columbia Land Records, 1792-1817

Party	What	Party	Year	Liber	Old	New
Gales, Joseph, Jr.	Mortgage to	Ewell, Thomas	1816	AM37	167	127
Gales, Joseph, Jr.	Deed to	Andrews, George	1816	AO39	027	021
Gales, Joseph, Jr.	Deed fr	Kerr, Alexander	1817	AN38	288	210
Gales, Joseph, Jr.	D. of T. to	Wallach, Richard	1817	AO39	257	185
Gallaher, Robert, of Martinsburgh	Lease fr	Van Ness, John P. & Marcia	1815	AI34	453	467
Galor, Thomas	Deed fr	Weatherall, John	1802	I9	293	481
Gamble, Thomas	Deed to	Woodward, John	1800	E5	147	136
Gamble, Thomas, of Montg. Co.	Deed fr	Balch, Stephen B., of Montg. Co.	1797	C3	136	111
Gamble, William	Marriage	Lee, Ann	1817	AN38	363	268
Gamble, William, insolvent	Deed to	Wheaton, Joseph, trustee	1810	Y24	266	244
Gammon, James, of Montg. Co.	Deed to	Beatty, Charles, of G'tn.	1796	B2B	423	096
Gannan, James, of G'tn.	Deed fr	Suttle, Henry, of G'tn.	1812	AC28	437	313
Gannon, James	Deed fr	Rezner, Elizabeth & Henry	1807	S18	291	328
Gannon, James	B. of S. fr	Greer, James	1808	T19	294	215
Gannon, James	Deed fr	Chandler, Walter Story	1808	V21	054	043
Gannon, James	Mortgage fr	Howard, John	1809	V21	302	220
Gannon, James	Mortgage to	Moore, George & George Clyver	1810	Y24	235	217
Gannon, James	Deed fr	Chandler, Walter Story	1810	Y24	070	062
Gannon, James	Mortgage to	Ott, John	1812	AD29	492	416
Gannon, James	Deed fr	Beatty, Charles A.	1812	AD29	089	067
Gannon, James	Release fr	Ott, John	1817	AN38	516	374
Gannon, James	D. of T. to	Ott, John	1817	AO39	501	344
Gannon, James	Deed to	Ott, John	1817	AN38	379	281
Gannon, James & John Ott	Assign fr	McMurray, Joseph	1810	Z25	241	188
Gannon, James & John Ott	B. of S. fr	McMurray, Joseph	1810	Y24	537	471
Gannon, James & James Moore	Deed fr	Murdock, John	1811	AC28	013	010
Gannon, James & John Ott, G'tn.	Assign to	Ritchie, Abner	1815	AI34	101	115
Gannon, James et al	B. of S. fr	Daugherty, Vincent	1811	Z25	556	442
Gannon, James, hairdresser	Deed fr	O'Reilly, Henry, merchant, of G'tn.	1800	E5	171	161
Gannon, James, of G'tn.	Deed fr	McClan, Robert, of G'tn.	1796	B2B	529	244
Gannon, James, of G'tn.	Deed fr	Rigdon, Thomas, of G'tn.	1797	C3	064	52
Gannon, James, of G'tn.	Deed to	O'Reilly, Henry, of G'tn.	1798	D4	082	069
Gannon, James, of G'tn.	Deed fr	Davidson, John	1798	C3	506	398
Gannon, James, of G'tn.	Deed to	Parrott, Richard, of Kent Co.	1798	D4	040	033
Gannon, James, of G'tn.	Deed to	Parrott, Richard, of G'tn.	1801	G7	375	507
Gannon, James, of G'tn.	Deed fr	Thecker, James et al	1804	M12	012	013
Gannon, James, of G'tn.	Deed fr	Kennedy, James, of G'tn.	1808	T19	194	139
Gannon, James, of G'tn.	Deed fr	Duncastle, Sarah, of G'tn.	1810	Y24	456	405
Gannon, James, of G'tn.	Deed to	Moore, James	1813	AE30	371	275
Gannon, James, of G'tn.	Deed fr	Johns, Richard H., of G'tn.	1815	AI34	401	424
Gannon, James, of G'tn.	Deed fr	Reizner, Henry	1815	AI34	538	542
Gannon, James, of G'tn.	Deed to	Ott, John, Dr.	1815	AI34	540	544
Gannon, James, trustee	Assign fr	McCutchens, James, insolvent	1808	V21	012	009
Gant, Francis et al	Deed fr	Templeman, John	1802	H8	375	349
Gant, John Mackall et al	Deed to	Hewitt, John	1802	H8	458	421
Gant, John Mackall	Deed fr	Beall, Thomas, of George	1802	H8	327	306
Gantt, Edward	Deed to	Forrest, Joseph	1805	N13	282	232
Gantt, Edward	Assign to	Herty, Thomas, trustee	1809	V21	140	102
Gantt, Edward, Dr.	Deed to	Cox, John	1804	L11	018	18
Gantt, Edward, Dr.	Deed fr	Magruder, Zadock, Sr. et al	1804	K10	164	174
Gantt, Edward N. et al	Assign to	Serra, Augustin	1813	AE30	376	279
Gantt, Edward, ship carpenter	Deed fr	Chandler, Walter Story	1809	V21	145	106
Gantt, Edward, to move to KY	P. of Atty. to	Smallwood, Samuel N.	1810	Z25	348	272
Gantt, Fielder, of P.G. Co.	Deed to	Williams, John S.	1813	AE30	360	267
Gantt, James M. et al	Deed fr	Maddox, Notley, sheriff	1798	D4	060	050

Party	What	Party	Year	Liber	Old	New
Gantt, James M. et al	Deed to	Pratt, Henry et al	1802	I9	568	920
Gantt, John M. & Thomas Beall	Deed fr	Beatty, Charles	1792	A1-1	025	38
Gantt, John M. & Thomas Beall	Deed fr	Johnson, Thomas & Daniel Carroll	1792	A1-1	044	66
Gantt, John M. & Thomas Beall	Deed fr	Smith, Amos, of Frederick Co.	1792	A1-1	080	117
Gantt, John M. & Thomas Beall	Deed fr	Woodard, Clement	1792	A1-1	015	23
Gantt, John M. & Thomas Beall	Deed fr	Price, Thomas & Michael Stooker	1792	A1-1	106	154
Gantt, John M. & Thomas Beall	Deed fr	Fisher, Margaret & John	1792	A1-1	078	115
Gantt, John M. & Thomas Beall	Deed fr	Bayer, Michael & Peter Engle	1792	A1-1	086	126
Gantt, John M. & Thomas Beall	Deed fr	Holmead, Anthony	1792	A1-1	007	12
Gantt, John M. & Thomas Beall	Deed fr	Walker, George	1792	A1-1	017	27
Gantt, John M. & Thoams Beall	Deed fr	Doll, Conrad, of Frederick Co.	1792	A1-1	084	123
Gantt, John M. & Thomas Beall	Deed fr	Peter, Robert	1792	A1-1	020	30
Gantt, John M. & Thomas Beall	Deed fr	Porter, Samuel & James Steret	1792	A1-1	141	205
Gantt, John M. & Thomas Beall	Deed fr	Hooe, Robert Townsend, Alexa.	1792	A1-1	055	81
Gantt, John M. & Thomas Beall	Deed fr	Schell, Charles, of Frederick Co.	1792	A1-1	135	196
Gantt, John M. & Thomas Beall	Deed fr	Stoddert, Benjamin	1792	A1-1	005	8
Gantt, John M. & Thomas Beall	Deed fr	Byer, Jacob	1792	A1-1	072	106
Gantt, John M. & Thomas Beall	Deed fr	Lingan, James McCubbin	1792	A1-1	022	34
Gantt, John M. & Thomas Beall	Deed fr	Conway, Richard & James Craik	1792	A1-1	057	85
Gantt, John M. & Thomas Beall	Deed fr	Myer, Henry & Frederick Reahl	1792	A1-1	090	131
Gantt, John M. & Thomas Beall	Deed fr	Grahame, Richard	1792	A1-1	061	90
Gantt, John M. & Thomas Beall	Deed fr	Markell, William, s/o Conrad	1792	A1-1	163	234
Gantt, John M. & Thomas Beall	Deed fr	Denton, Jacques	1792	A1-1	144	207
Gantt, John M. & Thomas Beall	Deed fr	Strever, Joachim, Frederick Co.	1792	A1-1	094	137
Gantt, John M. & Thomas Beall	Deed fr	Shellman, John, Sr., Frederick Co.	1792	A1-1	096	140
Gantt, John M. & Thomas Beall	Deed fr	Cramphin, Thomas	1792	A1-1	049	73
Gantt, John M. & Thomas Beall	Deed fr	Beall, William Murdock	1792	A1-1	159	227
Gantt, John M. & Thomas Beall	Deed fr	Beatty, Thomas, of Frederick Co.	1792	A1-1	100	146
Gantt, John M. & Thomas Beall	Deed fr	Neale, James, s/o Bernard	1792	A1-1	059	88
Gantt, John M.	Com. fr	Carroll, Daniel, Thos. Johnson	1792	A1-1	001	1
Gantt, John M. & Thomas Beall	Deed fr	Rench, John, of Washington Co.	1792	A1-1	137	199
Gantt, John M. & Thoams Beall	Deed fr	Miller, Samuel, of Frederick Co.	1792	A1-1	098	143
Gantt, John M. & Thomas Beall	Deed fr	Carroll, Daniel, of *Duddington*	1792	A1-1	012	19
Gantt, John M. & Thomas Beall	Deed fr	Murdock, George	1792	A1-1	133	193
Gantt, John M. & Thomas Beall	Deed fr	Young, Notley	1792	A1-1	010	16
Gantt, John M. & Thomas Beall	Deed fr	Kolb, Michael, Jr.	1792	A1-1	074	109
Gantt, John M. & Thomas Beall	Deed fr	Ott, Adam, of Washington Co.	1792	A1-1	131	190
Gantt, John M. & Thomas Beall	Deed fr	Raymer, Michael & Joseph Doll	1792	A1-1	076	112
Gantt, John M. & Thomas Beall	Deed fr	Young, Abraham	1792	A1-1	029	45
Gantt, John M. & Thomas Beall	Deed fr	Young, William	1792	A1-1	003	5
Gantt, John M. & Thomas Beall	Deed fr	McCleery, Henry, of Frederick Co.	1792	A1-1	139	202
Gantt, John M. & Thoams Beall	Deed fr	Lingenfelter, Ann, wid/o John	1792	A1-1	088	129
Gantt, John M. & Thomas Beall	Deed fr	Mantz, John, of Frederick Co.	1792	A1-1	070	103
Gantt, John M. & Thomas Beall	Deed fr	Magruder, John Read, merchant	1792	A1-1	119	173
Gantt, John M. & Thomas Beall	Deed fr	Young, Notley & George Digges	1792	A1-1	042	63
Gantt, John M. & Thomas Beall	Deed fr	Koontz, Henry, Low, & Kamp	1792	A1-1	102	148
Gantt, John M. et al	Deed fr	Davidson, Baire & Kirshimer	1792	A1-1	110	160
Gantt, John M. et al	Deed fr	Wishair, Appetonia, wid/o George	1792	A1-1	092	134
Gantt, John M. & Thomas Beall	Deed fr	Davidson, Samuel	1792	A1-1	027	41
Gantt, John M. & Thomas Beall	Deed fr	Pierce, James	1792	A1-1	035	52
Gantt, John M. & Thomas Beall	Deed fr	Boarman, Raphael	1792	A1-1	064	94
Gantt, John M. & Thomas Beall	Deed fr	Walter, Henry, of Frederick Co.	1792	A1-1	082	120
Gantt, John M. & Thomas Beall	Deed fr	Johnson, James & Roger	1792	A1-1	047	71
Gantt, John M. & Thomas Beall	Deed fr	Brent, George, of Stafford Co. VA	1792	A1-1	037	56
Gantt, John M. & Thomas Beall	Deed fr	Slater, Jonathan	1792	A1-1	032	48

Index to District of Columbia Land Records, 1792-1817

Party	What	Party	Year	Liber	Old	New
Gantt, John M. & Thomas Beall	Deed fr	Thomas, Zimmerman & Kemp	1792	A1-1	108	157
Gantt, John M. & Thomas Beall	Deed fr	Brogden, William & Tur. Wootton	1792	A1-1	052	77
Gantt, John M. et al	Deed fr	Burnes, David	1792	A1-1	002	1
Gantt, John M. & Thomas Beall	Deed fr	Shover, Barbara, wid/o Simon	1792	A1-1	104	152
Gantt, John M. & Thomas Beall	Deed fr	Thomas, Philip	1792	A1-1	147	212
Gantt, John M. & Thomas Beall	Deed fr	Beatty, Charles, Sr.	1792	A1-1	128	186
Gantt, John M. & Thomas Beall	D. of T. fr	Morton, Thomas	1792	A1-1	046	68
Gantt, John M. & Thomas Beall	Deed fr	Calvert, Elizabeth	1793	A1-1	220	306
Gantt, John M. & Thomas Beall	Deed fr	Warring, Marsham et al	1793	A1-1	371	478
Gantt, John M. & Thomas Beall	Deed fr	Scyle, John, of G'tn.	1793	A1-1	315	415
Gantt, John M. & Thomas Beall	Deed fr	Brookes, John Smith	1793	A1-1	305	404
Gantt, John M. & Thomas Beall	Deed fr	Anderson, George & G. Thompson	1793	A1-1	317	418
Gantt, John M. & Thomas Beall	Deed fr	Hairy, David, exr. of Martin	1793	A1-1	351	456
Gantt, John M. & Thomas Beall	Deed fr	Davidson, Samuel	1793	A1-1	358	464
Gantt, John M. & Thomas Beall	Deed fr	Hepburn, Samuel	1793	A1-1	329	432
Gantt, John M. & Thomas Beall	Deed fr	Beanes, William	1793	A1-1	300	399
Gantt, John M. & Thomas Beall	Deed fr	Beall, John	1793	A1-1	381	488
Gantt, John M. & Thomas Beall	Deed fr	Henderson, Richard	1793	A1-1	202	282
Gantt, John M. & Thomas Beall	Deed fr	Coolidge, Samuel Judson	1793	A1-1	307	406
Gantt, John M. & Thomas Beall	Deed fr	Flick, Andrew, of Orange Co. VA	1793	A1-1	296	393
Gantt, John M. & Thomas Beall	Deed fr	Tilghman, Richard, of Q.A. Co.	1793	A1-1	270	363
Gantt, John M. & Thomas Beall	Deed fr	Matthews, Daniel, of VA	1793	A1-1	261	354
Gantt, John M. & Thomas Beall	Deed fr	Steuart, John	1793	A1-1	204	285
Gantt, John M. & Thomas Beall	Deed fr	Dulaney, Walter	1793	A1-1	217	303
Gantt, John M. & Thomas Beall	Deed fr	Schnebley, Henry	1793	A1-1	364	471
Gantt, John M. & Thomas Beall	Deed fr	Garlick, Joseph	1793	A1-1	336	439
Gantt, John M. & Thomas Beall	Deed fr	Leeke, Ann	1793	A1-1	331	434
Gantt, John M. & Thomas Beall	Deed fr	Barclay, Petit, Poland	1793	A1-1	276	371
Gantt, John M. & Thomas Beall	Deed fr	Mackie, Lawson & Browne	1793	A1-1	292	389
Gantt, John M. & Thomas Beall	Deed fr	Klinger, Henry	1793	A1-1	369	476
Gantt, John M. & Thomas Beall	Deed fr	Hill, Henry, of Phila. PA	1793	A1-1	289	386
Gantt, John M. & Thomas Beall	Deed fr	Ross, David, Horatio & Archibald	1793	A1-1	254	345
Gantt, John M. & Thomas Beall	Deed fr	Earle, James, of Kent Co.	1793	A1-1	287	383
Gantt, John M. & Thomas Beall	Deed fr	Addison, Walter D.	1793	A1-1	211	294
Gantt, John M. & Thomas Beall	Deed fr	Williams, Thomas Owen	1793	A1-1	327	429
Gantt, John M. & Thomas Beall	Deed fr	Stuart, Charles	1793	A1-1	247	337
Gantt, John M. & Thomas Beall	Deed fr	Hollyday, James, of Q.A. Co.	1793	A1-1	284	380
Gantt, John M. & Thomas Beall	Deed fr	Fowler, Jubb, of Anne Arundel Co.	1793	A1-1	233	321
Gantt, John M. & Thomas Beall	Deed fr	Stewart, Charles & J. McCulloch	1793	A1-1	348	453
Gantt, John M. & Thomas Beall	Deed fr	Brice, John, of Annapolis	1793	A1-1	346	451
Gantt, John M. & Thomas Beall	Deed fr	Richmond, Christopher, in Phila.	1793	A1-1	279	374
Gantt, John M. & Thomas Beall	Deed fr	Tilghman, James, of Q.A. Co.	1793	A1-1	282	377
Gantt, John M. & Thomas Beall	Deed fr	Hall, Benjamin & Elizabeth C.	1793	A1-1	267	360
Gantt, John M. & Thomas Beall	Deed fr	Beall, James, s/o James	1793	A1-1	321	422
Gantt, John M. & Thomas Beall	Deed fr	Clagett, Hezekiah	1793	A1-1	249	339
Gantt, John M. & Thomas Beall	Deed fr	Hemsley, William & Sarah	1793	A1-1	251	342
Gantt, John M. & Thomas Beall	Deed fr	Millikin, Mark, of PA	1793	A1-1	187	265
Gantt, John M. & Thomas Beall	Deed fr	Magrath, William	1793	A1-1	313	412
Gantt, John M. & Thomas Beall	Deed fr	Mantz, Casper, reps. of	1793	A1-1	256	348
Gantt, John M. & Thomas Beall	Deed fr	Scott, Upton	1793	A1-1	208	291
Gantt, John M. & Thomas Beall	Deed fr	Ferrell, James	1793	A1-1	333	437
Gantt, John M. & Thomas Beall	Deed fr	Carroll, Charles, of *Carrollton*	1793	A1-1	215	300
Gantt, John M. & Thomas Beall	Deed fr	Adams, Margaret	1793	A1-1	272	366
Gantt, John M. & Thomas Beall	Deed fr	Addision, John, Jr. & Thomas G.	1793	A1-1	213	297
Gantt, John M. & Thomas Beall	Deed fr	Buchanan, Thomas	1793	A1-1	302	401

Party	What	Party	Year	Liber	Old	New
Gantt, John M. & Thomas Beall	Deed fr	Lee, Thomas Sim & Mary	1793	A1-1	259	351
Gantt, John M. & Thomas Beall	Deed fr	Medtart, Jacob, of Frederick	1793	A1-1	231	318
Gantt, John M. & Thomas Beall	Deed fr	Warring, Henry, devisee of Bazil	1793	A1-1	374	481
Gantt, John M. & Thomas Beall	Deed fr	Dick, Mason & Thomas	1793	A1-1	309	408
Gantt, John M. & Thomas Beall	Deed fr	Golden, Samuel, s/o Frederick	1793	A1-1	383	490
Gantt, John M. & Thomas Beall	Deed fr	Ridenhour, David	1793	A1-1	323	425
Gantt, John M. & Thomas Beall	Deed fr	Crawford, David & Nathaniel	1793	A1-1	298	396
Gantt, John M. & Thomas Beall	Deed fr	Tilghman, Peregrine	1793	A1-1	206	288
Gantt, John M. & Thoams Beall	Deed fr	Hill, Henry	1793	A1-1	354	460
Gantt, John M. & Thomas Beall	Deed fr	Johnson, Thomas & Ph. Thomas	1793	A1-1	389	496
Gantt, John M. & Thomas Beall	Deed fr	Campbell, Francis et al	1793	A1-1	274	369
Gantt, John M. & Thomas Beall	Deed fr	Davidson, John, of Annapolis	1793	A1-1	224	311
Gantt, John M. & Thomas Beall	Deed fr	Manavill, Patrick & Mary	1793	A1-1	361	468
Gantt, John M. & Thomas Beall	Deed fr	Ham, Peter	1793	A1-1	237	326
Gantt, John M. & Thomas Beall	Deed fr	Johns, Lingan, Deakins et al	1793	A1-1	227	314
Gantt, John M. & Thomas Beall	Deed fr	Wolgamoth, John	1793	A1-1	366	473
Gantt, John M. & Thomas Beall	Deed fr	Hoffman, Jacob, of Balto.	1793	A1-2	421	30
Gantt, John M. & Thomas Beall	Deed fr	Zeller, Jacob	1793	A1-2	413	22
Gantt, John M. & Thomas Beall	Deed fr	Peter, Robert	1793	A1-2	395	3
Gantt, John M. & Thomas Beall	Deed fr	Warring, Basil	1793	A1-2	429	37
Gantt, John M. & Thomas Beall	Deed fr	Bowie, Fielder et al	1793	A1-2	392	1
Gantt, John M. & Thomas Beall	Deed fr	King, William	1793	A1-2	433	42
Gantt, John M. & Thoams Beall	Deed fr	Fitzhugh, William	1793	A1-2	443	52
Gantt, John M. & Thomas Beall	Deed fr	Casey, John	1793	A1-2	406	15
Gantt, John M. & Thomas Beall	Deed fr	Jenifer, Daniel, Jr., devisee of D.	1793	A1-2	409	18
Gantt, John M. & Thomas Beall	Deed fr	Worman, Henry, of Frederick Co.	1793	A1-2	440	49
Gantt, John M. & Thomas Beall	Deed fr	Chiswell, Joseph N.	1793	A1-2	426	34
Gantt, John M. & Thomas Beall	Deed fr	Tilley, John	1793	A1-2	401	9
Gantt, John McDade & Thomas Beall	Deed fr	McDade, John W. & Milley	1794	A1-2	479	84
Gantt, John M.	Protest fr	Nicholson, John	1796	B2B	601	353
Gantt, John M.	Request fr	Washington, George, Pres.	1796	B2B	588	336
Gantt, John M. et al	Deed fr	Dulany, Matthew	1797	B2B	626	385
Gantt, John M. & Thomas Beall	Deed to	Commissioners of Washington	1797	B2B	616	372
Gantt, John M.	Division fr	Peter, Robert, of G'tn.	1799	D4	273	257
Gantt, John M. et al	Division btw	Thompson, James et al	1799	D4	267	251
Gantt, John M.	Deed to	Martin, Luther	1802	I9	208	326
Gantt, John M., of Bladensburgh	Deed to	Southgate, John, of Norfolk VA	1804	L11	252	232
Gantt, John M., of P.G. Co.	Deed fr	Beall, Thomas, of George, G'tn.	1804	L11	142	143
Gantt, John M., of P.G. Co.	Deed to	Southgate, John, of Norfolk VA	1804	L11	250	231
Gantt, John M., of P.G. Co.	Deed to	Southgate, John, of Norfolk VA	1804	L11	253	234
Gantt, John M., of P.G. Co.	Deed fr	Beall, Thomas, of George, G'tn.	1804	L11	143	144
Gantt, John M., of P.G. Co.	Deed to	Southgate, John, of Norfolk VA	1804	L11	255	235
Gantt, John M., of P.G. Co.	Deed to	Southgate, John, of VA	1804	L11	249	230
Gantt, John Mackall et al	Deed fr	Burnes, David	1792	A1-1	002	1
Gantt, John Mackall, of G'tn.	Deed fr	Davidson, Samuel	1797	C3	130	106
Gantt, John Mackall et al	Deed to	Livers, Anthony	1801	G7	463	599
Gantt, John Mackall	Deed fr	Davidson, Samuel	1801	G7	075	098
Gantt, John Mackall, of P.G. Co.	Deed to	Southgate, John, of Norfolk VA	1804	L11	256	236
Gantt, John Mackall, of P.G. Co.	Deed to	Shaaf, John Thomas, Annapolis	1807	R17	196	148
Gantt, Thomas	Deed fr	Lowndes, Charles	1802	I9	266	431
Gantt, Thomas T.	Deed fr	Stoddert, Benjamin	1802	I9	267	432
Gantt, Thomas T., of G'tn.	Deed fr	Robertson, Thomas, of G'tn.	1813	AF31	036	025
Gantt, Thomas T.	Slave	From Maryland	1813	AE30	291	221
Gantt, Thomas T.	Deed fr	Reintzel, Daniel, of G'tn.	1813	AE30	098	075
Gantt, Thomas T., of G'tn.	Deed to	Bogenreiff, Valentine, of G'tn.	1815	AI34	002	003

Index to District of Columbia Land Records, 1792-1817

Party	What	Party	Year	Liber	Old	New
Gantt, Thomas T., of G'tn.	Deed fr	Kingsbury, Horatio, of Montg. Co.	1815	AI34	001	001
Gantt, Thomas T.	D. of T. fr	Kelly, John	1816	AL36	029	031
Gantt, Thomas T.	Deed fr	Brookes, Joseph, of G'tn.	1816	AL36	032	034
Gantt, Thomas T.	Deed fr	West, Stephen et al	1816	AL36	035	036
Gantt, Thomas T., of G'tn.	Deed fr	Magruder, James A., of G'tn.	1816	AL36	330	324
Gantt, Thomas T.	Deed fr	Brookes, Joseph	1816	AM37	248	182
Gantt, Thomas T., of G'tn.	D. of T. fr	Hull, Jacob, of G'tn.	1816	AM37	499	365
Gantt, Thomas T., of G'tn.	Deed fr	Wagner, Jacob, of G'tn.	1816	AL36	328	321
Gantt, Thomas T., of G'tn.	Deed to	Ward, Ulysses, of G'tn.	1817	AN38	456	329
Gantt, William V., of G'tn. et al	Deed fr	Livres, Ignatius, of G'tn.	1816	AM37	007	006
Gardener, John & James C. King	Deed to	Smith, Samuel Harrison	1807	R17	387	293
Gardener, Thomas, of G'tn.	B. of S. to	Holliday, William, of G'tn.	1810	Z25	088	067
Gardiner, John	Mortgage to	King, James Carroll, of G'tn.	1801	G7	381	513
Gardiner, John	Lease fr	Davidson, Samuel	1801	G7	383	515
Gardiner, John	Mortgage to	Stockwell, Mark, of G'tn.	1802	I9	089	127
Gardiner, John	Lease fr	Underwood, Robert	1802	I9	549	892
Gardiner, John	Deed fr	Laird, John, exr. of J. Carleton	1816	AO39	040	033
Gardiner, John, of Phila. PA et al	Deed fr	Fitzsimons, Charles, Phila. et al	1805	N13	021	023
Gardiner, Peter	Deed fr	King, Ezekial	1802	I9	535	876
Gardiner, William P.	Mortgage fr	Hunt, Jeremiah	1814	AH33	216	192
Gardner, Esther	Deed fr	Aborn, Henry	1812	AC28	220	164
Gardner, Esther	Deed to	Nourse, Joseph	1813	AF31	515	377
Gardner, Esther	Deed fr	Boyd, Washington	1813	AF31	292	208
Gardner, Hetty	Slave	From Philadelphia PA	1809	W22	023	017
Gardner, Isaac S.	Slave Cert.	[ ], Sam (C), age 7	1811	AA26	007	005
Gardner, James et al	Agreement	Waugh, James, of VA	1802	I9	113	165
Gardner, John	Lease fr	Lovell, William	1802	G7	583	732
Gardner, John	Lease to	Stockwell, Mark	1802	G7	587	736
Gardner, John	Deed to	Stockwell, Mark	1802	H8	547	508
Gardner, John et al	Deed to	Waugh, James, Sr., Fairfax Co.	1804	L11	230	213
Gardner, John Frs., Charles Co.	Deed fr	Densley, Hugh et al	1802	G7	501	639
Gardner, John, of G'tn.	B. of S. to	Clark, Joseph, of G'tn.	1804	K10	216	226
Gardner, Mary	Slaves	From Charles Co. MD	1804	K10	214	
Gardner, Peter	Agreement	Bushby, William	1801	G7	080	104
Gardner, William P.	Convey fr	McDonald, Alexander et al	1811	AA26	181	124
Gardner, William P.	Deed fr	McDonald, Alexander, now Balto.	1812	AD29	270	222
Gardner, William P.	Deed fr	Ott, John, trustee, of G'tn.	1812	AD29	273	225
Gardner, William P.	Deed fr	Granger, Gideon	1814	AH33	177	164
Gardner, William P.	Deed to	Caldwell, Timothy, of Phila. PA	1814	AH33	278	242
Gardner, William P.	Deed fr	Smith, Walter, of G'tn., trustee	1816	AM37	052	043
Gardner, William P.	Deed to	Johnson, Thomas	1816	AL36	222	227
Garey, Ann	Deed fr	Wirt, John	1815	AI34	030	035
Garey, Ann, of G'tn.	Deed fr	Hedges, Nicholas, of G'tn.	1815	AI34	442	457
Garey, Everard	Deed fr	Renner, Daniel	1814	AH33	030	027
Garey, Everard	Deed to	Nixdorff, Samuel	1814	AH33	066	059
Garey, Everard	Deed fr	Beatty, Charles A.	1814	AH33	029	026
Garey, Everard & Anne et al	Deed to	Holmead, John	1810	Y24	180	165
Garey, Everard, of Montg. Co.	Deed fr	Forrest, Uriah, of Montg. Co.	1797	B2B	625	384
Garey, Everard, of G'tn.	Deed fr	Beatty, Charles, heirs of	1806	O14	283	187
Garey, Everard, of G'tn.	Deed to	Carter, Jacob, of G'tn.	1812	AC28	478	339
Garey, Everard, of G'tn.	Deed fr	Reintzel, Valentine, of G'tn.	1814	AH33	327	282
Garey, Everard, of G'tn.	Deed to	McChesney, William, of G'tn.	1814	AH33	222	196
Garey, Everard, of G'tn.	Lease to	Reintzel, Valentine, of G'tn.	1815	AH33	403	348
Garlick, Joseph	Deed to	Anderson, George, of G'tn.	1792	A1-1	054	80
Garlick, Joseph	Deed to	Beall, Thomas & John M. Gantt	1793	A1-1	336	439

Index to District of Columbia Land Records, 1792-1817

Party	What	Party	Year	Liber	Old	New
Garlick, Joseph, of G'tn.	Deed to	King, William, of G'tn.	1794	B2A	024	027
Garlick, Joseph, of G'tn.	Deed to	Neale, John Baptist, of Alexa.	1797	C3	070	57
Garner, Jesse	Deed fr	Stone, Edward	1814	AG32	092	069
Garner, Joseph, of G'tn.	D. of T. fr	Smith, Edward L., of G'tn.	1809	W22	136	097
Garner, Joseph, of G'tn.	Deed to	Stewart, William, of G'tn.	1810	Y24	020	017
Garretty, Murtaugh et al	Deed fr	Roe, Cornelius McDermot	1801	G7	379	511
Garretty, Timothy et al	Deed fr	Roe, Cornelius McDermot	1801	G7	379	511
Garrigues, Abraham et al	Deed to	Underwood, Robert	1810	Y24	133	121
Garrigues, Abraham M., et al	Deed to	Brooke, Samuel	1811	AB27	264	216
Gary, Ann, exrx. of Everard, G'tn.	Deed to	Reintzel, Valentine, of G'tn.	1815	AI34	477	487
Gary, Ann, of G'tn.	Lease to	Lacey, John, of G'tn.	1816	AL36	429	409
Gary, Ann, of G'tn.	Lease to	Thompson, Woodward, of G'tn.	1816	AL36	426	407
Gary, Ann, wid/o Everard of G'tn.	Deed to	Dial, Anna Statia, of G'tn.	1815	AI34	073	082
Gary, Everard	Deed fr	Bohrer, Mary	1802	I9	212	333
Gary, Everard	Deed fr	Dial, Annastatia	1806	Q16	197	133
Gary, Everard	B. of S. fr	Dial, Annastatia	1806	P15	319	211
Gary, Everard	Agreement	Shultz, Henry	1809	X23	183	136
Gary, Everard, of G'tn.	Deed fr	King, George, of G'tn.	1801	G7	401	534
Gary, Everard, of G'tn.	Deed to	Bussard, Daniel, of G'tn.	1804	K10	104	111
Gary, Everard, of G'tn.	Deed fr	Evans, Samuel & Hannah, of PA	1805	N13	161	149
Gary, Everard, of G'tn.	Deed fr	Cloud, Joseph, melter & refiner	1805	N13	164	151
Gary, Everard, of G'tn.	Deed fr	Waters, Jonathan, of A.A. Co.	1808	U20	014	009
Gary, Everard, of G'tn.	Deed fr	Baltzel, John, of Frederick Town	1809	W22	352	228
Gary, Everard, of G'tn.	Deed fr	Waters, Jonathan, of A.A. Co.	1811	AB27	325	268
Gassaway, Charles et al	Deed fr	Dawes, Isaac et al	1805	M12	147	143
Gassaway, Charles, exrs. of	Deed to	Peter, John, of G'tn.	1817	AO39	245	177
Gassaway, Charles, Montg. Co.	Deed to	Peter, John, of G'tn.	1817	AO39	245	177
Gates, Amelia, alias Rider	B. of S. fr	Rider, William	1809	W22	058	043
Gates, Elizabeth	Birth	December 29, 1782	1814	AH33	233	
Gates, Leonard	B. of S. to	Venable, Teresa	1814	AH33	119	112
Gates, Leonard	Deed to	Venable, Joseph	1815	AH33	422	363
Gates, Margaret, of Charles Co.	Marriage	Overton, Caleb (C)	1814	AH33	233	
Gatton, Azariah	B. of S. fr	Tompkins, James	1805	M12	185	186
Gatton, Azariah	Deed to	McKim, James & Thomas Herty	1806	Q16	181	121
Gatton, Azariah	B. of S. to	Baker, Samuel	1806	Q16	139	091
Gatton, Azariah	Deed fr	Baker, Samuel	1806	P15	281	185
Gatton, Azariah	B. of S. fr	Baker, Samuel	1806	P15	280	185
Gatton, Azariah	Deed to	McKim, James & Thomas Herty	1808	T19	053	039
Gatton, Azariah et al	Deed fr	Prout, William	1806	P15	229	152
Gatton, Azariah et al	Deed to	Serra, Augustin [Sara]	1806	Q16	104	068
Gatton, Azariah, of Alexa. Co.	B. of S. fr	Armstrong, Andrew	1808	T19	079	057
Gatton, Elisha, s/o Azariah	Indenture to	King, Benjamin, blacksmith, etc.	1811	AB27	271	222
Gearvis, Henry [Jearvis]	B. of S. to	Newton, Ignatius & Isaac Wilson	1817	AN38	339	249
Geary, Everard, of G'tn.	Deed fr	Pearce, Thomas, of G'tn.	1800	F6	106	065
Gebhart, John, of Frederick Co.	Deed to	Bohrer, George, of G'tn.	1812	AD29	145	113
Gellett, Hellen	Slaves	From VA	1809	W22	063	048
George, James	Deed to	Grose, Jacob	1802	I9	061	084
Georgetown, Beatty & Hawkins	Lots		1799	E5	466	
Georgetown Building Company	Deed fr	Melvin, James, of G'tn.	1808	T19	206	148
Georgetown Building Company	Deed fr	Green, Charles D., Somerset Co.	1808	T19	203	145
Georgetown Building Company	Deed fr	Beatty, Charles A.	1817	AO39	294	210
Georgetown College, President of	Deed fr	Young, Nicholas	1810	Y24	009	008
Georgetown, Corporation of	Cede fr	Dorsey, William H.	1797	B2B	619	376
Georgetown, Corporation of	Deed fr	Reintzel, Anthony	1797	B2B	619	377
Georgetown, Corporation of	Cede fr	Beatty, Thomas Jr.	1797	B2B	619	376

Index to District of Columbia Land Records, 1792-1817   175

Party	What	Party	Year	Liber	Old	New
Georgetown, Corporation of	Deed fr	Beall, Thomas, s/o George	1798	D4	145	127
Georgetown, Corporation of			1799	E5	406	
Georgetown, Corporation of	Deed fr	King, Adam, of G'tn.	1802	I9	129	192
Georgetown, Corporation of	Deed fr	Mitchell, John, of G'tn.	1802	I9	130	194
Georgetown, Corporation of	Deed fr	Magruder, George B. et al	1805	N13	091	083
Georgetown, Corporation of	Bond fr	Williams, Elisha O. et al	1805	N13	094	086
Georgetown, Corporation of	Deed fr	Beatty, John M. & Charles A.	1805	O14	001	001
Georgetown, Corporation of	Deed fr	Mason, John, of *Mason's Island*	1805	O14	051	030
Georgetown, Corporation of	Bond fr	Mackall, Leonard	1806	O14	392	262
Georgetown, Corporation of	Deed fr	Murdock, Addison	1806	P15	146	095
Georgetown, Corporation of	Bond fr	Magruder, George B.	1806	O14	394	263
Georgetown, Corporation of	Deed to	Beatty, John M. & Charles A.	1807	S18	387	308
Georgetown, Corporation of	Deed fr	Beatty, John M. & Charles A.	1807	R17	339	258
Georgetown, Corporation of	Bond fr	Mackall, Leonard et al	1808	T19	258	190
Georgetown Lancaster School	Deed fr	Bohrer, Jacob, of G'tn.	1812	AD29	107	082
Georgetown Lancaster School	Deed fr	Peter, George, of G'tn.	1812	AD29	109	083
Georgetown Lancaster School	Bond to	Mayor of Georgetown	1812	AC28	493	352
Georgetown Lots and Plats	Survey	Deakins, Francis et al	1803	K10	031	31
Georgetown, Mayor & Council	Deed to	Turner, Samuel, Jr.	1808	U20	330	178
Georgetown, Mayor & Aldermen	Deed to	Corcoran, Thomas, of G'tn.	1814	AG32	371	269
Georgetown, Mayor, Aldermen etc.	Deed to	Bowie, Washington	1814	AG32	179	127
Georgetown, Mayor of, et al	Deed to	Steuart, David	1808	U20	260	138
Gerrard, George	Deed fr	Prout, William	1814	AG32	245	175
Gerrard, George [Jarrad]	Deed fr	Prout, William	1814	AG32	245	175
Getty, Robert & Andrew Ross	Deed fr	Lee, Thomas S., of G'tn.	1810	Y24	045	039
Getty, Robert & Margaret, of G'tn.	Partition	Ross, Andrew & Hannah, of G'tn.	1811	AB27	240	196
Getty, Robert et al	Suit ads	Potomac Company	1812	AG32	258	183
Getty, Robert, of G'tn.	Deed to	Marbury, William	1811	AB27	243	199
Getty, Robert, of G'tn.	Partition	Ross, Andrew, of G'tn.	1812	AC28	247	182
Getty, Robert, of G'tn.	Lease to	Robb, John N., of G'tn.	1814	AG32	104	078
Getty, Robert, of G'tn.	Convey to	Clagett, Darius	1815	AK35	473	371
Getty, Robert, of G'tn.	Mortgage fr	Clagett, Darius, of G'tn.	1816	AM37	437	314
Geyer, Daniel	Deed fr	Burrows, Joseph	1802	I9	534	873
Geyer, Daniel	B. of S. to	Pringle, George	1807	R17	411	310
Geyer, Daniel, Sharpsburgh MD	Deed to	Granger, Gideon	1806	Q16	168	111
Gibbs, Nicholas, of G'tn.	Deed fr	Beall, John, of G'tn.	1793	A1-1	192	272
Gibbs, Nicholas, of Balto.	Deed to	Kaldenbauch, Andrew, of G'tn.	1796	B2B	611	365
Giberson, Eliza, of Phila. et al	Deed fr	Giberson, William & Jane, of Phila.	1811	AB27	141	117
Giberson, Mary, of Phila. et al	Deed fr	Giberson, William & Jane, of Phila.	1811	AB27	141	117
Giberson, Meribah, of Phila. et al	Deed fr	Giberson, William & Jane, of Phila.	1811	AB27	141	117
Giberson, William	Partition	Sandford, George	1805	M12	116	109
Giberson, William	Deed fr	Young, Notley	1810	Y24	446	396
Giberson, William & Jane, of Phila.	Deed to	Giberson, Mary et al	1811	AB27	141	117
Giberson, William et al	Deed fr	Van Ness, John P.	1802	I9	498	817
Gibson, Eleanor	B. of S. fr	Gibson, Robert	1809	X23	275	217
Gibson, Eleanor	B. of S. fr	Gibson, John	1809	X23	296	236
Gibson, Gerrard	B. of S. to	Bryan, Thomas	1808	U20	009	006
Gibson, John	B. of S. to	Gibson, Eleanor	1809	X23	296	236
Gibson, Joshua (C)	Manumis fr	Fenwick, Helena	1813	AF31	098	066
Gibson, Richard	B. of S. fr	Jones, Frederick P.	1816	AL36	226	231
Gibson, Richard, of G'tn.	Deed fr	Dixon, James, of G'tn.	1814	AG32	338	244
Gibson, Robert	B. of S. to	Gibson, Eleanor	1809	X23	275	217
Gibson, Thomas, of G'tn.	B. of S. fr	Sutorius, Mary Ann	1804	L11	101	107
Gideon, Jacob	D. of T. to	McClary, James	1815	AH33	414	357
Gilchrist, James	Cert fr	Commissioners of Washington	1800	F6	065	040

Index to District of Columbia Land Records, 1792-1817

Party	What	Party	Year	Liber	Old	New
Gilchrist, James, of Phila. PA	Cert fr	Commissioners of Washington	1792	B2A	285	398
Gildy, John	Qualify	Ensign 1st regiment	1813	AE30	472	351
Gilhart, John	Deed fr	Stoddert, Benjamin	1802	I9	524	858
Gillaspie, George, of Phila. et al	Deed fr	Bullus, John, Dr.	1804	L11	066	68
Gillaspie, George, of Phila. et al	Deed fr	Dorsey, William Hammond	1804	L11	064	66
Gillaspy, George et al	Deed to	Myer, Solomon	1807	R17	316	241
Gillespie, James	Deed to	Tuckfield, William H.P., trustee	1815	AI34	006	006
Gilless, Thomas H. et al	Deed fr	Bradley, Phineas	1801	G7	368	500
Gilless, Thomas Handy	Deed fr	Stoddert, Benjamin	1801	G7	081	104
Gilliam, Thomas	Lease fr	Farrell, Zephaniah	1817	AN38	093	071
Gillies, Thomas H.	Deed fr	Bently, Joseph	1804	L11	363	327
Gillingham, George	Mortgage fr	Lindo, Abraham	1810	Y24	286	262
Gillingham, George, in Alexa.	Deed fr	Aborn, Henry	1812	AC28	220	164
Gillingham, George, of Phila. PA	Assign to	Andrews, George & N. King	1810	Z25	109	084
Gillis, Thomas	Deed fr	Stoddert, Benjamin et al	1802	H8	483	444
Gillis, Thomas	Deed fr	Templeman, John	1802	H8	483	444
Gillis, Thomas	Release fr	Bank of Columbia	1802	H8	484	444
Gillis, Thomas	Manumis to	[ ], Peter (Negro)	1806	O14	071	043
Gillis, Thomas H.	Deed fr	Turner, Thomas	1802	I9	531	869
Gillis, Thomas H. et al	Deed to	Bradley, Phineas et al	1804	L11	365	329
Gillis, Thomas H. et al	Convey to	Van Ness, John P. et al	1804	L11	104	108
Gillis, Thomas H.	Deed to	Caldwell, Timothy	1805	O14	045	027
Gillis, Thomas H.	B. of S. fr	Byus, Stanley	1806	O14	071	043
Gillis, Thomas H.	Deed to	Davidson, John	1807	Q16	388	298
Gillis, Thomas H.	B. of S. to	Davidson, John	1807	Q16	398	306
Gillis, Thomas H. et al	Deed to	Thorpe, Thomas	1808	U20	410	229
Gillis, Thomas H.	Deed fr	Dorsey, William H., of Montg. Co.	1814	AH33	239	208
Gillis, Thomas H.	Deed fr	Murdock, John, of G'tn.	1814	AH33	237	207
Gillis, Thomas Handy	Deed fr	Saul, Joseph	1804	K10	407	422
Gillis, Thomas Handy	Deed to	Dorsey, William Hammond	1804	L11	262	241
Gillis, Thomas Handy	Deed to	Hyland, Lambert, Somerset Co.	1805	N13	168	153
Gilliss, Thomas H.	Deed to	Smith, Samuel et al	1802	I9	517	846
Gilliss, Thomas H. & M. Nourse	B. of S. fr	McLeod, John	1812	AD29	246	203
Gilliss, Thomas H.	Deed fr	Dorsey, William H., of Balto.	1813	AF31	110	074
Gilliss, Thomas H.	Deed fr	Murdock, John, of G'tn.	1813	AF31	113	076
Gilliss, Thomas H.	Deed to	Dawson, Joshua	1813	AF31	107	072
Gilliss, Thomas H.	B. of S. fr	Handy, James H.	1813	AE30	536	398
Gilliss, Thomas H.	Deed fr	Dorsey, William H., of Montg. Co.	1815	AI34	471	482
Gilliss, Thomas H.	Deed fr	Buchanan, Thomas, of MD	1815	AI34	468	480
Gilliss, Thomas H.	Agreement	McLean, Cornelius	1815	AK35	359	283
Gilliss, Thomas H.	Deed to	McLean, Cornelius	1815	AK35	356	281
Gilliss, Thomas H.	Deed fr	Murdock, John, of G'tn.	1815	AI34	472	483
Gilliss, Thomas H. et al	Deed fr	Bickley, Robert S., Bucks Co. PA	1817	AN38	564	411
Gilliss, Thomas Handy	Deed to	Willis, John	1802	H8	584	548
Gillman, Jacob	Cert. Free to	Franklin, Jane, c/o Nicholas et al	1814	AG32	303	220
Gilman, Nicholas, of Exeter NH	Manumis to	Dorsey, Andrew	1810	X23	253	197
Gilman, Peter, of Boston MA	Cert fr	Commissioners of Washington	1792	B2A	294	413
Gilmer, Robert, of Balto. et al	Deed to	Dorsey, William Hammond	1795	B2A	208	286
Gilmour, Helen, of Lancaster Co.	Deed fr	Keen, Frances, of Fairfax Co.	1814	AG32	109	083
Gilpin, Bernard	Deed to	Smith, William	1802	H8	115	111
Gilpin, Bernard	Deed to	Butler, Charles	1802	H8	125	121
Gilpin, Bernard	Deed fr	Brooke, Samuel	1802	H8	224	213
Gilpin, Bernard	Deed fr	Stoddert, Benjamin	1802	I9	375	623
Gilpin, Bernard	Deed fr	Prout, William	1802	I9	459	756
Gilpin, Bernard	Deed to	Butler, Thomas	1802	H8	228	217

Index to District of Columbia Land Records, 1792-1817

Party	What	Party	Year	Liber	Old	New
Gilpin, Bernard, of Montg. Co.	Lease to	Russ, Samuel	1806	P15	005	004
Gilpin, Bernard, of Montg. Co.	Deed to	Baum, John C. et al	1807	R17	376	286
Gilpin, Bernard, of Montg. Co.	Deed to	Johnson, Joseph	1812	AC28	237	176
Gilpin, Bernard, of Montg. Co.	Deed to	Brooke, Samuel	1813	AF31	273	192
Gilpin, Bernard, of Montg. Co.	Deed fr	Templeman, George, Allegany Co.	1816	AK35	486	382
Gilpin, George et al	Deed to	Beall, Thomas, of George	1795	B2A	166	222
Gioue, Don Jose Maria et al	Deed to	Prout, William	1817	AO39	474	325
Gird, Henry	B. of S. fr	Seeverman, John C.	1806	Q16	199	134
Gittings, Kinsey, estate of	Suit		1801	G7		122
Gittings, William	B. of S. fr	Cole, Jane, wid/o Bennet	1806	Q16	262	182
Gittings, William H., of Montg. Co.	Deed fr	Greenfield, Thomas, of P.G. Co.	1806	Q16	118	076
Gitzandanner, Christian	Deed to	Duvall, William	1805	M12	211	212
Gitzandanner, Christian, Montg.	Deed to	Goszler, John & George A.	1809	W22	259	173
Gitzandanner, Christian, of G'tn.	Deed to	Duvall, William, of G'tn.	1805	M12	209	211
Gitzendanner, Christian	Slaves	From Frederick Co. MD	1804	K10	352	
Gitzendanner, Christian	Deed fr	Delany, Matthew	1804	L11	145	146
Gitzendanner, Christian	Deed fr	Kennedy, Matthew	1804	K10	273	277
Gitzendanner, Christian, of G'tn.	Deed fr	Beatty, Charles, of G'tn.	1804	K10	271	276
Given, Thomas	Deed fr	Lovell, William, of Alexa.	1802	H8	337	315
Given, Thomas	Deed fr	Lovell, William	1802	I9	079	112
Given, Thomas	Cert fr	Munroe, Thomas, Supt.	1809	W22	391	255
Given, Thomas	Deed fr	Harbaugh, Samuel, of Phila.	1817	AO39	315	224
Given, Thomas	Deed to	Drane, Washington	1817	AO39	100	078
Glasco, John	Deed fr	Beale, William D. et al	1802	I9	220	348
Glasco, John	Release fr	Foxall, Henry, of G'tn.	1812	AD29	459	387
Glasco, John	Deed fr	Jones, Charles C., of Montg. Co.	1812	AD29	427	359
Glasco, John	Deed to	Mountz, John, of G'tn.	1813	AE30	146	114
Glasco, John	Deed fr	Mountz, John, of G'tn.	1813	AF31	357	254
Glasco, John	Release to	Owner, James	1814	AH33	169	157
Glasco, John	Cert fr	Munroe, Thomas, Supt.	1815	AI34	195	224
Glasco, John	Mortgage to	Murdock, John, of G'tn.	1817	AN38	147	108
Glasco, John et al	Deed fr	Brooke, Thomas A.	1802	I9	584	946
Glascoe, John, of G'tn.	Mortgage to	Owner, James [Onnar]	1810	Y24	453	402
Glascow, John	Deed fr	Caldwell, Timothy	1806	P15	159	105
Glascow, John	Deed to	Foxall, Henry	1807	S18	197	158
Glascow, John	Qualify	First Lieutenant in Militia	1808	V21	094	072
Glascow, John	Deed fr	Owner, James	1812	AD29	424	357
Glascow, John	Deed fr	Jones, Charles C., of Montg. Co.	1813	AE30	384	284
Glascow, John & Rachel	Deed to	Owner, James	1812	AD29	457	385
Glenn, Robert, insolvent	Assign to	Herty, Thomas, trustee	1808	V21	047	036
Glover, Charels	Deed fr	DeKrafft, Charles	1815	AH33	548	469
Glover, Charles	Cert fr	Thornton, William	1801	G7	191	256
Glover, Charles	Deed fr	Murdock, James	1802	I9	479	787
Glover, Charles	Deed fr	Murdock, John, of G'tn.	1804	K10	102	109
Glover, Charles	Deed to	Downes, George	1804	L11	286	262
Glover, Charles	Deed fr	Voss, Richard	1805	M12	159	157
Glover, Charles	Deed to	Travers, Esias	1806	Q16	121	078
Glover, Charles	Deed to	Voss, Nicholas	1808	U20	100	056
Glover, Charles	Release to	Voss, Nicholas	1809	V21	187	133
Glover, Charles	Certificate	Assistant Clerk, Circuit Court	1809	X23	276	218
Glover, Charles	Deed fr	McDonald, John G.	1810	Y24	358	323
Glover, Charles	Deed to	Dinmore, Richard	1811	AA26	032	024
Glover, Charles	Deed fr	Oden, Benjamin, of P.G. Co.	1812	AC28	375	273
Glover, Charles	Deed to	Renner, Daniel	1812	AC28	254	187
Glover, Charles	Deed fr	Macdaniel, Ezekiel	1812	AD29	113	086

Index to District of Columbia Land Records, 1792-1817

Party	What	Party	Year	Liber	Old	New
Glover, Charles	Deed fr	Ott, John, of G'tn.	1812	AD29	220	181
Glover, Charles	Deed fr	Macdaniel, Ezekiel	1812	AD29	358	301
Glover, Charles	Deed to	Bussard, Daniel	1812	AD29	504	425
Glover, Charles	Deed to	Butler, Silas	1812	AD29	159	126
Glover, Charles	D. of T. fr	Sweeny, George	1813	AF31	529	390
Glover, Charles	Deed fr	King, Robert	1813	AF31	284	201
Glover, Charles	Deed fr	Peltz, John	1814	AG32	209	146
Glover, Charles	Deed fr	Brent, William & Philip B. Key	1814	AG32	215	150
Glover, Charles	B. of S. fr	Burford, John A.	1814	AG32	377	273
Glover, Charles	Deed fr	Pratt, Henry et al	1814	AH33	302	261
Glover, Charles	Deed to	Campbell, William	1814	AH33	053	047
Glover, Charles	Deed to	Heath, Nathaniel H.	1814	AH33	089	081
Glover, Charles	D. of T. fr	Coyle, Andrew	1814	AH33	267	233
Glover, Charles	Deed to	Clarke, Isaac	1815	AH33	497	426
Glover, Charles	Deed fr	Bussard, Daniel, of G'tn.	1815	AH33	477	407
Glover, Charles	Deed fr	Corporation of Washington	1815	AI34	132	152
Glover, Charles	Deed fr	Corporation of Washington	1815	AI34	134	154
Glover, Charles	Deed fr	Corporation of Washington	1815	AI34	123	142
Glover, Charles	Deed fr	Isaacs, Ralph	1815	AI34	217	248
Glover, Charles	Deed fr	Corporation of Washington	1815	AI34	122	140
Glover, Charles	Release to	Coyle, Andrew	1815	AI34	490	497
Glover, Charles	Deed fr	Smith, Walter, of G'tn.	1815	AI34	011	012
Glover, Charles	Deed fr	Corporation of Washington	1815	AI34	120	137
Glover, Charles	Deed fr	Corporation of Washington	1815	AI34	118	135
Glover, Charles	Deed fr	Corporation of Washington	1815	AI34	116	133
Glover, Charles	D. of T. fr	Sweeny, George	1815	AI34	065	073
Glover, Charles	Deed fr	Corporation of Washington	1815	AI34	111	127
Glover, Charles	Deed fr	Corporation of Washington	1815	AI34	113	129
Glover, Charles	Deed fr	Corporation of Washington	1815	AI34	115	131
Glover, Charles	Deed fr	Corporation of Washington	1815	AK35	009	007
Glover, Charles	Deed fr	Corporation of Washington	1815	AK35	006	005
Glover, Charles	Deed fr	Corporation of Washington	1815	AK35	011	009
Glover, Charles	Convey fr	Randall, John & Henry Payson	1816	AK35	324	258
Glover, Charles	Deed to	Clarke, Joseph S.	1816	AL36	252	254
Glover, Charles	Deed fr	Holmead, Anthony	1816	AL36	208	215
Glover, Charles	Deed fr	Varden, Charles	1816	AL36	328	321
Glover, Charles	Deed fr	Phillips, Isaac, of Balto.	1816	AL36	347	338
Glover, Charles	Deed to	Walker, Zachariah	1816	AM37	337	245
Glover, Charles	Deed to	Randolph, William Beverly	1816	AM37	251	185
Glover, Charles	Deed fr	Hildreth, Ezekiel	1816	AM37	277	203
Glover, Charles	Deed fr	Munroe, Thomas, Supt.	1816	AO39	034	028
Glover, Charles	Deed to	Way, George	1816	AO39	009	007
Glover, Charles	Deed fr	Blanchard, William	1817	AN38	185	134
Glover, Charles	Deed fr	Bickley, Robert S., Bucks Co. PA	1817	AN38	333	243
Glover, Charles	D. of T. fr	Belt, Benjamin	1817	AN38	403	301
Glover, Charles	Deed to	Patterson, Thomas, Dr.	1817	AN38	236	173
Glover, Charles	Deed fr	Hopkins, David, of Balto.	1817	AN38	566	413
Glover, Charles	Confirm fr	Johnson, Joshua, of Fredk. Co.	1817	AO39	336	239
Glover, Charles & Rich. Forrest	Deed to	Young, Moses	1813	AF31	380	273
Glover, Charles & Rich. Forrest	Deed to	Parrott, Richard, of G'tn.	1813	AF31	378	272
Glover, Charles & Richard Forrest	Deed to	Davidson, James	1813	AF31	476	346
Glover, Charles & Wash. Boyd	Deed fr	Moriarty, Ambrose	1814	AG32	162	116
Glover, Charles & Jas. Davidson	Deed to	Carr, Overton	1815	AI34	347	378
Glover, Charles & Richard Forrest	Deed to	Tayloe, John	1815	AK35	120	093
Glover, Charles & David Ott	Deed fr	Hyatt, Seth & Jane Summerville	1816	AL36	163	163

Index to District of Columbia Land Records, 1792-1817

Party	What	Party	Year	Liber	Old	New
Glover, Charles et al	Bond fr	Broadwell, James	1804	K10	286	289
Glover, Charles, trustee	Deed to	Burgess, Samuel	1812	AC28	372	271
Glover, Charles, trustee	Deed to	Ladd, John G., of Alexa.	1812	AC28	113	085
Glover, Charles, trustee	Deed to	Patterson, Edgar, of G'tn.	1814	AG32	148	106
Glover, Charles, trustee	Deed to	Fresh, William, of G'tn.	1814	AG32	021	016
Glover, Charles, trustee	Deed to	Dair, Shadrack	1814	AH33	132	126
Glover, Charles, trustee	Assign fr	Varden, Ezra, insolvent	1814	AH33	096	088
Glover, Charles, trustee	Deed fr	Varden, Charles H., insolvent	1814	AG32	279	199
Glover, Charles, trustee	Deed fr	Ormsby, Robert	1815	AH33	537	459
Glover, Charles, trustee	Deed to	Arnot, John	1816	AL36	362	352
Glover, Charles, trustee	Deed to	Prout, William	1817	AN38	036	029
Glover, Richard, now of G'tn.	Manumis to	[ ], Harriott (C)	1812	AD29	040	029
Glover, William, of London	Deed fr	Munroe, Thomas, Supt.	1802	I9	039	051
Gloyd, Aminia, c/o Jonathan et al	B. of S. fr	Gloyd, George H. et al	1809	V21	304	222
Gloyd, Caroline, c/o Jonathan et al	B. of S. fr	Gloyd, George H. et al	1809	V21	304	222
Gloyd, Catherine	Deed fr	Threlkeld, John	1799	D4	355	342
Gloyd, George H., of G'tn.	Deed fr	Gloyd, Jonathan, of G'tn.	1808	U20	013	008
Gloyd, George H., of G'tn. et al	B. of S. to	Gloyd, Harriet et al	1809	V21	304	222
Gloyd, George H., trustee	Deed fr	Gobright, William, insolvent	1811	Z25	508	404
Gloyd, George H.	Manumis to	[ ], Milly (negro)	1811	Z25	457	361
Gloyd, George H.	Cert Free to	Purk, Benjamin	1813	AF31	433	312
Gloyd, George H., of G'tn.	Deed fr	Walker, Zachariah, collector	1816	AL36	039	040
Gloyd, George H., of G'tn.	B. of S. to	Newton, Ignatius	1816	AL36	467	441
Gloyd, George H., of G'tn.	Assign to	Renner, Daniel	1816	AK35	499	393
Gloyd, George Holland	Lease fr	Walker, George	1802	H8	416	384
Gloyd, George Holland	B. of S. fr	Balch, Stephen B.	1804	K10	198	207
Gloyd, George Holland	Deed fr	Quaid, Walter	1807	R17	257	195
Gloyd, Harriet, c/o Jonathan et al	B. of S. fr	Gloyd, George H. et al	1809	V21	304	222
Gloyd, James & George H.	B. of S. fr	Gloyd, Jonathan, of G'tn.	1808	U20	027	016
Gloyd, James, Hampshire Co. VA	B. of S. to	Gloyd, Harriet et al	1809	V21	304	222
Gloyd, Jonathan	Deed fr	Beatty, Charles, heirs of	1805	N13	180	161
Gloyd, Jonathan, of G'tn.	B. of S. to	Gloyd, James & George H.	1808	U20	027	016
Gloyd, Jonathan, of G'tn.	Deed to	Gloyd, George H., of G'tn.	1808	U20	013	008
Gloyd, William, c/o Jonathan et al	B. of S. fr	Gloyd, George H. et al	1809	V21	304	222
Gobright, William, insolvent	Deed to	Gloyd, George H., trustee	1811	Z25	508	404
Goddard, John B. & John, of G'tn.	Deed to	Holmead, Anthony	1811	AA26	245	167
Goddard, John B., of G'tn.	Deed fr	Walker, Nathan, of P.G. Co.	1811	AA26	247	168
Goddard, John B.	Qualify	Lieutant in militia	1813	AE30	472	351
Goddart, John B., of MD	Deed fr	Dove, Joseph	1806	Q16	092	059
Godefroy, Peter et al	Deed fr	Greenleaf, James, of NY	1794	B2A	065	083
Godefroy, Peter et al	Deed to	Greenleaf, James, New York NY	1796	B2B	493	188
Godfrey, William	Deed to	Tucker, Joseph et al	1801	G7	077	100
Godfrey, William	Cert fr	Munroe, Thomas, Supt.	1816	AM37	382	275
Goff, John	Lease fr	Prout, William	1804	L11	316	290
Goff, John	Deed to	Marshal, George	1808	T19	116	082
Goff, John	Deed to	Marshal, George	1808	T19	021	017
Golden, Samuel, s/o Frederick	Deed to	Beall, Thomas & John M. Gantt	1793	A1-1	383	490
Goldin, Sarah, wid/o Samuel et al	Deed to	Mountz, John	1815	AI34	351	382
Goldin, William, Montg. Co. et al	Deed to	Mountz, John	1815	AI34	351	382
Golding, John, Jr.	B. of S. to	Wannall, Thomas	1816	AL36	546	509
Goldsberry, John M.	Deed fr	Threlkeld, John	1807	S18	215	172
Goldsborough, Charles W.	Deed fr	Smallwood, Walter B.	1807	S18	053	044
Goldsborough, Charles W.	Deed fr	Abbott, John, of G'tn.	1809	X23	079	059
Goldsborough, Charles W.	Deed fr	Templeman, John	1809	X23	076	057
Goldsborough, Charles W.	Cert fr	Munroe, Thomas, Supt.	1811	AB27	065	055

Party	What	Party	Year	Liber	Old	New
Goldsborough, Charles W., G'tn.	Mortgage to	Smith, Edmund & E.H. Nicholl	1814	AH33	166	154
Goldsborough, Charles W.	Deed to	Smith, Edmund & E.H. Nicholl	1816	AL36	368	358
Goldsborough, Howe, of MD	Convey fr	Forrest, Joseph	1816	AL36	342	333
Goldsborough, John M.	Deed fr	Hutchins, Samuel	1807	S18	217	183
Goldsborough, John M.	Deed fr	Threlkeld, John	1812	AD29	027	019
Goldsborough, John M.	Deed fr	Hutchins, Samuel, of G'tn.	1813	AF31	309	220
Goldsborough, John M.	Manumis to	Bruce, Jacob	1813	AF31	003	002
Goldsmith, John, insolvent	Deed to	Tuckfield, William H.P., trustee	1813	AF31	334	238
Goldtwait, Samuel, of Balto.	Deed fr	Moscrop, Henry	1805	M12	141	136
Goodeberger, Adam, farmer	Deed to	Medtart, Jacob, Sr., Frederick Co.	1793	A1-1	230	317
Gooding, John, of Balto.	Deed fr	Dyer, Henry O., of G'tn.	1809	X23	022	015
Gooding, John, of Balto.	Deed to	Mackall, Leonard et al	1810	Y24	151	137
Gooding, John, of Balto.	Contract	Union Bank of Georgetown	1810	Y24	154	140
Goozler, John	Deed fr	Threlkeld, John, of G'tn.	1800	E5	266	259
Gordan, Elisha, of Phila. PA	Deed fr	Knowles, Henry	1808	T19	111	079
Gordon, Elisha & Elizabeth, Phila.	Deed to	Brannon, John & William Hunt	1815	AK35	101	078
Gordon, Elisha, late of Phila. PA	Deed fr	King, Robert	1813	AF31	127	085
Gordon, John, def.	Suit	Davidson, John, plt.	1797	C3	107	87
Gordon, John, of Annapolis	Deed to	Oden, Benjamin	1794	B2A	036	040
Gordon, Martha	Deed fr	Minchin, Patience	1816	AL36	386	373
Gore, Christopher, of Boston MA	Deed fr	Stoddert, Benjamin	1793	A1-1	199	280
Gore, Christopher, of Boston MA	Deed fr	Stoddert, Benjamin, of G'tn.	1805	M12	290	291
Gormley, Constantine	B. of S. to	Jordon, Hugh	1802	H8	269	255
Gosler, John	Deed fr	Beatty, Thomas, of MD	1810	Y24	382	345
Gosler, John, of G'tn.	Deed fr	Threlkeld, John, of G'tn.	1794	B2A	035	038
Goszler, George	Deed fr	Lowndes, Francis, of G'tn.	1802	I9	078	110
Goszler, George, of G'tn.	Deed fr	Magruder, Ninian, of G'tn.	1813	AE30	153	120
Goszler, Henry	Deed fr	Dorsey, William H.	1802	I9	403	669
Goszler, John	Deed fr	Waggoner, Adam	1802	H8	049	046
Goszler, John & George A.	Deed fr	Gitzandanner, Christian, Montg.	1809	W22	259	173
Goszler, John, of G'tn.	Deed to	Sanders, Thomas, of G'tn.	1798	C3	468	368
Goszler, John, of G'tn.	Deed to	King, George, of G'tn.	1802	H8	516	475
Goszler, John, of G'tn.	Deed fr	Boyd, Washington, marshal	1809	W22	325	211
Goszler, John, of G'tn.	Deed fr	Debow, Solomon, of NC	1809	W22	373	242
Goszler, John, of G'tn.	Deed to	Debow, Solomon, Caswell Co. NC	1809	W22	393	256
Goszler, John, of G'tn.	Deed fr	Bowie, Washington, of G'tn.	1812	AD29	465	391
Goszler, John, of G'tn.	Deed fr	Boyd, Washington, marshal	1812	AD29	466	394
Gouges, Arnaud, of Balto.	Deed fr	Washington, William A., of VA	1795	B2A	341	481
Gouges, Arnauld	Cert fr	Commissioners of Washington	1795	B2A	334	468
Gouges, Arnauld	Cert fr	Commissioners of Washington	1795	B2A	334	469
Goulding, John	Manumis to	[ ], Peter (Negro)	1806	O14	071	043
Goulding, John	Deed fr	Corporation of Washington	1816	AL36	268	268
Goulding, John	Deed fr	Corporation of Washington	1816	AL36	266	266
Gowans, John, of Petersburg VA	Deed fr	Murdock, John, of G'tn.	1804	L11	214	201
Gozler, John	Deed fr	Magruder, George, collector, G'tn.	1807	S18	078	064
Gozler, John, of G'tn.	Deed fr	Threlkeld, John, of G'tn.	1809	X23	046	034
Graff, John, s/o Michael, of PA	Deed to	Beatty, Charles	1799	D4	384	367
Graham, Charles, a free man	Deposition	Hepburn, Samuel	1807	S18	119	097
Graham, James	Deed to	Bryan, Benjamin	1804	L11	148	149
Graham, Jane	Slaves	From VA	1810	Z25	241	188
Graham, Jane	Deed fr	Smith, Walter, of G'tn.	1817	AO39	515	354
Graham, Jane [by John]	Slaves	From VA	1811	AB27	150	125
Graham, John	Slaves		1808	V21	113	084
Graham, John	Deed fr	Handy, Betsy G.	1814	AG32	195	136
Graham, John	Cert fr	Commissioner of Public Buildings	1817	AO39	335	239

Index to District of Columbia Land Records, 1792-1817

Party	What	Party	Year	Liber	Old	New
Graham, John et al	Deed fr	Jackson, John G., fr. Harrison Co.	1814	AG32	295	215
Graham, William, of Balto.	Deed to	French, George	1794	B2A	142	186
Graham, William, of G'tn.	B. of S. fr	Miles, Edward L.	1810	Y24	285	261
Grahame, Richard, Calvert Co.	Deed to	Beall, Thomas & John M. Gantt	1792	A1-1	061	90
Grammar, Frederick, of Annapolis	Deed fr	Hanson, Alexander Contee	1797	C3	045	35
Grammar, Frederick, of Annapolis	Deed fr	Burnes, David	1798	D4	153	135
Grammar, Frederick, of MD	Deed fr	Davidson, John, of MD	1802	H8	477	438
Grammar, Frederick, of Annapolis	Deed to	Davidson, Ann Maria, exrx.	1810	Z25	319	249
Grammar, Frederick, of Annapolis	Deed fr	Bassett, John et ux, Hanover Co.	1811	Z25	375	294
Grammar, Frederick, of Annapolis	Mortgage fr	Weiskopff, Charles Lewis et al	1812	AD29	350	293
Grammar, Frederick, of A.A. Co.	Mortgage fr	Peltz, John	1815	AI34	368	396
Grammar, Gotlieb C. et al	Deed fr	Hughes, Thomas	1814	AG32	060	047
Grammar, Gotlieb C.	Mortgage fr	Brush, John C.	1814	AH33	149	141
Grammar, Gottlieb C.	Assign fr	Underwood, John & Thomas	1815	AH33	544	466
Grammar, Gottlieb C.	Deed fr	Laird, John, exr. of J. Carleton	1816	AM37	047	038
Grammar, Gottlieb Christopher	Mortgage fr	Esenbeck, William	1814	AH33	124	118
Grammar, Gottlieb Christopher	Mortgage to	Mayer, Henry, of G'tn.	1814	AG32	381	277
Grammar, Gottlieb Christopher	Deed fr	Mayer, Henry, of G'tn.	1814	AG32	282	202
Grammar, Gottlieb Christopher	Deed fr	Mauro, Philip	1816	AM37	045	037
Grammer, Frederick, of A.A. Co.	Release to	Weiskopff, Lewis & J.F. Keller	1815	AI34	278	313
Grammer, G.C. & Geo. Kleiber	B. of S. fr	Estep, Alexander	1815	AI34	369	398
Grammer, Gotlieb C.	Mortgage fr	Prentiss, William & William H.	1817	AN38	373	275
Grammer, Gotlieb Christpher et al	Deed fr	Davidson, John	1812	AD29	234	193
Grammer, Gottlieb Christopher	Mortgage to	Hughes, Thomas	1812	AD29	387	326
Granberry, John	Deed fr	Wheeler, Luke & John Cowper	1812	AD29	531	448
Grander, Gideon	Deed fr	Caldwell, Timothy	1808	T19	259	191
Granger, Gideon	Deed fr	Geyer, Daniel, Sharpsburgh MD	1806	Q16	168	111
Granger, Gideon	Deed fr	Caldwell, Timothy	1808	T19	278	204
Granger, Gideon	Deed fr	Wilson, Samuel [Willson]	1808	T19	252	185
Granger, Gideon	Deed fr	Van Ness, John P.	1808	U20	205	112
Granger, Gideon	Deed to	Van Ness, John P.	1808	U20	304	162
Granger, Gideon	Deed fr	Holmead, Anthony	1810	X23	381	307
Granger, Gideon	Deed to	Ryan, Mary	1810	Y24	539	474
Granger, Gideon	Mortgage to	Tayloe, John & Thomas Munroe	1811	AB27	081	068
Granger, Gideon	Release fr	Tayloe, John & Thomas Munroe	1812	AE30	013	011
Granger, Gideon	Deed fr	Van Ness, John P.	1813	AF31	482	352
Granger, Gideon	Deed fr	Davidson, James, Jr.	1813	AF31	481	351
Granger, Gideon	Deed to	Gardner, William P.	1814	AH33	177	164
Granger, Gideon	D. of T. to	Howe, Robert F., of G'tn.	1814	AH33	294	254
Granger, Gideon & Mindwell P.	Deed to	Caldwell, Timothy, now of Phila.	1812	AE30	015	012
Granger, Gideon & Mindwell P.	Deed to	Varnum, James M.	1815	AK35	281	224
Granger, Gideon, of Oneida NY	Deed to	Varnum, James M. & Mary Pease	1815	AH33	461	394
Granger, Gideon, plt.	Suit	Wilson, William, def.	1808	T19	252	185
Granger, Gideon, postmaster	Deed fr	Aborn, Henry	1813	AE30	477	355
Grant, Charles	Manumis fr	Whipp, Reuben	1810	X23	355	284
Grant, Edward & James Kemp	Deed fr	Queen, Henry M., collector	1811	AA26	380	253
Grant, Edward M.	Deed to	McKim, James & Thomas Herty	1807	R17	115	090
Grant, Edward M.	Release fr	Herty, Thomas	1811	AB27	057	049
Grant, George	Deed fr	Prout, William	1812	AC28	475	337
Grant, George & Edward Bland	Deed fr	Dunlap, James, of G'tn.	1807	R17	103	080
Grant, William V., of G'tn. et al	Assign to	Burrows, John, of G'tn.	1817	AO39	137	104
Grantt, Edward & James Kemp	Mortgage fr	Picknoll, Richard H.	1811	AA26	081	057
Grantt, Edward & James Kemp	P. of Atty. fr	Picknoll, Richard H.	1811	AA26	010	008
Grantt, George	Deed to	Kemp, James	1811	Z25	390	307
Grantt, George	Agreement	Bland, Edward	1811	Z25	388	305

Party	What	Party	Year	Liber	Old	New
Grate, Jacob, of G'tn.	Deed to	Thompson, Josias, of G'tn.	1793	A1-1	243	332
Graves, Benjamin	B. of S. to	Fields, William	1810	Y24	364	329
Graves, Robert	B. of S. to	Pickerel, John	1811	AB27	483	395
Gray, Catharine, infant d/o Wm.	Deed fr	Bayne, Horatio & Elizabeth	1815	AI34	310	343
Gray, James W. (C), age 4	Cert Slave fr	Gustine, J.T. et al	1814	AH33	203	184
Gray, John, of London	Deed fr	Munroe, Thomas, Supt.	1802	I9	043	058
Gray, John, of London	Deed fr	Munroe, Thomas, Supt.	1802	I9	045	061
Gray, John, of London	Deed fr	Munroe, Thomas, Supt.	1802	I9	044	059
Gray, John, ship broker, of London	Deed fr	Lewis, Leyson, mer., of London	1804	K10	366	379
Gray, Judah Ann (C), age 1½	Cert Slave fr	Gustine, J.T. et al	1814	AH33	203	184
Gray, Nathan	Deed fr	Beatty, Charles, heirs of	1806	P15	359	238
Gray, Nathan	B. of S. fr	Osborn, Catharine	1813	AF30	102	078
Gray, Nathan	B. of S. fr	Bacchus, John	1817	AN38	272	199
Gray, Nathaniel	B. of S. to	Baltzer, Jacob	1806	P15	050	030
Gray, Nathaniel	Deed fr	Baker, John & Henry	1816	AL36	169	169
Gray, Robert M.R. (C), age 6	Cert Slave fr	Gustine, J.T. et al	1814	AH33	203	184
Gray, Stephen W., insolvent	Deed to	Speake, Samuel, trustee	1811	AA26	317	214
Gray, Stephen W.	B. of S. to	Bestor, Harvey	1814	AH33	375	325
Gray, Thomas et al	B. of S. fr	Collins, John	1805	M12	177	177
Gray, William	B. of S. to	Watterstone, David et al	1811	AC28	011	008
Gray, William	Lease fr	Law, Edmund, atty. of Thomas	1811	AA26	275	187
Gray, William	Assign to	Wagler, Frederick A.	1811	AB27	346	287
Gray, William	Deed fr	Prout, William	1814	AH33	123	116
Gray, William (C), age 24	Manumis fr	Digges, Edward	1813	AF31	393	284
Gray, William (C), as servant	Indenture to	Cox, John	1813	AF31	394	285
Grayson, John R. et al	B. of S. to	Davidson, John	1809	V21	319	234
Grayson, Mary E.	Slaves	From VA	1808	U20	246	132
Grayson, Mary E., reps. of	Manumis to	[ ], Alfred (C)	1811	AB27	298	244
Grayson, Mary E., reps. of	Manumis to	[ ], Jesse (C)	1811	AB27	298	244
Grayson, William	Deed fr	Clarke, Alben	1815	AK35	418	327
Grayson, William	Deed fr	Brown, Gustavus A., of Alexa.	1815	AK35	420	329
Grayson, William	Deed to	Bronaugh, John W.	1816	AM37	017	014
Grayson, William & wife, of G'tn.	Deed to	Bronaugh, John W., of G'tn.	1816	AM37	019	015
Grayson, William, Dr.	B. of S. fr	Threlkeld, John	1812	AC28	410	297
Grayson, William, Dr.	Deed fr	Belt, Joseph Sprigg	1813	AF31	037	026
Grayson, William, Dr., of G'tn.	Deed fr	Williams, John Stull	1815	AH33	381	330
Great, Jacob et al	Deed fr	Holmead, Anthony	1793	A1-1	244	333
Greate, Jacob, of G'tn.	Deed fr	Thompson, Josias, of G'tn.	1793	A1-1	245	335
Greate, Jacob, of G'tn.	Deed to	Walls, James, of Winchester VA	1793	A1-1	246	336
Green, Charles D., printer, et al	Deed fr	Lyles, William	1799	E5	059	048
Green, Charles D., printer, et al	Mortgage to	Lyles, William	1800	E5	184	175
Green, Charles D. et al	Deed fr	Commissioners of Washington	1800	E5	139	128
Green, Charles D. et al	Deed to	Claggett, Walter	1801	F6	181	115
Green, Charles D., printer, et al	Mortgage to	Lyles, William	1801	G7	188	252
Green, Charles D., Somerset Co.	Deed to	Corcoran, Thomas et al	1808	T19	203	145
Green, Charles D., Hunt. Co. NJ	Deed to	Melvin, James, of G'tn.	1810	X23	403	325
Green, Charles D., of NJ	Deed to	English, David	1812	AC28	193	147
Green, James	Deed fr	Frank, George	1802	H8	140	137
Green, James	B. of S. to	Carroll, James	1806	O14	213	141
Green, James (M)	Manumis fr	Hambleton, Samuel, of G'tn.	1815	AI34	394	418
Green, Jesse, of Sussex Co. DE	Deed fr	Lyles, George Noble & Elizabeth	1804	L11	337	307
Green, Jesse, of Sussex Co. DE	Deed fr	Lyles, George Noble & Eliz., Alexa.	1804	L11	046	46
Green, Jesse, of Sussex Co. DE	Deed to	Speake, Samuel	1809	W22	117	084
Green, John E.	B. of S. to	Moore, George	1814	AG32	102	077
Green, Levy	Deed fr	Greenleaf, James, of Phila.	1798	C3	421	332

Index to District of Columbia Land Records, 1792-1817

Party	What	Party	Year	Liber	Old	New
Green, Levy	Agreement	Simmons, James	1798	C3	420	331
Green, Simon	B. of S. to	Adams, George	1816	AL36	170	170
Greenfield, Gabriel	Deed fr	Beall, Thomas Brooke	1795	B2A	179	242
Greenfield, Gabriel	Deed to	King, Zephaniah	1795	B2A	181	244
Greenfield, Gerard T.	Slaves	From VA	1808	V21	128	094
Greenfield, Gerrard T.	Slave	From VA	1808	V21	092	070
Greenfield, James et al	Agreement	Waugh, James, of VA	1802	I9	113	165
Greenfield, Mary	B. of S. to	Porter, David, Com.	1815	AI34	518	523
Greenfield, Thomas	B. of S. to	Watterston, David	1808	V21	125	092
Greenfield, Thomas	B. of S. to	Marr, Philip	1808	V21	086	067
Greenfield, Thomas	Cert Free to	Reed, Letty, children of	1813	AE30	187	149
Greenfield, Thomas et al	D. of T. fr	Greenfield, Walter, of G'tn.	1813	AF31	367	263
Greenfield, Thomas, of P.G. Co.	Deed to	Gittings, William H., of Montg. Co.	1806	Q16	118	076
Greenfield, Thomas, of P.G. Co.	B. of S. to	Shaw, Mary	1810	Y24	475	420
Greenfield, Walter, of G'tn.	D. of T. to	Hyde, Thomas et al	1813	AF31	367	263
Greenfield, Walter, of G'tn.	D. of T. to	Hyde, Thomas, of G'tn.	1813	AF31	366	262
Greenfield, Walter T., of P.G. Co.	Deed fr	Beall, Joshua	1811	Z25	123	096
Greenfield, Walter T., of P.G. Co.	Deed to	Beall, Joshua	1811	Z25	126	098
Greenleaf, Ann Penn	Assign to	Lawrence, John et al	1809	V21	362	266
Greenleaf, James	Agreement	Johnson, Thomas et al	1794	B2A	070	090
Greenleaf, James	Deed to	Scott, Gustavus et al	1795	B2A	229	318
Greenleaf, James	Agreement	Commissioners of Washington	1796	B2B	544	267
Greenleaf, James	Transfer to	Barry, James, of Balto.	1796	B2B	454	141
Greenleaf, James	Deed fr	Godefroy, Peter et al	1796	B2B	493	188
Greenleaf, James	Agreement	Commissioners of Washington	1796	B2B	540	261
Greenleaf, James	Transfer to	Morris, Robert & John Nicholson	1796	B2B	452	140
Greenleaf, James	Deed to	Dalton, Tristram et al	1798	D4	055	046
Greenleaf, James	Deed to	Simpson, George	1799	E5	004	003
Greenleaf, James	Deed to	Sinclair, John	1804	L11	264	243
Greenleaf, James	P. of Atty. fr	Pratt, Henry et al	1804	K10	101	107
Greenleaf, James	Deed to	Barry, James	1804	L11	349	316
Greenleaf, James	P. of Atty. fr	Pratt, Henry et al	1805	M12	377	388
Greenleaf, James & Robert Morris	Agreement	Commissioners of Washington	1796	B2B	541	263
Greenleaf, James, Allen Town PA	Deed fr	Young, Thomas & Thomas Foyles	1814	AH33	299	259
Greenleaf, James, attorney in fact	Deed to	Sinclair, John	1805	M12	145	141
Greenleaf, James, attorney in fact	Deed to	May, Frederick	1805	N13	108	102
Greenleaf, James, by atty.	Deed to	Sinclair, John	1809	X23	141	
Greenleaf, James et al	Deed to	Pratt, Henry et al	1797	C3	154	127
Greenleaf, James et al	Deed fr	Maddox, Notley, sheriff	1799	D4	298	281
Greenleaf, James et al	B. in C. fr	Pratt, Henry et al	1799	E5	003	003
Greenleaf, James et al	Deed to	Ward, Joshua, of VA	1804	L11	175	170
Greenleaf, James et al	Deed to	Waugh, James, Sr., Fairfax Co.	1804	L11	230	213
Greenleaf, James et al	Deed to	Elliott, Samuel, Jr.	1806	O14	362	242
Greenleaf, James et al	Deed to	Eliot, Samuel, Jr.	1809	W22	293	193
Greenleaf, James et al	Consent fr	Anacostia Bridge Company	1815	AH33	450	386
Greenleaf, James, for 500 lots	Deed fr	Johnson, Stuart & Carroll	1794	B2A	044	052
Greenleaf, James, for 857 lots	Cert fr	Commissioners of Washington	1794	B2A	108	143
Greenleaf, James, for 1,000 lots	Cert fr	Johnson, Stuart & Carroll	1794	B2A	048	057
Greenleaf, James, for 500 lots	Cert fr	Johnson, Stuart & Carroll	1794	B2A	047	056
Greenleaf, James, for 1,000 lots	Cert fr	Johnson, Stuart & Carroll	1794	B2A	045	054
Greenleaf, James, New York NY	Deed fr	Buchanan, Thomas, Charles Co.	1794	B2A	120	161
Greenleaf, James, New York NY	Deed to	Carroll, Daniel et al	1794	B2A	137	181
Greenleaf, James, New York NY	Deed fr	Deakins, William, Jr., of G'tn.	1794	B2A	085	110
Greenleaf, James, New York NY	Deed fr	Young, Notley	1794	B2A	117	156
Greenleaf, James, New York NY	Deed fr	Lear, Tobias, of G'tn.	1794	B2A	152	201

Party	What	Party	Year	Liber	Old	New
Greenleaf, James, New York NY	Deed fr	Stoddert, Benjamin et al	1794	B2A	083	108
Greenleaf, James, New York NY	P. of Atty. to	Appleton, Nathaniel Walker	1794	B2A	080	103
Greenleaf, James, New York NY	Deed fr	Forrest, Uriah & Benj. Stoddert	1794	B2A	086	111
Greenleaf, James, New York NY	P. of Atty. to	Appleton, Nathaniel Walker	1794	B2A	081	105
Greenleaf, James, New York NY	Cert fr	Commissioners of Washington	1794	B2A	143	188
Greenleaf, James, New York NY	P. of Atty. fr	Carroll, Daniel, Scott & Thornton	1794	B2A	110	146
Greenleaf, James, New York NY	P. of Atty. to	Appleton, Nathaniel Walker	1794	B2A	077	100
Greenleaf, James, New York NY	Deed to	Young, Notley	1795	B2A	348	492
Greenleaf, James, New York NY	Agreement	Henderson, John, architect	1795	B2A	259	362
Greenleaf, James, New York NY	P. of Atty. to	Cranch, William, late of MA	1795	B2A	233	324
Greenleaf, James, New York NY	Deed to	Nicholson, John, of Phila.	1795	B2B	380	035
Greenleaf, James, New York NY	Bond	Henderson, John, architect	1795	B2A	262	365
Greenleaf, James, New York NY	Deed to	Duncanson, William M.	1795	B2A	273	382
Greenleaf, James, New York NY	Deed to	Morris, Robert & Jno. Nicholson	1796	B2B	579	323
Greenleaf, James, New York NY	Mortgage fr	Nicholson, John & Hannah et al	1796	B2B	592	341
Greenleaf, James, New York NY	Deed to	Morris, Robert, of Phila.	1796	B2B	388	047
Greenleaf, James, New York NY	Deed to	Morris, Robert, of Phila.	1796	B2B	387	044
Greenleaf, James, New York NY	Mortgage fr	Morris, Robert & Mary et al	1796	B2B	592	341
Greenleaf, James, New York NY	Deed fr	Boyd, Ann et al	1796	B2B	445	128
Greenleaf, James, New York NY	Deed fr	French, George, Scott & Boyd	1796	B2B	445	128
Greenleaf, James, now of Phila.	Deed fr	Morris, Robert & John Nicholson	1796	B2B	599	349
Greenleaf, James, now of NY	Deed to	Morris, Robert & Jno. Nicholson	1796	B2B	532	249
Greenleaf, James, now of NY	Deed to	Morris, Robert & John Nicholson	1796	B2B	562	296
Greenleaf, James, of NY	Deed fr	Warman, William Berry	1793	A1-2	464	72
Greenleaf, James, of NY	Deed to	Godefroy, Peter et al	1794	B2A	065	083
Greenleaf, James, of NY et al	Deed fr	Holmead, Anthony	1795	B2A	226	314
Greenleaf, James, of NY et al	Deed to	Law, Thomas, of New York NY	1795	B2B	377	030
Greenleaf, James, of NY et al	Deed to	Polock, Isaac, of Savannah GA	1796	B2B	505	206
Greenleaf, James, of NY et al	Mortgage to	Duncanson, William Mayme	1796	B2B	411	081
Greenleaf, James, of Phila. PA	Deed to	Deakins, William, Jr., of G'tn.	1797	B2B	615	371
Greenleaf, James, of Phila. PA	Deed to	Appleton, John, of Salem MA	1797	B2B	640	402
Greenleaf, James, of Phila. PA	Deed to	Appleton, John, of Salem MA	1797	B2B	696	478
Greenleaf, James, of Phila. PA	Deed to	Gridley, Richard, Jr., blacksmith	1797	C3	179	151
Greenleaf, James, of NY et al	Release fr	Law, Thomas	1797	C3	144	118
Greenleaf, James, of Phila. et al	Release fr	Law, Thomas	1797	C3	180	152
Greenleaf, James, of Phila. PA	P. of Atty. to	Cranch, William	1797	C3	251	206
Greenleaf, James, of Phila. PA	Deed to	Shanks, Michael, nailor	1797	C3	241	200
Greenleaf, James, of Phila. PA	Deed to	Simpson, George, of Phila.	1797	C3	160	132
Greenleaf, James, of Phila. PA	Deed to	Deakins, William, Jr., of G'tn.	1797	C3	169	141
Greenleaf, James, of Phila. et al	Deed to	Deakins, William, Jr., of G'tn.	1797	C3	218	183
Greenleaf, James, of Phila. et al	Deed to	Deakins, William, Jr., of G'tn.	1797	C3	221	186
Greenleaf, James, of Phila. PA	Deed to	Burrows, Edward	1797	C3	269	219
Greenleaf, James, of Phila. PA	Deed to	Dant, James	1798	C3	336	271
Greenleaf, James, of Phila. PA	Deed to	Green, Levy	1798	C3	421	332
Greenleaf, James, of Phila. PA	Deed to	Brickley, John	1798	C3	354	284
Greenleaf, James, of Phila. et al	Deed to	Pratt, Henry et al	1798	C3	301	243
Greenleaf, James, of Phila. PA	P. of Atty. fr	Cranch, William, judge	1804	K10	375	389
Greenleaf, James, of Phila. PA	P. of Atty. fr	Miller, John, Jr., of Phila.	1804	K10	377	391
Greenleaf, James, of Phila. PA	Deed to	Eliot, Samuel, Jr.	1806	Q16	232	159
Greenleaf, James, of Phila. PA	Deed to	Cranch, William	1806	Q16	229	157
Greenleaf, James, of Phila. PA	Deed to	Cranch, William	1808	T19	060	044
Greenleaf, James, of Phila. PA	D. of T. fr	Cook, Orlando, stone cutter	1809	W22	384	249
Greenleaf, James, of Phila. PA	D. of T. fr	Griffen, Launcelot, carpenter	1809	W22	385	250
Greenleaf, James, of Phila. PA	D. of T. fr	Toole, Patrick, carter	1809	W22	387	251
Greenleaf, James, of Phila. PA	D. of T. fr	Reed, Isaac	1809	W22	383	248

Party	What	Party	Year	Liber	Old	New
Greenleaf, James, of PA	Release fr	Cranch, William	1811	AB27	159	132
Greenleaf, James, of Phila.	Release fr	Reed, Isaac	1812	AB27	209	171
Greenleaf, James, of Phila. PA	Deed to	Standage, Eleazer	1812	AD29	128	099
Greenleaf, James, of Phila.	Deed fr	Free, John, sadler	1812	AB27	201	165
Greenleaf, James, of Phila.	Deed fr	Farrell, Zephaniah	1812	AB27	198	162
Greenleaf, James, of Phila. PA	Mortgage fr	Weightman, Roger C.	1813	AE30	074	056
Greenleaf, James, of Phila.	Release to	Weightman, Roger C.	1817	AN38	032	026
Greer, James	B. of S. to	Gannon, James	1808	T19	294	215
Greer, James	Deed fr	Reintzel, Anthony, of G'tn.	1812	AC28	178	134
Greer, James	Release fr	Bank of Columbia	1812	AC28	179	135
Greer, James, of G'tn.	Deed fr	Pickrell, John, of G'tn.	1816	AO39	031	026
Greer, James, of G'tn.	Deed fr	Ridgely, William G., of G'tn.	1816	AO39	030	024
Greer, James, of G'tn.	Deed fr	Smith, Richard, of G'tn.	1816	AO39	028	023
Greeves, Catharine, of Alexa.	B. of S. to	Davidson, John	1816	AK35	478	375
Gregg, Joshua	Mortgage to	Speake, Samuel	1802	I9	492	807
Gregg, Joshua	Deed to	Nicholls, Samuel	1802	I9	209	328
Gregg, Joshua, of G'tn.	Deed fr	Beall, Thomas, of George, of G'tn.	1793	A1-2	457	66
Gregg, Joshua, of G'tn.	Deed to	Morsell, James S.	1802	H8	218	208
Gregory, Nathaniel	Receipt to	Kedgly, John	1809	V21	318	234
Gregory, Nathaniel	Deed to	Gregory, William, King Wm. Co.	1809	W22	036	027
Gregory, Nathaniel	D. of T. to	Burch, Samuel	1809	V21	400	303
Gregory, Nathaniel, insolvent	Deed to	Burch, Benjamin, trustee	1810	X23	411	332
Gregory, William, King Wm. Co.	Deed fr	Gregory, Nathaniel	1809	W22	036	027
Gridley, Richard	Deed to	Harrison, William, of Balto.	1797	B2B	679	452
Gridley, Richard	Cert fr	Commissioners of Washington	1797	B2B	462	152
Gridley, Richard	Cert fr	Commissioners of Washington	1797	B2B	474	166
Gridley, Richard	Mortgage to	Law, Thomas	1798	D4	010	008
Gridley, Richard	P. of Atty. to	Moore, Benjamin, printer & editor	1798	D4	106	089
Gridley, Richard	Deed to	Whann, William, of G'tn.	1798	C3	353	283
Gridley, Richard, blacksmith	Deed fr	Law, Thomas	1798	D4	107	090
Gridley, Richard, Jr., blacksmith	Deed fr	Greenleaf, James, of Phila.	1797	C3	179	151
Gridley, Richard, Jr., blacksmith	Mortgage to	Law, Thomas	1798	D4	163	144
Gridly, Richard, Jr.	Agreement	Baker, Samuel	1795	B2B	358	006
Griffen, Launcelot, carpenter	D. of T. to	Greenleaf, James, of Phila. PA	1809	W22	385	250
Griffeth, Robert E., of Phila. PA	Deed fr	Smith, Andrew, of Richmond VA	1812	AD29	537	453
Griffeth, Robert E., of Phila. PA	Deed fr	Smith, Andrew, of Richmond VA	1812	AD29	539	455
Griffeth, Robert E., of Phila. PA	Deed fr	Smith, Andrew, of Richmond VA	1813	AE30	452	335
Griffeth, Robert E., of Phila. PA	Deed fr	Smith, Andrew, of Richmond VA	1813	AE30	450	334
Griffin, Edw.	Deed to	Prout, William	1802	I9	416	689
Griffin, Lancelot, constable	Deed to	Mallion, Vandourin	1816	AO39	047	039
Griffin, Martin & Bridget et al	Deed to	Wehrly, Jonathan, of Balto. Co.	1811	AB27	248	202
Griffin, Nehemiah et al	Deed fr	King, Elisha, of P.G. Co.	1809	W22	109	079
Griffith, Coombe	Deed fr	Law, Thomas	1807	S18	019	017
Griffith, Robert Eaglefield et al	Deed fr	Dalton, Tristram & Tobias Lear	1799	E5	061	049
Griffith, Robert Eaglefield et al	Deed fr	Commissioners of Washington	1800	E5	117	104
Griffith, Robert et al	Deed fr	Morris, Robert et al	1799	D4	186	168
Griffith, S., et al	Deed fr	McDonald, John G.	1808	T19	247	182
Griffith, Samuel G., of Alexa.	Deed fr	Bryan, Benjamin	1801	G7	092	118
Griffith, Samuel G., of Balto. et al	Deed to	McDonald, John G.	1810	Z25	223	175
Grigg, Joshua, of G'tn.	Deed to	Riggs, George W., of G'tn.	1802	G7	535	681
Grimes, Alice, of Montg. Co.	Deed fr	Lipscomb, John, of G'tn.	1817	AO39	440	301
Grimes, Alice, of Montg. Co.	Deed fr	Mountz, John, exr. of Wm. Fields	1817	AO39	442	302
Grimes, Ann, servant	Cert Free fr	Collins, William [Collings]	1814	AG32	054	042
Grimes, Ansey (C), d/o Allice	Cert Free fr	Reintzell, Daniel	1814	AG32	055	043
Grimes, Craven (C), s/o Allice	Cert Free fr	Reintzell, Daniel	1814	AG32	055	043

Party	What	Party	Year	Liber	Old	New
Grimes, Harriot (C), d/o Allice	Cert Free fr	Reintzell, Daniel	1814	AG32	055	043
Grimes, John, of G'tn.	B. of S. to	Grimes, Michael, of G'tn.	1804	L11	068	70
Grimes, Michael, insolvent	Deed to	Pryse, Thomas, trustee	1810	Z25	263	206
Grimes, Michael, of G'tn.	B. of S. fr	Grimes, John, of G'tn.	1804	L11	068	70
Grimes, Michael, of G'tn.	B. of S. to	Sands, William, of Montg. Co.	1805	N13	176	158
Grimes, Milly (C), d/o Allice	Cert Free fr	Reintzell, Daniel	1814	AG32	055	043
Grimes, Patty	B. of S. fr	Walker, John, of Francis	1812	AD29	426	358
Grimes, Polly (C), d/o Allice	Cert Free fr	Reintzell, Daniel	1814	AG32	055	043
Griswold, Chester, of OH	Deed to	Potter, Hosea E., of NY	1815	AH33	365	316
Griswold, Chester, Otsego Co. NY	Deed fr	Casteele, Edmund & Mary	1810	Z25	043	032
Groeneveldt, Gills et al	Deed fr	Bourne, Sylvanus	1796	B2B	496	192
Grose, Jacob	Deed fr	George, James	1802	I9	061	084
Grosh, Conrad, of Frederick Co.	Deed to	Thomas, Philip	1792	A1-1	067	99
Gross, Jacob	Deed to	French, Bernard	1802	H8	108	105
Gross, Jacob	Transfer to	French, Bernard	1802	H8	107	104
Gross, Jacob, an insolvent	Deed to	Threlkeld, John, trustee	1803	K10	097	103
Grout, Paul et al	Cert fr	Commissioners of Washington	1797	B2B	464	155
Grout, Paul, of Balto. et al	Deed fr	Burnes, David, of P.G. Co.	1797	C3	079	65
Grove, Elizabeth	Deed fr	Reinhart, Andrew	1804	K10	147	159
Groves, Elizabeth	Deed to	Lewis, Samuel, Jr.	1806	O14	243	160
Grundey, George, of Balto. et al	Deed fr	Stoddert, Benjamin	1806	P15	393	263
Grundy, George, Sr., of Balto.	Deed fr	Hoye, John, of Cumberland Co.	1816	AL36	525	491
Guest, John & wife, of Phila. PA	Deed to	Ewell, Thomas	1813	AE30	244	193
Guest, John, mer., of Phila. PA	D. of T. fr	Bancker, Charles N., of Phila. PA	1812	AC28	128	096
Guest, John, of Phila. Co. PA	Deed fr	Bancker, Chrales N., of Phila. PA	1812	AE30	019	015
Gunnell, Henry, of Fairfax Co. VA	Deed fr	Caldwell, Elias B., of G'tn.	1804	L11	029	28
Guss, Charles	B. of S. fr	Bayne, Elsworth, of P.G. Co.	1807	R17	353	269
Gustin, Justianna	Deed fr	Joy, John B.	1802	I9	560	908
Gustine, J.T. et al	Slaves	From Frederick Co. VA to G'tn.	1814	AH33	203	184
Guy, Everard	Release fr	Bussard, Daniel	1809	W22	354	229
Gwynn, Lucy	Slaves	From VA	1815	AH33	432	371

H

Party	What	Party	Year	Liber	Old	New
Haga, Godfrey, of Phila. PA	Deed fr	Cist, Charles, of Phila. PA	1805	N13	009	010
Hagan, Monica	B. of S. to	Abbott, John	1809	W22	070	052
Hagerty, John, Jr., of G'tn.	Deed fr	Holmead, John	1815	AH33	502	431
Hagerty, John, Jr.	Agreement	Riggs, Romulus	1815	AI34	027	031
Hagerty, John, Jr., of G'tn.	D. of T. to	Mountz, John, of G'tn.	1816	AO39	036	030
Hagner, Peter	Assign to	Simmons, William	1805	M12	295	296
Hagner, Peter	Lease fr	Melvin, James, of G'tn.	1806	O14	295	196
Hagner, Peter	B. of S. fr	Harrison, Elisha, of P.G. Co.	1806	O14	293	195
Hagner, Peter	B. of S. fr	Orr, Benjamin Grayson, of Montg.	1807	S18	410	327
Hagner, Peter	Deed fr	Boyd, Washington, marshal	1808	V21	067	053
Hagner, Peter	Deed fr	Kilty, John & Josias Wilson King	1809	V21	353	256
Hagner, Peter	Deed fr	Melvin, James, of G'tn.	1810	X23	164	121
Hagner, Peter	Cert fr	Munroe, Thomas, Supt.	1810	Y24	154	140
Hagner, Peter	Deed fr	Forrest, Joseph, agent	1810	Y24	202	185
Hagner, Peter	Deed fr	Dorsey, William H., of Balto.	1810	Y24	426	381
Hagner, Peter	Deed fr	Johns, Leonard H., of G'tn.	1810	Y24	200	184
Hagner, Peter	Deed to	Davidson, John	1811	AB27	504	412
Hagner, Peter	Deed fr	Davidson, John	1811	AB27	495	405
Hagner, Peter	Deed fr	Magruder, John Read, of P.G. Co.	1812	AC28	127	096
Hagner, Peter	B. of S. fr	Claytor, John & John Randall, Jr.	1814	AG32	422	306
Hagner, Peter	Deed fr	Corporation of Washington	1815	AI34	125	144
Hagner, Peter	Deed fr	Morsell, James S.	1815	AI34	146	167
Hagner, Peter	Cert fr	Munroe, Thomas, Supt.	1816	AM37	005	004
Hagner, Peter & Frances et al	Deed to	Bickley, Robert S., Phila. PA et al	1810	Y24	267	245
Hagner, Peter et al	Deed fr	Bickley, Robert S., Bucks Co. PA	1817	AN38	564	411
Hahn, Milly	Deed to	Wilson, Ann	1812	AC28	487	346
Haigh, Job & Elizabeth	Deed to	Lenox, Peter	1809	X23	130	093
Haigh, Job, carpenter	Deed fr	Van Ness, John & Marcia	1807	S18	115	094
Hairy, David, exr. of Martin	Deed to	Deakins, William, Jr. & B. Stoddert	1793	A1-1	338	442
Hairy, David, exr. of Martin	Deed to	Beall, Thomas & John M. Gantt	1793	A1-1	351	456
Haliday, Thomas	Deed fr	Prout, William	1806	O14	195	128
Haliday, Thomas	Deed fr	Alexander, John	1806	O14	196	129
Haliday, Thomas	B. of S. fr	Minitree, John, of G'tn.	1816	AK35	515	406
Haliday, Thomas et al	Deed to	Jones, Chalres	1807	T19	013	010
Hall, Ann, w/o John	P. of Atty. fr	Hall, John, of Richmond	1812	AC28	123	092
Hall, Benjamin & Elizabeth C.	Deed to	Beal, Thomas & John M. Gantt	1793	A1-1	267	360
Hall, Benjamin, of Q.A. Co.	Deed fr	Rozer, Henry, Carroll & Young	1795	B2B	366	017
Hall, Edward, of West River	Cert Free to	[ ], Milly (M)	1816	AK35	499	393
Hall, Elisha	B. of S. to	King, Enoch	1807	S18	164	134
Hall, Elisha, coachmaker, et ux	Deed to	Thompson, Rachel	1809	V21	157	113
Hall, Elisha, insolvent	D. of T. to	Thompson, John, trustee	1811	Z25	459	364
Hall, John	Deed fr	Burford, John A.	1804	K10	341	352
Hall, John	D. of T. to	Costigan, Joseph	1805	N13	085	078
Hall, John	Deed to	Cana, Frederick	1805	O14	094	058
Hall, John	Deed fr	Cana, Frederick	1810	X23	361	289
Hall, John, of Richmond	P. of Atty. to	Hall, Ann, w/o John	1812	AC28	123	092
Hall, Joseph C.	B. of S. fr	Hall, Richard, of Edward	1816	AM37	002	002
Hall, Joseph C.	D. ot T. to	Wallach, Richard	1817	AN38	228	166
Hall, Martha	Deposition		1807	R17	284	
Hall, Richard M.	Deed fr	Polkenhorn, Henry	1809	X23	293	233
Hall, Richard, of Edward	B. of S. to	Hall, Joseph C.	1816	AM37	002	002
Hall, William	Cert to	Hill, Susan	1808	U20	009	005
Hall, William, of G'tn. et al	Deed fr	Wools, George, of G'tn.	1804	K10	287	289
Halley, James	Cert. Free fr	Varnum, James M.	1814	AH33	228	200

Party	What	Party	Year	Liber	Old	New
Halliday, Thomas	Deed fr	Walker, Zachariah	1817	AN38	506	366
Halliday, Thomas et al	B. of S. fr	Moore, William	1815	AH33	423	364
Halsey, Henry	Deed fr	Halsey, John	1804	L11	139	141
Halsey, Henry	Deed fr	Lovejoy, Alexander	1804	L11	149	150
Halsey, Henry	Deed fr	Hughes, Theophilus	1807	R17	205	154
Halsey, Henry	Lease fr	Van Ness, John P. & Marcia	1817	AO39	267	191
Halsey, John	Deed to	Halsey, Henry	1804	L11	139	141
Halzall, of P.G. Co.	Convey fr	Lovejoy, Samuel	1808	T19	119	084
Ham, Peteer	Deed to	Forrest, Uriah	1801	G7	132	173
Ham, Peter	Deed fr	Lingenfelter, Abraham, of PA	1793	A1-1	240	328
Ham, Peter	Deed to	Beall, Thomas & John M. Gantt	1793	A1-1	237	326
Ham, Potor	Deed fr	Forrest, Uriah	1801	G7	131	171
Ham, Peter	Deed to	Forrest, Uriah	1801	G7	298	430
Hambden, William	Deed fr	Lambell, William	1812	AD29	155	122
Hambleton, Samuel	Deed fr	Hersey, John, of G'tn.	1816	AL36	149	149
Hambleton, Samuel, of G'tn.	Manumis to	[ ], Emanuel (C)	1815	AI34	395	419
Hambleton, Samuel, of G'tn.	Manumis to	Green, James (M)	1815	AI34	394	418
Hamilton, Absalom	B. of S. fr	Hurdle, Basil S.	1816	AM37	501	367
Hamilton, Alexander, P.G. Co.	Deed to	Patton, James, of Alexa.	1798	C3	345	277
Hamilton, Christiana	Release fr	Hamilton, John G.	1810	Y24	319	290
Hamilton, Christiana	Deed to	McCormick, Alexander et al	1811	AC28	035	026
Hamilton, Christiana	Deed fr	Boyd, Washington, marshal	1814	AG32	392	286
Hamilton, Christiana	Deed to	Coombe, Griffith	1814	AG32	394	287
Hamilton, Christina	Deed Gift to	Hamilton, Mary Christina, her dau.	1815	AI34	057	064
Hamilton, Christina, admx. of S.	B. of S. to	Meade, Simon	1809	W22	161	113
Hamilton, Francis P.	B. of S. to	Semmes, Tercia Henrietta	1808	V21	083	065
Hamilton, Francis P.	B. of S. to	Hamilton, Samuel S.	1808	V21	081	063
Hamilton, Francis P.	B. of S. to	White, Levi	1808	V21	049	038
Hamilton, Harriot S.	B. of S. fr	Semmes, Teresa H.	1811	AB27	422	348
Hamilton, John G.	Release to	Hamilton, Christiana	1810	Y24	319	290
Hamilton, John, of Loudoun Co.	Cert Slave	Pumphrey, James	1811	AA26	356	238
Hamilton, Letty H.	D. of T. to	Bates, David	1815	AK35	098	076
Hamilton, Louisa (C)	Cert Slave	Freeman, Constant	1816	AL36	431	411
Hamilton, Mary Christina	Deed Gift fr	Hamilton, Christina	1815	AI34	057	064
Hamilton, Mathew	Deed fr	Simpson, Josias	1817	AN38	534	388
Hamilton, Paul, of SC	Deed to	Ogeir, Thomas, of Charleston SC	1811	Z25	431	339
Hamilton, Samuel	Deposition re	Baker, Elizabeth (yellow)	1807	R17	062	
Hamilton, Samuel & Robert Brent	Convey to	Van Ness, John P.	1806	P15	271	178
Hamilton, Samuel S.	B. of S. fr	Hamilton, Francis P.	1808	V21	081	063
Hamilton, Samuel S.	B. of S. fr	Lindsay, George W.	1811	AB27	337	278
Hamilton, Samuel S.	Release to	Lindsay, Judith, admx. of George	1814	AH33	106	099
Hammond, A. et al	Release to	Nourse, Joseph	1813	AF31	011	008
Hammond, Hezekiah	B. of S. to	Worthington, William	1810	Y24	346	313
Hammond, Kitty (mulatto)	Manumis to	Addison, John	1805	M12	091	085
Hampton, Roderick, a black man	Deed fr	Suter, Alexander	1812	AB27	539	440
Hancock, James & Eliz., of Ire.	Deed to	Pleasonton, Stephen	1810	Z25	288	226
Hancock, James & Elizabeth	Deed to	Burns, George	1815	AH33	471	402
Hancock, James & Elizabeth	Deed to	Burns, George	1815	AH33	469	400
Hand, Ann	Deed fr	Corcoran, Thomas, of G'tn.	1812	AD29	461	388
Hand, Ann	Deed fr	Lenox, Peter & Margaret	1813	AF31	358	255
Hand, Anne, wid/o Charles	Deed fr	Van Ness, John P. & Marcia	1816	AO39	051	043
Handley, John	Deed fr	Commissioners of Washington	1801	G7	032	040
Handy, Betsy G.	Deed to	Graham, John	1814	AG32	195	136
Handy, James H.	B. of S. to	Gilliss, Thomas H.	1813	AE30	536	398
Handy, James H.	Convey fr	Vinson, Charles	1817	AO39	280	200

Index to District of Columbia Land Records, 1792-1817

Party	What	Party	Year	Liber	Old	New
Handy, Samuel W., of G'tn.	B. of S. fr	Richardson, Samuel, of MD	1817	AO39	286	204
Hankard, John	B. of S. to	Schultz, Henry	1802	G7	528	673
Hankart, John	B. of S. to	Thompson, William	1802	I9	508	833
Hanley, John	Deed to	Smith, John W.	1817	AN38	393	293
Hansenclever, Mary, wid., Phila.	Deed fr	Fitzsimmons, Thomas, Phila. et al	1810	X23	305	244
Hanson, Alexander Contee	Deed to	Queen, Joseph	1794	A1-2	490	93
Hanson, Alexander Contee	Deed to	Turner, Thomas, of G'tn.	1795	B2A	207	285
Hanson, Alexander Contee	Deed to	Deakins, William, Jr. et al	1797	C3	095	78
Hanson, Alexander Contee	Deed to	Grammar, Frederick, Annapolis	1797	C3	045	35
Hanson, Alexander Contee	C. Deed to	Dick, Thomas	1798	D4	017	015
Hanson, Alexander Contee	Deed to	Pratt, Henry et al	1798	C3	490	385
Hanson, Alexander Contee	Deed to	Mason, John	1799	D4	398	377
Hanson, Alexander Contee	Deed to	Beatty, Charles	1799	D4	234	216
Hanson, Alexander Contee	C. Deed to	Williams, James	1799	D4	253	237
Hanson, Alexander Contee	C. Deed to	Orme, Thomas	1799	D4	394	375
Hanson, Alexander Contee	Deed to	Dulany, Walter, of MD	1802	H8	553	515
Hanson, Alexander Contee	C. Deed to	Prout, William	1802	H8	480	441
Hanson, Alexander Contee	Deed to	Key, Philip B.	1802	H8	029	028
Hanson, Alexander Contee	Deed to	Minor, John, Fredericksburg VA	1805	M12	392	405
Hanson, Ann	B. of S. fr	Hanson, Isaac K.	1814	AH33	261	227
Hanson, Grafton, of Bladensburgh	B. of S. to	Miller, Peter	1809	W22	243	164
Hanson, Isaac K.	B. of S. to	Weightman, Roger C.	1814	AH33	261	227
Hanson, Isaac K.	B. of S. to	Hanson, Ann	1814	AH33	261	227
Hanson, Isaac Kay	B. of S. fr	Hanson, Marcia	1812	AC28	123	092
Hanson, Marcia	B. of S. to	Hanson, Isaac Kay	1812	AC28	123	092
Hanson, Maria, d/o Sam. & Mary	Deed fr	Hanson, Samuel, of Sam., et ux	1801	G7		521
Hanson, Rebecca, of G'tn.	Cert Free to	Lee, Patience	1810	Y24	054	047
Hanson, Samuel & Uriah Forrest	Deed to	Tingey, Thomas	1800	F6	092	056
Hanson, Samuel & Uriah Forrest	Deed to	Barry, James	1801	G7	003	004
Hanson, Samuel & Uriah Forrest	Deed to	Barry, James, heirs	1801	G7	002	003
Hanson, Samuel & Uriah Forrest	Deed to	Stoddert, Benjamin	1801	G7	330	461
Hanson, Samuel et al	Deed fr	Brown, Stuart	1802	H8	021	020
Hanson, Samuel et al	Deed to	Brown, Stewart	1802	H8	021	020
Hanson, Samuel et al	Deed to	Tousard, Louis	1802	I9	558	905
Hanson, Samuel et al	Deed fr	Childs, Henry	1802	H8	020	019
Hanson, Samuel, of Samuel	Deed to	Templeman, John	1801	G7	038	049
Hanson, Samuel, of Samuel et ux	Deed to	Hanson, Maria, d/o Sam. & Mary	1801	G7		521
Hanson, Samuel, of Samuel et al	Deed to	Law, Thomas	1801	G7	014	017
Hanson, Samuel, of Samuel et al	Deed to	Dinmore, Richard	1801	G7	287	398
Hanson, Samuel, of Samuel et al	Deed to	Butler, John	1802	H8	265	251
Hanson, Samuel, of Samuel et al	Deed to	Yeaton, William	1802	H8	204	195
Hanson, Samuel, of Samuel et al	Deed to	Hewitt, John	1802	H8	458	421
Hanson, Samuel, of Samuel et al	Deed to	Chandler, Walter Story	1802	I9	050	068
Hanson, Samuel, of Samuel et al	Deed to	Prout, William	1802	G7	576	725
Hanson, Samuel, of Samuel et al	Deed to	Thornton, William	1804	K10	116	125
Hanson, Samuel, of Samuel	B. of S. to	Munroe, Thomas	1806	Q16	111	072
Hanson, Samuel, of Samuel	Deed to	Dunlap, James et al	1807	R17	128	100
Hanson, Samuel, of Samuel	Deed to	Dunlap, James & Joseph Carlton	1807	R17	136	106
Hanson, Samuel, of Samuel	Deed to	Maddox, Notley, of P.G. Co.	1807	R17	131	101
Hanson, Samuel, of Samuel	Deed to	Venables, William et al	1807	R17	127	099
Hanson, Samuel, of Samuel	Deed to	Boyd, Washington	1809	V21	258	185
Hanson, Samuel, of Samuel	Manumis to	[ ], Caroline (C), age 12	1811	AA26	016	013
Hanson, Samuel, of Samuel	Deed to	Dunlap, James & John Laird	1816	AL36	324	318
Hanson, Thomas H. et al	Partition	Addison, Anthony & Daniel	1797	B2B	676	446
Hanson, Thomas, of P.G. Co.	Cert Free to	Ambush, Edward	1807	T19	016	013

Index to District of Columbia Land Records, 1792-1817

Party	What	Party	Year	Liber	Old	New
Happ, Andrew, of Shen. Co. VA	Deed to	Ridenour, David	1793	A1-1	344	448
Haraden, Nathaniel	B. of S. fr	Johnson, Archibald M.	1814	AG32	326	237
Harbaugh, Joseph	Mortgage fr	Cooper, George	1813	AF31	550	408
Harbaugh, Joseph	Release to	Cooper, George	1816	AL36	494	464
Harbaugh, Joseph & S. Bacon	B. of S. fr	Shuck, Elizabeth	1816	AL36	246	249
Harbaugh, Leonard	Transfer to	Cook, Thomas	1796	B2B	456	145
Harbaugh, Leonard	Cert fr	Commissioners of Washington	1796	B2B	456	144
Harbaugh, Leonard	Cert fr	Commissioners of Washington	1796	B2B	456	145
Harbaugh, Leonard	Deed to	Davidson, Samuel	1796	B2B	612	367
Harbaugh, Leonard	Deed to	Schneverly, Henry	1797	B2B	650	413
Harbaugh, Leonard	Deed to	Alt, Adam	1797	B2B	652	415
Harbaugh, Leonard	Cert fr	Commissioners of Washington	1798	B2B	482	175
Harbaugh, Leonard	Deed fr	Stoddert, Benjamin	1801	G7	314	439
Harbaugh, Leonard	Deed to	King, James C., of G'tn.	1801	G7	322	451
Harbaugh, Leonard	Deed fr	Mackall, Walter, of MD	1802	I9	074	104
Harbaugh, Leonard	Deed fr	Templeman, John	1802	I9	419	694
Harbaugh, Leonard	Deed to	Rinehart, Andrew	1802	I9	493	809
Harbaugh, Leonard	Deed fr	Commissioners of Washington	1802	H8	276	262
Harbaugh, Leonard	Mortgage to	Deakins, Francis et al	1804	L11	247	228
Harbaugh, Leonard et al, def.	Suit	Whann, William et al, plt.	1815	AK35	353	
Harbaugh, Leonard, of Balto. MD	D. of T. to	Hoye, John, of G'tn.	1812	AD29	443	
Harbaugh, Leonard, of Balto. et al	Deed to	Forrest, Benjamin S.	1813	AF31	491	358
Harbaugh, Leonard, of Balto. et al	Deed to	Whann, William & J.S. Morsell	1815	AK35	343	271
Harbaugh, Leonard, of Balto. et al	Deed to	Threlkeld, John	1817	AN38	295	215
Harbaugh, Samuel	Deed fr	Lovell, William	1804	K10	380	394
Harbaugh, Samuel & Elizabeth	Plat	11th Street	1817	AO39	318	
Harbaugh, Samuel, of Phila.	Deed to	Given, Thomas	1817	AO39	315	224
Harbough, Joseph	Cert Free to	Harris, Henry (negro)	1809	W22	113	082
Harbough, Joseph	Deed fr	Kid, Robert & Sarah, of Phila.	1817	AN38	555	404
Hardesty, Samuel	Assign to	Threlkeld, John	1801	G7	329	460
Hardesty, Samuel, Jr.	Deed fr	Brown, Robert	1798	D4	109	092
Hardey, William	Deed fr	Holmead, John	1805	O14	136	088
Harding, Edward, of Montg. Co.	Deed fr	Cramphin, Thomas, of Montg. Co.	1807	Q16	373	286
Harding, Edward, of Montg. Co.	Deed to	Heugh, Elizabeth, of G'tn.	1807	R17	042	034
Hardy, George & Priscilla	Deed to	Deakins, William, Jr.	1796	B2B	391	051
Hardy, Noah, of MD	Deed fr	Wigfield, Mathew	1806	Q16	011	007
Hardy, William	Deed to	Patterson, Edgar	1807	R17	214	160
Harkness, Samuel	Deed fr	Forrest, Uriah	1801	G7	024	031
Harkness, Samuel	Deed to	Higden, John S.	1805	M12	218	220
Harkness, Samuel	Manumis to	Barnes, Phebe (C), age 25	1812	AD29	285	234
Harkness, Samuel	Deed to	Briscoe, Edward, of Charles Co.	1814	AG32	093	070
Harlburt, Simeon	Deed fr	Prout, William	1801	G7	017	021
Harper & Lyles, merchants et al	Deed fr	Roberts, Owen	1802	H8	332	311
Harper, Alexander, trustee	Deed fr	McCormick, Benson, insolvent	1811	AB27	125	103
Harper, Ann (M)	Manumis fr	Coolidge, Charles & Hetty, of MA	1816	AM37	040	033
Harper, Thomas, of Phila. PA et al	Deed fr	Leamy, John & Eliz., of Phila. PA	1808	T19	227	167
Harriden, Nathaniel	B. of S. fr	Boswell, Rhody, of Charles Co.	1814	AG32	326	238
Harrington, Absolem	B. of S. fr	Chaney, Samuel	1808	T19	369	2264
Harris, Eleanor	C. Deed fr	Commissioners of Washington	1799	D4	226	208
Harris, Henry (negro)	Cert Free fr	Harbough, Joseph	1809	W22	113	082
Harris, John	Lease fr	Stoddert, Benjamin et al	1801	G7	194	259
Harris, John, insolvent	Assign to	Clare, Benjamin, trustee	1808	V21	134	098
Harris, Joseph	Lease to	Jones, Raphael, of G'tn.	1817	AN38	088	068
Harris, Joseph (C)	Lease fr	Beall, Samuel, of G'tn.	1815	AI34	525	529
Harris, Thomas et al	Deed to	Snowden, Thomas	1802	I9	381	632

Index to District of Columbia Land Records, 1792-1817

Party	What	Party	Year	Liber	Old	New
Harris, Thomas, Jr., of Annapolis	Lease to	Slye, Thomas G., of G'tn.	1810	Y24	413	372
Harris, Thomas, Jr., of Annapolis	Deed fr	Slye, Thomas G.	1814	AH33	374	324
Harrison, Benjamin, Jr.	Deed fr	Morris, Robert et al	1798	D4	069	058
Harrison, Elisha, of P.G. Co.	B. of S. to	Hagner, Peter	1806	O14	293	195
Harrison, George	Deed to	Sterret, Samuel	1802	I9	496	814
Harrison, George & wife Sophia	Deed to	Busti, Paul, merchant, of PA	1802	I9	119	174
Harrison, George et al	Release to	Nourse, Joseph	1813	AF31	011	008
Harrison, George, of PA et al	Deed fr	Nicholson, John & Hannah, of PA	1795	B2A	344	485
Harrison, Gustavus	Deed fr	Richards, George	1817	AO39	287	205
Harrison, Gustavus, of G'tn.	D. of T. fr	Cassin, James, of G'tn.	1816	AK35	496	390
Harrison, John	Deed fr	Dermott, James R.	1802	H8	266	252
Harrison, John	Assign to	Harrison, Robert	1805	N13	273	226
Harrison, John	Deed fr	Forrest, Joseph, trustee	1813	AE30	333	249
Harrison, Matthew, Jr.	D. of T. fr	Lewis, Joseph, Jr.	1810	Y24	547	480
Harrison, Richard	Deed fr	Chandler, Walter Story	1810	Y24	440	392
Harrison, Richard	Manumis to	[ ], Leonard (negro), age 36	1811	Z25	173	137
Harrison, Richard	Deed to	Nourse, Joseph	1817	AN38	228	168
Harrison, Richard H., of G'tn.	Deed to	Peter, David et al	1805	M12	327	331
Harrison, Richard, of Phila. PA	Cert fr	Commissioners of Washington	1797	B2B	463	155
Harrison, Richard, of Phila. PA	Deed fr	Commissioners of Washington	1799	D4	246	229
Harrison, Richard, of G'tn.	Deed fr	Chandler, Walter Story, of G'tn.	1807	Q16	399	307
Harrison, Richard, of Alexa. et al	Deed to	Muncaster, John, of Alexa.	1811	AB27	00½	001
Harrison, Robert	Assign fr	Harrison, John	1805	N13	273	226
Harrison, Robert	Deed to	Dermott, Alice, of Stafford VA	1806	P15	312	206
Harrison, William, of Balto.	Deed fr	Barry, James, of Balto.	1796	B2B	492	186
Harrison, William, of Balto.	Mortgage fr	Nicholson, John, of Phila.	1797	B2B	678	449
Harrison, William, of Balto.	Deed fr	Gridley, Richard	1797	B2B	679	452
Harrison, William, of Balto.	Deed fr	Barry, James & James R. Dermott	1800	E5	335	323
Harrison, William, of Balto.	Deed fr	Neale, John Baptist, Westm. Co.	1801	G7	296	411
Harry, David, of Washington Co.	C. Deed to	Deakins, William, Jr., of G'tn.	1795	B2A	204	280
Harshman, Henry	Deed fr	Barber, John, an insolvent	1803	K10	075	81
Harshman, Henry	Deed fr	Marshall, John	1804	L11	077	79
Harshman, Henry	Deed fr	Magruder, John & Rachael	1804	L11	239	219
Harshman, Henry	Mortgage fr	Vierse, Hezekiah, of Montg. Co.	1804	L11	078	80
Harshman, Henry	Deed to	Marshall, John	1804	L11	236	218
Harshman, Henry	B. of S. to	Cochran, Alexander, Jr.	1804	L11	245	227
Harshman, Henry	P. of Atty. fr	Southoron, Thomas L., in P.G. Co.	1804	L11	330	301
Harshman, Henry	Mortgage to	Cochran, Alexander, Jr.	1805	M12	098	091
Harshman, Henry	Receipt fr	Smith, Hugh	1813	AF31	312	223
Harshman, Henry & Susannah	Deed fr	Moore, John C., of P.G. Co.	1813	AF31	312	223
Harshman, Henry, insolvent	Assign to	Barber, John, trustee	1809	V21	420	321
Hartman, Charles	Deed fr	Johnson, Isaac, of G'tn.	1816	AL36	317	312
Hartman, Charles	Deed fr	Corcoran, Thomas	1817	AO39	213	155
Hartman, Charles	Manumis to	[ ], Blackston (C), age 28	1817	AN38	515	373
Hartman, Frederick	Deed fr	King, Charles, of G'tn.	1817	AN38	191	138
Harvey, Peter, of Phila. PA	Deed fr	Tingey, Thomas, Gent.	1804	L11	277	255
Harvey, Samuel, of Phila. PA	Deed fr	Dorsey, William H., of G'tn.	1806	Q16	305	232
Harvy, Peter, coachmaker, Phila.	Deed to	Cope, Jasper, mer., of Balto.	1807	S18	142	116
Harwood, Thomas, collector	Deed to	Williams, James, of Annapolis	1801	G7	085	110
Hasler, Joseph	Mortgage to	Baum & Pritchard	1802	I9	547	889
Hatfield, Jonathan, atty. for	B. of S. to	Thornton, William	1815	AH33	420	362
Hatfield, Jonathan, h/o Francis	Deed to	Cassin, James, of G'tn.	1815	AI34	305	
Hauser, Michael, Capt.	Deed fr	Ritchie, Abner	1811	AA26	214	147
Haw, John S., of G'tn.	Deed fr	Pleasonton, Stephen	1816	AK35	480	377
Hawker, John, of G'tn. et al	Deed to	Forrest, Uriah	1792	A1-1	169	242

Index to District of Columbia Land Records, 1792-1817

Party	What	Party	Year	Liber	Old	New
Hawker, Margaret, of G'tn.	Deed fr	Balch, Stephen B., of G'tn.	1796	B2B	504	204
Hawkins, George Fraser et al	Decree for	Deakins, William & Jane et al	1797	C3	015	12
Hawkins, George Fraser	N. of S.	Beatty, Charles, of Frederick Co.	1803	K10	006	6
Hawkins, James, of, of P.G. Co.	Mortgage fr	Addision, Thomas G., of P.G. Co.	1811	Z25	536	426
Hawkins, Matilda	B. of S. fr	Peter, Thomas & Mary Bromley	1812	AC28	159	118
Hay, Robert	Deed fr	Commissioners of Washington	1798	C3	494	389
Hay, Robert	Deed fr	Commissioners of Washington	1798	C3	493	387
Hay, Robert	Deed to	Cloakey, Samuel	1808	V21	053	041
Hay, Robert	Deed to	Clephan, Lewis	1809	X23	174	129
Hayman, William	Deed fr	Pickrell, John	1817	AO39	156	117
Hayman, William	Deed fr	Fitzhugh, Samuel, of G'tn.	1817	AN38	562	409
Hayne, Matthias	Deed fr	Dorsey, William H.	1802	I9	165	250
Haynes, Catharine	Deed fr	Van Ness, John P. & Marcia	1817	AN38	153	112
Hayre, John	B. of S. to	Jones, Charles	1811	AA26	083	059
Hays, Laurence	B. of S. to	Barry, Garret P.	1804	L11	020	19
Hays, Thomas, of P.G. Co.	Mortgage fr	Hughes, Theophilus	1809	V21	305	223
Haywood, Thomas, insolvent	Deed to	Caldwell, Elias B., trustee	1804	L11	082	83
Hazel, Henry, admr. of Jeremiah	B. of S. to	Morsell, James S.	1810	Y24	058	051
Hazel, Jeremiah	Deed fr	Walker, George	1804	K10	236	244
Hazel, Jeremiah	Deed to	Brooks, William H.	1804	K10	324	332
Hazel, Jeremiah	Deed fr	Beall, Alexander, of Frederick Co.	1804	K10	237	245
Hazel, Jeremiah	Deed fr	Threlkeld, John	1805	M12	129	124
Hazel, Jeremiah	Deed fr	Brown, Robert	1805	M12	128	123
Hazel, Jeremiah, of G'tn.	Deed fr	Brooks, William H., of G'tn.	1804	K10	234	243
Hazle, Henry	Manumis to	[ ], Austin (C), or Austin Queen	1812	AC28	381	277
Hazle, Jeremiah	Deed fr	Walker, George	1802	I9	425	703
Hazle, Jeremiah	Deed to	Walker, George	1802	I9	242	390
Hazle, Jeremiah	Deed fr	Doyle, Elizabeth, of G'tn.	1802	G7	532	676
Hazle, Jeremiah	Deed to	Turner, Samuel	1806	Q16	094	061
Hazle, Zachariah	Deed to	Mallion, Vandoren	1816	AM37	106	085
Hazle, Zachariah, of G'tn.	B. of S. to	Thompson, Lydia, of G'tn.	1806	Q16	066	042
Healy, Joseph & Nancy, of Balto.	Deed to	Carmical, Alexander, of G'tn.	1811	AB27	059	051
Healy, Patrick et al	B. of S. fr	Caffrey, Daniel	1802	H8	508	467
Heard, Edward	Cert Slave	From Chrales Co. MD	1816	AM37	194	144
Heard, James B., trustee	Deed fr	Fry, Thomas, insolvent	1806	P15	349	231
Heard, James B.	Deed to	Dobbyn, John	1808	U20	096	053
Hearn, Isaac, of A.A. Co.	Deed to	Ewell, James	1817	AN38	041	033
Hearn, John	B. of S. fr	Fitzgerald, William	1813	AE30	413	304
Hearn, John, s/o Wm., dec.	Assign to	Andrews, George, as atty.	1816	AL36	146	146
Hearn, William, of G'tn.	Deed to	Ownings, Patrick, of Balto.	1804	K10	401	415
Heater, Conrad	Lease to	Livers, Ignatius	1805	M12	108	101
Heater, Conrad [Heter], of G'tn.	Lease to	Fleet, Henry, of G'tn.	1804	L11	021	20
Heath, Nathaniel	Deed fr	Beall, Thomas, of George	1810	Z25	084	064
Heath, Nathaniel H	Deed to	Brent, Elizabeth, w/o Daniel	1815	AI34	333	366
Heath, Nathaniel H.	Deed fr	Beall, Thomas, of George	1808	U20	382	211
Heath, Nathaniel H. et al	Deed fr	Ringold, Tench et al	1810	Z25	083	063
Heath, Nathaniel H.	Deed to	Corcoran, Thomas	1811	Z25	507	402
Heath, Nathaniel H.	Release fr	Bank of Columbia	1812	AD29	356	299
Heath, Nathaniel H.	Deed fr	Dorsey, William H., of Balto. Co.	1812	AD29	355	298
Heath, Nathaniel H.	Deed to	King, William, Jr.	1812	AC28	202	143
Heath, Nathaniel H.	Deed fr	Murdock, John, of G'tn.	1812	AD29	354	297
Heath, Nathaniel H.	D. of T. to	Eliot, Samuel, Jr.	1813	AE30	276	213
Heath, Nathaniel H.	Deed fr	Pratt, Henry et al	1813	AE30	522	387
Heath, Nathaniel H.	Deed fr	Murdock, John, of G'tn.	1813	AF31	141	094
Heath, Nathaniel H.	Release fr	Bank of Columbia	1813	AF31	145	097

Index to District of Columbia Land Records, 1792-1817

Party	What	Party	Year	Liber	Old	New
Heath, Nathaniel H.	Deed fr	Dorsey, William H., of Balto.	1813	AF31	142	095
Heath, Nathaniel H.	Deed to	Ringgold, Tench	1814	AH33	057	051
Heath, Nathaniel H.	Deed fr	Glover, Charles	1814	AH33	089	081
Heath, Nathaniel H.	Deed to	Elliott, Samuel, Jr. [Eliot]	1815	AI34	458	470
Heath, Nathaniel H.	Release fr	Elliott, Samuel, Jr.	1815	AI34	332	365
Heath, William	Deed fr	Young, Thomas	1815	AI34	349	380
Heathcote, John, of Balto.	Deed fr	Riddle, Joseph, of Alexa.	1811	AB27	268	219
Hebb, William, of P.G. Co.	Deed fr	Cocking, William	1812	AE30	033	025
Hebb, William, of P.G. Co.	Deed fr	Cocking, William	1812	AE30	045	034
Hebb, William, of P.G. Co.	Deed fr	Kerr, Alexander	1813	AF31	298	212
Hebb, William, of P.G. Co.	Deed to	Somerville, Henry V. of St. M. Co.	1814	AG32	291	212
Hebb, William, of P.G. Co.	Deed fr	Prout, William	1814	AG32	176	125
Hebb, William, of P.G. Co.	Deed to	Somerville, Henry V., St. Mary's	1815	AH33	467	399
Hebb, William, of P.G. Co.	Deed to	Bradley, William Alfred	1816	AL36	117	118
Hebb, William, of P.G. Co.	Deed fr	Laird, John, exr. of J. Carleton	1817	AO39	209	153
Hebner, Michael	Mortgage fr	Schnively, Henry	1806	P15	112	070
Hebron, Abigail, of Petersburg	Lease to	Ellis, Samuel B.	1817	AO39	454	312
Hebron, John	Assign fr	Smallwood, Samuel N.	1810	Z25	229	180
Hedges, Hanson	Deed to	Dobbin, David	1812	AD29	286	235
Hedges, Nicholas	Deed fr	Ritchie, Mary, of Frederick Co.	1795	B2A	244	340
Hedges, Nicholas	Deed fr	Davidson, John, of Annapolis	1799	D4	367	353
Hedges, Nicholas	Deed fr	Ritchie, Abner	1802	I9	292	478
Hedges, Nicholas	Deed fr	Reintzel, Anthony	1802	I9	445	736
Hedges, Nicholas	Deed fr	Beall, Thomas	1802	I9	292	479
Hedges, Nicholas	Deed fr	Beatty, Charles, heirs of	1806	O14	199	130
Hedges, Nicholas	Deed fr	Fields, William	1806	P15	375	250
Hedges, Nicholas	Deed fr	Beatty, William, exrs. of	1807	T19	011	009
Hedges, Nicholas	Deed fr	Beatty, Charles, heirs of	1808	U20	184	102
Hedges, Nicholas	Deed to	Bussard, Daniel	1809	X23	288	229
Hedges, Nicholas	Deed fr	Beall, Thomas, of George	1810	Y24	468	414
Hedges, Nicholas	Deed fr	Peter, George	1813	AF31	227	156
Hedges, Nicholas	Deed to	Boarman, Raphael W.	1815	AK35	062	048
Hedges, Nicholas	Deed to	Smith, Mary	1815	AK35	060	046
Hedges, Nicholas	Deed to	Mountz, John, exr. of Wm. Fields	1817	AO39	429	293
Hedges, Nicholas	Deed to	Pierce, Abner	1817	AN38	115	085
Hedges, Nicholas, guardian	Deed to	Dawes, Isaac	1810	Z25	068	051
Hedges, Nicholas, of G'tn.	Deed to	Beale, Thomas, of George, of G'tn.	1794	A1-2	471	77
Hedges, Nicholas, of G'tn.	Deed fr	Hillary, Nicholas, of G'tn.	1806	Q16	109	071
Hedges, Nicholas, of G'tn. et al	Deed fr	Knowles, Henry, of G'tn.	1808	U20	033	019
Hedges, Nicholas, of G'tn.	Deed to	Garey, Ann, of G'tn.	1815	AI34	442	457
Hedges, William Ritchie, s/o Nich.	Indenture to	Bowie, Washington	1812	AD29	223	183
Hedrick, John	Deed fr	Forrest, Uriah	1801	G7	248	334
Hedrick, Margaret of NC	Deed to	Beatty, Charles, of G'tn.	1794	A1-2	494	97
Heeter, Conrad, Indiana Co. PA	Deed to	Livers, Ignatius, of G'tn.	1807	R17	221	166
Heeter, Conrad, of G'tn.	Deed to	Trundle, Horatio, of G'tn.	1806	Q16	170	113
Heeter, Conrad [Huter], of G'tn.	Lease to	Boarman, John B. et al	1796	B2B	602	353
Heigh, James	Letter fr	Blake, Betty H., w/o Dr. James H.	1807	S18	265	208
Heigh, James, of Balto. Co.	Deed to	Blake, James H., Dr.	1807	S18	265	208
Heighe, James, Calvert Co.	D. of T. fr	Blake, James Heighe, Dr., G'tn.	1796	B2B	549	276
Heighe, James, Capt., Calvert Co.	Deed fr	Blake, James Heighe, Dr., G'tn.	1799	D4	291	275
Heirshman, Matthias	Deed to	Deakins, William, Jr.	1792	A1-1	162	232
Heise, Christian	Deed to	Renner, Daniel & Daniel Bussard	1810	Z25	155	122
Heise, Christian, of G'tn.	Deed fr	Lucas, Henry	1809	X23	158	116
Heise, John C., of G'tn.	Lease fr	Wilson, John, of Henry, P.G. Co.	1814	AG32	255	182
Heisler, Joseph, of G'tn.	B. of S. to	Crawford, William	1809	W22	105	076

Party	What	Party	Year	Liber	Old	New
Helen, Walter	Deed to	Matthews, William, Rev.	1814	AG32	212	148
Hellen, Walter	Cert fr	Commissioners of Washington	1795	B2A	331	465
Hellen, Walter	Deed fr	Kerr, Alexander, of Alexa.	1800	F6	039	024
Hellen, Walter	Deed fr	Lovell, William, of Alexa.	1801	G7	445	581
Hellen, Walter	Deed to	Willing, Thomas, mer., of Phila.	1801	G7	323	453
Hellen, Walter	Deed fr	Munroe, Thomas, Supt.	1802	I9	175	267
Hellen, Walter	Deed fr	Munroe, Thomas, Supt.	1802	I9	178	271
Hellen, Walter	Deed fr	Munroe, Thomas, Supt.	1802	I9	177	270
Hellen, Walter	Deed fr	White, Alexander et al	1802	H8	016	015
Hellen, Walter	Deed fr	Munroe, Thomas, Supt.	1802	I9	176	268
Hellen, Walter	Deed to	Feltwell, William, of Hayes, Eng.	1804	L11	399	354
Hellen, Walter	Deed fr	Templeman, John, of Allegany Co.	1806	P15	364	242
Hellen, Walter	Deed fr	Johns, Richard & Leonard H., G'tn.	1806	Q16	035	023
Hellen, Walter	Deed fr	Munroe, Thomas, Supt.	1806	Q16	039	025
Hellen, Walter	Deed fr	Ardrey, John et al	1806	Q16	115	074
Hellen, Walter	Deed fr	Coles, John, now of G'tn.	1807	S18	125	103
Hellen, Walter	Deed fr	Threlkeld, John, of G'tn.	1807	S18	122	099
Hellen, Walter	D. of T. fr	Belt, Hiram	1810	X23	370	297
Hellen, Walter	Deed fr	Ardrey, William	1811	AB27	042	037
Hellen, Walter	Deed to	Forrest, Joseph & Edmund Law	1811	AB27	213	173
Hellen, Walter, exr. of	Cert Slave	From Calvert Co. MD	1817	AN38	483	349
Hellen, Walter, exr. of	Cert Slaves	From MD	1817	AO39	175	130
Hellen, Walter, mer., of Balto.	Deed fr	Whann, William, mer., of G'tn.	1800	E5	295	288
Hellen, Walter, of G'tn.	Deed to	Kolb, Michael [Culp]	1793	A1-2	416	25
Hellen, Walter, of G'tn.	Deed fr	Burnes, David, of P.G. Co.	1797	C3	100	82
Hellen, Walter, of G'tn.	Deed to	Johnson, Joshua	1799	D4	215	199
Hellriggle, Christian L.	Deed fr	Commissioners of Washington	1798	C3	503	395
Hembler, John H.	B. of S. to	[ ], Rachel (negro)	1809	W22	115	083
Hemler, John	Deed to	Tuckfield, William H.P.	1811	AB27	273	223
Hemler, John	B. of S. to	Jordan, William	1811	AA26	160	110
Hemsley, William & Sarah	Deed to	Gantt, John M. & Thomas Beall	1793	A1-1	251	342
Henderson, John	Mortgage fr	Bowman, Peter [Bauman]	1796	B2B	442	124
Henderson, John, architect	Bond	Greenleaf, James, New York NY	1795	B2A	262	365
Henderson, John, architect	Agreement	Greenleaf, James, New York NY	1795	B2A	259	362
Henderson, Richard	Deed to	Stoddert, Benjamin et al	1792	A1-1	168	240
Henderson, Richard	Deed to	Beall, Thomas & John M. Gantt	1793	A1-1	202	282
Henderson, Sara	Manumis to	[ ], Ara (Negro)	1804	L11	260	239
Henderson, Sarah	Deed fr	Lingan, James M., of Montg. Co.	1809	X23	198	149
Henderson, Sarah, of G'tn.	Deed to	Brookes, Joseph, of G'tn.	1815	AK35	116	089
Hendley, Richard	Deed to	Frank, Lewis	1814	AF31	496	363
Hendley, Richard	Deed fr	Sessford, John	1816	AM37	042	035
Hendley, Richard	Deed fr	Mauro, Philip	1816	AL36	506	475
Hendley, Richard	D. of T. to	Hewitt, James	1817	AO39	413	281
Hendley, Richard & Elkanah	Deed fr	Van Ness, John P.	1810	Z25	028	021
Henley, Elkanah	Deed to	Henley, Richard	1811	AB27	151	126
Henley, Richard	Deed fr	Henley, Elkanah	1811	AB27	151	126
Henley, Robert, Capt.	Cert fr	Munroe, Thomas, Supt.	1815	AI34	365	394
Henley, Robert, Capt.	Cert fr	Munroe, Thomas, Supt.	1815	AI34	364	392
Henley, Robert, Capt. U.S.N.	Plat		1815	AI34	367	
Henley, Robert, Capt. U.S.N.	Cert fr	Munroe, Thomas, Supt.	1815	AI34	366	394
Henley, Robert, U.S.N.	Mortgage to	Lear, Tobias	1815	AI34	386	411
Henley, Robert, U.S.N.	Deed fr	Carr, Overton	1815	AI34	398	422
Henly, Robert, Capt.	Cert fr	Munroe, Thomas, Supt.	1815	AI34	364	392
Henning, Thomas	Deed fr	Johnson, Joseph	1813	AE30	470	350
Henop & Co., creditors of	Memo fr	Henop, Philip	1802	I9	002	003

Index to District of Columbia Land Records, 1792-1817   195

Party	What	Party	Year	Liber	Old	New
Henop, Philip	Memo to	*Henop & Co.*, creditors of	1802	I9	002	003
Henry, John	Cert fr	Commissioners of Washington	1796	B2A	338	477
Henry, John	Transfer to	Robertson, Alexander	1796	B2A	338	447
Henry, Robert J. et al	Deed fr	Mountz, John, Sr., of G'tn.	1807	R17	278	212
Henry, Robert J. et al	Deed to	Olliver, Elizabeth	1808	U20	288	154
Henry, William	B. of S. fr	Walker, Samuel	1817	AN38	274	200
Henry, William (C), & wife	Manumis fr	Ball, Henry W.	1812	AD29	481	407
Henry, William (negro) & wife	Manumis fr	Ball, Henry W.	1811	Z25	172	136
Henry, William, of Hyatts Town	Deed fr	Rhoades, George, of Hyatts Town	1814	AG32	443	321
Hepburn, David	Deed fr	Carroll, Daniel, of Duddington	1802	I9	048	065
Hepburn, Samuel	Deed to	Beall, Thomas & John M. Gantt	1793	A1-1	329	432
Herbert, Francis, Jr.	Deed fr	Herbert, Francis, of St. Mary's Co.	1816	AM37	055	045
Herbert, Francis, of St. Mary's Co.	Deed fr	Threlkeld, John, of Montg. Co.	1796	B2B	501	200
Herbert, Francis, of St. Mary's Co.	Deed fr	Prout, William	1802	I9	016	022
Herbert, Francis, of St. Mary's Co.	Deed to	Jones, Monica, of St. Mary's Co.	1809	W22	289	191
Herbert, Francis, of St. Mary's Co.	Deed fr	Jones, Monica, of St. Mary's Co.	1815	AK35	382	301
Herbert, Francis, of St. Mary's Co.	Deed to	Herbert, Francis, Jr.	1816	AM37	055	045
Herbert, James	Deed fr	Brashears, Nathaniel	1815	AI34	416	437
Herbert, John (negro)	Manumis fr	Pearce, Catherine	1805	N13	362	291
Herbert, Polly (C), age 20	Manumis fr	Brackenridge, John	1816	AM37	223	164
Hereford, John	Deed fr	Dorsey, William H., of Balto.	1811	AA26	190	129
Herford, Henry	Deed to	McGowan, John et al	1816	AL36	445	423
Herford, Henry	D. of T. to	McGowen, John et al	1816	AM37	138	107
Herford, Henry	Deed to	McGowan, John et al	1816	AL36	450	426
Herford, Henry, trustee	Assign fr	Kean, William, insolvent	1808	V21	137	100
Herford, John	Deed fr	Munroe, Thomas	1802	H8	380	353
Herford, John	Deed fr	Murdock, John, of G'tn.	1811	AA26	192	131
Heron, William	Deed fr	Willson, Robert	1802	I9	026	034
Heron, William	Deed to	Brown, Robert	1810	X23	379	304
Heronimus, Pendleton	Slaves	From Winchester VA	1813	AE30	332	249
Heronimus, Pendleton	Deed fr	Newton, John S.	1814	AG32	446	323
Heronimus, Pendleton	Manumis to	[ ], Rachel (C)	1816	AL36	103	103
Heronimus, Pendleton	D. of T. to	Jenkins, Benjamin R.	1816	AM37	475	343
Heronimus, Pendleton	Deed to	Webster, Toppan & Geo. Andrews	1816	AL36	046	046
Heronimus, Pendleton	B. of S. to	Orr, Benjamin Grayson	1817	AO39	338	241
Heronimus, Pendleton, of G'tn.	Deed to	Holtzman, Jacob, of G'tn.	1814	AG32	447	324
Herron, Walter	Deed fr	Wheeler, Luke & John Cowper, VA	1817	AN38	136	100
Hersey, Benjamin & E. Eliason	Deed to	Foxall, Henry, of G'tn.	1814	AH33	192	175
Hersey, Benjamin, of Montg. Co.	Deed fr	Corporation of Georgetown	1810	Z25	328	256
Hersey, Benjamin, of Montg. Co.	Lease to	Foxall, Henry, of G'tn.	1810	Z25	332	259
Hersey, Benjamin, of Montg. Co.	Deed fr	Parrott, Richard, of G'tn.	1814	AG32	380	276
Hersey, John	Deed fr	Whann, William, of G'tn.	1816	AL36	129	130
Hersey, John, of G'tn.	Bond to	Williams, John S., trustee	1814	AG32	344	249
Hersey, John, of G'tn.	Deed fr	Nevitt, William, of P.G. Co.	1814	AH33	241	209
Hersey, John, of G'tn.	D. of T. to	Williams, John S., of G'tn.	1814	AG32	339	246
Hersey, John, of G'tn.	Deed to	Hambleton, Samuel	1816	AL36	149	149
Herstons, Charles, of G'tn.	Deed fr	Patterson, Edgar, of G'tn.	1808	V21	058	053
Herstons, Charles, of G'tn.	Deed to	Ross, John, of G'tn.	1810	Y24	065	057
Herstons, Charles, of G'tn.	Deed to	Patterson, Edgar, of G'tn.	1813	AF31	213	145
Herty, George et al	Deed fr	Munroe, Thomas, Supt.	1802	I9	151	229
Herty, Thomas	Deed fr	Densley, Hugh	1801	G7	480	617
Herty, Thomas	Deed fr	Dorsey, William H.	1802	I9	311	512
Herty, Thomas	Deed fr	Thompson, James	1802	G7	527	671
Herty, Thomas	Cert fr	Commissioners of Washington	1802	H8	201	192
Herty, Thomas	Lease fr	Johncherrez, Alexander L., G'tn.	1804	K10	342	354

Party	What	Party	Year	Liber	Old	New
Herty, Thomas	Deed fr	Kaldenbaugh, Andrew, of G'tn.	1805	M12	048	046
Herty, Thomas	Assign fr	Bodge, John, Allegany Co. et al	1805	N13	079	072
Herty, Thomas	Deed fr	Potts, James Bowman	1805	M12	132	127
Herty, Thomas	Deed fr	Serra, Augustin [Sarah]	1806	Q16	101	066
Herty, Thomas	Deed fr	Easton, David, insolvent	1806	P15	395	265
Herty, Thomas	D. of T. fr	Kaldenbach, Andrew, of G'tn.	1806	P15	057	034
Herty, Thomas	Deed to	Tayloe, John	1807	S18	148	121
Herty, Thomas	Convey fr	Banks, John	1807	S18	243	192
Herty, Thomas	B. of S. fr	Bridges, John	1807	R17	323	245
Herty, Thomas	Deed fr	McCutchen, James	1808	T19	055	041
Herty, Thomas	Release to	Serra, Augustin	1809	W22	195	136
Herty, Thomas	Release to	Grant, Edward M.	1811	AB27	057	049
Herty, Thomas	Deed to	Hurford, Henry	1812	AD29	042	030
Herty, Thomas	Convey to	Clarke, Walter	1814	AG32	308	225
Herty, Thomas & James McKim	Deed fr	Gatton, Azariah	1806	Q16	181	121
Herty, Thomas & James McKim	Deed fr	Washington, Lund & Sussnna	1806	Q16	205	139
Herty, Thomas & James McKim	Deed fr	Smoot, Alexander S.	1806	Q16	183	122
Herty, Thomas & James McKim	Assign fr	Washington, Lund & Susanna	1806	Q16	270	189
Herty, Thomas & James McKim	Deed fr	Grant, Edward M.	1807	R17	115	090
Herty, Thomas & James McKim	Deed fr	Smoot, Alexander	1807	R17	117	091
Herty, Thomas & James McKim	Deed fr	Bryan, Benjamin	1807	R17	179	137
Herty, Thomas & James McKim	Deed fr	Bryan, Benjamin	1807	R17	010	009
Herty, Thomas & James McKim	B. of S. fr	Washington, Lund	1807	R17	293	224
Herty, Thomas & James McKim	Deed fr	Gatton, Azariah	1808	T19	053	039
Herty, Thomas & James McKim	Assign fr	Bryan, Benjamin	1808	T19	050	038
Herty, Thomas et al	Deed to	Young, Thomas	1808	T19	031	024
Herty, Thomas, notary	Cert Free to	Ennis, Polly	1809	W22	373	241
Herty, Thomas, trustee	Deed fr	Washington, Lund, insolvent	1805	N13	320	258
Herty, Thomas, trustee	Deed fr	King, William R., insolvent	1806	O14	265	175
Herty, Thomas, trustee	Deed fr	Rutherford, William, insolvent	1807	R17	140	108
Herty, Thomas, trustee	Assign fr	Glenn, Robert, insolvent	1808	V21	047	036
Herty, Thomas, trustee	Assign fr	Gantt, Edward	1809	V21	140	102
Hessey, Caleb	B. of S. to	Brown, Blanch	1809	W22	206	142
Heugh, Elizabeth, of G'tn.	Deed fr	Harding, Edward, of Montg. Co.	1807	R17	042	034
Heugh, Harriot		Certificate of Slaves	1802	H8	319	299
Heugh, John		Certificate of Slaves	1802	H8	319	299
Heugh, John	Manumis to	[ ], Hezekiah (negro)	1805	O14	113	071
Heugh, John	Deed fr	Mackall, Benjamin & Christiana	1814	AG32	055	043
Heugh, John & John Murdock	Deed to	Smith, Clement, of P.G. Co.	1808	T19	310	226
Heugh, John & John Murdock	Deed to	Marbury, William	1808	T19	069	050
Heugh, John et al	Deed fr	Brent, William	1802	I9	279	455
Heugh, John et al	Deed fr	Addison, Anthony	1802	I9	272	452
Heugh, John et al	Deed fr	Addison, John	1802	I9	279	456
Heugh, John, of G'tn., trustee	Deed to	Worthington, William, Jr.	1815	AH33	547	468
Heugh, John, of G'tn., trustee	Deed to	Bowie, Washington et al	1815	AI34	091	104
Heugh, John, of G'tn.	Deed to	Adlum, John	1817	AN38	189	137
Heugh, Mary		Certificate of Slaves	1802	H8	319	299
Hewes, Archibald	Cert Free to	Butler, David (C)	1812	AD29	174	140
Hewit, James	Deed fr	Aiken, John	1804	L11	153	153
Hewit, John et al	Deed to	Gaines, Richard	1805	N13	202	176
Hewitt, James	B. of S. fr	Washington, Lund	1809	V21	327	241
Hewitt, James	D. of T. to	Bradley, Abraham, Jr.	1811	AA26	396	263
Hewitt, James	Deed fr	Bradley, Phineas	1811	AA26	389	259
Hewitt, James	Deed to	Varnum, James W.	1813	AF31	210	142
Hewitt, James	Release fr	Bradley, Abraham, Jr.	1813	AF31	209	141

Index to District of Columbia Land Records, 1792-1817 197

Party	What	Party	Year	Liber	Old	New
Hewitt, James	B. of S. to	Boyd, Washington	1814	AG32	402	293
Hewitt, James	Mortgage to	Hewitt, William	1815	AH33	458	392
Hewitt, James	D. of T. fr	Hendley, Richard	1817	AO39	413	281
Hewitt, John	Deed fr	Thornton, William et al	1802	H8	458	421
Hewitt, John	Deed fr	Hanson, Samuel, of Samuel et al	1802	H8	458	421
Hewitt, John	P. of Atty. fr	Phillebrown, John	1802	S18	400	
Hewitt, John	Deed fr	Gant, John Mackall et al	1802	H8	458	421
Hewitt, John	Deed to	Lingan, James M.	1806	Q16	328	252
Hewitt, John	Deed to	Martin, Honore, of Montg. Co.	1806	O14	325	216
Hewitt, John	Deed to	Maddox, Notley, of P.G. Co.	1807	S18	335	263
Hewitt, John	D. of T. fr	Warner, Osborn	1810	Z25	159	125
Hewitt, John	Deed to	Scholfield, Andrew, of Alexa.	1811	AA26	235	161
Hewitt, John	D. of T. fr	Warner, Osborn	1811	Z25	169	133
Hewitt, John	Release to	Weightman, Roger Chew	1813	AF31	441	317
Hewitt, John & Joseph Scholfield	D. of T. fr	Mayer, Frederick	1813	AF31	403	291
Hewitt, John & Jos. Scholfield	Deed to	Scholfield, Andrew, of Alexa.	1815	AK35	004	003
Hewitt, John, assignee	Deed to	Brown, Joel	1802	I9	054	074
Hewitt, John, assignee et al	Deed to	Perkins, Benjamin	1806	O14	170	111
Hewitt, John, assignee U. Forrest	Deed to	Shaw, John & James Birth	1807	S18	333	261
Hewitt, John et al	Deed to	Dinmore, Richard	1801	G7	287	398
Hewitt, John et al	Deed fr	Lanham, Elisha	1802	I9	372	617
Hewitt, John et al	Deed to	Stoddert, Benjamin	1802	I9	248	400
Hewitt, John et al	Deed to	Cozens, William R.	1802	I9	581	942
Hewitt, John et al	Deed fr	Forrest, Uriah	1802	I9	361	598
Hewitt, John et al	Deed to	Smith, Walter et al	1804	K10	247	254
Hewitt, John et al	Deed to	Smith, Walter, of G'tn.	1806	O14	245	161
Hewitt, John et al	D. of T. fr	McLeod, John, schoolmaster	1815	AK35	235	186
Hewitt, John, trustee et al	Deed to	Riggs, George W.	1806	O14	224	148
Hewitt, John, trustee	Deed fr	Schnively, Henry, insolvent	1806	P15	255	168
Hewitt, John, trustee et al	Deed to	Cozens, William R.	1806	O14	227	149
Hewitt, Mary	Deed fr	Travers, George	1814	AH33	307	265
Hewitt, Thomas	Deed fr	Easton, David	1806	P15	371	247
Hewitt, William	Mortgage fr	Hewitt, James	1815	AH33	458	392
Hewitt, William	Deed fr	Boyd, Washington	1815	AH33	478	408
Hewitt, William	Deed fr	Morsell, James S., trustee	1815	AH33	556	476
Hewitt, William	Cert Free to	Shorter, Jane (C), age 16	1817	AN38	493	356
Hewitt, William, register	Cert Free to	Crockett, Betsey (M)	1815	AI34	218	248
Hewitt, William, register	Cert Free to	Parnum, Benjamin (C), shoemaker	1816	AL36	044	045
Hews, Henry (C), age 28	Cert Free fr	Morris, Thomas Barton	1813	AE30	106	081
Hews, Milly	Cert. Free fr	Cassin, Joseph	1812	AC28	166	124
Hews, William	Cert. Free fr	Cassin, Joseph	1812	AC28	166	124
Heyle, William	Deed fr	Kerr, Alexander, of Alexa.	1801	G7	039	050
Hiat, Henry, attorney	Manumis to	[ ], Dole (negro) and others	1807	S18	076	062
Hickey, James	Deed fr	Bickley, Robert S., of Phila. PA	1810	Y24	256	235
Hickey, James	D. of T. to	Carroll, Daniel, of *Duddington* et al	1810	Y24	258	238
Hickey, James	Mortgage to	Dickson, John C. & George Burns	1811	AB27	233	190
Hickey, James	D. of T. to	Eliot, Samuel, Jr.	1813	AF31	218	149
Hickey, James & Mary Ann	Mortgage to	Mandeville, Joseph, of Alexa.	1811	AB27	120	098
Hickey, James & Mary	D. of T. to	Ingle, Henry	1811	AB27	299	246
Hicks, Elizabeth	B. of S. fr	Williams, James, of G'tn., her son	1812	AD29	200	163
Hicks, Elizabeth, of G'tn.	Deed fr	Knowles, Henry, of G'tn.	1812	AD29	201	163
Hicks, Elizabeth, of G'tn.	Deed to	Mountz, John, of G'tn.	1817	AO39	494	339
Hicks, George (M)	Manumis fr	Baker, Nancy H.	1816	AK35	201	157
Hicks, Lizzy	B. of S. fr	Williams, James	1812	AB27	537	438
Hiener, Michael [Kioner]	Deed to	Shaw, John	1808	T19	271	199

Party	What	Party	Year	Liber	Old	New
Higden, John S.	Deed fr	Harkness, Samuel	1805	M12	218	220
Higdon, Gustavus	Lease fr	Prout, William	1802	I9	479	788
Higdon, Gustavus	Deed fr	Prout, William	1806	P15	076	046
Higdon, Gustavus	Lease fr	Prout, William	1806	O14	123	079
Higdon, Gustavus	Deed fr	Prout, William	1807	R17	360	275
Higdon, Gustavus	B. of S. fr	Staines, John & Elizabeth Ireland	1807	R17	363	277
Higdon, Gustavus	Deed fr	Prout, William	1808	T19	300	220
Higdon, Gustavus	Deed fr	Nowland, John	1808	T19	298	218
Higdon, Gustavus	Deed fr	Adams, Margaret	1812	AD29	140	108
Higdon, Gustavus	Deed fr	Prout, William	1814	AH33	031	029
Hildreth, Ezekial	Deed fr	Van Ness, John P. & Maria	1816	AK35	523	413
Hildreth, Ezekiel	Lease fr	Van Ness, John P.	1815	AI34	009	009
Hildreth, Ezekiel	Deed to	Glover, Charles	1816	AM37	277	203
Hildreth, Ezekiel	Deed to	Fletcher, Noah & J.M. Varnum	1816	AL36	003	003
Hildreth, Ezekiel	Deed to	Patterson, Thomas, Dr.	1817	AN38	237	174
Hildreth, Ezekiel	Release fr	Flecher, Noah & James Varnum	1817	AO39	498	342
Hill, Clement & Notley Young	Deed fr	Bayly, William	1800	E5	315	305
Hill, Clement & Notley Young	Deed to	Reintzel, Anthony, of G'tn.	1800	E5	317	307
Hill, Dick (negro)	Manumis fr	Moore, Nathan	1810	Y24	280	256
Hill, Henry	Deed to	Beall, Thomas & John M. Gantt	1793	A1-1	354	460
Hill, Henry	Petition	Butler, Ignatius	1807	R17	140	108
Hill, Henry, Jr.	Deed fr	Rozer, Carroll & Young	1793	A1-1	360	466
Hill, Henry, of Phila. PA	Deed to	Beall, Thomas & John M. Gantt	1793	A1-1	289	386
Hill, Henry V.	Deed fr	Eliot, Samuel, Jr.	1817	AO39	082	066
Hill, John D.	Deed fr	Weightman, Roger C.	1816	AM37	432	310
Hill, Lethy (mulatto)	Manumis fr	Beall, George	1807	S18	180	146
Hill, Susan	Cert fr	Hall, William	1808	U20	009	005
Hill, William et al	Mortgage fr	Cooledge, Samuel J.	1811	AA26	096	068
Hillard, Samuel, of G'tn.	B. of S. fr	Hillard, Thomas, of G'tn.	1816	AO39	011	009
Hillard, Thomas	Assign to	Edmonson, James N.	1817	AO39	057	047
Hillard, Thomas, of G'tn.	Lease fr	Van Ness, John P. & Marcia	1816	AO39	012	010
Hillard, Thomas, of G'tn.	B. of S. to	Hillard, Samuel, of G'tn.	1816	AO39	011	009
Hillary, Lewis, of G'tn.	Lease fr	Magruder, Ninian, Dr., of G'tn.	1816	AM37	419	301
Hillary, Lewis, of G'tn.	Deed to	Magruder, Ninian, of G'tn.	1816	AM37	418	300
Hillary, Nicholas, of G'tn.	Deed to	Hedges, Nicholas, of G'tn.	1806	Q16	109	071
Hilleary, Lewis	Deed fr	Bussard, John R.	1813	AE30	165	131
Hillery, Lewis, of G'tn.	Deed fr	Pickerill, John, of G'tn.	1811	AA26	188	128
Hilliary, Eleanor Jackson	B. of S. to	Hilliary, Henry John	1806	Q16	244	169
Hilliary, Henry John	B. of S. fr	Hilliary, Eleanor Jackson	1806	Q16	244	169
Hillsimer, Elizabeth, a.k.a. Brown	Deed to	Wingard, John, of VA	1797	C3	066	54
Hilton, Samuel	Deed fr	Casteel, Edmund & Mary	1812	AD29	006	004
Hilton, Samuel	Deed fr	Forrest, Joseph, trustee	1817	AO39	115	089
Hilton, Samuel & Jere. Perkins	Deed fr	Holmead, Anthony	1812	AD29	052	037
Hiltzimer, Elizabeth, of G'tn.	Deed to	Winger, John, her son, of VA	1813	AE30	130	100
Hindman, William, of Balto.	Deed fr	Stoddert, Benjamin, of G'tn.	1807	R17	094	074
Hines, Christian & Matthew	Deed fr	Strong, Benjamin & Elizabeth	1817	AO39	193	142
Hines, Christopher	Qualify	Militia officer	1812	AD29	174	140
Hines, Daniel	Deed fr	Maynard, Benjamin & Susanna	1807	R17	367	280
Hines, Daniel, heirs of, Fredk. Co.	Deed fr	Hines, John	1812	AB27	542	443
Hines, Henry	Deed fr	Stoddert, Benjamin, of P.G. Co.	1812	AD29	463	490
Hines, John	Deed fr	Commissioners of Washington	1802	H8	209	200
Hines, John	Deed to	Kaldenbaugh, Andrew, of G'tn.	1805	M12	067	062
Hines, John	Deed to	Kaldenbaugh, Andrew	1806	O14	388	259
Hines, John	B. of S. fr	Kennedy, Matthew, of G'tn.	1806	O14	130	084
Hines, John	Deed fr	Stoddert, Benjamin, of G'tn.	1808	U20	308	164

Index to District of Columbia Land Records, 1792-1817

Party	What	Party	Year	Liber	Old	New
Hines, John	Deed to	Magruder, Ninian, of G'tn.	1808	U20	309	165
Hines, John	Deed to	Aurand, John et al	1812	AB27	542	443
Hines, John	Deed fr	Magruder, Ninian, of G'tn.	1812	AD29	309	254
Hines, John, of G'tn.	Deed fr	Davidson, John, of MD	1802	H8	497	457
Hines, John, of Liberty MD	Deed to	Nourse, Joseph, of G'tn.	1806	O14	355	237
Hines, John, of G'tn.	Deed fr	Deakins, Leonard M. & John Hoye	1813	AE30	220	177
Hines, Philip	Deed fr	Wagler, Frederick A.	1813	AE30	537	399
Hipkins, B.G.	Cert Slave	From VA	1816	AM37	141	109
Hitchborn, Benjamin	Deed fr	Walker, George	1802	I9	207	325
Hite, George, of Balto. et al	Deed fr	Barney, John H., of G'tn.	1805	M12	320	324
Hite, Isaac, of Frederick Co. VA	Deed to	Mason, John, of G'tn.	1795	B2A	244	341
Hite, Isaac, of Frederick Co. VA	Deed to	Mason, John, of G'tn.	1795	B2A	246	344
Hite, Isaac, of Frederick Co. VA	Deed to	Templeman, John, of G'tn.	1795	B2A	222	308
Hite, Isaac, of Frederick Co. VA	Deed to	Chandler, Walter Story, of G'tn.	1797	B2B	637	398
Hoban, James	Deed fr	White, James, Sr. & James, Jr.	1794	B2A	149	197
Hoban, James	Deed fr	White, James, Sr. & James, Jr.	1794	B2A	015	153
Hoban, James	Deed fr	Holmead, Anthony, Sr.	1796	B2B	429	105
Hoban, James	Deed to	Barclay, Thomas, of G'tn.	1797	B2B	697	479
Hoban, James	Deed to	Holmead, Anthony, Sr.	1797	C3	121	99
Hoban, James	Deed fr	Coghlan, William, of P.G. Co.	1797	C3	135	110
Hoban, James	Cert fr	Commissioners of Washington	1797	B2B	462	152
Hoban, James	Cert fr	Commissioners of Washington	1798	B2B	476	169
Hoban, James	Deed fr	Scott, Gustavus et al	1798	C3	319	257
Hoban, James	C. Deed fr	Commissioners of Washington	1798	C3	484	381
Hoban, James	Transfer fr	Coglan, Wm., of Charleston SC	1798	B2B	476	169
Hoban, James	Deed fr	Commissioners of Washington	1800	E5	161	150
Hoban, James	Deed to	Lovell, William	1800	F6	042	027
Hoban, James	Deed fr	Commissioners of Washington	1800	E5	383	361
Hoban, James	Mortgage fr	Voss, Nicholas	1801	G7	415	550
Hoban, James	Agreement	Johnson, James	1801	F6	232	152
Hoban, James	Deed fr	Brown, Robert	1801	G7	417	552
Hoban, James	Deed fr	Commissioners of Washington	1802	G7	577	726
Hoban, James	Deed fr	Purcell, Pierce	1802	H8	076	070
Hoban, James	Deed fr	Purcell, Pierce	1802	H8	074	069
Hoban, James	Cert fr	Munroe, Thomas, Supt.	1802	I9	222	352
Hoban, James	Deed fr	Purcell, Pierce	1802	I9	058	080
Hoban, James	Lease to	Lovell, William	1802	I9	211	331
Hoban, James	Cert fr	Munroe, Thomas, Supt.	1802	I9	222	351
Hoban, James	Deed fr	Taylor, John	1802	I9	234	374
Hoban, James	Cert fr	Munroe, Thomas, Supt.	1802	I9	221	350
Hoban, James	Deed to	Sappwaring, Marcus Sempronius	1805	M12	155	151
Hoban, James	Deed to	Brown, Robert, bricklayer	1805	M12	216	218
Hoban, James	Deed fr	Munroe, Thomas, Supt.	1807	R17	331	252
Hoban, James	Deed to	Sewall, Clement, of Alexa. Co.	1808	T19	321	234
Hoban, James	Agreement	Brent, William	1808	V21	045	034
Hoban, James	Deed to	Coolidge, Samuel J., of P.G. Co.	1809	W22	335	217
Hoban, James	Deed fr	McDonald, John G., trustee	1810	Y24	483	426
Hoban, James	Deed fr	Caffry, Anthony, Rev., Dublin, Ire.	1811	AA26	351	235
Hoban, James	Deed to	Clark, Francis	1811	AA26	207	142
Hoban, James	Lease to	Webster, Toppan	1811	AA26	167	115
Hoban, James	Lease to	Vallette, Peter	1811	AB27	333	274
Hoban, James	Deed to	Matthews, William, Rev.	1811	AC28	025	019
Hoban, James	Lease to	Webster, Toppan	1812	AD29	192	156
Hoban, James	Mortgage fr	Vallet, Peter	1814	AH33	357	309
Hoban, James	Lease to	Webster, Toppan	1815	AK35	375	295

Index to District of Columbia Land Records, 1792-1817

Party	What	Party	Year	Liber	Old	New
Hoban, James	Lease to	Littlejohn, Alexander S.	1817	AN38	547	398
Hoban, James & Peirce Purcell	Cert fr	Commissioners of Washington	1792	B2A	299	419
Hoban, James & Peirce Purcell	Cert fr	Commissioners of Washington	1792	B2A	299	419
Hoban, James & Peirce Purcell	Cert fr	Commissioners of Washington	1792	B2A	298	418
Hoban, James & Peirce Purcell	Cert fr	Commissioners of Washington	1792	B2A	290	406
Hoban, James & Peirce Purcell	Cert fr	Commissioners of Washington	1792	B2A	288	403
Hoban, James & Peirce Purcell	Cert fr	Commissioners of Washington	1792	B2A	299	420
Hoban, James & William Brent	Deed fr	Dent, Charles	1808	T19	241	177
Hoban, James & William Brent	Deed to	Mackey, William, of G'tn.	1809	X23	099	072
Hoban, James et al	Suit ads	Potomac Company	1812	AG32	258	183
Hobart, John Sloss	Petition fr	Jay, John	1797	C3	035	29
Hobart, John Sloss	Petition fr	Jay, John	1797	C3	024	20
Hobart, John Sloss	Petition fr	Jay, John	1797	C3	029	24
Hobart, John Sloss	Petition fr	Jay, John	1797	C3	040	32
Hobbs, William C. & Christiana	Deed to	Brengle, Lawrence, Frederick Co.	1805	M12	142	138
Hobson, Jonathan et al	Deed fr	Dalton, Tristram & Tobias Lear	1799	E5	061	049
Hobson, Jonathan, of NY et al	Deed fr	Dalton, Tristram et al	1798	D4	148	131
Hodge, George	B. of S. fr	Young, Thomas	1815	AH33	413	356
Hodges, Mathew C. et al	Deed fr	Calder, James, of G'tn.	1811	AA26	104	073
Hodges, Matthew C. & C. Varden	Mortgage to	Peltz, John	1812	AD29	436	366
Hodges, Thomas	Bond fr	Orme, Archibald	1808	U20	280	149
Hodges, Thomas C., of G'tn.	Deed fr	Craig, Robert, of G'tn.	1802	I9	014	019
Hodges, Thomas C., of G'tn.	Deed to	Williams, Thomas, of P.G. Co.	1807	Q16	397	305
Hodges, Thomas C., of G'tn.	Deed to	Pickrell, John, of G'tn.	1816	AL36	034	035
Hodges, Thomas Clagett, G'tn.	Deed fr	Lowndes, Francis, of G'tn.	1804	L11	038	37
Hodgsen, Joseph	Deed to	Lowry, Caesar	1805	M12	364	372
Hodgson, John, mer., in Eng.	Deed to	McCormick, Alexander	1811	AA26	403	268
Hodgson, John, of Balto.	Deed fr	Barclay, Thomas, of G'tn.	1797	B2B	701	485
Hodgson, Joseph	Cert fr	Commissioners of Washington	1795	B2A	330	462
Hodgson, Joseph	Deed fr	Scott, Gustavus et al	1798	C3	331	267
Hodgson, Joseph	Deed fr	Brown, Joel	1798	C3	514	403
Hodgson, Joseph	Deed to	Jackson, Jonathan	1800	E5	156	144
Hodgson, Joseph	Deed to	Mechlin, Joseph	1801	G7	004	005
Hodgson, Joseph	Lease to	Lowry, Caesar, of G'tn.	1802	H8	502	462
Hodgson, Joseph	Charge fr	Jefferson, Thomas	1802	I9	166	252
Hodgson, Joseph	Agreement	Sprogell, Thomas Y.	1802	G7	518	659
Hodgson, Joseph et al	Deed fr	Lingan, James McCubbin, of G'tn.	1797	C3	018	14
Hodgson, Joseph, hatter	Deed to	Sprogell, Thomas Y., hatter	1801	G7	005	007
Hodgson, Nicholson & Co.	Mortgage fr	Barclay, Thomas, of Montg. Co.	1796	B2B	582	327
Hodgson, Rebecca, wid/o Joseph	Deed to	Worthington, William	1816	AL36	177	177
Hodnett, James	Deed fr	Stoddert, Benjamin et al	1802	I9	163	247
Hodnett, James	Deed fr	Bank of Columbia	1802	I9	163	247
Hodnett, James	Deed to	Forrest, Joseph	1811	AB27	348	288
Hoff, Jacob, farmer, of MD	Deed to	Offutt, Ozias, physician, of MD	1802	I9	116	171
Hoffman, Jacob, of Balto.	Deed to	Beall, Thomas & John M. Gantt	1793	A1-2	421	30
Hoffman, John, of Fredk. Co.	Deed fr	Lingenfelter, John, of Fredk. Co.	1811	AB27	078	065
Hofman, Richard	Deed fr	Beall, Thomas B. et al	1802	I9	374	620
Hogan, Thady	Deed fr	Munroe, Thomas, Supt.	1802	I9	180	276
Hogan, Thady	B. of S. fr	Wheatley, Francis, of Charles Co.	1809	V21	269	192
Hogan, Thady	Deed fr	Dorsey, William H., of Balto.	1810	Y24	429	384
Hogan, Thady	Deed fr	Murdock, John, of G'tn.	1810	Y24	432	386
Hogan, Thady	Deed to	Cocking, William	1814	AG32	366	265
Hogan, Thady	Deed fr	Laird, John, exr. of J. Carleton	1816	AM37	060	049
Hogan, Thady, trustee	Deed fr	Berry, Hezekiah	1808	V21	136	099
Hogan, Thady [Thaddeus]	B. of S. fr	Ritchie, Abner	1809	V21	214	152

Party	What	Party	Year	Liber	Old	New
Hogland, Isaac	B. of S. fr	Howard, John	1816	AL36	159	159
Hoidel, Leonard [Hurdle]	B. of S. to	Browning & Renshaw, of G'tn.	1805	M12	184	185
Hoit, Samuel	Deed fr	Webster, Toppan	1814	AH33	083	075
Hoit, Samuel	Deed to	Webster, Toppan	1815	AH33	429	369
Holburne, William	Deed to	Tayloe, John	1806	O14	385	257
Holburne, William	Deed fr	McDonald, Andrew	1806	O14	379	252
Holburt, Simon	B. of S. to	Prout, William	1805	O14	030	019
Holcomb, John	B. of S. fr	Colvin, John B.	1812	AC28	394	286
Holiday, Elsworth, trustee	Deed fr	Morgan, Richard, insolvent	1806	O14	190	124
Holland, Edward	Deed fr	Boyd, Washington, marshal	1816	AL36	477	450
Holland, Edward	Deed to	Bradley, Phineas & John Davis	1817	AO39	225	163
Holland, Solomon, late sheriff	Deed to	Reintzel, Anthony	1795	B2A	275	385
Hollenback, William	Deed fr	Jones, Charles C., of Montg. Co.	1814	AG32	023	018
Hollenback, William	Deed to	Ford, Sarah	1814	AG32	184	130
Hollenback, William & Sarah	Deed to	Williams, John	1816	AL36	301	298
Holliday, Thomas	Deed fr	Prout, William	1807	R17	333	253
Holliday, Thomas & Sh. Davis	Release to	McLeod, John	1813	AF31	105	071
Holliday, Thomas & M. Jameson	Release to	Moore, William	1816	AM37	183	138
Holliday, William, of G'tn.	B. of S. fr	Gardener, Thomas, of G'tn.	1810	Z25	088	067
Holliday, William, of G'tn.	B. of S. fr	McClaren, Duncan, of G'tn.	1814	AG32	445	322
Hollingshead, James, Calvert Co.	Deed fr	Parrott, Richard, of Balto.	1798	C3	291	236
Hollingshead, James, Calvert Co.	B. of S. to	Kedgley, Ann	1811	AB27	430	354
Hollingshead, John	B. of S. fr	Jenkins, Robert D.	1809	V21	167	120
Hollingshead, John	D. of T. fr	Coulter, Peter	1810	Y24	469	416
Hollingshead, John	Deed fr	Lucas, Henry	1811	Z25	498	395
Hollingshead, John	Qualify	Captain in infanty of 1st regiment	1813	AE30	403	297
Hollingshead, John et al	Lease fr	Reintzel, Anthony	1811	Z25	490	389
Hollingshead, John et al	Deed to	Joncherez, Alexander L.	1812	AD29	383	323
Hollingshead, John et al	D. of T. fr	Greenfield, Walter, of G'tn.	1813	AF31	367	263
Hollingshead, John, mer., of G'tn.	Deed to	Magruder, Ninian, Dr., of G'tn.	1811	Z25	500	397
Hollingshead, John, of G'tn.	D. of T. fr	Lucas, Henry	1809	X23	223	172
Hollingshead, John, of G'tn.	Deed fr	Reintzel, Anthony, of G'tn.	1810	Z25	047	035
Hollingsworth, Paschal et al	Release to	Nourse, Joseph	1813	AF31	011	008
Hollowell & Augusta Bank	Deed fr	Snow, Gideon, of Boston MA	1817	AN38	183	133
Hollyday, Henry, of Talbot Co.	Deed fr	Hollyday, James, of Q.A. Co.	1795	B2B	361	011
Hollyday, James, of Q.A. Co.	Deed to	Beall, Thomas & John M. Gantt	1793	A1-1	284	380
Hollyday, James, of Q.A. Co.	Deed to	Hollyday, Henry, of Talbot Co.	1795	B2B	361	011
Hollyday, James, of Q.A. Co.	Release to	Earle, James, of Talbot Co.	1799	D4	182	163
Holmead, Anthony	Deed to	Beall, Thomas & John M. Gantt	1792	A1-1	007	12
Holmead, Anthony	Deed to	Great, Jacob & Josias Thompson	1793	A1-1	244	333
Holmead, Anthony	Deed to	Vermillion, John Robertson	1793	A1-1	242	330
Holmead, Anthony	Deed to	Scyle, John, of G'tn.	1794	B2A	140	185
Holmead, Anthony	Deed to	Peirce, Isaac	1794	B2A	151	199
Holmead, Anthony	Deed to	Scott, Gustavus	1795	B2A	170	227
Holmead, Anthony	Deed to	Dalton, Tristram & Tobias Lear	1795	B2A	226	314
Holmead, Anthony	Deed to	French, Arianna	1799	D4	199	182
Holmead, Anthony	Deed to	Beall, Lloyd et al	1800	E5	238	232
Holmead, Anthony	Deed to	Speake, Josias Milburn	1800	E5	324	314
Holmead, Anthony	Deed to	Deakins, Francis	1801	G7	227	303
Holmead, Anthony	Deed to	Abert, Philip	1801	G7	257	351
Holmead, Anthony	Deed to	Jones, John G.	1802	H8	018	017
Holmead, Anthony	Deed to	Dodge, Allen & Francis	1806	P15	271	179
Holmead, Anthony	Partition	Holmead, John	1807	R17	162	124
Holmead, Anthony	Deed to	Osburn, Archibald	1807	T19	016	013
Holmead, Anthony	Deed fr	Speake, Josias M. & Sarah	1808	U20	079	044

Party	What	Party	Year	Liber	Old	New
Holmead, Anthony	Deed to	Holmead, John	1808	V21	005	004
Holmead, Anthony	Deed to	Speake, Sarah, w/o Josias M.	1808	U20	083	046
Holmead, Anthony	Deed to	Fresh, William, of G'tn.	1809	W22	378	245
Holmead, Anthony	Deed to	Johnson, Roger, of Frederick Co.	1809	W22	153	108
Holmead, Anthony	Deed to	Barlow, Joel	1809	W22	402	262
Holmead, Anthony	Deed fr	Holmead, John	1810	X23	346	278
Holmead, Anthony	Deed to	Nourse, Michael	1810	Y24	339	308
Holmead, Anthony	Deed to	Granger, Gideon	1810	X23	381	307
Holmead, Anthony	Deed fr	Goddard, John B. & John, of G'tn.	1811	AA26	245	167
Holmead, Anthony	Deed to	Hilton, Samuel & Jere. Perkins	1812	AD29	052	037
Holmead, Anthony	Deed to	King, Vincent, of G'tn.	1814	AH33	234	204
Holmead, Anthony	Deed fr	Holmead, John	1814	AG32	151	109
Holmead, Anthony	Deed to	Thompson, James	1815	AH33	519	445
Holmead, Anthony	Deed to	Glover, Charles	1816	AL36	208	215
Holmead, Anthony	Deed to	Holmead, John	1816	AL36	224	230
Holmead, Anthony & Sarah	Deed to	Speake, Sarah, w/o Josias M.	1810	X23	225	173
Holmead, Anthony, devisees of	Partition		1807	R17	153	118
Holmead, Anthony et al	Deed fr	Davidson, John	1801	G7	142	187
Holmead, Anthony et al	Deed to	Lucas, Ignatius	1805	M12	401	415
Holmead, Anthony et al	Deed to	Speake, Sarah, w/o Josias M.	1807	R17	013	012
Holmead, Anthony, exrs. of	Deed to	Jones, John G., of G'tn.	1808	T19	283	208
Holmead, Anthony, heirs of	Partition	Holmead, Anthony, heirs of	1805	O14	015	010
Holmead, Anthony, Jr.	Deed fr	Holmead, Anthony, Sr.	1800	E5	361	344
Holmead, Anthony, of P.G. Co.	Deed to	Balch, Stephen Bloomer, of G'tn.	1796	B2B	402	067
Holmead, Anthony, of Montg. Co.	Deed to	Dove, Joseph	1797	C3	050	40
Holmead, Anthony, of G'tn.	Deed fr	Krous, Theodorus, of G'tn.	1801	G7	192	257
Holmead, Anthony, Sr.	Deed to	Hoban, James	1796	B2B	429	105
Holmead, Anthony, Sr.	Deed fr	Hoban, James	1797	C3	121	99
Holmead, Anthony, Sr.	Deed to	Holmead, Anthony, Jr.	1800	E5	361	344
Holmead, Anthony, Sr.	Deed to	Holmead, John	1801	G7	133	174
Holmead, Anthony, Sr.	Deed to	Thompson, James	1801	G7	325	455
Holmead, Anthony, Sr.	Deed to	Holmead, John & Anthony, Jr.	1802	I9	056	076
Holmead, James & Anthony et al	Deed fr	Fairfax, Ferdinando	1817	AO39	275	197
Holmead, John	Deed fr	Reintzel, Daniel	1801	G7	458	594
Holmead, John	Deed fr	Holmead, Anthony, Sr.	1801	G7	133	174
Holmead, John	Exchange	Reintzel, Daniel	1801	G7	456	593
Holmead, John	Qualify		1802	I9	484	796
Holmead, John	Qualify		1802	I9	465	766
Holmead, John	Deed fr	Buchanan, Loveday	1805	M12	299	301
Holmead, John	Deed fr	Beatty, Charles, heirs of	1805	N13	055	051
Holmead, John	Deed to	Patterson, Edgar	1805	N13	190	168
Holmead, John	D. of T. fr	Beatty, Charles, heirs of	1805	N13	053	049
Holmead, John	Deed to	Hardey, William	1805	O14	136	088
Holmead, John	Deed fr	Boyd, Washington, collector	1805	O14	008	007
Holmead, John	Deed fr	Butler, Edward Mann	1805	O14	003	004
Holmead, John	Deed to	Speake, Josiah M., of Alexa. Co.	1806	P15	060	036
Holmead, John	Deed to	Patterson, Edgar	1806	Q16	001	001
Holmead, John	Manumis to	[ ], Dinah (Negro)	1806	O14	317	210
Holmead, John	Lease fr	Speake, Josias M., of Alexa. Co.	1806	O14	270	179
Holmead, John	Deed to	Butler, Robert	1807	R17	168	128
Holmead, John	Deed to	Pairo, Thomas W.	1807	R17	002	002
Holmead, John	Partition	Holmead, Anthony	1807	R17	162	124
Holmead, John	Deed fr	Pairo, Thomas W.	1807	R17	175	134
Holmead, John	Deed to	Newton, John	1807	S18	226	180
Holmead, John	Deed fr	Speake, Josiah M. & Sarah	1808	T19	405	285

Index to District of Columbia Land Records, 1792-1817

Party	What	Party	Year	Liber	Old	New
Holmead, John	Deed fr	Speake, Josias M.	1808	U20	001	001
Holmead, John	Deed fr	Speake, Josias M.	1808	U20	004	003
Holmead, John	Deed to	Speake, Sarah	1808	U20	400	223
Holmead, John	Deed fr	Homead, Anthony	1808	V21	005	004
Holmead, John	Deed fr	Perkins, Benjamin & Elizabeth	1808	V21	002	002
Holmead, John	Deed to	Owens, Barak	1809	X23	157	115
Holmead, John	Convey to	Pairo, Loveday	1809	V21	394	298
Holmead, John	Deed to	Patterson, Edgar	1809	X23	053	040
Holmead, John	Deed fr	Lingan, James M., of Montg. Co.	1810	Y24	177	163
Holmead, John	Deed to	Holmead, Anthony	1810	X23	346	278
Holmead, John	Deed fr	Baley, Jesse & Mary et al	1810	Y24	180	165
Holmead, John	Deed to	Clare, Mary	1811	AB27	123	101
Holmead, John	Deed to	Wirt, John, of G'tn.	1811	AB27	324	266
Holmead, John	Deed to	Fox, Bartleson	1811	Z25	445	350
Holmead, John	Deed to	Waters, Draden	1811	Z25	411	323
Holmead, John	Deed to	Cox, John, of G'tn.	1812	AC28	116	087
Holmead, John	Deed to	Pairo, Loveday, form. Buchanan	1813	AF31	163	110
Holmead, John	Deed to	Pairo, Loveday	1813	AE30	135	104
Holmead, John	Deed fr	Cramphin, Watkins, of DE	1813	AE30	167	133
Holmead, John	Deed to	Holmead, Anthony	1814	AG32	151	109
Holmead, John	Deed fr	Cassin, James & Tabitha Marbury	1814	AH33	286	249
Holmead, John	D. of T. to	Ott, John	1814	AH33	289	251
Holmead, John	Deed to	Hagerty, John, Jr., of G'tn.	1815	AH33	502	431
Holmead, John	Deed to	Carrico, James & Mary	1815	AK35	337	267
Holmead, John	Deed fr	Carico, James & Mary	1815	AK35	426	334
Holmead, John	Deed fr	Chatelin, Anne, late Pic, of G'tn.	1815	AI34	280	316
Holmead, John	Deed to	Riggs, Romulus, of G'tn.	1816	AL36	098	098
Holmead, John	Deed fr	Holmead, Anthony	1816	AL36	224	230
Holmead, John	Deed to	Mountz, John	1816	AM37	324	235
Holmead, John & Anthony, Jr.	Deed fr	Holmead, Anthony, Sr.	1802	I9	056	076
Holmead, John & Anthony	Deed to	Jones, John G., of G'tn.	1808	T19	283	208
Holmead, John, Anthony & Susan	Deed to	French, Ariana	1804	L11	401	356
Holmead, John, Anthony & Susan	Deed to	French, Ariana	1804	L11	396	351
Holmead, John et al	Deed to	Lucas, Ignatius	1805	M12	401	415
Holmead, John et al	Partition		1807	R17	153	118
Holmead, John et al	Deed to	Pairo, Loveday	1807	R17	216	162
Holmead, John et al	Deed to	Speake, Sarah, w/o Josias M.	1807	R17	013	012
Holmead, Susanna et al	Deed to	Lucas, Ignatius	1805	M12	401	415
Holmes, Eleanor et al	Manumis fr	Law, Thomas	1807	R17	288	220
Holmes, Hugh, of Winchester VA	Deed fr	Forrest, Uriah	1801	F6	243	163
Holmes, Joseph	B. of S. to	Costine, William	1805	O14	028	018
Holmes, Nancy	Manumis to	Law, Thomas	1802	H8	413	382
Holmes, William		Certificate of Slaves	1802	H8	014	013
Holmes, William	Slave	From Charles Co.	1807	R17	176	135
Holmes, William, of Charles Co.	Deed fr	Stoddert, Benjamin, of G'tn.	1801	G7	248	335
Holmes, William, of Montg. Co.	Deed fr	Dorsey, William H., of G'tn.	1807	S18	082	067
Holstein, George & Elizabeth	Deed to	Forrest, Uriah & Benj. Stoddert	1792	A1-1	151	217
Holston, George M.	Receipt to	Stoddert, Benj. & Wm. Deakins	1796	B2B	382	038
Holt, Lawrence O., of G'tn.	Deed fr	Landes, Abraham, of G'tn.	1816	AL36	284	283
Holt, Theophilus	B. of S. to	McGrath, Thomas	1814	AH33	027	024
Holtzman, George	Deed fr	Creager, John	1810	X23	349	280
Holtzman, George	Deed fr	Beatty, Thomas, Sr.	1811	AB27	446	367
Holtzman, George	Deed fr	Bussard, Daniel	1816	AM37	428	307
Holtzman, George, of G'tn.	Deed to	Cox, John, Col., of G'tn.	1816	AL36	527	492
Holtzman, Jacob	Deed fr	McClan, Robert	1811	AA26	256	174

Party	What	Party	Year	Liber	Old	New
Holtzman, Jacob	Deed fr	Wineberger, Jacob	1812	AC28	459	327
Holtzman, Jacob	B. of S. fr	Holtzman, William F.	1812	AB27	232	189
Holtzman, Jacob	Deed fr	Newton, Ignatius	1814	AH33	342	296
Holtzman, Jacob et al	Suit ads	Potomac Company	1812	AG32	258	183
Holtzman, Jacob, heirs of	Agreement	Bussard, Daniel	1815	AI34	026	031
Holtzman, Jacob, heirs of	Deed fr	Newton, Ignatius	1815	AI34	249	281
Holtzman, Jacob, of G'tn.	Deed fr	Brengle, Lawrence, Frederick Co.	1808	U20	336	181
Holtzman, Jacob, of G'tn.	Assign fr	Ratrie, William, of G'tn.	1811	AA26	400	265
Holtzman, Jacob, of G'tn.	B. of S. fr	Ratrie, William, of G'tn.	1811	AA26	050	039
Holtzman, Jacob, of G'tn.	Deed fr	Bussard, Daniel, of G'tn.	1812	AE30	008	007
Holtzman, Jacob, of G'tn.	Deed to	McClan, Robert, of PA	1814	AH33	033	030
Holtzman, Jacob, of G'tn.	Deed fr	Herominus, Pendleton, of G'tn.	1814	AG32	447	324
Holtzman, John	Deed fr	Ratrie, William & James Ratrie	1816	AM37	486	353
Holtzman, Samuel & Sarah	Partition	Sweeny, George	1812	AD29	280	230
Holtzman, Samuel & E. Clarke	B. of S. fr	Hubbard, Dyer	1814	AG32	263	187
Holtzman, William F.	B. of S. to	Holtzman, Jacob	1812	AB27	232	189
Holyday, Thomas & Shad. Davis	Mortgage fr	McLeod, John	1812	AD29	205	167
Homans, Benjamin	B. of S. to	Wright, Thomas C.	1813	AF31	099	067
Homans, Benjamin	Mortgage to	Wright, Thomas C.	1813	AF31	099	067
Homans, Daniel	Agreement	Zantzinger, William P.	1817	AN38	502	363
Hooe, Mary C., d/o Bernard, Jr.	Marriage	Sweeny, George	1816	AK35	498	392
Hooe, Robert T.	Cert fr	Commissioners of Washington	1793	B2A	322	453
Hooe, Robert T., trustees of	Deed to	Muncaster, John, of Alexa.	1811	AB27	00½	001
Hooe, Robert Townsend, Alexa.	Deed to	Beall, Thomas & John M. Gantt	1792	A1-1	055	81
Hoof, John, heirs, Augusta Co. VA	Deed to	Dole, Conrad	1804	K10	360	373
Hoof, John, of Rockg. Co., heirs	Deed to	Doll, Conrad, of Frederick Co.	1804	K10	363	376
Hooper, Alexander	B. of S. fr	Hooper, Thomas, Jr.	1814	AH33	090	082
Hooper, Thomas, Jr.	B. of S. to	Hooper, Alexander	1814	AH33	090	082
Hoot, Samuel	Lease fr	Presbyterian Congregation of G'tn.	1811	AB27	221	179
Hoot, Samuel	Assign to	Mayne, Adam & John Brunner	1812	AC28	338	245
Hoot, Samuel	B. of S. fr	Reed, William F.	1814	AH33	024	022
Hoot, Samuel	Lease fr	Van Ness, John P. & Marcia	1815	AK35	069	053
Hoot, Samuel	Deed to	Moore, Mary et al	1816	AM37	464	334
Hoot, Samuel	Deed fr	Pratt, Henry et al	1816	AL36	122	124
Hoot, Samuel	Agreement	Forrest, Joseph	1817	AN38	010	008
Hoot, Samuel	Assign to	Hutchinson, Samuel	1817	AO39	290	206
Hoover, Andrew & Elijah Walker	Deed fr	McCutchen, Thomas, of G'tn.	1810	Y24	079	071
Hoover, Andrew, of G'tn.	Lease fr	Jones, John G., of G'tn.	1802	H8	489	449
Hoover, Andrew, of G'tn. et al	Deed fr	Knowles, Henry, of G'tn.	1808	U20	033	019
Hoover, Andrew, of G'tn.	Deed to	McCutchen, Thomas, of G'tn.	1809	X23	314	251
Hoover, Peter, of G'tn.	B. of S. to	Burrows, John, of G'tn.	1817	AO39	248	179
Hopewell, Dinah, of Calvert Co.	Cert Free fr	Blake, James H.	1816	AM37	347	252
Hopkins, David	Qualify	Justice of the Peace	1813	AE30	263	204
Hopkins, David	Deed fr	Johnson, Thomas, of Fredk. Co.	1817	AN38	124	092
Hopkins, David, of Balto.	Deed to	Glover, Charles	1817	AN38	566	413
Hopkins, John et al	Cert fr	Munroe, Thomas, Supt	1805	M12	047	045
Horsey, Outerbridge	Manumis to	[ ], Lucy, w/o Gerard, & children	1813	AF31	291	206
Horsey, Outerbridge, of DE	Manumis to	[ ], Henny (C) & Bernard (C)	1812	AC28	167	124
Horsey, Outerbridge, of DE	Manumis to	[ ], Robert, Eleanor & others	1812	AD29	399	336
Horsey, Outerbridge, of DE	B. of S. fr	Lee, John	1813	AF31	289	205
Horsey, Outerbridge, of DE	Manumis to	[ ], Pat (C)	1815	AG32	299	218
Horsey, Outerbridge, of DE	Manumis to	[ ], Emily (C)	1815	AG32	299	218
Hosack, John, of G'tn.	Deed fr	Carruthers, John & David, Balto.	1796	B2B	567	305
Hosack, John, of Montg. Co.	Deed fr	Brookes, Walter, of Montg. Co.	1796	B2B	417	088
Hoston, Stanislaus	Deed fr	Hoxton, Susanna, wid.	1800	E5	081	068

Index to District of Columbia Land Records, 1792-1817

Party	What	Party	Year	Liber	Old	New
Hourse, Charles J.	Deed fr	Lowndes, Francis	1810	Y24	211	194
House, David	Deed fr	Davis, Thomas M. & Sarah	1808	U20	255	136
House, David	Deed fr	Wigfield, James J.	1808	U20	254	135
Housman, John A.	Deed fr	Whetcroft, Henry & Sarah	1814	AG32	285	205
Howard, Cezar (C)	Manumis fr	Waters, John, of Cephas	1816	AM37	412	296
Howard, Gustavus	Mortgage to	Howard, Thomas	1807	Q16	355	257
Howard, Henry, s/o John	Deed fr	Moscrop, Henry, of MD	1802	H8	193	185
Howard, Jesse	B. of S. to	Howard, Peter	1805	N13	078	071
Howard, John	Mortgage to	Gannon, James	1809	V21	302	220
Howard, John	B. of S. to	Hogland, Isaac	1816	AL36	159	159
Howard, Joseph & Mary	Deed to	Thomas, John, 3rd	1809	X23	195	147
Howard, Peter	B. of S. fr	Howard, Jesse	1805	N13	078	071
Howard, Peter	B. of S. fr	Dougherty, Patrick	1805	O14	151	098
Howard, Peter	B. of S. fr	Richards, Benjamin	1807	S18	104	084
Howard, Peter	Deed fr	Prout, William	1812	AD29	238	197
Howard, Thomas	B. of S. fr	Templeman, John	1806	O14	210	138
Howard, Thomas	Mortgage fr	Howard, Gustavus	1807	Q16	355	272
Howard, Thomas	Deed fr	Law, John, attorney of Thoams	1809	W22	201	139
Howard, Thomas	Deed fr	Law, Thomas	1813	AE30	118	091
Howard, William	Deed fr	Jones, Jason	1806	Q16	083	053
Howe, Alban	B. of S. to	Boothe, Edward	1812	AD29	360	303
Howe, Albin	Lease fr	Law, Edmund, trustee of Thomas	1811	AA26	329	221
Howe, Ignatius	B. of S. fr	Parker, Fielder & Lawson Clarke	1811	AB27	497	406
Howe, Ignatius	B. of S. to	Teitizen, Henry	1812	AD29	340	284
Howe, Robert F., of G'tn.	Deed fr	Brent, Daniel Carroll, trustee et al	1807	S18	001	001
Howe, Robert F., of G'tn.	D. of T. fr	Granger, Gideon	1814	AH33	294	254
Howell, Benjamin B., of Phila.	Deed fr	Morris, Thomas, sons & devisees	1812	AD29	511	431
Howell, Benjamin B.	Deed to	Burd, Edward et al	1812	AD29	518	437
Howes, John, of G'tn.	Deed to	Thompson, John, of G'tn.	1798	D4	022	019
Hoxton, Stanislaus, of MD	Deed to	Barry, James	1802	G7	537	682
Hoxton, Stanislaus, of P.G. Co.	Deed fr	Semmes, George, of P.G. Co.	1806	O14	182	119
Hoxton, Stanislaus, of P.G. Co.	Deed to	Barry, James	1806	O14	183	120
Hoxton, Stanislaus, of P.G. Co.	Receipt to	Barry, James	1806	O14	186	121
Hoxton, Stanislaus, of P.G. Co.	B. of S. to	Costigan, Joseph	1811	Z25	555	441
Hoxton, Susanna, wid.	Deed to	Hoxton, Stanislaus	1800	E5	081	068
Hoy, John et al	Deed to	Dawes, Isaac	1805	M12	187	188
Hoye, John	Deed fr	Renner, Daniel & Daniel Bussard	1809	X23	210	159
Hoye, John	Deed to	Lehault, Louis Joseph et al	1810	Y24	023	020
Hoye, John	Deed fr	Johnson, George	1810	Y24	399	360
Hoye, John	Deed fr	White, James, of Montg. Co.	1810	Y24	041	035
Hoye, John	Deed fr	White, James, of Montg. Co.	1810	Y24	013	012
Hoye, John	Deed fr	Johnson, George, trustee, of G'tn.	1811	AA26	046	036
Hoye, John	Deed to	Smith, Walter	1811	AB27	002	004
Hoye, John	Certificate	List of 101 lots, Washington St.	1813	AF31	448	
Hoye, John	Plat	Washington St. & Virginia Ave.	1813	AF31	466	
Hoye, John & Leonard M. Deakins	Deed fr	Brent, William & Thomas Sim Lee	1809	V21	416	318
Hoye, John & Leonard M. Deakins	Deed fr	Beall, Thomas, of George	1809	W22	140	099
Hoye, John & Leonard M. Deakins	Deed fr	Threlkeld, John	1809	W22	132	094
Hoye, John & Leonard M. Deakins	Deed to	Riggs, George W., of G'tn.	1809	W22	193	135
Hoye, John & Leonard M. Deakins	Mortgage fr	Wallace, Charles, Annapolis et al	1809	W22	009	007
Hoye, John & Leomard M. Deakins	Deed to	Robertson, Thomas	1809	W22	026	020
Hoye, John & Leonard M. Deakins	Deed to	Robey, Theophilus & Jos. Nevitt	1809	W22	263	176
Hoye, John & Leonard M. Deakins	Deed to	Threlkeld, John	1809	W22	085	063
Hoye, John & Leonard M. Deakins	Deed to	Ober, Robert, of G'tn.	1809	X23	007	005
Hoye, John & Leonard M. Deakins	Deed to	Foxall, Henry	1809	X23	194	146

Index to District of Columbia Land Records, 1792-1817

Party	What	Party	Year	Liber	Old	New
Hoye, John & Leonard M. Deakins	Deed to	Williams, Elisha W.	1809	X23	206	156
Hoye, John & Leonard M. Deakins	Deed fr	Marbury, William, of G'tn.	1810	Y24	128	116
Hoye, John & William Crawford	B. of S. fr	Carter, John M., of G'tn. et al	1812	AD29	161	127
Hoye, John & Leonard M. Deakins	Deed to	Robertson, Thomas, of G'tn.	1812	AD29	441	370
Hoye, John & Leonard M. Deakins	Deed to	Livers, Ignatius	1812	AD29	398	335
Hoye, John & Leonard M. Deakins	Deed to	Hines, John, of G'tn.	1813	AE30	220	177
Hoye, John & Leonard M. Deakins	Deed to	Patterson, Edgar, of G'tn.	1813	AF31	215	146
Hoye, John & Leonard M. Deakins	Deed to	Thompson, Jonah, of Alexa. et al	1814	AH33	038	034
Hoye, John & Leonard M. Deakins	Deed to	Whann, William & J.S. Morsell	1815	AK35	343	271
Hoye, John & Leonard M. Deakins	D. of T. to	Morsell, James S. & Wm. Whann	1815	AK35	347	276
Hoye, John, Allegany Co. et al	Deed to	Threlkeld, John	1817	AN38	295	215
Hoye, John et al	Deed to	Hyde, Thomas	1805	O14	120	077
Hoye, John et al	Deed to	Foxall, Henry	1805	O14	117	075
Hoye, John et al	Deed to	Nourse, Joseph, of G'tn.	1806	O14	357	238
Hoye, John et al	Deed fr	Beatty, Charles, heirs of	1806	O14	334	222
Hoye, John et al	Deed to	Baker, John, exr. of John	1806	O14	160	104
Hoye, John et al	Deed to	Carroll, Patrick, of G'tn.	1807	R17	258	196
Hoye, John et al	Deed to	King, James C.	1807	S18	087	071
Hoye, John et al	Deed to	Benson, Eden, of G'tn.	1807	S18	060	050
Hoye, John et al	Deed to	Lucas, Bennet, of G'tn.	1807	S18	062	051
Hoye, John et al	Deed fr	Clagett, James	1807	R17	055	044
Hoye, John et al	Deed to	Lucas, Bennett	1809	V21	247	176
Hoye, John et al	Decree	Threlkeld, John	1817	AN38	295	215
Hoye, John, of Wash. Co.	Deed fr	Hoye, Paul, of Wash. Co.	1805	N13	015	016
Hoye, John, of G'tn. et al	Deed to	Craik, William, of Fairfax Co. VA	1805	M12	393	406
Hoye, John, of G'tn. et al	Deed to	Laird, John, of G'tn.	1806	Q16	294	223
Hoye, John, of G'tn. et al	Deed to	Coles, John, of Balto.	1807	S18	120	098
Hoye, John, of G'tn. et al	Deed to	Wright, Thomas C., of G'tn.	1807	S18	316	248
Hoye, John, of G'tn. et al	Deed to	Frush, William, of G'tn.	1807	R17	231	173
Hoye, John, of G'tn. et al	Deed to	Lehault, Louis Joseph et al	1807	R17	378	287
Hoye, John, of G'tn. et al	Deed fr	Brent, William	1808	T19	408	287
Hoye, John, of G'tn.	Deed to	Pritchard, Benjamin, of G'tn.	1808	U20	196	108
Hoye, John, of G'tn.	Deed fr	Mountz, Jacob, collector, G'tn.	1809	X23	208	158
Hoye, John, of G'tn.	Deed fr	Riggs, George W., of G'tn.	1809	W22	192	134
Hoye, John, of Montg. Co.	Deed fr	Maffit, Samuel, collector, G'tn.	1809	X23	211	160
Hoye, John, of Montg. Co.	Deed fr	McDonald, John G.	1810	Y24	409	368
Hoye, John, of Montg. Co.	Deed fr	Williams, Elisha W., of G'tn.	1810	Y24	086	077
Hoye, John, of G'tn.	Deed fr	Robertson, Thomas, of G'tn.	1811	AA26	149	103
Hoye, John, of G'tn.	Deed to	Bank of Columbia	1811	AB27	279	228
Hoye, John, of Montg. Co.	Deed fr	Orme, Richard J., of Montg. Co.	1811	AB27	433	356
Hoye, John, of G'tn.	Deed fr	Robertson, Thomas, of G'tn.	1812	AE30	039	029
Hoye, John, of G'tn.	Deed fr	Williams, Elisha W., of G'tn.	1812	AC28	361	261
Hoye, John, of G'tn.	D. of T. fr	Harbaugh, Leonard, of Balto. MD	1812	AD29	443	
Hoye, John, of G'tn.	Deed fr	Robertson, Thomas, of G'tn.	1813	AE30	044	033
Hoye, John, of G'tn.	Deed fr	Mountz, John, of G'tn.	1813	AE30	043	032
Hoye, John, of Allegany Co.	Deed to	Forrest, Benjamin S.	1813	AF31	491	358
Hoye, John, of Allegany Co.	Deed to	Lee, Thomas S., of Fredk. Co.	1813	AF31	446	321
Hoye, John, of Allegany Co.	Deed fr	Lee, Thomas S., of Fredk. Co.	1813	AF31	442	318
Hoye, John, of Allegany Co.	Deed fr	Lee, Thomas S., of Fredk. Co.	1813	AF31	443	319
Hoye, John, of Allegany Co.	Deed fr	Lee, Thomas S., of Fredk. Co.	1813	AF31	444	319
Hoye, John, of G'tn.	Deed to	Fresh, William, of G'tn.	1813	AF31	412	297
Hoye, John, of Allegany Co.	Deed fr	Forrest, Benjamin S.	1814	AH33	016	014
Hoye, John, of Allegany Co.	Deed to	Dawes, Isaac & Henry Baker	1814	AH33	003	002
Hoye, John, of Allegany Co.	Lease to	Brooks, Joseph	1815	AI34	072	081
Hoye, John, of G'tn.	Deed fr	Corporation of Washington	1815	AI34	220	251

Party	What	Party	Year	Liber	Old	New
Hoye, John, of Allegany Co. MD	Deed to	Stephenson, Thomas T.	1815	AI34	219	250
Hoye, John, of G'tn.	Deed fr	Corporation of Washington	1815	AI34	226	257
Hoye, John, of G'tn.	Deed fr	Corporation of Washington	1815	AI34	224	255
Hoye, John, of G'tn.	Deed fr	Corporation of Washington	1815	AI34	222	253
Hoye, John, of Allegany Co. MD	Deed to	Whann, William, of G'tn.	1815	AI34	295	329
Hoye, John, of Allegany Co. MD	Deed to	Neale, Francis, Rev., of G'tn.	1815	AI34	256	289
Hoye, John, of Allegany Co.	Deed to	Thompson, John C., of G'tn.	1815	AK35	274	218
Hoye, John, of Allegany Co.	D. of T. to	Whann, William & J.S. Morsell	1815	AK35	350	279
Hoye, John, of Allegany Co.	Deed to	Webster, Toppan	1815	AK35	371	293
Hoye, John, of Cumberland Co.	Deed to	Grundy, George, Sr., of Balto.	1816	AL36	525	491
Hoye, John, of Allegany Co.	Deed to	Forrest, Joseph	1816	AL36	064	065
Hoye, John, of Allegany Co.	Lease to	McKenney, William, of G'tn.	1817	AN38	368	271
Hoye, John, of Allegany Co.	Deed to	Kengla, Lewis, of G'tn.	1817	AN38	340	250
Hoye, John [Hoy]	Agreement	Coles, John	1807	S18	124	101
Hoye, Paul, of Wash. Co.	Deed to	Hoye, John, of Wash. Co.	1805	N13	015	016
Hoyt, Ephraim J.	B. of S. to	Suttle, Henry	1810	Y24	479	424
Hoyt, Ephraim J.	Deed to	Hoyt, James Thornton, his son	1813	AF31	263	184
Hoyt, James Thornton	Deed fr	Hoyt, Ephraim J., his father	1813	AF31	263	184
Hubbard, Dyer	B. of S. to	Clarke, Elizabeth & S. Holtzman	1814	AG32	263	187
Huber, Andrew, of G'tn.	Deed fr	Beall, Thomas B., of G'tn.	1808	V21	041	031
Huddleston, Joseph	Mortgage fr	Carpenter, Thomas	1806	O14	165	107
Huddleston, Joseph	Deed fr	Dorsey, William H., of Balto.	1809	W22	122	087
Huddleston, Joseph	Assign to	Somerville, David	1810	Z25	365	286
Huddleston, Joseph	Deed to	Cook, Orlando	1811	Z25	475	376
Huddleston, Joseph	Deed fr	Cook, Orlando	1811	Z25	469	372
Huddleston, Joseph	D. of T. to	Brent, William	1811	AC28	045	034
Huddleston, Joseph	Deed to	Edwards, Horace H. & H. Bestor	1812	AD29	300	246
Huddleston, Joseph	D. of T. to	Brown, Obadiah B. & Geo. Moore	1812	AC28	204	155
Huddleston, Joseph	Deed fr	Tuckfield, William H.P.	1816	AL36	364	353
Huddleston, Joseph	D. of T. fr	Bestor, Harvey	1816	AL36	518	485
Huddleston, Joseph & N. Fletcher	D. of T. fr	Edwards, Horace H. & H. Bestor	1812	AD29	277	229
Huddleston, Joseph & N. Fletcher	Deed to	Edwards, Horace H. & H. Bestor	1815	AK35	438	343
Huddleston, Joseph et al	Deed fr	Law, Thomas	1798	D4	155	137
Huddleston, Joseph et al	Lease fr	Law, Edmund, atty. of Thomas	1811	Z25	462	366
Huddleston, Joseph, stonecutter	D. of T. to	Brent, Robert & George Blagden	1810	Y24	242	223
Huddlestone, Joseph	B. of S. fr	Triplet, John	1804	K10	144	156
Huddlestone, Joseph	B. of S. fr	Toogood, Edward Fisher, of Balto.	1806	Q16	044	028
Huddlestone, Joseph	Deed to	Brent, William	1808	V21	024	018
Huddlestone, Joseph	Deed fr	Dorsey, William H., of Balto.	1810	Y24	448	398
Huddlestone, Joseph et al	Lease fr	Van Ness, John P. & Marcia	1806	Q16	124	081
Huddlestone, Joseph et al	Mortgage fr	Somerville, David	1810	Z25	362	284
Huff, Valentine, admr. of	Deed to	King, Nicholas	1804	K10	192	201
Huff, Valentine, Smith Co. TN	P. of Atty. to	Lane, John & Charles Hunter	1804	K10	195	
Hughes, Christopher	Deed fr	Etting, Solomon	1802	I9	431	713
Hughes, Christopher, of Balto.	Deed fr	Joncherez, Alexander L., of G'tn.	1816	AL36	044	045
Hughes, James & Mary, of KY	Mortgage to	Hughes, Martha, of Lexington KY	1816	AI34	447	462
Hughes, James & Mary, of KY	Mortgage to	Hughes, Martha, of Lexington KY	1816	AI34	445	460
Hughes, James, of Lexington KY	Bond to	Hughes, Martha, of Lexington KY	1816	AI34	450	464
Hughes, Martha, of Lexington KY	Mortgage fr	Hughes, James & Mary, of KY	1816	AI34	447	462
Hughes, Martha, of Lexington KY	Mortgage fr	Hughes, James & Mary, of KY	1816	AI34	445	460
Hughes, Martha, of Lexington KY	Bond fr	Hughes, James, of Lexington KY	1816	AI34	450	464
Hughes, Theophilus	Deed to	Halsey, Henry	1807	R17	205	154
Hughes, Theophilus	B. of S. fr	Masters, Ezekiel	1808	T19	100	071
Hughes, Theophilus	Mortgage to	Hays, Thomas, of P.G. Co.	1809	V21	305	223
Hughes, Theophilus	B. of S. to	Davis, John, of Able	1811	AB27	195	161

Party	What	Party	Year	Liber	Old	New
Hughes, Thomas	B. of S. fr	Kenner, James	1806	Q16	261	181
Hughes, Thomas	Lease to	Kiler, Daniel	1809	V21	241	172
Hughes, Thomas	Deed fr	McNamara, Roger & Mary	1809	V21	191	136
Hughes, Thomas	Deed to	Morin, Lewis	1810	Y24	047	041
Hughes, Thomas	Deed to	Burch, Henry	1812	AC28	165	122
Hughes, Thomas	D. of T. fr	Woodworth, Joseph	1812	AC28	356	258
Hughes, Thomas	Deed fr	Bussard, Daniel	1812	AC28	114	086
Hughes, Thomas	Release to	Woodworth, Joseph	1812	AD29	346	289
Hughes, Thomas	Mortgage fr	Grammar, G.C. & Henry Mayer	1812	AD29	387	326
Hughes, Thomas	Qualify	Captain in the militia	1812	AD29	361	303
Hughes, Thomas	Deed to	Grammar, Gotlieb C. et al	1814	AG32	060	047
Hughes, Thomas	Deed fr	Bradley, William A.	1816	AK35	498	392
Hughes, Thomas & W.A. Bradley	Deed fr	Munroe, Thomas & Frances	1815	AI34	250	283
Hughes, Thomas & W.A. Bradley	Manumis to	[ ], Minty (C)	1816	AM37	076	062
Hughes, Thomas et al	Suit ads	Potomac Company	1812	AG32	258	183
Hughes, Thomas et al	D. of T. fr	Polk, Charles P., insolvent	1813	AF31	071	048
Hughes, Thomas, trustee	Deed fr	Flaut, Joseph, insolvent	1806	P15	316	208
Hughes, Thomas, trustee	B. of S. fr	Belt, Richard W., insolvent	1808	V21	135	099
Hughs, Thomas	B. of S. fr	Lovering, William	1811	AA26	091	064
Huie, Helen Grant, Pr. Wm. Co.	Deed fr	Bullett, Thomas James, Talbot Co.	1806	P15	323	213
Huie, Hellen Grant, of Pr. Wm. Co.	Deed to	Boyle, David, of Pr. Wm. Co. VA	1809	V21	375	278
Hull, Jacob	Deed to	Hyde, Thomas	1816	AM37	346	251
Hull, Jacob, of G'tn.	D. of T. to	Gantt, Thomas T., of G'tn.	1816	AM37	499	365
Hummel, John, of Frederick Co.	Deed to	Meddert, Jacob, Frederick Town	1807	S18	042	035
Hunt, Jeremiah	B. of S. to	Lane, William	1802	I9	219	345
Hunt, Jeremiah	Mortgage to	Gardiner, William P.	1814	AH33	216	192
Hunt, Jeremiah	Deed to	Johnson, Samuel	1815	AK35	376	297
Hunt, Jeremiah	Cert fr	Munroe, Thomas, Supt.	1817	AO39	407	276
Hunt, William	Partition	Brannan, John	1817	AO39	460	316
Hunt, William & John Brannon	Deed fr	Gordon, Elisha & Elizabeth, Phila.	1815	AK35	101	078
Hunt, William et al	Deed to	Ingle, John P. & Eleazar Lindsley	1817	AO39	206	151
Hunter, Andrew	Manumis to	[ ], Sandy (C)	1813	AE30	183	146
Hunter, Charles, Rowan Co. NC	P. of Atty. fr	Huff, V. & Jacob Rowland	1804	K10	195	
Hunter, Charles, Rowan Co. NC	Deed to	King, Nicholas	1804	K10	192	210
Hunter, Elizabeth, wid.	Deposition		1804	L11	001	1
Hunter, George W., exr.	Cert Free to	[ ], Harriott (C), est. of A. Dow et al	1815	AK35	250	198
Hunter, John, of Alexa.	Deed fr	Slater, Joseph	1801	F6	161	100
Hunter, John, shipbuilder, Alexa.	Deed fr	Slater, Joseph	1801	F6	165	103
Hunter, Thomas	Deed fr	Carleton, Joseph, of G'tn.	1805	M12	222	223
Hunter, Thomas	Lease fr	Dunlap, James	1806	O14	376	250
Hurdell, Leonard, of G'tn.	B. of S. to	Trundle, Horatio, of G'tn. et al	1802	H8	408	378
Hurdell, Leonard, of G'tn.	B. of S. to	Weatherall, John, of G'tn et al	1802	H8	408	378
Hurdle, Ann, of G'tn.	B. of S. to	Fields, William	1810	Y24	157	144
Hurdle, Basil S.	B. of S. to	Hamilton, Absalom	1816	AM37	501	367
Hurdle, Leonard [Hoidel]	B. of S. to	Browning & Renshaw, of G'tn.	1805	M12	184	185
Hurdle, Noble	Deed fr	Ritchie, Abner	1811	AB27	429	353
Hurdle, Noble, of G'tn.	Deed fr	Nourse, Joseph, of G'tn.	1809	W22	355	230
Hurdle, Noble, of G'tn.	Deed to	Smith, Andrew, of G'tn.	1810	Y24	104	094
Hurdle, Noble, of G'tn.	Lease fr	Williamson, David, of Balto.	1813	AF31	348	248
Hurdle, Noble, of G'tn.	Assign to	Mayer, Henry, of G'tn.	1816	AL36	120	121
Hurdle, Thomas	B. of S. fr	Downes, Mary, of Montg. Co.	1806	P15	352	233
Hurdle, Thomas	Deed to	Blagden, George	1806	P15	374	249
Hurdle, Thomas	B. of S. to	Cochrane, Alexander	1807	S18	296	231
Hurdle, Thomas, insolvent	Convey to	Durity, William, trustee	1804	L11	279	257
Hurford, Henry	Deed fr	Van Ness, John P. & Marcia	1812	AD29	400	337

Party	What	Party	Year	Liber	Old	New
Hurford, Henry	Deed fr	Herty, Thomas	1812	AD29	042	030
Hurley, Daniel	Deed fr	Newman, Morris	1802	H8	587	553
Hurley, Daniel	Deed to	Densley, Hugh	1802	H8	585	551
Hurley, Daniel	Deed fr	Mackall, Walter	1802	H8	576	540
Hurley, Daniel	Deed fr	Voss, Nicholas	1802	H8	534	493
Hurley, Daniel	Deed fr	Densley, Hugh	1802	I9	036	048
Hurley, Daniel	Deed fr	Densley, Hugh	1802	I9	035	046
Hurley, Daniel	Deed to	Voss, Nicholas	1805	M12	059	055
Hurley, Daniel	Deed to	Kirby, John Baptist	1805	N13	324	262
Hurley, Daniel	Agreement	Voss, Nicholas	1809	V21	191	136
Hurley, Daniel et al	Mortgage to	Addison, Thomas Grafton et al	1804	K10	144	156
Hurley, Daniel et al	Deed to	Burnes, George	1805	N13	075	068
Hurley, John, of Montg. Co. MD	Deed to	Evans, Lucy (C), of G'tn.	1812	AD29	546	460
Hurley, Lanty, s/o Cornelius	Indenture to	Taylor, John, tobacconist	1811	AB27	322	265
Hurley, William	Mortgage to	Middleton, Isaac S.	1813	AF31	541	401
Hurley, William	Deed to	Criddle, Jonathan	1816	AL36	058	059
Hurly, Arnold	B. of S. fr	Adams, Henry	1809	W22	389	253
Hurly, Daniel	Deed to	Voss, Nicholas	1802	I9	346	570
Hurst, Thomas	B. of S. to	Wertz, Christian	1816	AL36	409	392
Husler, Caroline et al	Deed Gift fr	Husler, Joseph	1814	AG32	456	329
Husler, Eliza Anne et al	Deed Gift fr	Husler, Joseph	1814	AG32	456	329
Husler, Hellen et al	Deed Gift fr	Husler, Joseph	1814	AG32	456	329
Husler, John Thomas et al	Deed Gift fr	Husler, Joseph	1814	AG32	456	329
Husler, Joseph	B. of S. to	Crawford, William	1812	AD29	008	006
Husler, Joseph	Deed Gift to	Husler, Caroline et al	1814	AG32	456	329
Husler, Sarah Anne et al	Deed Gift fr	Husler, Joseph	1814	AG32	456	329
Hutchins, Samuel	Deed fr	Beatty, Charles, heirs of	1806	P15	084	051
Hutchins, Samuel	Deed to	Goldsborough, John M.	1807	S18	217	173
Hutchins, Samuel, of G'tn.	Deed to	Goldsborough, John M.	1813	AF31	309	220
Hutchinson, Benedict	B. of S. fr	Hutchinson, George	1815	AI34	512	517
Hutchinson, George	B. of S. to	Hutchinson, Benedict	1815	AI34	512	517
Hutchinson, Samuel	Manumis to	[ ], Betsey (Negro)	1804	K10	334	345
Hutchinson, Samuel	Deed fr	Threlkeld, John	1815	AI34	282	319
Hutchinson, Samuel	Assign fr	Hoot, Samuel	1817	AO39	290	206
Hutchinson, Samuel	Deed fr	Munroe, Thomas	1817	AO39	403	273
Hutchinson, Samuel	Release fr	Van Ness, John P. & Marcia	1817	AO39	405	275
Hutchinson, Samuel et al	Deed fr	Shoemaker, Jonathan	1808	T19	114	081
Hutchinson, Samuel, heirs of	Cert Free to	Dodson, Ann	1817	AO39	247	179
Hutchinson, Samuel, mer.	Deed fr	Mechlin, Joseph	1815	AI34	281	317
Huter, Conrad	Deed fr	Lucas, Henry	1795	B2A	168	224
Huter, Conrad [Heeter], of G'tn.	Lease to	Boarman, John B. et al	1796	B2B	602	353
Hutton, John	Deed fr	Belt, Joseph Sprigg	1813	AF31	433	312
Hutton, John, of Montg. Co.	Manumis to	[ ], Cecilia (negro)	1810	Y24	078	070
Hutton, John, of Montg. Co.	Manumis to	[ ], Mary (negro)	1810	Y24	078	070
Hutton, John, of Montg. Co.	Manumis to	[ ], Catherine (negro)	1810	Y24	078	070
Hyatt, Aquilla D.	Qualify	Militia officer	1812	AD29	361	304
Hyatt, Seth	Deed fr	Stockwell, John	1815	AI34	519	523
Hyatt, Seth & Jane Summerville	Deed to	Ott, David & Charles Glover	1816	AL36	163	163
Hyde, Thomas	B. of S. fr	Fenwick, Richard	1801	G7	365	497
Hyde, Thomas	Deed fr	Beatty, Charles, heirs of	1805	N13	103	097
Hyde, Thomas	Deed fr	Deakins, Leonard et al	1805	O14	120	077
Hyde, Thomas	Deed fr	Beatty, Charles, heirs of	1805	N13	102	095
Hyde, Thomas	B. of S. to	Fenwick, Richard	1805	N13	008	009
Hyde, Thomas	Deed to	Nourse, Michael	1808	V21	057	045
Hyde, Thomas	Agreement	Lingan, James M.	1809	V21	288	208

Index to District of Columbia Land Records, 1792-1817

Party	What	Party	Year	Liber	Old	New
Hyde, Thomas	Deed fr	Nourse, Michael	1809	V21	275	197
Hyde, Thomas	Deed fr	Lingan, James Macubin, Montg.	1809	V21	286	206
Hyde, Thomas	Bond to	Smith, John Kilty	1810	X23	367	295
Hyde, Thomas	Deed to	Wineberger, Jacob	1810	Y24	545	479
Hyde, Thomas	Deed to	Pickrell, John	1811	AB27	339	279
Hyde, Thomas	Deed to	Smith, John K.	1811	AB27	010	011
Hyde, Thomas	Deed fr	Livers, Anthony, Jr.	1812	AD29	079	058
Hyde, Thomas	Deed to	Riffle, George	1814	AG32	419	304
Hyde, Thomas	Deed fr	Miller, William, of G'tn., butcher	1815	AI34	236	268
Hyde, Thomas	Deed fr	Hull, Jacob	1816	AM37	346	251
Hyde, Thomas & Thos. Corcoran	Release to	Livers, Anthony	1812	AD29	080	059
Hyde, Thomas et al	Mortgage fr	Livers, Anthony, of G'tn.	1801	G7	466	603
Hyde, Thomas et al	D. of T. fr	Greenfield, Walter, of G'tn.	1813	AF31	367	263
Hyde, Thomas, of G'tn.	Deed to	Baltzer, Margaret, of G'tn.	1811	AB27	155	129
Hyde, Thomas, of G'tn.	Deed to	Presbyterian Congregation of Gtn.	1811	Z25	441	346
Hyde, Thomas, of G'tn.	Deed fr	Balch, Stephen B., of G'th.	1812	AD29	080	059
Hyde, Thomas, of G'tn.	D. of T. fr	Baker, Murray, of G'tn.	1812	AD29	129	099
Hyde, Thomas, of G'tn.	D. of T. fr	Greenfield, Walter, of G'tn.	1813	AF31	366	262
Hyde, Thomas, of G'tn.	Mortgage fr	Whelan, Nicholas, of G'tn.	1814	AH33	317	274
Hyde, Thomas, of G'tn.	Deed to	Corcoran, Thomas, of G'tn.	1814	AH33	280	244
Hyde, Thomas, of G'tn.	B. of S. fr	Donaldson, Thomas, of G'tn.	1817	AN38	531	386
Hyland, Lambert, Somerset Co.	Deed fr	Gillis, Thomas Handy	1805	N13	168	153

Party	What	Party	Year	Liber	Old	New
I						
Igan, Ephraim	B. of S. fr	Eliason, Ebenezer	1801	G7	170	227
Igan, Ephraim	Lease fr	Johnson, Thomas, Frederick Co.	1801	G7	067	087
Igan, Ephraim, of Balto.	Deed to	Reinhart, Andrew	1811	AA26	164	113
Igaw, Ephraim	Deed to	Rinehart, Andrew	1802	I9	357	590
Igaw, Ephraim	Deed to	Rinehart, Andrew	1802	I9	254	410
Igaw, Ephraim	Deed fr	Reinhart, Andrew	1802	H8	257	244
Ingle, Henry	Deed to	Pechin, Christianna, of PA	1802	H8	531	490
Ingle, Henry	Deed fr	Carroll, Daniel, of Duddington	1802	H8	396	366
Ingle, Henry	Deed fr	Law, Thomas	1807	R17	349	266
Ingle, Henry	B. of S. fr	Billing, Joseph	1807	R17	126	098
Ingle, Henry	Deed fr	Coombe, Griffith	1809	V21	142	105
Ingle, Henry	Deed fr	Carroll, Daniel, of *Duddington*	1809	W22	267	178
Ingle, Henry	D. of T. fr	Hickey, James & Mary	1811	AB27	299	246
Ingle, Henry	Deed to	Washington Parish Vestry	1812	AC28	245	181
Ingle, Henry, for graveyard	Cert fr	Munroe, Thomas, Supt.	1808	T19	219	160
Ingle, John & Eleazar Lindsley	Deed fr	Hunt, William et al	1817	AO39	206	151
Ingle, John P. [Engle]	D. of T. fr	Bailey, Robert	1817	AO39	183	135
Ingles, John P.	Qualify	Lieutenant in Militia	1812	AC28	493	
Ingraham, Alexander	Deed to	Vermillion, John	1805	M12	372	382
Ingraham, Alexander	Deed fr	Carroll, Daniel, of *Duddington*	1805	M12	382	383
Ingraham, John	Manumis fr	Dutton, Notley & Wm. O'Neale	1817	AN38	299	218
Ingraham, Nathaniel, of SC	Deed fr	Stoddert, Benjamin, of G'tn.	1804	K10	392	407
Ingram, Alexander	Deed fr	Chandler, Jacob	1802	I9	134	200
Ingram, Alexander & Mary	Deed to	Charles, Richard	1805	O14	025	016
Ingram, Alexander, chairmaker	Deed to	Parker, Fielder	1806	Q16	234	161
Ireland, Elizabeth	B. of S. to	Sisterson, William	1808	V21	022	016
Ireland, Elizabeth & John Staines	Deed to	Cummins, John	1806	Q16	259	180
Ireland, Elizabeth et al	Lease fr	Prout, William	1805	N13	235	199
Ireland, Elizabeth et al	Deed to	McCormick, Benson L.	1805	N13	240	202
Ireland, Elizabeth et al	Deed to	Vint, John	1806	P15	246	163
Ireland, Elizabeth et al	B. of S. to	Higdon, Gustavus	1807	R17	363	277
Irvine, Walter	Mortgage fr	Webster, Toppan	1802	G7	489	626
Irwin, Charles	B. of S. to	Dixon, John C.	1807	R17	347	264
Isaacs, Ralph	Deed to	Glover, Charles	1815	AI34	217	248
Ivey, Claybourn, Craven Co. NC	Deed to	Bradley, Phineas	1810	X23	339	272

Party	What	Party	Year	Liber	Old	New
J						
Jack, John	Assign to	Kerr, Alexander	1802	H8	543	504
Jack, John	Discharge	Bankruptcy	1802	I9	134	201
Jack, John	Deed to	Jack, Margaret	1802	H8	556	518
Jack, Margaret	Deed fr	Jack, John	1802	H8	556	518
Jackson, Agnes & William	Deed to	Worthington, William	1806	O14	258	170
Jackson, Agnes, trustee	Deed to	Bell, Samuel	1807	S18	406	325
Jackson, Alfred, infant	Release fr	Van Ness, John P. & Marcia	1815	AI34	198	226
Jackson, Alfred, s/o Peggy & Jos.	Baptism	St. Patrick's Church	1811	AB27	396	326
Jackson, Betsey (C) & children	Manumis fr	Rittenhouse, Harriet	1817	AN38	194	140
Jackson, Eliza, d/o Peggy & Jos.	Birth	St. Patrick's Church	1811	AB27	396	326
Jackson, Isaac, mer., of NY	Deed fr	Ober, Robert, mer.	1811	Z25	316	247
Jackson, John G., Harrison Co. VA	Deed fr	Fenwick, Mary Ann	1810	X23	350	281
Jackson, John G.	Deed fr	Commissioners of Washington	1810	X23	352	315
Jackson, John G., Harrison Co. VA	Mortgage to	Van Ness, John P.	1810	Y24	239	220
Jackson, John G., of VA	Mortgage to	Fenwick, Mary Ann, wid.	1810	Y24	171	157
Jackson, John G.	Release fr	Van Ness, John P.	1813	AF31	039	027
Jackson, John G., fr. Harrison Co.	Deed to	Bank of the Metropolis et al	1814	AG32	295	215
Jackson, Jonathan	Deed fr	Commissioners of Washington	1799	D4	231	213
Jackson, Jonathan	Deed fr	Hodgson, Joseph	1800	E5	156	144
Jackson, Jonathan, estate trustee	Deed to	Patterson, Benjamin	1805	O14	142	092
Jackson, Jonathan, trustees of	Deed to	Corcoran, Thomas	1805	O14	134	086
Jackson, Jonathan, trustees, et al	Deed to	Riggs, George W.	1806	O14	224	148
Jackson, Jonathan, trustees, et al	Deed to	Perkins, Benjamin	1806	O14	170	111
Jackson, Jonathan, trustees of	Deed to	Dorsey, William H.	1806	P15	064	039
Jackson, Jonathan, trustees, et al	Deed to	Worthington, William	1806	O14	258	170
Jackson, Jonathan, trustees, et al	Deed to	Cozens, William R.	1806	O14	227	149
Jackson, Joseph	Manumis to	[ ], Ned (negro) et al	1808	T19	374	267
Jackson, Joseph	Mortgage to	Moore, George	1813	AE30	063	048
Jackson, Joseph	Mortgage to	Moore, George	1813	AE30	062	046
Jackson, Joseph (C)	Lease fr	Van Ness, John P. & Marcia	1812	AD29	453	381
Jackson, Joseph, children of	Cert Free fr	Brent, Robert	1811	AB27	396	326
Jackson, Joseph, free black man	Lease fr	Van Ness, John P. & Marcia	1812	AD29	232	192
Jackson, Joseph, free black man	Lease fr	Van Ness, John P. & Marcia	1815	AI34	196	225
Jackson, Joseph, seaman, age 28	Cert Free		1811	Z25	416	327
Jackson, Nancy (C), and Maria	Manumis fr	Digges, Catherine	1812	AD29	440	370
Jackson, Samuel, mer., of G'tn.	Deed to	Shannon, William, mer., of Phila.	1800	E5		163
Jackson, Samuel, mer., of G'tn.	Deed to	Shannon, William, of Phila.	1800	E5	194	185
Jackson, Samuel, of Phila. PA	Deed fr	Polock, Isaac	1798	D4	001	001
Jackson, Samuel, of G'tn.	Deed fr	Craig, Robert	1799	D4	220	203
Jackson, Samuel, of G'tn.	Deed to	Shannon, William, mer., of Phila.	1799	D4	377	361
Jackson, Samuel, of G'tn.	Deed to	Fitzhugh, Philip	1800	F6	085	052
Jackson, William & Agnes et al	Deed fr	Morgan, William	1805	N13	299	243
Jacobs, John	Cert Free fr	Smothers, Francis	1809	X23	315	252
Jacques, Denton	Deed to	Beall, Thomas & John M. Gantt	1792	A1-1	144	207
Jacques, Denton	Deed to	Johnson, Thomas, Frederick Co.	1793	A1-2	450	59
Jameison, Marsham et al	B. of S. fr	Moore, William	1815	AH33	423	364
James, James	Deed to	Forrest, Uriah	1794	A1-2	501	
James, James	Mortgage fr	Pearce, Thomas, of G'tn.	1798	D4	043	036
James, James & Ann et al	Deed to	Forrest, Uriah & Benj. Stoddert	1792	A1-1	063	93
James, James & Anne	Deed to	Pearce, Thomas, of G'tn.	1798	C3	348	280
James, James, of G'tn.	Deed fr	Davidson, John, of Annapolis	1797	C3	117	96
James, James, of G'tn.	Deed to	Schultze, Henry, of G'tn.	1797	B2B	673	442
James, James, of P.G. Co.	Deed to	Schultze, Henry, of G'tn.	1798	C3	511	402
James, James, of MD	Deed fr	Polock, Isaac	1802	H8	234	223

Index to District of Columbia Land Records, 1792-1817

Party	What	Party	Year	Liber	Old	New
James, James, of MD	Deed to	Ward, William, of MD	1802	I9	083	118
James Knight & Co.	Agreement	Pearcy, Mr.	1797	C3	065	53
James, William	Deed fr	Thorn, Christopher S.	1802	I9	587	952
James, William et al	Suit ads	Potomac Company	1812	AG32	258	183
James, William, heirs of	Deed fr	Walker, Joseph, now of Richmond	1815	AK35	190	149
Jameson, Andrew, of Alexa.	Deed fr	Thompson, Jonah, of Alexa.	1802	I9	110	160
Jameson, Marsham	B. of S. fr	Jameson, Richard	1812	AD29	206	168
Jameson, Marsham & T. Holliday	Release to	Moore, William	1816	AM37	183	138
Jameson, Richard [Jameison]	B. of S. to	Jameson, Marsham	1812	AD29	206	168
Jameson, Walter, of Charles Co.	Deed fr	Brown, Joel	1805	O14	127	082
Jamieson, Andrew & Mary, Alexa.	Mortgage to	Thompson, Jonah, of Alexa.	1798	D4	140	123
Jamieson, Andrew et al	Cert fr	Commissioners of Washington	1796	B2B	455	142
Jamieson, Andrew, of Alexa.	Deed fr	Spencer, John Jonathan	1794	B2A	163	216
Jamieson, Andrew, of Alexa. Co.	Deed to	Noel, Jilson	1809	W22	282	187
Jamieson, Andrew, of Alexa.	D. of T. fr	Noel, Jilson	1809	W22	285	189
Jamison, Andrew	Deed to	Maitland, James, Sr. & James, Jr.	1802	H8	247	234
Jamison, Andrew	Deed fr	Maitland, James, Sr. & James, Jr.	1802	H8	238	227
Jamison, Andrew	Deed fr	Thompson, Jonah	1802	H8	239	228
Janney, Thomas, of Alexa.	Deed fr	Love, Charles & Ann, of G'tn.	1806	Q16	266	186
Jarber, Mary Ann	Marriage	Rodier, Philibert	1816	AM37	307	224
Jarber, Mary Ann & P. Rodier	B. of S. to	St. Victor, Louis de	1816	AM37	307	224
Jarboe, Bennet	Slaves	From MD	1810	Y24	317	288
Jarboe, Bennett	B. of S. to	Mills, Susanna, of St. Mary's Co.	1801	G7	307	428
Jarboe, Bennett	Deed to	Breshears, Richard B.	1802	H8	481	442
Jarboe, Bennett	Deed fr	Commissioners of Washington	1802	H8	036	035
Jarboe, Bennett	Deed to	Baker, Samuel	1802	H8	461	423
Jarboe, Charles	Cert fr	Munroe, Thomas, Supt.	1809	W22	345	223
Jarboe, Charles	Deed to	Magrath, Thomas	1811	AC28	001	001
Jarrad, George	Lease fr	Prout, William	1806	Q16	049	031
Jarrad, George	D. of T. to	Fowler, Samuel	1813	AE30	509	377
Jarrad, George	Deed fr	Prout, William	1813	AE30	370	274
Jarrad, George	D. of T. to	Fowler, Samuel	1815	AK35	049	038
Jarrad, George [Gerrard]	Deed fr	Prout, William	1814	AG32	245	175
Jarvis, Thomas	B. of S. fr	Picknoll, Richard H.	1811	Z25	174	138
Jay, John	Petition to	Hobart, John Sloss	1797	C3	024	26
Jay, John	Petition to	Hobart, John Sloss	1797	C3	035	29
Jay, John	Petition to	Hobart, John Sloss	1797	C3	029	24
Jay, John	Petition to	Hobart, John Sloss	1797	C3	040	32
Jay, Samuel, of Harford Co. MD	B. of S. to	Johnson, Archibald, of Balto.	1816	AK35	504	397
Jearvis, Henry [Gearvis]	B. of S. to	Newton, Ignatius & Isaac Wilson	1817	AN38	339	249
Jeffers, Matthias	Deed fr	May, Frederick	1810	X23	407	328
Jefferson, Thomas	Charge to	Hodgson, Joseph	1802	I9	166	252
Jefferson, Thomas	B. of S. fr	Baker, Philip Thomas [William]	1808	V21	030	022
Jenifer, Daniel, Jr., devisee of D.	Deed to	Beall, Thomas & John M. Gantt	1793	A1-2	409	18
Jenkins, Augustine, Rev. et al	Deed fr	Carroll, John, Rev. et al	1799	D4	286	268
Jenkins, Augustine, Rev. et al	Deed fr	Carroll, John, Rev. et al	1799	D4	283	265
Jenkins, Benjamin R.	D. of T. fr	Heronimus, Pendleton	1816	AM37	475	343
Jenkins, Benjamin R.	Cert Slave	From KY	1816	AM37	477	345
Jenkins, Creasy	Deed fr	Jenkins, Francis	1814	AG32	238	170
Jenkins, Daniel	B. of S. fr	Jenkins, Harriet	1810	Y24	257	237
Jenkins, Fabian	D. of T. fr	Jenkins, Francis	1814	AG32	383	279
Jenkins, Francis	Deed fr	Young, Mauduit	1808	T19	197	141
Jenkins, Francis	B. of S. to	O'Brian, William	1813	AE30	219	177
Jenkins, Francis	B. of S. to	Kneller, George	1813	AE30	279	214
Jenkins, Francis	Deed to	Jenkins, Creasy	1814	AG32	238	170

Party	What	Party	Year	Liber	Old	New
Jenkins, Francis	D. of T. to	Jenkins, Fabian	1814	AG32	383	279
Jenkins, Francis	Deed to	Jenkins, Susannah	1814	AG32	239	171
Jenkins, Francis	B. of S. to	Clarke, Eliza	1814	AG32	146	105
Jenkins, Francis & Fabian	Deed to	Renner, Daniel	1814	AH33	264	230
Jenkins, Francis, of G'tn.	Deed Gift to	Jenkins, Martha & Sarah	1814	AH33	362	314
Jenkins, Frank (Negro)	Manumis fr	Reintzel, Anthony, of G'tn.	1804	L11	271	250
Jenkins, Harriet	B. of S. fr	Selby, Martha	1810	X23	416	336
Jenkins, Harriet	B. of S. to	Jenkins, Daniel	1810	Y24	257	237
Jenkins, Hiram & A. McCerran	Lease fr	Van Ness, John P. & Marcia	1816	AM37	391	282
Jenkins, Hiram & A. McCerran	Lease fr	Van Ness, John P. & Marcia	1817	AO39	076	062
Jenkins, John	B. of S. fr	Ensey, William	1817	AO39	230	167
Jenkins, Josia, s/o Philip	Deed fr	Slater, Joseph, of Monroe Co. VA	1800	E5	086	074
Jenkins, Martha & Sarah	Deed Gift fr	Jenkins, Francis, of G'tn.	1814	AH33	362	314
Jenkins, Mary, of P.G. Co.	Deed to	Deakins, William, Jr., of G'tn.	1796	B2B	396	059
Jenkins, Robert D.	B. of S. to	Hollingshead, John	1809	V21	167	120
Jenkins, Susannah	Deed fr	Jenkins, Francisa	1814	AG32	239	171
Jenkins, Thomas	Deed fr	Beall, Thomas	1802	I9	290	476
Jenkins, Thomas	Deed to	Morris, Randal, of P.G. Co.	1806	P15	256	169
Jenkins, Thomas	Deed fr	Young, Mauduit	1807	R17	314	238
Jenkins, Thomas, of Charles Co.	Deed to	Beatty, Thomas J.	1795	B2A	196	267
Jenkins, Thomas, of Frs. P.G. Co.	Deed fr	Birch, Samuel Lewis & Jesse	1807	S18	279	219
Jenners, Abiel & Deborah	Deed to	Simpson, Solomon, Col.	1799	E5	001	001
Jenners, Abiel & Deborah	Deed to	Fairfax, Ferdinand, Berkeley Co.	1802	G7	557	706
Jenners, Abiel et al	Deed fr	Walker, George	1802	H8	070	065
Jennings, Thomas, Louisa Co. VA	Deed to	Balch, Stephen B., of G'tn.	1812	AD29	154	121
Joel, Ann, of Berkeley Co. VA	Deed to	Way, Andrew & George	1809	W22	371	240
Johncherrez, Alexander L., G'tn.	Lease to	Herty, Thomas	1804	K10	342	354
Johnes, Charles, mer., of Phila.	Deed fr	Lambert, Aaron, mer., of Phila.	1817	AN38	527	382
Johns, Acquila, of P.G. Co.	Deed fr	Masters, John	1805	N13	153	143
Johns, Acquilla	Deed fr	Magruder, George	1802	I9	526	860
Johns, Acquilla	Deed fr	Brent, Daniel C.	1802	I9	343	566
Johns, Aquila, of P.G. Co.	Deed to	Burrows, Edward	1807	S18	141	115
Johns, Aquila, of P.G. Co.	Deed To	Bowie, Washington	1808	U20	391	217
Johns, Aquila, of P.G. Co.	B. of S. fr	Orme, Archibald	1811	AA26	200	136
Johns, Hosea, of Balto.	B. of S. fr	Sprung, George, of Balto. [w/list]	1815	AI34	408	429
Johns, Leonard H.	B. of S. to	Simpson, Thomas, of MD	1802	H8	106	103
Johns, Leonard H. et al	Deed to	Williams, Jeremiah, of G'tn.	1805	M12	071	066
Johns, Leonard H. et al	Deed to	Deakins, Francis et al	1805	M12	069	064
Johns, Leonard H.	Deed fr	Stoddert, Benjamin	1807	Q16	362	277
Johns, Leonard H., of G'tn.	Deed to	Hagner, Peter	1810	Y24	200	184
Johns, Leonard H., of G'tn.	Mortgage fr	Williams, Elisha W., of G'tn.	1811	AB27	461	378
Johns, Leonard H.	D. of T. fr	Williams, Elisha W.	1812	AC28	384	280
Johns, Leonard H.	D. of T. fr	Williams, Jeremiah	1812	AC28	388	283
Johns, Leonard H., of G'tn.	Deed fr	Williams, Elisha W., of G'tn.	1812	AC28	329	239
Johns, Leonard H. et al	Deed to	Morsell, James S.	1815	AI34	086	098
Johns, Leonard H. et al	Deed to	Collins, William A.	1816	AL36	491	462
Johns, Leonard H. et al	Deed fr	Beatty, Charles A.	1817	AO39	294	210
Johns, Leonard Holliday et al	Deed fr	Lowndes, Francis & Charles	1804	K10	187	196
Johns, Leonard Holliday	Deed fr	Williams, Harriot	1813	AE30	365	271
Johns, Richard	Deed to	Davidson, Craik & Dorsey	1794	B2A	052	063
Johns, Richard	B. of S. fr	Orme, Thomas	1805	O14	087	054
Johns, Richard	Deed fr	Beatty, Charles, heirs of	1806	P15	068	041
Johns, Richard	Deed fr	Stoddert, Benjamin	1807	R17	086	068
Johns, Richard	Deed to	Suttle, Henry	1807	R17	276	210
Johns, Richard	Deed to	Suttle, Henry	1809	W22	049	036

Index to District of Columbia Land Records, 1792-1817

Party	What	Party	Year	Liber	Old	New
Johns, Richard	D. of T. fr	Rutherford, Alexander, of G'tn.	1816	AM37	125	097
Johns, Richard & Leonard	Deed to	Peter, David	1804	L11	226	210
Johns, Richard & Leonard H., G'tn.	Deed fr	Williams, Jeremiah, of G'tn.	1806	Q16	041	027
Johns, Richard & Leonard H., G'tn.	Deed to	Hellen, Walter	1806	Q16	035	023
Johns, Richard et al	Deed fr	Lowndes, Francis & Charles	1804	K10	187	196
Johns, Richard et al	Deed to	Deakins, Francis et al	1805	M12	069	064
Johns, Richard et al	Deed to	Williams, Jeremiah, of G'tn.	1805	M12	071	066
Johns, Richard H., of G'tn.	Deed fr	Morsell, James S., of G'tn.	1814	AG32	356	258
Johns, Richard H., of G'tn.	Deed to	Gannon, James, of G'tn.	1815	AI34	401	424
Johns, Richard, of G'tn.	Deed to	Renner, Daniel, of G'tn.	1806	P15	396	266
Johns, Richard, of G'tn.	Convey fr	Nourse, Charles J., of G'tn.	1811	AB27	026	024
Johns, Susanna	Deed fr	Keeler, David, of G'tn.	1805	O14	085	053
Johns, Susanna, of G'tn.	Mortgage fr	Coulter, Peter, of G'tn.	1809	V21	314	230
Johns, Susanna, of G'tn.	Release to	Coulter, Peter	1812	AC28	503	358
Johns, Susannah	Lease to	Scott, Sabret	1802	I9	355	587
Johns, Susannah & Richard	Manumis to	Ferguson, Charlotte & children	1815	AI34	079	089
Johns, Thomas et al	Deed to	Beall, Thomas & John M. Gantt	1793	A1-1	227	314
Johnson, Abraham (C)	Cert Free fr	Davis, Isaac, f/o Enos R.	1813	AE30	509	377
Johnson, Archibald M.	B. of S. to	Haraden, Nathaniel	1814	AG32	326	237
Johnson, Archibald, of Balto.	B. of S. fr	Jay, Samuel, of Harford Co. MD	1816	AK35	504	397
Johnson, Catherine	Deed to	Boyd, Washington & Wm. Brent	1801	G7	385	517
Johnson, Charles et al	Deed fr	Commissioners of Washington	1800	E5	154	143
Johnson, George	Deed fr	Mountz, Jacob, collector, of G'tn.	1810	Y24	391	353
Johnson, George	Deed to	Hoye, John	1810	Y24	399	360
Johnson, George	Convey to	Robertson, Thomas, mer.	1814	AG32	010	008
Johnson, George	Deed to	Coombe, Griffith	1815	AH33	417	359
Johnson, George	D. of T. to	Dunlop, James, Jr.	1817	AN38	108	081
Johnson, George, of G'tn.	Deed fr	Smith, Clement, of G'tn.	1816	AM37	250	184
Johnson, George, trustee, of G'tn.	Deed to	Hoye, John	1811	AA26	046	036
Johnson, George, trustee	Deed to	Robertson, Thomas	1814	AG32	068	052
Johnson, Isaac	Lease fr	Jones, John Godfrey	1804	K10	402	417
Johnson, Isaac, of G'tn.	Deed fr	Reintzel, Daniel, of G'tn.	1807	S18	171	139
Johnson, Isaac, of G'tn.	Deed to	Moxley, Charles, of G'tn.	1815	AI34	096	109
Johnson, Isaac, of G'tn.	Lease fr	Moxley, Charles, of G'tn.	1815	AI34	100	114
Johnson, Isaac, of G'tn.	Deed fr	McMurray, William	1816	AM37	498	364
Johnson, Isaac, of G'tn.	Deed to	Hartman, Charles	1816	AL36	317	312
Johnson, Isaac, trustee	Deed fr	Astin, David, insolvent	1805	N13	120	115
Johnson, James	Agreement	Hoban, James	1801	F6	232	152
Johnson, James	Deed fr	Prout, William	1808	T19	281	206
Johnson, James	Mortgage to	Burnes, George	1811	AC28	022	017
Johnson, James & Roger	Deed to	Beall, Thomas & John M. Gantt	1792	A1-1	047	71
Johnson, James et al	B. of S. fr	Gray, William	1811	AC28	011	008
Johnson, James, Frederick Co.	Deed to	Law, Thomas	1798	C3	299	242
Johnson, James W.	Deed fr	Pratt, Henry et al	1814	AH33	004	004
Johnson, James W.	Deed fr	Kelly, John	1816	AM37	094	075
Johnson, Jane, of Fredericksburg	Deed to	Cranch, William	1813	AE30	187	149
Johnson, Jemima	Cert Slave	From VA	1817	AO39	057	
Johnson, John	Deed fr	Burnes, David	1795	B2A	189	256
Johnson, John	B. of S. to	Johnson, Mary	1809	X23	309	247
Johnson, John, Attorney General	Deed to	Key, Philip Barton	1807	R17	373	284
Johnson, Joseph	B. of S. fr	Wheatley, Barnard	1802	I9	011	014
Johnson, Joseph	Deed fr	Boyd, Washington, collector	1805	M12	258	260
Johnson, Joseph	Assign fr	Russ, Samuel	1806	P15	010	006
Johnson, Joseph	Cert fr	Munroe, Thomas, Supt.	1811	AB27	151	125
Johnson, Joseph	Assign fr	Parker, Fielder, Sr.	1812	AD29	015	011

Party	What	Party	Year	Liber	Old	New
Johnson, Joseph	Deed fr	Gilpin, Bernard, of Montg. Co.	1812	AC28	237	176
Johnson, Joseph	Deed to	Henning, Thomas	1813	AE30	470	350
Johnson, Joseph	B. of S. fr	Boothe, Edward	1813	AF31	060	041
Johnson, Joseph	Deed fr	Law, Thomas	1814	AG32	157	113
Johnson, Joseph	B. of S. to	Mattingly, Joseph	1815	AH33	481	410
Johnson, Joseph et al	Deed fr	Barry, James	1806	Q16	310	237
Johnson, Joseph et al	Deed fr	Parker, Fielder	1812	AC28	125	094
Johnson, Joshua	Deed fr	Hellen, Walter, of G'tn.	1799	D4	215	199
Johnson, Joshua, late of London	Deed fr	Deakins, Francis, of G'tn.	1799	D4	213	197
Johnson, Joshua, of London et al	Deed to	Beatty, Thomas Johnson	1795	B2A	350	495
Johnson, Joshua, of G'tn.	Deed fr	Delius, Everhard	1799	D4	217	200
Johnson, Joshua, of Fredk. Co.	Confirm to	Glover, Charles	1817	AO39	336	239
Johnson, Joshua, of Fredk. Co.	Deed to	English, David, of G'tn.	1817	AO39	337	240
Johnson, Joshua, s/o Thomas	Deed fr	Johnson, Thomas, of Fredk. Co.	1817	AO39	200	147
Johnson, Mary	B. of S. fr	Johnson, John	1809	X23	309	247
Johnson, Morgan	Deed fr	O'Reilly, Henry, of G'tn.	1800	E5	204	197
Johnson, Renaldo, of P.G. Co.	Deed fr	Williams, Thomas, of P.G. Co.	1796	B2B	432	110
Johnson, Richard, of Frederick Co.	B. of S. fr	Weems, Nathaniel T., of G'tn.	1810	Y24	277	253
Johnson, Rinaldo, of P.G. Co.	Deed to	Egan, Thomas Henry, Calvert Co.	1796	B2B	548	273
Johnson, Roger, of Frederick Co.	Deed to	Appleton, John, of Salem MA	1797	B2B	683	461
Johnson, Roger, of Frederick Co.	Deed fr	Shoemaker, Jonathan	1809	W22	156	109
Johnson, Roger, of Frederick Co.	Deed fr	Holmead, Anthony	1809	W22	153	108
Johnson, Samuel	Deed fr	Hunt, Jeremiah	1815	AK35	376	297
Johnson, Thomas	Cert fr	Commissioners of Washington	1796	B2B	452	139
Johnson, Thomas	Deed to	Magruder, Ninian	1802	I9	307	504
Johnson, Thomas	B. of S. to	Dixon, Elizabeth	1811	AA26	199	135
Johnson, Thomas	Lease fr	Van Ness, John P. & Marcia	1813	AE30	497	368
Johnson, Thomas	B. of S. to	Shorter, John & John Freeman	1816	AM37	334	243
Johnson, Thomas	Deed fr	Gardner, William P.	1816	AL36	222	227
Johnson, Thomas (C), age 40	Manumis fr	Van Ness, John P., Gen.	1815	AH33	279	243
Johnson, Thomas (C)	Deed fr	Moxley, Charles, of G'tn.	1816	AM37	120	094
Johnson, Thomas (C)	Deed to	Moxley, Charles, of G'tn.	1816	AL36	223	229
Johnson, Thomas (mulatto)	Deposition		1806	Q16	303	231
Johnson, Thomas & Daniel Carroll	Deed to	Beall, Thomas & John M. Gantt	1792	A1-1	044	66
Johnson, Thomas C. et al	Assign to	Ross, Richard	1809	W22	248	167
Johnson, Thomas et al	Com to	Gantt, John M.	1792	A1-1	001	1
Johnson, Thomas et al	Deed to	Beall, Thomas & John M. Gantt	1793	A1-1	389	496
Johnson, Thomas et al	Cert to	Greenleaf, James, for 1,000 lots	1794	B2A	045	054
Johnson, Thomas et al	Cert to	Greenleaf, James, for 1,000 lots	1794	B2A	048	057
Johnson, Thomas et al	Assign to	United States for Seat of Gov.[2]	1794	B2A	121	162
Johnson, Thomas et al	Deed to	Greenleaf, James, for 500 lots	1794	B2A	044	052
Johnson, Thomas et al	Agreement	Greenleaf, James	1794	B2A	070	090
Johnson, Thomas, Frederick Co.	Deed fr	Stone, John, of Frederick Co.	1792	A1-1	057	84
Johnson, Thomas, Frederick Co.	Deed fr	Jacques, Denton	1793	A1-2	450	59
Johnson, Thomas, Frederick Co.	Deed fr	Peter, Robert, of G'tn.	1794	B2A	161	213
Johnson, Thomas, Frederick Co.	Deed to	Appleton, Nathaniel Walker	1794	B2A	057	070
Johnson, Thomas, Frederick Co.	Deed fr	Peter, Robert, of G'tn.	1795	B2A	175	235
Johnson, Thomas, Frederick Town	Deed to	Polock, Isaac, of G'tn.	1797	B2B	646	408
Johnson, Thomas, Frederick Co.	Deed fr	Stone, John Hoskins, of Balto.	1800	E5	334	322
Johnson, Thomas, Frederick Co.	Deed to	Lowery, Caesar, of G'tn.	1800	F6	033	021
Johnson, Thomas, Frederick Co.	Deed to	deBlock, Francis, of Balto.	1800	F6	104	064
Johnson, Thomas, Frederick Co.	Deed to	Barry, James, of Balto.	1800	E5	200	193

[2]For lots in Carrollsburgh and Hamburgh.

Index to District of Columbia Land Records, 1792-1817

Party	What	Party	Year	Liber	Old	New
Johnson, Thomas, Frederick Co.	Deed fr	Commissioners of Washington	1801	G7	071	092
Johnson, Thomas, Frederick Co.	Lease to	Igan, Ephraim	1801	G7	067	087
Johnson, Thomas, Frederick Co.	Deed fr	Commissioners of Washington	1801	G7	071	093
Johnson, Thomas, Jr.	Deed fr	Burnes, David	1794	B2A	026	029
Johnson, Thomas, Jr. et al	Deed fr	Blodget, Samuel	1794	B2A	009	010
Johnson, Thomas, Jr.	Deed fr	Burnes, David	1795	B2A	188	254
Johnson, Thomas, Jr.	Transfer to	Richmond, Christopher	1796	B2A	337	473
Johnson, Thomas, Jr.	Transfer fr	Edwards, Henry	1796	B2A	337	473
Johnson, Thomas, of Fredk. Co.	Deed to	Lawrence, John	1812	AD29	184	148
Johnson, Thomas, of Fredk. Co.	Deed to	Fitzhugh, Samuel, of G'tn.	1816	AM37	436	313
Johnson, Thomas, of Fredk. Co.	Deed to	Smoot, Samuel	1817	AN38	044	036
Johnson, Thomas, of Fredk. Co.	Deed to	Hopkins, David	1817	AN38	124	092
Johnson, Thomas, of Fredk. Co.	Deed to	Johnson, Joshua, s/o Thomas	1817	AO39	200	147
Johnson, Thomas, of Fredk. Co.	Deed to	Cummings, Mary	1817	AN38	028	023
Johnson, Tunis, Sr., Fauquier Co.	B. of G. to	Middleton, Hannah, w/o James	1801	G7	037	048
Johnson, Walter	Mortgage to	Miller, Peter	1809	V21	309	225
Johnson, Walter	B. of S. to	Knott, Ann	1811	AB27	103	084
Johnson, Walter	B. of S. to	Mattingly, Edward	1815	AI34	103	117
Johnson, William A., of B'burgh.	Deed fr	Brown, Joel	1800	E5	207	200
Johnson, William Andrew	Deed to	Coghlan, William	1802	G7	582	731
Johnston, Charles	Partition	Pollard, Robert & George Pickett	1810	Z25	272	214
Johnston, Charles & Eliza P., VA	Deed to	Pollard, Robert	1812	AC28	433	311
Johnston, Charles & Eliza et al	Deed to	Pickrell, George	1814	AH33	322	279
Johnston, Fanny	B. of S. fr	Johnston, James, of G'tn.	1816	AM37	177	134
Johnston, Jacob (C), age 35	Manumis fr	Winn, Timothy	1816	AM37	191	142
Johnston, James	Deed fr	Brent, Daniel C., marshall	1805	N13	252	211
Johnston, James	Release fr	Watterston, David	1811	AB27	331	272
Johnston, James	Assign to	Forrest, Alexander	1811	AB27	406	335
Johnston, James	B. of S. fr	Cox, Josias	1811	Z25	435	342
Johnston, James	Deed to	Wheaton, Joseph	1811	AB27	384	317
Johnston, James	B. of S. to	Carson, Thomas	1812	AD29	508	429
Johnston, James	B. of S. to	Burns, George	1812	AB27	527	430
Johnston, James & Robert Long	B. of S. fr	Boyert, P.C.F.	1811	AC28	046	035
Johnston, James, of G'tn.	B. of S. to	Johnston, Fanny	1816	AM37	177	134
Johnston, James W.	Deed to	Kelly, John	1814	AH33	008	007
Johnston, Margery	B. of S. fr	Cross, William	1802	H8	268	254
Johnston, Thomas, of Balto.	Deed fr	Loring, Israel	1802	H8	569	532
Johnston, Tunis, of VA	Deed to	Carter, John	1802	H8	127	123
Johnston, William	Deed fr	Walker, James	1808	T19	245	180
Johnston, William	Deed to	Walker, James	1813	AE30	352	263
Johnston, William, of B'burgh.	Deed to	Brown, Joel	1800	E5	215	209
Johnston, William, of VA	Deed fr	Polock, Isaac	1800	E5	215	209
Jolly, Elizabeth	Lease fr	Prout, William	1817	AN38	002	002
Joncherez, A.C.	Lease fr	Dorsey, William H.	1802	I9	312	514
Joncherez, Alex. Lewis et al	Deed fr	Feburier, Nicholas	1802	I9	252	407
Joncherez, Alexander L., trustee	B. of S. fr	Long, John, insolvent	1808	T19	201	144
Joncherez, Alexander L.	Deed fr	Patterson, Edgar, of G'tn.	1810	Y24	148	134
Joncherez, Alexander L., of G'tn.	Deed fr	Patterson, Edgar, of G'tn.	1810	Y24	471	469
Joncherez, Alexander L.	Release to	Patterson, Edgar	1810	Z25	312	244
Joncherez, Alexander L., of G'tn.	Release to	Patterson, Edgar, of G'tn.	1811	AB27	013	012
Joncherez, Alexander L. et al	Lease fr	Reintzel, Anthony	1811	Z25	490	389
Joncherez, Alexander L.	Deed fr	Forrest, Henry	1811	AB27	441	362
Joncherez, Alexander L.	Release to	Patterson, Edgar	1811	AB27	057	048
Joncherez, Alexander L., of G'tn.	B. of S. fr	Richardson, Thomas, of G'tn.	1812	AD29	341	285
Joncherez, Alexander L.	Deed fr	Hollingshead, John et al	1812	AD29	383	323

Party	What	Party	Year	Liber	Old	New
Joncherez, Alexander L., of G'tn.	Lease to	Riggs, Romulus	1813	AF31	121	081
Joncherez, Alexander L., of G'tn.	D. of T. to	Marbury, William, of G'tn.	1813	AF31	220	151
Joncherez, Alexander L., of G'tn.	Deed fr	Corporation of Washington	1815	AI34	319	352
Joncherez, Alexander L., of G'tn.	Deed fr	Corporation of Washington	1815	AI34	290	325
Joncherez, Alexander L., of G'tn.	Deed fr	Corporation of Washington	1815	AI34	292	327
Joncherez, Alexander L., of G'tn.	Deed fr	Corporation of Washington	1815	AI34	321	354
Joncherez, Alexander L., of G'tn.	Deed fr	Corporation of Washington	1815	AI34	296	330
Joncherez, Alexander L., of G'tn.	Deed fr	Corporation of Washington	1815	AI34	298	332
Joncherez, Alexander L., of G'tn.	Deed fr	Corporation of Washington	1815	AI34	300	334
Joncherez, Alexander L., of G'tn.	Deed fr	Corporation of Washington	1815	AI34	303	336
Joncherez, Alexander L., of G'tn.	Deed fr	Corporation of Washington	1815	AI34	305	339
Joncherez, Alexander L., of G'tn.	Deed fr	Corporation of Washington	1815	AI34	307	341
Joncherez, Alexander L., of G'tn.	Deed fr	Corporation of Washington	1815	AI34	311	344
Joncherez, Alexander L., of G'tn.	Deed fr	Corporation of Washington	1815	AI34	313	346
Joncherez, Alexander L., of G'tn.	Deed fr	Corporation of Washington	1815	AI34	315	348
Joncherez, Alexander L., of G'tn.	Deed fr	Corporation of Washington	1815	AI34	317	350
Joncherez, Alexander L., of G'tn.	Deed to	Hughes, Christopher, of Balto.	1816	AL36	044	045
Joncherez, Alexander L., of G'tn.	Deed to	Suter, Alexander	1816	AM37	032	026
Joncherez, Alexander L. et al	Lease fr	Peter, David, heirs of	1816	AM37	402	289
Joncherez, Alexander L., of G'tn.	D. of T. to	Ott, John, of G'tn.	1816	AL36	196	203
Joncherez, Alexander, of G'tn.	Deed fr	Marbury, William & John Peter	1813	AE30	315	237
Jones, Anthony	Deed fr	Smallwood, Samuel N.	1801	F6		106
Jones, Anthony	Deed to	Andrews, George et al	1802	H8	304	287
Jones, Anthony	Deed to	Brown, Robert et al	1802	H8	304	287
Jones, Anthony	Decree fr	Neale, Leonard	1805	N13	017	019
Jones, Anthony, of G'tn.	Deed fr	Threlkeld, John	1797	C3	115	94
Jones, Anthony, of G'tn.	Deed to	Threlkeld, John, of G'tn.	1799	E5	071	058
Jones, Anthony, of P.G. Co.	Deed to	Neale, Leonard, of G'tn.	1805	N13	018	019
Jones, Arthur, of Phila. PA	Deed fr	Dermott, James Reed	1797	B2B	620	378
Jones, Arthur, of Phila. PA	Relinquish fr	Brown, Samuel	1797	B2B	621	379
Jones, Benjamin & Horatio, G'tn.	D. of T. fr	Boyer, Richard Montgomery, G'tn.	1811	AA26	240	164
Jones, Benjamin W., late sheriff	Deed to	Upperman, Henry, of G'tn.	1801	G7		037
Jones, Benjamin W., of G'tn.	Deed fr	Mountz, Jacob, collector, G'tn.	1810	Z25	348	272
Jones, Benjamin W.	Bond	Tobacco Inspector, of G'tn.	1811	AA26	101	071
Jones, Benjamin W.	Deed fr	Presbyterian Congregation, G'tn.	1812	AC28	144	107
Jones, Benjamin W., of Montg. Co.	Deed to	Wells, John, Jr., of G'tn.	1815	AK35	312	248
Jones, Benjamin W.	Assign to	Bussard, Daniel	1815	AH33	396	342
Jones, Benjamin White, sheriff	Deed to	Carlton, Joseph, of G'tn.	1792	A1-1	051	76
Jones, Benjamin White	Deed to	Thompson, John, of G'tn.	1798	C3	376	300
Jones, Benjamin White, sheriff	Deed to	Laird, John	1801	G7	263	361
Jones, Benjamin White	Deed to	Magruder, Edward	1804	K10	250	257
Jones, Charles	Cert fr	Commissioners of Washington	1793	B2A	307	431
Jones, Charles	Transfer to	Sweeny, Mary	1797	B2B	459	148
Jones, Charles	B. of S. to	Cook, Orlando	1805	N13	090	082
Jones, Charles	Agreement	Cook, Orlando	1806	O14	297	197
Jones, Charles	Deed fr	Alexander, John et al	1807	T19	013	010
Jones, Charles	Deed fr	Flaut, Christian	1807	S18	200	160
Jones, Charles	B. of S. fr	Coombs, John	1809	W22	320	208
Jones, Charles	Deed fr	Dorsey, William H., of Balto.	1810	Y24	442	393
Jones, Charles	Deed to	Suttle, Henry, of G'tn.	1810	Y24	105	095
Jones, Charles	D. of T. fr	Warner, Osborn	1810	Z25	118	092
Jones, Charles	B. of S. fr	Wise, Samuel	1810	Y24	422	379
Jones, Charles	B. of S. fr	Hayre, John	1811	AA26	083	059
Jones, Charles	Lease fr	Law, Edmund, trustee of Thomas	1811	AA26	155	107
Jones, Charles C., of Montg. Co.	Deed fr	Starke, Belfield, of VA	1810	Y24	117	106

Party	What	Party	Year	Liber	Old	New
Jones, Charles C., of Montg. Co.	Deed fr	French, Arianna, wid/o Geo. et al	1810	Z25	086	065
Jones, Charles C., late Montg. Co.	Deed to	Smith, Samuel Harrison	1811	AA26	061	046
Jones, Charles C., of Montg. Co.	Deed to	Glasco, John	1812	AD29	427	359
Jones, Charles C., of Montg. Co.	Deed to	Shepperd, Lodowic, of G'tn.	1813	AE30	530	392
Jones, Charles C., of Montg. Co.	Deed to	Glascow, John	1813	AE30	384	284
Jones, Charles C., of Montg. Co.	Deed to	Hollenback, William	1814	AG32	023	018
Jones, Charles C., of Montg. Co.	Deed to	Lancaster, Stephen, of G'tn.	1815	AK35	041	032
Jones, Charles C., of Montg. Co.	Deed to	Beall, Samuel, of G'tn.	1815	AK35	037	029
Jones, Charles C., of Montg. Co.	Deed fr	Shepperd, Lowodic, of G'tn.	1815	AH33	554	475
Jones, Charles, Capt.	Qualify	Light Infantry	1808	U20	041	023
Jones, Charles Courts, Montg. Co.	Cert fr	Munroe, Thomas, Supt.	1809	W22	043	032
Jones, Charles Courts, Montg. Co.	Deed fr	Gaither, Henry, of Montg. Co.	1810	Y24	115	105
Jones, Charles et al	Deed fr	King, Nicholas	1805	M12	093	086
Jones, Charles, exrs. of	Deed to	Ward, William	1816	AL36	113	114
Jones, Charles, of Montg. Co.	Deed to	Beale, Samuel, of G'tn.	1812	AC28	299	218
Jones, Charles, trustee	Deed fr	Blaire, John A., insolvent	1805	N13	319	257
Jones, Charles, trustee	Deed fr	Dillon, Robert, insolvent	1805	N13	155	144
Jones, Cilla (C), age 27	Cert Free fr	Sims, Soddy (C)	1817	AO39	168	125
Jones, David, s/o David & Rachel	Cert Free fr	Brent, Robert	1811	AB27	395	325
Jones, Dennis, of G'tn.	Deed fr	Mitchell, John C., of G'tn.	1816	AL36	067	067
Jones, Edward	Assign to	Cox, John	1802	G7	522	665
Jones, Edward, children of	Deed Gift fr	Jones, Evan	1808	U20	202	111
Jones, Edward, of G'tn.	B. of S. to	Craig, Robert, of G'tn.	1809	X23	025	017
Jones, Edward, of G'tn.	Deed fr	Lingan, Nicholas, of G'tn.	1810	Z25	195	153
Jones, Edward, of G'tn.	Mortgage to	Lingan, Nicholas, of G'tn.	1811	Z25	453	358
Jones, Evan	Deed Gift to	Jones, Edward, children of	1808	U20	202	111
Jones, Frederick P.	B. of S. to	Gibson, Richard	1816	AL36	226	231
Jones, Frederick P.	Mortgage to	Jones, Philemon	1817	AO39	321	229
Jones, Henry, s/o David & Rachel	Cert Free fr	Brent, Robert	1811	AB27	395	325
Jones, Horatio & Susan	Deed fr	Magruder, George B.	1817	AO39	381	257
Jones, Jason	Deed to	Howard, William	1806	Q16	083	053
Jones, Jesson	B. of S. to	McDonald, Alspeth	1805	O14	105	066
Jones, John	D. of T. fr	Brooks, William & Margaret	1806	O14	268	177
Jones, John	Deed fr	Thompson, Arthur	1811	AB27	023	021
Jones, John	B. of S. fr	McDaniel, Nathaniel	1812	AD29	194	158
Jones, John Courts, Charles Co.	Deed to	Davidson, Samuel	1796	B2B	521	231
Jones, John Courts, Charles Co.	Deed fr	Lingan, James M., of G'tn.	1796	B2B	428	104
Jones, John G.	Lease to	Dove, Joseph	1802	I9	314	516
Jones, John G., of G'tn.	Lease to	Hoover, Andrew, of G'tn.	1802	H8	489	449
Jones, John G.	Deed fr	Holmead, Anthony	1802	H8	018	017
Jones, John G., of G'tn.	Deed fr	Holmes, John & Anthony	1808	T19	283	208
Jones, John G., of G'tn.	Agreement	Steuart, William	1808	U20	215	116
Jones, John G., of G'tn.	Deed to	Corcoran, Thomas, of G'tn.	1808	U20	065	037
Jones, John G.	Deed fr	Steuart, William	1808	U20	230	124
Jones, John G.	Deed fr	Steuart, William, of G'tn.	1809	W22	318	207
Jones, John G.	Deed to	Thompson, James, of MA	1809	X23	072	054
Jones, John G.	Deed to	Foxall, Henry	1811	AB27	108	088
Jones, John G., for son John A.	Indenture to	Reeder, John, turner	1811	AB27	237	194
Jones, John G.	Deed to	Foxall, Henry, of G'tn.	1813	AE30	141	110
Jones, John Godfrey	Lease to	Johnson, Isaac	1804	K10	402	417
Jones, John Godfrey	Lease to	Marquand, Charles	1809	W22	304	199
Jones, John, of G'tn.	Lease fr	Beatty, Charles, of G'tn.	1794	A1-2	476	81
Jones, John, of G'tn.	Deed to	Borer, Peter, of G'tn.	1794	B2A	164	218
Jones, John, of G'tn.	Lease to	Walter, Watta B., of G'tn.	1796	B2B	393	053
Jones, John, of MD	Deed fr	Elzey, Arnold	1802	H8	528	487

Party	What	Party	Year	Liber	Old	New
Jones, John, of Somerset Co.	Deed to	Leatherbury, John, of Robt.	1807	S18	286	224
Jones, Lewin, of P.G. Co.	Mortgage to	Reed, William, of Alexa. Co.	1808	V21	113	084
Jones, Mary	Cert. Free to	Astin, Nancy	1814	AG32	365	264
Jones, Maryan, d/o David & R.	Cert Free fr	Brent, Robert	1811	AB27	395	325
Jones, Matildy, d/o David & R.	Cert Free fr	Brent, Robert	1811	AB27	395	325
Jones, Maurice, of Frederick Co.	Deed fr	Mantz, Ezra, sheriff, Frederick Co.	1811	Z25	379	297
Jones, Monica, of St. Mary's Co.	Deed fr	Herbert, Francis, of St. Mary's Co.	1809	W22	289	191
Jones, Monica, of St. Mary's Co.	Deed to	Herbert, Francis, of St. Mary's Co.	1815	AK35	382	301
Jones, Moses W.	B. of S. to	Jones, Samuel	1806	Q16	272	190
Jones, Nathan	B. of S. to	Shorter, Charles	1808	V21	084	066
Jones, Philemon	Mortgage fr	Jones, Frederick P.	1817	AO39	321	229
Jones, Philip, of Phila.	Mortgage fr	Varden, Charles H.	1811	AB27	184	152
Jones, Prudence & N.L. Queen	Deed to	Ward, William	1816	AL36	113	114
Jones, Rachael	Deed fr	May, Frederick & Samuel Eliot, Jr.	1806	Q16	145	095
Jones, Rachel	Agreement	Eliot, Samuel, Jr.	1802	I9	282	461
Jones, Raphael	Deed fr	Gaines, Richard	1805	N13	215	186
Jones, Raphael	Deed to	Wright, Thomas C., of G'tn.	1807	R17	147	113
Jones, Raphael, insolvent	Assign to	Wright, Thomas C., trustee	1809	V21	414	316
Jones, Raphael, of G'tn.	Deed fr	Bowie, Washington, of G'tn.	1817	AN38	092	070
Jones, Raphael, of G'tn.	Lease fr	Harris, Joseph	1817	AN38	088	068
Jones, Richard	Deed fr	Prout, William	1817	AO39	422	287
Jones, Richard	Deed fr	Smallwood, Horatio, of G'tn.	1817	AN38	111	083
Jones, Richard, of G'tn.	Deed fr	Boyd, Washington, marshal	1817	AO39	211	154
Jones, Richard, of G'tn.	Deed fr	Ragan, Daniel, of G'tn.	1817	AN38	367	270
Jones, Samuel	B. of S. fr	Jones, Moses W.	1806	Q16	272	190
Jones, Sarah	Release fr	Thompson, Arthur	1815	AI34	129	148
Jones, Saryan, d/o David & R.	Cert Free fr	Brent, Robert	1811	AB27	395	325
Jones, Thomas	Mortgage fr	Frost, Amariah	1801	G7	394	528
Jones, Thomas	Deed fr	Carroll, Daniel, of *Duddington*	1802	G7	573	722
Jones, Thomas	Slave		1807	R17	306	233
Jones, Thomas D., of MD	P. of Atty. to	Waters, Benjamin, of Alexa.	1817	AN38	032	026
Jones, Thomas D., of MD	Deed to	Brodbeck, Jacob	1817	AN38	030	024
Jones, Thomas, Loudoun Co. VA	Convey to	Varden, Charles H.	1805	N13	098	091
Jones, Tristram F.	Deed fr	McNantz, Charles	1801	G7	069	089
Jones, Tristram F.	Deed to	Willson, David	1802	H8	181	174
Jones, Walter	Deed fr	Gales, Joseph & Sarah J.M.	1815	AI34	422	442
Jones, Walter	Deed fr	Carr, Overton	1817	AN38	303	222
Jones, Walter	Deed fr	Drane, Washington	1817	AO39	103	080
Jones, Walter	Deed fr	Carr, Overton	1817	AN38	310	227
Jones, Walter & John P. Van Ness	Mortgage fr	Underwood, John	1814	AH33	104	096
Jones, Walter, Jr.	Deed fr	Lingan, James M., of Montg. Co.	1809	X23	106	077
Jones, Walter, Jr.	B. of S. to	Smothers, Harry	1810	Y24	246	227
Jones, Walter, Jr.	Deed fr	Pratt, Henry et al	1812	AC28	400	290
Jones, Walter, Jr.	Deed fr	Van Ness, John P. & Marcia	1812	AD29	376	317
Jones, Walter, Jr.	Deed fr	Pratt, Henry et al	1813	AE30	328	246
Jones, Walter, Jr., trustee	Deed to	Crookshank, Richard et al	1814	AG32	219	153
Jones, Walter, Jr.	Deed to	Melvin, James, of G'tn.	1814	AG32	113	085
Jones, Walter, Jr. et al	Deed fr	Jackson, John G., fr. Harrison Co.	1814	AG32	295	215
Jones, Walter, Jr.	Deed fr	Ridgeway, Thomas S., of Phila.	1815	AI34	243	276
Jones, William	B. of S. to	Waterstone, David	1802	H8	535	495
Jones, William, of Thomas et al	Deed fr	King, Elisha, of P.G. Co.	1809	W22	109	079
Jones, William, s/o David & Rachel	Cert Free fr	Brent, Robert	1811	AB27	395	325
Jones, Willie Ann, of Balto. MD	Deed to	Nevitt, Mary	1813	AE30	502	372
Jordan, Hugh	B. of S. fr	Gormley, Constantine	1802	H8	269	255
Jordan, Hugh	Deed fr	Aiker, John	1802	I9	306	503

Party	What	Party	Year	Liber	Old	New
Jordan, William	B. of S. fr	Hemler, John	1811	AA26	160	110
Joy, Abraham	Deed fr	Thompson, William, of G'tn.	1804	L11	232	215
Joy, Absalom	Deed to	Woodward, William	1801	G7	009	011
Joy, Absalom	Deed fr	Commissioners of Washington	1801	G7		010
Joy, Absalom	Deed to	Nourse, Michael	1806	P15	023	014
Joy, Absalom, of G'tn.	Deed fr	Nourse, Michael	1806	O14	096	060
Joy, Barton	B. of S. to	Cannon, John	1802	I9	489	804
Joy, Henry B.	Deed fr	Cannon, Charles	1815	AI34	414	436
Joy, Henry B.	B. of S. to	Smith, William	1816	AL36	180	179
Joy, John B.	Deed to	Gustin, Justianna	1802	I9	560	908
Justine, J.T.	Cert Slave	From Frederick Co. VA to G'tn.	1815	AI34	248	281

Party	What	Party	Year	Liber	Old	New
K						
Kaegy, Abraham, of DE	Deed fr	Seyle, Ann Maria et al [Scyle]	1805	M12	157	154
Kain, Patrick	B. of S. fr	Cooper, John	1808	T19	131	093
Kain, Patrick	Lease fr	May, Frederick, physician	1808	V21	115	086
Kain, Patrick	Deed fr	Love, John	1813	AE30	182	145
Kain, Patrick	Lease fr	May, Frederick	1813	AF31	263	184
Kain, Patrick & John Love	Deed fr	May, Frederick, physician	1808	V21	119	088
Kain, Patrick & John Love	Deed fr	May, Frederick	1810	Y24	090	081
Kain, Patrick et al	Deed fr	King, Nicholas	1805	M12	093	086
Kain, Patrick et al	Mortgage fr	Spalding, John	1814	AG32	403	294
Kaldenbach, Andrew	Assign to	Clarke, Walter & Joseph	1806	O14	221	146
Kaldenbach, Androw	Assign to	Clarke, Robert	1806	P15	089	054
Kaldenbach, Andrew	Deed to	Nourse, Michael	1807	S18	246	194
Kaldenbach, Andrew, of G'tn.	Deed fr	Orme, Thomas, of MD	1802	H8	264	250
Kaldenbach, Andrew, of G'tn.	Deed fr	Davidson, John, of MD	1802	H8	474	435
Kaldenbach, Andrew, of G'tn.	Deed fr	Speerer, Nicholas, of G'tn.	1802	I9	088	126
Kaldenbach, Andrew, of G'tn.	Assign to	King, Adam, of G'tn.	1806	P15	054	033
Kaldenbach, Andrew, of G'tn.	D. of T. to	Herty, Thomas	1806	P15	057	034
Kaldenbach, Andrew, of G'tn.	D. of T. to	King, Adam, of G'tn.	1806	P15	107	067
Kaldenback, Andrew, of G'tn.	Deed fr	Davidson, John	1802	H8	378	351
Kaldenback, Andrew, of G'tn.	Deed fr	Davidson, John, of MD	1802	H8	475	436
Kaldenbauch, Andrew	Deed fr	Gibbs, Nicholas	1797	B2B	611	385
Kaldenbauch, Andrew, of G'tn.	Deed fr	Davidson, John, of Annapolis	1798	C3	407	323
Kaldenbaugh, Andrew	Release to	Dial, Annastatia	1804	K10	197	205
Kaldenbaugh, Andrew	Deed fr	Hines, John	1806	O14	388	259
Kaldenbaugh, Andrew, of G'tn.	Deed fr	Gibbs, Nicholas, of Balto.	1796	B2B	611	365
Kaldenbaugh, Andrew, of G'tn.	Deed fr	Wiley, Abel	1802	H8	359	334
Kaldenbaugh, Andrew, of G'tn.	Deed fr	Hines, John	1805	M12	067	062
Kaldenbaugh, Andrew, of G'tn.	Deed to	Herty, Thomas	1805	M12	048	046
Kaldenbaugh, Andrew, of G'tn.	Deed fr	Wayman, Charles	1805	N13	106	100
Kaldenbaugh, Andrew, of G'tn.	Deed to	King, Adam, of G'tn.	1805	N13	315	254
Kale, Jeremiah	B. of S. fr	Kale, John	1802	H8	007	007
Kale, John	Deed to	Street, Catherine	1802	H8	006	006
Kale, John	B. of S. to	Kale, Jeremiah	1802	H8	007	007
Kale, John	Deed to	Windle, Isaac	1802	H8	005	005
Kalklazer, Thomas, blacksmith	Deed fr	Bohrer, Mary, wid., of G'tn.	1803	K10	061	66
Kalkman, Charles Frederick, Balto.	Deed fr	Yeaton, William & Lucia, of Alexa.	1810	Z25	368	289
Kamp, John et al	Deed to	Beall, Thomas & John M. Gantt	1792	A1-1	102	148
Karrick, Joseph et al	Deed fr	Sprogell, Thomas Y.	1800	E5	166	156
Karrick, Joseph et al	Deed to	Wilmans, Frederick	1802	H8	080	074
Karrick, Joseph, of Phila. PA	Cert fr	Commissioners of Washington	1801	G7	185	248
Kastner, John	B. of S. fr	Miers, John	1809	V21	270	193
Keadle, John, of P.G. Co.	Deed fr	Keadle, Wiseman Gibson	1804	K10	129	139
Keadle, Wiseman Gibson	Deed to	Keadle, John, of P.G. Co.	1804	K10	129	139
Keagy, Abraham, of MD	Deed to	Brown, Joel	1812	AD29	439	368
Kealey, Daniel	B. of S. to	Brison, Sarah	1809	V21	285	205
Kealey, Daniel	Deed fr	Prout, William	1814	AG32	140	101
Kealey, Daniel	Lease fr	Prout, William	1814	AH33	163	152
Kealey, Daniel	Deed to	Bryson, Sarah	1816	AM37	009	007
Kealy, Daniel	Lease fr	Law, Edmund, trustee of Thomas	1811	AA26	019	015
Kealy, Daniel	Lease to	Moss, Philemon	1815	AK35	096	074
Kealy, Daniel	Deed fr	Bryson, Sarah	1816	AO39	033	027
Kean, William	Deed fr	Munroe, Thomas, Supt.	1805	M12	197	199
Kean, William	Slave	From Alexandria Co.	1807	S18	104	084
Kean, William, insolvent	Assign to	Herford, Henry, trustee	1808	V21	137	100

Index to District of Columbia Land Records, 1792-1817

Party	What	Party	Year	Liber	Old	New
Keane, Francis	Deed fr	Waugh, Alexander & Susanna P.	1810	Y24	343	
Kearnes, Francis, of G'tn.	B. of S. fr	French, Samuel	1801	G7	173	231
Kearney, James	Cert fr	Commissioners of Washington	1800	E5	381	359
Kearney, James	Lease fr	Law, John, atty. of Thomas	1810	Z25	052	039
Kearney, James	Deed fr	Law, Thomas	1816	AL36	339	331
Kearney, John	Deed fr	Commissioners of Washington	1799	E5	037	027
Kearney, John	Cert fr	Commissioners of Washington	1800	E5	403	376
Kearney, John	Deed to	Talton, Edward & John	1801	G7	056	072
Kearney, John	Agreement	Law, Thomas	1801	G7	084	109
Kearney, John	B. of S. fr	Robinson, Alexander	1801	G7	110	141
Kearney, John	Deed to	Ellis, Robert	1801	G7	396	530
Kearney, John	Bond to	Ellis, Robert	1801	G7	321	451
Kearney, John	Mortgage to	Ellis, Robert	1801	G7	319	447
Kearney, John	Deed to	McIntire, John et al	1801	G7	151	200
Kearney, John	Deed to	Fallon, Mary Ann	1802	I9	471	775
Kearney, John	Deed to	Fallon, Edward	1802	I9	404	671
Kearney, John	Deed to	Fallon, Edward	1802	I9	404	670
Kearney, John	Deed to	Fallon, Edward	1802	I9	405	672
Kearney, John	B. of S. fr	Peacock, Robert Ware	1802	H8	221	211
Kearney, John	Deed to	McIntire, John et al	1802	I9	474	780
Kearney, John & Edward Fallon	Deed to	Taylor, James N. & Henry Toland	1804	K10	139	151
Kearney, John & Edward Fallon	Deed to	Morris, Benjamin W. et al	1804	K10	114	123
Kearney, John & Edward Fallon	Deed to	Bartleman, William, of Alexa.	1804	K10	125	135
Kearney, John et al	Deed fr	Bradley, Phineas	1801	G7	368	500
Kearney, John et al	Deed fr	Baker, Samuel	1802	H8	324	304
Kearney, John et al	Deed to	McIntire, John et al	1802	I9	406	673
Kedgelie, Ann	B. of S. fr	Tayloe, John	1810	Y24	118	108
Kedgley, Ann	B. of S. fr	Hollingshead, James, Calvert Co.	1811	AB27	430	354
Kedgley, John	Deed fr	Reinhart, Andrew	1802	I9	092	131
Kedglie, Alexander	Assign to	Kedglie, John	1808	V21	048	036
Kedglie, Ann	B. of S. fr	Beall, Warring	1817	AN38	391	290
Kedglie, Ann	B. of S. fr	Shorter, John	1817	AN38	377	279
Kedglie, Ann	Deed fr	Shorter, John, free person	1817	AN38	204	149
Kedglie, John	Assign fr	Kedglie, Alexander	1808	V21	048	036
Kedgly, John	B. of S. fr	Porter, Charles, of Montg. Co.	1808	U20	226	122
Kedgly, John	Receipt fr	Gregory, Nathaniel	1809	V21	318	234
Keech, Chloe Tilda, of G'tn.	Deed fr	Keech, William, of G'tn.	1798	D4	049	041
Keech, William, of G'tn.	Deed to	Keech, Chloe Tilda, of G'tn.	1798	D4	049	041
Keef, William	Lease fr	Blodget, Samuel	1804	K10	274	279
Keeler, David, of G'tn.	Deed to	Johns, Susanna	1805	O14	085	053
Keeling, Edward A. & Ann et al	Deed to	Orr, Benjamin Grayson	1817	AN38	198	144
Keen, Frances, of Fairfax Co.	Deed to	Gilmour, Helen, of Lancaster Co.	1814	AG32	109	083
Keeper, Joseph, of Frederick Co.	Deed fr	Ragin, William, of Frederick Co.	1797	C3	059	48
Keepers, Joseph, Frederick Co.	Deed to	Ragan, Lurana, wid., Fredk. Co.	1798	C3	427	336
Keifer, Henry [Kefer]	Deed fr	Beatty, Charles, heirs of	1807	R17	260	197
Keiglar, John	Assign to	Tietjen, Henry	1804	L11	107	110
Keiglar, John	B. of S. to	Tietjen, Henry	1804	L11	108	112
Keigler, John	Deed fr	Law, Thomas	1802	H8	354	330
Keiler, Daniel	Release fr	Morin, Lewis	1811	AA26	204	139
Keith, James	Deed to	Lyles, George	1802	I9	297	487
Keith, James, of Alexa. et al	Deed fr	Roberts, Owen & Jane	1802	H8	332	311
Keithley, James	Deed fr	Keithley, Thomas	1813	AE30	136	106
Keithley, Thomas	Mortgage to	Young, Thomas	1812	AD29	395	333
Keithley, Thomas	Deed fr	Young, Thomas	1812	AD29	389	328
Keithley, Thomas	Deed to	Keithley, James	1813	AE30	136	106

Party	What	Party	Year	Liber	Old	New
Keithley, Thomas	B. of S. fr	Warren, Nahum	1815	AH33	398	344
Keithley, Thomas & Thos. Young	Deed to	White, Thomas	1813	AF31	494	360
Kellenberger, John H., of G'tn.	Deed fr	Ober, Robert, of G'tn.	1811	AB27	335	276
Kellenberger, John H., of G'tn.	Deed to	Smith, Walter, of G'tn.	1817	AO39	412	279
Keller, Frederick, of G'tn. et al	Deed fr	Lufborough, Nathan	1813	AE30	446	331
Keller, Frederick, of G'tn.	B. of S. to	Brauer, Frederick	1816	AL36	420	401
Keller, Frederick, of G'tn.	B. of S. fr	Weiskopff, C.L., of G'tn.	1816	AL36	421	402
Keller, Jacob, s/o Rudolph	Deed to	Thomas, Philip, of Frederick Co.	1792	A1-1	069	101
Keller, John et al	Convey fr	Riggs, George W., of Balto.	1810	Y24	495	436
Keller, John F., of G'tn. et al	Deed fr	Riggs, George W., of Balto. MD	1812	AD29	092	070
Keller, John Frederick, of G'tn.	Deed to	Weiskopff, Charles L., of G'tn.	1814	AH33	210	189
Keller, John Frederick et al	Release fr	Grammer, Frederick, of A.A. Co.	1815	AI34	278	313
Keller, Juliana, wid/o Rudolph	Deed to	Thomas, Philip, of Frederick Co.	1792	A1-1	069	101
Kelley, William	Mortgage fr	Nichols, Edward	1802	G7	544	691
Kelly, John	Deed fr	Wilson, Lanclot, of Henry	1814	AH33	148	140
Kelly, John	Deed fr	Johnston, James W.	1814	AH33	008	007
Kelly, John	Deed to	Johnson, James W.	1816	AM37	094	075
Kelly, John	D. of T. to	Gantt, Thomas T.	1816	AL36	029	031
Kelly, John, of G'tn.	Deed fr	Reintzel, Valentine, of G'tn.	1815	AI34	242	274
Kelly, John, of G'tn.	Deed to	Davis, John P., of G'tn.	1816	AL36	423	404
Kelly, Michael	B. of S. to	Warren, John	1806	O14	327	217
Kemp, Ann Margaret, Fredk. Co.	Deed to	Mayne, Adam, of G'tn.	1817	AO39	065	054
Kemp, Christian, of Frederick Co.	Deed fr	Baker, Walter, Jefferson Co. VA	1810	X23	394	317
Kemp, Henry	Deed fr	Beatty, John M. et al	1805	M12	179	179
Kemp, Henry	Deed fr	Beatty, Charles, heirs of	1807	R17	218	163
Kemp, Henry & Lodowick	Deed to	Beall, Thomas & John M. Gantt	1792	A1-1	108	157
Kemp, Henry & Christian	Deed fr	Kemp, Lodwick, of Frederick Co.	1801	G7	226	301
Kemp, Henry, of Frederick Co.	Deed to	Deakins, William, Jr., of G'tn.	1792	A1-1	122	179
Kemp, Henry, of Frederick Co.	Deed fr	Williams, Elisha W.	1809	W22	133	095
Kemp, James	Deed to	Wilcox, Thomas	1811	AC28	032	024
Kemp, James	Deed fr	Grantt, George	1811	Z25	390	307
Kemp, James & Edward Grant	Deed fr	Queen, Henry M., collector	1811	AA26	380	253
Kemp, James & Edward Grantt	P. of Atty. fr	Picknoll, Richard H.	1811	AA26	010	008
Kemp, James & Edward Grantt	Mortgage fr	Picknoll, Richard H.	1811	AA26	081	057
Kemp, James et al	Assign to	Serra, Augustin	1813	AE30	376	279
Kemp, Lodwick, of Frederick Co.	Deed to	Kemp, Henry & Christian	1801	G7	226	301
Kemp, Ludwick, of Frederick Co.	Deed fr	Davidson, John, of Annapolis	1800	E5	290	283
Kemp, Peter & Lodwick, s/o Fdk.	Deed to	Murdock, Eleanor, wid/o George	1806	Q16	061	039
Kendelback, Andrew, of G'tn.	Assign fr	Long, Frederick	1801	G7	178	238
Kendelback, Andrew, of G'tn.	B. of S. fr	Long, Frederick	1801	G7	180	240
Kengla, Joseph [Kingla]	Deed to	Ballzor, Elizabeth, Frederick Co.	1804	K10	321	328
Kengla, Lewis, of G'tn.	D. of T. to	English, David, cashier, of G'tn.	1817	AN38	342	251
Kengla, Lewis, of G'tn.	Deed fr	Hoye, John, of Allegany Co.	1817	AN38	340	250
Kennedy, James	Deed fr	Polock, Isaac	1802	I9	330	544
Kennedy, James	Deed fr	Beatty, Charles, heirs of	1805	O14	032	020
Kennedy, James	Deed fr	Beatty, Charles, heirs of	1806	P15	361	240
Kennedy, James	Deed fr	Beatty, John M. & Charles A.	1807	Q16	391	300
Kennedy, James	Deed to	Dodge, Francis	1813	AF31	551	409
Kennedy, James	Deed fr	Ober, Robert	1816	AL36	024	025
Kennedy, James	Deed fr	Beatty, Charles A.	1816	AL36	019	020
Kennedy, James	Deed to	Ott, John	1816	AL36	289	287
Kennedy, James, of G'tn.	Deed fr	McClan, Robert, of G'tn.	1797	B2B	682	456
Kennedy, James, of G'tn.	Deed to	Gannon, James, of G'tn.	1808	T19	194	139
Kennedy, James, of G'tn.	Deed fr	Davidson, Ann Maria, of G'tn.	1809	X23	176	131
Kennedy, James, of G'tn.	Deed to	Warring, Henry, of Montg. Co.	1815	AK35	110	085

Index to District of Columbia Land Records, 1792-1817

Party	What	Party	Year	Liber	Old	New
Kennedy, James, of G'tn.	Deed fr	Brundige, James, of Balto.	1816	AL36	021	022
Kennedy, James, of G'tn.	Deed to	Miles, William, of G'tn.	1817	AN38	391	291
Kennedy, John	Deed fr	Dalton, White et al	1802	H8	589	554
Kennedy, John	Deed to	Murdock, John et al	1802	I9	280	458
Kennedy, John	Deed fr	Alexander, William Thornton et al	1802	H8	589	554
Kennedy, Mathew, of G'tn.	Deed to	Reintzel, Anthony, of G'tn.	1800	F6	025	016
Kennedy, Matthew	Lease fr	Threlkeld, John	1798	D4	169	150
Kennedy, Matthew	Deed to	Gitzandanner, Christian	1804	K10	273	277
Kennedy, Matthew	B. of S. fr	Threlkeld, John	1805	M12	212	214
Kennedy, Matthew, of G'tn.	Deed fr	Peter, Robert, of G'tn.	1797	B2B	665	431
Kennedy, Matthew, of G'tn.	B. of S. to	Dodge, Francis, of G'tn.	1805	N13	177	159
Kennedy, Matthew, of G'tn.	B. of S. to	Hines, John	1806	O14	130	084
Kenner, James	B. of S. to	Hughes, Thomas	1806	Q16	261	181
Kenner, James	B. of S. to	Prout, William	1806	Q16	204	138
Kenner, James, trustee	Deed fr	McPherson, Samuel, insolvent	1804	L11	342	310
Kenner, James, trustee	B. of S. fr	Frost, John Thomas, insolvent	1805	M12	406	421
Kenner, James, trustee	B. of S. fr	Burch, Jane, insolvent	1805	N13	156	145
Kenner, James, trustee	Deed fr	Pollock, William, insolvent	1805	N13	112	106
Kenner, James, trustee	B. of S. fr	Connor, Jeremiah, insolvent	1805	M12	405	420
Kent, Luke et al	Deed to	Varden, Ezra	1809	X23	031	022
Kent, Luke, insolvent	Assign to	Callan, Nicholas, trustee	1811	AC28	050	038
Kent, Luke, trustee	D. of T. fr	Polkinhorn, Henry, insolvent	1810	Z25	350	274
Kent, Luke, trustee	Deed fr	Sciverman, John C., insolvent	1810	Z25	193	151
Kerby, Francis, of P.G. Co.	Deed fr	Collard, Samuel & Rachel of VA	1813	AE30	399	294
Kerby, John B.	Deed fr	Wigfield, Robert	1804	L11	212	199
Kerby, John B.	Deed fr	Wigfield, Matthew	1804	L11	210	198
Kerby, John Baptist [Kirby]	Deed fr	Wigfield, Mathew	1807	R17	089	071
Kerby, John Baptist	Deed to	Taylor, Thomas & Jonas	1809	V21	257	183
Kerby, John Baptist et al	Bond to	United States	1809	X23	316	253
Kerby, John Baptist	Deed fr	Minifie, Charles	1810	X23	384	309
Kerby, John Baptist	Deed fr	Farrell, Zephaniah	1811	Z25	442	348
Kerby, Robert B.	Slaves	From Fairfax Co. VA	1811	Z25	513	408
Kerr, A., w/o Alexander et al	Deed fr	Van Ness, John P. & Marcia	1809	X23	068	051
Kerr, Alexander	Cert fr	Commissioners of Washington	1800	F6		025
Kerr, Alexander	Deed fr	Templeman, John et al	1802	H8	348	324
Kerr, Alexander	Deed fr	Deakins, Francis	1802	H8	272	257
Kerr, Alexander	Deed fr	Forrest, Uriah et al	1802	H8	348	324
Kerr, Alexander	Assign fr	Jack, John	1802	H8	543	504
Kerr, Alexander	Deed to	Knapp, John	1806	Q16	250	172
Kerr, Alexander	Lease to	Little, Israel	1806	O14	253	167
Kerr, Alexander	Deed to	McCormick, James, Jr.	1807	S18	284	222
Kerr, Alexander	Assign fr	Speake, Samuel	1808	V21	094	072
Kerr, Alexander	Deed to	Costigan, Joseph	1808	U20	118	067
Kerr, Alexander	Deed fr	Whetcroft, Henry	1808	V21	095	073
Kerr, Alexander	Deed fr	Kilty, John & Josias Wilson King	1809	V21	412	314
Kerr, Alexander	Deed to	Tweedy, David	1810	Y24	491	433
Kerr, Alexander	L. of Atty. to	Kerr, Robert & James McConnell	1811	AB27	122	100
Kerr, Alexander	Qualify	Notary Public	1811	Z25	494	393
Kerr, Alexander	Cert fr	Munroe, Thomas, Supt.	1813	AE30	298	225
Kerr, Alexander	Partition	Whetcroft, William, heirs of	1813	AE30	196	157
Kerr, Alexander	Deed to	Hebb, William, of P.G. Co.	1813	AF31	298	212
Kerr, Alexander	Lease to	Donaldson, Ronald	1813	AE30	225	181
Kerr, Alexander	Cert fr	Munroe, Thomas, Supt.	1813	AE30	300	227
Kerr, Alexander	Deed to	Fletcher, Noah	1814	AG32	442	320
Kerr, Alexander	Deed fr	Corporation of Washington	1815	AK35	268	213

Party	What	Party	Year	Liber	Old	New
Kerr, Alexander	Deed fr	Corporation of Washington	1815	AK35	265	211
Kerr, Alexander	Deed fr	Corporation of Washington	1815	AK35	263	209
Kerr, Alexander	Deed fr	McNamara, Mary	1816	AM37	005	004
Kerr, Alexander	Deed to	Gales, Joseph, Jr.	1817	AN38	288	210
Kerr, Alexander	D. of T. fr	Ryan, Henry & Mary	1817	AO39	407	277
Kerr, Alexander	D. of T. fr	Shorter, John, a free man	1817	AN38	450	323
Kerr, Alexander & Anne et al	Deed to	Bradley, Abraham, Jr.	1811	AC28	069	052
Kerr, Alexander & Ann et al	Deed to	Bacon, Samuel & George Moore	1812	AD29	523	441
Kerr, Alexander & Jacob Wagner	Manumis to	[ ], Maria (C)	1812	AD29	289	238
Kerr, Alexander & Anne	Deed to	Kleiber, George	1813	AE30	302	228
Kerr, Alexander, of Alexa.	Deed fr	Commissioners of Washington	1799	E5	055	044
Kerr, Alexander, of Alexa.	Deed to	Oswald, John H., of Phila.	1800	E5	234	227
Kerr, Alexander, of Alexa.	Deed to	Hellen, Walter	1800	F6	039	024
Kerr, Alexander, of Alexa.	Deed to	Heyle, William	1801	G7	039	050
Kerr, Anne	Partition	Whetcroft, William, heirs of	1813	AE30	196	157
Kerr, Robert & James McConnell	L. of Atty. fr	Kerr, Alexander	1811	AB27	122	100
Kershmer, Martin et al	Deed to	Beall, Thomas & John M. Gantt	1792	A1-1	110	160
Kershner, Martin	Deed fr	Stoddert, Benj. & Wm. Deakins	1794	B2A	162	214
Ketland, Thomas	Cert fr	Commissioners of Washington	1798	B2B	480	173
Ketland, Thomas	Deed fr	Blodget, Samuel	1802	I9	184	283
Ketland, [Thomas], of Phila. PA	Cert fr	Commissioners of Washington	1792	B2A	296	415
Ketland, [Thomas], of Phila. PA	Cert fr	Commissioners of Washington	1792	B2A	293	411
Key, Francis S.	Manumis to	[ ], Joe (C), age 6m	1811	AC28	083	062
Key, Francis S.	Manumis to	[ ], James (C), age 2	1811	AC28	083	062
Key, Francis S. et al	Manumis to	[ ], Kitty (C), age 6, d/o Henny	1811	AC28	083	062
Key, Francis S.	Deed to	Law, John	1815	AK35	001	001
Key, Francis S.	Deed to	Campbell, William, of Fredk. Co.	1815	AH33	473	404
Key, Francis S.	Deed to	Coombe, Griffith	1816	AK35	505	398
Key, Francis S.	Deed to	Bowie, Washington	1816	AL36	482	455
Key, Francis S.	Deed to	Bowie, Washington	1816	AL36	281	280
Key, Francis S.	Deed to	Caldwell, Elias B.	1816	AK35	521	411
Key, Francis S. & William Brent	Deed fr	Williams, Elie, of G'tn.	1817	AN38	204	149
Key, Francis Scott, of G'tn.	Deed fr	Davidson, Ann Maria, of G'tn.	1810	X23	375	301
Key, Francis Scott, of G'tn.	Deed to	Smith, Clement	1811	Z25	479	380
Key, Francis Scott, of G'tn.	Deed fr	Turner, Mary, of Charles Co.	1811	Z25	487	387
Key, Philip B.	Deed fr	Stoddert, Benjamin, of G'tn.	1800	F6	083	051
Key, Philip B.	Deed fr	Forrest, Uriah	1802	H8	291	275
Key, Philip B.	Deed fr	Plater, John R.	1802	I9	452	747
Key, Philip B.	Deed fr	Stoddert, Benjamin	1802	I9	265	429
Key, Philip B.	Deed fr	Hanson, Akexander Contee	1802	H8	029	028
Key, Philip B. & W.S. Chandler	Deed fr	West, Stephen et al	1804	K10	112	120
Key, Philip B.	Deed fr	Van Ness, John P. & Marcia	1805	N13	141	134
Key, Philip B., of Montg. Co.	Deed fr	Chandler, Walter Story	1810	Y24	385	348
Key, Philip B., of Montg. Co.	Deed to	Parke, Thomas, of Phila.	1812	AB27	550	449
Key, Philip B., of Montg. Co. et al	Deed to	Peerce, Isaac	1812	AD29	507	427
Key, Philip B., of Montg. Co.	Deed fr	Ringgold, Tench	1813	AE30	206	167
Key, Philip B., of Montg. Co.	Deed fr	French, George, of G'tn., heirs of	1813	AE30	507	375
Key, Philip B. & Jos. W. Clagett	Deed to	Calder, William	1814	AH33	204	185
Key, Philip B., of Montg. Co. et al	Deed to	Stone, Edward, of G'tn.	1815	AK35	288	232
Key, Philip B.	Deed fr	Magruder, Middleton B. et al	1815	AI34	264	299
Key, Philip Barton, of Annapolis	Deed fr	Tyler, Robert Bradley & Dryden	1792	A1-1	155	222
Key, Philip Barton, of Annapolis	Deed fr	Beall, Zachariah & Samuel	1797	B2B	627	386
Key, Philip Barton, of Annapolis	Deed fr	O'Neale, William, of P.G. Co.	1797	C3	057	47
Key, Philip Barton, of Annapolis	Deed fr	Addison, Anthony	1800	E5	111	098
Key, Philip Barton, of Annapolis	Deed fr	Commissioners of Washington	1800	E5	322	312

Party	What	Party	Year	Liber	Old	New
Key, Philip Barton, of Annapolis	Deed to	Wilson, Samuel	1800	E5	320	309
Key, Philip Barton, of Annapolis	Deed to	O'Neale, William	1800	E5	321	310
Key, Philip Barton, of Annapolis	Deed	O'Neale, William	1800	E5	321	311
Key, Philip Barton	B. of S. fr	Forrest, Uriah	1802	H8	256	243
Key, Philip Barton	Deed to	Kilty, William	1802	I9	470	774
Key, Philip Barton	Deed to	Nourse, Joseph	1804	K10	311	317
Key, Philip Barton	Deed to	Pearce, Isaac	1804	K10	313	320
Key, Philip Barton	Deed fr	Templeman, John, of G'tn.	1804	K10	310	316
Key, Philip Barton	Deed to	Chandler, Walter Story	1804	L11	096	99
Key, Philip Barton et al	Deed fr	Diggs, William, of Montg. Co.	1805	N13	143	135
Key, Philip Barton	Deed fr	State of Maryland	1807	R17	373	284
Key, Philip Barton, of G'tn. et al	Deed to	Oden, Benjamin, of P.G. Co.	1807	R17	408	308
Key, Philip Barton, of Montg. Co.	Deed fr	Ross, Richard, of P.G. Co.	1809	W22	250	168
Key, Philip Barton	Assign fr	Soderstrom, Richard	1809	W22	094	068
Key, Philip Barton	Cert fr	Munroe, Thomas, Supr.	1809	W22	094	068
Key, Philip Barton, of Montg. Co.	Deed to	Chandler, Walter Story	1810	Y24	227	209
Key, Philip Barton, of Montg. Co.	Mortgage fr	Ringold, Tench	1810	X23	397	320
Key, Philip Barton & Wm. Brent	Deed to	Glover, Charles	1814	AG32	215	150
Key, Philip Barton & Wm. Brent	Deed to	Young, Moses	1814	AG32	217	152
Key, Philip Barton et al	Deed to	Bradley, Abraham, Jr., Montg. Co.	1815	AH33	401	346
Key, Philip Barton	D. of T. fr	Fitzhugh, Samuel	1815	AI34	480	489
Key, Philip Barton, of Montg. Co.	Deed to	Claggett, Joseph W., of P.G. Co.	1815	AH33	272	237
Keyne, Mathias	Deed fr	Dorsey, William H., of G'tn.	1805	O14	035	021
Keyne, Matthias	Deed fr	May, Frederick	1812	AD29	373	314
Kid, Robert & Sarah, of Phila.	Deed to	Harbough, Joseph	1817	AN38	555	404
Kid, Robert, mer., of Phila.	Deed to	Sweeny, George	1817	AO39	249	180
Kid, Robert, of Phila. PA	Cert fr	Commissioners of Washington	1793	B2A	312	439
Kid, Robert, of Phila. PA	Agreement	Dorsey, William H.	1800	E5	243	236
Kid, Robert, of Phila. PA	Deed fr	Dorsey, William H., of G'tn.	1805	N13	398	317
Kid, Robert, of Phila. PA	Deed to	Elliott, Samuel, Jr.	1806	O14	360	240
Kidd, Robert, of PA	Deed fr	Elliott, Samuel, Jr.	1802	I9	059	081
Kile, Alexander	Assign fr	Fleet, Henry	1812	AD29	180	145
Kile, Alexander	Deed fr	Richardson, Thomas R.H.	1812	AD29	182	147
Kile, Alexander, of G'tn.	Lease fr	Beall, Samuel, of G'tn.	1811	AB27	132	109
Kile, Alexander, of G'tn.	Deed fr	Fleet, Henry, of G'tn.	1812	AB27	541	441
Kile, Alexander, of G'tn.	Deed to	Wilson, Lancelot	1813	AF31	258	180
Kile, Alexander, of G'tn.	Deed fr	Fleet, Henry, of G'tn.	1815	AH33	526	451
Kile, Alexander, of G'tn.	Deed to	Foxall, Henry, of G'tn.	1815	AH33	528	452
Kile, Alexander, of G'tn.	Deed to	Lanham, Elisha, of G'tn.	1815	AK35	383	302
Kiler, Daniel	Deed fr	Roe, Cornelius McDermott	1807	S18	223	178
Kiler, Daniel	Lease fr	Hughes, Thomas	1809	V21	241	172
Kilty, John & Josias W. King	Deed to	O'Neale, William	1809	V21	344	248
Kilty, John & Josias Wilson King	Deed to	McCormick, Alexander	1809	V21	341	246
Kilty, John & Josias Wilson King	Deed to	Hagner, Peter	1809	V21	353	256
Kilty, John & Josias Wilson King	Deed to	Kerr, Alexander	1809	V21	412	314
Kilty, John & Josias W. King	Deed to	Duvall, Gabriel	1809	V21	409	311
Kilty, John & Josias Wilson King	Deed to	Randall, John, Jr.	1809	V21	355	258
Kilty, John & Jonas Wilson King	Deed to	Farrell, Zephaniah	1809	V21	339	243
Kilty, John & Josias W. King	Deed to	McCormick, James, Jr.	1809	W22	189	
Kilty, John & Josias Wilson King	Mortgage to	Davidson, James, Jr.	1809	W22	215	148
Kilty, John & Josias Wilson King	Deed to	Shaw, John & James Birth	1809	W22	052	039
Kilty, John & Josias Wilson King	Deed to	Munroe, Thomas, Supt.	1809	W22	253	170
Kilty, John & Josias Wilson King	Mortgage to	Lenox, Peter	1809	W22	244	164
Kilty, John & Josias Wilson King	Deed to	Wright, Thomas C.	1809	W22	055	041
Kilty, John & Josias Wilson King	Deed to	Stevenson, James	1809	W22	029	022

Party	What	Party	Year	Liber	Old	New
Kilty, John & Josias Wilson King	Mortgage to	Coombe, Griffith	1809	W22	208	143
Kilty, John & Josias Wilson King	Deed to	Young, Thomas	1809	X23	014	009
Kilty, John & Josias Wilson King	Deed to	Warner, Osborn, of VA	1809	X23	020	013
Kilty, John & Josias Wilson King	Deed to	Simmons, William	1809	X23	008	006
Kilty, John & Josias Wilson King	Deed to	Ober, Robert, of G'tn.	1809	X23	011	008
Kilty, John & Josias Wilson King	Deed to	Davidson, John	1809	X23	017	011
Kilty, John & Josias Wilson King	Deed to	Davidson, James	1810	Y24	296	271
Kilty, William	Deed fr	Key, Philip Barton	1802	I9	470	774
Kilty, William	Deed to	[ ], Sophia	1802	I9	525	869
Kilty, William	B. of S. fr	Wall, John	1804	M12	022	023
Kilty, William	Slave	From MD	1805	M12	390	402
Kilty, William	Mortgage fr	Nicholls, Edward	1806	O14	330	219
King, Acquilla et al	P. of Atty. to	King, James C.	1802	I9	237	379
King, Acquilla et al	Deed to	King, James Carrol	1805	M12	307	309
King, Adam	D. of T. fr	Conrad, Frederick	1801	G7	155	205
King, Adam	Deed	[ ], Sally (Negro)	1802	H8	206	196
King, Adam	Manumis to	[ ], Sally (Negro)	1802	H8	208	198
King, Adam	Manumis to	[ ], Robin (Negro)	1802	H8	208	198
King, Adam	Deed	[ ], Robin (Negro)	1802	H8	206	196
King, Adam	Deed fr	Wayman, Charles	1802	I9	170	258
King, Adam	Qualify		1802	I9	466	767
King, Adam	Deed to	Smith, Walter	1802	I9	171	261
King, Adam	Deed fr	Wayman, Charles, of G'tn. et al	1804	L11	073	75
King, Adam	Deed fr	Magruder, George, collector, G'tn.	1804	L11	235	217
King, Adam	Deed to	Wheaton, Joseph	1805	M12	235	237
King, Adam	Deed fr	Beatty, Charles, heirs of	1806	P15	096	059
King, Adam	Deed fr	Sharp, Mary, of York Co. PA	1807	S18	300	235
King, Adam	Qualify	Major in 1st regiment 1st brigade	1813	AE30	403	297
King, Adam	Deed to	Queen, Richard T.	1816	AM37	212	157
King, Adam & Grace	Deed to	Deakins, William, Jr. et al	1797	C3	262	214
King, Adam & George	Bond fr	Carcand, David, of Calvert Co.	1804	K10	118	127
King, Adam & Grace, of G'tn.	Deed to	Wingard, Adam, of G'tn.	1809	X23	212	162
King, Adam & Grace, of G'tn.	Deed to	Athey, George, of G'tn.	1810	Y24	299	273
King, Adam et al	Bond to	United States	1801	G7	012	015
King, Adam et al	Deed fr	Kearney, John & Edward Fallon	1804	K10	114	123
King, Adam et al	Suit ads	Potomac Company	1812	AG32	258	183
King, Adam, mer., of G'tn.	Deed fr	Beatty, Thomas Johnson, of G'tn.	1795	B2A	267	374
King, Adam, of Montg. Co.	Deed fr	Smith, Leonard, Richmond Co. GA	1796	B2B	570	308
King, Adam, of Montg. Co.	Deed fr	Davis, Charles, Montgomery Co.	1796	B2B	385	043
King, Adam, of G'tn.	Deed to	Forrest, Joseph, of G'tn.	1796	B2B	606	359
King, Adam, of G'tn.	Deed fr	Needham, William, of Montg. Co.	1797	B2B	698	481
King, Adam, of G'tn.	Deed fr	Doyle, Elizabeth, wid/o Alexander	1797	C3	084	69
King, Adam, of G'tn.	Deed fr	Smith, Benjamin, of KY	1798	D4	128	110
King, Adam, of G'tn.	Deed to	O'Reilly, Henry, of G'tn.	1799	D4	281	264
King, Adam, of G'tn.	Deed to	Corporation of Georgetown	1802	I9	129	192
King, Adam, of G'tn.	Deed fr	Lovell, William	1802	H8	517	476
King, Adam, of G'tn.	Deed fr	Kaldenbaugh, Andrew, of G'tn.	1805	N13	315	254
King, Adam, of G'tn.	D. of T. fr	Kaldenbach, Andrew, of G'tn.	1806	P15	107	067
King, Adam, of G'tn.	Assign fr	Kaldenbach, Andrew, of G'tn.	1806	P15	054	033
King, Adam, of G'tn.	Deed to	Bussard, Daniel, Gent., of G'tn.	1809	X23	148	107
King, Adam, of G'tn.	Release fr	Renner, Daniel & Daniel Bussard	1809	X23	283	224
King, Adam, of G'tn.	Deed to	Brookes, Joseph, of G'tn.	1810	Y24	530	465
King, Adam, of G'tn.	D. of T. fr	Livers, Ignatius, of G'tn.	1810	Y24	519	456
King, Adam, of G'tn.	Deed to	Mudd, Thomas J., of G'tn.	1811	Z25	511	406
King, Adam, of G'tn.	Deed to	Livers, Ignatius, of G'tn.	1812	AC28	398	289

Party	What	Party	Year	Liber	Old	New
King, Adam, of G'tn.	Deed to	King, George, of G'tn.	1812	AD29	256	212
King, Adam, of G'tn.	Deed to	Mudd, Thomas J., of G'tn.	1813	AE30	461	343
King, Adam, of G'tn.	Deed to	Kurtz, Daniel, of G'tn.	1815	AI34	489	496
King, Adam, of G'tn.	Deed to	King, Charles	1816	AL36	391	377
King, Adam, trustee	Deed fr	King, William, insolvent	1805	N13	121	116
King, Basil	P. of Atty. to	King, James C.	1802	I9	235	376
King, Basil, of Pr. Wm. Co. VA	Deed to	King, James Carrol	1805	M12	310	313
King, Benjamin	B. of S. fr	Clarke, William & Robert	1805	M12	239	240
King, Benjamin	Deed to	Davis, John, of Abel	1806	Q16	029	019
King, Benjamin	Deed fr	Tingey, Thomas	1806	P15	040	024
King, Benjamin	Deed fr	Tingey, Thomas	1806	Q16	027	018
King, Benjamin	Qualify	Captain in militia	1812	AD29	157	124
King, Benjamin	B. of S. to	Cassin, Joseph & J. Davis, of Abel	1813	AE30	276	212
King, Benjamin	Deed to	Winn, Timothy	1815	AI34	131	150
King, Benjamin, blacksmith	Apprentice fr	Ardrey, Wm., s/o John, age 16	1805	N13	307	249
King, Benjamin, blacksmith, etc.	Indenture fr	Gatton, Elisha, s/o Azariah	1811	AB27	271	222
King, Benjamin, of Balto.	Mortgage to	Coombe, Griffith	1816	AM37	444	319
King, Benjamin, trustee	Deed fr	Dove, Marmaduke	1811	AC28	031	023
King, C., W. & E.	P. of Atty. to	King, James C.	1802	I9	237	379
King, Charles	Deed fr	Ritchie, Abner	1812	AD29	365	307
King, Charles	Deed fr	Presbyterian Congregation, G'tn.	1812	AC28	457	325
King, Charles	D. of T. fr	Barron, Walter, of St. Mary's Co.	1813	AF31	373	268
King, Charles	Deed fr	Peter, George	1813	AE30	432	319
King, Charles	Deed to	Cox, John	1813	AF31	387	279
King, Charles	Deed to	Redman, James	1815	AI34	089	101
King, Charles	Deed fr	Dorsey, William H., of Montg. Co.	1815	AI34	327	359
King, Charles	B. of S. fr	Colclazer, Thomas, of G'tn.	1816	AL36	434	413
King, Charles	Deed fr	King, Adam, of G'tn.	1816	AL36	391	377
King, Charles	Deed to	Taylor, Robert	1817	AN38	001	001
King, Charles & Mary	Deed to	Beatty, Charles, of G'tn.	1797	C3	134	109
King, Charles & Mary	Deed to	O'Reilly, Henry	1798	C3	346	278
King, Charles & Mary	Deed to	Beatty, Thomas	1798	C3	416	328
King, Charles & James Thomson	Release to	Kirk, Militius Thomas, of G'tn.	1810	Z25	156	123
King, Charles & Hezekiah Langley	Deed fr	Van Ness, John P.	1816	AM37	326	237
King, Charles & Hezekiah Langley	Deed fr	Clarke, Albin	1816	AM37	090	072
King, Charles, of G'tn.	Deed fr	Dorsey, William H., of G'tn.	1807	R17	280	213
King, Charles, of G'tn. et al	D. of T. fr	Kirk, Miletius Thomas, of G'tn.	1809	W22	312	203
King, Charles, of G'tn.	D. of T. fr	Butler, Robert, of G'tn.	1810	Y24	517	454
King, Charles, of G'tn.	Deed fr	Ober, Robert, of G'tn.	1811	AB27	508	415
King, Charles, of G'tn.	Deed to	Riggs, Romulus, of G'tn.	1812	AC28	405	294
King, Charles, of G'tn.	Deed fr	Smith, Clement, of G'tn.	1812	AD29	106	081
King, Charles, of G'tn.	Deed fr	Bowie, Washington, of G'tn.	1812	AD29	367	309
King, Charles, of G'tn.	Deed to	Pickerill, John, of G'tn.	1812	AD29	210	171
King, Charles, of G'tn.	Deed fr	Moore, Alexander, of G'tn.	1812	AD29	366	308
King, Charles, of G'tn.	Deed fr	Mudd, Thomas I., of G'tn.	1814	AH33	062	055
King, Charles, of G'tn.	Deed fr	Lanham, Elisha, of G'tn.	1814	AH33	231	202
King, Charles, of G'tn.	Deed to	Lanham, Elisha, of G'tn.	1814	AH33	063	056
King, Charles, of G'tn.	Deed to	Rhoads, George, of Montg. Co.	1815	AH33	430	370
King, Charles, of G'tn.	Assign fr	Brookes, Joseph, of G'tn.	1816	AM37	192	143
King, Charles, of G'tn.	Deed to	Hartman, Frederick	1817	AN38	191	138
King, Cornelius et al	Deed to	King, James Carrol	1805	M12	307	309
King, Edward, of G'tn.	B. of S. fr	King, Henry, of G'tn.	1815	AI34	541	546
King, Elias et al	Deed to	King, James Carrol	1805	M12	307	309
King, Elisha, of P.G. Co.	Deed to	Jones, William, of Thomas et al	1809	W22	109	079
King, Eliza	Slaves	From Alexandria	1804	K10	401	

Party	What	Party	Year	Liber	Old	New
King, Enoch	B. of S. fr	Hall, Elisha	1807	S18	164	134
King, Enoch	Deed fr	Deakins, Leonard M. & John Hoye	1808	U20	293	156
King, Ezekial	Deed to	Gardiner, Peter	1802	I9	537	876
King, Ezekial	Discharge	Bankruptcy	1802	H8	091	083
King, Ezekiel	Deed to	Bridges, John, of G'tn.	1805	N13	193	170
King, Ezekiel	Deed fr	Brown, Robert	1813	AF31	548	406
King, Ezekiel	Deed to	Wannell, Thomas	1814	AG32	319	233
King, Ezekiel, insolvent	D. of T. to	Peacock, Robert	1803	K10	057	62
King, George	Deed fr	Robertson, William	1798	D4	076	064
King, George	Deed fr	Smith, Clement	1802	I9	560	908
King, George	Deed fr	Lingan, James Maccubbin	1802	I9	080	114
King, George	B. of S. to	Doyle, Elizabeth	1802	I9	128	192
King, George	Deed fr	Brookes, Joseph	1802	I9	268	435
King, George	Deed to	Brookes, Joseph	1802	I9	269	438
King, George	Deed fr	Wayman, Charles, of G'tn. et al	1804	L11	075	77
King, George	Agreement	Dodge, Allen & Francis	1805	N13	182	163
King, George	Deed fr	Beatty, Charles, heirs of	1806	P15	289	191
King, George	Deed to	Campbell, William, Frederick Co.	1806	Q16	156	103
King, George	Deed fr	Beatty, John M. & Charles A.	1806	P15	288	190
King, George	Convey fr	Long, John	1808	T19	144	103
King, George	Manumis to	[ ], Dorah (negroe)	1808	T19	129	091
King, George	Deed to	Brookes, Joseph	1808	U20	374	205
King, George	Deed fr	Brookes, Joseph	1808	U20	010	006
King, George	Bond to	Corporation of Georgetown	1808	T19	262	193
King, George	Deed to	Meddert, Jacob	1809	V21	377	280
King, George	Bond to	Corporation of Georgetown	1809	V21	399	302
King, George	Deed to	Meddert, Jacob	1809	W22	043	033
King, George	Deed to	Clarke, Robert & Ignatius Pearce	1810	Y24	109	099
King, George	Deed to	Baker, Zachariah	1812	AC28	490½	349
King, George & Margaret, G'tn.	Lease to	Waters, William, G'tn.	1795	B2A	340	479
King, George & Margaret	Deed to	Dunlop, James	1798	C3	356	286
King, George & Adam	Deed fr	French, Arianna, dev/o George	1804	K10	290	291
King, George & Charles, of G'tn.	Deed fr	Lewis, Samuel, Jr.	1805	O14	147	095
King, George & Adam	Deed fr	Chandler, Walter Story, of G'tn.	1805	N13	375	301
King, George & Charles, of G'tn.	Deed to	Lewis, Samuel, Jr.	1808	T19	149	105
King, George & Adam	Mortgage fr	Templeman, John, of G'tn.	1809	X23	281	223
King, George & Adam et al	Deed fr	Dodge, Allen & Francis	1810	Z25	049	036
King, George et al	Bond to	United States	1801	G7	011	014
King, George et al	Deed fr	Kearney, John & Edward Fallon	1804	K10	114	123
King, George et al	Deed to	Corporation of Georgetown	1805	N13	091	083
King, George et al	Deed fr	Beatty, John M. & Charles A.	1808	U20	300	160
King, George, mer., of G'tn.	Deed to	Weatherall, John, mechanic, G'tn.	1799	D4	203	186
King, George, mer.	Deed fr	Reintzel, Anthony, Gent. et al	1807	S18	131	107
King, George, mer.	Deed to	Whann, William, Gent.	1810	Y24	322	292
King, George, mer., of G'tn.	Deed to	Smith, Walter, mer., of G'tn.	1812	AC28	224	166
King, George, of G'tn.	Deed fr	Davidson, John, of Annapolis	1794	B2A	160	211
King, George, of G'tn.	Deed fr	Davidson, John, of Annapolis	1794	B2A	159	210
King, George, of G'tn.	Deed fr	King, William	1796	B2B	570	310
King, George, of Montg. Co.	Deed fr	Beatty, Charles, of Montg. Co.	1797	C3	138	112
King, George, of G'tn.	Deed fr	Doyle, Elizabeth, wid/o Alexander	1797	C3	129	105
King, George, of G'tn.	Agreement	Whann, William, of G'tn.	1797	C3	141	115
King, George, of Montg. Co.	Deed fr	Beatty, Charles, of Montg. Co.	1797	C3	139	114
King, George, of G'tn.	Deed to	Baily, Jesse, of G'tn.	1798	C3	341	274
King, George, of G'tn.	Deed fr	Beatty, Thomas Johnson, of G'tn.	1798	D4	073	061
King, George, of G'tn.	Deed to	Gary, Everard, of G'tn.	1801	G7	401	534

Index to District of Columbia Land Records, 1792-1817

Party	What	Party	Year	Liber	Old	New
King, George, of G'tn.	B. of S. to	Doyle, Elizabeth	1802	I9		192
King, George, of G'tn.	Deed fr	Goszler, John, of G'tn.	1802	H8	516	475
King, George, of G'tn.	Deed fr	Brooks, Joseph, of G'tn.	1804	L11	220	206
King, George, of G'tn.	Deed to	Brooks, Joseph, of G'tn.	1804	L11	300	275
King, George, of G'tn.	Deed to	Smith, Walter, of G'tn.	1805	M12	191	192
King, George, of G'tn.	Deed to	Dodge, Allen & Francis	1805	N13	173	157
King, George, of G'tn.	Deed fr	Dorsey, William H., of G'tn.	1807	R17	281	215
King, George, of G'tn.	Deed to	Renner, Daniel & Daniel Bussard	1808	U20	132	075
King, George, of G'tn.	Deed fr	King, Adam, of G'tn.	1812	AD29	256	212
King, George, of G'tn.	Lease fr	Carcand, David, of Calvert Co.	1813	AF31	484	353
King, George, of G'tn.	Release fr	Campbell, William, of Fredk. Co.	1815	AK35	021	016
King, George, of G'tn.	Deed to	Addison, Walter Dulaney, of G'tn.	1816	AL36	147	147
King, Henry, of G'tn.	B. of S. to	King, Edward, of G'tn.	1815	AI34	541	546
King, James C., of G'tn.	Deed to	Nourse, Michael, of G'tn.	1800	E5	076	063
King, James C., of G'tn.	Deed fr	Reintzel, Anthony, of G'tn.	1800	E5	075	062
King, James C., of G'tn.	Deed fr	Harbaugh, Leonard	1801	G7	322	451
King, James C., of G'tn.	Deed fr	Bussard, John R.	1801	G7	225	300
King, James C., lumber merchant	Deed to	Bussard, Daniel, of G'tn.	1801	G7	280	387
King, James C.	Deed to	Bussard, Daniel	1802	I9	239	384
King, James C.	P. of Atty. fr	Waters, James & D. et al	1802	I9	236	378
King, James C.	P. of Atty. fr	King, Acquilla et al	1802	I9	237	379
King, James C.	P. of Atty. fr	Turner, John	1802	I9	237	381
King, James C.	P. of Atty. fr	King, Basil	1802	I9	235	376
King, James C., of G'tn.	Lease to	Perkins, Benjamin	1802	G7	502	641
King, James C.	Manumis to	[ ], Peter (Negro)	1804	L11	045	46
King, James C.	Deed fr	Beatty, Charles, heirs of	1806	P15	102	062
King, James C.	Deed to	Beatty, John M. & Charles A.	1807	R17	277	211
King, James C.	Deed fr	Deakins, Leonard M. et al	1807	S18	087	071
King, James C.	Deed fr	Offutt, James, of William	1807	R17	256	194
King, James C. & John Gardener	Deed to	Smith, Samuel Harrison	1807	R17	387	293
King, James C., of G'tn.	Deed to	Foxall, Henry, of G'tn.	1808	T19	222	162
King, James C., of G'tn.	Deed to	Bussard, Daniel, of G'tn.	1808	U20	153	087
King, James C., insolvent	Deed to	Thorpe, Thomas, trustee	1810	Y24	061	054
King, James Carrol	Deed fr	King, Basil, of Pr. Wm. Co. VA	1805	M12	310	313
King, James Carrol	Deed fr	King, Acquilla et al	1805	M12	307	309
King, James Carrol	Deed to	Fenwick, George	1808	U20	138	079
King, James Carrol	Deed fr	Turner, John & Milesent, of NC	1808	U20	142	081
King, James Carroll, of G'tn.	Mortgage fr	Gardiner, John	1801	G7	381	513
King, James Carroll, mer., G'tn.	Deed to	Brookes, William H., of G'tn.	1804	K10	138	150
King, James Carroll	Deed fr	King, Vincent	1807	S18	084	069
King, John	Deed fr	McCormick, James, Jr.	1812	AC28	482	342
King, John, now of G'tn.	Deed fr	Van Ness, John P. & Marcia	1814	AG32	018	015
King, John, Sr.	Deed to	Aurand, David & Christianna	1816	AL36	382	369
King, Joseph	Slaves	From Delaware	1812	AD29	457	385
King, Josias W. & John Kilty	Mortgage to	McCormick, James, Jr.	1809	W22	189	132
King, Josias W. & John Kilty	Deed to	Duvall, Gabriel	1809	V21	409	311
King, Josias W. & Letitia et al	Deed to	Bradley, Abraham, Jr.	1811	AC28	069	052
King, Josias W. & Letitia et al	Deed to	Bacon, Samuel & George Moore	1812	AD29	523	441
King, Josias W.	Partition	Whetcroft, William, heirs of	1813	AE30	196	157
King, Josias W. & Mary	Deed to	Campbell, John	1815	AI34	508	513
King, Josias W.	Manumis to	[ ], Henny (C)	1816	AM37	054	044
King, Josias W. & Catharine	Deed to	Brent, Robert	1817	AN38	550	400
King, Josias Wilson & John Kilty	Deed to	Farrell, Zephaniah	1809	V21	339	243
King, Josias Wilson & John Kilty	Deed to	McCormick, Alexander	1809	V21	341	246
King, Josias Wilson & John Kilty	Deed to	Randall, John, Jr.	1809	V21	355	258

Party	What	Party	Year	Liber	Old	New
King, Josias Wilson & John Kilty	Deed to	Hagner, Peter	1809	V21	353	256
King, Josias Wilson & John Kilty	Deed to	Munroe, Thomas, Supt.	1809	W22	253	170
King, Josias Wilson & John Kilty	Deed to	Shaw, John & James Birth	1809	W22	052	039
King, Josias Wilson & John Kilty	Mortgage to	Coombe, Griffith	1809	W22	208	143
King, Josias Wilson & John Kilty	Mortgage to	Lenox, Peter	1809	W22	244	164
King, Josias Wilson & John Kilty	Deed to	Stevenson, James	1809	W22	029	022
King, Josias Wilson & John Kilty	Deed to	Wright, Thomas C.	1809	W22	055	041
King, Josias Wilson & John Kilty	Mortgage to	Davidson, James, Jr.	1809	W22	215	148
King, Josias Wilson & John Kilty	Deed to	Simmons, William	1809	X23	008	006
King, Josias Wilson & John Kilty	Deed to	Warner, Osborn, of VA	1809	X23	020	013
King, Josias Wilson & John Kilty	Deed to	Ober, Robert, of G'tn.	1809	X23	011	008
King, Josias Wilson & John Kilty	Deed to	Young, Thomas	1809	X23	014	009
King, Josias Wilson & John Kilty	Deed to	Davidson, John	1809	X23	017	011
King, Josias Wilson & John Kilty	Deed to	Davidson, James	1810	Y24	296	271
King, Letitia	Partition	Whetcroft, William, heirs of	1813	AE30	196	157
King, Letitia, w/o Josias W. et al	Deed fr	Van Ness, John P. & Marcia	1809	X23	068	051
King, Mary Gaunt, d/o Nicholas	Deed fr	Davidson, Samuel	1809	X23	264	207
King, Nicholas	Deed fr	Davidson, Samuel	1798	C3	434	341
King, Nicholas	P. of Atty. fr	Peter, Robert, of G'tn.	1798	C3	492	387
King, Nicholas	P. of Atty. fr	Brown, Samuel, of Lexington KY	1801	F6		088
King, Nicholas	Deed to	King, Robert	1804	K10	259	265
King, Nicholas	Deed fr	Lane, John	1804	K10	192	201
King, Nicholas	Cert fr	Munroe, Thomas, Supt.	1804	K10	398	412
King, Nicholas	Deed to	McCormick, Alexander et al	1805	M12	093	086
King, Nicholas	Deed to	Moore, George	1805	M12	293	294
King, Nicholas	D. of T. to	Brent, William	1805	O14	114	072
King, Nicholas	Release fr	Brent, William	1807	Q16	357	274
King, Nicholas	Cert fr	Munroe, Thomas, Supt.	1807	R17	105	082
King, Nicholas	P. of Atty. fr	Davidson, Samuel, of Balto.	1811	AB27	444	364
King, Nicholas & George Andrews	Deed fr	Lindo, Abraham	1810	Y24	366	331
King, Nicholas & G. Andrews	Assign fr	Gillingham, George, of Phila. PA	1810	Z25	109	084
King, Nicholas et al	Deed to	Wright, Thomas C.	1807	Q16	358	275
King, Nicholas, late of Charles Co.	Deed to	Fitzgerald, Thomas	1804	L11	171	167
King, Patrick	Deed fr	Prout, William	1801	G7	271	373
King, Richard	B. of S. to	Carroll, Daniel, of *Duddington*	1806	P15	114	072
King, Robert	Deed fr	King, Nicholas	1804	K10	259	265
King, Robert	Deed fr	Boyd, Washington, collector	1806	P15	200	134
King, Robert	Deed to	Smith, Amos, of KY	1806	Q16	085	054
King, Robert	Deed to	Varden, Ezra	1807	R17	098	077
King, Robert	Deed to	Cooper, William	1813	AF31	300	213
King, Robert	Deed to	Glover, Charles	1813	AF31	284	184
King, Robert	Deed fr	Laird, John, exr. of J. Carleton	1813	AF31	524	385
King, Robert	Convey to	Peltz, John	1813	AG32	001	001
King, Robert	Deed to	Gordon, Elisha, late of Phila. PA	1813	AF31	127	085
King, Robert	Deed to	Randolph, William B.	1814	AG32	098	074
King, Robert	Deed fr	Cocking, William	1815	AH33	507	435
King, Robert	Deed to	Pickford, John B.	1815	AK35	210	165
King, Robert	Deed to	Skyren, John, of Phila.	1816	AL36	013	014
King, Robert	Convey to	Reily, John H.	1817	AO39	398	270
King, Robert	Deed fr	Gaither, Benjamin & Daniel, MD	1817	AO39	176	130
King, Robert Fielder, s/o Nicholas	Deed fr	Davidson, Samuel	1809	X23	265	208
King, Robert, Sr. & Robert, Jr.	Deed fr	Commissioners of Washington	1801	G7	044	056
King, Robert, Sr. & Robert, Jr.	Deed to	Lenthall, John	1802	I9	160	242
King, Samuel Davidson, s/o N.	Deed fr	Davidson, Samuel	1807	R17	110	086
King, Samuel Davidson, s/o N.	Deed fr	Davidson, Samuel	1809	X23	267	209

Party	What	Party	Year	Liber	Old	New
King, Samuel, of NY et al	Deed fr	Templeman, John	1802	I9	126	186
King, Samuel, of Newport RI	Deed to	Blake, James H., Dr.	1816	AM37	314	229
King, Susan, d/o Nicholas	Deed fr	Davidson, Samuel	1809	X23	262	206
King, Timothy	Deed fr	Owen, Benjamin	1815	AH33	505	433
King, Timothy	Deed to	Owen, Benjamin	1815	AH33	538	460
King, Vincent	Deed to	King, James Carroll	1807	S18	084	069
King, Vincent	Deed fr	Pickrell, John	1813	AE30	088	067
King, Vincent	Deed fr	Smith, Jesse	1813	AE30	454	338
King, Vincent	Deed to	Lanham, Elisha	1813	AF31	257	179
King, Vincent	Deed fr	Waters, Draden	1813	AF31	057	039
King, Vincent	Deed fr	Lucas, Henry	1813	AF31	534	394
King, Vincent	Qualify	Second Lieutenant	1813	AE30	425	314
King, Vincent	Deed to	Magruder, James A.	1815	AI34	433	451
King, Vincent	Deed to	Fitzhugh, Samuel	1815	AH33	400	345
King, Vincent	Deed to	Thompson, James	1815	AK35	064	049
King, Vincent	Deed to	Peckham, Caleb	1816	AM37	088	071
King, Vincent	Deed to	Suter, Alexander	1816	AM37	033	027
King, Vincent	Deed to	Pickrell, John	1816	AL36	116	117
King, Vincent	B. of S. fr	Mudd, Walter, of G'tn.	1817	AO39	093	073
King, Vincent et al	P. of Atty. to	King, James C.	1802	I9	236	378
King, Vincent et al	Lease fr	Reintzel, Anthony	1811	Z25	490	389
King, Vincent et al	Deed to	Joncherez, Alexander L.	1812	AD29	383	323
King, Vincent, of G'tn.	Deed fr	Dorsey, William H., of Balto. Co.	1812	AC28	268	196
King, Vincent, of G'tn.	Assign fr	Lanham, Elisha, of G'tn.	1813	AE30	457	340
King, Vincent, of G'tn.	Deed fr	Pairo, Thomas W. & Loveday	1813	AE30	455	339
King, Vincent, of G'tn.	Deed fr	Holmead, Anthony	1814	AH33	234	204
King, Vincent, of G'tn.	Deed to	Pyfer, Henry, of G'tn.	1814	AH33	218	194
King, Vincent, of G'tn.	Deed fr	Priestley, James, of Nashville TN	1815	AI34	431	449
King, Walter et al	Deed to	King, James Carrol	1805	M12	307	309
King, William	Deed to	Beall, Thomas & John M. Gantt	1793	A1-2	433	42
King, William	Deed fr	Stoddert, Benj. & Wm. Deakins	1793	A1-2	419	28
King, William	Release fr	McClan, Robert, Montgomery Co.	1795	B2A	346	488
King, William	Deed to	King, George, of G'tn.	1796	B2B	570	310
King, William	Deed to	Nicholson, John, of Phila.	1796	B2B	537	256
King, William	Agreement	Taylor, Thomas	1797	C3	071	59
King, William	Deed fr	Fitzhugh, Samuel	1815	AK35	427	335
King, William & Elizabeth	Mortgage to	Vowell, Thomas, Jr., of Alexa.	1798	C3	295	239
King, William, cabinet maker, G'tn.	Deed fr	Bruff, Thomas	1805	M12	296	297
King, William, insolvent	Deed to	King, Adam, trustee	1805	N13	121	116
King, William, Jr. et al	Lease fr	Deakins, William et al	1796	B2B	508	211
King, William, Jr., of G'tn.	Deed to	Dorsey, William H., of G'tn.	1807	R17	060	048
King, William, Jr., of G'tn.	Deed fr	Dorsey, William H., of Balto.	1808	T19	386	275
King, William, Jr., of G'tn.	Deed fr	Dorsey, William Hammond, Balto.	1811	AB27	137	114
King, William, Jr.	Deed fr	Heath, Nathaniel H.	1812	AC28	202	153
King, William, Jr.	Deed fr	Robertson, Thomas, of G'tn.	1812	AD29	435	365
King, William, Jr., of G'tn.	Deed fr	Mountz, Jacob, collector, G'tn.	1812	AC28	214	161
King, William, Jr., of G'tn.	Deed fr	Watson, John, of Balto.	1815	AH33	553	473
King, William, of G'tn.	Deed fr	Casanave, Peter, of G'tn.	1794	B2A	062	079
King, William, of G'tn.	Deed to	McClann, Robert, of G'tn.	1794	A1-2	499	102
King, William, of G'tn.	Deed fr	Garlick, Joseph, of G'tn.	1794	B2A	024	027
King, William, of G'tn.	Deed to	Craig, Samuel, of Alexa.	1795	B2A	347	490
King, William, of Montgomery Co.	Deed fr	Young, Abraham, planter	1795	B2A	274	383
King, William, of G'tn.	Deed fr	Beall, Thomas, of George, G'tn.	1795	B2A	201	275
King, William, of G'tn.	Deed to	Carleton, Joseph, of G'tn.	1795	B2A	219	303
King, William, of G'tn.	Deed fr	Flaherty, James	1795	B2B	365	015

Party	What	Party	Year	Liber	Old	New
King, William, of G'tn. et al	Deed to	Dalton, Tristram, of G'tn.	1796	B2B	405	072
King, William, of G'tn.	Deed to	Pollock, Isaac, of Phila.	1796	B2B	560	292
King, William, of G'tn. et al	Deed to	Dalton, Tristram, of G'tn.	1796	B2B	407	074
King, William, of P.G. Co.	D. of T. to	French, George, of Montg. Co.	1798	C3	478	377
King, William, of P.G. Co.	Mortgage to	Vowell, Thomas, Jr., of Alexa.	1798	C3	324	262
King, William, of MD	Suit		1802	H8	186	
King, William, of G'tn.	B. of S. to	Williams, Stewart	1812	AD29	089	
King, William, of Fairfield Co. OH	Deed fr	Stoker, Michael & Mary, of OH	1812	AD29	379	319
King, William R., merchant	Mortgage to	Riddle, Robert, of Balto.	1804	K10	297	299
King, William R., insolvent	Deed to	Herty, Thomas, trustee	1806	O14	265	175
King, Zephaniah	Deed fr	Greenfield, Gabriel	1795	B2A	181	244
King, Zephaniah, of G'tn.	Deed fr	Threlkeld, John, of G'tn.	1795	B2A	243	338
King, Zepheniah, heirs of, by atty.	Deed to	Brookes, William H., of G'tn.	1804	K10	138	150
Kingla, Joseph [Kengla]	Deed to	Ballzor, Elizabeth, Frederick Co.	1804	K10	321	328
Kingsbury, Horatio, of G'tn.	Deed fr	Reintzel, Daniel, of G'tn.	1812	AD29	540	456
Kingsbury, Horatio, of Montg. Co.	Deed to	Gantt, Thomas T., of G'tn.	1815	AI34	001	001
Kioner, Michael [Hiener]	Deed to	Shaw, John	1808	T19	271	199
Kirby, Francis	Deed fr	Collard, George	1801	F6	178	113
Kirby, Francis	Assign fr	Thomas, Joseph	1810	X23	367	294
Kirby, Francis [Kerby]	Deed fr	Addison, Thomas G., of P.G. Co.	1815	AH33	432	371
Kirby, John B.	Deed fr	Macgill, Thomas, sheriff	1802	H8	186	179
Kirby, John B.	B. of S. to	Cranch, William	1806	O14	337	224
Kirby, John B.	Deed fr	Wigfield, Sarah	1807	S18	012	011
Kirby, John B.	Deed fr	Addison, Thomas Graton	1808	T19	224	164
Kirby, John B.	Deed fr	Brent, Daniel Carroll, marshal	1808	T19	268	197
Kirby, John B.	Deed to	Bean, John	1816	AL36	086	087
Kirby, John Baptist	Deed fr	Wigfield, Matthew	1804	L11	392	348
Kirby, John Baptist	Deed fr	Hurley, Daniel	1805	N13	324	262
Kirby, John Baptist	Deed fr	Newman, Morris et al	1805	M12	317	320
Kirby, John Baptist	Deed fr	Standage, Eleazer & Mary	1805	M12	090	083
Kirby, John Baptist	Deed fr	Cochran, Alexander, Jr.	1806	P15	179	119
Kirby, John Baptist	Deed to	Wigfield, Elizabeth	1806	P15	152	100
Kirby, John Baptist	Deed fr	Wigfield, Elizabeth	1806	P15	154	101
Kirby, John Baptist	Assign fr	May, Frederick	1806	Q16	176	117
Kirby, John Baptist [Kerby]	Deed fr	Wigfield, Mathew	1807	R17	089	071
Kirby, John Baptist	Assign to	Wigfield, Mathew	1807	R17	087	069
Kirby, John Baptist	Deed fr	Naylor, John Lawson	1807	R17	048	038
Kirby, John Baptist et al	Deed to	Addison, Daniel Dulaney	1808	T19	083	060
Kirby, John Baptist et al	Deed fr	Addison, Daniel Dulany, Annapolis	1808	T19	072	053
Kirby, John Baptist & Francis, plt.	Suit	Bayly, William, def.	1810	Z25	023	018
Kirby, John Baptist & Francis	Deed fr	Bayly, William, of P.G. Co.	1810	Z25	020	016
Kirk, John	Deed to	Cloakey, Samuel	1813	AE30	419	309
Kirk, John, carpenter et al	Deed fr	Van Ness, John P. & Marcia	1808	V21	051	040
Kirk, Milesius Thomas	Deed fr	Commissioners of Washington	1799	D4	362	348
Kirk, Milesius Thomas, of G'tn.	Deed to	Maguyre, Hugh, of Annapolis	1801	F6	195	126
Kirk, Milesius Thomas	Mortgage fr	Stephen, John	1807	R17	046	037
Kirk, Miletius Thomas, of G'tn.	D. of T. to	Thompson, James & Charles King	1809	W22	312	203
Kirk, Miletius Thomas, of G'tn.	D. of T. to	Ott, John, of G'tn.	1816	AM37	264	194
Kirk, Militius Thomas, of G'tn.	Deed fr	Mountz, John, Jr., of G'tn.	1809	X23	199	150
Kirk, Militius Thomas, of G'tn.	Release fr	Thomson, James & Charles King	1810	Z25	156	123
Kirk, Thomas, of G'tn.	Deed fr	Peter, John, of G'tn.	1817	AN38	334	245
Kirkland, George W., bankrupt	Discharge fr	Cranch, William	1802	G7	549	696
Kite, Alexander, of G'tn.	Deed to	Redman, James, of G'tn.	1812	AC28	452	322
Kitty, Rounds	Cert Free fr	Fry, Thomas	1814	AF31	517	379
Kleiber, George	Deed fr	Middleton, Joseph	1800	E5	264	258

Party	What	Party	Year	Liber	Old	New
Kleiber, George	Deed fr	Kerr, Alexander & Anne	1813	AE30	302	228
Kleiber, George	Deed fr	Whetcroft, William, heirs of	1813	AE30	304	229
Kleiber, George	Mortgage fr	Wilson, William	1814	AH33	333	288
Kleiber, George	Deed to	Varnum, James M.	1816	AM37	086	070
Kleiber, George	D. of T. to	Ott, David	1817	AO39	300	214
Kleiber, George & Jas. Moore, Sr.	B. of S. fr	Dove, Joseph	1815	AH33	488	418
Kleiber, George & G.C. Grammar	B. of S. fr	Estep, Alexander	1815	AI34	369	398
Kleiber, George, Jr.	Deed fr	Reinhart, Andrew	1802	I9	082	117
Kliber, James	Deed to	Rawlins, John	1802	I9	478	786
Klinger, Henry	Deed to	Beall, Thomas & John M. Gantt	1793	A1-1	369	476
Klinger, Henry	Cert fr	Commissioners of Washington	1793	B2A	317	445
Klinger, Henry	Cert fr	Commissioners of Washington	1793	B2A	316½	446
Klinger, Henry, joiner	Deed fr	Spiker, Henry, joiner	1793	A1-1	339	443
Klinger, Henry, joiner	Deed fr	Spyker, Benjamin & Marg. Barb.	1793	A1-1	342	446
Klinger, Henry, Washington Co.	Deed to	Deakins, William, Jr., of G'tn.	1795	B2A	212	293
Knapp, John	Deed to	Whetcroft, Henry	1802	I9	029	039
Knapp, John	Deed fr	Kerr, Alexander	1806	Q16	250	172
Knapp, John	Deed to	Munroe, Thomas	1807	R17	095	075
Knapp, John	B. of S. to	Stott, Ebenezer, of Petersburgh	1810	Z25	094	072
Knapp, John & Thomas Munroe	Deed to	Stott, Ebenezer, of Petersburg	1817	AO39	427	291
Kneller, Frederick et al	Mortgage to	Grammar, Frederick, of Annapolis	1812	AD29	350	293
Kneller, George	Deed fr	Van Ness, John P. & Marcia	1812	AC28	235	174
Kneller, George	Deed fr	Van Ness, John P. & Marcia	1812	AC28	233	171
Kneller, George	B. of S. fr	Jenkins, Francis	1813	AE30	279	214
Knepley, Solomon	B. of S. to	Knowles, Henry, of G'tn.	1815	AI34	441	456
Knight, James	Assign to	Frazier, Richard	1802	H8	374	348
Knight, James	B. of S. to	Smith, William H. et al	1804	L11	319	292
Knight, James	Deed to	Densly, Hugh	1804	L11	184	177
Knight, James	B. of S. to	Miller, Peter	1805	M12	087	081
Knight, James, insolvent	Deed to	Steene, Matthew, trustee	1804	L11	341	310
Knight, James, Jr. & Eleanor	B. of S. fr	Densley, Hugh	1804	L11	258	238
Knoblock, John	B. of S. fr	Beaven, Leonard, of Charles Co.	1811	AA26	084	059
Knoblock, John	B. of S. fr	Clarke, Abram	1813	AF31	311	222
Knoblock, John	Deed fr	Watson, James	1813	AF31	321	229
Knoblock, John	Deed fr	Mauro, Philip	1815	AK35	444	349
Knoblock, John	Convey fr	Belt, Benjamin M.	1815	AK35	094	073
Knoblock, John	Deed to	Davis, John P.	1817	AO39	465	319
Knott, Ann	B. of S. fr	Johnson, Walter	1811	AB27	103	084
Knowles, David, of G'tn.	B. of S. to	Smith, Anthony	1816	AO39	039	032
Knowles, Henry	Deed to	Gordan, Elisha, of Phila. PA	1808	T19	111	079
Knowles, Henry	B. of S. fr	Rumney, John	1808	T19	214	156
Knowles, Henry, of G'tn.	Deed fr	Mountz, John, Sr., of G'tn.	1797	C3	086	71
Knowles, Henry, of G'tn.	Deed fr	Balch, Stephen B., of G'tn.	1798	D4	086	073
Knowles, Henry, of G'tn.	Deed fr	Polock, Isaac	1801	G7	469	606
Knowles, Henry, of G'tn.	Deed fr	Mountz, John, Sr., of G'tn.	1806	Q16	296	225
Knowles, Henry, of G'tn.	Deed to	Patterson, Edgar, of G'tn.	1808	T19	250	184
Knowles, Henry, of G'tn.	Deed fr	Athey, Walter F., of G'tn.	1808	U20	012	007
Knowles, Henry, of G'tn.	Deed to	Hedges, Nicholas & A. Hoover	1808	U20	033	019
Knowles, Henry, of G'tn.	Deed to	Knowles, William	1810	Z25	258	202
Knowles, Henry, of G'tn.	Deed to	Hicks, Elizabeth, of G'tn.	1812	AD29	201	163
Knowles, Henry, of G'tn.	D. of T. to	Kurtz, John, of G'tn.	1813	AF31	181	122
Knowles, Henry, of G'tn.	B. of S. fr	Knepley, Solomon	1815	AI34	441	456
Knowles, Henry, of G'tn.	Manumis to	Scott, James	1816	AM37	027	022
Knowles, Henry, of G'tn.	Manumis to	Scott, James (C)	1816	AK35	278	221
Knowles, Henry, of G'tn.	D. of T. fr	Baker, John, of G'tn.	1817	AO39	198	145

Party	What	Party	Year	Liber	Old	New
Knowles, Joseph Evan	Deed fr	Cook, Thomas, of Frederick Co.	1804	M12	030	031
Knowles, William	Mortgage fr	Purcell, Pierce	1799	D4	335	321
Knowles, William	Deed fr	Lingan, James Macubbin, of G'tn.	1800	E5	141	129
Knowles, William	Mortgage to	Purcell, Pierce	1801	G7	386	519
Knowles, William	Deed fr	Lingan, James M.	1802	I9	414	686
Knowles, William	Deed fr	Knowles, Henry, of G'tn.	1810	Z25	258	202
Knowles, Williams	Mortgage fr	Purcell, Pierce	1799	D4	335	221
Knox, John & Thomas	B. of S. fr	Knox, William	1817	AN38	282	206
Knox, William	B. of S. to	Knox, John & Thomas	1817	AN38	282	206
Kogenderfer, Leonard et al	Deed fr	Pierce, Isaac & Elizabeth et al	1799	D4	239	221
Kokenderfer, Leonard, of G'tn.	Deed fr	Calder, James, of G'tn.	1809	X23	268	211
Kokenderfer, Leonard, of G'tn.	Deed to	Calder, James, of G'tn.	1809	W22	251	169
Kolb, Michael, Jr. [Culp]	Deed to	Beall, Thomas & John M. Gantt	1792	A1-1	074	109
Kolb, Michael, Jr. [Culp]	Deed to	Kolb, Michael Jr. [Culp]	1793	A1-1	177	252
Kolb, Michael, Jr. [Culp]	Deed to	Hellen, Walter, of G'tn.	1793	A1-2	416	25
Konig, Heinrich, of G'tn.	Cert fr	Commissioners of Washington	1793	B2A	307	430
Konig, Henry	Transfer to	Cook, Thomas & Jos. E. Rowles	1796	B2B	453	141
Koontz, Frederick	Assign fr	Craycroft, Thomas	1816	AL36	437	416
Koontz, Henry, Sr. et al	Deed to	Beall, Thomas & John M. Gantt	1792	A1-1	102	148
Koontz, Jacob	B. of S. to	Fry, Godfrey	1806	O14	352	235
Kortwright, James B.	Assign to	St. Clair, George	1809	W22	008	007
Kraft, John, d. 4 FEB 1817	Death	On board ship from Amsterdam	1817	AN38	193	140
Kraft, Regine Elizabeth, 12/24/16	Death	On board ship from Amsterdam	1817	AN38	193	140
Kramer, Henry	Deed fr	Munroe, Thomas, Supt.	1802	I9	268	436
Kramer, Henry	Mortgage fr	Blount, George	1804	K10	277	281
Kreager, John, of Frederick Co.	Deed fr	Williams, Elisha W., of G'tn.	1809	W22	134	096
Kreemer, John [Kramer]	B. of S. to	Thompson, Margaret	1813	AF31	330	235
Kremer, John	B. of S. to	Bentley, Joseph	1802	H8	199	191
Krous, Theodorus, of G'tn.	Deed to	Holmead, Anthony, of G'tn.	1801	G7	192	257
Krouz, Theodorus et al	Deed fr	Davidson, John	1801	G7	142	187
Kuhns, William	Deed fr	Balch, Stephen B., Rev.	1815	AI34	034	040
Kurtz, Benjamin et al, of G'tn.	Deed to	Kurtz, Daniel, of G'tn.	1815	AI34	486	494
Kurtz, Catharine	Deed to	Reintzel, Valentine	1815	AI34	247	279
Kurtz, Catharine et al	Deed to	Reintzel, Anthony	1809	W22	364	236
Kurtz, Catherine	Deed fr	Reintzell, Anthony	1810	Y24	129	117
Kurtz, Christian	Deed fr	Beall, Thomas, of George	1795	B2B	359	007
Kurtz, Christian	Deed fr	Beall, Thomas	1802	I9	521	852
Kurtz, Christian, of G'tn.	Deed fr	Reintzel, Daniel, of G'tn.	1807	S18	146	119
Kurtz, Christiana et al, of G'tn.	Deed to	Kurtz, Daniel, of G'tn.	1815	AI34	486	494
Kurtz, Daniel	D. of T. fr	Wirt, John	1813	AE30	459	341
Kurtz, Daniel	Deed fr	Stone, Edward	1815	AK35	290	232
Kurtz, Daniel	Deed fr	Parrott, Richard	1816	AM37	270	198
Kurtz, Daniel	D. of T. fr	Parrott, Richard	1817	AN38	405	303
Kurtz, Daniel & Thomas Robertson	Deed to	Davidson, Lewis Grant	1815	AK35	043	033
Kurtz, Daniel, gdn. of H. Reintzel	Deed to	McDaniel, John, of G'tn.	1814	AG32	453	327
Kurtz, Daniel, of G'tn.	Deed fr	Reintzel, Daniel & Anne, of G'tn.	1811	AB27	309	254
Kurtz, Daniel, of G'tn.	Deed fr	Robertson, Thomas, of G'tn.	1814	AH33	308	266
Kurtz, Daniel, of G'tn.	Deed fr	Reintzell, Daniel, of G'tn.	1814	AG32	095	072
Kurtz, Daniel, of G'tn.	Deed fr	King, Adam, of G'tn.	1815	AI34	489	496
Kurtz, Daniel, of G'tn.	Deed fr	Wirt, John, of G'tn.	1815	AK35	316	252
Kurtz, Daniel, of G'tn.	Deed fr	Kurtz, Mary et al, of G'tn.	1815	AI34	486	494
Kurtz, Daniel, of G'tn.	D. of T. fr	Lancaster, Stephen	1816	AM37	267	196
Kurtz, Daniel, of G'tn.	Deed fr	Thorpe, Thomas, of G'tn.	1816	AM37	155	118
Kurtz, Daniel, of G'tn.	D. of T. fr	McKelden, Andrew, of G'tn.	1816	AM37	151	116
Kurtz, Daniel, of G'tn.	Deed fr	Patterson, Edgar, of G'tn.	1817	AO39	189	139

Party	What	Party	Year	Liber	Old	New
Kurtz, Daniel, of G'tn.	D. of T. fr	Dunn, James C., of G'tn.	1817	AN38	411	308
Kurtz, David & Benjamin, bros.	Deed fr	Kurtz, Thomas, bro. of D. & B.	1815	AI34	478	488
Kurtz, David & Benjamin, of G'tn.	Deed fr	Turner, John & Elizabeth, of MD	1815	AI34	475	486
Kurtz, David et al, of G'tn.	Deed to	Kurtz, Daniel, of G'tn.	1815	AI34	486	494
Kurtz, Frederick, of Frederick Co.	Deed fr	Funk, Jacob, yeoman	1793	A1-1	186	263
Kurtz, George, of Phila. et al	Deed to	Brooke, Samuel	1811	AB27	264	216
Kurtz, John	B. of S. fr	Rutherford, Alexander, of G'tn.	1817	AN38	371	274
Kurtz, John & Washington Bowie	Deed fr	Smith, Andrew, of G'tn.	1812	AD29	542	457
Kurtz, John & Washington Bowie	Deed to	Smith, Andrew	1815	AI34	402	425
Kurtz, John et al	Deed fr	Heugh, John, of G'tn., trustee	1815	AI34	091	104
Kurtz, John, of G'tn.	D. of T. fr	Knowles, Henry, of G'tn.	1813	AF31	181	122
Kurtz, Mary et al, of G'tn.	Deed to	Kurtz, Daniel, of G'tn.	1815	AI34	486	494
Kurtz, Sarah et al, of G'tn.	Deed to	Kurtz, Daniel, of G'tn.	1815	AI34	486	494
Kurtz, Thomas, bro. of D. & B.	Deed to	Kurtz, David & Benjamin, bros.	1815	AI34	478	488
Kyne, Matthias	Deed fr	May, Frederick	1809	X23	171	127
Kyne, Matthias	Agreement	May, Frederick	1809	X23	172	128

Party	What	Party	Year	Liber	Old	New
L						
L'Enfant, Pierre Charles	Assign to	Soderstrom, Richard	1809	W22	094	068
Labille, Louis	Deed fr	Lucas, Henry	1808	U20	370	203
Labille, Louis, of G'tn.	D. of T. to	Mountz, John, Jr., of G'tn.	1812	AD29	101	076
Lacey, Benjamin, of G'tn.	Deed to	Cole, Bennet	1806	P15	328	216
Lacey, John, of G'tn.	Lease fr	Gary, Ann, of G'tn.	1816	AL36	429	409
Lacke, George et al	Lease fr	Carleton, Joseph	1804	L11	267	246
Ladd, John G., of Alexa.	Deed fr	Frost, Amariah	1800	E5	312	304
Ladd, John G., of Alexa.	Deed fr	Glover, Charles, trustee	1812	AC28	113	085
Ladd, John Gardiner, of Alexa.	Deed fr	Frost, Amariah & Esther	1800	E5	309	300
Laight, William & Charles et al	Deed fr	Walker, George	1802	G7	446	582
Laird, John	Deed fr	Beall, Thomas, of George	1793	A1-1	311	411
Laird, John	Deed fr	Dick, Thomas	1798	D4	016	014
Laird, John	Deed fr	Jones, Benjamin White, sheriff	1801	G7	263	361
Laird, John	Deed fr	Walker, George	1801	G7	309	431
Laird, John	Deed fr	Mason, John	1802	I9	509	834
Laird, John	Deed fr	Scott, Sabret	1802	I9	510	836
Laird, John	Deed fr	Murdock, John	1802	I9	562	911
Laird, John	Deed fr	Oakley, John, guard. of M. Burnes	1802	G7	510	650
Laird, John	B. of S. fr	Eliason, John	1814	AH33	129	123
Laird, John	Deed fr	Smith, Walter, of G'tn., trustee	1816	AM37	477	345
Laird, John & John Mason	Deed fr	Stoddert, Benjamin	1806	Q16	007	004
Laird, John & John Mason, G'tn.	Deed fr	Stoddert, Benjamin, of G'tn.	1812	AD29	306	251
Laird, John & James Dunlap	Deed fr	Hanson, Samuel, of Samuel	1816	AL36	324	318
Laird, John et al	Deed fr	Maddox, Notley, sheriff	1800	E5	090	077
Laird, John, exr. of Jos. Carleton	Convey to	Brashears, John W.	1812	AD29	468	395
Laird, John, exr. of J. Carleton	Deed to	Rice, George	1813	AE30	240	191
Laird, John, exr. of J. Carleton	Deed to	Rice, George	1813	AE30	242	192
Laird, John, exr. of J. Carleton	Deed to	King, Robert	1813	AF31	524	385
Laird, John, exr. of J. Carleton	Deed to	Elliott, Lynde, of G'tn.	1813	AF31	030	021
Laird, John, exr. of J. Carleton	Deed to	Cooper, Robert	1813	AF31	537	397
Laird, John, exr. of J. Carleton	Deed to	Brashears, John W.	1813	AF31	369	264
Laird, John, exr. of J. Carleton	Deed to	McGilton, William B.	1813	AF31	398	288
Laird, John, exr. of J. Carleton	Deed to	Curran, John	1814	AG32	076	057
Laird, John, exr. of J. Carleton	Deed to	McKim, James	1814	AG32	156	111
Laird, John, exr. of J. Carleton	Deed to	Little, Israel	1814	AG32	172	122
Laird, John, exr. of J. Carleton	Deed to	McLeod, John	1814	AG32	074	056
Laird, John, exr. of J. Carleton	Deed to	Beall, George	1814	AG32	046	037
Laird, John, exr. of J. Carleton	Deed to	Lake, George	1814	AG32	006	005
Laird, John, exr. of J. Carleton	Deed to	Bushby, Mary	1814	AG32	244	174
Laird, John, exr. of J. Carleton	Deed to	Smith, William	1814	AG32	301	219
Laird, John, exr. of J. Carleton	Deed to	Andrews, Timothy P.	1816	AM37	383	276
Laird, John, exr. of J. Carleton	Deed to	Fletcher, Noah	1816	AM37	427	306
Laird, John, exr. of J. Carleton	Deed to	Burford, Henry	1816	AM37	439	315
Laird, John, exr. of J. Carleton	Deed to	Hogan, Thady	1816	AM37	060	049
Laird, John, exr. of J. Carleton	Deed to	Andrews, George	1816	AM37	137	106
Laird, John, exr. of J. Carleton	Deed to	Grammer, Gottlieb C.	1816	AM37	047	038
Laird, John, exr. of J. Carleton	Deed to	Blake, James H.	1816	AM37	526	390
Laird, John, exr. of J. Carleton	Deed to	Campbell, John	1816	AM37	401	288
Laird, John, exr. of J. Carleton	Deed to	Gardiner, John	1816	AO39	040	033
Laird, John, exr. of J. Carleton	Deed to	Hebb, William, of P.G. Co.	1817	AO39	209	153
Laird, John, of G'tn.	Deed fr	Beall, Robert Lemar	1794	B2A	139	183
Laird, John, of G'tn.	Deed fr	Scott, William A. & Anne	1799	E5	065	053
Laird, John, of G'tn.	Deed fr	Peers, Nicholas & Valentine, VA	1801	F6	200	129
Laird, John, of G'tn.	Deed fr	Becraft, Benjamin	1801	G7	171	228

Party	What	Party	Year	Liber	Old	New
Laird, John, of G'tn.	Release fr	Burnes, Ann	1802	G7	512	652
Laird, John, of G'tn.	Deed fr	Furguson, William, P.G. Co.	1804	K10	328	337
Laird, John, of G'tn.	Deed to	Scott, Sabret, of G'tn.	1804	K10	126	136
Laird, John, of G'tn.	Deed fr	Deakins, Leonard M., of G'tn. et al	1806	Q16	294	223
Laird, John, of G'tn.	Deed fr	Murdock, John, of G'tn.	1806	Q16	138	090
Laird, John, of G'tn.	Convey to	Travers, Nicholas, of G'tn.	1810	Z25	257	201
Laird, John, of G'tn.	Deed to	Travers, Nicholas, of G'tn.	1811	AB27	454	373
Laird, John, of G'tn.	Deed fr	Meem, Peter, of G'tn.	1811	AB27	423	349
Laird, John, of G'tn.	Deed to	Crabb, John	1813	AE30	117	090
Laird, John, of G'tn.	Deed to	Farrell, Zephaniah	1813	AF31	322	230
Laird, John, of G'tn.	Deed to	Moss, Philemon	1813	AF31	520	382
Laird, John, of G'tn.	Deed to	Wingerd, Abraham, of G'tn.	1814	AH33	359	311
Laird, John, of G'tn.	Deed to	Forrest, Joseph	1814	AH33	019	017
Laird, John, of G'tn., exr.	Deed to	Steuart, Samuel	1816	AL36	211	218
Lake, George	Deed fr	Carleton, Joseph, of G'tn.	1805	M12	219	221
Lake, George	Deed fr	Carleton, Joseph, of G'tn.	1808	U20	238	128
Lake, George	Deed fr	Laird, John, exr. of J. Carleton	1814	AG32	006	005
Lake, George	B. of S. fr	Beeding, Mary	1817	AO39	171	127
Lake, George et al	Deed to	Carleton, Joseph, of G'tn.	1805	M12	148	145
Laland, John	Deed fr	Mountz, John, of G'tn.	1811	AA26	233	160
Laland, John	Deed to	McCann, Arthur, of G'tn.	1812	AC28	324	236
Lalor, Alice et al	Deed fr	Neale, Leonard, Rt. Rev., of G'tn.	1808	U20	283	151
Lalor, Alice et al	Confirm fr	Neale, Leonard, Rev.	1811	AB27	169	140
LaMarche, Mary de, of G'tn.	Deed fr	Potts, William, of Frederick Co.	1803	K10	090	87
Lambell, William	Mortgage fr	Thornton, William	1809	V21	254	181
Lambell, William	Deed to	Hambden, William	1812	AD29	155	122
Lambell, William et al	Lease fr	Carleton, Joseph, of G'tn.	1804	L11	273	251
Lambell, William, shipwright	Deed fr	Van Ness, John P.	1809	V21	246	175
Lambert, Aaron, mer., of Phila.	Deed to	Johnes, Charles, mer., of Phila.	1817	AN38	527	382
Lambert, Aaron, of Phila. PA	Deed fr	Willcox, Thomas, of Phila. PA	1813	AF31	374	269
Lambert, Moris, of G'tn.	Deed to	Foxall, Henry, of G'tn.	1815	AH33	534	457
Lambert, Moris, of G'tn.	Deed fr	Reintzel, Valentine, of G'tn.	1816	AL36	502	472
Lambert, Morris	Deed fr	Brown, Robert	1801	G7	061	078
Lambert, Morris	Manumis to	[ ], Charles (negro)	1807	S18	025	021
Lambert, Morris	Deed fr	Reintzel, Anthony, of G'tn.	1808	T19	159	112
Lambert, Morris, of G'tn.	Deed fr	Bradley, Phineas	1809	X23	284	225
Lambert, Morris, of G'tn.	Cert fr	Munroe, Thomas, Supt.	1817	AN38	052	042
Lamble, William	Release fr	Thornton, William	1812	AC28	476	338
Lambright, Bisa, of G'tn. et al	Deed to	Lipscomb, William C., of G'tn.	1817	AN38	085	066
Lancaster, Stephen	Lease fr	Pairo, Thomas W.	1816	AL36	547	510
Lancaster, Stephen	D. of T. to	Kurtz, Daniel, of G'tn.	1816	AM37	267	196
Lancaster, Stephen	D. of T. to	English, David, cashier	1816	AM37	360	261
Lancaster, Stephen	D. of T. to	Smith, Walter, of G'tn.	1817	AO39	416	283
Lancaster, Stephen	D. of T. to	Smith, Clement, of G'tn.	1817	AO39	132	100
Lancaster, Stephen	D. of T. to	Mountz, John, of G'tn.	1817	AN38	284	208
Lancaster, Stephen, of G'tn.	Deed fr	Jones, Charles C., of Montg. Co.	1815	AK35	041	032
Lancaster, Stephen, of G'tn.	Deed fr	Dodge, Francis, of G'tn.	1816	AL36	396	382
Lancaster, Stephen, of G'tn.	Deed to	Dodge, Francis, of G'tn.	1816	AL36	393	379
Landes, Abraham	Deed fr	Dunback, Elizabeth	1813	AF31	028	020
Landes, Abraham	D. of T. to	English, David, cashier	1815	AH33	407	351
Landes, Abraham, of G'tn.	Deed fr	Magruder, Ninian, of G'tn.	1815	AH33	405	350
Landes, Abraham, of G'tn.	Deed to	Holt, Lawrence O., of G'tn.	1816	AL36	284	283
Landes, Abraham, of G'tn.	Deed to	Mountz, John, of G'tn.	1816	AM37	331	241
Landes, Abraham, of G'tn.	Deed to	Traverse, George, of G'tn.	1816	AL36	093	094
Landis, David, of Bucks Co. PA	Deed to	Way, John, rep. of Nicholas	1811	AA26	372	248

Party	What	Party	Year	Liber	Old	New
Landrick, William (negro)	Manumis fr	Carroll, Elizabeth	1810	Y24	334	302
Lane, James S. et al	Deed fr	Jackson, John G., fr. Harrison Co.	1814	AG32	295	215
Lane, John, admr. of V. Huff	Deed to	King, Nicholas	1804	K10	192	201
Lane, Samuel & Rachel, of G'tn.	Deed to	Brown, Joel, of G'tn.	1810	X23	362	290
Lane, Samuel M. & Rachel	Deed fr	Smith, William	1808	T19	215	157
Lane, Samuel M. et al	Deed to	Brown, Joel, of G'tn.	1810	X23	362	290
Lane, William	Deed fr	Wood, Basil	1801	G7	147	194
Lane, William	B. of S. fr	Hunt, Jeremiah	1802	I9	219	345
Langley, Charles	B. of S. to	Robey, Thomas	1817	AO39	236	170
Langley, Edward	Deed fr	Commissioners of Washington	1799	D4	386	368
Langley, Edward	Deed fr	Carroll, Daniel, of *Duddington*	1800	E5	210	204
Langley, Edward	Deed fr	Lovell, William	1802	I9	011	015
Langley, Edward	Assign to	McClann, Robert, trustee	1809	W22	061	045
Langley, Edward, mer.	Deed to	Shute, John, mer., of Phila.	1797	C3	267	217
Langley, Hezekiah & Charles King	Deed fr	Clarke, Albin	1816	AM37	090	072
Langley, Hezekiah & Charles King	Deed fr	Van Ness, John P.	1816	AM37	326	237
Lanham, Asa	Receipt to	Ferguson, James	1804	L11	411	366
Lanham, Asa, h/o Notley	Deed to	Free, John, shoemaker	1804	K10	157	168
Lanham, Aza, of Wilkes Co. GA	Deed to	Ferguson, James	1807	R17	106	082
Lanham, Elisha	Lease to	Clarke, Robert	1801	G7	274	378
Lanham, Elisha	Deed fr	Forrest, Uriah et al	1802	I9	361	598
Lanham, Elisha	Lease to	Orme, Nathaniel	1802	I9	428	709
Lanham, Elisha	Lease to	Clarke, Joseph	1802	I9	427	707
Lanham, Elisha	Deed to	Hewitt, John	1802	I9	372	617
Lanham, Elisha	Deed to	Cozens, William R.	1810	Y24	166	152
Lanham, Elisha	B. of S. fr	McLearn, Duncan, of G'tn.	1813	AE30	164	130
Lanham, Elisha	Deed fr	King, Vincent	1813	AF31	257	179
Lanham, Elisha	Deed to	Waters, William	1816	AM37	041	034
Lanham, Elisha et al	Deed to	Gaines, Richard	1805	N13	202	176
Lanham, Elisha, of G'tn.	Agreement	O'Neale, William	1799	D4	358	345
Lanham, Elisha, of G'tn.	Deed to	Gaines, Richard, of G'tn.	1808	T19	030	023
Lanham, Elisha, of G'tn.	Deed to	Gains, Richard, of G'tn.	1809	W22	071	053
Lanham, Elisha, of G'tn.	Deed to	Davis, Jonas, of G'tn.	1810	Y24	224	206
Lanham, Elisha, of G'tn.	Deed to	Gains, Richard, of G'tn.	1810	Y24	279	255
Lanham, Elisha, of G'tn.	Deed fr	Beall, Thomas B., of G'tn.	1810	Y24	253	233
Lanham, Elisha, of G'tn.	Deed fr	Gaines, Richard, of G'tn.	1810	Y24	254	234
Lanham, Elisha, of G'tn.	Deed to	Gaines, Richard, of G'tn.	1810	Y24	096	078
Lanham, Elisha, of G'tn.	Lease fr	Dick, Margaret, of G'tn.	1810	Z25	076	057
Lanham, Elisha, of G'tn.	Deed to	Clarke, Joseph	1811	Z25	448	353
Lanham, Elisha, of G'tn.	Assign to	King, Vincent, of G'tn.	1813	AE30	457	340
Lanham, Elisha, of G'tn.	Deed fr	French, George, of G'tn.	1813	AE30	111	085
Lanham, Elisha, of G'tn.	B. of S. fr	Pickrell, John, of G'tn.	1814	AG32	400	292
Lanham, Elisha, of G'tn.	Lease fr	Beall, Thomas B., of G'tn.	1814	AG32	396	288
Lanham, Elisha, of G'tn.	Deed fr	French, George, of G'tn.	1814	AH33	243	211
Lanham, Elisha, of G'tn.	Deed fr	King, Charles, of G'tn.	1814	AH33	063	056
Lanham, Elisha, of G'tn.	Deed to	King, Charles, of G'tn.	1814	AH33	231	202
Lanham, Elisha, of G'tn.	Deed fr	Kile, Alexander, of G'tn.	1815	AK35	383	302
Lanham, Elisha, of G'tn.	Deed to	Bohrer, Jacob, of G'tn.	1815	AK35	215	169
Lanham, Elisha, of G'tn.	Deed to	Dodge, Francis, of G'tn.	1816	AL36	395	381
Lanham, Elisha, of G'tn.	Deed fr	Beall, Thomas B., of G'tn.	1816	AM37	158	121
Lanham, Elisha, of G'tn.	Deed to	Belt, James, of G'tn.	1816	AM37	474	342
Lanham, Elisha, of G'tn.	Deed fr	Calder, William, of G'tn.	1816	AL36	392	378
Lanham, Elisha, of G'tn.	Deed to	Smith, Anthony, of G'tn.	1817	AN38	370	273
Lanham, Jeremiah	Deed to	Worthington, Charles, of G'tn.	1793	A1-2	448	57
Lanham, Nathan N. et al	Deed to	Boucher, John Thomas	1794	B2A	011	012

Party	What	Party	Year	Liber	Old	New
Lanhan, Elisha	Lease to	Manning, Charles	1801	G7	478	615
Lansdale, Thomas, assignee	Deed fr	Oakley, John, guard.	1802	I9	007	009
Lansdale, Thomas, of P.G. Co.	Deed fr	Burnes, Ann, wid/o David	1802	I9	006	008
Lathrobe, Benjamin H.	Deed fr	Van Ness, John P. & Marcia	1812	AD29	062	044
Latrobe, Benjamin B.	D. of T. to	Tessier, John, pres. of Cath. Sem.	1812	AD29	103	079
Latrobe, Benjamin H.	Lease fr	Van Ness, John P.	1806	P15	173	115
Latrobe, Benjamin H. & J. Cassin	Mortgage fr	Alexander, Robert, New Orleans	1809	X23	270	212
Latrobe, Benjamin H.	Certificate	Commissioner of Turnpike Road	1810	Y24	292	267
Latrobe, Benjamin H.	Deed fr	Pratt, Henry et al	1812	AC28	445	318
Latrobe, Benjamin H.	B. of S. fr	Young, Mary	1814	AG32	310	226
Latrobe, Benjamin H. & Mary E.	D. of T. to	Caldwell, Elias B.	1816	AO39	021	017
Latrobe, Benjamin Henry	Lease fr	Van Ness, John P.	1812	AE30	024	018
Latrobe, Benjamin Henry	Lease to	Bowling, Robert, of Alexa.	1814	AG32	033	026
Lattimer, Arthur	Manumis to	Wilder, William (C)	1817	AN38	176	128
Laurence, John	B. of S. fr	Chester, Samuel	1817	AO39	096	076
Laurie, James, Rev.	Assign fr	Blount, George	1809	V21	228	162
Laurie, James, Rev.	Mortgage to	Smith, James R., of NY	1811	AC28	060	046
Laurie, James, Rev.	Deed fr	Dorsey, William H., of Balto	1811	Z25	450	355
Laurie, James, Rev.	Deed fr	Smith, James R., mer., of NY	1811	AC28	059	045
Lavely, Catherine, of Balto.	Deed fr	Commissioners of Washington	1800	E5	340	327
Laville, Nancy, only d/o Daniel	B. of S. fr	Burch, Jane	1804	K10	406	420
Law, Edmund	D. of T. fr	Caton, William, late of Alexa.	1809	X23	272	215
Law, Edmund	Deed to	McKim, James	1810	Z25	011	008
Law, Edmund	Deed fr	Law, John	1810	Y24	389	351
Law, Edmund	Agreement	M'Gilton, William B.	1811	AC28	037	027
Law, Edmund	Release to	Speake, Samuel	1811	AA26	050	039
Law, Edmund	Deed fr	Zantzinger, William P.	1817	AN38	496	358
Law, Edmund	Deed fr	Gadsden, James, Charleston SC	1817	AN38	297	217
Law, Edmund & Joseph Forrest	Deed fr	Hellen, Walter	1811	AB27	213	173
Law, Edmund & Thomas Law	Deed to	Carroll, Daniel, of *Duddington*	1811	AC28	067	051
Law, Edmund & Joseph Forrest	D. of T. to	Brent, William	1812	AD29	239	198
Law, Edmund & Buller Cocke	Deed to	Prout, William	1815	AK35	218	171
Law, Edmund & Joseph Forrest	Release fr	Law, Thomas & William Brent	1816	AL36	106	107
Law, Edmund & Joseph Forrest	Deed to	Wharton, Franklin	1816	AL36	107	108
Law, Edmund, atty. of Thomas	Deed to	Wilson, John A.	1810	Z25	264	207
Law, Edmund, atty. of Thomas	Lease to	Huddleston, Joseph et al	1811	Z25	462	366
Law, Edmund, atty. of Thomas	Lease to	Gray, William	1811	AA26	275	187
Law, Edmund et al	D. of T. fr	Hickey, James	1810	Y24	258	239
Law, Edmund et al	Deed fr	Jackson, John G., fr. Harrison Co.	1814	AG32	295	215
Law, Edmund, trustee	Lease to	Speake, Samuel	1810	Z25	099	077
Law, Edmund, trustee of Thomas	Lease to	Kealy, Daniel	1811	AA26	019	015
Law, Edmund, trustee of Thomas	Lease to	Howe, Albin	1811	AA26	329	221
Law, Edmund, trustee of Thomas	Lease to	Jones, Charles	1811	AA26	155	107
Law, Edmund, trustee of Thomas	Deed to	Cocke, Buller	1812	AC28	302	220
Law, Edmund, trustee of Thomas	Deed to	Watterston, David	1812	AB27	538	439
Law, Edward et al	Deed fr	Munroe, Thomas, Supt.	1811	AA26	259	176
Law, Elizabeth Park	Deed to	Peter, Thomas	1802	H8	392	363
Law, Elizabeth Park	Agreement	Peter, Thomas	1802	H8	391	362
Law, John	Deed fr	Law, Thomas	1807	S18	231	183
Law, John	Deed to	Brent, William	1808	T19	339	246
Law, John	Deed to	Tuckfield, William H.P. et al	1808	T19	139	099
Law, John	Deed fr	Law, Thomas	1808	T19	333	242
Law, John	Agreement	White, Levi	1808	U20	175	098
Law, John	Deed to	Allen, Thomas	1808	U20	357	195
Law, John	Deed to	Varden, Joseph	1808	U20	351	190

Party	What	Party	Year	Liber	Old	New
Law, John	Deed fr	Bradey, Nathaniel	1808	U20	355	193
Law, John	Deed to	Brent, William	1808	U20	234	126
Law, John	Lease to	Cunningham, Cornelius	1808	V21	061	048
Law, John	Deed to	Teitjen, Henry	1809	W22	095	069
Law, John	Deed fr	Maddox, Notley, of P.G. Co.	1809	W22	111	080
Law, John	Deed to	Lowe, John W.	1810	X23	356	285
Law, John	Deed to	Law, Edmund	1810	Y24	389	351
Law, John	B. of S. fr	Steuart, William	1811	Z25	535	425
Law, John	Deed fr	Davis, George S. & Ann	1811	AA26	150	104
Law, John	Deed fr	Maitland, James, Jr.	1812	AC28	295	215
Law, John	Deed to	Teitjen, Henry	1812	AD29	230	189
Law, John	Deed to	Orr, Benjamin G.	1812	AD29	011	008
Law, John	Deed fr	Connell, Catherine	1812	AC28	294	214
Law, John	Deed fr	Maitland, James	1813	AE30	154	121
Law, John	Deed fr	Boone, Ignatius	1813	AE30	344	257
Law, John	Assign fr	Bayly, Mountjoy	1813	AF31	201	136
Law, John	Deed fr	Orr, Benjamin G.	1813	AE30	223	179
Law, John	Deed to	O'Neale, William	1814	AG32	159	113
Law, John	Deed fr	Key, Francis S.	1815	AK35	001	001
Law, John	Marriage	Carter, Frances Ann	1815	AK35	260	207
Law, John	Cert Slave	From VA	1815	AK35	260	207
Law, John	Deed fr	Underwood, John & Thomas	1815	AI34	144	165
Law, John	Deed to	Clarke, Alban	1816	AL36	091	092
Law, John	Deed fr	May, Frederick	1816	AM37	070	057
Law, John	Deed fr	Carr, Overton	1817	AN38	354	260
Law, John, attorney of Thomas	Deed to	Thompson, James	1808	T19	236	173
Law, John, attorney of Thomas	Deed to	Howard, Thomas	1809	W22	201	139
Law, John, atty. of Thomas	Lease to	Kearney, James	1810	Z25	052	039
Law, John, atty. for Thomas	Lease to	Walker, Joseph	1810	Y24	208	191
Law, John, atty. for Thomas	Deed to	Nourse, Michael et al	1810	Y24	067	059
Law, John, by P. of Atty.	Deed to	Brady, Nathaniel	1807	S18	396	315
Law, Thomas	Transfer fr	Morris, Washington R. et al	1796	B2A	336	473
Law, Thomas	Agreement	Crocker, John, physician	1796	B2B	418	090
Law, Thomas	Deed to	Morris, Robert, of Phila.	1796	B2B	418	089
Law, Thomas	Deed to	Custis, Elizabeth Parke, of VA	1796	E5		224
Law, Thomas	Cert fr	Commissioners of Washington	1796	B2A	336	473
Law, Thomas	Cert fr	Commissioners of Washington	1797	B2B	472	165
Law, Thomas	Deed to	Piercy, James	1797	B2B	687	464
Law, Thomas	Mortgage fr	Piercy, James	1797	B2B	688	465
Law, Thomas	Transfer fr	Morris, Robert & James Greenleaf	1797	B2B	469	162
Law, Thomas	Mortgage fr	Crocker, John, physician	1797	B2B	630	390
Law, Thomas	Cert fr	Commissioners of Washington	1797	B2B	469	162
Law, Thomas	Release to	Morris, Robert, of Phila. et al	1797	C3	180	152
Law, Thomas	Deed fr	Morris, Robert & Mary, Phila. et al	1797	C3	074	61
Law, Thomas	Deed to	Carroll, Daniel, of *Duddington*	1797	C3	256	210
Law, Thomas	Release to	Morris, Robert, of Phila. et al	1797	C3	144	118
Law, Thomas	Deed fr	Johnson, James, Frederick Co.	1798	C3	299	242
Law, Thomas	Deed to	Barry, James, of Balto.	1798	C3	278	225
Law, Thomas	Deed to	Gridley, Richard, blacksmith	1798	D4	107	090
Law, Thomas	Agreement	Huddleston, Joseph et al	1798	D4	155	137
Law, Thomas	Agreement	Cook, Orlando et al	1798	D4	155	137
Law, Thomas	Mortgage fr	Gridley, Richard	1798	D4	010	008
Law, Thomas	Mortgage fr	Gridley, Richard, Jr., blacksmith	1798	D4	163	144
Law, Thomas	Mortgage fr	Miller, Peter	1799	D4	177	158
Law, Thomas	Deed to	Brown, Matthew, of Balto.	1799	D4	407	384

Party	What	Party	Year	Liber	Old	New
Law, Thomas	Mortgage to	Willings & Francis, of Phila.	1801	G7	172	229
Law, Thomas	Deed to	Moffat, William et al	1801	G7	362	493
Law, Thomas	Deed to	Scott, Michael	1801	G7	240	322
Law, Thomas	Deed fr	Forrest, Uriah et al	1801	G7	014	017
Law, Thomas	Deed to	Brown, Mathew, of Balto.	1801	G7	277	383
Law, Thomas	Agreement	Kearney, John	1801	G7	084	109
Law, Thomas	Deed to	Barry, Redmond & Garrett	1801	G7	140	184
Law, Thomas	Deed to	Bryan, Benjamin	1801	G7	091	117
Law, Thomas	Deed fr	Carroll, Daniel, of *Duddington*	1801	G7	087	112
Law, Thomas	Deed to	Moffat, William et al	1801	G7	359	490
Law, Thomas	B. of S. fr	Cochran, Alexander	1802	G7	508	647
Law, Thomas	Manumis to	[ ], William (Negro)	1802	H8	411	380
Law, Thomas	Manumis to	[ ], Jenny (Negro)	1802	H8	412	381
Law, Thomas	Agreement	Keigler, John	1802	H8	354	330
Law, Thomas	Lease to	Spearer, Nicholas, of G'tn.	1802	H8	366	341
Law, Thomas	Deed to	Miller, Peter	1802	H8	086	079
Law, Thomas	L. of Atty. fr	Blane, William	1802	H8	426	392
Law, Thomas	Deed fr	Willings, Thomas et al	1802	H8	351	327
Law, Thomas	Manumis to	[ ], Paul (Negro)	1802	H8	412	381
Law, Thomas	Agreement	Peter, Thomas	1802	H8	391	362
Law, Thomas	Agreement	Christian, John	1802	H8	190	182
Law, Thomas	P. of Atty. to	Brent, William	1802	H8	423	390
Law, Thomas	Lease to	Stettinius, Samuel, of G'tn.	1802	H8	364	339
Law, Thomas	Deed to	Combe, Griffith	1802	H8	175	168
Law, Thomas	Manumis to	Holmes, Nancy	1802	H8	413	382
Law, Thomas	D. of T. to	Brent, William	1802	H8	420	387
Law, Thomas	Deed to	Barry, James D.	1802	I9	441	729
Law, Thomas	Lease to	Miller, John M.	1802	I9	338	557
Law, Thomas	Agreement	Calvert, George, P.G. Co. et al	1804	L11	125	127
Law, Thomas	Deed to	Calvert, George, P.G. Co. et al	1804	L11	114	117
Law, Thomas	Deed to	Barry, James David	1804	L11	344	312
Law, Thomas	Cert fr	Munroe, Thomas, Supt.	1805	M12	260	262
Law, Thomas	Deed to	Company, W.B., trustee of	1805	N13	260	217
Law, Thomas	Convey to	McCormick, James, the younger	1805	N13	095	087
Law, Thomas	Deed to	Barry, Garret	1806	P15	034	021
Law, Thomas	Deed fr	Barry, Garret	1806	P15	036	022
Law, Thomas	Lease to	Middleton, James	1806	P15	047	029
Law, Thomas	Lease to	Thorpe, Thomas	1806	O14	256	169
Law, Thomas	Indemnify to	Barry, James	1806	Q16	302	230
Law, Thomas	Manumis to	Costen, George (negro)	1807	R17	289	220
Law, Thomas	Deed to	Ingle, Henry	1807	R17	349	266
Law, Thomas	Manumis to	Costen, Louisa	1807	R17	288	220
Law, Thomas	Manumis to	Costen, Jemima	1807	R17	288	220
Law, Thomas	Deed to	Carroll, Daniel, of *Duddington*	1807	R17	227	170
Law, Thomas	Manumis to	Holmes, Eleanor	1807	R17	288	220
Law, Thomas	Manumis to	Costen, Margaret	1807	R17	288	220
Law, Thomas	Manumis to	Costin, Delphy et al	1807	R17	409	309
Law, Thomas	P. of Atty. fr	Blane, William, of Eng.	1807	S18	236	
Law, Thomas	Deed to	Brent, Robert	1807	S18	228	181
Law, Thomas	Deed to	White, Joseph	1807	S18	163	132
Law, Thomas	Deed to	Coombe, Griffith	1807	S18	019	017
Law, Thomas	Deed fr	Wheat, Joseph	1807	S18	166	135
Law, Thomas	Deed fr	Brent, Daniel Carroll	1807	S18	007	006
Law, Thomas	Deed to	Douglass, John	1807	R17	001	001
Law, Thomas	Deed to	Law, John	1807	S18	231	183

Party	What	Party	Year	Liber	Old	New
Law, Thomas	Division	Carroll, Daniel Carroll	1807	S18	011	009
Law, Thomas	Deed to	Oliver, Robert, of Balto.	1807	T19	001	001
Law, Thomas	Lease to	Barry, John D. & Griffith Coombe	1808	T19	093	066
Law, Thomas	Deed to	Tunnicliff, William, of P.G. Co.	1808	T19	208	151
Law, Thomas	Deed to	Eliot, Samuel, Jr.	1808	S18	330	259
Law, Thomas	Deed to	Law, John	1808	T19	333	242
Law, Thomas	Deed to	Cocke, Buller	1810	X23	413	334
Law, Thomas	Deed to	Beall, Alfred, Uriah & Elizabeth	1812	AD29	337	281
Law, Thomas	Deed to	Docker, Gilbert	1812	AD29	038	027
Law, Thomas	Deed to	Way, Andrew & George	1812	AC28	314	229
Law, Thomas	Lease to	Cooke, David	1812	AC28	199	152
Law, Thomas	Deed to	May, John Frederick	1813	AE30	158	125
Law, Thomas	Deed to	Moore, John	1813	AE30	395	291
Law, Thomas	Deed to	Lyles, William H., of P.G. Co.	1813	AE30	122	094
Law, Thomas	Deed to	Howard, Thomas	1813	AE30	118	091
Law, Thomas	Deed to	Young, James	1813	AF31	169	114
Law, Thomas	Deed to	Beale, George	1813	AF31	003	002
Law, Thomas	Deed to	Johnson, Joseph	1814	AG32	157	113
Law, Thomas	Deed fr	Moore, George	1815	AH33	512	439
Law, Thomas	Deed to	Ott, David	1815	AH33	464	396
Law, Thomas	Deed to	Cooper, William	1815	AH33	514	441
Law, Thomas	Deed to	Ott, John, of G'tn.	1815	AH33	466	398
Law, Thomas	Deed to	McLean, Cornelius	1815	AI34	241	273
Law, Thomas	Deed to	Meade, Simon	1815	AI34	008	008
Law, Thomas	Deed to	Moore, George	1815	AI34	165	189
Law, Thomas	Deed to	Moore, George	1815	AK35	461	361
Law, Thomas	Deed to	Walker, Joseph	1816	AL36	531	496
Law, Thomas	Deed to	Bean, Arey Minty	1816	AL36	501	470
Law, Thomas	Deed to	Claxton, Thomas	1816	AL36	305	301
Law, Thomas	Deed to	Young, James	1816	AL36	277	276
Law, Thomas	Deed to	Kearney, James	1816	AL36	339	331
Law, Thomas	Deed to	Tims, Henry	1816	AL36	436	415
Law, Thomas	Deed to	Coombe, Griffith	1816	AL36	275	275
Law, Thomas	Deed fr	Coombe, Griffith	1816	AL36	274	273
Law, Thomas	Lease to	Webster, Toppan	1816	AL36	133	134
Law, Thomas	Lease to	Stevens, Samuel	1816	AM37	502	368
Law, Thomas	Lease to	Brooks, Charles	1816	AM37	505	370
Law, Thomas	Deed to	Meade, Simon	1816	AO39	053	044
Law, Thomas	Lease to	Stewart, David	1817	AN38	318	232
Law, Thomas	Deed to	Moore, John	1817	AN38	250	183
Law, Thomas	Deed to	Moore, Thomas	1817	AN38	246	180
Law, Thomas	Convey to	Ott, David & Thomas Coote	1817	AO39	303	216
Law, Thomas	Deed to	Marshall, Barbary	1817	AN38	034	028
Law, Thomas & Elizabeth Parke	Deed fr	Peter, Thomas	1800	E5	228	221
Law, Thomas & Eliza Park	Deed to	Calvert, George, P.G. Co. et al	1804	L11	127	129
Law, Thomas & Edmund Law	Deed to	Carroll, Daniel, of *Duddington*	1811	AC28	067	051
Law, Thomas & Edmund Law	Deed fr	Carroll, Daniel	1811	AA26	153	106
Law, Thomas & Edmund	Deed to	Barry, James D.	1811	AB27	355	294
Law, Thomas & Edmund	Deed to	Thruston, Buckner	1812	AD29	013	009
Law, Thomas & Edmund	Deed to	Ewell, Thomas	1812	AE30	006	005
Law, Thomas & Edmund	Deed to	Mead, Simon	1812	AC28	281	204
Law, Thomas & Edmund	Deed to	McCormick, James	1813	AE30	159	126
Law, Thomas & William Brent	Release to	Forrest, Joseph & Edmund Law	1816	AL36	106	107
Law, Thomas & Griffith Coombe	Agreement	Young, James	1816	AL36	278	277
Law, Thomas et al	Mortgage fr	Piercy, James	1797	B2B	690	468

Party	What	Party	Year	Liber	Old	New
Law, Thomas et al	Deed fr	Walker, George	1798	D4	156	138
Law, Thomas et al	Deed to	Peter, Thomas	1802	H8	392	363
Law, Thomas, Gent.	Deed to	Miller, Peter	1798	D4	047	039
Law, Thomas, of New York NY	Deed fr	Greenleaf, Morris & Nicholson	1795	B2B	377	030
Lawrance, John et al	Deed fr	Pratt, Henry et al	1808	T19	086	061
Lawrason & Fowle, plt.	Suit	Patton, James, exr., def.	1810	Y24	006	
Lawrason, Thomas, of Alexa.	Deed fr	Wadsworth, Charles & Elizabeth	1810	Y24	003	003
Lawrence, Clement, of Phila. PA	Deed fr	Commissioners of Washington	1801	G7	033	042
Lawrence, John	Deed fr	Johnson, Thomas, of Fredk. Co.	1812	AD29	184	148
Lawrence, John et al	Assign fr	Greenleaf, Ann Penn	1809	V21	362	266
Lawrence, John, morocco finisher	Indenture fr	Lucas, Ignatius, s/o John	1812	AD29	186	150
Lawrie, James, Rev.	Deed to	Smith, James R., of New York NY	1810	X23	285	226
Lawson, Alexander	Deed to	Scott, Gustavus	1796	B2B	404	071
Lawson, Alexander et al	Deed to	Beall, Thomas & John M. Gantt	1793	A1-1	292	389
Lawwell, Samuel	Deed fr	McLaughlin, James	1806	Q16	134	088
Lay & Cruttenden	Deed fr	Smallwood, Horatio	1815	AI34	054	062
Lay, Richard, of G'tn.	B. of S. fr	Reemney, John, of G'tn.	1815	AK35	239	189
Lazenby, Cephas, of Montg. Co.	Deed to	Smith, Samuel H.	1814	AH33	047	043
Leach, Asel, of Charles Co.	B. of S. to	Casteel, Edmond [Casseel]	1817	AN38	180	131
Leach, John	B. of S. to	Moore, James	1816	AL36	517	484
Leager, Nathaniel	Deed to	Sothoron, Thomas L.	1802	I9	501	823
Leakin, Thomas I., of G'tn. et al	Mortgage to	Patterson, Edgar, of G'tn.	1810	Z25	111	086
Leamy, John & Eliz., of Phila. PA	Deed to	Harper, Thomas et al	1808	T19	227	167
Leamy, John, mer.	Deed fr	FitzSimons, Thomas, Phila. et al	1808	T19	153	108
Leamy, John, of Phila. PA	Deed fr	Threlkeld, John	1799	D4	248	232
Lear, Benjamin L.	Convey fr	Cottman, William	1815	AK35	457	358
Lear, Benjamin L.	Deed fr	Coltman, William	1816	AM37	479	347
Lear, Tobias	Cert fr	Commissioners of Washington	1795	B2A	330	463
Lear, Tobias	Cert fr	Commissioners of Washington	1797	B2B	464	156
Lear, Tobias	Deed fr	Wagner, Jacob, of G'tn.	1815	AI34	089	102
Lear, Tobias	Mortgage fr	Henley, Robert, U.S.N.	1815	AI34	386	411
Lear, Tobias	Convey fr	Calder, James, of G'tn.	1815	AK35	455	355
Lear, Tobias	Deed fr	Andrews, Christopher	1815	AK35	232	183
Lear, Tobias & Co.	Cert fr	Commissioners of Washington	1793	B2A	308	432
Lear, Tobias & Co.	Cert fr	Commissioners of Washington	1793	B2A	308	432
Lear, Tobias & Tristram Dalton	Deed to	Hobson, Jonathan et al	1799	E5	061	049
Lear, Tobias & Tristram Dalton	Deed to	Griffith, Robert Eaglefield et al	1799	E5	061	049
Lear, Tobias & Tristram Dalton	Deed to	Coles, John et al	1799	E5	061	049
Lear, Tobias et al	Deed to	Deakins, William, Jr., of G'tn.	1797	C3	221	186
Lear, Tobias et al	Deed fr	Greenleaf, James	1798	D4	055	046
Lear, Tobias et al	Deed to	Hobson, Jonathan, of NY et al	1798	D4	148	131
Lear, Tobias et al	Deed to	Deakins, William, Jr., of G'tn.	1798	D4	062	052
Lear, Tobias et al	Deed fr	Peter, Robert, of G'tn.	1799	D4	321	305
Lear, Tobias et al	Deed to	Deakins, William, Jr.	1800	E5	163	152
Lear, Tobias, mer.	Deed to	Dalton, Tristram, mer.	1798	C3	317	256
Lear, Tobias, of Portsmouth NH	Cert fr	Commissioners of Washington	1792	B2A	284	398
Lear, Tobias, of Phila. PA	Cert fr	Commissioners of Washington	1793	B2A	306	430
Lear, Tobias, of G'tn.	Deed fr	Peter, Robert, of G'tn.	1794	B2A	143	189
Lear, Tobias, of G'tn.	Deed to	Dalton, Tristram & J. Greenleaf	1794	B2A	152	201
Lear, Tobias, of G'tn. et al	Deed fr	Holmead, Anthony	1795	B2A	226	314
Lear, Tobias, of P.G. Co. et al	Deed to	Deakins, William, Jr., of G'tn.	1797	C3	218	183
Lear, Tobias, of P.G. Co. et al	Deed to	Deakins, William, Jr., of G'tn.	1797	C3	223	187
Lear, Tobias, of Fairfax Co. VA	P. of Atty. to	Dalton, Tristram	1800	E5		154
Lear, Tobias, of Fairfax Co. VA	P. of Atty. to	Thornton, William	1800	E5		365
Lear, Tobias, of Fairfax Co. VA	Deed to	Chandler, Walter Story	1800	E5	386	363

Party	What	Party	Year	Liber	Old	New
Leatherbury, John & Sarah	Deed to	Elsey, Arnold	1807	S18	288	225
Leatherbury, John, of Robt.	Deed fr	Jones, John, of Somerset Co.	1807	S18	286	224
Leatherman, Henry, Frederick Co.	Deed fr	Pearce, Thomas, of G'tn.	1805	N13	092	084
Leatherman, Henry, Frederick Co.	Deed Gift to	Sanderson, William R., Fredk. Co.	1809	W22	270	180
Ledan, Nicholas	B. of S. fr	Crowley, Bartholomew	1812	AD29	132	102
Lee, Ann	Marriage	Gamble, William	1817	AN38	363	268
Lee, Ann et al	Deed to	Threlkeld, John	1812	AD29	448	377
Lee, Ann, of Charles Co.	Deed to	Threlkeld, John	1811	AA26	048	037
Lee, Edmund Jennings, of Alexa.	Deed to	Peter, David, of G'tn.	1808	U20	076	043
Lee, Edmund Jennings, of Alexa.	Deed to	French, George, of G'tn.	1812	AD29	338	282
Lee, Edward Jennings, exr.	Deed to	Bearcroft, William, of G'tn.	1809	V21	243	173
Lee, Eliza	Deed fr	Lee, Thomas Sim & Mary	1802	H8	055	052
Lee, Eliza et al	Deed fr	Lee, Thomas Sim et ux	1802	H8	053	050
Lee, Henry	Cert fr	Brent, Daniel C.	1806	Q16	314	240
Lee, Henry & Anne, Westm. Co.	Deed to	Fairfax, Ferdinand, Berkeley Co.	1799	E5	067	055
Lee, Henry, Gen., of VA	Deed fr	French, George, of G'tn.	1798	D4	166	147
Lee, Henry, of VA	Deed fr	Polock, Isaac	1798	D4	083	070
Lee, Henry, of Westm. Co. VA	Deed to	Bond, Joshua B., of Phila.	1801	G7	001	001
Lee, Henry, of VA	Deed to	Tayloe, John, of VA	1807	S18	152	124
Lee, James Clerk et al	Deed fr	Contee, Benjamin & Sarah R.	1809	V21	361	264
Lee, John	B. of S. to	Horsey, Outerbridge, of DE	1813	AF31	289	205
Lee, John	Deed fr	Lee, Thomas Sim, of Fredk. Co.	1813	AF31	431	310
Lee, John	B. of S. fr	Sewall, Clement, of Alexa. Co.	1813	AF31	288	204
Lee, John	Deed to	Reinagle, Anna	1815	AI34	048	054
Lee, John, of G'tn.	Deed fr	Mountz, Jacob, collector, of G'tn.	1813	AE30	079	060
Lee, John, of G'tn.	Deed to	Milligan, Joseph, of G'tn.	1813	AF31	353	252
Lee, John, of G'tn.	Deed fr	Carroll, Patrick, of G'tn.	1813	AF31	426	306
Lee, John, of G'tn.	Deed fr	Carroll, Patrick & Susanna, G'tn.	1813	AF31	428	308
Lee, John, of G'tn.	Deed fr	Mountz, Jacob, collector, G'tn.	1814	AG32	090	068
Lee, John, of G'tn.	Deed to	Beverly, Robert	1815	AI34	163	187
Lee, Margaret Russell Clerk et al	Deed fr	Contee, Benjamin & Sarah R.	1809	V21	361	264
Lee, Maria (M)	Manumis fr	Dawson, John	1812	AC28	130	098
Lee, Mary	B. of S. to	Maffitt, Samuel	1809	V21	204	144
Lee, Mary	B. of S. to	Burch, Susan	1811	AA26	328	220
Lee, Mary, late wid/o H. Butler	Deed to	Bussard, John R., of P.G. Co.	1809	W22	225	153
Lee, May, wid/o Henry Butler	Deed to	Bussard, Daniel	1805	N13	396	316
Lee, Patience	Cert Free fr	Hanson, Rebecca, of G'tn.	1810	Y24	054	047
Lee, Peter (negro)	Cert Free fr	Stoddert, Benjamin	1810	Y24	247	228
Lee, Peter, insolvent	Deed to	Collard, George, trustee	1810	Y24	025	021
Lee, Richard B., of VA	Transfer to	Scott, Sabret	1797	B2B	468	161
Lee, Richard Bland, of VA	Cert fr	Commissioners of Washington	1792	B2A	289	405
Lee, Richard Bland & Elizabeth	Manumis to	Ludwell, Bearer	1817	AN38	125	092
Lee, Richard Bland	D. of T. to	Bank of United States	1817	AN38	248	181
Lee, Richard, of *Blenheim*, gd/o	Deed to	Threlkeld, John	1810	Y24	538	472
Lee, Russell, heirs of	Agreement		1812	AD29	433	
Lee, Theoderick, of VA	Mortgage to	Stoddert, Benjamin	1804	K10	372	386
Lee, Theodorick	Convey to	Stoddert, Benjamin	1807	S18	103	083
Lee, Thomas, of A.A. Co.	Deed fr	Lee, Thomas Sim, of Fredk. Co.	1814	AG32	360	261
Lee, Thomas S., of Annapolis	Deed to	Stoddert, Benjamin, of G'tn.	1794	B2A	029	031
Lee, Thomas S. et al	Deed fr	Dorsey, William H.	1795	B2A	235	327
Lee, Thomas S. et al	Deed to	Beall, Thomas, of George	1795	B2A	166	222
Lee, Thomas S.	Deed fr	Brookes, Henry	1801	G7	341	472
Lee, Thomas S.	Deed to	Riggs, George W.	1802	I9	316	519
Lee, Thomas S.	Deed to	Warring, Marsham et al	1802	I9	261	422
Lee, Thomas S.	Deed to	Gaither, Henry	1802	I9	360	596

Party	What	Party	Year	Liber	Old	New
Lee, Thomas S., of G'tn.	Deed to	Ross, Andrew & Robert Getty	1810	Y24	045	039
Lee, Thomas S., of G'tn.	Deed to	Shepperd, Lodowick, of G'tn.	1811	AB27	100	082
Lee, Thomas S., of G'tn.	Deed to	Crawford, William, of G'tn.	1811	AB27	098	080
Lee, Thomas S.	Agreement	Ringgold, Tench, trustee	1811	AC28	100	075
Lee, Thomas S., of Fredk. Co.	Deed to	Deakins, Leonard M., of P.G. Co.	1813	AF31	443	319
Lee, Thomas S., of Fredk. Co.	Deed to	Deakins, Leonard M., of P.G. Co.	1813	AF31	444	320
Lee, Thomas S., of Fredk. Co.	Deed fr	Deakins, Leonard M. & John Hoye	1813	AF31	446	321
Lee, Thomas S., of Fredk. Co.	Deed to	Smith, Walter & Clement Smith	1813	AE30	421	310
Lee, Thomas S., of Fredk. Co.	Deed to	Deakins, Leonard M., of P.G. Co.	1813	AF31	442	318
Lee, Thomas S., of Fredk. Co.	Deed to	Corcoran, Thomas, of G'tn.	1814	AG32	373	271
Lee, Thomas S., of Fredk. Co.	Deed to	Carter, John M., of G'tn.	1815	AI34	064	072
Lee, Thomas Sim & Mary	Deed to	Beall, Thomas & John M. Gantt	1793	A1-1	259	351
Lee, Thomas Sim	Cert fr	Commissioners of Washington	1795	B2A	330	463
Lee, Thomas Sim et al	Deed to	Beatty, Charles, Sr., of G'tn.	1795	B2A	242	336
Lee, Thomas Sim et al	Deed fr	Warring, Marsham	1795	B2A	253	353
Lee, Thomas Sim, of G'tn.	Deed fr	Beall, Thomas, of George, of G'tn.	1796	B2B	607	360
Lee, Thomas Sim, of G'tn.	Deed fr	Boucher, John Thomas, P.G. Co.	1796	B2B	526	239
Lee, Thomas Sim	Deed fr	Stoddert, Benjamin	1798	D4	134	116
Lee, Thomas Sim	Deed fr	Stoddert, Benjamin	1798	D4	132	115
Lee, Thomas Sim, of G'tn.	Deed fr	Beall, Thomas, of George, of G'tn.	1798	C3	423	333
Lee, Thomas Sim, of G'tn.	Deed fr	Beall, Thomas et al	1799	D4	190	173
Lee, Thomas Sim	Deed fr	Magruder, Eleanor, rel/o Charles	1801	G7	342	473
Lee, Thomas Sim & Mary	Deed to	Lee, Eliza	1802	H8	055	052
Lee, Thomas Sim et ux	Deed to	Ringold, Mary C. et al	1802	H8	053	050
Lee, Thomas Sim et al	Deed fr	Beatty, John M. et al	1805	N13	011	012
Lee, Thomas Sim, of G'tn.	Deed fr	Beall, Thomas, of George, of G'tn.	1805	N13	378	303
Lee, Thomas Sim	Deed fr	Beall, Thomas, of George	1805	M12	061	057
Lee, Thomas Sim & William Brent	Deed to	Deakins, Leonard M. & John Hoye	1809	V21	416	318
Lee, Thomas Sim	Deed to	Mackey, William	1810	Y24	173	158
Lee, Thomas Sim	Deed to	Lutz, John	1810	Y24	175	161
Lee, Thomas Sim, of Fredk. Co.	Deed fr	Lee, William, of Montg. Co.	1813	AE30	100	077
Lee, Thomas Sim, of Fredk. Co.	Deed to	Lee, John	1813	AF31	431	310
Lee, Thomas Sim, of Fredk. Co.	Convey to	Adams, Henry (C), of G'tn.	1813	AF31	122	082
Lee, Thomas Sim	Plat	Washington St. & Virginia Ave.	1813	AF31	466	
Lee, Thomas Sim	Certificate	List of 101 lots, Washington St.	1813	AF31	448	322
Lee, Thomas Sim, of Fredk. Co.	Deed to	Ringgold, Tench & Mary C.	1813	AF31	424	305
Lee, Thomas Sim, of Fredk. Co.	Deed to	Corcoran, Thomas, of G'tn.	1813	AF31	318	227
Lee, Thomas Sim, of *Needwood*	Deed to	Foxall, Henry, of G'tn.	1814	AH33	190	173
Lee, Thomas Sim, of *Needwood*	Deed to	Crawford, William, of G'tn.	1814	AH33	330	285
Lee, Thomas Sim, of Fredk. Co.	Deed to	Shepherd, Lodowick, of G'tn.	1814	AG32	088	066
Lee, Thomas Sim, of Fredk. Co.	Deed to	Lee, Thomas, of A.A. Co.	1814	AG32	360	261
Lee, Thomas Sim, of G'tn.	Deed to	Ross, Andrew, of G'tn.	1815	AI34	283	320
Lee, Thomas Sim, of G'tn.	Deed to	Ross, Andrew, of G'tn.	1815	AI34	285	321
Lee, Thomas Sim, of Fredk. Co.	Deed to	Wilson, John A., of G'tn.	1815	AI34	033	038
Lee, Thomas Sim, of Fredk. Co.	Deed to	Adams, Henry, of G'tn	1815	AK35	252	200
Lee, Thomas Simm & Mary	Deed to	Ringold, Mary C.	1802	H8	052	049
Lee, Thomas, Sr., Pr. Wm. Co.	Mortgage fr	Moscrop, Henry	1804	L11	048	49
Lee, William	Slaves		1808	V21	113	084
Lee, William	Deed fr	Mountz, Jacob, collector, of G'tn.	1809	X23	344	275
Lee, William, of G'tn.	Deed fr	Mountz, Jacob, collector, of G'tn.	1810	Y24	261	240
Lee, William, of Montg. Co.	Deed to	Lee, Thomas Sim, of Fredk. Co.	1813	AE30	100	077
Lee, William, of G'tn.	Deed fr	Bowie, Washington, of G'tn.	1815	AH33	550	471
Leeke, Ann	Deed to	Beall, Thomas & John M. Gantt	1793	A1-1	331	434
Lefevre, Lewis, of G'tn.	B. of S. fr	Fox, Bartleson, of G'tn.	1807	Q16	224	152
Lehault, Louis Joseph et al	Deed fr	Deakins, Leonard M. et al	1807	R17	378	287

Party	What	Party	Year	Liber	Old	New
Lehault, Louis Joseph et al	Deed fr	Hoye, John	1810	Y24	023	020
Lehault, Marie Francoise et al	Deed fr	Deakins, Leonard M. et al	1807	R17	378	287
Lehault, Marie Francoise et al	Deed fr	Hoye, John	1810	Y24	023	020
Lehault, Marie Magdalene et al	Deed fr	Deakins, Leonard M. et al	1807	R17	378	287
Lehault, Marie Magdelene et al	Deed fr	Hoye, John	1810	Y24	023	020
Leiper, George R., of P.G. Co.	Assign to	Burch, Samuel	1811	AB27	270	221
Leiper, George R., late P.G. Co.	Manumis to	Scott, Louisa (M)	1815	AK35	181	141
LeKoy, Adam & Anna M., of PA	Deed to	Moyer, Jacob	1792	A1-1	174	247
Lenmon, Isiah	B. of S. fr	Drane, David	1809	V21	155	112
Lennis, Samuel	Deed to	Simmons, William	1802	I9	559	906
Lenox, David	Deed fr	Willing, Thomas, of Phila. et al	1811	AA26	333	223
Lenox, David et al	Release to	Nourse, Joseph	1813	AF31	011	008
Lenox, Peter	Deed to	Crook, Bernard	1798	C3	298	241
Lenox, Peter	Deed fr	Commissioners of Washington	1798	C3	471	371
Lenox, Peter	Deed fr	Commissioners of Washington	1801	G7	136	179
Lenox, Peter	Deed fr	Munroe, Thomas, Supt.	1802	I9	149	225
Lenox, Peter	B. of S. fr	Murray, William	1804	K10	211	222
Lenox, Peter	Deed fr	Murdock, John, of G'tn.	1804	L11	313	287
Lenox, Peter	B. of S. fr	Fenwick, Richard	1805	N13	008	009
Lenox, Peter	Deed fr	Birth, James	1807	R17	269	205
Lenox, Peter	Deed to	Birth, James	1807	R17	036	030
Lenox, Peter	Deed fr	Carroll, Daniel Carroll, trustee et al	1807	R17	271	206
Lenox, Peter	Deed fr	Murdock, John, of G'tn.	1808	U20	365	199
Lenox, Peter	Deed fr	Dorsey, William H., of Balto.	1808	U20	367	200
Lenox, Peter	Mortgage fr	Kilty, John & Josias Wilson King	1809	W22	244	164
Lenox, Peter	Deed fr	Haigh, Job & Elizabeth	1809	X23	130	093
Lenox, Peter	Deed to	Bennett, James	1811	Z25	412	324
Lenox, Peter	Deed to	Varden, Charles	1811	Z25	421	330
Lenox, Peter	Deed fr	Van Ness, John & Marcia	1812	AD29	374	315
Lenox, Peter	Deed to	Corcoran, Thomas, of G'tn.	1812	AD29	472	399
Lenox, Peter	Deed fr	Van Ness, John P. & Marcia	1813	AE30	494	366
Lenox, Peter	Deed fr	Van Ness, John P. & Marcia	1815	AI34	103	118
Lenox, Peter	Deed fr	Porter, Sarah, wid/o Thomas et al	1815	AI34	105	119
Lenox, Peter	Deed fr	Corporation of Warhington	1815	AI34	106	121
Lenox, Peter	Deed fr	Campbell, John	1815	AK35	449	352
Lenox, Peter	Deed fr	Van Ness, John P. & Marcia	1817	AN38	121	089
Lenox, Peter	Release fr	Perkins, Joseph, admrs. or	1817	AN38	123	091
Lenox, Peter	Deed fr	Carr, Overton	1817	AN38	263	192
Lenox, Peter & Margaret	Deed to	Hand, Ann	1813	AF31	358	255
Lenox, Peter et al	Deed fr	Morton, Thomas, of Montg. Co.	1796	B2B	559	290
Lenox, Peter, house joiner	Deed to	Washington, Bailey	1807	R17	301	229
Lenox, Peter, of P.G. Co.	Deed fr	Bruner, Stephen & Barbara	1796	B2B	569	307
Lenox, Peter [Lynox]	Mortgage fr	Schnively, Henry	1806	P15	206	138
Lenthall, John	Deed fr	Deakins, Francis et al	1800	E5	308	299
Lenthall, John	Deed fr	Stoddert, Benjamin et al	1800	E5	308	299
Lenthall, John	Deed fr	King, Robert, Sr. & Robert, Jr.	1802	I9	160	242
Lenthall, John	Deed to	Francis, William, of Phila. PA	1808	V21	075	059
Leonard, Jacob	Qualify	Lieutenant of infantry	1813	AE30	531	394
Leonard, Jacob	D. of T. to	Lowe, Enoch M.	1816	AM37	074	060
Leonard, Jacob	D. of T. to	Smith, Clement, of G'tn.	1816	AM37	048	039
Leonard, Jacob, of G'tn.	Deed fr	Lufborough, Nathan	1813	AF31	089	060
Leonard, Jacob, of G'tn.	D. of T. to	Smith, Clement, of G'tn.	1813	AF31	092	062
Leonx, Peter	Deed fr	Corcoran, Thomas, of G'tn.	1812	AE30	050	037
Lettler, Nathan, exrs. of, of VA	Deed to	Morgan, William, of G'tn.	1815	AK35	078	060
Levy, David, of Frederick Co.	Deed to	McCleary, Henry	1792	A1-1	066	98

Party	What	Party	Year	Liber	Old	New
Lewis, Edward S.	B. of S. fr	Lewis, Henry C.	1815	AH33	475	406
Lewis, Elizabeth, insolvent	Deed to	Crawford, Jacob, trustee	1804	L11	179	173
Lewis, Frederick	Cert Free fr	Paulding, John K.	1817	AO39	228	165
Lewis, George, mer., of NY	Deed fr	Lynch, Dominick et ux, et al	1797	C3	026	21
Lewis, George, of New York NY	Deed to	Taylor, James, late of Phila.	1806	Q16	153	101
Lewis, George, of New York NY	Deed to	Martin, James, of Long Island NY	1809	W22	175	123
Lewis, Henry	Deed fr	Bussard, Daniel	1816	AK35	533	421
Lewis, Henry	Deed fr	Smallwood, Horatio	1816	AM37	027	022
Lewis, Henry	Deed fr	Clarke, Edward	1816	AM37	030	025
Lewis, Henry C.	B. of S. to	Lewis, Edward S.	1815	AH33	475	406
Lewis, John	B. of S. to	Wheeler, Thomas, Fairfax Co. VA	1810	Y24	225	207
Lewis, Joseph, Jr.	D. of T. to	Harrison, Matthew, Jr.	1810	Y24	547	480
Lewis, Joseph S. et al	Deed fr	Howell, Benjamin B.	1812	AD29	519	
Lewis, Joseph S., of Phila. PA	Deed fr	Davidson, James	1813	AF31	479	349
Lewis, Joseph S., of Phila. PA	Deed fr	Davidson, John	1813	AF31	538	398
Lewis, Joseph S., agent, of Phila.	Deed to	Waln, Robert, Jr., of Phila., mer.	1815	AK35	150	115
Lewis, Joseph S. et al	Deed fr	Waln, Robert, Jr., of Phila., mer.	1815	AK35	152	118
Lewis, Joseph S., of Phila. PA	Deed fr	Davidson, James et al	1815	AI34	345	377
Lewis, Joseph Saunders, of PA	Deed fr	Brent, William, trustee	1816	AM37	224	165
Lewis, Kendall M., Sussex Co. DE	Deed fr	Dorsey, William H.	1801	G7	094	121
Lewis, Kendall M., Sussex Co. DE	Deed fr	Dorsey, William H., of Balto.	1810	Z25	207	163
Lewis, Lawrence, of VA	Deed fr	Commissioners of Washington	1799	E5	046	036
Lewis, Leyson, of London	Deed fr	Munroe, Thomas, Supt.	1802	I9	040	053
Lewis, Lucy (negro)	Manumis fr	Dearborn, Henry	1806	O14	116	074
Lewis, Nelly (M), age 22	Cert free fr	Carr, Overton	1812	AD29	302	248
Lewis, Robert	B. of S. fr	Spotwood, John A.	1810	Y24	143	130
Lewis, Samuel, Jr.	Deed fr	Munroe, Thomas, Supt.	1802	H8	575	539
Lewis, Samuel, Jr.	Deed to	King, George & Charles, of G'tn.	1805	O14	147	095
Lewis, Samuel, Jr.	Deed fr	Groves, Elizabeth	1806	O14	243	160
Lewis, Samuel, Jr.	Deed fr	King, George & Charles, of G'tn.	1808	T19	149	105
Lewis, Samuel, Jr.	Cert fr	Munroe, Thomas, Supt.	1811	Z25	449	354
Lewis, Samuel, Jr.	Deed fr	Borrows, Joseph	1812	AD29	136	105
Lewis, Samuel, Jr.	D. of T. to	Burrows, Joseph	1812	AD29	214	175
Lewis, Samuel, Jr.	Deed fr	Corporation of Washington	1816	AM37	493	359
Lewis, Samuel, Jr.	Release fr	Borrows, Joseph	1816	AM37	471	340
Lewis, Winslow, of Boston MA	Deed fr	Wilson, Offa	1812	AB27	360	299
Lewis, Winslow, of Boston MA	B. of S. fr	Wilson, Offa	1815	AH33	455	390
Ley, Michael & Magdalena	Deed to	Forrest, Uriah & Benj. Stoddert	1792	A1-1	151	217
Leyson, Lewis, mer., of London	Deed to	Gray, John, ship broker, of London	1804	K10	366	379
Lighty, Samuel, Frederick Town	Deed to	Meddert, Jacob, Frederick Town	1795	B2A	218	302
Linday, John	Cert Free to	Shorter, John (C)	1817	AO39	421	287
Lindenberger, Jacob, Balto. et al	Deed to	Olliver, Elizabeth	1808	U20	288	154
Lindenberger, Jacob et al	Deed fr	Mountz, John, Sr., of G'tn.	1807	R17	278	212
Lindo, Abraham	Cert fr	Munroe, Thomas, Supt.	1807	S18	329	258
Lindo, Abraham	Deed to	Andrews, George & Nicholas King	1810	Y24	365	331
Lindo, Abraham	Mortgage to	Gillingham, George	1810	Y24	286	262
Lindsay, Adam	Deed fr	Brent, Daniel Carroll, trustee et al	1807	R17	251	190
Lindsay, Adam	B. of S. fr	Way, Andrew, Jr.	1813	AF31	187	126
Lindsay, Adam	Deed fr	Corporation of Washington	1815	AI34	201	230
Lindsay, Adam	Deed fr	Corporation of Washington	1815	AI34	206	235
Lindsay, Adam	Deed fr	Corporation of Washington	1815	AI34	208	237
Lindsay, Adam	Deed fr	Corporation of Washington	1815	AI34	210	239
Lindsay, Adam	Deed fr	Corporation of Washington	1815	AI34	211	241
Lindsay, Adam	Deed fr	Corporation of Washington	1815	AI34	213	243
Lindsay, Adam	Deed fr	Corporation of Washington	1815	AI34	215	245

Party	What	Party	Year	Liber	Old	New
Lindsay, Adam	Deed fr	Corporation of Washington	1815	AI34	203	232
Lindsay, Adam	Deed fr	Slater, David H., of TN	1815	AK35	381	300
Lindsay, George W., insolvent	Deed to	Washington, Lund, trustee	1811	AA26	318	214
Lindsay, George W.	B. of S. to	Hamilton, Samuel S.	1811	AB27	337	278
Lindsay, Judith, admx. of George	Release fr	Hamilton, Samuel S.	1814	AH33	106	099
Lindsey, Adam	Deed fr	Blodgett, Samuel et al	1801	G7	267	367
Lindsey, Adam	Deed fr	Blodget, Samuel et al	1801	G7	268	371
Lindsey, Adam	Deed fr	Burford, John A.	1804	L11	194	186
Lindsey, George W.	B. of S. to	McCormick, Alexander et al	1810	Z25	191	150
Lindsley, Eleazar & John Ingle	Deed fr	Hunt, William et al	1817	AO39	206	151
Lingan, James, Gen., estate of	Plat	Harlem, part of Spring Hill	1815	AI34	373a	
Lingan, James M. et al	Deed to	Beall, Thomas & John M. Gantt	1793	A1-1	227	314
Lingan, James M., of G'tn.	Deed fr	Magruder, Charles, of G'tn.	1794	B2A	055	069
Lingan, James M. et al	Deed to	Beall, Thomas, of George	1795	B2A	166	222
Lingan, James M., of G'tn.	Deed fr	Bayly, William	1795	B2A	192	261
Lingan, James M., of G'tn.	Deed to	Jones, John Courts, Charles Co.	1796	B2B	428	104
Lingan, James M., of G'tn.	Deed to	Eno, Edward, of G'tn.	1797	C3	185	156
Lingan, James M., of G'tn.	Deed fr	Threlkeld, John, of G'tn.	1797	C3	004	3
Lingan, James M. et al	Deed to	Davidson, Samuel	1797	B2B	613	369
Lingan, James M. et al	Deed fr	Davidson, Samuel	1797	B2B	614	370
Lingan, James M., of G'tn.	Deed to	Faw, Abraham, of Alexa.	1799	D4	263	248
Lingan, James M., of G'tn.	Deed fr	Commissioners of Washington	1799	D4	392	373
Lingan, James M., of G'tn.	Deed to	Rae, John	1799	D4	176	157
Lingan, James M.	Deed fr	Forrrest, Uriah	1801	G7	290	403
Lingan, James M., of G'tn.	Deed to	Williams, Thomas O.	1801	G7	422	557
Lingan, James M.	Deed fr	Threlkeld, John	1802	I9	587	951
Lingan, James M. et al	Deed fr	Forrest, Uriah	1802	I9	075	106
Lingan, James M.	Deed to	Knowles, William	1802	I9	414	686
Lingan, James M.	Deed to	Threlkeld, John	1802	I9	566	917
Lingan, James M.	Deed fr	McCubbin, Thomas	1804	L11	042	42
Lingan, James M.	Deed to	Foxall, Henry	1804	L11	005	5
Lingan, James M. et al	Deed to	Parrott, Richard	1804	K10	369	382
Lingan, James M. et al	Deed to	Parrott, Richard	1805	N13	218	187
Lingan, James M.	Deed to	Mechlin, Joseph [Mecklin]	1806	Q16	226	154
Lingan, James M.	Deed fr	Murdock, John	1806	O14	157	102
Lingan, James M.	Deed fr	Hewitt, John	1806	Q16	328	252
Lingan, James M., of Montg. Co.	Deed to	Smith, Walter	1807	S18	340	267
Lingan, James M., now of G'tn.	Deed to	Bank of Columbia	1807	R17	380	289
Lingan, James M.	Deed to	Smith, Walter	1807	S18	361	285
Lingan, James M., of Mont. Co.	Deed to	Munroe, Thomas, Supt.	1808	T19	019	015
Lingan, James M.	Agreement	Hyde, Thomas	1809	V21	288	208
Lingan, James M., of Montg. Co.	Deed to	Worthington, William	1809	X23	082	061
Lingan, James M., of Montg. Co.	Deed to	Cope, Israel, of Balto.	1809	X23	051	038
Lingan, James M., of Montg. Co.	Deed to	Henderson, Sarah	1809	X23	198	149
Lingan, James M., of Montg. Co.	Deed to	Jones, Walter, Jr.	1809	X23	106	077
Lingan, James M., of Montg. Co.	Deed to	Foxall, Henry	1810	Y24	195	179
Lingan, James M., of Montg. Co.	Deed to	Holmead, John	1810	Y24	177	163
Lingan, James M., of Montg. Co.	Deed to	Worthington, Charles	1810	Y24	164	149
Lingan, James M., of Montg. Co.	Deed to	Meem, Peter, of G'tn.	1811	AB27	426	351
Lingan, James M.	Convey to	Crown, Trueman	1814	AH33	235	205
Lingan, James Maccubbin, of G'tn.	Deed fr	O'Neall, Bernard, of MD	1795	B2A	268	375
Lingan, James Maccubbin	Deed to	Burnes, David	1796	B2B	580	325
Lingan, James Maccubbin, of G'tn.	Deed fr	Reid, James, of G'tn.	1796	B2B	503	203
Lingan, James Maccubbin, of G'tn.	Deed to	Mason, George, of Fairfax Co. VA	1796	B2B	585	332
Lingan, James Maccubbin	Deed fr	Deakins, Francis	1798	C3	485	382

Index to District of Columbia Land Records, 1792-1817

Party	What	Party	Year	Liber	Old	New
Lingan, James Maccubbin, of G'tn.	Mortgage fr	Polock, Isaac	1799	D4	365	351
Lingan, James Maccubbin, of G'tn.	Deed fr	Beall, Thomas & John Peter, G'tn.	1800	F6	001	001
Lingan, James Maccubbin, of G'tn.	Deed to	Bullus, John, M.D.	1802	H8	309	292
Lingan, James Maccubbin	Deed to	Caldwell, Timothy	1802	H8	572	536
Lingan, James Maccubbin	Deed to	Coombe, Benjamin	1802	H8	579	543
Lingan, James Maccubbin, of G'tn.	Deed to	Mechlin, Joseph	1802	H8	306	288
Lingan, James Maccubbin	Deed to	King, George	1802	I9	080	114
Lingan, James Maccubbin	Deed fr	Beall, Thomas, of George	1802	H8	319	300
Lingan, James Maccubbin et al	Deed to	Mayor & Council of Georgetown	1807	R17	232	
Lingan, James Maccubbin, of MD	Deed to	Threlkeld, John	1811	AB27	104	085
Lingan, James Macubbin, of G'tn.	Deed to	Templeman, John, Esq., of Boston	1793	A1-1	200	281
Lingan, James Macubbin, of G'tn.	Deed to	Smith, Samuel, of Balto.	1799	E5	035	025
Lingan, James Macubbin, of G'tn.	Deed to	Bayly, William	1800	E5	079	066
Lingan, James Macubbin, of G'tn.	Deed to	Knowles, William	1800	E5	141	129
Lingan, James Macubbin, of G'tn.	Deed to	Caldwell, Timothy	1805	M12	396	409
Lingan, James Macubin, Montg.	Deed to	Hyde, Thomas	1809	V21	286	206
Lingan, James McCubbin	Deed to	Beall, Thomas & John M. Gantt	1792	A1-1	022	34
Lingan, James McCubbin, of G'tn.	Deed to	Beatty, Thomas J.	1795	B2A	194	263
Lingan, James McCubbin, of G'tn.	Deed to	Hodgson, Joseph et al	1797	C3	018	14
Lingan, James McCubbin	Deed to	Polock, Isaac	1800	E5	105	093
Lingan, James McCubbin	Deed fr	Dorsey, Joshua, of Frederick	1801	G7	235	315
Lingan, James McCubbin	Deed to	Loring, Isaac	1801	G7	200	267
Lingan, James McCubbin, of G'tn.	Deed fr	Bayly, Mountjoy, Gen., Frederick	1801	G7	234	313
Lingan, John McCubbin	Deed to	Dennis, John & Samuel Wilson	1801	G7	118	152
Lingan, Nicholas	Deed fr	Beall, Thomas, of George	1796	B2B	441	122
Lingan, Nicholas	Deed fr	Beall, Thomas, of George	1801	F6	157	098
Lingan, Nicholas	Deed to	[ ], Dick & Polly (Negroes)	1802	H8	581	546
Lingan, Nicholas	Manumis to	[ ], Dick & Polly (negro)	1807	R17	174	133
Lingan, Nicholas et al	Receipt fr	Moore, James	1807	S18	376	299
Lingan, Nicholas et al	Manumis to	[ ], Henny (C)	1812	AB27	481	394
Lingan, Nicholas, mer.	Deed fr	Beatty, Charles, of G'tn.	1795	B2A	173	233
Lingan, Nicholas, of G'tn.	Deed fr	Beatty, Thomas, Jr., of G'tn.	1795	B2A	202	276
Lingan, Nicholas, of Montg. Co.	Deed fr	Queen, Joseph & James Simpson	1796	B2B	400	065
Lingan, Nicholas, of P.G. Co.	Deed to	Polock, Isaac, of G'tn.	1798	C3	372	297
Lingan, Nicholas, of G'tn.	Deed to	Craig, Robert, of G'tn.	1802	H8	410	379
Lingan, Nicholas, of Montg. Co.	Deed fr	Scott, Gustavus, of Montg. Co.	1805	N13	183	164
Lingan, Nicholas, of G'tn.	Deed fr	Reintzel, Anthony, of G'tn.	1806	Q16	122	079
Lingan, Nicholas, of G'tn.	Deed fr	Dorsey, William H., of G'tn.	1807	Q16	333	256
Lingan, Nicholas, of G'tn.	Deed to	Morgan, William, of G'tn.	1808	T19	345	250
Lingan, Nicholas, of G'tn.	Deed fr	Morgan, William, of G'tn.	1808	T19	304	222
Lingan, Nicholas, of G'tn.	Deed fr	Turner, Thomas, of G'tn.	1808	U20	020	012
Lingan, Nicholas, of G'tn.	Deed to	Jones, Edward, of G'tn.	1810	Z25	195	153
Lingan, Nicholas, of G'tn.	Deed to	Dodge, Francis, of G'tn.	1811	Z25	393	308
Lingan, Nicholas, of G'tn.	Deed to	Smith, Clement, of G'tn.	1811	AB27	438	361
Lingan, Nicholas, of G'tn.	Mortgage fr	Jones, Edward, of G'tn.	1811	Z25	453	358
Lingenfelter, Abraham, of PA	Deed to	Ham, Peter	1793	A1-1	240	328
Lingenfelter, Ann, wid/o John	Deed to	Beall, Thomas & John M. Gantt	1792	A1-1	088	129
Lingenfelter, John, Frederick Co.	Deed fr	Lingenfelter, Michael, Fredk. Co.	1798	C3	351	282
Lingenfelter, John, of Fredk. Co.	Deed to	Hoffman, John, of Fredk. Co.	1811	AB27	078	065
Lingenfelter, Michael, Fredk. Co.	Deed to	Lingenfelter, John, Frederick Co.	1798	C3	351	282
Link, Adam & Jane, Jefferson Co.	Deed to	Thompson, John C. et al	1811	AB27	128	105
Link, Adam, of Frederick Co.	Deed fr	Davidson, John, of Annapolis	1800	E5	267	261
Link, Adam, of Jefferson Co. VA	Partition	Link, Thomas, of Frederick Co.	1807	R17	181	138
Link, Adam, Sr., of Frederick Co.	Deed to	Murdock, George, Frederick Co.	1794	B2A	069	089
Link, Daniel, of Frederick Co.	Deed to	Link, George, of Frederick Co.	1807	R17	402	304

Party	What	Party	Year	Liber	Old	New
Link, George	Deed to	Lutz, John	1808	U20	116	066
Link, George, of Frederick Co.	Deed fr	Link, Daniel, of Frederick Co.	1807	R17	402	304
Link, George, s/o Adam et al	Partition	Link, Daniel, s/o Adam et al	1807	R17	181	138
Link, Thomas	Deed to	Lutz, John	1810	Z25	194	153
Link, Thomas, of Frederick Co.	Partition	Link, Adam, of Jefferson Co. VA	1807	R17	181	138
Link, Thomas, of MD	Deed to	Lutz, John	1810	Z25	080	060
Linkins, Henry, of G'tn.	Deed fr	Linkins, Thomas, of G'tn.	1809	X23	313	252
Linkins, Henry, of G'tn.	Deed to	Pickerel, John, of G'tn.	1813	AF31	001	001
Linkins, James, of G'tn.	Deed fr	Wirt, John, of G'tn.	1808	U20	074	041
Linkins, James, of G'tn.	Deed fr	Foxall, Henry, of G'tn.	1816	AL36	292	290
Linkins, Thomas, of G'tn.	Deed to	Linkins, Henley, of G'tn.	1809	X23	313	252
Linn, Philip, of Frederick Co.	Deed to	Dulaney, Matthew, of G'tn.	1804	K10	179	188
Linscott, Edward	B. of S. fr	Antrim, Parnell	1809	V21	214	151
Lipscomb, John & J. Pickrell	Lease fr	Renner, Daniel	1815	AI34	093	106
Lipscomb, John, of G'tn.	Deed fr	Beall, Thomas B.	1809	X23	167	123
Lipscomb, John, of G'tn.	D. of T. fr	Quabbs, William, of G'tn.	1811	AA26	006	004
Lipscomb, John, of G'tn.	Deed fr	Fields, William, of G'tn.	1812	AC28	140	105
Lipscomb, John, of G'tn.	Deed fr	McDaniel, James (C), of G'tn.	1813	AE30	065	049
Lipscomb, John, of G'tn.	Cert fr	Munroe, Thomas, Supt.	1817	AN38	079	062
Lipscomb, John, of G'tn.	Manumis to	[ ], Bill (C)	1817	AN38	402	300
Lipscomb, John, of G'tn.	Deed to	Lipscomb, William C., of G'tn.	1817	AN38	081	063
Lipscomb, John, of G'tn.	Deed fr	Bruner, Jacob & Eleanor	1817	AN38	082	064
Lipscomb, John, of G'tn.	Deed fr	Pickrell, John, of G'tn.	1817	AN38	079	062
Lipscomb, John, of G'tn.	Deed to	Mackall, Benjamin F., of G'tn.	1817	AN38	166	121
Lipscomb, John, of G'tn.	Deed to	Grimes, Alice, of Montg. Co.	1817	AO39	440	301
Lipscomb, William C., of G'tn.	Deed fr	Lipscomb, John, of G'tn.	1817	AN38	081	063
Lipscomb, William C., of G'tn.	Deed fr	Davis, Charles B. et al	1817	AN38	085	066
Lipscomb, William Curry	Deed fr	Waters, Thomas G.	1815	AK35	379	299
Lisle, John, of Phila. et al	Deed to	Brooke, Samuel	1811	AB27	264	216
Litle, John	Deed to	Nourse, Michael	1810	Z25	217	171
Litle, John, plt.	Suit	Sutton, Robert & Catharine, def.	1809	V21	178	128
Little, Israel	Slaves	From Charles Co. MD	1804	K10	226	
Little, Israel	B. of S. to	Bryan, Wilson	1806	O14	352	235
Little, Israel	Deed to	Middleton, James	1806	P15	328	217
Little, Israel	B. of S. to	Pumfrey, James, of P.G. Co.	1806	P15	192	129
Little, Israel	Lease fr	Kerr, Alexander	1806	O14	253	167
Little, Israel	Lease to	Brady, Nathaniel	1808	T19	210	152
Little, Israel	Assign to	Brady, Nathaniel	1811	AB27	065	056
Little, Israel	Deed fr	Laird, John, exr. of J. Carleton	1814	AG32	172	122
Little, Israel	Deed to	Perry, Caleb, of P.G. Co.	1817	AN38	006	005
Littlejohn, Alexander S.	Lease fr	Hoban, James	1817	AN38	547	398
Littler, Nathan, Frederick Co. VA	Deed fr	Beall, Ely & Octavia, Fred. Co. VA	1806	P15	015	009
Liverpool, John, b. 26 OCT 1808	Cert Free fr	Cassin, Joseph	1817	AN38	503	363
Liverpool, Louisa, b. 22 DEC 1809	Cert Free fr	Cassin, Joseph	1817	AN38	503	363
Liverpool, Moses	Lease fr	Prout, William	1806	Q16	131	086
Liverpool, Moses	Deed fr	Spooner, William	1807	T19	003	002
Liverpool, Moses & George Beall	Deed to	Adams, Henry & Nicholas Franklin	1810	Y24	301	274
Liverpool, Moses & George Beall	Deed to	Franklin, Nicholas	1814	AG32	165	118
Liverpool, Moses, b. 25 JAN 1801	Cert Free fr	Cassin, Joseph	1817	AN38	503	363
Liverpool, Sophia, b. 7 NOV 1802	Cert Free fr	Cassin, Joseph	1817	AN38	503	363
Liverpoole, Moses & George Beall	Deed fr	Chandler, Jacob	1810	Y24	068	061
Livers, Anthony	Release fr	Corcoran, Thomas & Thos. Hyde	1812	AD29	080	059
Livers, Anthony et al	Deed fr	Mason, John Thomson et al	1801	G7	463	599
Livers, Anthony, Jr.	Deed to	Hyde, Thomas	1812	AD29	079	058
Livers, Anthony, of G'tn.	Mortgage to	Corcoran, Thomas et al	1801	G7	466	603

Party	What	Party	Year	Liber	Old	New
Livers, Anthony, of G'tn.	Deed fr	Rigdon, Thomas, admr. of T., G'tn.	1809	W22	067	050
Livers, Ignatious	B. of S. fr	Miller, Jacob, of Frederick Co.	1808	T19	315	230
Livers, Ignatius	Lease fr	Heater, Conrad	1805	M12	108	101
Livers, Ignatius	Deed fr	Deakins, Leonard M. & John Hoye	1812	AD29	398	335
Livers, Ignatius, of G'tn.	Deed fr	Heeter, Conrad, Indiana Co. PA	1807	R17	221	166
Livers, Ignatius, of G'tn.	D. of T. to	King, Adam, of G'tn.	1810	Y24	519	456
Livers, Ignatius, of G'tn.	Deed to	Wilson, John, of Hy., of P.G. Co.	1812	AD29	121	093
Livers, Ignatius, of G'tn.	Deed fr	King, Adam, of G'tn.	1812	AC28	398	289
Livers, Ignatius, of G'tn.	Lease fr	Robertson, Joseph, of G'tn.	1814	AH33	068	061
Livres,. Ignatius, of G'tn.	Deed to	Gantt, William V., of G'tn. et al	1816	AM37	007	006
Lloyd, James, of Boston MA	Agreement	Webster, Daniel, of Occoquan VA	1810	Z25	107	083
Lloyd, William A., of Fredk. Town	Deed to	Young, Sarah H., of North. Co. PA	1814	AH33	249	216
Lockerman, John	Ship List	Stull, John J. & John S. Williams	1817	AN38	143	105
Lockwood, Levi	B. of S. to	Smith, Henry	1807	S18	394	314
Lodge, William, Montg. Co. et al	Deed fr	Mountz, Jacob, collector, of G'tn.	1811	AB27	008	009
Lodge, William, of Montg. Co.	Deed to	Smith, Clement, of G'tn.	1811	AB27	001	003
Logan, George W.	Deed fr	Bird, Alice	1812	AD29	535	451
Long, Frederick	B. of S. to	Kendelback, Andrew, of G'tn.	1801	G7	180	240
Long, Frederick	Assign to	Kendelback, Andrew, of G'tn.	1801	G7	178	238
Long, Frederick	Deed fr	Templeman, John, of G'tn.	1801	G7	040	051
Long, Frederick	Deed fr	Templeman, John	1805	M12	177	178
Long, Frederick	Deed to	Nourse, Michael	1806	Q16	194	130
Long, Frederick	Release fr	Bank of Columbia	1808	U20	298	159
Long, James, of G'tn.	Deed fr	Riley, William	1801	G7	010	012
Long, John	Convey to	King, George	1808	T19	144	103
Long, John, hatter, of G'tn.	Deed fr	Beatty, Charles, of G'tn.	1797	C3	110	90
Long, John, insolvent	B. of S. to	Joncherez, Alexander L., trustee	1808	T19	201	144
Long, John, of G'tn.	Deed to	Merriken, John et al	1799	D4	209	192
Long, John, of G'tn.	Deed fr	Beall, Elijah, of Loudoun Co. VA	1808	T19	148	104
Long, Robert	Assign fr	Boyert, P.C.F.	1811	AC28	048	036
Long, Robert	Assign to	Varden, Charles	1812	AD29	315	258
Long, Robert & James Johnston	B. of S. fr	Boyert, P.C.F.	1811	AC28	046	034
Long, Robert, insolvent debtor	Deed to	McCormick, Alexander, trustee	1812	AD29	312	256
Long, Robert, tavern keeper, et al	Deed to	Young, James, trustee	1813	AE30	094	072
Longden, John et al	Deed to	Whann, William, of Montg. Co.	1796	B2B	551	279
Longden, Susan, admx. of Abel	Assign to	Spalding, John	1813	AF31	230	159
Longdon, Abel	Lease fr	Prout, William	1805	M12	262	263
Longdon, Anne, of G'tn. et al	Deed to	Lipscomb, William C., of G'tn.	1817	AN38	085	066
Longley, Walker G.	Deed fr	Osborn, Archibald	1802	H8	358	334
Loockerman, John	D. of T. fr	Stull, John J. & John S. Williams	1817	AN38	130	096
Loring, Isaac	Deed fr	Lingan, James McCubbin	1801	G7	200	267
Loring, Isaac	Deed to	Burrows, William W.	1801	G7	199	266
Loring, Israel	B. of S. to	Thompson, James	1802	H8	472	433
Loring, Israel	Release fr	Burrows, William E.	1802	H8	508	467
Loring, Israel	Deed to	Johnston, Thomas, of Balto. MD	1802	H8	569	532
Loring, Israel	Mortgage to	Wadsworth, Charles	1802	I9	075	105
Loring, Israel	Deed to	Chandler, Walter	1802	I9	417	691
Loring, Israel	Mortgage to	Eliason, Ebenezer	1802	I9	193	301
Loring, Israel	Mortgage to	Chandler, Walter S., of G'tn.	1802	I9	049	066
Loring, Israel	B. of S. to	May, Frederick	1802	I9	190	294
Lorman, William	Deed fr	Walker, Mary, of Balto.	1817	AO39	121	093
Lorman, William, of Balto.	Deed fr	Sands, Louis, of NY	1802	H8	098	090
Lorman, William, of Balto. et al	Deed fr	Bussard, Daniel, of G'tn.	1810	X23	327	261
Lorman, William, of Balto.	Deed fr	Crawford, William, of G'tn.	1816	AM37	286	209
Lorman, William, of Balto.	Deed fr	Crawford, William, of G'tn.	1816	AM37	288	211

Party	What	Party	Year	Liber	Old	New
Lorman, William, of Balto.	Deed fr	Walker, Archibald, heirs of	1817	AO39	117	090
Loundes, Charles	Deed to	Smith, Walker	1802	I9	199	310
Loundes, Charles	Deed to	Smith, Walter	1802	I9	285	466
Loundes, Charles	Deed to	Gantt, Thomas	1802	I9	266	431
Loundes, Charles	Deed to	Tool, Patrick	1802	I9	331	545
Loundes, Charles, of G'tn.	Deed fr	Polock, Isaac	1802	G7	530	675
Loundes, Charles, of G'tn.	Mortgage fr	Polock, Isaac	1802	G7	533	678
Loundes, Francis	Deed to	Stoddert, Benjamin	1805	M12	336	340
Loundes, Francis	Deed to	Bowie, Washington	1809	W22	411	267
Loundes, Francis & Charles, G'tn.	Deed to	Templeman, John, of G'tn.	1800	E5	381	360
Loundes, Richard T.	Deed fr	Turner, Samuel	1802	I9	259	418
Loundes, Richard T.	Deed to	Peter, David et al	1805	M12	343	349
Lounds, Charles	Deed to	Smith, Walter	1802	I9	540	880
Louwdes, Richard T., of MD	Deed fr	Lowndes, Francis	1802	H8	448	412
Love, Charles	Discharge	Bankruptcy	1802	H8	042	040
Love, Charles	B. of S. to	Cox, John, merchant	1804	L11	017	17
Love, Charles	Deed fr	Browning, Joseph	1806	Q16	072	045
Love, Charles & Ann, of G'tn.	Deed to	Janney, Thomas, of Alexa.	1806	Q16	266	154
Love, Charles I.	Deed to	Wingard, Abraham	1801	G7	198	264
Love, Charles, of G'tn.	Deed fr	Doughty, William, of G'tn.	1806	P15	137	089
Love, Charles, of G'tn.	Deed to	Raborg, William et al	1806	P15	135	088
Love, Charles, of G'tn.	Deed to	Waters, William	1807	Q16	372	285
Love, John	Deed to	Kain, Patrick	1813	AE30	182	145
Love, John	D. of T. fr	Burford, John A.	1813	AF31	050	034
Love, John & Patrick Kain	Deed fr	May, Frederick, physician	1808	V21	119	088
Love, John & Patrick Kain	Deed fr	May, Frederick	1810	Y24	090	081
Love, Sarah	Deed fr	Beall, Thomas, of George	1805	M12	374	384
Love, Sarah	B. of S. to	Whann, William	1810	Y24	321	291
Love, Sarah	Deed to	Burke, John	1816	AL36	105	106
Love, Sarah, gdn. of Henry	Slaves	From Fairfax Co. VA	1815	AH33	411	355
Lovejoy, Alexander	Deed to	Halsey, Henry	1804	L11	149	150
Lovejoy, John N., of G'tn.	B. of S. to	Blake, James H., Dr.	1802	H8	437	401
Lovejoy, Samuel	Convey to	Halzall, of P.G. Co.	1808	T19	119	084
Loveless, William	Deed fr	Sparrow, John W.	1813	AE30	401	296
Lovell, William	Deed fr	Hoban, James	1800	F6	042	027
Lovell, William	Deed fr	Commissioners of Washington	1801	G7		539
Lovell, William	Deed fr	Commissioners of Washington	1801	G7	404	537
Lovell, William	Deed fr	Stoddert, Benjamin, of G'tn.	1801	G7	443	579
Lovell, William	Deed fr	Commissioners of Washington	1801	G7		010
Lovell, William	Deed fr	Commissioners of Washington	1801	G7		538
Lovell, William	Lease to	Gardner, John	1802	G7	583	732
Lovell, William	Deed to	Munroe, Thomas	1802	H8	434	399
Lovell, William	Deed to	Willis, John	1802	H8	164	158
Lovell, William	Deed to	Burford, Henry	1802	H8	161	155
Lovell, William	Mortgage to	Orr, Benjamin G.	1802	H8	295	279
Lovell, William	Deed to	King, Adam, of G'tn.	1802	H8	517	476
Lovell, William	Deed fr	Carroll, Daniel, of Duddington	1802	H8	568	531
Lovell, William	Deed fr	Murdock, John	1802	H8	571	534
Lovell, William	Mortgage to	Webster, Toppan	1802	H8	402	372
Lovell, William	Lease to	Andrews, George	1802	H8	281	266
Lovell, William	Deed to	Andrews, George	1802	I9	057	078
Lovell, William	Deed to	Given, Thomas	1802	I9	079	112
Lovell, William	Lease to	Hoban, James	1802	I9	211	331
Lovell, William	Deed fr	Orr, Benjamin G.	1802	I9	423	701
Lovell, William	Deed to	Thorn, Christopher	1802	I9	332	547

Index to District of Columbia Land Records, 1792-1817 255

Party	What	Party	Year	Liber	Old	New
Lovell, William	Lease to	Beall, Thomas K.	1802	I9	503	825
Lovell, William	Deed to	Clarke, Joseph	1802	I9	168	256
Lovell, William	Deed to	Underwood, Robert	1802	I9	547	890
Lovell, William	Deed to	Orr, Benjamin G.	1802	I9	408	677
Lovell, William	Release fr	Orr, Benjamin G.	1802	I9	224	356
Lovell, William	Deed to	Langley, Edward	1802	I9	011	015
Lovell, William	Convey to	Reed, Alexander	1803	K10	081	88
Lovell, William	Deed to	Lovering, William, of Alexa.	1804	L11	406	361
Lovell, William	Deed to	Harbaugh, Samuel	1804	K10	380	394
Lovell, William	Deed to	Shoemaker, David	1804	L11	025	24
Lovell, William	B. of S. to	Lovering, William, of Alexa.	1805	M12	176	176
Lovell, William	Deed to	Wheaton, Joseph	1805	M12	241	243
Lovell, William	Manumis to	[ ], Forrester (Negro)	1805	M12	048	046
Lovell, William et al	Deed to	Dorsey, William H. et al	1802	I9	364	604
Lovell, William, of Alexa.	Deed to	Hellen, Walter	1801	G7	445	581
Lovell, William, of Alexa.	Deed to	Given, Thomas	1802	H8	337	315
Lovell, William, of Balto.	Assign to	Webster, Toppan	1806	P15	086	052
Lovell, William, of Balto.	Deed to	Webster, Toppan & Lewis Ford	1807	R17	075	061
Lovell, William, of Balto.	D. of T. to	Webster, Toppan	1809	W22	222	151
Lovell, William, of Balto.	Deed fr	Lovering, William, of Balto. et al	1811	Z25	467	370
Lovell, William, Sr., of Balto.	Mortgage fr	Lovering, Susannah, Balto. et al	1814	AH33	112	104
Lovely, John V.	B. of S. fr	Chester, Samuel	1811	AA26	183	125
Lovely, William, of Balto. MD	Deed to	Randall, John, of Balto. MD	1813	AE30	067	051
Lovering, Charles Fox, s/o Wm.	Deed fr	Davidson, Samuel	1801	G7	364	496
Lovering, Charles Fox, of Phila.	Deed to	Natt, Thomas, of Phila.	1817	AO39	517	356
Lovering, Susannah, Balto. et al	Mortgage to	Lovell, William, Sr., of Balto.	1814	AH33	112	104
Lovering, William	Deed to	Darnall, John	1800	E5	393	368
Lovering, William	Deed fr	Densley, Hugh	1804	L11	099	101
Lovering, William	B. of S. to	Hughs, Thomas	1811	AA26	091	064
Lovering, William & Susannah et al	Deed to	Rowles, Joseph E., of G'tn.	1809	X23	067	050
Lovering, William & Sarah	Deed to	Potts, John	1817	AO39	372	251
Lovering, William, architect	Agreement	Nicholson & Prentiss	1797	B2B	622	380
Lovering, William, of Alexa.	Deed to	McDono, William	1804	L11	384	342
Lovering, William, of Alexa.	Deed fr	Lovell, William	1804	L11	406	361
Lovering, William, of Alexa.	B. of S. fr	Lovell, William	1805	M12	176	176
Lovering, William, of Balto.	Deed to	Webster, Toppan & Lewis Ford	1809	W22	101	073
Lovering, William, of Balto. et al	Deed to	Lovell, William, of Balto.	1811	Z25	467	370
Low, Andrew et al	Deed to	Beall, Thomas & John M. Gantt	1792	A1-1	102	148
Low, Andrew, of Frederick Co.	Deed to	French, George, of Montg. Co.	1796	B2B	394	056
Low, Nicholas, of P.G. Co.	Deed to	Watterston, David	1807	S18	315	247
Lowe, Barbara	B. of S. to	Claggett, Hezekiah, of Balto. Co.	1813	AE30	367	272
Lowe, Elizabeth & Henrietta	B. of S. fr	Lowe, Michael	1809	V21	398	301
Lowe, Enoch M.	D. of T. fr	Leonard, Jacob	1816	AM37	074	060
Lowe, Henry H.	D. of T. to	Magruder, Dennis, of P.G. Co.	1810	Y24	081	072
Lowe, Henry H. et al	B. of S. fr	Finigan, Rosannah	1816	AM37	145	112
Lowe, John W.	Deed fr	Law, John	1810	X23	356	285
Lowe, Lloyd Magruder	Deed fr	McClelland, John	1815	AI34	466	478
Lowe, Loyd M.	D. of T. to	McClelland, John	1815	AI34	379	406
Lowe, Martha	B. of S. to	Mattingly, Margaret	1816	AL36	299	296
Lowe, Michael	B. of S. to	Lowe, Elizabeth & Henrietta	1809	V21	398	301
Lowe, Michael	Bond	Tobacco Inspector	1810	Y24	331	300
Lowe, Michael et al	B. of S. fr	Cooper, John	1807	S18	047	039
Lowe, Michael, inspector	Bond to	Corporation of Washington	1809	W22	079	059
Lowe, Nicholas	Manumis to	[ ], Patty & children Kitty & Henry	1802	H8	555	517
Lowe, Samuel P.	Slaves	From Fairfax Co. VA	1804	K10	222	

Party	What	Party	Year	Liber	Old	New
Lower, Christian & Barbara	Deed to	Forrest, Uriah & Benj. Stoddert	1792	A1-1	151	217
Lowery, Caesar, of G'tn.	Deed fr	Johnson, Thomas, Frederick Co.	1800	F6	033	021
Lowndes, Ann, of Bladensburg	Deed fr	Lowndes, Francis, of G'tn.	1814	AH33	206	186
Lowndes, Anne, Bladensburgh	Deed fr	Lowndes, Francis, of G'tn.	1804	L11	382	341
Lowndes, Charles	Deed fr	Forrest, Uriah	1802	I9	075	106
Lowndes, Charles, Jefferson Co.	Agreement	Stoddert, Benjamin	1807	S18	112	
Lowndes, Charles, Jefferson Co.	Deed to	Stoddert, Benjamin	1807	R17	328	249
Lowndes, Charles, Jefferson Co.	Deed to	Lowndes, Francis	1808	T19	122	086
Lowndes, Charles, Jefferson Co.	Deed to	Lowndes, Francis	1808	T19	120	085
Lowndes, Charles, of G'tn.	Deed fr	Polock, Isaac	1802	H8	515	474
Lowndes, Charles, of G'tn.	Deed fr	Templeman, John, of G'tn.	1802	I9	079	111
Lowndes, Francis	Deed fr	Beall, Thomas, of George	1794	B2A	019	019
Lowndes, Francis	Deed to	Lowndes, Richard T., of MD	1802	H8	448	412
Lowndes, Francis	Deed fr	Blodget, Samuel	1802	H8	012	011
Lowndes, Francis	Deed to	Peter, Thomas	1805	M12	379	390
Lowndes, Francis	Deed fr	Lowndes, Charles, Jefferson Co.	1808	T19	122	086
Lowndes, Francis	Deed fr	Lowndes, Charles, Jefferson Co.	1808	T19	120	085
Lowndes, Francis	Deed to	Nourse, Charles J.	1810	Y24	211	194
Lowndes, Francis & Charles	Deed to	Deakins, Francis	1800	E5	351	336
Lowndes, Francis & Charles	Deed to	Bayly, William	1800	E5	237	230
Lowndes, Francis & Charles et al	Deed fr	Templeman, John	1802	H8	375	349
Lowndes, Francis & Charles	Deed to	Johns, Richard & Leonard H.	1804	K10	187	196
Lowndes, Francis & Jane, of G'tn.	Deed to	Bank of Columbia	1817	AN38	300	219
Lowndes, Francis et al	Deed to	Smith, Walter	1807	S18	343	270
Lowndes, Francis et al	Deed to	Smith, Walter	1807	S18	354	275
Lowndes, Francis et al	Deed to	Stoddert, Benjamin	1807	S18	359	
Lowndes, Francis et al	Deed to	Stoddert, Benjamin	1807	S18	341	268
Lowndes, Francis, Jr.	Deed to	Lowndes, Jane, w/o Francis, Sr.	1812	AC28	292	212
Lowndes, Francis, Jr.	Deed fr	Lowndes, Francis, Sr.	1812	AC28	290	210
Lowndes, Francis, of G'tn.	Deed to	Goszler, George	1802	I9	078	110
Lowndes, Francis, of G'tn.	Lease to	Thomson, George, of G'tn.	1804	K10	396	411
Lowndes, Francis, of G'tn.	Deed to	Lowndes, Anne, Bladensburgh	1804	L11	382	341
Lowndes, Francis, of G'tn.	Deed to	Hodges, Thomas Clagett, G'tn.	1804	L11	038	37
Lowndes, Francis, of Montg. Co.	Manumis to	Thompson, Semus	1805	M12	366	375
Lowndes, Francis, of G'tn.	Deed to	Swann, Thomas, of Alexa.	1810	Z25	144	114
Lowndes, Francis, of G'tn.	Deed to	Magruder, Ninian, Dr., of G'tn.	1812	AD29	066	047
Lowndes, Francis, of G'tn.	Deed to	Lowndes, Ann, of Bladensburg	1814	AH33	206	186
Lowndes, Francis, Sr.	Release fr	Nourse, Charles J.	1811	AC28	084	064
Lowndes, Francis, Sr.	Deed to	Lowndes, Francis, Jr.	1812	AC28	290	210
Lowndes, Francis, trustee	Deed to	McCleary, Henry	1802	H8	352	328
Lowndes, Jane, w/o Francis, Sr.	Deed fr	Lowndes, Francis, Jr.	1812	AC28	292	212
Lowry, Caesar	Deed fr	Stoddert, Benjamin	1802	I9	422	699
Lowry, Caesar	Deed fr	Hodgson, Joseph	1805	M12	364	372
Lowry, Caesar	B. of S. fr	Andrews, Benjamin	1805	N13	101	094
Lowry, Caesar et al	Lease fr	Threlkeld, John	1799	D4	173	154
Lowry, Caesar, of G'tn.	Lease fr	Hodgson, Joseph	1802	H8	502	462
Lowry, Caesar, of G'tn.	Deed fr	Balch, Stephen B., of G'tn.	1802	H8	500	460
Lowry, Ceasar, of G'tn.	Assign to	Lowry, William, of Alexa.	1802	H8	314	295
Lowry, Ceasar, of G'tn.	Deed fr	Stoddert, Benjamin, of G'tn.	1802	H8	487	448
Lowry, Ceasar, of G'tn.	Deed to	Bain, Quinton, of G'tn.	1802	H8	222	212
Lowry, Cesar, heirs of	Deed to	Dawes, Isaac	1810	Z25	068	051
Lowry, John	Deed to	Smoot, Samuel, of G'tn.	1817	AN38	042	034
Lowry, Mary or Cooper	Deed fr	Threlkeld, John	1810	Z25	244	191
Lowry, Mary [John]	Deed fr	Corporation of Washington	1815	AI34	417	439
Lowry, William, of Alexa.	Assign fr	Lowry, Ceasar, of G'tn.	1802	H8	314	295

Index to District of Columbia Land Records, 1792-1817   257

Party	What	Party	Year	Liber	Old	New
Lucas, Bennet, of G'tn.	Deed fr	Deakins, Leonard M. et al	1807	S18	062	051
Lucas, Bennett	Deed fr	Deakins, Francis, exors. of	1809	V21	247	176
Lucas, Henry	Deed to	Huter, Conrad	1795	B2A	168	224
Lucas, Henry	Deed to	Sanford, Hector	1802	I9	420	696
Lucas, Henry	Deed fr	Threlkeld, John	1804	K10	156	167
Lucas, Henry	Deed to	Smith, Jesse	1807	R17	143	110
Lucas, Henry	Deed to	Labille, Louis	1808	U20	370	203
Lucas, Henry	Deed to	Heise, Christian, of G'tn.	1809	X23	158	116
Lucas, Henry	D. of T. to	Hollingshead, John, of G'tn.	1809	X23	223	172
Lucas, Henry	Deed to	Hollingshead, John	1811	Z25	498	395
Lucas, Henry	Deed to	Smith, Jesse	1812	AD29	250	207
Lucas, Henry	Deed to	King, Vincent	1813	AF31	534	394
Lucas, Henry	Deed to	Renner, Daniel, of G'tn.	1816	AL36	480	452
Lucas, Henry, of G'tn.	Deed to	Bowman, John B., of G'tn.	1795	B2A	250	349
Lucas, Henry, of G'tn.	Deed fr	Beall, Thomas, of George, G'tn.	1795	B2B	354	001
Lucas, Henry, of G'tn.	Deed to	Threlkeld, John	1808	T19	234	172
Lucas, Ignatius	Deed fr	Holmead, Susanna et al	1805	M12	401	415
Lucas, Ignatius	Cert Free to	Dempsie, Lavinia, alias Cooper	1813	AE30	190	152
Lucas, Ignatius	Deed to	Way, Andrew, Jr.	1816	AL36	042	043
Lucas, Ignatius, s/o John	Indenture to	Lawrence, John, morocco finisher	1812	AD29	186	150
Luddington, Henry, of NY	Mortgage fr	Pratt, Carey	1801	G7	259	354
Ludlow, Daniel, mer., of NY	Deed to	Ludlow, Gulian, mer., of NY	1811	AB27	275	225
Ludlow, Daniel, of NY	Deed fr	FitzSimmons, Thomas et al	1807	Q16	217	147
Ludlow, Gulian, mer., of NY	Deed fr	Ludlow, Daniel, mer., of NY	1811	AB27	275	225
Ludwell, Bearer	Manumis fr	Lee, Richard Bland & Elizabeth	1817	AN38	125	092
Lufborough, Nathan	Deed fr	Riggs, Elisha, of G'tn.	1810	Z25	033	025
Lufborough, Nathan	D. of T. fr	Morris, Gerrard (C)	1812	AD29	261	216
Lufborough, Nathan	Release fr	French, Charles & Mariamne	1812	AD29	050	036
Lufborough, Nathan	Deed fr	Suttle, Henry, of G'tn.	1812	AD29	343	286
Lufborough, Nathan	Mortgage to	Crawford, William, of G'tn.	1812	AD29	344	288
Lufborough, Nathan	Deed to	Leonard, Jacob, of G'tn.	1813	AF31	089	060
Lufborough, Nathan	Deed to	Brown, Joel, of G'tn.	1813	AF31	082	056
Lufborough, Nathan	D. of T. fr	Morris, Gerard (C), of G'tn.	1813	AF31	145	097
Lufborough, Nathan	Release fr	Crawford, William, of G'tn.	1813	AE30	489	363
Lufborough, Nathan	Deed to	Weiskopff, Charles L., of G'tn.	1813	AE30	446	531
Lufborough, Nathan	D. of T. fr	Shepperd, Lodowick, of G'tn.	1815	AK35	408	321
Lufborough, Nathan	Deed to	Forrest, Joseph	1817	AO39	446	306
Lufborough, Nathan & Mary	Deed to	Riggs, Elisha, merchant	1802	H8	384	357
Lufborough, Nathan, of G'tn.	Mortgage fr	Bridges, John, of G'tn.	1804	K10	245	252
Lufborough, Nathan, of G'tn.	Lease to	Patterson, Benjamin, of G'tn.	1804	K10	386	401
Lufborough, Nathan, of G'tn.	Deed fr	Murdock, Addison, of G'tn.	1805	O14	098	061
Lufborough, Nathan, of G'tn.	Mortgage fr	Murdock, Addison, of G'tn.	1805	O14	101	063
Lufborough, Nathan, of Phila. PA	Deed fr	Rumsey, Jane, Wilmington DE	1807	S18	021	018
Lufborough, Nathan, of G'tn.	Deed fr	Patterson, Benjamin	1808	U20	295	157
Luffborough, Nathan	Deed fr	Williams, Edward O. et al	1801	G7	282	391
Luffborough, Nathan, of G'tn.	Deed fr	Beall, Thomas, of George, G'tn.	1804	M12	010	011
Lukens, Samuel et al	Deed fr	Shoemaker, Jonathan	1808	T19	114	081
Lukens, Samuel, Montg. Co. et al	Cert fr	Munroe, Thomas, Supr.	1808	T19	349	252
Lutz, John	Lease fr	Beatty, Charles, heirs of	1806	O14	296	196
Lutz, John	Deed f	Beatty, Charles A. et al	1806	Q16	016	010
Lutz, John	Deed fr	Link, George	1808	U20	116	066
Lutz, John	Release fr	Reeder, Benjamin, assignees of	1810	Y24	497	438
Lutz, John	Deed fr	Beatty, Charles A., Dr.	1810	Y24	496	437
Lutz, John	Deed fr	Beatty, Charles A., Dr.	1810	Z25	270	212
Lutz, John	Deed fr	Link, Thomas, of MD	1810	Z25	080	060

Index to District of Columbia Land Records, 1792-1817

Party	What	Party	Year	Liber	Old	New
Lutz, John	Release fr	Davidson, Ann Maria, wid/o John	1810	Z25	269	211
Lutz, John	Deed fr	Link, Thomas	1810	Z25	194	153
Lutz, John	Deed fr	Lee, Thomas Sim	1810	Y24	175	161
Lutz, John	Deed to	Bailey, Mary, wid/o Jesse	1811	AB27	044	038
Lutz, John	Deed fr	Thompson, John C.	1814	AG32	044	035
Lutz, John & John S. Miller	Deed fr	Botner, Elias, of Alexa. Co.	1811	AB27	359	297
Lutz, John & John S. Miller	Deed to	Miller, Frederick	1815	AI34	505	510
Lutz, John et al	D. of T. fr	Foxall, Henry	1816	AL36	357	348
Lutz, John, mantua maker	Apprentice fr	Marks, William G., of Alexa. Co.	1806	P15	332	219
Lutz, John, of G'tn.	Deed fr	Magruder, Middleton B. et al	1815	AI34	372	400
Lutz, John, of G'tn.	Deed to	Mackey, William, of G'tn.	1816	AM37	164	125
Lydick, Francis	Deed fr	Van Ness, John P.	1817	AN38	145	106
Lyle, James et al	Deed fr	Polock, Isaac	1798	D4	003	002
Lyles, George	Deed fr	Keith, James	1802	I9	297	487
Lyles, George Noble & Elizabeth	Deed to	Green, Jesse, of Sussex Co. DE	1804	L11	337	307
Lyles, George Noble & Eliz., Alexa.	Deed to	Green, Jesse, of Sussex Co. DE	1804	L11	046	46
Lyles, Isaac (negro)	Manumis fr	Brady, Joshua	1807	R17	038	031
Lyles, Thomas C.	Mortgage to	Brooke, James B.	1814	AH33	136	129
Lyles, William	Assign to	Carr, Overton	1799	E5	154	
Lyles, William	Deed to	Green, Charles D., printer, et al	1799	E5	059	048
Lyles, William	Deed to	English, David, printer, et al	1799	E5	059	048
Lyles, William	Mortgage fr	Green, Charles D. & D. English	1800	E5	184	175
Lyles, William	Mortgage fr	Green, Charles D. & D. English	1801	G7	188	252
Lyles, William	Mortgage fr	English, David & Chas. D. Green	1801	G7	188	252
Lyles, William H., of P.G. Co.	Deed fr	Law, Thomas	1813	AE30	122	094
Lyles, William, of P.G. Co.	Deed fr	Deakins, Francis, of G'tn.	1798	C3	406	321
Lyles, William, of P.G. Co.	Deed fr	Thornton, William	1813	AE30	441	327
Lynch, Dominick & Jane, of NY	Deed fr	Lewis, George, mer., of NY	1797	C3	026	21
Lynch, Dominick & Jane, of NY	Deed fr	Covachick, Joseph, mer., of NY	1797	C3	021	17
Lynch, Dominick & Jane, of NY	Deed to	Atkinson, John, mer., of NY	1797	C3	037	30
Lynch, Dominick & Jane, of NY	Deed to	Atkinson, Francis, mer., of NY	1797	C3	032	26
Lynch, Dominick & Jane, of NY	Deed to	Oden, Benjamin, of P.G. Co.	1797	C3	047	37
Lynch, Dominick et al	P. of Atty. to	Covachiche, Joseph	1796	B2B	450	136
Lynch, Dominick et al	Deed fr	Burnes, David, of P.G. Co.	1796	B2B	489	181
Lynch, Dominick et al	P. of Atty. to	Dorsey, William H., of G'tn.	1796	B2B	523	234
Lynch, Dominick, of NY et al	Deed fr	Bayly, William	1796	B2B	384	040
Lynch, Dominick, of NY et al	Deed fr	Oden, Benjamin, of P.G. Co.	1797	C3	043	34
Lynn, Adam	Cert fr	Commissioners of Washington	1800	F6	014	010
Lynn, Adan	Deed fr	Munroe, Thomas, Supt.	1802	I9	207	324
Lynn, James	Mortgage to	Westcott, James D.	1802	I9	187	290
Lynn, John & Eleanor et al	Deed to	Dorsey, Joshua, of Frederick Co.	1799	E5	069	056
Lynn, John & Eleanor et al	Deed to	Beatty, Charles, Sr.	1800	E5	115	102
Lyon, James	Lease fr	Nourse, Joseph, of G'tn.	1802	I9	065	090
Lyon, James, printer	Deed to	Dinmore, Richard, of Alexa.	1804	L11	191	183
Lyon, John	Deed to	Baker, Samuel et al	1802	I9	442	731
Lyon, John	Deed to	Eastburn, Jane	1804	L11	203	192
Lyon, John	Mortgage fr	Eliason, Ebenezer	1815	AI34	095	108
Lyons, Charles	Lease fr	Van Ness, John P. & Marcia	1817	AN38	239	176
Lyons, John	Deed fr	Willson, Robert	1802	H8	577	541
Lyons, John	Deed fr	Heugh, John, of G'tn., trustee	1815	AI34	091	104
Lytton, John Williams, a bankrupt	Discharge		1804	K10	202	211

M

Party	What	Party	Year	Liber	Old	New
M'Connell, John & Francis Clarke	Release fr	Van Ness, John P.	1811	AC28	002	002
M'Gilton, William B.	Agreement	Law, Edmund	1811	AC28	037	027
MacCreery, William, of Balto.	Deed to	Forrest, Joseph	1808	T19	212	154
Maccubbin, Thomas	Slaves		1802	H8	211	202
Macdaniel, Elizabeth	Deed fr	Macdaniel, Ezekiel	1815	AI34	427	446
Macdaniel, Ezekiel	Deed to	Glover, Charles	1812	AD29	113	086
Macdaniel, Ezekiel	Deed to	Glover, Charles	1812	AD29	358	301
Macdaniel, Ezekiel	Deed fr	Brackenridge, John & Eleanor	1814	AG32	231	164
Macdaniel, Ezekiel	Deed to	Macdaniel, Elizabeth	1815	AI34	427	446
Macdaniel, Ezekiel	Deed fr	Edwards, Horace H.	1815	AK35	462	363
Macdaniel, Ezekiel	Deed to	O'Neale, William	1815	AI34	088	100
Macdaniel, Ezekiel	Deed fr	Davidson, Lewis G.	1817	AN38	164	120
Macdaniel, George	Deed fr	Simmons, William	1816	AM37	482	349
Macdaniel, John, Jr.	Deed to	Bussard, Daniel	1812	AC28	185	140
Macdaniel, John, Jr., secretary	Deed to	Mayer, Henry	1815	AK35	075	058
Macdaniel, Walter & Sarah Cannon	P. of Atty. to	Adams, George	1817	AN38	503	364
Macdonald, Archabald	Deed to	Tuell, Henry	1804	L11	314	288
Macdonald, Janet, d/o Archabald	Deed fr	Tuell, Henry	1804	L11	315	289
MacDonald, John G.	Qualify	Deputy Clerk, Circuit Court	1805	N13	098	090
Macgill, Thomas, sheriff	Deed to	Kirby, John B.	1802	H8	186	179
Machen, Lewis H.	B. of S. fr	Washington, Susan, of G'tn.	1811	AB27	411	339
Machen, Lewis H.	Deed fr	Eliot, Samuel, Jr.	1817	AN38	013	011
Mackall, Ann Maria & Benjamin T.	Convey to	Ward, Ulysses, of G'tn.	1817	AO39	187	138
Mackall, Benjamin & Christianna	Deed to	Beall, Lewis	1803	K10	089	95
Mackall, Benjamin & Christianna	Deed to	Williams, Elisha O. & Harriot	1804	K10	190	199
Mackall, Benjamin & Christiana	Deed to	Steuart, William, of G'tn.	1804	L11	198	189
Mackall, Benjamin & Christiana	Deed fr	Mackall, Leonard et al	1804	K10	226	235
Mackall, Benjamin & Christiana	Deed to	Heugh, John	1814	AG32	055	043
Mackall, Benjamin F.	Deed fr	Clarke, William	1810	Y24	216	198
Mackall, Benjamin F.	Deed fr	Smith, Clement	1811	AA26	070	051
Mackall, Benjamin F., of G'tn.	Deed to	Mackall, Leonard, of G'tn.	1813	AE30	308	231
Mackall, Benjamin F.	Deed fr	Whann, William	1814	AG32	017	014
Mackall, Benjamin F., of G'tn.	Deed fr	Cox, John, of G'tn.	1814	AG32	016	012
Mackall, Benjamin F., of G'tn.	Deed to	Brooks, Joseph, of G'tn.	1816	AL36	529	495
Mackall, Benjamin F., of G'tn.	Deed to	Parrott, Richard, of G'tn.	1816	AM37	441	316
Mackall, Benjamin F.	Deed fr	Bohrer, Jacob	1816	AO39	043	034
Mackall, Benjamin F.	Deed fr	Bohrer, Jacob	1816	AO39	041	
Mackall, Benjamin F., of G'tn.	Deed fr	Lipscomb, John, of G'tn.	1817	AN38	166	121
Mackall, Benjamin, of G'tn.	Deed fr	Mackall, Leonard, of G'tn.	1807	T19	008	006
Mackall, Benjamin, of G'tn.	Deed to	Mackall, Catherine, of G'tn.	1807	T19	010	008
Mackall, Benjamin T.	Deed fr	Whann, William, of G'tn.	1816	AK35	529	418
Mackall, Catherine, of G'tn.	Deed fr	Mackall, Benjamin, oif G'tn.	1807	T19	010	008
Mackall, Christiana, of P.G. Co.	Deed fr	Stewart, William & Hellen	1804	L11	200	190
Mackall, Christianna, d/o Benj.	Deed fr	Beall, Thomas, of George	1805	O14	083	051
Mackall, Leonard	Slaves		1802	H8	129	
Mackall, Leonard	Deed fr	Mackall, Walter	1802	I9	370	614
Mackall, Leonard	Deed fr	Parrott, Richard	1804	K10	260	266
Mackall, Leonard	Bond to	Corporation of Georgetown	1806	O14	392	262
Mackall, Leonard	Manumis to	[ ], Tom (negro)	1809	V21	253	180
Mackall, Leonard	Deed fr	Speake, Josias M.	1811	AA26	301	203
Mackall, Leonard	Manumis to	[ ], Delaware (C)	1812	AC28	486	345
Mackall, Leonard	Assign fr	Davis, Edward, of G'tn.	1815	AI34	323	356
Mackall, Leonard	Agreement	Holmead, John	1815	AI34	027	031
Mackall, Leonard	Deed fr	Carroll, Richard	1815	AI34	404	427

Index to District of Columbia Land Records, 1792-1817

Party	What	Party	Year	Liber	Old	New
Mackall, Leonard	Deed fr	Parrott, Richard	1817	AN38	167	122
Mackall, Leonard & Catherine	Deed to	Stuart, William & Hellen	1804	K10	185	194
Mackall, Leonard & Catharine	Deed to	Williams, Elisha O. & Harriot	1804	K10	190	199
Mackall, Leonard & Catharine	Deed to	Mackall, Benjamin & Christiana	1804	K10	226	235
Mackall, Leonard et al	Bond to	United States	1801	G7	013	016
Mackall, Leonard et al	Bond to	United States	1801	G7	013	016
Mackall, Leonard et al	Bond to	United States	1802	H8	519	478
Mackall, Leonard et al	Deed fr	Beall, Upton & Lewis	1802	I9	576	933
Mackall, Leonard et al	Deed to	Beall, Lewis	1803	K10	089	095
Mackall, Leonard et al	Bond to	Corporation of Georgetown	1805	N13	094	086
Mackall, Leonard et al	Bond to	Corporation of Georgetown	1808	T19	258	190
Mackall, Leonard et al	Deed fr	Eliason, Ebenezer & Ann	1809	V21	290	210
Mackall, Leonard et al	Deed fr	Gooding, John, of Balto.	1810	Y24	151	137
Mackall, Leonard, of G'tn.	Manumis to	[ ], Sciss (Negro)	1804	L11	280	258
Mackall, Leonard, of G'tn.	Manumis to	[ ], Toby (negro)	1807	S18	170	139
Mackall, Leonard, of G'tn.	Manumis to	[ ], Priscilla (negro)	1807	R17	134	104
Mackall, Leonard, of G'tn.	Deed fr	Stewart, William, of G'tn.	1807	S18	297	233
Mackall, Leonard, of G'tn.	Manumis to	[ ], Polly (negro)	1807	S18	170	138
Mackall, Leonard, of G'tn.	Deed to	Mackall, Benjamin, of G'tn.	1807	T19	008	006
Mackall, Leonard, of G'tn.	Manumis to	[ ], Luke (negro)	1807	Q16	310	236
Mackall, Leonard, of G'tn.	Deed to	Owens, Isaac, of G'tn.	1808	T19	296	217
Mackall, Leonard, of G'tn.	Manumis to	[ ], Murray (negro)	1809	X23	173	129
Mackall, Leonard, of G'tn.	Lease fr	Beal, Samuel, of G'tn.	1811	AA26	303	205
Mackall, Leonard, of G'tn.	Deed to	Ratcliffe, Joseph, of G'tn.	1811	AA26	297	200
Mackall, Leonard, of G'tn.	Deed fr	Mackall, Benjamin F., of G'tn.	1813	AE30	308	231
Mackall, Leonard, of G'tn.	Deed fr	Smith, Clement, of G'tn.	1813	AF31	337	241
Mackall, Leonard, of G'tn.	Deed to	Shepperd, Lodowick, of G'tn.	1815	AK35	411	323
Mackall, Leonard, of G'tn.	Deed fr	Smith, Clement, of G'tn.	1815	AK35	050	039
Mackall, Leonard, trustee et al	Deed fr	Morgan, William, of G'tn.	1814	AH33	010	009
Mackall, Thomas, inspector	Bond	New Georgetown Warehouse	1808	T19	258	190
Mackall, Walter	Deed to	Hurley, Daniel	1802	H8	576	540
Mackall, Walter	Deed to	Mackall, Leonard	1802	I9	370	614
Mackall, Walter	Mortgage fr	Shoemaker, Jonathan	1803	K10	058	62
Mackall, Walter	Deed to	Shoemaker, Jonathan	1804	K10	109	117
Mackall, Walter, Esq., Calvert Co.	Deed fr	Stoddert, Benjamin, Esq., of G'tn.	1801	F6	154	095
Mackall, Walter et al	Deed to	Marbury, William	1802	H8	362	337
Mackall, Walter, of Calvert Co.	Deed fr	Beall, Thomas, of George, of G'tn.	1800	E5	128	116
Mackall, Walter, of Calvert Co.	Deed fr	Bayly, William	1800	F6	002	002
Mackall, Walter, of MD	Deed to	Harbaugh, Leonard	1802	I9	074	104
Mackall, William, admr. of	Release to	Shoemaker, Jonathan	1809	W22	159	112
Mackay, James, stage driver, G'tn.	B. of S. to	McMurray, Joseph, of G'tn.	1806	Q16	097	063
Mackay, William, mer., of PA	Deed fr	Burnes, David, Gent.	1795	B2A	254	354
Mackey, Alexander	Deed fr	Mackey, William	1811	AB27	263	215
Mackey, Alexander et al	Deed to	Underwood, Robert	1810	Y24	133	121
Mackey, Alexander, of G'tn.	Deed fr	Mackey, William, of G'tn.	1811	AB27	260	213
Mackey, Mary Butler, s/o	Indenture to	Newton, Ignatius, of G'tn.	1811	AB27	418	345
Mackey, William	Deed fr	Lee, Thomas Sim	1810	Y24	173	158
Mackey, William	Deed to	Mackey, Alexander	1811	AB27	263	215
Mackey, William et al	Deed fr	Law, John, atty. for Thomas	1810	Y24	067	059
Mackey, William, of G'tn.	Deed fr	Brent, William & James Hoban	1809	X23	099	072
Mackey, William, of Berkeley Co.	Deed to	Potterfield, John, of Berkeley Co.	1811	AB27	328	270
Mackey, William, of G'tn.	Deed to	Mackey, Alexander, of G'tn.	1811	AB27	260	213
Mackey, William, of G'tn.	Deed fr	Peckham, Caleb, of G'tn.	1816	AL36	414	396
Mackey, William, of G'tn.	Deed fr	Lutz, John, of G'tn.	1816	AM37	164	125
Mackey, William, of G'tn.	Deed to	Dean, Charles, of G'tn.	1816	AL36	415	397

Index to District of Columbia Land Records, 1792-1817

Party	What	Party	Year	Liber	Old	New
Mackie, Ebenezer et al	Deed to	Beall, Thomas & John M. Gantt	1793	A1-1	292	389
Macpherson, Samuel	B. of S. to	Bond, William	1802	I9	005	007
Madden, Hezekiah	B. of S. to	Steuart, David	1814	AG32	147	105
Maddox, Lanta	Deed to	Posey, Benjamin, of Charles Co.	1801	G7	291	404
Maddox, Notley	Lease to	Clarke, James	1801	G7	115	146
Maddox, Notley	Deed fr	Darnall, John	1801	G7	297	412
Maddox, Notley, of P.G. Co.	Deed fr	Hewitt, John	1807	S18	335	263
Maddox, Notley, of P.G. Co.	Deed fr	Hanson, Samuel, of Samuel	1807	R17	131	101
Maddox, Notley, of P.G. Co.	Deed to	Law, John	1809	W22	111	080
Maddox, Notley, of P.G. Co.	Deed to	McLeod, John, schoolmaster	1814	AG32	407	297
Maddox, Notley, of P.G. Co.	Convey fr	McLeod, John, schoolmaster	1816	AM37	495	362
Maddox, Notley, of P.G. Co.	Lease to	Franks, Mary	1816	AM37	067	055
Maddox, Notley, sheriff	Deed to	Dorsey, William Hammond et al	1798	D4	060	050
Maddox, Notley, sheriff	Deed to	Brown, Matthew, printer, of Balto.	1799	D4	342	330
Maddox, Notley, sheriff	Deed to	Darnall, John	1800	E5	279	273
Maddox, Notley, sheriff	Deed to	Laird, John et al	1800	E5	090	077
Maddox, Notley, sheriff	Deed to	Dorsey, William Hammond et al	1800	E5	090	077
Maddox, Notley, sheriff	Deed to	Deakins, Francis	1802	I9	140	211
Maddox, Notley, sherrif	Deed to	Dorsey, William H.	1799	D4	298	281
Maddox, Thomas R.	Lease fr	Allen, Thomas	1815	AK35	047	037
Maffit, Samuel, collector, G'tn.	Deed to	Hoye, John, of Montg. Co.	1809	X23	211	160
Maffitt, Samuel	B. of S. fr	Lee, Mary	1809	V21	204	144
Maffitt, Samuel, collector, of G'tn.	Deed to	Magruder, Greenbury, of G'tn.	1809	X23	303	241
Maffitt, Samuel, of G'tn.	Deed to	Renner, Daniel & Daniel Bussard	1809	X23	256	201
Maffitt, Sarah	Deed fr	Parrott, Richard	1810	Z25	004	003
Magan, Michael Joseph	Deed fr	Davidson, Samuel, Esq., of G'tn.	1800	E5	363	345
Magill, William	B. of S. to	Talbert, Alexander	1815	AI34	179	204
Magrath, Thomas	Deed fr	Jarboe, Charles	1811	AC28	001	001
Magrath, William	Deed to	Beall, Thomas & John M. Gantt	1793	A1-1	313	412
Magrath, William	Deed to	Wilson, Joseph	1793	A1-2	412	21
Magruder, Adelina et al	Deed Gift fr	Magruder, Patrick	1816	AL36	251	253
Magruder, Brooke	Bond to	Magruder, Charles	1811	AC28	106	079
Magruder, Charles	Deed fr	Berry, William Warman & Lucy	1793	A1-1	194	274
Magruder, Charles	Deed fr	Willson, William & Sarah	1793	A1-1	195	275
Magruder, Charles	Bond fr	Magruder, Brooke	1811	AC28	106	079
Magruder, Charles, heirs	Deed fr	Beall, Thomas, of George	1809	W22	396	258
Magruder, Charles, of G'tn.	Deed to	Lingan, James M., of G'tn.	1794	B2A	055	069
Magruder, Dennis, of P.G. Co.	D. of T. fr	Lowe, Henry H.	1810	Y24	081	072
Magruder, Edw.	Deed to	Reintzel, Anthony	1802	I9	349	576
Magruder, Edward	Deed to	Magruder, Ninian	1802	I9	354	585
Magruder, Edward	Deed to	Wingard, Abraham	1804	K10	121	130
Magruder, Edward	Deed fr	Jones, Benjamin White	1804	K10	250	257
Magruder, Edward, of Montg. Co.	Deed fr	Beatty, Thomas J., of G'tn.	1795	B2B	373	026
Magruder, Edward, of Montg. Co.	Deed to	Magruder, Ninian, Dr., of G'tn.	1804	L11	370	332
Magruder, Edward, of Montg. Co.	Deed to	Magruder, Ely, of G'tn.	1805	M12	227	228
Magruder, Eleanor et al	Deed fr	Lee, Thomas Sim	1801	G7	341	472
Magruder, Eleanor et al	Deed fr	Davidson, Samuel	1802	I9	453	748
Magruder, Eleanor, rel/o Charles	Deed to	Lee, Thomas Sim	1801	G7	342	473
Magruder, Eleanora et al	Deed fr	Beall, Thomas, of George	1809	W22	396	258
Magruder, Eliza Lidia Mary, d/o N.	Deed fr	Beatty, Charles A., Dr.	1811	AA26	185	126
Magruder, Ely, of G'tn.	Deed fr	Magruder, Edward, of Montg. Co.	1805	M12	227	228
Magruder, George	Deed to	Johns, Acquilla	1802	I9	526	860
Magruder, George	Deed fr	Eton, John	1807	R17	293	223
Magruder, George	Deed to	Beatty, John M. & Charles A.	1807	Q16	385	296
Magruder, George	Bond to	Corporation of Georgetown	1808	T19	258	190

Party	What	Party	Year	Liber	Old	New
Magruder, George	Deed fr	Beall, Thomas, of George	1808	T19	133	094
Magruder, George	Bond to	Corporation of Georgetown	1808	T19	262	193
Magruder, George	Qualify	Colonel 1st Regiment of Militia	1813	AE30	364	270
Magruder, George	D. of T. fr	Cassin, James, of G'tn.	1816	AK35	494	389
Magruder, George	D. of T. to	Smith, Clement	1817	AN38	388	288
Magruder, George & Patrick, G'tn.	Deed to	Turner, Samuel, Jr., of G'tn.	1795	B2A	176	237
Magruder, George & Wm. Lodge	Deed fr	Mountz, Jacob, collector, of G'tn.	1811	AB27	008	009
Magruder, George B. et al	Bond to	United States	1801	G7	011	014
Magruder, George B., of G'tn.	Deed fr	Beatty, Charles A., of G'tn.	1805	N13	178	160
Magruder, George B. et al	Deed to	Corporation of Georgetown	1805	N13	091	083
Magruder, George B.	Bond to	Corporation of Georgetown	1806	O14	394	263
Magruder, George B.	B. of S. fr	Beall, Basil D.	1807	R17	087	069
Magruder, George B., inspector	Bond	Central Warehouse	1808	T19	262	193
Magruder, George B.	Bond to	Corporation of Georgetown	1808	T19	262	193
Magruder, George B., inspector	Bond to	Corporation of Georgetown	1809	V21	399	302
Magruder, George B.	Bond	Tobacco Inspector, of G'tn.	1811	AA26	099	070
Magruder, George B.	Deed fr	Brooks, William H.	1817	AN38	261	191
Magruder, George B.	Deed to	Jones, Horatio & Susan	1817	AO39	381	257
Magruder, George Beall	Bond to	United States	1802	I9	091	130
Magruder, George Beall, of G'tn.	Deed fr	Yost, Henry, of Bladensburgh	1808	T19	041	032
Magruder, George Beall	Deed fr	Maynard, Brice, h/o Thomas	1810	Y24	275	252
Magruder, George, collector, G'tn.	Deed to	King, Adam	1804	L11	235	217
Magruder, George, collector, G'tn.	Deed to	Offutt, Ozias, Dr., of Montg. Co.	1804	L11	304	279
Magruder, George, collector, G'tn.	Deed to	Eastburn, Jane, of G'tn.	1804	K10	402	416
Magruder, George, collector, G'tn.	Deed to	Offutt, Ozias, Dr., of Montg. Co.	1804	L11	303	278
Magruder, George, collector, G'tn.	Deed to	Ritchie, Abner	1805	M12	082	075
Magruder, George, collector, G'tn.	Deed to	Smith, Walter, of G'tn.	1805	M12	189	191
Magruder, George, collector, G'tn.	Deed to	Magruder, Ninian, of G'tn.	1805	M12	409	425
Magruder, George, collector, G'tn.	Deed to	Gozler, John	1807	S18	078	064
Magruder, George, collector, G'tn.	Deed to	McClane, Robert	1807	S18	036	029
Magruder, George, collector, G'tn.	Deed to	Beatty, Thomas, Jr.	1807	S18	239	189
Magruder, George, collector, G'tn.	Deed to	Suter, Alexander	1807	S18	037	030
Magruder, George, collector, G'tn.	Deed to	Renner, Daniel & Daniel Bussard	1807	S18	203	163
Magruder, George, collector, G'tn.	Deed to	Forrest, Joseph	1809	W22	092	067
Magruder, George, collector, G'tn.	Deed to	Steuart, William et al	1810	Z25	205	161
Magruder, George, collector, G'tn.	Deed to	Smith, Walter & Clement	1811	AB27	006	008
Magruder, George et al	Deed to	Corporation of Georgetown	1805	N13	091	083
Magruder, George, of G'tn.	Deed fr	Bayly, William	1798	D4	146	128
Magruder, George, of G'tn.	Deed fr	Beall, Thomas, of George, of G'tn.	1809	V21	159	114
Magruder, George, of G'tn. et al	Mortgage fr	Turner, Samuel, Jr., of G'tn.	1811	Z25	514	408
Magruder, Greenbury et al	Deed fr	Mason, George, of Fairfax Co. VA	1797	B2B	698	482
Magruder, Greenbury, of G'tn.	Deed fr	Maffitt, Samuel, collector, of G'tn.	1809	X23	303	241
Magruder, Henry B. et al	Deed fr	Davidson, Samuel	1802	I9	453	748
Magruder, Henry B. et al	Deed fr	Beall, Thomas, of George	1809	W22	396	258
Magruder, Henry B. et al	Deed to	Lutz, John, of G'tn.	1815	AI34	372	400
Magruder, Henry B. et al	Deed to	Crawford, William, of G'tn.	1815	AI34	141	161
Magruder, Henry B. et al	Deed to	Key, Philip B.	1815	AI34	264	299
Magruder, Henry et al	Deed fr	Lee, Thomas Sim	1801	G7	341	472
Magruder, Hezekiah et al	Bond to	United States	1801	G7	011	014
Magruder, James A., of G'tn.	D. of T. to	Ott, John, of G'tn.	1815	AK35	304	243
Magruder, James A., of G'tn.	Deed fr	Magruder, Ninian, of G'tn.	1815	AK35	057	044
Magruder, James A.	Deed fr	King, Vincent	1815	AI34	433	451
Magruder, James A., of G'tn.	Deed to	Yerby, John	1816	AL36	089	090
Magruder, James A., of G'tn.	Deed to	Bowie, Washington, of G'tn.	1816	AM37	233	171
Magruder, James A., of G'tn.	Deed fr	Pairo, Thomas W. & Loveday	1816	AM37	105	084

Index to District of Columbia Land Records, 1792-1817

Party	What	Party	Year	Liber	Old	New
Magruder, James A., of G'tn.	Deed to	Gantt, Thomas T., of G'tn.	1816	AL36	330	324
Magruder, James A., of G'tn.	B. of S. fr	Wright, William, of KY	1817	AO39	247	178
Magruder, John et al	Deed fr	Mason, George, of Fairfax Co. VA	1797	B2B	698	482
Magruder, John R.	Cert to	Deakins, William, Jr.	1795	B2A	171	230
Magruder, John R.	Cert to	Deakins, William, Jr.	1795	B2A	171	229
Magruder, John R. et al	Manumis to	[ ], Henny (C)	1812	AB27	481	394
Magruder, John Read, mer.	Deed to	Beall, Thomas & John M. Gantt	1792	A1-1	119	173
Magruder, John Read, P.G. Co.	Deed to	Carroll, Daniel, of *Duddington*	1795	B2B	372	024
Magruder, John Read, Jr. et al	Mortgage fr	Cooledge, Samuel J.	1811	AA26	096	068
Magruder, John Read, of P.G. Co.	Deed to	Hagner, Peter	1812	AC28	127	096
Magruder, John Reed, Jr.	Cert to	Cramphin, Thomas	1797	B2B	643	405
Magruder, John Smith	Deed fr	Burnes, David	1794	B2A	006	006
Magruder, John Smith, P.G. Co.	Deed to	Pratt, John Wilkes	1806	P15	196	131
Magruder, Joseph et al	Deed fr	Mason, George, of Fairfax Co. VA	1797	B2B	698	482
Magruder, Middleton B. et al	Deed fr	Davidson, Samuel	1802	I9	453	748
Magruder, Middleton B. et al	Deed fr	Beall, Thomas, of George	1809	W22	396	258
Magruder, Middleton B. et al	Deed to	Key, Philip B.	1815	AI34	264	299
Magruder, Middleton B. et al	Deed to	Lutz, John, of G'tn.	1815	AI34	372	400
Magruder, Middleton B. et al	Deed to	Crawford, William, of G'tn.	1815	AI34	141	161
Magruder, Middleton et al	Deed fr	Lee, Thomas Sim	1801	G7	341	472
Magruder, Nathaniel	Deed to	Ditty, Roger, of Ann Arundel Co.	1796	B2B	590	339
Magruder, Nathaniel, carpenter	Deed fr	Davidson, John, of Annapolis	1795	B2A	183	245
Magruder, Nathaniel Edwards	Deed to	Thomas, Gustavus, free black	1807	R17	091	072
Magruder, Ninian	Deed fr	Wise, John	1802	I9	308	505
Magruder, Ninian	Deed fr	Orme, Thomas	1802	I9	202	316
Magruder, Ninian	Deed fr	Johnson, Thomas	1802	I9	307	504
Magruder, Ninian	Deed fr	Magruder, Edward	1802	I9	354	585
Magruder, Ninian	Mortgage fr	Wright, Thomas C.	1810	Z25	325	254
Magruder, Ninian	Deed fr	Suter, Alexander	1814	AG32	276	196
Magruder, Ninian	Deed fr	Rigden, Thomas, of G'tn.	1816	AL36	076	077
Magruder, Ninian	Deed fr	Dant, Thomas, of G'tn.	1816	AL36	017	018
Magruder, Ninian, Dr., of G'tn.	Deed fr	Wistar, William, mer., of Phila.	1800	E5	176	166
Magruder, Ninian, Dr., of G'tn.	Deed fr	Forrest, Uriah	1800	E5	303	295
Magruder, Ninian, Dr., of G'tn.	Deed fr	Magruder, Edward, of Montg. Co.	1804	L11	370	332
Magruder, Ninian, Dr.	Deed fr	Beatty, Charles, heirs of	1806	P15	199	133
Magruder, Ninian, Dr.	Deed fr	Offutt, Ozias, Dr.	1806	P15	198	132
Magruder, Ninian, Dr.	Deed to	Collins, Hezekiah	1809	X23	295	235
Magruder, Ninian, Dr.	Deed to	Bussard, Daniel	1810	Y24	501	441
Magruder, Ninian, Dr., of G'tn.	Deed fr	Bussard, Daniel, of G'tn.	1810	Y24	356	322
Magruder, Ninian, Dr., of G'tn.	Deed fr	Hollingshead, John, mer., of G'tn.	1811	Z25	500	397
Magruder, Ninian, Dr., of G'tn.	Deed fr	Dorsey, William H., of Balto.	1811	AA26	013	010
Magruder, Ninian, Dr., of G'tn.	Deed to	Walker, Archibald, of Easton MD	1811	AA26	194	132
Magruder, Ninian, Dr., of G'tn.	Deed fr	Swann, Thomas, of Alexa.	1812	AD29	071	051
Magruder, Ninian, Dr.	Deed fr	Ritchie, Abner	1812	AD29	368	310
Magruder, Ninian, Dr.	Lease to	Wilson, Levi G.	1812	AD29	369	311
Magruder, Ninian, Dr., of G'tn.	Deed fr	Lowndes, Francis, of G'tn.	1812	AD29	066	047
Magruder, Ninian, Dr., of G'tn.	Deed to	Walker, Archibald, Rev., of Easton	1812	AD29	150	117
Magruder, Ninian, Dr., of G'tn.	Deed fr	Pickrell, John, of G'tn.	1812	AD29	072	052
Magruder, Ninian, Dr., of G'tn.	Deed fr	Wilson, Levi G., of G'tn.	1813	AE30	467	348
Magruder, Ninian, Dr.	Deed to	Wilson, Levi G.	1814	AH33	099	091
Magruder, Ninian, Dr., of G'tn.	Deed to	Dant, Thomas	1816	AK35	370	291
Magruder, Ninian, Dr., of G'tn.	Lease to	Bunnell, Eliab & W.B. Robertson	1816	AL36	084	086
Magruder, Ninian, Dr.	Deed fr	Rigden, James, of G'tn.	1816	AL36	231	236
Magruder, Ninian, Dr., of G'tn.	Deed fr	Riley, Martha, of Montg. Co.	1816	AL36	079	081
Magruder, Ninian, Dr., of G'tn.	Deed fr	Rigden, Henry	1816	AL36	080	082

Party	What	Party	Year	Liber	Old	New
Magruder, Ninian, Dr., of G'tn.	Surrender fr	Smallwood, Horatio, of G'tn.	1816	AM37	077	063
Magruder, Ninian, Dr., of G'tn.	Deed to	Smallwood, Horatio, of G'tn.	1816	AM37	003	003
Magruder, Ninian, Dr., of G'tn.	Lease to	Smallwood, Horatio, of G'tn.	1816	AM37	079	064
Magruder, Ninian, Dr., of G'tn.	Lease to	Hillary, Lewis, of G'tn.	1816	AM37	419	301
Magruder, Ninian, Dr., of G'tn.	Deed fr	Rigden, Henry, of G'tn.	1817	AN38	523	379
Magruder, Ninian, Dr., of G'tn.	Deed to	Bunnel, Eliab & Wm. Robertson	1817	AN38	027	022
Magruder, Ninian, of G'tn.	Deed fr	Orme, Thomas, of MD	1802	I9	087	124
Magruder, Ninian, of G'tn.	Deed fr	Dorsey, William H., of G'tn.	1805	M12	408	423
Magruder, Ninian, of G'tn.	Deed fr	Magruder, George, collector, G'tn.	1805	M12	409	425
Magruder, Ninian, of G'tn.	Deed fr	Hines, John	1808	U20	309	164
Magruder, Ninian, of G'tn.	Deed fr	Davidson, Ann Maria, late of A.	1809	W22	357	231
Magruder, Ninian, of G'tn.	Deed fr	Turner, Mary, of Charles Co.	1811	Z25	502	398
Magruder, Ninian, of G'tn.	Deed to	Foxall, Henry, of G'tn.	1811	AA26	079	056
Magruder, Ninian, of G'tn.	Deed to	Hines, John	1812	AD29	309	254
Magruder, Ninian, of G'tn.	Deed to	Foxall, Henry, of G'tn.	1813	AE30	138	107
Magruder, Ninian, of G'tn.	Deed to	Weeden, Henry, of G'tn.	1813	AE30	464	345
Magruder, Ninian, of G'tn.	Deed to	Goszler, George, of G'tn.	1813	AE30	153	120
Magruder, Ninian, of G'tn.	Deed fr	Mountz, Jacob, collector, of G'tn.	1813	AE30	465	346
Magruder, Ninian, of G'tn.	Deed to	John K. Smith, of G'tn.	1814	AG32	048	038
Magruder, Ninian, of G'tn.	Deed fr	Wingert, Charles, Harrisburg PA	1814	AH33	109	102
Magruder, Ninian, of G'tn.	Deed to	McGowan, John	1814	AH33	195	177
Magruder, Ninian, of G'tn.	Deed fr	Claggett, William, of G'tn.	1814	AG32	274	194
Magruder, Ninian, of G'tn.	Lease to	Smallwood, Horatio	1815	AI34	043	049
Magruder, Ninian, of G'tn.	Deed fr	Bussard, Daniel, of G'tn.	1815	AI34	044	050
Magruder, Ninian, of G'tn.	Deed to	Landes, Abraham, of G'tn.	1815	AH33	405	350
Magruder, Ninian, of G'tn.	Deed to	Magruder, James A., of G'tn.	1815	AK35	057	044
Magruder, Ninian, of G'tn.	Deed fr	Wingart, John, of Harrisburg PA	1816	AL36	081	083
Magruder, Ninian, of G'tn.	Deed fr	Hillary, Lewis, of G'tn.	1816	AM37	418	300
Magruder, Ninian, of G'tn.	Deed fr	Rigdon, Stephen, of Jefferson Co.	1816	AM37	342	248
Magruder, Ninian, of G'tn.	Deed to	Davis, John P.	1816	AL36	100	100
Magruder, Ninian, of G'tn.	Deed fr	Rigden, Thomas	1817	AN38	521	378
Magruder, Ninian, of G'tn.	Deed fr	Mountz, Jacob, collector, of G'tn.	1817	AN38	519	376
Magruder, Ninian, of G'tn.	Deed to	Smith, Lewis, of G'tn.	1817	AN38	499	360
Magruder, Ninian, physic, of G'tn.	Deed fr	Davidson, Ann Maria, exrx.	1810	Z25	307	240
Magruder, Ninian, physic, of G'tn.	Deed fr	Reintzel, Daniel, of G'tn.	1811	Z25	532	422
Magruder, Patrick	B. of S. fr	Ewell, James	1811	AB27	412	340
Magruder, Patrick	Slave	From VA	1811	AC28	034	026
Magruder, Patrick	Slave		1812	AD29	460	388
Magruder, Patrick	Deed Gift to	Magruder, Adelina et al	1816	AL36	251	253
Magruder, Patrick & George	Deed to	Smith, Clement	1813	AF31	531	391
Magruder, Patrick et al	Deed fr	Shepperd, James G., of NC	1810	Z25	147	116
Magruder, Patrick et al	Deed fr	Magruder, George, collector, G'tn.	1810	Z25	205	161
Magruder, Patrick et al	Deed fr	Mountz, Jacob, collector, of G'tn.	1811	AA26	052	041
Magruder, Patrick, of G'tn.	Deed fr	Beall, Thomas, of George, of G'tn.	1798	C3	443	348
Magruder, Patrick, of G'tn.	Deed to	Thompson, Jonah & Rich. Veitch	1799	D4	344	333
Magruder, Patrick, of G'tn. et al	Deed to	Shepperd, James G., of G'tn.	1810	Z25	175	139
Magruder, Samuel B., Montg. Co.	B. of S. to	Barker, Murray	1815	AH33	440	377
Magruder, Samuel B.	B. of S. to	Barker, Murry, of G'tn.	1817	AO39	090	071
Magruder, William B.	R. of M. fr	Pollard, William, of Phila. et al	1794	B2A	039	045
Magruder, William B.	Deed fr	Beall, Thomas	1795	B2B	355	002
Magruder, William B., of Balto.	Deed to	Yates, John, of Balto.	1798	D4	122	105
Magruder, William B., of Balto.	Deed to	Bowie, Washington, of G'tn.	1800	E5	136	124
Magruder, William B., of Balto.	Deed to	Bowie, Washington, of G'tn.	1800	E5	133	121
Magruder, William B., Balto. et al	Deed to	Chesley, Anne, of G'tn.	1804	L11	372	333
Magruder, Zadock, Sr. et al	Deed to	Gantt, Edward, Dr.	1804	K10	164	174

Index to District of Columbia Land Records, 1792-1817

Party	What	Party	Year	Liber	Old	New
Maguire, Hugh et al	B. of S. fr	Callen, Henry	1808	U20	072	040
Maguyre, Hugh, of Annapolis	Deed fr	Kirk, Milesius Thomas, of G'tn.	1801	F6	195	126
Mahone, John, of G'tn. [Mehone]	Assign to	Fields, William, of G'tn.	1805	M12	192	194
Mahoney, Barney, age 40, others	Manumis fr	Sprigg, Osborn, of P.G. Co.	1813	AE30	221	178
Mahony, Barney, of P.G. Co.	Deed fr	Parsons, Barney & Samuel Bond	1812	AC28	501	357
Mahony, Benjamin et al	B. of S. fr	Mahony, John, bricklayer	1809	V21	162	116
Mahony, John, bricklayer	B. of S. to	Mahony, Benjamin & Teresa	1809	V21	162	116
Mahony, John, of G'tn.	Lease fr	Threlkeld, John, of G'tn.	1804	K10	346	358
Mahony, Teresa et al	B. of S. fr	Mahony, John, bricklayer	1809	V21	162	116
Mahorney, Charles	D. of T. fr	Pearl, Daniel & Thomas Williams	1817	AN38	220	161
Mahorney, Charles & Barney	Manumis to	[ ], Alley & Charles	1817	AO39	438	299
Mailey, Jacob, of Phila. PA	Deed fr	Deakins, William, Jr. et al	1797	B2B	667	434
Mailey, Robert, cordwainer, Phila.	Deed to	Polock, Isaac, late of GA	1797	C3	081	66
Main, Thomas	Cert	Stray	1802	G7		634
Main, Thomas, of Montg. Co.	Lease fr	Cloud, Abner, of Montg. Co.	1797	C3	248	204
Main, Thomas, of Montg. Co.	Deed fr	Cloud, Abner, of Montg. Co.	1797	C3	148	122
Maitland, James	Cert fr	Commissioners of Washington	1796	B2B	455	143
Maitland, James	Transfer to	Jamieson, Andrew, of Alexa.	1796	B2B	455	142
Maitland, James	Deed fr	Templeman, John, of Allegany Co.	1808	V21	129	095
Maitland, James	Deed to	Law, John	1813	AE30	154	121
Maitland, James, bricklayer	Deed to	Maitland, Mary, spinster	1799	D4	346	334
Maitland, James et al	Cert fr	Commissioners of Washington	1796	B2B	455	142
Maitland, James, et al	Lease fr	Stoddert, Benjamin et al	1801	G7	276	381
Maitland, James, Jr.	Deed fr	Maitland, James, Sr.	1801	G7	249	337
Maitland, James, Jr.	Release fr	Maitland, Mary	1802	H8	220	210
Maitland, James, Jr.	Deed to	Law, John	1812	AC28	295	215
Maitland, James, Sr.	Deed to	Maitland, James, Jr.	1801	G7	249	337
Maitland, James, Sr. & James, Jr.	Deed to	Jamieson, Andrew	1802	H8	238	228
Maitland, James, Sr. & James, Jr.	Deed fr	Jamieson, Andrew	1802	H8	247	234
Maitland, Mary	Release to	Maitland, James, Jr.	1802	H8	220	210
Maitland, Mary, spinster	Deed fr	Maitland, James, bricklayer	1799	D4	346	334
Major, John	Lease fr	Van Ness, John P. & Marcia	1813	AF31	542	402
Major, John, carpenter	Lease fr	Van Ness, John P. & Marcia	1804	K10	167	177
Majors, John	Lease to	Edmonston, Brooke	1813	AF31	324	231
Maker, Matthew et al	Deed to	Gardner, James	1802	I9	506	829
Mallion, Jane	Agreement	Mallion, Vandouren	1817	AN38	223	163
Mallion, Vandoren	Deed fr	Hazle, Zachariah	1816	AM37	106	085
Mallion, Vandouren	Agreement	Mallion, Jane	1817	AN38	223	163
Mallion, Vandourin	Deed fr	Griffin, Lancelot, constable	1816	AO39	047	039
Maltby, Sarah	Deed fr	Munroe, Thomas, Supt.	1802	I9	144	217
Maltby, Sarah, now of Phila.	Deed to	Beale, George, mer.	1814	AG32	388	282
Man, George, of Annapolis	Deed fr	Beall, Thomas, of George, G'tn.	1793	A1-1	265	358
Man, George, of Annapolis	Deed fr	Beall, Thomas, of George	1793	A1-2	445	54
Manavill, Patrick & Mary	Deed to	Beall, Thomas & John M. Gantt	1793	A1-1	361	468
Mandell, Daniel, insolvent	Deed to	Burns, William, trustee	1810	Y24	463	410
Mandeville, Joseph, of Alexa.	Mortgage fr	Hickey, James & Mary Ann	1811	AB27	120	098
Mane, Adam, of John	Deed fr	Ritchie, Abner	1810	Z25	262	205
Maniville, Mary, w/o Patrick	Cert fr	Commissioners of Washington	1794	B2A	324	455
Mann, John, of Balto. Co.	Deed to	West, Jacob, of Balto. Co.	1816	AL36	373	361
Mann, Mary, of Annapolis	Deed to	Neth, Lewis, of Annapolis	1809	V21	359	262
Manning, Charles	Lease fr	Lanham, Elisha	1801	G7	478	615
Manning, Charles	Assign to	Gaines, Richard	1804	K10	305	309
Manning, Ignatius, St. Mary's Co.	B. of S. to	Mayer, Henry	1815	AI34	179	204
Mantz, Casper, of Fredk. Co.	Deed fr	Mantz, John, of Fredk. Co.	1814	AH33	055	049
Mantz, Casper, reps. of	Deed to	Beall, Thomas & John M. Gantt	1793	A1-1	256	348

Party	What	Party	Year	Liber	Old	New
Mantz, Ezra, sheriff, Frederick Co.	Deed to	Jones, Maurice, of Frederick Co.	1811	Z25	379	297
Mantz, John, of Frederick Co.	Deed to	Beall, Thomas & John M. Gantt	1792	A1-1	070	103
Mantz, John, of Fredk. Co.	Deed to	Mantz, Casper, of Fredk. Co.	1814	AH33	055	049
Mantz, Peter, of Frederick Co.	Deed fr	Ritchie, Abner	1804	L11	035	35
Mara, Catherine, amx. of Philip	Deed to	Ross, James	1812	AC28	426	307
Mara, Philip	Deed fr	Spencer, John J.	1796	B2B	440	120
Mara, Philip	Deed fr	McDaniel, Ezekiel, collector	1811	AB27	179	147
Mara, Philip O.	Deed fr	Pratt, Henry, trustee, et al	1810	Z25	340	266
Maran, Jesse	B. of S. fr	Burch, Jane	1805	M12	343	348
Marbury, John, of G'tn.	Deed fr	Morsell, James S., of G'tn.	1815	AH33	425	366
Marbury, William	Deed to	Deakins, Francis	1802	H8	111	107
Marbury, William	Dood fr	Mackall, Walter et al	1802	H8	362	337
Marbury, William	Deed fr	Addison, Thomas Grafton, of P.G.	1804	K10	359	371
Marbury, William	Deed to	Worthington, Charles	1804	L11	044	44
Marbury, William	Deed fr	Addison, Anthony, of P.G. Co.	1808	T19	066	048
Marbury, William	Deed fr	Moore, James D.	1808	T19	101	072
Marbury, William	Deed fr	Murdock, John & John Heugh	1808	T19	069	050
Marbury, William	Release to	Addison, Thomas G.	1809	W22	184	129
Marbury, William	Release to	Davidson, Ann Maria, exrx.	1810	Z25	324	253
Marbury, William	Deed fr	Getty, Robert, of G'tn.	1811	AB27	243	199
Marbury, William	Deed fr	Beatty, Charles A., Dr., et al	1811	Z25	377	296
Marbury, William	Deed to	Beatty, Charles A., Dr.	1811	AA26	077	055
Marbury, William	Deed fr	Mountz, Jacob, collector, of G'tn.	1811	AB27	086	071
Marbury, William	Deed fr	Smith, Clement, Dr., of P.G. Co.	1812	AD29	487	412
Marbury, William	D. of T. fr	Peter, John, of G'tn.	1812	AD29	197	160
Marbury, William	Deed fr	Nevitt, William	1812	AC28	321	234
Marbury, William	Deed fr	Brookes, Walter, of Montg. Co.	1814	AG32	322	235
Marbury, William	Release to	Clagett, Darius	1815	AK35	477	374
Marbury, William & John Peter	Deed to	Joncherez, Alexander, of G'tn.	1813	AE30	315	237
Marbury, William & John Peter	Deed to	Ridgely, William G., of G'tn.	1813	AF31	132	089
Marbury, William et al	Deed fr	Davidson, John	1804	K10	219	228
Marbury, William et al	Deed fr	Davidson, John, of Annapolis	1804	L11	089	91
Marbury, William, Jr., of P.G. Co.	Deed fr	Wigfield, Robert	1809	W22	080	060
Marbury, William, Naval agent	Deed fr	Templeman, John, of G'tn.	1801	F6	183	117
Marbury, William, of G'tn.	Deed fr	Campbell, William, Frederick Co.	1801	G7	015	018
Marbury, William, of G'tn.	Deed to	Deakins, Leonard M. & John Hoye	1810	Y24	128	116
Marbury, William, of G'tn.	Deed fr	Davidson, Ann Maria, of Annapolis	1811	Z25	372	292
Marbury, William, of G'tn.	Deed fr	Mountz, Jacob, collector, G'tn.	1812	AC28	148	111
Marbury, William, of G'tn.	Deed fr	Dorsey, William H., of Balto.	1813	AF31	346	246
Marbury, William, of G'tn. et al	Deed to	English, David, of G'tn.	1813	AF31	279	197
Marbury, William, of G'tn. et al	Deed to	Washington, George C., of G'tn.	1813	AF31	277	195
Marbury, William, of G'tn. et al	Deed to	Washington, George C., of G'tn.	1813	AF31	275	194
Marbury, William, of G'tn.	Deed fr	Murdock, John, of G'tn.	1813	AF31	344	245
Marbury, William, of G'tn.	D. of T. fr	Joncherez, Alexander L., of G'tn.	1813	AF31	220	151
Marbury, William, of G'tn.	Deed to	Washington, George C.	1816	AL36	068	069
Marbury, William, trustee	Deed to	Davidson, Anna Maria, Annapolis	1811	AB27	219	178
Marche, Maria dela	Deed fr	Threlkeld, John	1800	E5	298	291
Marche, Mary dela	Deed fr	Threlkeld, John	1800	E5	299	292
Markell, William, s/o Conrad	Deed to	Beall, Thomas & John M. Gantt	1792	A1-1	163	234
Markland, John, of Charles Co.	B. of S. to	Brown, Matthew	1808	U20	044	025
Marks, Sarah	B. of S. fr	Mulloy, John	1817	AN38	415	311
Marks, William G., of Alexa. Co.	Apprentice to	Lutz, John, mantua maker	1806	P15	332	219
Markward, William	Deed fr	Munroe, Thomas, Supt.	1802	H8	539	500
Markward, William	Deed to	Simmons, William	1802	I9	318	524
Marlborough, John (C), age 27	Manumis fr	Renner, Daniel, of G'tn.	1816	AM37	313	228

Index to District of Columbia Land Records, 1792-1817

Party	What	Party	Year	Liber	Old	New
Marquand, Charles	Lease fr	Jones, John Godfrey	1809	W22	304	199
Marquand, Charles, of G'tn.	Deed fr	Reintzel, Anthony, of G'tn.	1809	W22	233	158
Marquand, Charles, of G'tn.	Deed fr	Mountz, John, Jr., of G'tn.	1810	Z25	031	023
Marquand, Charles, of G'tn.	D. of T. to	Mountz, John, Jr., of G'tn.	1810	Y24	505	445
Marr, John, Henry Co. VA et al	Deed fr	Watson, John, of Henry Co. VA	1793	A1-2	431	39
Marr, John, Henry Co. VA et al	Deed fr	Stoddert, Benj. & Wm. Deakins	1793	A1-2	432	40
Marr, John, of Henry Co. VA, heirs	Cert fr	Commissioners of Washington	1793	B2A	321	451
Marr, John, of Henry Co. VA, heirs	Cert fr	Commissioners of Washington	1793	B2A	322	452
Marr, Philip	B. of S. fr	Greenfield, Thomas	1808	V21	086	067
Marshal, George	Deed fr	Goff, John	1808	T19	021	017
Marshal, George	Deed fr	Goff, John	1808	T19	116	082
Marshall, Barbara	Deed fr	Boyd, Washington, collector	1805	N13	006	006
Marshall, Barbary	Deed fr	Law, Thomas	1817	AN38	034	028
Marshall, Charles	Deed to	Walker, Zachariah	1817	AN38	554	403
Marshall, George	Deed fr	Prout, William	1813	AF31	477	348
Marshall, James et al	Cert fr	Munroe, Thomas, Supt.	1805	M12	047	045
Marshall, John	Deed to	Harshman, Henry	1804	L11	077	79
Marshall, John	Deed fr	Harshman, Henry	1804	L11	236	218
Marshall, John & Rachael	Deed to	Harshman, Henry	1804	L11	239	221
Marshall, John & Rachael et al	Partition		1804	K10	131	141
Marshall, John & Rachael	Deed to	Marshall, John, Jr. & Charles	1804	L11	237	219
Marshall, John et al	Cert fr	Munroe, Thomas, Supt.	1805	M12	047	045
Marshall, John, Jr. & Charles	Deed fr	Marshall, John & Rachael	1804	L11	237	219
Marshall, Richard et al	Mortgage fr	Cooledge, Samuel J.	1811	AA26	096	068
Marshall, Samuel, of London	Deed fr	Munroe, Thomas, Supt.	1802	I9	042	056
Marshall, Samuel, of London	Deed fr	Munroe, Thomas, Supt.	1802	I9	041	054
Marshall, Samuel, of London	Lease to	Stanton, Patrick	1813	AE30	239	190
Marsteller, Philip G., of Alexa.	Deed fr	Craven, Tunis	1808	U20	106	059
Martell, William, of G'tn.	B. of S. to	Campbell, Mary, of G'tn.	1816	AM37	456	329
Martin, Hanore, of Montg. Co.	Deed fr	Dorsey, William H., of G'tn.	1807	R17	080	064
Martin, Honore	B. of S. fr	Dashiell, George	1811	AA26	002	002
Martin, Honore & Sarah et al	Deed to	Luffborough, Nathan	1801	G7	282	391
Martin, Honore, of Montg. Co.	Deed fr	Polock, Isaac, of G'tn.	1797	C3	264	215
Martin, Honore, of Montg. Co.	B. of S. fr	Evans, Charles	1804	L11	285	261
Martin, Honore, of Montg. Co.	Deed fr	Hewitt, John	1806	O14	325	216
Martin, Honore, of Rockville MD	B. of S. to	Coyle, Andrew	1815	AI34	491	499
Martin, James	Deed fr	Carroll, Daniel, of *Duddington*	1805	M12	380	391
Martin, James, of Long Island NY	Deed fr	Lewis, George, of New York NY	1809	W22	175	123
Martin, John & Nancy	Cert Free fr	Turner, Walker	1813	AE30	152	119
Martin, Luther	Deed fr	Gantt, John M.	1802	I9	208	326
Martin, Luther, of Balto.	Deed to	Thompson, John, of G'tn.	1810	Y24	158	144
Martin, Maria & Eleanora	Deed fr	Burnes, David, of P.G. Co.	1796	B2B	530	245
Maryland, State of	Deed to	Murdock, John	1797	C3	095	78
Maryland, State of	Deed fr	Forrest, Uriah	1800	E5	305	298
Mason, Edward	Assign to	Davis, John, of Abel	1813	AF31	472	342
Mason, George, of Fairfax Co. VA	Deed fr	Lingan, James Maccubbin, of G'tn.	1796	B2B	585	332
Mason, George, of Fairfax Co. VA	Deed to	Magruder, Joseph et al	1797	B2B	698	482
Mason, John	Deed fr	Hanson, Alexander Contee	1799	D4	398	377
Mason, John	Deed fr	Deakins, William, Jr., of G'tn.	1800	E5	260	253
Mason, John	Deed fr	Deakins, William, Jr.	1800	E5	257	251
Mason, John	Deed fr	Deakins, Francis	1800	E5	261	255
Mason, John	Deed fr	Oakley, John, guard.	1802	H8	077	071
Mason, John	Deed to	Laird, John	1802	I9	509	834
Mason, John	Slaves	From Alexandria Co.	1810	Y24	433	387
Mason, John	Slaves	From Alexandria Co.	1810	Y24	158	144

Party	What	Party	Year	Liber	Old	New
Mason, John	Deed to	Way, Andrew, Jr.	1817	AO39	453	311
Mason, John & Benjamin Stoddert	D. of T. fr	Taney, Francis Lewis, of G'tn.	1796	B2B	571	311
Mason, John & John Laird	Deed fr	Stoddert, Benjamin	1806	Q16	007	004
Mason, John & John Laird, G'tn.	Deed fr	Stoddert, Benjamin, of G'tn.	1812	AD29	306	251
Mason, John, Gen.	Deed fr	Foxall, Henry	1816	AM37	239	175
Mason, John, mer., of G'tn.	Deed fr	Taney, Francis Lewis, mer., G'tn.	1796	B2B	444	127
Mason, John, mer.	Deed fr	French, George, of G'tn.	1799	D4	181	162
Mason, John, of G'tn.	Deed fr	Thompson, George, of G'tn.	1794	B2A	107	142
Mason, John, of G'tn.	Deed fr	Orme, James & Lucy	1794	B2A	057	072
Mason, John, of G'tn.	Deed fr	Peter, Robert, of G'tn.	1794	B2A	106	140
Mason, John, of G'tn.	Deed fr	Hite, Isaac, of Frederick Co. VA	1795	B2A	244	341
Mason, John, of G'tn.	Deed fr	Hite, Isaac, of Frederick Co. VA	1795	B2A	246	344
Mason, John, of G'tn.	Deed fr	Burnes, Ann	1802	H8	082	076
Mason, John, of *Mason's Island*	Deed to	Corporation of Georgetown	1805	O14	051	030
Mason, John, of G'tn.	Deed fr	Suttle, Henry, of G'tn.	1813	AE30	106	081
Mason, John T. et al	Deed fr	Dulany, Matthew	1797	B2B	626	385
Mason, John T.	Deed fr	Beatty, Charles	1802	I9	519	849
Mason, John T.	Deed fr	Polock, Isaac	1802	I9	259	419
Mason, John T.	Deed to	Worthington, Charles, Dr.	1812	AE30	051	038
Mason, John Thompson	Deed fr	Threlkeld, John	1804	K10	241	249
Mason, John Thomson, of G'tn.	Deed fr	Threlkeld, John, of G'tn.	1798	D4	085	071
Mason, John Thomson, attorney	Deed fr	Threlkeld, John	1799	D4	248	231
Mason, John Thomson	Deed to	Gantt, John M. et al	1801	G7	467	599
Mason, John Thomson, Wash. Co.	Deed to	Teackle, John, Jr., now of G'tn.	1808	T19	036	028
Mason, John Thomson, late G'tn.	Deed to	Teakle, John, Sr., Accomack Co.	1811	AA26	017	013
Masonic Lodge No. 35, members	Deed fr	King, Nicholas	1805	M12	093	086
Masonic Lodge No. 15, members	Deed fr	King, Nicholas	1805	M12	093	086
Massey, Henry, of Chilicothe	Deed fr	Munroe, Thomas, Supt.	1802	H8	565	528
Massey, Thomas	Deed fr	Brooks, William H.	1802	H8	312	293
Massey, Thomas, of G'tn.	Deed fr	Brooks, William H., of G'tn.	1804	K10	117	126
Massey, Thomas, of G'tn.	Deed fr	Athey, George, of G'tn.	1813	AF31	059	040
Masters, Benjamin et al	Deed to	Walker, Zachariah	1815	AI34	435	452
Masters, Ezekiel	B. of S. to	O'Brien, William	1806	Q16	264	184
Masters, Ezekiel	B. of S. to	O'Brien, William	1806	Q16	263	183
Masters, Ezekiel	B. of S. to	Hughes, Theophilus	1808	T19	100	071
Masters, Ezekiel	Mortgage to	Cannon, John & Richard Spalding	1812	AD29	313	257
Masters, Ezekiel	B. of S. to	Walker, Zachariah	1816	AM37	452	325
Masters, Ezekiel	B. of S. to	Walker, Zachariah	1816	AM37	453	326
Masters, George et al	Deed to	Spalding, Enoch	1815	AI34	097	110
Masters, George et al	Deed to	Walker, Zachariah	1815	AI34	435	452
Masters, George et al	Deed to	Spalding, Enoch	1815	AI34	110	126
Masters, John	Deed to	Johns, Acquila, of P.G. Co.	1805	N13	153	143
Masters, John	B. of S. to	Murray, Thomas	1807	R17	375	284
Masters, John	Deed to	Burrows, Edward	1807	S18	137	112
Masters, John, heirs of	Deed to	Spalding, Enoch	1815	AI34	097	110
Masters, John, heirs, Scioto OH	Deed to	Walker, Zachariah	1815	AI34	435	452
Masters, John, Jr.	Deed to	Walker, Zachariah	1817	AO39	439	300
Masters, Priscilla, Scioto Co. OH	Release to	Spalding, Enoch	1815	AI34	098	112
Masters, Priscilla, wid/o John, OH	Dower to	Walker, Zachariah	1816	AM37	297	217
Mathers, James	Deed fr	Brent, Daniel Carroll, trustee et al	1807	R17	022	019
Mathers, James	Deed fr	Varden, Charles H.	1807	R17	020	017
Mathers, James	Deed fr	McDonald, John G., trustee	1810	Z25	009	007
Mathers, James	Deed to	McDonald, John G.	1810	Z25	018	014
Mathers, James	Deed fr	Varden, Charles H.	1811	AA26	365	243
Matten, Ann	B. of S. fr	Beall, Benjamin	1814	AH33	177	163

Index to District of Columbia Land Records, 1792-1817

Party	What	Party	Year	Liber	Old	New
Matthews, Daniel, of VA	Deed to	Beall, Thomas & John M. Gantt	1793	A1-1	261	354
Matthews, William	Manumis to	[ ], Suckey (mulatto)	1808	T19	224	164
Matthews, William	Deed fr	Van Ness, John P. & Marcia	1811	AB27	157	130
Matthews, William	Deed to	Neale, Francis, Rev.	1815	AI34	257	290
Matthews, William Penrose, Balto.	Transfer fr	Ralph, George, Rev.	1798	B2B	478	171
Matthews, William Penrose, Balto.	Cert fr	Commissioners of Washington	1798	B2B	478	171
Matthews, William, Rev.	Deed fr	Pratt, Henry, of Phila. et al	1811	AB27	342	282
Matthews, William, Rev.	Deed fr	Hoban, James	1811	AC28	025	019
Matthews, William, Rev.	Deed fr	Cox, John, of G'tn.	1813	AE30	345	258
Matthews, William, Rev.	Deed fr	Helen, Walter	1814	AG32	212	148
Matthews, William, Rev.	Assign fr	Caffry, Daniel	1814	AG32	317	232
Matthews, William, Rev.	Deed fr	Dunlop, James, of G'tn.	1814	AG32	311	227
Mattingley, Edward	B. of S. fr	Church, Lewis	1817	AO39	071	058
Mattingly, Edward	Deed to	Mattingly, Wm., of St. Mary's Co.	1812	AD29	267	221
Mattingly, Edward	Deed fr	Carroll, Daniel, of *Duddington*	1815	AI34	182	209
Mattingly, Edward	B. of S. fr	Johnson, Walter	1815	AI34	103	117
Mattingly, Joseph	B. of S. fr	Johnson, Joseph	1815	AH33	481	410
Mattingly, Margaret	B. of S. fr	Lowe, Martha	1816	AL36	299	296
Mattingly, Stephen, trustee	B. of S. fr	Murray, William, insolvent	1805	N13	116	111
Mattingly, Thomas	B. of S. to	Eliason, Ebenezer	1808	T19	151	106
Mattingly, Wm., of St. Mary's Co.	Deed fr	Mattingly, Edward	1812	AD29	267	221
Maul, John P.	Deed fr	Owens, Isaac, of G'tn.	1815	AK35	175	135
Maul, John P.	Deed to	Davis, Charles B., of G'tn.	1816	AM37	232	170
Maul, John P.	Agreement	Druet, James	1817	AO39	120	092
Maupin, Catharine	Agreement	Wilson, John A.	1810	Y24	043	038
Mauro, P., of Balto.	Deed to	Ott, John, of G'tn.	1814	AG32	341	247
Mauro, P., of Balto.	D. of T. to	Ott, John, of G'tn.	1814	AH33	049	044
Mauro, Philip	Cert fr	Munroe, Thomas, Supt.	1809	X23	081	060
Mauro, Philip	Deed fr	Wright, Thomas C.	1809	V21	152	111
Mauro, Philip	Deed fr	Stoddert, Benjamin	1811	AC28	054	041
Mauro, Philip	Deed to	Knoblock, John	1815	AK35	444	349
Mauro, Philip	Deed to	Stinger, Frederick	1815	AK35	447	350
Mauro, Philip	Plat	Pennsylvania Ave. & 10th St.	1816	AL36	509	
Mauro, Philip	Deed to	Hendley, Richard	1816	AL36	506	475
Mauro, Philip	Deed fr	Ott, David	1816	AM37	146	113
Mauro, Philip	Deed to	Grammer, Gottlieb Christopher	1816	AM37	045	037
Mauro, Philip & Conradt Schwartz	Deed fr	Dorsey, William H.	1811	AB27	223	181
Mauro, Philip & Conrad Schwartz	Deed fr	Murdock, John	1811	AB27	227	185
Mauro, Philip & Conrad Schwartz	Deed fr	Murdock, John, of G'tn.	1812	AC28	257	188
Mauro, Philip & Conrad Schwartz	Deed fr	Dorsey, William H., of Balto. Co.	1812	AC28	258	189
Mauro, Philip & Elizabeth	Deed to	Clarke, Alban	1815	AI34	514	519
Mauro, Philip, of Balto.	Deed fr	Schwarz, Conrad, of Balto.	1815	AI34	151	173
Mauro, Philip, of Balto.	Deed to	Fielius, Jacob	1815	AI34	060	060
Mauro, Philip, of Balto. et al	Deed to	Riley, William	1815	AI34	012	013
Mauro, Philip, of Balto.	Plat	Squares 292 and 349	1815	AI34	062	
Mauro, Philip, of Balto.	Release fr	Ott, John, of G'tn.	1815	AI34	007	007
Maus, John H.	Deed fr	Cozens, William R.	1815	AH33	483	413
Maus, John N.	Deed fr	Riggs, George W., of Balto. MD	1812	AD29	168	134
Maxwell, George	Assign fr	Wade, Robert P.	1809	V21	371	275
Maxwell, George	Convey to	Stewart, William	1809	V21	405	308
Maxwell, George	Deed fr	Brooke, Henry, of P.G. Co.	1809	V21	370	273
Maxwell, George	D. of T. to	McClann, Robert & Robt. P. Wade	1809	W22	150	106
Maxwell, George	Deed to	Beall, Thomas B.	1811	AB27	431	355
Maxwell, George	B. of S. to	Miller, George	1812	AD29	142	110
Maxwell, George P.	Lease fr	Van Ness, John P. & Marcia	1815	AI34	462	474

Party	What	Party	Year	Liber	Old	New
Maxwell, George P.	Lease fr	Van Ness, John P. & Marcia	1816	AM37	240	176
May, Frederick	Deed fr	Brent, Daniel Carroll, marshall	1802	H8	446	410
May, Frederick	Deed fr	Steele, John	1802	I9	462	761
May, Frederick	Deed fr	Loring, Israel	1802	I9	190	294
May, Frederick	Deed to	Wayman, Charles	1802	I9	539	879
May, Frederick	Deed to	Middleton, James	1802	I9	182	279
May, Frederick	Deed fr	Munroe, Thomas, Supt.	1802	I9	461	760
May, Frederick	Agreement	Fletcher, Betsey	1802	I9	282	460
May, Frederick	Assign fr	Eliot, Samuel	1802	I9	457	755
May, Frederick	Deed to	Dempsey, John	1803	K10	059	64
May, Frederick	Deed to	Bowen, Thomas	1805	M12	305	307
May, Frederick	Deed fr	Greenleaf, James, attorney in fact	1805	N13	108	102
May, Frederick	Deed to	Wayman, Charles, of G'tn.	1805	N13	147	137
May, Frederick	Deed fr	Eliot, Samuel, Jr.	1805	N13	152	142
May, Frederick	Deed fr	Eliot, Samuel, Jr.	1805	N13	150	140
May, Frederick	Deed to	Middleton, Electus	1805	N13	056	052
May, Frederick	Deed to	Bell, George (mulatto)	1805	M12	306	308
May, Frederick	Assign to	Kirby, John Baptist	1806	Q16	176	117
May, Frederick	Mortgage fr	Wigfield, Mathew	1806	P15	149	097
May, Frederick	Deed fr	Bell, George (mulatto)	1806	P15	003	002
May, Frederick	Deed to	Tippitt, Cartwright	1807	R17	356	271
May, Frederick	Deed fr	Barry, James & Johanna, of NY	1807	S18	320	251
May, Frederick	Deed fr	Elliot, Samuel, Jr.	1808	T19	366	262
May, Frederick	Deed to	Cranch, William	1808	T19	098	069
May, Frederick	Deed to	Bowen, Thomas	1808	T19	057	042
May, Frederick	Deed to	Caton, John	1809	X23	169	125
May, Frederick	Deed to	Kyne, Matthias	1809	X23	171	127
May, Frederick	Deed to	Young, Moses	1809	X23	133	096
May, Frederick	Agreement	Kyne, Matthias	1809	X23	172	128
May, Frederick	Deed to	Tippett, Cartwright	1809	V21	255	182
May, Frederick	Deed to	Jeffers, Matthias	1810	X23	407	328
May, Frederick	B. of S. fr	Middleton, Electius	1810	Y24	174	159
May, Frederick	Deed to	McKee, James	1810	Y24	373	337
May, Frederick	Deed to	Love, John & Patrick Kain	1810	Y24	090	081
May, Frederick	Deed to	Middleton, Electius	1810	Y24	058	051
May, Frederick	Deed to	Patterson, James	1810	Y24	191	175
May, Frederick	Deed to	Coombe, Griffith	1810	Z25	242	189
May, Frederick	Lease to	Wason, Edward	1810	Z25	294	231
May, Frederick	Lease to	White, Ambrose	1810	Z25	211	166
May, Frederick	Release fr	Cranch, William	1811	AB27	493	403
May, Frederick	Deed to	White, Levi	1811	AC28	021	016
May, Frederick	Deed to	Smallwood, Samuel N.	1811	AB27	511	418
May, Frederick	Deed fr	Smallwood, Samuel N.	1811	AB27	513	420
May, Frederick	Lease to	Bury, James	1812	AB27	516	422
May, Frederick	Mortgage fr	Young, James	1812	AB27	525	428
May, Frederick	Deed to	Keyne, Matthias	1812	AD29	373	314
May, Frederick	Deed to	Middleton, Electius	1812	AD29	138	107
May, Frederick	Deed to	Cocke, Buller	1812	AD29	482	407
May, Frederick	Lease to	Elliott, Robert	1812	AD29	176	141
May, Frederick	Deed to	Miller, Samuel	1813	AF31	223	152
May, Frederick	Lease to	Kain, Patrick	1813	AF31	263	184
May, Frederick	Deed to	McGowan, John	1813	AE30	517	384
May, Frederick	Deed to	Bury, James	1814	AH33	139	132
May, Frederick	Release fr	Elliott, Robert	1815	AI34	014	015
May, Frederick	Deed to	Scott, William A.	1816	AM37	219	162

Index to District of Columbia Land Records, 1792-1817

Party	What	Party	Year	Liber	Old	New
May, Frederick	Deed to	Law, John	1816	AM37	070	057
May, Frederick & Samuel Eliot, Jr.	Deed to	Jones, Rachael	1806	Q16	145	095
May, Frederick, Dr.	Deed fr	Commissioners of Washington	1801	G7	019	025
May, Frederick, Dr.	Deed to	Barry, James	1802	H8	445	409
May, Frederick, Dr.	Deed to	Young, James	1812	AB27	189	155
May, Frederick et al	Cert fr	Commissioners of Washington	1798	B2B	477	170
May, Frederick et al	Cert fr	Commissioners of Washington	1798	B2B	477	171
May, Frederick et al	Cert fr	Commissioners of Washington	1798	B2B	477	170
May, Frederick et al	Agreement	Burrows, Edward	1799	E5	050	040
May, Frederick et al	Deed to	Patterson, James	1802	H8	260	247
May, Frederick et al	Deed to	Wade, Anne	1802	H8	504	464
May, Frederick et al	Deed fr	Barry, James David	1804	L11	346	313
May, Frederick et al	Deed to	Fletcher, Betsey	1808	U20	128	073
May, Frederick, physician	Deed fr	Dempsie, John, Gent.	1801	G7	022	027
May, Frederick, physician	Deed to	Dempsie, John, Gent.	1801	G7	020	026
May, Frederick, physician	Release fr	Dempsie, John, Gent.	1807	S18	016	014
May, Frederick, physician	Lease to	Kain, Patrick	1808	V21	115	086
May, Frederick, physician	Deed to	Love, John & Patrick Kain	1808	V21	119	088
May, Frederick, s/o John	Deed fr	May, John, of Boston MA	1804	L11	241	223
May, George et al	Cert fr	Munroe, Thomas, Supt.	1808	U20	345	187
May, George W.	Deed fr	Turner, Robert, of Balto. Co.	1815	AI34	045	051
May, John Frederick	Deed fr	Law, Thomas	1813	AE30	158	125
May, John, of Boston MA	Deed fr	Commissioners of Washington	1800	F6	036	023
May, John, of MA	Deed fr	Commissioners of Washington	1802	H8	273	259
May, John, of Boston MA	Deed to	May, Frederick, s/o John	1804	L11	241	223
Mayer & Wetzel	Mortgage fr	Williams, Philip, of G'tn.	1809	W22	321	209
Mayer, Frederick	D. of T. to	Hewitt, John & Joseph Scholfield	1813	AF31	403	291
Mayer, Frederick	Deed fr	Scholfield, Andrew, of Alexa. Co.	1814	AG32	204	142
Mayer, Henry	B. of S. fr	Saunders, Thomas	1809	W22	214	147
Mayer, Henry	B. of S. fr	Baker, John	1810	Y24	150	136
Mayer, Henry	Deed to	Baker, John	1813	AE30	213	173
Mayer, Henry	Convey fr	Sanderson, William R., Fredk. Co.	1814	AH33	091	083
Mayer, Henry	B. of S. to	Beatty, Thomas, Jr.	1814	AH33	020	018
Mayer, Henry	Deed fr	Bohrer, Jacob, of G'tn.	1814	AG32	167	119
Mayer, Henry	Convey to	Beatty, Thomas, Jr.	1814	AH33	020	018
Mayer, Henry	B. of S. fr	Manning, Ignatius, St. Mary's Co.	1815	AI34	179	204
Mayer, Henry	Assign fr	Brunner, John, of Henry, of G'tn.	1815	AI34	503	509
Mayer, Henry	Assign fr	Mayne, Adam, of G'tn.	1815	AK35	077	059
Mayer, Henry	Deed fr	Presbyterian Congregation of G'tn.	1815	AK35	075	058
Mayer, Henry	Deed fr	Bohrer, Jacob, of G'tn.	1816	AL36	183	182
Mayer, Henry & G.C. Grammar	Mortgage to	Hughes, Thomas	1812	AD29	387	326
Mayer, Henry et al	B. of S. fr	Talbert, Bazil, of P.G. Co.	1808	T19	324	236
Mayer, Henry et al	Deed fr	Hughes, Thomas	1814	AG32	060	047
Mayer, Henry, of G'tn.	Deed fr	Davidson, John	1812	AD29	234	193
Mayer, Henry, of G'tn.	Deed fr	Beatty, Thomas, Jr., of G'tn.	1813	AE30	126	098
Mayer, Henry, of G'tn.	Deed to	Grammar, Gottlieb Christopher	1814	AG32	282	202
Mayer, Henry, of G'tn.	Mortgage fr	Grammar, Gottlieb Christopher	1814	AG32	381	277
Mayer, Henry, of G'tn.	Deed fr	Sanderson, William R., Fredk. Co.	1815	AK35	249	197
Mayer, Henry, of G'tn.	Assign fr	Hurdle, Noble, of G'tn.	1816	AL36	120	121
Mayhew, Clement	B. of S. to	Smiller, Margaret	1816	AL36	092	093
Mayhew, James	Deed fr	Wigfield, Mathew	1808	T19	108	077
Mayhue, Clement & Mary	Deed to	Foyles, Thomas & J. Middleton	1816	AM37	099	079
Mayhue, James	Deed to	Free, John	1811	AB27	114	093
Mayn, Adam	Lease fr	Presbyterian Congregation of G'tn.	1811	AB27	471	385
Mayn, Adam	B. of S. fr	Mudd, Walter	1813	AF31	070	048

Party	What	Party	Year	Liber	Old	New
Mayn, Adam, of G'tn.	Deed fr	Brooke, William H., of G'tn.	1814	AH33	072	064
Mayn, Adam, s/o John, of G'tn.	Deed fr	Fouke, George & Elizabeth	1812	AD29	152	119
Mayn, Adam, s/o John, of G'tn.	Deed to	Renner, Daniel	1814	AH33	137	131
Maynard, Benjamin & Susanna	Deed to	Hines, Daniel	1807	R17	367	280
Maynard, Brice, h/o Thomas	Deed to	Magruder, George Beall	1810	Y24	275	252
Maynard, Thomas	Deed fr	Davidson, John	1802	I9	289	474
Mayne, Adam	Deed to	Edmonston, Thomas	1817	AN38	552	402
Mayne, Adam	Deed to	Erskine, Elizabeth	1817	AN38	203	147
Mayne, Adam & John Brunner	Assign fr	Hoot, Samuel	1812	AC28	338	245
Mayne, Adam, of G'tn.	Assign to	Mayer, Henry	1815	AK35	077	059
Mayne, Adam, of G'tn.	Deed fr	Kemp, Ann Margaret, Fredk. Co.	1817	AO39	065	054
Mayne, Adan et al	Lease fr	Schultze, Henry	1816	AK35	502	396
Mayo, Joseph, late of Henrico Co.	Manumis to	[ ], Tom (negro)	1805	N13	284	
Mayor & Corporation Washington	Cert fr	Munroe, Thomas, Supt.	1807	S18	013	012
Mayor & Council of Washington	Deed fr	Carroll, Daniel, of *Duddington*	1807	R17	228	172
Mayor & Council of Georgetown	Deed fr	Peter, Robert et al	1807	R17	232	
Mayor, Henry	Deed fr	Esenbeck, William	1815	AK35	073	057
Mayor of Georgetown	Deed fr	Deakins, William, Jr., of G'tn.	1793	A1-2	461	69
Mayor of Georgetown et al	Deed to	Turner, Samuel, Jr.	1808	U20	330	178
Mayor of Georgetown et al	Deed to	Steuart, David	1808	U20	260	138
Mayor of Georgetown	Bond fr	Georgetown Lancaster School	1812	AC28	493	352
McAlister, Richard	Deed fr	Beall, Thomas	1793	A1-1	359	
McCaffrey, William	Lease fr	Carroll, Daniel, of *Duddington*	1816	AO39	024	019
McCall, Archibald et al	Release to	Nourse, Joseph	1813	AF31	011	008
McCann, Arthur, of G'tn.	Deed fr	Laland, John	1812	AC28	324	236
McCann, Arthur, of G'tn.	Deed fr	Simms, Francis, of P.G. Co.	1813	AE30	156	123
McCarthy, John	Deed fr	Carroll, Daniel, of Duddington	1802	H8	567	529
McCarthy, John	Deed fr	Carroll, Daniel, of Duddington	1802	H8	563	526
McCauley, George	Deed fr	Chandler, Walter Story	1808	U20	385	213
McCauley, George	Deed fr	Chandler, Walter Story	1813	AE30	503	373
McCauley, George	Qualify	Lieutant in 2nd Regiment	1814	AH33	117	110
McCauley, George	Deed fr	Cocke, Buller	1814	AH33	116	108
McCauley, George	D. of T. to	Young, James	1815	AI34	464	476
McCauley, George	Release fr	Young, James	1816	AL36	153	153
McCawley, George	B. of S. fr	Soper, Leven	1810	Y24	226	208
McCerran, Andrew & H. Jenkins	Lease fr	Van Ness, John P. & Marcia	1816	AM37	391	282
McCerran, Andrew & H. Jenkins	Lease fr	Van Ness, John P. & Marcia	1817	AO39	076	062
McChesney, William, of G'tn.	Deed to	English, David, of G'tn.	1814	AH33	224	198
McChesney, William, of G'tn.	Deed fr	Garey, Everard, of G'tn.	1814	AH33	222	196
McClain, George, s/o John of NC	Deed to	Beatty, Charles, of G'tn.	1794	A1-2	494	97
McClain, Thomas	Deed to	Cassin, Joseph	1808	U20	161	091
McClain, Thomas	Deed to	Cassin, Joseph	1809	V21	223	158
McClan, Elizabeth	Deed fr	Beatty, Charles, heirs of	1807	Q16	341	261
McClan, Robert	Deed fr	Doll, Jacob	1795	B2A	271	379
McClan, Robert	Deed fr	Munroe, Thomas, Supt.	1802	I9	502	824
McClan, Robert	Deed fr	Wingard, Abraham	1802	I9	511	837
McClan, Robert	Deed fr	Segur, Nathaniel	1802	I9	232	369
McClan, Robert	Deed fr	Bastian, Charles, an insolvent	1804	K10	200	208
McClan, Robert	Deed fr	Ames, Benjamin	1804	K10	221	230
McClan, Robert	Deed fr	Beatty, Charles, heirs of	1806	O14	236	155
McClan, Robert	Deed to	Boyd, Washington	1809	V21	267	191
McClan, Robert	Deed to	Holtzman, Jacob	1811	AA26	256	174
McClan, Robert, of G'tn.	Deed to	McClan, William, of G'tn.	1794	B2A	033	037
McClan, Robert, of Montg. Co.	Release to	King, William	1795	B2A	346	488

Party	What	Party	Year	Liber	Old	New
McClan, Robert, of G'tn.	Deed to	Shanks, Michael, of G'tn.	1795	B2A	272	380
McClan, Robert, of G'tn.	Deed to	Gannon, James, of G'tn.	1796	B2B	529	244
McClan, Robert, of G'tn.	Deed to	French, George, of G'tn.	1796	B2B	528	242
McClan, Robert, of G'tn.	Deed to	Kennedy, James, of G'tn.	1797	B2B	682	456
McClan, Robert, of PA	Deed fr	Holtzman, Jacob, of G'tn.	1814	AH33	033	030
McClan, Robert, trustee	Deed fr	Evans, Evan, insolvent	1804	L11	139	
McClan, William, of G'tn.	Deed fr	McClan, Robert, of G'tn.	1794	B2A	033	037
McClane, Robert	B. of S. fr	Thomson, George	1806	Q16	010	006
McClane, Robert	Deed fr	Magruder, George, collector, G'tn.	1807	S18	036	029
McClann, Andrew	Deed fr	Elford, John	1806	P15	336	222
McClann, Robert & Robt. P. Wade	D. of T. fr	Maxwell, George	1809	W22	150	106
McClann, Robert, of G'tn.	Deed fr	King, William, of G'tn.	1794	A1-2	499	102
McClann, Robert, of G'tn.	Deed fr	Beatty, John M. et al	1805	M12	363	371
McClann, Robert, of G'tn.	Deed to	Renner, Daniel & Daniel Bussard	1809	X23	292	232
McClann, Robert, trustee	Assign fr	Langley, Edward	1809	W22	061	045
McClaren, Duncan, of G'tn.	B. of S. to	Holliday, William, of G'tn.	1814	AG32	445	322
McClary, Henry, of Frederick Co.	Deed fr	Deakins, Francis	1792	A1-1	123	180
McClary, Henry, of Frederick Co.	Deed fr	Balch, Stephen B.	1795	B2A	189	253
McClary, James	D. of T. fr	Gideon, Jacob	1815	AH33	414	357
McClean, Cornelius	Deed to	Triplett, Thomas	1807	Q16	370	283
McCleary, Henry	Deed fr	Levy, David, of Frederick Co.	1792	A1-1	066	98
McCleary, Henry	Deed fr	Lowndes, Francis, trustee	1802	H8	352	328
McCleary, Henry	Deed fr	Beall, Thomas	1802	I9	513	840
McCleary, Henry	Deed fr	Beall, Thomas	1802	I9	542	884
McCleary, Henry	Deed fr	Brent, Robert	1802	H8	352	328
McCleary, Henry	Deed to	Waters, William	1804	L11	091	93
McCleary, Henry	Deed fr	Stoner, Stephen, Col., s/o John	1812	AC28	490	348
McCleary, Henry, of Frederick Co.	Deed fr	Davidson, John	1798	D4	050	042
McCleery, Andrew & Robert	Deed fr	Ritchie, Abner	1811	AA26	213	146
McCleery, Henry	Deed fr	Brother, Henry, of Frederick Co.	1794	B2A	021	023
McCleery, Henry	Deed fr	Beatty, Charles, Col.	1804	K10	266	272
McCleery, Henry	Deed to	Waters, William, of G'tn.	1805	M12	291	292
McCleery, Henry	Deed to	Brengle, Lawrence	1806	P15	306	199
McCleery, Henry	Deed fr	Smith, Andrew & Isabella	1812	AC28	170	126
McCleery, Henry	Deed fr	Smith, Andrew	1812	AC28	169	126
McCleery, Henry, of Frederick Co.	Deed to	Beall, Thomas & John M. Gantt	1792	A1-1	139	202
McCleery, Henry, of Frederick Co.	Deed fr	Beall, Thomas & Elijah, of G'tn.	1801	G7	088	114
McCleery, Henry, of Frederick Co.	Deed fr	Brengle, Lawrence, Frederick Co.	1806	P15	303	199
McCleery, Henry, of MD	Deed to	Newton, Ignatius	1814	AH33	321	277
McCleery, William, of Balto.	Deed fr	Commissioners of Washington	1801	G7	090	116
McCleland, John	Deed fr	Caldwell, Timothy	1805	M12	407	422
McCleland, John	Manumis to	[ ], Benjamin (negro)	1810	Y24	419	376
McClellan, John et al	Release to	deKrafft, Edward B.	1813	AF31	532	393
McClelland, John	B. of S. fr	Murdock, John, of G'tn.	1807	S18	161	131
McClelland, John	Deed to	Bacon, Samuel	1807	S18	005	004
McClelland, John	Deed fr	Davidson, John	1808	V21	065	052
McClelland, John	Deed fr	Murdock, John, of G'tn.	1808	U20	339	183
McClelland, John	Mortgage fr	Daugherty, Joseph & Mary	1810	X23	333	266
McClelland, John	Deed to	Appler, David & Jonathan	1811	Z25	313	245
McClelland, John	Deed fr	Dorsey, William H., of Balto.	1811	AA26	003	002
McClelland, John	Deed to	Daugherty, Joseph	1814	AH33	122	115
McClelland, John	Deed to	Campbell, John	1815	AI34	506	511
McClelland, John	D. of T. fr	Lowe, Loyd M.	1815	AI34	379	406
McClelland, John	Deed to	Lowe, Lloyd Magruder	1815	AI34	466	478
McClelland, John	Deed fr	Campbell, John	1815	AI34	382	408

Index to District of Columbia Land Records, 1792-1817

Party	What	Party	Year	Liber	Old	New
McClelland, John	Deed fr	Davidson, Samuel, of Balto.	1816	AO39	018	014
McClelland, John et al	Mortgage fr	Ryan, Henry & Mary	1809	X23	298	237
McClelland, John et al	Release to	deKrafft, Edward B.	1813	AF31	280	198
McClelland, John, trustee	Mortgage fr	deKrafft, Edward B.	1813	AE30	234	187
McClery, James	Qualify	Deputy Clerk County Court	1802	H8	545	506
McCloskey, William	Mortgage to	Rice, Edmund	1814	AG32	358	259
McCloskey, William, of P.G. Co.	B. of S. to	Fletcher, William	1805	N13	205	178
McClure, John	Discharge	Private in Capt. Littlejohn's troop	1815	AH33	451	386
McConnell, James & Robert Kerr	L. of Atty. fr	Kerr, Alexander	1811	AB27	122	100
McConnell, John	Deed to	Clarke, Frances et al	1813	AE30	326	244
McCormick, Alex. & C. Varden	D. of T. fr	Varden, Charles H.	1813	AE30	355	265
McCormick, Alexander	Deed fr	Dermott, James Reed	1796	B2B	576	319
McCormick, Alexander	Deed to	Riddle, Joseph, of Alexa. et al	1798	D4	053	044
McCormick, Alexander	Deed fr	Dunlop, Henry	1802	I9	086	123
McCormick, Alexander	Deed fr	Sothoron, Thomas L.	1802	I9	334	551
McCormick, Alexander	B. of S. fr	Brown, Robert	1804	K10	331	341
McCormick, Alexander	B. of S. fr	Staines, John	1805	O14	090	056
McCormick, Alexander	Deed to	Wigfield, James	1808	U20	252	135
McCormick, Alexander	D. of T. fr	Wigfield, Robert & Mary	1809	X23	125	090
McCormick, Alexander	Deed fr	Kilty, John & Josias Wilson King	1809	V21	341	246
McCormick, Alexander	Deed to	Cassin, Joseph	1809	W22	130	093
McCormick, Alexander	B. of S. fr	Veitch, James	1810	Y24	316	287
McCormick, Alexander	B. of S. fr	Boyd, Richard D.	1810	Y24	511	449
McCormick, Alexander	B. of S. fr	Stelle, Portius D.	1810	Y24	314	286
McCormick, Alexander	Deed fr	Hodgson, John, mer., in Eng.	1811	AA26	403	268
McCormick, Alexander	B. of S. fr	Frost, John T.	1812	AC28	306	223
McCormick, Alexander	B. of S. fr	Orr, Benjamin G.	1813	AE30	252	197
McCormick, Alexander	Qualify	First Lieutenant of artillery	1813	AE30	384	283
McCormick, Alexander	D. of T. fr	Cassin, Joseph	1813	AE30	253	198
McCormick, Alexander	D. of T. fr	Young, James	1813	AF31	487	355
McCormick, Alexander	Deed fr	Watterston, George	1813	AE30	266	206
McCormick, Alexander	B. of S. fr	Smoot, Alexander S.	1814	AH33	098	090
McCormick, Alexander	B. of S. fr	Moore, William	1814	AG32	124	091
McCormick, Alexander	Deed fr	Middleton, Isaac	1814	AG32	427	309
McCormick, Alexander	B. of S. fr	Ball, Henry W.	1815	AH33	380	329
McCormick, Alexander	Release to	Moore, William	1816	AM37	247	182
McCormick, Alexander	Deed fr	Walker, Zachariah, collector	1817	AN38	178	129
McCormick, Alexander	Deed to	Campbell, John, agent	1817	AN38	208	152
McCormick, Alexander, *Cap. Hill*	Deed fr	Threlkeld, James	1804	K10	265	271
McCormick, Alexander et al	Deed to	Gannon, James, of G'tn.	1804	M12	012	013
McCormick, Alexander et al	Deed fr	King, Nicholas	1805	M12	093	086
McCormick, Alexander et al	Deed to	Wigfield, James	1807	S18	305	239
McCormick, Alexander et al	B. of S. fr	Lindsey, George W.	1810	Z25	191	150
McCormick, Alexander et al	Deed fr	Hamilton, Christiana	1811	AC28	035	026
McCormick, Alexander et al	Manumis to	[ ], Kitty (C), age 6, d/o Henny	1811	AC28	083	063
McCormick, Alexander et al	D. of T. fr	Caldwell, Timothy, of Phila. PA	1812	AE30	017	014
McCormick, Alexander et al	Release to	Caldwell, Timothy, of Phila. PA	1813	AF31	243	168
McCormick, Alexander et al	Deed to	Young, James, trustee	1813	AE30	094	072
McCormick, Alexander et al	Deed fr	Jackson, John G., fr. Harrison Co.	1814	AG32	295	215
McCormick, Alexander, mer.	Deed fr	Young, Moses, Gent.	1810	Z25	361	283
McCormick, Alexander, trustee	Deed fr	Barclay, Thomas, an insolvent	1804	K10	311	315
McCormick, Alexander, trustee	Deed fr	Suter, John, insolvent	1806	P15	360	239
McCormick, Alexander, trustee	Deed fr	Long, Robert, insolvent debtor	1812	AD29	312	256
McCormick, Benson, insolvent	Deed to	Harper, Alexander, trustee	1811	AB27	125	103
McCormick, Benson L.	Deed fr	Ireland, Elizabeth et al	1805	N13	240	202

Party	What	Party	Year	Liber	Old	New
McCormick, Benson L.	Deed fr	Wigfield, James	1805	N13	119	114
McCormick, Benson L.	Deed fr	Wigfield, James	1805	M12	163	160
McCormick, Benson L.	B. of S. to	Bean, George	1806	O14	162	106
McCormick, Benson L. et al	Deed to	Vint, John	1806	P15	246	163
McCormick, Benson L. et al	Deed to	Wigfield, James	1807	S18	305	239
McCormick, George	Deed to	Waters, William	1806	O14	334	299
McCormick, George, of G'tn.	Deed fr	Smith, William, of G'tn.	1804	L11	395	350
McCormick, George, of G'tn.	Deed to	Waters, William, of VA	1806	O14	344	229
McCormick, James	Deed fr	McIntire, Samuel	1807	S18	028	024
McCormick, James	Deed fr	Boyd, Washington, marshal	1808	U20	346	187
McCormick, James	Deed fr	Munroe, Thomas, Supt.	1811	AC28	054	041
McCormick, James	Deed fr	Mercer, John, of Fredericksburg	1813	AE30	092	071
McCormick, James	Deed fr	Law, Thomas & Edmund	1813	AE30	159	126
McCormick, James	Deed fr	Corporation of Washington	1816	AM37	514	379
McCormick, James	Deed fr	Corporation of Washington	1816	AM37	519	383
McCormick, James	Deed fr	Corporation of Washington	1816	AM37	522	386
McCormick, James	Deed fr	Corporation of Washington	1816	AM37	512	377
McCormick, James	Deed fr	Corporation of Washington	1816	AM37	510	375
McCormick, James	Deed fr	Corporation of Washington	1816	AM37	517	381
McCormick, James	Deed fr	Corporation of Washington	1816	AM37	527	391
McCormick, James	Deed fr	Corporation of Washington	1816	AM37	524	388
McCormick, James	Deed fr	Corporation of Washington	1816	AO39	006	005
McCormick, James	Deed fr	Corporation of Washington	1816	AO39	001	001
McCormick, James	Deed fr	Corporation of Washington	1816	AO39	003	003
McCormick, James, Jr.	Deed fr	Kerr, Alexander	1807	S18	284	222
McCormick, James, Jr.	Deed fr	Van Ness, John P. & Marcia	1808	T19	215	156
McCormick, James, Jr.	Mortgage fr	Kilty, John & Josias W. King	1809	W22	189	132
McCormick, James, Jr.	Deed to	Young, Moses	1810	Y24	112	102
McCormick, James, Jr. et al	Deed fr	Oden, Benjamin, of P.G. Co.	1811	AB27	490	401
McCormick, James, Jr.	Deed to	Tayloe, John	1811	AB27	093	076
McCormick, James, Jr.	Assign fr	Webster, Toppan	1812	AD29	118	090
McCormick, James, Jr.	Deed to	King, John	1812	AC28	482	342
McCormick, James, Jr.	Deed fr	Webster, Toppan	1812	AD29	116	089
McCormick, James, Jr., Balto. Co.	Deed to	Webster, Toppan	1814	AH33	094	086
McCormick, James, Jr., Balto. Co.	Assign to	Webster, Toppan	1814	AG32	084	063
McCormick, James, of P.G. Co.	Deed fr	Scholfield, Issachar & M.	1797	B2B	664	429
McCormick, James, the younger	Convey fr	Law, Thomas	1805	N13	095	087
McCormick, Michael	B. of S. to	Cochran, Alexander & Robert	1806	P15	223	149
McCormick, Morgan	Deed fr	Munroe, Thomas, Supt.	1803	K10	072	78
McCoull, Neil, of Richmond VA	Deed fr	Stewart, Sarah, of Balto.	1808	T19	141	101
McCoy, Henry	B. of S. to	Prout, William	1811	AB27	171	141
McCoy, Henry	D. of T. to	Wheatley, Bernard	1815	AI34	017	018
McCoy, Jesse	Lease fr	Dunlap, James	1806	O14	373	248
McCoy, Jesse	Deed to	Dunlop, James	1809	W22	315	205
McCoy, Robert	Deed fr	Deakins, Francis et al	1801	G7	224	299
McCoy, Robert	Deed to	Shepherd, John	1802	I9	034	045
McCreery, William, of Balto.	Deed fr	Brent, Daniel Carroll, marshal	1805	M12	229	230
McCrery, William, of Balto. et al	Deed to	Chesley, Anne, of G'tn.	1804	L11	372	333
McCubbin, Thomas	Deed to	Lingan, James M.	1804	L11	042	42
McCue, Owen	Lease fr	Casanave, Ann	1808	V21	032	024
McCue, Owen	Assign to	Connell, Catharine et al	1808	V21	089	069
McCue, Owen, trustee	Deed fr	Selby, Henry, insolvent	1809	X23	166	122
McCulloch, James et al	Deed to	Beall, Thomas & John M. Gantt	1793	A1-1	348	453
McCutchen, James	Deed to	Herty, Thomas	1808	T19	055	041
McCutchen, John	Lease fr	Prout, William	1805	M12	199	200

Party	What	Party	Year	Liber	Old	New
McCutchen, John, of G'tn.	Deed fr	Prout, William	1808	T19	256	189
McCutchen, Thomas	Lease fr	Beall, Thomas Brooke, of G'tn.	1812	AD29	235	195
McCutchen, Thomas, of G'tn.	Deed fr	Trundel, Horatio, of G'tn.	1808	T19	289	212
McCutchen, Thomas, of G'tn.	Deed fr	Hoover, Andrew, of G'tn.	1809	X23	314	251
McCutchen, Thomas, of G'tn.	Deed to	Hoover, Andrew & Elijah Walker	1810	Y24	079	071
McCutchen, Thomas, of G'tn.	Deed fr	Beall, Thomas B., of G'tn.	1813	AF31	384	276
McCutchen, Thomas, of G'tn.	Deed to	Patterson, Edgar, of G'tn.	1813	AF31	385	277
McCutchens, James, insolvent	Assign to	Gannon, James, trustee	1808	V21	012	009
McCutchin, James	Bond fr	Fields, William	1807	R17	012	011
McCutchin, John	Lease fr	Prout, William	1806	P15	295	194
McCutchin, John, of G'tn.	Deed fr	Dorsey, William Hammond, G'tn.	1801	G7	336	466
McCutchin, Thomas, of G'tn.	B. of S. fr	Barnes, Reason	1809	W22	370	239
McDade, John & Milley, of Balto.	Deed to	Beall, Thomas & John M. Gantt	1794	A1-2	479	84
McDade, Stephen, Monongalia Co.	Deed to	Milligan, Joseph, of G'tn.	1813	AF31	535	396
McDaniel, Ezekiel	Deed fr	Bradley, Phineas	1811	Z25	527	419
McDaniel, Ezekiel	B. of S. fr	Smoot, Alexander S.	1814	AH33	070	063
McDaniel, Ezekiel, collector	Deed to	Mara, Philip	1811	AB27	179	147
McDaniel, George G.	Deed fr	Wayman, Charles, of G'tn.	1804	L11	100	102
McDaniel, George G.	Deed to	Murdock, George, Frederick Town	1804	L11	405	359
McDaniel, James	Deed fr	Beall, Thomas B.	1807	R17	298	227
McDaniel, James (C), of G'tn.	Deed to	Lipscomb, John, of G'tn.	1813	AE30	065	049
McDaniel, James (mulatto)	Discharge	Barney, John H.	1805	M12	319	322
McDaniel, John	Deed fr	Bohrer, George, of G'tn.	1815	AK35	471	370
McDaniel, John	Deed to	Rind, William A., Sr.	1816	AM37	123	096
McDaniel, John, of G'tn.	Deed fr	Kurtz, Daniel, gdn. of H. Reintzel	1814	AG32	453	327
McDaniel, John, s/o Leonard	Cert Free fr	Corcoran, Thomas	1809	V21	379	283
McDaniel, Leonard	Deed fr	Beall, Thomas B.	1807	R17	299	228
McDaniel, Martin N.	Cert Slave	From Loudoun Co.	1816	AM37	299	218
McDaniel, Mary	B. of S. fr	Reilly, William	1808	U20	064	036
McDaniel, Nathan	B. of S. to	Jones, John	1812	AD29	194	158
McDaniel, William, s/o Leonard	Cert Free fr	Corcoran, Thomas	1809	V21	379	283
McDermot, Maria et al	Deed fr	Neale, Leonard, Rt. Rev., of G'tn.	1808	U20	283	151
McDermott, Maria et al	Confirm fr	Neale, Leonard, Rev.	1811	AB27	169	140
McDonald, Alexander	Assign fr	McDonald, Charles	1802	H8	259	246
McDonald, Alexander	Deed fr	Eliason, Ebenezer	1807	S18	275	215
McDonald, Alexander	Release fr	Brodeau, Ann	1811	AB27	177	146
McDonald, Alexander	Deed fr	Thornton, William	1811	AB27	164	136
McDonald, Alexander	Agreement	Davidson, Samuel, of Balto. MD	1812	AD29	169	135
McDonald, Alexander	Deed fr	Davidson, Samuel, of Balto.	1816	AL36	510	478
McDonald, Alexander et al	Convey to	Gardner, William P.	1811	AA26	181	124
McDonald, Alexander, now Balto.	Deed to	Gardner, William P.	1812	AD29	270	222
McDonald, Alexander, of MD	Deed fr	Smith, Walter & Clement, of G'tn.	1806	Q16	088	056
McDonald, Alexander, of G'tn.	Deed to	Eliason, Ebenezer, late of G'tn.	1807	S18	370	293
McDonald, Alexander, of Balto.	Convey to	Gardner, William P.	1811	AA26	181	124
McDonald, Alspeth	B. of S. fr	Jones, Jesson	1805	O14	105	066
McDonald, Andrew	Deed fr	Scott, Gustavus	1799	D4	249	233
McDonald, Andrew	Deed fr	Dorsey, William Hammond	1802	H8	399	370
McDonald, Andrew	Deed to	Clephan, Lewis	1802	I9	379	629
McDonald, Andrew	Deed to	Holburne, William	1806	O14	379	252
McDonald, Andrew	B. of S. fr	Finnicum, Benjamin	1808	T19	344	248
McDonald, Andrew	B. of S. fr	Finnicum, Benjamin, of G'tn.	1808	T19	342	248
McDonald, Andrew & Catherine	D. of T. to	Clephan, Lewis	1808	T19	395	20
McDonald, Andrew & L. Clephan	Deed to	Wright, Matthew	1812	AC28	150	112
McDonald, Andrew & L. Clephan	Deed to	Wright, Matthew	1812	AD29	275	227
McDonald, Andrew, of G'tn.	Release fr	Clephane, Lewis	1805	O14	145	094

Party	What	Party	Year	Liber	Old	New
McDonald, Archibald	Deed fr	Brackenridge, John	1811	AB27	131	108
McDonald, Archibald	Deed to	Shoemaker, David	1811	AB27	126	103
McDonald, Charles	Assign to	McDonald, Alexander	1802	H8	259	246
McDonald, James, bankrupt	Discharge		1804	K10	302	306
McDonald, John G.	Deed to	Roberts, John & S. Griffith	1808	T19	247	182
McDonald, John G.	Deed to	Hoye, John, of Montg. Co.	1810	Y24	409	368
McDonald, John G., trustee	Deed to	Snow, Gideon, of Boston MA	1810	Y24	168	154
McDonald, John G.	Deed to	Glover, Charles	1810	Y24	358	323
McDonald, John G., trustee	Deed to	Hoban, James	1810	Y24	483	426
McDonald, John G., trustee	Deed to	Whelan, Nicholas	1810	Z25	103	080
McDonald, John G., trustee	Deed to	Mathers, James	1810	Z25	009	007
McDonald, John G.	Deed fr	Mathers, James	1810	Z25	018	014
McDonald, John G.	Deed fr	Roberts, John, of Alexa. et al	1810	Z25	223	175
McDonald, John G.	Deed to	Wharton, Franklin	1812	AD29	254	210
McDonald, John G.	Deed to	Wilson, John A.	1815	AK35	234	185
McDonald, John G.	Deed fr	Clerklee, James, of Charles Co.	1816	AM37	253	186
McDonald, Walter	Deed fr	Cannon, Abial	1817	AN38	270	197
McDono, William	Deed to	Connelly, Patrick, of G'tn.	1804	L11	227	211
McDono, William	Deed fr	Lovering, William, of Alexa.	1804	L11	384	342
McDono, William	Deed to	Mechlin, Joseph	1804	L11	386	344
McDonough, William	Sale to	Brown, Samuel	1805	O14	123	
McDougall, Duncan Stewart et ux	Deed to	Bradey, Francis	1801	G7	070	091
McElden, William	B. of S. fr	Rowland, George	1815	AI34	324	357
McElwee, John	Deed fr	Munroe, Thomas, Supt.	1802	I9	138	208
McElwee, John	Deed fr	Munroe, Thomas, Supt.	1802	I9	139	209
McElwee, John	Deed to	Young, Moses	1809	X23	122	088
McElwee, John	Deed to	Young, Moses	1810	Y24	111	101
McElwee, John, mer., of Balto.	Lease fr	Etting, Solomon, of Balto. Co.	1804	L11	033	32
McElwee, John, of Balto.	Deed fr	Munroe, Thomas, Supt.	1802	H8	491	452
McElwee, John, of Balto.	Deed fr	Munroe, Thomas, Supt.	1802	H8	490	451
McElwee, John, of Balto.	Deed to	Roy, John, of Balto.	1805	M12	270	271
McElwee, John, of Balto.	Deed fr	Roy, John, of Balto.	1809	X23	108	078
McElwee, Rebecca, of Phila. PA	Release to	Young, Moses	1812	AD29	187	151
McElwee, Rebecca, wid/o John	Deed fr	Etting, Solomon, of Balto. MD	1812	AD29	086	064
McElwee, Rebecca, wid/o John	Deed to	Webster, Toppan	1812	AD29	082	060
McFarland, Henry	Deed to	Cole, Bennett	1802	I9	373	618
McFerson, Alexander	Manumis fr	McVicker, Esther & M. Thomson	1815	AI34	015	016
McGilton, William B.	Deed fr	Laird, John, exr. of J. Carleton	1813	AF31	398	288
McGlue, Owen	Deed fr	Van Ness, John P. & Marcia	1816	AL36	165	165
McGowan, Ann, wid/o Barney	Deed fr	Van Ness, John P. & Marcia	1809	X23	025	017
McGowan, John	Assign fr	Stephen, John, insolvent	1809	W22	077	057
McGowan, John	Bond	President, Commercial Co.	1810	Z25	143	114
McGowan, John	P. of Atty. fr	McLachlin, James, Sr.	1812	AC28	164	122
McGowan, John	Deed fr	May, Frederick	1813	AE30	517	384
McGowan, John	Deed fr	Magruder, Ninian, of G'tn.	1814	AH33	195	177
McGowan, John	Deed to	Cana, Frederick	1815	AK35	207	162
McGowan, John	B. of S. fr	Bailey, Robert	1817	AO39	229	165
McGowan, John & Eliz. Clarke	Deed to	Patterson, James	1813	AF31	376	270
McGowan, John & Eliza Clarke	Assign to	Sutherland, Thomas Janey	1814	AH33	316	273
McGowan, John et al	Deed fr	Caldwell, Timothy	1802	I9	571	925
McGowan, John et al	Deed fr	Caldwell, Timothy	1802	I9	570	923
McGowan, John et al	Deed to	Caldwell, Timothy	1808	T19	269	198
McGowan, John et al	B. of S. fr	Sprogell, Thomas Yorke	1808	T19	400	282
McGowan, John et al	Deed fr	Law, John, atty. for Thomas	1810	Y24	067	059
McGowan, John et al	B. of S. fr	Webster, Toppan	1814	AH33	130	123

Party	What	Party	Year	Liber	Old	New
McGowan, John et al	Deed fr	Jackson, John G., fr. Harrison Co.	1814	AG32	295	215
McGowan, John et al	Deed fr	Herford, Henry	1816	AL36	450	426
McGowan, John et al	D. of T. fr	Herford, Henry	1816	AM37	138	107
McGowan, John et al	Deed fr	Herford, Henry	1816	AL36	445	423
McGowan, John et al	Deed fr	Webster, Toppan	1817	AO39	307	218
McGrath, Jane, of G'tn.	Deed Gift to	McGrath, Margaret, d/o Jane	1805	M12	358	366
McGrath, Margaret, d/o Jane	Deed Gift fr	McGrath, Jane, of G'tn.	1805	M12	358	366
McGrath, Thomas	Lease fr	Beatty, John M. et a;	1805	M12	165	164
McGrath, Thomas	Assign to	Brunner, John, of Henry	1811	AA26	355	237
McGrath, Thomas	B. of S. fr	Holt, Theophilus	1814	AH33	027	024
McGrath, Thomas	Deed fr	Murdock, John, of G'tn.	1817	AO39	389	263
McGrath, Thomas	Dood fr	Dorsey, William H., of Montg. Co.	1817	AO39	388	262
McHenry, James	Deed fr	Commissioners of Washington	1802	H8	066	061
McHenry, James, Sec., of Phila.	Deed fr	Commissioners of Washington	1799	D4	352	340
McIntire, Alexander & Sarah	Deed Gift fr	McIntire, Samuel	1808	U20	381	210
McIntire, John et al	Deed fr	Fallon, Edw. et al	1802	I9	406	673
McIntire, John et al	Deed fr	Kearney, John	1802	I9	474	780
McIntire, John et al	Deed fr	Armstrong, James	1802	I9	476	783
McIntire, John, of Balto. et al	Deed fr	Kearney, John	1801	G7	151	200
McIntire, John, of Balto.	Deed to	Steele, Pontius D.	1808	V21	013	010
McIntire, Samuel	Deed fr	Corcoran, Thomas, of G'tn.	1802	H8	244	232
McIntire, Samuel	Deed fr	Ramsay, John, of PA	1802	H8	242	231
McIntire, Samuel	Deed to	Underwood, Robert	1805	N13	129	124
McIntire, Samuel	Deed fr	Underwood, Robert	1806	P15	128	062
McIntire, Samuel	Deed to	McCormick, James	1807	S18	028	024
McIntire, Samuel	Deed Gift to	McIntire, Alexander & Sarah	1808	U20	381	210
McIntire, Samuel	Deed fr	Brumley, Joseph, collector	1813	AF31	422	304
McIntire, Samuel	B. of S. fr	Moore, Eliza, wid/o Joshua John	1814	AG32	389	283
McIntosh, Thomas	Deed fr	Fenwick, George & Margaret	1810	Y24	313	284
McKale, Leonard et al	D. of T. fr	Foxall, Henry	1816	AL36	357	348
McKee, James	B. of S. to	McQuillan, Eleanor, of Balto.	1806	O14	266	176
McKee, James	B. of S. fr	McQuillan, Eleanor, of Balto.	1806	Q16	201	135
McKee, James	Qualify	First Lieutenant in Militia	1808	V21	094	072
McKee, James	Deed fr	May, Frederick	1810	Y24	373	337
McKee, James	B. of S. fr	Smith, Job	1810	Y24	466	413
McKee, James	Deed to	Campbell, Arthur	1811	AB27	256	209
McKee, Samuel, Garrad Co. KY	Cert. Free to	Bowe, Kitty (M)	1815	AH33	451	386
McKelden, Andrew, of G'tn.	D. of T. to	Kurtz, Daniel, of G'tn.	1816	AM37	151	116
McKelden, Andrew, of G'tn.	Deed fr	Brookes, Joseph, of G'tn.	1816	AM37	148	114
McKelden, John	B. of S. to	McKelden, William	1815	AK35	424	333
McKelden, John, s/o John	Gift Deed fr	McKelden, William	1817	AN38	127	094
McKelden, William	B. of S. fr	McKelden, John	1815	AK35	424	333
McKelden, William	Gift Deed to	McKelden, William, s/o John	1817	AN38	127	094
McKelden, William	Gift Deed to	McKelden, John, s/o John	1817	AN38	127	094
McKelden, William, s/o John	Gift Deed fr	McKelden, William	1817	AN38	127	094
McKeldon, William	Deed fr	Payne, John	1810	Y24	423	380
McKenney, Benson	B. of S. to	McKenney, Edward	1816	AM37	213	158
McKenney, Edward	B. of S. fr	McKenney, Benson	1816	AM37	213	158
McKenney, William, of G'tn.	D. of T. to	Cox, John, of G'tn.	1815	AK35	301	240
McKenney, William, of G'tn.	B. of S. fr	Robertson, Henry B., of G'tn.	1816	AM37	305	223
McKenney, William, of G'tn.	Lease fr	Hoye, John, of Allegany Co.	1817	AN38	368	271
McKenny, Samuel et al	D. of T. fr	Foxall, Henry	1816	AL36	357	348
McKenny, William	Qualify	Lieutenant 1st regiment	1813	AE30	472	351
McKim, James	Deed fr	Armstrong, Andrew et al	1807	R17	082	066
McKim, James	Deed fr	Law, Edmund	1810	Z25	011	008

Party	What	Party	Year	Liber	Old	New
McKim, James	Mortgage fr	Provott, Peter P.	1810	Z25	012	010
McKim, James	Deed fr	Sewall, Robert, of P.G. Co.	1810	Y24	360	225
McKim, James	Deed fr	Delphy, Richard	1810	Y24	084	075
McKim, James	Deed fr	Laird, John, exr. of J. Carleton	1814	AG32	156	111
McKim, James	Deed fr	Brumley, Joseph, collector	1814	AG32	293	213
McKim, James & Thomas Herty	Deed fr	Smoot, Alexander	1806	Q16	183	122
McKim, James & Thomas Herty	Assign fr	Washington, Lund & Susanna	1806	Q16	270	189
McKim, James & Thomas Herty	Deed fr	Washington, Lund & Susanna	1806	Q16	205	130
McKim, James & Thomas Herty	Deed fr	Gatton, Azariah	1806	Q16	181	121
McKim, James & Thomas Herty	Deed fr	Smoot, Alexander	1807	R17	117	091
McKim, James & Thomas Herty	Deed fr	Bryan, Benjamin	1807	R17	010	009
McKim, James & Thomas Herty	B. of S. fr	Washington, Lund	1807	R17	293	223
McKim, James & Thomas Herty	Deed fr	Bryan, Benjamin	1807	R17	179	137
McKim, James & Thomas Herty	Deed fr	Grant, Edward M.	1807	R17	115	090
McKim, James & Thomas Herty	Assign fr	Bryan, Benjamin	1808	T19	050	038
McKim, James & Thomas Herty	Deed fr	Gatton, Azariah	1808	T19	053	039
McKim, James, of Marine Corps	Deed fr	Russ, Samuel	1805	N13	209	181
McKin, James, Sr. et al	B. of S. fr	Parry, Stephen	1814	AG32	305	222
McKoy, Robert, of P.G. Co.	Mortgage to	Smith, Thomas, of P.G. Co.	1808	T19	219	161
McLachlin, James, Sr.	P. of Atty. to	McGowan, John	1812	AC28	164	122
McLain, John & Joseph, of NC	Deed to	Beatty, Charles, of G'tn.	1793	A1-2	397	6
McLan, Cornelius	Deed fr	Van Ness, John P.	1802	I9	188	292
McLann, Robert, Cumb. Co. PA	Convey to	Coppersmith, Henry, of G'tn.	1816	AL36	403	387
McLaughlin, Charles	Deed fr	Aubert, Henry	1802	I9	482	792
McLaughlin, Charles	Deed fr	Beall, Thomas	1802	I9	196	305
McLaughlin, Charles	Qualify		1802	I9	467	769
McLaughlin, Charles	Manumis to	[ ], Rachel (negro)	1805	O14	033	021
McLaughlin, Charles, of G'tn.	Deed fr	Brent, Daniel Carroll, marshal	1804	L11	260	
McLaughlin, James	B. of S. to	Robertson, Alexander	1802	H8	545	506
McLaughlin, James	Lease fr	Roe, Cornelius McDermott	1802	G7	515	656
McLaughlin, James	Assign to	Fletcher, William	1804	K10	205	215
McLaughlin, James	Deed to	Lawwell, Samuel	1806	Q16	134	088
McLaughlin, John	B. of S. to	Way, George	1817	AO39	284	202
McLean, Cornelius	Assign to	Shoemaker, David	1802	I9	243	391
McLean, Cornelius	Lease fr	Dorsey, William H.	1802	I9	240	386
McLean, Cornelius	Deed fr	Speake, Samuel	1807	R17	326	248
McLean, Cornelius	Deed fr	Davidson, John	1807	S18	282	221
McLean, Cornelius	Deed to	Cochrane, Alexander	1809	X23	261	204
McLean, Cornelius	Deed fr	Davidson, John	1810	Y24	094	085
McLean, Cornelius	D. of T. to	Burch, Samuel	1811	AC28	097	075
McLean, Cornelius	Release fr	Burch, Samuel	1812	AD29	417	351
McLean, Cornelius	Deed fr	Davidson, John	1813	AF31	396	286
McLean, Cornelius	Release fr	Bradley, Phineas	1814	AH33	358	310
McLean, Cornelius	D. of T. to	Bradley, Phineas	1814	AH33	180	166
McLean, Cornelius	Deed fr	Law, Thomas	1815	AI34	241	273
McLean, Cornelius	Deed fr	Davidson, John	1815	AI34	240	272
McLean, Cornelius	D. of T. to	Bradley, Phineas	1815	AI34	412	435
McLean, Cornelius	Receipt fr	Sprigg, Benjamin	1815	AI34	237	269
McLean, Cornelius	Deed fr	Murdock, John, of G'tn.	1815	AI34	237	269
McLean, Cornelius	Deed fr	Gilliss, Thomas H.	1815	AK35	356	281
McLean, Cornelius	Agreement	Gilliss, Thomas H.	1815	AK35	359	283
McLean, Cornelius	Deed to	Reitz, Frederick	1816	AL36	227	232
McLean, Cornelius	Agreement	Reitz, Frederick	1816	AL36	228	233
McLean, Cornelius [Maclean]	Deed fr	Dorsey, William H., of Montg. Co.	1815	AI34	239	271
McLearn, Duncan, of G'tn.	B. of S. to	Lanham, Elisha	1813	AE30	164	130

Party	What	Party	Year	Liber	Old	New
McLeod, John	Deed to	Smith, Hugh, of Alexa.	1808	U20	362	197
McLeod, John	Deed fr	Cochrane, Alexander & Eleanor	1810	Z25	023	018
McLeod, John	B. of S. to	Nourse, Michael & Thos. H. Gilliss	1812	AD29	246	203
McLeod, John	Mortgage to	Holyday, Thomas & Shad. Davis	1812	AD29	205	167
McLeod, John	Release fr	Holliday, Thomas & Sh. Davis	1813	AF31	105	071
McLeod, John	Deed to	Dye, Reuben, of Fairfax Co. VA	1813	AE30	495	367
McLeod, John	Deed fr	Laird, John, exr. of J. Carleton	1814	AG32	074	056
McLeod, John	D. of T. to	Brent, William	1815	AH33	426	367
McLeod, John	D. of T. to	Caldwell, Elias B.	1816	AL36	384	371
McLeod, John	Deed to	Crabb, John	1816	AM37	116	091
McLeod, John	Lease fr	Van Ness, John P. & Marcia	1816	AM37	394	284
McLeod, John	Deed to	Miller, Samuel	1816	AL36	550	513
McLeod, John, plt.	Suit	Cochrane, Alexr. & Eleanor, def.	1810	Z25	023	018
McLeod, John, schoolmaster	Deed fr	Maddox, Notley, of P.G. Co.	1814	AG32	407	297
McLeod, John, schoolmaster	D. of T. to	Scholfield, Andrew, of Alexa. et al	1815	AK35	235	186
McLeod, John, schoolmaster	Convey to	Maddox, Notley, of P.G. Co.	1816	AM37	495	362
McMahon, Robert	Deed fr	Carroll, Daniel, of *Duddington*	1807	R17	304	232
McMantz, Charles	Deed fr	Commissioners of Washington	1800	E5	223	216
McMantz, Charles	Receipt fr	Wilson, John C.	1800	F6	068	042
McMantz, Charles	Deed to	Jones, Tristram F.	1801	G7	069	089
McMantz, Charles	Deed fr	Commissioners of Washington	1801	G7	050	064
McMinn, Thomas	Deed fr	Clockey, Samuel	1801	G7	148	195
McMullin, Archibald	Deed to	Currill, James	1811	AA26	307	207
McMurray, Joseph	Dissolved	McMurray, William	1810	Y24	051	045
McMurray, Joseph	Assign to	Ott, John & James Gannon	1810	Z25	241	188
McMurray, Joseph	B. of S. to	Ott, John & James Gannon	1810	Y24	537	471
McMurray, Joseph & William	Deed fr	Cramphin, Thomas, of Montg. Co.	1806	Q16	245	169
McMurray, Joseph, of G'tn.	B. of S. fr	Mackay, James, stage driver, G'tn.	1806	Q16	097	063
McMurray, Joseph, of G'tn.	Deed fr	McMurray, William, of G'tn.	1810	Y24	198	182
McMurray, William	Dissolved	McMurray, Joseph	1810	Y24	051	045
McMurray, William	Deed fr	Pratt, Henry et al	1814	AH33	171	159
McMurray, William	Deed to	Johnson, Isaac, of G'tn.	1816	AM37	498	364
McMurray, William & Joseph	Deed fr	Cramphin, Thomas, of Montg. Co.	1806	Q16	245	169
McMurray, William, of G'tn.	Deed to	McMurray, Joseph, of G'tn.	1810	Y24	198	182
McMurrey, William	Deed fr	Sandford, George	1816	AM37	321	233
McNamara, Mary	Deed to	Kerr, Alexander	1816	AM37	005	004
McNamara, Roger & Mary	Deed to	Hughes, Thomas	1809	V21	191	136
McNantz, Charles	Lease fr	Prout, William	1804	L11	109	112
McNantz, Charles	Deed to	Moss, Philemon	1807	S18	098	080
McNantz, Charles	Cert. fr	Brent, Daniel C.	1812	AC28	239	177
McNantz, Charles	Deed fr	Brent, Eleanor & Robert Y.	1812	AC28	229	170
McNantz, Charles, trustee	B. of S. fr	Betterton, Benjamin, insolvent	1810	Y24	516	454
McNeal, James	Lease fr	Carroll, Daniel, of *Duddington*	1816	AM37	181	136
McNeill, James	D. of T. to	Radcliff, William S.	1816	AM37	037	030
McNeill, James	B. of S. to	Milligan, Joseph, of G'tn.	1816	AM37	039	032
McNemara, Mary	Deed fr	Brent, William	1816	AL36	498	459
McNemara, Roger	Deed to	Davis, George L., trustee	1810	X23	380	306
McNemara, Roger & Mary	B. of S. to	Roe, Edward McDermott	1809	X23	034	025
McNemara, Roger & Mary	Deed to	Roe, Edward McDermott	1809	W22	247	166
McNemara, Roger & Mary	B. of S. to	Callan, Nicholas	1809	X23	035	025
McPherson, Dorathy	Deed Gift to	Barber, Mary	1807	R17	359	273
McPherson, Henry, of G'tn.	Deed fr	Connelly, John, Jr., of G'tn.	1814	AH33	340	294
McPherson, John	Deed fr	Eliason, Ebenezer	1814	AH33	087	079
McPherson, John & Sarah, of MD	Deed to	Pierce, Isaac	1815	AI34	158	181
McPherson, John, Frederick MD	Lease to	Riggs, Romulus	1813	AF31	121	081

Index to District of Columbia Land Records, 1792-1817

Party	What	Party	Year	Liber	Old	New
McPherson, Samuel, insolvent	Deed to	Kenner, James, trustee	1804	L11	342	310
McQuillan, Eleanor, of Balto.	B. of S. fr	McKee, James	1806	O14	266	176
McQuillan, Eleanor, of Balto.	B. of S. to	McKee, James	1806	Q16	201	135
McVicken, Esther	Slaves	From VA	1808	T19	369	264
McVicker, Esther et al	Manumis to	McFerson, Alexander	1815	Al34	015	016
McVickir, Esther & M. Thompson	Manumis to	Thompson, Charity (C), age 38	1813	AE30	255	199
McWilliams, Alex	Cert Free to	Butler, Bill	1809	W22	349	226
McWilliams, Alexander	Slaves	From MD	1807	S18	185	150
McWilliams, Alexander	Slave		1808	U20	073	041
McWilliams, Alexander	Lease fr	Prout, William	1811	Z25	495	393
McWilliams, Alexander	D. of T. to	Forrest, Alexander	1813	AE30	057	043
McWilliams, Alexander	B. of S. to	Smallwood, Samuel N.	1815	Al34	148	170
Mead, Simon	B. of S. fr	Davis, Francis	1812	AD29	471	398
Mead, Simon	Deed fr	Law, Thomas & Edmund	1812	AC28	281	204
Meade, Simon	Lease fr	Stoddert, Benjamin et al	1801	G7	202	269
Meade, Simon	Deed fr	Edelin, Ignatius & J.C. Palmer	1808	U20	112	063
Meade, Simon	B. of S. fr	Hamilton, Christina, admx. of S.	1809	W22	161	113
Meade, Simon	Deed fr	Law, Thomas	1815	Al34	008	008
Meade, Simon	Deed fr	Law, Thomas	1816	AO39	053	044
Meamy, John, mariner, of Phila.	Deed fr	Ball, Joseph & Standish Forde	1800	E5	343	330
Meany, John, mariner, of Phila.	Deed fr	Ball, Joseph & Standish Forde	1800	E5	347	333
Mecahan, Samuel et al	Deed to	Dial, Annastatia	1804	K10	310	314
Mecahon, Samuel et al	Deed fr	Wert, Joseph F.	1802	I9	298	490
Mechlin, Joseph	Deed fr	Hodgson, Joseph	1801	G7	004	005
Mechlin, Joseph	Deed fr	Lingan, James Maccubbin, of G'tn.	1802	H8	306	288
Mechlin, Joseph	Deed fr	McDono, William	1804	L11	386	344
Mechlin, Joseph	Deed to	Pairo, Thomas W.	1805	N13	139	132
Mechlin, Joseph	B. of S. fr	Brown, Samuel	1805	N13	181	162
Mechlin, Joseph	B. of S. fr	Tilly, Ann	1812	AC28	227	169
Mechlin, Joseph	Deed to	Hutchinson, Samuel, mer.	1815	Al34	281	317
Mechlin, Joseph et al	B. of S. fr	Yeamans, Royal	1817	AO39	147	111
Mechlin, Joseph, late of Phila. PA	Deed fr	Forrest, Uriah	1800	E5	367	349
Mechlin, Joseph [Mecklin]	Deed fr	Lingan, James M.	1806	Q16	226	154
Meddart, Jacob, of Frederick Co.	Deed fr	Stoker, Michael, of Frederick Co.	1798	C3	480	378
Meddert, Jacob	Deed fr	Beatty, John M. & Charles A.	1806	O14	346	231
Meddert, Jacob	Deed fr	Davidson, John, Gen., exrx. of	1807	S18	241	190
Meddert, Jacob	Deed fr	King, George	1809	W22	043	033
Meddert, Jacob	Deed fr	King, George	1809	V21	377	280
Meddert, Jacob	Deed fr	Mudd, Thomas James	1811	AB27	259	212
Meddert, Jacob, Frederick Town	Deed fr	Lighty, Samuel, Frederick Town	1795	B2A	218	302
Meddert, Jacob, Frederick Town	Deed fr	Hummel, John, of Frederick Co.	1807	S18	042	035
Medley, Bernard et al	Deed to	Fenwick, Francis & Eleanor	1809	V21	303	221
Medley, Bernard, Montgomery Co.	Deed fr	Threlkeld, John, Montgomery Co.	1795	B2A	270	377
Medley, Bernard, of Montg. Co.	Deed fr	Threlkeld, John, of Montg. Co.	1796	B2B	512	217
Medley, Bernard, of Montg. Co.	Deed to	Sewall, Clement, of Montg. Co.	1796	B2B	525	237
Medley, Bernard, St. Mary's Co.	Deed fr	Threlkeld, John	1806	P15	166	110
Medtart, Jacob, of Frederick Co.	Deed to	Beall, Thomas & John M. Gantt	1793	A1-1	231	318
Medtart, Jacob, of Fredk. Co.	Deed fr	Taylor, Thomas & Josiah	1817	AN38	544	396
Medtart, Jacob, Sr., Frederick Co.	Deed fr	Goodeberger, Adam, farmer	1793	A1-1	230	317
Meem, Ann et al	Deed fr	Meem, Peter, of G'tn.	1813	AE30	089	068
Meem, Elizabeth et al	Deed fr	Meem, Peter, of G'tn.	1813	AE30	089	068
Meem, George et al	Deed fr	Meem, Peter, of G'tn.	1813	AE30	089	068
Meem, John et al et al	Deed fr	Meem, Peter, of G'tn.	1813	AE30	089	068
Meem, Peter, of G'tn.	Deed to	Laird, John, of G'tn.	1811	AB27	423	349

Party	What	Party	Year	Liber	Old	New
Meem, Peter, of G'tn.	Deed fr	Lingan, James M., of Montg. Co.	1811	AB27	426	351
Meem, Peter, of G'tn.	Deed to	Meem, Elizabeth et al	1813	AE30	089	068
Meem, Polly et al	Deed fr	Meem, Peter, of G'tn.	1813	AE30	089	068
Mees, Rudolph et al	Deed fr	Bourne, Sylvanus, Boston MA	1796	B2B	496	192
Mehone, John, of G'tn. [Mahone]	Assign to	Fields, William, of G'tn.	1805	M12	192	194
Meigs, Jane Clarke et al	D. of T. to	Meigs, Josiah & J. Forsyth	1815	AK35	421	330
Meigs, Josiah & J. Forsyth	D. of T. fr	Meigs, Samuel William et al	1815	AK35	421	330
Meigs, Return J., Jr., postmaster	Deed to	Osbourn, James, of Balto.	1817	AO39	313	223
Meigs, Samuel William et al	D. of T. to	Meigs, Josiah & J. Forsyth	1815	AK35	421	330
Melvin, James	Deed fr	English, David	1802	I9	150	226
Melvin, James	Mortgage to	English, David	1802	I9	233	373
Melvin, James	D. of T. to	Smith, Walter et al	1806	O14	307	203
Melvin, James	Deed fr	Smith, Walter & John Cox, of G'tn.	1810	X23	162	119
Melvin, James	Lease to	Fitzhugh, Samuel	1813	AF31	282	199
Melvin, James	Deed fr	Jones, Walter, Jr.	1814	AG32	113	085
Melvin, James	Deed to	Stretch, Joseph	1816	AL36	361	350
Melvin, James, Jr.	Deed fr	Presbyterian Congregation, G'tn.	1812	AC28	242	179
Melvin, James, of G'tn.	Lease to	Hagner, Peter	1806	O14	295	196
Melvin, James, of G'tn.	Deed to	Shaw, John, trustee et al	1808	T19	206	148
Melvin, James, of G'tn.	Deed to	Hagner, Peter	1810	X23	164	121
Melvin, James, of G'tn.	Deed fr	Green, Charles D., Hunt. Co. NJ	1810	X23	403	325
Mercer, John Francis	Deed fr	Commissioners of Washington	1799	D4	418	393
Mercer, John Francis	Deed fr	Commissioners of Washington	1799	D4	412	389
Mercer, John Francis, of A.A. Co.	Deed to	Munroe, Thomas	1816	AL36	504	473
Mercer, John, of Fredericksburg	Deed fr	Commissioners of Washington	1799	D4	415	391
Mercer, John, of Fredericksburg	Deed to	McCormick, James	1813	AE30	092	071
Merky, David	Deed fr	Read, Leonard	1795	B2A	351	497
Merriken, John et al	Deed fr	Long, John, of G'tn.	1799	D4	209	192
Merrill, Jeremiah	Cert Free to	[ ], Charity (negroe)	1808	T19	141	101
Mersen, Jacobus, of Holland	Deed fr	Young, Notley	1794	B2A	119	159
Metcalf, Thomas	Cert fr	Commissioners of Washington	1796	B2B	452	140
Metcalf, Thomas, of Phila. PA	Cert fr	Commissioners of Washington	1792	B2A	293	410
Methodist E. Church, trustees of	Deed fr	Prout, William	1813	AF31	184	124
Methodist Episcopal Church, Gtn.	Deed fr	Morgan, William, of G'tn.	1814	AH33	010	009
Methodist Meeting House, trustees	Deed fr	Prout, William	1810	Z25	134	105
Meyer, Philip, insolvent	B. of S. to	Burnes, George, trustee	1805	M12	068	063
Mickle, John, of Balto.	Deed fr	Commissioners of Washington	1800	E5	221	214
Mickle, John, of Balto.	Deed to	Cox, John, of G'tn.	1811	AB27	389	321
Mickle, John, of Balto.	Deed to	Cox, John, of G'tn.	1812	AC28	216	162
Middagh, John, Fredrick Co. et al	Deed to	O'Reilly, Henry	1798	C3	346	278
Middagh, John Gaither et al	Deed to	Beatty, Thomas	1798	C3	416	328
Middagh, John, s/o John	Deed to	Beatty, Charles, of Montg. Co.	1797	C3	126	103
Middleton, Electius	Deed fr	Munroe, Thomas, Supt.	1802	I9	181	277
Middleton, Electius	B. of S. to	May, Frederick	1810	Y24	174	159
Middleton, Electius	Deed fr	May, Frederick	1810	Y24	058	051
Middleton, Electius	Deed fr	May, Frederick	1812	AD29	138	107
Middleton, Electius & Ann	Deed to	Middleton, Isaac Smallwood	1811	AA26	162	111
Middleton, Electius, trustee of	Deed to	Smallwood, Samuel N.	1817	AO39	329	234
Middleton, Electus	Deed fr	May, Frederick	1805	N13	056	052
Middleton, Electus	Manumis to	[ ], Arianna (negress)	1806	Q16	236	162
Middleton, Electus et al	B. of S. fr	Cooper, John	1807	S18	047	039
Middleton, Elexius, trustee	Deed fr	Prout, William	1813	AF31	184	124
Middleton, Elizabeth	Deed fr	Brumley, Joseph, collector	1811	AA26	257	175
Middleton, Hannah, w/o James	B. of G. fr	Johnson, Tunis, Sr., Fauquier Co.	1801	G7	037	048
Middleton, Ignatius, of Charles Co.	Deed fr	Boone, Edward, of Charles Co.	1799	D4	195	178

Party	What	Party	Year	Liber	Old	New
Middleton, Ignatius, of Charles Co.	Deed fr	Boone, Ignatius, of Nicholas	1800	E5	201	194
Middleton, Ignatius, of Charles Co.	Deed to	Dawes, Edward, of G'tn.	1815	AK35	394	310
Middleton, Isaac	Deed to	McCormick, Alexander	1814	AG32	427	309
Middleton, Isaac S.	Mortgage fr	Hurley, William	1813	AF31	541	401
Middleton, Isaac S.	Deed to	Reynolds, Thomas	1815	AK35	368	290
Middleton, Isaac S.	Deed fr	Walker, Zachariah	1815	AK35	189	147
Middleton, Isaac S.	Deed to	Steuart, Philip, Gen., Charles Co.	1816	AL36	549	512
Middleton, Isaac Smallwood	Deed fr	Middleton, Electius & Ann	1811	AA26	162	111
Middleton, James	Deed fr	Commissioners of Washington	1800	E5	108	095
Middleton, James	Deed fr	May, Frederick	1802	I9	182	279
Middleton, James	Deed fr	Munroe, Thomas, Supt.	1805	N13	087	079
Middleton, James	Deed to	Dempsie, John	1805	N13	089	080
Middleton, James	Deed fr	Little, Israel	1806	P15	328	217
Middleton, James	Lease fr	Law, Thomas	1806	P15	047	029
Middleton, James	D. of T. to	Eliot, Samuel, Jr.	1814	AH33	254	220
Middleton, James	Manumis to	Simpson, James & Mariah	1815	AH33	446	382
Middleton, James & D. Carroll	Deed to	Smallwood, Samuel N.	1816	AL36	161	161
Middleton, James & T. Foyles	Deed fr	Mayhue, Clement & Mary	1816	AM37	099	079
Middleton, Joseph	Deed to	Dowens, George	1800	E5	263	256
Middleton, Joseph	Deed to	Kleiber, George	1800	E5	264	258
Middleton, Joseph	Deed fr	Commissioners of Washington	1800	E5	189	180
Middleton, Joseph	Deed to	Cist, Charles, of Phila.	1801	G7	223	298
Middleton, Joseph	Deed fr	Porter, James A., trustee	1808	V21	087	067
Middleton, Joseph	Deed to	O'Neale, William	1810	Y24	140	127
Middleton, Joseph	B. of S. to	Middleton, William, of Richmond	1810	Z25	074	056
Middleton, Joseph et al	Lease fr	Deakins, William, Jr. et al	1796	B2B	508	211
Middleton, Joseph, of Norfolk	Manumis to	[ ], Phoebe (M)	1816	AL36	005	005
Middleton, Smallwood C.	Deed fr	Ewell, Thomas	1815	AK35	126	097
Middleton, William, of Richmond	B. of S. fr	Middleton, Joseph	1810	Z25	074	056
Miers, John	B. of S. to	Kastner, John	1809	V21	270	193
Miles, Edward	Deed to	Tuckfield, William H.P.	1816	AM37	174	131
Miles, Edward L.	B. of S. to	Graham, William, of G'tn.	1810	Y24	285	261
Miles, Henry, of St. Mary's Co.	Deed fr	Threlkeld, John, of Montg. Co.	1797	C3	216	182
Miles, Henry, of St. Mary's Co.	Deed to	Dawes, Isaac	1808	U20	148	085
Miles, Henry, of St. Mary's Co.	Deed fr	Dawes, Isaac	1808	U20	151	086
Miles, Henry, of St. Mary's Co.	Deed fr	Dawes, Isaac	1808	U20	146	083
Miles, Stanislaus	B. of S. to	Smith, Lewis	1814	AG32	045	036
Miles, William, of G'tn.	Deed fr	Kennedy, James, of G'tn.	1817	AN38	391	291
Miliken, Mark	Deed to	Stephen, John, of G'tn.	1799	D4	395	376
Miller, Ann Maria, of G'tn.	Deed fr	Myers, John, of G'tn., house carp.	1811	Z25	383	300
Miller, Barbara	Deed fr	Miller, Jacob	1813	AE30	444	330
Miller, Daniel, of G'tn.	B. of S. to	Smith, Walter H. & Abm. Wingard	1812	AD29	217	177
Miller, Edward et al	Partition		1804	K10	306	310
Miller, Elizabeth, of G'tn.	Deed fr	Threlkeld, John, of G'tn.	1804	K10	354	366
Miller, Frederick	Deed fr	Lutz, John & John S. Miller	1815	AI34	505	510
Miller, George	Lease fr	Beatty, Charles	1804	K10	398	413
Miller, George	Deed fr	Dooling, Michael	1807	R17	365	278
Miller, George	Deed to	Williamson, David	1809	W22	046	034
Miller, George	B. of S. fr	Maxwell, George	1812	AD29	142	110
Miller, George	D. of T. to	Burch, Samuel	1812	AE30	053	040
Miller, Hezekiah, of G'tn.	Deed to	Nicholls, William S., of G'tn.	1817	AO39	342	243
Miller, Jacob	Deed fr	Clephan, Lewis	1812	AD29	001	001
Miller, Jacob	Deed to	Miller, Barbara	1813	AE30	444	330
Miller, Jacob, innholder, of G'tn.	B. of S. to	Staley, Jacob, currier, of G'tn.	1812	AC28	286	207
Miller, Jacob, of Frederick Co.	B. of S. to	Livers, Ignatious	1808	T19	315	230

Index to District of Columbia Land Records, 1792-1817

Party	What	Party	Year	Liber	Old	New
Miller, Jacob, of P.G. Co.	Deed fr	Bohrer, George, of G'tn.	1813	AF31	355	253
Miller, James, by his attorney	Deed to	Patton, James, of Alexa.	1798	C3	345	277
Miller, James, of Glasgow, Scot.	Deed to	Patton, James, of Alexa.	1805	N13	363	292
Miller, John et al	Deed fr	Hanson, Alexander Contee	1798	C3	490	385
Miller, John et al	Deed fr	Morris, Robert et al	1798	D4	030	025
Miller, John et al	Deed fr	Tingey, Thomas	1802	I9	572	927
Miller, John et al	Deed fr	Dorsey, William H. et al	1802	I9	568	920
Miller, John, Jr. et al	D. of T. fr	Morris, Robert, of Phila. et al	1797	C3	204	172
Miller, John, Jr. et al	Deed fr	Greenleaf, James, of Phila. et al	1797	C3	154	127
Miller, John, Jr. et al	D. of T. fr	Morris, Robert, of Phila. et al	1797	C3	192	161
Miller, John, Jr. et al	Deed fr	Morris, Robert, of Phila. et al	1798	C3	301	243
Miller, John, Jr.	Deed fr	Commissioners of Washington	1800	E5	369	350
Miller, John, Jr. et al	Deed fr	Commissioners of Washington	1800	E5	372	353
Miller, John, Jr. et al	Deed fr	Commissioners of Washington	1800	ES	369	350
Miller, John, Jr.	Deed fr	Commissioners of Washington	1801	F6	202	131
Miller, John, Jr. et al	Deed fr	Commissioners of Washington	1801	G7	281	389
Miller, John, Jr.	Deed to	Underwood, Robert et al	1802	I9	217	342
Miller, John, Jr. et al	Deed fr	Dorsey, William H.	1802	I9	263	426
Miller, John, Jr.	Deed to	Tingey, Thomas	1802	I9	213	336
Miller, John, Jr. et al	Deed to	Yeates, William	1802	H8	056	053
Miller, John, Jr., of Phila. PA	P. of Atty. to	Greenleaf, James, of Phila.	1804	K10	377	391
Miller, John, Jr. et al	P. of Atty. to	Greenleaf, James	1804	K10	101	107
Miller, John, Jr. et al	Deed to	May, Frederick	1805	N13	108	102
Miller, John, Jr. et al	P. of Atty. to	Greenleaf, James	1805	M12	377	388
Miller, John, Jr. et al	Deed fr	Sewall, Robert, of P.G. Co.	1805	N13	081	074
Miller, John, Jr. et al	Deed to	Van Ness, John P.	1806	P15	105	065
Miller, John, Jr. et al	Deed to	Elliott, Samuel, Jr.	1806	O14	362	242
Miller, John, Jr. et al	Deed to	Voss, Nicholas	1807	S18	025	021
Miller, John, Jr. et al	Quit to	Eliot, Samuel, Jr.	1809	W22	293	193
Miller, John, Jr. et al	Deed to	Cook, Orlando	1809	X23	245	190
Miller, John, Jr. et al	Quit to	Toole, Patrick	1809	X23	135	097
Miller, John, Jr. et al	B. of S. fr	Prout, William	1809	W22	380	247
Miller, John, Jr., trustee, et al	Deed to	Mara, Philip O.	1810	Z25	340	266
Miller, John, Jr. et al	Deed to	Griffin, Lancelot	1810	X23	319	256
Miller, John, Jr. et al	Deed fr	Munroe, Thomas, Supt.	1811	Z25	472	274
Miller, John, Jr., of Phila. et al	Deed to	Weightman, Roger C.	1811	AB27	228	186
Miller, John, Jr., of Phila. et al	Deed to	Matthews, William, Rev.	1811	AB27	342	282
Miller, John, Jr. et al	Deed to	Varnum, James M.	1812	AC28	508	363
Miller, John, Jr. et al	Deed to	Jones, Walter, Jr.	1812	AC28	400	290
Miller, John, Jr. et al	Deed to	Aborn, Henry	1812	AC28	470	334
Miller, John, Jr. et al	Deed to	Latrobe, Benjamim H.	1812	AC28	445	318
Miller, John, Jr. et al	Deed to	Tingey, Thomas	1812	AC28	428	308
Miller, John, Jr., of Phila. PA et al	Deed to	Weightman, Roger C.	1812	AD29	402	339
Miller, John, Jr., of Phila. PA et al	Deed to	Weightman, Roger C.	1812	AD29	406	342
Miller, John, Jr., of Phila. PA et al	Deed to	Weightman, Roger C.	1812	AD29	409	346
Miller, John, Jr. et al	Deed to	Gales, Joseph, Jr.	1812	AE30	001	001
Miller, John, Jr. et al	Deed to	Tuckfield, William H.P.	1813	AE30	230	184
Miller, John, Jr. et al	Deed to	Van Ness, John P.	1813	AE30	485	360
Miller, John, Jr. et al	Deed to	Smallwood, Samuel N.	1813	AF31	032	022
Miller, John, Jr. et al	Deed to	Jones, Walter, Jr.	1813	AE30	328	246
Miller, John, Jr. et al	Deed to	Heath, Nathaniel H.	1813	AE30	522	387
Miller, John, Jr. & Wm. Cranch	Deed to	Pratt, Henry et al	1814	AG32	330	240
Miller, John, Jr. et al	Deed to	Van Ness, John P.	1814	AG32	313	229
Miller, John, Jr. et al	Deed to	Wayne, Francis	1814	AH33	377	326
Miller, John, Jr. et al	Deed to	McMurray, William	1814	AH33	171	159

Party	What	Party	Year	Liber	Old	New
Miller, John, Jr. et al	Deed to	Glover, Charles	1814	AH33	302	261
Miller, John, Jr. et al	Deed to	Johnson, James W.	1814	AH33	004	004
Miller, John, Jr. et al	Deed to	Gales, Joseph, Jr.	1815	AK35	400	314
Miller, John, Jr. et al	Deed to	Walker, Zachariah	1815	AK35	404	317
Miller, John, Jr. et al	Deed to	Brent, Robert	1816	AL36	538	502
Miller, John, Jr. et al	Deed to	Eliot, Samuel, Jr.	1816	AL36	171	171
Miller, John, Jr. et al	Deed to	Hoot, Samuel	1816	AL36	122	124
Miller, John, Jr., of Phila.	Assign to	Eliot, Samuel, Jr.	1817	AN38	418	313
Miller, John M.	Deed fr	Law, Thomas	1802	I9	338	557
Miller, John Moore	Assign to	Moore, James & John	1806	P15	164	108
Miller, John Moore	B. of S. to	Moore, James & John	1806	P15	165	109
Miller, John S. & John Lutz	Deed fr	Botner, Elias, of Alexa. Co.	1811	AB27	359	297
Miller, John S. & John Lutz	Deed to	Miller, Frederick	1815	AI34	505	510
Miller, John, the younger et al	Deed to	Tilghman, William, of Phila. et al	1808	T19	086	061
Miller, Peter	Deed fr	Law, Thomas, Gent.	1798	D4	047	039
Miller, Peter	Mortgage to	Law, Thomas	1799	D4	177	158
Miller, Peter	Deed fr	Law, Thomas	1802	H8	086	079
Miller, Peter	Deed to	Waters, Benjamin	1802	I9	302	496
Miller, Peter	B. of S. fr	Knight, James	1805	M12	087	081
Miller, Peter	Deed fr	Waters, Benjamin, of Montg. Co.	1805	M12	357	364
Miller, Peter	Deed fr	Carroll, Daniel, of *Duddington*	1806	P15	167	111
Miller, Peter	Assign fr	Eno, Edward, butcher	1806	Q16	257	178
Miller, Peter	B. of S. fr	Frost, John T.	1806	Q16	070	044
Miller, Peter	D. of T. to	Stelle, Pontius D.	1808	V21	020	015
Miller, Peter	B. of S. fr	Addison, Thomas G., admr. of T.	1809	W22	059	044
Miller, Peter	Mortgage fr	Johnson, Walter	1809	V21	309	225
Miller, Peter	B. of S. fr	Hanson, Grafton, of Bladensburgh	1809	W22	243	164
Miller, Peter	Mortgage fr	Stelle, Pontius D.	1810	Y24	049	043
Miller, Peter	Deed fr	Stelle, Pontius D. & wife	1811	Z25	455	359
Miller, Peter	Deed fr	Carroll, Daniel, of *Duddington*	1813	AE30	282	216
Miller, Peter & Thomas Tingey	Deed fr	Prout, William	1807	Q16	377	289
Miller, Peter et al	Deed fr	Holmead, Anthony	1800	E5	238	232
Miller, Peter et al	Mortgage fr	Alexander, Robert	1807	S18	212	169
Miller, Peter, of Wash. Co. MD	Deed fr	Baird, Margaret, wid.	1798	C3	429	337
Miller, Robert	Mortgage to	Suttle, Henry, of G'tn.	1805	N13	359	289
Miller, Robert	Slave	From Alexandria	1812	AD29	310	
Miller, Robert	Slave	From Alexandria	1816	AL36	018	020
Miller, Robert	Deed fr	Ward, William	1817	AO39	333	237
Miller, Samuel	Deed fr	May, Frederick	1813	AF31	223	152
Miller, Samuel	Deed fr	McLeod, John	1816	AL36	550	513
Miller, Samuel	Deed fr	Tingey, Thomas	1816	AM37	414	297
Miller, Samuel	Plat		1816	AL36	552	
Miller, Samuel, Maj.	Deed to	Tingey, Thomas, Com.	1817	AN38	259	189
Miller, Samuel, of Frederick Co.	Deed to	Beall, Thomas & John M. Gantt	1792	A1-1	098	143
Miller, William	Deed fr	Orr, Benjamin G., of Montg. Co.	1804	K10	122	131
Miller, William	Cert Free to	[ ], Austin	1808	T19	318	232
Miller, William & James Craig	Deed fr	Wagner, Jacob, of G'tn.	1813	AF31	203	137
Miller, William, Jr.	B. of S. to	Miller, William, Sr.	1813	AF31	274	193
Miller, William, of Phila. PA	Deed to	Andrews, George	1810	Y24	037	032
Miller, William, of Phila. PA et al	Deed to	Underwood, Robert	1810	Y24	133	121
Miller, William, of G'tn.	Deed fr	Corcoran, Thomas, of G'tn.	1815	AI34	235	267
Miller, William, of G'tn., butcher	Deed to	Hyde, Thomas	1815	AI34	236	268
Miller, William, Sr.	B. of S. fr	Miller, William, Jr.	1813	AF31	274	193
Milligan, Joseph & William Steuart	Deed to	Vinson, Charles	1812	AE30	027	021
Milligan, Joseph, of G'tn.	B. of S. fr	Dashiell, George, of G'tn.	1811	AB27	356	295

Party	What	Party	Year	Liber	Old	New
Milligan, Joseph, of G'tn.	Deed fr	McDade, Stephen, Monongalia Co.	1813	AF31	535	396
Milligan, Joseph, of G'tn.	Deed fr	Calder, James, of G'tn.	1813	AF31	026	018
Milligan, Joseph, of G'tn.	Deed fr	Lee, John, of G'tn.	1813	AF31	353	252
Milligan, Joseph, of G'tn.	D. of T. to	Ott, John, of G'tn.	1814	AH33	313	270
Milligan, Joseph, of G'tn.	Deed fr	Wilson, Anne, of Balto.	1814	AH33	194	177
Milligan, Joseph, of G'tn.	Deed to	Reinagle, Ann, of G'tn.	1814	AG32	267	190
Milligan, Joseph, of G'tn.	B. of S. fr	McNeill, James	1816	AM37	039	032
Milligan, Joseph, of G'tn.	Convey to	Beall, Gustavus, of G'tn.	1817	AN38	344	253
Milliken, Mark, carpenter	Deed to	Taylor, Samuel, of PA	1798	D4	126	109
Milliken, Mark, carpenter	Mortgage fr	Taylor, Samuel, farmer, of PA	1798	D4	138	121
Milliken, Mark, of PA	Deed to	Beall, Thomas & John M. Gantt	1793	A1-1	187	265
Mills, Ephraim	Agreement	Baker, Samuel	1795	B2B	357	005
Mills, John	B. of S. to	Nicholson, John	1809	W22	226	154
Mills, Peter	Deed to	Belknap, Stephen, trustee	1813	AF31	235	162
Mills, Susanna, of St. Mary's Co.	B. of S. fr	Jarboe, Bennett	1801	G7	307	428
Mills, William G., of G'tn.	Deed to	Mountz, John, of G'tn.	1817	AO39	492	337
Mimm, Peter, of G'tn.	Deed to	Morsell, James Sewall, of G'tn.	1806	O14	347	232
Mincher, William	B. of S. to	Cheney, Jesse	1805	M12	292	293
Minchin, John	Deed fr	Carroll, Daniel	1802	I9	166	253
Minchin, John	Qualify	Ensign in Militia	1808	V21	056	044
Minchin, John	Deed fr	Carroll, Daniel, of *Duddington*	1811	AA26	265	180
Minchin, Patience	Deed to	Gordon, Martha	1816	AL36	386	373
Minifee, Charles	Transfer to	Farrell, Zephaniah	1813	AE30	469	349
Minifee, Charles & James Ewell	Deed to	Boyd, Washington	1814	AG32	173	123
Minifie, Charles	Deed fr	Commissioners of Washington	1801	G7	045	057
Minifie, Charles	B. of S. fr	Calvert, Edward H., of P.G. Co.	1805	N13	107	101
Minifie, Charles	Deed fr	Davis, George S.	1809	V21	189	134
Minifie, Charles	Mortgage fr	Myer, Solomon, of Alexa.	1809	V21	147	107
Minifie, Charles	Deed to	Kerby, John Baptist	1810	X23	384	309
Minifie, Charles	Mortgage to	Ewell, James, Dr. et al	1811	AA26	273	185
Minifie, Charles et al	Deed fr	Walker, George	1799	D4	305	289
Minifie, Charles, of Phila. PA	Deed fr	Walker, George	1799	D4	304	288
Minifie, Charles, of Phila. PA	Deed fr	Walker, George	1800	F6	009	007
Minitree, John	B. of S. fr	Picknall, Richard H.	1809	X23	044	032
Minitree, John	Deed fr	Chandler, Walter Story	1813	AE30	193	154
Minitree, John	Mortgage to	Walker, Zachariah	1814	AH33	037	033
Minitree, John	Mortgage to	Davis, John, of Abel et al	1814	AH33	035	031
Minitree, John & George Cox	Mortgage fr	Bland, Edward	1813	AF31	514	376
Minitree, John & George Cox	Release to	Walker, Zachariah	1815	AI34	155	178
Minitree, John, of G'tn.	Release fr	Davis, John, of Abel	1815	AK35	255	202
Minitree, John, of G'tn.	B. of S. to	Haliday, Thomas	1816	AK35	515	406
Minitree, John, of G'tn.	Deed to	Young, Thomas	1816	AK35	257	204
Minor, Daniel	B. of S. to	Boyd, Washington	1816	AL36	068	069
Minor, John, of Fredericksburg VA	Deed fr	Dermott, James Reed	1800	E5	253	247
Minor, John, of Fredericksburg VA	Deed fr	Hanson, Alexander Contee	1805	M12	392	405
Minor, Lucy L., exrs. of John	Deed to	Eliot, Samuel, Jr.	1817	AN38	558	406
Minturn, Benjamin G. et al	Deed fr	Polock, Isaac	1802	H8	011	010
Mirky, David, wheelwright, of PA	Deed fr	Read, Leonard & Eliz. O. of PA	1795	B2A	351	497
Mitchell, James & Eleanor	Deed fr	Cole, Bennett	1802	I9	429	711
Mitchell, John	Bond to	United States	1802	I9		130
Mitchell, John	Deed fr	Reintzel, Valentine, heirs of	1802	H8	405	374
Mitchell, John	B. of S. fr	Febririer, N. et al	1804	K10	246	253
Mitchell, John C., of G'tn.	Mortgage to	Smith, Jesse, of G'tn.	1816	AM37	083	067
Mitchell, John C., of G'tn.	Deed to	Jones, Dennis, of G'tn.	1816	AL36	067	067
Mitchell, John, Capt., trustee	Deed fr	Tompkins, Charles, insolvent	1806	O14	264	175

Index to District of Columbia Land Records, 1792-1817 287

Party	What	Party	Year	Liber	Old	New
Mitchell, John et al	Bond to	United States	1801	G7	012	015
Mitchell, John, of G'tn.	Deed fr	Peter, Robert, of Montg. Co.	1796	B2B	517	226
Mitchell, John, of G'tn.	Deed fr	Swearingen, Elemeleck	1797	B2B	669	436
Mitchell, John, of G'tn.	Deed to	Corporation of Georgetown	1802	I9	130	194
Mitchell, John, of G'tn.	Deed fr	Brent, Daniel Carroll, marshal	1804	L11	281	258
Mitchell, John, of G'tn.	Deed to	Corcoran, Thomas et al	1806	P15	144	093
Mitchell, John, of G'tn.	Deed to	Calder, James, of G'tn.	1808	U20	053	030
Mitchell, John, of G'tn.	Deed fr	Turner, Samuel, Jr., of G'tn.	1810	Z25	026	020
Mitchell, John, of Montg. Co.	Deed fr	Beckwith, Charles & Cassandra	1813	AF31	270	189
Mitchell, John, of G'tn.	Deed fr	Scott, Sabret, of G'tn. [Cebart]	1816	AK35	488	383
Mitchell, Maria & Matilda	Deed fr	Weatherall, John	1802	I9	341	562
Mitchell, Mary, plt.	Suit	Turner, Samuel, Jr., def.	1810	Z25	025	019
Mitchell, Mary, wid/o Capt. John	Deed fr	Beatty, John M., Dr.	1810	Y24	054	048
Mitchell, Thomas L.	B. of S. fr	Brooks, Joseph	1801	G7	007	009
Mitchell, Walter	B. of S. fr	Thompson, Andrew	1809	V21	368	270
Mitchell, Walter & Matilda et al	Deed to	Walker, Zachariah	1815	AI34	435	452
Mitchell, Walter & Matilda et al	Deed to	Spalding, Enoch	1815	AI34	110	126
Mitchell, Walter & Matilda et al	Deed to	Spalding, Enoch	1815	AI34	097	110
Moffat, William	Deed to	Nesmith, Ebenezer	1802	H8	094	086
Moffat, William	Deed to	Nesmith, Ebenezer	1802	H8	092	084
Moffat, William et al	Deed fr	Law, Thomas	1801	G7	362	493
Moffat, William et al	Deed fr	Law, Thomas	1801	G7	359	490
Mollyneux, Robert et al	Deed fr	Threlkeld, John, of Montg. Co.	1796	B2B	500	197
Molyneux, Robert, Rev. et al	Deed to	Walton, James, Rev. et al	1799	D4	286	268
Molyneux, Robert, St. Mary's Co.	Deed to	Walton, James, Rev. et al	1799	D4	283	265
Moncreiff, Archibald, of Balto et al	Deed to	Dorsey, William Hammond	1795	B2A	208	286
Monroe, Thomas	B. of S. fr	Coningham, Cornelius	1805	O14	089	055
Monroe, Thomas, Supt.	Cert to	Young, Moses	1809	X23	033	023
Montgomery, James, trustee	Deed fr	Smith, Amos, insolvent	1805	N13	041	041
Moody, John & Betsey	Deed to	Cannon, Sarah	1817	AN38	163	119
Moore, Alexander	Lease fr	Brooks, Joseph	1810	Z25	180	142
Moore, Alexander	Deed to	Bohrer, Jacob	1814	AH33	320	276
Moore, Alexander, house joiner	Deed fr	Ober, Robert, mer.	1812	AE30	026	020
Moore, Alexander, of G'tn.	Deed fr	Brookes, Joseph, of G'tn.	1811	AB27	486	398
Moore, Alexander, of G'tn.	Deed fr	Brookes, Joseph, of G'tn.	1811	AB27	074	062
Moore, Alexander, of G'tn.	Deed to	Brookes, Joseph, of G'tn.	1811	AB27	415	342
Moore, Alexander, of G'tn.	Deed to	Pickrell, John, of G'tn.	1811	AB27	340	280
Moore, Alexander, of G'tn.	Deed to	King, Charles, of G'tn.	1812	AD29	366	308
Moore, Ann Maria et al	Deed fr	Hoot, Samuel	1816	AM37	464	334
Moore, Benjamin, printer & editor	P. of Atty. fr	Gridley, Richard	1798	D4	106	089
Moore, Eliza, wid/o Joshua John	B. of S. to	McIntire, Samuel	1814	AG32	389	283
Moore, Elizabeth	B. of S. to	Brown, Obadiah B.	1813	AF31	232	152
Moore, George	Deed fr	Brent, Daniel Carroll, marshal	1804	L11	368	331
Moore, George	Deed fr	King, Nicholas	1805	M12	293	294
Moore, George	Deed fr	Bentley, Joseph	1806	P15	258	170
Moore, George	Deed fr	Downes, George, Loudoun Co. VA	1806	Q16	151	099
Moore, George	Deed to	Van Ness, John P.	1807	R17	251	190
Moore, George	Deed to	Bacon, Samuel	1808	U20	387	215
Moore, George	Convey to	Van Ness, John P.	1808	T19	046	034
Moore, George	Assign fr	Smith, Robert R.	1808	T19	400	282
Moore, George	Deed fr	Caldwell, Timothy	1808	U20	097	054
Moore, George	Cert fr	Munroe, Thomas, Supt.	1808	U20	102	057
Moore, George	Lease to	Mudd, Theodore	1809	W22	309	202
Moore, George	B. of S. fr	Thorpe, Thomas	1810	Y24	234	215
Moore, George	Assign fr	Burch, Henry	1811	AA26	049	038

Party	What	Party	Year	Liber	Old	New
Moore, George	Assign fr	Speake, Samuel	1811	Z25	398	313
Moore, George	Deed fr	Burch, Henry	1812	AC28	167	124
Moore, George	Deed fr	Van Ness, John P. & Marcia	1812	AD29	212	174
Moore, George	Deed to	Queen, Nicholas L.	1813	AE30	292	222
Moore, George	Deed fr	Woodworth, Joseph	1813	AE30	108	083
Moore, George	Mortgage fr	Jackson, Joseph	1813	AE30	063	048
Moore, George	Assign fr	Speake, Samuel	1813	AE30	178	142
Moore, George	Mortgage fr	Jackson, Joseph	1813	AE30	062	046
Moore, George	Deed to	Sutherland, Thomas J.	1813	AF31	526	387
Moore, George	B. of S. fr	Green, John E.	1814	AG32	102	077
Moore, George	Deed to	Law, Thomas	1815	AH33	512	439
Moore, George	Deed fr	Belt, Benjamin M.	1815	AI34	523	527
Moore, George	Release fr	Van Ness, John P. & Marcia	1815	AI34	522	526
Moore, George	Deed to	Bacon, Samuel	1815	AI34	020	021
Moore, George	Deed to	Cooper, William	1815	AI34	325	357
Moore, George	Deed fr	Webster, Toppan	1815	AI34	164	188
Moore, George	Deed to	Woodworth, Joseph	1815	AI34	081	092
Moore, George	Deed fr	Law, Thomas	1815	AI34	165	189
Moore, George	Deed to	Belt, Benjamin M.	1815	AK35	458	359
Moore, George	Deed fr	Law, Thomas	1815	AK35	461	361
Moore, George & Samuel Bacon	Assign fr	Thorpe, Thomas	1809	V21	419	320
Moore, George & George Clyver	Mortgage fr	Gannon, James	1810	Y24	235	217
Moore, George & O.B. Brown	D. of T. fr	Huddleston, Joseph	1812	AC28	204	155
Moore, George & John M. Wight	Assign fr	Connell, Catherine	1812	AD29	024	017
Moore, George & Samuel Bacon	Deed fr	Whetcroft, William & Sarah et al	1812	AD29	523	441
Moore, George & John M. Wightt	Assign fr	Fitzgerald, William	1812	AC28	512	366
Moore, George & Samuel Bacon	B. of S. to	Campbell, John	1815	AI34	510	515
Moore, George & Verlinda	Deed to	Edmonston, Enoch, of Montg. Co.	1815	AK35	216	175
Moore, George et al	Manumis to	[ ], Hanson (negro)	1808	T19	126	089
Moore, George et al	B. of S. fr	Edelen, Ignatius	1812	AD29	019	014
Moore, George et al	Release to	deKrafft, Edward B.	1813	AF31	280	198
Moore, James	Deed fr	Threlkeld, John, of G'tn.	1802	H8	252	240
Moore, James	Assign fr	Doughty, William	1802	H8	248	236
Moore, James	Deed fr	Munroe, Thomas, Supt.	1802	H8	545	506
Moore, James	Deed to	Doughty, William	1802	H8	251	238
Moore, James	Deed fr	Munroe, Thomas, Supt.	1805	M12	240	241
Moore, James	Deed to	Underwood, Robert	1807	S18	219	175
Moore, James	Receipt to	Lingan, Nicholas et al	1807	S18	376	299
Moore, James	Deed fr	Reed, Alexander	1807	S18	260	205
Moore, James	Deed fr	Bacon, Samuel	1809	V21	407	309
Moore, James	Deed fr	Dorsey, William H., of Balto. Co.	1810	Z25	072	054
Moore, James	Deed fr	Murdock, John, of G'tn.	1810	Z25	070	053
Moore, James	Deed fr	Wheaton, Joseph	1811	AB27	498	407
Moore, James	Deed fr	Boyd, Washington, marshal	1811	AA26	312	211
Moore, James	Assign to	Worthington, William	1812	AC28	108	081
Moore, James	Deed fr	Worthington, William	1812	AC28	226	167
Moore, James	Release fr	Bank of Columbia	1812	AD29	498	420
Moore, James	Deed fr	Dorsey, William H., of Balto. Co.	1812	AD29	495	418
Moore, James	Deed fr	Murdock, John, of G'tn.	1812	AD29	496	419
Moore, James	Deed fr	Worthington, William	1812	AC28	226	167
Moore, James	Deed fr	Gannon, James, of G'tn.	1813	AE30	371	275
Moore, James	B. of S. fr	Smoot, Alexander S.	1813	AG32	005	004
Moore, James	Deed fr	Connell, Catharine	1813	AE30	375	277
Moore, James	Deed fr	Beatty, Charles A.	1814	AG32	207	144
Moore, James	Deed fr	Dick, Margaret	1815	AI34	051	058

Party	What	Party	Year	Liber	Old	New
Moore, James	Deed to	District of Columbia	1815	AH33	543	465
Moore, James	B. of S. fr	Leach, John	1816	AL36	517	484
Moore, James	Deed fr	Billmyer, Thomas	1816	AM37	308	225
Moore, James	Release to	Billmyer, Thomas	1817	AN38	540	392
Moore, James & John	B. of S. fr	Miller, John Moore	1806	P15	165	109
Moore, James & John	Assign fr	Miller, John Moore	1806	P15	164	108
Moore, James & James Gannon	Deed fr	Murdock, John	1811	AC28	013	010
Moore, James, butcher, of G'tn.	Mortgage to	Threlkeld, John	1799	D4	335	322
Moore, James D.	Deed to	Marbury, William	1808	T19	101	072
Moore, James D.	D. of T. to	Thomas, Joseph	1809	V21	184	131
Moore, James et al	B. of S. fr	Bootes, Samuel	1805	N13	383	307
Moore, James et al	B. of S. fr	Daugherty, Vincent	1811	Z25	556	442
Moore, James, of G'tn.	Deed fr	Threlkeld, John, of Montg. Co.	1798	C3	327	264
Moore, James, Sr. & G. Kleiber	B. of S. fr	Dove, Joseph	1815	AH33	488	418
Moore, John	B. of S. fr	Varden, Richard	1805	M12	316	319
Moore, John	Deed fr	Law, Thomas	1813	AE30	395	291
Moore, John	Deed fr	Law, Thomas	1817	AN38	250	183
Moore, John, brickmaker, of Phila.	Mortgage fr	Caldwell, Timothy, of Phila. PA	1813	AF31	245	170
Moore, John C., of P.G. Co.	Deed fr	Wigfield, Robert & Mary	1812	AD29	455	383
Moore, John C., of P.G. Co.	Deed to	Harshman, Henry & Susannah	1813	AF31	312	223
Moore, John et al	B. of S. to	Varden, Joseph	1808	U20	351	190
Moore, John O.	B. of S. to	Evans, Philip	1810	Y24	163	148
Moore, Joseph	Cert Free to	Moore, Peggy [Indian Peg]	1808	U20	025	014
Moore, Joseph	B. of S. to	Traverse, Nicholas	1817	AO39	252	182
Moore, Mary et al	Deed fr	Hoot, Samuel	1816	AM37	464	334
Moore, Nathan	Manumis to	Hill, Dick (negro)	1810	Y24	280	256
Moore, Nathan	B. of S. to	Newton, John S.	1810	Y24	323	293
Moore, Nicholas	Deed fr	Dial, Annastatia	1804	K10	393	408
Moore, Nicholas	Deed to	Brady, Michael	1808	V21	036	026
Moore, Nicholas	Deed to	Brady, Michael	1808	V21	127	093
Moore, Nicholas et al	Deed fr	Wert, Joseph D.	1802	I9	298	490
Moore, Nicholas et al	Deed to	Dial, Annastatia	1804	K10	310	314
Moore, Peggy [Indian Peg]	Cert Free fr	Moore, Joseph	1808	U20	025	014
Moore, Peter Dent	Deed fr	Van Ness, John P. & Marcia	1808	V21	123	090
Moore, Peter Dent	Deed fr	Skam, John	1809	W22	040	030
Moore, Peter Dent	B. of S. fr	Reid, William F.	1810	Y24	288	263
Moore, Thomas	Deed fr	Law, Thomas	1817	AN38	246	180
Moore, Thomas & James	Cert fr	Munroe, Thomas, Supt.	1815	AI34	427	446
Moore, Thomas L., of Phila. PA	Cert fr	Commissioners of Washington	1793	B2A	301	423
Moore, Thomas L., of Phila. PA	Cert fr	Commissioners of Washington	1793	B2A	301	422
Moore, Warren, of St. Mary's Co.	B. of S. to	Watterston, David	1812	AC28	377	274
Moore, William	Lease fr	Young, Nicholas	1814	AG32	119	088
Moore, William	B. of S. to	McCormick, Alexander	1814	AG32	124	091
Moore, William	B. of S. to	Jameison, Marsham et al	1815	AH33	423	364
Moore, William	Release fr	McCormick, Alexander	1816	AM37	247	182
Moore, William	Release fr	Holliday, Thomas & M. Jameson	1816	AM37	183	138
Moore, William	B. of S. to	Walker, Zachariah	1817	AN38	100	076
Moore, William & John L. Naylor	Mortgage fr	Fry, Thomas	1811	AC28	041	030
Moore, William Horace et al	Deed fr	Hoot, Samuel	1816	AM37	464	334
Moran, Jesse	B. of S. to	Bussard, Daniel, of G'tn.	1815	AK35	066	051
Moran, Jesse	Cert Slave	From Allegany Co. MD	1815	AI34	074	083
More, James	Assign fr	Blount, George, sadler	1803	K10	068	74
Morgan, Benjamin, New Orleans	Manumis to	[ ], Toby, age 45	1817	AN38	361	265
Morgan, Nelly (negro)	Agreement	Baker, Zachariah, of G'tn.	1809	V21	300	218
Morgan, Richard, insolvent	Deed to	Holliday, Elsworth, trustee	1806	O14	190	124

Party	What	Party	Year	Liber	Old	New
Morgan, William	Deed fr	Ray, Benjamin, Jr.	1802	I9	238	382
Morgan, William	Deed fr	Dorsey, William H.	1804	K10	358	370
Morgan, William	Deed fr	Beall, Thomas, of George et al	1805	N13	299	243
Morgan, William	Lease fr	Baker, Henry	1811	AB27	050	042
Morgan, William	Deed to	Foxall, Henry	1811	AC28	062	047
Morgan, William	Deed to	Pickrell, John	1812	AD29	208	169
Morgan, William	Deed fr	Peter, George	1813	AE30	321	241
Morgan, William	Deed fr	Wirt, John, of G'tn.	1813	AE30	209	170
Morgan, William	D. of T. fr	Thornton, William	1813	AF31	505	368
Morgan, William	D. of T. fr	Doughty, William	1813	AF31	078	054
Morgan, William et al	B. of S. fr	Cooper, John	1810	X23	409	330
Morgan, William, mer., of G'tn.	Deed fr	Wright, Thomas C., of G'tn.	1808	U20	177	099
Morgan, William, mer.	Deed fr	Beatty, Charles A., Dr.	1811	AB27	052	044
Morgan, William, of G'tn.	Deed fr	Myer, Solomon	1805	M12	385	397
Morgan, William, of G'tn.	Deed to	Myer, Solomon	1805	M12	138	134
Morgan, William, of G'tn.	Deed to	Cocking, William	1807	R17	068	055
Morgan, William, of G'tn.	Deed to	Lingan, Nicholas, of G'tn.	1808	T19	304	222
Morgan, William, of G'tn.	Deed fr	Lingan, Nicholas, of G'tn.	1808	T19	345	250
Morgan, William, of G'tn. et al	Cert fr	Munroe, Thomas, Supr.	1808	T19	349	252
Morgan, William, of G'tn.	Deed fr	Reintzel, Anthony, of G'tn.	1809	V21	381	285
Morgan, William, of G'tn.	D. of T. fr	Williams, James, of G'tn.	1810	Y24	141	128
Morgan, William, of G'tn.	D. of T. fr	Fox, Josiah	1813	AE30	323	243
Morgan, William, of G'tn.	Deed to	Methodist Episcopal Church, G'tn.	1814	AH33	010	009
Morgan, William, of G'tn.	Release to	Doughty, William	1815	AI34	184	211
Morgan, William, of G'tn.	Deed fr	Lettler, Nathan, exrs. of, of VA	1815	AK35	078	060
Morgan, William, of G'tn.	Deed to	Woodward, Thomas & G. Cooke	1815	AK35	415	325
Morgan, William, of G'tn.	Deed to	Bowie, John, of Montg. Co.	1816	AL36	536	500
Morgan, William, of G'tn.	Lease fr	Bowie, John, of Montg. Co.	1816	AL36	533	498
Moriarty, Ambrose	Deed fr	Munroe, Thomas	1802	H8	495	455
Moriarty, Ambrose	Deed to	Boyd, Washington & C. Glover	1814	AG32	162	116
Morin, Lewis	Mortgage to	Stockwell, Mark	1801	G7	366	498
Morin, Lewis	Mortgage to	Stockwell, Mark	1802	I9	072	101
Morin, Lewis	Release fr	Stockwell, Mark	1804	K10	308	312
Morin, Lewis	Deed fr	Dorsey, William H.	1806	Q16	047	030
Morin, Lewis	Deed fr	Coltman, William	1806	Q16	047	030
Morin, Lewis	Deed fr	Hughes, Thomas	1810	Y24	047	041
Morin, Lewis	Release to	Keiler, Daniel	1811	AA26	204	135
Morin, Lewis et al	Mortgage fr	Ryan, Henry & Mary	1809	X23	298	237
Morris & Nicholson	Deed to	Harrison, Benjamin, Jr.	1798	D4	069	058
Morris & Nicholson	Deed to	Thornton, Presley	1798	D4	030	025
Morris, Benjamin W., of Phila. PA	Deed fr	Thompson, James	1801	F6	171	107
Morris, Benjamin W. et al	Deed fr	Kearney, John & Edward Fallon	1804	K10	114	123
Morris, Benjamin W., late of Phila.	Deed to	Morris, Samuel, exrs. of	1814	AG32	277	197
Morris, Caspar W. et al	Deed to	Thompson, James	1816	AL36	488	459
Morris, George	Deed fr	Mountz, John, exr. of Wm. Fields	1817	AO39	431	294
Morris, George	Deed to	Riggs, Elisha	1817	AO39	432	295
Morris, George, of G'tn.	Deed fr	Fields, William, of G'tn.	1815	AI34	425	445
Morris, Gerard (C), of G'tn.	D. of T. to	Lufborough, Nathan	1813	AF31	145	097
Morris, Gerrard (C) et al	Deed fr	Beall, Thomas	1805	M12	164	162
Morris, Gerrard (C), of G'tn.	Deed fr	Suter, Alexander, of G'tn.	1812	AD29	423	356
Morris, Gerrard (C)	D. of T. to	Lufborough, Nathan	1812	AD29	261	216
Morris, Gerrard & John Shorter	Deed to	Suter, Alexander	1812	AD29	291	240
Morris, Henry B., of Charles Co.	Manumis to	[ ],.Mason	1816	AK35	300	240
Morris, Henry Bishop, by will of	Manumis to	Morris, Sarah (M), age 20	1816	AM37	247	181
Morris, Isaac W. et al	Deed to	Thompson, James	1816	AL36	488	459

Index to District of Columbia Land Records, 1792-1817

Party	What	Party	Year	Liber	Old	New
Morris, Israel et al	Deed fr	Kearney, John & Edward Falon	1804	K10	114	123
Morris, Israel W. et al	Deed fr	Kearney, John & Edward Fallon	1804	K10	114	123
Morris, Israel W. et al	Deed to	Thompson, James	1816	AL36	488	459
Morris, Joseph et al	D. of T. fr	Burd, Edward Shippen, Phila. PA	1809	V21	365	268
Morris, Joseph S. et al	Partition	Young, Moses	1810	X23	216	165
Morris, Joseph S. et al	Deed fr	Howell, Benjamin B.	1812	AD29	519	
Morris, Joseph S., of Phila. et al	Deed to	Howell, Benjamin B., of Phila.	1812	AD29	511	431
Morris, Joseph S. et al	Deed fr	Waln, Robert, Jr., of Phila., mer.	1815	AK35	152	118
Morris, Luke W. et al	Deed to	Thompson, James	1816	AL36	488	459
Morris, Mary, w/o Robert et al	R. of D. to	Duncanson, William M. et al	1798	C3	364	292
Morris, Nathaniel, of G'tn.	Deed fr	Beall, Thomas B., of G'tn.	1808	U20	130	074
Morris, Randal	Deed to	Beck, Richard, Jr.	1802	I9	273	446
Morris, Randal, of Montg. Co.	Deed fr	Beall, Thomas Brooke, Montg. Co.	1797	C3	190	160
Morris, Randal, of P.G. Co.	Deed fr	Jenkins, Thomas	1806	P15	256	169
Morris, Randal, of G'tn.	Deed to	Cox, John, of G'tn.	1811	AA26	035	027
Morris, Robert & John Nicholson	Deed to	Forrest, Uriah, of G'tn.	1796	B2B	577	320
Morris, Robert & James Greenleaf	Transfer to	Scott, Gustavus	1796	B2B	457	145
Morris, Robert & James Greenleaf	Agreement	Commissioners of Washington	1796	B2B	544	267
Morris, Robert & James Greenleaf	Agreement	Commissioners of Washington	1796	B2B	541	263
Morris, Robert & John Nicholson	Deed fr	Scott, Gustavus, of G'tn.	1796	B2B	603	355
Morris, Robert & John Nicholson	Deed fr	Greenleaf, James, New York NY	1796	B2B	579	323
Morris, Robert & John Nicholson	Deed fr	Greenleaf, James, now of NY	1796	B2B	562	296
Morris, Robert & John Nicholson	Deed fr	Deakins, William, Jr., of G'tn.	1796	B2B	604	356
Morris, Robert & Mary, et al	Mortgage to	Greenleaf, James, New York NY	1796	B2B	592	341
Morris, Robert & John Nicholson	Deed to	Duncanson, William et al	1796	B2B	566	302
Morris, Robert & John Nicholson	Agreement	Bickley, John, bricklayer	1796	B2B	584	330
Morris, Robert & James Greenleaf	Transfer to	Dermott, James Reed	1796	B2B	457	146
Morris, Robert & John Nicholson	Deed to	Greenleaf, James, now of Phila.	1796	B2B	599	349
Morris, Robert & John Nicholson	Deed to	Dermott, James Reed	1796	B2B	560	293
Morris, Robert & James Greenleaf	Transfer to	Peter, Robert	1797	B2B	461	150
Morris, Robert & James Greenleaf	Transfer to	Deakins, Wm., Jr. & U. Forrest	1797	B2B	473	166
Morris, Robert & James Greenleaf	Transfer to	Edwards, Henry	1797	B2B	458	148
Morris, Robert & James Greenleaf	Transfer to	Philips, Grout & West	1797	B2B	464	155
Morris, Robert & James Greenleaf	Transfer to	Forrest, Uriah	1797	B2B	472	164
Morris, Robert & James Greenleaf	Transfer to	Crocker, John	1797	B2B	464	155
Morris, Robert & James Greenleaf	Transfer to	Law, Thomas	1797	B2B	469	162
Morris, Robert & Mary, of Phila.	Deed to	Ball, Joseph, of Phila. et al	1797	C3	007	5
Morris, Robert & Mary et al	Deed to	Duncanson, William Mayne	1797	C3	238	197
Morris, Robert & Mary, Phila. et al	Deed to	Law, Thomas	1797	C3	074	61
Morris, Robert et al	Cert fr	Commissioners of Washington	1796	B2B	452	140
Morris, Robert et al	Deed to	Dickinson, Philemon	1798	D4	034	028
Morris, Robert et al	Deed to	Pratt, Henry et al	1798	D4	030	025
Morris, Robert et al	P. of Atty. to	Scott, Gustavus	1799	D4	188	170
Morris, Robert et al	Deed to	Nicklin, Philip & E. Griffith	1799	D4	186	168
Morris, Robert et al	Oblig. to	Dunlop, James et al	1802	H8	100	091
Morris, Robert, of Phila. PA et al	Deed to	Law, Thomas, of New York NY	1795	B2B	377	030
Morris, Robert, of Phila. PA et al	Deed to	Polock, Isaac, of Savannah GA	1796	B2B	505	206
Morris, Robert, of Phila. PA et al	Mortgage to	Duncanson, William Mayne	1796	B2B	411	081
Morris, Robert, of Phila. PA	Deed fr	Law, Thomas	1796	B2B	418	089
Morris, Robert, of Phila. PA	Agreement	Reed, Isaac, painter & glazier	1796	B2B	554	281
Morris, Robert, of Phila. PA	Deed fr	Commissioners of Washington	1796	B2B	419	091
Morris, Robert, of Phila. PA	Deed fr	Greenleaf, James, New York NY	1796	B2B	387	044
Morris, Robert, of Phila. PA	P. of Atty. to	Cranch, William	1796	B2B	390	049
Morris, Robert, of Phila. PA et al	Deed fr	Greenleaf, James	1796	B2B	532	249
Morris, Robert, of Phila. PA	Deed fr	Greenleaf, James, New York NY	1796	B2B	388	047

Party	What	Party	Year	Liber	Old	New
Morris, Robert, of Phila. PA	Deed to	Deakins, William, Jr.	1797	B2B	684	453
Morris, Robert, of Phila. PA	Deed to	Dunlap, James, of G'tn.	1797	B2B	674	444
Morris, Robert, of Phila. PA	Deed to	Deakins, William, Jr.	1797	B2B	676	447
Morris, Robert, of Phila. PA	P. of Atty. to	Cranch, William	1797	B2B	663	428
Morris, Robert, of Phila. PA et al	Release fr	Law, Thomas	1797	C3	180	152
Morris, Robert, of Phila. PA et al	Release fr	Law, Thomas	1797	C3	144	118
Morris, Robert, of Phila. PA et al	D. of T. to	Pratt, Henry et al	1797	C3	192	161
Morris, Robert, of Phila. PA et al	D. of T. to	Pratt, Henry et al	1797	C3	204	172
Morris, Robert, of Phila. PA et al	Deed to	Baker, Jacob et al	1798	C3	301	243
Morris, Robert, of Phila. PA et al	Deed to	Duncanson, William M. et al	1798	C3	362	289
Morris, Robert, of Phila. PA et al	Deed to	Forrest, Uriah	1798	C3	517	406
Morris, Samuel, exrs. of	Deed fr	Morris, Benjamin W., late of Phila.	1814	AG32	277	197
Morris, Samuel, of PA, exrs. of	Deed to	Thompson, James	1816	AL36	488	459
Morris, Sarah (M), age 20	Manumis fr	Morris, Henry Bishop, by will of	1816	AM37	247	181
Morris, Thomas B., of P.G. Co.	B. of S. to	Prout, William	1810	Z25	338	265
Morris, Thomas B., of P.G. Co.	B. of S. to	Pumphrey, William	1817	AN38	087	067
Morris, Thomas Barton	Cert Free to	Hews, Henry (C), age 28	1813	AE30	106	081
Morris, Thomas, devisees of	Partition	Young, Moses	1810	X23	216	165
Morris, Thomas et al	D. of T. fr	Burd, Edward Shippen, Phila. PA	1809	V21	365	268
Morris, Thomas, of Phila. et al	Deed to	Howell, Benjamin B., of Phila.	1812	AD29	511	431
Morris, Thomas, sons & devisees	Deed to	Howell, Benjamin B., of Phila.	1812	AD29	511	431
Morris, Washington R. et al	Cert fr	Commissioners of Washington	1796	B2A	337	473
Morris, Washington R. et al	Transfer to	Law, Thomas	1796	B2A	336	473
Morrow, John, of Balto. MD	Deed fr	Fallon, Edward & Mary Anne	1813	AE30	417	307
Morsell, James S.	Deed fr	Barclay, Thomas	1799	D4	279	262
Morsell, James S.	P. of Atty. fr	Thompson, John	1799	D4	270	254
Morsell, James S.	Deed fr	Forrest, Richard	1799	D4	255	240
Morsell, James S.	Deed fr	Gregg, Joshua, of G'tn.	1802	H8	218	208
Morsell, James S.	Deed to	Speake, Josias M.	1802	I9	300	493
Morsell, James S.	Deed fr	Simpson, James	1802	G7	504	643
Morsell, James S. et al	Deed fr	Turner, Thomas	1805	M12	339	344
Morsell, James S. et al	Deed fr	Etting, Solomon	1805	M12	329	333
Morsell, James S. et al	Deed fr	Harrison, Richard H., of G'tn.	1805	M12	327	331
Morsell, James S. et al	Deed fr	Brodean, Ann	1805	M12	337	342
Morsell, James S. et al	Deed fr	Loundes, Richard T.	1805	M12	343	349
Morsell, James S. et al	Deed fr	Weems, John	1805	M12	346	352
Morsell, James S. et al	Deed fr	Stoddert, Benjamin	1805	M12	321	325
Morsell, James S., of G'tn.	Release to	Shoemaker, Jonathan	1809	W22	159	112
Morsell, James S., of G'tn.	Deed to	Williams, Elisha W., mer., G'tn.	1809	X23	235	182
Morsell, James S., of G'tn. et al	Deed to	Beall, Thomas B., of G'tn.	1809	W22	083	061
Morsell, James S., trustee	Deed to	Wilson, Joseph	1810	X23	300	239
Morsell, James S.	B. of S. fr	Hazel, Henry, admr. of Jeremioah	1810	Y24	058	051
Morsell, James S., of G'tn.	Deed to	Corcoran, Thomas, of G'tn.	1811	Z25	530	421
Morsell, James S.	Deed fr	Chandler, Walter S.	1811	AB27	397	327
Morsell, James S.	Deed fr	Naylor, John L.	1811	AC28	008	006
Morsell, James S., of G'tn.	Deed to	Brashears, Trueman, of Alexa. Co.	1812	AB27	531	433
Morsell, James S., of G'tn.	Deed to	Nicholls, William S. et al	1812	AC28	288	209
Morsell, James S., trustee, of G'tn.	Deed to	Chandler, Walter S.	1812	AD29	075	055
Morsell, James S., trustee, of G'tn.	Deed to	Chandler, Walter S.	1812	AD29	074	053
Morsell, James S., of G'tn.	Deed to	Marbury, William	1812	AD29	487	412
Morsell, James S., of G'tn.	Deed to	Johns, Richard H., of G'tn.	1814	AG32	356	258
Morsell, James S., of G'tn.	Deed to	Marbury, John, of G'tn.	1815	AH33	425	366
Morsell, James S., trustee	Deed to	Hewitt, William	1815	AH33	556	476
Morsell, James S.	Deed to	Hagner, Peter	1815	AI34	146	167
Morsell, James S.	Deed fr	Williams, H. & Leonard H. Johns	1815	AI34	086	098

Party	What	Party	Year	Liber	Old	New
Morsell, James S.	B. of S. fr	Beall, Thomas Brooke	1815	AI34	032	037
Morsell, James S. & Wm. Whann	D. of T. fr	Hoye, John, of Allegany Co.	1815	AK35	350	279
Morsell, James S. & Wm. Whann	D. of T. fr	Deakins, Leonard M. & John Hoye	1815	AK35	347	276
Morsell, James S. & Wm. Whann	Deed fr	Harbaugh, Leonard et al	1815	AK35	343	271
Morsell, James S., of G'tn.	Manumis to	[ ], Serena (M)	1816	AL36	433	412
Morsell, James S.	B. of S. fr	Beall, Thomas B., of G'tn.	1816	AL36	432	412
Morsell, James S., trustee	Deed to	Edwards, Lewis	1817	AN38	008	007
Morsell, James Sewall, of G'tn.	Deed to	Renner, Daniel	1801	G7	158	209
Morsell, James Sewall, trustee	Deed to	Barry, James	1804	K10	214	224
Morsell, James Sewall, of G'tn.	Deed fr	Mimm, Peter, of G'tn.	1806	O14	347	232
Morsell, James Sewall, of G'tn.	Deed to	Beck, Richard, of G'tn.	1806	P15	032	019
Morsell, James Sewall, of G'tn.	Deed fr	Creager, Mary et al	1810	Y24	056	049
Morsell, James Sewell, of G'tn.	Deed fr	Densley, Hugh	1802	G7	554	702
Morton, Thomas	D. of T. to	Beall, Thomas & John M. Gantt	1792	A1-1	046	68
Morton, Thomas, of Montg. Co.	Deed to	Lenox, Peter & Bernard Crook	1796	B2B	559	290
Morton, William	D. of T. fr	Thomson, James & Marg. Smith	1810	Z25	291	228
Morton, William	Deed fr	Bussard, Daniel	1816	AL36	062	063
Morton, William, of G'tn.	D. of T. fr	Thomson, George, of G'tn.	1810	Y24	126	114
Morton, William, of G'tn.	Deed fr	Duvall, William N., of G'tn.	1816	AL36	040	041
Morton, William, trustee	Deed to	Clark, Isaac	1817	AO39	448	307
Moscrop, Henry	Deed fr	Polock, Isaac, in MD	1802	H8	380	353
Moscrop, Henry	Deed to	Piercy, Israel	1802	I9	500	821
Moscrop, Henry	Deed to	Neale, John B.	1802	I9	353	582
Moscrop, Henry	B. of S. to	Wayman, Charles	1802	I9	538	878
Moscrop, Henry	Receipt to	Fitzhugh, Philip	1802	I9	088	125
Moscrop, Henry	Mortgage to	Lee, Thomas, Sr., Pr. Wm. Co.	1804	L11	048	49
Moscrop, Henry	Deed to	Goldthwait, Samuel, of Balto.	1805	M12	141	136
Moscrop, Henry	Deed to	Foxall, Henry, of Alexa.	1805	N13	135	129
Moscrop, Henry & Elizabeth, NY	Deed to	Nicholson, John, of Balto.	1816	AM37	184	138
Moscrop, Henry et al	Agreement	Schofield, J. & M.	1799	D4	241	224
Moscrop, Henry, of A.A. Co.	Deed fr	Young, Samuel W., s/o Abraham	1801	G7	298	415
Moscrop, Henry, of MD	Deed to	Friese, Philip R.I., of Balto. MD	1802	H8	514	472
Moscrop, Henry, of MD	Deed to	Howard, Henry, s/o John	1802	H8	193	185
Moscrop, Henry, of MD	Deed to	Schroeder, Henry, of Balto. MD	1802	H8	524	483
Moscrop, Henry, of MD	Deed to	Schroeder, Henry, of Balto. MD	1802	H8	262	249
Moscrop, Henry, of MD	Deed to	Cole, Samuel, of Balto. MD	1802	H8	308	290
Moscrop, Henry, of Alexa.	Deed fr	Whetcroft, Henry	1805	N13	133	127
Mosher, Jeremiah, of G'tn.	B. of S. fr	Porter, Isaiah, of G'tn.	1813	AF31	440	316
Moss, Philemon	Deed fr	McNantz, Charles	1807	S18	098	080
Moss, Philemon	Deed fr	Laird, John, of G'tn.	1813	AF31	520	382
Moss, Philemon	Lease fr	Kealy, Daniel	1815	AK35	096	074
Motts, Bacchus (negro)	Manumis fr	Nourse, Joseph	1807	S18	260	205
Moulder, John M.	B. of S. fr	Suter, Alexander, of G'tn.	1816	AL36	103	103
Moulder, John N.	Deed fr	Stretch, Joseph	1817	AO39	126	096
Mountz, George et al	Deed to	Henry, Robert J. et al	1807	R17	278	212
Mountz, George, of G'tn.	Deed fr	Mountz, John, Sr., of G'tn.	1807	R17	191	145
Mountz, George, of G'tn.	Deed fr	Mountz, John, Sr., of G'tn.	1807	R17	188	143
Mountz, Henry et al	Deed to	Beall, Thomas & John M. Gantt	1792	A1-1	102	148
Mountz, Jacob	Deed fr	Thompson, Josias	1802	I9	358	592
Mountz, Jacob	Deed to	Mountz & Wehrly	1802	I9	359	594
Mountz, Jacob, collector, G'tn.	Deed to	Renner, Daniel & Daniel Bussard	1809	X23	289	230
Mountz, Jacob, collector, of G'tn.	Deed to	Lee, William	1809	X23	344	275
Mountz, Jacob, collector, G'tn.	Deed to	Hoye, John, of G'tn.	1809	X23	208	158
Mountz, Jacob, collector, of G'tn.	Deed to	Corcoran, Thomas, of G'tn.	1810	X23	325	260
Mountz, Jacob, collector, of G'tn.	Deed to	Johnson, George	1810	Y24	391	353

Index to District of Columbia Land Records, 1792-1817

Party	What	Party	Year	Liber	Old	New
Mountz, Jacob, collector, of G'tn.	Deed to	Lee, William, of G'tn.	1810	Y24	261	240
Mountz, Jacob, collector, of G'tn.	Deed to	Corcoran, Thomas, of G'tn.	1810	Y24	523	460
Mountz, Jacob, collector, G'tn.	Deed to	Reintzel, John, of G'tn.	1810	Z25	233	182
Mountz, Jacob, collector, G'tn.	Deed to	Thomas, John, Sr., of Montg. Co.	1810	Z25	259	203
Mountz, Jacob, collector, G'tn.	Deed to	Shepperd, James Glasgow, of NC	1810	Z25	228	178
Mountz, Jacob, collector, G'tn.	Deed to	Jones, Benjamin W., of G'tn.	1810	Z25	348	272
Mountz, Jacob, collector, of G'tn.	Deed to	Robertson, Thomas, of G'tn.	1811	AA26	370	246
Mountz, Jacob, collector, of G'tn.	Deed to	Turner, Samuel et al	1811	AA26	052	041
Mountz, Jacob, collector, of G'tn.	Deed to	Williams, Elisha W., of G'tn.	1811	AA26	094	066
Mountz, Jacob, collector, of G'tn.	Deed to	Smith, Clement, of G'tn.	1811	AB27	002	005
Mountz, Jacob, collector, of G'tn.	Deed to	Reintzel, Valentine & J. Thompson	1811	AB27	458	376
Mountz, Jacob, collector, of G'tn.	Deed to	Marbury, William	1811	AB27	086	071
Mountz, Jacob, collector, of G'tn.	Deed to	Mountz, John, Jr. et al	1811	AB27	456	374
Mountz, Jacob, collector, of G'tn.	Deed to	Magruder, George & Wm. Lodge	1811	AB27	008	009
Mountz, Jacob, collector, of G'tn.	Deed to	Smith, Clement, of G'tn.	1811	Z25	485	385
Mountz, Jacob, collector, G'tn.	Deed to	King, William, Jr., of G'tn.	1812	AC28	214	161
Mountz, Jacob, collector, G'tn.	Deed to	Williams, Elisha W., of G'tn.	1812	AC28	333	242
Mountz, Jacob, collector, G'tn.	Deed to	Threlkeld, John	1812	AC28	191	145
Mountz, Jacob, collector, G'tn.	Deed to	Marbury, William, of G'tn.	1812	AC28	148	111
Mountz, Jacob, collector, G'tn.	Deed to	Williams, Elisha W., of G'tn.	1812	AC28	336	243
Mountz, Jacob, collector, of G'tn.	Deed to	Mountz, John, of G'tn.	1813	AE30	041	030
Mountz, Jacob, collector, of G'tn.	Deed to	Lee, John, of G'tn.	1813	AE30	079	060
Mountz, Jacob, collector, of G'tn.	Deed to	Magruder, Ninian, of G'tn.	1813	AE30	465	346
Mountz, Jacob, collector, G'tn.	Deed to	Lee, John, of G'tn.	1814	AG32	090	068
Mountz, Jacob, collector, of G'tn.	Deed to	Magruder, Ninian, of G'tn.	1817	AN38	519	376
Mountz, Jacob, collector	Deed to	Threlkeld, John	1817	AO39	094	074
Mountz, Jacob, collector, of G'tn.	Deed to	Renner, Daniel, mer., of G'tn.	1817	AN38	507	367
Mountz, Jacob, of G'tn.	Deed to	Renner, Daniel, of G'tn.	1813	AF31	153	103
Mountz, Jacob, of G'tn., collector	Deed to	Bussard, Daniel, of G'tn.	1815	AI34	053	060
Mountz, Jacob, of G'tn.	Deed to	Thompson, John C., of G'tn. et al	1815	AI34	049	056
Mountz, Jacob, of G'tn., collector	Deed to	Shaw, Lemuel, of G'tn.	1816	AL36	254	256
Mountz, John	D. of T. fr	Braiden, Elizabeth	1813	AE30	541	401
Mountz, John	Deed fr	Goldin, Sarah & William	1815	AI34	351	382
Mountz, John	Deed fr	Holmead, John	1816	AM37	324	235
Mountz, John & Richard Parrott	Deed fr	Adams, Thomas	1809	W22	001	001
Mountz, John & Maria Eliz. et al	Deed to	Reintzel, Anthony	1809	W22	364	236
Mountz, John & John Thompson	Deed fr	Skinner, Adderton, of P.G. Co.	1812	AC28	253	186
Mountz, John et al	Deed to	Oden, Benjamin, of P.G. Co.	1815	AI34	376	403
Mountz, John, exr. of Wm. Fields	Deed to	Morris, George	1817	AO39	431	294
Mountz, John, exr. of Wm. Fields	Deed fr	Hedges, Nicholas	1817	AO39	429	293
Mountz, John, exr. of Wm. Fields	Deed to	Grimes, Alice, of Montg. Co.	1817	AO39	442	302
Mountz, John, Jr. et al	Deed fr	Mountz, John, Sr.	1805	M12	243	244
Mountz, John, Jr., of G'tn.	Deed fr	Mountz, John, Sr., of G'tn.	1806	Q16	299	227
Mountz, John, Jr., of G'tn.	Deed to	Kirk, Militius Thomas, of G'tn.	1809	X23	199	150
Mountz, John, Jr.	D. of T. fr	West, John	1809	W22	003	002
Mountz, John, Jr., of G'tn.	D. of T. fr	Marquand, Charles, of G'tn.	1810	Y24	505	445
Mountz, John, Jr., of G'tn.	Deed to	Marquand, Charles, of G'tn.	1810	Z25	031	023
Mountz, John, Jr., of G'tn.	Deed fr	Reintzel, Anthony, of G'tn.	1810	X23	359	288
Mountz, John, Jr., of G'tn.	Deed fr	Smith, Anthony, of G'tn.	1811	AA26	353	236
Mountz, John, Jr., et al	Deed fr	Mountz, Jacob, collector, of G'tn.	1811	AB27	456	374
Mountz, John, Jr., of G'tn.	Deed fr	Wehrly, David, of G'tn.	1811	AB27	254	207
Mountz, John, Jr., of G'tn.	D. of T. fr	Gaines, Richard, of G'tn.	1811	AA26	298	201
Mountz, John, Jr., of G'tn.	Deed fr	Mountz, Joseph, of G'tn.	1812	AD29	167	133
Mountz, John, Jr., of G'tn.	D. of T. fr	Labille, Louis, of G'tn.	1812	AD29	101	076
Mountz, John, Jr. & R. Parrott	Deed to	Foxall, Henry	1812	AD29	143	111

Index to District of Columbia Land Records, 1792-1817

Party	What	Party	Year	Liber	Old	New
Mountz, John, Jr. et al	Deed fr	White, James, of Montg. Co.	1812	AC28	251	185
Mountz, John, of G'tn.	Deed to	Corcoran, Thomas, of G'tn.	1800	E5	271	264
Mountz, John, of G'tn. et al	Deed to	Wehrly, David, of G'tn.	1805	M12	130	125
Mountz, John, of G'tn.	P. of Atty. fr	Stoddert, Benjamin	1809	X23	076	057
Mountz, John, of G'tn.	D. of T. fr	Stephen, John	1809	V21	265	189
Mountz, John, of G'tn.	Deed to	Laland, John	1811	AA26	233	160
Mountz, John, of G'tn. et al	Deed to	Snowden, Gerrard H., of A.A. Co.	1812	AD29	378	318
Mountz, John, of G'tn.	Deed fr	Mountz, Jacob, collector, of G'tn.	1813	AE30	041	030
Mountz, John, of G'tn.	Deed to	Hoye, John, of G'tn.	1813	AE30	043	032
Mountz, John, of G'tn.	Deed to	Gaines, Richard, Hamilton Co. OH	1813	AE30	317	238
Mountz, John, of G'tn.	Deed fr	Glasco, John	1813	AE30	146	114
Mountz, John, of G'tn.	D. of T. fr	Fahey, Mark, of G'tn.	1813	AF31	340	242
Mountz, John, of G'tn.	Deed to	Glasco, John	1813	AF31	357	254
Mountz, John, of G'tn.	Deed fr	Wilson, Elizabeth, of Montg. Co.	1815	AI34	350	381
Mountz, John, of G'tn.	Cert fr	Munroe, Thomas, Supt.	1816	AM37	325	236
Mountz, John, of G'tn.	D. of T. fr	Hagerty, John, Jr., of G'tn.	1816	AO39	036	030
Mountz, John, of G'tn.	Deed fr	Landes, Abraham, of G'tn.	1816	AM37	331	241
Mountz, John, of G'tn.	D. of T. fr	Lancaster, Stephen	1817	AN38	284	208
Mountz, John, of G'tn.	Deed fr	Wehrby, Jonathan, of Balto.	1817	AN38	513	372
Mountz, John, of G'tn.	Deed to	Wehrby, Jonathan, of Balto.	1817	AN38	518	375
Mountz, John, of G'tn.	Deed fr	Mills, William G., of G'tn.	1817	AO39	492	337
Mountz, John, of G'tn.	Deed fr	Hicks, Elizabeth, of G'tn.	1817	AO39	494	339
Mountz, John, Sr., of G'tn.	Deed to	Walker, Elijah, of G'tn.	1796	B2B	524	236
Mountz, John, Sr., of G'tn.	Deed to	Knowles, Henry, of G'tn.	1797	C3	086	71
Mountz, John, Sr.	Deed to	Mountz, John, Jr. et al	1805	M12	243	244
Mountz, John, Sr., of G'tn.	Deed to	Knowles, Henry, of G'tn.	1806	Q16	296	225
Mountz, John, Sr., of G'tn.	Deed to	Mountz, John, Jr., of G'tn.	1806	Q16	299	227
Mountz, John, Sr., of G'tn.	Deed to	Mountz, George, of G'tn.	1807	R17	188	143
Mountz, John, Sr., of G'tn. et al	Deed to	Henry, Robert J. et al	1807	R17	278	212
Mountz, John, Sr., of G'tn.	B. of S. to	Walker, Elijah, of G'tn.	1807	R17	235	177
Mountz, John, Sr., of G'tn.	Deed to	Mountz, George, of G'tn.	1807	R17	191	145
Mountz, Joseph	Qualify	Deputy Clerk County Court	1802	H8	545	506
Mountz, Joseph, of G'tn.	Deed to	Mountz, John, Jr., of G'tn.	1812	AD29	167	133
Mountz, Joseph, of G'tn.	Mortgage to	Traverse, Nicholas, of G'tn.	1817	AN38	241	177
Moutz, Jacob	Deed to	Williams, Elisha W.	1811	AB27	041	035
Movin, Lewis	Deed fr	Commissioners of Washington	1800	E5	337	324
Moxley, Charles	Deed to	Thompson, James, Col.	1814	AH33	248	215
Moxley, Charles et al	Deed fr	Fields, William, of G'tn.	1808	U20	227	122
Moxley, Charles, of G'tn.	Deed fr	Thompson, John, of G'tn.	1810	Z25	226	177
Moxley, Charles, of G'tn.	Deed fr	Connely, John, of G'tn.	1813	AF31	521	383
Moxley, Charles, of G'tn. et al	Deed fr	Mountz, Jacob, of G'tn.	1815	AI34	049	056
Moxley, Charles, of G'tn.	Deed fr	Johnson, Isaac, of G'tn.	1815	AI34	096	109
Moxley, Charles, of G'tn.	Lease to	Johnson, Isaac, of G'tn.	1815	AI34	100	114
Moxley, Charles, of G'tn.	Deed fr	Murdock, John, of G'tn.	1816	AL36	218	224
Moxley, Charles, of G'tn.	Deed to	Adams, Henry (C), of G'tn.	1816	AL36	220	225
Moxley, Charles, of G'tn.	Deed fr	Dorsey, William H., of Montg. Co.	1816	AL36	216	223
Moxley, Charles, of G'tn.	Deed fr	Johnson, Thomas (C)	1816	AL36	223	229
Moxley, Charles, of G'tn.	Deed to	Johnson, Thomas (C)	1816	AM37	120	094
Moxley, Charles, of G'tn.	Deed fr	Reintzel, Valentine, of G'tn.	1816	AK35	512	404
Moxley, Daniel	Deed fr	Addison, Thomas Grafton	1809	V21	349	252
Moxley, Daniel, of P.G. Co.	Deed to	Talbert, McKenzie	1816	AL36	441	419
Moyer, Jacob	Deed fr	LeKoy, Adam & Anna M., of PA	1792	A1-1	174	247
Moyers, John	Deed fr	Dunlop, James et al	1801	G7	242	325
Moylan, Jasper, of Phila. PA	Deed fr	Crawford, James, Jr., of Phila. PA	1808	T19	354	255
Mudd, Jeremiah, exr. of	B. of S. to	Smith, Henry	1816	AL36	525	490

Party	What	Party	Year	Liber	Old	New
Mudd, Joseph, Dr. et al	Deed fr	Ritchie, Abner	1810	Y24	460	408
Mudd, Joseph, Dr.	Deed to	Mudd, Thomas James	1811	AC28	015	012
Mudd, Theodore	Lease fr	Moore, George	1809	W22	309	202
Mudd, Theodore, of Charles Co.	Assign to	Sutherland, Thomas Jenny	1811	AC28	079	060
Mudd, Thomas I., of G'tn.	Deed to	King, Charles, of G'tn.	1814	AH33	062	055
Mudd, Thomas J.	Slaves	From Alexandria Co.	1806	P15	350	
Mudd, Thomas J.	Slaves	From Alexandria C.	1807	Q16	338	259
Mudd, Thomas J., of G'tn.	Deed fr	Clarke, William, of G'tn.	1809	V21	323	238
Mudd, Thomas J., of G'tn.	Deed fr	Brookes, Joseph, of G'tn.	1810	Y24	278	254
Mudd, Thomas J.	Deed fr	Simpson, John	1811	AB27	258	211
Mudd, Thomas J., of G'tn.	Deed fr	King, Adam, of G'tn.	1811	Z25	511	406
Mudd, Thomas J., of G'tn.	Deed fr	King, Adam, of G'tn.	1813	AE30	461	343
Mudd, Thomas J.	Deed fr	Bussard, Daniel	1813	AE30	462	344
Mudd, Thomas James et al	Deed fr	Ritchie, Abner	1810	Y24	460	408
Mudd, Thomas James	Deed to	Meddert, Jacob	1811	AB27	259	212
Mudd, Thomas James	Deed fr	Mudd, Joseph, Dr.	1811	AC28	015	012
Mudd, Thomas James	Deed to	Smith, Clement	1813	AE30	210	171
Mudd, Walter	B. of S. to	Mayn, Adam	1813	AF31	070	048
Mudd, Walter, of G'tn.	B. of S. to	King, Vincent	1817	AO39	093	073
Muir, John, of Annapolis et al	Deed to	Beatty, Thomas Johnson	1795	B2A	350	495
Muir, John, of Annapolis et al	Mortgage to	Hoye, John & Leonard M. Deakins	1809	W22	009	007
Mullany, Michael	B. of S. to	Cassin, Joseph	1808	T19	311	227
Mulloy, John	Deed fr	Brent, William	1815	AK35	341	270
Mulloy, John	D. of T. to	Brent, Robert	1816	AL36	087	089
Mulloy, John	B. of S. to	Marks, Sarah	1817	AN38	415	311
Mulloy, John, of Montg. Co.	Deed to	Williams, Jeremiah & Elisha W.	1807	Q16	394	303
Munay, Peter	Lease fr	Dorsey, William H.	1802	I9	468	772
Muncaster, John	Deed fr	Simms, Charles	1811	AB27	000½	001
Munro, Robert	B. of S. fr	Washington, Lund, of G'tn.	1812	AD29	476	403
Munro, Robert	D. of T. fr	Ringgold, Tench	1817	AO39	296	211
Munroe, F.	Partition	Whetcroft, William, heirs of	1813	AE30	196	157
Munroe, Frances, w/o Thomas	Deed fr	Van Ness, John P. & Marcia	1809	X23	068	051
Munroe, Jane	Slaves	From St. Mary's Co.	1814	AG32	058	045
Munroe, Jane, of St. Mary's Co.	B. of S. to	Boyd, Washington	1804	K10	142	154
Munroe, Jonathan	B. of S. to	Ball, Thomas, of MD	1802	H8	419	386
Munroe, Jonathan, trustee	Deed fr	Betz, Frederick, insolvent	1805	M12	402	416
Munroe, Thomas	Deed fr	Burnes, David	1798	D4	063	053
Munroe, Thomas	Receipt to	Roe, Cornelius McDermott	1799	D4	381	365
Munroe, Thomas	Deed fr	Cunningham, Cornelius	1800	E5	159	148
Munroe, Thomas	Deed to	Fenwick, Mary Ann, of G'tn.	1801	G7	427	562
Munroe, Thomas	P. of Atty. fr	Denison, Robert, Jr., of Phila.	1801	G7	207	277
Munroe, Thomas	Deed to	Fenwick, Mary Ann	1802	G7	520	662
Munroe, Thomas	Deed to	Coningham, Cornelius	1802	G7	591	740
Munroe, Thomas	Deed to	Waring, Marsham, of G'tn.	1802	G7	593	742
Munroe, Thomas	Deed to	Moriarty, Ambrose	1802	H8	495	455
Munroe, Thomas	Deed to	Stoddert, Benjamin, of G'tn.	1802	H8	431	396
Munroe, Thomas	Deed fr	Lovell, William	1802	H8	434	399
Munroe, Thomas	Deed to	Stoddert, Benjamin, of G'tn.	1802	H8	429	395
Munroe, Thomas	Deed to	Herford, John	1802	H8	380	353
Munroe, Thomas	Assign fr	Coningham, Cornelius	1803	K10	079	85
Munroe, Thomas	B. of S. fr	Cunningham, Cornelius	1804	L11	061	62
Munroe, Thomas	Suit	Blagden, George	1804	L11	116	119
Munroe, Thomas	Deed fr	Neale, Francis, of G'tn. College	1804	K10	213	223
Munroe, Thomas	Deed fr	Clarke, Francis	1806	P15	190	127
Munroe, Thomas	B. of S. fr	Hanson, Samuel, of Samuel	1806	Q16	111	072

Party	What	Party	Year	Liber	Old	New
Munroe, Thomas	Deed fr	Knapp, John	1807	R17	095	075
Munroe, Thomas	Receipt fr	Coolidge, Samuel J.	1809	V21	318	234
Munroe, Thomas	Partition	Whetcroft, William, heirs of	1813	AE30	196	157
Munroe, Thomas	Deed to	Nourse, Joseph	1813	AE30	396	292
Munroe, Thomas	Deed to	Varnum, James M.	1815	AI34	230	261
Munroe, Thomas	Deed fr	Cox, John, of G'tn.	1815	AI34	230	261
Munroe, Thomas	Cert. to	Roe, Bernard McDermott	1815	AH33	442	380
Munroe, Thomas	Deed fr	Mercer, John Francis, of A.A. Co.	1816	AL36	504	473
Munroe, Thomas	Deed fr	Craven, John	1816	AL36	350	340
Munroe, Thomas	Deed fr	Ringgold, Tench	1817	AN38	386	287
Munroe, Thomas	Deed fr	Carroll, Daniel, of *Duddington*	1817	AN38	384	285
Munroe, Thomas	Deed to	Hutchinson, Samuel	1817	AO39	403	273
Munroe, Thomas	Deed fr	Dearborn, Henry, of Boston	1817	AO39	423	288
Munroe, Thomas & John Tayloe	Mortgage fr	Granger, Gideon	1811	AB27	081	068
Munroe, Thomas & Fanny et al	Deed to	Bradley, Abraham, Jr.	1811	AC28	069	052
Munroe, Thomas & John Tayloe	Release to	Granger, Gideon	1812	AE30	013	011
Munroe, Thomas & Frances et al	Deed to	Bacon, Samuel & George Moore	1812	AD29	523	441
Munroe, Thomas & Frances	Deed to	Hughes, Thomas & W.A. Bradley	1815	AI34	250	283
Munroe, Thomas & Frances	Deed to	Ott, David	1815	AI34	194	223
Munroe, Thomas & John Knapp	Deed to	Stott, Ebenezer, of Petersburg	1817	AO39	427	291
Munroe, Thomas et al	Deed to	Dorsey, William H. et al	1802	I9	364	604
Munroe, Thomas et al	Deed fr	Woodward, Augustus B.	1804	L11	244	225
Munroe, Thomas et al	Deed fr	Wadsworth, Charles, in Norfolk VA	1804	L11	327	299
Munroe, Thomas et al	Deed fr	Wadsworth, Charles, Hartford CN	1804	L11	326	298
Munroe, Thomas et al	Deed to	Bickley, Robert S., of Phila. PA	1807	R17	026	022
Munroe, Thomas et al	Deed to	Varden, Charles H.	1807	R17	016	014
Munroe, Thomas et al	Deed to	Bradley, Phineas	1815	AI34	076	085
Munroe, Thomas, Supt.	Deed to	Templeman, John	1802	H8	598	564
Munroe, Thomas, Supt.	Deed to	Markward, William	1802	H8	539	500
Munroe, Thomas, Supt.	Deed to	McElwee, John, of Balto. MD	1802	H8	491	452
Munroe, Thomas, Supt.	Deed to	Moore, James	1802	H8	545	506
Munroe, Thomas, Supt.	Deed to	Doughty, William	1802	H8	550	512
Munroe, Thomas, Supt.	Deed to	Lewis, Samuel, Jr.	1802	H8	575	539
Munroe, Thomas, Supt.	Deed to	McElwee, John, of Balto. MD	1802	H8	490	451
Munroe, Thomas, Supt.	Deed to	Stoddert, Benjamin	1802	H8	541	501
Munroe, Thomas, Supt.	Deed to	Doughty, William	1802	H8	552	513
Munroe, Thomas, Supt.	Deed to	Templeman, John	1802	H8	597	563
Munroe, Thomas, Supt.	Deed to	Templeman, John, of G'tn.	1802	H8	596	562
Munroe, Thomas, Supt.	Deed to	Stockwell, Mark	1802	H8	544	504
Munroe, Thomas, Supt.	Deed to	Massey, Henry, of Chilicothe	1802	H8	565	528
Munroe, Thomas, Supt.	Deed to	Caldwell, David, of PA	1802	H8	493	453
Munroe, Thomas, Supt.	Deed to	Burrows, Joseph	1802	H8	538	498
Munroe, Thomas, Supt.	Deed to	Willis, John, Dr.	1802	H8	582	547
Munroe, Thomas, Supt.	Deed to	Van Ness, John P.	1802	I9	158	239
Munroe, Thomas, Supt.	Deed to	Maltby, Sarah	1802	I9	144	217
Munroe, Thomas, Supt.	Deed to	Underwood, Robert et al	1802	I9	062	085
Munroe, Thomas, Supt.	Deed to	Stoddert, Benjamin, of G'tn.	1802	I9	095	137
Munroe, Thomas, Supt.	Deed to	Boyd, Washington et al	1802	I9	374	621
Munroe, Thomas, Supt.	Deed to	Cutter, Nathaniel, of NH	1802	I9	053	073
Munroe, Thomas, Supt.	Deed to	Fickfield, William H.	1802	I9	132	198
Munroe, Thomas, Supt.	Deed to	Stoddert, Benjamin, of G'tn.	1802	I9	104	151
Munroe, Thomas, Supt.	Cert to	Craig, Robert	1802	I9	068	095
Munroe, Thomas, Supt.	Cert to	Hoban, James	1802	I9	222	352
Munroe, Thomas, Supt.	Deed to	Brodeau, Ann	1802	I9	136	205
Munroe, Thomas, Supt.	Deed to	Lenox, Peter	1802	I9	149	225

Index to District of Columbia Land Records, 1792-1817

Party	What	Party	Year	Liber	Old	New
Munroe, Thomas, Supt.	Deed to	Marshall, Samuel, of London	1802	I9	041	054
Munroe, Thomas, Supt.	Deed to	Stoddert, Benjamin, of G'tn.	1802	I9	105	153
Munroe, Thomas, Supt.	Deed to	McClan, Robert	1802	I9	502	824
Munroe, Thomas, Supt.	Deed to	Hellen, Walter	1802	I9	176	268
Munroe, Thomas, Supt.	Deed to	Bullus, John	1802	I9	060	082
Munroe, Thomas, Supt.	Deed to	Gray, John, of London	1802	I9	044	059
Munroe, Thomas, Supt.	Cert to	Hoban, James	1802	I9	222	352
Munroe, Thomas, Supt.	Deed to	Simmons, William	1802	I9	320	527
Munroe, Thomas, Supt.	Deed fr	Speake, Samuel	1802	I9	486	799
Munroe, Thomas, Supt.	Deed to	Hellen, Walter	1802	I9	177	270
Munroe, Thomas, Supt.	Deed to	Waters, William	1802	I9	068	095
Munroe, Thomas, Supt.	Deed to	Simmons, William	1802	I9	323	532
Munroe, Thomas, Supt.	Deed to	Taylor, Joseph	1802	I9	208	327
Munroe, Thomas, Supt.	Deed to	Wayman, Charles	1802	I9	451	745
Munroe, Thomas, Supt.	Deed to	Chandler, Jacob	1802	I9	131	196
Munroe, Thomas, Supt.	Deed to	Stoddert, Benjamin, of G'tn.	1802	I9	094	135
Munroe, Thomas, Supt.	Deed to	Stoddert, Benjamin, of G'tn.	1802	I9	096	138
Munroe, Thomas, Supt.	Deed to	Fletcher, William et al	1802	I9	153	230
Munroe, Thomas, Supt.	Deed to	Simmons, William	1802	I9	319	525
Munroe, Thomas, Supt.	Deed to	Bailey, Daniel	1802	I9	004	006
Munroe, Thomas, Supt.	Deed to	Stoddert, Benjamin, of G'tn.	1802	I9	101	146
Munroe, Thomas, Supt.	Deed to	Stoddert, Benjamin, of G'tn.	1802	I9	106	154
Munroe, Thomas, Supt.	Deed to	Stoddert, Benjamin, of G'tn.	1802	I9	102	148
Munroe, Thomas, Supt.	Deed to	Stoddert, Benjamin	1802	I9	098	143
Munroe, Thomas, Supt.	Deed to	Tabbs, Barton	1802	I9	052	071
Munroe, Thomas, Supt.	Cert to	Bloor, John	1802	I9	200	313
Munroe, Thomas, Supt.	Deed to	Turner, Thomas	1802	I9	274	447
Munroe, Thomas, Supt.	Deed to	Lewis, Leyson, of London	1802	I9	040	053
Munroe, Thomas, Supt.	Deed to	Stoddert, Benjamin, of G'tn.	1802	I9	100	145
Munroe, Thomas, Supt.	Deed to	Turner, Samuel	1802	I9	250	403
Munroe, Thomas, Supt.	Deed to	Dempsie, John, gardener	1802	I9	048	065
Munroe, Thomas, Supt.	Deed to	Wayman, Charles	1802	I9	412	682
Munroe, Thomas, Supt.	Deed to	Brent, Daniel	1802	I9	258	416
Munroe, Thomas, Supt.	Deed to	Bailey, Daniel	1802	I9	003	004
Munroe, Thomas, Supt.	Deed to	Marshall, Samuel, of London	1802	I9	042	056
Munroe, Thomas, Supt.	Cert to	Hoban, James	1802	I9	222	351
Munroe, Thomas, Supt.	Deed to	Gray, John, of London	1802	I9	043	058
Munroe, Thomas, Supt.	Deed to	Turner, Thomas	1802	I9	276	451
Munroe, Thomas, Supt.	Cert to	Hoban, James	1802	I9	221	350
Munroe, Thomas, Supt.	Deed to	Van Ness, John P.	1802	I9	157	237
Munroe, Thomas, Supt.	Deed to	Stoddert, Benjamin, of G'tn.	1802	I9	098	141
Munroe, Thomas, Supt.	Deed to	Wayman, Charles	1802	I9	504	827
Munroe, Thomas, Supt.	Deed to	Kramer, Henry	1802	I9	268	436
Munroe, Thomas, Supt.	Deed to	Gray, John, of London	1802	I9	045	061
Munroe, Thomas, Supt.	Deed to	Van Ness, John P.	1802	I9	156	235
Munroe, Thomas, Supt.	Deed to	Summers, Lewis	1802	I9	178	273
Munroe, Thomas, Supt.	Deed to	Van Ness, John P.	1802	I9	155	234
Munroe, Thomas, Supt.	Deed to	Stockwell, Mark et al	1802	I9	062	085
Munroe, Thomas, Supt.	Deed to	Stoddert, Benjamin, of G'tn.	1802	I9	099	143
Munroe, Thomas, Supt.	Deed to	Hogan, Thady	1802	I9	180	276
Munroe, Thomas, Supt.	Deed to	Wayman, Charles	1802	I9	169	256
Munroe, Thomas, Supt.	Deed to	Craven, Tunis	1802	I9	128	190
Munroe, Thomas, Supt.	Deed to	Evans, Evan	1802	I9	028	037
Munroe, Thomas, Supt.	Deed to	Stewart, William	1802	I9	170	259
Munroe, Thomas, Supt.	Deed to	Lynn, Adam	1802	I9	207	324

Party	What	Party	Year	Liber	Old	New
Munroe, Thomas, Supt.	Deed to	Stoddert, Benjamin, of G'tn.	1802	I9	103	150
Munroe, Thomas, Supt.	Deed to	Stoddert, Benjamin, of G'tn.	1802	I9	097	140
Munroe, Thomas, Supt.	Deed to	Turner, Samuel	1802	I9	249	401
Munroe, Thomas, Supt.	Deed fr	Stoddert, Benjamin	1802	I9	304	498
Munroe, Thomas, Supt.	Deed to	Simmons, William	1802	I9	321	528
Munroe, Thomas, Supt.	Deed to	Van Ness, John P.	1802	I9	154	232
Munroe, Thomas, Supt.	Deed to	May, Frederick	1802	I9	461	760
Munroe, Thomas, Supt.	Deed to	Dunlop, James	1802	I9	229	364
Munroe, Thomas, Supt.	Deed to	Alexander, Robert, Jr., P.W. Co.	1802	I9	017	023
Munroe, Thomas, Supt.	Deed to	McElwee, John	1802	I9	139	209
Munroe, Thomas, Supt.	Deed to	Steele, John	1802	I9	206	322
Munroe, Thomas, Supt.	Deed to	Simmonds, William	1802	I9	413	684
Munroe, Thomas, Supt.	Deed to	Hellen, Walter	1802	I9	175	267
Munroe, Thomas, Supt.	Deed to	Fletcher, William et al	1802	I9	151	229
Munroe, Thomas, Supt.	Deed to	Glover, William, of London	1802	I9	039	051
Munroe, Thomas, Supt.	Deed to	Turner, Thomas	1802	I9	275	449
Munroe, Thomas, Supt.	Deed to	McElwee, John	1802	I9	138	208
Munroe, Thomas, Supt.	Deed to	Hellen, Walter	1802	I9	178	271
Munroe, Thomas, Supt.	Deed to	Thorn, Christopher S.	1802	I9	414	687
Munroe, Thomas, Supt.	Deed to	Simmons, William	1802	I9	322	530
Munroe, Thomas, Supt.	Deed to	Dupuy, William	1802	I9	111	162
Munroe, Thomas, Supt.	Deed to	Brent, William	1802	I9	257	415
Munroe, Thomas, Supt.	Deed to	Middleton, Electius	1802	I9	181	277
Munroe, Thomas, Supt.	Deed to	Stoddert, Benjamin, of G'tn.	1802	I9	107	156
Munroe, Thomas, Supt.	Deed to	McCormick, Morgan	1803	K10	072	78
Munroe, Thomas, Supt.	Cert to	Davidson, John	1804	K10	316	322
Munroe, Thomas, Supt.	Deed to	Thornton, William	1804	K10	298	300
Munroe, Thomas, Supt.	Deed to	Shoemaker, David	1804	K10	304	308
Munroe, Thomas, Supt.	Cert to	Avidh, J.B.	1804	K10	230	238
Munroe, Thomas, Supt.	Deed to	Carroll, Daniel, of *Duddington*	1804	K10	335	346
Munroe, Thomas, Supt.	Deed to	Thornton, William	1804	K10	299	302
Munroe, Thomas, Supt.	Cert to	King, Nicholas	1804	K10	398	412
Munroe, Thomas, Supt.	Deed to	Willis, John, Dr.	1804	L11	023	23
Munroe, Thomas, Supt.	Cert to	Bickley, Robert S., of Phila.	1804	L11	408	363
Munroe, Thomas, Supt.	Cert to	Collard, George	1804	L11	331	302
Munroe, Thomas, Supt.	Cert fo	Fitzgerald, William	1804	L11	094	96
Munroe, Thomas, Supt.	Deed to	French, Ariana	1804	L11	158	157
Munroe, Thomas, Supt.	Deed to	Caldwell, Elias B., trustee	1804	L11	291	267
Munroe, Thomas, Supt.	Cert to	Collard, George	1804	L11	332	303
Munroe, Thomas, Supt.	Cert to	Dearborn, Henry, Gen.	1804	L11	037	36
Munroe, Thomas, Supt.	Deed to	Sandford, William, of Alexa.	1804	M12	038	038
Munroe, Thomas, Supt.	Deed to	Steele, John, of Balto.	1804	M12	013	013
Munroe, Thomas, Supt.	Cert to	Law, Thomas	1805	M12	260	262
Munroe, Thomas, Supt.	Cert to	Marshall, John et al	1805	M12	047	045
Munroe, Thomas, Supt.	Cert to	Daugherty, Joseph	1805	M12	270	271
Munroe, Thomas, Supt.	Deed to	Kean, William	1805	M12	197	199
Munroe, Thomas, Supt.	Deed to	Cutts, Ann, w/o Hon. Richard	1805	M12	051	049
Munroe, Thomas, Supt.	Deed to	Moore, James	1805	M12	240	241
Munroe, Thomas, Supt.	Cert to	Esenbeck, William	1805	M12	146	143
Munroe, Thomas, Supt.	Deed to	Cox, John, of G'tn.	1805	M12	360	368
Munroe, Thomas, Supt.	Deed to	Middleton, James	1805	N13	087	079
Munroe, Thomas, Supt.	Cert to	Dulany, Benjamin, of Alexa.	1806	Q16	145	095
Munroe, Thomas, Supt.	Deed to	Hellen, Walter	1806	Q16	039	025
Munroe, Thomas, Supt.	Cert to	Barry, James	1806	O14	382	255
Munroe, Thomas, Supt.	Deed to	Barry, James	1806	O14	383	255

Party	What	Party	Year	Liber	Old	New
Munroe, Thomas, Supt.	Cert to	Roe, Cornelius McDermott	1807	R17	243	183
Munroe, Thomas, Supt.	Cert to	King, Nicholas	1807	R17	105	082
Munroe, Thomas, Supt.	Deed to	Way, Andrew, Jr. et al	1807	R17	315	239
Munroe, Thomas, Supt. et al	Deed to	Lenox, Peter	1807	R17	271	206
Munroe, Thomas, Supt. et al	Deed to	Lindsay, Adam	1807	R17	251	190
Munroe, Thomas, Supt.	Deed to	Hoban, James	1807	R17	331	252
Munroe, Thomas, Supt.	Cert to	Traverse, Esias	1807	S18	243	192
Munroe, Thomas, Supt.	Cert to	Lindo, Abraham	1807	S18	329	258
Munroe, Thomas, Supt.	Cert to	Mayor & Corporation Washington	1807	S18	013	012
Munroe, Thomas, Supt.	Deed to	Thornton, William	1807	S18	094	076
Munroe, Thomas, Supt.	Cert to	Moore, George	1808	U20	102	057
Munroe, Thomas, Supt.	Cert to	Rapine, Daniel	1808	T19	164	116
Munroe, Thomas, Supt.	Cert to	Easenbeck, William	1808	U20	052	029
Munroe, Thomas, Supt.	Cert to	Ingle, Henry, for graveyard	1808	T19	219	160
Munroe, Thomas, Supt.	Deed fr	Lingan, James M., of Montg. Co.	1808	T19	019	015
Munroe, Thomas, Supt.	Cert to	Way, Andrew, Jr. et al	1808	U20	345	187
Munroe, Thomas, Supt.	Cert to	Morgan, William et al	1808	T19	349	252
Munroe, Thomas, Supt.	Cert to	Caldwell, Elias B.	1808	V21	055	044
Munroe, Thomas, Supt.	Cert to	Warner, Osborn, of P.G. Co.	1809	V21	352	255
Munroe, Thomas, Supt.	Cert to	Caldwell, Elias B.	1809	V21	389	293
Munroe, Thomas, Supt.	Cert to	Carroll, Daniel, of *Duddington*	1809	V21	388	292
Munroe, Thomas, Supt.	Cert to	Given, Thomas	1809	W22	391	255
Munroe, Thomas, Supt.	Cert to	Key, Philip Barton	1809	W22	094	068
Munroe, Thomas, Supt.	Cert to	Jarboe, Charles	1809	W22	345	223
Munroe, Thomas, Supt.	Deed to	O'Neale, William	1809	W22	050	037
Munroe, Thomas, Supt.	Cert to	Jones, Charles Courts, Montg. Co.	1809	W22	043	032
Munroe, Thomas, Supt.	Cert to	Smothers, Henry	1809	W22	018	014
Munroe, Thomas, Supt.	Deed to	Davidson, James	1809	W22	274	183
Munroe, Thomas, Supt.	Deed fr	Kilty, John & Josias Wilson King	1809	W22	253	170
Munroe, Thomas, Supt.	Cert to	Mauro, Philip	1809	X23	081	060
Munroe, Thomas, Supt.	Deed to	Young, Moses	1809	X23	213	163
Munroe, Thomas, Supt.	Cert to	Purcell, Pierce	1809	X23	162	119
Munroe, Thomas, Supt.	Cert to	Brent, William	1809	X23	063	048
Munroe, Thomas, Supt.	Deed to	Boyd, Washington	1810	Y24	332	301
Munroe, Thomas, Supt.	Cert to	Hagner, Peter	1810	Y24	154	140
Munroe, Thomas, Supt.	Cert to	Sessford, John	1810	Y24	168	153
Munroe, Thomas, Supt.	Cert to	Shorter, John	1810	X23	406	327
Munroe, Thomas, Supt.	Deed to	Blagden, George	1810	Y24	476	421
Munroe, Thomas, Supt.	Cert to	Burch, Susan	1811	AA26	045	035
Munroe, Thomas, Supt.	Deed to	Forrest, Joseph et al	1811	AA26	259	176
Munroe, Thomas, Supt.	Cert to	Way, Andrew & George	1811	AB27	358	297
Munroe, Thomas, Supt.	Cert to	Goldsborough, Charles W.	1811	AB27	065	055
Munroe, Thomas, Supt.	Cert to	Sioussa, John	1811	AB27	350	290
Munroe, Thomas, Supt.	Cert to	Johnson, Joseph	1811	AB27	151	125
Munroe, Thomas, Supt.	Deed to	Carroll, Daniel, of *Duddington*	1811	AC28	071	054
Munroe, Thomas, Supt.	Deed to	McCormick, James	1811	AC28	054	041
Munroe, Thomas, Supt.	Cert to	Lewis, Samuel, Jr.	1811	Z25	449	354
Munroe, Thomas, Supt.	Deed to	Pratt, Henry et al	1811	Z25	472	372
Munroe, Thomas, Supt.	Deed to	Webster, Toppan	1812	AC28	349	252
Munroe, Thomas, Supt.	Cert. to	Vinson, Charles	1812	AC28	495	353
Munroe, Thomas, Supt.	Release to	Gaither, Henry	1812	AD29	258	213
Munroe, Thomas, Supt.	Cert. to	Elliott, Richard	1812	AD29	044	032
Munroe, Thomas, Supt.	Cert. to	Waring, Patrick	1812	AD29	124	095
Munroe, Thomas, Supt.	Cert. to	Carroll, Daniel, of *Duddington*	1812	AD29	010	007
Munroe, Thomas, Supt.	Cert. to	Gales, Joseph	1812	AC28	514	367

Index to District of Columbia Land Records, 1792-1817

Party	What	Party	Year	Liber	Old	New
Munroe, Thomas, Supt.	Deed to	Webster, Toppan	1812	AC28	348	252
Munroe, Thomas, Supt.	Deed to	Cochrane, William et al	1813	AE30	426	314
Munroe, Thomas, Supt.	Cert to	Caldwell, Elias B. et al	1813	AE30	350	262
Munroe, Thomas, Supt.	Cert to	Kerr, Alexander	1813	AE30	300	227
Munroe, Thomas, Supt.	Cert to	Kerr, Alexander	1813	AE30	298	225
Munroe, Thomas, Supt.	Cert to	Sioussa, John	1813	AF31	314	224
Munroe, Thomas, Supt.	Lease to	Bayly, Mountjoy	1813	AF31	192	130
Munroe, Thomas, Supt.	Cert. to	Whann, William	1814	AG32	290	211
Munroe, Thomas, Supt.	Cert to	Siousa, John	1815	AI34	373	373
Munroe, Thomas, Supt.	Cert to	Traverse, Nicholas, of G'tn.	1815	AI34	461	474
Munroe, Thomas, Supt.	Cert to	Henley, Robert, Capt. U.S.N.	1815	AI34	366	394
Munroe, Thomas, Supt.	Cert to	Henley, Robert, Capt.	1815	AI34	365	394
Munroe, Thomas, Supt.	Cert to	Henley, Robert, Capt.	1815	AI34	364	393
Munroe, Thomas, Supt.	Cert to	Henly, Robert, Capt.	1815	AI34	364	392
Munroe, Thomas, Supt.	Cert to	Glasco, John	1815	AI34	195	224
Munroe, Thomas, Supt.	Cert to	Moore, Thomas & James	1815	AI34	427	446
Munroe, Thomas, Supt.	Cert to	Carroll, Daniel, of *Duddington*	1816	AL36	303	299
Munroe, Thomas, Supt.	Cert to	Siousa, John	1816	AL36	238	242
Munroe, Thomas, Supt.	Cert to	Allen, William, of G'tn.	1816	AL36	413	396
Munroe, Thomas, Supt.	Cert to	Godfrey, William	1816	AM37	382	275
Munroe, Thomas, Supt.	Deed to	Carroll, Daniel, of *Duddington*	1816	AM37	417	299
Munroe, Thomas, Supt.	Cert to	Ringgold, Tench	1816	AM37	274	201
Munroe, Thomas, Supt.	Cert to	Ringgold, Tench	1816	AM37	274	201
Munroe, Thomas, Supt.	Cert to	Hagner, Peter	1816	AM37	005	004
Munroe, Thomas, Supt.	Cert to	Mountz, John, of G'tn.	1816	AM37	325	236
Munroe, Thomas, Supt.	Deed to	Nicholls, Edward H. & W. Floyd	1816	AM37	115	091
Munroe, Thomas, Supt.	Deed to	Glover, Charles	1816	AO39	034	028
Munroe, Thomas, Supt.	Cert to	Lipscomb, John, of G'tn.	1817	AN38	080	062
Munroe, Thomas, Supt.	Cert to	Lambert, Morris, of G'tn.	1817	AN38	052	042
Munroe, Thomas, Supt.	Cert to	Blanchard, William	1817	AN38	016	013
Munroe, Thomas, Supt.	Cert to	Sandiford, Thomas, Jr. & Samuel	1817	AN38	283	207
Munroe, Thomas, Supt.	Cert to	Cutts, Richard	1817	AO39	242	174
Munroe, Thomas, Supt.	Cert to	Cutts, Richard	1817	AO39	241	174
Munroe, Thomas, Supt.	Cert to	Hunt, Jeremiah	1817	AO39	407	276
Murdock, Addison	Deed to	Cox, John, mer., of G'tn.	1806	P15	274	180
Murdock, Addison	Deed to	Cox, John et al	1806	Q16	057	036
Murdock, Addison	Deed to	Corporation of Georgetown	1806	P15	146	095
Murdock, Addison	Deed to	Corcoran, Thomas, of G'tn.	1807	R17	324	247
Murdock, Addison	Deed to	Clagett, Jane, of G'tn.	1807	S18	393	313
Murdock, Addison	Deed to	Thompson, Semus	1807	R17	045	036
Murdock, Addison, Gent.	Deed to	Riggs, Elisha, mer., of G'tn.	1806	P15	367	244
Murdock, Addison, Gent.	Deed to	Williams, Elisha W.	1806	P15	343	227
Murdock, Addison, Gent.	Deed to	Dyer, Henry O., mer., of G'tn.	1806	P15	345	229
Murdock, Addison, heirs of	Deed to	Risener, Henry	1812	AD29	445	375
Murdock, Addison, of G'tn.	Deed to	Baltzer, John, of G'tn.	1805	M12	375	386
Murdock, Addison, of G'tn.	Mortgage to	Lufborough, Nathan, of G'tn.	1805	O14	101	063
Murdock, Addison, of G'tn.	Deed to	Lufborough, Nathan, of G'tn.	1805	O14	098	061
Murdock, Eleanor, wid/o George	Deed fr	Kemp, Peter & Lodowick, s/o Fdk.	1806	Q16	061	039
Murdock, George	Deed to	Beall, Thomas & John M. Gantt	1792	A1-1	133	193
Murdock, George	Deed fr	Wayman, Charles	1802	I9	213	335
Murdock, George, Frederick Co.	Deed fr	Link, Adam, Sr., Frederick Co.	1794	B2A	069	089
Murdock, George, Frederick Town	Deed fr	McDaniel, George G.	1804	L11	405	359
Murdock, James	Deed to	Glover, Charles	1802	I9	479	787
Murdock, John	Deed fr	Commissioners of Washington	1802	G7	540	686
Murdock, John	Deed to	Lovell, William	1802	H8	571	534

Party	What	Party	Year	Liber	Old	New
Murdock, John	Deed fr	Polock, Isaac	1802	H8	033	031
Murdock, John	Deed to	Laird, John	1802	I9	562	912
Murdock, John	Deed to	Laird, John	1802	I9	562	911
Murdock, John	Deed to	Smith, Walter	1805	M12	172	171
Murdock, John	Deed to	Lingan, James M.	1806	O14	157	102
Murdock, John	Deed to	Cope, Jasper, of Phila. PA	1810	X23	387	311
Murdock, John	Deed to	Gannon, James & James Moore	1811	AC28	013	010
Murdock, John	Deed to	Mauro, Philip & Conrad Schwartz	1811	AB27	227	185
Murdock, John	Deed fr	Boyd, Washington, marshal	1814	AG32	440	318
Murdock, John	Deed fr	Dodge, Francis, of G'tn.	1817	AO39	320	228
Murdock, John & John Heugh	Deed to	Marbury, William	1808	T19	069	050
Murdock, John & John Heugh	Deed to	Smith, Clement, of P.G. Co.	1808	T19	310	226
Murdock, John A. & Margaret	Deed to	Thruston, Buckner	1815	AI34	396	419
Murdock, John, alias Barker	Deed to	Threlkeld, John	1815	AI34	495	502
Murdock, John, Col., exrs. of	Lease to	Middleton, Joseph et al	1796	B2B	508	211
Murdock, John et al	Deed to	Davidson, John	1802	I9	575	932
Murdock, John et al	Deed fr	Brent, William	1802	I9	279	455
Murdock, John et al	Deed fr	Addison, Anthony	1802	I9	277	452
Murdock, John et al	Deed fr	Kennedy, John	1802	I9	280	458
Murdock, John et al	Deed fr	Addison, John	1802	I9	279	456
Murdock, John et al	Quit to	Brookes, Joseph, of G'tn.	1809	V21	312	228
Murdock, John, of G'tn.	Deed to	Rineheart, Andrew	1802	H8	254	241
Murdock, John, of G'tn.	Deed fr	Austin, David, of G'tn.	1802	I9	080	113
Murdock, John, of G'tn.	Deed fr	Commissioners of Washington	1802	G7	542	689
Murdock, John, of G'tn.	Deed to	Gowans, John, of Petersburg VA	1804	L11	214	201
Murdock, John, of G'tn.	Deed to	Lenox, Peter	1804	L11	313	287
Murdock, John, of G'tn. et al	Deed to	Peacock, Robert Ware	1804	L11	012	12
Murdock, John, of G'tn.	Deed to	Glover, Charles	1804	K10	102	109
Murdock, John, of G'tn.	Deed fr	Brookes, William H., of G'tn.	1805	M12	053	050
Murdock, John, of G'tn.	Deed to	Wayman, Charles	1805	N13	051	048
Murdock, John, of G'tn.	Deed fr	Taney, Arsene Berenice, wid/o L.	1805	M12	102	095
Murdock, John, of G'tn.	Deed to	Laird, John, of G'tn.	1806	Q16	138	090
Murdock, John, of G'tn.	Deed fr	Dorsey, William H., of G'tn.	1807	R17	414	313
Murdock, John, of G'tn.	B. of S. to	McClelland, John	1807	S18	161	131
Murdock, John, of G'tn.	Deed to	Shoemaker, David	1807	R17	208	156
Murdock, John, of G'tn.	Deed to	Clephan, Lewis	1807	R17	206	155
Murdock, John, of G'tn.	Deed to	McClelland, John	1808	U20	339	183
Murdock, John, of G'tn.	Deed to	Lenox, Peter	1808	U20	365	199
Murdock, John, of G'tn.	B. of S. to	Smith, Clement, of G'tn.	1809	V21	312	228
Murdock, John, of G'tn.	Deed fr	Smith, Clement, of G'tn.	1809	V21	346	249
Murdock, John, of G'tn.	Deed to	Travers, Nicholas	1810	Z25	245	192
Murdock, John, of G'tn.	Deed to	Moore, James	1810	Z25	070	053
Murdock, John, of G'tn.	Deed to	Hogan, Thady	1810	Y24	432	386
Murdock, John, of G'tn.	Deed to	Underwood, Robert	1811	AA26	306	206
Murdock, John, of G'tn.	Deed fr	Dorsey, William H., of Balto.	1811	Z25	407	320
Murdock, John, of G'tn.	Deed to	Borrows, Joseph	1811	Z25	437	343
Murdock, John, of G'tn.	Deed to	Herford, John	1811	AA26	192	131
Murdock, John, of G'tn.	Deed to	Moore, James	1812	AD29	496	419
Murdock, John, of G'tn.	Deed to	Fletcher, Noah	1812	AD29	303	249
Murdock, John, of G'tn.	Deed to	Doughty, William, of G'tn.	1812	AD29	391	329
Murdock, John, of G'tn.	Deed to	Heath, Nathaniel H.	1812	AD29	354	297
Murdock, John, of G'tn.	Deed to	Mauro, Philip & Conrad Schwartz	1812	AC28	257	188
Murdock, John, of G'tn.	Deed to	Reintzel, Valentine, of G'tn.	1813	AE30	313	236
Murdock, John, of G'tn.	Deed to	Gilliss, Thomas H.	1813	AF31	113	076
Murdock, John, of G'tn.	Deed to	Bussard, Daniel, of G'tn.	1813	AF31	134	090

Party	What	Party	Year	Liber	Old	New
Murdock, John, of G'tn.	Deed to	Heath, Nathaniel H.	1813	AF31	141	094
Murdock, John, of G'tn.	Deed to	Marbury, William, of G'tn.	1813	AF31	344	245
Murdock, John, of G'tn.	Deed to	Shuck, Frederick	1813	AF31	051	035
Murdock, John, of G'tn.	Deed to	Reintzel, Valentine, of G'tn.	1814	AG32	181	128
Murdock, John, of G'tn.	Deed to	Gillis, Thomas H.	1814	AH33	237	207
Murdock, John, of G'tn.	Deed to	Smoot, Samuel, of G'tn.	1814	AH33	258	224
Murdock, John, of G'tn.	Deed to	Brent, Robert	1814	AH33	079	071
Murdock, John, of G'tn.	Deed to	Way, Andrew & George	1814	AG32	236	168
Murdock, John, of G'tn.	Deed to	Gilliss, Thomas H.	1815	AI34	472	483
Murdock, John, of G'tn.	Deed to	Buchannan, Thomas	1815	AI34	037	043
Murdock, John, of G'tn.	Deed to	McLean, Cornelius	1815	AI34	237	269
Murdock, John, of G'tn.	Deed to	Bussard, Daniel, of G'tn.	1815	AI34	025	029
Murdock, John, of G'tn.	Deed to	Andrews, Timothy P.	1815	AK35	364	287
Murdock, John, of G'tn.	Deed to	Wilson, John A.	1815	AK35	183	142
Murdock, John, of G'tn.	Deed to	Dorsey, William H., of Montg. Co.	1815	AK35	452	354
Murdock, John, of G'tn.	Deed to	Smith, Clement & John Pickrell	1815	AK35	105	081
Murdock, John, of G'tn.	Deed to	Fitzhugh, Samuel, of G'tn.	1816	AK35	517	407
Murdock, John, of G'tn.	Deed to	Williams, John S., of G'tn.	1816	AL36	316	311
Murdock, John, of G'tn.	Deed to	Plater, John R., of St. Mary's Co.	1816	AL36	011	012
Murdock, John, of G'tn.	Deed to	Moxley, Charles, of G'tn.	1816	AL36	218	224
Murdock, John, of G'tn.	Deed to	Smith, Clement & John Pickrell	1816	AL36	468	442
Murdock, John, of G'tn.	D. of T. fr	Fenwick, Francis, of G'tn.	1816	AL36	459	433
Murdock, John, of G'tn.	Deed to	McGrath, Thomas	1817	AO39	389	263
Murdock, John, of G'tn.	Deed to	Randall, Daniel	1817	AO39	068	056
Murdock, John, of G'tn.	Deed to	Ott, David	1817	AO39	064	053
Murdock, John, of G'tn.	Mortgage fr	Glasco, John	1817	AN38	147	108
Murdock, John, trustee of the late	Deed to	Luffborough, Nathan, of G'tn.	1804	M12	010	011
Murdock, John, trustees of	Deed fr	Hanson, Alexander Contee	1797	C3	095	78
Murdock, John, trustees of	Deed to	Nourse, Joseph	1801	G7	116	148
Murdock, John, trustees of	Lease to	Corcoran, Thomas	1801	G7	175	233
Murdock, William, mer., London	Deed to	Slater, Jonathan	1793	A1-1	222	309
Murphey, Benjamin	B. of S. to	Scott, Henry	1816	AM37	022	018
Murphy, William, of G'tn.	Deed to	Dulany, Matthew, of G'tn.	1795	B2A	225	312
Murray, Peter, of Harford Co.	Deed to	Thorpe, Thomas	1807	R17	100	078
Murray, Peter, of Balto.	B. of S. fr	Murray, William	1807	S18	181	147
Murray, Thomas	B. of S. fr	Masters, John	1807	R17	375	285
Murray, Thomas	Deed fr	Walker, Zachariah	1812	AD29	241	200
Murray, Thomas	Assign fr	Webster, Toppan	1815	AI34	046	053
Murray, Thomas	B. of S. fr	Burdine, William	1815	AH33	463	396
Murray, Wiliam, insolvent	B. of S. to	Mattingly, Stephen, trustee	1805	N13	116	111
Murray, William	B. of S. to	Lenox, Peter	1804	K10	211	222
Murray, William	B. of S. to	Murray, Peter, of Balto.	1807	S18	181	147
Murray, William, of A.A. Co.	Deed to	Thomas, John, of Montg. Co.	1811	AB27	450	369
Murrell, Bennett	B. of S. to	Bainbridge, Richard C.	1813	AE30	154	121
Murry, Rachel, d/o Sarah	Deed Gift fr	Walker, Sarah	1809	X23	184	138
Murry, Thomas	B. of S. fr	Walker, Sarah	1809	X23	183	137
Murry, William, Dr., of G'tn.	Deed fr	Boucher, John Thomas, P.G. Co.	1796	B2B	397	060
Murry, William, of A.A. Co.	Deed to	Thomas, Samuel, Jr., Montg. Co.	1806	P15	169	112
Muse, Lawrence, of Tappa. VA	Deed to	Pleasant, Israel & John P., Balto.	1805	M12	301	303
Muse, Lawrence, of Essex Co. VA	Deed fr	Ward, Joshua, Middlesex Co. VA	1805	M12	161	159
Muse, Lawrence, of VA	Deed to	Ross, James	1809	W22	197	137
Mustin, Thomas	Cert Slave	From VA	1816	AM37	495	361
Myer, Henry & Frederick Reahl	Deed to	Beall, Thomas & John M. Gantt	1792	A1-1	090	131
Myer, Jacob, of Balto. et al	Deed to	Myer, John Jeremiah [Myers]	1813	AF31	136	091
Myer, John Jeremiah, of Balto.	Deed fr	Myer, Jacob & C. Brensinger	1813	AF31	136	091

Party	What	Party	Year	Liber	Old	New
Myer, John, s/o John, age 15	Apprentice to	Davis, Shadrack	1805	N13	305	247
Myer, Solomon	Deed to	Morgan, William, of G'tn.	1805	M12	385	397
Myer, Solomon	Deed fr	Morgan, William, of G'tn.	1805	M12	138	134
Myer, Solomon	Deed to	Way, Andrew, Jr. & George	1807	Q16	363	278
Myer, Solomon	Deed fr	Gillaspy, George & Joseph Strong	1807	R17	316	241
Myer, Solomon	Deed to	Way, Andrew, Jr. & George	1807	S18	050	042
Myer, Solomon, of Alexa.	Mortgage to	Minifie, Charles	1809	V21	147	107
Myers, John	Slave	From Loudoun Co. VA	1810	X23	398	321
Myers, John	B. of S. fr	Doughty, William	1810	Y24	474	419
Myers, John	Qualify	Ensign 1st regiment	1813	AE30	472	351
Myers, John	B. of S. to	Camillier, Vincent	1815	AK35	374	295
Myers, John, of G'tn., house carp.	Deed to	Miller, Ann Maria, of G'tn.	1811	Z25	383	300
Myers, Levi, Dr. et al	Bond fr	Myers, Moses	1802	H8	155	150
Myers, Moses	Bond to	Myers, Levi, Dr. et al	1802	H8	155	150
Myers, Moses	Bond to	Polock, Isaac et al	1802	H8	155	150
Myers, Moses	Deed fr	Wheeler, Luke & John Cowper	1812	AD29	527	444

Index to District of Columbia Land Records, 1792-1817

Party	What	Party	Year	Liber	Old	New
N						
Nalley, John	B. of S. to	Downes, George	1805	M12	088	081
Nally, Aaron	Bond fr	O'Neale, William	1813	AE30	114	087
Nally, Jane	B. of S. fr	Nally, Rebecca	1806	Q16	162	107
Nally, Jane	B. of S. to	Nally, Susannah, d/o Jane	1815	AH33	484	414
Nally, John	Deed to	Nally, Rebecca	1805	N13	033	035
Nally, Rebecca	Deed fr	Nally, John	1805	N13	033	035
Nally, Rebecca	B. of S. to	Nally, Susannah	1806	Q16	165	109
Nally, Rebecca	B. of S. to	Nally, Jane	1806	Q16	162	107
Nally, Rebecca, exr. of	B. of S. to	Davis, John, of Abel	1809	X23	302	242
Nally, Susannah	B. of S. fr	Nally, Rebecca	1806	Q16	165	109
Nally, Susannah, d/o Jane	B. of S. fr	Nally, Jane	1815	AH33	484	414
Nardin, Baptist	Assign to	Pic, Francis	1815	AH33	492	421
Nardin, Baptist	D. of T. to	Pic, Francis	1815	AH33	493	422
Natt, Thomas, of Phila.	Deed fr	Lovering, Charles Fox, of Phila.	1817	AO39	517	356
Naylor, George	Agreement	Templeman, John	1795	B2A	216	299
Naylor, George, of Augusta GA	Agreement	Templeman, John, of G'tn.	1795	B2A	215	297
Naylor, John L. et al	Manumis fr	Voss, Nicholas	1806	P15	313	207
Naylor, John L.	Deed fr	Wigfield, Robert & Mary	1807	R17	200	152
Naylor, John L. & William Moore	Mortgage fr	Fry, Thomas	1811	AC28	041	030
Naylor, John L.	Deed to	Morsell, James S.	1811	AC28	008	006
Naylor, John Lawson	Deed to	Kirby, John Baptist	1807	R17	048	038
Naylor, John S.	D. Gift to	Naylor, Verlinder, his daughter	1813	AF31	297	211
Naylor, Verlinder	D. Gift fr	Naylor, John S., her father	1813	AF31	297	211
Neale, Charles, Rev. et al	Deed fr	Neale, Leonard, Rev.	1814	AG32	029	023
Neale, Charles, Rev. et al	Deed fr	Neale, Francis I., Rev., of G'tn.	1814	AG32	025	020
Neale, Francis	Deposition	Sanders, Ann & Thomas	1806	P15	187	126
Neale, Francis	Deed fr	Whetzel, John	1817	AN38	490	354
Neale, Francis I., Rev., of G'tn.	Deed to	Carroll, John, Rev. et al	1814	AG32	025	020
Neale, Francis Ignatius, Rev.	Deed fr	Threlkeld, John, of Montg. Co.	1798	C3	447	351
Neale, Francis, of G'tn. College	Deed to	Munroe, Thomas	1804	K10	213	223
Neale, Francis, Rev., of Montg. Co.	Deed fr	Threlkeld, John, of Montg. Co.	1796	B2B	502	201
Neale, Francis, Rev. et al	Deed fr	Carroll, John, Rev. et al	1799	D4	286	268
Neale, Francis, Rev. et al	Deed fr	Carroll, John, Rev. et al	1799	D4	283	265
Neale, Francis, Rev.	Deed fr	Deakins, Francis, of William, Jr.	1802	H8	463	425
Neale, Francis, Rev.	Deed fr	Threlkeld, John	1802	H8	136	132
Neale, Francis, Rev.	Deed fr	Butler, Mann	1805	O14	041	025
Neale, Francis, Rev.	Deed fr	Threlkeld, John	1810	Y24	283	259
Neale, Francis, Rev.	Deed fr	Clarke, Robert	1811	AC28	089	068
Neale, Francis, Rev.	Deed fr	Threlkeld, John	1814	AG32	351	254
Neale, Francis, Rev., of G'tn.	Release fr	Van Ness, John P. & Marcia	1815	AI34	252	285
Neale, Francis, Rev., of G'tn.	Lease fr	Van Ness, John P.	1815	AI34	254	287
Neale, Francis, Rev.	Deed fr	Matthews, William	1815	AI34	257	290
Neale, Francis, Rev., of G'tn.	Deed fr	Hoye, John, of Allegany Co. MD	1815	AI34	256	287
Neale, Francis, Rev., of G'tn.	Deed fr	Boyd, Washington, marshal	1816	AL36	279	278
Neale, Henry	Slave		1807	R17	136	105
Neale, James, s/o Bernard	Deed to	Beall, Thomas & John M. Gantt	1792	A1-1	059	88
Neale, John B.	Deed fr	Moscrop, Henry	1802	I9	353	582
Neale, John Baptist, of Alexa.	Deed fr	Garlick, Joseph, of G'tn.	1797	C3	070	57
Neale, John Baptist, of Westm. Co.	Deed to	Harrison, William, of Balto.	1801	G7	296	411
Neale, Leonard	Decree to	Jones, Anthony	1805	N13	017	019
Neale, Leonard, of G'tn.	Deed fr	Jones, Anthony, of P.G. Co.	1805	N13	018	019
Neale, Leonard, of G'tn.	Deed fr	Rochefoucolt, Celeste LeBlonde dela	1805	N13	380	305
Neale, Leonard, Rev.	Deed fr	Threlkeld, John	1805	N13	019	021
Neale, Leonard, Rev.	Deed fr	Rochefaucolt, Celeste LeBlonde de la	1805	N13	031	033

Party	What	Party	Year	Liber	Old	New
Neale, Leonard, Rev.	Assign fr	Carrere, John	1808	T19	328	239
Neale, Leonard, Rev.	B. of S. fr	Fenwick, Richard	1808	T19	327	238
Neale, Leonard, Rev.	Confirm to	Lalor, Alice et al	1811	AB27	169	140
Neale, Leonard, Rev.	Deed to	Carroll, John, Most Rev. et al	1814	AG32	029	023
Neale, Leonard, Rt. Rev.	Deed fr	Rochfoucolt, Celeste LeBlonde dela	1805	N13	067	061
Neale, Leonard, Rt. Rev.	Deed fr	Doughty, William, of G'tn.	1805	N13	366	295
Neale, Leonard, Rt. Rev., of G'tn.	Deed to	Lalor, Alice et al	1808	U20	283	151
Neale, Leonard, Rt. Rev. et al	Deed fr	Neale, Francis I., Rev., of G'tn.	1814	AG32	025	020
Neale, Mary et al	Deed fr	Neale, Leonard, Rt. Rev., of G'tn.	1808	U20	283	151
Neale, Mary et al	Confirm fr	Neale, Leonard, Rev.	1811	AB27	169	140
Neale, Richard S.	Deed fr	Beatty, Charles	1802	I9	435	719
Neale, William, Jr., St. Mary's Co.	Deed to	Carberry, Thomas & James	1816	AL36	434	414
Neale, William O.	Deed fr	Key, Philip Barton, of Annapolis	1800	E5	321	310
Neale, William, of MD	Deed to	Brent, William C., of MD	1802	H8	432	398
Needham, William, of Montg. Co.	Deed to	Thompson, George, of G'tn.	1796	B2B	586	333
Needham, William, of Montg. Co.	Deed to	King, Adam, of G'tn.	1797	B2B	698	481
Nesbit, Henry	Deed fr	Prout, William	1805	N13	170	154
Nesmith, Ebenezer	Deed fr	Moffat, William	1802	H8	094	086
Nesmith, Ebenezer	Deed fr	Moffat, William	1802	H8	092	084
Nesmith, Ebenezer	Deed to	Wheat, Joseph	1806	P15	390	261
Nesmith, Ebenezer	Deed to	St. Clair, George	1813	AE30	535	397
Nesmith, Ebenezer, carpenter	Deed fr	Tingey, Thomas, Gent.	1804	L11	059	61
Nesmith, Ebenezer et al	Deed fr	Law, Thomas	1801	G7	362	492
Nesmith, Ebenezer et al	Deed fr	Law, Thomas	1801	G7	362	493
Neswmith, Ebenezer et al	Deed fr	Law, Thomas	1801	G7	359	490
Neth, Lewis, of Annapolis	Deed fr	Mann, Mary, of Annapolis	1809	V21	359	262
Nevitt, Charles & Levinah	Agreement	Peacock, Robert Ware	1801	G7	124	160
Nevitt, John B., of MD	B. of S. fr	Nevitt, John, of MD	1802	H8	071	066
Nevitt, John B.	Certificate of Slaves		1802	H8	072	067
Nevitt, John, of MD	B. of S. to	Nevitt, John B., of MD	1802	H8	071	066
Nevitt, Joseph	Partition	Robey, Theophilus	1813	AF31	173	117
Nevitt, Joseph	Deed to	Belt, Joseph Sprigg	1813	AF31	237	163
Nevitt, Joseph & Theo. Robey	Deed fr	Hoye, John & Leomard M. Deakins	1809	W22	263	176
Nevitt, Joseph et al	Deed fr	Beatty, Charles, heirs of	1808	T19	393	279
Nevitt, Joseph, Jr. et al	Deed fr	Beatty, Charles A., Dr.	1811	Z25	384	302
Nevitt, Lousiana	Deed Gift to	Nevitt, Thomas Francis	1815	AI34	424	444
Nevitt, Mary	Deed fr	Jones, Willie Ann, of Balto. MD	1813	AE30	502	372
Nevitt, Thomas Francis	Deed Gift fr	Nevitt, Louisiana	1815	AI34	424	444
Nevitt, William	Deed fr	Dorsey, William H.	1805	M12	074	068
Nevitt, William	Deed to	Marbury, William	1812	AC28	321	234
Nevitt, William, of G'tn.	Deed fr	Voss, Nicholas	1806	P15	320	211
Nevitt, William, of G'tn.	Deed to	Wright, Matthew	1811	AB27	372	307
Nevitt, William, of G'tn.	Deed fr	Dorsey, William H., of Balto. Co.	1811	AB27	281	230
Nevitt, William, of P.G. Co.	Deed fr	Parrott, Richard, of G'tn.	1814	AG32	150	108
Nevitt, William, of P.G. Co.	Deed to	Hersey, John, of G'tn.	1814	AH33	241	209
Nevitt, William, of P.G. Co.	Deed fr	Suter, Alexander	1817	AN38	197	143
Newman, Francis	B. of S. fr	Brooke, Thomas A., of Montg. Co.	1812	AC28	308	224
Newman, Morris	Deed fr	Hurley, Daniel	1802	H8	587	553
Newman, Morris	Deed to	Wheeler, Eleanor	1804	L11	169	165
Newman, Morris	Deed fr	Wheeler, Leonard	1804	K10	406	
Newman, Morris et al	Mortgage to	Addison, Thomas Grafton et al	1804	K10	144	156
Newman, Morris et al	Deed fr	Addison, Thomas Grafton	1804	L11	215	202
Newman, Morris et al	Deed to	Kirby, John Baptist	1805	M12	317	320
Newman, Thomas, of P.G. Co.	B. of S. fr	Barrett, John	1813	AF31	483	353
Newton, Charles, of Zachariah	B. of S. fr	Newton, James	1815	AG32	457	331

Index to District of Columbia Land Records, 1792-1817

Party	What	Party	Year	Liber	Old	New
Newton, Ignatius	B. of S. fr	Brown, George G.	1805	O14	044	027
Newton, Ignatius	B. of S. to	Ritchie, Abner	1806	Q16	255	176
Newton, Ignatius	B. of S. fr	Broome, George G.	1806	O14	164	107
Newton, Ignatius	Deed to	Holtzman, Jacob	1814	AH33	342	296
Newton, Ignatius	Deed fr	McCleery, Henry, of MD	1814	AH33	321	277
Newton, Ignatius	Deed to	Holtzman, Jacob, heirs of	1815	AI34	249	281
Newton, Ignatius	Deed to	Wineberger, Jacob	1816	AL36	294	291
Newton, Ignatius	B. of S. fr	Gloyd, George H., of G'tn.	1816	AL36	467	441
Newton, Ignatius & Isaac Wilson	B. of S. fr	Jearvis, Henry	1817	AN38	339	249
Newton, Ignatius, of G'tn.	B. of S. to	Bussard, Daniel	1805	O14	043	026
Newton, Ignatius, of G'tn.	Deed fr	Brooks, William H., of G'tn.	1805	N13	229	195
Newton, Ignatius, of G'tn.	Indenture fr	Butler, Joseph, s/o Mary	1811	AB27	418	345
Newton, Ignatius, of G'tn.	Deed to	Wineberger, Jacob	1812	AC28	301	219
Newton, James	B. of S. to	Newton, Charles, of Zachariah	1815	AG32	457	331
Newton, John	B. of S. to	Soderstrom, Richard, of Phila.	1801	G7	402	536
Newton, John	Deed fr	Holmead, John	1807	S18	226	180
Newton, John	Manumis to	[ ], Kate (negress)	1807	R17	336	256
Newton, John S.	B. of S. fr	Busey, Samuel	1810	Y24	324	294
Newton, John S.	B. of S. fr	Moore, Nathan	1810	Y24	323	293
Newton, John S.	Deed to	Heronimus, Pendleton	1814	AG32	446	323
Nichlin, Philip, of Phila. PA	Cert fr	Commissioners of Washington	1793	B2A	304	427
Nicholl, Edward H. & E. Smith	Mortgage fr	Goldsborough, Charles W., G'tn.	1814	AH33	166	154
Nicholl, Edward H. & Edm. Smith	Deed fr	Goldsborough, Charles W.	1816	AL36	368	358
Nicholl, Edward H. & Edm. Smith	Mortgage fr	Freeman, Constant	1816	AM37	280	206
Nicholls & Co., William S. et al	Deed fr	Beck, Richard, of G'tn.	1805	M12	123	117
Nicholls, Edward	Mortgage to	Kilty, William	1802	G7	544	691
Nicholls, Edward	B. of S. to	Smith, Robert	1802	I9	148	224
Nicholls, Edward	Slaves		1805	N13	104	098
Nicholls, Edward	Mortgage to	Kilty, William	1806	O14	330	219
Nicholls, Edward H. & W. Floyd	Deed fr	Munroe, Thomas, Supt.	1816	AM37	115	091
Nicholls, Henry	Cert fr	Commissioners of Washington	1795	B2A	332	466
Nicholls, Henry, of Balto.	Cert fr	Commissioners of Washington	1793	B2A	300	421
Nicholls, Henry, of Balto.	Cert fr	Commissioners of Washington	1793	B2A	300	420
Nicholls, Henry, of Balto.	Deed to	Carroll, Daniel, of *Duddington*	1815	AK35	413	324
Nicholls, Robert H.	B. of S. to	Davidson, John	1806	O14	209	138
Nicholls, Samuel	Deed fr	Gregg, Joshua	1802	I9	209	328
Nicholls, William S., of G'tn. et al	Deed to	Beck, Richard, mer.	1806	Q16	264	184
Nicholls, William S., of G'tn.	B. of S. fr	Beall, William D.	1809	V21	353	255
Nicholls, William S., of G'tn. et al	Deed fr	Cocking, William	1812	AD29	498	420
Nicholls, William S. et al	Deed fr	Morsell, James S., of G'tn.	1812	AC28	288	209
Nicholls, William S., of G'tn.	D. of T. fr	Deveney, Daniel, of G'tn.	1817	AO39	340	243
Nicholls, William S., of G'tn.	Deed fr	Miller, Hezekiah, of G'tn.	1817	AO39	342	243
Nicholls, Wm. S. & Romulus Riggs	Award fr	Claggett, Walter, reps. of	1813	AF31	073	050
Nicholls, Wm. S. & Romulus Riggs	Bond fr	Claggett, Walter, reps. of	1813	AF31	072	049
Nicholson, Charity	B. of S. to	Nicholson, Edward	1816	AO39	049	041
Nicholson, Edward	B. of S. fr	Nicholson, Charity	1816	AO39	049	041
Nicholson, Hannah et al	R. of D. to	Duncanson, William M. et al	1798	C3	364	292
Nicholson, John	Protest to	Gantt, John M.	1796	B2B	601	353
Nicholson, John	P. of Atty. R	DeBois, Lewis & Wm. Cranch	1796	B2B	591	340
Nicholson, John	Agreement	Prentiss, William, merchant	1797	B2B	622	380
Nicholson, John	B. of S. fr	Mills, John	1809	W22	226	154
Nicholson, John & Hannah, Phila.	Deed to	Ball, Joseph, of Phila.	1795	B2A	276	387
Nicholson, John & Hannah, of PA	Deed to	Harrison, George, of PA et al	1795	B2A	344	485
Nicholson, John & Robert Morris	Deed fr	Greenleaf, James, New York NY	1796	B2B	579	323
Nicholson, John & Robert Morris	Deed fr	Greenleaf, James, now of NY	1796	B2B	562	296

Index to District of Columbia Land Records, 1792-1817

Party	What	Party	Year	Liber	Old	New
Nicholson, John & Robert Morris	Agreement	Bickley, John, bricklayer	1796	B2B	584	330
Nicholson, John & Robert Morris	Deed to	Greenleaf, James, now of Phila.	1796	B2B	599	349
Nicholson, John & Robert Morris	Deed to	Dermott, James Reed	1796	B2B	560	293
Nicholson, John & Hannah, et al	Mortgage to	Greenleaf, James, New York NY	1796	B2B	592	341
Nicholson, John & Robert Morris	Deed to	Duncanson, William et al	1796	B2B	566	302
Nicholson, John & Robert Morris	Deed fr	Deakins, William, Jr., of G'tn.	1796	B2B	604	356
Nicholson, John & Robert Morris	Deed to	Forrest, Uriah, of G'tn.	1796	B2B	577	320
Nicholson, John & Robert Morris	Deed fr	Scott, Gustavus, of G'tn.	1796	B2B	603	355
Nicholson, John & Hannah et al	Deed to	Duncanson, William Mayne	1797	C3	238	197
Nicholson, John & Hannah	Deed to	Ashley, John	1797	B2B	692	471
Nicholson, John & Hannah	Deed to	Ashley, John	1797	B2B	693	473
Nicholson, John et al	Cert fr	Commissioners of Washington	1796	B2B	452	140
Nicholson, John et al	Deed to	Harrison, Benjamin	1798	D4	069	058
Nicholson, John et al	Deed to	Pratt, Henry et al	1798	D4	030	025
Nicholson, John et al	Deed to	Dickinson, Philemon	1798	D4	034	028
Nicholson, John et al	P. of Atty. to	Scott, Gustavus	1799	D4	188	170
Nicholson, John et al	Deed to	Nicklin, Philip & E. Griffith	1799	D4	186	168
Nicholson, John et al	Oblig. to	Dunlap, James et al	1802	H8	100	091
Nicholson, John, of Phila. PA et al	Deed to	Law, Thomas, of New York NY	1795	B2B	377	030
Nicholson, John, of Phila. PA	Deed fr	Greenleaf, James, New York NY	1795	B2B	380	035
Nicholson, John, of Phila. PA	Mortgage to	Corporation of the Poor, Presby.	1795	B2A	278	390
Nicholson, John, of Phila. PA et al	Deed fr	Greenleaf, James, now of NY	1796	B2B	532	249
Nicholson, John, of Phila. PA et al	Deed to	Polock, Isaac, of Savannah GA	1796	B2B	505	206
Nicholson, John, of Phila. PA	Deed fr	Walker, George, Gent.	1796	B2B	536	254
Nicholson, John, of Phila. PA et al	Mortgage to	Duncanson, William M.	1796	B2B	411	081
Nicholson, John, of Phila. PA	Agreement	Bickley, John, bricklayer	1796	B2B	584	330
Nicholson, John, of Phila. PA	Deed fr	Walker, George	1796	B2B	605	358
Nicholson, John, of Phila. PA	Deed fr	King, William	1796	B2B	537	256
Nicholson, John, of Phila. PA	Mortgage to	Wilkinson, Joseph, Calvert Co.	1797	B2B	671	439
Nicholson, John, of Phila. PA	Mortgage to	Harrison, William, of Balto.	1797	B2B	678	449
Nicholson, John, of Phila. PA	Mortgage to	Wilkinson, Joseph, Calvert Co.	1797	B2B	670	438
Nicholson, John, of Phila. PA	P. of Atty.	Turnicliff, William	1797	B2B	691	471
Nicholson, John, of Phila. PA et al	D. of T. to	Pratt, Henry et al	1797	C3	204	172
Nicholson, John, of Phila. PA et al	Release fr	Law, Thomas	1797	C3	144	118
Nicholson, John, of Phila. PA et al	Deed to	Law, Thomas	1797	C3	074	81
Nicholson, John, of Phila. PA et al	Release fr	Law, Thomas	1797	C3	180	152
Nicholson, John, of Phila. PA et al	D. of T. to	Pratt, Henry et al	1797	C3	192	161
Nicholson, John, of Phila. PA	Mortgage to	Duncanson, William Mayne	1797	C3	011	8
Nicholson, John, of Phila. PA et al	Deed to	Baker, Jacob et al	1798	C3	301	243
Nicholson, John, of Phila. PA et al	Deed to	Forrest, Uriah	1798	C3	517	406
Nicholson, John, of Phila. PA et al	Deed to	Duncanson, William M. et al	1798	C3	362	289
Nicholson, John, of Balto.	Deed fr	Moscrop, Henry & Elizabeth, NY	1816	AM37	184	138
Nicholson, Philip et al	Deed fr	Morris, Philip et al	1799	D4	186	168
Nicklin, Philip & E. Griffith	Deed fr	Nicholson, John et al	1799	D4	186	168
Nicklin, Philip et al	Deed fr	Commissioners of Washington	1800	E5	117	104
Nickolson, Joseph Hopper	Deed fr	Richmond, William, Q. Anne's C.	1799	D4	256	241
Nicoll, Edward H. & Wm. Floyd	Deed fr	Ringgold, Tench	1816	AM37	025	020
Nicoll, Edward H. & Edm. Smith	Deed to	Freeman, Constant	1816	AM37	354	256
Nixdorf, Samuel, of Fredk. Co.	B. of S. to	Woltz, Susanna, of G'tn.	1813	AF31	234	161
Nixdorff, Samuel	Deed fr	Garey, Everard	1814	AH33	066	059
Noel, Gilson	Deed to	Varnum, James M.	1815	AI34	494	501
Noel, Jilson	Deed fr	Jamieson, Andrew, of Alexa. Co.	1809	W22	282	187
Noel, Jilson	D. of T. to	Jamieson, Andrew, of Alexa.	1809	W22	285	189
Norris, Benjamin et al	Deed fr	Norris, Benjamin, of G'tn.	1814	AH33	185	169
Norris, Benjamin, of G'tn.	Deed to	Norris, Lloyd et al	1814	AH33	185	169

Party	What	Party	Year	Liber	Old	New
Norris, Daniel & Catherine, of MD	Deed fr	Clements, Joseph, of G'tn.	1812	AD29	288	237
Norris, Isaac	Deed to	Wilson, Henry	1805	M12	354	361
Norris, Isaac	Deed to	Norris, Sarah	1807	R17	004	003
Norris, Isaac	Release to	Ritchie, Abner	1807	S18	253	199
Norris, Isaac, of G'tn.	Deed fr	Eastburn, Isaac Washington, G'tn.	1799	D4	409	386
Norris, Isaac, of G'tn.	Deed fr	Ritchie, Abner, of G'tn.	1805	M12	083	077
Norris, Isaac, of G'tn.	Deed to	Dawes, Isaac et al	1806	Q16	118	076
Norris, John et al	Deed fr	Norris, Benjamin, of G'tn.	1814	AH33	185	169
Norris, Lloyd et al	Deed fr	Norris, Benjamin, of G'tn.	1814	AH33	185	169
Norris, Lydia Ann et al	Deed fr	Norris, Benjamin, of G'tn.	1814	AH33	185	169
Norris, Sarah	Deed fr	Norris, Isaac	1807	R17	004	003
Norris, Sarah et al	Deed fr	Norris, Benjamin, of G'tn.	1814	AH33	185	169
Norris, Sarah et al	Convey to	Redman, James, of G'tn.	1816	AL36	463	437
Norris, Stephen	Lease fr	Smith, Richard, of G'tn.	1816	AM37	300	219
Norris, Stephen	Surrender to	Smith, Richard, of G'tn.	1816	AM37	302	221
Norris, Stephen, of G'tn.	Deed fr	Bussard, Daniel, of G'tn.	1812	AC28	282	205
Norris, Stephen, of Hagerstown	Deed to	Smith, Richard, of G'tn.	1814	AH33	274	239
Norris, Stephen, Wash. Co. MD	Lease fr	Smith, Richard, of G'tn.	1814	AH33	153	145
Norris, William, insolvent	B. of S. to	Bastian, Charles, trustee	1805	M12	405	429
North Capitol Street	Road Survey		1815	AH33	543	
North, Richard, of Phila. PA	Deed fr	Ramsay, John, of Phila. PA	1805	N13	059	054
Norton, Thomas & Catherine	Deed to	Beatty, Charles, of G'tn.	1794	A1-2	494	97
Nourse, Charles J., of G'tn.	Deed fr	Lowndes, Francis	1810	Y24	211	194
Nourse, Charles J., of G'tn.	Agreement	Suter, Alexander, of G'tn.	1810	Y24	213	195
Nourse, Charles J.	Deed fr	Beall, Thomas, of George	1810	Y24	214	196
Nourse, Charles J., of G'tn.	Convey to	Johns, Richard, of G'tn.	1811	AB27	026	024
Nourse, Charles J.	Release to	Lowndes, Francis, Sr.	1811	AC28	084	064
Nourse, Charles J., of G'tn.	Deed to	Davidson, William	1811	AA26	179	122
Nourse, Joseph	Deed fr	Armat, Thomas & Elizabeth, of PA	1799	D4	244	227
Nourse, Joseph	Deed fr	Murdock, John, trustees of	1801	G7	116	148
Nourse, Joseph	Deed fr	Peter, John et al	1801	G7	073	095
Nourse, Joseph	Deed fr	Beall, Thomas, of George et al	1801	G7	073	095
Nourse, Joseph	Deed fr	Beall, Thomas, of George et al	1801	G7	372	504
Nourse, Joseph	Deed fr	O'Riley, Henry	1802	G7	570	719
Nourse, Joseph	Deed fr	Beatty, Charles	1802	G7	567	716
Nourse, Joseph	Deed fr	Forrest, Uriah	1804	K10	313	319
Nourse, Joseph	Deed fr	Key, Philip Barton	1804	K10	311	317
Nourse, Joseph	Deed fr	Wayman, Charles et al	1804	K10	183	192
Nourse, Joseph	Deed fr	Beatty, John M. & Charles A.	1806	O14	353	236
Nourse, Joseph	Manumis to	Motts, Bacchus (negro)	1807	S18	260	205
Nourse, Joseph	Deed fr	Armat, Thomas, of Phila. PA	1809	X23	178	132
Nourse, Joseph	Deed to	Davidson, James	1811	AA26	209	143
Nourse, Joseph	Deed fr	Beall, Thomas, of Geo.	1811	AB27	204	167
Nourse, Joseph	Deed to	Smith, Clement	1812	AC28	120	090
Nourse, Joseph	Deed fr	Munroe, Thomas	1813	AE30	396	292
Nourse, Joseph	Release fr	Bowie, Washington	1813	AE30	397	292
Nourse, Joseph	Deed fr	Gardner, Esther	1813	AF31	515	377
Nourse, Joseph	Deed to	Carroll, Charles, of *Bellevue*	1813	AF31	013	010
Nourse, Joseph	Release fr	Lenox, David et al	1813	AF31	011	008
Nourse, Joseph	Deed fr	Davidson, James	1813	AF31	012	009
Nourse, Joseph	Deed to	English, David, cashier	1814	AG32	223	156
Nourse, Joseph	Release fr	English, David, cashier	1816	AL36	243	247
Nourse, Joseph	Assign fr	Brumley, Joseph, collector	1816	AI34	451	464
Nourse, Joseph	D. of T. to	Pleasonton, Stephen	1817	AN38	231	170
Nourse, Joseph	Deed fr	Harrison, Richard	1817	AN38	230	168

Party	What	Party	Year	Liber	Old	New
Nourse, Joseph	Deed fr	Andrews, George, admrs. of	1817	AN38	423	317
Nourse, Joseph	Deed fr	Bassett, John, Hanover Co. VA	1817	AN38	425	318
Nourse, Joseph	Agreement	Andrews, George	1817	AN38	426	320
Nourse, Joseph, agent	Lease to	Stanton, Patrick	1813	AE30	239	190
Nourse, Joseph et al	Deed fr	Law, John, atty. for Thomas	1810	Y24	067	059
Nourse, Joseph, of Phila. PA	Deed fr	Beatty, Charles	1799	D4	184	165
Nourse, Joseph, of Phila. PA	Deed fr	Commissioners of Washington	1799	D4	302	286
Nourse, Joseph, of G'tn.	Deed fr	Turner, Samuel, Jr., of G'tn.	1800	F6	023	015
Nourse, Joseph, of G'tn.	Lease to	Lyon, James	1802	I9	065	090
Nourse, Joseph, of G'tn.	Lease to	Ellis, Robert	1802	I9	092	133
Nourse, Joseph, of G'tn.	Deed to	Weems, John, of G'tn.	1804	L11	011	10
Nourse, Joseph, of G'tn.	Mortgage to	United States	1805	M12	234	235
Nourse, Joseph, of G'tn.	Deed fr	Duvall, Gabriel	1805	M12	286	287
Nourse, Joseph, of G'tn.	Deed fr	Hines, John, of Liberty MD	1806	O14	355	237
Nourse, Joseph, of G'tn.	Deed fr	Hoye, John et al	1806	O14	357	238
Nourse, Joseph, of G'tn.	Mortgage to	United States	1808	U20	275	146
Nourse, Joseph, of G'tn.	Deed to	Hurdle, Noble, of G'tn.	1809	W22	355	230
Nourse, Joseph, of G'tn.	Mortgage fr	Smith, Andrew, of G'tn.	1809	W22	236	160
Nourse, Joseph, of G'tn.	Deed fr	Beall, Thomas, of George, of G'tn.	1809	W22	239	162
Nourse, Joseph, of G'tn.	Deed to	Smith, Andrew, of G'tn.	1810	Z25	059	044
Nourse, Joseph, of G'tn.	Deed to	Smith, Andrew, of G'tn.	1810	Z25	055	041
Nourse, Joseph, of G'tn.	D. of T. to	Smith, Walter, of G'tn.	1811	AB27	045	039
Nourse, Joseph, of G'tn.	Deed to	Brooke, Thomas A., of G'tn.	1811	AA26	196	134
Nourse, Joseph, of G'tn.	Deed to	Bowie, Washington, of G'tn.	1812	AC28	117	088
Nourse, Michael	Deed fr	Woodward, William	1802	I9	311	510
Nourse, Michael	Cert fr	Commissioners of Washington	1802	H8	105	102
Nourse, Michael	Deed to	Reintzel, Anthony	1805	M12	110	103
Nourse, Michael	Deed fr	Joy, Abraham	1806	P15	023	014
Nourse, Michael	Deed fr	Beatty, John M.	1806	Q16	189	127
Nourse, Michael	Deed fr	Long, Frederick	1806	Q16	194	130
Nourse, Michael	Deed fr	Beatty, John M. & Charles A.	1806	Q16	192	128
Nourse, Michael	Deed to	Joy, Abraham, of G'tn.	1806	O14	096	060
Nourse, Michael	Deed fr	Kaldenbach, Andrew	1807	S18	246	194
Nourse, Michael	Deed to	Sandiford, Thomas	1807	S18	249	196
Nourse, Michael	Qualify	Captain in Militia	1808	V21	056	044
Nourse, Michael	Deed fr	Hyde, Thomas	1808	V21	057	045
Nourse, Michael	Deed fr	Pairo, Thomas W. & Loveday	1809	W22	013	011
Nourse, Michael	Deed fr	Webster, Toppan	1809	W22	006	005
Nourse, Michael	Deed to	Hyde, Thomas	1809	V21	275	197
Nourse, Michael	Deed fr	Holmead, Anthony	1810	Y24	339	308
Nourse, Michael	Deed to	Rittenhouse, John Bull	1810	Y24	379	342
Nourse, Michael	Deed to	Rittenhouse, John Bull	1810	Y24	380	344
Nourse, Michael	Lease to	Fleet, Henry, of G'tn.	1810	Z25	045	034
Nourse, Michael	Deed fr	Litle, John	1810	Z25	217	171
Nourse, Michael	Deed to	Webster, Toppan	1812	AC28	343	248
Nourse, Michael	Qualify	Notary Public	1817	AN38	189	136
Nourse, Michael & Thos. H. Gilliss	B. of S. fr	McLeod, John	1812	AD29	246	203
Nourse, Michael & George Clarke	D. of T. fr	Webster, Toppan	1817	AO39	310	221
Nourse, Michael et al	Bond to	Smallwood, Samuel N. et al	1810	Z25	143	114
Nourse, Michael et al	Deed fr	Law, John, atty. for Thomas	1810	Y24	067	059
Nourse, Michael, of G'tn.	Deed fr	King, James C., of G'tn.	1800	E5	076	063
Nowlan, Edward, of Phila. PA	Mortgage fr	Brown, John	1801	G7	262	359
Nowland, John	Deed fr	Carleton, Joseph, of G'tn.	1804	L11	205	194
Nowland, John	Deed to	Higdon, Gustavus	1808	T19	298	218

Index to District of Columbia Land Records, 1792-1817

Party	What	Party	Year	Liber	Old	New
O						
O'Brian, John	Deed fr	Costigan, Joseph	1811	AB27	214	174
O'Brian, William	B. of S. fr	Jenkins, Francis	1813	AE30	219	177
O'Brien, James	Mortgage to	Barry, James	1802	H8	235	224
O'Brien, James	Deed fr	Barry, James	1802	H8	346	323
O'Brien, James, of Balto.	B. of S. fr	Fitzpatrick, Nicholas	1815	AH33	560	479
O'Brien, William	Deed fr	Prout, William	1804	L11	162	160
O'Brien, William	Deed to	Brent, Robert et al	1805	M12	095	085
O'Brien, William	B. of S. fr	Masters, Ezekiel	1806	Q16	264	184
O'Brien, William	B. of S. fr	Clephan, Lewis	1806	P15	081	049
O'Brien, William	B. of S. fr	Masters, Ezekiel	1806	Q16	263	183
O'Brien, William	Deed fr	Prout, William	1810	Y24	486	429
O'Brien, William	Record	Prout, William	1812	AD29	159	124
O'Brien, William	Deed fr	Prout, William	1812	AC28	124	093
O'Connell, John, insolvent	D. of T. to	Bristed, Richard, trustee	1811	Z25	526	417
O'Conner, Dennis	Deed to	Criddle, Jonathan	1812	AD29	056	040
O'Connor, Dennis	Lease fr	Prout, William	1810	Z25	278	218
O'Connor, Honora, of Balto. et al	P. of Atty. to	O'Connor, John, of Balto.	1813	AF31	148	099
O'Connor, John, of Balto.	P. of Atty. fr	O'Connor, Honora & S.M. Tyson	1813	AF31	148	099
O'Connor, Lawrence, Montg. Co.	Deed fr	Dorsey, William H., of G'tn.	1807	S18	077	063
O'Connor, Lawrence, of NY	Deed to	Donohoe, James	1807	S18	168	136
O'Hara, James, of Pittsburgh PA	Deed fr	Davidson, John	1805	M12	181	182
O'Hare, Christopher	Lease fr	Prout, William	1807	Q16	335	257
O'Hare, Christopher	Assign to	Prout, William	1810	Y24	118	108
O'Mara, Catharine	B. of S. to	Toole, Matthew	1815	AH33	440	378
O'Neal, William	B. of S. fr	Templeman, John	1808	V21	060	048
O'Neale, Bernard, Montg. Co. et al	Deed to	Thomson, William, of Montg. Co.	1797	C3	098	81
O'Neale, Henry	Deed fr	Davidson, Ann Maria, of G'tn.	1809	X23	200	152
O'Neale, Lawrence, of Montg. Co.	Deed to	Dorsey, William Hammond	1798	C3	332	268
O'Neale, Sarah, of Montg. Co.	Deed to	Adams, Alexander & R. West	1811	AC28	106	080
O'Neale, William	Cert fr	Commissioners of Washington	1795	B2A	334	469
O'Neale, William	Cert fr	Commissioners of Washington	1797	B2B	465	157
O'Neale, William	Cert fr	Commissioners of Washington	1797	B2B	467	159
O'Neale, William	Cert fr	Commissioners of Washington	1797	B2B	467	159
O'Neale, William	Deed to	Wilson, Samuel	1798	C3	285	231
O'Neale, William	Agreement	Lanham, Elisha, of G'tn.	1799	D4	358	345
O'Neale, William	Deed to	Key, Philip Barton, of Annapolis	1800	E5	321	311
O'Neale, William	Deed fr	Frost, Amariah	1802	H8	027	026
O'Neale, William	Deed fr	Munroe, Thomas, Supt.	1809	W22	050	037
O'Neale, William	Deed fr	Boyd, Washington, marshal	1809	W22	343	221
O'Neale, William	Deed fr	Kilty, John & Josias W. King	1809	V21	344	248
O'Neale, William	Deed fr	Middleton, Joseph	1810	Y24	140	127
O'Neale, William	D. of T. fr	Peltz, John	1811	AC28	028	021
O'Neale, William	Deed to	Speake, Samuel	1812	AD29	125	096
O'Neale, William	Bond to	Nally, Aaron	1813	AE30	114	087
O'Neale, William	Deed fr	Law, John	1814	AG32	159	113
O'Neale, William	Deed fr	Speake, Samuel	1814	AG32	228	162
O'Neale, William	Deed fr	Corporation of Washington	1815	AI34	275	310
O'Neale, William	Deed fr	Corporation of Washington	1815	AI34	273	308
O'Neale, William	Deed fr	Corporation of Washington	1815	AI34	271	306
O'Neale, William	Deed fr	Macdaniel, Ezekiel	1815	AI34	088	100
O'Neale, William	Deed fr	Corporation of Washington	1815	AI34	269	304
O'Neale, William	Deed fr	Corporation of Washington	1815	AI34	268	302
O'Neale, William	Deed fr	Corporation of Washington	1815	AI34	266	300
O'Neale, William & Rhoda	Deed to	Brown, Joel	1804	K10	254	261

Party	What	Party	Year	Liber	Old	New
O'Neale, William et al	Deed fr	Hamilton, Christiana	1811	AC28	035	026
O'Neale, William et al	D. of T. fr	Caldwell, Timothy, of Phila. PA	1812	AE30	017	014
O'Neale, William et al	Deed to	Young, James, trustee	1813	AE30	094	072
O'Neale, William et al	Release to	Caldwell, Timothy, of Phila. PA	1813	AF31	243	168
O'Neale, William et al	Manumis to	Ingraham, John	1817	AN38	299	218
O'Neale, William, of P.G. Co.	Deed to	Key, Philip Barton, of Annapolis	1797	C3	057	47
O'Neall, Bernard, of MD	Deed to	Lingan, James Maccubbin, G'tn.	1795	B2A	268	375
O'Neall, William	B. of S. fr	Coolidge, Margaret, of P.G. Co.	1808	V21	060	048
O'Reiley, Henry	Deed to	Thomson, George, of G'tn.	1810	Y24	458	407
O'Reilly, Henry	Deed fr	Middagh, John, Frederick Co. et al	1798	C3	346	278
O'Reilly, Henry	Deed fr	Beall, Thomas of Samuel et al	1799	D4	290	273
O'Roilly, Henry	Cert fr	Commissioners of Washington	1801	F6	134	083
O'Reilly, Henry	Convey fr	Patterson, Capt.	1808	V21	045	034
O'Reilly, Henry	Deed to	Mackey, William	1809	X23	095	070
O'Reilly, Henry, mer,, of G'tn.	Deed to	Gannon, James, hairdresser	1800	E5	171	161
O'Reilly, Henry, of G'tn.	Deed fr	Gannon, James, of G'tn.	1798	D4	082	069
O'Reilly, Henry, of G'tn.	Deed fr	King, Adam, of G'tn.	1799	D4	281	264
O'Reilly, Henry, of G'tn.	Deed to	Johnson, Morgan	1800	E5	204	197
O'Reilly, Johnson Michael	Deed fr	Davidson, John, of Annapolis MD	1797	B2B	658	422
O'Reilly, Johnson Michael et ux	Deed to	Scott, Sabret	1800	E5	180	170
O'Reilly, Michael J., of P.G. Co.	Convey to	Scott, Sabret, of Montg. Co.	1797	C3	092	76
O'Reily, Henry & Thomas Beatty	Deed fr	Downes, Henry & Winefred	1793	A1-1	175	249
O'Reily, Henry, of G'tn.	Deed fr	Beatty, Charles, of G'tn.	1795	B2A	231	321
O'Reily, Henry, of G'tn.	Deed to	Dunlap, John, of G'tn.	1795	B2A	239	333
O'Reily, Henry, of G'tn.	D. of T. to	Brent, William	1806	O14	167	109
O'Riely, Thomas, of Alexa. Co.	Deed to	Patterson, Edgar, of G'tn.	1807	R17	043	035
O'Riley, Henry	Deed to	Nourse, Joseph	1802	G7	570	719
Oakley, John	Deed to	Stephenson, Clotworthy	1802	H8	240	229
Oakley, John, guard.	Deed to	Lansdale, Thomas, assignee	1802	I9	007	009
Oakley, John, guard.	Deed to	Dorsey, William H.	1802	I9	009	011
Oakley, John, guard. of M. Burnes	Deed to	Laird, John	1802	G7	510	650
Oakley, John, guard.	Deed to	Mason, John	1802	H8	077	071
Ober, Richard	Cert fr	Commissioners of Washington	1795	B2A	329	461
Ober, Richard	Assign to	Somervill, James et al	1795	B2A	329	461
Ober, Richard, of G'tn.	Cert fr	Commissioners of Washington	1792	B2A	291	407
Ober, Richard, of G'tn.	Cert fr	Commissioners of Washington	1792	B2A	290	406
Ober, Richard, of G'tn.	Cert fr	Commissioners of Washington	1792	B2A	291	407
Ober, Richard, of G'tn.	Cert fr	Commissioners of Washington	1792	B2A	289	404
Ober, Robert	Deed fr	Beall, Thomas B.	1808	T19	161	113
Ober, Robert	Deed to	Whann, William	1810	Z25	005	004
Ober, Robert	Deed to	Wirt, John	1811	AB27	091	075
Ober, Robert	Deed to	Wright, Thomas C.	1813	AE30	174	139
Ober, Robert	Deed to	Wright, Thomas C.	1813	AE30	172	137
Ober, Robert	Deed fr	Wright, Thomas C.	1813	AF31	042	029
Ober, Robert	Deed to	Cromwell, Jesse, of Montg. Co.	1814	AF31	503	366
Ober, Robert	Deed to	Kennedy, James	1816	AL36	024	025
Ober, Robert & Isaac Tenny	Deed fr	Beatty, John M. & Charles A.	1808	U20	090	050
Ober, Robert & Isaac Tenny	Deed fr	Beall, Thomas, of George	1809	X23	089	066
Ober, Robert et al	Deed fr	Beatty, Charles, heirs of	1807	Q16	383	294
Ober, Robert, Gent.	Deed to	Steuart, David R., Gent.	1811	AB27	197	161
Ober, Robert, mer.	Deed fr	Reintzel, Anthony, Gent. et al	1807	S18	129	105
Ober, Robert, mer.	Deed to	Whann, William, Gent.	1808	U20	379	209
Ober, Robert, mer.	Deed to	Jackson, Isaac H., mer., of NY	1811	Z25	316	247
Ober, Robert, mer.	Deed fr	Beatty, Charles A., Dr.	1812	AD29	226	186
Ober, Robert, mer.	Deed to	Moore, Alexander, house joiner	1812	AE30	026	020

Index to District of Columbia Land Records, 1792-1817

Party	What	Party	Year	Liber	Old	New
Ober, Robert, of G'tn.	Deed fr	Kilty, John & Josias Wilson King	1809	X23	011	008
Ober, Robert, of G'tn.	Deed fr	Deakins, Leonard M. & John Hoye	1809	X23	007	005
Ober, Robert, of G'tn.	Deed fr	Reintzel, Anthony, of G'tn.	1810	Y24	335	303
Ober, Robert, of G'tn.	Deed to	Kellenberger, John H., of G'tn.	1811	AB27	335	276
Ober, Robert, of G'tn.	Deed to	King, Charles, of G'tn.	1811	AB27	508	415
Ober, Robert, of G'tn.	Deed fr	Reintzel, Anthony, of G'tn.	1811	Z25	458	362
Ober, Robert, of G'tn.	D. of T. to	Smith, Clement, of G'tn.	1811	Z25	545	433
Ober, Robert, of G'tn.	Deed to	Foxall, Henry	1811	AA26	215	147
Ober, Robert, of G'tn.	Deed fr	Tenny, Isaac, of Newburyport MA	1811	AA26	218	149
Ober, Robert, of G'tn.	Deed to	Union Bank of Georgetown	1814	AG32	367	266
Ober, Robert, of G'tn.	D. of T. to	Ott, John, of G'tn.	1814	AG32	368	267
Ober, Robert, of G'tn.	D. of T. to	Brundige, James	1814	AG32	270	191
Ober, Robert [Tenny & Ober]	Deed to	Smith, Walter	1816	AL36	321	315
Ochenbrod, William	Deed fr	Beatty, Thomas J., of G'tn.	1793	A1-1	197	277
Oddlin, Eleanor	B. of S. fr	Ellis, Robert	1802	I9	456	752
Oden, Benjamin	Deed fr	Gordon, John, of Annapolis	1794	B2A	036	040
Oden, Benjamin	P. of Atty. to	Dorsey, William H., of G'tn.	1796	B2B	558	289
Oden, Benjamin	Deed to	Sands, Mary	1798	C3	329	265
Oden, Benjamin & Sophia et al	Deed to	Chandler, Walter S. et al	1804	K10	112	120
Oden, Benjamin & Sophia et al	Deed to	Smith, Walter & Clement, of G'tn.	1804	K10	127	138
Oden, Benjamin & Harriet B. et al	Deed to	Gantt, Thomas T.	1816	AL36	035	036
Oden, Benjamin et al	Deed fr	Jackson, John G., fr. Harrison Co.	1814	AG32	295	215
Oden, Benjamin, of P.G. Co.	Deed to	Lynch, Dominick, of NY et al	1797	C3	043	34
Oden, Benjamin, of P.G. Co.	Deed fr	Lynch, Dominick & Jane, of NY	1797	C3	047	37
Oden, Benjamin, of P.G. Co.	Deed fr	Robertson, William, of Montg. Co.	1798	C3	334	270
Oden, Benjamin, of P.G. Co.	Deed fr	Key, Philip Barton, of G'tn. et al	1807	R17	408	308
Oden, Benjamin, of P.G. Co.	Deed to	Dodge, Allen & Francis, of G'tn.	1807	R17	406	307
Oden, Benjamin, of P.G. Co.	Deed to	Shoemaker, David et al	1811	AB27	490	401
Oden, Benjamin, of P.G. Co.	Deed to	Young, Moses	1812	AD29	133	103
Oden, Benjamin, of P.G. Co.	Deed to	Peltz, John	1812	AD29	421	354
Oden, Benjamin, of P.G. Co.	Deed to	Glover, Charles	1812	AC28	375	273
Oden, Benjamin, of P.G. Co.	Deed fr	Mountz, John et al	1815	AI34	376	403
Oden, Benjamin, of P.G. Co.	Deed fr	Reintzell, Val. & John Thompson	1815	AI34	375	403
Oden, Benjamin, of P.G. Co.	Bond to	Gantt, Thomas T.	1816	AL36	038	039
Offult, Ozear	Deed fr	Beatty, Charles	1802	H8	072	067
Offut, Thomas B. & Lydia et al	Deed fr	Kogenderfer, Leonard et al	1799	D4	239	221
Offutt, Aaron & Ann et al	Deed to	Riggs, George W., of Balto.	1814	AH33	017	016
Offutt, James, of William	Deed to	King, James C.	1807	R17	256	194
Offutt, James, of William	Deed to	Beatty, John M. & Charles A.	1807	R17	337	257
Offutt, Ozeas, Dr., of Montg. Co.	Deed fr	Magruder, George, collector, G'tn.	1804	L11	304	279
Offutt, Ozeas, of Montg. Co. et al	Deed to	Templeman, John, of G'tn.	1804	L11	185	178
Offutt, Ozias, Dr., of Montg. Co.	Deed fr	Magruder, George, collector, G'tn.	1804	L11	303	278
Offutt, Ozias, Dr.	Deed to	Brookes, Joseph	1806	O14	249	164
Offutt, Ozias, Dr.	Deed to	Magruder, Ninian, Dr.	1806	P15	198	132
Offutt, Ozias, Dr., admr. of	Deed to	Beatty, John M. & Charles A.	1807	R17	337	257
Offutt, Ozias, Dr., of Montg. Co.	Deed to	Beatty, Charles	1807	R17	341	260
Offutt, Ozias, physician, of MD	Deed fr	Hoff, Jacob, farmer, of MD	1802	I9	116	171
Offutt, Rezin, of Fairfax Co. VA	Deed fr	Threlkeld, John, of G'tn.	1800	E5	296	289
Offutt, Rezin, of Fairfax Co. VA	Mortgage to	Threlkeld, John	1808	U20	173	097
Offutt, Thomas, Montg. Co. et al	Deed to	Holmead, John	1810	Y24	180	165
Ogdon, David, of G'tn.	Deed to	Thomas, John, 3rd, trustee	1811	AA26	269	182
Ogeir, Thomas, of Charleston SC	Deed fr	Hamilton, Paul, of SC	1811	Z25	431	339
Ogle, Benjamin	Deed fr	Brookes, Joseph	1802	I9	260	420
Ogle, Benjamin	Deed to	Wiley, Daniel	1802	I9	339	558
Ogle, Benjamin, Frederick Town	Deed to	Chandler, Walter Story, of G'tn.	1795	B2A	185	251

Party	What	Party	Year	Liber	Old	New
Oglevie, David	Deed fr	Rutherford, Andrew & A. Reid	1800	E5	089	076
Okely, John, of G'tn.	B. of S. to	Webster, John A., of Balto.	1817	AN38	195	141
Oliver, Benjamin, Jr., Hanover VA	Deed fr	Turner, Thomas, of G'tn.	1804	K10	153	165
Oliver, Elizabeth et al	Release fr	English, David, cashier	1817	AO39	394	267
Oliver, Elizabeth et al	D. of T. to	English, David, cashier, of G'tn.	1817	AN38	352	259
Oliver, John, of Balto.	Release to	Barry, James D.	1811	AB27	475	388
Oliver, Robert, of Balto.	Deed fr	Law, Thomas	1807	T19	001	001
Oliver, Thomas (C), 12 FEB 1807	Marriage	Davis, Heney (C)	1808	V21	070	055
Olliver, Elizabeth	D. of T. fr	Henry, Robert J. et al	1808	U20	288	154
Olliver, John, of Balto.	Deed fr	Barry, James D.	1809	W22	091	066
Olliver, Thomas	Manumis to	Davidson, Henry	1808	V21	070	055
Orme, Archibald	Deed to	Orme, Thomas	1794	B2A	030	033
Orme, Archibald	Bond to	Hodges, Thomas	1808	U20	280	149
Orme, Archibald	B. of S. to	Johns, Aquila, of P.G. Co.	1811	AA26	200	136
Orme, James & Lucy	Deed to	Stoddert, Benjamin	1793	A1-2	463	70
Orme, James & Lucy	Deed to	Mason, John, of G'tn.	1794	B2A	057	072
Orme, James, of Montg. Co.	Deed to	Orme, Thomas, of Montg. Co.	1795	B2A	211	290
Orme, John	B. of S. to	Belt, Joseph Sprigg	1810	Y24	317	289
Orme, Lucy	Deed to	Peter, John	1794	A1-2	488	92
Orme, Lucy	Deed fr	Beall, Thomas, of George	1794	B2A	043	051
Orme, Moses, of A.A. Co.	D. of T. fr	Van Ness, John P. & Marcisa	1814	AG32	449	325
Orme, Nathan	B. of S. to	Clarke, Joseph & Robert	1808	T19	370	264
Orme, Nathan, of G'tn.	Deed fr	Cook, Charles	1801	G7	254	345
Orme, Nathaniel	Deed fr	Rinehart, Andrew	1802	H8	467	429
Orme, Nathaniel	Lease fr	Lanham, Elisha	1802	I9	428	709
Orme, Polly, Montg. Co. et al	Deed to	Reinhart, Andrew	1806	O14	088	055
Orme, Richard J., of Montg. Co.	Deed to	Hoye, John, of Montg. Co.	1811	AB27	433	356
Orme, Richard Johns, Dr.	Deed fr	Orme, Thomas, of Montg. Co.	1806	O14	237	156
Orme, Thomas	Lease fr	Belt, Joseph S.	1794	B2A	031	035
Orme, Thomas	Deed fr	Orme, Archibald	1794	B2A	030	033
Orme, Thomas	Deed fr	Deakins, William, Jr., of G'tn.	1795	B2A	210	289
Orme, Thomas	Deed fr	Hanson, Alexander Contee	1799	D4	394	375
Orme, Thomas	Deed to	Chandler, Walter Story	1801	G7	107	137
Orme, Thomas	Deed to	Wiley, David	1801	G7	043	055
Orme, Thomas	Deed to	Magruder, Ninian	1802	I9	202	316
Orme, Thomas	Deed fr	Davidson, John	1802	I9	203	317
Orme, Thomas	B. of S. to	Johns, Richard	1805	O14	087	054
Orme, Thomas, of Montg. Co.	Deed fr	Faw, Abraham, Montgomery Co.	1795	B2A	212	292
Orme, Thomas, of Montg. Co.	Deed fr	Orme, James, Montgomery Co.	1795	B2A	211	290
Orme, Thomas, of Montg. Co.	Deed fr	Troutman, Michael, Bullett Co. KY	1798	C3	496	390
Orme, Thomas, of Montg. Co.	Deed fr	Davidson, John, of Annapolis	1798	C3	438	344
Orme, Thomas, of G'tn.	Deed to	Corcoran, Thomas, of G'tn.	1800	E5	244	238
Orme, Thomas, of MD	Deed to	Kaldenbach, Andrew, of G'tn.	1802	H8	264	250
Orme, Thomas, of MD	Deed to	Magruder, Ninian, of G'tn.	1802	I9	087	124
Orme, Thomas, of Montg. Co.	Deed to	Orme, Richard Johns, Dr.	1806	O14	237	156
Ormsby, Robert	Deed to	Glover, Charles, trustee	1815	AH33	537	459
Orr, Benjamin G.	Mortgage fr	Lovell, William	1802	H8	295	279
Orr, Benjamin G. et al	Deed to	Van Ness, John P.	1802	I9	326	536
Orr, Benjamin G.	Deed to	Lovell, William	1802	I9	423	701
Orr, Benjamin G.	Deed fr	Lovell, William	1802	I9	408	677
Orr, Benjamin G. et al	Deed fr	Beale, Thomas K.	1802	I9	145	219
Orr, Benjamin G.	Release to	Lovell, William	1802	I9	224	356
Orr, Benjamin G., of Montg. Co.	Deed to	Miller, William	1804	K10	122	131
Orr, Benjamin G.	Deed fr	Law, John	1812	AD29	011	008
Orr, Benjamin G.	Deed to	Law, John	1813	AE30	223	179

Index to District of Columbia Land Records, 1792-1817

Party	What	Party	Year	Liber	Old	New
Orr, Benjamin G.	B. of S. to	McCormick, Alexander	1813	AE30	252	197
Orr, Benjamin G.	Deed fr	Underwood, Thomas & John, PA	1817	AN38	219	160
Orr, Benjamin Grayson, of Montg.	B. of S. to	Hagner, Peter	1807	S18	410	327
Orr, Benjamin Grayson	Deed fr	Slater, Henry & David H.	1816	AL36	310	305
Orr, Benjamin Grayson	Deed fr	Tingey, Thomas	1816	AL36	300	297
Orr, Benjamin Grayson	Deed fr	Slater, Henry, of TN	1816	AL36	311	307
Orr, Benjamin Grayson	Deed fr	Slater, Henry et al	1817	AN38	198	144
Orr, Benjamin Grayson	Deed fr	Eliot, Samuel, Jr.	1817	AO39	073	060
Orr, Benjamin Grayson	B. of S. fr	Heronimus, Pendleton	1817	AO39	338	241
Orr, Benjamin Grayson	D. of T. to	Eliot, Samuel, Jr.	1817	AO39	400	272
Orr, John	Deed fr	Corporation of Washington	1815	AK35	338	268
Osborn, Archibald	Deed to	Longley, Walter G.	1802	H8	358	334
Osborn, Archibald	Deed to	Worthington, Charles	1810	Z25	358	280
Osborn, Catharine	B. of S. to	Gray, Nathan	1813	AE30	102	078
Osborn, Joshua, of P.G. Co.	B. of S. fr	Stallings, James	1814	AH33	028	025
Osborne, Mary W. [Osbourne]	B. of S. fr	Osborne, Stephen	1806	P15	066	040
Osborne, Stephen	B. of S. to	Osborne, Mary W.	1806	P15	066	040
Osbourn, James, of Balto.	Deed fr	Meigs, Return J., Jr., postmaster	1817	AO39	313	223
Osburn, Archibald	Deed to	Worthington, Charles	1807	S18	380	302
Osburn, Archibald	Deed fr	Holmead, Anthony	1807	T19	016	013
Osterday, Christian, Jr. & Jacob	Deed to	Osterday, Daniel	1806	P15	310	204
Osterday, Daniel	Deed fr	Osterday, Christian, Jr. & Jacob	1806	P15	310	204
Oswald, John H., of Phila. PA	Deed fr	Kerr, Alexander, of Alexa.	1800	E5	234	227
Otis, Samuel Allyne, of Phila. PA	Deed fr	Walker, George	1801	G7	018	023
Ott, Adam	Deed to	Vermonnet, John	1794	A1-2	473	78
Ott, Adam, of Wash. Co. MD	Deed to	Beall, Thomas & John M. Gantt	1792	A1-1	131	190
Ott, David	Qualify	Militia officer	1812	AD29	174	140
Ott, David	Deed to	Pairo, Thomas W.	1813	AF31	161	109
Ott, David	Deed fr	Whetcroft, Henry & Sarah	1813	AF31	159	107
Ott, David	Deed fr	Whetcroft, Henry & Sarah	1813	AE30	112	086
Ott, David	Mortgage fr	Ewell, Thomas	1814	AH33	134	127
Ott, David	Deed fr	Law, Thomas	1815	AH33	464	396
Ott, David	Deed fr	Munroe, Thomas & Frances	1815	AI34	194	223
Ott, David	D. of T. fr	Clarke, Isaac	1815	AH33	498	427
Ott, David	Deed to	Mauro, Philip	1816	AM37	146	113
Ott, David	Deed fr	Ewell, Thomas	1817	AN38	453	326
Ott, David	Deed fr	Murdock, John, of G'tn.	1817	AO39	064	052
Ott, David	D. of T. fr	Kleiber, George	1817	AO39	300	214
Ott, David	Deed fr	Dorsey, William H., of Montg. Co.	1817	AO39	061	051
Ott, David & Charles Glover	Deed fr	Hyatt, Seth & Jane Summerville	1816	AL36	163	163
Ott, David & Thomas Coote	Assign fr	Collet, Ann, of Paterson NJ	1817	AO39	305	217
Ott, David & Thomas Coote	Convey fr	Law, Thomas	1817	AO39	303	216
Ott, David et al	Deed fr	Jackson, John G., fr. Harrison Co.	1814	AG32	295	215
Ott, David et al	Deed to	Thompson, Julia [Kaine]	1816	AL36	523	489
Ott, David et al	Deed fr	Herford, Henry	1816	AL36	450	426
Ott, David et al	Deed fr	Herford, Henry	1816	AL36	445	423
Ott, David et al	D. of T. fr	Herford, Henry	1816	AM37	138	107
Ott, John	B. of S. fr	Schnively, Henry	1806	P15	183	122
Ott, John	Deed fr	Schnively, Henry	1806	P15	184	123
Ott, John	Deed to	Shaw, John & James Birth	1807	R17	058	046
Ott, John	Deed fr	Doll, Conrad	1809	W22	265	177
Ott, John	Qualify	Justice of the Peace	1812	AD29	462	389
Ott, John	Mortgage fr	Gannon, James	1812	AD29	492	416
Ott, John	Deed fr	Baltzer, George	1813	AE30	534	396
Ott, John	D. of T. fr	Holmead, John	1814	AH33	289	251

Index to District of Columbia Land Records, 1792-1817

Party	What	Party	Year	Liber	Old	New
Ott, John	Deed fr	Wineberg, Jacob, of G'tn.	1815	AI34	155	177
Ott, John	Deed fr	Dulany, Michael	1815	AI34	154	176
Ott, John	Deed fr	Schwarz, Conrad, of Balto.	1815	AI34	152	174
Ott, John	D. of T. fr	Bridge, John, of G'tn.	1815	AI34	259	292
Ott, John	Cert Free to	Smith, William (M), age 23	1816	AK35	172	133
Ott, John	Deed fr	Beatty, Violletta, wid/o Dr. John	1816	AL36	418	400
Ott, John	Deed fr	Kennedy, James	1816	AL36	289	287
Ott, John	Deed fr	Chandler, Walter Story	1816	AM37	133	104
Ott, John	Deed fr	Chandler, Walter S.	1816	AM37	130	101
Ott, John	D. of T. fr	Beatty, Charles A., Dr., of G'tn.	1817	AN38	525	380
Ott, John	Deed fr	Gannon, James	1817	AN38	379	281
Ott, John	Deed fr	Balch, Stephen B.	1817	AN38	511	370
Ott, John	Release to	Gannon, James	1817	AN38	516	374
Ott, John	D. of T. fr	Gannon, James	1817	AO39	501	344
Ott, John	Deed fr	Whann, William	1817	AO39	452	310
Ott, John & James Gannon	B. of S. fr	McMurray, Joseph	1810	Y24	537	471
Ott, John & James Gannon	Assign fr	McMurray, Joseph	1810	Z25	241	188
Ott, John & Thomas C. Wright	Mortgage fr	Pic, Francis	1812	AD29	258	214
Ott, John & James Gannon, G'tn.	Assign to	Ritchie, Abner	1815	AI34	101	115
Ott, John, Dr.	Deed fr	Beatty, Charles, heirs of	1806	O14	180	118
Ott, John, Dr., Gent.	Deed fr	Bohrer, George	1807	S18	136	110
Ott, John, Dr., of G'tn.	Deed fr	Bayley, Robert, s/o William	1808	T19	172	123
Ott, John, Dr.	Deed to	Winebergh, Jacob	1808	U20	285	152
Ott, John, Dr., of G'tn.	Deed fr	Bayley, William, Jr., of Balto.	1808	T19	173	122
Ott, John, Dr.	Deed fr	Bayley, William, Sr.	1808	T19	170	120
Ott, John, Dr.	Deed fr	Ritchie, Abner	1810	Z25	142	113
Ott, John, Dr.	Deed fr	Crown, Samuel T.	1810	Z25	138	109
Ott, John, Dr.	Deed fr	Wright, Thomas C., of G'tn.	1810	Z25	139	110
Ott, John, Dr., of G'tn.	Deed fr	Patterson, Edgar, of G'tn.	1815	AK35	333	264
Ott, John, Dr.	Deed fr	Gannon, James, of G'tn.	1815	AI34	540	544
Ott, John, Dr., of G'tn.	Assign fr	Ritchie, Abner, of G'tn.	1817	AN38	102	077
Ott, John et al	Deed fr	Beatty, Charles, heirs of	1807	Q16	383	294
Ott, John, Gen. et al	Deed to	Ober, Robert, mer.	1807	S18	129	105
Ott, John, Gent. et al	Deed to	Bohrer, George	1807	S18	134	109
Ott, John, Gent. et al	Deed to	King, George, mer.	1807	S18	131	107
Ott, John, Gent. et al	Deed to	Ritchie, Abner	1807	S18	132	108
Ott, John, of G'tn.	Deed fr	Brent, Daniel Carroll, marshal	1804	L11	057	58
Ott, John, of G'tn.	B. of S. fr	Foxall, Henry, of G'tn.	1810	X23	406	328
Ott, John, of G'tn.	B. of S. fr	Stewart, William, of G'tn.	1810	Z25	132	103
Ott, John, of G'tn.	D. of T. fr	Clark, Francis	1811	AA26	172	118
Ott, John, of G'tn.	Deed to	Glover, Charles	1812	AD29	220	181
Ott, John, of G'tn.	D. of T. fr	Baltzer, George, of G'tn.	1813	AE30	532	394
Ott, John, of G'tn., trustee	Deed to	Wright, Thomas C.	1813	AE30	177	141
Ott, John, of G'tn.	Deed fr	Mauro, P., of Balto.	1814	AG32	341	247
Ott, John, of G'tn.	D. of T. fr	Milligan, Joseph, of G'tn.	1814	AH33	313	270
Ott, John, of G'tn.	D. of T. fr	Wright, Thomas C., of G'tn.	1814	AH33	310	268
Ott, John, of G'tn.	D. of T. fr	Mauro, P., of Balto.	1814	AH33	049	044
Ott, John, of G'tn.	D. of T. fr	Ober, Robert, of G'tn.	1814	AG32	368	267
Ott, John, of G'tn. et al	Deed to	Riley, William	1815	AI34	012	013
Ott, John, of G'tn.	Release to	Mauro, Philip, of Balto.	1815	AI34	007	007
Ott, John, of G'tn.	D. of T. fr	French, Robert, of G'tn.	1815	AI34	261	294
Ott, John, of G'tn.	D. of T. fr	Scott, Jesse, of G'tn.	1815	AI34	149	171
Ott, John, of G'tn.	Deed fr	Law, Thomas	1815	AH33	466	398
Ott, John, of G'tn.	D. of T. fr	Ewell, Thomas, of G'tn.	1815	AK35	298	238
Ott, John, of G'tn.	D. of T. fr	Magruder, James A., of G'tn.	1815	AK35	304	243

Index to District of Columbia Land Records, 1792-1817

Party	What	Party	Year	Liber	Old	New
Ott, John, of G'tn.	Deed to	Roy, James H., of Richmond VA	1816	AM37	430	308
Ott, John, of G'tn.	Plat	Penna. Ave., D and 13th streets	1816	AM37		310
Ott, John, of G'tn.	D. of T. fr	Kirk, Miletius Thomas, of G'tn.	1816	AM37	264	194
Ott, John, of G'tn.	D. of T. fr	Joncherez, Alexander L., of G'tn.	1816	AL36	196	203
Ott, John, of G'tn.	D. of T. fr	Ewell, Thomas, of G'tn.	1817	AN38	104	078
Ott, John, of G'tn.	Deed to	Whann, William, of G'tn.	1817	AN38	196	142
Ott, John, plt.	Suit	Scott, Sabret, def.	1816	AK35	487	383
Ott, John, trustee, of G'tn.	Deed to	Gardner, William P.	1812	AD29	273	225
Ott, John, trustee, of G'tn.	Deed to	Walker, Zachariah	1812	AD29	221	182
Otterback, Philip	Deed fr	Prout, William	1813	AF31	336	239
Otterback, Phillip	Deed fr	Prout, William	1817	AN38	275	200
Ould, Robert	Deed fr	Smith, Anthony	1816	AL36	260	261
Overton, Caleb (C)	Birth	July 14, 1750	1814	AH33	233	204
Overton, Caleb (C)	Marriage	Gates, Margaret, of Charles Co.	1814	AH33	233	204
Overton, Caleb (C), s/o Caleb	Birth	September 1, 1790	1814	AH33	233	204
Overton, John (C), s/o Caleb	Birth	February 25, 1792	1814	AH33	233	204
Overton, Margaret (C), d/o Caleb	Birth	May 13, 1796	1814	AH33	233	204
Overton, Mary Magdalene (C)	Birth	July 28, 1788	1814	AH33	233	204
Overton, Patrick (C), s/o Caleb	Birth	May 12, 1798	1814	AH33	233	204
Overton, Richard (C), s/o Caleb	Birth	January 23, 1800	1814	AH33	233	204
Overton, Samuel (C), s/o Caleb	Birth	July 6, 1786	1814	AH33	233	204
Overton, Susan (C), d/o Caleb	Birth	January 23, 1803	1814	AH33	233	204
Ovington, Caleb	Cert Free		1810	Z25	115	089
Owen, Benjamin	Deed fr	King, Timothy	1815	AH33	538	460
Owen, Benjamin	Deed to	King, Timothy	1815	AH33	505	433
Owen, Isaac, of G'tn.	Deed fr	Chandler, Walter S., of G'tn.	1805	M12	254	255
Owen, Robert	Deed fr	Commissioners of Washington	1802	H8	127	124
Owens, Barak	Deed fr	Holmead, John	1809	X23	157	115
Owens, Barrach & J. Thompson	D. of T. fr	Curran, Eleanor, of G'tn.	1812	AD29	253	209
Owens, Barrak, of G'tn.	Deed to	Davis, Edward	1816	AL36	247	250
Owens, Benjamin & Joseph Dove	Mortgage to	Brown, John, of Balto.	1808	V21	063	050
Owens, Charity	B. of S. to	Shaw, Joseph	1813	AF31	402	391
Owens, Isaac	Deed fr	Weatherall, John	1806	O14	340	227
Owens, Isaac	Deed to	Foxall, Henry	1812	AC28	413	299
Owens, Isaac	Deed fr	Speake, Josias M.	1817	AN38	216	158
Owens, Isaac et al	Deed fr	Holmead, Anthony	1800	E5	238	232
Owens, Isaac et al	D. of T. fr	Foxall, Henry	1816	AL36	357	348
Owens, Isaac, of G'tn.	Deed fr	Walker, Nathan, of G'tn.	1797	C3	183	155
Owens, Isaac, of G'tn.	Deed fr	Parrott, Richard, of Kent Co.	1798	D4	042	035
Owens, Isaac, of G'tn.	Deed fr	Parrott, Richard, of Kent Co.	1799	D4	180	160
Owens, Isaac, of G'tn.	Deed fr	Weatherall, John & D. Ferguson	1807	R17	344	262
Owens, Isaac, of G'tn.	Manumis to	[ ], Rachel (negro)	1808	T19	295	216
Owens, Isaac, of G'tn.	Deed fr	Mackall, Leonard, of G'tn.	1808	T19	296	217
Owens, Isaac, of G'tn.	Deed fr	Speake, Josias M. & Sarah	1808	T19	302	221
Owens, Isaac, of G'tn.	Deed to	Patterson, Edgar, of G'tn.	1809	V21	209	148
Owens, Isaac, of G'tn.	Deed to	Maul, John P.	1815	AK35	175	135
Owens, Isaac, of G'tn.	Deed fr	Corcoran, Thomas, of G'tn.	1816	AL36	174	175
Owens, Isaac, trustee et al	Deed fr	Morgan, William, of G'tn.	1814	AH33	010	009
Owens, Josiah	Deed to	Stone, Zephaniah, of P.G. Co.	1807	R17	172	132
Owings, Beale & Elenora B. et al	Deed to	Crawford, William, of G'tn.	1815	AI34	141	161
Owings, Beale & Eleanor B. et al	Deed to	Lutz, John, of G'tn.	1815	AI34	372	400
Owings, Beale & Eleonora B. et al	Deed to	Key, Philip B.	1815	AI34	264	299
Owings, Christopher	Slaves		1804	K10	315	
Owings, Christopher, of G'tn.	Assign fr	Walker, Nathan, of P.G. Co.	1804	L11	004	4
Owings, Christopher, of G'tn.	Deed to	Beall, Samuel, of G'tn.	1805	N13	385	308

Party	What	Party	Year	Liber	Old	New
Owings, Isaac	Deed fr	Williams, William, of G.B., s/o S.	1805	N13	128	122
Owings, Isaac et al	Deed fr	Eliason, Ebenezer & Ann	1809	V21	290	210
Owings, Isaac, of G'tn.	Deed fr	Williams, John S., of G'tn.	1816	AL36	462	436
Owner, Hannah	B. of S. fr	Picknoll, Richard H.	1810	Z25	008	006
Owner, James	Deed to	Glascow, John	1812	AD29	424	357
Owner, James	Deed fr	Glascow, John & Rachel	1812	AD29	457	385
Owner, James	Release fr	Glasco, John	1814	AH33	169	157
Owner, James [Onnar]	Mortgage fr	Glascoe, John	1810	Y24	453	402
Ownings, Patrick, of Balto.	Deed fr	Hearn, William, of G'tn.	1804	K10	401	415

Index to District of Columbia Land Records, 1792-1817

Party	What	Party	Year	Liber	Old	New
P						
Pairo, Loveday	Deed fr	Holmead, John et al	1807	R17	216	162
Pairo, Loveday	Convey fr	Holmead, John	1809	V21	394	298
Pairo, Loveday	Deed fr	Holmead, John	1813	AE30	135	105
Pairo, Loveday, form. Buchanan	Deed fr	Holmead, John	1813	AF31	163	110
Pairo, Thomas W.	Deed fr	Mechlin, Joseph	1805	N13	139	132
Pairo, Thomas W. & Loveday	Manumis to	[ ], Dianna (Negro)	1806	P15	388	259
Pairo, Thomas W.	B. of S. to	Burnes, Thomas	1806	O14	277	183
Pairo, Thomas W.	Deed to	Holmead, John	1807	R17	175	134
Pairo, Thomas W.	Deed fr	Holmead, John	1807	R17	002	002
Pairo, Thomas W. & Loveday et al	Deed to	Speake, Sarah, w/o Josias M.	1807	R17	013	012
Pairo, Thomas W.	Deed fr	Van Ness, John P. & Marcia	1809	X23	185	138
Pairo, Thomas W. & Loveday	Deed to	Nourse, Michael	1809	W22	013	011
Pairo, Thomas W.	Deed fr	Thornton, William & Ann Calvert	1809	X23	187	140
Pairo, Thomas W.	Manumis to	[ ], Rezin (negro)	1810	X23	408	329
Pairo, Thomas W.	Deed fr	Van Ness, John P. & Marcia	1810	Y24	363	228
Pairo, Thomas W.	Deed fr	Thornton, William	1810	Y24	362	327
Pairo, Thomas W.	Deed fr	Stoddert, Benjamin	1810	Y24	455	404
Pairo, Thomas W. & Loveday	Deed to	King, Vincent, of G'tn.	1813	AE30	455	339
Pairo, Thomas W. & Loveday	Deed to	Patterson, Edgar, of G'tn.	1813	AF31	331	236
Pairo, Thomas W.	Deed fr	Ott, David	1813	AF31	161	109
Pairo, Thomas W.	Deed to	Barry, Richard	1813	AE30	287	219
Pairo, Thomas W.	Deed fr	Barry, Richard	1813	AE30	343	256
Pairo, Thomas W.	Assign fr	Webster, Toppan	1814	AG32	082	062
Pairo, Thomas W.	Deed fr	Brashears, Richard B.	1815	AH33	480	410
Pairo, Thomas W. & Loveday	Deed to	Magruder, James A., of G'tn.	1816	AM37	105	084
Pairo, Thomas W.	Lease to	Lancaster, Stephen	1816	AL36	547	510
Pairo, Thomas W.	Deed fr	Walker, Joseph	1817	AN38	362	267
Pairo, Thomas William, of G'tn.	Deed fr	Stoddert, Benjamin, of G'tn.	1804	K10	173	182
Pairo, Thomas William	Deed fr	Buchanan, Loveday	1805	M12	299	301
Paleske, Charles G., of Phila. et al	Deed fr	Fitzsimmons, Thomas, Phila. et al	1805	N13	021	023
Palmer, Eliakum	Deed fr	Smith, Walter, of G'tn., trustee	1815	AH33	486	416
Palmer, Jesse C.	Deed fr	Edelin, Ignatius	1808	T19	134	095
Palmer, Jesse C. et al	Deed to	Meade, Simon	1808	U20	112	063
Palmer, Jesse C.	Deed fr	Edelin, Ignatius	1808	T19	136	095
Palmer, Jesse C., insolvent	Deed to	Wood, William, trustee	1811	AA26	268	182
Paradise, Sarah Ann, d/o Wm.	Convey fr	Paradise, William, of G'tn.	1816	AL36	099	100
Paradise, William, of G'tn.	Convey to	Paradise, Sarah Ann	1816	AL36	099	100
Parburt, George [Parvert]	B. of S. to	Bussard, Daniel	1812	AD29	035	025
Parke, Thomas, of Phila.	Deed fr	Key, Philip B., of Montg. Co.	1812	AB27	550	449
Parker, Eleanor P.	Cert Free to	Butler, Abraham	1817	AO39	319	227
Parker, Fielder	Deed fr	Ingram, Alexander, chairmaker	1806	Q16	234	161
Parker, Fielder	Deed fr	Cochrane, Alexander, Jr.	1807	S18	411	328
Parker, Fielder	B. of S. fr	Thompson, William	1809	W22	409	266
Parker, Fielder	Lease to	Craycroft, Thomas	1812	AC28	172	129
Parker, Fielder	Deed to	Parker, F., Sr. & Jos. Johnson	1812	AC28	125	094
Parker, Fielder & Lawson Clarke	B. of S. to	Howe, Ignatius	1811	AB27	497	406
Parker, Fielder, Sr.	Assign to	Johnson, Joseph	1812	AD29	015	011
Parker, Fielder, Sr. et al	Deed fr	Parker, Fielder	1812	AC28	125	094
Parker, George, trustee	Deed to	Beall, Gustavus, of G'tn.	1816	AL36	212	219
Parkinson, Edward, of MD	Deed to	Bussard, Daniel	1806	Q16	090	058
Parnum, Benjamin (C), age 24	Cert Free fr	Hewitt, William, register	1816	AL36	044	045
Parritt, Richard et al	Deed fr	Eliason, Ebenezer & Ann	1809	V21	290	210
Parrott, Richard	Deed fr	Beall, Thomas B.	1802	I9	356	588
Parrott, Richard	Deed to	Lingan, James M. et al	1804	K10	369	382

Party	What	Party	Year	Liber	Old	New
Parrott, Richard	Deed fr	Beall, Thomas, of George	1804	L11	052	53
Parrott, Richard	Deed to	Mackall, Leonard	1804	K10	260	266
Parrott, Richard	Deed fr	Lingan, James M. et al	1805	N13	218	187
Parrott, Richard	Mortgage to	Dorsey, William H.	1805	N13	074	067
Parrott, Richard	Deed to	Smith, Clement	1805	N13	070	063
Parrott, Richard	Deed fr	Dorsey, William H.	1807	R17	135	104
Parrott, Richard	Deed fr	Van Ness, John P.	1807	S18	089	073
Parrott, Richard	Cert Free to	Carter, Stacy	1807	S18	066	
Parrott, Richard	Deed fr	Beatty, John M. & Charles A.	1808	U20	018	011
Parrott, Richard	Deed fr	Dorsey, William H., of Balto.	1808	T19	232	170
Parrott, Richard	Deed fr	Reintzel, Anthony	1808	T19	162	115
Parrott, Richard	Deed fr	Caldwell, Elias B., exr.	1809	V21	251	179
Parrott, Richard	Deed to	Corcoran, Thomas, Esq.	1810	Y24	522	459
Parrott, Richard	Deed to	Beall, Thomas, of George	1810	Y24	188	173
Parrott, Richard	Deed fr	Banning, Anthony	1810	Y24	281	257
Parrott, Richard	Deed fr	Whann, William	1810	Y24	548	481
Parrott, Richard	Deed fr	Ritchie, Abner	1810	Y24	282	258
Parrott, Richard	Deed to	Maffitt, Sarah	1810	Z25	004	003
Parrott, Richard	Deed to	Wineberger, George	1810	Z25	266	208
Parrott, Richard	Mortgage to	Foxall, Henry	1812	AC28	411	298
Parrott, Richard	Deed fr	Foxall, Henry	1812	AC28	407	295
Parrott, Richard	Deed to	Foxall, Henry	1812	AC28	416	301
Parrott, Richard	Deed fr	Beall, Thomas, of Geo.	1813	AE30	085	065
Parrott, Richard	Mortgage to	Foxall, Henry	1814	AH33	188	172
Parrott, Richard	Deed to	Mackall, Leonard	1815	AI34	404	427
Parrott, Richard	Deed fr	Reintzel, Anthony	1816	AK35	231	182
Parrott, Richard	Deed to	Kurtz, Daniel	1816	AM37	270	198
Parrott, Richard	Deed to	Thorpe, Thomas	1816	AM37	276	202
Parrott, Richard	Deed fr	Varnum, James M.	1816	AK35	525	414
Parrott, Richard	Deed to	Mackall, Leonard	1817	AN38	167	122
Parrott, Richard	Deed to	Pickrell, John	1817	AN38	098	075
Parrott, Richard	D. of T. to	Kurtz, Daniel	1817	AN38	405	303
Parrott, Richard & John Mountz	D. of T. fr	Adams, Thomas	1809	W22	001	001
Parrott, Richard & Jno. Mountz, Jr.	Deed to	Foxall, Henry	1812	AD29	143	111
Parrott, Richard et al	Deed fr	Holmead, Anthony	1800	E5	238	232
Parrott, Richard et al	Deed to	Hofman, Richad	1802	I9	374	620
Parrott, Richard, Gent.	Deed fr	Ritchie, Abner	1808	T19	065	047
Parrott, Richard, of Montg. Co.	Deed fr	Davidson, Samuel, of Montg. Co.	1797	C3	093	77
Parrott, Richard, of Balto.	Deed to	Hollingshead, James, Calvert Co.	1798	C3	291	236
Parrott, Richard, of Balto.	Deed to	Barry, John, of Montg. Co.	1798	C3	293	237
Parrott, Richard, of Balto.	Deed to	Berry, John Wilkes, of Montg. Co.	1798	C3	418	330
Parrott, Richard, of Balto.	Deed to	Banning, Anthony, of Talbot Co.	1798	C3	289	234
Parrott, Richard, of Kent Co.	Deed fr	Gannon, James, of G'tn.	1798	D4	040	033
Parrott, Richard, of Kent Co.	Deed to	Owens, Isaac, of G'tn.	1798	D4	042	035
Parrott, Richard, of Kent Co.	Deed to	Owens, Isaac, of G'tn.	1799	D4	180	160
Parrott, Richard, of G'tn.	Deed fr	Gannon, James, of G'tn.	1801	G7	375	507
Parrott, Richard, of G'tn.	Deed fr	Reintzel, Anthony, of G'tn.	1811	AA26	064	047
Parrott, Richard, of G'tn.	Deed to	Foxall, Henry, of G'tn.	1813	AE30	143	111
Parrott, Richard, of G'tn.	Deed fr	Forrest, Richard & Chas. Glover	1813	AF31	378	272
Parrott, Richard, of G'tn.	Deed to	Eliason, Ebenezer & B. Hersey	1814	AG32	380	240
Parrott, Richard, of G'tn.	Deed to	Nevitt, William, of P.G. Co.	1814	AG32	150	108
Parrott, Richard, of G'tn.	Deed to	Pickrell, John, of G'tn.	1814	AG32	039	031
Parrott, Richard, of G'tn.	Deed fr	Mackall, Benjamin F., of G'tn.	1816	AM37	441	316
Parrott, Richard, trustee	B. of S. fr	English, Joseph, insolvent	1805	M12	106	099
Parry, Edward, Portsmouth NH	Deed fr	Cutter, Nathaniel, Portsmouth NH	1806	P15	384	256

Index to District of Columbia Land Records, 1792-1817

Party	What	Party	Year	Liber	Old	New
Parry, Stephen	Deed fr	Prout, William	1802	I9	367	607
Parry, Stephen	Lease fr	Prout, William	1803	K10	097	104
Parry, Stephen	B. of S. to	Prout, William	1809	W22	351	227
Parry, Stephen	B. of S. to	Brashears, John W. et al	1814	AG32	305	222
Parsons, Barney	Deed fr	Prout, William	1800	F6	101	062
Parsons, Barney & Samuel Bond	Deed to	Mahony, Barney, of P.G. Co.	1812	AC28	501	357
Parsons, Bernard	Lease fr	Dunlap, James et al	1806	O14	370	246
Parsons, James	Qualify	Militia officer	1812	AD29	361	304
Parsons, Joseph B.	Lease fr	Prout, William	1807	R17	120	093
Parsons, Joseph B.	Deed to	Boyd, Washington et al	1807	R17	123	095
Parsons, Joseph Baker	Deed fr	Queen, Nicholas L. et al	1808	T19	023	018
Parsons, William	Deed fr	Prout, William	1805	N13	121	116
Parsons, William	Deed fr	Boyd, Washington, marshal	1813	AE30	415	306
Patison, Mary, of Dorchester Co.	Deed to	Breckenridge, James, Gen., of VA	1816	AL36	377	366
Patterson, Benjamin	Qualify		1802	I9	464	765
Patterson, Benjamin	Deed fr	Beall, Thomas B., trustee	1805	O14	142	092
Patterson, Benjamin, of G'tn.	Lease fr	Lufborough, Nathan, of G'tn.	1804	K10	386	401
Patterson, Benjamin, of G'tn.	B. of S. to	Bootes, Samuel, innkeeper, G'tn.	1806	O14	248	163
Patterson, Benjamin, of G'tn.	Deed to	Lufborough, Nathan, of G'tn.	1808	U20	295	157
Patterson, Capt.	Convey to	O'Reilly, Henry	1808	V21	045	034
Patterson, Charles M.	Mortgage fr	Patterson, William	1817	AN38	066	052
Patterson, Edgar	Qualify		1802	I9	465	766
Patterson, Edgar	Deed fr	Holmead, John	1805	N13	190	168
Patterson, Edgar	Deed fr	Beatty, John M. et al	1805	N13	249	208
Patterson, Edgar	Deed fr	Caldwell, Elias B., trustee	1806	P15	402	270
Patterson, Edgar	Deed fr	Holmead, John	1806	Q16	001	001
Patterson, Edgar	Deed fr	Hardy, William	1807	R17	214	160
Patterson, Edgar	Deed fr	Brent, William, trustee	1808	V21	045	034
Patterson, Edgar	Deed fr	Holmead, John	1809	X23	053	040
Patterson, Edgar	Deed fr	Scott, Margaret, of Fairfax Co. VA	1809	V21	374	277
Patterson, Edgar	Release fr	Joncherez, Alexander L.	1810	Z25	312	244
Patterson, Edgar	Release fr	Joncherez, Alexander L.	1811	AB27	057	048
Patterson, Edgar	Deed fr	Dunlap, Henry	1813	AE30	081	061
Patterson, Edgar et al	Deed to	Scholfield, Joseph L.	1810	Y24	073	065
Patterson, Edgar et al	Deed to	Clark, Francis	1810	Y24	374	338
Patterson, Edgar et al	Deed to	Donohoo, Patrick	1810	Y24	062	055
Patterson, Edgar, of G'tn.	Deed fr	O'Riely, Thomas, of Alexa. Co.	1807	R17	043	035
Patterson, Edgar, of G'tn.	Deed fr	Knowles, Henry, of G'tn.	1808	T19	250	184
Patterson, Edgar, of G'tn.	Deed to	Herstons, Charles, of G'tn.	1808	V21	058	046
Patterson, Edgar, of G'tn.	Deed fr	Peter, John, of G'tn.	1809	V21	207	146
Patterson, Edgar, of G'tn.	Deed fr	Suter, Alexander, of G'tn.	1809	V21	205	144
Patterson, Edgar, of G'tn.	Deed fr	Owens, Isaac, of G'tn.	1809	V21	209	148
Patterson, Edgar, of G'tn.	Deed fr	Balch, Stephen B., of G'tn.	1809	V21	211	149
Patterson, Edgar, of G'tn.	Deed to	Joncherez, Alexander L.	1810	Y24	148	134
Patterson, Edgar, of G'tn.	Deed to	Joncherez, Alexander L., of G'tn.	1810	Y24	471	417
Patterson, Edgar, of G'tn.	Mortgage fr	Thomas, John, 3rd & Thos. Leakin	1810	Z25	111	086
Patterson, Edgar, of G'tn.	Deed to	Davidson, James	1810	Z25	250	196
Patterson, Edgar, of G'tn.	Deed to	Williams, Elie et al	1811	AC28	093	070
Patterson, Edgar, of G'tn.	Release fr	Joncherez, Alexander L., of G'tn.	1811	AB27	013	012
Patterson, Edgar, of G'tn.	Release fr	Davidson, James	1811	AC28	091	069
Patterson, Edgar, of G'tn.	Deed fr	Hoye, John & Leonard M. Deakins	1813	AF31	215	146
Patterson, Edgar, of G'tn.	Deed fr	Gaines, Richard, of Cincinnati OH	1813	AF31	332	237
Patterson, Edgar, of G'tn.	B. of S. fr	Crossfield, Ichiel	1813	AF31	164	111
Patterson, Edgar, of G'tn.	Deed fr	McCutchen, Thomas, of G'tn.	1813	AF31	385	277
Patterson, Edgar, of G'tn.	Deed fr	Pairo, Thomas W. & Loveday	1813	AF31	331	236

Index to District of Columbia Land Records, 1792-1817

Party	What	Party	Year	Liber	Old	New
Patterson, Edgar, of G'tn.	Deed fr	Herstons, Charles, of G'tn.	1813	AF31	213	145
Patterson, Edgar, of G'tn.	Deed fr	Glover, Charles, trustee	1814	AG32	148	106
Patterson, Edgar, of G'tn.	Deed to	Foxall, Henry, of G'tn.	1814	AG32	037	030
Patterson, Edgar, of G'tn.	Deed to	Foxall, Henry, of G'tn.	1814	AG32	036	028
Patterson, Edgar, of G'tn.	Deed to	Clagett, William, of G'tn.	1814	AG32	050	039
Patterson, Edgar, of G'tn.	Deed to	Crawford, William, of G'tn.	1814	AH33	082	074
Patterson, Edgar, of G'tn.	Deed to	Ott, John, Dr., of G'tn.	1815	AK35	333	264
Patterson, Edgar, of G'tn.	Deed fr	Renner, Daniel, of G'tn.	1816	AO39	055	045
Patterson, Edgar, of G'tn.	Deed fr	Corporation of Washington	1816	AL36	074	075
Patterson, Edgar, of G'tn.	Deed to	Kurtz, Daniel, of G'tn.	1817	AO39	189	139
Patterson, James	Deed fr	Elliot, Samuel et al	1802	H8	260	247
Patterson, James	Deed fr	May, Frederick	1802	H8	260	247
Patterson, James	Manumis to	[ ], Suck (negro)	1807	R17	125	097
Patterson, James	Deed fr	May, Frederick	1810	Y24	191	175
Patterson, James	Deed fr	Clarke, Eliz. & John McGowan	1813	AF31	376	270
Patterson, James	Deed to	Patterson, William	1817	AN38	057	047
Patterson, James	Assign fr	Blodget, R., wid/o Samuel	1817	AN38		049
Patterson, James et al	Deed fr	Eliason, Ebenezer & Ann	1809	V21	290	210
Patterson, James et al	B. of S. fr	Webster, Toppan	1814	AH33	130	123
Patterson, James et al	Deed fr	Webster, Toppan	1817	AO39	307	218
Patterson, Thomas, Dr.	Deed fr	Glover, Charles	1817	AN38	236	173
Patterson, Thomas, Dr.	Deed fr	Hildreth, Ezekiel	1817	AN38	237	174
Patterson, William	Deed fr	Patterson, James	1817	AN38	057	047
Patterson, William	Mortgage to	Patterson, Charles M.	1817	AN38	066	052
Patton, James & Mary Ann, Alexa.	Deed to	Sayre, Daniel, of Amelia Co. VA	1799	D4	212	195
Patton, James, exr., def.	Suit	Lawrason & Fowle, plt.	1810	Y24	006	
Patton, James, mer., of Alexa.	Deed to	Barry, James, of Balto.	1798	C3	448	352
Patton, James, of Alexa.	Deed fr	Hamilton, Alexander	1798	C3	345	277
Patton, James, of Alexa.	Deed to	Barry, James, of Balto.	1799	E5	043	033
Patton, James, of Alexa.	Deed to	Sayre, Daniel, of Amelia Co. VA	1799	D4	299	283
Patton, James, of Alexa.	Deed fr	Miller, James, of Glasgow, Scot.	1805	N13	363	292
Paul, Nicholas	Deed fr	Wilson, Levi G.	1816	AM37	144	111
Paul, Nicholas, Jr.	Deed fr	Ritchie, Abner	1809	V21	263	188
Paulding, John K.	Cert Free to	Lewis, Frederick	1817	AO39	228	165
Paxton, Samuel & Amos Cloud	Deed to	Way, Nicholas, of Wilmington DE	1793	A1-2	403	12
Payne, John	Deed to	McKeldon, William	1810	Y24	423	380
Payne, John, of Leesburg VA	Deed fr	Bain, Quinton, of G'tn.	1809	X23	102	074
Payne, Nathan, of Fayette Co. KY	Sale fr	Chapman, William, of G'tn.	1805	M12	295	
Payson, Henry, of Balto. Co. et al	Convey to	Glover, Charles	1816	AK35	324	258
Peacock, James Green	B. of S. fr	Smallwood, Walter B.	1804	L11	259	239
Peacock, Robert	D. of T. fr	King, Ezekiel, an insolvent	1803	K10	057	62
Peacock, Robert Green	Deed fr	Peacock, Robert Ware	1801	G7	167	222
Peacock, Robert Green	Bond fr	Peacock, Robet Ware	1801	G7	167	221
Peacock, Robert W.	Deed fr	Ellis, Robert	1802	I9	579	939
Peacock, Robert Ward, trustee	Deed fr	Wade, Robert P., an insolvent	1804	K10	176	184
Peacock, Robert Ware	Bond to	Peacock, Robert Green	1801	G7	167	221
Peacock, Robert Ware, attorney	Deed fr	Davidson, John	1801	G7	105	134
Peacock, Robert Ware	Deed to	Peacock, Robert Green	1801	G7	167	222
Peacock, Robert Ware	Agreement	Nevitt, Charles & Lavinah	1801	G7	124	160
Peacock, Robert Ware	Assign to	Fletcher, William	1801	G7	243	328
Peacock, Robert Ware	B. of S. to	Kearney, John	1802	H8	221	211
Peacock, Robert Ware	Mortgage to	Densley, Hugh	1802	H8	255	242
Peacock, Robert Ware	Mortgage to	English, Robert, of Winchester	1802	H8	506	466
Peacock, Robert Ware	Deed fr	Dowson, Joseph, an insolvent	1803	K10	096	102
Peacock, Robert Ware, attorney	B. of S. to	Boyd, Washington	1804	K10	142	154

Index to District of Columbia Land Records, 1792-1817

Party	What	Party	Year	Liber	Old	New
Peacock, Robert Ware, trustee	Deed fr	Shoemaker, Charles, insolvent	1804	K10	291	293
Peacock, Robert Ware	Deed fr	Dunlop, Henry	1804	K10	262	268
Peacock, Robert Ware	Deed fr	Thomson, George et al	1804	L11	012	12
Peacock, Robert Ware, trustee	Deed fr	Brown, George, insolvent	1804	L11	197	188
Peacock, Robert Ware	Deed to	Davidson, John	1804	L11	014	14
Peacock, Robert Ware	Agreement	Thomson, William	1804	L11	298	273
Peacock, Robert Ware	Mortgage to	Thornton, William	1804	L11	111	114
Peacock, Robert Ware, trustee	Deed fr	Sheperd, William, insolvent	1804	L11	401	355
Peacock, Robert Ware	Deed fr	Sheperd, Henry	1804	L11	298	274
Peacock, Robert Ware, trustee	Deed fr	Polk, Charles Peale, insolvent	1804	L11	343	311
Peacock, Robert Ware, trustee	Convey fr	Queen, Walter, insolvent	1804	M12	037	038
Peacock, Robert Ware et al	Release fr	Crow, John et al	1805	M12	209	210
Pearce, Catherine	Manumis to	Herbert, John (negro)	1805	N13	362	291
Pearce, Catherine, rel/o Benj. N.	Deed to	Forrest, Uriah & Benj. Stoddert	1792	A1-1	063	93
Pearce, G.	Receipt fr	Brewer, Joseph	1809	W22	184	128
Pearce, Ignatius & Robert Clarke	Deed fr	King, George	1810	Y24	109	099
Pearce, Isaac	Deed fr	Peter, John et al	1801	G7	143	189
Pearce, Isaac	Deed fr	Forrest, Uriah	1804	K10	315	321
Pearce, Isaac	Deed fr	Key, Philip Barton	1804	K10	313	320
Pearce, Isaac	Deed fr	Beatty, Charles A., Dr.	1810	X23	364	292
Pearce, Mathew et al	Deed to	Leamy, John, mer.	1808	T19	153	108
Pearce, Mathew, of Phila. PA et al	Deed to	Ludlow, Daniel, of NY	1807	Q16	217	148
Pearce, Mathew, of Phila. PA et al	Deed to	Crawford, James, younger, Phila.	1807	R17	062	050
Pearce, Matthew, of Phila. PA et al	Deed to	Crawford, James, younger, Phila.	1804	L11	131	133
Pearce, Matthew, of Phila. PA et al	Deed to	Crawford, James, younger, Phila.	1804	L11	135	137
Pearce, Matthew, of Phila. PA et al	Deed to	Read, William, mer., of Phila.	1805	M12	125	119
Pearce, Matthew, of Phila. PA et al	Deed to	Paleske, Charles G., Phila. et al	1805	N13	021	023
Pearce, Matthew, Phila. PA et al	Deed to	Read, William, mer., of Phila. PA	1809	V21	276	198
Pearce, Matthew, Phila. et al	Deed to	Hansenclever, Mary, wid., Phila.	1810	X23	305	244
Pearce, Thomas, Isle of Wight Co.	Deed fr	Stoddert, Benjamin, of G'tn.	1795	B2A	215	296
Pearce, Thomas, of G'tn.	Deed fr	James, James & Anne	1798	C3	348	280
Pearce, Thomas, of G'tn.	Mortgage to	James, James	1798	D4	043	036
Pearce, Thomas, of G'tn.	Deed to	Geary, Everard, of G'tn.	1800	F6	106	065
Pearce, Thomas, of G'tn.	Deed to	Leatherman, Henry, Frederick Co.	1805	N13	092	084
Pearcy, Mr.	Agreement	*James Knight & Co.*	1797	C3	065	53
Pearl, Daniel	Lease fr	Van Ness, John P. & Marcia	1817	AO39	269	193
Pearl, Daniel & Thomas Williams	D. of T. to	Mahorney, Charles	1817	AN38	220	161
Pearson, Joseph et al	Deed fr	Casanave, Ann	1817	AO39	079	064
Pearson, Lawson	B. of S. to	Alexander, Robert	1806	P15	307	202
Pearson, Lawson	Deed fr	Alexander, Robert, New Orleans	1811	AC28	103	077
Pearson, Lawson & Joseph Dove	Deed to	Brown, William	1801	G7	128	167
Pearson, Lawson, bricklayer	Mortgage to	Alexander, Robert	1806	O14	205	135
Peck, Joseph	Deed to	Chapman, Winifred	1808	U20	181	100
Peck, Joseph	B. of S. to	Walker, George & S. Tophouse	1808	U20	390	216
Peck, Joseph	Release fr	Walker, George & S. Tophouse	1814	AG32	125	092
Peck, Joseph, of Alexa.	Deed fr	Wright, John, of G'tn.	1797	C3	233	193
Peck, Joseph, of G'tn.	Deed fr	Peck, Winifred, of G'tn.	1810	Y24	155	141
Peck, Winifred, of G'tn.	Deed to	Peck, Joseph, of G'tn.	1810	Y24	155	141
Peckham, Caleb	Deed fr	King, Vincent	1816	AM37	088	071
Peckham, Caleb, of G'tn.	Deed fr	Beall, Thomas, of Geo., of G'tn.	1813	AE30	386	285
Peckham, Caleb, of G'tn.	Deed to	Mackey, William, of G'tn.	1816	AL36	414	396
Peckin, Christianna, of PA	Deed fr	Ingle, Henry	1802	H8	531	490
Peerce, Ignatius, of G'tn.	Deed to	Renner, Daniel, of G'tn.	1817	AO39	087	069
Peerce, Isaac	Deed fr	Beatty, John M. & Charles A.	1809	W22	410	266
Peerce, Isaac	Deed fr	Key, Philip B., of Montg. Co.	1812	AD29	507	427

Party	What	Party	Year	Liber	Old	New
Peerce, William, s/o Edw., of Balto.	Deed fr	Davidson, Samuel	1799	D4	266	250
Peirce, Isaac	Deed fr	Holmead, Anthony	1794	B2A	151	199
Peirce, Isaac	Deed fr	Deakins, William, Jr.	1794	B2A	156	206
Peirce, Thomas, of Smithfield VA	Cert fr	Commissioners of Washington	1792	B2A	285	399
Peltz, John	D. of T. to	Coombe, Griffith	1810	X23	337	269
Peltz, John	Mortgage to	Cloakey, Samuel	1811	AA26	270	184
Peltz, John	D. of T. to	O'Neale, William	1811	AC28	028	021
Peltz, John	Mortgage fr	Varden, Charles & M.C. Hodges	1812	AD29	436	366
Peltz, John	Deed fr	Oden, Benjamin, of P.G. Co.	1812	AD29	421	354
Peltz, John	Assign fr	Tuckfield, William H.P.	1812	AC28	139	104
Peltz, John	Deed fr	Van Ness, John P. & Marcia	1812	AD29	195	159
Peltz, John	Deed fr	Bussard, Daniel, of G'tn.	1813	AE30	472	351
Peltz, John	Convey fr	King, Robert	1813	AG32	001	001
Peltz, John	Deed to	Glover, Charles	1814	AG32	209	146
Peltz, John	Mortgage to	Grammer, Frederick, of A.A. Co.	1815	AI34	368	396
Peltz, John	Deed fr	Boyd, Washington, marshal	1815	AK35	397	313
Peltz, John	Deed to	Young, Moses	1815	AK35	195	152
Peltz, John	Deed to	Wallach, Richard	1815	AK35	354	275
Peltz, John	Deed to	Thruston, Buckner	1816	AM37	364	263
Peltz, John	Mortgage to	Davis, John	1817	AN38	170	124
Pembroke, Jack (negro)	Manumis fr	Addison, John	1810	Y24	013	011
Pennock, Isaac et al	Deed fr	Bailey, Daniel	1805	M12	063	059
Pennock, Isaac, of PA et al	Deed fr	Bailey, Daniel, of PA	1807	S18	372	295
Perceval, Joshua et al	Deed fr	Sprogell, Thomas Y.	1800	E5	166	156
Percival, Joshua et ux, et al	Deed to	Wilmans, Frederick	1802	H8	080	074
Percival, Joshua, of Phila. PA	Cert fr	Commissioners of Washington	1801	G7	185	248
Perkins, Abigail, of Boston MA	Deed to	Snow, Gideon, mer., of Boston MA	1810	Y24	485	428
Perkins, Benjamin	Lease fr	King, James C., of G'tn.	1802	G7	502	641
Perkins, Benjamin	Deed to	Bullus, John	1806	Q16	141	092
Perkins, Benjamin	Deed fr	Hewitt, John, assignee et al	1806	O14	170	111
Perkins, Benjamin	Deed to	Davidson, James, Jr.	1807	R17	248	187
Perkins, Benjamin & Elizabeth	Deed to	Holmead, John	1808	V21	002	002
Perkins, Benjamin, carpenter	Deed fr	Bullus, John, M.D.	1806	Q16	074	047
Perkins, Hannah S., of Boston MA	Rel. Dower	Snow, Gideon, mer., of Boston MA	1815	AG32	401	293
Perkins, Jeremiah	Deed fr	Carleton, Joseph, of G'tn.	1804	L11	275	253
Perkins, Jeremiah	Lease to	Quigley, Michael	1812	AC28	265	193
Perkins, Jeremiah & Sam. Hilton	Deed fr	Holmead, Anthony	1812	AD29	052	037
Perkins, Jeremiah et al	Deed fr	Bates, David, constable	1811	AA26	084	060
Perkins, Joseph & Isaac	Deed fr	Bond, Nathaniel, of Portland MA	1801	F6	234	154
Perkins, Joseph & Isaac	Deed fr	Bond, Nathan, of Portland MA	1801	G7	289	401
Perkins, Joseph, admrs. of	Release to	Lenox, Peter	1817	AN38	123	091
Perot, John, of Phila. et al	Deed fr	Bank of the United States	1811	AA26	344	230
Perot, John, of Phila. et al	Deed to	Lenox, David	1811	AA26	333	223
Perry, Caleb, of P.G. Co.	Deed fr	Little, Israel	1817	AN38	006	005
Perry, Elisha	Deed to	Reed, William F., trustee	1814	AH33	306	264
Perry, Erasmus	B. of S. to	Reintzel, Daniel, of G'tn.	1801	G7	192	256
Perry, James, of *Trinidad*	Deed fr	Barry, James	1802	I9	032	042
Peter, David	Deed fr	Johns, Richard & Leonard	1804	L11	226	210
Peter, David	B. of S. fr	Tuel, Henry	1807	S18	160	130
Peter, David & Sarah et al	Deed to	Mayor & Council of Georgetown	1807	R17	232	
Peter, David et al	Deed fr	Charlton, Ralph	1804	L11	378	338
Peter, David et al	Deed fr	Stoddert, Benjamin	1805	M12	321	325
Peter, David et al	Deed fr	Turner, Thomas	1805	M12	339	344
Peter, David et al	Deed fr	Brodeau, Ann	1805	M12	337	342
Peter, David et al	Deed fr	Harrison, Richard H., of G'tn.	1805	M12	327	331

Index to District of Columbia Land Records, 1792-1817

Party	What	Party	Year	Liber	Old	New
Peter, David et al	Deed fr	Weems, John	1805	M12	346	352
Peter, David et al	Deed fr	Loundes, Richard T.	1805	M12	343	349
Peter, David et al	Deed fr	Etting, Solomon	1805	M12	329	333
Peter, David et al	Deed fr	Stewart, William & Helen	1809	X23	277	219
Peter, David et al	Deed to	Corporation of Georgetown	1811	AB27	135	112
Peter, David, heirs of et al	Deed to	Walker, David	1815	AH33	436	374
Peter, David, heirs of	Lease to	Joncherez, Alexander L. et al	1816	AM37	402	289
Peter, David, of G'tn.	Deed fr	Barwin, Thomas	1807	R17	194	147
Peter, David, of G'tn.	Deed fr	Lee, Edmund Jennings, of Alexa.	1808	U20	076	043
Peter, David, of G'tn. et al	Deed to	Thompson, James, of Boston MA	1810	Z25	301	236
Peter, David, of G'tn.	Lease to	Gains, Richard, of G'tn.	1810	Y24	093	083
Peter, David, of G'tn.	Deed to	Union Bank of Georgetown	1811	AA26	357	238
Peter, David, of G'tn.	D. of T. fr	Steuart, William, of G'tn.	1811	AA26	383	254
Peter, David, Thomas & Robert	Deed fr	Stoddert, Benjamin	1802	H8	301	284
Peter, David, trustee	Deed to	Charlton, Ralph	1804	L11	347	315
Peter, David, trustee	Deed to	Costigan, Joseph	1806	Q16	017	011
Peter, Eleanor et al	Deed to	Smith, Clement	1811	Z25	478	379
Peter, Elizabeth Margaret et al	Deed to	Walker, David	1815	AH33	436	374
Peter, Elizabeth, of G'tn.	Deed fr	Peter, John, of G'tn.	1810	Y24	289	265
Peter, Elizabeth, of G'tn. et al	Deed to	Smith, Clement, of G'tn.	1815	AH33	386	334
Peter, George	Deed fr	Beall, Thomas, of Geo.	1811	AB27	361	300
Peter, George	Deed fr	Peter, Thomas & David Peter	1811	AA26	007	006
Peter, George	Deed to	Elliott, Richard	1812	AD29	045	032
Peter, George	Deed to	Robertson, Thomas	1812	AD29	058	042
Peter, George	Deed to	King, Charles	1813	AE30	432	319
Peter, George	Deed to	Thompson, John	1813	AE30	545	404
Peter, George	Deed to	Hedges, Nicholas	1813	AF31	227	156
Peter, George	Deed to	Crawford, William	1813	AF31	151	102
Peter, George	Deed to	Morgan, William	1813	AE30	321	241
Peter, George	Deed fr	Reinagle, Ann	1815	AK35	259	206
Peter, George	Cert Slave	From VA	1815	AI34	460	473
Peter, George	Deed to	Smoot, Samuel	1816	AL36	286	284
Peter, George	Deed to	Pickrell, John	1817	AO39	108	084
Peter, George & Thomas David	Deed to	Peter, John, of G'tn.	1810	Z25	038	028
Peter, George & Sarah et al	Deed to	Collins, William A.	1816	AL36	491	462
Peter, George et al	Deed fr	Stewart, William & Helen	1809	X23	277	219
Peter, George et al	Deed to	Corporation of Georgetown	1811	AB27	135	112
Peter, George Hamilton et al	Deed to	Walker, David	1815	AH33	436	374
Peter, George, of G'tn. et al	Deed to	Thompson, James, of Boston MA	1810	Z25	301	236
Peter, George, of G'tn.	Deed to	Union Bank of Georgetown	1811	AA26	361	241
Peter, George, of G'tn.	Deed to	Georgetown Lancaster School	1812	AD29	109	083
Peter, George, of G'tn.	Deed to	Union Bank of Georgetown	1814	AG32	227	161
Peter, George, of G'tn.	Deed to	Yerby, David, of G'tn.	1815	AI34	085	097
Peter, George, of G'tn.	Deed to	Clark, Satterlee	1816	AL36	454	429
Peter, George, of G'tn.	Deed to	Robertson, Thomas & Sarah, G'tn.	1816	AL36	007	008
Peter, George, of G'tn.	Deed to	Pickrell, John, of G'tn.	1817	AO39	111	086
Peter, James et al	Deed to	Walker, David	1815	AH33	436	374
Peter, Jane Johns et al	Deed to	Walker, David	1815	AH33	436	374
Peter, John	Deed fr	Orme, Lucy	1794	A1-2	488	92
Peter, John	Deed to	Renner, Daniel & Daniel Bussard	1809	V21	383	286
Peter, John	Deed fr	Beall, Thomas, of Geo.	1811	AC28	043	032
Peter, John	Deed to	Whann, William	1812	AD29	416	350
Peter, John	Qualify	Justice of the Peace	1816	AL36	148	148
Peter, John & William Marbury	Deed to	Joncherez, Alexander, of G'tn.	1813	AE30	315	237
Peter, John & Wm. Marbury, G'tn.	Deed to	Ridgely, William G., of G'tn.	1813	AF31	132	089

Party	What	Party	Year	Liber	Old	New
Peter, John & Mariamne C. French	Deed to	Wetzel, Frederick	1817	AN38	280	205
Peter, John, admr. of John	Deed to	Beall, Thomas, of George	1805	N13	231	196
Peter, John et al	Deed to	Bowman, Peter	1795	B2A	355	499
Peter, John et al	Deed to	Lee, Thomas Sim, of G'tn.	1799	D4	190	173
Peter, John et al	Lease to	Corcoran, Thomas	1801	G7	175	233
Peter, John et al	Deed to	Nourse, Joseph	1801	G7	073	095
Peter, John et al	Deed to	Nourse, Joseph	1801	G7	372	504
Peter, John et al	Deed to	Pearce, Isaac	1801	G7	143	189
Peter, John et al	Deed to	Risener, Henry	1812	AD29	445	374
Peter, John et al	Deed to	Wetzel, Frederick	1812	AD29	017	012
Peter, John, mayor	Cert Free to	Williams, Fanny & children	1816	AL36	113	114
Poter, John, mer., of G'tn.	Mortgage to	Beall, Hezekiah, Jefferson Co. VA	1809	W22	276	184
Peter, John, mer., of G'tn.	Deed fr	Beall, Hezekiah, Jefferson Co. VA	1809	W22	327	212
Peter, John, mer., of G'tn.	Mortgage to	Beall, Thomas B., of G'tn.	1809	W22	279	186
Peter, John, mer., of G'tn.	Deed fr	Rose, John & Ann, Loudoun Co.	1809	W22	331	215
Peter, John, of Frederick Co. et al	Lease to	Middleton, Joseph et al	1796	B2B	508	211
Peter, John, of Montg. Co. et al	Deed fr	Hanson, Alexander Contee	1797	C3	095	078
Peter, John, of G'tn. et al	Deed to	Lingan, James Maccubbin, of G'tn.	1800	F6	001	001
Peter, John, of G'tn.	Deed fr	Brent, Daniel Carroll, marshal	1808	U20	007	004
Peter, John, of G'tn.	Deed to	Patterson, Edgar, of G'tn.	1809	V21	207	146
Peter, John, of G'tn.	Deed to	Adams, Thomas, of G'tn.	1809	V21	380	283
Peter, John, of G'tn.	Deed fr	Balch, Stephen B. & Eliza., of G'tn.	1809	W22	023	018
Peter, John, of G'tn.	Deed fr	Williams, Benjamin, of Montg. Co.	1809	V21	369	271
Peter, John, of G'tn.	Deed fr	David, Thomas & George Peter	1810	Z25	038	028
Peter, John, of G'tn.	Deed to	Peter, Elizabeth, of G'tn.	1810	Y24	289	265
Peter, John, of G'tn.	Deed to	Yerby, John, of G'tn.	1811	AB27	033	029
Peter, John, of G'tn.	Lease to	Wirt, John, of G'tn.	1811	AB27	089	073
Peter, John, of G'tn.	D. of T. to	Marbury, William	1812	AD29	197	160
Peter, John, of G'tn.	Deed to	English, David, of G'tn.	1812	AD29	414	349
Peter, John, of G'tn.	Deed to	Yerby, John, of G'tn.	1812	AD29	551	463
Peter, John, of G'tn.	Deed to	Yerby, John, of G'tn.	1812	AD29	413	
Peter, John, of G'tn. et al	Deed to	Washington, George C., of G'tn.	1813	AF31	275	194
Peter, John, of G'tn. et al	Deed to	Washington, George C., of G'tn.	1813	AF31	277	195
Peter, John, of G'tn.	Deed to	Wirt, John, of G'tn.	1813	AF31	096	064
Peter, John, of G'tn. et al	Deed to	English, David, of G'tn.	1813	AF31	279	197
Peter, John, of G'tn.	Deed to	Pickerill, John, of G'tn.	1813	AE30	184	146
Peter, John, of G'tn.	Deed to	Washington, George C., of G'tn.	1814	AG32	299	218
Peter, John, of G'tn. et al	Deed to	Smith, Clement, of G'tn.	1815	AH33	386	334
Peter, John, of G'tn.	Deed to	Whann, William, of G'tn.	1816	AL36	497	467
Peter, John, of G'tn.	Deed to	Yerby, John, of G'tn.	1817	AO39	378	255
Peter, John, of G'tn.	Deed fr	Gassaway, Charles, exrs. of	1817	AO39	245	177
Peter, John, of G'tn.	Deed to	Kirk, Thomas, of G'tn.	1817	AN38	334	245
Peter, Mary & Elizabeth, of G'tn.	Deed to	Washington, George C., of MD	1816	AL36	126	127
Peter, Mary & Elizabeth, of G'tn.	Release to	Cox, John	1816	AL36	199	206
Peter, Mary & Elizabeth, of G'tn.	Deed to	Pickrell, John, of G'tn.	1816	AM37	111	088
Peter, Mary, of G'tn. et al	Deed to	Smith, Clement, of G'tn.	1815	AH33	386	334
Peter, Miller	Deed fr	Stelle, Pontius D. et ux	1808	V21	017	013
Peter, Robert	Deed to	Beall, Thomas & John M. Gantt	1792	A1-1	020	30
Peter, Robert	Deed to	Beall, Thomas & John M. Gantt	1793	A1-2	395	3
Peter, Robert	Deed to	Clark, Thomas & W.S. Chandler	1795	B2A	199	273
Peter, Robert	Cede to	Corporation of Georgetown	1797	B2B	619	377
Peter, Robert	Cert fr	Commissioners of Washington	1797	B2B	461	150
Peter, Robert	Transfer fr	Morris, Robert & James Greenleaf	1797	B2B	461	150
Peter, Robert	Division	Thompson, James et al	1799	D4	267	251
Peter, Robert	Deed to	Smith, Clement	1800	F6	027	017

Index to District of Columbia Land Records, 1792-1817

Party	What	Party	Year	Liber	Old	New
Peter, Robert	Deposition		1801	G7		122
Peter, Robert	Deed fr	Cook, Charles	1801	G7	432	567
Peter, Robert	Deed fr	Beall, Thomas, of George	1801	G7	302	421
Peter, Robert	Deed to	Dunlap, Elizabeth	1801	G7	461	598
Peter, Robert	Deed to	Wilcoxon, Lewis, of KY	1802	H8	440	405
Peter, Robert	Deed fr	Duer, James, of Snow Hill	1802	H8	109	105
Peter, Robert	Manumis to	[ ], Agey (Negro)	1802	H8	443	407
Peter, Robert	B. of S. fr	Steele, Jesse	1802	I9	537	877
Peter, Robert	Deed fr	Wilcoxen, Lewis, Pend. Co. KY	1804	L11	188	181
Peter, Robert, assignee of Wells	Deed fr	Stoddert, Benj. & Wm. Deakins	1793	A1-1	386	493
Peter, Robert et al	Deed to	Templeman, John, of G'tn.	1794	B2A	063	080
Peter, Robert et al	Deed to	Beall, Thomas, of George	1795	B2A	166	222
Peter, Robert et al	R. of S. to	Mayor of Georgetown	1803	K10	031	31
Peter, Robert et al	Deed to	Mayor & Council of Georgetown	1807	R17	232	
Peter, Robert et al	Deed fr	Stewart, William & Helen	1809	X23	277	219
Peter, Robert et al, defs.	Suit	Scholfield, Andrew, plt.	1809	V21	326	240
Peter, Robert, heirs of	Partition		1812	AD29	319	262
Peter, Robert, of G'tn.	Deed to	Johnson, Thomas, Frederick Co.	1794	B2A	161	213
Peter, Robert, of G'tn.	Deed to	Mason, John, of G'tn.	1794	B2A	106	140
Peter, Robert, of G'tn.	Deed to	Lear, Tobias, of G'tn.	1794	B2A	143	189
Peter, Robert, of G'tn.	Deed to	Johnson, Thomas, Frederick Co.	1795	B2A	175	235
Peter, Robert, of G'tn.	Deed to	Washington, George, Pres.	1795	B2A	214	295
Peter, Robert, of G'tn.	Deed fr	Beall, Thomas Brooke, of G'tn.	1796	B2B	547	272
Peter, Robert, of Montg. Co.	Deed to	Mitchell, John, of G'tn.	1796	B2B	517	226
Peter, Robert, of G'tn.	Deed to	Reintzel, Anthony, of G'tn.	1796	B2B	426	101
Peter, Robert, of G'tn.	Deed to	Reid, James, of G'tn.	1796	B2B	436	115
Peter, Robert, of G'tn.	Deed to	Kennedy, Matthew, of G'tn.	1797	B2B	665	431
Peter, Robert, of G'tn.	P. of Atty. to	King, Nicholas	1798	C3	492	387
Peter, Robert, of G'tn.	Deed to	Deakins, Francis, of G'tn.	1798	C3	505	396
Peter, Robert, of G'tn.	Deed to	Thompson, James, mer., of G'tn.	1799	D4	275	258
Peter, Robert, of G'tn.	Deed to	Gantt, John M.	1799	D4	273	257
Peter, Robert, of G'tn.	Deed to	Lear, Tobias et al	1799	D4	321	305
Peter, Robert, of G'tn.	Deed to	Thompson, James, mer., of G'tn.	1799	D4	348	336
Peter, Robert, of G'tn.	Deef r	Thompson, James, mer., of G'tn.	1799	D4	272	255
Peter, Robert, of G'tn.	Deed fr	Dalton, Tristram	1799	D4	309	293
Peter, Robert, of G'tn.	Deed to	Dalton, Tristram et al	1799	D4	321	305
Peter, Robert, of G'tn.	Deed fr	Commissioners of Washington	1800	E5	198	190
Peter, Robert, of G'tn.	Deed fr	Stone, John Hoskins, of Balto.	1800	E5		325
Peter, Robert, of G'tn.	Deed to	Stone, John Hoskins, of Balto.	1800	E5	389	365
Peter, Robert, of G'tn.	Deed fr	Wayman, Charles, of G'tn.	1801	G7	292	405
Peter, Robert, of G'tn.	Deed to	Thompson, James, of G'tn.	1801	G7	398	531
Peter, Robaff, of G'tn.	Deed to	Shaaff, Arthur, of Annapolis	1801	G7	239	321
Peter, Robert, of G'tn. et al	Deed to	Brumly, Mary	1804	L11	323	296
Peter, Robert, trustee	Deed fr	Feburier, Nicholas, insolvent	1805	N13	233	198
Peter, Sarah et al	Lease to	Joncherez, Alexander L. et al	1816	AM37	402	289
Peter, Sarah, wid/o David, of G'tn.	Deed fr	Bowie, Washington & Margaret C.	1814	AH33	353	305
Peter, Sarah, wid/o David et al	Deed to	Walker, David	1815	AH33	436	374
Peter, Thomas	Deed fr	Law, Thomas & Elizabeth Parke	1800	E5	228	221
Peter, Thomas	Deed to	Law, Thomas et al	1802	H8	392	363
Peter, Thomas	Agreement	Law, Thomas	1802	H8	391	362
Peter, Thomas	Deed fr	Lowndes, Francis	1805	M12	379	390
Peter, Thomas	Deed to	Smith, Clement	1812	AC28	277	201
Peter, Thomas & David Peter	Deed to	Peter, George	1811	AA26	007	006
Peter, Thomas & Mary Bromley	B. of S. to	Hawkins, Matilda	1812	AC28	159	118
Peter, Thomas & Mary Bromley	Manumis to	[ ], Matilda (C)	1812	AC28	159	119

Party	What	Party	Year	Liber	Old	New
Peter, Thomas & Mary Brumley	Manumis to	[ ], Maria (C)	1816	AL36	127	128
Peter, Thomas et al	Deed fr	Blodget, Samuel, Jr.	1794	B2A	009	010
Peter, Thomas et al	Agreement	Law, Thomas	1804	L11	125	127
Peter, Thomas et al	Deed fr	Law, Thomas & Eliza Park	1804	L11	127	129
Peter, Thomas et al	Deed fr	Law, Thomas	1804	L11	114	117
Peter, Thomas et al	Deed to	Bickley, Robert S., of Phila.	1805	L11	410	364
Peter, Thomas et al	Deed to	Varden, Ezra	1807	Q16	404	311
Peter, Thomas et al	Deed to	Lenox, Peter	1807	R17	271	206
Peter, Thomas et al	Deed to	Varden, Charles H.	1807	R17	016	014
Peter, Thomas et al	Deed to	Mathers, James	1807	R17	022	019
Peter, Thomas et al	Deed to	Lindsay, Adam	1807	R17	251	190
Peter, Thomas et al	Deed to	Bickley, Robert S., of Phila. PA	1807	R17	026	022
Peter, Thomas et al	Deed to	Thornton, William	1807	S18	094	076
Peter, Thomas et al	Deed to	Howe, Robert F., of G'tn.	1807	S18	001	001
Peter, Thomas et al	Deed fr	Stewart, William & Helen	1809	X23	277	219
Peter, Thomas et al	Deed to	Craven, John et al	1811	AA26	280	190
Peter, Thomas et al	Deed to	Corporation of Georgetown	1811	AB27	135	112
Peter, Thomas, exr. of Robert	Deed to	Bowie, Washington	1812	AC28	325	237
Peter, Thomas, of G'tn. et al	Deed to	Thompson, James, of Boston MA	1810	Z25	301	236
Peter, Thomas, of G'tn.	Deed to	Union Bank of Georgetown	1814	AG32	224½	159
Peter, Thomas, of G'tn.	Lease to	Colclazer, Jacob, of G'tn.	1816	AM37	072	058
Peter, Thomas, of G'tn.	Lease to	Broadwell, James, of G'tn.	1816	AL36	486	457
Peter, William Henry et al	Deed to	Walker, David	1815	AH33	436	374
Peters, David		Certificate of Slaves	1802	H8	070	065
Peters, Janet, wid/o Geo., cooper	Deposition		1804	L11	001	1
Peters, Samuel, of NY	Deed to	Wright, Mary, wid., of NY	1817	AN38	473	341
Peters, Samuel, of NY	Deed to	Wright, Solomon, of NY	1817	AN38	470	339
Peters, Samuel, of NY	Deed to	Wright, Reuben, of NY	1817	AN38	480	346
Peters, Samuel, of NY	Deed to	Wright, Mercy, wid., of NY	1817	AN38	476	344
Peters, Samuel, of NY	Deed to	Wright, John, of NY	1817	AN38	466	336
Petit, Charles et al	Deed to	Beall, Thomas & John M. Gantt	1793	A1-1	276	371
Peyton, T.W., of Alexa.	Deed to	Bloxham, James, of Alexa.	1817	AO39	149	112
Peyton, Thomas W., of Alexa.	Deed fr	Williams, Elisha W., of G'tn.	1813	AE30	133	104
Peyton, Valentine	Mortgage fr	Deakins, Francis	1800	E5		177
Philips, Isaac	Deed fr	Philips, John N.	1814	AG32	242	173
Philips, Isaac et al	Cert fr	Commissioners of Washington	1797	B2B	464	155
Philips, Isaac et al	Deed fr	Burnes, David, of P.G. Co.	1797	C3	079	65
Philips, John N.	Deed to	Philips, Isaac	1814	AG32	242	173
Philips, Nathaniel, of Phila. PA	Cert fr	Commissioners of Washington	1793	B2A	304	427
Phillebrown, John	P. of Atty. to	Hewitt, John	1802	S18	400	
Phillips, Isaac, of Balto.	Deed to	Glover, Charles	1816	AL36	347	338
Phillips, John	Deed fr	Durety, William	1802	I9	411	681
Phillips, John	B. of S. to	Durity, Francis	1805	N13	124	120
Pic, Anne, now Chatelin, of G'tn.	Deed to	Holmead, John	1815	AI34	280	316
Pic, Francis	Deed fr	Feburier, Nicholas	1802	I9	252	407
Pic, Francis	Inventory		1806	Q16	273	
Pic, Francis	Lease fr	Carroll, Daniel, of *Duddington*	1812	AD29	163	129
Pic, Francis	Mortgage to	Wright, Thomas C. & John Ott	1812	AD29	258	214
Pic, Francis	Mortgage to	Wright, Thomas C., of G'tn.	1813	AE30	169	135
Pic, Francis	D. of T. fr	Nardin, Baptist	1815	AH33	493	422
Pic, Francis	Assign fr	Nardin, Baptist	1815	AH33	492	421
Pic, Francis & Mary A. Pic, G'tn.	Dissolution		1810	X23	254	198
Pic, Francis, of G'tn.	B. of S. to	Reintzel, Daniel, of G'tn.	1806	Q16	292	191
Pic, Mary A.	B. of S. fr	Dulany, Anne	1809	W22	166	116
Pic, Mary A., trustee of	Agreement	Lee, Thomas S.	1811	AC28	100	075

Index to District of Columbia Land Records, 1792-1817 329

Party	What	Party	Year	Liber	Old	New
Pickerall, Elizabeth et al	Deed to	Varden, Ezra	1809	X23	031	022
Pickerel, Benjamin	B. of S. fr	Rhodes, John	1811	AB27	480	393
Pickerel, Benjamin	B. of S. fr	Rhodes, Cassandra	1817	AN38	053	043
Pickerel, John	B. of S. fr	Graves, Robert	1811	AB27	483	395
Pickerel, John, of G'tn.	Deed fr	Linkins, Henry, of G'tn.	1813	AF31	001	001
Pickerell, John	Deed fr	Chandler, Walter S., of G'tn.	1808	T19	063	046
Pickerell, John, of G'tn.	Deed to	Dixon, Thomas, of G'tn.	1812	AC28	240	177
Pickerell, John, of G'tn.	Deed to	Suter, Alexander, of G'tn.	1813	AF31	171	115
Pickerell, John, of G'tn.	Deed to	Stone, Edward, of G'tn.	1814	AG32	233	166
Pickerell, John, of G'tn.	Deed to	Bowie, Washington, of G'tn.	1814	AG32	142	102
Pickerill, Benjamin	Deed fr	Wirt, John	1808	T19	238	175
Pickerill, Benjamin & Alethe	Deed to	Gaines, Richard	1809	V21	357	260
Pickerill, John, of G'tn.	Deed fr	Dixon, Thomas, of G'tn.	1810	Y24	176	161
Pickerill, John, of G'tn.	Deed to	Hillery, Lewis, of G'tn.	1811	AA26	188	128
Pickerill, John, of G'tn.	Deed fr	English, David, of G'tn.	1811	Z25	519	412
Pickerill, John, of G'tn.	Deed fr	King, Charles, of G'tn.	1812	AD29	210	171
Pickerill, John, of G'tn.	Deed fr	Wirt, John, of G'tn.	1813	AE30	185	148
Pickerill, John, of G'tn.	Deed fr	Peter, John, of G'tn.	1813	AE30	184	146
Pickett, George	Partition	Johnston, Chas. & Robert Pollard	1810	Z25	272	214
Pickett, George	Deed fr	Pollard, Robert & Chas. Johnston	1814	AH33	322	279
Pickett, George et al	Deed fr	Commissioners of Washington	1800	E5	154	143
Pickford, John B.	Deed fr	King, Robert	1815	AK35	210	165
Picknal, John	Deed fr	Chandler, Walter S., of G'tn.	1807	Q16	343	273
Picknall, Richard H.	B. of S. to	Brown, Henry	1809	X23	034	024
Picknall, Richard H.	B. of S. to	Boyd, Richard D.	1809	X23	159	117
Picknall, Richard H.	B. of S. to	Minitree, John	1809	X23	044	032
Picknall, Richard Henry	Deed fr	Carleton, Joseph, of G'tn.	1807	Q16	345	264
Picknall, Richard Henry	Deed to	Bond, Samuel & Richard D. Boyd	1809	X23	045	033
Picknoll, Richard	Discharge	Private in Light Dragons	1815	AI34	020	021
Picknoll, Richard H.	B. of S. to	Prout, William	1809	X23	131	094
Picknoll, Richard H.	Deed fr	Prout, William	1810	Y24	480	425
Picknoll, Richard H.	B. of S. to	Owner, Hannah	1810	Z25	008	006
Picknoll, Richard H.	Mortgage to	Kemp, James & Edward Grantt	1811	AA26	081	057
Picknoll, Richard H.	B. of S. to	Jarvis, Thomas	1811	Z25	174	138
Picknoll, Richard H.	B. of S. to	Scott, Watkins, of Bladensburgh	1811	Z25	527	418
Picknoll, Richard H.	P. of Atty. to	Grantt, Edward & James Kemp	1811	AA26	010	008
Picknoll, Richard H. et al	Assign to	Serra, Augustin	1813	AE30	376	279
Pickrell, Benjamin	Deed fr	Pickrell, John, of G'tn.	1809	X23	121	086
Pickrell, Benjamin	B. of S. to	Rhoades, Cassandra	1814	AH33	227	199
Pickrell, John	Deed fr	Chandler, Walter Story & Margaret	1810	Y24	011	010
Pickrell, John	Deed fr	Hyde, Thomas	1811	AB27	339	279
Pickrell, John	Deed fr	Wineberger, George	1811	Z25	402	316
Pickrell, John	Deed fr	Morgan, William	1812	AD29	208	169
Pickrell, John	Deed to	Cox, John	1813	AF31	391	282
Pickrell, John	Deed to	King, Vincent	1813	AE30	088	067
Pickrell, John	D. of T. fr	Weeden, Henry	1814	AH33	363	315
Pickrell, John	Deed fr	Weeden, Henry, of G'tn.	1815	AI34	128	147
Pickrell, John	Deed fr	King, Vincent	1816	AL36	116	117
Pickrell, John	Deed fr	Parrott, Richard	1817	AN38	098	075
Pickrell, John	Deed fr	Peter, George	1817	AO39	108	084
Pickrell, John	Deed to	Hayman, William	1817	AO39	156	117
Pickrell, John & Clement Smith	Deed fr	Dorsey, William H., of Montg. Co.	1815	AK35	106	082
Pickrell, John & Clement Smith	Deed fr	Murdock, John, of G'tn.	1815	AK35	105	081
Pickrell, John & J. Lipscomb	Lease fr	Renner, Daniel	1815	AI34	093	106
Pickrell, John & Clement Smith	Deed fr	Dorsey, William H., of Montg. Co.	1816	AL36	470	443

Index to District of Columbia Land Records, 1792-1817

Party	What	Party	Year	Liber	Old	New
Pickrell, John & Clement Smith	Deed fr	Murdock, John, of G'tn.	1816	AL36	468	442
Pickrell, John & Joel Brown, G'tn.	Deed fr	Stout, Jacob, of G'tn.	1816	AM37	470	339
Pickrell, John, of G'tn.	Deed to	Pickrell, Benjamin	1809	X23	121	086
Pickrell, John, of G'tn.	Deed fr	Brookes, Joseph, of G'tn.	1811	AB27	341	281
Pickrell, John, of G'tn.	Deed to	Robertson, Joseph, of G'tn.	1811	AA26	322	217
Pickrell, John, of G'tn.	Deed fr	Moore, Alexander, of G'tn.	1811	AB27	340	280
Pickrell, John, of G'tn.	Deed to	Robey, Leonard, of G'tn.	1812	AC28	310	226
Pickrell, John, of G'tn.	Deed to	Magruder, Ninian, Dr., of G'tn.	1812	AD29	072	052
Pickrell, John, of G'tn.	Deed to	Smallwood, Horatio, of G'tn.	1812	AD29	070	050
Pickrell, John, of G'tn.	B. of S. to	Lanham, Elisha, of G'tn.	1814	AG32	400	292
Pickrell, John, of G'tn.	Deed fr	Parrott, Richard, of G'tn.	1814	AG32	039	031
Pickrell, John, of G'tn.	Deed fr	Rhodes, George, of Montg. Co.	1815	AH33	496	425
Pickrell, John, of G'tn.	Deed fr	Hodges, Thoams C., of G'tn.	1816	AL36	034	035
Pickrell, John, of G'tn.	Deed to	Cox, John, of G'tn.	1816	AL36	101	102
Pickrell, John, of G'tn.	Deed to	Smith, Clement, of G'tn.	1816	AL36	474	447
Pickrell, John, of G'tn.	Deed to	Smith, Clement, of G'tn.	1816	AL36	471	443
Pickrell, John, of G'tn.	Deed fr	Riggs, Romulus, of G'tn.	1816	AM37	109	087
Pickrell, John, of G'tn.	Deed fr	Ridgely, William G., of G'tn.	1816	AM37	114	090
Pickrell, John, of G'tn.	Deed fr	Peter, Mary & Elizabeth, of G'tn.	1816	AM37	111	088
Pickrell, John, of G'tn.	Deed to	Greer, James, of G'tn.	1816	AO39	031	026
Pickrell, John, of G'tn.	Deed to	Wetzell, William Y., of G'tn.	1816	AO39	042	034
Pickrell, John, of G'tn.	Deed to	Lipscomb, John, of G'tn.	1817	AN38	079	062
Pickrell, John, of G'tn.	Deed fr	Brookes, Joseph, of G'tn.	1817	AO39	152	114
Pickrell, John, of G'tn.	Lease to	Bunnell, Eliab, of G'tn. et al	1817	AO39	154	116
Pickrell, John, of G'tn.	Deed fr	Peter, George, of G'tn.	1817	AO39	111	086
Pierce, Abner	Deed fr	Hedges, Nicholas	1817	AN38	114	085
Pierce, Humphrey, of Balto. et al	Deed to	Chesley, Anne, of G'tn.	1804	L11	372	333
Pierce, Ignatius [Peerce]	Deed to	Clarke, Robert	1812	AC28	404	293
Pierce, Isaac	Deed to	Forrest, Uriah	1794	B2A	027	030
Pierce, Isaac	Deed to	Forrest, Uriah	1795	B2A	190	257
Pierce, Isaac	Deed to	Bailey, Jesse	1801	G7	459	595
Pierce, Isaac	Deed fr	Bayley, Jesse	1808	T19	287	210
Pierce, Isaac	Deed fr	McPherson, John & Sarah, of MD	1815	AI34	158	181
Pierce, Isaac	Assign fr	Smith, John Kilty	1817	AN38	114	085
Pierce, Isaac	Deed to	Smith, John Kilty	1817	AO39	172	128
Pierce, Isaac	Deed fr	Beatty, Charles A.	1817	AN38	116	086
Pierce, Isaac & Elizabeth et al	Deed to	Kogenderfer, Leonard et al	1799	D4	239	221
Pierce, Isaac & Elizabeth	Deed to	Townsend, Henry	1801	G7	218	291
Pierce, Isaac & Elizabeth	Deed to	Smith, John R.	1817	AO39	060	049
Pierce, James	Deed to	Beall, Thomas & John M. Gantt	1792	A1-1	035	52
Pierce, James	Deed to	Davidson, Samuel, of G'tn.	1792	A1-1	039	58
Pierce, Thomas	Cert fr	Commissioners of Washington	1795	B2A	332	465
Pierce, Thomas, of G'tn.	Deed to	Baltzell, George, Frederick Co.	1804	L11	404	358
Piercy, George	Qualify	Ensign in 2nd Regiment	1814	AH33	117	110
Piercy, Israel	Deed fr	Moscrop, Henry	1802	I9	500	821
Piercy, James	Mortgage to	Law, Thomas et al	1797	B2B	690	468
Piercy, James	Mortgage to	Law, Thomas	1797	B2B	688	465
Piercy, James	Deed to	Law, Thomas	1797	B2B	687	464
Piercy, James	Release to	Ray, James	1798	C3	280	227
Piercy, James	Agreement	Commissioners of Washington	1800	E5	192	183
Piercy, James et al	Deed fr	Ray, James, mer.	1797	C3	176	149
Piercy, James, sugar refiner	Deed to	Treat, Samuel	1800	E5	196	187
Piercy, James, sugar refiner	Agreement	Piercy, James, Sr. et al	1800	E5	196	187
Piercy, James, sugar refiner	Deed to	Ray, James	1800	F6	015	010
Piercy, James, sugar refiner	Deed to	Prout, William et al	1800	E5	197	189

Index to District of Columbia Land Records, 1792-1817

Party	What	Party	Year	Liber	Old	New
Piers, Nicholas & Valentine, VA	Deed to	Laird, John, of G'tn.	1801	F6	200	129
Pigott, Edward, of Phila. PA	Deed fr	Davidson, Samuel	1801	F6	206	133
Plat		Lot 76, Georgetown	1797	C3	143	
Plat		Square 38; L & 24th streets west	1798	D4		190
Plat		Beatty & Hawkins Addition to G.T.	1798	K10	004	
Plat		Tract called Fox	1798	C3	451	
Plat		Lots 60-61, Bridge & Jefferson sts.	1799	D4	267	251
Plat		Square 38	1800	E5		273
Plat		Square 156	1800	E5	275	269
Plat		Square 193	1800	E5	275	269
Plat			1801	G7		505
Plat		Tract called *Friendship*	1801	G7		097
Plat		10th street west	1801	G7		195
Plat		Tract called *Friendship*	1801	G7		150
Plat		Wigfield, R. & James et al	1803	K10	131	141
Plat		Lot 80	1803	K10	100	
Plat		Wigfield, Matthew et al	1803	K10	131	141
Plat		Square 348, Lot 7 part	1804	K10	381	
Plat		Tract called *Friendship*, part	1805	O14	104	
Plat		G'tn. Lots 1,4,6,8,10,12	1805	N13	014	
Plat		Frederick St., G'tn., part	1805	O14	002	
Plat			1806	P15	107	
Plat		Part of Discovery	1807	S18	140	
Plat		B St. and New Jersey Ave.	1807	S18	010	
Plat		Birch's Venture	1807	S18	281	
Plat		Southern Section of Georgetown	1808	T19	146	
Plat		Georgia Ave., 12th and L sts.	1809	W22	382	
Plat		11th Street west, Lot 12	1810	X23	406	
Plat		Square 459, Lot 3	1810	Y24	453	
Plate, Adolphus F.	Lease fr	Van Ness, John P. & Marcia	1810	Y24	463	411
Plater, John R.	Deed fr	Forrest, Uriah	1802	H8	288	272
Plater, John R. et al	Deed fr	Forrest, Uriah	1802	I9	075	106
Plater, John R.	Deed to	Key, Philip B.	1802	I9	452	747
Plater, John R.	Mortgage fr	Forrest, Uriah	1802	H8	292	276
Plater, John R., of St. Mary's Co.	Deed fr	Murdock, John, of G'tn.	1816	AL36	011	012
Plater, John Rousby	Deed to	Forrest, Uriah	1801	G7	082	106
Plater, John Rousby	Deed fr	Beall, Thomas, of George	1802	H8	320	301
Plater, John Rousby & Elizabeth	Deed to	Chandler, Walter Story	1810	Y24	231	213
Plater, John Rousby, St. Mary's	Deed to	Chandler, Walter Story	1810	Y24	229	211
Plater, John Rowlsby, of G'tn.	Deed to	Deakins, Francis	1800	E5	353	337
Plater, John Rowsby, of G'tn.	Deed to	Forrest & Deakins	1799	D4	194	177
Plater, John Rowsby, of G'tn.	Deed fr	Forrest, Uriah & Francis Deakins	1800	E5	325	315
Plater, John Rowsly, of G'tn.	Deed fr	Deakins, Francis et al	1798	D4	104	088
Plater, Thomas	Deed to	Dunlap, John	1793	A1-2	418	26
Plater, Thomas	Deed fr	Beall, Thomas, of George	1798	C3	436	342
Plater, Thomas et al	Deed to	Peerce, Isaac	1812	AD29	507	427
Plater, Thomas, of Montg. Co.	Deed fr	Chandler, Walter Story, of G'tn.	1806	P15	052	031
Plater, Thomas, of Montg. Co.	Deed to	Chandler, Walter Story	1806	P15	278	183
Pleasanton, Stephen	P. of Atty. fr	Purcell, Pierce	1802	I9	233	372
Pleasants, Israel & John P., Balto.	Deed fr	Muse, Lawrence, of Tappa. VA	1805	M12	301	303
Pleasonton, Stephen	Deed fr	Stockwell, Mark	1801	G7	419	553
Pleasonton, Stephen	Deed fr	Polock, David	1803	K10	070	76
Pleasonton, Stephen	Deed to	Brent, Daniel	1806	Q16	020	013
Pleasonton, Stephen	Manumis to	[ ], Kitty (negro)	1807	R17	234	176
Pleasonton, Stephen	Deed fr	Hancock, James & Eliz., of Ire.	1810	Z25	288	226

Party	What	Party	Year	Liber	Old	New
Pleasonton, Stephen	Deed fr	Williams, John S., of G'tn.	1814	AH33	126	119
Pleasonton, Stephen	Deed to	Ross, Andrew, of G'tn.	1815	AI34	262	296
Pleasonton, Stephen	Deed to	Haw, John S., of G'tn.	1816	AK35	480	377
Pleasonton, Stephen	D. of T. fr	Nourse, Joseph	1817	AN38	231	170
Pleasonton, Stephen & J.D. Barry	Deed fr	Bowie, Washington	1816	AL36	484	456
Pleasonton, Stephen et al	Deed fr	Purcell, Pierce	1801	G7	377	509
Pleasonton, Stephen et al	Mortgage fr	Purcell, Pierce	1802	I9	066	092
Pleasonton, Stephen et al	Deed to	Purcell, Pierce	1803	K10	056	61
Pleasonton, Stephen, of G'tn. et al	Deed fr	Gaither, Benjamin & Daniel	1814	AH33	336	290
Plowden, Edward, St. Mary's Co.	Deed fr	Commissioners of Washington	1799	D4	340	327
Plunkett, Robert, Rev. et al	Deed fr	Neale, Leonard, Rev.	1814	AG32	029	023
Plunkett, Robert, Rev. et al	Deed fr	Neale, Francis I., Rev., of G'tn.	1814	AG32	025	020
Poland, William et al	Deed to	Beall, Thomas & John M. Gantt	1793	A1-1	276	371
Polk, Charles P.	Deed fr	Templeman, John	1802	I9	210	330
Polk, Charles P.	Deed to	Craven, John	1802	I9	533	871
Polk, Charles P., insolvent	D. of T. to	Reilly, William et al	1813	AF31	071	048
Polk, Charles P.	D. of T. to	Brown, Obadiah B.	1813	AF31	154	104
Polk, Charles P.	Slaves	From VA	1817	AN38	318	232
Polk, Charles Peale, insolvent	Deed to	Peacock, Robert Ware, trustee	1804	L11	343	311
Polk, Robert	Slave	From Virginia	1812	AD29	473	400
Polkenhorn, Henry	Deed to	Hall, Richard M.	1809	X23	293	233
Polkinhorn, Henry, insolvent	D. of T. to	Kent, Luke, trustee	1810	Z25	350	274
Polkinhorn, Henry, of G'tn. et al	Deed fr	Wools, George, of G'tn.	1804	K10	287	289
Pollard, Robert	Partition	Pickett, George & Chas. Johnston	1810	Z25	272	214
Pollard, Robert	Deed fr	Johnston, Charles & Eliza P.	1812	AC28	433	311
Pollard, Robert & wife, Richmond	Deed to	Roberts, John & Lucy, Culpeper	1813	AF31	370	265
Pollard, Robert & Jael et al	Deed to	Pickett, George	1814	AH33	322	279
Pollard, Robert et al	Deed fr	Commissioners of Washington	1800	E5	154	143
Pollard, William et al	R. of M. to	Magruder, William B.	1794	B2A	039	045
Pollock, Isaac	Deed to	Van Ness, John P.	1802	I9	545	552
Pollock, Isaac	Deed fr	Fairfax, Ferdinando, of VA	1802	I9	081	115
Pollock, Isaac, of Phila. PA	Deed fr	King, William, of G'tn.	1796	B2B	560	292
Pollock, William, insolvent	Deed to	Kenner, James, trustee	1805	N13	112	106
Polock, Abigail	Deed fr	Polock, Isaac	1802	I9	305	501
Polock, Abigail	Deed fr	Polock, Isaac	1802	I9	225	356
Polock, Abigail, late of MD	Deed to	Polock, Isaac	1806	P15	216	144
Polock, Abigail, of Montg. Co.	Deed to	Tayloe, John	1804	K10	148	160
Polock, Abigail, of Montg. Co.	Deed to	Waters, William, of G'tn.	1804	L11	092	94
Polock, Abigail, of Montg. Co.	Deed to	Waters, William, of G'tn.	1804	M12	025	025
Polock, Abigail, of Montg. Co.	Deed to	Clark, Samuel, of G'tn.	1805	M12	085	079
Polock, David	Deed to	Denison, Robert, Jr., of Phila.	1801	G7	062	080
Polock, David	Deed fr	Dennison, Robert, Jr., of Phila.	1801	G7	210	281
Polock, David	Deed fr	Polock, Isaac	1802	I9	378	627
Polock, David	Deed fr	Polock, Isaac	1802	I9	379	628
Polock, David	Deed to	Pleasonton, Stephen	1803	K10	070	76
Polock, David	Deed to	Van Ness, John P.	1804	L11	097	100
Polock, David	Deed to	Thorpe, Thomas	1804	K10	281	284
Polock, David, of Phila. PA	Deed fr	Polock, Isaac	1800	E5	277	271
Polock, David, of G'tn.	Deed to	Traverse, Nicholas, of G'tn.	1804	L11	031	31
Polock, David, of G'tn.	Deed to	Thompson, Arthur	1804	K10	351	363
Polock, Isaac	Agreement	Templeman, John	1795	B2A	216	299
Polock, Isaac	Deed fr	Stoddert, Benjamin	1797	B2B	649	411
Polock, Isaac	Deed fr	Forrest, Uriah, of Montg. Co.	1797	C3	123	101
Polock, Isaac	Deed fr	Forrest, Uriah, of Montg. Co.	1797	B2B	647	410
Polock, Isaac	D. of T. to	Deakins, William, Jr., of G'tn.	1798	C3	395	314

Index to District of Columbia Land Records, 1792-1817

Party	What	Party	Year	Liber	Old	New
Polock, Isaac	Deed to	Denison, Robert, Jr., of Phila.	1798	C3	392	311
Polock, Isaac	Deed fr	Forrest, Uriah	1798	C3	385	306
Polock, Isaac	Deed to	Thompson, Jonah, of Alexa. et al	1798	C3	444	349
Polock, Isaac	Deed to	Carmichael, Alexander et al	1798	D4	003	002
Polock, Isaac	Deed to	Craig, Robert	1798	D4	147	129
Polock, Isaac	Deed to	Lee, Henry, of VA	1798	D4	083	070
Polock, Isaac	Release fr	Tebbs, William P.	1798	D4	114	098
Polock, Isaac	Deed to	Cook, Charles	1798	D4	045	038
Polock, Isaac	Deed fr	Commissioners of Washington	1798	D4	097	082
Polock, Isaac	Deed to	Jackson, Samuel, of Phila. PA	1798	D4	001	001
Polock, Isaac	Deed to	French, George	1798	D4	160	141
Polock, Isaac	Deed to	Weatherall, John	1798	D4	028	023
Polock, Isaac	Mortgage to	Tebbs, William P.	1798	D4	023	019
Polock, Isaac	Deed to	Dennison, Robert, Jr., of Phila.	1799	D4	205	188
Polock, Isaac	Deed to	Lingan, James Maccubbin, G'tn.	1799	D4	365	351
Polock, Isaac	Deed to	Veitch, Richard	1800	E5	396	371
Polock, Isaac	Deed to	Foster, John, of Alexa.	1800	E5	169	159
Polock, Isaac	Deed to	Steuart, William, of B'burgh.	1800	E5	212	206
Polock, Isaac	Deed to	Deakins, William, Jr.	1800	E5	396	371
Polock, Isaac	Deed fr	Lingan, James McCubbin	1800	E5	105	093
Polock, Isaac	Deed to	Polock, David, of Phila.	1800	E5	277	271
Polock, Isaac	Deed to	Johnston, William, of VA	1800	E5	215	209
Polock, Isaac	Deed to	Thompson, Jonah	1800	E5	396	371
Polock, Isaac	Deed to	Knowles, Henry, of G'tn.	1801	G7	469	606
Polock, Isaac	Deed to	Loundes, Charles, of G'tn.	1802	G7	530	675
Polock, Isaac	Deed to	Templeman, John, of G'tn.	1802	G7	498	636
Polock, Isaac	Mortgage to	Loundes, Charles, of G'tn.	1802	G7	533	678
Polock, Isaac	Deed to	Templeman, John, of G'tn.	1802	G7	496	635
Polock, Isaac	Deed to	Lowndes, Charles, of G'tn.	1802	H8	515	474
Polock, Isaac	Deed to	Brown, Stewart	1802	H8	021	020
Polock, Isaac	Lease to	Tharpe, Thomas	1802	H8	145	140
Polock, Isaac	Deed to	Childs, Henry	1802	H8	020	019
Polock, Isaac	Deed to	Minturn, Benjamin G. et al	1802	H8	011	010
Polock, Isaac	Deed to	Travis, Nicholas & Elias C.	1802	H8	043	041
Polock, Isaac	Deed to	James, James, of MD	1802	H8	234	223
Polock, Isaac	Deed to	Bigham, Hugh	1802	H8	153	148
Polock, Isaac	Lease to	Thompson, Arthur	1802	H8	143	139
Polock, Isaac	Deed to	Porter, Sarah, admx. of Thomas	1802	H8	279	264
Polock, Isaac	Release fr	Burnes, Anne	1802	H8	141	137
Polock, Isaac	Deed to	Willis, John	1802	H8	345	321
Polock, Isaac	Deed to	Porter, Sarah, of Alexa.	1802	H8	278	263
Polock, Isaac	Deed fr	Burnes, Marcia, by her guard.	1802	H8	147	143
Polock, Isaac	Deed to	Murdock, John	1802	H8	033	031
Polock, Isaac	Deed fr	Stoddert, Benjamin et al	1802	I9	198	308
Polock, Isaac	Deed to	Mason, John T.	1802	I9	259	419
Polock, Isaac	Deed to	Doll, James	1802	I9	205	321
Polock, Isaac	Deed to	Templeman, John	1802	I9	147	221
Polock, Isaac	Deed to	Sprigg, William O.	1802	I9	318	522
Polock, Isaac	Deed to	Armstrong, William	1802	I9	363	601
Polock, Isaac	Deed to	Taylor, Jon	1802	I9	194	302
Polock, Isaac	Deed to	Anderson, John B.	1802	I9	136	203
Polock, Isaac	Deed to	Fairfax, Ferdinando, of VA	1802	I9	027	036
Polock, Isaac	Discharge		1802	I9	230	367
Polock, Isaac	Deed to	Polock, Abigail	1802	I9	225	356
Polock, Isaac	Deed to	Polock, David	1802	I9	402	667

Party	What	Party	Year	Liber	Old	New
Polock, Isaac	Deed to	Kennedy, James	1802	I9	330	544
Polock, Isaac	Deed to	Polock, David	1802	I9	378	627
Polock, Isaac	Deed fr	Anderson, John B.	1802	I9	159	240
Polock, Isaac	Deed to	Fox, Joseph, Jr.	1802	I9	410	680
Polock, Isaac	Deed to	Polock, David	1802	I9	379	628
Polock, Isaac	Deed to	Polock, Abigail	1802	I9	305	501
Polock, Isaac	Deed to	Brady, Michael	1802	I9	303	497
Polock, Isaac	Cert fr	Commissioners of Washington	1804	K10	382	396
Polock, Isaac	Cert fr	Commissioners of Washington	1804	K10	382	396
Polock, Isaac	Deed fr	Polock, Abigail, late of MD	1806	P15	216	144
Polock, Isaac	Deed to	Teakle, Littleton Dennis, Som. Co.	1806	P15	220	147
Polock, Isaac et al	Bond fr	Myers, Moses	1802	H8	155	150
Polock, Isaac, in MD	Deed to	Moscrop, Henry	1802	H8	380	353
Polock, Isaac, late of GA	Deed fr	Mailey, Robert, cordwainer, Phila.	1797	C3	081	66
Polock, Isaac, mer., of GA	Deed fr	Burnes, David, of P.G. Co.	1796	B2B	507	210
Polock, Isaac, of Savannah GA	Deed to	Templeman, John, of G'tn.	1795	B2B	375	028
Polock, Isaac, of Savannah GA	Deed fr	Morris, Robert et al	1796	B2B	505	206
Polock, Isaac, of G'tn.	Deed fr	Johnson, Thomas, Frederick Town	1797	B2B	646	408
Polock, Isaac, of Savannah GA	Deed fr	Davidson, Samuel, of G'tn.	1797	B2B	645	407
Polock, Isaac, of G'tn.	Deed to	Forrest, Uriah	1797	C3	088	072
Polock, Isaac, of G'tn.	Deed to	Blodget, Samuel, Jr., of Phila.	1797	C3	077	64
Polock, Isaac, of G'tn.	Deed to	Martin, Honore, of Montg. Co.	1797	C3	264	215
Polock, Isaac, of G'tn.	Deed fr	Lingan, Nicholas, of P.G. Co.	1798	C3	372	297
Polock, Isaac, of G'tn.	Deed to	Barney, John H., of G'tn.	1802	H8	522	482
Ponsonby, John, Glasgow Co. NC	Deed to	Sheppard, Benjamin, of NC	1792	A1-1	157	225
Ponsonby, John, Glasgow Co. NC	Deed fr	Townsend, Henry	1792	A1-1	156	224
Poor, John	Assign to	Burford, John A. et al	1810	X23	415	335
Poor, John	B. of S. fr	Swann, William T., of Alexa. Co.	1812	AD29	133	102
Poor, John	Deed fr	Burchan, John, of New York NY	1815	AK35	246	195
Pope, Fielder	B. of S. to	Pope, Joshua (bro.)	1802	H8	582	546
Pope, Joshua (bro.)	B. of S. fr	Pope, Fielder	1802	H8	582	546
Porter, Charles, of Montg. Co.	B. of S. to	Kedgly, John	1808	U20	226	122
Porter, Daniel P. et al	Deed to	Lenox, Peter	1815	AI34	105	119
Porter, David, Com.	B. of S. fr	Greenfield, Mary	1815	AI34	518	523
Porter, David, Com.	Deed fr	Bowie, Washington, of G'tn.	1816	AL36	166	167
Porter, Isaiah, of G'tn.	B. of S. to	Mosher, Jeremiah, of G'tn.	1813	AF31	440	316
Porter, James A., trustee	Deed to	Middleton, Joseph	1808	V21	087	067
Porter, James A., trustee	Deed fr	Templeman, John	1808	U20	315	168
Porter, James A., trustee	B. of S. fr	Banks, John, insolvent	1808	U20	183	102
Porter, James A.	B. of S. fr	Belle, Benjamin (C)	1811	AB27	069	058
Porter, Marcy Maria et al	Deed to	Lenox, Peter	1815	AI34	105	119
Porter, Nancy McCarty et al	Deed to	Lenox, Peter	1815	AI34	105	119
Porter, Porter et al	Deed to	French, George, of G'tn.	1795	B2B	371	022
Porter, Samuel & James Sterrett	Cert fr	Commissioners of Washington	1793	B2A	316	444
Porter, Samuel et al	Deed to	Beall, Thomas & John M. Gantt	1792	A1-1	141	205
Porter, Sarah & children, Alexa.	Deed to	Yeates, William	1816	AM37	406	292
Porter, Sarah, admx. of Thomas	Deed fr	Polock, Isaac	1802	H8	279	264
Porter, Sarah, of Alexa.	Deed fr	Polock, Isaac	1802	H8	278	263
Porter, Sarah, wid/o Thomas et al	Deed to	Lenox, Peter	1815	AI34	105	119
Porterfield, John, of Berkeley Co.	Deed to	Bell, Charles	1815	AI34	074	084
Portersfield, John, Berkeley Co.	Deed fr	Faulkner, James, Berkeley Co.	1808	T19	124	087
Portugal, the Queen of	Deed fr	Commissioners of Washington	1798	C3	474	374
Posey, Benjamin, of Charles Co.	Deed fr	Maddox, Lanta	1801	G7	290	404
Posey, Richard (negro)	Manumis fr	Wightt, John Magruder	1810	Z25	037	028
Poston, Bartholomew	Manumis to	[ ], Jesse (negro)	1808	T19	384	273

Party	What	Party	Year	Liber	Old	New
Poston, Bartholomew	Deed fr	Brashears, John W.	1809	W22	186	130
Poston, Fielder B., of G'tn.	B. of S. to	Edd, John, of G'tn.	1817	AO39	177	132
Potomac Company	Suit vs	Sundry Persons	1812	AG32	258	183
Potomac Masonic Lodge No. 43	Lease fr	Reintzel, Anthony	1811	Z25	490	389
Potter, Hosea E., of NY	Deed fr	Griswold, Chester, of OH	1815	AH33	365	316
Potterfield, John, of Berkeley Co.	Deed fr	Mackey, William, of Berkeley Co.	1811	AB27	328	270
Potts, James B.	Deed fr	Prout, William	1808	T19	039	029
Potts, James Bowman	Deed to	Herty, Thomas	1805	M12	132	127
Potts, James Bowman et al	Deed to	Young, Thomas	1808	T19	031	024
Potts, John	D. of T. to	Richter, John	1809	W22	375	243
Potts, John	Deed fr	Lovering, William & Sarah	1817	AO39	372	251
Potts, John, plt.	Suit	Voss, Nicholas, def.	1809	W22	375	243
Potts, William	Deed fr	Fenwick, George, of G'tn.	1802	H8	407	376
Potts, William, of Frederick Co.	Deed to	LaMache, Mary de, of G'tn.	1803	K10	090	97
Powell, Adam	B. of S. to	Young, Charles, of Montg. Co.	1811	Z25	525	416
Powell, Cuthbert	Cert fr	Commissioners of Washington	1800	E5		158
Powell, Cuthbert et al	Deed fr	Wadsworth, Charles & Elizabeth	1810	Y24	001	001
Powell, Cuthbert, of Alexa. et al	Deed to	Butler, Silas	1810	Y24	326	296
Powell, Nichlas	Deed fr	Busey, Charles	1802	I9	230	366
Power, Francis, of G'tn.	Deed to	Power, Joseph, s/o Francis	1805	M12	353	360
Power, Joseph, s/o Francis	Deed fr	Power, Francis, of G'tn.	1805	M12	353	360
Pratt, Carey	Mortgage to	Luddington, Henry, of NY	1801	G7	259	354
Pratt, Carey, of Winchester VA	Deed fr	Commissioners of Washington	1799	D4	185	167
Pratt, Henry & George Budd	P. of Atty. to	Bickley, Robert S.	1806	Q16	178	118
Pratt, Henry et al	D. of T. fr	Morris, Robert, of Phila. et al	1797	C3	204	172
Pratt, Henry et al	D. of T. fr	Morris, Robert, of Phila. et al	1797	C3	192	161
Pratt, Henry et al	Deed fr	Greenleaf, James, of Phila. et al	1797	C3	154	127
Pratt, Henry et al	Deed fr	Morris, Robert, of Phila. et al	1798	C3	301	243
Pratt, Henry et al	Deed fr	Hanson, Alexander Contee	1798	C3	490	385
Pratt, Henry et al	B. in C. to	Greenleaf, James et al	1799	E5	003	003
Pratt, Henry et al	Deed fr	Commissioners of Washington	1800	E5	369	350
Pratt, Henry et al	Deed fr	Commissioners of Washington	1800	E5	372	353
Pratt, Henry et al	Deed fr	Commissioners of Washington	1801	G7	281	389
Pratt, Henry et al	Deed fr	Commissioners of Washington	1801	F6	202	131
Pratt, Henry et al	Deed fr	Dorsey, William H. et al	1802	I9	568	920
Pratt, Henry et al	Deed fr	Tingey, Thomas	1802	I9	572	927
Pratt, Henry et al	Deed to	Tingey, Thomas	1802	I9	213	336
Pratt, Henry et al	Deed to	Underwood, Robert et al	1802	I9	217	342
Pratt, Henry et al	Deed fr	Dorsey, William H.	1802	I9	263	426
Pratt, Henry et al	Deed to	Yeates, William	1802	H8	056	053
Pratt, Henry et al	P. of Atty. to	Greenleaf, James	1804	K10	101	107
Pratt, Henry et al	Deed to	Sewall, Robert, of P.G. Co.	1805	N13	081	074
Pratt, Henry et al	P. of Atty. to	Greenleaf, James	1805	M12	377	390
Pratt, Henry et al	Deed to	May, Frederick	1805	N13	108	102
Pratt, Henry et al	Deed to	Elliott, Samuel, Jr.	1806	O14	362	242
Pratt, Henry et al	Deed to	Van Ness, John P.	1806	P15	105	065
Pratt, Henry et al	Deed to	Tilghman, William, of Phila. et al	1808	T19	086	061
Pratt, Henry et al	Deed to	Cook, Orlando	1809	X23	245	190
Pratt, Henry et al	B. of S. fr	Prout, William	1809	W22	380	247
Pratt, Henry et al	Quit to	Toole, Patrick	1809	X23	135	097
Pratt, Henry et al	Deed to	Griffin, Lancelot	1810	X23	319	256
Pratt, Henry et al	Deed fr	Munroe, Thomas, Supt.	1811	Z25	472	374
Pratt, Henry et al	Deed to	Aborn, Henry	1812	AC28	470	334
Pratt, Henry et al	Deed to	Varnum, James M.	1812	AC28	508	363
Pratt, Henry et al	Deed to	Latrobe, Benjamim H.	1812	AC28	445	318

Party	What	Party	Year	Liber	Old	New
Pratt, Henry et al	Deed to	Tingey, Thomas	1812	AC28	428	308
Pratt, Henry et al	Deed to	Jones, Walter, Jr.	1812	AC28	400	290
Pratt, Henry et al	Deed to	Gales, Joseph, Jr.	1812	AE30	001	001
Pratt, Henry et al	Deed to	Tuckfield, William H.P.	1813	AE30	230	184
Pratt, Henry et al	Deed to	Van Ness, John P.	1813	AE30	485	360
Pratt, Henry et al	Deed to	Jones, Walter, Jr.	1813	AE30	328	246
Pratt, Henry et al	Release to	Nourse, Joseph	1813	AF31	011	008
Pratt, Henry et al	Deed to	Smallwood, Samuel N.	1813	AF31	032	022
Pratt, Henry et al	Deed to	Heath, Nathaniel H.	1813	AE30	522	387
Pratt, Henry et al	Deed to	Van Ness, John P.	1814	AG32	313	229
Pratt, Henry et al	Deed fr	Miller, John, Jr. & Wm. Cranch	1814	AG32	330	240
Pratt, Henry et al	Deed to	McMurray, William	1814	AH33	171	159
Pratt, Henry et al	Deed to	Wayne, Francis	1814	AH33	377	326
Pratt, Henry et al	Deed to	Johnson, James W.	1814	AH33	004	004
Pratt, Henry et al	Deed to	Glover, Charles	1814	AH33	302	261
Pratt, Henry et al	Deed to	Gales, Joseph, Jr.	1815	AK35	400	314
Pratt, Henry et al	Deed to	Walker, Zachariah	1815	AK35	404	317
Pratt, Henry et al	Deed to	Hoot, Samuel	1816	AL36	122	124
Pratt, Henry et al	Deed to	Brent, Robert	1816	AL36	538	502
Pratt, Henry et al	Deed to	Eliot, Samuel, Jr.	1816	AL36	171	171
Pratt, Henry, of Phila. PA et al	Deed to	Voss, Nicholas	1807	S18	025	021
Pratt, Henry, of Phila. et al	Deed to	Weightman, Roger C.	1811	AB27	228	186
Pratt, Henry, of Phila. et al	Deed to	Matthews, William, Rev.	1811	AB27	342	282
Pratt, Henry, of Phila. PA et al	Deed to	Weightman, Roger C.	1812	AD29	406	342
Pratt, Henry, of Phila. PA et al	Deed to	Weightman, Roger C.	1812	AD29	409	346
Pratt, Henry, of Phila. PA et al	Deed to	Weightman, Roger C.	1812	AD29	402	339
Pratt, Henry, trustee et al	Quit to	Eliot, Samuel, Jr.	1809	W22	293	193
Pratt, Henry, trustee, et al	Deed to	Mara, Philip O.	1810	Z25	340	266
Pratt, John Wilkes	Deed fr	Burnes, David	1794	B2A	006	006
Pratt, John Wilkes	Deed fr	Magruder, John Smith, P.G. Co.	1806	P15	196	131
Pratt, John Wilks	Deed to	Underwood, Robert	1806	Q16	031	020
Pratt, Rachel, of P.G. Co.	B. of S. to	Daugherty, Joseph	1810	Y24	369	334
Pravotte, Peter	Deed fr	Chandler, Walter Story	1807	S18	314	246
Prentiss, William & William H.	Mortgage to	Grammer, Gotlieb C.	1817	AN38	373	275
Prentiss, William, mer.	B. of S. to	Cranch, William, Gent.	1796	B2B	532	248
Prentiss, William, mer.	Agreement	Nicholson, John	1797	B2B	622	380
Presbyterian Congregation, G'tn.	Deed to	Bussard, Daniel	1812	AC28	185	140
Presbyterian Congregation, G'tn.	Lease to	Craig, Robert	1812	AC28	186	142
Presbyterian Congregation, G'tn.	Deed to	Robertson, Thomas	1812	AC28	275	200
Presbyterian Congregation, G'tn.	Deed to	English, David	1812	AC28	197	150
Presbyterian Congregation, G'tn.	Deed to	Jones, Benjamin W.	1812	AC28	144	107
Presbyterian Congregation, G'tn.	Deed to	English, David	1812	AC28	196	149
Presbyterian Congregation, G'tn.	Deed to	King, Charles	1812	AC28	457	325
Presbyterian Congregation, G'tn.	Lease to	Whann, David	1812	AC28	141	106
Presbyterian Congregation, G'tn.	Deed to	Melvin, James, Jr.	1812	AC28	242	179
Presbyterian Congregation of G'tn.	Deed fr	Beatty, Charles	1802	H8	562	525
Presbyterian Congregation of G'tn.	Deed fr	Deakins, Francis	1802	H8	558	520
Presbyterian Congregation of G'tn.	Lease to	Renner, Daniel	1811	AB27	367	304
Presbyterian Congregation of G'tn.	Lease to	Mayn, Adam	1811	AB27	471	385
Presbyterian Congregation of G'tn.	Lease to	Hoot, Samuel	1811	AB27	221	179
Presbyterian Congregation of G'tn.	Lease to	Renner, Daniel	1811	AB27	364	302
Presbyterian Congregation of G'tn.	Deed to	Cox, John	1811	AB27	392	323
Presbyterian Congregation of G'tn.	Deed fr	Hyde, Thomas, of G'tn.	1811	Z25	441	346
Presbyterian Congregation of G'tn.	Deed to	Bussard, Daniel	1812	AD29	521	439
Presbyterian Congregation of G'tn.	Deed to	Mayer, Henry	1815	AK35	075	058

Party	What	Party	Year	Liber	Old	New
Presbyterian Congregation of G'tn.	Deed to	Wilson, John A.	1815	AI34	277	312
Preston, John	B. of S. to	Sutherland, Thomas J.	1814	AH33	014	013
Price, Handley	B. of S. to	Clarke, Horatio D.	1817	AO39	279	199
Price, Handley	B. of S. to	Clarke, Horatio D.	1817	AO39	277	198
Price, Thomas & Michael Stooker	Deed to	Beall, Thomas & John M. Gantt	1792	A1-1	106	154
Price, Thomas [Pryse]	Qualify	Lieutenant of light infantry	1812	AD29	190	155
Priestley, James, of Nashville TN	Deed to	King, Vincent, of G'tn.	1815	AI34	431	449
Prime, William	Mortgage to	Tuckfield, William H.P.	1805	O14	048	029
Prime, William	B. of S. to	Corning, Zephorah	1806	O14	350	234
Prime, William	Assign to	Corning, Zephorah	1806	O14	349	233
Prince, Isaac, of Phila. PA	Deed fr	Vanzandt, Nicholas B.	1807	R17	071	057
Pringle, George	B. of S. fr	Geyer, Daniel	1807	R17	411	310
Pritchard, Benjamin et al	Deed fr	Gilpin, Bernard, of Montg. Co.	1807	R17	376	286
Pritchard, Benjamin, Montg. Co.	Assign to	Wilson, John A.	1817	AN38	494	357
Pritchard, Benjamin, of G'tn.	Deed fr	Hoye, John, of G'tn.	1808	U20	196	108
Procter, Ann	Cert Free to	Savoy, William, s/o Archibald	1810	Y24	032	027
Proctor, Alexander (M)	Cert Free fr	Proctor, Ann	1811	AB27	123	101
Proctor, Ann	Cert Free to	Savoy, Archibald, Jr.	1809	V21	406	309
Proctor, Ann	Cert Free to	Proctor, Alexander (M)	1811	AB27	123	101
Proctor, Ann & Susannah Collins	Cert Free to	Wiseman, Thomas S. (M), age 23	1817	AO39	092	073
Proctor, Sarah (C)	Cert Free to	Butler, Betsy	1812	AD29	552	464
Profit, William et al	Deed to	Dalton, Tristram, of G'tn.	1796	B2B	407	074
Prouse, Peregrine	Affidavit	Gale, Joseph T. (C)	1804	K10	187	
Prout, Anna (M), age 17	Cert Free fr	Dowrey, James	1813	AF31	242	168
Prout, James, a man of color	Cert fr	Quynn, Allen	1805	M12	342	347
Prout, William	Deed to	Dalton, Tristram, of G'tn.	1796	B2B	408	076
Prout, William	Deed fr	Woodward, Augustine, of VA	1797	B2B	661	425
Prout, William	Deed to	Woodward, Augustine, of VA	1797	B2B	659	423
Prout, William	Deed fr	Woodward, Frances, wid/o C.	1798	C3	284	230
Prout, William	Deed fr	Woodward, J., A., C., H. & F.	1798	D4	129	112
Prout, William	Deed fr	Deblois, Lewis	1798	D4	103	087
Prout, William	Deed fr	Slater, Jonathan	1798	D4	009	007
Prout, William	Deed to	Venable, William & Elizabeth	1798	C3	282	229
Prout, William	Deed fr	Deblois, Lewis	1799	D4	198	181
Prout, William	Deed to	Deblois, Lewis	1799	D4	343	331
Prout, William	Deed fr	Stater, Joseph & David	1799	D4	374	359
Prout, William	Deed to	Slater, David Harris, of VA	1800	E5	098	086
Prout, William	Deed to	Slater, Sarah, d/o Joseph, of VA	1800	E5	096	084
Prout, William	Deed to	Tictzen, Henry, Jr.	1800	E5	219	212
Prout, William	Deed to	Slater, Jonathan, s/o Joseph	1800	E5	095	082
Prout, William	Deed to	Slater, Charles, of Monroe Co. VA	1800	E5	099	087
Prout, William	Deed to	Slater, Joseph, of Monroe Co. VA	1800	E5	101	089
Prout, William	Deed to	Slater, David	1800	E5	082	069
Prout, William	Deed to	Slater, Anna, d/o Joseph, of VA	1800	E5	093	081
Prout, William	Deed to	Slater, Henry, s/o Joseph, of VA	1800	E5	092	079
Prout, William	Deed to	Parsons, Barney	1800	F6	101	062
Prout, William	Release fr	Slater, Sarah, w/o Joseph	1801	F6	167	104
Prout, William	Deed to	Shaw, Alexander	1801	G7	251	341
Prout, William	Deed to	Voss, Nicholas	1801	G7	420	555
Prout, William	Deed to	King, Patrick	1801	G7	271	373
Prout, William	Deed fr	Davidson, John	1801	G7	154	204
Prout, William	Lease to	Swank, John	1801	G7	441	577
Prout, William	Deed to	Harlburt, Simeon	1801	G7	017	021
Prout, William	Deed to	Tingey, Thomas	1801	G7	246	331
Prout, William	Deed fr	Commissioners of Washington	1801	G7	253	343

Index to District of Columbia Land Records, 1792-1817

Party	What	Party	Year	Liber	Old	New
Prout, William	Deed to	Simms, William	1801	G7	327	457
Prout, William	Deed fr	Tingey, Thomas	1801	G7	228	304
Prout, William	Lease to	Bunyie, William	1801	G7	485	622
Prout, William	Lease to	Dempsey, John	1801	G7	176	235
Prout, William	Deed to	Thomas, Joseph	1801	G7	057	073
Prout, William	Deed fr	Commissioners of Washington	1802	G7	575	724
Prout, William	Deed fr	Forrest, Uriah et al	1802	G7	576	725
Prout, William	Lease to	Fry, James	1802	G7	546	693
Prout, William	Deed to	Fuller, Oliver et al	1802	H8	217	207
Prout, William	Deed fr	Hanson, Alexander C., Hon.	1802	H8	480	441
Prout, William	Deed to	Brown, Amos et al	1802	H8	217	207
Prout, William	Lease to	Brown, Jesse	1802	I9	450	743
Prout, William	Lease to	White, Levi	1802	I9	369	612
Prout, William	Deed to	Smallwood, Samuel N.	1802	I9	530	867
Prout, William	Deed to	Waugh, James, Jr. of VA	1802	I9	108	158
Prout, William	Deed to	Ford, Joseph, of MD et al	1802	I9	016	022
Prout, William	Deed to	Herbert, Francis, St. Mary's Co.	1802	I9	016	022
Prout, William	Deed to	Gilpin, Bernard	1802	I9	459	756
Prout, William	Lease to	White, Levi	1802	I9	368	610
Prout, William	Deed to	Dunlap, Henry	1802	I9	085	121
Prout, William	Lease to	Higdon, Gustavus	1802	I9	479	788
Prout, William	Deed fr	Griffin, Edw.	1802	I9	416	689
Prout, William	Lease to	Rose, Robert	1802	I9	566	919
Prout, William	Lease to	Brown, Robert	1802	I9	183	281
Prout, William	Deed to	Parry, Stephen	1802	I9	367	607
Prout, William	Lease to	Parry, Stephen	1803	K10	097	104
Prout, William	Lease to	Fry, James	1803	K10	094	100
Prout, William	Lease to	Adams, William	1804	K10	325	335
Prout, William	Deed to	Woodward, Augustus Brevoost	1804	L11	084	86
Prout, William	Deed fr	Walker, George	1804	L11	152	152
Prout, William	Deed fr	Woodward, Augustus Brevoost	1804	L11	085	87
Prout, William	Lease to	McNantz, Charles	1804	L11	109	112
Prout, William	Deed to	Woodward, Augustus Brevoost	1804	L11	087	89
Prout, William	Deed to	Forrest, Alexander	1804	L11	177	172
Prout, William	Deed to	Vint, John	1804	L11	361	325
Prout, William	Lease to	Brinyie, Robert	1804	L11	306	281
Prout, William	B. of S. fr	Vermillion, Caleb	1804	L11	007	7
Prout, William	Deed to	O'Brien, William	1804	L11	162	160
Prout, William	Lease to	Goff, John	1804	L11	316	290
Prout, William	Deed to	Clarke, Bailey Erles, of P.G. Co.	1804	M12	028	029
Prout, William	Mortgage fr	Vint, John	1804	M12	036	036
Prout, William	Lease to	McCutchen, John	1805	M12	199	200
Prout, William	Lease to	Spooner, William	1805	M12	387	399
Prout, William	Deed to	Edelin, Electus, of P.G. Co.	1805	M12	075	069
Prout, William	B. of S. fr	Thompson, William	1805	M12	288	288
Prout, William	Deed to	Walker, James	1805	M12	225	226
Prout, William	Deed to	Adams, Henry	1805	M12	117	111
Prout, William	Lease to	Longdon, Abel	1805	M12	262	263
Prout, William	B. of S. fr	Boone, Ignatius	1805	N13	115	110
Prout, William	Lease to	Smitson, Hezekiah	1805	N13	206	179
Prout, William	B. of S. fr	Adams, Henry	1805	N13	400	318
Prout, William	Deed to	Parsons, William	1805	N13	121	116
Prout, William	Deed to	Spalding, Philip, of P.G. Co.	1805	N13	116	111
Prout, William	Deed to	Nesbit, Henry	1805	N13	170	154
Prout, William	Deed to	Russ, Samuel	1805	N13	212	183

Index to District of Columbia Land Records, 1792-1817

Party	What	Party	Year	Liber	Old	New
Prout, William	Deed fr	Vint, John	1805	N13	402	320
Prout, William	Lease to	Ireland, Elizabeth et al	1805	N13	235	199
Prout, William	Deed fr	Holburt, Simon	1805	O14	030	019
Prout, William	Deed to	Haliday, Thomas	1806	O14	195	128
Prout, William	Lease to	Higdon, Gustavus	1806	O14	123	079
Prout, William	Deed to	Dougherty, Barney	1806	O14	323	214
Prout, William	Lease to	Young, Thomas et al	1806	P15	139	090
Prout, William	Lease to	Delphy, Richard	1806	P15	250	165
Prout, William	B. of S. fr	Smith, Cornelius	1806	P15	151	099
Prout, William	Lease to	Bryan, Thomas	1806	P15	353	234
Prout, William	Lease to	McCutchin, John	1806	P15	295	194
Prout, William	Deed to	Queen, Nicholas Lewes et al	1806	P15	229	152
Prout, William	Deed to	Higdon, Gustavus	1806	P15	076	046
Prout, William	Lease to	Brown, Thomas	1806	P15	267	176
Prout, William	Lease to	Brady, Nathaniel	1806	Q16	237	163
Prout, William	B. of S. fr	Baker, Samuel	1806	Q16	143	094
Prout, William	Deed to	Vidler, Edward	1806	Q16	080	051
Prout, William	B. of S. fr	Kenner, James	1806	Q16	204	138
Prout, William	Lease to	Jarrad, George	1806	Q16	049	031
Prout, William	Lease to	Liverpool, Moses	1806	Q16	131	086
Prout, William	Lease to	Drummond, John	1806	Q16	148	097
Prout, William	Deed to	Tingey, Thomas & Peter Miller	1807	Q16	377	289
Prout, William	Lease to	O'Hare, Christopher	1807	Q16	335	258
Prout, William	Deed to	Bryan, Benjamin	1807	R17	176	135
Prout, William	Deed to	Bryan, Benjamin	1807	R17	007	007
Prout, William	Lease to	Parsons, Joseph B.	1807	R17	120	093
Prout, William	Deed to	Holliday, Thomas	1807	R17	333	253
Prout, William	Deed to	Higdon, Gustavus	1807	R17	360	375
Prout, William	B. of S. fr	Russ, Samuel	1807	R17	031	026
Prout, William	Deed to	Farrell, Patrick	1807	S18	308	241
Prout, William	Deed to	Cox, George	1807	S18	195	156
Prout, William	Deed to	Tippett, Cartwright	1808	U20	220	119
Prout, William	Deed to	Charles, Richard	1808	T19	199	142
Prout, William	Lease to	Bryan, Benjamin	1808	T19	380	271
Prout, William	Deed fr	Ratcliff, William	1808	U20	093	052
Prout, William	B. of S. fr	Sheckles, Richard	1808	T19	359	258
Prout, William	Deed to	Johnson, James	1808	T19	281	206
Prout, William	Deed to	Higdon, Gustavus	1808	T19	300	220
Prout, William	Deed to	Rose, Robert	1808	U20	211	114
Prout, William	Deed to	Brashears, Nathaniel	1808	U20	068	038
Prout, William	Deed to	Farrington, Lewis, Somerset Co.	1808	T19	104	074
Prout, William	B. of S. fr	Cross, William	1808	U20	372	204
Prout, William	Deed to	Summers, Thomas	1808	U20	055	032
Prout, William	Deed to	Collard, George	1808	U20	342	185
Prout, William	Deed to	Potts, James B.	1808	T19	039	029
Prout, William	Deed to	Brice, Thomas P.	1808	U20	271	144
Prout, William	D. of T. to	Cooke, Thomas, Frederick Co.	1808	T19	168	119
Prout, William	Deed to	McCutchen, John, of G'tn.	1808	T19	256	189
Prout, William	Lease to	Spooner, Holder	1808	V21	099	075
Prout, William	Deed fr	Russ, Samuel	1808	V21	038	029
Prout, William	B. of S. fr	Sarratt, Henry B.	1808	V21	037	028
Prout, William	B. of S. fr	Cassin, Joseph	1809	V21	223	158
Prout, William	Deed to	Fowler, Samuel	1809	V21	289	209
Prout, William	Deed to	Cassin, Joseph	1809	V21	225	160
Prout, William	Lease to	Cassin, Joseph	1809	V21	219	156

Party	What	Party	Year	Liber	Old	New
Prout, William	Lease to	Wood, William	1809	V21	351	254
Prout, William	Deed to	Serra, Augustin	1809	V21	316	232
Prout, William	B. of S. fr	Parry, Stephen	1809	W22	351	227
Prout, William	B. of S. fr	Vint, John	1809	W22	350	226
Prout, William	B. of S. to	Pratt, Henry et al	1809	W22	380	247
Prout, William	B. of S. fr	Watkins, John	1809	W22	167	118
Prout, William	Deed to	Catalano, Salvadora	1809	X23	086	064
Prout, William	Deed to	Smith, William	1809	X23	039	029
Prout, William	B. of S. fr	Bryan, Benjamin	1809	X23	049	036
Prout, William	Deed to	Wickham, James, of Phila. PA	1809	X23	112	080
Prout, William	B. of S. fr	Drummond, John	1809	X23	087	065
Prout, William	B. of S. fr	Picknoll, Richard H.	1809	X23	131	094
Prout, William	Deed to	Forrest, Alexander	1810	Y24	186	171
Prout, William	Deed to	Clarke, Robert	1810	Y24	156	142
Prout, William	Deed to	O'Brien, William	1810	Y24	486	429
Prout, William	Deed to	Picknoll, Richard H.	1810	Y24	480	425
Prout, William	Deed to	Forrest, Alexander	1810	Y24	185	171
Prout, William	Lease to	Bowen, John	1810	Y24	145	132
Prout, William	Assign fr	O'Hare, Christopher	1810	Y24	118	108
Prout, William	Lease to	O'Connor, Dennis	1810	Z25	278	218
Prout, William	Deed to	Methodist Meeting House, trustees	1810	Z25	134	105
Prout, William	B. of S. fr	Morris, Thomas B., of P.G. Co.	1810	Z25	338	265
Prout, William	B. of S. fr	McCoy, Henry	1811	AB27	171	141
Prout, William	Deed to	Wharton, Franklin	1811	AB27	218	177
Prout, William	Lease to	McWilliams, Alexander	1811	Z25	495	393
Prout, William	Lease to	Townshend, Lemuel	1811	AA26	073	053
Prout, William	Deed to	Spooner, Holder	1812	AC28	408	296
Prout, William	Deed to	O'Brien, William	1812	AC28	124	093
Prout, William	Deed to	Grant, George	1812	AC28	475	337
Prout, William	Deed to	Wharton, Franklin, Col.	1812	AC28	504	360
Prout, William	Deed to	Howard, Peter	1812	AD29	238	197
Prout, William	Record	O'Brien, William	1812	AD29	159	125
Prout, William	B. of S. fr	Craver, Philip	1812	AD29	123	094
Prout, William	Deed fr	White, Levi	1812	AC28	480	341
Prout, William	Deed to	Jarrad, George	1813	AE30	370	274
Prout, William	Deed to	Friend, James et al	1813	AF31	184	124
Prout, William	Deed to	Otterback, Philip	1813	AF31	336	239
Prout, William	Deed to	Marshall, George	1813	AF31	477	348
Prout, William	Lease to	Vermillion, Henrietta	1813	AF31	115	078
Prout, William	Lease to	Serra, Augustin	1813	AE30	380	281
Prout, William	Deed to	Kealey, Daniel	1814	AG32	140	101
Prout, William	Deed to	Cocking, William	1814	AG32	160	115
Prout, William	Deed to	Hebb, William, of P.G. Co.	1814	AG32	176	125
Prout, William	B. of S. fr	Delphy, Richard	1814	AG32	290	211
Prout, William	Deed to	Gerrard, George	1814	AG32	245	175
Prout, William	Deed to	Venable, Charles	1814	AG32	318	232
Prout, William	Deed to	Gray, William	1814	AH33	123	116
Prout, William	Deed to	Higdon, Gustavus	1814	AH33	031	029
Prout, William	Deed to	Cox, George	1814	AH33	276	241
Prout, William	Lease to	Kealey, Daniel	1814	AH33	163	152
Prout, William	Deed to	Evans, Philip	1815	AH33	453	389
Prout, William	Deed to	Evans, Philip	1815	AH33	452	387
Prout, William	Deed fr	Cocke, Buller & Edmund Law	1815	AK35	218	171
Prout, William	Deed to	Friend, James	1815	AK35	396	311
Prout, William	Lease to	Brashears, Nathaniel	1815	AH33	389	337

Index to District of Columbia Land Records, 1792-1817　341

Party	What	Party	Year	Liber	Old	New
Prout, William	Deed to	Ensey, William	1816	AL36	110	112
Prout, William	Deed to	Fowler, Joseph	1816	AM37	001	001
Prout, William	Deed to	Bryson, Sarah	1816	AM37	011	009
Prout, William	Deed to	Bryson, Sarah	1816	AM37	013	010
Prout, William	Deed to	Forrest, John B.	1816	AM37	066	054
Prout, William	Lease to	Chalmers, John, Jr.	1817	AN38	399	297
Prout, William	Deed fr	Glover, Charles, trustee	1817	AN38	036	029
Prout, William	Deed to	Charles, Richard	1817	AN38	149	109
Prout, William	Deed to	Otterback, Phillip	1817	AN38	275	200
Prout, William	Lease to	Jolly, Elizabeth	1817	AN38	002	002
Prout, William	Deed to	Jones, Richard	1817	AO39	422	287
Prout, William	Deed fr	De Arce, Don Manual et al	1817	AO39	474	325
Prout, William	Deed fr	Slater, Sarah, wid/o David	1817	AO39	216	157
Prout, William & wife Sarah	Deed to	Davidson, James	1811	AC28	038	028
Prout, William, et al	Deed to	Dalton, Tristram, of G'tn.	1796	B2B	405	072
Prout, William et al	Deed fr	Piercy, James, sugar refiner	1800	E5	197	189
Prout, William, of Montg. Co.	Deed fr	Beatty, Charles, of Montg. Co.	1795	B2A	280	392
Prout, William, trustee	Deed fr	Walker, George, insolvent	1804	L11	280	257
Provott, Peter	Deed to	Wright, Matthew	1808	T19	360	259
Provott, Peter P.	Mortgage to	McKim, James	1810	Z25	012	010
Pryse, Thomas, trustee	Deed fr	Reid, William F., insolvent	1810	Z25	197	155
Pryse, Thomas, trustee	Deed fr	Grimes, Michael, insolvent	1810	Z25	263	206
Pryse, Thomas [Price]	Qualify	Lieutenant of light infantry	1812	AD29	190	155
Pumfrey, James, of P.G. Co.	B. of S. fr	Little, Israel	1806	P15	192	129
Pumphrey, James	Cert Slave	Hamilton, John, of Loudoun Co.	1811	AA26	356	238
Pumphrey, James, of P.G. Co.	Manumis to	[ ], Eliza (C), and others	1813	AE30	091	070
Pumphrey, James, of P.G. Co.	Manumis to	[ ], Thamer (C), and others	1813	AE30	091	070
Pumphrey, William	B. of S. fr	Morris, Thomas B., of P.G. Co.	1817	AN38	087	067
Pumphrey, William, of P.G. Co.	B. of S. to	Reynolds, Thomas	1816	AM37	295	216
Purcell, Peirce & James Hoban	Cert fr	Commissioners of Washington	1792	B2A	298	418
Purcell, Peirce & James Hoban	Cert fr	Commissioners of Washington	1792	B2A	298	419
Purcell, Peirce & James Hoban	Cert fr	Commissioners of Washington	1792	B2A	290	406
Purcell, Peirce & James Hoban	Cert fr	Commissioners of Washington	1792	B2A	288	403
Purcell, Peirce & James Hoban	Cert fr	Commissioners of Washington	1792	B2A	299	419
Purcell, Peirce & James Hoban	Cert fr	Commissioners of Washington	1792	B2A	299	420
Purcell, Pierce	Transfer fr	Beatty, Thomas J.	1796	B2B	451	138
Purcell, Pierce	Cert fr	Commissioners of Washington	1796	B2B	452	138
Purcell, Pierce	Cert fr	Commissioners of Washington	1796	B2B	452	138
Purcell, Pierce	Transsfer fr	Beatty, Thomas J.	1796	B2B	452	138
Purcell, Pierce	Deed to	Purcell, Redmond	1799	D4	322	307
Purcell, Pierce	Deed fr	Burnes, David	1799	D4	311	295
Purcell, Pierce	Mortgage to	Knowles, William	1799	D4	335	321
Purcell, Pierce	Release fr	Purcell, Redmond	1801	G7	460	596
Purcell, Pierce	Deed to	Stockwell, Mark et al	1801	G7	377	509
Purcell, Pierce	Mortgage fr	Knowles, William	1801	G7	386	519
Purcell, Pierce	Deed to	Hoban, James	1802	H8	076	070
Purcell, Pierce	Deed fr	Commissioners of Washington	1802	H8	089	082
Purcell, Pierce	Deed to	Hoban, James	1802	H8	074	069
Purcell, Pierce	Mortgage to	Pleasonton, Stephen et al	1802	I9	066	092
Purcell, Pierce	P. of Atty. to	Stockwell, Mark et al	1802	I9	233	372
Purcell, Pierce	Deed to	Hoban, James	1802	I9	058	080
Purcell, Pierce	Deed to	Purcell, Redmond	1802	I9	495	812
Purcell, Pierce	Mortgage to	Stockwell, Mark et al	1802	I9	066	092
Purcell, Pierce	Deed fr	Pleasonton, Stephen et al	1803	K10	056	61
Purcell, Pierce	Deed fr	Stockwell, Mark et al	1803	K10	056	61

Party	What	Party	Year	Liber	Old	New
Purcell, Pierce	Deed to	Carroll, Mary et al	1809	X23	160	118
Purcell, Pierce	Cert fr	Munroe, Thomas, Supt.	1809	X23	162	119
Purcell, Pierce	D. of T. to	Brent, William	1810	Y24	052	046
Purcell, Pierce	Deed fr	Corporation of Washington	1815	AK35	453	355
Purcell, Pierce et al	Deed to	Scholfield, Joseph L.	1810	Y24	073	065
Purcell, Pierce et al	Deed to	Donohoo, Patrick	1810	Y24	062	055
Purcell, Pierce et al	Deed to	Clark, Francis	1810	Y24	374	338
Purcell, Redmond	Deed fr	Purcell, Pierce	1799	D4	322	307
Purcell, Redmond	Release to	Purcell, Pierce	1801	G7	460	596
Purcell, Redmond	Deed fr	Purcell, Pierce	1802	I9	495	812
Purk, Benjamin	Marriage	Anderson, Hannah	1813	AF31	433	312
Purk, Benjamin	Cert Free fr	Gloyd, George H.	1813	AF31	433	312
Putnam, Ernestus, of G'tn.	Lease fr	Bohrer, George, of G'tn.	1816	AL36	070	071
Pyfer, Henry, of G'tn.	Manumis to	Brown, Amy, age 48	1813	AF31	140	094
Pyfer, Henry, of G'tn.	Deed fr	King, Vincent, of G'tn.	1814	AH33	218	194

Index to District of Columbia Land Records, 1792-1817   343

Party	What	Party	Year	Liber	Old	New
Q						
Quabbs, William, of G'tn.	D. of T. to	Lipscomb, John, of G'tn.	1811	AA26	006	004
Quables, William, of G'tn.	Deed fr	Balch, Stephen B., of G'tn.	1809	W22	062	046
Quaid, Walter	Deed to	Gloyd, George Holland	1807	R17	257	195
Quaid, Walter & Ruth, of G'tn.	Deed to	Thompson, Rachel, of G'tn.	1810	X23	412	333
Queen, Amon E.	Division		1802	H8	230	219
Queen, Ann E. Gardner	Division		1802	H8	230	219
Queen, Ann Edwardina, P.G. Co.	Deed fr	Queen, Samuel	1811	AB27	235	192
Queen, Austin (C), or Austin [ ]	Manumis fr	Hazel, Henry	1812	Ac28	381	277
Queen, Catherine F. et al	Deed fr	Queen, Louisa	1815	AK35	085	065
Queen, Charles T. et al	Deed fr	Queen, Louisa	1815	AK35	085	065
Queen, Eleanor	Division		1802	H8	230	219
Queen, Henry M.	Qualify		1802	I9	442	731
Queen, Henry M., collector	Deed to	Kemp, James & Edward Grant	1811	AA26	380	253
Queen, James	Division		1802	H8	230	219
Queen, James, of KY	Assign to	Queen, Samuel	1802	H8	231	220
Queen, John	Qualify	Lieutenant of militia	1813	AE30	287	219
Queen, Joseph	Deed fr	Hanson, Alexander Contee	1794	A1-2	490	93
Queen, Joseph	Deed fr	Brent, Daniel Carroll, marshall	1801	G7	370	502
Queen, Joseph	Division		1802	H8	230	219
Queen, Joseph, of P.G. Co. et al	Deed to	Lingan, Nicholas, of Montg. Co.	1796	B2B	400	065
Queen, Louisa	Deed to	Queen, Richard T. et al	1815	AK35	085	065
Queen, Louisa	Mortgage fr	Queen, Richard T. et al	1816	AK35	489	385
Queen, Marsham	Division		1802	H8	230	219
Queen, Marsham, of Charles Co.	Deed to	St. Clair, George	1812	AC28	271	198
Queen, Milley	Manumis fr	Bond, William	1802	H8	343	319
Queen, Nichlas L. et al	Deed fr	Parsons, Joseph B.	1807	R17	123	095
Queen, Nicholas L. et al	Deed to	Serra, Augustin [Sara]	1806	Q16	104	068
Queen, Nicholas L.	Deed fr	Carroll, Daniel, of *Duddington*	1806	P15	377	252
Queen, Nicholas L. et al	Deed to	Parsons, Joseph Baker	1808	T19	023	018
Queen, Nicholas L.	Certificate	Captain in 1st Legion of Militia	1809	X23	007	005
Queen, Nicholas L.	Deed fr	Edelen, Ignatius	1811	AB27	510	417
Queen, Nicholas L.	B. of S. fr	Rider, William	1811	Z25	554	441
Queen, Nicholas L. et al	Suit ads	Potomac Company	1812	AG32	258	183
Queen, Nicholas L.	Deed fr	Moore, George	1813	AE30	292	222
Queen, Nicholas L.	B. of S. to	Campbell, John	1814	AH33	092	085
Queen, Nicholas L.	Deed fr	Corporation of Washington	1815	AI34	536	541
Queen, Nicholas L. et al	Mortgage fr	Bacon, Samuel	1815	AI34	193	221
Queen, Nicholas L. & Prud. Jones	Deed to	Ward, William	1816	AL36	113	114
Queen, Nicholas L.	Deed to	Blake, James H.	1817	AO39	436	298
Queen, Nicholas Lewes et al	Deed fr	Prout, William	1806	P15	229	152
Queen, Nicholas Lewis	Release to	Cooper, William	1815	AH33	516	443
Queen, Nichols L. et al	B. of S. fr	Lindsey, George W.	1810	Z25	191	150
Queen of Portugal, the	Deed fr	Commissioners of Washington	1798	C3	474	374
Queen, Richard	Deed fr	Young, Notley	1793	A1-1	236	324
Queen, Richard T. et al	Deed fr	Queen, Louisa	1815	AK35	085	065
Queen, Richard T.	Deed fr	King, Adam	1816	AM37	212	157
Queen, Richard T. et al	Mortgage to	Queen, Lpuisa	1816	AK35	489	385
Queen, Samuel	Division		1802	H8	230	219
Queen, Samuel	Assign fr	Queen, James, of KY	1802	H8	231	220
Queen, Samuel	Deed to	Queen, Ann Edwardina, P.G. Co.	1811	AB27	235	192
Queen, Samuel, of P.G. Co.	Deed to	St. Clare, George	1814	AG32	116	087
Queen, Susanna (C)	Cert Free fr	Rapine, Daniel	1816	AL36	243	246
Queen, Walter	Lease to	Sparrow, Joseph et ux	1792	A1-1	041	62
Queen, Walter et al	Release fr	Boone, Joseph, sheriff	1799	E5	053	042

Index to District of Columbia Land Records, 1792-1817

Party	What	Party	Year	Liber	Old	New
Queen, Walter, insolvent	Convey to	Peacock, Robert Ware, trustee	1804	M12	037	038
Quigley, Michael	Lease fr	Perkins, Jeremiah	1812	AC28	265	193
Quigley, Patrick	Deed fr	Van Ness, John P. & Marcia	1817	AN38	257	188
Quinn, Edward	Deed to	Fitzgerrald, William	1810	Y24	143	130
Quinn, Edward et al	Deed fr	McCue, Owen	1808	V21	089	069
Quyn, Allen et al	Deed to	Beall, Thomas & John M. Gantt	1793	A1-1	274	369
Quynn, Allen	Cert to	Prout, James, a man of color	1805	M12	342	347

Index to District of Columbia Land Records, 1792-1817

Party	What	Party	Year	Liber	Old	New
R						
Raborg, William et al	Deed fr	Love, Charles, of G'tn.	1806	P15	135	086
Radcliff, William	Deed fr	Fry, James	1806	Q16	224	153
Radcliff, William S.	Deed fr	Van Ness, John P. & Marcia	1815	AK35	124	096
Radcliff, William S.	D. of T. fr	McNeill, James	1816	AM37	037	030
Radcliffe, Sarah, of Worcester Co.	Deed fr	Stoddert, Benjamin, of G'tn.	1801	G7	318	446
Rae, John	Deed fr	Lingan, James M., of G'tn.	1799	D4	176	157
Ragan, Daniel et al	Convey to	Redman, James, of G'tn.	1816	AL36	463	437
Ragan, Daniel, of G'tn.	Deed to	Jones, Richard, of G'tn.	1817	AN38	367	270
Ragan, Edward, of G'tn.	P. of Atty. fr	Dawes, Mordecai, of Harford Co.	1816	AL36	466	439
Ragan, Edward, of G'tn.	P. of Atty. fr	Dawes, Abraham, of Fauquier Co.	1816	AL36	464	438
Ragan, Lurana, of Frederick Co.	Deed to	Shellman, Jacob, of Frederick Co.	1799	D4	314	297
Ragan, Lurana, wid., Fredk. Co.	Deed fr	Keepers, Joseph, Frederick Co.	1798	C3	427	336
Ragan, Mary et al	Convey to	Redman, James, of G'tn.	1816	AL36	463	437
Ragan, Susanna, of Frederick Co.	Deed to	Shellman, Jacob, of Frederick Co.	1799	D4	193	175
Ragin, William, of Frederick Co.	Deed to	Keeper, Joseph, of Frederick Co.	1797	C3	059	48
Ragon, Daniel, of Frederick Co.	Deed to	Thompson, George	1792	A1-1	065	97
Ragon, Daniel, of G'tn.	Deed fr	Davidson, John, of Annapolis	1795	B2A	165	220
Ragon, John	B. of S. to	Crookshank, John, of G'tn.	1802	G7	488	625
Ragon, John	Deed to	Ritchie, Abner	1807	S18	255	201
Ragon, John, of G'tn.	Deed fr	Ritchie, Abner, of G'tn.	1805	M12	084	078
Ralph, George, Rev.	Transfer to	Matthews, William Penrose, Balto.	1798	B2B	478	171
Ralph, Lewis & Mary, of NC	Deed to	Beatty, Charles, of G'tn.	1794	A1-2	494	97
Ramsay, A.	Slaves		1810	Y24	279	255
Ramsay, John, of PA	Deed to	McIntire, Samuel	1802	H8	242	231
Ramsay, John, of Phila. PA	Deed to	North, Richard, of Phila. PA	1805	N13	059	054
Ramsberg, Jacob, exr. V. Steckle	Deed to	Brengle, Lawrence, Frederick Co.	1805	N13	372	299
Ramsberg, Sebastian & Eliz. et al	Deed to	Stoner, Stephen, of Frederick Co.	1810	Z25	182	144
Ramsbergher, John, Fredk. Co.	Deed to	Thomas, Philip	1792	A1-1	146	210
Ramsey, Andrew & Catherine	B. of S. to	Forrest, Joseph	1816	AL36	059	060
Ramsey, John, by Nicholas King	Deed to	Corcoran, Thomas, of G'tn.	1801	F6	238	158
Ramsey, John, of Phila. PA	Deed fr	Corcoran, Thomas, of G'tn.	1801	F6	240	160
Randall, Daniel	Deed fr	Dorsey, William H., of Montg. Co.	1817	AO39	069	057
Randall, Daniel	Deed fr	Murdock, John, of G'tn.	1817	AO39	068	056
Randall, John	Partition	Whetcroft, William, heirs of	1813	AE30	196	157
Randall, John, Jr.	Deed fr	Kilty, John & Josias Wilson King	1809	V21	355	258
Randall, John, Jr. & John Clayton	B. of S. to	Hagner, Peter	1814	AG32	422	306
Randall, John, of Annapolis	Release to	Renner & Bussard	1808	V21	067	053
Randall, John, of Annapolis	Deed fr	Davidson, Ann Marcia, of G'tn.	1809	X23	042	031
Randall, John, of Annapolis	Deed fr	Whetcroft, William, of Annapolis	1811	AB27	016	015
Randall, John, of Balto. MD	Deed fr	Lovely, William, of Balto. MD	1813	AE30	067	051
Randall, John, of Annapolis	Deed to	Varnum, James M.	1814	AH33	101	093
Randall, John, of Annapolis	Deed to	Campbell, John	1815	AI34	038	044
Randall, John, of Balto. Co. et al	Convey to	Glover, Charles	1816	AK35	324	258
Randall, John, of Annapolis	Deed to	Campbell, John	1816	AK35	531	419
Randolph, William B.	Qualify	Cornet in cavalry	1813	AE30	440	326
Randolph, William B.	Deed fr	King, Robert	1814	AG32	098	074
Randolph, William Beverly	Deed fr	Glover, Charles	1816	AM37	251	185
Rankin, Elizabeth M., d/o W.W.N.	B. of S. fr	Rankin, Walter W.M.	1810	Y24	338	306
Rankin, Robert & Elizabeth	Deed to	Gunnell, Henry, of Fairfax Co. VA	1804	L11	029	28
Rankin, Walter W.M.	B. of S. to	Rankin, Elizabeth M., d/o W.W.M.	1810	Y24	338	306
Ransburg, John D.	Deed fr	Bussard, John R.	1801	G7		076
Ransburgh, John D.	Deed to	Bussard, Daniel	1802	I9	554	898
Rapine, Daniel	Slave		1807	R17	344	
Rapine, Daniel	Cert fr	Munroe, Thomas, Supt.	1808	T19	164	116

Index to District of Columbia Land Records, 1792-1817

Party	What	Party	Year	Liber	Old	New
Rapine, Daniel	Deed fr	Webster, Toppan	1809	X23	003	002
Rapine, Daniel	Cert. Free to	Crockett, Betty	1811	AC28	055	042
Rapine, Daniel	Cert Free to	Thompson, Joe (M)	1812	AB27	504	412
Rapine, Daniel	Release to	Webster, Toppan	1812	AC28	345	250
Rapine, Daniel	Cert Free to	Queen, Susanna (C)	1816	AL36	243	246
Rapine, Daniel et al	B. of S. fr	Webster, Toppan	1814	AH33	130	123
Rapine, Daniel et al	Deed fr	Webster, Toppan	1817	AO39	307	218
Ratcliff, Joseph	Manumis to	[ ], Frank (C), age 25	1811	AA26	072	052
Ratcliff, Joseph, of G'tn.	D. of T. to	Threlkeld, John	1817	AN38	045	037
Ratcliff, William	Deed to	Prout, William	1808	U20	093	052
Ratcliff, William, trustee	Deed fr	Prout, William	1813	AF31	184	124
Ratcliffe, Joseph, of G'tn.	Deed fr	Mackall, Leonard, of G'tn.	1811	AA26	297	200
Ratcliffe, Joseph, of G'tn.	D. of T. to	Eliason, John, of G'tn.	1811	AA26	291	195
Ratcliffe, Joseph, of G'tn.	D. of T. to	Eliason, John, of G'tn.	1811	AA26	294	199
Ratcliffe, Joseph, of G'tn.	Deed to	Threlkeld, John, of G'tn.	1814	AG32	192	134
Ratcliffe, Joseph, of G'tn.	B. of S. fr	Adams, Henry, ship carp., G'tn.	1817	AO39	490	336
Ratcliffe, Joseph, of G'tn.	Deed to	Wilson, John A.	1817	AO39	520	358
Ratcliffe, Richard, chan. comr.	Deed to	Blake, James H.	1814	AG32	436	315
Ratcliffe, William	Deed to	Fry, James	1806	P15	263	174
Rathie, John B., of Loudoun Co.	Deed fr	Commissioners of Washington	1801	G7	474	611
Ratrie, James & William Ratrie	Deed to	Holtzman, John	1816	AM37	486	353
Ratrie, William	Plat	High Street	1816	AM37		356
Ratrie, William & James Ratrie	Deed to	Holtzman, John	1816	AM37	486	353
Ratrie, William, Jr.	Deed fr	Creager, Michael	1816	AM37	197	146
Ratrie, William, of G'tn.	Deed to	Craig, Robert, of G'tn.	1804	K10	337	348
Ratrie, William, of G'tn.	Assign to	Holtzman, Jacob, of G'tn.	1811	AA26	400	265
Ratrie, William, of G'tn.	B. of S. to	Holtzman, Jacob, of G'tn.	1811	AA26	050	039
Ratrie, William, taylor, of G'tn.	Deed fr	Beatty, Charles, of G'tn.	1797	C3	112	92
Ratrie, William [Rattery]	Plat		1811	AA26	403	
Rattrie, James	Deed fr	Rattrie, William	1816	AL36	308	303
Rattrie, William	Deed to	Rattrie, James	1816	AL36	308	303
Rawlings, Betsey (M)	Deposition fr	Shanks, Elizabeth, G'tn.	1817	AN38	221	161
Rawlins, John	Deed fr	Kliber, James	1802	I9	478	786
Rawlins, John	Deed to	Brown, Frederick	1815	AK35	038	030
Rawn, David, of G'tn.	Deed fr	Coombe, Benjamin	1804	K10	231	239
Ray, Anne, s/o Josiah	B. of S. fr	Ray, Josiah	1805	M12	195	197
Ray, Benjamin	Deed to	Morgan, William	1802	I9	238	382
Ray, Benjamin, Jr.	Deed fr	Schoolfield, Joseph et al	1802	H8	526	485
Ray, Benjamin, Jr.	Deed fr	Schoolfield, Joseph	1802	H8	426	485
Ray, George & Sarah et al	Deed to	Riggs, George W., of Balto.	1814	AH33	017	016
Ray, James	Release fr	Piercy, James	1798	C3	280	227
Ray, James	Deed to	Caton, James, of Balto.	1799	D4	313	296
Ray, James	Deed fr	Piercy, James, sugar refiner	1800	F6	015	010
Ray, James et al	Mortgage fr	Piercy, James	1797	B2B	690	468
Ray, James, mer.	Deed to	Piercy, James et al	1797	C3	176	149
Ray, James, of Lamberton NJ	Deed fr	Duncanson, William Mayne	1797	C3	068	56
Ray, James, of Montg. Co.	Deed to	Ray, Josias, Mary & Sarah	1816	AL36	144	144
Ray, Josiah	B. of S. to	Ray, Anne, s/o Josiah	1805	M12	195	197
Ray, Josias, Mary & Sarah	Deed fr	Ray, James, of Montg. Co.	1816	AL36	144	144
Raymer, Michael et al	Deed to	Beall, Thomas & John M. Gantt	1792	A1-1	076	112
Raymer, Michael, Frederick Town	Deed to	French, George, of G'tn.	1796	B2B	395	058
Rea, William	Lease fr	Van Ness, John P.	1817	AO39	379	255
Read, Leonard & Eliz. O., of PA	Deed to	Merky, David, wheelwright, of PA	1795	B2A	351	497
Read, Thomas, of Montg. Co.	B. of S. fr	Ferguson, James	1805	N13	404	321
Read, William & Ann, of Phila. PA	Deed to	Dale, Richard, mer., of Phila. PA	1812	AC28	439	315

Party	What	Party	Year	Liber	Old	New
Read, William, mer., of Phila. PA	Deed fr	Fitzsimons, Thomas, Phila. et al	1805	M12	125	119
Read, William, mer., of Phila. PA	Deed fr	Fitzsimons, Thomas, Phila. et al	1809	V21	276	198
Reahle, Frederick & Henry Myer	Deed to	Beall, Thomas & John M. Gantt	1792	A1-1	090	131
Redman, James	Slave		1812	AC28	452	322
Redman, James	Deed fr	King, Charles	1815	AI34	089	101
Redman, James, of G'tn.	Deed fr	Kite, Alexander, of G'tn.	1812	AC28	452	322
Redman, James, of G'tn.	Convey fr	Ragan, Mary et al	1816	AL36	463	437
Reed, Alexander	Convey fr	Lovell, William	1803	K10	081	88
Reed, Alexander	Deed to	Moore, James	1807	S18	260	205
Reed, Crissa (C), b. 5/5/03	Cert Free fr	Greenfield, Thomas	1813	AE30	187	149
Reed, Delila (C), b. 12/6/99	Cert Free fr	Greenfield, Thomas	1813	AE30	187	149
Reed, Eliz. (C), b. 9/13/12	Cert Free fr	Greenfield, Thomas	1813	AE30	187	149
Reed, Isaac	Agreement	Simmons, James	1801	F6	143	088
Reed, Isaac	D. of T. to	Greenleaf, James, of Phila. PA	1809	W22	383	248
Reed, Isaac	Release to	Greenleaf, James, of Phila.	1812	AB27	209	171
Reed, Isaac, painter & glazier	Agreement	Morris, Robert, of Phila.	1796	B2B	553	281
Reed, John (C), b. 4/8/10	Cert Free fr	Greenfield, Thomas	1813	AE30	187	149
Reed, Julet A. (C), b. 12/14/08	Cert Free fr	Greenfield, Thomas	1813	AE30	187	149
Reed, Kitty (C), b. 7/7/97	Cert Free fr	Greenfield, Thomas	1813	AE30	187	149
Reed, Letty, children of	Cert Free fr	Greenfield, Thomas	1813	AE30	187	149
Reed, Mitilday (C), b. 4/5/05	Cert Free fr	Greenfield, Thomas	1813	AE30	187	149
Reed, Osten, of G'tn.	Mortgage to	Fields, William, of G'tn.	1812	AD29	003	002
Reed, Wash. (C), b. 7/13/02	Cert Free fr	Greenfield, Thomas	1813	AE30	187	149
Reed, William F., trustee	Deed fr	Blount, George, insolvent	1809	X23	205	155
Reed, William F.	B. of S. to	Hoot, Samuel	1814	AH33	024	022
Reed, William F., trustee	Deed fr	Perry, Elisha	1814	AH33	306	264
Reed, William, of Alexa. Co.	Mortgage fr	Jones, Lewin, of P.G. Co.	1808	V21	113	084
Reeder, Benjamin & Eleanor	Release to	Renner, Daniel & Daniel Bussard	1807	R17	401	303
Reeder, Benjamin, assignees of	Release to	Lutz, John	1810	Y24	497	438
Reeder, Benjamin, of Morgantown	Deed to	Renner, Daniel & Daniel Bussard	1807	R17	224	168
Reeder, Charles, of Balto.	B. of S. fr	Yeamons, Royal	1817	AN38	375	278
Reeder, John, turner	Indenture fr	Taylor, Mary, for son Cornelious	1811	AB27	238	195
Reeder, John, turner	Indenture fr	Jones, John G., for son John A.	1811	AB27	237	194
Reemney, John, of G'tn.	B. of S. to	Lay, Richard, of G'tn.	1815	AK35	239	189
Reeves, Thomas C., Charles Co.	Deed to	Spalding, Bernard, of G'tn.	1811	AB27	386	318
Reeves, Thomas Courtney, of MD	Deed fr	Threlkeld, John, of G'tn.	1802	H8	137	133
Reid, Alexander	Deed to	Rutherford, Andrew	1800	E5	341	328
Reid, Alexander	Deed to	Watterston, George	1809	X23	155	113
Reid, Alexander et al	Deed fr	Burnes, David	1799	D4	174	155
Reid, Alexander et al	Deed to	Oglevie, David	1800	E5	089	076
Reid, Alexander, stonecutter	Deed fr	Robertson, Alexander, stonecutter	1800	E5	088	075
Reid, James	Deed fr	Walker, George	1802	I9	219	346
Reid, James, mer., of G'tn.	Deed to	Taney, Francis Lewis, of G'tn.	1799	D4	328	314
Reid, James, of G'tn.	Deed to	Chandler, Walter S., of G'tn.	1796	B2B	438	117
Reid, James, of G'tn.	Deed to	Lingan, James Maccubbin, G'tn.	1796	B2B	503	203
Reid, James, of Dumfries VA	Deed fr	Walker, George	1796	B2B	431	109
Reid, James, of G'tn.	Deed fr	Peters, Robert, of G'tn.	1796	B2B	436	115
Reid, William F.	B. of S. to	Moore, Peter Dent	1810	Y24	288	263
Reid, William F., insolvent	Deed to	Pryse, Thomas, trustee	1810	Z25	197	155
Reilly, William	B. of S. to	McDaniel, Mary	1808	U20	064	036
Reilly, William et al	D. of T. fr	Polk, Charles P., insolvent	1813	AF31	071	048
Reily, Hugh	Deed fr	Davidson, John, of Annapolis	1799	D4	189	171
Reily, John H.	Convey fr	King, Robert	1817	AO39	398	270
Reily, Sarah, of Phila. PA	B. of S. fr	Carpenter, Thomas	1805	N13	138	131
Reinagle, Ann	Deed to	Peter, George	1815	AK35	259	206

Index to District of Columbia Land Records, 1792-1817

Party	What	Party	Year	Liber	Old	New
Reinagle, Ann, of G'tn.	Deed fr	Milligan, Joseph, of G'tn.	1814	AG32	267	190
Reinagle, Anna	Deed fr	Lee, John	1815	AI34	048	054
Reinagle, Anna	Deed fr	Beall, Thomas, of Geo., of G'tn.	1816	AL36	096	097
Reinhart, Andrew	Deed to	Kleiber, George, Jr.	1802	I9	082	117
Reinhart, Andrew	Deed to	Kedgley, John	1802	I9	092	131
Reinhart, Andrew	Deed to	Grove, Elizabeth	1804	K10	147	159
Reinhart, Andrew	Deed fr	Orme, Polly, Montg. Co. et al	1805	O14	088	055
Reinhart, Andrew	Deed to	Bussard, Daniel, of G'tn.	1805	N13	131	125
Reinhart, Andrew	Deed fr	Igan, Ephraim, of Balto.	1811	AA26	164	113
Reinhart, Andrew	Deed to	Barclay, John D. & Mary Ann	1813	AE30	188	150
Reintzel, Alexander	Deed fr	Davidson, John, of Annapolis	1798	C3	469	369
Reintzel, Andrew	Deed to	Rowles, Joseph E. et al	1802	I9	256	414
Reintzel, Andrew et al	Deed to	Reintzel, Anthony	1809	W22	364	236
Reintzel, Andrew, now of G'tn.	Deed to	Brashear, Ann et al	1800	E5	251	244
Reintzel, Andrew, of Fairfax Co.	Deed fr	Beatty, Charles	1800	E5	085	072
Reintzel, Andrew, of Fairfax Co.	Deed fr	Bayly, William	1800	E5		139
Reintzel, Anthony	Deed fr	Belt, Joseph Sprigg	1793	A1-1	179	254
Reintzel, Anthony	Deed fr	Holland, Samuel, late sheriff	1795	B2A	275	385
Reintzel, Anthony	Cede to	Corporation of Georgetown	1797	B2B	619	377
Reintzel, Anthony	Deed to	Chandler, Walter S.	1802	I9	200	313
Reintzel, Anthony	Deed fr	Magruder, Edw.	1802	I9	349	576
Reintzel, Anthony	Deed to	Hodges, Nicholas	1802	I9	445	736
Reintzel, Anthony	Deed fr	Beall, Elijah	1802	I9	446	747
Reintzel, Anthony	Deed to	Travers, Nicholas	1802	I9	288	472
Reintzel, Anthony	Deed fr	Nourse, Michael	1805	M12	110	103
Reintzel, Anthony	Deed to	Parrott, Richard	1808	T19	162	115
Reintzel, Anthony	Deed fr	Reintzel, Andrew et al	1809	W22	364	236
Reintzel, Anthony	Deed fr	Beatty, John M. & Charles A.	1809	W22	361	234
Reintzel, Anthony	Release to	Reintzel, Valentine	1810	Y24	245	225
Reintzel, Anthony	Deed to	Bogenrieff, Margaret	1810	Y24	018	015
Reintzel, Anthony	Lease to	Joncherez, Alexander L. et al	1811	Z25	490	389
Reintzel, Anthony	Deed to	Smith, Richard	1811	Z25	492	391
Reintzel, Anthony	Release fr	Bank of Columbia	1811	AB27	466	381
Reintzel, Anthony	Deed to	Parrott, Richard	1816	AK35	231	182
Reintzel, Anthony & Daniel et al	Deed fr	Mitchell, John, of G'tn.	1806	P15	144	093
Reintzel, Anthony et al	Deed fr	Johns, Richard et al	1805	M12	069	064
Reintzel, Anthony et al	Deed to	Williams, Jeremiah, of G'tn.	1805	M12	071	066
Reintzel, Anthony et al	Deed fr	Beatty, Charles, heirs of	1807	Q16	383	294
Reintzel, Anthony et al	Deed fr	Green, Charles D., Somerset Co.	1808	T19	203	145
Reintzel, Anthony, Gent. et al	Deed to	Bohrer, George	1807	S18	134	109
Reintzel, Anthony, Gent. et al	Deed to	Ober, Robert, mer.	1807	S18	129	105
Reintzel, Anthony, Gent. et al	Deed to	King, George, mer.	1807	S18	131	107
Reintzel, Anthony, Gent.	Deed fr	Bohrer, George, Sr.	1807	S18	135	110
Reintzel, Anthony, of G'tn.	Deed to	Deakins, William, Jr. et al	1793	A1-1	183	259
Reintzel, Anthony, of G'tn.	Deed fr	Peter, Robert, of G'tn.	1796	B2B	426	101
Reintzel, Anthony, of G'tn.	Deed to	Beatty, Thomas J.	1796	B2B	486	178
Reintzel, Anthony, of G'tn.	Deed fr	Kennedy, Mathew, of G'tn.	1800	F6	025	016
Reintzel, Anthony, of G'tn.	Deed fr	Hill, Clement & Notley Young	1800	E5	317	307
Reintzel, Anthony, of G'tn.	Deed to	King, James C., of G'tn.	1800	E5	075	062
Reintzel, Anthony, of G'tn.	Deed fr	Campbell, William, Frederick Co.	1801	F6	163	101
Reintzel, Anthony, of G'tn.	Deed to	Reintzel, John, of G'tn.	1802	H8	457	419
Reintzel, Anthony, of G'tn.	Deed to	Carmichael, Alexander, of G'tn.	1802	G7	487	624
Reintzel, Anthony, of G'tn.	Deed fr	Turner, Thomas, of G'tn.	1802	H8	371	345
Reintzel, Anthony, of G'tn.	Deed to	Traverse, Nicholas, of G'tn.	1803	K10	088	94
Reintzel, Anthony, of G'tn.	Manumis to	Jenkins, Frank (Negro)	1804	L11	271	250

Index to District of Columbia Land Records, 1792-1817

Party	What	Party	Year	Liber	Old	New
Reintzel, Anthony, of G'tn.	Deed fr	Reintzel, Jacob, of Hardy Co. VA	1805	M12	113	106
Reintzel, Anthony, of G'tn.	Deed fr	Dorsey, William H., of G'tn.	1805	M12	114	107
Reintzel, Anthony, of G'tn.	Deed to	Beck, Rezin, of P.G. Co.	1805	M12	156	152
Reintzel, Anthony, of G'tn.	Deed to	Lingan, Nicholas, of G'tn.	1806	Q16	122	079
Reintzel, Anthony, of G'tn.	Deed to	Smith, Walter, of G'tn.	1807	Q16	347	267
Reintzel, Anthony, of G'tn.	Deed to	Carmichaell, Alexander, of G'tn.	1807	R17	202	153
Reintzel, Anthony, of G'tn.	Deed to	Lambert, Morris	1808	T19	159	112
Reintzel, Anthony, of G'tn.	Deed fr	Smith, Walter, of G'tn.	1808	T19	059	
Reintzel, Anthony, of G'tn.	Deed to	Smith, Walter, of G'tn.	1808	U20	325	174
Reintzel, Anthony, of G'tn.	Deed to	Morgan, William, of G'tn.	1809	V21	381	285
Reintzel, Anthony, of G'tn.	Deed to	Marquand, Charles, of G'tn.	1809	W22	233	158
Reintzel, Anthony, of G'tn.	Deed to	Hollingshead, John, of G'tn.	1810	Z25	047	035
Reintzel, Anthony, of G'tn.	Deed to	Reintzel, John, of G'tn.	1810	Z25	235	183
Reintzel, Anthony, of G'tn.	Deed fr	Bogenrieff, Margaret, of G'tn.	1810	Z25	237	185
Reintzel, Anthony, of G'tn.	Deed to	Mountz, John, Jr., of G'tn.	1810	X23	359	288
Reintzel, Anthony, of G'tn.	Deed to	Ober, Robert, of G'tn.	1810	Y24	335	303
Reintzel, Anthony, of G'tn.	Deed to	Parrott, Richard, of G'tn.	1811	AA26	064	047
Reintzel, Anthony, of G'tn.	Mortgage to	English, David, of G'tn.	1811	AA26	039	030
Reintzel, Anthony, of G'tn.	Lease to	Boone, Arnold, of G'tn.	1811	AB27	470	384
Reintzel, Anthony, of G'tn.	Deed to	Smith, Walter, of G'tn.	1811	AB27	314	259
Reintzel, Anthony, of G'tn.	Deed fr	English, David, of G'tn.	1811	AB27	302	249
Reintzel, Anthony, of G'tn.	Deed to	Dodge, Francis, of G'tn.	1811	AB27	467	383
Reintzel, Anthony, of G'tn.	Deed to	Ober, Robert, of G'tn.	1811	Z25	458	362
Reintzel, Anthony, of G'tn.	Deed to	Bogenrieff, Margaret, of G'tn.	1811	Z25	418	329
Reintzel, Anthony, of G'tn.	Deed to	Bogenrieff, Valentine, of G'tn.	1811	Z25	417	327
Reintzel, Anthony, of G'tn.	Deed to	Greer, James	1812	AC28	178	134
Reintzel, Anthony, of G'tn.	Deed to	Reintzel, Valentine, of G'tn.	1813	AE30	448	333
Reintzel, Anthony, of G'tn.	Deed to	Reintzel, Valentine, of G'tn.	1813	AE30	501	371
Reintzel, Anthony [Reintzell]	Deed to	Adams, Thomas	1808	T19	254	187
Reintzel, Daniel	Deed fr	Beall, Thomas, of George	1795	B2B	363	012
Reintzel, Daniel	Deed fr	Beall, Thomas, of George	1796	B2B	522	233
Reintzel, Daniel	Deed to	Holmead, John	1801	G7	458	594
Reintzel, Daniel	Exchange	Holmead, John	1801	G7	456	593
Reintzel, Daniel	Deed fr	Forrest, Uriah	1802	G7	523	666
Reintzel, Daniel	Manumis to	Afterly, Abraham (negro)	1806	O14	122	078
Reintzel, Daniel	Deed to	Williams, Elisha W.	1809	W22	163	115
Reintzel, Daniel	Cert. Free to	Overton, Samuel et al	1814	AH33	232	203
Reintzel, Daniel	Cert Free to	Grimes, Allice, children of	1814	AG32	055	043
Reintzel, Daniel & Anne, of G'tn.	Deed to	Kurtz, Daniel, of G'tn.	1811	AB27	309	254
Reintzel, Daniel et al	P. of Atty. fr	Blodget, Samuel	1796	B2B	524	235
Reintzel, Daniel et al	Deed fr	Green, Charles D., Somerset Co.	1808	T19	203	145
Reintzel, Daniel et al	Deed to	Reintzel, Anthony	1809	W22	364	236
Reintzel, Daniel et al	Deed fr	Gooding, John, of Balto.	1810	Y24	151	137
Reintzel, Daniel, of G'tn.	Deed fr	Forrest, Uriah, of Montg. Co.	1798	C3	386	308
Reintzel, Daniel, of G'tn.	B. of S. fr	Perry, Erasmus	1801	G7	192	256
Reintzel, Daniel, of G'tn.	Deed fr	Riggs, George W., of G'tn.	1806	Q16	325	249
Reintzel, Daniel, of G'tn.	B. of S. fr	Pic, Francis, of G'tn.	1806	Q16	292	191
Reintzel, Daniel, of G'tn.	Deed to	Johnson, Isaac, of G'tn.	1807	S18	171	139
Reintzel, Daniel, of G'tn.	Deed to	Kurtz, Christian, of G'tn.	1807	S18	146	119
Reintzel, Daniel, of G'tn.	Deed to	Dodge, Francis, of G'tn.	1809	W22	231	157
Reintzel, Daniel, of G'tn.	Deed fr	Riggs, George W., of G'tn.	1809	W22	228	155
Reintzel, Daniel, of G'tn.	Deed to	Magruder, Ninian, physic, of G'tn.	1811	Z25	532	422
Reintzel, Daniel, of G'tn.	Deed to	Smith, Clement	1811	AB27	004	006
Reintzel, Daniel, of G'tn.	Deed to	Davis, Edward, of G'tn.	1811	AB27	096	079
Reintzel, Daniel, of G'tn.	Deed to	Kingsbury, Horatio, of G'tn.	1812	AD29	540	456

Party	What	Party	Year	Liber	Old	New
Reintzel, Daniel, of G'tn.	Deed to	Gantt, Thomas T.	1813	AE30	098	075
Reintzel, Daniel, of G'tn.	D. of T. to	Corcoran, Thomas, of G'tn.	1814	AG32	040	032
Reintzel, Daniel, trustee et al	Deed fr	Melvin, James, of G'tn.	1808	T19	206	148
Reintzel, Henry, minor, by atty.	Deed to	McDaniel, John, of G'tn.	1814	AG32	453	327
Reintzel, Jacob, of Hardy Co. VA	Deed to	Reintzel, Anthony, of G'tn.	1805	M12	113	106
Reintzel, John, Dr.	Deed fr	Beatty, John M. et al	1805	M12	384	396
Reintzel, John et al	Deed to	Reintzel, Anthony	1809	W22	364	236
Reintzel, John, of G'tn.	Deed fr	Reintzel, Anthony, of G'tn.	1802	H8	457	419
Reintzel, John, of G'tn.	Deed to	Boarman, Richard B.A., of G'tn.	1810	Z25	016	012
Reintzel, John, of G'tn.	Deed fr	Reintzel, Anthony, of G'tn.	1810	Z25	235	183
Reintzel, John, of G'tn.	Deed fr	Mountz, Jacob, collector, G'tn.	1810	Z25	233	182
Reintzel, Valentine	Deed to	Thornton, William	1795	B2A	221	307
Reintzel, Valentine	Release fr	Reintzel, Anthony	1810	Y24	245	225
Reintzel, Valentine	Deed to	Threlkeld, John	1814	AG32	187	132
Reintzel, Valentine	Deed to	Davis, Richard	1815	AI34	057	065
Reintzel, Valentine	Deed fr	Kurtz, Catharine	1815	AI34	247	279
Reintzel, Valentine	Deed fr	English, David, of G'tn.	1815	AI34	055	063
Reintzel, Valentine & J. Thompson	Deed fr	Mountz, Jacob, collector, of G'tn.	1811	AB27	458	376
Reintzel, Valentine & J. Thompson	Deed fr	Sheppard, Benjamin et al	1812	AD29	430	361
Reintzel, Valentine et al	Deed to	Reintzel, Anthony	1809	W22	364	236
Reintzel, Valentine, et al	Deed fr	Mountz, Jacob, collector, of G'tn.	1811	AB27	456	374
Reintzel, Valentine et al	Deed fr	White, James, of Montg. Co.	1812	AC28	251	185
Reintzel, Valentine et al	Deed fr	Sheppard, Abraham, of NC	1817	AO39	478	328
Reintzel, Valentine, heirs of	Deed to	Mitchell, John	1802	H8	405	374
Reintzel, Valentine, of G'tn.	Deed to	Deakins, William, of G'tn.	1793	A1-1	376	483
Reintzel, Valentine, of G'tn.	D. of T. to	Bowie, Washington, of G'tn.	1810	Z25	121	094
Reintzel, Valentine, of G'tn.	Deed fr	Dorsey, William H., of Balto.	1811	AA26	377	356
Reintzel, Valentine, of G'tn. et al	Deed to	Cooper, Isaac, of G'tn.	1812	AD29	041	029
Reintzel, Valentine, of G'tn. et al	Deed to	Snowden, Gerrard H., of A.A. Co.	1812	AD29	378	318
Reintzel, Valentine, of G'tn.	Deed fr	Murdock, John, of G'tn.	1813	AE30	313	236
Reintzel, Valentine, of G'tn.	Deed fr	Reintzel, Anthony, of G'tn.	1813	AE30	501	371
Reintzel, Valentine, of G'tn.	B. of S. to	Bowie, Washington	1813	AE30	546	405
Reintzel, Valentine, of G'tn.	Deed to	Thompson, John, of G'tn.	1813	AF31	267	187
Reintzel, Valentine, of G'tn.	Deed fr	Fahey, Mark, of G'tn.	1814	AH33	337	292
Reintzel, Valentine, of G'tn.	Deed to	Garey, Everard, of G'tn.	1814	AH33	327	282
Reintzel, Valentine, of G'tn.	Deed fr	Murdock, John, of G'tn.	1814	AG32	181	128
Reintzel, Valentine, of G'tn.	Deed fr	Thomson, John, of G'tn.	1814	AG32	183	129
Reintzel, Valentine, of G'tn.	Lease fr	Garey, Everard, of G'tn.	1815	AH33	403	348
Reintzel, Valentine, of G'tn.	Deed fr	Gary, Ann, exrx. of Everard, G'tn.	1815	AI34	477	487
Reintzel, Valentine, of G'tn.	Deed to	Threlkeld, John	1815	AI34	483	492
Reintzel, Valentine, of G'tn.	Deed to	Kelly, John, of G'tn.	1815	AI34	242	274
Reintzel, Valentine, of G'tn.	Deed to	Cox, John, of G'tn.	1815	AK35	093	072
Reintzel, Valentine, of G'tn.	Deed to	Lambert, Moris, of G'tn.	1816	AL36	502	472
Reintzel, Valentine, of G'tn.	Deed to	Moxley, Charles, of G'tn.	1816	AK35	512	404
Reintzel, Valentine, of G'tn.	Deed to	Dunn, James C., of G'tn.	1817	AN38	410	306
Reintzel, Valentine, reps.	Deed to	Reintzel, Anthony	1809	W22	364	236
Reintzell, Anthony	Deed to	Kurtz, Catherine	1810	Y24	129	117
Reintzell, Daniel	D. of T. fr	Scott, James	1816	AM37	027	022
Reintzell, Daniel et al	Deed fr	Burnett, Charles A.	1806	Q16	320	245
Reintzell, Daniel et al	Deed to	Riggs, Elisha	1806	Q16	322	246
Reintzell, Daniel, of G'tn.	Deed to	Kurtz, Daniel, of G'tn.	1814	AG32	095	072
Reintzell, Valentine et al	Deed to	Oden, Benjamin, of P.G. Co.	1815	AI34	376	403
Reintzell, Valentine et al	Deed to	Oden, Benjamin, of P.G. Co.	1815	AI34	375	403
Reitnzel, Anthony, Gent. et al	Deed to	Ritchie, Abner	1807	S18	132	108
Reitnzel, Valentine, of G'tn.	Deed fr	Reintzel, Anthony, of G'tn.	1813	AE30	448	333

Index to District of Columbia Land Records, 1792-1817   351

Party	What	Party	Year	Liber	Old	New
Reitz, Frederick	Agreement	McLean, Cornelius	1816	AL36	228	233
Reitz, Frederick	Deed fr	McLean, Cornelius	1816	AL36	227	232
Reizner, Henry	Deed to	Gannon, James, of G'tn.	1815	AI34	538	542
Reizner, Henry	Release fr	Traverse, Nicholas	1815	AI34	542	546
Reizner, Henry	Deed fr	Tolson, Alexander	1817	AN38	287	209
Rench, John, of Wash. Co. MD	Deed to	Beall, Thomas & John M. Gantt	1792	A1-1	137	199
Renner & Bussard	Release fr	Randall, John, of Annapolis	1808	V21	067	053
Renner, Daniel	Deed fr	Commissioners of Washington	1801	G7	160	211
Renner, Daniel	Deed fr	Morsell, James Sewall, of G'tn.	1801	G7	158	209
Renner, Daniel	Deed to	Bussard, Daniel	1802	H8	044	042
Renner, Daniel	Deed to	Bussard, Daniel	1802	H8	046	043
Renner, Daniel	Deed to	Stewart, John	1802	H8	047	045
Renner, Daniel	Mortgage fr	Schley, Daniel	1805	M12	136	131
Renner, Daniel	Deed to	Simpson, John	1807	S18	211	168
Renner, Daniel	Deed fr	Ritchie, Abner	1807	S18	202	162
Renner, Daniel	Slaves	From Frederick Co. VA	1810	Z25	226	177
Renner, Daniel	Deed fr	Duffy, Bryan	1810	X23	386	311
Renner, Daniel	Lease fr	Presbyterian Congregation of G'tn.	1811	AB27	367	204
Renner, Daniel	Lease fr	Presbyterian Congregation of G'tn.	1811	AB27	364	302
Renner, Daniel	Deed fr	Bussard, Daniel, of G'tn.	1812	AC28	382	278
Renner, Daniel	Deed to	Brook, Joseph	1812	AE30	009	007
Renner, Daniel	Deed fr	Glover, Charles	1812	AC28	254	187
Renner, Daniel	Deed fr	Dixon, Thomas	1814	AH33	262	229
Renner, Daniel	Deed to	Dixon, Thomas	1814	AH33	301	260
Renner, Daniel	Deed fr	Mayn, Adam, s/o John, of G'tn.	1814	AH33	137	131
Renner, Daniel	Deed fr	Jenkins, Francis & Fabian	1814	AH33	264	230
Renner, Daniel	Deed to	Garey, Everard	1814	AH33	030	027
Renner, Daniel	Lease to	Lipscomb, John & J. Pickrell	1815	AI34	093	106
Renner, Daniel	Assign fr	Gloyd, George H., of G'tn.	1816	AK35	499	393
Renner, Daniel	Assign fr	Young, Patrick C.	1816	AK35	501	395
Renner, Daniel	Deed fr	Cooms, Sarah, of Charles Co.	1816	AM37	199	148
Renner, Daniel & Daniel Bussard	Deed to	Bussard, John R.	1804	K10	108	115
Renner, Daniel & Daniel Bussard	Deed fr	Deakins, Francis, of G'tn.	1804	K10	103	110
Renner, Daniel & Daniel Bussard	Deed fr	Beall, Thomas B., of G'tn.	1804	K10	107	114
Renner, Daniel & Daniel Bussard	Release fr	Reeder, Benjamin & Eleanor	1807	R17	401	303
Renner, Daniel & Daniel Bussard	Deed fr	Beatty, Charles, heirs of	1807	R17	404	305
Renner, Daniel & Daniel Bussard	Deed fr	King, George, of G'tn.	1808	U20	132	075
Renner, Daniel & Daniel Bussard	Deed fr	Peter, John	1809	V21	383	286
Renner, Daniel & Daniel Bussard	Deed fr	McClann, Robert, of G'tn.	1809	X23	292	232
Renner, Daniel & Daniel Bussard	Deed fr	Wright, Thomas C.	1809	X23	256	200
Renner, Daniel & Daniel Bussard	Deed to	Hoye, John	1809	X23	210	159
Renner, Daniel & Daniel Bussard	Deed fr	Maffitt, Samuel, of G'tn.	1809	X23	256	201
Renner, Daniel & Daniel Bussard	Release to	King, Adam, of G'tn.	1809	X23	283	224
Renner, Daniel & Daniel Bussard	Deed fr	Mountz, Jacob, collector, G'tn.	1809	X23	289	230
Renner, Daniel & Daniel Bussard	Deed fr	Heise, Christian	1810	Z25	155	122
Renner, Daniel & Daniel Bussard	Release to	Smith, Walter	1810	Y24	202	186
Renner, Daniel & Daniel Bussard	Deed to	Bayley, Mary	1812	AD29	175	140
Renner, Daniel et al	Lease fr	Beatty, Charles	1802	H8	191	183
Renner, Daniel et al	Deed fr	Nicholls, Samuel	1802	I9	551	895
Renner, Daniel et al	B. of S. fr	Fowler, Benjamin	1804	L11	054	55
Renner, Daniel et al	Deed fr	Easterday, Daniel	1806	P15	308	203
Renner, Daniel et al	Deed fr	Magruder, George, collector, G'tn.	1807	S18	203	163
Renner, Daniel et al	Deed to	Bussard, Daniel	1815	AH33	397	343
Renner, Daniel, mer., of G'tn.	Deed fr	Mountz, Jacob, collector, of G'tn.	1817	AN38	507	367
Renner, Daniel, of G'tn.	Deed fr	Johns, Richard, of G'tn.	1806	P15	396	266

Index to District of Columbia Land Records, 1792-1817

Party	What	Party	Year	Liber	Old	New
Renner, Daniel, of G'tn. et al	Deed fr	Easterday, Daniel, of G'tn.	1806	P15	399	268
Renner, Daniel, of G'tn. et al	Deed fr	Reeder, Benjamin, of Morgantown	1807	R17	224	168
Renner, Daniel, of G'tn.	Deed fr	Brent, Daniel Carroll, marshal	1808	U20	028	017
Renner, Daniel, of G'tn.	Deed fr	Duvall, Samuel, of G'tn.	1810	X23	410	331
Renner, Daniel, of G'tn.	Deed fr	Brooke, Joseph, of G'tn.	1810	Z25	335	262
Renner, Daniel, of G'tn.	Deed to	Bussard, Daniel, of G'tn.	1810	Z25	337	264
Renner, Daniel, of G'tn.	Deed fr	Beatty, Charles A., Dr., of G'tn.	1811	AB27	063	054
Renner, Daniel, of G'tn.	Deed to	Duffey, Bryan, of G'tn.	1811	AC28	042	032
Renner, Daniel, of G'tn.	Deed fr	Bayley, Mary, of G'tn.	1812	AD29	147	115
Renner, Daniel, of G'tn.	Deed to	Bussard, Daniel, of G'tn.	1813	AF31	308	220
Renner, Daniel, of G'tn.	Deed fr	Mountz, Jacob, of G'tn.	1813	AF31	153	103
Renner, Daniel, of G'tn.	Deed fr	Bussard, Daniel, of G'tn.	1814	AG32	196	137
Renner, Daniel, of G'tn.	Deed fr	Lucas, Henry	1816	AL36	480	452
Renner, Daniel, of G'tn.	Deed to	English, David, of G'tn.	1816	AL36	054	055
Renner, Daniel, of G'tn.	Manumis to	Marlborough, John (C), age 27	1816	AM37	313	228
Renner, Daniel, of G'tn.	Deed to	Patterson, Edgar, of G'tn.	1816	AO39	055	045
Renner, Daniel, of G'tn.	Deed fr	Peerce, Ignatius, of G'tn.	1817	AO39	087	069
Renock, Renith	C. Deed to	State of Maryland	1799	D4	253	237
Renshaw & Browning	B. of S. to	Eliason, John & Richard Beck	1806	Q16	147	097
Renshaw, Thomas S., of G'tn. et al	B. of S. to	Cochrane, Alexander	1807	S18	296	232
Rentch, Jacob, exr. of John	Deed to	Young, Ludwick	1809	W22	145	103
Reynolds, Enoch & O.B. Brown	D. of T. fr	Van Ness, John P.	1816	AM37	175	132
Reynolds, James & Hannah, DE	Deed to	Way, John, of New Castle Co. DE	1815	AK35	220	173
Reynolds, Thomas	B. of S. to	Thorn, Bennet, of P.G. Co.	1806	P15	134	086
Reynolds, Thomas	Deed fr	Sewall, Clement, of Alexa. Co.	1815	AK35	187	146
Reynolds, Thomas	Deed fr	Middleton, Isaac S.	1815	AK35	368	290
Reynolds, Thomas	B. of S. fr	Pumphrey, William, of P.G. Co.	1816	AM37	295	216
Rezner, Elizabeth & Henry	Deed to	Gannon, James	1807	S18	291	228
Rhinehart, Andrew	Deed to	Stretch, Joseph	1805	N13	323	260
Rhoades, Cassandra	B. of S. fr	Pickrell, Benjamin	1814	AH33	227	199
Rhoades, George, of Hyatts Town	Deed to	Henry, William, of Hyatts Town	1814	AG32	443	321
Rhoads, George, of Montg. Co.	Deed fr	King, Charles, of G'tn.	1815	AH33	430	370
Rhodes, Cassandra	B. of S. to	Pickerel, Benjamin	1817	AN38	053	043
Rhodes, George, of Montg. Co.	Deed to	Pickrell, John, of G'tn.	1815	AH33	496	425
Rhodes, John	B. of S. to	Pickerel, Benjamin	1811	AB27	480	393
Rhodes, William	B. of S. to	Davidson, John, Capt.	1805	M12	158	156
Rhodes, William	Mortgage to	Davidson, John	1806	O14	211	139
Rhodes, William & Anne	Deed to	Simms, Edward, of Charles Co.	1801	G7	256	349
Rice, Edmund	Mortgage fr	McCloskey, William	1814	AG32	358	259
Rice, George	Deed fr	Laird, John, exr. of J. Carleton	1813	AE30	240	191
Rice, George	Deed fr	Laird, John, exr. of J. Carleton	1813	AE30	242	192
Richards, Benjamin	B. of S. to	Howard, Peter	1807	S18	104	084
Richards, G.	Cert Slave	Bias, Samuel (C), age 24y 5m	1817	AN38	016	014
Richards, George	B. of S. to	Wagner, Jacob	1816	AL36	006	006
Richards, George	Marriage	Saunders, Ann B., Mrs.	1816	AM37	323	235
Richards, George	Cert Slave	From VA	1816	AM37	323	235
Richards, George	Deed to	Bowie, Washington	1817	AO39	058	048
Richards, George	Deed to	Harrison, Gustavus	1817	AO39	287	205
Richards, George, bookseller	B. of S. to	Watts, Richard K., Sr., Montg. Co.	1817	AN38	508	368
Richards, John, in Can.	P. of Atty. fr	Richards, Mary, of Glasgow, Scot.	1804	L11	002	2
Richards, Mary, of Glasgow, Scot.	P. of Atty. to	Richards, John, in Can.	1804	L11	002	2
Richardson, Allison et al	B. of S. fr	Richardson, Esther	1809	V21	411	313
Richardson, David K.	B. of S. fr	Beall, Basil D.	1807	R17	287	219
Richardson, Esther	B. of S. to	Richardson, Judson et al	1809	V21	411	313
Richardson, Hannah, w/o John	Release to	Steuart, William	1804	K10	349	361

Party	What	Party	Year	Liber	Old	New
Richardson, John	R. of D. fr	Eastburn, Sarah, w/o Robinson	1804	K10	350	362
Richardson, John, of NY	Deed fr	Eastburn, Robinson, Frederick Co.	1803	K10	099	106
Richardson, John, of NY	Agreement	Steuart, William	1804	K10	347	360
Richardson, John, of NY	Deed to	Steuart, William, of G'tn.	1804	K10	119	129
Richardson, Judson et al	B. of S. fr	Richardson, Esther	1809	V21	411	313
Richardson, Samuel, of MD	B. of S. to	Handy, Samuel W., of G'tn.	1817	AO39	286	204
Richardson, Thomas, of G'tn.	B. of S. to	Joncherez, Alexander L., of G'tn.	1812	AD29	341	285
Richardson, Thomas R.	D. of T. fr	Thomas, George N., insolvent	1811	AC28	027	020
Richardson, Thomas R.H.	Deed fr	Wigfield, Sarah	1812	AC28	297	216
Richardson, Thomas R.H.	Deed to	Kile, Alexander	1812	AD29	182	147
Richardson, Tracy et al	B. of S. fr	Richardson, Esther	1809	V21	411	313
Richmond, Braddock	Manumis to	[ ], Wesley (negro)	1810	Z25	041	031
Richmond, Braddock	B. of S. to	Wayne, Isaac	1810	Z25	041	031
Richmond, Braddock	B. of S. to	Frost, John T., trustee	1811	AB27	304	250
Richmond, Christopher	Cert fr	Commissioners of Washington	1795	B2A	334	470
Richmond, Christopher	Cert fr	Commissioners of Washington	1796	B2A	337	473
Richmond, Christopher	Transfer fr	Johnson, Thomas, Jr.	1796	B2A	337	473
Richmond, Christopher, in Phila.	Deed to	Beall, Thomas & John M. Gantt	1793	A1-1	279	374
Richmond, Christopher, of Eng.	Deed to	Davidson, John	1810	Y24	221	204
Richmond, Eliz., of Durham, Eng.	Deed to	Davidson, John	1810	Y24	218	201
Richmond, William, of Q.A. Co.	Deed to	Nicholson, Joseph Hopper	1799	D4	256	241
Richmond, William, trustee	Deed to	Davidson, James, of Q.A. Co.	1800	E5	203	196
Richter, John	D. of T. fr	Potts, John	1809	W22	375	243
Ricks, Elizabeth	B. of S. fr	Ricks, Joseph	1805	N13	239	201
Ricks, Joseph	B. of S. to	Ricks, Elizabeth	1805	N13	239	201
Ricks, Joseph, insolvent	B. of S. to	Foxon, William, trustee	1808	T19	218	159
Riddle, Joseph	Deed fr	Cook, Thomas, of Frederick Town	1805	M12	201	203
Riddle, Joseph, of Alexa. et al	Deed fr	McCormick, Alexander	1798	D4	053	044
Riddle, Joseph, of Alexa. et al	Deed to	Dunlap, John	1805	M12	370	380
Riddle, Joseph, of Alexa.	Deed to	Heathcote, John, of Balto.	1811	AB27	268	219
Riddle, Joseph, of Alexa. et al	Deed fr	Steuart, William, of G'tn.	1811	Z25	385	303
Riddle, Robert, of Balto.	Mortgage fr	King, William R., merchant	1804	K10	297	299
Ridenhour, David	Deed fr	Happ, Andrew, Shenandoah Co.	1793	A1-1	344	448
Ridenhour, David	Deed to	Beall, Thomas & John M. Gantt	1793	A1-1	323	425
Rider, William	B. of S. to	Stonestreet, Eleanor	1805	M12	319	323
Rider, William	B. of S. to	Gates, Amelia, alias Rider	1809	W22	058	043
Rider, William	B. of S. to	Queen, Nicholas L.	1811	Z25	554	441
Ridgate, Thomas Hew, trustee of	Deed to	Wayman, Charles, of G'tn.	1805	M12	256	258
Ridgely, William G.	Qualify	Captain in cavalry	1813	AE30	425	313
Ridgely, William G., of G'tn.	Deed fr	Marbury, William & John Peter	1813	AF31	132	089
Ridgely, William G., of G'tn.	Deed to	Greer, James, of G'tn.	1816	AO39	030	024
Ridgely, William G., of G'tn.	Deed to	Pickrell, John, of G'tn.	1816	AM37	114	090
Ridgeway, Eleanor, d/o Robert	Deed Gift fr	Ridgeway, Robert	1814	AH33	371	322
Ridgeway, Robert	Deed Gift to	Ridgeway, Eleanor, d/o Robert	1814	AH33	371	322
Ridgeway, Thomas S., of Phila.	Deed to	Jones, Walter, Jr.	1815	AI34	243	276
Ridgley, William G.	D. of T. fr	Fitzhugh, Samuel	1817	AN38	328	240
Ridgway, James	B. of S. to	Ridgway, Mordecai	1802	I9	542	883
Ridgway, Mordecai	B. of S. fr	Ridgway, James	1802	I9	542	883
Riffel, George	Deed fr	Balch, Stephen B.	1812	AD29	348	292
Riffle, George	Qualify	Ensign 1st regiment	1813	AE30	472	351
Riffle, George	Deed to	Dant, Thomas [Dantt]	1814	AG32	154	110
Riffle, George	Deed fr	Hyde, Thomas	1814	AG32	419	304
Riffle, George [Riffel]	Deed to	Dant, Thomas	1816	AL36	160	160
Rigden, Henry	Deed to	Magruder, Ninian, Dr., of G'tn.	1816	AL36	080	082
Rigden, Henry, of G'tn.	Deed to	Magruder, Ninian, Dr., of G'tn.	1817	AN38	523	379

Index to District of Columbia Land Records, 1792-1817

Party	What	Party	Year	Liber	Old	New
Rigden, James, of G'tn.	Deed to	Magruder, Ninian, Dr.	1816	AL36	231	236
Rigden, John E.	Qualify		1802	I9	466	768
Rigden, Thomas	Deed to	Magruder, Ninian, of G'tn.	1817	AN38	521	378
Rigden, Thomas, of G'tn.	Deed to	Magruder, Ninian	1816	AL36	076	077
Rigdon, John E. et al	Mortgage fr	Rigdon, Thomas	1802	H8	009	008
Rigdon, John Edward et al	Deed fr	Threlkeld, John, coroner	1799	D4	351	338
Rigdon, Stephen, of Jefferson Co.	Deed to	Magruder, Ninian, of G'tn.	1816	AM37	342	248
Rigdon, Thomas	Deed fr	Beall, Thomas, of George	1801	G7	255	347
Rigdon, Thomas	Deed to	Bruce, Thomas	1801	G7	255	
Rigdon, Thomas	Mortgage to	Burnet, Charles A. et al	1802	H8	009	008
Rigdon, Thomas, admr. of T., G'tn.	Deed to	Livers, Anthony, of G'tn.	1809	W22	067	050
Rigdon, Thomas, of G'tn.	Deed fr	Davidson, John, of Annapolis	1795	B2B	365	016
Rigdon, Thomas, of G'tn.	Deed to	Gannon, James, of G'tn.	1797	C3	064	52
Riggs, Elisha	Deed fr	Beall, Thomas, of George, of G'tn.	1806	P15	369	246
Riggs, Elisha	Deed fr	Reintzell, Daniel et al	1806	Q16	322	246
Riggs, Elisha	Deed fr	Heugh, John, of G'tn., trustee	1815	AI34	091	104
Riggs, Elisha	Deed fr	Morris, George	1817	AO39	432	295
Riggs, Elisha, mer.	Deed fr	Lufborough, Nathan & Mary	1802	H8	384	357
Riggs, Elisha, mer., of G'tn.	Deed fr	Murdock, Addison, Gent.	1806	P15	367	244
Riggs, Elisha, of G'tn.	Deed to	Riggs, George W., of G'tn.	1806	Q16	324	248
Riggs, Elisha, of G'tn.	Deed to	Lufborough, Nathan	1810	Z25	033	025
Riggs, Elisha, of G'tn.	Deed to	Riggs, George W., of Balto. MD	1812	AD29	091	068
Riggs, Elisha, of G'tn.	Deed fr	Anderson, Richard, of John, G'tn.	1816	AO39	014	011
Riggs, George, of G'tn.	Deed fr	Scholfield, Joseph	1801	F6	226	147
Riggs, George W., of G'tn.	Deed fr	Dorsey, William H., of G'tn.	1801	G7	206	275
Riggs, George W.	Deed fr	Lee, Thomas S.	1802	I9	316	519
Riggs, George W.	Deed fr	Beall, Thomas	1802	I9	315	518
Riggs, George W., of G'tn.	Deed fr	Grigg, Joshua, of G'tn.	1802	G7	535	681
Riggs, George W., of G'tn.	Deed fr	Riggs, Elisha, of G'tn.	1806	Q16	324	248
Riggs, George W., of G'tn.	Deed to	Reintzel, Daniel, of G'tn.	1806	Q16	325	249
Riggs, George W. et al	Deed fr	Burnett, Charles A.	1806	Q16	320	245
Riggs, George W. et al	Deed to	Riggs, Elisha	1806	Q16	322	246
Riggs, George W.	Deed fr	Hewitt, John, trustee et al	1806	O14	224	148
Riggs, George W., of G'tn.	Deed fr	Deakins, Leonard M. & John Hoye	1809	W22	193	135
Riggs, George W., of G'tn.	Deed to	Hoye, John, of G'tn.	1809	W22	192	134
Riggs, George W., of G'tn.	Deed to	Reintzel, Daniel, of G'tn.	1809	W22	228	155
Riggs, George W., of Balto.	Convey to	Weiskopff, Charles L. et al	1810	Y24	495	436
Riggs, George W., of G'tn.	Deed to	Crawford, William, of G'tn.	1810	Y24	026	022
Riggs, George W., of Balto. MD	Deed to	Maus, John N.	1812	AD29	168	134
Riggs, George W., of Balto. MD	Deed to	Weiskoff, Charles L., of G'tn. et al	1812	AD29	092	070
Riggs, George W., of Balto. MD	Deed fr	Riggs, Elisha, of G'tn.	1812	AD29	091	068
Riggs, George W., of Balto.	Deed fr	Ray, George & Sarah et al	1814	AH33	017	016
Riggs, George W., of Balto.	Deed to	Crawford, William, of G'tn.	1814	AH33	328	283
Riggs, George Washington	Deed fr	Beall, Thomas, of George	1809	W22	363	235
Riggs, Romulus	Deed fr	Thomas, John, Sr., of Montg. Co.	1812	AC28	495	353
Riggs, Romulus	B. of S. fr	Sim, Thomas	1812	AC28	497	355
Riggs, Romulus	Lease fr	Joncherez, Alexander L., of G'tn.	1813	AF31	121	081
Riggs, Romulus	Deed fr	Rittenhouse, Harriet, exrx.	1815	AI34	023	027
Riggs, Romulus	Agreement	Hagerty, John, Jr.	1815	AI34	027	032
Riggs, Romulus & Wm. S. Nicholls	Bond fr	Claggett, Walter, reps. of	1813	AF31	072	050
Riggs, Romulus & Wm. S. Nicholls	Award fr	Claggett, Walter, reps. of	1813	AF31	073	050
Riggs, Romulus et al	Deed fr	Morsell, James S., of G'tn.	1812	AC28	288	209
Riggs, Romulus, of G'tn. et al	Deed fr	Cocking, William	1812	AD29	498	420
Riggs, Romulus, of G'tn.	Deed fr	King, Charles, of G'tn.	1812	AC28	405	294
Riggs, Romulus, of G'tn.	Deed fr	Beall, Thomas, of Geo., of G'tn.	1814	AH33	500	429

Index to District of Columbia Land Records, 1792-1817

Party	What	Party	Year	Liber	Old	New
Riggs, Romulus, of G'tn.	Deed fr	Cocking, William	1815	AH33	481	411
Riggs, Romulus, of G'tn.	Deed to	Pickrell, John, of G'tn.	1816	AM37	109	087
Riggs, Romulus, of G'tn.	Deed fr	Holmead, John	1816	AL36	098	098
Riley, George R.	Slave	From VA	1808	U20	131	074
Riley, Henry O.	Deed to	Nourse, Joseph	1802	G7	570	719
Riley, Martha, of Montg. Co.	Deed to	Magruder, Ninian, Dr., of G'tn.	1816	AL36	079	081
Riley, Mary, of Montg. Co.	Deed to	Cox, John, of G'tn.	1815	AK35	092	071
Riley, William	Deed to	Long, James, of G'tn.	1801	G7	010	012
Riley, William	D. of T. to	Eliot, Samuel, Jr.	1815	AK35	365	288
Riley, William	Deed fr	Ott, John, of G'tn. et al	1815	AI34	012	013
Rind, William A., Sr.	Deed fr	McDaniel, John	1816	AM37	123	096
Rinehart, Andrew	Deed to	Orme, Nathaniel	1802	H8	467	429
Rinehart, Andrew	Deed fr	Forrest, Uriah	1802	H8	542	503
Rinehart, Andrew	Deed to	Smith, Henry, of MD	1802	H8	465	427
Rinehart, Andrew	Deed fr	Igan, Ephraim	1802	I9	357	590
Rinehart, Andrew	Deed fr	Smith, Henry	1802	I9	225	358
Rinehart, Andrew	Deed fr	Harbaugh, Leonard	1802	I9	493	809
Rinehart, Andrew	Deed fr	Stretch, Joseph	1802	I9	421	698
Rinehart, Andrew	Deed fr	Igan, Ephraim	1802	I9	254	410
Rinehart, Andrew	Deed fr	Evans, Evan	1802	I9	494	811
Rineheart, Andrew	Deed to	Igaw, Ephraim	1802	H8	257	244
Rineheart, Andrew	Deed fr	Murdock, John, of G'tn.	1802	H8	254	241
Ringgold, Tench	Deed fr	Wayman, Charles, of G'tn.	1803	K10	064	69
Ringgold, Tench	Mortgage fr	Ball, Henry W.	1811	AB27	053	045
Ringgold, Tench	Manumis to	Brown, Monica (C)	1813	AF31	305	217
Ringgold, Tench	Deed to	Key, Philip B., of Montg. Co.	1813	AE30	206	167
Ringgold, Tench	Deed fr	Heath, Nathaniel H.	1814	AH33	057	051
Ringgold, Tench	Cert fr	Munroe, Thomas, Supt.	1816	AM37	275	201
Ringgold, Tench	Deed to	Nicoll, Edward H. & Wm. Floyd	1816	AM37	025	020
Ringgold, Tench	Cert fr	Munroe, Thomas, Supt.	1816	AM37	274	201
Ringgold, Tench	Deed to	Munroe, Thomas	1817	AN38	386	287
Ringgold, Tench	D. of T. to	Munro, Robert	1817	AO39	296	211
Ringgold, Tench & Robert Brent	Agreement	French, Daniel	1811	AB27	379	314
Ringgold, Tench & Mary C.	Deed fr	Lee, Thomas Sim, of Fredk. Co.	1813	AF31	424	305
Ringgold, Tench, trustee	Agreement	Lee, Thomas S.	1811	AC28	100	075
Ringgold, Thomas, of Kent Co.	Deed to	Washington, William A., of VA	1804	K10	284	287
Ringold, Mary C. et al	Deed fr	Lee, Thomas Sim et ux	1802	H8	053	050
Ringold, Mary C.	Deed fr	Lee, Thomas Simm & Mary	1802	H8	052	049
Ringold, Tench	Mortgage to	Key, Philip Barton, of Montg. Co.	1810	X23	397	320
Ringold, Tench et al	Deed fr	Carroll, Daniel, of *Duddington*	1810	Z25	083	063
Risener, Henry	Deed to	Travers, Nicholas	1812	AD29	449	378
Risener, Henry	Deed fr	Peter, John et al	1812	AD29	445	374
Riszner, Elizabeth & Henry	Deed to	Gannon, James	1807	S18	291	228
Ritchie, Abner	Deed fr	Davidson, John, of Annapolis	1798	C3	452	356
Ritchie, Abner	Deed fr	Beatty, William, Frederick Co. et al	1801	G7	205	274
Ritchie, Abner	Deed fr	Davidson, John, of Annapolis	1802	G7	551	699
Ritchie, Abner	Deed fr	Beatty, Thomas	1802	H8	130	126
Ritchie, Abner	Deed fr	Beatty, Charles	1802	H8	442	406
Ritchie, Abner	Deed fr	Beatty, Thomas	1802	H8	131	128
Ritchie, Abner	Deed fr	Wingard, Abraham	1802	I9	434	718
Ritchie, Abner	Lease fr	Beatty, Charles	1802	I9	046	062
Ritchie, Abner	Deed fr	Spochrer, Nicholas	1802	I9	514	841
Ritchie, Abner	Deed to	Hedges, Nicholas	1802	I9	292	478
Ritchie, Abner	Deed fr	Beatty, Charles	1802	I9	512	838
Ritchie, Abner	Deed fr	Beall, Thomas	1802	I9	512	839

Index to District of Columbia Land Records, 1792-1817

Party	What	Party	Year	Liber	Old	New
Ritchie, Abner	B. of S. fr	Esterday, Daniel	1804	K10	183	191
Ritchie, Abner	Deed to	Mantz, Peter, of Frederick Co.	1804	L11	035	35
Ritchie, Abner	Deed fr	Dole, Conrad	1804	K10	267	273
Ritchie, Abner	Deed to	Dole, Conrad	1804	K10	268	274
Ritchie, Abner	Deed fr	Magruder, George, collector, G'tn.	1805	M12	082	075
Ritchie, Abner	B. of S. fr	Newton, Ignatius	1806	Q16	255	176
Ritchie, Abner	Deed fr	Beatty, Charles, heirs of	1806	Q16	254	176
Ritchie, Abner	Deed to	Beatty, Charles A. & John M.	1807	Q16	342	262
Ritchie, Abner	Deed to	Simpson, John	1807	Q16	387	297
Ritchie, Abner	Release fr	Norris, Isaac	1807	S18	253	199
Ritchie, Abner	Deed to	Simpson, John	1807	S18	210	167
Ritchie, Abner	Deed fr	Davidson, Ann Maria, exrx. John	1807	S18	278	217
Ritchie, Abner	Deed to	Renner, Daniel	1807	S18	202	162
Ritchie, Abner	Deed fr	Reintzel, Anthony, Gent. et al	1807	S18	132	108
Ritchie, Abner	Deed fr	Ragon, John	1807	S18	255	201
Ritchie, Abner	Deed to	Wingard, Abraham	1808	U20	045	025
Ritchie, Abner	Deed fr	Wingerd, Abraham	1808	U20	049	028
Ritchie, Abner	Deed to	Parrott, Richard, Gent.	1808	T19	065	047
Ritchie, Abner	Deed to	Crown, Samuel T.	1808	V21	050	039
Ritchie, Abner	Deed to	Winebergh, Jacob	1808	U20	287	153
Ritchie, Abner	D. of T. to	Debow, Solomon	1809	W22	113	082
Ritchie, Abner	Deed to	Paul, Nicholas, Jr.	1809	V21	263	188
Ritchie, Abner	B. of S. to	Hogan, Thady [Thaddeus]	1809	V21	214	152
Ritchie, Abner	Deed fr	Cooke, William, of Balto.	1810	Y24	310	282
Ritchie, Abner	Deed to	Mudd, Joseph, Dr. et al	1810	Y24	460	408
Ritchie, Abner	Deed to	Clarke, Robert	1810	Y24	304	277
Ritchie, Abner	Deed to	Parrott, Richard	1810	Y24	282	258
Ritchie, Abner	Deed fr	Schneitzell, George, of MD	1810	Y24	499	439
Ritchie, Abner	Deed fr	Davidson, John, Gen., exrx. of	1810	Y24	308	280
Ritchie, Abner	Deed to	Mane, Adam, of John	1810	Z25	262	205
Ritchie, Abner	Deed to	Ott, John, Dr.	1810	Z25	142	113
Ritchie, Abner	Deed fr	Davidson, John, Gen., exrx. of	1810	Z25	267	210
Ritchie, Abner	Deed to	Hauser, Michael, Capt.	1811	AA26	214	147
Ritchie, Abner	Deed to	Hurdle, Noble	1811	AB27	429	353
Ritchie, Abner	Deed fr	Dent, Lewis W., of Charles Co.	1811	AB27	173	142
Ritchie, Abner	Deed fr	Dent, George Washington, of GA	1811	AB27	167	138
Ritchie, Abner	Deed fr	Dent, Patrick, of P.G. Co.	1811	AB27	175	145
Ritchie, Abner	Deed to	Simpson, John	1811	AB27	163	135
Ritchie, Abner	Deed to	McCleery, Andrew & Robert	1811	AA26	213	146
Ritchie, Abner	Deed to	Ritchie, John T.	1812	AD29	112	085
Ritchie, Abner	Deed to	Wilson, Levi G.	1812	AD29	224	185
Ritchie, Abner	Deed to	Magruder, Ninian, Dr.	1812	AD29	368	310
Ritchie, Abner	Deed to	King, Charles	1812	AD29	365	307
Ritchie, Abner	Release fr	Smith, Richard	1815	AH33	421	362
Ritchie, Abner	Assign fr	Ott, John & James Gannon, G'tn.	1815	AI34	101	115
Ritchie, Abner et al	Deed fr	Beatty, Charles, heirs of	1807	Q16	383	294
Ritchie, Abner, of G'tn.	Deed fr	Davidson, John, of MD	1802	H8	470	432
Ritchie, Abner, of G'tn.	Deed fr	Beatty, Thomas, of MD	1802	H8	601	548
Ritchie, Abner, of G'tn.	Deed to	Schley, Daniel, of G'tn.	1804	M12	024	024
Ritchie, Abner, of G'tn.	Deed fr	Beatty, Charles, heirs of	1805	N13	077	070
Ritchie, Abner, of G'tn.	Deed to	Norris, Isaac, of G'tn.	1805	M12	083	077
Ritchie, Abner, of G'tn.	Deed to	Ragon, John, of G'tn.	1805	M12	084	078
Ritchie, Abner, of G'tn.	Lease fr	Williamson, David, of Balto.	1809	W22	064	048
Ritchie, Abner, of G'tn.	Assign to	Ott, John, Dr., of G'tn.	1817	AN38	102	077
Ritchie, Abner, sheriff	Deed to	Rohr, Philip & Henry Bontz	1800	E5	379	358

Index to District of Columbia Land Records, 1792-1817

Party	What	Party	Year	Liber	Old	New
Ritchie, John T.	Deed fr	Ritchie, Abner	1812	AD29	112	085
Ritchie, Mary, of Frederick Co.	Deed to	Hedges, Nicholas	1795	B2A	244	340
Ritchie, William, of Frederick Co.	Deed fr	Davidson, John, of Annapolis	1799	D4	326	311
Rittenhouse, Harriet	Manumis to	Jackson, Betsey (C) & children	1817	AN38	194	140
Rittenhouse, Harriet et al	Deed to	Morsell, James S.	1815	AI34	086	098
Rittenhouse, Harriet, exrx.	Deed to	Riggs, Romulus	1815	AI34	023	027
Rittenhouse, John B.	Slave Births	From VA	1810	Z25	207	163
Rittenhouse, John B., of G'tn.	Deed to	Smith, Richard, of G'tn.	1812	AC28	352	255
Rittenhouse, John Bull	Deed fr	Nourse, Michael	1810	Y24	379	342
Rittenhouse, John Bull	Deed fr	Nourse, Michael	1810	Y24	380	344
Ritter, Peter	Deed fr	Beatty, Charles A., of G'tn.	1816	AL36	210	217
Ritter, Peter, of G'tn.	Deed fr	Eastburn, Jane, of G'tn.	1810	Y24	481	425
Roach, Mahlon & Elizabeth, of VA	Deed to	Young, Thomas	1816	AL36	401	485
Roach, Mahlon & Elizabeth, of VA	Deed to	Clarke, Joseph S.	1816	AL36	256	258
Roane, John, of King William Co.	Manumis to	[ ], Simon (M), age 22	1815	AH33	504	433
Robb, John N., of G'tn.	Lease fr	Getty, Robert, of G'tn.	1814	AG32	104	078
Robb, John N.	B. of S. fr	Davis, Briscoe, of G'tn.	1816	AL36	195	202
Roberson, William et al	Deed to	Riggs, George W., of Balto.	1814	AH33	017	016
Roberts, Ann	Separation	Roberts, Charles	1815	AI34	342	374
Roberts, Charles	Separation	Roberts, Ann	1815	AI34	342	374
Roberts, John & Lucy, Culpeper	Deed fr	Pollard, Robert & wife, Richmond	1813	AF31	370	265
Roberts, John et al	Deed fr	McDonald, John G.	1808	T19	247	182
Roberts, John, of Alexa.	Deed fr	Bryan, Benjamin & Mary	1801	G7	092	118
Roberts, John, of Alexa. et al	Deed to	McDonald, John G.	1810	Z25	223	175
Roberts, Owen	Deed to	Wadsworth, Charles, U.S.N.	1801	G7	186	248
Roberts, Owen	Deed to	Clagett, Thomas John, Rev.	1801	G7	126	163
Roberts, Owen	Deed fr	Commissioners of Washington	1801	G7	127	165
Roberts, Owen	Deed to	Beale, Thomas K.	1802	H8	051	048
Roberts, Owen & Jane	Deed to	Harper & Lyles, merchants et al	1802	H8	332	311
Roberts, Owen & Jane	Deed to	Keith, James, of Alexa. et al	1802	H8	332	311
Roberts, Thomas et al	Deed fr	Brooke, Thomas A.	1802	I9	584	946
Roberts, William	B. of S. to	Vermillion, Ann	1806	P15	121	078
Robertson, Alexander	Transfer fr	Henry, John	1796	B2A	338	447
Robertson, Alexander	Deed fr	Commissioners of Washington	1801	G7	130	170
Robertson, Alexander	B. of S. fr	McLaughlin, James	1802	H8	545	506
Robertson, Alexander, stonecutter	Cert fr	Commissioners of Washington	1799	D4	379	363
Robertson, Alexander, stonecutter	Deed fr	Watkins, Thomas, carpenter	1799	D4	207	190
Robertson, Alexander, stonecutter	Deed to	Reid, Alexander, stonecutter	1800	E5	088	075
Robertson, Charles et al	Deed fr	Beale, William D.	1802	I9	220	348
Robertson, Henry B. et al	Lease fr	Dodge, Francis	1813	AF31	552	409
Robertson, Henry B., of G'tn. et al	Deed to	Dodge, Francis, of G'tn.	1815	AI34	543	548
Robertson, Henry B., of G'tn.	B. of S. to	McKenney, William, of G'tn.	1816	AM37	305	223
Robertson, Henry, s/o Wm.	Deed fr	Davidson, Samuel	1801	G7	153	201
Robertson, James, sadler, wid/o	Deposition		1804	L11	001	1
Robertson, John, of G'tn.	Lease fr	Smith, Clement, of G'tn.	1817	AN38	020	017
Robertson, John Starkes, of NY	Deed fr	Duncanson, William Mayne	1796	B2B	613	368
Robertson, John Stearkes, of NY	Deed to	Duncanson, William Mayne	1800	E5	241	234
Robertson, Joseph, of G'tn.	Deed fr	Pickrell, John, of G'tn.	1811	AA26	322	217
Robertson, Joseph, of G'tn.	Lease fr	Dixon, Thomas, of G'tn.	1811	AB27	134	111
Robertson, Joseph, of G'tn.	Lease to	Livers, Ignatius, of G'tn.	1814	AH33	068	061
Robertson, Samuel	Deed fr	Debow, Solomon, now of VA	1815	AI34	459	472
Robertson, Samuel	Deed fr	Clagett, Jane	1815	AI34	063	071
Robertson, Samuel, 3rd et al	Deed to	Riggs, George W., of Balto.	1814	AH33	017	016
Robertson, Thomas	Deed fr	Deakins, Leonard M. & John Hoye	1809	W22	026	020
Robertson, Thomas	Deed fr	Whann, William, of G'tn.	1812	AC28	363	263

Party	What	Party	Year	Liber	Old	New
Robertson, Thomas	Deed fr	Peter, George	1812	AD29	058	042
Robertson, Thomas	Deed fr	Presbyterian Congregation, G'tn.	1812	AC28	275	200
Robertson, Thomas	Deed fr	Smith, Walter	1812	AC28	362	263
Robertson, Thomas	Deed fr	Johnson, George, trustee	1814	AG32	068	052
Robertson, Thomas	Deed to	Davidson, Lewis Grant	1814	AH33	012	011
Robertson, Thomas & Daniel Kurtz	Deed to	Davidson, Lewis Grant	1815	AK35	043	033
Robertson, Thomas & Sarah, G'tn.	Deed fr	Peter, George, of G'tn.	1816	AL36	007	008
Robertson, Thomas, mer.	Convey fr	Johnson, George	1814	AG32	010	008
Robertson, Thomas, of G'tn.	Deed to	Deakins, Leonard M., of G'tn.	1809	W22	078	058
Robertson, Thomas, of G'tn.	Deed fr	Williams, Elisha W., of G'tn.	1810	Y24	347	315
Robertson, Thomas, of G'tn.	Deed fr	Mountz, Jacob, collector, of G'tn.	1811	AA26	370	246
Robertson, Thomas, of G'tn.	Deed to	Thomas, John, Sr., of Montg. Co.	1811	AB27	101	083
Robertson, Thomas, of G'tn.	Deed to	Hoye, John, of G'tn.	1811	AA26	149	103
Robertson, Thomas, of G'tn.	Deed to	King, William, Jr.	1812	AD29	435	365
Robertson, Thomas, of G'tn.	Deed fr	Deakins, Leonard M. & John Hoye	1812	AD29	441	370
Robertson, Thomas, of G'tn.	Deed to	Hoye, John, of G'tn.	1812	AE30	039	029
Robertson, Thomas, of G'tn.	B. of S. to	Abbott, John, of G'tn.	1812	AC28	147	109
Robertson, Thomas, of G'tn.	Deed to	Williams, John S., of G'tn.	1813	AF31	040	028
Robertson, Thomas, of G'tn.	Deed to	Hoye, John, of G'tn.	1813	AE30	044	033
Robertson, Thomas, of G'tn.	Deed to	Gantt, Thomas T., of G'tn.	1813	AF31	036	025
Robertson, Thomas, of G'tn.	Deed to	Kurtz, Daniel, of G'tn.	1814	AH33	308	266
Robertson, Thomas [Jane B.]	Slave	From VA	1810	Z25	261	204
Robertson, William	Deed to	Dorsey, William H.	1794	A1-2	483	87
Robertson, William	Deed to	King, George	1798	D4	076	064
Robertson, William B. et al	Lease fr	Dodge, Francis	1813	AF31	552	409
Robertson, William B. & E. Bunnell	Lease fr	Smith, Clement	1814	AH33	156	147
Robertson, William B. & E. Bunnell	D. of T. fr	Smith, Clement	1814	AH33	157	148
Robertson, William B., of G'tn. et al	Deed to	Dodge, Francis, of G'tn.	1815	AI34	543	548
Robertson, William B. & E. Bunnell	Lease fr	Magruder, Ninian, Dr., of G'tn.	1816	AL36	084	086
Robertson, William B. et al	Deed to	Smith, Clement, of G'tn.	1817	AN38	025	021
Robertson, William B., G'tn. et al	Lease fr	Pickrell, John, of G'tn.	1817	AO39	154	116
Robertson, William B. & E. Bunnel	Deed fr	Magruder, Ninian, Dr., of G'tn.	1817	AN38	027	022
Robertson, William, of G'tn.	Deed fr	Stoddert, Benjamin, of G'tn.	1798	C3	277	224
Robertson, William, of Montg. Co.	Deed to	Oden, Benjamin, of P.G. Co.	1798	C3	334	270
Robertson, William, of G'tn.	Deed to	Brookes, Joseph, of G'tn.	1811	AB27	417	344
Robertson, Wm. B. & E. Bunnell	B. of S. fr	Weeden, Henry, of G'tn.	1813	AF31	172	116
Robey, Elizabeth, of G'tn.	Deed fr	Robey, Leonard, of G'tn.	1814	AH33	103	095
Robey, John et al	Deed to	Robey, William, of Scioto Co. OH	1805	N13	369	297
Robey, Leonard, of G'tn.	Deed fr	Pickrell, John, of G'tn.	1812	AC28	310	226
Robey, Leonard, of G'tn.	Deed to	Robey, Elizabeth, of G'tn.	1814	AH33	103	095
Robey, Theophilus	Partition	Nevitt, Joseph	1813	AF31	173	117
Robey, Theophilus & Jos. Nevitt	Deed fr	Deakins, Leonard M. & John Hoye	1809	W22	263	176
Robey, Theophilus et al	Deed fr	Beatty, Charles, heirs of	1808	T19	393	279
Robey, Theophilus et al	Deed fr	Beatty, Charles A., Dr.	1811	Z25	384	302
Robey, Thomas	B. of S. fr	Langley, Charles	1817	AO39	236	170
Robey, Thomas et al	Deed to	Robey, William, of Scioto Co. OH	1805	N13	369	297
Robey, William et al	Deed to	Robey, William, of Scioto Co. OH	1805	N13	369	297
Robey, William, of Scioto Co. OH	Deed fr	Robey, William et al	1805	N13	369	297
Robinson, Alexander	B. of S. to	Kearney, John	1801	G7	110	141
Robinson, Susan	Cert Free fr	Gardner, Hetty	1809	W22	023	017
Robinson, William, of G'tn.	Deed fr	Brooks, Joseph, of G'tn.	1810	Z25	178	141
Robinson, Zadock	B. of S. fr	Townshend, Leonard, of P.G. Co.	1816	AI34	453	466
Roby, Theophilus	Deed to	Dial, Anastasia	1802	H8	015	014
Roby, Theophilus, of G'tn.	Deed fr	Weems, John, Dr. of G'tn.	1796	B2B	403	069
Rochester, Nathaniel, Col. et al	Deed to	Hedges, Nicholas	1807	T19	011	009

Index to District of Columbia Land Records, 1792-1817

Party	What	Party	Year	Liber	Old	New
Rochfoucolt, Celeste LeBlonde dela	Deed fr	Neale, Leonard, of G'tn.	1805	N13	380	305
Rochfoucolt, Celeste LeBlonde dela	Deed to	Neale, Leonard, Rev.	1805	N13	031	033
Rochfoucolt, Celeste LeBlonde dela	Deed to	Neale, Leonard	1805	N13	067	061
Rodes, George	Deed fr	Crown, Samuel T.	1807	S18	382	304
Rodier, Philibert	Marriage	Jarber, Mary Ann	1816	AM37	307	224
Rodier, Philibert & Mary A. Jarber	B. of S. to	St. Victor, Louis de	1816	AM37	307	224
Roe, Bernard McDermot	Cert fr	Commissioners of Washington	1801	G7	433	569
Roe, Bernard McDermott	D. of T. to	Brent, William	1809	W22	389	253
Roe, Bernard McDermott	Cert. fr	Munroe, Thomas	1815	AH33	442	380
Roe, C. McD.	Lease to	Cessford, John	1802	I9	223	353
Roe, Charles & Cornelius McD.	Deed fr	Roe, Owen McDermott	1801	G7	266	366
Roe, Charles McDermot, of Ire.	P. of Atty. to	Roe, Cornelius McDermot, arch.	1800	E5	361	344
Roe, Charles McDermott	Receipt fr	Roe, Owen McDermott	1798	C3	356	286
Roe, Cornelius McD., children of	B. of S. fr	Callan, Nicholas	1810	Y24	524	461
Roe, Cornelius McDermot, of G'tn.	Cert fr	Commissioners of Washington	1792	B2A	292	409
Roe, Cornelius McDermot, of G'tn.	Cert fr	Commissioners of Washington	1792	B2A	292	409
Roe, Cornelius McDermot, of G'tn.	Cert fr	Commissioners of Washington	1792	B2A	291	408
Roe, Cornelius McDermot, of G'tn.	Cert fr	Commissioners of Washington	1792	B2A	292	408
Roe, Cornelius McDermot, arch.	P. of Atty. fr	Roe, Charles McDermot, of Ire.	1800	E5	361	344
Roe, Cornelius McDermot	Lease to	Garrety, Timothy et al	1801	G7	379	511
Roe, Cornelius McDermott	Receipt fr	Munroe, Thomas	1799	D4	381	365
Roe, Cornelius McDermott	Lease to	McLaughlin, James	1802	G7	515	656
Roe, Cornelius McDermott	Deed to	Deery, Patrick	1802	H8	521	480
Roe, Cornelius McDermott	Deed to	Fletcher, William	1804	K10	208	218
Roe, Cornelius McDermott	Deed to	Deiry, Patrick	1806	O14	191	125
Roe, Cornelius McDermott	Cert fr	Munroe, Thomas, Supt.	1807	R17	243	183
Roe, Cornelius McDermott	Deed to	Anderson, Catharine	1807	S18	268	211
Roe, Cornelius McDermott	Deed to	Sessford, John	1807	S18	048	041
Roe, Cornelius McDermott	Deed to	Kiler, Daniel	1807	S18	223	178
Roe, Cornelius McDermott	Deed to	Deery, Patrick	1807	S18	044	036
Roe, Edward McDermott	Deed fr	Commissioners of Washington	1799	D4	381	365
Roe, Edward McDermott	Deed fr	McNemara, Roger & Mary	1809	W22	247	166
Roe, Edward McDermott	B. of S. fr	McNemara, Roger & Mary	1809	X23	034	025
Roe, Edward McDermott et al	B. of S. fr	Callan, Nicholas	1810	Y24	524	461
Roe, Margaret McDermott et al	B. of S. fr	Callan, Nicholas	1810	Y24	524	461
Roe, Mary McDermott	Deed to	Anderson, Catherine	1808	T19	325	237
Roe, Mary McDermott et al	B. of S. fr	Callan, Nicholas	1810	Y24	524	461
Roe, Norah McDermott et al	B. of S. fr	Callan, Nicholas	1810	Y24	524	461
Roe, Owen McDermot	Receipt to	Deakins, William, Jr.	1795	B2A	281	394
Roe, Owen McDermot	Assign fr	Burnes, David	1795	B2A	248	347
Roe, Owen McDermot	Assign fr	Roe, Patrick McDermott	1795	B2A	251	351
Roe, Owen McDermott	Receipt to	Roe, Charles McDermott	1798	C3	356	286
Roe, Owen McDermott	Deed fr	Burnes, David	1798	C3	498	391
Roe, Owen McDermott	Agreement	Roe, Patrick McDermott	1798	D4	020	016
Roe, Owen McDermott	Deed to	Roe, Charles & Cornelius McD.	1801	G7	266	366
Roe, Patrick McDermot, of G'tn.	Cert fr	Commissioners of Washington	1792	B2A	298	417
Roe, Patrick McDermott	Assign to	Roe, Owen McDermot	1795	B2A	251	351
Roe, Patrick McDermott	Agreement	Roe, Owen McDermott	1798	D4	020	016
Roe, Sarah McDermott et al	B. of S. fr	Callan, Nicholas	1810	Y24	524	461
Roger, M.	Cert Free to	Shorter, Rachel and children	1807	S18	219	175
Rogers, Charles	B. of S. to	Soderstrom, Richard	1801	G7	438	573
Rogers, Daniel, of Balto. Co.	Deed to	Chandler, Walter Story	1810	Y24	071	063
Rogers, Matthew, of New York NY	Deed to	Deakins, William, Jr., of G'tn.	1792	A1-1	154	221
Rogers, Thomas, of Balto.	Deed to	Chandler, Walter Story	1809	V21	261	186
Rogers, William	Deed fr	Chandler, Walter Story, of G'tn.	1801	G7	156	207

Index to District of Columbia Land Records, 1792-1817

Party	What	Party	Year	Liber	Old	New
Rogers, William	P. of Atty. to	Chandler, Walter Story	1802	H8	063	059
Rogers, William	Deed fr	Van Ness, John P. & Marcia	1804	K10	113	122
Rogers, William, of New Orleans	Deed to	Chandler, Walter Story	1808	V21	027	020
Rogers, Wm., Thos., Marg. & Dan.	Deed fr	Davidson, John, of Annapolis	1800	E5	077	064
Rohr, Philip & Henry Bontz	Deed fr	Ritchie, Abner, sheriff	1800	E5	379	358
Rohrer, Frederick, s/o John	Deed fr	Bachtel, Isaac, of Bedford Co. PA	1792	A1-1	165	236
Roland, Jacob, Harrison Co. KY	P. of Atty. to	Lane, John & Charles Hunter	1804	K10	195	
Rollins, Bob (C), age 35	Cert Free fr	Carr, Overton	1813	AF31	240	166
Rollins, John	B. of S. to	Van Ness, John P.	1814	AG32	365	264
Rose, John & Ann, Loudoun Co.	Deed to	Peter, John, mer., of G'tn.	1809	W22	331	215
Rose, Robert	Deed fr	Weatherall, John, of G'tn.	1798	D4	117	101
Rose, Robert	Lease fr	Prout, William	1802	I9	566	919
Rose, Robert	Deed fr	Prout, William	1808	U20	211	114
Rose, Robert	Deed fr	Chandler, Walter S.	1809	X23	168	124
Ross, Andrew	Qualify	Captain of militia	1812	AD29	204	167
Ross, Andrew & Robert Getty	Deed fr	Lee, Thomas S., of G'tn.	1810	Y24	045	039
Ross, Andrew & Hannah, of G'tn.	Partition	Getty, Robert & Margaret, of G'tn.	1811	AB27	240	196
Ross, Andrew, of G'tn.	Partition	Getty, Robert, of G'tn.	1812	AC28	247	182
Ross, Andrew, of G'tn. et al	Deed fr	Gaither, Benjamin & Daniel	1814	AH33	336	290
Ross, Andrew, of G'tn.	Deed fr	Lee, Thomas Sim, of G'tn.	1815	AI34	285	321
Ross, Andrew, of G'tn.	Deed fr	Pleasonton, Stephen	1815	AI34	262	296
Ross, Andrew, of G'tn.	Deed fr	Lee, Thomas Sim, of G'tn.	1815	AI34	283	320
Ross, Andrew, of G'tn.	Deed to	Anderson, Richard	1816	AK35	270	215
Ross, Andrew, of G'tn.	Plat		1816	AK35	273	
Ross, Andrew, of G'tn.	Deed fr	Anderson, Richard, of John, G'tn.	1816	AM37	095	076
Ross, Charles & John Simpson	Deed fr	Barry, James	1801	G7	145	191
Ross, Charles et al	Deed fr	Barry, James, of Balto.	1800	E5	187	178
Ross, Charles et al	Deed to	Craig, John et al	1802	H8	120	117
Ross, Charles et al	Deed to	Craig, John et al	1806	P15	230	153
Ross, Charles, of Phila. et al	Deed to	Barry, James D.	1809	W22	087	064
Ross, David, Horatio & Archibald	Deed to	Beall, Thomas & John M. Gantt	1793	A1-1	254	345
Ross, David, of MD, exr.	Deed to	Barry, James	1802	H8	232	221
Ross, James	Deed fr	Muse, Lawrence, of VA	1809	W22	197	137
Ross, James	Deed fr	Mara, Catherine, amx. of Philip	1812	AC28	426	307
Ross, James, Fredericksburg VA	Assign fr	Beverly, Munford, Culpeper Co.	1806	O14	108	068
Ross, John, of G'tn.	Deed fr	Herstons, Charles, of G'tn.	1810	Y24	065	057
Ross, Nancy (negro) & child	Manumis fr	DeCow, Rachel	1811	Z25	187	147
Ross, Richard	Cert fr	Commissioners of Washington	1796	B2B	455	144
Ross, Richard	Assign fr	Commissioners of Washington	1809	W22	248	167
Ross, Richard	Manumis to	[ ], Airy (C), d/o Cassandra, age 5	1814	AH33	127	121
Ross, Richard	Manumis to	Briarwood, Giles (C) & wife Henny	1814	AH33	221	195
Ross, Richard	Manumis to	[ ], Cassandra (C), age 43	1814	AH33	127	121
Ross, Richard, of Bladensburgh	Cert fr	Commissioners of Washington	1793	B2A	313	441
Ross, Richard, of P.G. Co.	Deed to	Key, Philip Barton, of Montg. Co.	1809	W22	250	168
Ross, Richard, of Montg. Co.	Deed fr	Crawford, William, of G'tn.	1816	AM37	290	212
Ross, William, of G'tn.	Deed fr	Deakins, Francis, of G'tn.	1801	G7	029	035
Rounds, Hezekiah (M)	Cert Free fr	Tippett, Cartwright	1812	AD29	503	425
Rounds, Off (M)	Cert Free fr	Tippett, Cartwright	1812	AD29	502	424
Rowland, George	B. of S. to	McElden, William	1815	AI34	324	357
Rowles, Joseph E. et al	Cert fr	Commissioners of Washington	1796	B2B	453	141
Rowles, Joseph E., mer., et al	Deed to	Schneily, Henry, merchant	1800	E5	152	141
Rowles, Joseph E. et al	Deed to	Schnibly, Henry	1800	E5	175	165
Rowles, Joseph E. et al	Deed fr	Reintzel, Andrew	1802	I9	256	414
Rowles, Joseph E. et al	Deed fr	Beatty, Charles	1802	I9	255	412
Rowles, Joseph E.	Slaves	From Fairfax Co. VA	1804	L11	017	

Index to District of Columbia Land Records, 1792-1817

Party	What	Party	Year	Liber	Old	New
Rowles, Joseph E.	Slaves	From VA	1805	N13	002	002
Rowles, Joseph E.	Slaves	From VA	1807	R17	398	301
Rowles, Joseph E., of G'tn.	Deed fr	Stoddert, Benjamin, of G'tn.	1807	Q16	402	309
Rowles, Joseph E., for mill dam	Agreement	Beall, Thomas, of George	1808	T19	178	126
Rowles, Joseph E.	Deed fr	Beall, Thomas, of George	1808	U20	376	207
Rowles, Joseph E., of G'tn.	Slaves	From VA	1809	X23	066	
Rowles, Joseph E., of G'tn.	Deed fr	Lovering, William & Susannah et al	1809	X23	067	050
Rowles, Joseph Evan	Deed to	Cook, Thomas, of Frederick Co.	1805	M12	247	249
Roy, James H., of Richmond VA	Deed fr	Ott, John, of G'tn.	1816	AM37	430	308
Roy, John, of Balto.	Deed fr	McElwee, John, of Balto.	1805	M12	270	271
Roy, John, of Balto.	Deed to	McElwee, John, of Balto.	1809	X23	108	078
Rozer, Henry	Deed fr	Cooledge, Samuel Judson	1794	B2A	144	191
Rozer, Henry et al	Deed to	Carroll, Henry Hill, of Balto. Co.	1793	A1-1	353	459
Rozer, Henry et al	Deed to	Davidson, Samuel	1793	A1-1	356	463
Rozer, Henry et al	Deed to	Hill, Henry, Jr.	1793	A1-1	360	466
Rozer, Henry, P.G. Co. et al	Deed to	Hall, Benjamin, of Q.A. Co.	1795	B2B	366	017
Rumney, John	B. of S. to	Knowles, Henry	1808	T19	214	156
Rumsey, Jane, Wilmington DE	Deed to	Lufborough, Nathan, of Phila. PA	1807	S18	021	018
Rush, Richard, of PA	Deed fr	Chandler, Walter Story	1816	AM37	377	272
Rush, Richard, of PA	Deed fr	Davidson, Lewis Grant	1816	AM37	374	270
Rush, Richard, of PA	Deed fr	Davidson, Lewis Grant	1816	AM37	369	266
Rush, Richard, of PA	Deed fr	Davidson, Lewis Grant	1817	AO39	481	330
Rusk, William et al	Deed fr	Ross, John et al	1806	P15	230	153
Russ, Samuel	Mortgage to	Tingey, Thomas et al	1804	K10	390	405
Russ, Samuel	B. of S. fr	French, James	1804	K10	329	339
Russ, Samuel	Deed fr	Prout, William	1805	N13	212	183
Russ, Samuel	Deed to	McKim, James, of Marine Corps	1805	N13	209	181
Russ, Samuel	B. of S. to	Alexander, Robert	1806	O14	242	159
Russ, Samuel	Assign to	Johnson, Joseph	1806	P15	010	006
Russ, Samuel	Lease fr	Gilpin, Bernard, of Montg. Co.	1806	P15	005	004
Russ, Samuel	Mortgage to	Tinsley, Thomas et al	1806	P15	012	007
Russ, Samuel	Deed fr	Smallwood, Samuel N. et al	1806	Q16	107	069
Russ, Samuel	Deed to	Smallwod, Samuel N.	1806	Q16	098	063
Russ, Samuel	B. of S. to	Prout, William	1807	R17	031	026
Russ, Samuel	Deed to	Prout, William	1808	V21	038	029
Russ, Samuel et al	Deed fr	Voss, Nicholas	1806	P15	313	207
Russ, Samuel, insolvent	Deed to	Bryan, Benjamin, trustee	1810	Y24	182	167
Russel, Frederick A., of G'tn.	B. of S. fr	Bixby, Nathaniel P., of G'tn.	1817	AO39	205	150
Russell, Joseph	B. of S. to	Deblois, Lewis	1810	Z25	141	112
Russell, William, def.	Suit	Skinner, John, plt.	1799	D4	342	330
Rustin, Lawson (negro)	Manumis fr	Stone, Mathew, of Charles Co.	1806	P15	266	175
Rustin, Mary Ann (negro)	Manumis fr	Stone, Mathew, of Charles Co.	1806	P15	266	175
Rustin, Thomas (negro)	Manumis fr	Stone, Mathew, of Charles Co.	1806	P15	266	175
Ruth, Henry	Qualify	Captain of light infantry	1812	AD29	216	177
Rutherford, Alexander et al	Deed to	Oglevie, David	1800	E5	089	076
Rutherford, Alexander, of G'tn.	D. of T. to	Johns, Richard	1816	AM37	125	097
Rutherford, Alexander, of G'tn.	B. of S. to	Kurtz, John	1817	AN38	371	274
Rutherford, Andrew	Deed fr	Reid, Alexander	1800	E5	341	328
Rutherford, Andrew et al	Deed fr	Burnes, David	1799	D4	174	155
Rutherford, William	Deed to	Burford, Henry	1804	L11	216	203
Rutherford, William, insolvent	Deed to	Herty, Thomas, trustee	1807	R17	140	108
Rutter, Thomas, of Balto.	Deed fr	Commissioners of Washington	1801	F6	125	078
Rutter, Thomas, of Balto.	Deed to	Williams, Sarah B.	1817	AO39	179	133
Ryan, Henry & Mary [Caldwell]	Deed to	Caldwell, Timothy	1808	T19	269	198
Ryan, Henry & Mary	Mortgage to	Morin, Lewis et al	1809	X23	298	237

Party	What	Party	Year	Liber	Old	New
Ryan, Henry & Mary	Deed to	deKraft, Edward B.	1812	AE30	010	008
Ryan, Henry & Mary et al	Release to	deKraftt, Edward B.	1813	AF31	532	393
Ryan, Henry & Mary	Deed to	Brook, Samuel	1816	AM37	214	158
Ryan, Henry & Mary	D. of T. to	Kerr, Alexander	1817	AO39	407	277
Ryan, Mary	Deed fr	Granger, Gideon	1810	Y24	539	474
Ryan, Mary	B. of S. fr	Shuck, Elizabeth	1817	AN38	395	294
Ryan, Mary, trustee of	Mortgage fr	deKrafft, Edward B.	1813	AE30	234	187

Party	What	Party	Year	Liber	Old	New
S						
Saintclere, George [St. Clair]	Assign fr	Adams, William	1804	K10	326	335
Salmon, Margaret (negro)	Cert Free fr	Winsett, Kezia N.	1807	R17	292	
Samuel, Griffen (C)	Manumis fr	Beverly, Maria	1812	AC28	305	222
Sanborius, Mary Ann	Deed to	Coates, James et al	1802	I9	578	937
Sanders, Ann & Thomas	Deposition	Neale, Francis	1806	P15	187	126
Sanders, Anne	Deed to	Sanders, Thomas	1805	N13	264	220
Sanders, Catherine	B. of S. fr	Flaut, Joseph	1809	X23	133	095
Sanders, Thomas	Qualify		1802	I9	465	767
Sanders, Thomas	Deed fr	Sanders, Anne	1805	N13	264	220
Sanders, Thomas	Deed to	French, John B.	1806	Q16	113	073
Sanders, Thomas	B. of S. to	Flaut, Joseph	1809	X23	105	076
Sanders, Thomas, of G'tn.	Deed fr	Goszler, John, of G'tn.	1798	C3	468	368
Sanderson, James, of Alexa.	D. of T. fr	Taylor, Robert I., of Alexa.	1813	AE30	070	053
Sanderson, William R., Fredk. Co.	Deed Gift fr	Leatherman, Henry, Frederick Co.	1809	W22	270	180
Sanderson, William R., Fredk. Co.	Convey to	Mayer, Henry	1814	AH33	091	083
Sanderson, William R., Fredk. Co.	Deed to	Mayer, Henry, of G'tn.	1815	AK35	249	197
Sandford, George	Partition	Giberson, William	1805	M12	116	109
Sandford, George	Mortgage fr	Boyld, Eghtane M.	1808	V21	126	093
Sandford, George	Deed to	McMurrey, William	1816	AM37	321	233
Sandford, George, carpenter	Deed fr	Van Ness, John P. & Marcia	1805	M12	174	173
Sandford, Hector, of G'tn.	Deed to	Beck, Richard, of G'tn.	1805	N13	227	193
Sandford, William, of Alexa.	Deed fr	Munroe, Thomas, Supt.	1804	M12	038	038
Sandhagan, Frederick	B. of S. to	Dixon, John C.	1807	R17	316	240
Sandiford, James	Deed to	Sandiford, Samuel	1812	AD29	229	189
Sandiford, Samuel	Deed fr	Sandiford, James	1812	AD29	229	189
Sandiford, Samuel et al	Deed fr	Sandiford, Thomas, Sr.	1813	AF31	055	038
Sandiford, Thomas	Deed fr	Nourse, Michael	1807	S18	249	176
Sandiford, Thomas, Jr. et al	Deed fr	Sandiford, Thomas, Sr.	1813	AF31	055	038
Sandiford, Thomas, Jr. & Samuel	Cert fr	Munroe, Thomas, Supt.	1817	AN38	283	207
Sandiford, Thomas, Sr.	Deed to	Sandiford, Thomas, Jr. et al	1813	AF31	055	038
Sands, Comfort et al	P. of Atty. to	Covachiche, Joseph	1796	B2B	450	136
Sands, Comfort et al	Deed fr	Burnes, David, of P.G. Co.	1796	B2B	489	181
Sands, Comfort et al	P. of Atty. to	Dorsey, William H., of G'tn.	1796	B2B	523	234
Sands, Comfort et al	Deed to	Atkinson, John, mer., of NY	1797	C3	037	30
Sands, Comfort, mer., of NY et al	Deed to	Atkinson, Francis	1797	C3	032	26
Sands, Comfort, mer. et al	Deed to	Covachick, Joseph, mer., of NY	1797	C3	021	17
Sands, Comfort, mer., of NY et al	Deed to	Lewis, George, mer., of NY	1797	C3	026	21
Sands, Comfort, mer., of NY	Deed to	Sands, Robert C., s/o Comfort	1815	AH33	447	383
Sands, Comfort, of NY et al	Deed fr	Bayly, William, of P.G. Co.	1796	B2B	384	040
Sands, Comfort, of NY et al	Deed to	Oden, Benjamin, of P.G. Co.	1797	C3	047	37
Sands, Comfort, of NY et al	Deed fr	Oden, Benjamin	1797	C3	043	34
Sands, Comfort, of Flatbush NY	Deed to	Sands, Louis, of Brooklyn NY	1800	F6	112	069
Sands, Francis	Deed fr	Walker, George	1802	H8	023	022
Sands, Louis, of Brooklyn NY	Deed fr	Sands, Comfort, of Flatbush NY	1801	F6	112	069
Sands, Louis, of NY	Deed to	Lorman, William, of Balto. MD	1802	H8	098	090
Sands, Mary	Deed fr	Oden, Benjamin	1798	C3	329	265
Sands, Mary, of G'tn.	Deed fr	Davidson, John, of Annapolis	1798	C3	323	260
Sands, Robert C., s/o Comfort	Deed fr	Sands, Comfort, mer., of NY	1815	AH33	447	383
Sands, William, of Montg. Co.	B. of S. fr	Grimes, Michael, of G'tn.	1805	N13	176	158
Sanford, Daniel, of Norfolk VA	Deed fr	Cowper, William et al, by atty.	1811	AB27	319	263
Sanford, George	Deed fr	Carroll, Daniel, of *Duddington*	1812	AD29	211	172
Sanford, George	Deed fr	Coombe, Griffith	1816	AL36	288	286
Sanford, George et al	Deed fr	Van Ness, John P.	1802	I9	498	817
Sanford, Hector	Deed fr	Lucas, Henry	1802	I9	420	696

Party	What	Party	Year	Liber	Old	New
Sanford, Hector	Manumis to	[ ], Rhodam (Negro)	1802	I9		135
Sappwaring, Marcus Sempronius	Deed fr	Hoban, James	1805	M12	155	151
Sardo, Michael	Deed fr	Catolina, Salvadora	1812	AB27	226	183
Sardo, Michael	Deed to	Catalano, Salvadora	1812	AC28	303	221
Sarratt, Henry B.	B. of S. to	Prout, William	1808	V21	037	028
Saul, Joseph	Deed to	Gillis, Thomas Handy	1804	K10	407	422
Saunders, Ann B., Mrs.	Marriage	Richards, George	1816	AM37	323	235
Saunders, John (negro)	Manumis fr	Van Ness, John P.	1809	W22	139	099
Saunders, Joseph	B. of S. to	Clubb, Druey Ann	1812	AD29	311	255
Saunders, Thomas	B. of S. to	Mayer, Henry	1809	W22	214	147
Savoy, Archibald, Jr.	Cert Free fr	Proctor, Ann	1809	V21	406	309
Savoy, William, s/o Archibald	Cert Free fr	Procter, Ann	1810	Y24	032	027
Sayre, Daniel, of Amelia Co. VA	Deed fr	Patton, James, of Alexa.	1799	D4	299	283
Sayre, Daniel, of Amelia Co. VA	Deed fr	Patton, James & Mary Ann, Alexa.	1799	D4	212	195
Scace, Shadrick & Ellender	Deed to	Beatty, Charles, of G'tn.	1794	A1-2	494	97
Scallan, James	Agreement	Boyd, Washington, agent	1816	AL36	500	469
Scamm, John [Shamm]	Mortgage to	Taylor, Elizabeth	1804	K10	258	264
Schaffer, Frederick	Deed fr	Fitzhugh, Philip	1801	G7	237	318
Schell, Charles, of Frederick Co.	Deed to	Beall, Thomas & John M. Gantt	1792	A1-1	135	196
Schenebely, Henry, Dr.	Cert fr	Commissioners of Washington	1797	B2B	461	151
Schimmelpennick, Rutger Jan	Deed to	Greenleaf, James, New York NY	1796	B2B	493	188
Schimmelpenninck, Rutger Jan	Deed fr	Greenleaf, James	1794	B2A	065	083
Schley, Daniel	Mortgage to	Renner, Daniel	1805	M12	136	131
Schley, Daniel, of G'tn.	Deed fr	Ritchie, Abner, of G'tn.	1804	M12	024	024
Schley, George Jacob, of MD	Deed to	Smith, Clement	1810	Z25	287	225
Schnebley, Henry	Deed to	Beall, Thomas & John M. Gantt	1793	A1-1	364	471
Schneily, Henry, mer.	Deed fr	Rowles, Joseph E. & Thos. Cook	1800	E5	152	141
Schneitzell, George, of MD	Deed to	Ritchie, Abner	1810	Y24	499	439
Schnertzel, George	Deed to	Bringle, Lawrence	1802	I9	589	954
Schnertzel, George, Sr., Fredk.	Deed to	Brengle, Laurence, Frederick Co.	1804	K10	181	189
Schneverly, Henry	Deed fr	Harbaugh, Leonard	1797	B2B	650	413
Schnider, Abraham	Deed fr	Beatty, Charles	1802	I9	030	040
Schnively, Henry	Deed fr	Cook, Thomas et al	1800	E5	175	165
Schnively, Henry	Deed to	Ott, John	1806	P15	184	123
Schnively, Henry	Mortgage to	Hebner, Michael	1806	P15	112	070
Schnively, Henry	B. of S. to	Ott, John	1806	P15	183	122
Schnively, Henry	Mortgage to	Lenox, Peter [Lynox]	1806	P15	206	138
Schnively, Henry, insolvent	Deed to	Hewitt, John, trustee	1806	P15	255	168
Schnivley, Henry	Deed fr	Vermillion, John Robertson, G'tn.	1794	B2A	060	075
Scholfield, Andrew, of Alexa.	Deed fr	Hewitt, John	1811	AA26	235	161
Scholfield, Andrew, of Alexa.	Assign fr	Stettinius, Samuel	1811	AB27	255	208
Scholfield, Andrew, of Alexa. Co.	Deed to	Mayer, Frederick	1814	AG32	204	142
Scholfield, Andrew, of Alexa.	Deed fr	Corporation of Washington	1815	AI34	500	507
Scholfield, Andrew, of Alexa.	Deed fr	Corporation of Washington	1815	AI34	498	505
Scholfield, Andrew, of Alexa.	Deed fr	Hewitt, John & Jos. Scholfield	1815	AK35	004	003
Scholfield, Andrew, of Alexa. et al	D. of T. fr	McLeod, John, schoolmaster	1815	AK35	235	186
Scholfield, Andrew, plt.	Suit	Peter, Robert et al, defs.	1809	V21	326	240
Scholfield, Isachar	Deed to	Ewell, Thomas	1814	AH33	366	317
Scholfield, Isachar et al	Mortgage to	Ewell, Thomas	1813	AE30	260	202
Scholfield, Isachar, of P.G. Co.	Deed fr	Ewell, Thomas & Elizabeth	1813	AE30	256	200
Scholfield, Issachar	Partition	Scholfield, Joseph Leonard	1815	AK35	197	154
Scholfield, Issachar	Deed fr	Corporation of Washington	1816	AL36	232	237
Scholfield, Issachar	Deed fr	Corporation of Washington	1816	AL36	234	239
Scholfield, Issachar & Mahlon	Deed fr	Wells, Joseph, of PA	1796	B2B	539	259
Scholfield, Issachar & Mahlon	Deed to	McCormick, James, of P.G. Co.	1797	B2B	664	429

Party	What	Party	Year	Liber	Old	New
Scholfield, Issachar & Mahlon	Deed to	Evans, Evan, of N.C. Co. DE	1797	B2B	666	433
Scholfield, Issachar & Mahlon	Deed fr	Creager, Michael, Alexa., et al	1799	D4	289	271
Scholfield, Issachar, of P.G. Co.	Deed fr	Ewell, Thomas	1813	AE30	527	390
Scholfield, Issachar, of P.G. Co.	Mortgage to	Ewell, Thomas	1813	AF31	076	052
Scholfield, J. & M.	Agreement	Moscrop, Henry et al	1799	D4	241	224
Scholfield, Joseph	Deed to	Riggs, George, of G'tn.	1801	F6	226	147
Scholfield, Joseph & John Hewitt	D. of T. fr	Mayer, Frederick	1813	AF31	403	291
Scholfield, Joseph & John Hewitt	Deed to	Scholfield, Andrew, of Alexa.	1815	AK35	004	003
Scholfield, Joseph et al	B. of S. fr	Cooper, John	1810	X23	409	330
Scholfield, Joseph L.	Deed fr	Patterson, Edgar et al	1810	Y24	073	065
Scholfield, Joseph L., et al	Deed fr	Ewell, Thomas & Elizabeth	1813	AE30	256	200
Scholfield, Joseph L. et al	Mortgage to	Ewell, Thomas	1813	AE30	260	202
Scholfield, Joseph L. & I.	Deed to	Ewell, Thomas	1814	AG32	202	141
Scholfield, Joseph L. & Isachar	Deed to	Ewell, Thomas	1814	AH33	368	319
Scholfield, Joseph L. & Issachar	Release fr	Ewell, Thomas	1815	AI34	353	384
Scholfield, Joseph Leonard	Partition	Scholfield, Issachar	1815	AK35	197	154
Scholfield, Mahlon, of Alexa. et al	D. of T. fr	McLeod, John, schoolmaster	1815	AK35	235	186
Scholfield, Mahlon, of Alexa.	Deed fr	Corporation of Washington	1817	AN38	486	350
Schoolfield, Andrew	Deed to	Ray, Benjamin, Jr.	1802	H8	526	485
Schoolfield, Issachar	Deed to	Ray, Benjamin, Jr.	1802	H8	526	485
Schoolfield, Joseph	Deed to	Ray, Benjamin, Jr.	1802	H8	526	485
Schoolfield, Joseph et al	Deed fr	Shoemaker, Jonathan	1808	T19	114	081
Schoolfield, Mahlon	Deed to	Ray, Benjamin, Jr.	1802	H8	526	485
Schroeder, Henry, of Balto. MD	Deed fr	Moscrop, Henry, of MD	1802	H8	262	249
Schroeder, Henry, of Balto. MD	Deed fr	Moscrop, Henry, of MD	1802	H8	524	483
Schroeder, Henry, of Balto.	Deed fr	Washington, Bailey	1808	U20	317	169
Schroeder, Henry, of Balto.	Assign to	Coyle, John	1810	Z25	161	128
Schultz, Henry	B. of S. fr	Hankard, John	1802	G7	528	673
Schultz, Henry	Deed to	Tracey, Thomas	1805	N13	157	145
Schultz, Henry, of G'tn.	Deed fr	Beatty, Thomas J., Jr., of G'tn.	1796	B2B	589	337
Schultze, Henry	Mortgage fr	Smith, Lewis, of G'tn.	1814	AG32	353	256
Schultze, Henry	Lease to	Mayne, Adam et al	1816	AK35	502	396
Schultze, Henry, of G'tn.	Deed fr	James, James, of G'tn.	1797	B2B	673	442
Schultze, Henry, of G'tn.	Deed fr	James, James, of P.G. Co.	1798	C3	511	402
Schultze, Henry, of G'tn.	Deed fr	Davidson, John, of Annapolis	1800	E5	333	321
Schultze, Henry, of G'tn.	Deed to	Smith, Lewis, of G'tn.	1814	AG32	286	206
Schultze, Henry, of G'tn.	Deed fr	Tracy, Thomas, of Fairfax Co.	1816	AL36	297	294
Schultze, J.L. Henry	Deed to	Wingard, Abraham	1808	U20	048	027
Schultze, J.L. Henry	Deed fr	Wingerd, Abraham	1808	U20	046	026
Schwartz, Conrad & Philip Mauro	Deed fr	Murdock, John	1811	AB27	227	185
Schwartz, Conrad & Philip Mauro	Deed fr	Dorsey, William H., of Balto. Co.	1812	AC28	258	189
Schwartz, Conrad & Philip Mauro	Deed fr	Murdock, John, of G'tn.	1812	AC28	257	188
Schwartz, Conradt & Philip Mauro	Deed fr	Dorsey, William H.	1811	AB27	223	181
Schwarz, Conrad, of Balto.	Deed to	Mauro, Philip, of Balto.	1815	AI34	151	173
Schwarz, Conrad, of Balto.	Plat	13th St. and Pennsylvania Ave.	1815	AI34	153	
Schwarz, Conrad, of Balto.	Deed to	Ott, John	1815	AI34	152	174
Sciverman, John C., insolvent	Deed to	Kent, Luke, trustee	1810	Z25	193	151
Scott, Alexander	Manumis to	Smith, Will	1808	V21	098	075
Scott, Allen	Slaves	From Fairfax Co. VA	1810	Y24	097	088
Scott, Allen	D. of T. to	Darne, Simon	1815	AI34	146	167
Scott, Eleanor		Certificate of Slaves	1802	H8	026	025
Scott, Eleanor	Slaves		1804	K10	182	
Scott, Elizabeth C. et al	Bond to	United States	1801	G7	347	478
Scott, Elizabeth, d/o Jane	B. of S. fr	Scott, Jane	1805	N13	137	131
Scott, George, exr. of George	Deed to	French, George et al	1795	B2B	368	020

Party	What	Party	Year	Liber	Old	New
Scott, George, of Wash. Co. MD	Deed to	Turner, Thomas, of G'tn.	1795	B2A	224	311
Scott, Gusstavus	Transfer fr	Morris, Robert & James Greenleaf	1796	B2B	457	145
Scott, Gustavus	Deed fr	Forrest, Uriah	1795	B2A	263	367
Scott, Gustavus	Deed fr	Blodget, Samuel	1795	B2A	262	366
Scott, Gustavus	Deed fr	Holmead, Anthony	1795	B2A	170	227
Scott, Gustavus	Deed fr	Stoddert, Benjamin	1795	B2A	169	226
Scott, Gustavus	Cert fr	Commissioners of Washington	1796	B2B	457	145
Scott, Gustavus	Deed fr	Lawson, Alexander	1796	B2B	404	071
Scott, Gustavus	Deed to	Tayloe, John, of VA	1797	B2B	683	457
Scott, Gustavus	Deed fr	Forrest, Uriah	1799	D4	371	356
Scott, Gustavus	Deed fr	Forrest, Uriah	1799	D4	369	354
Scott, Gustavus	Deed to	Forrest, Uriah	1799	D4	388	370
Scott, Gustavus	P. of Atty. fr	Morris, Robert et al	1799	D4	188	170
Scott, Gustavus	Deed to	Macdonald, Andrew	1799	D4	249	233
Scott, Gustavus	Deed fr	Forrest, Uriah	1799	D4	373	358
Scott, Gustavus	Deed fr	Beatty, Charles, Col.	1800	E5	224	217
Scott, Gustavus	Deed to	Forrest, Uriah	1800	E5	200	192
Scott, Gustavus & Marg., exr. of	Deed to	Parrott, Richard	1809	V21	251	179
Scott, Gustavus, estate, trustee of	Deed fr	Munroe, Thomas, Supt.	1804	L11	291	267
Scott, Gusstavus et al	Cert to	Young, Notley	1794	B2A	109	145
Scott, Gusstavus et al	P. of Atty. to	Greenleaf, James, New York NY	1794	B2A	110	146
Scott, Gusstavus et al	Cert to	Greenleaf, James	1794	B2A	108	143
Scott, Gusstavus et al	Deed to	Greenleaf, James, New York NY	1794	B2A	137	181
Scott, Gusstavus et al	Deed fr	Greenleaf, James, New York NY	1795	B2A	229	318
Scott, Gusstavus et al	Deed to	Dermott, James Reed	1797	B2B	672	440
Scott, Gusstavus et al	Deed to	Hoban, James	1798	C3	319	257
Scott, Gusstavus et al	Deed to	Hodgson, Joseph	1798	C3	331	267
Scott, Gusstavus et al	Deed to	Sherrard, Francis	1798	C3	464	365
Scott, Gustavus, of G'tn.	Deed to	Morris, Robert & John Nicholson	1796	B2B	603	355
Scott, Gustavus, of Montg. Co.	Deed to	Stone, John Hoskins, Annapolis	1796	B2B	520	230
Scott, Gustavus, of G'tn.	Deed to	Barry, James, of Balto.	1796	B2B	489	182
Scott, Gustavus, of Montg. Co.	Deed to	Lingan, Nicholas, of Montg. Co.	1805	N13	183	164
Scott, Henry	B. of S. fr	Murphey, Benjamin	1816	AM37	022	018
Scott, Henry	B. of S. fr	Boothe, George	1817	AN38	162	118
Scott, Isabella	B. of S. fr	Boyd, George	1811	AB27	500	409
Scott, Isabella et al	Deed fr	Scott, George, exr. of George	1795	B2B	368	020
Scott, Isabella et al	Deed to	Greenleaf, James, New York NY	1796	B2B	445	128
Scott, James	D. of T. to	Reintzell, Daniel	1816	AM37	027	022
Scott, James	Manumis fr	Knowles, Henry, of G'tn.	1816	AM37	027	022
Scott, James (C)	Manumis fr	Knowles, Henry, of G'tn.	1816	AK35	278	221
Scott, Jane	B. of S. to	Scott, Elizabeth, d/o Jane	1805	N13	137	131
Scott, Jesse, of G'tn.	Deed fr	Wright, Thomas C., of G'tn.	1815	AH33	485	414
Scott, Jesse, of G'tn.	D. of T. to	Ott, John, of G'tn.	1815	AI34	149	171
Scott, John C. et al	Bond to	United States	1801	G7	347	478
Scott, Leonard (C), of Annapolis	B. of S. fr	Belt, Joseph S.	1801	G7	338	468
Scott, Louisa (M)	Manumis fr	Leiper, George R., late P.G. Co.	1815	AK35	183	141
Scott, Margaret, by E.B. Caldwell	B. of S. to	Shorter, Moses	1806	Q16	293	223
Scott, Margaret et al	Deed fr	Scott, George, exr. of George	1795	B2B	368	020
Scott, Margaret et al	Deed to	Greenleaf, James, New York NY	1796	B2B	445	128
Scott, Margaret et al	Bond to	United States	1801	G7	347	478
Scott, Margaret, of Fairfax Co. VA	Deed to	Patterson, Edgar	1809	V21	374	277
Scott, Margaret, wid/o Gustavus	Deed to	Washington, William A.	1804	K10	252	259
Scott, Margaret, wid/o Gustavus	Deed to	Corcoran, Thomas	1806	P15	171	118
Scott, Mary et al	Bond to	United States	1801	G7	347	478
Scott, Michael	Deed to	Law, Thomas	1801	G7	240	322

Index to District of Columbia Land Records, 1792-1817

Party	What	Party	Year	Liber	Old	New
Scott, Michael, now of Balto.	Deed to	Barry, Garret	1805	N13	222	190
Scott, Nancy (M)	Cert Free fr	Tippett, Cartwright	1812	AD29	503	424
Scott, Sabre, def.	Suit	Ott, John, plt.	1816	AK35	487	383
Scott, Sabret	Cert fr	Commissioners of Washington	1797	B2B	468	161
Scott, Sabret	Transfer fr	Lee, Richard B., of VA	1797	B2B	468	161
Scott, Sabret	Deed fr	O'Reilly, Johnson Michael et ux	1800	E5	180	170
Scott, Sabret	Deed to	Foxall, Henry	1802	I9	471	776
Scott, Sabret	Deed to	Laird, John	1802	I9	510	836
Scott, Sabret	Deed fr	Stewart, Deborah	1802	I9	425	705
Scott, Sabret	Deed fr	Stewart, Deborah	1802	I9	187	289
Scott, Sabret	Deed fr	Stewart, Deborah	1802	I9	186	286
Scott, Sabret	Lease fr	Johns, Susannah	1802	I9	355	587
Scott, Sabret, of Montg. Co.	Convey fr	O'Reilly, Michael J., of P.G. Co.	1797	C3	092	76
Scott, Sabret, of G'tn.	Deed fr	Laird, John, of G'tn.	1804	K10	126	136
Scott, Sabret, of G'tn.	Deed to	Fox, Bartleson, of G'tn.	1804	K10	229	237
Scott, Sabret, of G'tn.	Deed to	Bowie, Washington, of G'tn.	1816	AL36	283	281
Scott, Sabret, of G'tn. [Cebart]	Deed to	Mitchell, John, of G'tn.	1816	AK35	488	383
Scott, Sabrett	Slave	From VA	1807	R17	278	212
Scott, Treasy (C), alias Rounds	Cert Free fr	Tippett, Cartwright	1812	AD29	503	424
Scott, Upton	Deed to	Beall, Thomas & John M. Gantt	1793	A1-1	208	291
Scott, Watkins, of Bladensburgh	B. of S. fr	Picknoll, Richard H.	1811	Z25	527	418
Scott, William A. & Anne	Deed to	Laird, John, of G'tn.	1799	E5	065	053
Scott, William A. & Anne, P.G. Co.	Deed to	Corcoran, Thomas, of G'tn.	1805	O14	131	084
Scott, William A.	Deed fr	May, Frederick	1816	AM37	219	162
Scott, William et al	Deed to	Ray, Benjamin, Jr.	1802	H8	526	485
Scovell, Hope	Deed fr	Wordworth, Joseph [Ann]	1814	AG32	240	172
Scoville, Hope	Deed fr	Woodworth, Joseph	1814	AH33	236	206
Scyle, Ann Maria, wid/o J. [Seyle]	Deed to	Kaegy, Abraham, of DE	1805	M12	157	154
Scyle, John, of G'tn.	Deed to	Beall, Thomas & John M. Gantt	1793	A1-1	315	415
Scyle, John, of G'tn.	Deed fr	Holmead, Anthony	1794	B2A	140	185
Seager, Nathaniel	Deed to	Sothoron, Thomas L.	1802	I9	501	823
Seaton, Thomas, trustees of	Deed fr	Reintzel, Anthony, of G'tn.	1793	A1-1	183	259
Seeverman, John C.	B. of S. to	Gird, Henry	1806	Q16	199	134
Segur, Nathaniel	Deed to	McClan	1802	I9	232	369
Selbey, Adeline et al	Deed fr	Estep, Joseph	1814	AG32	349	253
Selby, Henry	B. of S. to	Smallwood, Benjamin	1806	P15	350	232
Selby, Henry	B. of S. to	Bryan, Benjamin	1808	T19	097	069
Selby, Henry Estep et al	Deed fr	Estep, Joseph	1814	AG32	349	253
Selby, Henry, insolvent	Deed to	McCue, Owen, trustee	1809	X23	166	122
Selby, Martha	B. of S. to	Jenkins, Harriet	1810	X23	416	336
Selby, Philip	Manumis to	Butler, Philis (negro)	1808	U20	137	078
Selby, Philip B.	B. of S. to	Estep, Joseph	1811	Z25	404	317
Selby, Philip Butler	Manumis to	Butler, Philice	1806	Q16	069	043
Selby, Philip, children of et al	Deed fr	Estep, Joseph	1814	AG32	349	253
Selby, Samuel Washington et al	Deed fr	Estep, Joseph	1814	AG32	349	253
Semes, Jesse M.	B. of S. fr	Speake, Samuel & Mary Anne et al	1813	AF31	229	157
Semmes, Francis X., of P.G> Co.	Deed to	Semmes, Joseph M., of G'tn.	1814	AG32	221	155
Semmes, George, of P.G. Co.	Deed to	Hoxton, Stanislaus, of P.G. Co.	1806	O14	182	119
Semmes, Jesse M. [Simmes]	Lease fr	Van Ness, John P. & Marcia	1817	AO39	392	266
Semmes, Joseph	Bond to	United States	1801	G7	013	016
Semmes, Joseph et al	Bond to	United States	1802	H8	520	479
Semmes, Joseph et al	Bond to	Corporation of Georgetown	1805	N13	094	086
Semmes, Tercia Henrietta	B. of S. fr	Hamilton, Francis P.	1808	V21	083	065
Semmes, Teresa H.	B. of S. to	Hamilton, Harriot S.	1811	AB27	422	348
Serra, Augustin	Release fr	Herty, Thomas	1809	W22	195	136

Index to District of Columbia Land Records, 1792-1817

Party	What	Party	Year	Liber	Old	New
Serra, Augustin	Deed fr	Prout, William	1809	V21	316	232
Serra, Augustin	Lease fr	Prout, William	1813	AE30	380	281
Serra, Augustin	Assign fr	Kemp, James et al	1813	AE30	376	279
Serra, Augustin [Sarah]	Deed to	Herty, Thomas	1806	Q16	101	066
Serra, Augustin [Sara]	Deed fr	Gatton, Azariah et al	1806	Q16	104	068
Serra, Augustin [Sara]	Deed fr	Queen, Nicholas L. et al	1806	Q16	104	068
Sessford, John	Deed fr	Roe, Cornelius McDermott	1807	S18	048	041
Sessford, John	Deed to	Bacon, Samuel	1807	S18	040	033
Sessford, John	Deed fr	Bacon, Samuel	1809	X23	116	082
Sessford, John	Cert fr	Munroe, Thomas, Supt.	1810	Y24	168	153
Sessford, John	Deed to	Hendley, Richard	1816	AM37	042	035
Sessford, John, Lt.	Qualify	Light Infantry	1808	U20	041	
Sessford, John [Cessford]	Lease fr	Roe, C. McD.	1802	I9	223	353
Sewall, Charles, Rev. et al	Deed fr	Carroll, John, Rev. et al	1799	D4	282	265
Sewall, Charles, Rev. et al	Deed fr	Carroll, John, Rev. et al	1799	D4	286	268
Sewall, Clement et al	Deed to	Fenwick, Francis & Eleanor	1809	V21	303	221
Sewall, Clement, of Montg. Co.	Deed fr	Medley, Bernard, of Montg. Co.	1796	B2B	525	237
Sewall, Clement, of Alexa. Co.	Deed fr	Hoban, James	1808	T19	321	234
Sewall, Clement, of Alexa. Co.	B. of S. to	Lee, John	1813	AF31	288	204
Sewall, Clement, of Alexa. Co.	Deed to	Reynolds, Thomas	1815	AK35	187	146
Sewall, Lewis	Slaves	From Alexandria Co. to G'tn.	1816	AL36	018	019
Sewall, Robert	Deed fr	Commissioners of Washington	1799	D4	252	236
Sewall, Robert	Deed fr	Carroll, Daniel, of *Duddington*	1799	D4	359	346
Sewall, Robert, of P.G. Co.	Deed fr	Pratt, Henry et al	1805	N13	081	074
Sewall, Robert, of P.G. Co.	Deed to	McKim, James	1810	Y24	360	325
Sexton, Francis, of NY	Deed fr	Boyd, Washington, marshal	1816	AL36	443	421
Seyle, Ann Maria, wid/o J. [Scyle]	Deed to	Kaegy, Abraham, of DE	1805	M12	157	154
Seyle, George et al	Deed to	Kaegy, Abraham, of DE	1805	M12	157	154
Seyle, John et al	Deed to	Kaegy, Abraham, of DE	1805	M12	157	154
Seyle, Lewis et al	Deed to	Kaegy, Abraham, of DE	1805	M12	157	154
Shaaf, John Thomas, Annapolis	Deed fr	Gantt, John Mackall, of P.G. Co.	1807	R17	196	148
Shaaff, Arthur, of Annapolis	Deed fr	Peter, Robert, of G'tn.	1801	G7	239	321
Shaaff, Arthur, of Annapolis	Deed fr	Davidson, Samuel	1801	G7	076	099
Shaaff, John T., Dr.	Deed fr	Smith, Walter & Clement	1817	AO39	504	346
Shaaff, John Thomas, Annapolis	Deed fr	Wayman, Charles, of G'tn.	1805	N13	049	046
Shaaff, John Thomas, Annapolis	Deed fr	Addison, John	1805	M12	297	299
Shaaff, John Thomas, Annapolis	Deed fr	Addison, John	1809	X23	027	019
Shaaff, John Thomas, of A.A. Co.	Deed fr	Addison, Thomas G., of P.G. Co.	1811	AA26	028	021
Shaaff, Thomas, M.D., Annapolis	Deed fr	Addison, Thomas Grafton	1807	R17	149	115
Shamm, John [Scamm]	Mortgage to	Taylor, Elizabeth	1804	K10	258	264
Shanks, Elizabeth, of G'tn.	Deposition		1817	AN38	221	161
Shanks, Michael	Mortgage to	Cranch, William	1809	W22	031	024
Shanks, Michael, nailor	Deed fr	Greenleaf, James, of Phila.	1797	C3	241	200
Shanks, Michael, of G'tn.	Deed fr	McClan, Robert, of G'tn.	1795	B2A	272	380
Shannon, Luke	Deed to	Andrews, George	1802	I9	560	907
Shannon, Luke	B. of S. to	Wade, Ann	1802	I9	491	806
Shannon, William	Assign to	Wolcott, Oliver	1800	E5	172	163
Shannon, William, mer., of Phila.	Mortgage fr	Jackson, Samuel, of G'tn.	1799	D4	377	361
Shannon, William, mer., of Phila.	Deed fr	Jackson, Samuel, merchant, G'tn.	1800	E5		163
Shannon, William, of Phila. PA	Deed fr	Jackson, Samuel, mer., of G'tn.	1800	E5	194	185
Sharp, Mary, of York Co. PA	Deed to	King, Adam	1807	S18	300	235
Shaw, Alexander	Deed fr	Prout, William	1801	G7	251	341
Shaw, Alexander, of Balto. MD	Deed to	Dempsie, John	1802	I9	114	167
Shaw, Ann	Deed fr	Dempsey, John	1802	I9	527	861
Shaw, Anne, of Annapolis	Deed fr	Stoddert, Benjamin, Bladensburg	1810	Z25	064	047

Index to District of Columbia Land Records, 1792-1817

Party	What	Party	Year	Liber	Old	New
Shaw, James	B. of S. fr	Fenwick, Richard	1807	S18	001	001
Shaw, James	B. of S. to	Wharton, Franklin	1809	V21	415	317
Shaw, John	Deed fr	Dorsey, William H.	1802	I9	373	619
Shaw, John	Deed fr	Hiener, Michael [Kioner]	1808	T19	271	199
Shaw, John & James Birth	Deed fr	Hewitt, John, assignee U. Forrest	1807	S18	333	261
Shaw, John & James Birth	Deed fr	Ott, John	1807	R17	058	046
Shaw, John & James Birth	Deed fr	Kilty, John & Josias Wilson King	1809	W22	052	039
Shaw, John & Thomas Corcoran	Deed to	Bowie, Washington	1813	AF31	437	314
Shaw, John et al	Deed fr	Cooke, Thomas	1802	H8	038	036
Shaw, John, of Phila. PA	Deed fr	Stoddert, Benjamin	1801	F6	214	139
Shaw, John, of Phila. PA	Deed fr	Stoddert, Benjamin	1801	F6	224	145
Shaw, John, of Phila. PA	Deed fr	Stoddert, Benjamin	1801	F6	221	144
Shaw, John, of Phila. PA	Deed fr	Stoddert, Benjamin	1801	F6	219	142
Shaw, John, of Phila. PA	Deed fr	Stoddert, Benjamin	1801	F6	217	141
Shaw, John, trustee et al	Deed fr	Melvin, James, of G'tn.	1808	T19	206	148
Shaw, Joseph	B. of S. fr	Owens, Charity	1813	AF31	402	291
Shaw, Lemuel	Deed to	Foxall, Henry	1811	AA26	221	151
Shaw, Lemuel, of G'tn.	Deed fr	Davis, Thomas, of G'tn.	1805	M12	185	186
Shaw, Lemuel, of G'tn.	Deed fr	Mountz, Jacob, of G'tn., collector	1816	AL36	254	256
Shaw, Mary	B. of S. fr	Greenfield, Thomas, of P.G. Co.	1810	Y24	475	420
Shaw, Polly, of G'tn.	Deed to	Bussard, Daniel, of G'tn.	1812	AD29	148	116
Shearrard, Francis	Deed fr	Scott, Gustavus et al	1798	C3	464	365
Sheckles, Richard	B. of S. to	Prout, William	1808	T19	359	258
Sheele, Augustua Daniel	Deed fr	Coulter, Peter	1817	AN38	536	389
Shellman, Jacob, of Frederick Co.	Deed fr	Ragan, Susanna, of Frederick Co.	1799	D4	193	175
Shellman, Jacob, of Frederick Co.	Deed fr	Ragan, Laurana, of Frederick Co.	1799	D4	314	297
Shellman, Jacob, of Frederick MD	Deed to	Way, Andrew & George	1812	AD29	469	396
Shellman, John, of Frederick Co.	Deed fr	Deakins, William, Jr.	1792	A1-1	149	215
Shellman, John, Sr., Frederick Co.	Deed to	Beall, Thomas & John M. Gantt	1792	A1-1	096	140
Shellman, John, Sr., Fredk. Co.	P. of Atty. to	Beall, Thomas	1793	A1-2	409	18
Sheperd, Henry	Deed to	Peacock, Robert Ware	1804	L11	298	274
Sheperd, William, insolvent	Deed to	Peacock, Robert Ware, trustee	1804	L11	401	355
Shepherd, John	Deed fr	McCoy, Robert	1802	I9	034	045
Shepherd, Lodowick, of G'tn.	Deed fr	Lee, Thomas Sim, of Fredk. Co.	1814	AG32	088	066
Shepherd, Walter, trustee	Deed fr	Fowler, Thomas, insolvent	1804	L11	343	312
Sheppard, Abraham, of NC	Deed to	Reintzel, Valentine & J. Thompson	1817	AO39	478	328
Sheppard, Benjamin, of NC	Deed fr	Ponsonby, John, Glasgow Co. NC	1792	A1-1	157	225
Sheppard, Benjamin, of NC et al	Deed to	Thompson, John & V. Reintzel	1812	AD29	430	361
Sheppard, James Glasco, of NC	Deed to	Thompson, John & V. Reintzel	1812	AD29	430	361
Shepperd, James G., of G'tn.	Deed fr	Steuart, William, of G'tn. et al	1810	Z25	175	139
Shepperd, James Glascow, of NC	Release to	Steuart, William et al	1810	Z25	150	118
Shepperd, James Glascow, of NC	Deed to	Steuart, William et al	1810	Z25	147	116
Shepperd, James Glasgow, of NC	Deed fr	Mountz, Jacob, collector, G'tn.	1810	Z25	228	178
Shepperd, Lodowic, of G'tn.	Deed fr	Jones, Charles C., of Montg. Co.	1813	AE30	530	392
Shepperd, Lodowic, of G'tn.	Deed to	Jones, Charles C., of Montg. Co.	1815	AH33	554	475
Shepperd, Lodowick	Deed fr	Beall, Thomas, of Geo.	1814	AH33	044	040
Shepperd, Lodowick, of G'tn.	Deed fr	Lee, Thomas S., of G'tn.	1811	AB27	100	082
Shepperd, Lodowick, of G'tn.	D. of T. to	Lufborough, Nathan	1815	AK35	408	321
Shepperd, Lodowick, of G'tn.	Deed fr	Mackall, Leonard, of G'tn.	1815	AK35	411	323
Shepperd, Lowodick, of G'tn.	Deed fr	Burbeck, Henry, New London CN	1814	AH33	046	041
Sherrard, Francis & Eleanor	Deed to	Ardery, John, of G'tn.	1798	D4	065	055
Shields, Easter	Deed fr	Willson, Joseph	1802	H8	370	344
Shiplen, Ellenor, w/o Rezin	Deed fr	Brook, William H., of G'tn.	1815	AH33	435	373
Shippen, Thomas Lee, Phila. PA	Cert fr	Commissioners of Washington	1791	B2A	283	396
Shippen, Thomas Lee, Phila. PA	Cert fr	Commissioners of Washington	1791	B2A	283	396

Party	What	Party	Year	Liber	Old	New
Shoemaker, Charles	Discharge	Bankruptcy	1802	H8	212	202
Shoemaker, Charles, insolvent	Deed to	Peacock, Robert Ware, trustee	1804	K10	291	293
Shoemaker, Charles, of MD	Deed to	Bayly, Mountjoy, of NY	1802	I9	071	100
Shoemaker, Daniel	Convey fr	Washington Building Company	1812	AD29	036	026
Shoemaker, David	Assign fr	McLean, Cornelius	1802	I9	243	391
Shoemaker, David	Deed fr	Lovell, William	1804	L11	025	24
Shoemaker, David	Deed fr	Andrews, George	1804	L11	027	27
Shoemaker, David	Deed fr	Munroe, Thomas, Supt.	1804	K10	304	308
Shoemaker, David	Deed fr	Van Ness, John P. & Marcia	1807	S18	105	085
Shoemaker, David	Deed fr	Murdock, John, of G'tn.	1807	R17	208	156
Shoemaker, David	Deed to	Van Ness, John P. & Marcia	1807	S18	073	085
Shoemaker, David	Deed to	Clephan, Lewis	1809	X23	001	001
Shoemaker, David	Lease to	Frazier, Patrick	1810	Y24	527	463
Shoemaker, David	Deed fr	McDonald, Archibald	1811	AB27	126	103
Shoemaker, David	Deed fr	Stoddert, Benjamin, Bladensburg	1811	AA26	326	219
Shoemaker, David	Deed fr	Van Ness, John P. & Marcia	1812	AD29	356	299
Shoemaker, David	Deed fr	Washington Building Company	1812	AD29	381	321
Shoemaker, David	Deed fr	Corporation of Washington	1815	AI34	228	259
Shoemaker, David et al	Deed to	Van Ness, John P. et al	1804	M12	027	027
Shoemaker, David et al	Convey fr	Gillis, Thomas H. et al	1804	L11	104	108
Shoemaker, David et al	Deed fr	Law, Thomas	1805	N13	260	217
Shoemaker, David et al	Release fr	Van Ness, John P. et al	1806	P15	062	037
Shoemaker, David et al	Deed fr	Tingey, Thomas	1810	Y24	406	366
Shoemaker, David et al	Deed fr	Oden, Benjamin, of P.G. Co.	1811	AB27	490	401
Shoemaker, David et al	Deed to	Boyd, Washington	1812	AC28	498	356
Shoemaker, David et al	Deed to	Thompson, Julia [Kaine]	1816	AL36	523	489
Shoemaker, Jonathan	Mortgage to	Mackall, Walter	1803	K10	058	62
Shoemaker, Jonathan	Deed fr	Mackall, Walter	1804	K10	109	117
Shoemaker, Jonathan	Deed to	Lukens, Samuel et al	1808	T19	114	081
Shoemaker, Jonathan	Release fr	Morsell, James S., of G'tn.	1809	W22	159	112
Shoemaker, Jonathan	Deed to	Johnson, Roger, of Frederick Co.	1809	W22	156	109
Shoemaker, Rachel	Deed fr	Van Ness, John P. & Maria	1802	I9	515	843
Shoemaker, Rachel, w/o David	Deed fr	Commissioners of Washington	1801	G7	476	613
Shoemaker, Rachel, w/o David	Deed fr	Van Ness, John P. & Marcia	1805	M12	100	093
Short, Ann (Negro)	Manumis fr	Stone, Mathew, of Charles Co.	1806	P15	266	175
Shorter, Ann (C)	Manumis fr	Foxall, Henry	1816	AL36	355	345
Shorter, Anna (C)	Cert Free fr	Cooper, Molly (C)	1811	AB27	095	078
Shorter, Catharine & children	Cert. Free		1806	P15	025	015
Shorter, Catherine & children	Cert Free fr	Dangerfield, M.H.	1808	U20	361	197
Shorter, Catherine et al	Cert Free		1806	P15	025	15
Shorter, Charles	B. of S. fr	Jones, Nathan	1808	V21	084	066
Shorter, Charles	Cert Free fr	Brent, Robert	1809	W22	126	090
Shorter, Charles (C), age 26	Cert Free	Matthews, W.	1811	AA26	288	195
Shorter, Henny (yellow)	Cert Free fr	Duvall, G.	1808	T19	205	148
Shorter, James	Cert Free		1810	Z25	141	112
Shorter, Jane (C), age 16	Cert Free fr	Hewitt, William	1817	AN38	493	356
Shorter, Jenny	Cert Free	Lucas, Henry	1807	R17	136	105
Shorter, Jenny (C)	Cert Free to	Butler, Mary (C)	1817	AO39	063	052
Shorter, John	Cert fr	Munroe, Thomas, Supt.	1810	X23	406	327
Shorter, John	Deed fr	Suter, Alexander, of G'tn.	1812	AD29	293	241
Shorter, John	B. of S. fr	Crocket, Elizabeth	1817	AO39	107	083
Shorter, John	B. of S. to	Kedglie, Ann	1817	AN38	377	279
Shorter, John (C) et al	Deed fr	Beall, Thomas, of George	1805	M12	164	162
Shorter, John (C)	Cert Free fr	Linday, John	1817	AO39	421	287
Shorter, John & Gerrard Morris	Deed to	Suter, Alexander	1812	AD29	291	240

Index to District of Columbia Land Records, 1792-1817 371

Party	What	Party	Year	Liber	Old	New
Shorter, John & John Freeman	B. of S. fr	Johnson, Thomas	1816	AM37	334	243
Shorter, John, a free man	D. of T. to	Kerr, Alexander	1817	AN38	450	323
Shorter, John, free person	Deed to	Kedglie, Ann	1817	AN38	204	149
Shorter, Kate	Cert Free		1806	P15	085	52
Shorter, Martha (C)	Manumis fr	Foxall, Henry	1816	AL36	353	344
Shorter, Mary, grandchildren of	Cert Free fr	Brent, Robert	1811	AB27	395	
Shorter, Mary, grandchildren of	Cert Free fr	Brent, Robert	1811	AB27	395	
Shorter, Moses	B. of S. fr	Scott, Margaret	1806	Q16	293	223
Shorter, Nancy	Cert Free		1810	Z25	141	112
Shorter, Nancy (negro)	Manumis fr	Casanave, Ann	1808	U20	393	219
Shorter, Nelly	Cert Free fr	Dickson, John C.	1810	Z25	368	288
Shorter, Peggy	Cert Free		1806	P15	070	42
Shorter, Peggy	Cert Free		1806	P15	070	042
Shorter, Rachel and children	Cert Free fr	Roger, M.	1807	S18	219	175
Shorter, Samuel	Cert Free		1810	Z25	141	112
Shorter, Terressa	Affidavit		1807	R17	344	262
Shorter, Thomas	Deed fr	White, Patrick	1815	AK35	208	164
Shorter, Thomas	Deed to	Blake, James H., Dr.	1816	AL36	157	158
Shorter, Thomas et al	Manumis to	[ ], Kate (C), w/o Thomas	1815	AI34	004	004
Shorter, Trecy	Cert Free		1810	Z25	141	112
Shover, Barbara, wid/o Simon	Deed to	Beall, Thomas & John M. Gantt	1792	A1-1	104	152
Shreeve, Barlie et al	Deed fr	Templeman, John	1802	I9	226	359
Shreve, Benjamin	Slave	From Alexandria	1812	AC28	317	230
Shuck, Elizabeth	B. of S. to	Bacon, Samuel & Jos. Harbaugh	1816	AL36	246	249
Shuck, Elizabeth	B. of S. to	Ryan, Mary	1817	AN38	395	294
Shuck, Frederick	Deed fr	Dorsey, William H., of Balto. Co.	1813	AF31	053	036
Shuck, Frederick	Deed fr	Murdock, John, of G'tn.	1813	AF31	051	035
Shuck, Frederick	D. of T. to	Young, Moses	1814	AH33	145	138
Shuck, Frederick, of Alexa. Co.	Bond to	Young, Moses et al	1813	AE30	436	322
Shultz, Henry	Agreement	Gary, Everard	1809	X23	183	136
Shultze, John Earnest Christian	Deed to	Deluis, Frederick, of Bremen	1807	Q16	210	142
Shute, John, mer., of Phila.	Deed fr	Langley, Edward, mer.	1797	C3	267	217
Shute, John, Sr., of Exeter, Eng.	Cert fr	Commissioners of Washington	1799	D4	386	368
Siemen, Paul et al	Release to	Nourse, Joseph	1813	AF31	011	008
Sim, Patrick	Deed fr	Brent, J.C. & Robert	1802	I9	417	691
Sim, Patrick	Deed to	Young Thomas & John Arnott	1808	U20	114	065
Sim, Patrick, Jr.	Deed to	Young, Thomas	1802	I9	448	740
Sim, Patrick, Jr.	Deed to	Cherry, Robert	1802	I9	438	725
Sim, Patrick, Jr.	Deed to	Varden, Charles	1802	I9	430	712
Sim, Patrick, Sr.	Deed to	Sim, William, midshipman, U.S.N.	1804	K10	130	140
Sim, Patrick, Sr.	Mortgage to	Young, Thomas	1806	P15	147	096
Sim, Thomas	Slaves	From VA	1809	V21	322	237
Sim, Thomas	B. of S. to	Riggs, Romulus	1812	AC28	497	355
Sim, Thomas	Deed to	Calvert, George, of P.G. Co.	1816	AL36	238	243
Sim, William, midshipman, U.S.N.	Deed fr	Sim, Patrick, Sr.	1804	K10	130	140
Simmes, George, of P.G. Co.	Deed to	Addison, John	1805	M12	154	150
Simmes, George, of P.G. Co.	Deed fr	Brent, Daniel Carroll, marshal	1805	M12	152	148
Simmes, Jesse M. [Semmes]	Lease fr	Van Ness, John P. & Marcia	1817	AO39	392	266
Simmonds, William	Deed fr	Munroe, Thomas, Supt.	1802	I9	412	684
Simmons, James	Agreement	Bickley, John	1795	B2B	372	024
Simmons, James	Agreement	Baker, Samuel	1795	B2B	357	005
Simmons, James	Agreement	Green, Levy	1798	C3	420	331
Simmons, James	Agreement	Reed, Isaac	1801	F6	143	088
Simmons, John	B. of S. fr	Thomas, Elizabeth	1809	X23	154	113
Simmons, Walter	Deed fr	Caldwell, Elias B., trustee	1806	P15	317	209

Index to District of Columbia Land Records, 1792-1817

Party	What	Party	Year	Liber	Old	New
Simmons, William	Deed fr	Whann, William, of G'tn.	1802	G7	579	728
Simmons, William	Deed fr	Lewis, Samuel	1802	I9	559	906
Simmons, William	Deed fr	Markward, William	1802	I9	318	524
Simmons, William	Deed fr	Munroe, Thomas, Supt.	1802	I9	323	532
Simmons, William	Deed fr	Munroe, Thomas, Supt.	1802	I9	322	530
Simmons, William	Deed fr	Munroe, Thomas, Supt.	1802	I9	319	525
Simmons, William	Deed fr	Munroe, Thomas, Supt.	1802	I9	321	528
Simmons, William	Deed fr	Munroe, Thomas, Supt.	1802	I9	320	527
Simmons, William	Deed fr	Feltwell, William, Jr., of Hays, Eng.	1805	N13	349	281
Simmons, William	Assign fr	Hagner, Peter	1805	M12	295	296
Simmons, William	Deed fr	Kilty, John & Josias Wilson King	1809	X23	008	006
Simmons, William	Deed fr	Corporation of Washington	1815	AI34	389	414
Simmons, William	Deed fr	Corporation of Washington	1815	AI34	391	416
Simmons, William	Deed to	Macdaniel, George	1816	AM37	482	349
Simmons, William	Deed to	Bomford, George, Col.	1816	AM37	243	178
Simmons, William	Deed to	Bomford, George, Col.	1816	AM37	244	179
Simmons, William	Deed to	Bomford, George, Col.	1816	AM37	246	180
Simms, Charles, of Alexa. et al	Deed to	Muncaster, John, of Alexa.	1811	AB27	00½	001
Simms, Edward		Certificate of Slaves	1802	H8	034	033
Simms, Edward	Deed to	Clarke, Robert	1802	I9	354	584
Simms, Edward, of Charles Co.	Deed fr	Rhodes, William & Anne	1801	G7	256	349
Simms, Francis, of P.G. Co.	Deed to	McCann, Arthur, of G'tn.	1813	AE30	156	123
Simms, Francis X., of P.G. Co.	Deed to	Simms, Joseph Milbourne, of G'tn.	1814	AG32	221	155
Simms, Henry, of G'tn.	Assign fr	Spalding, John, of Jefferson Co.	1816	AM37	107	085
Simms, Joseph M.	Slaves	From Prince George's Co. MD	1804	K10	316	
Simms, Joseph Milbourne, of G'tn.	Deed fr	Threlkeld, John, of G'tn.	1794	B2A	003	004
Simms, Joseph Milbourne, of G'tn.	Deed fr	Simms, Francis X., of P.G. Co.	1814	AG32	221	155
Simms, Sarah	Slaves	From Alexandria Co.	1807	R17	054	043
Simms, William	Deed fr	Prout, William	1801	G7	327	457
Simpson, George	Deed fr	Greenleaf, James	1799	E5	004	003
Simpson, George, cashier, et al	Deed to	Pratt, Henry et al	1797	C3	154	127
Simpson, George et al	B. in C. fr	Pratt, Henry et al	1799	E5	003	003
Simpson, George, of Phila.	Deed fr	Greenleaf, James, of Phila.	1797	C3	160	132
Simpson, James	Deed to	Morsell, James S.	1802	G7	504	643
Simpson, James & Mariah	Manumis fr	Middleton, James	1815	AH33	446	382
Simpson, James, Mont. Co. et al	Deed to	Lingan, Nicholas, of Montg. Co.	1796	B2B	400	065
Simpson, John	Deed fr	Ritchie, Abner	1807	S18	210	167
Simpson, John	Deed fr	Renner, Daniel	1807	S18	211	168
Simpson, John	Deed fr	Ritchie, Abner	1807	Q16	387	297
Simpson, John	Deed to	Mudd, Thomas J.	1811	AB27	258	211
Simpson, John	Deed fr	Ritchie, Abner	1811	AB27	163	135
Simpson, John & Charles Ross	Deed fr	Barry, James	1801	G7	145	191
Simpson, John, of Phila.	Deed fr	Barry, James, of Balto.	1796	B2B	491	185
Simpson, John, of Phila. et al	Deed fr	Barry, James	1800	E5	187	178
Simpson, John, of G'tn.	Deed to	Beall, William M., Jr., of Fredk. Co.	1814	AG32	289	210
Simpson, Josias	Deed fr	Templeman, John, of G'tn.	1800	F6	010	007
Simpson, Josias	Deed fr	Van Ness, John P. & Marcia	1815	AH33	541	463
Simpson, Josias	Deed fr	Eliot, Samuel, Jr. & wife Mary	1816	AM37	371	268
Simpson, Josias	Deed to	Hamilton, Mathew	1817	AN38	534	388
Simpson, Josias	Deed to	Simpson, Lidia	1817	AN38	532	387
Simpson, Josias, Sr.	B. of S. fr	Stevens, Eleanor	1816	AL36	258	259
Simpson, Lidia	Deed fr	Simpson, Josias	1817	AN38	532	387
Simpson, Solomon, Col.	Deed fr	Jenners, Abiel & Deborah	1799	E5	001	001
Simpson, Thomas, of MD	B. of S. fr	Johns, Leonard H.	1802	H8	106	103
Simpson, Tobias	Deed fr	Crown, William	1817	AN38	224	164

Index to District of Columbia Land Records, 1792-1817

Party	What	Party	Year	Liber	Old	New
Simpson, William	Cert Free	[ ], Toby (negro) and others	1807	S18	259	139
Simpson, William	Will		1807	S18	259	
Simpson, William	Manumis to	[ ], Tobias (negro)	1808	U20	384	213
Sims, H. et al	Release to	Nourse, Joseph	1813	AF31	011	008
Sims, Henry	B. of S. to	Frost, John T.	1802	H8	382	355
Sims, Soddy (C)	Cert Free to	Jones, Cilla (C), age 27	1817	AO39	168	125
Simson, George, of Phila. PA et al	Deed fr	Skyrin, John, of Frankford PA	1806	O14	012	009
Simson, John et al	Deed to	Craig, John et al	1806	P15	230	153
Simson, John, of PA et al	Deed to	Craig, John et al	1802	H8	120	117
Simson, John, of Phila. et al	Deed to	Barry, James D.	1809	W22	087	064
Sinclair, Arthur, Lt., U.S.N.	Deed fr	Cocke, Buller & Eliza	1811	AB27	452	371
Sinclair, George	Deed fr	Friend, James	1804	M12	034	035
Sinclair, John	Deed fr	Greenleaf, James	1804	L11	264	243
Sinclair, John	Deed fr	Greenleaf, James, attorney in fact	1805	M12	145	141
Sinclair, John	Deed fr	Greenleaf, James, by atty.	1809	X23	141	
Sinclair, John et al	Deed fr	King, Nicholas	1805	M12	093	086
Siousa, John	Plat	Harlem, part of Spring Hill	1815	AI34	373a	
Siousa, John	Cert fr	Munroe, Thomas, Supt.	1815	AI34	373	401
Siousa, John	Cert fr	Munroe, Thomas, Supt.	1816	AL36	238	242
Sioussa, John	Cert fr	Munroe, Thomas, Supt.	1811	AB27	350	290
Sioussa, John	Cert fr	Munroe, Thomas, Supt.	1813	AF31	314	224
Sisterson, William	B. of S. fr	Ireland, Elizabeth	1808	V21	022	016
Skam, John	Deed fr	Yeates, William	1809	W22	016	012
Skam, John	Deed to	Moore, Peter Dent	1809	W22	040	030
Skelly, Thomas	B. of S. fr	Banks, John	1802	I9	424	702
Skinner, Adderton, of P.G. Co.	Deed to	Mountz, John & John Thompson	1812	AC28	253	186
Skinner, Edward, in PA	Deed to	Bachman, Jacob	1814	AH33	348	301
Skinner, John, plt..	Suit	Russell, William, def.	1799	D4	342	330
Skyren, John, of Phila.	Deed fr	King, Robert	1816	AL36	013	014
Skyrin, John, of Phila. PA	Deed fr	Foster, John, of Alexa.	1804	L11	055	55
Skyrin, John, of Frankford PA	Deed to	Barclay, James, of Phila. et al	1806	O14	012	009
Slater, Anna, d/o Joseph, of VA	Deed fr	Prout, William	1800	E5	093	081
Slater, Charles, of Monroe Co. VA	Deed fr	Prout, William	1800	E5	099	087
Slater, Charles, of Wmsn. Co. TN	Deed to	Bates, David	1812	AD29	048	035
Slater, Charles, of TN et al	Deed to	Orr, Benjamin Grayson	1817	AN38	198	144
Slater, Cornelius et al	D. of G. fr	Slater, Thomas	1798	C3	520	409
Slater, David	Deed fr	Prout, William	1800	E5	082	069
Slater, David	Deed to	Contee, Thomas	1802	I9	272	442
Slater, David & Sarah	Deed to	Clerklee, James, of P.G. Co.	1808	T19	330	240
Slater, David H., of TN	Deed to	Lindsay, Adam	1815	AK35	381	300
Slater, David H., of TN et al	Deed to	Orr, Benjamin Grayson	1817	AN38	198	144
Slater, David Harris, of VA	Deed fr	Prout, William	1800	E5	098	086
Slater, David, of P.G. Co.	Deed fr	Slater, Jonathan, of Montg. Co.	1797	B2B	642	403
Slater, David, of P.G. Co.	Deed to	Vint, John	1808	T19	028	021
Slater, Henry & David H.	Deed to	Orr, Benjamin Grayson	1816	AL36	310	305
Slater, Henry et al	Deed Gift fr	Slater, Sarah, wid/o Joseph, of TN	1815	AK35	193	151
Slater, Henry, of TN	Deed to	Orr, Benjamin Grayson	1816	AL36	311	307
Slater, Henry, of TN et al	Deed to	Orr, Benjamin Grayson	1817	AN38	198	144
Slater, Henry, s/o Joseph, of VA	Deed fr	Prout, William	1800	E5	092	079
Slater, Jonathan	Deed to	Beall, Thomas & John M. Gantt	1792	A1-1	032	48
Slater, Jonathan	Deed to	Murdock, William, mer., London	1793	A1-1	222	309
Slater, Jonathan	Deed to	Prout, William	1798	D4	009	007
Slater, Jonathan, of Montg. Co.	Deed to	Slater, David, of P.G. Co.	1797	B2B	642	403
Slater, Jonathan, s/o Joseph	Deed fr	Prout, William	1800	E5	095	082
Slater, Joseph	Deed to	Williams, Jeremiah, of G'tn.	1800	E5	293	286

Index to District of Columbia Land Records, 1792-1817

Party	What	Party	Year	Liber	Old	New
Slater, Joseph	Deed to	Hunter, John, of Alexa. VA	1801	F6	161	100
Slater, Joseph	Deed to	Hunter, John, shipbuilder, Alexa.	1801	F6	165	103
Slater, Joseph, of Monroe Co. VA	Deed to	Jenkins, Josia, s/o Philip	1800	E5	086	074
Slater, Joseph, of Monroe Co. VA	Deed fr	Prout, William	1800	E5	101	089
Slater, Lucy	B. of S. fr	White, John B.	1814	AH33	144	137
Slater, Lucy, d/o Stephen et al	D. of G. fr	Slater, Thomas	1798	C3	520	409
Slater, Mary, d/o Stephen et al	D. of G. fr	Slater, Thomas	1798	C3	520	409
Slater, Rachel, d/o Stephen et al	D. of G. fr	Slater, Thomas	1798	C3	520	409
Slater, Sarah	Deed fr	Contee, Thomas	1802	I9	308	507
Slater, Sarah & Henry, Montg. Co.	Bond to	Stanton, Patrick	1813	AE30	237	189
Slater, Sarah, d/o Joseph, of VA	Deed fr	Prout, William	1800	E5	096	084
Slater, Sarah, w/o Joseph	Release to	Prout, William	1801	F6	167	104
Slater, Sarah, wid/o Joseph, of TN	Deed Gift to	Slater, Henry et al	1815	AK35	193	151
Slater, Sarah, wid/o David	Deed to	Prout, William	1817	AO39	216	157
Slater, Sarah, wid/o David, P.G.	Deed to	Wayne, Francis	1817	AO39	331	236
Slater, Sarah, wid/o David, P.G.	Deed to	Blake, James H.	1817	AO39	468	321
Slater, Stephen et al	D. of G. fr	Slater, Thomas	1798	C3	520	409
Slater, Thomas	Deed fr	Beall, Thomas, of George	1798	C3	466	367
Slater, Thomas, of G'tn.	D. of G. to	Slater, Stephen	1798	C3	520	409
Slimmer, Christian & Ann	Bond to	Bridges, John, of G'tn.	1804	K10	288	290
Sluby, Nicholas	Cert fr	Commissioners of Washington	1795	B2A	331	464
Sluby, Nicholas, of Balto.	Deed fr	Stoddert, Benjamin	1795	B2A	216	298
Slye, Ann, of G'tn.	B. of S. to	Williams, Elisha W., of G'tn.	1807	R17	061	049
Slye, John, of Charles Co.	B. of S. to	Slye, Thomas G., of G'tn.	1804	L11	238	221
Slye, Thomas G.	Qualify	Lieutenant of Infantry	1804	L11	061	63
Slye, Thomas G., of G'tn.	B. of S. fr	Slye, John, of Charles Co.	1804	L11	238	221
Slye, Thomas G., of G'tn.	Deed to	Contee, Dorah (negro)	1804	L11	213	200
Slye, Thomas G., of G'tn., trustee	Deed to	Threlkeld, John, of G'tn.	1810	Z25	167	132
Slye, Thomas G., of G'tn.	Lease fr	Harris, Thomas, Jr., of Annapolis	1810	Y24	413	372
Slye, Thomas G.	Mortgage to	Wilson, John A.	1813	AE30	388	286
Slye, Thomas G.	Deed to	Harris, Thomas, Jr., of Annapolis	1814	AH33	374	324
Slye, Thomas G.	Cert Free to	Contee, Mariah	1815	AI34	331	364
Slye, Thomas G.	Cert Free to	Contee, Mariah	1816	AK35	259	205
Small, George, of York Co. PA	Deed fr	Stoddert, Benjamin, of G'tn.	1801	G7	059	077
Small, William, trustee	D. of T. fr	Adlington, Daniel, insolvent	1811	Z25	447	352
Smallwood, Benjamin	B. of S. fr	Selby, Henry	1806	P15	350	232
Smallwood, Elizabeth	B. of S. fr	Smallwood, James	1807	S18	080	066
Smallwood, George	Manumis fr	Davidson, John	1816	AK35	480	376
Smallwood, Horatio	Deed to	Lay & Cruttenden	1815	AI34	054	062
Smallwood, Horatio	Lease fr	Magruder, Ninian, of G'tn.	1815	AI34	043	049
Smallwood, Horatio	Deed to	Brooks, William H.	1816	AM37	458	330
Smallwood, Horatio	Deed to	Lewis, Henry	1816	AM37	027	022
Smallwood, Horatio	Deed fr	Bussard, Daniel	1817	AO39	091	072
Smallwood, Horatio & Charlotte	Deed to	Clarke, Alban	1814	AG32	327	238
Smallwood, Horatio, of G'tn.	Deed fr	Pickrell, John, of G'tn.	1812	AD29	070	050
Smallwood, Horatio, of G'tn.	Surrender to	Magruder, Ninian, Dr., of G'tn.	1816	AM37	077	063
Smallwood, Horatio, of G'tn.	Deed fr	Clements, Thomas, of G'tn.	1816	AM37	483	351
Smallwood, Horatio, of G'tn.	Lease fr	Magruder, Ninian, Dr., of G'tn.	1816	AM37	079	064
Smallwood, Horatio, of G'tn.	Deed fr	Magruder, Ninian, Dr., of G'tn.	1816	AM37	003	003
Smallwood, Horatio, of G'tn.	Deed to	Jones, Richard	1817	AN38	111	083
Smallwood, James	B. of S. to	Smallwood, Elizabeth	1807	S18	080	066
Smallwood, Leavan, of G'tn.	Deed to	Bussard, Daniel, of G'tn.	1805	N13	394	314
Smallwood, Leven	Deed to	Athey, Walter F.	1802	I9	585	948
Smallwood, Leven	Deed fr	Dorsey, William H.	1802	I9	586	950
Smallwood, S.N. & Thos. Tingey	D. of T. fr	Voss, Nicholas, of VA	1813	AE30	115	089

Index to District of Columbia Land Records, 1792-1817   375

Party	What	Party	Year	Liber	Old	New
Smallwood, Samuel & E. Boothe	D. of T. to	Caldwell, Elias B.	1816	AM37	229	168
Smallwood, Samuel et al	Mortgage fr	Russ, Samuel	1804	K10	390	405
Smallwood, Samuel N.	Deed fr	Commissioners of Washington	1800	E5	143	132
Smallwood, Samuel N.	Deed fr	Commissioners of Washington	1800	F6	081	050
Smallwood, Samuel N.	Deed to	Jones, Anthony	1801	F6		106
Smallwood, Samuel N.	Deed fr	Prout, William	1802	I9	530	867
Smallwood, Samuel N.	Deed fr	Ellis, Robert	1802	I9	529	865
Smallwood, Samuel N.	Deed fr	Duckworth, George	1802	I9	528	863
Smallwood, Samuel N.	Deed fr	Brown, Robert	1802	I9	329	542
Smallwood, Samuel N.	Release to	Brown, Robert, carpenter N. yard	1805	N13	312	253
Smallwood, Samuel N. et al	Mortgage fr	Russ, Samuel	1806	P15	012	007
Smallwood, Samuel N.	Deed fr	Russ, Samuel	1806	Q16	098	063
Smallwood, Samuel N. et al	Deed to	Russ, Samuel	1806	Q16	107	069
Smallwood, Samuel N., trustee	Deed fr	Tuckfield, William H.P.	1807	R17	267	203
Smallwood, Samuel N. et al	Mortgage fr	Alexander, Robert	1807	S18	212	169
Smallwood, Samuel N.	Deed fr	Tingey, Thomas	1809	V21	231	165
Smallwood, Samuel N., exr.	B. of S. to	Davis, John, of Abel	1809	X23	302	242
Smallwood, Samuel N.	Deed fr	Cherry, Robert	1810	X23	393	316
Smallwood, Samuel N.	P. of Atty. fr	Dempsie, Elizabeth	1810	X23	392	316
Smallwood, Samuel N. & T. Tingey	Mortgage fr	Voss, Nicholas	1810	Y24	240	222
Smallwood, Samuel N.	P. of Atty. fr	Gantt, Edward, to move to KY	1810	Z25	348	272
Smallwood, Samuel N.	Assign to	Hebron, John	1810	Z25	229	180
Smallwood, Samuel N.	Deed fr	Carroll, Daniel, of *Duddington*	1811	AA26	058	044
Smallwood, Samuel N.	Deed to	May, Frederick	1811	AB27	513	420
Smallwood, Samuel N.	Mortgage fr	Voss, Nicholas, of VA	1811	AB27	482	394
Smallwood, Samuel N. et al	Deed to	Wright, Matthew	1811	AB27	377	312
Smallwood, Samuel N.	Deed fr	May, Frederick	1811	AB27	511	418
Smallwood, Samuel N.	Deed to	Carroll, Daniel, of *Duddington*	1811	AC28	065	050
Smallwood, Samuel N.	P. of Atty. fr	Voss, Nicholas	1811	AA26	102	071
Smallwood, Samuel N.	Qualify	Justice of the Peace	1812	AD29	451	380
Smallwood, Samuel N.	Deed fr	Pratt, Henry et al	1813	AF31	032	022
Smallwood, Samuel N.	Deed to	Travers, George	1813	AE30	268	207
Smallwood, Samuel N.	Release to	Voss, Nicholas, of VA	1813	AE30	148	116
Smallwood, Samuel N.	Deed fr	Carroll, Daniel, of *Duddington*	1815	AI34	513	518
Smallwood, Samuel N.	B. of S. fr	McWilliams, Alexander	1815	AI34	148	170
Smallwood, Samuel N.	Marriage to	Dempsie, Elizabeth, of Phila. PA	1815	AI34	173	198
Smallwood, Samuel N.	Deed fr	Carroll, Daniel & Jas. Middleton	1816	AL36	161	161
Smallwood, Samuel N.	Deed fr	Walker, Zachariah, trustee	1817	AO39	329	234
Smallwood, Samuel N.	Deed fr	Carroll, Daniel, of *Duddington*	1817	AO39	326	232
Smallwood, Samuel N. et al	D. of T. to	Caldwell, Elias B.	1817	AN38	396	296
Smallwood, Velinder	Deed Gift fr	Tench, Eleanor	1809	W22	170	119
Smallwood, Walter B.	Deed fr	Templeman, John, of G'tn.	1805	M12	264	265
Smallwood, Walter B.	Deed to	Goldsborough, Charles W.	1807	S18	053	044
Smallwood, William B.	B. of S. to	Peacock, James Green	1804	L11	259	239
Smiller, Margaret	B. of S. fr	Mahew, Clement	1816	AL36	092	093
Smith, Amos, insolvent	Deed to	Montgomery, James, trustee	1805	N13	041	041
Smith, Amos, of Frederick Co.	Deed to	Beall, Thomas & John M. Gantt	1792	A1-1	080	117
Smith, Amos, of KY	Deed fr	King, Robert	1806	Q16	085	054
Smith, Andrew	Naturalize	Chase, Samuel	1795	B2A	281	394
Smith, Andrew	Deed fr	Beall, Thomas, of George	1810	Y24	217	199
Smith, Andrew	Deed to	McCleery, Henry	1812	AC28	169	126
Smith, Andrew	Deed fr	Bowie, Washington & John Kurtz	1815	AI34	402	425
Smith, Andrew & Isabella	Deed to	McCleery, Henry	1812	AC28	170	126
Smith, Andrew, of New York NY	Deed fr	Walker, George	1801	F6	233	153
Smith, Andrew, of G'tn.	Mortgage to	Nourse, Joseph, of G'tn.	1809	W22	236	160

Party	What	Party	Year	Liber	Old	New
Smith, Andrew, of G'tn.	Deed fr	Hurdle, Noble, of G'tn.	1810	Y24	104	094
Smith, Andrew, of G'tn.	Deed fr	Nourse, Joseph, of G'tn.	1810	Z25	059	044
Smith, Andrew, of G'tn.	Deed fr	Nourse, Joseph, of G'tn.	1810	Z25	055	041
Smith, Andrew, of Richmond VA	Plat	Congress and West streets	1812	AD29	538a	
Smith, Andrew, of G'tn.	Deed to	Bowie, Washington & John Kurtz	1812	AD29	542	457
Smith, Andrew, of Richmond VA	Deed to	Griffeth, Robert E., of Phila. VA	1812	AD29	537	450
Smith, Andrew, of Richmond VA	Deed to	Griffeth, Robert E., of Phila. PA	1812	AD29	539	453
Smith, Andrew, of Richmond VA	Deed to	Griffeth, Robert E., of Phila. PA	1813	AE30	450	334
Smith, Andrew, of Richmond VA	Deed to	Griffeth, Robert E., of Phila. PA	1813	AE30	452	335
Smith, Andrew, of Richmond VA	Plat	Beall and Congress streets	1813	AE30	453a	
Smith, Andrew, of Richmond	Deed to	Dodge, Francis, of G'tn.	1815	AK35	430	338
Smith, Ann, of G'tn.	B. of S. fr	Turner, Ann, of G'tn.	1801	G7	426	561
Smith, Anthony	B. of S. fr	Knowles, David, of G'tn.	1816	AO39	039	032
Smith, Anthony	Deed to	Ould, Robert	1816	AL36	260	261
Smith, Anthony, of G'tn.	Deed fr	Smith, William, of G'tn.	1805	M12	213	215
Smith, Anthony, of P.G. Co.	Deed fr	Beall, Thomas Brooke, of G'tn.	1807	S18	324	254
Smith, Anthony, of G'tn.	Deed to	Mountz, John, Jr., of G'tn.	1811	AA26	353	236
Smith, Anthony, of G'tn.	Deed fr	Lanham, Elisha, of G'tn.	1817	AN38	370	273
Smith, Benjamin, of KY	Deed to	King, Adam, of G'tn.	1798	D4	128	110
Smith, Caroline, w/o John K.	Deed fr	Williams, Brooke	1814	AG32	250	178
Smith, Clement	Deed fr	Peter, Robert	1800	F6	027	017
Smith, Clement	Deed to	Bank of Columbia	1802	I9	142	214
Smith, Clement	Deed to	King, George	1802	I9	560	908
Smith, Clement	Deed fr	Andrews, George	1805	M12	237	238
Smith, Clement	Deed fr	Parrott, Richard	1805	N13	070	063
Smith, Clement	Deed fr	Whann, William	1806	O14	311	206
Smith, Clement	Convey fr	Beall, William Dent, bookkeeper	1807	S18	366	289
Smith, Clement	B. of S. fr	Addison, Anthony	1808	T19	307	224
Smith, Clement	Deed fr	Williams, Benjamin, of MD	1810	Z25	283	222
Smith, Clement	Deed fr	Schley, George Jacob, of MD	1810	Z25	287	225
Smith, Clement	Deed fr	Davidson, John, Gen., exrx. of	1810	Z25	285	224
Smith, Clement	Deed fr	Thomas, John, 3rd	1810	Z25	284	223
Smith, Clement	Deed fr	Beall, Thomas, of George et al	1811	Z25	478	379
Smith, Clement	Deed to	Mackall, Benjamin F.	1811	AA26	070	051
Smith, Clement	Deed fr	Key, Francis Scott, of G'tn.	1811	Z25	479	380
Smith, Clement	Deed fr	Davidson, Ann Maria, of Annapolis	1811	Z25	481	382
Smith, Clement	Deed fr	Reintzel, Daniel, of G'tn.	1811	AB27	004	006
Smith, Clement	B. of S. fr	Steuart, David, of G'tn.	1812	AC28	174	131
Smith, Clement	Deed fr	Nourse, Joseph	1812	AC28	120	090
Smith, Clement	Deed fr	Peter, Thomas	1812	AC28	277	201
Smith, Clement	Deed fr	Mudd, Thomas James	1813	AE30	210	171
Smith, Clement	Deed fr	Magruder, Patrick & George	1813	AF31	531	391
Smith, Clement	Lease to	Bunnell, Eliab & W.B. Robertson	1814	AH33	156	147
Smith, Clement	D. of T. to	Bunnell, Eliab & W.B. Robertson	1814	AH33	157	148
Smith, Clement	Deed fr	Stull, John J., of G'tn.	1816	AM37	473	341
Smith, Clement	D. of T. fr	Magruder, George	1817	AN38	388	288
Smith, Clement & Walter Smioth	Deed fr	Lee, Thomas S., of Fredk. Co.	1813	AE30	421	310
Smith, Clement & A. Addison	Receipt to	Calder, James	1813	AE30	342	255
Smith, Clement & John Pickrell	Deed fr	Dorsey, William H., of Montg. Co.	1815	AK35	106	082
Smith, Clement & John Pickrell	Deed fr	Murdock, John, of G'tn.	1815	AK35	105	081
Smith, Clement & John Pickrell	Deed fr	Murdock, John, of G'tn.	1816	AL36	468	442
Smith, Clement & John Pickrell	Deed fr	Dorsey, William H., of Montg. Co.	1816	AL36	470	443
Smith, Clement, Dr., of P.G. Co.	Deed to	Marbury, William	1812	AD29	487	412
Smith, Clement, of G'tn.	Deed fr	Brodhag, Charles F., of G'tn.	1805	M12	077	071
Smith, Clement, of G'tn.	Deed fr	Stoddert, Benjamin, of G'tn.	1806	Q16	128	083

Index to District of Columbia Land Records, 1792-1817

Party	What	Party	Year	Liber	Old	New
Smith, Clement, of G'tn.	Deed to	Whann, William, of G'tn.	1807	S18	364	288
Smith, Clement, of P.G. Co.	Deed fr	Addison, Anthony, of P.G. Co.	1808	T19	313	228
Smith, Clement, of P.G. Co.	Deed fr	Murdock, John & John Heugh	1808	T19	310	226
Smith, Clement, of G'tn.	Deed to	Murdock, John, of G'tn.	1809	V21	346	249
Smith, Clement, of G'tn.	B. of S. fr	Murdock, John, of G'tn.	1809	V21	312	228
Smith, Clement, of G'tn.	D. of T. fr	Thompson, George, of G'tn.	1810	Y24	028	024
Smith, Clement, of P.G. Co.	D. of T. fr	Addison, Anthony, of P.G. Co.	1810	Y24	487	430
Smith, Clement, of G'tn.	Deed fr	Mountz, Jacob, collector, of G'tn.	1811	AB27	002	005
Smith, Clement, of G'tn.	Deed fr	Lodge, William, of Montg. Co.	1811	AB27	001	003
Smith, Clement, of G'tn.	Deed fr	Lingan, Nicholas, of G'tn.	1811	AB27	438	361
Smith, Clement, of G'tn.	Deed fr	Mountz, Jacob, collector, of G'tn.	1811	Z25	485	385
Smith, Clement, of G'tn.	D. of T. fr	Ober, Robert, of G'tn.	1811	Z25	545	433
Smith, Clement, of G'tn.	Deed fr	Bussard, Daniel, of G'tn.	1812	AD29	034	024
Smith, Clement, of G'tn.	Deed to	King, Charles, of G'tn.	1812	AD29	106	081
Smith, Clement, of G'tn.	Deed fr	Brooks, Joseph, of G'tn.	1813	AE30	389	287
Smith, Clement, of G'tn.	Deed to	Foxall, Henry, of G'tn.	1813	AE30	144	112
Smith, Clement, of G'tn.	D. of T. fr	Brown, Joel, of G'tn.	1813	AF31	085	058
Smith, Clement, of G'tn.	D. of T. fr	Leonard, Jacob, of G'tn.	1813	AF31	092	062
Smith, Clement, of G'tn.	Deed to	Mackall, Leonard, of G'tn.	1813	AF31	337	241
Smith, Clement, of G'tn.	Deed fr	Forrest, Joseph	1814	AG32	051	040
Smith, Clement, of G'tn.	D. of T. fr	Colclazer, Thomas, of G'tn.	1814	AG32	264	188
Smith, Clement, of G'tn.	Deed fr	Peter, John, of G'tn. et al	1815	AH33	386	334
Smith, Clement, of G'tn.	D. of T. fr	Williams, John Stull, of G'tn.	1815	AH33	383	332
Smith, Clement, of G'tn.	Deed to	Mackall, Leonard, of G'tn.	1815	AK35	050	039
Smith, Clement, of G'tn.	Deed fr	Bussard, Daniel, of G'tn.	1815	AK35	108	083
Smith, Clement, of G'tn.	Deed fr	Bussard, Daniel, of G'tn.	1815	AK35	109	084
Smith, Clement, of G'tn.	Deed to	Brookes, Joseph, of G'tn.	1815	AK35	119	092
Smith, Clement, of G'tn.	Deed fr	Fitzhugh, Samuel, of G'tn.	1816	AL36	473	446
Smith, Clement, of G'tn.	Deed fr	Pickrell, John, of G'tn.	1816	AL36	474	447
Smith, Clement, of G'tn.	Deed fr	Pickrell, John, of G'tn.	1816	AL36	471	444
Smith, Clement, of G'tn.	D. of T. fr	Leonard, Jacob	1816	AM37	048	039
Smith, Clement, of G'tn.	Deed to	Johnson, George, of G'tn.	1816	AM37	250	184
Smith, Clement, of G'tn.	Deed fr	Williams, John S., of G'tn.	1816	AM37	085	068
Smith, Clement, of G'tn.	Lease to	Vonessen, Peter, of G'tn.	1816	AM37	058	048
Smith, Clement, of G'tn.	Deed fr	Bunnel, Eliab & Wm. Robertson	1817	AN38	025	021
Smith, Clement, of G'tn.	Lease to	Brown, Joel, of G'tn.	1817	AN38	018	015
Smith, Clement, of G'tn.	D. of T. fr	French, George	1817	AN38	023	019
Smith, Clement, of G'tn.	D. of T. fr	Lancaster, Stephen	1817	AO39	132	100
Smith, Clement, of G'tn.	Deed fr	Brookes, Joseph, of G'tn.	1817	AO39	135	102
Smith, Clement, of G'tn.	Lease to	Robertson, John, of G'tn.	1817	AN38	020	017
Smith, Cornelius	B. of S. to	Prout, William	1806	P15	151	099
Smith, Dennis	Assign to	Bury, James	1812	AB27	520	425
Smith, Edmund & E.H. Nicholl	Mortgage fr	Goldsborough, Charles W., G'tn.	1814	AH33	166	154
Smith, Edmund & E.H. Nicholl	Mortgage fr	Freeman, Constant	1816	AM37	280	206
Smith, Edmund & Edw. H. Nicoll	Deed to	Freeman, Constant	1816	AM37	354	256
Smith, Edmund & E.H. Nicholl	Deed fr	Goldsborough, Charles W.	1816	AL36	368	358
Smith, Edward L., of G'tn.	B. of S. fr	Thompson, Charles	1807	S18	023	019
Smith, Edward L., of G'tn.	D. of T. to	Garner, Joseph, of G'tn.	1809	W22	136	097
Smith, Edward Lowe, of G'tn.	Deed fr	Carmichael, Alexander, of G'tn.	1807	R17	261	199
Smith, Harriot	B. of S. fr	Suter, Barbara	1816	AM37	227	167
Smith, Henry	Deed to	Rinehart, Andrew	1802	I9	225	358
Smith, Henry	B. of S. fr	Lockwood, Levi	1807	S18	394	314
Smith, Henry	Deed fr	Washington Building Company	1813	AE30	434	321
Smith, Henry	B. of S. fr	Adams, George, exr.	1816	AL36	525	490
Smith, Henry, of MD	Deed fr	Rinehart, Andrew	1802	H8	465	427

Index to District of Columbia Land Records, 1792-1817

Party	What	Party	Year	Liber	Old	New
Smith, Hugh	Receipt to	Harshman, Henry	1813	AF31	312	223
Smith, Hugh, of Alexa.	P. of Atty. fr	Cochran, Alexander, Jr., to Ire.	1809	V21	403	306
Smith, Hugh, of Alexa.	Deed to	Farrell, Zephaniah	1809	X23	037	027
Smith, Hugh, of Alexa.	Deed to	Dye, Reuben, of Fairfax Co.	1814	AH33	361	313
Smith, Hugh, oif Alexa.	Deed fr	McLeod, John	1808	U20	362	197
Smith, Ignatius	Deed to	Casanave, Peter	1794	B2A	092	120
Smith, Isaac, of NY et al	Deed fr	Van Cortland, Philip, of NY	1804	M12	001	
Smith, Isaac, of NY et al	Deed to	Van Cortland, Philip, of NY	1804	M12	002	
Smith, James	B. of S. to	Spunogle, George	1805	N13	304	246
Smith, James	Mortgage fr	Smith, Job, of St. Mary's Co.	1816	AM37	485	352
Smith, James, of *Cedar Grove* VA	Deed fr	Walker, George	1796	B2B	430	107
Smith, James, of Frederick Co.	Lease to	Cox, John, of G'tn.	1800	E5	178	169
Smith, James, of Pr. Wm. Co. VA	Deed fr	Walker, George	1817	AN38	529	384
Smith, James R., of New York NY	Deed fr	Lawrie, James, Rev.	1810	X23	285	226
Smith, James R., mer., of NY	Deed to	Laurie, James, Rev.	1811	AC28	059	045
Smith, James R., of NY	Mortgage fr	Laurie, James, Rev.	1811	AC28	060	046
Smith, Jesse	Deed fr	Lucas, Henry	1807	R17	143	110
Smith, Jesse	Deed fr	Lucas, Henry	1812	AD29	250	207
Smith, Jesse	Deed to	King, Vincent	1813	AE30	454	338
Smith, Jesse, of G'tn.	Mortgage fr	Mitchell, John C., of G'tn.	1816	AM37	083	067
Smith, Job	B. of S. to	McKee, James	1810	Y24	466	413
Smith, Job, as baker	Apprentice fr	Wimsett, John & father James	1805	M12	233	235
Smith, Job, baker	Manumis to	[ ], Phillis (Negro)	1804	L11	167	164
Smith, Job, of St. Mary's Co.	Mortgage to	Smith, James	1816	AM37	485	352
Smith, John K.	Deed fr	Hyde, Thomas	1811	AB27	010	011
Smith, John K.	Deed to	Williams, Brooke	1814	AG32	248	177
Smith, John K., of G'tn.	Deed fr	Magruder, Ninian, of G'tn.	1814	AG32	048	038
Smith, John K. & Caroline, G'tn.	Deed to	Williams, Brooke, of G'tn.	1817	AO39	128	098
Smith, John Kilty	Bond fr	Hyde, Thomas	1810	X23	367	295
Smith, John Kilty	Assign fr	Steuart, William	1811	AB27	010	011
Smith, John Kilty	Deed fr	Pierce, Isaac	1817	AO39	172	128
Smith, John Kilty, of G'tn.	Deed fr	Brooke, Thomas A., Montg. Co.	1817	AO39	139	106
Smith, John Kilty	Assign to	Pierce, Isaac	1817	AN38	114	085
Smith, John R.	Deed fr	Pierce, Isaac & Elizabeth	1817	AO39	060	049
Smith, John W.	Deed fr	Hanley, John	1817	AN38	393	293
Smith, Leonard, Richmond Co. GA	Deed to	King, Adam, of Montg. Co.	1796	B2B	570	308
Smith, Lewis	B. of S. fr	Miles, Stanislaus	1814	AG32	045	036
Smith, Lewis, of G'tn.	Mortgage to	Schultze, Henry	1814	AG32	353	256
Smith, Lewis, of G'tn.	Deed fr	Schultze, Henry, of G'tn.	1814	AG32	286	206
Smith, Lewis, of G'tn.	Deed fr	Magruder, Ninian, of G'tn.	1817	AN38	499	360
Smith, Lewis, of G'tn.	Deed to	Coppersmith, Magdalena et al	1817	AN38	500	361
Smith, Margaret, of G'tn. et al	D. of T. to	Morton, William	1810	Z25	291	228
Smith, Mary	Deed fr	Davidson, John, of Annapolis	1799	D4	363	350
Smith, Mary	Deed fr	Hedges, Nicholas	1815	AK35	060	046
Smith, Philip & Isaac	Deed fr	Bailey, Theodorus et al	1802	G7	465	601
Smith, Rachael (mulatto)	B. of S. fr	Dyer, Henry O., mer., of G'tn.	1806	Q16	060	038
Smith, Richard	Deed fr	Reintzel, Anthony	1811	Z25	492	391
Smith, Richard	Deed fr	Wingart, Abraham	1811	Z25	493	392
Smith, Richard	Deed fr	Davidson, Lewis Grant	1815	AK35	018	014
Smith, Richard	Release to	Ritchie, Abner	1815	AH33	421	362
Smith, Richard	Deed fr	Bussard, Daniel, of G'tn.	1816	AL36	176	176
Smith, Richard, cashier	D. of T. fr	Lee, Richard Bland	1817	AN38	248	181
Smith, Richard, of G'tn.	Deed fr	Rittenhouse, John B., of G'tn.	1812	AC28	352	255
Smith, Richard, of G'tn.	Lease to	Norris, Stephen, Wash. Co. MD	1814	AH33	153	145
Smith, Richard, of G'tn.	Deed fr	French, George, of G'tn.	1814	AH33	292	253

Index to District of Columbia Land Records, 1792-1817

Party	What	Party	Year	Liber	Old	New
Smith, Richard, of G'tn.	Deed fr	Norris, Stephen, of Hagerstown	1814	AH33	274	239
Smith, Richard, of G'tn.	Deed fr	French, George, of G'tn.	1814	AH33	199	181
Smith, Richard, of G'tn.	B. of S. to	Davis, Benjamin	1815	AH33	439	377
Smith, Richard, of G'tn.	Deed to	Fleet, Henry, of G'tn.	1815	AH33	524	449
Smith, Richard, of G'tn.	Deed fr	French, George	1815	AK35	016	013
Smith, Richard, of G'tn.	Deed fr	Suter, Barbara	1816	AM37	466	335
Smith, Richard, of G'tn.	Lease to	Norris, Stephen	1816	AM37	300	219
Smith, Richard, of G'tn.	Surrender fr	Norris, Stephen	1816	AM37	302	221
Smith, Richard, of G'tn.	Deed to	Greer, James, of G'tn.	1816	AO39	028	023
Smith, Richard, of G'tn.	Deed fr	Belt, Benjamin M.	1816	AM37	207	153
Smith, Robert	B. of S. fr	Nicholls, Edward	1802	I9	148	224
Smith, Robert	Slaves	From Montgomery Co. MD	1810	Y24	114	104
Smith, Robert	Manumis to	Fletcher, Michael	1811	AB27	516	422
Smith, Robert & Samuel, Balto.	Deed to	Barry, James	1804	K10	256	262
Smith, Robert, attorney, of Balto.	Deed to	Barry, James, merchant, of Balto.	1799	D4	171	152
Smith, Robert et al	Release to	Nourse, Joseph	1813	AF31	011	008
Smith, Robert R.	Assign to	Moore, George	1808	T19	400	282
Smith, Robert, Sec. U.S.N.	Release to	Templeman, John, of G'tn.	1805	M12	275	275
Smith, Samuel	B. of S. to	Way, Andrew, Jr.	1812	AD29	162	128
Smith, Samuel et al	Deed fr	Gilliss, Thomas H.	1802	I9	517	846
Smith, Samuel H.	Mortgage fr	Coombe, Griffith	1807	R17	039	032
Smith, Samuel H.	Release to	Coombe, Griffith	1811	AB27	289	237
Smith, Samuel H.	Deed fr	Lazenby, Cephas, of Montg. Co.	1814	AH33	047	043
Smith, Samuel Harrison	Bond fr	Duly, Jonathan & Wm., Montg.	1804	K10	404	419
Smith, Samuel Harrison	Deed fr	Gardener, John & James C. King	1807	R17	387	293
Smith, Samuel Harrison	Deed fr	Duley, Joseph Ford & Rebecca	1807	S18	293	225
Smith, Samuel Harrison	Deed fr	Davidson, Samuel	1807	R17	383	291
Smith, Samuel Harrison	Deed fr	Duley, William & Ann, Montg. Co.	1808	T19	190	135
Smith, Samuel Harrison	Deed fr	Duly, Zadock & Susanna, of KY	1808	T19	178	127
Smith, Samuel Harrison	Deed fr	Duley, Hezekiah, of Calvert Co.	1808	T19	192	137
Smith, Samuel Harrison	Deed fr	Duley, Jonathan & Catharine	1808	T19	182	129
Smith, Samuel Harrison	Deed fr	Wells, Nathan & Sophia, of KY	1808	T19	187	133
Smith, Samuel Harrison	Deed fr	Beall, Daniel & Ann, of Montg. Co.	1808	T19	184	131
Smith, Samuel Harrison	Deed fr	Duley, John, of Mason Co. KY	1810	Y24	183	168
Smith, Samuel Harrison	Deed fr	Jones, Charles C., late Montg. Co.	1811	AA26	061	046
Smith, Samuel, of Balto.	Deed fr	Bodget, Samuel, Jr., of Phila.	1799	D4	424	396
Smith, Samuel, of Balto.	Deed fr	Lingan, James Macubbin, of G'tn.	1799	E5	035	025
Smith, Samuel, of Balto.	Cert fr	Commissioners of Washington	1800	F6	089	054
Smith, Sarah, w/o William	Relinquish to	Stevens, John	1801	G7	305	426
Smith, Sophia, of G'tn.	Deed fr	Cox, John, of G'tn.	1814	AG32	053	041
Smith, Sophia, of G'tn.	Deed to	Waters, Thomas Gibbons, of G'tn.	1815	AK35	015	012
Smith, Thomas	Deed fr	Taylor, Thomas, Jr.	1816	AL36	319	314
Smith, Thomas (M)	Cert free fr	Digges, Susannah	1812	AD29	211	172
Smith, Thomas, of P.G. Co.	Mortgage fr	McKoy, Robert, of P.G. Co.	1808	T19	219	161
Smith, Walter	Deed fr	Loundes, Charles	1802	I9	285	466
Smith, Walter	Qualify		1802	I9	464	765
Smith, Walter	Deed fr	King, Adam	1802	I9	171	261
Smith, Walter	Deed fr	Templeman, John	1802	I9	283	463
Smith, Walter	Deed fr	Loundes, Charles	1802	I9	540	880
Smith, Walter	Deed fr	Deakins, Francis	1802	I9	173	264
Smith, Walter	Deed fr	Davidson, John	1802	I9	172	263
Smith, Walter	Deed fr	Loundes, Charles	1802	I9	199	310
Smith, Walter	Deed fr	Murdock, John	1805	M12	172	171
Smith, Walter	Deed fr	Dorsey, William Hammond	1805	N13	268	223
Smith, Walter	Release to	Templeman, John	1805	M12	278	279

Index to District of Columbia Land Records, 1792-1817

Party	What	Party	Year	Liber	Old	New
Smith, Walter	Deed to	Stoddert, Benjamin	1805	M12	171	169
Smith, Walter	Deed fr	Thomson, William, of G'tn.	1806	Q16	002	002
Smith, Walter	Deed fr	Lowndes, Francis et al	1807	S18	354	279
Smith, Walter	Deed fr	Lowndes, Francis et al	1807	S18	343	270
Smith, Walter	Deed fr	Lingan, James M., of Montg. Co.	1807	S18	340	267
Smith, Walter	Deed fr	Templeman, John, of Allegany Co.	1807	S18	349	275
Smith, Walter	Deed fr	Lingan, James M.	1807	S18	361	285
Smith, Walter	Deed fr	Templeman, John	1807	S18	351	277
Smith, Walter	Release fr	Renner, Daniel & Daniel Bussard	1810	Y24	202	186
Smith, Walter	Deed fr	Hoye, John	1811	AB27	002	004
Smith, Walter	Deed to	Robertson, Thomas	1812	AC28	362	263
Smith, Walter	D. of T. fr	Webster, Toppan	1812	AC28	463	329
Smith, Walter	Convey fr	Crown, Mary Ann	1815	AK35	277	221
Smith, Walter	Deed fr	Ober, Robert [Tenny & Ober]	1816	AL36	321	315
Smith, Walter & Clement	Deed fr	Bowie, Washington, mer., of G'tn.	1800	E5	144	133
Smith, Walter & Clement, of G'tn.	Deed fr	West, Stephen et al	1804	K10	127	138
Smith, Walter & Clement	Deed fr	Wayman, Charles, of G'tn.	1805	N13	388	310
Smith, Walter & Clement, of G'tn.	Deed to	McDonald, Alexander, of MD	1806	Q16	088	056
Smith, Walter & John Cox, of G'tn.	Deed to	Melvin, James	1810	X23	162	119
Smith, Walter & Clement	Deed fr	Magruder, George, collector, G'tn.	1811	AB27	006	008
Smith, Walter & Clement	Deed to	Turner, Samuel, Jr.	1811	Z25	540	430
Smith, Walter & Clement Smith	Deed fr	Lee, Thomas S., of Fredk. Co.	1813	AE30	421	310
Smith, Walter & Clement	Deed to	Shaaff, John T., Dr.	1817	AO39	504	346
Smith, Walter, agent	Deed fr	Foxall, Henry, of G'tn.	1816	AM37	204	151
Smith, Walter et al	Deed fr	Beatty, Charles, of G'tn.	1803	K10	062	67
Smith, Walter et al	Deed fr	Caldwell, Eliase B. et al	1804	K10	247	254
Smith, Walter et al	Deed to	King, Adam	1804	L11	073	75
Smith, Walter et al	Deed to	King, George	1804	L11	075	77
Smith, Walter et al	Deed to	Baltzer, John, Jr.	1804	L11	079	81
Smith, Walter et al	Deed to	Dorsey, William H.	1804	L11	071	73
Smith, Walter et al	Deed to	Nourse, Joseph	1804	K10	183	192
Smith, Walter et al	Mortgage fr	Calder, James	1806	O14	300	199
Smith, Walter et al	Deed fr	Melvin, James	1806	O14	307	203
Smith, Walter et al	D. of T. fr	Calder, James	1806	O14	303	201
Smith, Walter H. & Abm. Wingard	B. of S. fr	Miller, Daniel, of G'tn.	1812	AD29	217	172
Smith, Walter, mer., of G'tn.	Deed fr	King, George, mer., of G'tn.	1812	AC28	224	166
Smith, Walter, of G'tn.	Deed fr	Magruder, George, collector, G'tn.	1805	M12	189	191
Smith, Walter, of G'tn.	Deed fr	King, George, of G'tn.	1805	M12	191	192
Smith, Walter, of G'tn.	Deed fr	Caldwell, Elias B. et al	1806	O14	245	161
Smith, Walter, of G'tn.	Deed to	Stoddert, Benjamin, of G'tn.	1807	S18	110	089
Smith, Walter, of G'tn.	Deed fr	Reintzel, Anthony, of G'tn.	1807	Q16	347	267
Smith, Walter, of G'tn.	Deed fr	Reintzel, Anthony, of G'tn.	1808	U20	325	174
Smith, Walter, of G'tn.	Deed to	Reintzel, Anthony, of G'tn.	1808	T19	059	
Smith, Walter, of G'tn.	Deed fr	Templeman, John, of G'tn.	1810	Y24	121	111
Smith, Walter, of G'tn.	D. of T. fr	Nourse, Joseph, of G'tn.	1811	AB27	045	039
Smith, Walter, of G'tn.	Deed fr	Reintzel, Anthony, of G'tn.	1811	AB27	314	259
Smith, Walter, of G'tn.	Deed fr	Wiley, David, of G'tn.	1812	AD29	166	132
Smith, Walter, of G'tn.	Deed to	Crawford, William, of G'tn.	1814	AH33	059	052
Smith, Walter, of G'tn.	Deed to	Glover, Charles	1815	AI34	011	012
Smith, Walter, of G'tn.	Deed fr	Cox, John, of G'tn.	1815	AI34	029	033
Smith, Walter, of G'tn., trustee	Deed to	Palmer, Eliakum	1815	AH33	486	416
Smith, Walter, of G'tn.	D. of T. fr	Webster, Toppan	1815	AK35	307	245
Smith, Walter, of G'tn.	D. of T. fr	Bogenrieff, Valentine, of G'tn.	1815	AK35	320	255
Smith, Walter, of G'tn.	Deed to	Cox, John, of G'tn.	1815	AI34	018	019
Smith, Walter, of G'tn., trustee	Deed to	Laird, John	1816	AM37	477	345

Index to District of Columbia Land Records, 1792-1817

Party	What	Party	Year	Liber	Old	New
Smith, Walter, of G'tn.	Deed to	Barclay, Susan, w/o Thos., of NY	1816	AM37	102	082
Smith, Walter, of G'tn.	Deed to	Clarke, George	1816	AM37	284	208
Smith, Walter, of G'tn., trustee	Deed to	Gardner, William P.	1816	AM37	052	043
Smith, Walter, of G'tn.	Deed to	Graham, Jane	1817	AO39	515	354
Smith, Walter, of G'tn.	Deed fr	Kellenberger, John H., of G'tn.	1817	AO39	412	279
Smith, Walter, of G'tn.	D. of T. fr	Lancaster, Stephen	1817	AO39	416	283
Smith, Walter, plt.	Suit	Templeman, John, def.	1810	Y24	120	109
Smith, Walter, trustee of J. Lingan	Deed to	Foxall, Henry, of G'tn.	1815	AH33	529	453
Smith, Walter, trustee of J. Lingan	Deed to	Foxall, Henry, of G'tn.	1815	AH33	532	455
Smith, Will	Manumis fr	Scott, Alexander	1808	V21	098	075
Smith, William	Deed fr	Beall, Thomas B., of G'tn.	1802	H8	003	003
Smith, William	Deed fr	Gilpin, Bernard	1802	H8	115	111
Smith, William	Deed fr	Carleton, Joseph, of G'tn.	1804	L11	207	196
Smith, William	Deed fr	Beall, Thomas B.	1805	M12	215	217
Smith, William	Deed fr	Balch, Alfred	1807	S18	327	256
Smith, William	Deed to	Lane, Samuel M. & Rachel	1808	T19	216	157
Smith, William	Deed fr	Prout, William	1809	X23	039	029
Smith, William	Certificate	Captain in 1st Legion of Militia	1809	X23	007	005
Smith, William	Deed fr	Laird, John, exr. of J. Carleton	1814	AG32	301	219
Smith, William	Deed to	Carson, George, of Alexa.	1816	AL36	439	417
Smith, William	B. of S. fr	Joy, Henry B.	1816	AL36	180	179
Smith, William (M), age 23	Cert Free fr	Ott, John	1816	AK35	172	133
Smith, William (mulatto)	Cert Free fr	Brent, Robert	1809	W22	227	155
Smith, William & Sarah, of Alexa.	B. of S. to	Blakeney, Abel, of Alexa.	1802	G7		697
Smith, William H., of Balto. et al	B. of S. fr	Knight, James	1804	L11	319	292
Smith, William, joiner	Deed to	Carleton, George, bricklayer	1804	M12	009	009
Smith, William, joiner	Deed fr	Beall, Thomas, of George	1804	L11	353	319
Smith, William, joiner	Deed fr	Beall, Thomas, of George	1807	Q16	338	259
Smith, William, Loudoun Co. VA	Deed fr	Blakeney, Abel & Mary, of Alexa.	1807	Q16	366	281
Smith, William M.	Deed fr	Blodget, Samuel	1802	I9	179	274
Smith, William, of Alexa.	Deed fr	Crook, Bernard & Agnes	1800	E5	280	274
Smith, William, of Alexa.	Deed to	Stevens, John	1801	G7	229	306
Smith, William, of G'tn.	Deed to	McCormick, George, of G'tn.	1804	L11	395	350
Smith, William, of G'tn.	Deed to	Smith, Anthony, of G'tn.	1805	M12	213	215
Smith, William, of Loudoun Co. VA	Deed fr	Blakeney, Abel, of Alexa.	1807	S18	385	307
Smith, William, of Loudoun Co. VA	Deed to	Swift, Jonathan, of Alexa.	1807	S18	092	075
Smitson, Hezekiah	Lease fr	Prout, William	1805	N13	206	179
Smitson, Hezekiah	Assign to	St. Clare [Saintclere]	1806	O14	188	123
Smoot, Alexander	Deed to	McKim, James & Thomas Herty	1806	Q16	183	122
Smoot, Alexander	Deed to	McKim, James & Thomas Herty	1807	R17	117	091
Smoot, Alexander	P. of Atty. fr	Contee, P.A.L.	1813	AG32	005	004
Smoot, Alexander S.	Deed to	Duvall, Gabriel	1805	M12	282	283
Smoot, Alexander S.	Release fr	Duvall, Gabriel	1811	AB27	045	039
Smoot, Alexander S.	B. of S. to	Moore, James	1813	AG32	005	004
Smoot, Alexander S.	B. of S. to	McDaniel, Ezekiel	1814	AH33	070	063
Smoot, Alexander S.	B. of S. to	McCormick, Alexander	1814	AH33	098	090
Smoot, John N.	Cert Free to	Swann, Margaret	1810	Z25	114	089
Smoot, Samuel	Release fr	Bank of Columbia	1814	AH33	260	227
Smoot, Samuel	Deed to	Williams, John S., of G'tn.	1816	AL36	313	308
Smoot, Samuel	Deed fr	Peter, George	1816	AL36	286	284
Smoot, Samuel	Deed to	Wilson, John, of Henry, P.G. Co.	1817	AO39	390	264
Smoot, Samuel	Deed fr	Johnson, Thomas, of Fredk. Co.	1817	AN38	044	036
Smoot, Samuel, of G'tn.	Deed fr	Murdock, John, of G'tn.	1814	AH33	258	224
Smoot, Samuel, of G'tn.	Deed fr	Dorsey, William H., of Montg. Co.	1814	AH33	259	226
Smoot, Samuel, of G'tn.	Deed fr	Dorsey, William H., of Montg. Co.	1816	AM37	166	126

Party	What	Party	Year	Liber	Old	New
Smoot, Samuel, of G'tn.	Deed fr	Lowry, John	1817	AN38	042	034
Smothers, Flora (negro)	Manumis fr	Smothers, Henry	1805	O14	127	081
Smothers, Francis	Cert Free to	Jacobs, John	1809	X23	315	252
Smothers, Harry	B. of S. fr	Jones, Walter, Jr.	1810	Y24	246	227
Smothers, Henry	Manumis to	Smothers, Flora (negro)	1805	O14	127	081
Smothers, Henry	B. of S. fr	Wright, William B.	1809	V21	316	232
Smothers, Henry	Cert fr	Munroe, Thomas, Supt.	1809	W22	018	014
Snider, Abraham	Lease fr	Veal, Richard S.	1802	I9	543	883
Snow, Gideon, mer., of Boston MA	Deed fr	Perkins, Abigail, of Boston MA	1810	Y24	485	428
Snow, Gideon, mer., of Boston MA	Rel. Dower	Perkins, Hannah S., of Boston MA	1815	AG32	401	293
Snow, Gideon, of Boston MA	Deed fr	McDonald, John G., trustee	1810	Y24	168	154
Snow, Gideon, of Boston MA	Deed to	Hollowell & Augusta Bank	1817	AN38	183	133
Snow, Martha	Cert Free to	Snow, Mary (M), age 20	1816	AM37	371	268
Snow, Mary (M), age 20	Cert Free fr	Snow, Martha	1816	AM37	371	268
Snowden, Ann Maria et al	Release fr	Corcoran, Thomas, of G'tn.	1810	Y24	263	242
Snowden, Gerard H. et al	Release fr	Corcoran, Thomas, of G'tn.	1810	Y24	263	242
Snowden, Gerrard H., of A.A. Co.	Deed fr	Mountz, John, of G'tn. et al	1812	AD29	378	318
Snowden, Margaret Hopkins et al	Release fr	Corcoran, Thomas, of G'tn.	1810	Y24	263	242
Snowden, Rachel et al	Release fr	Corcoran, Thomas, of G'tn.	1810	Y24	263	242
Snowden, Rezen Hammond et al	Release fr	Corcoran, Thomas, of G'tn.	1810	Y24	263	242
Snowden, Richard J. et al	Release fr	Corcoran, Thomas, of G'tn.	1810	Y24	263	242
Snowden, Richard P. et al	Release fr	Corcoran, Thomas, of G'tn.	1810	Y24	263	242
Snowden, Samuel et al	Deed fr	Shoemaker, Jonathan	1808	T19	114	081
Snowden, Samuel, of A.A. Co. et al	Cert fr	Munroe, Thomas, Supr.	1808	T19	349	252
Snowden, Thomas	Deed fr	Chapman, Henry H. et al	1802	I9	381	632
Snowden, Thomas, of P.G. Co.	Mortgage fr	Stoddert, Benjamin	1797	B2B	623	381
Snyder, Abraham	Deed to	Gaither, Henry, Col.	1806	O14	202	133
Snyder, Jacob	Deed to	Crookshank & Thompson	1800	F6	053	033
Snyder, Jacob	Deed fr	Commissioners of Washington	1800	F6	047	030
Snyder, Jacob, of VA	Deed to	Flaut, Christian	1807	S18	190	154
Society of Friends	Deed fr	Shoemaker, Jonathan	1808	T19	114	081
Soderstrom, Richard	B. of S. fr	Rogers, Charles	1801	G7	438	573
Soderstrom, Richard	Assign to	Key, Philip Barton	1809	W22	094	068
Soderstrom, Richard	Assign fr	L'Enfant, Pierre Charles	1809	W22	094	068
Soderstrom, Richard, of Phila. PA	B. of S. fr	Newton, John	1801	G7	402	536
Soleather, Betsey, b. 2/23/83	Cert of Birth		1804	K10	331	
Solomon, Lewis	Transfer to	Burden, Henry R.	1817	AO39	458	314
Somers, Nathan, oif P.G. Co.	Mortgage fr	Ayres, Thomas	1809	V21	165	119
Somervill, James et al	Assign fr	Ober, Richard	1795	B2A	329	461
Somerville, David	Deed fr	Flaut, Christian & Hannah	1807	S18	256	202
Somerville, David	Mortgage to	Watterston, David et al	1810	Z25	362	285
Somerville, David	Assign fr	Huddleston, Joseph	1810	Z25	365	286
Somerville, David et al	Lease fr	Van Ness, John P. & Marcia	1806	Q16	124	081
Somerville, David, stone cutter	Deed to	Cranch, William	1810	Y24	417	375
Somerville, Henry V., of St. M. Co.	Deed fr	Hebb, William, of P.G. Co.	1814	AG32	291	212
Somerville, Henry V., St. Mary's	Deed fr	Hebb, William, of P.G. Co.	1815	AH33	467	399
Somerville, James, mer., of Balto.	Deed fr	Duguid, William, mer., of Balto.	1801	F6	208	134
Somerville, Jane, late Underwood	Deed fr	Underwood, Robert	1811	AA26	011	009
Sommerville, David	Deed fr	Van Ness, John P. & Marcia	1811	Z25	460	364
Sommerville, Hugh, grocer	Lease fr	Van Ness, John P.	1804	K10	161	171
Soper, Alexander, of P.G. Co.	B. of S. fr	Brashears, Jeremiah	1811	AA26	089	063
Soper, Henry, of P.G. Co.	B. of S. to	Watterston, George	1813	AE30	364	270
Soper, Leven	B. of S. to	McCawley, George	1810	Y24	226	208
Sorton, Susan (M), age 9	Cert Slave fr	Gustine, J.T. et al	1814	AH33	203	184
Sothoron, Thomas L.	Deed to	Seager, Nathaniel	1802	I9	501	823

Index to District of Columbia Land Records, 1792-1817

Party	What	Party	Year	Liber	Old	New
Sothoron, Thomas L.	Deed to	McCormick, Alexander	1802	I9	334	551
Southerland, Thomas J.	Deed fr	Bird, Alice	1815	AI34	443	459
Southgate, John, of VA	Deed fr	Gantt, John M., of P.G. Co.	1804	L11	249	230
Southgate, John, of Norfolk VA	Deed fr	Gantt, John M., of P.G. Co.	1804	L11	253	234
Southgate, John, of Norfolk VA	Deed fr	Gantt, John M., Bladensburgh	1804	L11	252	232
Southgate, John, of Norfolk VA	Deed fr	Gantt, John Mackall, of P.G. Co.	1804	L11	256	236
Southgate, John, of Norfolk VA	Deed fr	Gantt, John M., of P.G. Co.	1804	L11	250	231
Southgate, John, of Norfolk VA	Deed fr	Gantt, John M., of P.G. Co.	1804	L11	255	235
Southgate, John, of Norfolk	Deed to	Williams, John Stull, of G'tn.	1814	AG32	065	050
Southgate, John, of Norfolk	Deed to	Wagner, Jacob, of G'tn.	1814	AG32	133	096
Southgate, John, of Norfolk	Deed to	Wagner, Jacob & John Williams	1814	AG32	136	098
Southoron, Thomas L., in P.G. Co.	P. of Atty. to	Harshman, Henry	1804	L11	330	301
Spalding, Bernard	Deed fr	Threlkeld, John	1809	W22	098	071
Spalding, Bernard	B. of S. fr	Ford, Edward	1811	AA26	034	026
Spalding, Bernard	Release to	Ford, Edward	1812	AD29	124	095
Spalding, Bernard, of G'tn.	Deed fr	Reeves, Thomas C., Charles Co.	1811	AB27	386	318
Spalding, Electius	B. of S. fr	Wells, John, of P.G. Co.	1811	Z25	544	432
Spalding, Enoch	B. of S. fr	Brown, George Washington	1811	AA26	316	213
Spalding, Enoch	Release fr	Masters, Priscilla, Scioto Co. OH	1815	AI34	098	112
Spalding, Enoch	Deed fr	Masters, John, heirs of	1815	AI34	097	110
Spalding, Enoch	Deed fr	Mitchell, Walter & Matilda et al	1815	AI34	110	121
Spalding, Enoch & Elizabeth et al	Deed to	Walker, Zachariah	1815	AI34	435	452
Spalding, Enoch, Scioto Co. OH	Deed to	Walker, Zachariah	1815	AI34	099	113
Spalding, John	Assign fr	Longden, Susan, admx. of Abel	1813	AF31	230	159
Spalding, John	Mortgage to	Davis, John, of Abel et al	1814	AG32	403	294
Spalding, John et al	Release fr	Boone, Joseph, sheriff	1799	E5	053	042
Spalding, John, of Piscataway MD	Deed to	May, Frederick & Samuel Eliot, Jr.	1803	K10	066	71
Spalding, John, of Jefferson Co.	Assign to	Simms, Henry, of G'tn.	1816	AM37	107	085
Spalding, Philip, of P.G. Co.	Deed fr	Prout, William	1805	N13	116	111
Spalding, Richard	B. of S. to	Brent, William	1817	AN38	383	285
Spalding, Richard & John Cannon	Mortgage fr	Masters, Ezekiel	1812	AD29	313	
Spalding, Richard, constable	Deed to	Tippitt, Cartwright	1807	R17	353	269
Spalding, William	Deed fr	Templeman, John	1802	I9	376	624
Sparrow, John W.	Deed to	Loveless, William	1813	AE30	401	296
Sparrow, Joseph et ux	Lease fr	Queen, Walter	1792	A1-1	041	62
Sparrow, William	B. of S. fr	Berron, Jerome	1817	AN38	455	328
Spaulding, John	Agreement	May, Frederick et al	1799	E5	060	
Spaulding, John et al	Agreement	Burrows, Edward	1799	E5	050	040
Speake, Edward	B. of S. to	Clarke, Robert	1809	V21	352	254
Speake, Eleanor	Cert	Negroes	1802	H8	017	016
Speake, Eleanor	Slaves	From Charles Co. MD	1804	K10	155	
Speake, Josiah M. & Sarah et al	Deed to	Pairo, Loveday	1807	R17	216	162
Speake, Josiah M. & Sarah	Deed to	Holmead, John	1808	T19	405	285
Speake, Josias M.	Lease to	Walker, Nathan, of G'tn.	1801	G7	357	489
Speake, Josias M.	Deed fr	Morsell, James S.	1802	I9	300	493
Speake, Josias M.	Deed to	Beale, Thomas B.	1802	I9	304	500
Speake, Josias M. & Sarah et al	Deed to	French, Ariana	1804	L11	396	351
Speake, Josias M. & Sarah et al	Deed to	French, Arianna	1804	L11	401	356
Speake, Josias M., of Alexa. Co.	Lease to	Holmead, Jon	1806	O14	270	179
Speake, Josias M., of Alexa. Co.	Deed fr	Holmead, John	1806	P15	060	036
Speake, Josias M. & Sarah	Deed to	Holmead, Anthony	1808	U20	079	044
Speake, Josias M.	Deed to	Holmead, John	1808	U20	001	001
Speake, Josias M. & Sarah	Deed to	Owens, Isaac, of G'tn.	1808	T19	302	221
Speake, Josias M.	Deed to	Holmead, John	1808	U20	004	003
Speake, Josias M. & Sarah	Deed to	Barlow, Joel	1809	W22	399	260

Party	What	Party	Year	Liber	Old	New
Speake, Josias M.	Manumis to	Carroll, Airy (mulatto)	1810	Z25	133	104
Speake, Josias M.	Deed to	Mackall, Leonard	1811	AA26	301	203
Speake, Josias M. et al	Suit ads	Potomac Company	1812	AG32	258	183
Speake, Josias M.	D. of T. fr	Speakle, Samuel	1812	AD29	265	219
Speake, Josias M., trustee	B. of S. to	Semmes, Jesse M.	1813	AF31	229	157
Speake, Josias M.	Deed to	Owens, Isaac	1817	AN38	216	158
Speake, Josias Milburn	Deed fr	Holmead, Anthony	1800	E5	324	314
Speake, Samuel	Deed fr	Munroe, Thomas, Supt	1802	I9	486	799
Speake, Samuel	Mortgage fr	Gregg, Joshua	1802	I9	492	807
Speake, Samuel	B. of S. fr	Bently, Joseph	1806	P15	225	150
Speake, Samuel	Slaves	From Charles Co. MD	1806	P15	267	176
Speake, Samuel	Slave	From Alexandria Co.	1806	P15	371	
Speake, Samuel	Deed to	McLean, Cornelius	1807	R17	326	248
Speake, Samuel	Assign to	Kerr, Alexander	1808	V21	094	072
Speake, Samuel	Deed fr	Green, Jesse, of Sussex Co. DE	1809	W22	117	084
Speake, Samuel	Agreement	Dant, James	1810	Y24	108	098
Speake, Samuel	Lease fr	Law, Edmund, trustee	1810	Z25	099	077
Speake, Samuel	Qualify	Captain of Militia	1811	AB27	179	
Speake, Samuel	Assign to	Moore, George	1811	Z25	398	313
Speake, Samuel	Release fr	Law, Edmund	1811	AA26	050	039
Speake, Samuel	D. of T. to	Speake, Josias M.	1812	AD29	265	219
Speake, Samuel	Mortgage to	Cloakey, Samuel	1812	AD29	094	071
Speake, Samuel	Deed fr	O'Neale, William	1812	AD29	125	096
Speake, Samuel	Assign to	Moore, George	1813	AE30	178	142
Speake, Samuel	Release fr	Cloakey, Samuel	1813	AF31	512	374
Speake, Samuel	Deed to	O'Neale, William	1814	AG32	228	162
Speake, Samuel	Lease fr	Van Ness, John P. & Marcia	1815	AK35	132	102
Speake, Samuel & Mary Anne et al	B. of S. to	Semmes, Jesse M.	1813	AF31	229	157
Speake, Samuel, trustee	Deed fr	Davis, Thomas, insolvent	1805	N13	004	004
Speake, Samuel, trustee	Deed fr	Vernon, William W., insolvent	1811	Z25	510	405
Speake, Samuel, trustee	Deed fr	Gray, Stephen W., insolvent	1811	AA26	317	214
Speake, Sarah	Deed fr	Holmead, John	1808	U20	400	223
Speake, Sarah, w/o Josias M.	Deed fr	Holmead, John et al	1807	R17	013	012
Speake, Sarah, w/o Josias M.	Deed fr	Holmead, Anthony	1808	U20	083	046
Speake, Sarah, w/o Josias M.	Deed fr	Holmead, Anthony & Sarah	1810	X23	225	173
Speakes, Eleanor	Slaves		1802	G7		693
Spear, Joseph	Deed fr	Etting, Solomon	1802	I9	245	394
Speerer, Nicholas, of G'tn.	Lease fr	Law, Thomas	1802	H8	366	341
Spellman, Abram	Cert Free fr	Wilson, William, clerk	1817	AO39	467	321
Spellman, George	Cert Free fr	Wilson, William, clerk	1817	AO39	467	321
Spelman, William (C)	Cert Slave	Freeman, Constant	1816	AL36	431	411
Spencer, John J.	Deed to	Mara, Philip	1796	B2B	440	120
Spencer, John Jonathan	Deed to	Jamieson, Andrew, of Alexa.	1794	B2A	163	216
Spiker, Henry, of Berks Co. PA	Deed to	Klinger, Henry [Clinger]	1793	A1-1	339	443
Spochrer, Nicholas	B. of S. to	Ritchie, Adam	1802	I9	514	841
Spooner, Holder	Lease fr	Prout, William	1808	V21	099	075
Spooner, Holder	Deed fr	Prout, William	1812	AC28	408	296
Spooner, William	Lease fr	Prout, William	1805	M12	387	399
Spooner, William	Deed to	Liverpool, Moses	1807	T19	003	002
Spooner, William	Deed fr	Baily, Daniel	1808	T19	109	078
Spooner, William	Deed fr	Chandler, Jacob	1809	X23	084	062
Spotwood, John A.	B. of S. to	Lewis, Robert	1810	Y24	143	130
Spreerer, Nicholas, of G'tn.	Deed fr	Kaldenbach, Andrew, of G'tn.	1802	I9	088	126
Sprigg, Benjamin	Receipt to	McLean, Cornelius	1815	AI34	237	269
Sprigg, Benjamin	Deed fr	Carr, Overton, trustee	1817	AN38	155	113

Index to District of Columbia Land Records, 1792-1817

Party	What	Party	Year	Liber	Old	New
Sprigg, Margaret	Deed fr	Commissioners of Washington	1799	D4	421	394
Sprigg, Osborn, of P.G. Co.	Manumis to	[ ], Caroline (C), age 10	1813	AE30	221	178
Sprigg, Osborn, of P.G. Co.	Manumis to	Mahoney, Barney, age 40, others	1813	AE30	221	178
Sprigg, Osborn, of P.G. Co.	Manumis to	[ ], Barney (C), age 1	1813	AE30	221	178
Sprigg, Osborn, of P.G. Co.	Manumis to	[ ], Susan (C), age 6	1813	AE30	221	178
Sprigg, Osborn, of P.G. Co.	Manumis to	[ ], Linda (C), age 40	1813	AE30	221	178
Sprigg, Osborn, of P.G. Co.	Manumis to	[ ], Mary (C), age 9	1813	AE30	221	178
Sprigg, Osborn, of P.G. Co.	Manumis to	[ ], Ann (C), age 12	1813	AE30	221	178
Sprigg, Osborn, of P.G. Co.	Manumis to	[ ], Daniel (C), age 4	1813	AE30	221	178
Sprigg, Osborn, of P.G. Co.	Manumis to	[ ], Patsey (C), age 20	1813	AE30	221	178
Sprigg, Osborne, of P.G. Co.	Deed to	Sprigg, Samuel, of P.G. Co.	1811	AB27	419	346
Sprigg, Osburn, of P.G. Co.	Deed fr	Sprigg, William Osburn	1806	P15	356	236
Sprigg, Samuel, of P.G. Co.	Deed fr	Sprigg, Osborne, of P.G. Co.	1811	AB27	419	346
Sprigg, William O., of G'tn.	Deed fr	Carr, Overton	1801	G7	204	272
Sprigg, William O.	Qualify		1802	I9	465	766
Sprigg, William O.	Deed fr	Polock, Isaac	1802	I9	318	522
Sprigg, William Osburn	Deed to	Sprigg, Osburn, of P.G. Co.	1806	P15	356	236
Sprogell, John Lodwick	Convey to	Brown, Joel	1801	G7	064	083
Sprogell, John Lodwick	Agreement	Brown, Joel	1801	G7	065	084
Sprogell, Thomas Y.	Deed to	Karrick, Joseph et al	1800	E5	166	156
Sprogell, Thomas Y.	Deed to	Perceval, Joshua et al	1800	E5	166	156
Sprogell, Thomas Y.	Agreement	Brown, Joel	1801	G7	065	084
Sprogell, Thomas Y., hatter	Deed fr	Hodgson, Joseph, hatter	1801	G7	005	007
Sprogell, Thomas Y.	Agreement	Hodgson, Joseph	1802	G7	518	659
Sprogell, Thomas Y.	Deed fr	Doughty, William	1802	H8	172	165
Sprogell, Thomas Y.	Deed to	Doughty, William	1802	H8	096	087
Sprogell, Thomas Y.	Deed fr	Caldwell, Timothy	1802	H8	183	175
Sprogell, Thomas Y.	B. of S. to	Davidson, John	1805	M12	274	274
Sprogell, Thomas Y., insolvent	Assign to	Wheaton, Joseph, trustee	1808	V21	133	097
Sprogell, Thomas Yorke	Convey to	Brown, Joel	1801	G7	064	083
Sprogell, Thomas Yorke	B. of S. to	Stretch, Joseph et al	1808	T19	400	283
Sprung, George, of Balto. [w/list]	B. of S. to	Johns, Hosea, of Balto.	1815	AI34	408	429
Spunogle, Catharine	B. of S. fr	Spunogle, George	1809	W22	096	070
Spunogle, George	B. of S. fr	Smith, James	1805	N13	304	246
Spunogle, George	B. of S. to	Spunogle, Catharine	1809	W22	096	070
Spunogle, Margaret	B. of S. fr	Conner, William	1807	S18	175	142
Spyker, Benj., Jr. & Catherine	Deed to	Forrest, Uriah & Benj. Stoddert	1792	A1-1	151	217
Spyker, Benjamin	Letter to	Spyker, Daniel	1797	C3	062	050
Spyker, Benjamin & Marg. Barb.	Deed to	Klinger, Henry, joiner [Clinger]	1793	A1-1	342	446
Spyker, Benjamin, of Reading PA	Deed to	Stoddert, Benjamin, of G'tn.	1798	C3	273	222
Spyker, Daniel	Letter fr	Spyker, Benjamin	1797	C3	062	050
St. Clair, George [Saintclere]	Assign fr	Adams, William	1804	K10	326	335
St. Clair, George [Saintclere]	Assign to	Adams, William	1805	O14	074	046
St. Clair, George	Assign fr	Kortwright, James B.	1809	W22	008	007
St. Clair, George	Deed fr	Queen, Marsham, of Charles Co.	1812	AC28	271	198
St. Clair, George	Deed fr	Nesmith, Ebenezer	1813	AE30	535	397
St. Clair, George	Deed to	Forrest, John B.	1816	AM37	491	358
St. Clair, George	Deed fr	Thomas, John V. & Deborah	1817	AO39	195	144
St. Clare, George	Cert fr	Commissioners of Washington	1802	I9	071	099
St. Clare, George	Deed fr	Wilson, Joseph	1802	I9	124	185
St. Clare, George [Saintclere]	Assign fr	Smitson, Hezekiah	1806	O14	188	123
St. Clare, George	Deed fr	Queen, Samuel, of P.G. Co.	1814	AG32	116	087
St. Cleare, Reason	B. of S. fr	Brown, Robert & Elizabeth	1812	AC28	380	277
St. John, Leonard, of G'tn.	Deed fr	Williams, Brooke, of G'tn.	1817	AO39	471	
St. John's Church, vestrymen et al	Deed fr	Bickley, Robert S., Bucks Co. PA	1817	AN38	564	411

Index to District of Columbia Land Records, 1792-1817

Party	What	Party	Year	Liber	Old	New
St. Victor, Louis de	B. of S. fr	Rodier, Philibert & Mary A. Jarber	1816	AM37	307	224
Staines, John	B. of S. to	McCormick, Alexander	1805	O14	090	056
Staines, John & Elizabeth Ireland	Deed to	Cummins, John	1806	Q16	259	180
Staines, John et al	Deed to	McCormick, Benson L.	1805	N13	240	202
Staines, John et al [Stanes]	Lease fr	Prout, William	1805	N13	235	199
Staines, John et al	Deed to	Vint, John	1806	P15	246	163
Staines, John et al	B. of S. to	Higdon, Gustavus	1807	R17	363	277
Stains, Thomas	Deed to	Williams, Elisha W., Gent.	1809	V21	396	299
Staley, Jacob, currier, of G'tn.	B. of S. fr	Miller, Jacob, innholder, of G'tn.	1812	AC28	286	207
Staley, Jacob, of G'tn.	B. of S. fr	Dorman, Samuel C.	1812	AD29	090	068
Staley, Jacob, of G'tn.	B. of S. to	Bishop, Charles, of Balto. MD	1812	AE30	004	003
Staley, Jacob, of G'tn.	Manumis to	Butler, Henry (C)	1815	AI34	371	399
Stallings, James	B. of S. to	Osborn, Joshua, of P.G. Co.	1814	AH33	028	025
Stamp, Francis	Deed fr	Charles, Richard	1817	AN38	150	110
Stanard, Edward C.	Slaves	From Richmond VA	1810	Y24	205	189
Standage, Eleazer	Deed to	Bayly, William	1795	B2A	266	372
Standage, Eleazer	Deed to	Bayly, William	1796	B2B	421	094
Standage, Eleazer	Deed to	Free, Sarah & her son John, Jr.	1811	AB27	106	087
Standage, Eleazer	Deed fr	Greenleaf, James, of Phila. PA	1812	AD29	128	099
Standage, Eleazer & Mary	Deed to	Kirby, John Baptist	1805	M12	090	083
Standage, Eleazer & Mary	Deed to	Wigfield, Robert	1805	M12	368	378
Standage, Eleazer & Mary	Deed to	Cochrane, Alexander, Jr.	1807	S18	176	143
Standage, Eleazer, of Montg. Co.	Partition		1804	K10	131	141
Standage, Eleazer, of Montg. Co.	Deed to	Wigfield, James et al	1805	M12	367	376
Standage, Eleazor & Mary	Deed to	Farrell, Zephaniah	1809	W22	019	014
Stanes, John et al [Staines]	Lease fr	Prout, William	1805	N13	235	199
Stanton, Patrick	Deed fr	Carleton, Joseph, of G'tn.	1809	W22	169	119
Stanton, Patrick	Lease fr	Marshall, Samuel, of London	1813	AE30	239	190
Stanton, Patrick	Bond fr	Slater, Sarah & Henry, Montg. Co.	1813	AE30	237	189
Starke, Belfield	Deed fr	Brooke, Samuel, trustee	1802	G7	509	649
Starke, Belfield, of VA	Deed to	Jones, Charles C., of Montg. Co.	1810	Y24	117	106
State of Maryland	Deed to	Key, Philip Barton	1807	R17	373	284
Stater, Joseph & David	Deed to	Prout, William	1799	D4	374	359
Steel, Matthew	Deed fr	Balch, Stephen B.	1797	C3	246	203
Steele, Charles	Manumis fr	Addison, John	1809	W22	167	117
Steele, Jesse	B. of S. to	Peter, Robert	1802	I9	537	877
Steele, John	Deed fr	Munroe, Thomas, Supt.	1802	I9	206	322
Steele, John	Deed to	May, Frederick	1802	I9	462	761
Steele, John, of Balto.	Deed to	Van Bibber, Abraham, Gent.	1804	M12	014	015
Steele, John, of Balto.	Deed fr	Munroe, Thomas, Supt.	1804	M12	013	013
Steele, John, of Balto. Co.	Deed to	Van Bibber, Abraham, Balto. Co.	1805	M12	390	403
Steene, Matthew, of Balto. et al	B. of S. fr	Knight, James	1804	L11	319	292
Steene, Matthew, trustee	Deed fr	Knight, James, insolvent	1804	L11	341	310
Steiner, Henry M.	Deed fr	Cocking, William	1816	AL36	521	487
Stelle, Pontius D.	D. of T. fr	Miller, Peter	1808	V21	020	015
Stelle, Pontius D. et ux	Deed to	Miller, Peter	1808	V21	017	013
Stelle, Pontius D.	Deed fr	McIntire, John, of Balto.	1808	V21	013	010
Stelle, Pontius D.	Manumis to	Douglas, John (negro)	1809	W22	174	122
Stelle, Pontius D.	Mortgage to	Miller, Peter	1810	Y24	049	043
Stelle, Pontius D. & wife	Deed to	Miller, Peter	1811	Z25	455	359
Stelle, Pontius Delare	Mortgage to	Tunnicliffe, William	1804	L11	122	125
Stelle, Pontius Delare	Deed fr	Walker, George et al	1804	M12	019	020
Stelle, Portius D.	B. of S. to	McCormick, Alexander	1810	Y24	314	286
Stephen, John	Mortgage to	Kirk, Milesius Thomas	1807	R17	046	037
Stephen, John	D. of T. to	Mountz, John, of G'tn.	1809	V21	265	189

Index to District of Columbia Land Records, 1792-1817

Party	What	Party	Year	Liber	Old	New
Stephen, John, involvent	Assign to	McGowan, John	1809	W22	077	057
Stephen, John, of G'tn.	Deed fr	Milliken, Mark	1799	D4	395	376
Stephens, John	Deed to	Travers, Eseas	1809	W22	039	029
Stephens, Stephen et al	Lease fr	Heeter, Conrad, of G'tn.	1796	B2B	602	353
Stephenson, Clotworthy	Cert fr	Commissioners of Washington	1796	B2B	457	147
Stephenson, Clotworthy	Cert fr	Commissioners of Washington	1796	B2B	458	147
Stephenson, Clotworthy	Deed to	Burnes, David	1798	D4	015	012
Stephenson, Clotworthy	Deed fr	Oakley, John	1802	H8	240	229
Stephenson, Clotworthy	Lease fr	Davidson, John	1802	I9	459	758
Stephenson, Clotworthy	Assign to	Davidson, John	1804	K10	279	283
Stephenson, Clotworthy	B. of S. to	Boyd, Washington	1812	AC28	383	279
Stephenson, Clotworthy et al	Deed to	Wheaton, Sally	1807	Q16	307	234
Stephenson, Clotworthy, P.G. Co.	Deed fr	Burnes, David, of P.G. Co.	1798	C3	501	394
Stephenson, James S.	Deed fr	Chandler, Walter Story	1809	X23	301	240
Stephenson, James S. et al	Deed fr	Bates, David, constable	1811	AA26	084	060
Stephenson, James S.	Deed to	Wharton, Franklin	1811	AB27	060	052
Stephenson, Thomas T.	Deed fr	Hoye, John, of Allegany Co. MD	1815	AI34	219	250
Steret, James et al	Deed to	Beall, Thomas & John M. Gantt	1792	A1-1	141	205
Sterret, James et al	Deed to	French, George, of G'tn.	1795	B2B	371	022
Sterret, Samuel	Deed fr	Harrison, George	1802	I9	496	814
Sterret, Samuel, of PA et al	Deed fr	Nicholson, John & Hannah, of PA	1795	B2A	344	485
Sterrett, James & Samuel Porter	Cert fr	Commissioners of Washington	1793	B2A	316	444
Sterrett, Samuel, of Balto, MD	Deed to	Buste, Paul	1802	I9	119	174
Stettenius, Samuel	Deed fr	Van Ness, John P. & Marcia	1810	Y24	433	387
Stettenius, Samuel	B. of S. fr	Balding, William, oif P.G. Co.	1810	Z25	105	081
Stettinius, Samuel	Mortgage fr	Warner, Osborn	1810	Y24	076	068
Stettinius, Samuel	Assign to	Scholfield, Andrew, of Alexa.	1811	AB27	255	208
Stettinius, Samuel, of G'tn.	Lease fr	Law, Thomas	1802	H8	364	339
Steuart, David	Deed fr	Mayor of Georgetown et al	1808	U20	260	138
Steuart, David	Agreement	Steuart, William	1811	AA26	051	040
Steuart, David	B. of S. fr	Madden, Hezekiah	1814	AG32	147	105
Steuart, David, of G'tn.	Deed fr	Steuart, William, of G'tn.	1811	AA26	044	034
Steuart, David, of G'tn.	B. of S. to	Whann, William	1812	AC28	175	131
Steuart, David, of G'tn.	B. of S. to	Smith, Clement	1812	AC28	174	131
Steuart, David, of G'tn.	Deed fr	Steuart, William, of G'tn.	1812	AC28	136	102
Steuart, David, of G'tn.	Deed fr	Steuart, William, of G'tn.	1812	AC28	133	100
Steuart, David R., Gent.	Deed fr	Ober, Robert, Gent.	1811	AB27	197	161
Steuart, John	Deed to	Beall, Thomas & John M. Gantt	1793	A1-1	204	285
Steuart, Philip, Gen., Charles Co.	Deed fr	Middleton, Isaac S.	1816	AL36	549	512
Steuart, Samuel	Deed fr	Laird, John, of G'tn., exr.	1816	AL36	211	218
Steuart, William	Release fr	Richardson, Hannah, w/o John	1804	K10	349	361
Steuart, William	Agreement	Richardson, John, of NY	1804	K10	347	360
Steuart, William	Agreement	Jones, John G., of G'tn.	1808	U20	215	116
Steuart, William	Convey fr	Forrest, Joseph, trustee	1808	U20	247	132
Steuart, William	Deed to	Jones, John G.	1808	U20	230	124
Steuart, William	B. of S. to	Law, John	1811	Z25	535	425
Steuart, William	Agreement	Steuart, David	1811	AA26	051	040
Steuart, William	Assign to	Smith, John Kilty	1811	AB27	010	011
Steuart, William & Hellen et al	Deed to	Beall, Lewis	1803	K10	089	095
Steuart, William & Hellen	Deed to	Williams, Elisha O. & Harriot	1804	K10	190	199
Steuart, William & Hellen	Deed to	Mackall, Benjamin & Christiana	1804	K10	226	235
Steuart, William & Hellen	Deed to	Mackall, Christiana, of P.G. Co.	1804	L11	200	190
Steuart, William & Joseph Milligan	Deed to	Vinson, Charles	1812	AE30	027	021
Steuart, William et al	Deed fr	Shepperd, James G., of NC	1810	Z25	147	116
Steuart, William et al	Release fr	Shepperd, James Glascow, of NC	1810	Z25	150	118

Party	What	Party	Year	Liber	Old	New
Steuart, William et al	Deed fr	Magruder, George, collector, G'tn.	1810	Z25	205	161
Steuart, William et al	Deed fr	Mountz, Jacob, collector, of G'tn.	1811	AA26	052	041
Steuart, William, of B'burgh.	Deed fr	Polock, Isaac	1800	E5	212	206
Steuart, William, of G'tn.	Deed fr	Richardson, John, of NY	1804	K10	119	129
Steuart, William, of G'tn.	Bond fr	Williams, Elisha Owen, of G'tn.	1804	K10	225	234
Steuart, William, of G'tn.	Deed fr	Mackall, Benjamin & Christianna	1804	L11	198	189
Steuart, William, of G'tn.	Deed to	Jones, John G.	1809	W22	318	207
Steuart, William, of G'tn.	Deed to	Weems, Nathaniel T., of G'tn.	1810	Y24	021	018
Steuart, William, of G'tn. et al	Deed to	Shepperd, James G., of G'tn.	1810	Z25	175	139
Steuart, William, of G'tn.	D. of T. to	Peter, David, of G'tn.	1811	AA26	383	254
Steuart, William, of G'tn.	Deed to	Steuart, David, of G'tn.	1811	AA26	044	034
Steuart, William, of G'tn.	Deed to	Riddle, Joseph, of Alexa. et al	1811	Z25	385	303
Steuart, William, of G'tn.	Deed to	Steuart, David, of G'tn.	1812	AC28	133	100
Steuart, William, of G'tn.	Deed to	Steuart, David of G'tn.	1812	AC28	136	102
Stevens, Eleanor	B. of S. to	Simpson, Josias, Sr.	1816	AL36	258	259
Stevens, John	Deed fr	Smith, William, of Alexa.	1801	G7	229	306
Stevens, John	Relinquish fr	Smith, Sarah, w/o William	1801	G7	305	426
Stevens, John	Deed fr	Wayman, Charles	1802	I9	463	762
Stevens, John	Deed fr	Stoddert, Benjamin et al	1804	K10	269	275
Stevens, John, of Worcester Co.	Deed to	Elzey, Arnold	1805	N13	333	269
Stevens, John, of MD	Deed to	Elzey, Arnold	1806	Q16	022	014
Stevens, Samuel	Deed fr	Carroll, Daniel, of *Duddington*	1814	AG32	378	275
Stevens, Samuel	Lease fr	Law, Thomas	1816	AM37	502	368
Stevenson, James	Deed fr	Kilty, John & Josias Wilson King	1809	W22	029	022
Stewart, Adam Duncan, of VA	B. of S. fr	Stewart, William M., of G'tn.	1817	AN38	484	349
Stewart, Adam, of Liverpool, Eng.	Deed to	Afflick, Thomas, of G'tn.	1797	B2B	653	417
Stewart, Catherine	Cert Free to	Crusey, Betsey (C), age 33	1813	AF31	230	159
Stewart, Charles et al	Deed to	Beall, Thomas & John M. Gantt	1793	A1-1	348	453
Stewart, David	Lease fr	Law, Thomas	1817	AN38	318	232
Stewart, David, of Balto. et al	Deed to	Dorsey, William Hammond	1795	B2A	208	286
Stewart, David, of G'tn.	Deed fr	Beatty, John M. & Charles A.	1807	S18	023	020
Stewart, David, of G'tn.	Deed to	Stewart, William M., of G'tn.	1812	AC28	188	143
Stewart, David R.	Manumis to	[ ], Jim (Negro)	1802	I9		064
Stewart, David, trustee of Wm.	Mortgage to	Bowie, Washington	1812	AD29	509	430
Stewart, Deborah	Deed to	Scot, Sabret	1802	I9	425	705
Stewart, Deborah	Release to	Templeman, John et al	1806	P15	337	222
Stewart, John	Deed to	Williams, Jeremiah	1801	G7	297	414
Stewart, John	Deed fr	Renner, Daniel	1802	H8	047	045
Stewart, John	Lease fr	Thompson, Arthur	1814	AG32	007	006
Stewart, John	Lease fr	Van Ness, John P.	1815	AI34	528	532
Stewart, John	Deed to	Barron, James	1817	AO39	443	304
Stewart, John, of Frederick Co.	Deed fr	Bussard, Daniel, of G'tn.	1804	L11	147	148
Stewart, Richard	B. of S. to	Watterston, David	1809	V21	321	236
Stewart, Richard	Mortgage to	Caldwell, Elias B.	1816	AL36	271	270
Stewart, Sarah, of Balto.	Deed to	McCoull, Neil, of Richmond VA	1808	T19	141	101
Stewart, Walter, of Phila. PA	Cert fr	Commissioners of Washington	1793	B2A	300	421
Stewart, Walter, of Phila. PA	Deed fr	Chandler, Walter Story	1795	B2A	197	269
Stewart, Walter, of Phila. PA	Deed fr	Stoddert, Benjamin, of G'tn.	1795	B2A	240	335
Stewart, Walter, of Phila. PA	Deed fr	Stoddert, Benjamin, of G'tn.	1795	B2A	220	305
Stewart, William	Deed fr	Munroe, Thomas, Supt.	1802	I9	170	259
Stewart, William	Deed fr	Brent, Daniel C.	1802	I9	552	896
Stewart, William	Deed fr	Deakins, Francis	1802	I9	267	433
Stewart, William	Deed fr	Beatty, Charles, heirs of	1806	O14	274	181
Stewart, William	Cert Free to	[ ], Margaret (negro) and children	1807	S18	254	200
Stewart, William	B. of S. fr	Davis, Otho H., of G'tn.	1808	U20	404	226

Index to District of Columbia Land Records, 1792-1817

Party	What	Party	Year	Liber	Old	New
Stewart, William	Deed fr	Dorsey, William H., of Balto.	1809	W22	376	244
Stewart, William	Convey fr	Maxwell, George	1809	V21	405	308
Stewart, William	Deed to	Worthington, William	1810	Z25	129	101
Stewart, William & Helen	Deed to	Peter, Thomas et al	1809	X23	277	219
Stewart, William M.	Slave	From Fairvax Co. VA	1812	AC28	478	339
Stewart, William M., of G'tn.	Deed fr	Stewart, David, of G'tn.	1812	AC28	188	143
Stewart, William M., of G'tn.	B. of S. to	Stewart, Adam Duncan, of VA	1817	AN38	484	349
Stewart, William, of G'tn.	B. of S. fr	Wilson, Richard	1801	G7	219	293
Stewart, William, of G'tn.	Deed to	Barry, James	1802	H8	232	221
Stewart, William, of G'tn.	Deed to	Mackall, Leonard, of G'tn.	1807	S18	297	233
Stewart, William, of G'tn.	Deed fr	Beall, Margery, Frederick Co. VA	1808	T19	080	057
Stewart, William, of G'tn.	Deed fr	Garner, Joseph, of G'tn.	1810	Y24	020	017
Stewart, William, of G'tn.	B. of S. to	Ott, John, of G'tn.	1810	Z25	132	103
Stickell, Solomon	Deed fr	Doll, Margaret, d/o Conrad	1815	AI34	031	036
Stickney, John	Discharge	Bankruptcy	1802	H8	316	297
Stickney, John	Deed to	Stickney, Thomas, of MA	1802	H8	180	172
Stickney, John et al	P. of Atty. fr	Blodget, Samuel	1796	B2B	524	235
Stickney, John et al	Deed fr	Blodgett, Samuel, of Phila.	1801	G7	097	125
Stickney, Thomas, of MA	Deed fr	Stickney, John	1802	H8	180	172
Stille, John et al	Release to	Nourse, Joseph	1813	AF31	011	008
Stiner, Jacob, Jr.	Cert fr	Commissioners of Washington	1795	B2A	333	468
Stinger, Frederick	Deed fr	Mauro, Philip	1815	AK35	447	350
Stinger, Frederick	Deed fr	Burch, Samuel	1816	AM37	340	247
Stinger, Solomon	Deed to	Way, Andrew, Jr. et al	1808	U20	243	130
Stockwell, John	Deed to	Hyatt, Seth	1815	AI34	519	523
Stockwell, John	Deed to	Forrest, Joseph	1816	AM37	063	052
Stockwell, John, elder, of Amagh	Convey to	Stockwell, John, younger	1807	S18	069	058
Stockwell, John, younger	Convey fr	Stockwell, John, elder, of Armagh	1807	S18	069	058
Stockwell, Mark	Deed to	Pleasonton, Stephen	1801	G7	419	553
Stockwell, Mark	Deed fr	Worman, George, of Balto. Co.	1801	G7	315	441
Stockwell, Mark	Mortgage fr	Morin, Lewis	1801	G7	366	498
Stockwell, Mark	Lease fr	Gardner, John	1802	G7	587	736
Stockwell, Mark	Deed fr	Gardner, John	1802	H8	547	508
Stockwell, Mark	Deed fr	Munroe, Thomas, Supt.	1802	H8	544	504
Stockwell, Mark	Deed fr	Morin, Lewis	1802	I9	072	101
Stockwell, Mark	Deed to	Craver, Jacob	1804	K10	395	409
Stockwell, Mark	Release to	Morin, Lewis	1804	K10	308	312
Stockwell, Mark et al	Deed fr	Purcell, Pierce	1801	G7	377	509
Stockwell, Mark et al	Deed fr	Munroe, Thomas, Supt.	1802	I9	062	085
Stockwell, Mark et al	Deed fr	Pratt, Henry et al	1802	I9	217	342
Stockwell, Mark et al	Mortgage fr	Purcell, Pierce	1802	I9	066	092
Stockwell, Mark et al	P. of Atty. fr	Purcell, Pierce	1802	I9	233	372
Stockwell, Mark et al	Deed to	Purcell, Pierce	1803	K10	056	61
Stockwell, Mark, of G'tn.	Deed fr	Gardiner, John	1802	I9	089	127
Stockwell, Sarah, of Ire.	Deed to	Forrest, Joseph	1816	AM37	062	050
Stoddert, Benjamin	Deed fr	Tillotson, Thomas, of NY	1792	A1-1	113	165
Stoddert, Benjamin	Deed to	Beall, Thomas & John M. Gantt	1792	A1-1	005	8
Stoddert, Benjamin	Deed fr	Bachtel, Isaac, Washington Co.	1792	A1-1	166	238
Stoddert, Benjamin	Deed to	Gore, Christopher, of Boston	1793	A1-1	199	280
Stoddert, Benjamin	Deed fr	Orme, James & Lucy	1793	A1-2	463	70
Stoddert, Benjamin	Deed to	Beall, Thomas, of George	1794	A1-2	491	94
Stoddert, Benjamin	Deed fr	Beall, Thomas, s/o George	1794	B2A	059	074
Stoddert, Benjamin	Deed to	Sluby, Nicholas, of Balto.	1795	B2A	216	298
Stoddert, Benjamin	Deed to	Scott, Gustavus	1795	B2A	169	226
Stoddert, Benjamin	Freedom to	[ ], George (M) & Lizza	1795	B2A	204	279

Party	What	Party	Year	Liber	Old	New
Stoddert, Benjamin	Deed to	Polock, Isaac	1797	B2B	649	411
Stoddert, Benjamin	Mortgage to	Snowden, Thomas, of P.G. Co.	1797	B2B	623	381
Stoddert, Benjamin	Deed to	Beall, Thomas, of George	1798	C3	450	353
Stoddert, Benjamin	Agreement	Duncanson, William M.	1798	C3	451	355
Stoddert, Benjamin	Deed to	Lee, Thomas Sim	1798	D4	132	115
Stoddert, Benjamin	Deed to	Lee, Thomas Sim	1798	D4	134	116
Stoddert, Benjamin	Deed to	Foxall, Henry	1800	F6	090	055
Stoddert, Benjamin	Warrant to	Wadsworth, Charles	1800	F6	035	022
Stoddert, Benjamin	Deed to	Shaw, John, of Phila.	1801	F6	219	142
Stoddert, Benjamin	Deed fr	Commissioners of Washington	1801	F6	226	147
Stoddert, Benjamin	Deed to	Shaw, John, of Phila.	1801	F6	224	145
Stoddert, Benjamin	Deed to	Shaw, John, of Phila.	1801	F6	217	141
Stoddert, Benjamin	Deed to	Shaw, John, of Phila.	1801	F6	221	144
Stoddert, Benjamin	Deed fr	Commissioners of Washington	1801	G7	181	242
Stoddert, Benjamin	Deed fr	Commissioners of Washington	1801	G7	182	244
Stoddert, Benjamin	Deed fr	Commissioners of Washington	1801	G7	187	250
Stoddert, Benjamin	Deed fr	Commissioners of Washington	1801	G7	190	254
Stoddert, Benjamin	Deed fr	Commissioners of Washington	1801	G7	184	246
Stoddert, Benjamin	Relinquish fr	Forrest, Uriah	1801	G7	265	364
Stoddert, Benjamin	Deed fr	Forrest, Uriah & Samuel Hanson	1801	G7	330	461
Stoddert, Benjamin	Deed to	Wheeler, Luke & John Cowper	1801	G7	410	544
Stoddert, Benjamin	Deed to	Caucand, David, of Calvert Co.	1801	G7	241	323
Stoddert, Benjamin	Deed fr	Commissioners of Washington	1801	G7	455	591
Stoddert, Benjamin	Deed to	Gilless, Thomas Handy	1801	G7	081	104
Stoddert, Benjamin	Deed to	Bank of Columbia	1801	G7	353	484
Stoddert, Benjamin	Deed fr	Forrest, Uriah et al	1801	G7	113	144
Stoddert, Benjamin	Deed to	Harbaugh, Leonard	1801	G7	314	439
Stoddert, Benjamin	Deed fr	Commissioners of Washington	1802	H8	087	080
Stoddert, Benjamin	Deed fr	Commissioners of Washington	1802	H8	084	077
Stoddert, Benjamin	Release fr	Bank of Columbia	1802	H8	452	415
Stoddert, Benjamin	Deed fr	Templeman, John	1802	H8	451	414
Stoddert, Benjamin	Deed to	Peter, David, Thomas & Robert	1802	H8	301	284
Stoddert, Benjamin	Deed to	Williams, Thomas Owen	1802	H8	040	039
Stoddert, Benjamin	Deed fr	Commissioners of Washington	1802	H8	226	215
Stoddert, Benjamin	Deed fr	Munroe, Thomas, Supt.	1802	H8	541	501
Stoddert, Benjamin	Deed to	Evans, Evan	1802	H8	025	023
Stoddert, Benjamin	Manumis to	[ ], Phillis (Negro)	1802	H8	318	299
Stoddert, Benjamin	Deed fr	Commissioners of Washington	1802	H8	060	056
Stoddert, Benjamin	Deed fr	Munroe, Thomas, Supt.	1802	I9	304	498
Stoddert, Benjamin	Deed to	Gilhart, John	1802	I9	524	858
Stoddert, Benjamin	Deed fr	Deakins, Francis et al	1802	I9	248	400
Stoddert, Benjamin	Deed to	Armstrong, Andrew et al	1802	I9	523	856
Stoddert, Benjamin	Deed to	Cannon, John	1802	I9	224	355
Stoddert, Benjamin	Deed to	Voss, Nicholas	1802	I9	557	903
Stoddert, Benjamin	Deed fr	Lowry, Caesar	1802	I9	422	699
Stoddert, Benjamin	Deed to	Williamson, Catherine	1802	I9	337	556
Stoddert, Benjamin	Deed to	Gilpin, Bernard	1802	I9	375	623
Stoddert, Benjamin	Deed fr	Munroe, Thomas, Supt.	1802	I9	098	141
Stoddert, Benjamin	Deed to	Evans, Evan	1802	I9	288	471
Stoddert, Benjamin	Deed to	Gantt, Thomas T.	1802	I9	267	432
Stoddert, Benjamin	Deed to	Thomas, Richard	1802	I9	310	509
Stoddert, Benjamin	Deed fr	Turner, Thomas	1802	I9	333	550
Stoddert, Benjamin	Deed to	Key, Philip B.	1802	I9	265	429
Stoddert, Benjamin	Deed to	Clephan, Lewis	1802	I9	296	485
Stoddert, Benjamin	Deed fr	Beatty, Thomas J.	1802	I9	485	798

Index to District of Columbia Land Records, 1792-1817

Party	What	Party	Year	Liber	Old	New
Stoddert, Benjamin	Mortgage fr	Lee, Theoderick, of VA	1804	K10	372	386
Stoddert, Benjamin	Deed to	Van Bibber, Abraham, of Balto.	1804	K10	210	221
Stoddert, Benjamin	Deed to	Craig, John, of Phila.	1804	L11	321	294
Stoddert, Benjamin	Deed to	Thompson, William	1804	L11	160	158
Stoddert, Benjamin	Deed fr	Threlkeld, John	1804	M12	032	033
Stoddert, Benjamin	Deed fr	Voss, Nicholas	1804	K10	233	241
Stoddert, Benjamin	Deed to	Ward, John, of Charleston SC	1804	K10	292	293
Stoddert, Benjamin	Deed to	Peter, David et al	1805	M12	321	325
Stoddert, Benjamin	Deed fr	Bank of Columbia	1805	M12	334	338
Stoddert, Benjamin	Deed fr	Loundes, Francis	1805	M12	336	340
Stoddert, Benjamin	Deed fr	Smith, Walter	1805	M12	171	169
Stoddert, Benjamin	Deed to	Forrest, Uriah	1805	N13	001	001
Stoddert, Benjamin	Deed to	Laird, John & John Mason	1806	Q16	007	004
Stoddert, Benjamin	Deed fr	Beatty, Charles, heirs of	1806	P15	094	058
Stoddert, Benjamin	Deed to	West, Joseph	1806	P15	158	104
Stoddert, Benjamin	Deed to	Chandler, Walter S.	1807	Q16	392	301
Stoddert, Benjamin	Deed to	Johns, Leonard H.	1807	Q16	362	277
Stoddert, Benjamin	Deed fr	Lowndes, Charles, Jefferson Co.	1807	R17	328	249
Stoddert, Benjamin	Deed to	Johns, Richard	1807	R17	086	068
Stoddert, Benjamin	Deed fr	Bullus, John	1807	R17	330	251
Stoddert, Benjamin	Cert Free to	Cupid, Betzy and child	1807	S18	185	150
Stoddert, Benjamin	Deed fr	Lowndes, Francis et al	1807	S18	359	283
Stoddert, Benjamin	Deed fr	Lowndes, Francis et al	1807	S18	341	268
Stoddert, Benjamin	Agreement	Lowndes, Charles, Jefferson Co.	1807	S18	112	
Stoddert, Benjamin	Convey fr	Lee, Theodorick	1807	S18	103	083
Stoddert, Benjamin	P. of Atty. to	Mountz, John, of G'tn.	1809	X23	076	057
Stoddert, Benjamin	Cert to	Templeman, John	1809	X23	075	056
Stoddert, Benjamin	Deed to	Pairo, Thomas W.	1810	Y24	455	404
Stoddert, Benjamin	Cert Free to	Lee, Peter (negro)	1810	Y24	247	228
Stoddert, Benjamin	Deed fr	Blodget, Samuel	1811	AB27	022	021
Stoddert, Benjamin	Deed to	Mauro, Philip	1811	AC28	054	041
Stoddert, Benjamin & U. Forrest	Deed to	Carcand, David, of Calvert Co.	1792	A1-1	121	176
Stoddert, Benjamin & U. Forrest	Deed fr	Lower, Holstein, Ley & Spyker	1792	A1-1	151	217
Stoddert, Benjamin & John Mason	D. of T. fr	Taney, Francis Lewis, of G'tn.	1796	B2B	571	311
Stoddert, Benjamin & Rebecca	Deed to	Swan, Caleb	1801	G7	356	487
Stoddert, Benjamin, Bladensburg	Deed to	Shaw, Anne, of Annapolis	1810	Z25	064	047
Stoddert, Benjamin, Bladensburg	Deed to	Shoemaker, David	1811	AA26	326	219
Stoddert, Benjamin, Bladensburg	Release to	Wright, Matthew	1811	AB27	370	306
Stoddert, Benjamin, Bladensburg	Deed to	Foxall, Henry	1812	AC28	418	302
Stoddert, Benjamin, Esq., of G'tn.	Deed to	Mackall, Walter, Esq., Calvert Co.	1801	F6	154	095
Stoddert, Benjamin et al	Deed fr	Henderson, Richard	1792	A1-1	168	240
Stoddert, Benjamin et al	Deed fr	Pearce, Catherine, rel/o Benj. N.	1792	A1-1	063	93
Stoddert, Benjamin et al	Deed to	Beall, Thomas & John M. Gantt	1793	A1-1	227	314
Stoddert, Benjamin et al	Deed to	Beall, William Murdock	1793	A1-1	379	486
Stoddert, Benjamin et al	Deed to	French, William & John Marr	1793	A1-2	432	40
Stoddert, Benjamin et al	Deed to	Beall, John	1793	A1-1	378	485
Stoddert, Benjamin et al	Deed to	Thomas, Philip, of Frederick Co.	1793	A1-1	387	494
Stoddert, Benjamin et al	Deed fr	Funk, Jacob, of Jefferson Co. KY	1793	A1-1	189	268
Stoddert, Benjamin et al	Deed to	Flick, Andrew, of Orange Co. VA	1793	A1-1	294	392
Stoddert, Benjamin et al	Deed to	Hairy, David, exr. of Martin	1793	A1-1	338	442
Stoddert, Benjamin et al	Deed to	Williams, Thomas Owen	1793	A1-1	325	428
Stoddert, Benjamin et al	Deed to	Beall, James, s/o James	1793	A1-1	319	421
Stoddert, Benjamin et al	Deed to	King, William	1793	A1-2	419	28
Stoddert, Benjamin et al	Deed to	Chiswell, Joseph N.	1793	A1-2	424	33
Stoddert, Benjamin et al	Deed to	Peter, Robert, assignee of Wells	1793	A1-1	386	493

Party	What	Party	Year	Liber	Old	New
Stoddert, Benjamin et al	Deed to	Greenleaf, James, New York NY	1794	B2A	086	111
Stoddert, Benjamin et al	Deed to	Greenleaf, James, New York NY	1794	B2A	083	108
Stoddert, Benjamin et al	Deed to	Kershner, Martin	1794	B2A	162	214
Stoddert, Benjamin et al	Deed to	Thomas, Evan	1794	B2A	093	121
Stoddert, Benjamin et al	Deed to	Stone, John H.	1795	B2A	172	230
Stoddert, Benjamin et al	Deed fr	Blodget, Samuel, now of Phila.	1795	B2A	265	371
Stoddert, Benjamin et al	Deed to	Beall, Thomas, of George	1795	B2A	166	222
Stoddert, Benjamin et al	Receipt fr	Holston, George M.	1796	B2B	382	038
Stoddert, Benjamin et al	Deed fr	Threlkeld, John	1797	C3	260	213
Stoddert, Benjamin et al	Deed fr	King, Adam	1797	C3	262	214
Stoddert, Benjamin et al	Deed to	Davidson, Samuel	1797	B2B	613	369
Stoddert, Benjamin et al	Deed to	Mailey, Jacob, of Phila. PA	1797	B2B	667	434
Stoddert, Benjamin et al	Deed to	Waters, Jonathan	1799	D4	236	219
Stoddert, Benjamin et al	Deed to	Lenthall, John	1800	E5	308	299
Stoddert, Benjamin et al	Deed to	Thomas, Evan	1801	F6	168	105
Stoddert, Benjamin et al	Deed to	Shaw, John, of Phila.	1801	F6	214	139
Stoddert, Benjamin et al	Deed to	Wilson, John Custis, Somerset Co.	1801	G7	119	153
Stoddert, Benjamin et al	Lease to	Maitland, James & Thomas Taylor	1801	G7	276	381
Stoddert, Benjamin et al	Deed fr	Blodgett, Samuel, of Phila.	1801	G7	097	125
Stoddert, Benjamin et al	Deed to	Wilson, Samuel & John Dennis	1801	G7	117	150
Stoddert, Benjamin et al	Deed to	Lindsey, Adam	1801	G7	267	367
Stoddert, Benjamin et al	Lease to	Harris, John	1801	G7	194	259
Stoddert, Benjamin et al	Deed to	Alexander, John	1801	G7	150	198
Stoddert, Benjamin et al	Bond to	United States	1801	G7	347	478
Stoddert, Benjamin et al	Deed to	Forrest, Uriah	1802	G7	529	674
Stoddert, Benjamin et al	Deed to	Worthington, Charles	1802	H8	533	492
Stoddert, Benjamin et al	Deed to	Gillis, Thomas	1802	H8	483	444
Stoddert, Benjamin et al	Deed to	Bank of Columbia	1802	H8	386	358
Stoddert, Benjamin et al	Deed to	Polock, Isaac	1802	I9	198	308
Stoddert, Benjamin et al	Deed to	Hodnett, James	1802	I9	163	247
Stoddert, Benjamin et al	Deed to	Abbot, John	1802	I9	013	016
Stoddert, Benjamin et al	Deed to	Davidson, John	1804	L11	062	64
Stoddert, Benjamin et al	Deed to	Stevens, John	1804	K10	269	275
Stoddert, Benjamin et al	Deed fr	Carlon, James	1804	K10	370	384
Stoddert, Benjamin et al	Deed fr	Stewart, Deborah	1806	P15	337	222
Stoddert, Benjamin et al	Bond to	Commercial Co. of Washington	1808	U20	037	021
Stoddert, Benjamin et al	Deed to	Thompson, Mary	1813	AF31	045	031
Stoddert, Benjamin et al	Deed to	Ardrey, Robert	1813	AF31	007	005
Stoddert, Benjamin, of G'tn.	Deed fr	Beall, George	1793	A1-1	180	255
Stoddert, Benjamin, of G'tn.	Deed fr	Bayly, William	1794	B2A	099	129
Stoddert, Benjamin, of G'tn.	Deed fr	Lee, Thomas S., of Annapolis	1794	B2A	029	031
Stoddert, Benjamin, of G'tn.	Deed fr	Deakins, William, Jr., of G'tn.	1794	B2A	096	125
Stoddert, Benjamin, of G'tn.	Deed to	Pearce, Thomas, Isle of Wight Co.	1795	B2A	215	296
Stoddert, Benjamin, of G'tn.	Deed to	Stewart, Walter, of Phila.	1795	B2A	220	305
Stoddert, Benjamin, of G'tn.	Deed to	Stewart, Walter, of Phila.	1795	B2A	240	335
Stoddert, Benjamin, of G'tn.	Deed fr	Deakins, William, Jr., of G'tn.	1795	B2A	264	369
Stoddert, Benjamin, of G'tn.	Deed to	Taney, Francis Lewis, of G'tn.	1795	B2B	370	021
Stoddert, Benjamin, of G'tn.	Deed to	Casanave, Peter, of G'tn.	1796	B2B	519	228
Stoddert, Benjamin, of G'tn.	Deed to	Campbell, William, Frederick Co.	1797	C3	132	107
Stoddert, Benjamin, of G'tn.	Deed to	Campbell, William, of A.A. Co.	1797	B2B	684	458
Stoddert, Benjamin, of Montg. Co.	Deed fr	Beall, Patrick, of P.G. Co.	1797	B2B	656	419
Stoddert, Benjamin, of G'tn.	Deed fr	Spyker, Benjamin, of Reading PA	1798	C3	273	222
Stoddert, Benjamin, of G'tn.	Deed to	Forrest, Uriah, of Montg. Co.	1798	C3	453	357
Stoddert, Benjamin, of G'tn.	Deed to	Robertson, William, of G'tn.	1798	C3	277	224
Stoddert, Benjamin, of G'tn.	Deed to	Bayly, William, of P.G. Co.	1798	C3	515	405

Index to District of Columbia Land Records, 1792-1817

Party	What	Party	Year	Liber	Old	New
Stoddert, Benjamin, of G'tn.	Deed to	Forrest, Uriah, of Montg. Co.	1798	C3	379	303
Stoddert, Benjamin, of G'tn.	Deed to	Forrest, Uriah, of Montg. Co.	1798	C3	458	360
Stoddert, Benjamin, of G'tn.	Deed to	Key, Philip B.	1800	F6	083	051
Stoddert, Benjamin, of G'tn. et al	Lease to	Meade, Simon	1801	G7	202	269
Stoddert, Benjamin, of G'tn.	Deed to	Small, George, of York Co. PA	1801	G7	059	077
Stoddert, Benjamin, of G'tn.	Deed fr	Commissioners of Washington	1801	G7	312	435
Stoddert, Benjamin, of G'tn.	Deed fr	Commissioners of Washington	1801	G7	407	541
Stoddert, Benjamin, of G'tn.	Deed to	Boyer, Augustine & Richard M.	1801	G7	284	394
Stoddert, Benjamin, of G'tn.	Deed to	Deakins, Francis, devisee of Wm.	1801	G7		283
Stoddert, Benjamin, of G'tn.	Deed to	Deakins, Francis, devisee of Wm.	1801	G7	214	285
Stoddert, Benjamin, of G'tn.	Deed fr	Commissioners of Washington	1801	G7	310	433
Stoddert, Benjamin, of G'tn.	Deed to	Carmick, Daniel, Capt., of PA	1801	G7	333	463
Stoddert, Benjamin, of G'tn.	Deed fr	Commissioners of Washington	1801	G7	405	539
Stoddert, Benjamin, of G'tn.	Deed to	Stretch, Joseph	1801	G7	305	425
Stoddert, Benjamin, of G'tn.	Deed to	Holmes, William, of Charles Co.	1801	G7	248	335
Stoddert, Benjamin, of G'tn.	Deed to	Radcliffe, Sarah, Worcester Co.	1801	G7	318	446
Stoddert, Benjamin, of G'tn.	Deed to	Lovell, William	1801	G7	443	579
Stoddert, Benjamin, of G'tn.	Deed to	Duckworth, George	1802	G7	562	711
Stoddert, Benjamin, of G'tn.	Deed to	Thompson, William, of G'tn.	1802	H8	357	332
Stoddert, Benjamin, of G'tn.	Deed to	Berry, Zachariah, of MD	1802	H8	469	430
Stoddert, Benjamin, of G'tn.	Deed fr	Munroe, Thomas	1802	H8	431	396
Stoddert, Benjamin, of G'tn.	Deed to	Lowry, Ceasar, of G'tn.	1802	H8	487	448
Stoddert, Benjamin, of G'tn.	Deed fr	Munroe, Thomas	1802	H8	429	395
Stoddert, Benjamin, of G'tn.	Deed fr	Munroe, Thomas, Supr.	1802	I9	100	145
Stoddert, Benjamin, of G'tn.	Deed fr	Munroe, Thomas, Supt.	1802	I9	099	143
Stoddert, Benjamin, of G'tn.	Deed fr	Munroe, Thomas, Supt.	1802	I9	096	138
Stoddert, Benjamin, of G'tn.	Deed fr	Munroe, Thomas, Supr.	1802	I9	106	154
Stoddert, Benjamin, of G'tn.	Deed fr	Munroe, Thomas, Supt.	1802	I9	097	140
Stoddert, Benjamin, of G'tn.	Deed fr	Munroe, Thomas, Supr.	1802	I9	104	151
Stoddert, Benjamin, of G'tn.	Deed fr	Munroe, Thomas, Supr.	1802	I9	107	156
Stoddert, Benjamin, of G'tn.	Deed fr	Munroe, Thomas, Supr.	1802	I9	102	148
Stoddert, Benjamin, of G'tn.	Deed fr	Munroe, Thomas, Supt.	1802	I9	095	137
Stoddert, Benjamin, of G'tn.	Deed fr	Munroe, Thomas, Supr.	1802	I9	105	153
Stoddert, Benjamin, of G'tn.	Deed fr	Munroe, Thomas, Supr.	1802	I9	103	150
Stoddert, Benjamin, of G'tn.	Deed fr	Munroe, Thomas, Supt.	1802	I9	094	135
Stoddert, Benjamin, of G'tn.	Deed fr	Munroe, Thomas, Supr.	1802	I9	101	146
Stoddert, Benjamin, of G'tn.	Deed to	Ingraham, Nathaniel, of SC	1804	K10	392	407
Stoddert, Benjamin, of G'tn.	Deed to	Ward, John, of Charleston SC	1804	K10	293	293
Stoddert, Benjamin, of G'tn.	Deed to	Pairo, Thomas William, of G'tn.	1804	K10	173	182
Stoddert, Benjamin, of G'tn. et al	Deed to	Carlon, James	1804	K10	344	355
Stoddert, Benjamin, of G'tn.	Deed to	Bussard, Daniel, of G'tn.	1804	K10	106	113
Stoddert, Benjamin, of G'tn.	Deed to	Brown, Joel, of G'tn.	1804	L11	305	280
Stoddert, Benjamin, of G'tn. et al	Deed to	Backer, Henry, of G'tn.	1804	L11	389	346
Stoddert, Benjamin, of G'tn. et al	Deed to	Daws, Isaac, of G'tn.	1804	L11	390	347
Stoddert, Benjamin, of G'tn.	Deed to	Davis, Thomas, of G'tn.	1804	M12	033	034
Stoddert, Benjamin, of G'tn.	Deed fr	Templeman, John, of G'tn.	1805	M12	169	168
Stoddert, Benjamin, of G'tn.	Deed to	Gore, Christopher, of Boston MA	1805	M12	290	291
Stoddert, Benjamin, of G'tn.	Deed fr	Templeman, John, of G'tn.	1805	M12	167	166
Stoddert, Benjamin, of G'tn.	Deed fr	Chandler, Walter Story, of G'tn.	1805	M12	304	305
Stoddert, Benjamin, of G'tn.	Deed to	Alexander, Robert	1805	N13	220	189
Stoddert, Benjamin, of G'tn.	Deed to	Templeman, John, of G'tn.	1805	M12	151	147
Stoddert, Benjamin, of G'tn.	Deed fr	Caldwell, Elias B.	1806	P15	392	260
Stoddert, Benjamin, of G'tn.	Deed to	Smith, Clement, of G'tn.	1806	Q16	128	083
Stoddert, Benjamin, of G'tn.	Deed to	White, Patrick	1806	Q16	014	009
Stoddert, Benjamin, of G'tn.	Deed to	Grundey, George, of Balto. et al	1806	P15	393	263

Party	What	Party	Year	Liber	Old	New
Stoddert, Benjamin, of G'tn.	Deed fr	Smith, Walter, of G'tn.	1807	S18	110	089
Stoddert, Benjamin, of G'tn.	Deed to	Hindman, William, of Balto.	1807	R17	094	074
Stoddert, Benjamin, of G'tn.	Deed to	Rowles, Joseph E., of G'tn.	1807	Q16	402	309
Stoddert, Benjamin, of G'tn.	Deed to	Hines, John	1808	U20	308	164
Stoddert, Benjamin, of P.G. Co.	Deed to	Hines, Henry	1812	AD29	463	390
Stoddert, Benjamin, of G'tn.	Deed to	Mason, John & John Laird, G'tn.	1812	AD29	306	251
Stoker, Michael & Mary, of OH	Deed to	King, William, of Fairfield Co. OH	1812	AD29	379	319
Stoker, Michael, of Frederick Co.	Deed to	Meddart, Jacob, of Frederick Co.	1798	C3	480	378
Stokes, John	B. of S. to	Cross, Elie	1816	AL36	122	123
Stokes, John & James Ambush	B. of S. to	Cooper, John	1811	AB27	162	134
Stone, Ann, of G'tn.	Mortgage fr	Balmain, Nancy C., Fairfax Co. VA	1813	AE30	505	374
Stone, Edward	Deed fr	Balmain, Andrew	1807	S18	402	321
Stone, Edward	Deed fr	Beatty, Charles A.	1813	AF31	510	373
Stone, Edward	Deed fr	Upperman, Henry, Jr.	1813	AF31	525	386
Stone, Edward	Deed to	Corcoran, James, of G'tn.	1814	AG32	375	272
Stone, Edward	Deed to	Garner, Jesse	1814	AG32	092	069
Stone, Edward	Deed to	Kurtz, Daniel	1815	AK35	290	232
Stone, Edward	B. of S. to	Threlkeld, John	1817	AN38	048	039
Stone, Edward, of G'tn.	Deed fr	Pickerell, John, of G'tn.	1814	AG32	233	166
Stone, Edward, of G'tn.	Deed fr	Key, Philip B. & J.W. Clagett	1815	AK35	288	230
Stone, John H.	Deed fr	Stoddert, Benjamin et al	1795	B2A	172	230
Stone, John Hoskins, Annapolis	Deed fr	Scott, Gustavus, of Montg. Co.	1796	B2B	520	230
Stone, John Hoskins, of Balto.	Deed to	Johnson, Thomas, Frederick Co.	1800	E5	334	322
Stone, John Hoskins, of Balto.	Deed to	Peter, Robert, of G'tn.	1800	E5		325
Stone, John Hoskins, of Balto.	Deed to	Chandler, Walter Story	1800	E5	391	367
Stone, John Hoskins, of Balto.	Deed fr	Peter, Robert, of G'tn.	1800	E5	389	365
Stone, John, of Frederick Co.	Deed to	Johnson, Thomas, Frederick Co.	1792	A1-1	057	84
Stone, Mathew, of Charles Co.	Manumis to	[ ], Ann [Short] (Negro)	1806	P15	266	175
Stone, Mathew, of Charles Co.	Manumis to	[ ], David [Baise] (Negro)	1806	P15	266	175
Stone, Mathew, of Charles Co.	Manumis to	[ ], Peter (Negro)	1806	P15	266	175
Stone, Mathew, of Charles Co.	Manumis to	[ ], Thomas [Rustin] (Negro)	1806	P15	266	175
Stone, Zephaniah, of P.G. Co.	Deed fr	Owens, Josiah	1807	R17	172	132
Stoner, Christian et al	Deed to	Stoner, Stephen, of Frederick Co.	1810	Z25	182	144
Stoner, David, of Frederick Co.	Deed to	Stoner, Stephen, of Frederick Co.	1810	Z25	188	148
Stoner, Frederick et al	Deed to	Stoner, Stephen, of Frederick Co.	1810	Z25	182	144
Stoner, Henry & Stephen	Deed fr	Davidson, John, of Annapolis	1807	Q16	379	291
Stoner, Henry et al	Deed to	Stoner, Stephen, of Frederick Co.	1810	Z25	182	144
Stoner, Stephen & Henry	Deed fr	Davidson, John, of Annapolis	1807	Q16	379	291
Stoner, Stephen, Col., s/o John	Deed to	McCleary, Henry	1812	AC28	490	348
Stoner, Stephen, Frederick Co.	Deed fr	Wisenall, Bernard, Jefferson Co.	1811	AA26	174	120
Stoner, Stephen, of Frederick Co.	Deed fr	Stoner, Henry et al	1810	Z25	182	144
Stoner, Stephen, of Frederick Co.	Deed fr	Stoner, David, of Frederick Co.	1810	Z25	188	148
Stonestreet, Eleanor	B. of S. fr	Rider, William	1805	M12	319	323
Stooker, Michael & Thomas Price	Deed to	Beall, Thomas & John M. Gantt	1792	A1-1	106	154
Stott, Ebenezer, of Petersburgh	B. of S. fr	Knapp, John	1810	Z25	094	072
Stott, Ebenezer, of Petersburg	Deed fr	Knapp, John & Thomas Munroe	1817	AO39	427	291
Stout, Jacob, of G'tn.	Deed to	Brown, Joel & John Pickrell, G'tn.	1816	AM37	470	339
Stras, George F., of VA	Deed fr	Bayly, William	1799	D4	339	326
Stras, George Fredk. & Martha	Deed to	Currie, James	1807	Q16	215	145
Street, Catherine	B. of S. fr	Kale, John	1802	H8	006	006
Stretch, Joseph	Deed fr	Stoddert, Benjamin, of G'tn.	1801	G7	305	425
Stretch, Joseph	Deed fr	Commissioners of Washington	1801	G7	034	044
Stretch, Joseph	Deed fr	Rinehart, Andrew	1802	I9	421	698
Stretch, Joseph	Deed fr	Rinehart, Andrew	1805	N13	323	260
Stretch, Joseph	Deed fr	Melvin, James	1816	AL36	361	350

Index to District of Columbia Land Records, 1792-1817

Party	What	Party	Year	Liber	Old	New
Stretch, Joseph	Deed to	Moulder, John N.	1817	AO39	126	096
Stretch, Joseph et al	B. of S. fr	Sprogell, Thomas Yorke	1808	T19	400	283
Stretch, Joseph et al	Deed fr	Sutton, Robert & Catharine	1809	V21	178	128
Strever, Joachim, of Frederick Co.	Deed to	Beall, Thomas & John M. Gantt	1792	A1-1	094	137
Stricker, George, of Frederick Co.	Deed fr	Funk, Jacob, of P.G. Co., yeoman	1811	Z25	425	333
Stricker, George, of Ohio Co. VA	Deed to	Stricker, John, of Balto.	1811	Z25	428	336
Stricker, John, of Balto.	Deed fr	Stricker, George, of Ohio Co. VA	1811	Z25	428	336
Stringer, Solomon et al	Deed fr	Munroe, Thomas, Supt.	1807	R17	315	239
Strong, Benjamin & Elizabeth	Deed to	Hines, Christian & Matthew	1817	AO39	193	142
Strong, Joseph et al	Deed to	Myer, Solomon	1807	R17	316	240
Strong, Joseph, of Phila. et al	Deed fr	Dorsey, William Hammond	1804	L11	064	66
Strong, Joseph, of Phila. et al	Deed fr	Bullus, John, Dr.	1804	L11	066	68
Stuart, Charles	Deed to	Beall, Thomas & John M. Gantt	1793	A1-1	247	337
Stuart, David et al	Com to	Gantt, John M.	1792	A1-1	001	1
Stuart, David et al	Agreement	Greenleaf, James	1794	B2A	070	090
Stuart, David et al	Assign to	United States for Seat of Gov.	1794	B2A	121	162
Stuart, David, of G'tn.	Deed to	Brashears, Trueman, of Alexa.	1812	AB27	529	432
Stuart, Deborah	Deed to	Scott, Deborah	1802	I9	187	289
Stuart, Deborah	Deed to	Scott, Sabret	1802	I9	186	286
Stuart, Walter, of Phila. PA	Cert fr	Commissioners of Washington	1793	B2A	302	424
Stuart, Walter, of Phila. PA	Cert fr	Commissioners of Washington	1793	B2A	303	425
Stuart, Walter, of Phila. PA	Cert fr	Commissioners of Washington	1793	B2A	303	425
Stuart, Walter, of Phila. PA	Cert fr	Commissioners of Washington	1793	B2A	302	423
Stuart, Walter, of Phila. PA	Cert fr	Commissioners of Washington	1793	B2A	303	426
Stuart, Walter, of Phila. PA	Cert fr	Commissioners of Washington	1793	B2A	301	422
Stuart, Walter, of Phila. PA	Cert fr	Commissioners of Washington	1793	B2A	302	424
Stuart, William & Hellen	Deed fr	Williams, Elisha O. et al	1804	K10	185	194
Stull, John J., of G'tn.	Deed to	Smith, Clement	1816	AM37	473	341
Stull, John J. & John S. Williams	Ship List	Loockerman, John	1817	AN38	143	105
Stull, John J. & John S. Williams	D. of T. to	Loockerman, John	1817	AN38	130	096
Sullivan, Murto, of VA	Deed fr	Commissioners of Washington	1802	I9	063	087
Summers, Lewis	Deed fr	Munroe, Thomas, Supt.	1802	I9	178	271
Summers, Thomas	Lease fr	Carleton, Joseph, of G'tn.	1806	P15	072	044
Summers, Thomas	Deed fr	Prout, William	1808	U20	055	032
Summers, Thomas	Deed to	Young, Thomas	1810	Z25	081	061
Summers, Thomas	Release to	Carleton, Joseph, of G'tn.	1813	AE30	158	124
Suter, Alexander	Deed fr	Thomson, George, of G'tn. et al	1806	Q16	316	242
Suter, Alexander	Deed fr	Thomson, George, of G'tn.	1806	Q16	318	243
Suter, Alexander	Deed fr	Magruder, George, collector, G'tn.	1807	S18	037	030
Suter, Alexander	Deed to	Hampton, Roderick, a black man	1812	AB27	539	440
Suter, Alexander	Deed fr	Shorter, John & Gerrard Morris	1812	AD29	291	240
Suter, Alexander	Deed fr	Davidson, Lewis Grant	1814	AH33	351	304
Suter, Alexander	Deed to	Clagett, William W.	1814	AH33	293	254
Suter, Alexander	Deed to	Magruder, Ninian	1814	AG32	276	196
Suter, Alexander	Deed to	English, David	1815	AH33	409	353
Suter, Alexander	D. of T. to	English, David	1816	AL36	052	053
Suter, Alexander	Deed fr	King, Vincent	1816	AM37	033	027
Suter, Alexander	Deed fr	Joncherez, Alexander L., of G'tn.	1816	AM37	032	026
Suter, Alexander	Deed to	English, David	1816	AM37	179	135
Suter, Alexander	Deed to	Nevitt, William, of P. G. Co.	1817	AN38	197	143
Suter, Alexander et al	Cert fr	Commissioners of Washington	1797	B2B	463	154
Suter, Alexander, of G'tn.	Deed to	Patterson, Edgar, of G'tn.	1809	V21	205	144
Suter, Alexander, of G'tn.	Agreement	Nourse, Charles J., of G'tn.	1810	Y24	213	195
Suter, Alexander, of G'tn.	Deed fr	Doughty, William, of G'tn.	1811	Z25	505	401
Suter, Alexander, of G'tn.	Deed to	Shorter, John	1812	AD29	293	241

Party	What	Party	Year	Liber	Old	New
Suter, Alexander, of G'tn.	Deed to	Morris, Gerrard (C), of G'tn.	1812	AD29	423	356
Suter, Alexander, of G'tn.	Deed fr	Pickerell, John, of G'tn.	1813	AF31	171	115
Suter, Alexander, of G'tn.	Deed fr	Webster, Toppan	1813	AF31	005	003
Suter, Alexander, of G'tn.	Deed to	Barker, Thomas (C), of G'tn.	1813	AF31	119	080
Suter, Alexander, of G'tn.	Deed fr	Fresh, William, of G'tn.	1814	AG32	201	140
Suter, Alexander, of G'tn.	B. of S. to	Moulder, John M.	1816	AL36	103	103
Suter, Barbara	Deed to	Smith, Richard, of G'tn.	1816	AM37	466	335
Suter, Barbara	B. of S. to	Smith, Harriot	1816	AM37	227	167
Suter, John	Deed to	Thomson, George	1802	I9	556	901
Suter, John	Deed to	Davidson, Samuel	1802	I9	590	956
Suter, John	Deed to	Thomson, George	1802	I9	554	899
Suter, John & Richard his son	Deed fr	Davidson, Samuel, of G'tn.	1806	Q16	243	167
Suter, John et al	Deed fr	King, Nicholas	1805	M12	093	086
Suter, John, insolvent	Deed to	McCormick, Alexander, trustee	1806	P15	360	239
Suter, John, Jr. et al	Cert fr	Commissioners of Washington	1797	B2B	463	154
Suter, John, of G'tn.	Assign fr	Contee, Richard	1797	B2B	463	154
Suter, John, of G'tn. et al	Deed to	Suter, Alexander	1806	Q16	316	242
Suter, Jon	Deed fr	Davidson, Samuel	1802	H8	026	025
Suter, Margaret et al	Cert fr	Commissioners of Washington	1797	B2B	463	154
Suter, Robert et al	Cert fr	Commissioners of Washington	1797	B2B	463	154
Sutherland, George	B. of S. to	Cochrane, Alexander	1808	T19	103	073
Sutherland, Thomas J.	Deed fr	Moore, George	1813	AF31	526	387
Sutherland, Thomas J.	B. of S. fr	Preston, John	1814	AH33	014	013
Sutherland, Thomas Janey	Assign fr	Clarke, Eliza & John McGowan	1814	AH33	316	273
Sutherland, Thomas Jenny	Assign fr	Mudd, Theodore, of Charles Co.	1811	AC28	079	060
Sutorius, Mary Ann	B. of S. to	Sutorius, Thomas, s/o Mary Ann	1804	L11	104	107
Sutorius, Mary Ann	B. of S. to	Gibson, Thomas, of G'tn.	1804	L11	101	107
Sutorius, Thomas, s/o Mary Ann	B. of S. fr	Sutorius, Mary Ann	1804	L11	104	107
Suttle, Henry	Deed fr	Johns, Richard	1807	R17	276	210
Suttle, Henry	Deed fr	Johns, Richard	1809	W22	049	036
Suttle, Henry	B. of S. fr	Hoyt, Ephraim J.	1810	Y24	479	424
Suttle, Henry, of G'tn.	Mortgage fr	Miller, Robert	1805	N13	359	289
Suttle, Henry, of G'tn.	Deed fr	Dermott, James R.	1810	X23	391	314
Suttle, Henry, of G'tn.	Deed fr	Jones, Charles	1810	Y24	105	095
Suttle, Henry, of G'tn.	Deed to	Gannan, James, of G'tn.	1812	AC28	437	313
Suttle, Henry, of G'tn.	Deed to	Lufborough, Nathan	1812	AD29	343	286
Suttle, Henry, of G'tn.	Deed to	Mason, John, of G'tn.	1813	AE30	106	081
Suttle, Henry, plt.	Suit	Bird, Thomas & Alice et al, def.	1810	X23	390	314
Suttle, Henry, trustee	Deed to	Washington, George C.	1811	AA26	038	029
Sutton, John, Jr.	Deed to	Sutton, Robert	1805	M12	183	184
Sutton, Margaret, d/o Thomas	Deed Gift fr	Sutton, Thomas	1814	AH33	207	187
Sutton, Robert	Deed fr	Commissioners of Washington	1798	C3	482	380
Sutton, Robert	Deed fr	Abert, Philip	1804	L11	155	154
Sutton, Robert	Deed fr	Clephan, Lewis	1804	L11	041	40
Sutton, Robert	Deed fr	Sutton, John, Jr.	1805	M12	183	184
Sutton, Robert	Deed to	Bussard, Daniel	1805	N13	390	311
Sutton, Robert & Catharine	Deed to	Stretch, Joseph et al	1809	V21	178	128
Sutton, Robert & Catharine, def.	Suit	Litle, John, plt.	1809	V21	178	128
Sutton, Robert, of PA	Deed to	Crandell, George & Ninian Beall	1810	Y24	303	276
Sutton, Thomas	Deed Gift to	Sutton, Margaret, d/o Thomas	1814	AH33	207	187
Swan, Caleb	Deed fr	Stoddert, Benjamin & Rebecca	1801	G7	356	487
Swan, Caleb et al	Partition		1804	K10	306	310
Swan, John	Deed fr	Balch, Stephen B.	1807	R17	390	295
Swan, Maria	Convey to	Thomas, Mathew	1807	S18	059	049
Swank, John	Lease fr	Prout, William	1801	G7	441	577

Party	What	Party	Year	Liber	Old	New
Swann, John, Esq., of Balto.	Deed fr	Forrest, Uriah	1800	E5	400	374
Swann, John, of Balto.	Deed fr	Commissioners of Washington	1800	E5	397	372
Swann, Margaret	Cert Free fr	Smoot, John N.	1810	Z25	114	089
Swann, Mary	Cert Free fr	Dent, William, Sr.	1810	Z25	114	089
Swann, Thomas, of Alexa.	Deed fr	Lowndes, Francis, of G'tn.	1810	Z25	144	114
Swann, Thomas, of Alexa. et al	Deed to	Muncaster, John, of Alexa.	1811	AB27	00½	001
Swann, Thomas, of Alexa.	Deed to	Magruder, Ninian, Dr., of G'tn.	1812	AD29	071	051
Swann, Thomas, of Alexa.	Deed fr	Veitch, Richard & Eliz., of Alexa.	1814	AG32	385	280
Swann, William T., of P.G. Co.	Mortgage fr	Compton, Henry T.	1810	Y24	494	435
Swann, William T., of P.G. Co.	D. of T. fr	Compton, Henry T.	1810	Y24	492	434
Swann, William T., of Alexa. Co.	B. of S. to	Poor, John	1812	AD29	133	102
Swearingan, Elemeleck	Deed to	Mitchell, John, of G'tn.	1797	B2B	669	436
Swearingan, Thomas, Sr.	Deed to	Carleton, Joseph, of G'tn.	1794	A1-2	497	100
Sweeny, George	Deed fr	Blagden, George	1810	Y24	532	467
Sweeny, George	Partition	Holtzman, Samuel & Sarah	1812	AD29	280	230
Sweeny, George	D. of T. to	Glover, Charles	1813	AF31	529	390
Sweeny, George	D. of T. to	Glover, Charles	1815	AI34	065	073
Sweeny, George	Cert Slave	From Prince William Co. VA	1816	AK35	498	392
Sweeny, George	Marriage	Hooe, Mary S.C., d/o Bernard, Jr.	1816	AK35	498	392
Sweeny, George	Deed fr	Kid, Robert, mer., of Phila.	1817	AO39	249	180
Sweeny, George & Sarah	Cert fr	Commissioners of Washington	1797	B2B	459	148
Sweeny, Mary	Transfer fr	Jones, Charles	1797	B2B	459	148
Swett, Samuel	B. of S. to	Woodward, Salem	1817	AN38	451	324
Swift, Jonathan, of Alexa.	Deed fr	Smith, William, of Loudoun Co. VA	1807	S18	092	075
Swinton, Archibald, in Scot.	P. of Atty. to	Traquair, James, Phila. et al	1808	U20	312	166
Symmons, John	B. of S. to	Thomas, Elizabeth & James	1809	W22	360	233

Party	What	Party	Year	Liber	Old	New
T						
Tabbs, Barton	Deed fr	Munroe, Thomas, Supt.	1802	I9	052	071
Tailor, George	B. of S. fr	Tailor, Moses	1814	AH33	281	245
Tailor, Moses	B. of S. to	Tailor, George	1814	AH33	281	245
Talbert, Alexander	Slaves	From Anne Arundel Co. MD	1812	AC28	241	179
Talbert, Alexander	B. of S. fr	Magill, William	1815	AI34	179	204
Talbert, Bazil, of P.G. Co.	B. of S. to	Mayer, Henry & Wm. Y. Wetzell	1808	T19	324	236
Talbert, Lewin & Osborn Warner	Deed fr	Davis, George S. & Ann	1811	AA26	001	001
Talbert, McKenzie	Deed fr	Moxley, Daniel, of P.G. Co.	1816	AL36	441	419
Talbot, Bazil et al	Deed fr	Willson, James	1802	H8	495	455
Talbot, George W., of NY	Deed to	Blake, James H.	1816	AM37	317	231
Talbott, Basil	Deed fr	Wilson, James	1802	I9	137	206
Talbott, Charles	Cert fr	Commissioner of Public Buildings	1817	AO39	464	319
Talbott, George W., of NY et al	Deed fr	Templeman, John	1802	I9	126	186
Talbott, Lewin et al	Mortgage to	Addison, Thomas Grafton et al	1804	K10	144	156
Talburt, Lewin	Deed to	Talburt, Zadock	1809	X23	059	044
Talburt, Lewin	Deed fr	Talburt, Zadock	1809	X23	058	043
Talburt, Lewin et al	Deed fr	Hanson, Samuel, of Samuel	1807	R17	127	099
Talburt, Lewin et al	Deed fr	Addison, Daniel Dulany, Annapolis	1808	T19	072	053
Talburt, Lewis et al	Deed to	Addison, Daniel Dulaney	1808	T19	083	060
Talburt, Zadock	Deed to	Talburt, Lewin	1809	X23	058	043
Talburt, Zadock	Deed fr	Talburt, Lewin	1809	X23	059	044
Talburtt, Lewin	Deed fr	Venable, William	1811	AB27	211	172
Talbutt, Levin	Deed fr	Venable, William	1809	W22	033	025
Talbutt, Lewin	B. of S. fr	Venable, William	1809	W22	127	091
Talton, Edward & John	Deed fr	Kearney, John	1801	G7	056	072
Taney, Arsene Berenice, wid/o L.	Deed to	Murdock, John, of G'tn.	1805	M12	102	095
Taney, Francis Lewis, of G'tn.	Deed fr	Stoddert, Benjamin, of G'tn.	1795	B2B	370	021
Taney, Francis Lewis, Montg. Co.	Deed fr	Deakins, William, Jr., Montg. Co.	1796	B2B	514	220
Taney, Francis Lewis, of G'tn.	D. of T. to	Stoddert, Benjamin & John Masn	1796	B2B	571	311
Taney, Francis Lewis, mer., G'tn.	Deed to	Mason, John, mer., G'tn.	1796	B2B	444	127
Taney, Francis Lewis, of G'tn.	Deed fr	Reid, James, merchant, of G'tn.	1799	D4	328	314
Taney, Francis Lewis	Cert fr	Cranch, William	1801	G7	337	468
Tanner, Lethe (yellow)	Manumis fr	Daugherty, Joseph	1810	Y24	370	335
Tanner, Mary Ann, of G'tn.	B. of S. fr	Crocken, James, of G'tn.	1817	AN38	538	391
Tanner, Pierce L., of Alexa.	Deed fr	Dermott, James R.	1802	H8	574	537
Tate, Andrew	Deed fr	Bradley, Phineas	1814	AG32	283	203
Tate, Andrew	Deed to	Brown, Obadiah Bruen	1816	AL36	514	482
Tayler, Thomas et al	Lease fr	Prout, William	1806	P15	139	090
Tayloe, John	Deed fr	Deakins, Francis, devisee of Wm.	1801	G7	409	543
Tayloe, John	Deed fr	Deakins, Francis	1802	H8	068	063
Tayloe, John		Certificate of Slaves	1802	H8	374	347
Tayloe, John	Deed fr	Polock, Abigail, of Montg. Co.	1804	K10	148	160
Tayloe, John	Deed fr	Dorsey, William H., of G'tn.	1804	K10	263	269
Tayloe, John	Deed fr	Holburne, William	1806	O14	385	257
Tayloe, John	Deed to	Dorsey, William H., of G'tn.	1806	P15	362	241
Tayloe, John	B. of S. to	Kedgelie, Ann	1810	Y24	118	108
Tayloe, John	Release to	Dorsey, William H., of Balto. Co.	1810	Z25	014	011
Tayloe, John	Deed fr	McCormick, James, Jr.	1811	AB27	093	076
Tayloe, John	Deed fr	Glover, Charles & Richard Forrest	1815	AK35	120	093
Tayloe, John	Deed fr	Webster, Toppan	1816	AM37	490	357
Tayloe, John	Deed fr	Webster, Toppan	1816	AL36	229	234
Tayloe, John & Thomas Munroe	Mortgage fr	Granger, Gideon	1811	AB27	081	068
Tayloe, John & Thomas Munroe	Release to	Granger, Gideon	1812	AE30	013	011
Tayloe, John, Col.	Deed fr	Brodeau, Ann	1815	AK35	100	077

Party	What	Party	Year	Liber	Old	New
Tayloe, John, Col.	Deed fr	Worthington, William, Jr.	1816	AM37	188	141
Tayloe, John, Col.	Deed to	Worthington, William, Jr.	1816	AM37	329	239
Tayloe, John et al	Deed fr	Bickley, Robert S., Bucks Co. PA	1817	AN38	564	411
Tayloe, John, of VA	Deed fr	Scott, Gustavus	1797	B2B	683	457
Tayloe, John, of VA	Deed fr	White, James, of Montg. Co.	1804	K10	165	176
Tayloe, John, of G'tn.	Deed fr	Dorsey, William H., of G'tn.	1806	Q16	129	084
Tayloe, John, of VA	Deed fr	Lee, Henry, of VA	1807	S18	152	124
Tayloe, John, Richmond Co. VA	Deed fr	Thompson, Jonah et al	1804	K10	150	162
Tayloe, John, Richmond Co. VA	Deed to	Worthington, Charles, of G'tn.	1808	U20	120	069
Tayloe, William et al	Deed fr	Love, Charles, of G'tn.	1806	P15	135	088
Taylor, Elizabeth	Mortgage fr	Scamm, John	1804	K10	258	264
Taylor, George et al	Deed fr	Wadsworth, Charles & Elizabeth	1810	Y24	001	001
Taylor, George, of Fairfax Co. VA	Deed to	Butler, Silas	1810	Y24	326	296
Taylor, James	Slaves	From NC	1814	AH33	299	258
Taylor, James, late of Phila. PA	Deed fr	Lewis, George, of New York NY	1806	Q16	153	101
Taylor, James M., of Phila. et al	Deed fr	Underwood, Robert	1807	S18	117	095
Taylor, James N., of Phila. et al	Mortgage fr	Ellis, Robert	1801	G7	390	523
Taylor, James N. & Henry Toland	Deed fr	Kearney, John & Edward Fallon	1804	K10	139	151
Taylor, James N., of Phila. et al	Deed fr	Brent, Daniel Carroll, marshal	1805	O14	140	091
Taylor, James N. et al	Deed fr	Underwood, Robert	1806	P15	142	092
Taylor, James, of Southwark	Deed to	Cotterill, Thomas, mer., of NY	1810	Y24	247	228
Taylor, John	Deed fr	Polock, Isaac	1802	I9	194	302
Taylor, John	Deed to	Hoban, James	1802	I9	234	374
Taylor, John	Deed fr	Dorsey, William H.	1802	I9	195	303
Taylor, John	Deed fr	Herty, Thomas	1807	S18	148	121
Taylor, John & Margaret	Deed to	Brady, Nathaniel	1811	AB27	070	059
Taylor, John, late of Charles Co.	B. of S. to	Coombe, Griffith	1815	AI34	377	404
Taylor, John, tobacconist	Indenture fr	Hurley, Lanty, s/o Cornelius	1811	AB27	322	265
Taylor, John, trustee	Deed fr	Prout, William	1813	AF31	184	124
Taylor, Josias & Thomas	Deed fr	Corporation of Washington	1815	AI34	354	385
Taylor, Josias & Thomas	Deed fr	Corporation of Washington	1815	AI34	356	387
Taylor, Josias et al	Deed fr	Templeman, John, of Allegany Co.	1807	S18	311	244
Taylor, Mary, for son Cornelious	Indenture to	Reeder, John, turner	1811	AB27	238	195
Taylor, Robert	Deed fr	King, Charles	1817	AN38	001	001
Taylor, Robert I., of Alexa.	D. of T. fr	Brashears, Trueman, of Alexa.	1812	AB27	533	435
Taylor, Robert I., of Alexa.	D. of T. to	Sanderson, James, of Alexa.	1813	AE30	070	053
Taylor, Samuel, farmer, of PA	Mortgage to	Milliken, Mark, carpenter	1798	D4	138	121
Taylor, Samuel, of PA	Deed fr	Milliken, Mark, carpenter	1798	D4	126	109
Taylor, Thomas	Agreement	King, William	1797	C3	071	59
Taylor, Thomas	Deed fr	Corporation of Washington	1815	AI34	361	391
Taylor, Thomas	Deed fr	Corporation of Washington	1815	AI34	359	389
Taylor, Thomas & Thomas Young	Deed fr	Vidler, Edward	1807	R17	311	236
Taylor, Thomas & Jonas	Deed fr	Kerby, John Baptist	1809	V21	257	183
Taylor, Thomas & Josias	Deed fr	Corporation of Washington	1815	AI34	354	385
Taylor, Thomas & Sarah	Deed to	Way, John, of New Castle Co. DE	1815	AK35	224	176
Taylor, Thomas & Josias	Deed fr	Corporation of Washington	1815	AI34	356	387
Taylor, Thomas & Josiah	Deed to	Medtart, Jacob, of Fredk. Co.	1817	AN38	544	396
Taylor, Thomas et al	Lease fr	Stoddert, Benjamin et al	1801	G7	276	381
Taylor, Thomas, Jr. et al	Deed fr	Templeman, John, of Allegany Co.	1807	S18	311	244
Taylor, Thomas, Jr.	Deed to	Smith, Thomas	1816	AL36	319	314
Taylor, William	Deed to	Eliason, Ebenezer	1802	I9	458	755
Teackle, John	Slaves	From Accomack Co. VA	1808	T19	371	265
Teackle, John, Jr., now of G'tn.	Deed fr	Mason, John Thomson, Wash. Co.	1808	T19	036	028
Teackle, John, of G'tn.	Deed to	Worthington, Charles, Dr., of G'tn.	1810	Z25	356	278
Teackle, Littleton D., of MD	Deed fr	Walker, Zachariah	1813	AF31	294	209

Index to District of Columbia Land Records, 1792-1817

Party	What	Party	Year	Liber	Old	New
Teackle, Littleton Dennis, Som.	Mortgage to	Campbell, William, Frederick Co.	1806	Q16	207	140
Teackle, Littleton Dennis, Som.	Deed to	Banker, Charles Nicole, of Phila.	1808	T19	165	117
Teackle, Littleton Dennis, Som.	Deed to	Banker, Charles Nicole, Phila. Co.	1808	T19	034	026
Teackle, Littleton Dennis, of MD	Deed to	Banker, Charles Nicole, Phila. Co.	1810	Y24	396	358
Teakle, John, Sr., Accomack Co.	Deed fr	Mason, John Thomson, late G'tn.	1811	AA26	017	013
Teakle, Littleton Dennis, Som. Co.	Deed fr	Polock, Isaac	1806	P15	220	147
Teakle, Littleton Dennis, Som. Co.	Deed fr	Campbell, William, Frederick Co.	1806	P15	227	151
Tebbs, William P.	Release to	Polock, Isaac	1798	D4	114	098
Tebbs, William P.	Mortgage fr	Polock, Isaac	1798	D4	023	019
Teitizen, Henry	B. of S. fr	Howe, Ignatius	1812	AD29	340	284
Teitjen, Henry	Deed fr	Law, John	1809	W22	095	069
Teitjen, Henry	Deed fr	Law, John	1812	AD29	230	189
Templeman, George, Allegany Co.	Deed fr	Boyd, Washington, collector	1815	AI34	335	367
Templeman, George, Allegany Co.	Deed to	Gilpin, Bernard, of Montg. Co.	1816	AK35	486	382
Templeman, John	Deed fr	Bayly, William & William Deakins	1794	B2A	097	127
Templeman, John	Agreement	Polock, Isaac	1795	B2A	216	299
Templeman, John	Cert fr	Commissioners of Washington	1795	B2A	335	471
Templeman, John	Deed fr	Commissioners of Washington	1798	C3	287	232
Templeman, John	Lease to	Harris, John	1801	G7	194	259
Templeman, John	Agreement	Tillotson, Thomas, of NY	1801	G7	120	154
Templeman, John	Lease to	Maitland, James & Thomas Taylor	1801	G7	276	381
Templeman, John	Deed fr	Forrest, Uriah et al	1801	G7	038	049
Templeman, John	Lease fr	Deterly, John	1801	G7	345	476
Templeman, John	D. of T. fr	Duncanson, William Mayne	1801	G7	338	469
Templeman, John	Deed fr	Forrest, Uriah	1801	G7	111	141
Templeman, John	Deed fr	Forrest, Uriah et al	1801	G7	113	144
Templeman, John	Deed fr	Duncanson, William Mayne	1802	G7	499	637
Templeman, John	Deed to	Cox, John	1802	H8	174	167
Templeman, John	Deed to	Lowndes, Francis & Charles et al	1802	H8	375	349
Templeman, John	Deed to	Stoddert, Benjamin	1802	H8	451	414
Templeman, John	Deed fr	Munroe, Thomas, Supt.	1802	H8	597	563
Templeman, John	Deed to	Gant, Francis et al	1802	H8	375	349
Templeman, John	Deed fr	Commissioners of Washington	1802	H8	178	170
Templeman, John	Deed to	Gillis, Thomas	1802	H8	483	444
Templeman, John	B. of S. fr	Wheeler, Samuel	1802	H8	023	022
Templeman, John	Deed to	Washington Building Company	1802	H8	401	371
Templeman, John	Deed fr	Munroe, Thomas, Supt.	1802	H8	598	564
Templeman, John	Deed to	Tousard, Louis	1802	I9	574	930
Templeman, John	Deed to	Smith, Walter	1802	I9	283	463
Templeman, John	Deed fr	Polock, Isaac	1802	I9	147	221
Templeman, John	Deed fr	Cozens, William R.	1802	I9	371	615
Templeman, John	Deed to	Van Ness, John P.	1802	I9	148	223
Templeman, John	Deed to	King, Samuel, of NY et al	1802	I9	126	186
Templeman, John	Deed to	Spalding, William	1802	I9	376	624
Templeman, John	Deed to	Chandler, William S.	1802	I9	418	692
Templeman, John	Deed to	Shreeve, Barlie et al	1802	I9	226	359
Templeman, John	Deed to	Talbott, George W., of NY	1802	I9	126	186
Templeman, John	Deed to	Craven, John	1802	I9	204	320
Templeman, John	Deed to	Harbaugh, Leonard	1802	I9	419	694
Templeman, John	Deed to	Polk, Charles P.	1802	I9	210	330
Templeman, John	Deed to	Polock, Isaac	1802	I9	198	308
Templeman, John	Deed fr	Deakins, Francis	1802	I9	264	428
Templeman, John	Deed to	Craven, John	1805	M12	251	252
Templeman, John	Deed to	Long, Frederick	1805	M12	177	178
Templeman, John	Release fr	Smith, Walter	1805	M12	278	279

Index to District of Columbia Land Records, 1792-1817

Party	What	Party	Year	Liber	Old	New
Templeman, John	B. of S. to	Howard, Thomas	1806	O14	210	138
Templeman, John	Deed to	Bank of Columbia	1807	S18	356	281
Templeman, John	Deed to	Smith, Walter	1807	S18	354	279
Templeman, John	Deed to	Smith, Walter	1807	S18	351	277
Templeman, John	Deed to	Porter, James A., trustee	1808	U20	315	168
Templeman, John	B. of S. to	O'Neal, William	1808	V21	060	048
Templeman, John	B. of S. to	Caldwell, Elias B.	1808	U20	232	125
Templeman, John	Cert fr	Stoddert, Benjamin	1809	X23	075	056
Templeman, John	Deed to	Goldsborough, Charles W.	1809	X23	076	057
Templeman, John	B. of S. fr	Forrest, Uriah	1810	Y24	114	104
Templeman, John	Deed to	Voss, Nicholas	1813	AE30	103	079
Templeman, John & B. Stoddert	Deed to	Ardrey, Robert	1813	AF31	007	005
Templeman, John, Allegany Co.	B. of S. to	Templeman, Sarah	1808	U20	038	022
Templeman, John, defl	Suit	Smith, Walter, plt.	1810	Y24	120	109
Templeman, John, Esq., of Boston	Deed fr	Lingan, James Macubin, G'tn.	1793	A1-1	200	281
Templeman, John et al	Deed to	Alexander, John	1801	G7	150	198
Templeman, John et al	Deed to	Forrest, Uriah	1802	G7	529	674
Templeman, John et al	Deed to	Worthington, Charles	1802	H8	533	492
Templeman, John et al	Deed to	Bank of Columbia	1802	H8	386	358
Templeman, John et al	Deed to	Kerr, Alexander	1802	H8	348	324
Templeman, John et al	Deed fr	Worhington, Charles	1802	H8	536	496
Templeman, John et al	Deed to	Abbot, John	1802	I9	013	016
Templeman, John et al	Deed to	Hodnett, James	1802	I9	163	247
Templeman, John et al	Deed fr	Carlon, James	1804	K10	370	384
Templeman, John et al	Deed to	Davidson, John	1804	L11	062	64
Templeman, John et al	Deed to	Stevens, John	1804	K10	269	275
Templeman, John et al	Release fr	Stewart, Deborah	1806	P15	337	222
Templeman, John et al	Deed to	Smith, Walter	1807	S18	343	270
Templeman, John et al	Deed to	Stoddert, Benjamin	1807	S18	359	283
Templeman, John et al	Deed to	Stoddert, Benjamin	1807	S18	341	268
Templeman, John et al	Deed to	Thompson, Mary	1813	AF31	045	031
Templeman, John, G'tn. et al	Deed to	Carlin, James	1804	K10	344	355
Templeman, John, mer., of G'tn.	Mortgage fr	Dawes, Isaac, tanner, of G'tn.	1794	B2A	038	044
Templeman, John, of Boston MA	Cert fr	Commissioners of Washington	1792	B2A	297	417
Templeman, John, of Boston MA	Cert fr	Commissioners of Washington	1792	B2A	293	410
Templeman, John, of Boston MA	Cert fr	Commissioners of Washington	1792	B2A	297	417
Templeman, John, of Boston MA	Cert fr	Commissioners of Washington	1792	B2A	297	416
Templeman, John, of G'tn.	Deed fr	Peter, Robert & Wm. Deakins, Jr.	1794	B2A	063	080
Templeman, John, of G'tn.	Deed fr	Deakins, William, Jr., of G'tn.	1794	B2A	064	082
Templeman, John, of G'tn.	Deed fr	Hite, Isaac, of Frederick Co. VA	1795	B2A	222	308
Templeman, John, of G'tn.	Deed to	Polock, Isaac, of Savannah GA	1795	B2B	375	028
Templeman, John, of G'tn.	Agreement	Naylor, George, of Augusta GA	1795	B2A	215	297
Templeman, John, of G'tn.	Deed fr	Beckwith, Charles, of Montg. Co.	1796	B2B	424	097
Templeman, John, of G'tn.	Deed fr	Deakins, William, Jr., of G'tn.	1797	C3	235	195
Templeman, John, of G'tn.	Deed fr	Loundes, Francis & Charles, G'tn.	1800	E5	381	360
Templeman, John, of G'tn.	Deed to	Simpson, Josias	1800	F6	010	007
Templeman, John, of G'tn.	Deed to	Marbury, William, Naval agent	1801	F6	183	117
Templeman, John, of G'tn.	Deed to	Deakins, Francis, of G'tn.	1801	F6	115	071
Templeman, John, of G'tn.	Deed to	Long, Frederick	1801	G7	040	051
Templeman, John, of G'tn. et al	Lease to	Meade, Simon	1801	G7	202	269
Templeman, John, of G'tn.	Deed to	Elliott, Richard	1801	G7	101	129
Templeman, John, of G'tn.	Deed fr	Blodgett, Samuel, of Phila.	1801	G7	220	295
Templeman, John, of G'tn.	Deed fr	Commissioners of Washington	1801	G7	313	437
Templeman, John, of G'tn.	Deed fr	Polock, Isaac	1802	G7	498	636
Templeman, John, of G'tn.	Deed fr	Commissioners of Washington	1802	G7	492	630

Party	What	Party	Year	Liber	Old	New
Templeman, John, of G'tn.	Deed fr	Commissioners of Washington	1802	G7	490	628
Templeman, John, of G'tn.	Deed fr	Commissioners of Washington	1802	G7	494	632
Templeman, John, of G'tn.	Deed fr	Polock, Isaac	1802	G7	496	635
Templeman, John, of G'tn.	Deed fr	Munroe, Thomas, Supt.	1802	H8	596	562
Templeman, John, of G'tn.	Lease to	Voss, Nicholas	1802	H8	340	317
Templeman, John, of G'tn.	Deed to	Cox, John, of G'tn.	1802	H8	368	342
Templeman, John, of G'tn.	Deed to	Baptist Church of Washington	1802	H8	509	468
Templeman, John, of G'tn.	Deed to	Lowndes, Charles, of G'tn.	1802	I9	079	111
Templeman, John, of G'tn.	Deed to	Burford, John A.	1804	K10	339	351
Templeman, John, of G'tn.	Deed to	Key, Philip Barton	1804	K10	310	316
Templeman, John, of G'tn.	Deed to	Foxall, Henry, of G'tn.	1804	L11	009	9
Templeman, John, of G'tn.	Deed to	Thompson, William, of G'tn.	1804	L11	167	164
Templeman, John, of G'tn.	Deed fr	Beatty, Charles, of G'tn. et al	1804	L11	185	178
Templeman, John, of G'tn.	Deed to	Caldwell, Timothy	1804	L11	129	131
Templeman, John, of G'tn.	Deed to	Williams, Jeremiah & Elisha W.	1804	L11	333	304
Templeman, John, of G'tn.	Deed to	Baltzer, John, Jr., of G'tn.	1804	L11	173	169
Templeman, John, of G'tn.	Deed to	Voss, Nicholas	1804	M12	040	040
Templeman, John, of G'tn.	Deed to	Williams, Jeremiah & Elisha W.	1805	M12	280	281
Templeman, John, of G'tn.	Deed to	Stoddert, Benjamin, of G'tn.	1805	M12	169	168
Templeman, John, of G'tn.	Deed to	Smallwood, Walter B.	1805	M12	264	265
Templeman, John, of G'tn.	Deed fr	Stoddert, Benjamin, of G'tn.	1805	M12	151	147
Templeman, John, of G'tn.	Deed to	Stoddert, Benjamin, of G'tn.	1805	M12	167	166
Templeman, John, of G'tn.	Release fr	Smith, Robert, Sec. U.S.N.	1805	M12	275	275
Templeman, John, of G'tn.	Deed to	Cope, Israel & Jasper, of Balto.	1805	O14	149	097
Templeman, John, of Allegany Co.	Deed to	Hellen, Walter	1806	P15	364	242
Templeman, John, of Allegany Co.	Deed to	Caldwell, Timothy	1806	P15	161	106
Templeman, John, of G'tn.	Mortgage to	Breck, Samuel	1806	P15	001	001
Templeman, John, of Allegany Co.	Deed to	Smith, Walter	1807	S18	349	275
Templeman, John, of Allegany Co.	Deed to	Bank of Columbia	1807	S18	346	272
Templeman, John, of Allegany Co.	Deed to	Taylor, Thomas, Jr. et al	1807	S18	311	244
Templeman, John, of Allegany Co.	B. of S. fr	Caldwell, Timothy	1808	U20	127	072
Templeman, John, of Allegany Co.	Deed to	Maitland, James	1808	V21	129	095
Templeman, John, of G'tn.	Deed to	Cope, Israel & Jasper, of Balto.	1809	V21	249	177
Templeman, John, of G'tn.	Mortgage to	King, George & Adam	1809	X23	281	223
Templeman, John, of G'tn.	Deed to	Smith, Walter, of G'tn.	1810	Y24	121	111
Templeman, Sarah	B. of S. fr	Templeman, John, Allegany Co.	1808	U20	038	022
Tench, Eleanor	Deed Gift to	Smallwood, Velinder	1809	W22	170	119
Tennally, Sarah	Deed fr	Weems, John, Dr., of G'tn.	1796	B2B	398	062
Tenny, Arianna (C), b. 12/19/12	Cert Free fr	Thompson, John	1813	AF31	312	223
Tenny, Isaac & Robert Ober	Deed fr	Beatty, John M. & Charles A.	1808	U20	090	050
Tenny, Isaac & Robert Ober	Deed fr	Beall, Thomas, of George	1809	X23	089	066
Tenny, Isaac, of Newburyport MA	Deed to	Ober, Robert, of G'tn.	1811	AA26	218	149
Tessier, John, pres. of Cath. Sem.	D. of T. fr	Latrobe, Benjamin B.	1812	AD29	103	079
Tharpe, Thomas	Lease fr	Polock, Isaac	1802	H8	145	140
Tharpe, Thomas	Lease fr	Dowling, Michael	1802	I9	112	163
Thaw, Joseph	Deed fr	Worthington, William, Jr.	1815	AK35	229	180
Thecker, James et al	Deed to	Gannon, James, of G'tn.	1804	M12	012	013
Theker, James, insolvent	B. of S. to	Dolan, Bernard, trustee	1808	U20	117	067
Thiker, James	B. of S. fr	Delphy, Richard	1802	G7	526	669
Thom, Christopher S.	T. of M. fr	Webster, Toppan	1802	I9	051	069
Thomas, Ann (M), & children	Cert free fr	Briscoe, Richard S.	1813	AF31	230	158
Thomas, Augustus	Manumis to	[ ], Patty (negro)	1806	Q16	019	012
Thomas, Caroline (black)	Manumis fr	Thomas, Mathew	1807	S18	059	049
Thomas, Clement	Cert Free fr	Barnes, John, clerk Charles Co.	1816	AL36	424	405
Thomas, Elizabeth	Manumis to	[ ], John (negro)	1809	X23	153	112

Index to District of Columbia Land Records, 1792-1817

Party	What	Party	Year	Liber	Old	New
Thomas, Elizabeth	B. of S. to	Simmons, John	1809	X23	154	113
Thomas, Elizabeth & James	B. of S. fr	Symmons, John	1809	W22	360	233
Thomas, Elizabeth et al	Deed to	Bentley, Caleb & Henrietta T.	1809	X23	091	067
Thomas, Evan	Deed fr	Stoddert, Benj. & Wm. Deakins	1794	B2A	093	121
Thomas, Evan	Deed fr	Stoddert, Benjamin	1801	F6	168	105
Thomas, Evan et al	Deed to	Gantt, Edward, Dr.	1804	K10	164	174
Thomas, George N.	Slave	From MD	1809	V21	183	131
Thomas, George N., trustee	Deed fr	Boyd, Richard D., insolvent	1810	Z25	168	133
Thomas, George N.	B. of S. fr	Boyd, Richard D.	1810	Z25	137	108
Thomas, George N., insolvent	D. of T. to	Richardson, Thomas R.	1811	AC28	027	020
Thomas, George Naylor	B. of S. to	Brightwell, John L., of P.G. Co.	1809	V21	325	240
Thomas, Gerrard, age 22	Cert free fr	Briscoe, Richard S.	1813	AF31	230	158
Thomas, Gustavus, free black	Deed fr	Magruder, Nathaniel Edwards	1807	R17	091	072
Thomas, Gustavus, free black	Deed to	Brooke, Samuel, Gent.	1807	R17	034	028
Thomas, Gustavus, trustee of	Deed to	Bohrer, Jacob	1809	V21	162	117
Thomas, Henry, age 15	Cert free fr	Briscoe, Richard S.	1813	AF31	230	158
Thomas, John, 3rd	Deed fr	Howard, Joseph & Mary	1809	X23	195	147
Thomas, John, 3rd	Deed to	Smith, Clement	1810	Z25	284	223
Thomas, John, 3rd et al	Mortgage to	Patterson, Edgar, of G'tn.	1810	Z25	111	086
Thomas, John, 3rd	B. of S. to	Calder, James	1810	Y24	032	028
Thomas, John, 3rd, trustee	Deed fr	Ogdon, David, of G'tn.	1811	AA26	269	182
Thomas, John, age 28	Cert free fr	Briscoe, Richard S.	1813	AF31	230	158
Thomas, John, of Montg. Co.	Deed fr	Murray, William, of A.A. Co.	1811	AB27	450	369
Thomas, John, Sr., of Montg. Co.	Deed fr	Mountz, Jacob, collector, G'tn.	1810	Z25	259	203
Thomas, John, Sr., of Montg. Co.	Deed fr	Robertson, Thomas, of G'tn.	1811	AB27	101	083
Thomas, John, Sr., of Montg. Co.	Deed to	Riggs, Romulus	1812	AC28	495	353
Thomas, John V. & Deborah	Deed to	St. Clair, George	1817	AO39	195	144
Thomas, John Valentine	Deed fr	Forrest, Joseph, trustee	1815	AK35	214	168
Thomas, Joseph	Deed fr	Prout, William	1801	G7	057	073
Thomas, Joseph	D. of T. fr	Moore, James D.	1809	V21	184	131
Thomas, Joseph	Assign to	Kirby, Francis	1810	X23	367	294
Thomas, Joseph	Assign fr	Thomas, Notley	1811	AB27	291	238
Thomas, Lewis, age 12	Cert free fr	Briscoe, Richard S.	1813	AF31	230	158
Thomas, Mathew	Manumis to	Thomas, Caroline (black)	1807	S18	059	049
Thomas, Mathew	Convey fr	Swan, Maria	1807	S18	059	049
Thomas, Matilda, age 17	Cert free fr	Briscoe, Richard S.	1813	AF31	230	158
Thomas, Nathan P.	Lease fr	Van Ness, John P. & Marcia	1817	AO39	272	195
Thomas, Notley	Assign to	Thomas, Joseph	1811	AB27	291	238
Thomas, Philip	Deed fr	Ramsbergher, John, Fredk. Co.	1792	A1-1	146	210
Thomas, Philip	Deed to	Beall, Thomas & John M. Gantt	1792	A1-1	147	212
Thomas, Philip, Dr. et al	Deed to	Beall, Thomas & John M. Gantt	1793	A1-1	389	496
Thomas, Philip et al	Deed to	Beall, Thomas & John M. Gantt	1792	A1-1	108	157
Thomas, Philip, of Frederick Co.	Deed fr	Keller, Juliana, wid/o Rudolph	1792	A1-1	069	101
Thomas, Philip, of Frederick Co.	Deed fr	Grosh, Conrad et al	1792	A1-1	067	99
Thomas, Philip, of Frederick Co.	Deed fr	Stoddert, Benj. & Wm. Deakins	1793	A1-1	387	494
Thomas, Richard	Deed fr	Stoddert, Benjamin	1802	I9	310	509
Thomas, Richard, age 20	Cert free fr	Briscoe, Richard S.	1813	AF31	230	158
Thomas, Richard, of Montg. Co.	Deed fr	Wayman, Charles, of G'tn.	1804	K10	222	231
Thomas, Samuel & Mary et al	Deed to	Bentley, Caleb & Henrietta T.	1809	X23	091	067
Thomas, Samuel 3rd	Deed to	Davidson, Craik & Dorsey	1794	B2A	051	062
Thomas, Samuel, Jr., Montg. Co.	Deed fr	Murry, William, of A.A. Co.	1806	P15	169	112
Thomas, William	Cert Free to	[ ], Dick (C)	1816	AL36	293	291
Thomas, William et al	Deed fr	Shoemaker, Jonathan	1808	T19	114	081
Thompkins, James	B. of S. to	Gatton, Azariah	1805	M12	185	186
Thompson, Andrew	B. of S. to	Mitchell, Walter	1809	V21	368	270

Index to District of Columbia Land Records, 1792-1817

Party	What	Party	Year	Liber	Old	New
Thompson, Arthur	Lease fr	Polock, Isaac	1802	H8	143	139
Thompson, Arthur	Deed fr	Polock, David, of G'tn.	1804	K10	351	363
Thompson, Arthur	Deed to	Jones, John	1811	AB27	023	021
Thompson, Arthur	Lease to	Stewart, John	1814	AG32	007	006
Thompson, Arthur	Release to	Jones, Sarah	1815	AI34	129	148
Thompson, Charity (C), age 38	Manumis fr	Thompson, Mary & Est. McVickir	1813	AE30	255	199
Thompson, Charles	B. of S. to	Smith, Edward L., of G'tn.	1807	S18	023	019
Thompson, Elizabeth Lund, of VA	Deed fr	Walker, George	1796	B2B	421	093
Thompson, Ezra	Deed fr	Bailey, Theodorus et al	1802	G7	465	601
Thompson, Ezra, of NY et al	Deed fr	Van Cortland, Philip, of NY	1804	M12	001	001
Thompson, Ezra, of NY et al	Deed to	Van Cortland, Philip, of NY	1804	M12	002	002
Thompson, George	Deed fr	Ragon, Daniel, of Frederick Co.	1792	A1-1	065	97
Thompson, George	Deed fr	Davidson, John, of Annapolis	1800	E5	375	354
Thompson, George	Deed fr	Snyder, Jacob	1800	F6	053	033
Thompson, George	Deed fr	Emess, Barton	1802	H8	354	329
Thompson, George	Deed fr	Beall, Thomas B., trustee	1805	N13	262	218
Thompson, George et al	Deed to	Beall, Thomas & John M. Gantt	1793	A1-1	317	418
Thompson, George et al	Deed fr	Commissioners of Washington	1800	E5	131	119
Thompson, George et al	Cert fr	Commissioners of Washington	1801	G7	453	589
Thompson, George et al	Deed fr	Kennedy, John	1802	I9	280	458
Thompson, George et al	Deed to	Mayor & Council of Georgetown	1807	R17	232	
Thompson, George, of G'tn.	Deed to	Mason, John, of G'tn.	1794	B2A	107	142
Thompson, George, of G'tn.	Deed fr	Needham, William, of Montg. Co.	1796	B2B	586	333
Thompson, George, of G'tn.	Deed fr	Afflick, Thomas, of G'tn.	1797	B2B	635	396
Thompson, George, of G'tn.	Deed to	Brookes, Joseph, of G'tn.	1809	V21	313	229
Thompson, George, of G'tn.	B. of S. fr	Finagen, Rosanna	1809	V21	311	227
Thompson, George, of G'tn.	Deed to	Baird, Mary, of G'tn.	1810	Y24	368	332
Thompson, George, of G'tn.	D. of T. to	Smith, Clement, of G'tn.	1810	Y24	028	024
Thompson, Henry	Deed fr	Child, Henry H.	1802	I9	347	573
Thompson, Henry, of Balto. et al	Deed to	Chesley, Anne, of G'tn.	1804	L11	372	333
Thompson, Henry, of Balto.	Deed to	Brent, Robert Young	1816	AL36	026	027
Thompson, Hillery, of Balto. MD	Lease fr	Corporation of Georgetown	1813	AE30	408	301
Thompson, Hugh, of Balto.	Deed to	Commissioners of Washington	1799	D4	227	210
Thompson, James	Division	Peter, Robert	1799	D4	267	251
Thompson, James	Deed fr	Commissioners of Washington	1800	F6	071	044
Thompson, James	Deed fr	Commissioners of Washington	1800	F6	068	042
Thompson, James	Deed fr	Holmead, Anthony, Sr.	1801	G7	325	455
Thompson, James	Deed fr	Densey, Hugh	1801	G7	453	590
Thompson, James	Deed to	Morris, Benjamin W., of Phila.	1801	F6	171	107
Thompson, James	B. of S. fr	Loring, Israel	1802	H8	472	433
Thompson, James	Deed to	Burrows, William W.	1802	I9	432	715
Thompson, James	Deed to	Herty, Thomas	1802	G7	527	671
Thompson, James	Deed to	Burrows, William W. & W.	1804	L11	308	283
Thompson, James	Deed fr	Law, John, attorney of Thomas	1808	T19	236	173
Thompson, James	Lease to	Clarke, William	1811	AA26	022	017
Thompson, James	Deed to	Braden, Elizabeth [Braiden]	1812	AC28	369	268
Thompson, James	Deed to	Clarke, William	1812	AC28	370	269
Thompson, James	Qualify	Major in militia	1812	AD29	171	137
Thompson, James	D. of T. fr	Fields, William, of G'tn.	1812	AD29	252	208
Thompson, James	Deed to	Clarke, William	1813	AF31	342	244
Thompson, James	Qualify	Lt. Col. of 1st Regiment 1st Brigade	1813	AE30	359	267
Thompson, James	Deed to	Braden, Elizabeth, of G'tn.	1813	AE30	515	382
Thompson, James	Deed fr	Brown, Joel	1815	AH33	522	447
Thompson, James	Deed fr	King, Vincent	1815	AK35	064	049
Thompson, James	Deed fr	Holmead, Anthony	1815	AH33	519	445

Party	What	Party	Year	Liber	Old	New
Thompson, James	Deed fr	Morris, Caspar W. et al	1816	AL36	488	459
Thompson, James	Deed to	Yerby, John, of G'tn.	1816	AM37	507	373
Thompson, James, Col.	Deed fr	Moxley, Charles	1814	AH33	248	215
Thompson, James, Col.	Deed fr	Fields, William, of G'tn.	1814	AH33	245	213
Thompson, James et al	Deed to	Blake, John, of Charleston SC	1804	L11	120	122
Thompson, James et al	Deed fr	Bickley, Robert S., Bucks Co. PA	1817	AN38	564	411
Thompson, James, mer., of G'tn.	Deed fr	Peter, Robert, of G'tn.	1799	D4	275	258
Thompson, James, mer., of G'tn.	Deed fr	Peter, Robert, of G'tn.	1799	D4	349	336
Thompson, James, mer., of G'tn.	Deed to	Peter, Robert, of G'tn.	1799	D4	272	255
Thompson, James, of G'tn.	Deed fr	Thompson, John, Capt., of NY	1799	D4	269	253
Thompson, James, of G'tn.	Deed fr	Peter, Robert, of G'tn.	1801	G7	398	531
Thompson, James, of MA	Deed fr	Jones, John G.	1809	X23	072	043
Thompson, James, of G'tn. et al	D. of T. fr	Kirk, Miletius Thomas, of G'tn.	1809	W22	312	203
Thompson, James, of Boston MA	Deed fr	Peter, Thomas, of G'tn. et al	1810	Z25	301	236
Thompson, James, of G'tn.	Deed to	Thompson, Rachel, his mother	1810	Z25	102	079
Thompson, Jay, of G'tn.	Deed fr	Anderson, George, of G'tn.	1794	B2A	002	002
Thompson, Jay, of Fayette Co. PA	Deed to	Deakins, William, of G'tn.	1795	B2B	358	006
Thompson, Joe (M)	Cert Free fr	Rapine, Daniel	1812	AB27	504	412
Thompson, John	Deed fr	Howes, John	1798	D4	022	019
Thompson, John	P. of Atty. to	Morsell, James S.	1799	D4	270	254
Thompson, John	Deed to	Beall, Thomas B.	1802	I9	162	245
Thompson, John	Deed to	Bruff, Thomas	1803	K10	076	82
Thompson, John	Manumis to	[ ], Jane (negro)	1810	Z25	317	248
Thompson, John	Cert Free to	Tenny, Arianna (C), b. 12/19/12	1813	AF31	312	223
Thompson, John	Deed fr	Peter, George	1813	AE30	545	404
Thompson, John	Mortgage fr	Williams, John S. & Jacob Wagner	1814	AH33	322	278
Thompson, John & V. Reintzel	Deed fr	Mountz, Jacob, collector, of G'tn.	1811	AB27	458	376
Thompson, John & B. Owens	D. of T. fr	Curran, Eleanor, of G'tn.	1812	AD29	253	209
Thompson, John & John Mountz	Deed fr	Skinner, Adderton, of P.G. Co.	1812	AC28	253	186
Thompson, John & V. Reintzel	Deed fr	Sheppard, Benjamin et al	1812	AD29	430	361
Thompson, John C. et al	Deed fr	Link, Adam & Jane, Jefferson Co.	1811	AB27	128	105
Thompson, John C.	B. of S. fr	Berry, Richard	1812	AD29	444a	374
Thompson, John C., of G'tn.	Deed fr	Bausman, Benjamin, of Balto.	1813	AF31	124	084
Thompson, John C.	B. of S. fr	Berry, Richard	1813	AE30	208	169
Thompson, John C.	Deed to	Lutz, John	1814	AG32	044	035
Thompson, John C., of G'tn.	Deed fr	Hoye, John, of Allegany Co.	1815	AK35	274	218
Thompson, John C., of G'tn. et al	Deed fr	Mountz, Jacob, of G'tn.	1815	AI34	049	056
Thompson, John, Capt., of NY	Deed to	Thompson, James, of G'tn.	1799	D4	269	253
Thompson, John, Capt., G'tn.	Deed to	Beall, Thomas B., of George, G'tn.	1800	E5	268	262
Thompson, John et al	Deed fr	Fields, William, of G'tn.	1808	U20	227	122
Thompson, John, et al	Deed fr	Mountz, Jacob, collector, of G'tn.	1811	AB27	456	374
Thompson, John et al	Deed fr	White, James, of Montg. Co.	1812	AC28	251	185
Thompson, John et al	Deed to	Oden, Benjamin, of P.G. Co.	1815	AI34	375	403
Thompson, John et al	Deed to	Oden, Benjamin, of P.G. Co.	1815	AI34	376	403
Thompson, John et al	Deed fr	Sheppard, Abraham, of NC	1817	AO39	478	328
Thompson, John, of G'tn.	Deed fr	Jones, Benjamin White	1798	C3	376	300
Thompson, John, of G'tn.	Deed fr	Howes, John, of G'tn.	1798	D4	022	019
Thompson, John, of G'tn.	Deed fr	Ferguson, William, of P.G. Co.	1798	C3	441	346
Thompson, John, of G'tn.	D. of T. fr	Fields, William, of G'tn.	1809	X23	128	092
Thompson, John, of G'tn.	Release to	Fields, William, of G'tn.	1810	Z25	310	243
Thompson, John, of G'tn.	Deed to	Moxley, Charles, of G'tn.	1810	Z25	226	177
Thompson, John, of G'tn.	Deed fr	Fields, William, of G'tn.	1810	Z25	300	235
Thompson, John, of G'tn.	Deed fr	Martin, Luther, of Balto.	1810	Y24	158	145
Thompson, John, of G'tn. et al	Deed to	Snowden, Gerrard H., of A.A. Co.	1812	AD29	378	318
Thompson, John, of G'tn.	Deed to	Wagner, Jacob & J.S. Williams	1813	AF31	493	359

Party	What	Party	Year	Liber	Old	New
Thompson, John, of G'tn.	Deed fr	Reintzel, Valentine, of G'tn.	1813	AF31	267	187
Thompson, John, trustee	B. of S. fr	Dunlap, Henry, insolvent	1805	M12	107	100
Thompson, John, trustee	D. of T. fr	Hall, Elisha, insolvent	1811	Z25	459	364
Thompson, Jonah	Deed fr	Polock, Isaac	1800	E5	396	371
Thompson, Jonah	Deed to	Jamison, Andrew	1802	H8	239	228
Thompson, Jonah & Margaret et al	Deed to	Tayloe, John, Richmond Co. VA	1804	K10	150	162
Thompson, Jonah & Margaret	Deed to	Veitch, Richard, of Alexa.	1814	AH33	073	065
Thompson, Jonah et ux, of Alexa.	Deed to	Veitch, Richard, of Alexa.	1809	V21	170	122
Thompson, Jonah et ux, of Alexa.	Deed to	Veitch, Richard, of Alexa.	1809	V21	174	125
Thompson, Jonah, of Alexa.	Mortgage fr	Jamieson, Andrew & Mary, Alexa.	1798	D4	140	123
Thompson, Jonah, of Alexa. et al	Deed fr	Polock, Isaac	1798	C3	444	349
Thompson, Jonah, of Alexa. et al	Deed fr	Magruder, Patrick, of G'tn.	1799	D4	344	333
Thompson, Jonah, of Alexa.	Deed to	Jameson, Andrew, of Alexa.	1802	I9	110	160
Thompson, Jonah, of Alexa. et al	Deed fr	Brent, Daniel Carroll, marshal	1813	AF31	261	182
Thompson, Jonah, of Alexa. et al	Deed fr	Deakins, Leonard M. & John Hoye	1814	AH33	038	034
Thompson, Joseph	Deed fr	Corporation of Washington	1816	AM37	201	149
Thompson, Josias	Deed to	Mountz, Jacob	1802	I9	358	592
Thompson, Josias et al	Deed fr	Holmead, Anthony	1793	A1-1	244	333
Thompson, Josias, of G'tn.	Deed fr	Greate, Jacob, of G'tn.	1793	A1-1	243	332
Thompson, Josias, of G'tn.	Deed to	Greate, Jacob, of G'tn.	1793	A1-1	245	335
Thompson, Josias, of G'tn. et al	Lease fr	Corporation of Georgetown	1813	AE30	408	301
Thompson, Julia [Kaine]	Deed fr	Appler, David et al	1816	AL36	523	489
Thompson, Lydia, of G'tn.	B. of S. fr	Hazle, Zachariah, of G'tn.	1806	Q16	066	042
Thompson, Margaret	B. of S. fr	Kreemer, John [Kramer]	1813	AF31	330	235
Thompson, Mary	Deed fr	Stoddert, B. & J. Templeman	1813	AF31	045	031
Thompson, Mary & Est. McVickir	Manumis to	Thompson, Charity (C), age 38	1813	AE30	255	199
Thompson, Moses	Deed to	Wells, John, of Annapolis	1817	AN38	276	202
Thompson, Moses	Deed fr	Balch, Stephen B., Rev.	1817	AN38	119	088
Thompson, Moses, b. 9/20/70	Cert of Birth		1804	K10	330	341
Thompson, Rachel	Deed fr	Hall, Elisha & Catharine	1809	V21	157	113
Thompson, Rachel	B. of S. fr	Fowler, Elisha, her father	1816	AL36	343	334
Thompson, Rachel, his mother	Deed fr	Thompson, James, of G'tn.	1810	Z25	102	079
Thompson, Rachel, of G'tn.	Deed fr	Quaid, Walter & Ruth, of G'tn.	1810	X23	412	333
Thompson, Semus	Deed fr	Murdock, Addison	1807	R17	045	036
Thompson, Semus, yellow	Manumis to	Dowry, Hercules (C), under 45	1813	AE30	430	317
Thompson, Simms	Manumis fr	Lowndes, Francis, of Montg. Co.	1805	M12	366	375
Thompson, William	Deed fr	Commissioners of Washington	1802	H8	355	331
Thompson, William	B. of S. fr	Hankart, John	1802	I9	508	833
Thompson, William	Deed fr	Turner, Samuel	1802	I9	251	405
Thompson, William	Deed fr	Stoddert, Benjamin	1804	L11	160	158
Thompson, William	B. of S. to	Prout, William	1805	M12	288	288
Thompson, William	Deed fr	Ferguson, David, Ontario Co. NY	1806	O14	067	040
Thompson, William	B. of S. to	Parker, Fielder	1809	W22	409	266
Thompson, William et al	Deed fr	Long, John, of G'tn.	1799	D4	209	192
Thompson, William et al	Deed fr	Upperman, Henry	1801	G7	030	038
Thompson, William, Fairfax Co.	Deed fr	Walker, George	1796	B2B	420	092
Thompson, William, of G'tn.	Deed fr	Stoddert, Benjamin, of G'tn.	1802	H8	357	332
Thompson, William, of G'tn.	Deed fr	Templeman, John, of G'tn.	1804	L11	167	164
Thompson, William, of G'tn.	Deed to	Joy, Abraham	1804	L11	232	215
Thompson, Woodward, of G'tn.	Lease fr	Gary, Ann, of G'tn.	1816	AL36	426	407
Thomson, Andrew	Agreement	Thompson, George	1801	F6	197	127
Thomson, George	Deed fr	Deakins, William, Jr.	1800	E5	255	249
Thomson, George	Agreement	Thompson, Andrew	1801	F6	197	127
Thomson, George	Deed fr	Suter, John	1802	I9	556	901
Thomson, George	Deed fr	Suter, John	1802	I9	554	899

Index to District of Columbia Land Records, 1792-1817

Party	What	Party	Year	Liber	Old	New
Thomson, George	Deed fr	Threlkeld, John	1803	K10	056	060
Thomson, George	Deed fr	Beatty, Charles, heirs of	1806	P15	326	216
Thomson, George	B. of S. to	McClane, Robert	1806	Q16	010	006
Thomson, George, of G'tn.	Lease fr	Lowndes, Francis, of G'tn.	1804	K10	396	411
Thomson, George, of G'tn.	Deed to	Thornbrough, Joseph, of PA	1804	K10	356	369
Thomson, George, of G'tn. et al	Deed to	Peacock, Robert Ware	1804	L11	012	12
Thomson, George, of G'tn. et al	Deed to	Suter, Alexander	1806	Q16	316	242
Thomson, George, of G'tn.	Deed fr	Brooke, Samuel, of Montg. Co.	1806	P15	193	129
Thomson, George, of G'tn.	Deed to	Suter, Alexander	1806	Q16	318	243
Thomson, George, of G'tn.	D. of T. to	Morton, William, of G'tn.	1810	Y24	126	114
Thomson, George, of G'tn.	Deed fr	O'Reiley, Henry	1810	Y24	458	407
Thomson, James & Charles King	Release to	Kirk, Militius Thomas, of G'tn.	1810	Z25	156	123
Thomson, James, of G'tn. et al	D. of T. to	Morton, William	1810	Z25	291	228
Thomson, John, of G'tn.	Deed to	Reintzel, Valentine, of G'tn.	1814	AG32	183	129
Thomson, Joseph (free)	Slave	From Charles Co.	1807	R17	284	
Thomson, Mary et al	Manumis to	McFerson, Alexander	1815	AI34	015	016
Thomson, Wiliam	Agreement	Peacock, Robert Ware	1804	L11	298	273
Thomson, William	Lease fr	Turner, Samuel	1808	V21	039	029
Thomson, William, Jr., of G'tn.	B. of S. fr	Thomson, William, of G'tn.	1815	AH33	412	355
Thomson, William, of Montg. Co.	Deed fr	Deakins, William, Jr. et al	1797	C3	098	81
Thomson, William, of G'tn.	Deed to	Smith, Walter	1806	Q16	002	002
Thomson, William, of G'tn.	Deed to	Wright, Thomas Crafts, of G'tn.	1806	O14	320	212
Thomson, William, of G'tn.	Lease to	Duffy, Bryan, of G'tn.	1809	W22	147	104
Thomson, William, of G'tn.	B. of S. to	Thomson, William, Jr., of G'tn.	1815	AH33	412	355
Thorburn, James	Deed fr	Wheeler, Luke & John Cowper, VA	1817	AN38	140	103
Thorn, Bennet, of P.G. Co.	B. of S. fr	Reynolds, Thomas	1806	P15	134	086
Thorn, Christopher S.	Deed to	James, William	1802	I9	587	952
Thorn, Christopher S.	Deed fr	Lovell, William	1802	I9	332	547
Thorn, Christopher S.	Deed fr	Munroe, Thomas, Supt.	1802	I9	414	687
Thorn, Christopher S.	B. of S. fr	Webster, Toppan	1802	H8	001	001
Thornbrough, Joseph, of PA	Deed fr	Thomson, George, of G'tn.	1804	K10	356	369
Thornbrough, Joseph, of PA	Deed fr	Brooke, Samuel, of Montg. Co.	1804	K10	355	367
Thornbrough, Joseph, of PA	Deed to	Crawford, William, heirs of	1817	AO39	370	249
Thornton, Ann G. al	B. of S. to	Bomford, George, Col.	1817	AO39	105	082
Thornton, Anthony	Slaves	From Fairfax Co. VA	1810	Y24	114	104
Thornton, Anthony & Jane	B. of S. to	Watterstone, George	1816	AM37	328	238
Thornton, Anthony [Jane]	Slaves	From Fairfax Co. VA	1810	Y24	547	480
Thornton, Jane E.B. et al	B. of S. to	Bomford, George, Col.	1817	AO39	105	082
Thornton, Jane et al	B. of S. to	Bomford, George, Col.	1817	AO39	105	082
Thornton, Presley	Deed fr	Morris & Nicholson	1798	D4	030	025
Thornton, William	Deed fr	Reintzel, Valentine	1795	B2A	221	307
Thornton, William	Deed to	Hoban, James	1798	C3	319	257
Thornton, William	P. of Atty. fr	Lear, Tobias, of Fairfax Co. VA	1800	E5		365
Thornton, William	Cert to	Glover, Charles	1801	G7	191	256
Thornton, William	Deed to	Pratt, Henry et al	1801	F6	202	131
Thornton, William	Deed fr	Fitzhugh, Philip	1801	G7	243	327
Thornton, William	Deed to	Blagdon, George	1802	H8	529	489
Thornton, William	Deed to	Chandler, Walter S., of G'tn.	1802	G7	521	663
Thornton, William	Deed to	Calvert, Joseph	1802	H8	511	470
Thornton, William	Deed fr	Munroe, Thomas, Supt.	1804	K10	298	300
Thornton, William	Deed fr	Forrest, Uriah et al	1804	K10	116	125
Thornton, William	Deed fr	Munroe, Thomas, Supt.	1804	K10	299	302
Thornton, William	Mortgage fr	Peacock, Robert Ware	1804	L11	111	114
Thornton, William	Deed fr	Brent, Daniel Carroll, marshal	1804	L11	358	323
Thornton, William	Deed to	Brodeau, Ann	1805	N13	104	098

Party	What	Party	Year	Liber	Old	New
Thornton, William	Release to	Crow, John et al	1805	M12	207	208
Thornton, William	B. of S. to	Edelen, Edward	1805	M12	355	362
Thornton, William	Deed fr	Brent, Daniel Carroll, trustee et al	1807	S18	094	076
Thornton, William	Mortgage to	Lambell, William	1809	V21	254	181
Thornton, William	B. of S. to	Davidson, Samuel	1809	X23	182	136
Thornton, William	Deed fr	Van Ness, John P. & Marcia	1810	Y24	349	316
Thornton, William	D. of T. to	Eliot, Samuel, Jr. et al	1810	Z25	198	156
Thornton, William	Deed to	Pairo, Thomas W.	1810	Y24	362	327
Thornton, William	Deed to	Blagden, George	1811	AA26	054	042
Thornton, William	Deed to	McDonald, Alexander	1811	AB27	164	136
Thornton, William	Release to	Lamble, William	1812	AC28	476	338
Thornton, William	Deed to	Lyles, William, of P.G. Co.	1813	AE30	441	327
Thornton, William	D. of T. to	Morgan, William	1813	AF31	505	368
Thornton, William	Deed to	Barry, Richard	1813	AE30	289	220
Thornton, William	B. of S. fr	Armitage, Benjamin, atty.	1815	AH33	420	362
Thornton, William	Deed to	Forrest, Julius	1816	AM37	468	337
Thornton, William & Ann Calvert	Deed to	Pairo, Thomas W.	1809	X23	187	140
Thornton, William & S. Eliot, Jr.	Deed fr	Cranch, William	1810	Z25	200	157
Thornton, William, Dr.	Cert fr	Commissioners of Washington	1797	B2B	475	168
Thornton, William, Dr. et al	Mortgage to	Bank of Columbia	1801	G7	162	215
Thornton, William, Dr.	Mortgage to	Bank of Columbia	1801	G7	161	213
Thornton, William et al	Cert to	Young, Notley	1794	B2A	109	145
Thornton, William et al	P. of Atty. to	Greenleaf, James, New York NY	1794	B2A	110	146
Thornton, William et al	Cert to	Greenleaf, James	1794	B2A	108	143
Thornton, William et al	Deed fr	Greenleaf, James, New York NY	1795	B2A	229	318
Thornton, William et al	Deed to	Dermott, James Reed	1797	B2B	672	440
Thornton, William et al	Deed to	Hodgson, Joseph	1798	C3	331	267
Thornton, William et al	Deed to	Sherrard, Francis	1798	C3	464	365
Thornton, William et al	Deed fr	Blodgett, Samuel, of Phila.	1801	G7	097	125
Thornton, William et al	Deed to	Hewitt, John	1802	H8	458	421
Thornton, William F.	Qualify	Cornet in cavalry	1813	AE30	425	314
Thorp, John, of Balto. Co.	Lease fr	Betz, George, of Balto.	1804	K10	204	213
Thorpe, Thomas	Deed fr	Dowling, Michael	1802	I9	348	574
Thorpe, Thomas	Deed to	Bradley, Phinease et al	1804	L11	365	329
Thorpe, Thomas	Deed fr	Polock, David	1804	K10	281	284
Thorpe, Thomas	Deed to	Bussard, Daniel, of G'tn.	1805	M12	134	129
Thorpe, Thomas	Deed fr	Bigham, Hugh, of Adams Co. PA	1806	O14	390	260
Thorpe, Thomas	Lease fr	Law, Thomas	1806	O14	256	169
Thorpe, Thomas	Deed fr	Murray, Peter, of Harford Co.	1807	R17	100	078
Thorpe, Thomas	Deed to	Wilson, John, of Henry	1808	U20	407	228
Thorpe, Thomas	Deed to	Dodge, Allen & Francis, of G'tn.	1808	T19	371	265
Thorpe, Thomas	Deed fr	Gillis, Thomas H. et al	1808	U20	410	229
Thorpe, Thomas	Assign to	Bacon, Samuel & George Moore	1809	V21	419	320
Thorpe, Thomas	Assign to	Walker, Joseph	1810	Y24	508	447
Thorpe, Thomas	B. of S. to	Moore, George	1810	Y24	234	215
Thorpe, Thomas	Deed to	Barlow, Joel	1810	Z25	095	073
Thorpe, Thomas	Deed to	Wilson, John A.	1810	Z25	035	026
Thorpe, Thomas	Assign to	Davidson, John	1810	X23	189	142
Thorpe, Thomas	Deed fr	Parrott, Richard	1816	AM37	276	202
Thorpe, Thomas & Daniel Bussard	Deed to	Davidson, John	1810	Z25	090	068
Thorpe, Thomas, of G'tn.	Deed to	Kurtz, Daniel, of G'tn.	1816	AM37	155	118
Thorpe, Thomas, storekeeper	Lease fr	Van Ness, John P. & Marcia	1806	P15	027	016
Thorpe, Thomas, trustee	Deed fr	King, James C., insolvent	1810	Y24	061	054
Threcker, James	B. of S. to	Brown, Robert	1802	I9	443	732
Threcker, James	Deed to	McCormick, Alexander, *Cap. Hill*	1804	K10	265	271

Index to District of Columbia Land Records, 1792-1817

Party	What	Party	Year	Liber	Old	New
Threlkeld, Elizabeth et al	Deed to	Deakins, Francis	1802	H8	361	336
Threlkeld, Elizabeth, w/o John	Deed fr	Deakins, William, Jr.	1794	B2A	050	060
Threlkeld, John	Deed to	Dawes, Isaac	1794	B2A	037	042
Threlkeld, John	Deed to	Fenwick, George	1794	B2A	007	008
Threlkeld, John	Deed fr	Deakins, William, Jr.	1794	B2A	049	058
Threlkeld, John	Deed fr	Bayly, William	1795	B2A	177	239
Threlkeld, John	Deed to	Kennedy, Matthew	1798	D4	169	150
Threlkeld, John	Deed to	Mason, John Thomson, attorney	1799	D4	248	231
Threlkeld, John	Deed to	Gloyd, Catherine	1799	D4	355	342
Threlkeld, John	Lease to	Lowry, Caesar et al	1799	D4	173	154
Threlkeld, John	Deed to	Leamy, John, of Phila.	1799	D4	248	232
Threlkeld, John	Deed to	Fenwick, George	1800	E5	127	115
Threlkeld, John	Deed to	Clarke, Robert	1800	E5	302	295
Threlkeld, John	Deed to	Marche, Mary dela	1800	E5	299	292
Threlkeld, John	Deed to	Marche, Maria dela	1800	E5	298	291
Threlkeld, John	Deed to	Boone, Ignatius, of Nicholas	1800	E5	138	126
Threlkeld, John	Deed fr	Brown, Robert, house joiner	1801	G7	334	465
Threlkeld, John	Assign fr	Hardesty, Samuel	1801	G7	329	460
Threlkeld, John	B. of S. to	Cox, John	1801	G7	153	203
Threlkeld, John	Deed to	Threlkeld, Mary & Jane (daus.)	1802	H8	328	307
Threlkeld, John	Deed to	Neale, Francis, Rev.	1802	H8	136	132
Threlkeld, John	Deed to	Dulany, Michael	1802	I9	581	941
Threlkeld, John	Deed to	Neale, Leonard	1802	I9	592	959
Threlkeld, John	Deed to	Neale, Leonard	1802	I9	591	957
Threlkeld, John	Deed to	Lingan, James M.	1802	I9	587	951
Threlkeld, John	Deed fr	Lingan, James M.	1802	I9	566	917
Threlkeld, John	Deed to	Crookshank, John	1802	I9	579	938
Threlkeld, John	Deed to	Fenwick, George	1803	K10	055	59
Threlkeld, John	Deed to	Thomson, George	1803	K10	056	060
Threlkeld, John	Deed to	Lucas, Henry	1804	K10	156	167
Threlkeld, John	Deed to	Mason, John Thompson	1804	K10	241	249
Threlkeld, John	Deed fr	Deakins, Francis	1804	L11	295	271
Threlkeld, John	Manumis to	[ ], Lucy (Negro)	1804	L11	037	37
Threlkeld, John	Deed to	Collins, Hezekiah	1804	L11	151	151
Threlkeld, John	Deed fr	Deakins, Francis	1804	L11	293	269
Threlkeld, John	Deed to	Stoddert, Benjamin	1804	M12	032	033
Threlkeld, John	B. of C. to	Kennedy, Matthew	1805	M12	212	214
Threlkeld, John	Deed to	Neale, Leonard, Rev.	1805	N13	019	021
Threlkeld, John	Deed to	Foxall, Henry	1805	N13	037	038
Threlkeld, John	Deed to	Bussard, Daniel	1805	O14	027	017
Threlkeld, John	Deed to	Hazel, Jeremiah	1805	M12	129	124
Threlkeld, John	Deed to	Medley, Bernard, St. Mary's Co.	1806	P15	166	110
Threlkeld, John	Deed fr	Dorsey, William Hammond et al	1807	R17	073	059
Threlkeld, John	Deed to	Goldsberry, John M.	1807	S18	215	172
Threlkeld, John	Deed to	Collins, Hezekiah	1807	R17	400	302
Threlkeld, John	Mortgage fr	Offutt, Rezin, of Fairfax Co. VA	1808	U20	173	097
Threlkeld, John	Deed to	Foxall, Henry	1808	V21	069	054
Threlkeld, John	Deed fr	Lucas, Henry, of G'tn.	1808	T19	234	172
Threlkeld, John	Deed to	Deakins, Leonard M. & John Hoye	1809	W22	132	094
Threlkeld, John	Deed fr	Deakins, Leonard M. & John Hoye	1809	W22	085	063
Threlkeld, John	Deed to	Spalding, Bernard	1809	W22	098	071
Threlkeld, John	Deed to	Addison, Walter D., Rev.	1810	Y24	534	469
Threlkeld, John	Deed fr	Clerklee, James & Margaret R.	1810	Y24	538	472
Threlkeld, John	Deed to	Cooper, Mary or Lowry	1810	Z25	244	191
Threlkeld, John	Deed to	Neale, Francis, Rev.	1810	Y24	283	259

Party	What	Party	Year	Liber	Old	New
Threlkeld, John	Deed fr	West, Joseph D.	1811	AB27	474	387
Threlkeld, John	Deed fr	Lingan, James Maccubbin, of MD	1811	AB27	104	085
Threlkeld, John	Deed fr	Lee, Ann, of Charles Co.	1811	AA26	048	037
Threlkeld, John	Deed fr	Mountz, Jacob, collector, G'tn.	1812	AC28	191	145
Threlkeld, John	Deed to	Goldsborough, John M.	1812	AD29	027	019
Threlkeld, John	Deed to	Bussard, Daniel	1812	AD29	149	117
Threlkeld, John	Deed fr	Dawson, William & Ann Lee	1812	AD29	448	377
Threlkeld, John	B. of S. to	Grayson, William, Dr.	1812	AC28	410	297
Threlkeld, John	Deed to	Boarman, Charles	1813	AF31	466	338
Threlkeld, John	Deed to	Barron, Walter	1813	AE30	443	329
Threlkeld, John	Deed fr	Reintzel, Valentine	1814	AG32	187	132
Threlkeld, John	Deed to	Neale, Francis, Rev.	1814	AG32	351	254
Threlkeld, John	Deed to	Waters, William	1814	AG32	423	307
Threlkeld, John	Deed fr	Murdock, John, alias Barker	1815	AI34	495	502
Threlkeld, John	Deed fr	Reintzel, Valentine, of G'tn.	1815	AI34	483	492
Threlkeld, John	Deed to	Hutchinson, Samuel	1815	AI34	282	319
Threlkeld, John	Deed to	Cochran, Eleanor	1816	AM37	171	130
Threlkeld, John	Deed to	Bronaugh, John W.	1816	AM37	020	016
Threlkeld, John	Deed to	Brookes, Joseph	1817	AN38	461	332
Threlkeld, John	D. of T. fr	Ratcliff, Joseph, of G'tn.	1817	AN38	045	037
Threlkeld, John	Deed fr	Harbaugh, Leonard et al	1817	AN38	295	215
Threlkeld, John	B. of S. fr	Stone, Edward	1817	AN38	048	039
Threlkeld, John	Decree	Harbaugh, Leonard et al	1817	AN38	295	215
Threlkeld, John	B. of S. fr	Bradley, Phineas	1817	AO39	254	183
Threlkeld, John	B. of S. fr	Wathen, Charles [Worthen]	1817	AO39	411	279
Threlkeld, John	Deed fr	Mountz, Jacob, collector	1817	AO39	094	074
Threlkeld, John & Elizabeth et al	Decree agt	Beatty, Charles et al	1797	C3	015	12
Threlkeld, John & Jane	Deed fr	Deakins, Francis	1798	D4	088	074
Threlkeld, John & Elizabeth	Deed to	Duffy, Bryan	1807	S18	113	093
Threlkeld, John, coroner	Deed to	Burnett, Charles & J.E. Rigdon	1799	D4	351	338
Threlkeld, John et al	Deed to	Deakins, Francis	1802	H8	361	336
Threlkeld, John et al	R. of S. to	Mayor of Georgetown	1803	K10	031	31
Threlkeld, John, Gent.	Deed to	Beatty, John M. et al	1805	N13	302	245
Threlkeld, John, *Knaves Disapp.*	Deed fr	Davidson, John, of Annapolis	1795	B2A	178	240
Threlkeld, John, Montgomery Co.	Deed to	Medley, Bernard, Montgomery Co.	1795	B2A	270	377
Threlkeld, John, of G'tn.	Deed to	Simms, Joseph Milbourne, of G'tn.	1794	B2A	003	004
Threlkeld, John, of G'tn.	Deed to	Bayly, Jesse, of G'tn.	1794	B2A	145	192
Threlkeld, John, of G'tn.	Deed to	Gosler, John, of G'tn.	1794	B2A	035	038
Threlkeld, John, of G'tn.	Deed to	King, Zephaniah, of G'tn.	1795	B2A	243	338
Threlkeld, John, of Montg. Co.	Deed to	Medley, Bernard, of Mongt. Co.	1796	B2B	512	217
Threlkeld, John, of Montg. Co.	Deed fr	Deakins, Francis, of Montg. Co.	1796	B2B	486	177
Threlkeld, John, of Montg. Co.	Deed to	Carroll, John et al	1796	B2B	500	197
Threlkeld, John, of Montg. Co.	Deed to	Neale, Francis, Rev., Montg. Co.	1796	B2B	502	201
Threlkeld, John, of Montg. Co.	Deed to	Fenwick, George, of Montg. Co.	1796	B2B	501	199
Threlkeld, John, of Montg. Co.	Deed to	Herbert, Francis, St. Mary's Co.	1796	B2B	501	200
Threlkeld, John, of Montg. Co.	Deed fr	Bayly, William, of P.G. Co.	1796	B2B	382	038
Threlkeld, John, of Montg. Co.	Deed to	Boone, Edward, of G'tn.	1797	C3	175	147
Threlkeld, John, of Montg. Co.	Deed to	Miles, Henry, of St. Mary's Co.	1797	C3	216	182
Threlkeld, John, of G'tn.	Deed to	Lingan, James M., of G'tn.	1797	C3	004	3
Threlkeld, John, of G'tn.	Deed to	Jones, Anthony	1797	C3	115	94
Threlkeld, John, of Montg. Co.	Deed to	Deakins, William, Jr. et al	1797	C3	260	213
Threlkeld, John, of Montg. Co.	Deed to	Neale, Francis Ignatius, Rev.	1798	C3	447	351
Threlkeld, John, of Montg. Co.	Deed to	Moore, James, of G'tn.	1798	C3	327	264
Threlkeld, John, of G'tn.	Deed to	Carroll, Patrick, taylor, of G'tn.	1798	C3	463	364
Threlkeld, John, of G'tn.	Deed to	Mason, John Thomson, of G'tn.	1798	D4	085	071

Party	What	Party	Year	Liber	Old	New
Threlkeld, John, of G'tn.	Deed fr	Jones, Anthony, of G'tn.	1799	E5	071	058
Threlkeld, John, of G'tn.	Deed to	Offutt, Rezin, of Fairfax Co. VA	1800	E5	296	289
Threlkeld, John, of G'tn.	Deed to	Goozler, John	1800	E5	266	259
Threlkeld, John, of G'tn.	Deed to	Deakins, Francis, of G'tn.	1802	G7	589	739
Threlkeld, John, of G'tn.	Deed to	Reeves, Thomas Courtney, of MD	1802	H8	137	133
Threlkeld, John, of G'tn.	Deed to	Moore, James	1802	H8	252	240
Threlkeld, John, of G'tn.	Deed to	Deakins, Francis, of G'tn.	1802	G7	589	738
Threlkeld, John, of G'tn.	Lease to	Mahony, John, of G'tn.	1804	K10	346	358
Threlkeld, John, of G'tn.	Deed to	Miller, Elizabeth, of G'tn.	1804	K10	354	366
Threlkeld, John, of G'tn.	Deed fr	Brent, Daniel Carroll, marshal	1804	K10	319	326
Threlkeld, John, of G'tn.	Deed to	Turner, Samuel, of G'tn.	1804	K10	384	399
Threlkeld, John, of G'tn.	Agreement	Coles, John	1806	O14	218	144
Threlkeld, John, of G'tn.	Deed to	Hellen, Walter	1807	S18	122	099
Threlkeld, John, of G'tn.	Deed to	Coles, John, now of G'tn.	1807	S18	173	141
Threlkeld, John, of G'tn.	Deed to	Gozler, John, of G'tn.	1809	X23	046	034
Threlkeld, John, of G'tn.	Deed fr	Slye, Thomas G., of G'tn., trustee	1810	Z25	167	132
Threlkeld, John, of G'tn.	Deed to	Duvall, William, innkeeper, of G'tn.	1813	AE30	128	099
Threlkeld, John, of G'tn.	Deed to	Addison, Walter D., Rev., of G'tn.	1814	AG32	306	224
Threlkeld, John, of G'tn.	Deed fr	Ratcliffe, Joseph, of G'tn.	1814	AG32	192	134
Threlkeld, John, of G'tn.	Deed fr	Wells, John, Jr., of G'tn.	1815	AK35	313	250
Threlkeld, John, of G'tn.	Deed fr	Dawson, William & Eleanor, Eng.	1816	AM37	169	128
Threlkeld, John, trustee	Deed fr	Gross, Jacob, an insolvent	1803	K10	097	103
Threlkeld, Mary & Jane (daus.)	Deed fr	Threlkeld, John	1802	H8	328	307
Threlkeld, Sarah	Deed fr	Beall, Thomas, of George	1798	C3	477	376
Thruston, Bucker	Deed fr	Murdock, John A. & Margaret	1815	AI34	396	419
Thruston, Buckner	Deed fr	Carroll, Daniel, of *Duddington* et ux	1812	AD29	004	003
Thruston, Buckner	Deed fr	Law, Thoma & Edmund	1812	AD29	013	009
Thruston, Buckner	Mortgage to	Brent, William	1813	AF31	474	345
Thruston, Buckner	Deed fr	Carroll, Daniel, of *Duddington*	1813	AF31	435	313
Thruston, Buckner	Deed fr	Peltz, John	1816	AM37	364	263
Tictzen, Henry, Jr.	Deed fr	Prout, William	1800	E5	219	212
Tidgen, Henry	Deed to	Cochran, Aleander, Jr.	1806	P15	070	043
Tiethy, Edw.	Deed fr	Dorsey, William H.	1802	I9	186	287
Tietjen, Henry	B. of S. fr	Keiglar, John	1804	L11	108	112
Tietjen, Henry	Assign fr	Keiglar, John	1804	L11	107	110
Tiffin, Edward	Cert Free to	[ ], Sukey (C) & daughters	1817	AO39	182	134
Tilghman, James, of Q.A. Co.	Deed to	Beall, Thomas & John M. Gantt	1793	A1-1	282	377
Tilghman, Lloyd, of MD et al	Deed to	Barry, James	1802	H8	599	566
Tilghman, Matthew et al	Deed to	Barry, James	1802	H8	599	566
Tilghman, Peregrine	Deed to	Beall, Thomas & John M. Gantt	1793	A1-1	206	288
Tilghman, Richard et al	Deed to	Barry, James	1802	H8	599	566
Tilghman, Richard, of Q.A. Co.	Deed to	Beall, Thomas & John M. Gantt	1793	A1-1	270	353
Tilghman, William et al	Deed fr	Pratt, Henry et al	1808	T19	086	061
Tilghman, William et al	Convey fr	Greenleaf, Ann Penn	1809	V21	362	266
Tilley, John	Deed to	Beall, Thomas & John M. Gantt	1793	A1-2	401	9
Tilley, John, of P.G. Co.	B. of S. fr	Tilley, Robert	1807	R17	119	093
Tilley, Robert	B. of S. to	Bennet, Charles, of Alexa.	1807	R17	198	150
Tilley, Robert	B. of S. to	Tilley, John, of P.G. Co.	1807	R17	119	093
Tillotson, Thomas & Margaret, def.	Suit	Foxall, Henry, plt.	1816	AN38	073	057
Tillotson, Thomas & Margaret, NY	Deed to	Foxall, Henry	1817	AN38	076	059
Tillotson, Thomas, of NY	Deed to	Stoddert, Benjamin	1792	A1-1	113	165
Tillotson, Thomas, of NY	Deed fr	Bayly, William & William Deakins	1794	B2A	094	123
Tillotson, Thomas, of NY	Deed fr	Deakins, William, Jr. et al	1795	B2A	255	356
Tillotson, Thomas, of NY	Agreement	Templeman, John	1801	G7	120	154
Tilly, Ann	B. of S. to	Mechlin, Joseph	1812	AC28	227	169

Party	What	Party	Year	Liber	Old	New
Tilman, Nice (C)	Cert Free fr	Coombe, Griffith	1815	AI34	388	413
Tims, Henry	Deed fr	Law, Thomas	1816	AL36	436	415
Tims, Henry	D. of T. to	Burch, Samuel	1817	AN38	226	165
Tingey, Thomas	Deed fr	Forrest, Uriah & Samuel Hanson	1800	F6	092	056
Tingey, Thomas	Deed fr	Hanson, Samuel & Uriah Forrest	1800	F6	092	056
Tingey, Thomas	Deed to	Prout, William	1801	G7	228	304
Tingey, Thomas	Deed fr	Prout, William	1801	G7	246	331
Tingey, Thomas	Deed fr	Deblois, Louis	1802	I9	217	340
Tingey, Thomas	Deed to	Pratt, Henry et al	1802	I9	572	927
Tingey, Thomas	Deed fr	Pratt, Henry et al	1802	I9	213	336
Tingey, Thomas	Deed fr	Yeates, William	1802	H8	184	177
Tingey, Thomas	Deed to	Woodward, William	1803	K10	092	99
Tingey, Thomas	Deed fr	Woodward, William	1803	K10	060	65
Tingey, Thomas	Deed to	Yates, William, of Alexa.	1805	M12	349	355
Tingey, Thomas	Deed to	Beck, Richard, of G'tn.	1805	M12	196	197
Tingey, Thomas	Deed to	King, Benjamin	1806	P15	040	024
Tingey, Thomas	Deed to	Cocke, Butler	1806	Q16	064	040
Tingey, Thomas	Deed to	Underwood, Robert	1806	O14	398	266
Tingey, Thomas	Deed to	King, Benjamin	1806	Q16	027	018
Tingey, Thomas	Deed fr	Voss, Nicholas	1807	S18	107	047
Tingey, Thomas	Deed to	Davis, Shadrach	1807	R17	052	042
Tingey, Thomas	Deed fr	Voss, Nicholas	1807	S18	056	087
Tingey, Thomas	Convey fr	Craven, Tunis	1808	U20	267	142
Tingey, Thomas	Deed fr	Voss, Nicholas	1809	V21	196	139
Tingey, Thomas	Manumis to	[ ], Abraham (negro)	1809	W22	213	146
Tingey, Thomas	Deed to	Smallwood, Samuel N.	1809	V21	231	165
Tingey, Thomas	Release to	Davis, Shadrick	1810	Z25	203	160
Tingey, Thomas	Deed to	Brent, Daniel et al	1810	Y24	406	366
Tingey, Thomas	Deed fr	Pratt, Henry et al	1812	AC28	428	308
Tingey, Thomas	Agreement	Davis, John	1813	AF31	507	370
Tingey, Thomas	Release to	Voss, Nicholas, of VA	1813	AE30	149	117
Tingey, Thomas	Deed to	Truxton, Thomas, Capt., of NJ	1813	AF31	507	370
Tingey, Thomas	Deed to	Winn, Timothy	1815	AI34	183	210
Tingey, Thomas	Mortgage fr	Winn, Timothy	1815	AK35	123	095
Tingey, Thomas	Deed to	Miller, Samuel	1816	AM37	414	297
Tingey, Thomas	Deed to	Orr, Benjamin Grayson	1816	AL36	300	297
Tingey, Thomas & Peter Miller	Deed fr	Prout, William	1807	Q16	377	289
Tingey, Thomas & S.N. Smallwood	Mortgage fr	Voss, Nicholas	1810	Y24	240	222
Tingey, Thomas & S.N. Smallwood	Deed to	Wright, Matthew	1811	AB27	377	312
Tingey, Thomas & S.N. Smallwood	D. of T. fr	Voss, Nicholas, of VA	1813	AE30	115	089
Tingey, Thomas, Capt. U.S.N.	Deed fr	Beck, Richard, mer., of G'tn.	1805	M12	313	316
Tingey, Thomas, Capt.	Deed fr	Davis, Shadrach	1807	R17	265	202
Tingey, Thomas, Capt.	Deed to	Beck, Richard, of G'tn.	1807	S18	375	297
Tingey, Thomas, Com.	Deed fr	Miller, Samuel, Maj.	1817	AN38	259	189
Tingey, Thomas et al	Mortgage fr	Russ, Samuel	1804	K10	390	405
Tingey, Thomas et al	Mortgage fr	Russ, Samuel	1806	P15	012	007
Tingey, Thomas et al	Deed to	Russ, Samuel	1806	Q16	107	069
Tingey, Thomas, Gent.	Deed to	Harvey, Peter, of Phila.	1804	L11	277	255
Tingey, Thomas, Gent.	Deed to	Friend, James, baker	1804	L11	039	39
Tingey, Thomas, Gent.	Deed to	Nesmith, Ebenezer, carpenter	1804	L11	059	61
Tippett, Ann	B. of S. fr	Tippett, Thomas, her son	1813	AF31	304	217
Tippett, Cartwright	Deed fr	Boyd, Washington, marshal	1808	U20	353	192
Tippett, Cartwright	Deed fr	Prout, William	1808	U20	220	119
Tippett, Cartwright	Deed fr	May, Frederick	1809	V21	255	182
Tippett, Cartwright	Cert Free to	Scott, Treasy (C), alias Rounds	1812	AD29	503	424

Index to District of Columbia Land Records, 1792-1817

Party	What	Party	Year	Liber	Old	New
Tippett, Cartwright	Cert Free to	Rounds, Hezekiah (M)	1812	AD29	503	425
Tippett, Cartwright	Cert Free to	Scott, Nancy (M)	1812	AD29	503	424
Tippett, Cartwright	Cert Free to	Rounds, Off (M)	1812	AD29	502	424
Tippett, Cartwright	Deed fr	Young, Moses	1813	AF31	291	206
Tippett, Thomas	B. of S. to	Tippett, Ann, his mother	1813	AF31	304	217
Tippit, Cartwright	Deed fr	Carroll, Daniel, of *Duddington*	1806	P15	397	266
Tippitt, Cartwright	Deed fr	May, Frederick	1807	R17	356	271
Tippitt, Cartwright	Deed fr	Spalding, Richard, constable	1807	R17	353	269
Toland, Henry & James Taylor	Deed fr	Kearney, John & Edward Fallon	1804	K10	139	151
Toland, Henry, of Phila. et al	Mortgage fr	Ellis, Robert	1801	G7	390	523
Toland, Henry, of Phila. et al	Deed fr	Brent, Daniel Carroll, marshal	1805	O14	140	091
Toland, Henry, of Phila. et al	Deed fr	Underwood, Robert	1806	P15	142	092
Toland, Henry, of Phila. et al	Deed fr	Underwood, Robert	1807	S18	117	095
Tolmie, Alice, d/o Robert et al	Deed fr	Van Ness, John P. & Marcia	1807	Q16	375	288
Tolmie, James, s/o Robert et al	Deed fr	Van Ness, John P. & Marcia	1807	Q16	375	288
Tolmie, Margaret, d/o Robert et al	Deed fr	Van Ness, John P. & Marcia	1807	Q16	375	288
Tolmie, Robert, of G'tn.	Deed fr	Wilson, Alexander	1800	E5	130	118
Tolmie, Robert, of G'tn.	Deed to	Dove, Joseph	1801	G7	103	132
Tolson, Alexander	Deed to	Reizner, Henry	1817	AN38	287	209
Tolson, Alexander, of G'tn.	Lease fr	Allen, Samuel (C), of Montg. Co.	1816	AL36	481	453
Tomlinson, B.H.	Qualify	Lieutenant of militia	1813	AE30	376	278
Tompkins, Charles, insolvent	Deed to	Mitchell, John, Capt., trustee	1806	O14	264	175
Toogood, Edward Fisher, of Balto.	B. of S. to	Huddlestone, Joseph	1806	Q16	044	028
Tool, Patrick	Deed fr	Lowndes, Charles	1802	I9	331	545
Tool, Philip	Lease fr	Dempsey, John	1801	G7	481	618
Toole, James	B. of S. fr	White, John	1805	N13	002	003
Toole, James	B. of S. fr	Toole, Patrick	1813	AE30	526	390
Toole, John	Assign fr	Whelan, Peter	1805	N13	125	120
Toole, Matthew	B. of S. fr	O'Mara, Catharine	1815	AH33	440	378
Toole, Patrick	B. of S. to	Toole, Philip	1802	I9	449	742
Toole, Patrick	Bond fr	Baker, Samuel	1806	O14	315	209
Toole, Patrick	Bond fr	Baker, Samuel	1806	O14	313	208
Toole, Patrick	Quit fr	Pratt, Henry et al	1809	X23	135	097
Toole, Patrick	B. of S. to	Toole, James	1813	AE30	526	390
Toole, Patrick, carter	D. of T. to	Greenleaf, James, of Phila. PA	1809	W22	387	251
Toole, Philip	B. of S. fr	Toole, Philip	1802	I9	449	742
Tophouse, Samuel & G. Walker	Release to	Peck, Joseph	1814	AG32	125	092
Tophouse, Samuel et al	B. of S. fr	Peck, Joseph	1808	U20	390	216
Tousard, Lewis	Deed to	Dunlap, James et al	1802	H8	138	134
Tousard, Lewis	Deed to	Carleton, Joseph et al	1802	H8	138	134
Tousard, Louis	Deed fr	Templeman, John	1802	I9	574	930
Tousard, Louis	Deed fr	Forrest, Uriah et al	1802	I9	558	905
Tousard, Louis	Deed fr	Forrest, Uriah	1802	I9	558	904
Townsend, Henry	Deed to	Ponsonby, John, Glasgow Co. NC	1792	A1-1	156	224
Townsend, Henry	Deed fr	Cloud, Amos, heirs of	1801	G7	218	291
Townsend, Henry	Deed fr	Evans, Samuel et a;	1801	G7	216	288
Townsend, Henry et al	Lease fr	Threlkeld, John	1799	D4	173	154
Townsend, Henry, of G'tn.	Deed to	Townsend, Hy., Thos. & George	1804	L11	224	209
Townsend, Henry, Thos. & Geo.	Deed fr	Townsend, Henry, of G'tn.	1804	L11	224	209
Townsend, Jesse J.	B. of S. to	Ward, John W., of Montg. Co.	1815	AK35	053	041
Townsend, John, of P.G.	Assign to	Burch, Samuel	1811	AB27	270	221
Townshend, Henry et al	Deed fr	Sentorius, Mary Ann	1802	I9	578	937
Townshend, Lemuel	Lease fr	Prout, William	1811	AA26	073	053
Townshend, Leonard, of P.G. Co.	B. of S. to	Robinson, Zadock	1816	Al34	453	466
Townshnd, Leonard et al	Release fr	Boone, Joseph, sheriff	1799	E5	053	042

Party	What	Party	Year	Liber	Old	New
Tracey, Thomas	Deed fr	Schultz, Henry	1805	N13	157	145
Tracy, Thomas, of Fairfax Co.	Deed to	Shultze, Henry, of G'tn.	1816	AL36	297	294
Traquair, James, Phila. et al	P. of Atty. fr	Swinton, Archibald, in Scot.	1808	U20	312	166
Travers, Elias	Deed fr	Dorsey, William H., of G'tn.	1806	Q16	256	177
Travers, Elias	Deed to	Travers, Nicholas, of G'tn.	1812	AD29	111	085
Travers, Elias Erl	Deed fr	Balch, Stephen B., Rev.	1805	O14	036	022
Travers, Eseas	Deed fr	Stephens, John	1809	W22	039	029
Travers, Esias	Deed fr	Glover, Charles	1806	Q16	121	078
Travers, Esias	Deed to	Travers, Nicholas, of G'tn.	1808	T19	127	090
Travers, Esias	Deed to	Travers, Nicholas	1812	AC28	207	156
Travers, George	Deed fr	Smallwood, Samuel N.	1813	AE30	268	207
Travers, George	Deed to	Hewitt, Mary	1814	AH33	307	265
Travers, John	Deed to	Schnively, Henry	1800	E5	175	165
Travers, Nicholas	Deed fr	Reintzel, Anthony	1802	I9	288	472
Travers, Nicholas	Deed fr	Chandler, Walter Story	1804	K10	389	404
Travers, Nicholas	Deed fr	Murdock, John, of G'tn.	1810	Z25	245	192
Travers, Nicholas	Deed fr	Travers, Elias	1812	AC28	207	156
Travers, Nicholas	Deed fr	Risener, Henry	1812	AD29	449	378
Travers, Nicholas, of G'tn.	Deed fr	Tyler, Dryden, wid/o Robert	1796	B2B	587	335
Travers, Nicholas, of G'tn.	Deed fr	Travers, Esias	1808	T19	127	090
Travers, Nicholas, of G'tn.	Deed fr	Dorsey, William H., of Balto.	1810	Z25	246	193
Travers, Nicholas, of G'tn.	Convey fr	Laird, John, of G'tn.	1810	Z25	257	201
Travers, Nicholas, of G'tn.	Deed fr	Laird, John, of G'tn.	1811	AB27	454	373
Travers, Sidney	Deed fr	Dorsey, William H., of Balto.	1811	AC28	051	039
Travers, Thomas, of G'tn.	Deed fr	Travers, Elias	1812	AD29	111	085
Traverse, Elias E.	Deed fr	Traverse, Esias	1808	V21	044	033
Traverse, Elias E.	Deed fr	Traverse, Esias	1808	V21	042	032
Traverse, Esias	Cert fr	Munroe, Thomas, Supt.	1807	S18	243	192
Traverse, Esias	Deed to	Traverse, Elias E.	1808	V21	044	033
Traverse, Esias	Deed to	Traverse, Elias E.	1808	V21	042	032
Traverse, George, of G'tn.	Deed fr	Landes, Abraham, of G'tn.	1816	AL36	093	094
Traverse, Mary, w/o Capt. Geo.	Cert Free to	[ ], Milley (C)	1816	AL36	143	143
Traverse, Nichlas, of G'tn.	Mortgage fr	Mountz, Joseph, of G'tn.	1817	AN38	241	177
Traverse, Nicholas	Release to	Reizner, Henry	1815	AI34	542	546
Traverse, Nicholas	B. of S. fr	Moore, Joseph	1817	AO39	252	182
Traverse, Nicholas & Elias E.	Deed to	Commissioners of Washington	1800	F6	110	068
Traverse, Nicholas, of G'tn.	Deed fr	Reintzel, Anthony, of G'tn.	1803	K10	088	94
Traverse, Nicholas, of G'tn.	Deed fr	Polock, David, of G'tn.	1804	L11	031	31
Traverse, Nicholas, of G'tn.	Cert fr	Munroe, Thomas, Supt.	1815	AI34	461	474
Traverse, Nicholas, of G'tn.	Deed fr	Clarke, Edward, of G'tn.	1816	AM37	442	317
Travis, Elizabeth, admx. of John	D. of T. to	Bond, Phineas & Thos. Astley	1808	V21	102	077
Travis, John, mer., of Phila. PA	Deed fr	Ashley, John, mer., of Phila.	1803	K10	085	91
Travis, Nicholas & Elias C.	Deed fr	Polock, Isaac	1802	H8	043	041
Treat, Samuel	Deed fr	Piercy, James, sugar refiner	1800	E5	196	187
Treat, Samuel et al	Deed fr	Piercy, James, sugar refiner	1800	E5	197	189
Trezevant, Peter	Deposition		1806	Q16	303	231
Triplet, John	B. of S. to	Huddleston, Joseph	1804	K10	144	156
Triplet, Thomas	Inventory		1802	H8	032	30
Triplett, Sarah	B. of S. fr	Crossfield, Jeheel	1808	V21	019	014
Triplett, Thomas	Division		1802	H8	032	030
Triplett, Thomas	Deed fr	McClean, Cornelius	1807	Q16	370	283
Troutman, Michael, Bullett Co. KY	Deed to	Orme, Thomas, of Montg. Co.	1798	C3	496	390
Trudeau, Maria Josepha Laveau	Deed to	Wilkerson, Maria Celesta Laveau	1815	AI34	288	324
Trundel, Horatio, of G'tn.	Deed to	McCutchen, Thomas, of G'tn.	1808	T19	289	212
Trundle, Horatio, of G'tn. et al	B. of S. fr	Hurdell, Leonard, of G'tn.	1802	H8	408	378

Party	What	Party	Year	Liber	Old	New
Trundle, Horatio, of G'tn.	Deed fr	Heeter, Conrad, of G'tn.	1806	Q16	170	113
Trundle, Horatio, of G'tn.	Lease fr	Beall, Thomas B., of G'tn.	1813	AF31	315	225
Trundle, Horatio, of G'tn.	Deed fr	Gaines, Richard, Hamilton Co. OH	1813	AF31	317	226
Trundle, Horatio, of G'tn.	Deed to	Beall, Thomas	1816	AL36	416	399
Truxton, Thomas	Deed fr	Commissioners of Washington	1799	D4	412	388
Truxton, Thomas	Deed fr	Commissioners of Washington	1799	D4	411	388
Truxton, Thomas, Capt., of NJ	Deed fr	Tingey, Thomas	1813	AF31	507	370
Tucker, Joseph	Deed to	Tucker, Sarah & Mary	1802	I9	455	752
Tucker, Joseph et al	Deed fr	Godfrey, William	1801	G7	077	100
Tucker, Sarah & Mary	Deed fr	Tucker, Joseph	1802	I9	455	752
Tuckfield, William H.	Convey to	Fletcher, William	1804	K10	207	216
Tuckfield, William H.P.	B. of S. to	Frost, John T.	1802	I9	489	803
Tuckfield, William H.P.	Deed to	Chandler, Jacob	1802	I9	183	280
Tuckfield, William H.P.	Mortgage fr	Prime, William	1805	O14	048	029
Tuckfield, William H.P.	Deed to	Smallwood, Samuel N., trustee	1807	R17	267	203
Tuckfield, William H.P.	Deed to	Cochrane, Alexander, Jr.	1808	T19	137	097
Tuckfield, William H.P.	Deed to	Wright, Matthew	1808	T19	363	260
Tuckfield, William H.P. et al	Deed fr	Law, Thomas	1808	T19	139	099
Tuckfield, William H.P.	Assign to	Young, Thomas	1809	W22	202	140
Tuckfield, William H.P.	Deed fr	Hemler, John	1811	AB27	273	223
Tuckfield, William H.P.	Assign to	Peltz, John	1812	AC28	139	104
Tuckfield, William H.P., trustee	Deed fr	Goldsmith, John, insolvent	1813	AF31	334	238
Tuckfield, William H.P.	Lease fr	Bayly, Mountjoy	1813	AF31	197	133
Tuckfield, William H.P.	Deed fr	Chandler, Walter Story	1813	AF31	545	404
Tuckfield, William H.P.	Deed fr	Pratt, Henry et al	1813	AE30	230	184
Tuckfield, William H.P.	Deed to	Davis, Shadrach	1814	AG32	086	065
Tuckfield, William H.P., trustee	Deed fr	Gillespie, James	1815	AI34	006	006
Tuckfield, William H.P.	Deed fr	Miles, Edward	1816	AM37	174	131
Tuckfield, William H.P.	Deed to	Huddleston, Joseph	1816	AL36	364	353
Tudor, William, of Boston MA	Deed fr	Blodget, Samuel, Jr., of Phila.	1800	F6	079	049
Tuel, Henry	B. of S. to	Peter, David	1807	S18	160	130
Tuell, Henry	Deed fr	Macdonald, Archabald	1804	L11	314	288
Tuell, Henry	Deed to	Macdonald, Janet, d/o Archabald	1804	L11	315	289
Tunnicliff, William	Deed fr	Walker, George	1804	M12	022	022
Tunnicliff, William	B. of S. fr	Fenwick, Richard	1807	R17	360	274
Tunnicliff, William et al	Deed to	Stelle, Pontius Delare	1804	M12	019	020
Tunnicliff, William, of P.G. Co.	Deed fr	Law, Thomas	1808	T19	208	151
Tunnicliffe, William	Mortgage fr	Stelle, Pontius Delare	1804	L11	122	125
Turner, Ann, of G'tn.	B. of S. to	Smith, Ann, of G'tn.	1801	G7	426	561
Turner, Catherine et al	Deed to	Forrest, Uriah, of G'tn.	1792	A1-1	168	242
Turner, Catherine, wid/o Edmund	Deed to	White, James, Jr.	1794	B2A	103	135
Turner, Celia (C), age 23	Cert Free fr	Cooper, Lavinia	1813	AE30	225	181
Turner, Elleck (C), age 43	Manumis fr	Dodge, Francis	1813	AE30	550	408
Turner, John	P. of Atty. to	King, James C.	1802	I9	237	381
Turner, John & Milesent, of NC	Deed to	King, James Carrol	1808	U20	142	081
Turner, John & Elizabeth, of MD	Deed to	Kurtz, David & Benjamin, of G'tn.	1815	AI34	475	486
Turner, Mary, exrx. of Zephaniah	Deed to	Key, Francis Scott, of G'tn.	1811	Z25	487	387
Turner, Mary, of Charles Co.	Deed to	Magruder, Ninian, of G'tn.	1811	Z25	502	398
Turner, Nancy	B. of S. to	Bridges, John	1802	I9	201	315
Turner, Nanny	B. of S. to	Bridges, John, of G'tn.	1802	H8	313	295
Turner, Nanny	Exchange	Conkling, Augustine	1802	I9	001	001
Turner, Nanny	B. of S. to	Worsley, John	1802	I9	001	002
Turner, Nanny	B. of S. to	Bridges, John	1802	I9	001	001
Turner, Robert, of Balto. Co.	Deed fr	Weightman, Roger C.	1815	AG32	348	252
Turner, Robert, of Balto. Co.	Deed to	May, George W.	1815	AI34	045	051

Party	What	Party	Year	Liber	Old	New
Turner, Samuel	Deed to	Lowndes, Richard T.	1802	I9	259	418
Turner, Samuel	Deed fr	Munroe, Thomas, Supt.	1802	I9	249	401
Turner, Samuel	Deed to	Thompson, William	1802	I9	251	405
Turner, Samuel	Deed to	Wagner, Jacob	1802	I9	345	569
Turner, Samuel	Deed fr	Munroe, Thomas, Supr.	1802	I9	250	403
Turner, Samuel	Deed fr	Bank of Columbia	1802	I9	342	563
Turner, Samuel	Deed fr	Hazle, Jeremiah	1806	Q16	094	061
Turner, Samuel	Lease to	Thomson, William	1808	V21	039	029
Turner, Samuel et al	Deed fr	Shepperd, James G., of NC	1810	Z25	147	116
Turner, Samuel et al	Deed fr	Magruder, George, collector, G'tn.	1810	Z25	205	161
Turner, Samuel et al	Deed fr	Mountz, Jacob, collector, of G'tn.	1811	AA26	052	041
Turner, Samuel, Jr., of G'tn.	Deed fr	Magruder, George & Patrick, G'tn.	1795	B2A	176	237
Turner, Samuel, Jr.	Deed to	Bank of Columbia, President of	1800	E5	181	171
Turner, Samuel, Jr., of G'tn.	Deed fr	Beall, Thomas, of George, of G'tn.	1800	E5	192	184
Turner, Samuel, Jr., of G'tn.	Deed to	Nourse, Joseph, of G'tn.	1800	F6	023	015
Turner, Samuel, Jr.	Deed fr	Beatty, Charles, heirs of	1806	P15	021	013
Turner, Samuel, Jr., of G'tn.	Deed to	Turner, Thomas, of G'tn.	1806	Q16	314	240
Turner, Samuel, Jr.	Deed to	Bank of Columbia	1807	R17	145	112
Turner, Samuel, Jr.	Deed fr	Mayor of Georgetown et al	1808	U20	330	178
Turner, Samuel, Jr., def.	Suit	Mitchell, Mary, plt.	1810	Z25	025	019
Turner, Samuel, Jr., of G'tn.	Deed to	Mitchell, John, of G'tn.	1810	Z25	026	020
Turner, Samuel, Jr., of G'tn.	Mortgage to	Magruder, George, of G'tn. et al	1811	Z25	514	408
Turner, Samuel, Jr.	Deed fr	Smith, Walter & Clement	1811	Z25	540	430
Turner, Samuel, Jr.	D. of T. to	Union Bank of Georgetown	1813	AF31	399	289
Turner, Samuel, Jr., of G'tn.	Deed fr	Wooten, Richard, of Montg. Co.	1816	AL36	206	213
Turner, Samuel, of G'tn.	Deed fr	Threlkeld, John, of G'tn.	1804	K10	384	399
Turner, Samuel, of G'tn. et al	Deed to	Shepperd, James G., of G'tn.	1810	Z25	175	139
Turner, Thomas	Deed fr	Munroe, Thomas, Supt.	1802	I9	275	449
Turner, Thomas	Deed to	Stoddert, Benjamin	1802	I9	333	550
Turner, Thomas	Deed to	Gillis, Thomas H.	1802	I9	531	869
Turner, Thomas	Deed to	Vogeler, Rudolph	1802	I9	572	926
Turner, Thomas	Deed fr	Munroe, Thomas, Supt.	1802	I9	274	447
Turner, Thomas	Deed fr	Munroe, Thomas, Supt.	1802	I9	276	451
Turner, Thomas	Deed to	Benson, John	1802	I9	455	750
Turner, Thomas	Deed to	Peter, David et al	1805	M12	339	344
Turner, Thomas	Deed fr	Weems, Elizabeth, wid/o John	1815	AK35	202	158
Turner, Thomas	Deed fr	Weems, Elizabeth, gdn.	1815	AK35	203	159
Turner, Thomas & Samuel	Deed fr	Forrest, Rebecca	1810	Y24	203	187
Turner, Thomas, of G'tn.	Deed fr	Hanson, Alexander Contee	1795	B2A	207	285
Turner, Thomas, of G'tn.	Deed fr	Scott, George, Washington Co.	1795	B2A	224	311
Turner, Thomas, of G'tn.	Deed fr	Beall, William Murdock, Frdk. Co.	1800	E5	246	239
Turner, Thomas, of G'tn.	Deed to	Darnall, John	1800	E5	291	285
Turner, Thomas, of G'tn.	B. of S. to	Reintzel, Anthony, of G'tn.	1802	H8	371	345
Turner, Thomas, of G'tn.	Deed to	Oliver, Benjamin, Jr., Hanover VA	1804	K10	153	165
Turner, Thomas, of G'tn.	Deed fr	Turner, Samuel, Jr., of G'tn.	1806	Q16	314	240
Turner, Thomas, of G'tn.	Deed to	Lingan, Nicholas, of G'tn.	1808	U20	020	012
Turner, Thomas, of G'tn.	Deed fr	Chandler, Walter S. & Margaret	1815	AK35	205	160
Turner, Walker	Cert Free to	Martin, John & Nancy	1813	AE30	152	119
Turnicliff, William	P. of Atty. fr	Nicholson, John, of Phila.	1797	B2B	691	471
Turnpike Roads Company	Deed to	Fenwick, Thomas & Eleanor	1812	AC28	263	192
Tweedy, David	Deed fr	Kerr, Alexander	1810	Y24	491	433
Tweedy, David, trustee	Deed fr	Cox, Josias	1813	AF31	065	044
Tydings, John, of A.A. Co.	Mortgage fr	Tydings, Thomas	1813	AF31	268	188
Tydings, Thomas	Mortgage to	Tydings, John, of A.A. Co.	1813	AF31	268	188
Tyler, Dryden, wid/o Robert	Deed to	Travers, Nicholas, of G'tn.	1796	B2B	587	335

Party	What	Party	Year	Liber	Old	New
Tyler, Robert Bradley & Dryden	Deed to	Key, Philip Barton, of Annapolis	1792	A1-1	155	222
Tyson, Sabina Maria et al	P. of Atty. to	O'Connor, John, of Balto.	1813	AF31	148	099

Party	What	Party	Year	Liber	Old	New
U						
Underwood, John	Mortgage to	Jones, Walter & John P. Van Ness	1814	AH33	104	096
Underwood, John	Deed fr	Brush, John C.	1816	AM37	132	103
Underwood, John & Thomas	Deed to	Law, John	1815	AI34	144	165
Underwood, John & Thomas	Assign to	Grammar, Gottlieb C.	1815	AH33	544	466
Underwood, Robert	Assign fr	Burford, Henry	1802	I9	563	912
Underwood, Robert	Deed fr	Lovell, William	1802	I9	547	890
Underwood, Robert	Lease fr	Gardiner, John	1802	I9	549	892
Underwood, Robert	Deed fr	Brent, Daniel Carroll, marshal	1805	O14	138	090
Underwood, Robert	Deed fr	McIntire, Samuel	1805	N13	129	124
Underwood, Robert	Agreement	Woodward, William	1806	O14	404	270
Underwood, Robert	Deed fr	Tingey, Thomas	1806	O14	398	266
Underwood, Robert	Deed to	Taylor, James N. & Henry Toland	1806	P15	142	092
Underwood, Robert	Deed to	McIntire, Samuel	1806	P15	128	082
Underwood, Robert	Deed fr	Pratt, John Wilks	1806	Q16	031	020
Underwood, Robert	Deed fr	Woodward, William	1806	O14	396	264
Underwood, Robert	Deed to	Taylor, James M., of Phila. et al	1807	S18	117	095
Underwood, Robert	Deed fr	Moore, James	1807	S18	219	175
Underwood, Robert	Deed fr	Miller, William, of Phila. PA	1810	Y24	133	121
Underwood, Robert	Deed to	Somerville, Jane, late Underwood	1811	AA26	011	009
Underwood, Robert	Deed fr	Dorsey, William H., of Balto.	1811	AA26	309	208
Underwood, Robert	Deed fr	Murdock, John, of G'tn.	1811	AA26	306	206
Underwood, Robert	Deed to	Walker, Archibald, Rev., of MD	1812	AD29	337	280
Underwood, Robert et al	Deed fr	Munroe, Thomas, Supt.	1802	I9	062	085
Underwood, Robert et al	Deed fr	Pratt, Henry et al	1802	I9	217	342
Underwood, Thomas & John, PA	Deed to	Orr, Benjamin G.	1817	AN38	219	160
Union Bank of Georgetown	Contract	Gooding, John, of Balto.	1810	Y24	154	140
Union Bank of Georgetown	Deed fr	Peter, George, of G'tn.	1811	AA26	361	241
Union Bank of Georgetown	Deed fr	Peter, David, of G'tn.	1811	AA26	357	238
Union Bank of Georgetown	D. of T. fr	Turner, Samuel, Jr.	1813	AF31	399	289
Union Bank of Georgetown	Deed fr	Peter, George, of G'tn.	1814	AG32	227	161
Union Bank of Georgetown	Deed fr	Peter, Thomas, of G'tn.	1814	AG32	224½	159
Union Bank of Georgetown	Deed fr	Ober, Robert, of G'tn.	1814	AG32	367	266
United States	Cert fr	Commissioners of Washington	1794	B2A	327	459
United States	Cert fr	Commissioners of Washington	1794	B2A	329	461
United States	Cert fr	Commissioners of Washington	1794	B2A	328	460
United States	Cert fr	Commissioners of Washington	1794	B2A	327	458
United States	Assign fr	Commissioners of Washington	1794	B2A	121	162
United States	Cert fr	Commissioners of Washington	1794	B2A	327	458
United States	Cert fr	Commissioners of Washington	1794	B2A	328	460
United States	Cert fr	Commissioners of Washington	1794	B2A	328	460
United States	Cert fr	Commissioners of Washington	1794	B2A	327	459
United States	Cert fr	Commissioners of Washington	1794	B2A	326	457
United States	Notice fr	Commissioners of Washington	1798	C3	321	306
United States	Deed fr	Commissioners of Washington	1800	E5	149	137
United States	Surveys	Commissioners of Washington	1800	E5	406	379
United States	Bond fr	Caldwell, Elias B. et al	1801	G7	347	478
United States	Deed fr	Commissioners of Washington	1801	G7	157	208
United States	Bond fr	Williams, Elisha Owen et al	1801	G7	013	016
United States	Bond fr	Mitchell, John et al	1801	G7	012	015
United States	Bond fr	Magruder, George B. et al	1801	G7	011	014
United States	Bond fr	Mackall, Leonard et al	1801	G7	013	016
United States	Bond fr	Mackall, Leonard et al	1802	H8	519	478
United States	Bond fr	Williams, Elisha O. et al	1802	H8	520	479
United States	Bond fr	Williams, Jeremiah et al	1802	H8	519	478

Index to District of Columbia Land Records, 1792-1817

Party	What	Party	Year	Liber	Old	New
United States	Bond fr	Magruder, George Beall	1802	I9	091	130
United States	Bond fr	Mitchell, John	1802	I9		130
United States	Bond fr	Boyd, Washington, as coroner	1802	I9	116	170
United States	Bond fr	Semmes, Joseph et al	1802	H8	520	479
United States	Mortgage fr	Nourse, Joseph, of G'tn.	1805	M12	234	235
United States	Mortgage fr	Nourse, Joseph, of G'tn.	1808	U20	275	146
United States	Bond fr	Bayne, Horatio et al	1809	X23	316	253
United States	Bond fr	Kerby, John Baptist et al	1809	X23	316	253
United States	Bond fr	Edmonston, Edward, constable	1810	X23	346	277
United States	Deed to	Bickley, Robert S., Phila. PA et al	1810	Y24	267	245
United States [George Bumford]	Deed fr	Brooke, Thomas A., of Montg. Co.	1815	AK35	003	002
Updegraff, Mary, wid/o Josiah et al	Deed to	Way, John, of New Castle Co. DE	1815	AK35	224	176
Upperman, George	Deed fr	Davidson, John	1802	I9	450	743
Upperman, George	Deed fr	Beatty, Charles	1802	I9	244	393
Upperman, Henry	Deed fr	Beall, Thomas, of George	1794	B2A	154	203
Upperman, Henry	Deed fr	Beatty, Charles	1802	H8	113	109
Upperman, Henry, Jr.	Deed fr	Beall, Thomas, of George	1805	M12	400	413
Upperman, Henry, Jr.	Deed fr	Beatty, Charles, heirs of	1806	O14	278	184
Upperman, Henry, Jr.	Deed to	Bowie, Washington, mer.	1810	Y24	102	093
Upperman, Henry, Jr.	Deed to	Stone, Edward	1813	AF31	525	386
Upperman, Henry, of G'tn.	Deed to	Bayly, Jesse et al	1801	G7	030	038
Upperman, Henry, of G'tn.	Deed fr	Jones, Benjamin W., late sheriff	1801	G7		037

Party	What	Party	Year	Liber	Old	New
V						
Vallet, Peter	B. of S. to	Boyd, Washington	1814	AH33	356	308
Vallet, Peter	Mortgage to	Hoban, James	1814	AH33	357	309
Vallet, Peter	Lease to	Wright, Barzeller, of NJ	1817	AN38	106	079
Vallett, Peter	B. of S. to	Dixon, John C.	1807	R17	275	209
Vallette, Peter	Lease fr	Hoban, James	1811	AB27	333	274
Van Bibber, Abraham, Gent.	Deed fr	Steele, John, of Balto.	1804	M12	014	015
Van Bibber, Abraham, of Balto.	Deed fr	Stoddert, Benjamin	1804	K10	210	221
Van Bibber, Abraham, Balto. Co.	Deed fr	Steele, John, of Balto. Co.	1805	M12	390	403
Van Cortland, Philip, of NY	Deed to	Thompson, Ezra et al	1802	G7	465	601
Van Cortland, Philip, of NY	Deed fr	Bailey, Theodorus & Rebecca, NY	1804	M12	005	005
Van Cortland, Philip, of NY	Deed fr	Smith, Isaac et al	1804	M12	002	002
Van Cortland, Philip, of NY	Deed to	Smith, Isaac et al	1804	M12	001	001
Van Cortlandt, Philip, of NY	Deed fr	Forrest, Uriah	1801	G7	079	102
Van Horne, Gabriel P., of P.G. Co.	Cert fr	Commissioners of Washington	1792	B2A	289	404
Van Mannierck, Anthony, Phila.	Deed to	Corless, Matthias, grocer, Phila.	1801	G7	348	479
Van Mannierck, Anthony, Phila.	Deed to	Corless, Matthias, grocer, Phila.	1801	G7	350	481
Van Maunierck, Anthony, of PA	Deed fr	Commissioners of Washington	1799	D4	330	316
Van Ness, John P.	Lease to	Beale, Thomas K.	1802	I9	327	539
Van Ness, John P.	Deed fr	Munroe, Thomas, Supt.	1802	I9	157	237
Van Ness, John P.	Deed fr	Munroe, Thomas, Supt.	1802	I9	158	239
Van Ness, John P.	Deed fr	Templeman	1802	I9	148	223
Van Ness, John P.	Deed fr	Orr, Benjamin G.	1802	I9	326	536
Van Ness, John P.	Deed fr	Brent, Daniel C.	1802	I9	545	887
Van Ness, John P. & Marcia	Deed to	Shoemaker, Rachel	1802	I9	515	843
Van Ness, John P.	Qualify		1802	I9	477	785
Van Ness, John P.	Deed fr	Munroe, Thomas, Supt.	1802	I9	154	232
Van Ness, John P.	Deed fr	Munroe, Thomas, Supt.	1802	I9	156	235
Van Ness, John P.	Deed fr	Munroe, Thomas, Supt.	1802	I9	155	234
Van Ness, John P.	Lease to	Sanford, George et al	1802	I9	498	817
Van Ness, John P.	Deed fr	McLan, Cornelius	1802	I9	188	292
Van Ness, John P.	Deed fr	Chandler, Walter Story	1803	K10	073	79
Van Ness, John P. & Marcia	Lease to	Willis, John	1804	K10	373	387
Van Ness, John P. & Marcia	Deed to	Rogers, William	1804	K10	113	122
Van Ness, John P.	Lease to	Sommerville, Hugh, grocer	1804	K10	161	171
Van Ness, John P. & Marcia	Lease to	Major, John, carpenter	1804	K10	167	177
Van Ness, John P. et al	Deed fr	Woodward, Augustus B.	1804	L11	244	225
Van Ness, John P.	Deed fr	Polock, David	1804	L11	097	100
Van Ness, John P. et al	Convey fr	Gillis, Thomas H.	1804	L11	104	108
Van Ness, John P. & Marcia	Deed to	Fields, William	1804	L11	069	70
Van Ness, John P. et al	Deed fr	Brent, Daniel et al	1804	M12	027	027
Van Ness, John P & Marcia.	Deed to	White, John	1805	M12	180	180
Van Ness, John P. & Marcia	Deed to	Brent, Daniel	1805	M12	350	356
Van Ness, John P. & Marcia	Deed to	Sanford, George, carpenter	1805	M12	174	173
Van Ness, John P. & Marcia	Deed to	Shoemaker, Rachel, w/o David	1805	M12	100	093
Van Ness, John P. & Marcia	Deed to	Dorsey, William Hammond, G'tn.	1805	N13	242	204
Van Ness, John P.	Assign fr	Dorsey, William Hammond	1805	N13	044	043
Van Ness, John P. & Marcia	Deed to	Key, Philip B.	1805	N13	141	134
Van Ness, John P. et al	Deed fr	Law, Thomas	1805	N13	260	217
Van Ness, John P.	Mortgage fr	Dorsey, William H., of G'tn.	1805	N13	042	041
Van Ness, John P. & Marcia	Deed to	Williamson, John	1805	O14	092	057
Van Ness, John P.	Deed fr	Williamson, John	1806	O14	339	226
Van Ness, John P.	Mortgage fr	Williamson, John	1806	O14	338	225
Van Ness, John P. & Marcia	Lease to	Thorpe, Thomas, storekeeper	1806	P15	027	016
Van Ness, John P.	Lease to	Latrobe, Benjamin H.	1806	P15	173	115

Index to District of Columbia Land Records, 1792-1817 421

Party	What	Party	Year	Liber	Old	New
Van Ness, John P.	Convey fr	Brent, Robert & Samuel Hamilton	1806	P15	271	178
Van Ness, John P. et al	Release to	Brent, Daniel & William et al	1806	P15	062	037
Van Ness, John P.	Deed fr	Pratt, Henry et al	1806	P15	105	065
Van Ness, John P. et ux	Deed to	Donnahue, Morgan	1806	Q16	025	016
Van Ness, John P. & Marcia	Lease to	Huddlestone, Joseph et al	1806	Q16	124	081
Van Ness, John P. & Marcia	Deed to	Tolmie, Margaret et al	1807	Q16	375	288
Van Ness, John P. & Marcia et al	Deed to	Wheaton, Sally	1807	Q16	307	234
Van Ness, John P.	Deed fr	Moore, George	1807	R17	251	190
Van Ness, John P. & Marcia	Deed to	Waterston, David	1807	R17	306	233
Van Ness, John P. & Marcia	Deed to	Shoemaker, David	1807	S18	105	085
Van Ness, John P.	Deed fr	Brent, Daniel Carroll, marshal	1807	S18	030	025
Van Ness, John P. & Marcia	Deed to	Haigh, Job, carpenter	1807	S18	115	094
Van Ness, John P.	Deed to	Parrott, Richard	1807	S18	089	073
Van Ness, John P. & Marcia	Deed fr	Shoemaker, David	1807	S18	073	085
Van Ness, John P. & Marcia	Deed to	McCormick, James, Jr.	1808	T19	215	156
Van Ness, John P.	Deed to	Granger, Gideon	1808	U20	205	112
Van Ness, John P. & Marcia	Deed to	Bassett, John, of VA	1808	U20	190	105
Van Ness, John P.	Deed fr	Granger, Gideon	1808	U20	304	162
Van Ness, John P.	Deed fr	Davidson, James, Jr.	1808	U20	103	058
Van Ness, John P. & Marcia	Deed to	Moore, Peter Dent	1808	V21	123	090
Van Ness, John P. & Marcia	Deed to	Cloakey, Samuel & John Kirk	1808	V21	051	040
Van Ness, John P.	Convey fr	Moore, George	1808	T19	046	034
Van Ness, John P.	Release to	Beverly, Robert, of G'tn.	1809	W22	060	045
Van Ness, John P.	Manumis to	Saunders, John (negro)	1809	W22	139	099
Van Ness, John P. & Marcia	Deed to	King, Letitia et al	1809	X23	068	051
Van Ness, John P. & Marcia	Deed to	McGowan, Ann, wid/o Barney	1809	X23	025	017
Van Ness, John P. & Marcia	Deed to	Pairo, Thomas W.	1809	X23	185	138
Van Ness, John P.	Deed to	Lambell, William, shipwright	1809	V21	246	175
Van Ness, John P. & Marcia	Deed to	Thornton, William	1810	Y24	349	316
Van Ness, John P.	Release fr	Brodeau, Ann	1810	Y24	325	295
Van Ness, John P. & Marcia	Lease to	Plate, Adolphus F.	1810	Y24	463	411
Van Ness, John P. & Marcia	Deed to	Stettenius, Samuel	1810	Y24	433	387
Van Ness, John P.	Mortgage fr	Jackson, John G., Harrison Co. VA	1810	Y24	239	220
Van Ness, John Peter et ux et al	Deed to	Bickley, Robert S., Phila. PA et al	1810	Y24	267	245
Van Ness, John P. & Marcia	Deed to	Pairo, Thomas W.	1810	Y24	363	328
Van Ness, John P.	Release to	Dorsey, William Hammond, Balto.	1810	Z25	281	221
Van Ness, John P.	Deed to	Hendley, Richard & Elkanah	1810	Z25	028	021
Van Ness, John P. & Marcia	Release to	Bullus, John, of NY	1810	Z25	001	001
Van Ness, John P. & Marcia	Release to	Way, Andrew & George	1811	AA26	157	109
Van Ness, John P.	Mortgage fr	Cloakey, Samuel, builder	1811	AB27	143	119
Van Ness, John P. & Marcia	Deed to	Matthews, William	1811	AB27	157	130
Van Ness, John P. & Maria	Deed to	Cloakey, Samuel	1811	AB27	305	251
Van Ness, John P.	Deed fr	Boyd, Washington, marshal	1811	AB27	154	127
Van Ness, John P. & Marcia	Deed to	Cloakey, Samuel	1811	AB27	312	257
Van Ness, John P. & Marcia	Deed to	Clarke, Robert, painter	1811	AB27	484	396
Van Ness, John P. & Marcia	Deed to	Clarke, Walter, painter	1811	AB27	191	157
Van Ness, John P. & Maria	Deed to	Cloakey, Samuel	1811	AB27	307	252
Van Ness, John P.	Deed fr	Whelan, Nicholas	1811	AC28	012	009
Van Ness, John P.	Release to	Clarke, Francis & John M'Connell	1811	AC28	002	002
Van Ness, John P. & Marcia	Deed to	Sommerville, David	1811	Z25	460	364
Van Ness, John P. & Marcia	Deed to	Woodworth, Joseph	1812	AC28	358	260
Van Ness, John P. & Marcia	Deed to	Kneller, George	1812	AC28	235	174
Van Ness, John P. & Marcia	Deed to	Kneller, George	1812	AC28	233	173
Van Ness, John P. & Marcia	Deed to	Shoemaker, David	1812	AD29	356	299
Van Ness, John P.	Deed fr	Clephan, Lewis et ux	1812	AD29	452	380

Party	What	Party	Year	Liber	Old	New
Van Ness, John P. & Marcia	Lease to	Jackson, Joseph (C)	1812	AD29	453	381
Van Ness, John P. & Marcia	Deed to	Lathrobe, Benjamin H.	1812	AD29	062	044
Van Ness, John P. & Marcia	Deed to	Moore, George	1812	AD29	212	174
Van Ness, John P. & Marcia	Deed to	Jones, Walter, Jr.	1812	AD29	376	317
Van Ness, John P. & Marcia	Lease to	Jackson, Joseph, free black man	1812	AD29	232	192
Van Ness, John P. & Marcia	Deed to	Hurford, Henry	1812	AD29	400	337
Van Ness, John P. & Marcia	Deed to	Peltz, John	1812	AD29	195	159
Van Ness, John P. & Marcia	Deed to	Lenox, Peter	1812	AD29	374	315
Van Ness, John P.	Lease to	Latrobe, Benjamin Henry	1812	AE30	024	018
Van Ness, John P. & Marcia	Lease to	Johnson, Thomas	1813	AE30	497	368
Van Ness, John P. & Marcia	Deed to	Lenox, Peter	1813	AE30	494	366
Van Ness, John P. & Marcia	Lease to	Major, John	1813	AF31	542	402
Van Ness, John P.	Deed to	Granger, Gideon	1813	AF31	482	352
Van Ness, John P.	Release to	Jackson, John G.	1813	AF31	039	027
Van Ness, John P. & Marcia	Deed to	Belt, Benjamin M.	1813	AF31	382	275
Van Ness, John P.	Deed fr	Pratt, Henry et al	1813	AE30	485	360
Van Ness, John P.	Deed fr	Pratt, Henry et al	1814	AG32	313	229
Van Ness, John P. & Marcia	Deed to	King, John, now of G'tn.	1814	AG32	018	015
Van Ness, John P. & Marcia	D. of T. to	Orme, Moses, of A.A. Co.	1814	AG32	449	325
Van Ness, John P. et al	Deed fr	Jackson, John G. & wife	1814	AG32	295	215
Van Ness, John P.	B. of S. fr	Rollins, John	1814	AG32	365	264
Van Ness, John P. & Walter Jones	Mortgage fr	Underwood, John	1814	AH33	104	096
Van Ness, John P. et al	Deed fr	Jackson, John G., fr. Harrison Co.	1814	AG32	295	215
Van Ness, John P. & Marcia	Deed to	Simpson, Josias	1815	AH33	541	463
Van Ness, John P., Gen.	Manumis to	Johnson, Thomas (C), age 40	1815	AH33	279	243
Van Ness, John P.	Lease to	Hildreth, Ezekiel	1815	AI34	009	009
Van Ness, John P. & Marcia	Deed to	Lenox, Peter	1815	AI34	103	118
Van Ness, John P. & Marcia	Lease to	Jackson, Joseph, free black man	1815	AI34	196	225
Van Ness, John P. & Marcia	Release to	Jackson, Alfred, infant	1815	AI34	198	226
Van Ness, John P.	Lease to	Stewart, John	1815	AI34	528	532
Van Ness, John P.	Lease to	Walker, James, joiner	1815	AI34	527	531
Van Ness, John P. & Marcia	Deed to	Varnum, James M.	1815	AI34	231	262
Van Ness, John P. & Marcia	Release to	Neale, Francis, Rev., of G'tn.	1815	AI34	252	285
Van Ness, John P.	Lease to	Neale, Francis, Rev., of G'tn.	1815	AI34	254	287
Van Ness, John P. & Marcia	Release to	Moore, George	1815	AI34	522	526
Van Ness, John P. & Marcia	Lease to	Gallaher, Robert, of Martinsburgh	1815	AI34	453	467
Van Ness, John P. & Marcia	Lease to	Maxwell, George P.	1815	AI34	462	474
Van Ness, John P. & Marcia	Deed to	Radcliff, William S.	1815	AK35	124	096
Van Ness, John P. & Marcia	Lease to	Speake, Samuel	1815	AK35	132	102
Van Ness, John P. & Marcia	Deed to	Andrews, Christopher	1815	AK35	244	193
Van Ness, John P. & Marcia	Lease to	Hoot, Samuel	1815	AK35	069	053
Van Ness, John P. & Maria	Deed to	Andrews, George	1815	AK35	058	045
Van Ness, John P. & Maria	Deed to	Hildreth, Ezekial	1816	AK35	523	413
Van Ness, John P. & Marcia	Deed to	Young, Moses	1816	AK35	514	405
Van Ness, John P.	B. of S. fr	Bacchus, John, of G'tn.	1816	AL36	376	364
Van Ness, John P. & Marcia	Deed to	Billmyer, Thomas	1816	AL36	241	245
Van Ness, John P. & Marcia	Deed to	Bradley, William A.	1816	AL36	119	120
Van Ness, John P. & Marcia	Deed to	McGlue, Owen	1816	AL36	165	165
Van Ness, John P. & Marcia	Deed to	Clarke, Joseph S.	1816	AM37	035	028
Van Ness, John P. & Marcia	Lease to	White, John B.	1816	AM37	398	286
Van Ness, John P. & Marcia	Lease to	McLeod, John	1816	AM37	394	284
Van Ness, John P. & Marcia	Lease to	McCerran, Andrew & H. Jenkins	1816	AM37	391	282
Van Ness, John P.	D. of T. to	Brown, Obediah B. & E. Reynolds	1816	AM37	175	132
Van Ness, John P. & Marcia	Lease to	Maxwell, George P.	1816	AM37	240	176
Van Ness, John P.	Deed to	King, Charles & Hezekiah Langley	1816	AM37	326	237

Index to District of Columbia Land Records, 1792-1817 423

Party	What	Party	Year	Liber	Old	New
Van Ness, John P. et al	B. of S. fr	Willis, Perrin	1816	AM37	366	265
Van Ness, John P. & Marcia	Lease to	Burch, Remigius	1816	AM37	379	273
Van Ness, John P.	Lease to	Gales, Joseph, Jr.	1816	AM37	385	277
Van Ness, John P.	Lease to	Gales, Joseph, Jr.	1816	AM37	388	279
Van Ness, John P. & Marcia	Deed to	Hand, Anne, wid/o Charles	1816	AO39	051	043
Van Ness, John P. & Marcia	Lease to	Hillard, Thomas, of G'tn.	1816	AO39	012	010
Van Ness, John P.	B. of S. fr	Conley, Charles	1817	AN38	101	076
Van Ness, John P.	Deed fr	Boyd, Washington, marshal	1817	AN38	070	055
Van Ness, John P.	Petition		1817	AN38	069	054
Van Ness, John P. & Marcia	Deed to	Lenox, Peter	1817	AN38	121	089
Van Ness, John P.	Deed to	Lydick, Francis	1817	AN38	145	106
Van Ness, John P. & Marcia	Deed to	Haynes, Catharine	1817	AN38	153	112
Van Ness, John P. & Marcia	Lease to	Lyons, Charles	1817	AN38	239	176
Van Ness, John P. & Marcia	D. of T. to	Brown, Obadian B., Rev. et al	1817	AN38	252	185
Van Ness, John P. & Marcia	Deed to	Quigley, Patrick	1817	AN38	257	188
Van Ness, John P. & Marcia	Deed to	Cocking, William	1817	AN38	592	355
Van Ness, John P. et al	Deed fr	Bickley, Robert S., Bucks Co. PA	1817	AN38	564	411
Van Ness, John P. & Marcia	Lease to	McCerran, Andrew & H. Jenkins	1817	AO39	075	062
Van Ness, John P. & Marcia	Release to	Hutchinson, Samuel	1817	AO39	405	285
Van Ness, John P. & Marcia	Release to	Edmonson, James N.	1817	AO39	191	141
Van Ness, John P. & Marcia	Lease to	Durr, John, Jr.	1817	AO39	243	175
Van Ness, John P. & Marcia	Lease to	Durr, John, Jr.	1817	AO39	261	188
Van Ness, John P. & Marcia	Lease to	Baltimore, Theresa [Trecy] (C)	1817	AO39	264	189
Van Ness, John P. & Marcia	Lease to	Halsey, Henry	1817	AO39	267	191
Van Ness, John P. & Marcia	Lease to	Pearl, Daniel	1817	AO39	269	193
Van Ness, John P. & Marcia	Lease to	Thomas, Nathan P.	1817	AO39	272	195
Van Ness, John P. & Marcia	Lease to	Simmes, Jesse M. [Semmes]	1817	AO39	392	266
Van Ness, John P.	Lease to	Rea, William	1817	AO39	379	255
Van Vollenhoven, Peter et al	Deed fr	Bourne, Sylvanus	1796	B2B	496	192
Van Zandt, Nicholas B.	B. of S. to	Weightman, Roger C. & L. Deblois	1810	Z25	002	002
Van Zandt, Nicholas B.	Assign to	Van Zant, James	1810	Y24	371	335
Van Zandt, Nicholas B.	Slave	From VA	1812	AC28	350	253
Van Zant, James	Assign fr	Van Zandt, Nicholas B.	1810	Y24	371	335
Vance, Robert & Mazy et al	Deed to	Stewart, William, of G'tn.	1808	T19	080	057
Vanhorn, Archibald & Elizabeth A.	Deed fr	Beall, William T. & Eleanor	1806	P15	240	160
Vanhorn, Archibald, of P.G. Co.	Deed fr	Cecil, Mary & Ann Aud	1816	AL36	262	263
Vanzandt, Nicholas B.	Deed to	Prince, Isaac, of Phila. PA	1807	R17	071	057
Varden, Charles	Deed fr	Simm, Patrick, Jr.	1802	I9	430	712
Varden, Charles	Deed fr	Boyd, Washington, collector	1806	P15	116	074
Varden, Charles	Deed fr	Lenox, Peter	1811	Z25	421	330
Varden, Charles	Assign fr	Long, Robert	1812	AD29	315	258
Varden, Charles	B. of S. fr	Varden, Charles H.	1813	AE30	295	224
Varden, Charles	Mortgage to	Bennett, James	1816	AL36	249	252
Varden, Charles	Deed to	Glover, Charles	1816	AL36	328	321
Varden, Charles	Deed to	Bestor, Harvey	1816	AL36	333	326
Varden, Charles & M.C. Hodges	Mortgage to	Peltz, John	1812	AD29	436	366
Varden, Charles & A. McCormick	D. of T. fr	Varden, Charles H.	1813	AE30	355	265
Varden, Charles et al	Deed fr	Calder, James, of G'tn.	1811	AA26	104	073
Varden, Charles H.	Convey fr	Jones, Thomas, Loudoun Co. VA	1805	N13	098	091
Varden, Charles H.	Deed fr	Brent, Daniel Carroll, trustee et al	1807	R17	016	014
Varden, Charles H.	Deed to	Mathers, James	1807	R17	020	017
Varden, Charles H.	Assign fr	Varden, Ezra	1809	W22	171	120
Varden, Charles H.	Deed to	Mathers, James	1811	AA26	365	243
Varden, Charles H.	Mortgage to	Jones, Philip, of Phila.	1811	AB27	184	152
Varden, Charles H.	D. of T. to	Varden, Charles & A. McCormick	1813	AE30	355	265

Party	What	Party	Year	Liber	Old	New
Varden, Charles H.	B. of S. to	Varden, Charles	1813	AE30	295	224
Varden, Charles H., insolvent	Deed to	Glover, Charles, trustee	1814	AG32	279	199
Varden, Ezra	Deed fr	Boyd, Washington, collector	1805	N13	196	172
Varden, Ezra	Assign fr	Frethy, Edward, of OH	1807	R17	132	102
Varden, Ezra	Deed fr	King, Robert	1807	R17	098	077
Varden, Ezra	Deed fr	Brent, Daniel Carroll, trustee et al	1807	Q16	404	311
Varden, Ezra	Assign to	Varden, Charles H.	1809	W22	171	120
Varden, Ezra	Deed fr	Kent, Luke & Elizabeth Pickerall	1809	X23	031	022
Varden, Ezra	Deed fr	Carpenter, Thomas, Jr., insolvent	1812	AC28	396	288
Varden, Ezra, insolvent	Assign to	Glover, Charles, trustee	1814	AH33	096	088
Varden, Joseph	Mortgage fr	Varden, Richard	1806	P15	260	172
Varden, Joseph	B. of S. fr	Moore, John & Richard Varden	1808	U20	351	190
Varden, Joseph	Deed fr	Law, John	1808	U20	351	190
Varden, Joseph	Deed fr	Carroll, Daniel, of *Duddington*	1809	X23	029	020
Varden, Richard	B. of S. to	Moore, John	1805	M12	316	319
Varden, Richard	Mortgage to	Varden, Joseph	1806	P15	260	172
Varden, Richard et al	B. of S. to	Varden, Joseph	1808	U20	351	196
Varnum, James & Noah Flecher	Release to	Hildreth, Ezekiel	1817	AO39	498	342
Varnum, James M.	Agreement	Young, Thomas	1811	Z25	484	385
Varnum, James M.	Deed fr	Pratt, Henry et al	1812	AC28	508	363
Varnum, James M.	Qualify	Captain in the militia	1812	AD29	361	304
Varnum, James M.	Cert. Free to	Halley, James	1814	AH33	228	200
Varnum, James M.	Cert Free to	Adams, Joseph (C), age 27	1814	AG32	116	087
Varnum, James M.	Deed fr	Randall, John, of Annapolis	1814	AH33	101	093
Varnum, James M. & Mary Pease	Deed fr	Granger, Gideon, of Oneida NY	1815	AH33	461	394
Varnum, James M.	Deed fr	Wagler, Frederick Augustus	1815	AH33	459	393
Varnum, James M.	Cert. Free to	Curtis, Eliza (M), age 16	1815	AH33	558	477
Varnum, James M.	Deed fr	Bradley, Phineas	1815	AI34	492	499
Varnum, James M.	Deed fr	Noel, Gilson	1815	AI34	494	501
Varnum, James M.	Deed to	Bradley, Phineas	1815	AI34	496	503
Varnum, James M.	Deed to	Young, Thomas	1815	AI34	374	401
Varnum, James M.	Deed fr	Van Ness, John P. & Marcia	1815	AI34	231	262
Varnum, James M.	Deed fr	Munroe, Thomas	1815	AI34	230	261
Varnum, James M.	Deed fr	Granger, Gideon	1815	AK35	281	224
Varnum, James M. & N. Fletcher	Deed fr	Hildreth, Ezekiel	1816	AL36	003	003
Varnum, James M.	D. of T. fr	Fletcher, Noah	1816	AL36	001	001
Varnum, James M.	Deed fr	Kleiber, George	1816	AM37	086	070
Varnum, James M.	Manumis to	Davis, Kitty (C), age 35	1816	AM37	119	094
Varnum, James M.	Deed to	Parrott, Richard	1816	AK35	525	414
Varnum, James W.	Deed fr	Hewitt, James	1813	AF31	210	142
Varnum, Joseph B., of MA	Manumis to	[ ], Adam (C)	1813	AF31	103	069
Vaughan, John, mer., of Phila. PA	Deed fr	Ehrenzeller, George & Henrietta	1810	Y24	351	318
Vaughan, John, mer., of Phila. PA	Deed fr	Ehrenzeller, George & Henrietta	1810	Y24	354	320
Veal, Richard S.	Lease to	Snider, Abraham	1802	I9	543	885
Veitch, James	Qualify		1802	I9	467	769
Veitch, James	B. of S. to	McCormick, Alexander	1810	Y24	316	287
Veitch, Richard	Deed fr	Polock, Isaac	1080	E5	396	371
Veitch, Richard & Elizabeth et al	Deed to	Tayloe, John, Richmond Co. VA	1804	K10	150	162
Veitch, Richard & Eliz., of Alexa.	Deed to	Swann, Thomas, of Alexa.	1814	AG32	385	280
Veitch, Richard, of Alexa. et al	Deed fr	Polock, Isaac	1798	C3	444	349
Veitch, Richard, of Alexa. et al	Deed fr	Magruder, Patrick, of G'tn.	1799	D4	344	333
Veitch, Richard, of Alexa.	Deed fr	Thompson, Jonah & Margaret	1809	V21	170	122
Veitch, Richard, of Alexa.	Deed fr	Thompson, Jonah & Margaret	1809	V21	174	125
Veitch, Richard, of Alexa. et al	Deed fr	Brent, Daniel Carroll, marshal	1813	AF31	261	182
Veitch, Richard, of Alexa.	Deed fr	Thompson, Jonah & Margaret	1814	AH33	073	065

Index to District of Columbia Land Records, 1792-1817

Party	What	Party	Year	Liber	Old	New
Veitch, Richard, of Alexa. et al	Deed fr	Deakins, Leonard M. & John Hoye	1814	AH33	038	034
Veitch, William	Deed fr	Commissioners of Washington	1800	E5	109	097
Venable, Charles	Deed fr	Prout, William	1814	AG32	318	232
Venable, Clement	B. of S. fr	Venable, William	1809	W22	035	026
Venable, Joseph	Deed to	Callan, Patrick	1814	AF31	522	384
Venable, Joseph	Deed fr	Gates, Leonard	1815	AH33	422	363
Venable, Teresa	B. of S. fr	Gates, Leonard	1814	AH33	119	112
Venable, William	Deed to	Talbutt, Levin	1809	W22	033	025
Venable, William	B. of S. to	Venable, Clement	1809	W22	035	026
Venable, William	B. of S. to	Talbutt, Lewin	1809	W22	127	091
Venable, William	Deed to	Talburtt, Lewin	1811	AB27	211	172
Venable, William	Cert Free to	Woodward, John, yellow, age 30	1813	AF31	360	257
Venable, William & Elizabeth	Deed to	Prout, William	1798	C3	282	229
Venables, William et al	Deed fr	Hanson, Samuel, of Samuel	1807	R17	127	099
Veneble, William	Lease fr	Wheeler, Acquilla	1794	B2A	073	094
Vermillion, Anne	B. of S. fr	Roberts, William	1806	P15	121	078
Vermillion, Caleb	B. of S. to	Prout, William	1804	L11	007	7
Vermillion, Giles, of P.G. Co.	B. of S. fr	Vermillion, Osburn	1814	AH33	253	220
Vermillion, Henrietta	Lease fr	Prout, William	1813	AF31	115	078
Vermillion, John	Deed fr	Ingraham, Alexander	1805	M12	372	382
Vermillion, John Robertson	Deed fr	Holmead, Anthony	1793	A1-1	242	330
Vermillion, John Robertson, G'tn.	Deed to	Schnively, Henry	1794	B2A	060	075
Vermillion, Osburn	B. of S. to	Vermillion, Giles, of P.G. Co.	1814	AH33	253	220
Vermonnet, John	Deed fr	Ott, Adam	1794	A1-2	473	78
Vermonnet, John	Deed to	Fitzhugh, Philip	1798	C3	365	292
Vernon, William W.	B. of S. to	Davis, Ann	1809	V21	328	242
Vernon, William W., insolvent	Deed to	Speake, Samuel, trustee	1811	Z25	510	405
Vidler, Edward	Deed fr	Prout, William	1806	Q16	080	051
Vidler, Edward	Deed to	Young, Thomas & Thomas Taylor	1807	R17	311	236
Vierse, Hezekiah, of Montg. Co.	Mortgage to	Harshman, Henry	1804	L11	078	80
Villard, Andrew J.	B. of S. fr	Fenwick, Richard	1809	X23	119	085
Villard, Andrew J.	B. of S. fr	Willson, John A.	1809	X23	117	084
Villard, Andrew J.	Release to	Fenwick, Richard	1810	Z25	203	159
Villard, Andrew J.	D. of T. fr	Franc, Lewis [Frank]	1811	AA26	260	177
Villard, Andrew Joseph	Deed fr	Fitzhugh, Philip, of MD	1802	I9	084	120
Villard, Andrew Joseph	Deed to	Frank, Lewis [Franc]	1811	AC28	005	004
Villard, Andrew Joseph	Release to	Franc, Lewis, of Balto. MD	1812	AD29	173	138
Villard, Andrew Joseph	Deed fr	Frank, Lewis & Mary Ann	1817	AO39	281	200
Villard, Joseph	Deed fr	Fitzhugh, Philip, of P.G. Co.	1807	R17	395	299
Vinson, Charles	Deed fr	Steuart, William & Joseph Miligan	1812	AE30	027	021
Vinson, Charles	Cert. fr	Munroe, Thomas, Supt.	1812	AC28	495	353
Vinson, Charles	Deed fr	Burgess, Samuel	1813	AE30	083	063
Vinson, Charles	Convey to	Handy, James H.	1817	AO39	280	200
Vinson, Charles	Deed fr	Gaither, Benjamin & Henry, MD	1817	AO39	113	088
Vinson, Charles, mer., of G'tn.	Deed to	Vinson, William, of Montg. Co.	1810	Z25	115	090
Vinson, William, of Montg. Co.	Deed fr	Vinson, Charles, mer., of G'tn.	1810	Z25	115	090
Vint, John	Deed fr	Prout, William	1804	L11	361	325
Vint, John	Deed fr	Foyle, Thomas	1804	L11	380	339
Vint, John	Mortgage to	Prout, William	1804	M12	036	036
Vint, John	Deed fr	Baker, Samuel et al	1805	N13	185	165
Vint, John	Deed to	Prout, William	1805	N13	402	320
Vint, John	B. of S. fr	Clephan, Lewis	1805	N13	321	259
Vint, John	Mortgage to	Clephan, Lewis	1805	N13	352	283
Vint, John	Deed fr	Ireland, Elizabeth et al	1806	P15	246	163
Vint, John	Deed to	Cocking, William	1808	T19	025	020

Party	What	Party	Year	Liber	Old	New
Vint, John	Deed fr	Slater, David, of P.G. Co.	1808	T19	028	021
Vint, John	Deed fr	Bryan, Benjamin	1808	U20	086	048
Vint, John	Deed to	Wright, Thomas C.	1809	X23	229	177
Vint, John	Deed to	Wright, Thomas C.	1809	X23	231	178
Vint, John	B. of S. to	Prout, William	1809	W22	350	226
Vint, John	Deed to	Wright, Thomas C.	1809	X23	233	180
Vint, John	Deed to	Wright, Thomas C.	1810	X23	227	175
Vogeler, Randolph	Deed fr	Turner, Thomas	1802	I9	572	926
Vonessen, Peter, of G'tn.	Lease fr	Smith, Clement, of G'tn.	1816	AM37	058	048
Voss, Nicholas	Assign to	Williamson, David, of Balto.	1801	G7	082	106
Voss, Nicholas	Deed fr	Prout, William	1801	G7	420	555
Voss, Nicholas	Deed fr	Commissioners of Washington	1801	G7	082	106
Voss, Nicholas	Mortgage to	Hoban, James	1801	G7	415	550
Voss, Nicholas	Lease to	Costigan, Joseph	1801	G7	440	576
Voss, Nicholas	Lease fr	Templeman, John, of G'tn.	1802	H8	340	317
Voss, Nicholas	Deed to	Hurley, Daniel	1802	H8	534	493
Voss, Nicholas	Deed fr	Stoddert, Benjamin	1802	I9	557	903
Voss, Nicholas	Deed fr	Hurly, Daniel	1802	I9	346	570
Voss, Nicholas	Deed to	Costigan, Joseph	1802	I9	317	521
Voss, Nicholas	Deed to	Chandler, Walter S.	1804	L11	095	97
Voss, Nicholas	Deed fr	Templeman, John, of G'tn.	1804	M12	040	040
Voss, Nicholas	Deed to	Alexander, Robert	1804	K10	239	247
Voss, Nicholas	Deed to	Stoddert, Benjamin	1804	K10	233	241
Voss, Nicholas	Deed fr	Chandler, Walter Story, of G'tn.	1805	M12	057	054
Voss, Nicholas	Deed fr	Hurley, Daniel	1805	M12	059	055
Voss, Nicholas	Slaves	From VA	1806	P15	024	015
Voss, Nicholas	Deed to	Naylor, John L. et al	1806	P15	313	207
Voss, Nicholas	Deed to	Nevitt, William, of G'tn.	1806	P15	320	211
Voss, Nicholas	Deed to	Tingey, Thomas	1807	S18	056	047
Voss, Nicholas	Deed fr	Pratt, Henry, of Phila. PA et al	1807	S18	025	021
Voss, Nicholas	Deed to	Tingey, Thomas	1807	S18	107	087
Voss, Nicholas	Deed fr	Glover, Charles	1808	U20	100	056
Voss, Nicholas	Agreement	Hurley, Daniel	1809	V21	191	136
Voss, Nicholas	Deed to	Tingey, Thomas	1809	V21	196	139
Voss, Nicholas	Release fr	Glover, Charles	1809	V21	187	133
Voss, Nicholas	Release fr	Alexander, Robert	1810	Z25	076	057
Voss, Nicholas	Slaves	From Culpeper Co. VA	1810	Y24	208	191
Voss, Nicholas	Mortgage to	Tingey, Thomas & S.N. Smallwood	1810	Y24	240	222
Voss, Nicholas	P. of Atty. to	Smallwood, Samuel N.	1811	AA26	102	071
Voss, Nicholas	Deed fr	Templeman, John	1813	AE30	103	079
Voss, Nicholas & wife, of VA	Deed to	Wright, Matthew	1811	AB27	374	310
Voss, Nicholas, def.	Suit	Potts, John, plt.	1809	W22	375	243
Voss, Nicholas et al	Deed fr	Alexander, Robert	1807	S18	212	179
Voss, Nicholas, of VA	Mortgage to	Smallwood, Samuel N.	1811	AB27	482	394
Voss, Nicholas, of VA	Release fr	Tingey, Thomas	1813	AE30	149	117
Voss, Nicholas, of VA	D. of T. to	Tingey, Thomas & S.N. Smallwood	1813	AE30	115	089
Voss, Nicholas, of VA	Release fr	Smallwood, Samuel N.	1813	AE30	148	116
Voss, Nicholas, of VA	Deed to	Way, Andrew & George	1813	AE30	150	118
Voss, Richard	Deed to	Glover, Charles	1805	M12	159	157
Vowell, Thomas, Jr., of Alexa.	Mortgage fr	King, William, of P.G. Co.	1798	C3	324	262
Vowell, Thomas, Jr., of Alexa.	Mortgage fr	King, William & Elizabeth	1798	C3	295	239

Index to District of Columbia Land Records, 1792-1817

Party	What	Party	Year	Liber	Old	New
W						
Waddington, John, of Phila. et al	Deed fr	Leamy, John & Eliz., of Phila. PA	1808	T19	227	167
Wade, Ann	B. of S. fr	Shannon, Luke	1802	I9	491	806
Wade, Anne	Deed fr	Elliot, Samuel, Jr. et al	1802	H8	504	464
Wade, Anne	Deed fr	May, Frederick et al	1802	H8	504	464
Wade, Robert P., an insolvent	Deed to	Peacock, Robert Ward, trustee	1804	K10	176	184
Wade, Robert P.	Deed to	Brooke, Henry, s/o Nicholas, P.G.	1805	M12	355	363
Wade, Robert P.	B. of S. to	Burrows, Edward & T. Connor	1808	V21	092	071
Wade, Robert P.	Assign to	Maxwell, George	1809	V21	371	275
Wade, Robert P. & Robt. McClann	Deed fr	Maxwell, George	1809	W22	150	106
Wadsworth, Charles	Deed fr	Commissioners of Washington	1800	F6	030	019
Wadsworth, Charles	Warranty fr	Stoddert, Benjamin	1800	F6	035	022
Wadsworth, Charles	Mortgage fr	Loring, Israel	1802	I9	075	105
Wadsworth, Charles & Elizabeth	Deed to	Lawrason, Thomas, of Alexa.	1810	Y24	003	003
Wadsworth, Charles & Elizabeth	Deed to	Powell, Cuthbert et al	1810	Y24	001	001
Wadsworth, Charles, Alexa. Co.	Deed fr	Ford, Lewis, of St. Mary's Co.	1809	V21	298	216
Wadsworth, Charles, Hartford CN	Deed to	Bullus, John et al	1804	L11	326	298
Wadsworth, Charles, in Norfolk VA	Deed to	Bullus, John et al	1804	L11	327	299
Wadsworth, Charles, of Alexa.	Deed to	Powell, Cuthbert et al	1810	Y24	001	001
Wadsworth, Charles, U.S.N.	Deed fr	Roberts, Owen	1801	G7	186	248
Wadsworth, Elizabeth	Deed to	Winn, Timothy & Silas Butler	1814	AH33	120	113
Wadsworth, Elizabeth	Manumis to	Beall, Betsey (C)	1814	AH33	001	001
Wadsworth, Elizabeth, rel/o Chas.	R. Dower to	Butler, Silas	1814	AH33	119	112
Waggoner, Adam	Deed to	Goszler, John	1802	H8	049	046
Wagler, Frederick A.	Assign fr	Gray, William	1811	AB27	346	287
Wagler, Frederick A.	Deed to	Hines, Philip	1813	AE30	537	399
Wagler, Frederick A.	Deed fr	Woodworth, Joseph	1815	AI34	005	005
Wagler, Frederick Augustus	Deed fr	Whetcroft, William, heirs of	1813	AE30	310	233
Wagler, Frederick Augustus	Deed to	Varnum, James M.	1815	AH33	459	393
Wagner, Jacob	Deed fr	Turner, Samuel	1802	I9	345	569
Wagner, Jacob	Deed fr	Dorsey, William H.	1806	Q16	045	029
Wagner, Jacob	Mortgage fr	Washington, Thomas	1806	P15	363	241
Wagner, Jacob	Deed to	Dorsey, William Hammond, G'tn.	1806	Q16	331	254
Wagner, Jacob	Deed to	Williams, John S.	1814	AH33	355	307
Wagner, Jacob	Deed fr	Williams, John S., of G'tn.	1814	AH33	209	188
Wagner, Jacob	B. of S. fr	Richard, George	1816	AL36	006	006
Wagner, Jacob & Alexander Kerr	Manumis to	[ ], Maria (C)	1812	AD29	289	238
Wagner, Jacob & J.S. Williams	Deed fr	Thompson, John, of G'tn.	1813	AF31	493	359
Wagner, Jacob & John S. Williams	Mortgage to	Thompson, John	1814	AH33	322	278
Wagner, Jacob & John Williams	Deed fr	Southgate, John, of Norfolk	1814	AG32	136	098
Wagner, Jacob, of G'tn.	Deed to	Miller, William & James Craig	1813	AF31	203	137
Wagner, Jacob, of G'tn.	Deed fr	Williams, John S., of G'tn.	1813	AF31	207	140
Wagner, Jacob, of G'tn.	Deed fr	Southgate, John, of Norfolk	1814	AG32	133	096
Wagner, Jacob, of G'tn.	Deed to	Lear, Tobias	1815	AI34	089	102
Wagner, Jacob, of G'tn.	Deed to	Gantt, Thomas T., of G'tn.	1816	AL36	328	322
Wailes, John	Slaves	From Norfolk VA	1808	T19	377	269
Walker, Alexander E. et al	Deed to	Lorman, William, of Balto.	1817	AO39	117	090
Walker, Arch., Rev., of Easton MD	Deed fr	Underwood, Robert	1812	AD29	336a	280
Walker, Arch., Rev., of Easton MD	Deed fr	Magruder, Ninian, Dr., of G'tn.	1812	AD29	150	117
Walker, Archibald E. et al	Deed to	Lorman, William, of Balto.	1817	AO39	117	090
Walker, Archibald, heirs of	Deed to	Lorman, William, of Balto.	1817	AO39	117	090
Walker, Archibald, of Easton MD	Deed fr	Magruder, Ninian, Dr., of G'tn.	1811	AA26	194	132
Walker, Archibald, Rev., Kent Co.	Deed fr	Woodward, William	1806	P15	210	140
Walker, Cyrus, trustee	B. of S. fr	Walker, George, insolvent	1809	V21	140	102
Walker, David	Cert fr	Commissioners of Washington	1802	H8	124	121

Party	What	Party	Year	Liber	Old	New
Walker, David	Deed to	Foxall, Henry	1815	AH33	535	458
Walker, David	Deed fr	Peter, Sarah et al	1815	AH33	436	374
Walker, Elijah & Andrew Hoover	Deed fr	McCutchen, Thomas, of G'tn.	1810	Y24	079	071
Walker, Elijah, of G'tn.	Deed fr	Mountz, John, Sr., of G'tn.	1796	B2B	524	236
Walker, Elijah, of G'tn.	B. of S. fr	Mountz, John, Sr., of G'tn.	1807	R17	235	177
Walker, Elijah, of G'tn.	Deed to	Bridges, John, of G'tn.	1811	AB27	149	124
Walker, George	Deed to	Beall, Thomas & John M. Gantt	1792	A1-1	017	27
Walker, George	Deed to	Davidson, Samuel, of G'tn.	1793	A1-1	176	251
Walker, George	Deed to	Willink, Wilhem & Jan, Amsterdam	1796	B2B	435	113
Walker, George	Deed to	Nicholson, John, of Phila.	1796	B2B	605	358
Walker, George	Deed to	Reid, James, of Dumfries VA	1796	B2B	431	109
Walker, George	Deed to	Smith, James, of *Cedar Grove* VA	1796	B2B	430	107
Walker, George	Deed to	Thompson, William, Fairfax Co.	1796	B2B	420	092
Walker, George	Deed to	Thompson, Elizabeth Lund, of VA	1796	B2B	421	093
Walker, George	Deed to	Fry, John, Jr., of Phila.	1797	B2B	694	475
Walker, George	Deed to	Carr, Overton	1798	D4	091	077
Walker, George	Deed to	Law, Thomas et al	1798	D4	156	138
Walker, George	Deed fr	Washington, Lund	1798	D4	113	097
Walker, George	Deed fr	Carr, Overton	1798	D4	090	076
Walker, George	Deed to	Minifie, Charles, of Phila.	1799	D4	304	288
Walker, George	Deed to	Minifie, Charles et al	1799	D4	305	289
Walker, George	Deed fr	Commissioners of Washington	1799	D4	254	238
Walker, George	Mortgage to	Crawford, David	1800	E5	073	060
Walker, George	Deed to	Minifie, Charles. of Phila.	1800	F6	009	007
Walker, George	Deed to	Smith, Andrew, of New York NY	1801	F6	233	153
Walker, George	Deed to	Elliott, Barnard, of Charleston SC	1801	F6	198	128
Walker, George	Deed fr	Commissioners of Washington	1801	G7	247	333
Walker, George	Deed fr	Dorsey, William H.	1801	G7	230	308
Walker, George	Deed to	Laird, John	1801	G7	309	431
Walker, George	Deed to	Otis, Samuel Allyne, of Phila.	1801	G7	018	023
Walker, George	Deed fr	Carr, Overton	1801	F6	173	109
Walker, George	Release fr	Carr, Overton	1802	G7	559	708
Walker, George	Deed to	Young, William & Alexander et al	1802	H8	070	065
Walker, George	Lease fr	Beatty, Charles	1802	H8	413	382
Walker, George	Deed to	Carr, Overton	1802	H8	439	404
Walker, George	Deed fr	Walker, Nathaniel & David	1802	H8	338	316
Walker, George	Lease to	Gloyd, George Holland	1802	H8	416	384
Walker, George	Deed to	Sands, Francis	1802	H8	023	022
Walker, George	Deed fr	Young, William et al	1802	H8	030	029
Walker, George	Deed fr	Commissioners of Washington	1802	H8	444	408
Walker, George	Deed to	Hazle, Jeremiah	1802	I9	425	703
Walker, George	Deed to	Reid, James	1802	I9	219	346
Walker, George	Deed fr	Hazle, Jeremiah	1802	I9	242	390
Walker, George	Deed fr	Beatty, Charles	1802	I9	242	388
Walker, George	Deed to	Hitchborn, Benjamin	1802	I9	207	325
Walker, George	Deed to	Blagg, John	1802	I9	233	371
Walker, George	Deed to	Prout, William	1804	L11	152	152
Walker, George	Deed to	Tunnicliff, William	1804	M12	022	022
Walker, George	Deed to	Walker, James, mer., of Britain	1804	K10	209	220
Walker, George	Deed to	Hazel, Jeremiah	1804	K10	236	244
Walker, George	Deed fr	Davidson, Lewis Grant	1815	AH33	518	444
Walker, George	Deed to	Smith, James, of Pr. Wm. Co. VA	1817	AN38	529	384
Walker, George & S. Tophouse	Release to	Peck, Joseph	1814	AG32	125	092
Walker, George, butcher, G'tn.	Deed fr	Deakins, Francis, of G'tn.	1800	E5	249	242
Walker, George et al	B. of S. fr	Godfrey, William	1801	G7	077	100

Party	What	Party	Year	Liber	Old	New
Walker, George et al	Deed to	Stelle, Pontius Delare	1804	M12	019	020
Walker, George et al	B. of S. fr	Peck, Joseph	1808	U20	390	216
Walker, George, Gent.	Deed to	Nicholson, John, of Phila.	1796	B2B	536	254
Walker, George, Gent.	Ded to	Bryden, James, of Balto.	1801	G7	285	395
Walker, George, Gent.	Deed to	Blagge, John, of NY et al	1802	G7	446	582
Walker, George, insolvent	Deed to	Prout, William, trustee	1804	L11	280	257
Walker, George, insolvent	B. of S. to	Walker, Cyrus, trustee	1809	V21	140	102
Walker, George, Jr.	Deed to	Watson, Thomas	1801	G7	231	309
Walker, George, Jr.	Bond to	Mitchell, John	1804	K10	246	253
Walker, George, of Phila. PA	Deed to	Carr, Overton, of P.G. Co.	1797	C3	171	144
Walker, Hales E. et al	Deed to	Lorman, William, of Balto.	1817	AO39	117	090
Walker, James	Deed fr	Prout, William	1805	M12	225	226
Walker, James	Deed to	Johnston, William	1808	T19	245	180
Walker, James	Deed fr	Johnston, William	1813	AE30	352	263
Walker, James	Deed to	Cook, Mary	1817	AN38	336	246
Walker, James, joiner	Lease fr	Van Ness, John P.	1815	AI34	527	531
Walker, James, Jr.	Deed fr	Walker, James, Sr.	1808	V21	010	007
Walker, James, mer., of Britain	Deed fr	Walker, George	1804	K10	209	220
Walker, James, Sr.	Deed to	Walker, James, Jr.	1808	V21	010	007
Walker, John E. et al	Deed to	Lorman, William, of Balto.	1817	AO39	117	090
Walker, John, of Francis	B. of S. to	Grimes, Patty	1812	AD29	426	368
Walker, Joseph	Assign fr	Thorpe, Thomas	1810	Y24	508	447
Walker, Joseph	Lease fr	Law, John, atty. for Thomas	1810	Y24	208	191
Walker, Joseph	Deed fr	Elliott, Samuel, Jr.	1815	AI34	456	469
Walker, Joseph	Deed fr	Law, Thomas	1816	AL36	531	496
Walker, Joseph	Manumis to	[ ], Betsey (C)	1816	AM37	210	156
Walker, Joseph	Deed to	Pairo, Thomas W.	1817	AN38	362	267
Walker, Joseph, now of Richmond	Deed to	James, William, heirs of	1815	AK35	190	149
Walker, Mary, of Balto.	Deed to	Lorman, William	1817	AO39	121	093
Walker, Nathan	Deed to	French, George	1798	D4	020	017
Walker, Nathan, of G'tn.	Deed fr	Beck, John, of G'tn.	1796	B2B	447	131
Walker, Nathan, of G'tn.	Deed fr	Balch, Stephen B., of G'tn.	1797	B2B	632	392
Walker, Nathan, of G'tn.	Deed to	Owens, Isaac, of G'tn.	1797	C3	183	155
Walker, Nathan, of G'tn.	Lease fr	Speake, Josias M.	1801	G7	357	489
Walker, Nathan, of P.G. Co.	Assign to	Owings, Christopher, of G'tn.	1804	L11	004	4
Walker, Nathan, of MD	Deed fr	Beall, Thomas B.	1811	AC28	004	003
Walker, Nathan, of P.G. Co.	Deed to	Goddard, John B., of G'tn.	1811	AA26	247	168
Walker, Samuel	B. of S. to	Henry, William	1817	AN38	274	200
Walker, Sarah	Slaves	From Montgomery Co. MD	1805	M12	217	219
Walker, Sarah	B. of S. to	Murry, Thomas	1809	X23	183	137
Walker, Sarah	Deed Gift to	Murry, Rachel, d/o Sarah	1809	X23	184	138
Walker, Sarah	B. of S. to	Bland, Delilah, her daughter	1810	Z25	157	124
Walker, Sarah	B. of S. to	Davis, Sarah & John	1810	Z25	239	187
Walker, Sarah	B. of S. to	Walker, Zachariah, her son	1810	Z25	158	124
Walker, Sarah	Deed to	Walker, Zachariah	1812	AD29	486	411
Walker, Sarah	B. of S. to	Walker, Zachariah	1812	AD29	487	411
Walker, William E. et al	Deed to	Lorman, William, of Balto.	1817	AO39	117	090
Walker, Zachariah	Bond	Deputy Clerk, Circuit Court	1810	X23	359	287
Walker, Zachariah	B. of S. fr	Walker, Sarah, his mother	1810	Z25	158	124
Walker, Zachariah	B. of S. fr	Walker, Sarah	1812	AD29	487	411
Walker, Zachariah	Deed fr	Ott, John, trustee, of G'tn.	1812	AD29	221	182
Walker, Zachariah	Deed to	Murray, Thomas	1812	AD29	241	200
Walker, Zachariah	Deed fr	Walker, Sarah	1812	AD29	486	411
Walker, Zachariah	Deed to	Teackle, Littleton D., of MD	1813	AF31	294	209
Walker, Zachariah	Deed to	Coxon, Jesse W.	1813	AF31	272	191

Party	What	Party	Year	Liber	Old	New
Walker, Zachariah	Deed to	Dobbins, David	1813	AE30	500	370
Walker, Zachariah	B. of S. fr	Bland, Edward	1814	AH33	060	054
Walker, Zachariah	Mortgage fr	Minitree, John	1814	AH33	037	033
Walker, Zachariah	Deed fr	Masters, John, heirs, Scioto OH	1815	AI34	435	452
Walker, Zachariah	Release fr	Minitree, John & George Cox	1815	AI34	155	177
Walker, Zachariah	Deed fr	Spalding, Enoch, Scioto Co. OH	1815	AI34	099	113
Walker, Zachariah	Deed fr	Pratt, Henry et al	1815	AK35	404	317
Walker, Zachariah	Deed fr	Young, Moses	1815	AK35	185	144
Walker, Zachariah	Deed to	Middleton, Isaac S.	1815	AK35	189	147
Walker, Zachariah	B. of S. fr	Masters, Ezekiel	1816	AM37	452	325
Walker, Zachariah	B. of S. fr	Masters, Ezekiel	1816	AM37	453	326
Walker, Zachariah	Deed fr	Glover, Charles	1816	AM37	337	245
Walker, Zachariah	Dower fr	Masters, Priscilla, wid/o John, OH	1816	AM37	297	217
Walker, Zachariah	Deed to	Halliday, Thomas	1817	AN38	506	366
Walker, Zachariah	Deed fr	Marshall, Charles	1817	AN38	554	403
Walker, Zachariah	B. of S. fr	Moore, William	1817	AN38	100	076
Walker, Zachariah	Deed fr	Masters, John, Jr.	1817	AO39	439	300
Walker, Zachariah, collector	Deed to	Gloyd, George H., of G'tn.	1816	AL36	039	040
Walker, Zachariah, collector	Deed to	McCormick, Alexander	1817	AN38	178	129
Walker, Zachariah, trustee	Deed to	Carroll, Daniel, of *Duddington*	1816	AL36	028	029
Walker, Zachariah, trustee	Deed to	Smallwood, Samuel N.	1817	AO39	329	234
Walker, Zachariah, trustee	Deed to	Allen, Henry J.	1817	AN38	255	187
Wall, John	B. of S. to	Kilty, William	1804	M12	022	023
Wallace, Charles, Annapolis et al	Deed to	Beatty, Thomas Johnson	1795	B2A	350	495
Wallace, Charles, Annapolis et al	Mortgage to	Hoye, John & Leonard M. Deakins	1809	W22	009	007
Wallach, Richard	B. of S. to	Whitehill, James	1813	AF31	365	261
Wallach, Richard	Manumis to	[ ], Phil (C), age 8	1813	AF31	364	260
Wallach, Richard	Deed fr	Wilson, William	1814	AH33	343	297
Wallach, Richard	Deed fr	White, Patrick	1815	AK35	080	062
Wallach, Richard	Deed fr	Peltz, John	1815	AK35	354	279
Wallach, Richard	D. of T. fr	Gales, Joseph, Jr.	1817	AO39	257	185
Wallach, Richard	D. of T. fr	Hall, Joseph C.	1817	AN38	228	166
Wallach, Richard, trustee	B. of S. fr	Warner, Osborn, insolvent	1811	AA26	093	065
Walls, Elizabeth, w/o James	Relinquish	Dower	1809	V21	284	
Walls, George, of P.G. Co.	Deed to	Brady, Francis	1812	AC28	180	136
Walls, James, Frederick Co. VA	Deed to	Foxall, Henry	1809	V21	281	202
Walls, James, of Winchester VA	Deed fr	Greate, Jacob, of G'tn.	1793	A1-1	246	336
Waln, Robert, Jr., of Phila., mer.	Deed fr	Lewis, Joseph S., agent, of Phila.	1815	AK35	150	115
Waln, Robert, Jr., of Phila., mer.	Deed to	Burd, Edward et al	1815	AK35	152	118
Walter, Henry, of Frederick Co.	Deed to	Beall, Thomas & John M. Gantt	1792	A1-1	082	120
Walter, Thomas R.	B. of S. to	Etter, Joseph	1817	AN38	290	212
Walter, Watta & Anna et al	P. of Atty. to	King, James C.	1802	I9	237	379
Walter, Watta B., of G'tn.	Lease fr	Jones, John, of G'tn.	1796	B2B	393	053
Walter, Watta B.	Deed fr	White, Benjamin, of P.G. Co.	1796	B2B	518	227
Walter, Watta B. & A.	Deed to	King, James	1805	M12	307	309
Walton, James, Rev. et al	Deed fr	Carroll, John, Rev. et al	1799	D4	283	265
Wand, Thomas	Deed fr	Commissioners of Washington	1801	G7	473	609
Wannall, Thomas	B. of S. fr	Golding, John, Jr.	1816	AL36	546	509
Wannell, Thomas	Deed fr	King, Ezekiel	1814	AG32	319	233
Wannell, Thomas	Deed fr	Fletcher, William, now of MD	1815	AK35	385	303
Ward, James, of Charleston SC	Deed fr	Stoddert, Benjamin, of G'tn.	1804	K10	293	294
Ward, John, of Charleston SC	Deed fr	Stoddert, Benjamin	1804	K10	292	293
Ward, John W., of Montg. Co.	B. of S. fr	Townsend, Jesse J.	1815	AK35	053	041
Ward, Joshua, Middlesex Co. VA	Deed to	Muse, Laurence, of Essex Co. VA	1805	M12	161	159
Ward, Joshua, of VA	Deed fr	Greenleaf, James et al	1804	L11	175	170

Index to District of Columbia Land Records, 1792-1817

Party	What	Party	Year	Liber	Old	New
Ward, Matthias, bookseller, of NY	Deed fr	Cotterill, Thomas, mer., of NY	1810	Y24	250	230
Ward, Matthias, of NY	Deed to	Eastburn, James, mer., of NY	1812	AC28	364	264
Ward, Nancy	B. of S. fr	Ward, Thomas	1815	AK35	184	143
Ward, Thomas	B. of S. to	Ward, Nancy	1815	AK35	184	143
Ward, Ulysses, of G'tn.	Deed fr	Gantt, Thomas T., of G'tn.	1817	AN38	456	329
Ward, Ulysses, of G'tn.	Convey fr	Mackall, Ann Maria & Benjamin T.	1817	AO39	187	138
Ward, William	Deed to	Beall, James	1802	I9	380	631
Ward, William	Deed fr	Bird, Thomas & Alice	1811	AA26	319	215
Ward, William	Deed fr	Jones, Charles, exrs. of	1816	AL36	113	114
Ward, William	Deed fr	Delaney, George	1816	AL36	050	051
Ward, William	Deed to	Miller, Robert	1817	AO39	333	237
Ward, William H.	Qualify	Ensign in first legion of militia	1812	AD29	397	335
Ward, William, of MD	Deed fr	James, James, of MD	1802	I9	083	118
Warder, Jeremiah, Jr. et al	Deed fr	Atkinson, John & Elizabeth, of NY	1811	AB27	110	089
Warder, John Head, Phila. et al	Deed fr	Atkinson, John & Elizabeth, of NY	1811	AB27	110	089
Ware, Gustavus M., of Lynchburg	P. of Atty. to	Cox, Walter	1811	AB27	409	337
Waring, Henry, of Montg. Co.	Deed to	Cox, John, of G'tn.	1815	AK35	090	069
Waring, Marsham, of G'tn.	B. of S. fr	Coningham, Cornelius	1801	G7	438	574
Waring, Marsham, of G'tn.	Deed fr	Munroe, Thomas	1802	G7	593	742
Waring, Patrick	Cert. fr	Munroe, Thomas, Supt.	1812	AD29	124	095
Warley, George	Cert fr	Commissioners of Washington	1794	B2A		457
Warman, William Berry	Deed to	Greenleaf, James, of NY	1793	A1-2	464	72
Warner, Nicholas, of G'tn. et al	Deed fr	Livres, Ignatius, of G'tn.	1816	AM37	007	006
Warner, Nicholas, of G'tn. et al	Assign to	Burrows, John, of G'tn.	1817	AO39	137	104
Warner, Osborn	Mortgage to	Stettinius, Samuel	1810	Y24	076	068
Warner, Osborn	D. of T. to	Hewitt, John	1810	Z25	159	125
Warner, Osborn	D. of T. to	Jones, Charles	1810	Z25	118	092
Warner, Osborn	B. of S. to	Dove, Joseph	1810	Z25	371	291
Warner, Osborn	D. of T. to	Hewitt, John	1811	Z25	169	133
Warner, Osborn & Lewin Talbert	Deed fr	Davis, George S. & Ann	1811	AA26	001	001
Warner, Osborn, insolvent	B. of S. to	Wallach, Richard, trustee	1811	AA26	093	065
Warner, Osborn, of P.G. Co.	Cert fr	Munroe, Thomas, Supr.	1809	V21	352	255
Warner, Osborn, of VA	Deed fr	Kilty, John & Josias Wilson King	1809	X23	020	013
Warner, Zebulon, a bankrupt	Discharge		1804	K10	200	209
Warren, John	B. of S. fr	Kelly, Michael	1806	O14	327	217
Warren, Marshan et al	Deed to	Mayor & Council of Georgetown	1807	R17	232	
Warren, Nahum	B. of S. to	Keithley, Thomas	1815	AH33	398	344
Warring, Basil	Deed to	Beall, Thomas & John M. Gantt	1793	A1-2	429	37
Warring, Henry, devisee of Bazil	Deed to	Beall, Thomas & John M. Gantt	1793	A1-1	374	481
Warring, Henry, of Montg. Co.	Deed fr	Kennedy, James, of G'tn.	1815	AK35	110	085
Warring, Marsham	P. of Atty. fr	Dorsey, Joshua	1801	G7		317
Warring, Marsham	P. of Atty. fr	Bayly, Mountjoy	1801	G7		314
Warring, Marsham et al	Deed to	Beall, Thomas & John M. Gantt	1793	A1-1	371	478
Warring, Marsham, of G'tn.	Cert fr	Commissioners of Washington	1793	B2A	313	441
Warring, Marsham, of G'tn.	Deed to	Lee, Thomas Sim et al	1795	B2A	253	353
Warring, Marsham, of G'tn.	Deed fr	Beatty, Charles et al	1795	B2A	252	351
Washington, B., Jr.	Slave	From VA	1807	R17	005	004
Washington, Bailey	Deed fr	Lenox, Peter, house joiner	1807	R17	301	229
Washington, Bailey	Deed to	Schroeder, Henry, of Balto.	1808	U20	317	169
Washington Building Company	Deed fr	Bradley, Phineas	1801	G7	368	500
Washington Building Company	Deed fr	Baker, Samuel et al	1802	H8	321	302
Washington Building Company	Deed fr	Templeman, John	1802	H8	401	371
Washington Building Company	Deed fr	Densley, Hugh et al	1802	H8	321	302
Washington Building Company	Convey fr	Gillis, Thomas H. et al	1804	L11	104	108
Washington Building Company	Deed to	Van Ness, John P. et al	1804	M12	027	027

Party	What	Party	Year	Liber	Old	New
Washington Building Company	Deed fr	Law, Thomas	1805	N13	260	217
Washington Building Company	Deed fr	Dorsey, William H., of Balto.	1809	X23	239	186
Washington Building Company	Deed fr	Tingey, Thomas	1810	Y24	406	366
Washington Building Company	Convey to	Shoemaker, Daniel	1812	AD29	036	026
Washington Building Company	Deed to	Shoemaker, David	1812	AD29	381	321
Washington Building Company	Deed to	Boyd, Washington	1812	AC28	498	356
Washington Building Company	Convey to	Clarke, Abram	1813	AE30	430	318
Washington Building Company	Deed to	Smith, Henry	1813	AE30	434	321
Washington Building Company	Deed to	Boyd, Washington	1815	AI34	156	179
Washington Building Company	Convey to	Davis, John	1816	AM37	292	214
Washington, Corporation of		(see Corporation of Washington)				
Washington, George	Deed fr	Walker, George	1798	D4	156	138
Washington, George	B. of S. to	Washington, Susanna	1806	Q16	268	187
Washington, George C.	Slave	From Westmoreland Co. VA	1808	U20	404	225
Washington, George C.	Deed fr	Suttle, Henry, trustee	1811	AA26	038	029
Washington, George C. et al	Deed to	Beverly, Robert	1811	AA26	036	028
Washington, George C., of G'tn.	Deed fr	Marbury, Wm. & John Peter, G'tn.	1813	AF31	275	194
Washington, George C., of G'tn.	Deed fr	Marbury, Wm. & John Peter, G'tn.	1813	AF31	277	195
Washington, George C., of G'tn.	Deed fr	Peter, John, of G'tn.	1814	AG32	299	218
Washington, George C.	Deed fr	Marbury, William, of G'tn.	1816	AL36	068	069
Washington, George C., of MD	Deed to	Cox, John, of G'tn.	1816	AL36	202	210
Washington, George C., of MD	Deed fr	Peter, Mary & Elizabeth, of G'tn.	1816	AL36	126	127
Washington, George, Esq.	Cert fr	Commissioners of Washington	1798	B2B	481	175
Washington, George, Esq.	Cert fr	Commissioners of Washington	1798	B2B	482	175
Washington, George, Esq.	Cert fr	Commissioners of Washington	1798	B2B	481	174
Washington, George, Gen.	Deed fr	Carroll, Daniel, of *Duddington*	1798	D4	121	104
Washington, George, Pres.	Cert fr	Commissioners of Washington	1793	B2A	310	436
Washington, George, Pres.	Cert fr	Commissioners of Washington	1793	B2A	311	437
Washington, George, Pres.	Deed fr	Peter, Robert, of G'tn.	1795	B2A	214	295
Washington, George, Pres.	Request to	Commissioners of Washington	1796	B2B	588	336
Washington, George, Pres.	Request to	Commissioners of Washington	1796	B2B	588	336
Washington, Lund	Transfer fr	Dermott, James Reed	1797	B2B	467	160
Washington, Lund	Cert fr	Commissioners of Washington	1797	B2B	467	160
Washington, Lund	Deed to	Walker, George	1798	D4	113	097
Washington, Lund	Deed fr	Dermott, James R.	1799	D4	233	215
Washington, Lund	Slaves		1804	K10	180	
Washington, Lund	B. of S. to	McKim, James & Thomas Herty	1807	R17	293	224
Washington, Lund	B. of S. to	Hewitt, James	1809	V21	327	241
Washington, Lund	Cert Free to	Winters, William (C), age 42	1816	AM37	023	019
Washington, Lund & Susanna	Deed to	McKim, James & Thomas Herty	1806	Q16	205	139
Washington, Lund & Susanna	Assign to	Herty, Thomas & James McKim	1806	Q16	270	189
Washington, Lund & Susanna	D. of T. to	Davidson, John	1809	V21	319	234
Washington, Lund & Susanna	B. of S. to	Eliot, Samuel, Jr.	1811	AB27	288	236
Washington, Lund, insolvent	Deed to	Herty, Thomas, trustee	1805	N13	320	258
Washington, Lund, of Colchester	Deed to	Dermott, James R.	1800	E5	149	138
Washington, Lund, of G'tn.	D. of T. to	Cochrane, Alexander	1811	AB27	447	367
Washington, Lund, of G'tn.	B. of S. to	Munro, Robert	1812	AD29	476	403
Washington, Lund, trustee	Deed fr	Lindsay, George W., insolvent	1811	AA26	318	214
Washington Parish Vestry	Deed fr	Ingle, Henry	1812	AC28	245	181
Washington, Sarah	Slave	From VA	1813	AE30	190	152
Washington, Sarah, w/o Aug.	Manumis to	[ ], Betsey (C), and others	1813	AE30	351	262
Washington, Susan, of G'tn.	B. of S. to	Machen, Lewis H.	1811	AB27	411	339
Washington, Susanna	B. of S. fr	Washington, George	1806	Q16	268	187
Washington, Susanna, w/o Lund	B. of S. to	Winters, William	1812	AD29	491	415
Washington, Thomas	Slaves	From Stafford Co. VA	1805	M12	291	292

Party	What	Party	Year	Liber	Old	New
Washington, Thomas	Mortgage to	Wagner, Jacob	1806	P15	363	241
Washington, Thomas Lund, P.G.	Deed fr	Casey, John, of GA	1805	M12	403	417
Washington, William	Slaves	From Westmoreland Co. VA	1804	L11	313	
Washington, William A.	Cert fr	Commissioners of Washington	1792	B2A	287	401
Washington, William A.	Cert fr	Commissioners of Washington	1792	B2A	287	401
Washington, William A.	Cert fr	Commissioners of Washington	1793	B2A	315	442
Washington, William A.	Cert fr	Commissioners of Washington	1793	B2A	315	443
Washington, William A.	Cert fr	Commissioners of Washington	1793	B2A	317½	446
Washington, William A.	Cert fr	Commissioners of Washington	1793	B2A	319	449
Washington, William A.	Cert fr	Commissioners of Washington	1793	B2A	320	450
Washington, William A.	Cert fr	Commissioners of Washington	1793	B2A	319	449
Washington, William A.	Cert fr	Commissioners of Washington	1793	B2A	318	447
Washington, William A.	Assign to	Gouges, Arnauld	1795	B2A	334	469
Washington, William A.	Assign to	Gouges, Arnauld	1795	B2A	334	468
Washington, William A., of VA	Deed to	Gouges, Arnaud, of Balto.	1795	B2A	341	481
Washington, William A.	Deed fr	Caldwell, Elias B., of G'tn. et al	1804	K10	252	259
Washington, William A., of VA	Deed fr	Ringgold, Thomas, of Kent Co.	1804	K10	284	287
Washington, William Augustine	Deed to	Barlow, Joel	1809	W22	404	263
Washington, William Augustine	B. of S. to	Bradley, Arthur	1810	Y24	143	130
Wason, Edward	Lease fr	May, Frederick	1810	Z25	294	231
Waterman, Thomas	B. of S. to	Barney, John H., of Balto.	1801	G7	437	573
Waterman, Thomas, bankrupt	Discharge		1802	S18	400	319
Waters, Benjamin	Deed fr	Miller, Peter	1802	I9	302	496
Waters, Benjamin	B. of S. fr	Finigan, Rosanna	1805	M12	099	092
Waters, Benjamin, of Montg. Co.	Deed to	Miller, Peter	1805	M12	357	364
Waters, Benjamin, of Alexa.	P. of Atty. fr	Jones, Thomas D., of MD	1817	AN38	032	026
Waters, Draden	Deed fr	Holmead, John	1811	Z25	411	323
Waters, Draden	Deed to	King, Vincent	1813	AF31	057	039
Waters, James & Dradon et al	P. of Atty. to	King, James C.	1802	I9	236	378
Waters, John, of Cephas	Manumis to	Howard, Cezar (C)	1816	AM37	412	296
Waters, Jonathan	Deed fr	Forrest, Uriah et al	1799	D4	236	219
Waters, Jonathan, of A.A. Co.	Deed to	Gary, Everard, of G'tn.	1808	U20	014	009
Waters, Jonathan, of A.A. Co.	Deed to	Gary, Everard, of G'tn.	1811	AB27	325	268
Waters, Thomas G.	Deed to	Lipscomb, William Curry	1815	AK35	379	299
Waters, Thomas Gibbons	Deed fr	Wirt, John	1811	AB27	506	414
Waters, Thomas Gibbons, of G'tn.	Deed fr	Smith, Sophia, of G'tn.	1815	AK35	015	012
Waters, William	Deed fr	Munroe, Thomas, Supt.	1802	I9	068	095
Waters, William	Deed fr	Beall, Thomas	1802	I9	522	853
Waters, William	Deed fr	McCleery, Henry	1804	L11	091	93
Waters, William	Deed fr	Love, Charles, of G'tn.	1807	Q16	372	285
Waters, William	Manumis to	[ ], Susannah (negress) & child	1808	U20	167	094
Waters, William	Deed fr	Coombe, Benjamin, of Smyrna DE	1811	AB27	352	291
Waters, William	Deed fr	Threlkeld, John	1814	AG32	423	307
Waters, William	Deed fr	Lanham, Elisha	1816	AM37	041	034
Waters, William, Gent.	Deed to	Bowie, Washington, Gent.	1810	Y24	101	092
Waters, William, of G'tn.	Lease fr	King, George & Margaret, G'tn.	1795	B2A	340	479
Waters, William, of G'tn.	Deed fr	Beatty, Charles, of G'tn.	1802	I9	069	097
Waters, William, of G'tn.	Deed fr	Polock, Abigail, of Montg. Co.	1804	L11	092	94
Waters, William, of G'tn.	Deed fr	Polock, Abigail, of Montg. Co.	1804	M12	025	025
Waters, William, of G'tn.	Deed fr	McCleery, Henry	1805	M12	291	292
Waters, William, of Fairfax Co. VA	Deed fr	Beall, Thomas B., of G'tn.	1806	O14	342	228
Waters, William, of VA	Deed fr	McCormick, George, of G'tn.	1806	O14	344	229
Waters, William, of G'tn.	Deed fr	Beatty, John M. & Charles A.	1808	T19	044	033
Waterston, David	Deed to	Wheaton, Sally	1807	R17	309	235
Waterston, David	Deed fr	Van Ness, John P. & Marcia	1807	R17	306	233

Party	What	Party	Year	Liber	Old	New
Waterstone, David	B. of S. fr	Jones, William	1802	H8	535	495
Wathen, Charles [Worthen]	B. of S. to	Threlkeld, John	1817	AO39	411	270
Watkins, John	B. of S. to	Prout, William	1809	W22	167	118
Watkins, Richard	Manumis to	Watkins, Susan (C), age c.35	1815	AI34	331	364
Watkins, Susan (C), age c.35	Manumis fr	Watkins, Richard	1815	AI34	331	364
Watkins, Thomas, carpenter	Deed to	Robertson, Alexander, stone cutter	1799	D4	207	190
Watson, Elizabeth	B. of S. fr	Wilson, Joseph	1805	N13	048	045
Watson, Elizabeth et al	Convey fr	Wilson, Joseph	1805	N13	046	044
Watson, James	Mortgage to	Evans, Evan	1811	AB27	388	320
Watson, James	Deed to	Knoblock, John	1813	AF31	321	229
Watson, James, of NY	Cert fr	Commissioners of Washington	1793	B2A		429
Watson, James, of NY	Cert fr	Commissioners of Washington	1793	B2A	305	428
Watson, James Wilson et al	Convey to	Wilson, Joseph	1805	N13	046	044
Watson, John	Deed fr	Watson, Thomas	1806	Q16	187	126
Watson, John	Deed to	Foxall, Henry	1806	Q16	184	124
Watson, John, of Henry Co. VA	Deed to	French, William & John Marr	1793	A1-2	431	39
Watson, John, of Balto.	Deed to	King, William, Jr., of G'tn.	1815	AH33	553	473
Watson, John, of Balto.	Release fr	Foxall, Henry, of G'tn.	1815	AH33	551	472
Watson, Thomas	Deed fr	Walker, George, Jr.	1801	G7	231	309
Watson, Thomas	Deed to	Watson, John	1806	Q16	187	126
Watterson, David	B. of S. fr	Bullock, Richard	1810	Z25	367	287
Watterston, David	Deed fr	Williamson, John	1806	P15	020	012
Watterston, David	Deed fr	Low, Nicholas, of P.G. Co.	1807	S18	315	247
Watterston, David	B. of S. fr	Greenfield, Thomas	1808	V21	125	092
Watterston, David	B. of S. fr	Stewart, Richard	1809	V21	321	236
Watterston, David	Release to	Johnston, James	1811	AB27	331	272
Watterston, David	Manumis to	[ ], Rachel (C)	1812	AC28	203	154
Watterston, David	B. of S. fr	Moore, Warren, of St. Mary's Co.	1812	AC28	377	274
Watterston, David	Deed fr	Law, Edmund, trustee of Thomas	1812	AB27	538	439
Watterston, David et al	Mortgage fr	Somerville, David	1810	Z25	362	284
Watterston, George	Deed fr	Reid, Alexander	1809	X23	155	113
Watterston, George	Mortgage fr	Brady, Nathaniel	1812	AD29	352	295
Watterston, George	B. of S. fr	Soper, Henry, of P.G. Co.	1813	AE30	364	270
Watterston, George	Deed to	McCormick, Alexander	1813	AE30	266	206
Watterston, George	B. of S. fr	Ellicott, William	1814	AG32	123	091
Watterstone, David	B. of S. fr	Ford, Athanasius [Lewis]	1815	AI34	516	521
Watterstone, David et al	B. of S. fr	Gray, William	1811	AC28	011	008
Watterstone, George	B. of S. fr	Thornton, Anthony & Jane	1816	AM37	328	238
Watts, Richard K., Sr., Montg. Co.	B. of S. fr	Richards, George, bookseller	1817	AN38	508	368
Waugh, Alexander & Susanna P.	Deed to	Keane, Francis	1810	Y24	343	310
Waugh, Alexander, Fairfax Co. VA	Deed fr	Waugh, James, Jr. & Sr.	1807	R17	240	181
Waugh, Alexander, of Fairfax Co.	Deed fr	Waugh, James, Jr.	1808	T19	274	202
Waugh, James, Jr. of VA	Deed fr	Prout, William	1802	I9	108	158
Waugh, James, Jr., Fairfax Co.	Deed to	Waugh, Alexander, Fairfax Co. VA	1807	R17	240	181
Waugh, James, Jr.	Deed to	Waugh, Alexander, of Fairfax Co.	1808	T19	274	202
Waugh, James, of VA	Agreement	Greenfield, James et al	1802	I9	113	165
Waugh, James, Sr., Fairfax Co.	Deed fr	Greenleaf, James et al	1804	L11	230	213
Waugh, James, Sr., Fairfax Co.	Deed to	Waugh, Alexander, Fairfax Co. VA	1807	R17	240	181
Way, Andrew & George	Deed fr	Edwards, Horace Hampden	1809	V21	402	305
Way, Andrew & George	Deed fr	Joel, Ann, of Berkeley Co. VA	1809	W22	371	240
Way, Andrew & George	Release fr	Edwards, Horace H.	1810	Y24	160	146
Way, Andrew & George	Release fr	Van Ness, John P. & Marcia	1811	AA26	157	109
Way, Andrew & George	Cert fr	Munroe, Thomas, Supt.	1811	AB27	358	297
Way, Andrew & George	Deed fr	Ardrey, William	1811	AC28	072	055
Way, Andrew & George	Deed fr	Law, Thomas	1812	AC28	314	229

Index to District of Columbia Land Records, 1792-1817

Party	What	Party	Year	Liber	Old	New
Way, Andrew & George	Deed fr	Shellman, Jacob, of Frederick MD	1812	AD29	469	396
Way, Andrew & George	Deed fr	Cox, Thomas Cambell, of SC	1813	AE30	480	357
Way, Andrew & George	Deed fr	Voss, Nicholas, of VA	1813	AE30	150	118
Way, Andrew & George	Deed fr	Dorsey, William H., of Montg. Co.	1814	AG32	234	167
Way, Andrew & George	Deed fr	Murdock, John, of G'tn.	1814	AG32	236	168
Way, Andrew & George	Deed fr	Blake, James H., mayor of Wash.	1815	AI34	108	123
Way, Andrew, Jr. et al	Deed fr	Baker, Samuel	1802	H8	324	304
Way, Andrew, Jr. et al	Convey to	Van Ness, John P. et al	1804	L11	104	108
Way, Andrew, Jr. & George	Deed fr	Myer, Solomon	1807	S18	050	042
Way, Andrew, Jr. & George	Deed fr	Myer, Solomon	1807	Q16	363	278
Way, Andrew, Jr. et al	Deed fr	Munroe, Thomas, Supt.	1807	R17	315	239
Way, Andrew, Jr. et al	Deed fr	Cist, Jacob	1808	T19	070	051
Way, Andrew, Jr. et al	Deed fr	Ardery, Alexander & William	1808	U20	256	137
Way, Andrew, Jr. et al	Deed fr	Stinger, Solomon	1808	U20	243	130
Way, Andrew, Jr. et al	Cert fr	Munroe, Thomas, Supt.	1808	U20	345	187
Way, Andrew, Jr.	B. of S. fr	Smith, Samuel	1812	AD29	162	128
Way, Andrew, Jr.	B. of S. to	Lindsay, Adam	1813	AF31	187	126
Way, Andrew, Jr.	Deed fr	Lucas, Ignatius	1816	AL36	042	043
Way, Andrew, Jr. et al	Deed fr	Herford, Henry	1816	AL36	450	426
Way, Andrew, Jr. et al	Deed fr	Herford, Henry	1816	AL36	445	423
Way, Andrew, Jr. et al	D. of T. fr	Herford, Henry	1816	AM37	138	107
Way, Andrew, Jr.	Deed fr	Mason, John	1817	AO39	453	311
Way, Andrew, Jr.	Deed fr	Carr, Overton, trustee	1817	AN38	321	235
Way, Andrew, the younger et al	Deed fr	Bradley, Phineas	1801	G7	368	500
Way, George	Deed fr	Glover, Charles	1816	AO39	009	007
Way, George	Deed fr	Elliott, Samuel, Jr.	1816	AL36	048	048
Way, George	B. of S. fr	McLaughlin, John	1817	AO39	284	202
Way, George & Andrew, Jr.	Deed fr	Myer, Solomon	1807	S18	050	042
Way, George & Andrew, Jr.	Deed fr	Myer, Solomon	1807	Q16	363	278
Way, George et al	Deed fr	Munroe, Thomas, Supt.	1807	R17	315	239
Way, George et al	Deed fr	Stinger, Solomon	1808	U20	243	130
Way, George et al	Deed fr	Ardery, Alexander & William	1808	U20	256	137
Way, George et al	Deed fr	Cist, Jacob	1808	T19	070	051
Way, John & Jane, of DE	Deed to	Whann, William, of G'tn.	1816	AK35	508	400
Way, John, of New Castle Co. DE	Deed fr	Reynolds, James & Hannah, DE	1815	AK35	220	173
Way, John, of New Castle Co. DE	Deed fr	Updegraff, Mary, wid/o Josiah et al	1815	AK35	224	176
Way, John, rep. of Nicholas	Deed fr	Landis, David, of Bucks Co. PA	1811	AA26	372	248
Way, Nicholas, of Wilmington DE	Deed fr	Cloud, Amos & Samuel Paxton	1793	A1-2	403	12
Way, Nicholas, physic, of DE	Deed fr	Cloud, Amos	1793	A1-2	405	14
Wayman, Charles	Deed to	Murdock, George	1802	I9	213	335
Wayman, Charles	Deed to	Callahan, John	1802	I9	167	254
Wayman, Charles	Deed fr	Munroe, Thomas, Supt.	1802	I9	169	256
Wayman, Charles	Deed fr	Munroe, Thomas, Supt.	1802	I9	504	827
Wayman, Charles	Deed to	Caldwell, Elias B.	1802	I9	344	568
Wayman, Charles	B. of S. fr	Moscrop, Henry	1802	I9	538	878
Wayman, Charles	Deed fr	Munroe, Tomas, Supt.	1802	I9	451	745
Wayman, Charles	Deed to	Campbell, William	1802	I9	197	307
Wayman, Charles	Deed to	Beatty, Thomas J.	1802	I9	574	931
Wayman, Charles	Deed fr	Munroe, Thomas, Supt.	1802	I9	412	682
Wayman, Charles	Deed to	Stevens, John	1802	I9	463	762
Wayman, Charles	Deed fr	May, Frederick	1802	I9	539	879
Wayman, Charles	Deed to	King, Adam	1802	I9	170	258
Wayman, Charles	Deed to	Kaldenbaugh, Andrew, of G'tn.	1805	N13	106	100
Wayman, Charles	Deed fr	Davidson, John	1805	M12	255	256
Wayman, Charles	Deed fr	Murdock, John, of G'tn.	1805	N13	051	048

Party	What	Party	Year	Liber	Old	New
Wayman, Charles et al	Deed fr	Duncanson, William Mayne	1797	C3	103	84
Wayman, Charles et al	Bond to	United States	1801	G7	347	478
Wayman, Charles et al	Deed fr	Beall, Thomas H.	1802	I9	145	219
Wayman, Charles et al	Deed to	Nourse, Joseph	1804	K10	183	192
Wayman, Charles et al	Deed fr	Caldwell, Elias B. et al	1804	K10	247	254
Wayman, Charles et al	Deed fr	Charlton, Ralp	1804	L11	378	338
Wayman, Charles, of G'tn.	Deed to	Peter, Robert, of G'tn.	1801	G7	292	405
Wayman, Charles, of G'tn.	Deed fr	Commissioners of Washington	1801	G7	258	353
Wayman, Charles, of G'tn.	Deed to	Corcoran, Thomas	1802	H8	195	186
Wayman, Charles, of G'tn.	Deed to	Ringgold, Tench	1803	K10	064	69
Wayman, Charles, of G'tn.	Deed to	Thomas, Richard, of Montg. Co.	1804	K10	222	231
Wayman, Charles, of G'tn.	Deed to	McDaniel, George G.	1804	L11	100	102
Wayman, Charles, of G'tn. et al	Deed to	King, Adam	1804	L11	073	75
Wayman, Charles, of G'tn. et al	Deed to	Baltzer, John, Jr.	1804	L11	079	81
Wayman, Charles, of G'tn. et al	Deed to	King, George	1804	L11	075	77
Wayman, Charles, of G'tn. et al	Deed to	Dorsey, William H.	1804	L11	071	73
Wayman, Charles, of G'tn.	Deed to	Smith, Walter & Clement	1805	N13	388	310
Wayman, Charles, of G'tn.	Deed to	Shaaff, John Thomas, Annapolis	1805	N13	049	046
Wayman, Charles, of G'tn.	Deed fr	Fendall, Philip Richard, of Alexa.	1805	M12	256	258
Wayman, Charles, of G'tn.	Deed fr	May, Frederick	1805	N13	147	137
Wayman, Henry	Manumis to	[ ], Rachel (Negro)	1806	O14	207	137
Wayman, Henry	Manumis to	[ ], Amy, and son Peter	1806	Q16	301	229
Wayman, Henry	B. of S. to	Dyer, Henry O.	1806	O14	156	102
Wayman, John	Deed to	Deakins, Francis	1800	E5	146	135
Wayne, Francis	Deed fr	Pratt, Henry et al	1814	AH33	377	326
Wayne, Francis	Deed fr	Slater, Sarah, wid/o David, P.G.	1817	AO39	331	236
Wayne, Isaac	B. of S. fr	Richmond, Braddock	1810	Z25	041	031
Weaden, Henry	Mortgage to	Craig, Robert	1812	AD29	362	304
Weatheral, John, of G'tn.	Deed fr	Balch, Stephen B., of G'tn.	1796	B2B	409	077
Weatheral, John, of G'tn.	Deed to	Douglas, Edward, of G'tn.	1799	E5	057	047
Weatherall, John	Deed fr	Polock, Isaac	1798	D4	028	023
Weatherall, John	Deed fr	French, George	1798	D4	168	149
Weatherall, John	Deed to	Barron, Walter & Hezekiah Berry	1799	D4	426	398
Weatherall, John	Deed to	Mitchell, Maria & Matilda	1802	I9	341	562
Weatherall, John	Deed to	Galor, Thomas	1802	I9	293	481
Weatherall, John	Deed to	Owens, Isaac	1806	O14	340	227
Weatherall, John et al	Deed to	Owens, Isaac, of G'tn.	1807	R17	344	262
Weatherall, John, mechanic, G'tn.	Deed fr	King, George, merchant, of G'tn.	1799	D4	203	186
Weatherall, John, of Montg. Co.	Deed fr	Balch, Stephen B., of Montg. Co.	1796	B2B	517	224
Weatherall, John, of Montg. Co.	Deed to	Bulger, Margaret, of P.G. Co.	1796	B2B	561	294
Weatherall, John, of G'tn.	Deed to	Rose, Robert	1798	D4	117	101
Weatherall, John, of G'tn. et al	B. of S. fr	Hurdell, Leonard, of G'tn.	1802	H8	408	378
Weatherall, John, of G'tn.	B. of S. to	Ferguson, David, Ontario Co. NY	1806	P15	381	255
Weatherall, John, of G'tn.	Deed to	Ferguson, David, Ontario Co. NY	1806	Q16	252	174
Weaver, George	Slaves	From VA	1809	X23	031	022
Weaver, George F., of G'tn.	B. of S. to	Weaver, William A., Lt.	1817	AN38	505	365
Weaver, William A., Lt.	B. of S. fr	Weaver, George F., of G'tn.	1817	AN38	505	365
Webb, Thomas	Deed fr	Whann, William, of G'tn.	1798	D4	012	010
Webb, Thomas	Deed fr	Whann, William, of G'tn.	1800	E5	394	369
Webb, Thomas	Mortgage to	Brent, Robert et al	1802	I9	190	295
Webb, Thomas et al	Deed to	Burnes, George	1805	N13	075	068
Webb, Thomas, of Montg. Co.	Mortgage fr	Densley, Hugh	1805	M12	104	097
Webb, Thomas, of P.G. Co. et al	Deed to	Burrows, Edward	1805	N13	250	209
Webb, Thomas, of Montg. Co.	Deed to	Densley, Hugh	1817	AO39	232	167
Webster, Daniel, of Occoquan VA	Agreement	Lloyd, James, of Boston MA	1810	Z25	107	083

Index to District of Columbia Land Records, 1792-1817   437

Party	What	Party	Year	Liber	Old	New
Webster, John A., of Balto.	B. of S. fr	Okely, John, of G'tn.	1817	AN38	195	141
Webster, Toppan	Mortgage fr	Lovell, William	1802	H8	402	372
Webster, Toppan	B. of S. to	Thorn, Christopher S.	1802	H8	001	001
Webster, Toppan	T. of M. to	Thom, Christopher S.	1802	I9	051	069
Webster, Toppan	Mortgage to	Irvine, Walter	1802	G7	489	626
Webster, Toppan	Assign fr	Lovell, William, of Balto.	1806	P15	086	052
Webster, Toppan	D. of T. fr	Lovell, William, of Balto.	1809	W22	222	151
Webster, Toppan	D. of T. fr	Ford, Lewis, of St. Mary's Co.	1809	W22	219	150
Webster, Toppan	Deed to	Nourse, Michael	1809	W22	006	005
Webster, Toppan	Deed to	Rapine, Daniel	1809	X23	003	002
Webster, Toppan	Deed fr	Beall, Samuel, of G'tn.	1809	V21	347	251
Webster, Toppan	Lease fr	Hoban, James	1811	AA26	167	115
Webster, Toppan	D. of T. to	Smith, Walter	1812	AC28	463	329
Webster, Toppan	Release fr	Rapine, Daniel	1812	AC28	345	250
Webster, Toppan	Deed fr	Boyd, Washington, marshal	1812	AC28	340	246
Webster, Toppan	Deed fr	Munroe, Thomas, Supt.	1812	AC28	349	252
Webster, Toppan	Deed fr	Munroe, Thomas, Supt.	1812	AC28	348	252
Webster, Toppan	Deed fr	Nourse, Michael	1812	AC28	343	248
Webster, Toppan	Deed fr	English, David, of G'tn.	1812	AD29	115	088
Webster, Toppan	Lease fr	Hoban, James	1812	AD29	192	156
Webster, Toppan	Assign to	McCormick, James, Jr.	1812	AD29	118	090
Webster, Toppan	Deed to	McCormick, James, Jr.	1812	AD29	116	089
Webster, Toppan	Deed fr	McElwee, Rebecca, wid/o John	1812	AD29	082	060
Webster, Toppan	Deed to	Suter, Alexander, of G'tn.	1813	AF31	005	003
Webster, Toppan	Mortgage to	Foxall, Henry, of G'tn.	1813	AE30	139	108
Webster, Toppan	Deed fr	Gaines, Richard, of Cincinnati OH	1813	AE30	543	402
Webster, Toppan	Assign to	Pairo, Thomas W.	1814	AG32	082	062
Webster, Toppan	Assign fr	McCormick, James, Jr., Balto. Co.	1814	AG32	084	063
Webster, Toppan	Deed to	Baily, John	1814	AG32	198	138
Webster, Toppan	Deed fr	McCormick, James, Jr., Balto. Co.	1814	AH33	094	086
Webster, Toppan	Deed to	Hoit, Samuel	1814	AH33	083	075
Webster, Toppan	B. of S. to	Rapine, Daniel et al	1814	AH33	130	123
Webster, Toppan	Deed fr	Hoit, Samuel	1815	AH33	429	369
Webster, Toppan	Deed to	Moore, George	1815	AI34	164	188
Webster, Toppan	Assign to	Murray, Thomas	1815	AI34	046	053
Webster, Toppan	Lease fr	Hoban, James	1815	AK35	375	295
Webster, Toppan	Deed fr	Hoye, John, of Allegany Co.	1815	AK35	371	293
Webster, Toppan	D. of T. to	Smith, Walter, of G'tn.	1815	AK35	307	245
Webster, Toppan	Deed to	Tayloe, John	1816	AL36	229	234
Webster, Toppan	Deed to	Tayloe, John	1816	AM37	490	357
Webster, Toppan	Lease fr	Law, Thomas	1816	AL36	133	134
Webster, Toppan	Deed to	McGowan, John et al	1817	AO39	307	218
Webster, Toppan	D. of T. to	Nourse, Michael & George Clarke	1817	AO39	310	221
Webster, Toppan & Lewis Ford	Deed fr	Lovell, William, of Balto.	1807	R17	075	061
Webster, Toppan & Lewis Ford	Deed fr	Lovering, William, of Balto.	1809	W22	101	073
Webster, Toppan & Geo. Andrews	Deed fr	Heronimus, Pendleton	1816	AL36	046	046
Webster, Toppan et al	Deed fr	Law, John, atty. for Thomas	1810	Y24	067	059
Wedding, James H. & Nancy et al	Deed to	Walker, Zachariah	1815	AI34	435	452
Wedding, James H. & Ann et al	Deed to	Spalding, Enoch	1815	AI34	097	110
Wedding, James H. & Ann et al	Deed to	Spalding, Enoch	1815	AI34	110	110
Weeden, Henry	D. of T. to	Pickrell, John	1814	AH33	363	315
Weeden, Henry	Deed fr	Wilson, Levi G.	1815	AI34	127	146
Weeden, Henry, of G'tn.	Deed fr	Magruder, Ninian, of G'tn.	1813	AE30	464	345
Weeden, Henry, of G'tn.	B. of S. to	Bunnell, Elias & W.B. Robertson	1813	AF31	172	116
Weeden, Henry, of G'tn.	Deed to	Davis, John P., of G'tn.	1814	AH33	174	162

Party	What	Party	Year	Liber	Old	New
Weeden, Henry, of G'tn.	Deed to	Pickrell, John	1815	AI34	128	147
Weems, Elizabeth	Deed fr	Weems, Elizabeth, of G'tn., exrx.	1813	AE30	390	288
Weems, Elizabeth	Deed fr	French, George et al	1813	AF31	253	176
Weems, Elizabeth et al	Deed to	Jones, Charles C.	1810	Z25	086	065
Weems, Elizabeth et al	Deed to	French, George	1813	AF31	247	171
Weems, Elizabeth et al	Deed to	French, Robert	1813	AF31	250	174
Weems, Elizabeth et al	Deed to	French, Charles	1813	AF31	249	173
Weems, Elizabeth, gdn.	Deed to	Turner, Thomas	1815	AK35	203	159
Weems, Elizabeth, of G'tn., exrx.	Deed to	French, George et al	1813	AE30	390	288
Weems, Elizabeth, wid/o John	Deed to	Turner, Thomas	1815	AK35	202	158
Weems, George et al	Deed fr	Chandler, Walter Story	1812	AD29	500	422
Weems, John	Deed to	Peter, David et al	1805	M12	346	352
Weems, John, Dr., of G'tn.	Cert fr	Commissioners of Washington	1793	B2A	309	434
Weems, John, Dr.	Deed fr	Beall, Thomas, of George	1795	B2A	258	360
Weems, John, Dr., of G'tn.	Deed fr	Bayly, William	1795	B2A	256	358
Weems, John, Dr., of G'tn.	Deed to	Roby, Theophilus, of G'tn.	1796	B2B	403	069
Weems, John, Dr., of G'tn.	Deed to	Tennally, Sarah	1796	B2B	398	062
Weems, John, Dr., of G'tn.	Deed fr	Chandler, Walter Story, G'tn.	1801	G7	261	358
Weems, John, Dr., of G'tn.	Deed fr	French, Ariana, exrx. of George	1806	P15	237	157
Weems, John, Dr., heirs of	Deed fr	Chandler, Walter Story	1812	AD29	500	422
Weems, John, Dr., exrx. of	Deed to	French, George et al	1813	AE30	390	288
Weems, John et al	Deed fr	Chandler, Walter Story	1812	AD29	500	422
Weems, John, of G'tn.	Deed to	West, Joseph D., of MD	1802	H8	571	535
Weems, John, of G'tn.	Deed fr	Nourse, Joseph, of G'tn.	1804	L11	011	10
Weems, John, of G'tn.	Deed fr	Chandler, Walter Story, of G'tn.	1804	L11	007	7
Weems, John, physician, of G'tn.	Deed to	Chandler, Walter S., of G'tn.	1802	H8	286	270
Weems, John, physician, of G'tn.	Deed fr	Corcoran, Thomas	1802	H8	283	268
Weems, Mason L.	B. of S. fr	Ewell, James	1814	AH33	025	023
Weems, Nathaniel T., of G'tn.	B. of S. to	Johnson, Richard, of Frederick Co.	1810	Y24	277	253
Weems, Nathaniel T., of G'tn.	Deed fr	Steuart, William, of G'tn.	1810	Y24	021	018
Weems, Rolla et al	Deed fr	Chandler, Walter Story	1812	AD29	500	422
Weems, William	Mortgage fr	Chalmers, John, Sr. & Jr.	1812	AC28	449	321
Wehrby, Jonathan, of Balto.	Deed fr	Mountz, John, of G'tn.	1817	AN38	518	375
Wehrby, Jonathan, of Balto.	Deed to	Mountz, John, of G'tn.	1817	AN38	513	372
Wehrly, David	Deed to	Clarke, William	1806	Q16	033	021
Wehrly, David, of G'tn.	Deed fr	Wehrly, Jonathan, of G'tn. et al	1805	M12	130	125
Wehrly, David, of G'tn. [Wherly]	Deed to	Carmical, Alexander, of G'tn.	1811	AB27	058	050
Wehrly, David, of G'tn.	Deed to	Mountz, John, Jr., of G'tn.	1811	AB27	254	207
Wehrly, David, of G'tn.	Deed to	Wehrly, Jonathan, of Balto. Co.	1811	AB27	253	206
Wehrly, Jonathan et al	Deed fr	Mountz, John, Sr.	1805	M12	243	244
Wehrly, Jonathan, of G'tn. et al	Deed to	Wehrly, David, of G'tn.	1805	M12	130	125
Wehrly, Jonathan, of Balto. Co.	Deed to	Wehrly, David, of G'tn.	1811	AB27	252	205
Wehrly, Jonathan, of Balto. Co.	Deed fr	Wehrly, David, of G'tn.	1811	AB27	253	206
Wehrly, Jonathan, of Balto. Co.	Deed fr	Griffin, Martin & Bridget et al	1811	AB27	248	202
Weightman, Henry T.	B. of S. fr	Weightman, John	1817	AO39	142	108
Weightman, John	B. of S. to	Weightman, Henry T.	1817	AO39	142	108
Weightman, Roger C. & L. Deblois	B. of S. fr	Van Zandt, Nicholas B.	1810	Z25	002	002
Weightman, Roger C.	Deed fr	Pratt, Henry et al	1811	AB27	228	186
Weightman, Roger C.	Slaves	From Alexandria	1812	AC28	317	228
Weightman, Roger C.	Deed fr	Pratt, Henry, of Phila. PA et al	1812	AD29	409	346
Weightman, Roger C.	Deed fr	Pratt, Henry, of Phila. PA et al	1812	AD29	406	342
Weightman, Roger C.	Deed fr	Pratt, Henry, of Phila. PA et al	1812	AD29	402	339
Weightman, Roger C.	Plat	North D Street	1813	AE30	075	
Weightman, Roger C.	Mortgage to	Greenleaf, James, of Phila. PA	1813	AE30	074	056
Weightman, Roger C.	Deed fr	Clokey, Samuel	1813	AE30	348	260

Index to District of Columbia Land Records, 1792-1817

Party	What	Party	Year	Liber	Old	New
Weightman, Roger C.	B. of S. fr	Hanson, Isaac K.	1814	AH33	261	227
Weightman, Roger C.	Release to	Crawford, William	1815	AI34	138	159
Weightman, Roger C.	Deed to	Turner, Robert, of Balto. Co.	1815	AG32	348	252
Weightman, Roger C. et al	Deed fr	Herford, Henry	1816	AL36	450	426
Weightman, Roger C.	Deed to	Hill, John D.	1816	AM37	432	310
Weightman, Roger C. et al	D. of T. fr	Herford, Henry	1816	AM37	138	107
Weightman, Roger C. et al	B. of S. fr	Willis, Perrin	1816	AM37	366	265
Weightman, Roger C.	Qualify	Justice of the Peace	1816	AM37	530	393
Weightman, Roger C. et al	Deed fr	Herford, Henry	1816	AL36	445	423
Weightman, Roger C. et al	Deed fr	Bickley, Robert S., Bucks Co. PA	1817	AN38	564	411
Weightman, Roger C.	Release fr	Greenleaf, James, of Phila.	1817	AN38	032	026
Weightman, Roger C.	B. of S. fr	Davis, John	1817	AO39	125	096
Weightman, Roger Chew	Mortgage fr	Duane, William, of Phila.	1812	AB27	521	425
Weightman, Roger Chew et al	Deed fr	Wilson, William	1813	AE30	194	156
Weightman, Roger Chew	Release fr	Hewitt, John	1813	AF31	441	317
Weightman, Roger Chew	Deed fr	Eliot, Samuel, Jr.	1817	AO39	168	125
Weiskoff, Charles L., of G'tn. et al	Deed fr	Riggs, George W., of Balto. MD	1812	AD29	092	070
Weiskopff & Keller	B. of S. fr	Cox, Josiah	1809	W22	414	269
Weiskopff, C.L., of G'tn.	B. of S. to	Keller, Frederick, of G'tn.	1816	AL36	421	402
Weiskopff, Charles L. et al	Convey fr	Riggs, George W., of Balto.	1810	Y24	495	436
Weiskopff, Charles L., of G'tn.	Deed fr	Lufborough, Nathan	1813	AE30	446	331
Weiskopff, Charles L., of G'tn.	Deed fr	Keller, John Frederick, of G'tn.	1814	AH33	210	189
Weiskopff, Charles Lewis et al	Mortgage to	Grammer, Frederick, of Annapolis	1812	AD29	350	293
Weiskopff, Lewis & J.F. Keller	Release fr	Grammer, Frederick, of A.A. Co.	1815	AI34	278	313
Welch, Bridget et al	Deed fr	Purcell, Pierce	1809	X23	160	118
Welch, Jacob, of Lunenburg MA	Cert fr	Commissioners of Washington	1792	B2A	285	399
Welch, Mary Ann et al	Deed fr	Purcell, Pierce	1809	X23	160	118
Welch, Mary Ann	Relinquish fr	Welch, Valentine	1817	AO39	386	261
Welch, Mary Ann	Relinquish fr	Welch, Valentine	1817	AO39	385	260
Welch, Valentine	Relinquish to	Welch, Mary Ann	1817	AO39	386	261
Welch, Valentine	Relinquish to	Welch, Mary Ann	1817	AO39	385	260
Welch, Valentine & Mary Ann	Deed to	Burdine, Reubin	1817	AO39	383	259
Welch, Valentine et al	Deed fr	Purcell, Pierce	1809	X23	160	118
Wells, John, Jr., of G'tn.	Deed fr	Jones, Benjamin W., of Montg. Co.	1815	AK35	312	248
Wells, John, Jr., of G'tn.	Deed to	Threlkeld, John, of G'tn.	1815	AK35	313	250
Wells, John, of P.G. Co.	B. of S. to	Spalding, Electius	1811	Z25	544	432
Wells, John, of Annapolis	Deed to	Wetzel, John, of G'tn.	1817	AN38	278	203
Wells, John, of Annapolis	Deed fr	Thompson, Moses	1817	AN38	276	202
Wells, Joseph et al, defs.	Suit	Scholfield, Andrew, plt.	1809	V21	326	240
Wells, Joseph, of PA	Deed to	Scholfield, Issachar & Mahlon	1796	B2B	539	259
Wells, Nathan	P. of Atty. to	Boyd, Abraham	1800	E5	162	151
Wells, Nathan & Sophia, of KY	Deed to	Duley, William, of Montg. Co.	1805	N13	309	250
Wells, Nathan & Sophia, of KY	Deed to	Smith, Samuel Harrison	1808	T19	187	133
Welsh, Jacob, of Lunenburg MA	Cert fr	Commissioners of Washington	1792	B2A	284	397
Welsh, Jacob, of Lunenburg MA	Cert fr	Commissioners of Washington	1792	B2A	286	400
Welsh, William & Hannah et al	Deed to	Way, John, of New Castle Co. DE	1815	AK35	224	176
Wenrly, David, of G'tn.	Deed fr	Wehrly, Jonathan & A. Carmical	1811	AB27	252	205
Wert, Joseph D.	Deed to	Moore, Nicholas et al	1802	I9	298	490
Wertz, Christian	B. of S. fr	Hurst, Thomas	1816	AL36	409	392
Wertz, Henry, Jr.	Mortgage to	Ewell, Thomas	1813	AF31	179	120
Wertz, Henry, Jr.	Mortgage to	Cocke, Buller	1813	AF31	224	154
West, Harriet Black et al	Deed to	Chandler, Walter S. et al	1804	K10	112	120
West, Harriet Black et al	Deed to	Smith, Walter & Clement, of G'tn.	1804	K10	127	138
West, Jacob, of Balto. Co.	Deed fr	Mann, John, of Balto. Co.	1816	AL36	373	361
West, Joel et al	Deed fr	Burnes, David, of P.G. Co.	1797	C3	079	65

Party	What	Party	Year	Liber	Old	New
West, Joel et al	Cert fr	Commissioners of Washington	1797	B2B	464	155
West, John	D. of T. to	Mountz, John, Jr.	1809	W22	003	002
West, John	D. of T. to	Dougherty, James, trustee	1810	Y24	139	126
West, John, New Castle Co. DE	B. of S. fr	Clayton, Rachel, Newc. Co. DE	1809	V21	307	224
West, Joseph	Deed fr	Stoddert, Benjamin	1806	P15	158	104
West, Joseph	Deed fr	French, Ariana, exrx. of George	1806	P15	156	102
West, Joseph D., of MD	Deed fr	Weems, John, of G'tn.	1802	H8	571	535
West, Joseph D.	Deed fr	Dorsey, William H.	1805	M12	112	105
West, Joseph D.	Deed to	Threlkeld, John	1811	AB27	474	387
West, Joseph D.	Deed to	Willett, John, of Montg. Co.	1816	AL36	296	293
West, Richard & Alex. Adams	Deed fr	O'Neale, Sarah, of Montg. Co.	1811	AC28	106	080
West, Richard W., of P.G. Co.	Deed to	Gantt, Thomas T.	1816	AL36	035	036
West, Richard William et al	Deed to	Smith, Walter & Clement, of G'tn.	1804	K10	127	138
West, Richard William et al	Deed to	Chandler, Walter S. & P.B. Key	1804	K10	112	120
West, Stephen et al	Deed to	Chandler, Walter S. et al	1804	K10	112	120
West, Stephen et al	Deed to	Smith, Walter & Clement, of G'tn.	1804	K10	127	138
West, Stephen et al	Deed to	Gantt, Thomas T.	1816	AL36	035	036
Westcott, James D.	Mortgage fr	Lyon, James	1802	I9	187	290
Westcott, James D., of NJ	Deed fr	Wright, Thomas C., of G'tn.	1813	AF31	211	144
Westerfield, David et al	B. of S. fr	Finigan, Rosannah	1816	AM37	145	112
Wetherall, Charles	B. of S. to	Boothe, Benjamin	1817	AO39	151	114
Wetzel, Frederick	Deed fr	French, Mariamnc C. et al	1812	AD29	017	012
Wetzel, Frederick	Deed fr	French, Mariamne C. & John Peter	1817	AN38	280	205
Wetzel, John	Slave	From VA	1812	AC28	407	295
Wetzel, John, of G'tn.	Deed fr	Wells, John, of Annapolis	1817	AN38	278	203
Wetzell, Frederick	Deed fr	Beatty, Charles A., Dr.	1815	AH33	510	438
Wetzell, William Y. et al	B. of S. fr	Talbert, Bazil, of P.G. Co.	1808	T19	324	236
Wetzell, William Y., of G'tn.	Deed fr	Pickrell, John, of G'tn.	1816	AO39	042	034
Weyenberger, George	Deed fr	Beatty, Charles, of G'tn.	1800	E5	157	146
Whalan, Nicholas	Deed fr	Chandler, Walter Story	1809	W22	107	077
Whann, Adam, of Elkton MD	Deed fr	Chesley, Ann, of G'tn.	1807	S18	199	159
Whann, Adam, of G'tn.	Deed fr	Davidson, Anna Maria, of G'tn.	1809	X23	317	254
Whann, Adam, of Cecil Co. MD	Deed to	Whann, Ann Maria, of G'tn.	1812	AD29	077	056
Whann, Ann M., d/o William	Deed Gift fr	Whann, William, of G'tn.	1810	Z25	006	005
Whann, Ann Maria, of G'tn.	Deed fr	Whann, Adam, of Cecil Co. MD	1812	AD29	077	056
Whann, Daniel	Cert		1802	I9	338	557
Whann, David	Deed fr	Brooks, Joseph	1812	AD29	098	074
Whann, David	Deed fr	Brooks, Joseph	1812	AD29	191	155
Whann, David	Lease fr	Presbyterian Congregation, G'tn.	1812	AC28	141	106
Whann, David, of G'tn.	Mortgage fr	Ball, Henry W.	1811	AB27	187	154
Whann, William	Deed fr	Commissioners of Washington	1799	D4	277	260
Whann, William	Deed fr	Beatty, Charles, heirs of	1806	O14	312	207
Whann, William	Deed to	Smith, Slement	1806	O14	311	206
Whann, William	Deed to	Eliason, Ebenezer	1807	S18	367	291
Whann, William	Deed fr	Brookes, Joseph	1808	T19	337	245
Whann, William	Deed to	Parrott, Richard	1810	Y24	548	481
Whann, William	Deed fr	Ober, Robert	1810	Z25	005	004
Whann, William	B. of S. fr	Love, Sarah	1810	Y24	321	291
Whann, William	B. of S. fr	Steuart, David, of G'tn.	1812	AC28	175	131
Whann, William	Deed fr	Peter, John	1812	AD29	416	350
Whann, William	Cert. fr	Munroe, Thomas, Supt.	1814	AG32	290	211
Whann, William	Release to	Beatty, Charles, heirs of	1814	AG32	106	080
Whann, William	Deed to	Mackall, Benjamin F.	1814	AG32	017	014
Whann, William	Lease to	Brooks, Joseph, of G'tn.	1815	AI34	070	079
Whann, William	Lease to	Brooks, Joseph, of G'tn.	1815	AI34	068	077

Party	What	Party	Year	Liber	Old	New
Whann, William	Lease to	Brooks, Joseph, of G'tn.	1815	AI34	066	075
Whann, William	Deed to	Ott, John	1817	AO39	452	310
Whann, William	Deed to	Brookes, Joseph	1817	AO39	142	107
Whann, William & J.S. Morsell	D. of T. fr	Deakins, Leonard M. & John Hoye	1815	AK35	347	274
Whann, William & J.S. Morsell	Deed fr	Harbaugh, Leonard et al	1815	AK35	343	271
Whann, William & J.S. Morsell	D. of T. fr	Hoye, John, of Allegany Co.	1815	AK35	350	279
Whann, William et al	Deed fr	Beatty, John M. & Charles A.	1808	U20	300	160
Whann, William et al, plt.	Suit	Harbaugh, Leonard et al, def.	1815	AK35	353	279
Whann, William et al	Deed fr	Beatty, Charles A.	1817	AO39	294	210
Whann, William, Gent.	Deed fr	Ober, Robert, mer.	1808	U20	379	209
Whann, William, Gent.	Deed fr	King, George, mer.	1810	Y24	322	292
Whann, William, mer., of G'tn.	Deed to	Hellen, Walter, mer., of Balto.	1800	E5	295	288
Whann, William, of Montg. Co.	Deed fr	Davis, Charles B., Sr. & Jr.	1796	B2B	551	279
Whann, William, of G'tn.	Agreement	King, George, of G'tn.	1797	C3	141	115
Whann, William, of G'tn.	Deed to	Webb, Thomas	1798	D4	012	010
Whann, William, of G'tn.	Deed fr	Gridley, Richard	1798	C3	353	283
Whann, William, of G'tn.	Deed to	Webb, Thomas	1800	E5	394	369
Whann, William, of G'tn.	Deed to	Simmons, William	1802	G7	579	728
Whann, William, of G'tn.	Deed fr	Smith, Clement, of G'tn.	1807	S18	364	288
Whann, William, of G'tn. et al	B. of S. to	[ ], Rachel (negro)	1809	W22	115	083
Whann, William, of G'tn.	Deed Gift to	Whann, Ann M., d/o William	1810	Z25	006	005
Whann, William, of G'tn.	Deed to	Robertson, Thomas	1812	AC28	363	263
Whann, William, of G'tn.	Deed fr	Hoye, John, of Allegany Co. MD	1815	AI34	295	329
Whann, William, of G'tn.	Deed fr	Corporation of Washington	1815	AK35	240	190
Whann, William, of G'tn.	Deed fr	Corporation of Washington	1815	AK35	242	191
Whann, William, of G'tn.	Deed to	Brookes, Joseph, of G'tn.	1815	AK35	113	087
Whann, William, of G'tn.	Lease to	Brookes, Joseph, of G'tn.	1815	AK35	442	347
Whann, William, of G'tn.	Deed to	Brookes, Joseph, of G'tn.	1815	AK35	111	086
Whann, William, of G'tn.	Deed to	Barclay, John D. & Mary Ann	1816	AK35	530	419
Whann, William, of G'tn.	Deed fr	Way, John & Jane, of DE	1816	AK35	508	400
Whann, William, of G'tn.	Deed to	Hersey, John	1816	AL36	129	130
Whann, William, of G'tn.	Deed to	Beatty, Charles A., of G'tn.	1816	AL36	136	136
Whann, William, of G'tn.	Deed fr	Peter, John, of G'tn.	1816	AL36	497	467
Whann, William, of G'tn.	Deed to	Mackall, Benjamin T.	1816	AK35	529	418
Whann, William, of G'tn.	Deed fr	Bussard, Daniel, of G'tn.	1817	AN38	195	141
Whann, William, of G'tn.	Deed fr	Ott, John, of G'tn.	1817	AN38	196	142
Wharton, Franklin	Deed fr	Bullus, John	1807	S18	251	198
Wharton, Franklin	B. of S. fr	Shaw, James	1809	V21	415	317
Wharton, Franklin	Assign fr	Cassin, James	1809	X23	149	108
Wharton, Franklin	Assign fr	Cox, John, of G'tn	1810	Y24	034	030
Wharton, Franklin	Deed fr	Prout, William	1811	AB27	218	177
Wharton, Franklin	Deed fr	Stephenson, James S.	1811	AB27	060	052
Wharton, Franklin	Deed fr	McDonald, John G.	1812	AD29	254	210
Wharton, Franklin	Deed fr	Campbell, Arthur	1812	AD29	317	260
Wharton, Franklin	Deed fr	Costigan, Joseph	1812	AC28	506	362
Wharton, Franklin	Deed fr	Boyd, Washington, marshal	1812	AC28	503	359
Wharton, Franklin	Deed fr	Collard, George, trustee	1813	AE30	334	250
Wharton, Franklin	Deed to	Coombe, Griffith	1816	AL36	411	394
Wharton, Franklin	Deed fr	Law, Edmund & Joseph Forrest	1816	AL36	107	108
Wharton, Franklin, Col.	Deed fr	Prout, William	1812	AC28	504	360
Wharton, Zephaniah	B. of S. fr	Davis, Francis	1816	AL36	007	007
Whealey, Bernard	D. of T. fr	McCoy, Henry	1815	AI34	017	018
Wheat, Joseph	Deed fr	Nesmith, Ebenezer	1806	P15	390	261
Wheat, Joseph	Mortgage fr	Barry, James	1807	Q16	351	270
Wheat, Joseph	Deed to	Law, Thomas	1807	S18	166	135

Party	What	Party	Year	Liber	Old	New
Wheatley, Barnard	B. of S. to	Johnson, Joseph	1802	I9	011	014
Wheatley, Francis, of Charles Co.	B. of S. to	Hogan, Thady	1809	V21	269	192
Wheaton, Joseph	Deed fr	King, Adam	1805	M12	235	237
Wheaton, Joseph	Deed fr	Dorsey, William H., of G'tn.	1805	N13	112	107
Wheaton, Joseph	Deed fr	Lovell, William	1805	M12	241	243
Wheaton, Joseph	Deed fr	Johnston, James	1811	AB27	384	317
Wheaton, Joseph	B. of S. fr	Barlow, Joel	1811	AB27	351	291
Wheaton, Joseph	Deed to	Moore, James	1811	AB27	498	407
Wheaton, Joseph	Deed to	Caldwell, Elias B.	1811	AB27	487	399
Wheaton, Joseph	D. of T. to	Eliot, Samuel, Jr.	1812	AC28	160	120
Wheaton, Joseph	Deed to	Elliott, Samuel, Jr.	1812	AC28	210	158
Wheaton, Joseph	Qualify	Captain of Militia	1813	AF31	227	155
Wheaton, Joseph, trustee	Assign fr	Sprogell, Thomas Y., insolvent	1808	V21	133	097
Wheaton, Joseph, trustee	Deed fr	Gamble, William, insolvent	1810	Y24	266	244
Wheaton, Nicholas	B. of S. fr	Crowley, Thomas	1807	Q16	340	261
Wheaton, Sally	Deed fr	Waterston, David	1807	R17	309	235
Wheaton, Sally	Deed fr	Stephenson, Clotworthy et al	1807	Q16	307	234
Wheelan, Nicholas	Agreement	Crowley, Thomas & Edward	1807	S18	081	067
Wheelan, Nicholas	Deed fr	Dorsey, William H., of G'tn.	1807	R17	056	045
Wheeler, Acquilla	Lease to	Veneble, William	1794	B2A	073	094
Wheeler, Edward	B. of S. to	Cocker, William	1811	AA26	223	153
Wheeler, Eleanor	Deed fr	Newman, Morris	1804	L11	169	165
Wheeler, Elizabeth	Deed fr	Young, John	1799	D4	197	180
Wheeler, Leonard	Deed to	Newman, Morris	1804	K10	406	
Wheeler, Leonard T.	Deed to	Berry, William, of P.G. Co.	1807	R17	322	245
Wheeler, Luke & John Cooper	Deed to	Willock, William	1812	AC28	422	304
Wheeler, Luke & John Cowper	Deed to	Myers, Moses	1812	AD29	528	444
Wheeler, Luke & John Cowper	Deed to	Granberry, John	1812	AD29	531	448
Wheeler, Luke & John Cowper	Deed to	Cammack, William	1812	AC28	154	115
Wheeler, Luke & John Cowper	Deed to	Campbell, James	1814	AG32	127	093
Wheeler, Luke & John Cowper, VA	Deed to	Thorburn, James	1817	AN38	140	103
Wheeler, Luke & John Cowper	D. of T. to	Wilson, Alexander	1817	AN38	062	049
Wheeler, Luke & John Cowper, VA	Deed to	Herron, Walter	1817	AN38	136	100
Wheeler, Luke, of Norfolk VA et al	Deed fr	Stoddert, Benjamin	1801	G7	410	544
Wheeler, Luke, of Norfolk et al	Deed to	Wright, Stephen	1814	AG32	459	332
Wheeler, Samuel	B. of S. to	Templeman, John	1802	H8	023	022
Wheeler, Thomas, Fairfax Co. VA	B. of S. fr	Lewis, John	1810	Y24	225	207
Whelan, Nicholas	L. of Atty. fr	Whelan, Patrick, in Galway Ire.	1802	H8	373	346
Whelan, Nicholas	B. of S. fr	Crowley, Thomas	1808	T19	316	231
Whelan, Nicholas	Deed fr	McDonald, John G., trustee	1810	Z25	103	080
Whelan, Nicholas	Deed to	Van Ness, John P.	1811	AC28	012	009
Whelan, Nicholas	D. of T. to	Brent, William	1813	AF31	062	043
Whelan, Nicholas	D. of T. to	Brent, William & John Davidson	1814	AG32	169	120
Whelan, Nicholas, of G'tn.	Mortgage to	Hyde, Thomas, of G'tn.	1814	AH33	317	274
Whelan, Patrick, in Galway Ire.	L. of Atty. to	Whelan, Nicholas	1802	H8	373	346
Whelan, Peter	Assign to	Toole, James	1805	N13	125	120
Whelan, Thomas	Deed fr	Dorsey, William H., of G'tn.	1807	R17	331	252
Whetcroft, Burton	Deed fr	Davidson, Lewis Grant, of G'tn.	1814	AH33	128	122
Whetcroft, Burton et al	Deed fr	Davidson, John, of Annapolis	1804	L11	089	91
Whetcroft, Burton et al	Deed fr	Davidson, John	1804	K10	219	228
Whetcroft, Burton, of Annapolis	Release to	Davidson, Ann Maria, exrx.	1810	Z25	321	251
Whetcroft, Catharine	Partition	Whetcroft, William, heirs of	1813	AE30	196	157
Whetcroft, Catharine	Bond to	Brent, Robert	1817	AN38	549	400
Whetcroft, Catherine, d/o Wm.	Deed fr	Van Ness, John P. & Marcia	1809	X23	068	051
Whetcroft, Catherine et al	Deed to	Bradley, Abraham, Jr.	1811	AC28	069	052

Index to District of Columbia Land Records, 1792-1817

Party	What	Party	Year	Liber	Old	New
Whetcroft, Catherine et al	Deed to	Bacon, Samuel & George Moore	1812	AD29	524	441
Whetcroft, Henry	Deed fr	Knapp, John	1802	I9	029	039
Whetcroft, Henry	Deed to	Moscrop, Henry, of Alexa.	1805	N13	133	127
Whetcroft, Henry	Deed to	Kerr, Alexander	1808	V21	095	073
Whetcroft, Henry	Partition	Whetcroft, William, heirs of	1813	AE30	196	157
Whetcroft, Henry	Mortgage to	Boyd, Washington	1816	AK35	484	380
Whetcroft, Henry & Sarah et al	Deed to	Bradley, Abraham, Jr.	1811	AC28	069	052
Whetcroft, Henry & Sarah	Deed to	Ott, David	1813	AE30	112	086
Whetcroft, Henry & Sarah	Deed to	Ott, David	1813	AF31	159	107
Whetcroft, Henry & Sarah	Deed to	Coyle, Andrew	1814	AH33	142	135
Whetcroft, Henry & Sarah	Deed to	Housman, John A.	1814	AG32	285	205
Whetcroft, Henry & Sarah	Deed to	Eliot, Samuel, Jr. & W.A. Bradley	1816	AM37	410	294
Whetcroft, Henry, trustee	Assign fr	Crossfield, Jehiel, insolvent	1809	V21	379	282
Whetcroft, Sarah	Partition	Whetcroft, William, heirs of	1813	AE30	196	157
Whetcroft, Sarah, w/o Henry et al	Deed fr	Van Ness, John P. & Marcia	1809	X23	068	051
Whetcroft, William	Partition	Whetcroft, William, heirs of	1813	AE30	196	157
Whetcroft, William et al	Deed fr	Van Ness, John P. & Marcia	1809	X23	068	051
Whetcroft, William, heirs of	Deed to	Kleiber, George	1813	AE30	304	229
Whetcroft, William, heirs of	Plat	11th Street West, New York Ave.	1813	AE30	204a	
Whetcroft, William, heirs of	Plat	8th Street West	1813	AE30	204b	
Whetcroft, William, heirs of	Plat	Pennsylvania Ave., 7th Street West	1813	AE30	204c	
Whetcroft, William, heirs of	Plat	9th Street West	1813	AE30	204a	
Whetcroft, William, heirs of	Plat	North D Street, 7th Street West	1813	AE30	204b	
Whetcroft, William, heirs of	Plat	North F Street, New York Ave.	1813	AE30	204c	
Whetcroft, William, heirs of	Deed to	Wagler, Frederick Augustus	1813	AE30	310	233
Whetcroft, William, heirs of	Partition		1813	AE30	196	157
Whetcroft, William, heirs of	Deed to	Bradley, Phineas	1815	AI34	076	085
Whetcroft, William, of Annapolis	Deed to	Randall, John, of Annapolis	1811	AB27	016	015
Whetcroft, Wm. & Sarah, Annap.	Deed to	Bacon, Samuel & George Moore	1812	AD29	524	441
Whetzel, John	Deed to	Neale, Francis	1817	AN38	490	354
Whipp, Reuben	Manumis to	Grant, Charles	1810	X23	355	284
Whips, Reuben	B. of S. fr	Digges, William	1817	AO39	306	218
Whitcroft, Henry et al	Deed fr	Munroe, Thomas	1802	I9	374	621
White, Alexander et al	Deed to	Dermott, James Reed	1797	B2B	672	440
White, Alexander et al	Deed to	Sherrard, Francis	1798	C3	464	365
White, Alexander et al	Deed to	Hodgson, Joseph	1798	C3	331	267
White, Alexander et al	Deed to	Hoban, James	1798	C3	319	257
White, Alexander et al	Deed to	Pratt, Henry et al	1801	F6	202	131
White, Alexander et al	Deed to	Hellen, Walter	1802	H8	016	015
White, Ambrose	Lease fr	May, Frederick	1810	Z25	211	166
White, Ambrose	Qualify	Captain of Infantry	1813	AF31	042	029
White, Andrew, of G'tn.	Deed fr	Beall, Thomas, of George, of G'tn.	1796	B2B	566	303
White, Benjamin, of P.G. Co.	Deed to	Walter, Watta B.	1796	B2B	518	227
White, Israel, of Cecil Co. MD	Deed fr	White, Levi	1813	AE30	125	096
White, James et al	Deed to	Boucher, John Thomas	1794	B2A	011	012
White, James, Jr. & James, Sr.	Deed to	Hoban, James	1794	B2A	149	197
White, James, Jr. & James, Sr.	Deed to	Davidson, Samuel	1794	B2A	114	151
White, James, Jr.	Deed fr	Turner, Catherine, wid/o Edmund	1794	B2A	103	135
White, James, Jr. & James, Sr.	Deed to	Hoban, James	1794	B2A	115	153
White, James, Jr., of Montg. Co.	Deed to	Breckenridge, Nelly, w/o John	1813	AF31	413	298
White, James, of Montg. Co.	Deed fr	Beall, Thomas, of George	1803	K10	065	70
White, James, of Montg. Co.	Deed to	Tayloe, John, of VA	1804	K10	165	176
White, James, of Montg. Co.	Deed to	Deakins, Leonard M. & John Hoye	1807	S18	271	213
White, James, of Montg. Co.	Deed to	Hoye, John	1810	Y24	013	012
White, James, of Montg. Co.	Deed to	Hoye, John	1810	Y24	041	035

Party	What	Party	Year	Liber	Old	New
White, James, of Montg. Co.	Deed to	Mountz, John, Jr. et al	1812	AC28	251	185
White, James, of Mong. Co.	Deed to	Drane, James Haddock & Mary	1813	AF31	502	365
White, James, Sr. & James, Jr.	Deed to	Davidson, Samuel	1794	B2A	147	194
White, James, Sr.	Deed to	Casanave, Peter	1795	B2A	232	323
White, James, Sr.	Deed to	Boucher, John Thomas	1796	B2B	516	223
White, James, Sr., of P.G. Co.	Deed to	Brakenridge, John, clerk, P.G. Co.	1798	C3	343	276
White, Jane, d/o Joseph S.	Deed Gift fr	White, Joseph S., of G'tn.	1805	M12	224	225
White, John	Deed fr	Van Ness, John P. & Marcia	1805	M12	180	180
White, John	B. of S. to	Toole, James	1805	N13	002	003
White, John B.	B. of S. to	Slater, Lucy	1814	AH33	144	137
White, John B.	Lease fr	Van Ness, John P. & Marcia	1816	AM37	398	286
White, John B. & Lucy	Deed to	Clarke, Robert, of G'tn.	1817	AN38	244	179
White, John et al	B. of S. fr	Edelen, Ignatius	1812	AD29	019	014
White, Joseph	Deed fr	Law, Thomas	1807	S18	163	132
White, Joseph S., of G'tn.	Deed Gift to	White, Jane, s/o Joseph S.	1805	M12	224	225
White, Levi	Lease fr	Prout, William	1802	I9	369	612
White, Levi	Lease fr	Prout, William	1802	I9	368	610
White, Levi	Assign to	Cox, John, of G'tn.	1805	M12	248	250
White, Levi	B. of S. fr	Hamilton, Francis P.	1808	V21	049	038
White, Levi	Agreement	Law, John	1808	U20	175	098
White, Levi	Deed fr	Brent, William	1810	Z25	253	198
White, Levi	Deed fr	May, Frederick	1811	AC28	021	016
White, Levi	Mortgage to	Fitzhugh, Samuel, of G'tn.	1811	AA26	393	261
White, Levi	B. of S. to	Deblois, Lewis	1811	AB27	191	156
White, Levi	Deed to	Prout, William	1812	AC28	480	341
White, Levi	Deed to	White, Israel, of Cecil Co. MD	1813	AE30	125	096
White, Patrick	Deed fr	Stoddert, Benjamin, of G'tn.	1806	Q16	014	009
White, Patrick	Deed to	Wallach, Richard	1815	AK35	080	062
White, Patrick	Deed to	Shorter, Thomas	1815	AK35	208	164
White, Patrick, painter	Deed to	Young, Moses	1811	AA26	087	062
White, Richard	B. of S. to	Andrews, George	1807	S18	014	013
White, Susanna, d/o W. Lovering	Deed to	Rowles, Joseph E., of G'tn.	1809	X23	067	050
White, Thomas	Deed to	Young, Thomas	1813	AF31	497	362
Whitehill, James	B. of S. fr	Wallach, Richard	1813	AF31	365	261
Wickam, James, of Phila. PA	B. of S. fr	Brown, Matthew	1809	W22	413	268
Wickem, James, of Phila. PA	Mortgage fr	Brown, Mathew	1809	V21	149	109
Wickham, James, of Phila. PA	Deed fr	Prout, William	1809	X23	112	080
Wicoff, Isaac, of Phila. PA	Deed fr	Carleton, Joseph, of G'tn.	1792	A1-1	114	167
Wier, Edward, Sr.	B. of S. fr	Williams, Thomas	1802	H8	317	298
Wigfield, Ann	Deed to	Buntin, Aaron	1806	P15	342	226
Wigfield, Ann et al	Deed fr	Standage, Eleazer, of Montg. Co.	1805	M12	367	376
Wigfield, Anne	Deed to	Buntin, Aaron	1805	N13	255	213
Wigfield, Elizabeth	Deed fr	Kirby, John Baptist	1806	P15	152	100
Wigfield, Elizabeth	Deed to	Buntin, Aaron	1806	P15	347	230
Wigfield, Elizabeth	Deed to	Kirby, John Baptist	1806	P15	154	101
Wigfield, James	Deed fr	Wigfield, Matthew	1805	N13	225	192
Wigfield, James	Deed to	McCormick, Benson L.	1805	M12	163	160
Wigfield, James	Deed to	McCormick, Benson L.	1805	N13	119	114
Wigfield, James	Deed to	Dyer, John	1806	P15	292	192
Wigfield, James	Deed fr	Dyer, John, seaman	1806	P15	293	193
Wigfield, James	Deed fr	McCormick, Benson L. et al	1807	S18	305	239
Wigfield, James	Deed fr	McCormick, Alexander	1808	U20	252	135
Wigfield, James	D. of T. fr	Wigfield, Sarah	1810	Y24	170	155
Wigfield, James & Ann	Deed to	Free, John	1808	U20	157	089
Wigfield, James et al	Deed fr	Standage, Eleazer, of Montg. Co.	1805	M12	367	376

Party	What	Party	Year	Liber	Old	New
Wigfield, James, insolvent	D. of T. to	Davis, George S., trustee	1810	Y24	544	478
Wigfield, James J.	Deed fr	Wigfield, Sarah	1807	S18	299	234
Wigfield, James J.	Deed to	Wigfield, Sarah	1807	S18	304	238
Wigfield, James J.	Deed to	Davis, George S.	1808	U20	030	018
Wigfield, James J.	Deed to	House, David	1808	U20	254	135
Wigfield, James J., et al	Deed to	Collard, George	1810	Y24	131	119
Wigfield, Mathew	Deed to	Hardy, Noah, of MD	1806	Q16	011	007
Wigfield, Mathew	Mortgage to	May, Frederick	1806	P15	149	097
Wigfield, Mathew	Deed to	Young, Thomas	1806	P15	132	085
Wigfield, Mathew	Assign fr	Kirby, John Baptist	1807	R17	087	069
Wigfield, Mathew	Deed to	Kirby, John Baptist [Kerby]	1807	R17	089	071
Wigfield, Mathew	Deed to	Mayhew, James	1808	T19	108	077
Wigfield, Mathew et al	Plat		1804	K10	136	
Wigfield, Mathew et al	Partition		1804	K10	131	141
Wigfield, Matthew	Deed to	Kirby, John Baptist	1804	L11	392	348
Wigfield, Matthew	Deed to	Kerby, John B.	1804	L11	210	198
Wigfield, Matthew	Deed to	Wigfield, James	1805	N13	225	192
Wigfield, Matthew	Deed fr	Wigfield, Robert	1805	N13	126	121
Wigfield, Matthew	Deed to	Kirby, John Baptist	1808	T19	268	197
Wigfield, Matthew	Deed to	Young, Thomas & Thos. Foyales	1808	U20	208	113
Wigfield, Robert	Deed to	Kerby, John B.	1804	L11	212	199
Wigfield, Robert	Deed to	Wigfield, Matthew	1805	N13	126	121
Wigfield, Robert	Deed fr	Standage, Eleazer & Mary	1805	M12	368	378
Wigfield, Robert	Agreement	Cochran, Alexander	1805	N13	034	036
Wigfield, Robert	Deed to	Marbury, William, Jr., of P.G. Co.	1809	W22	080	060
Wigfield, Robert & Mary	Deed to	Naylor, John L.	1807	R17	200	152
Wigfield, Robert & Mary	D. of T. to	McCormick, Alexander	1809	X23	125	090
Wigfield, Robert & Mary	Deed to	Casteel, Edmund	1810	Z25	214	168
Wigfield, Robert & Mary	Deed to	Moore, John C., of P.G. Co.	1812	AD29	455	383
Wigfield, Sara et al	Deed fr	Standage, Eleazer, of Montg. Co.	1805	M12	367	376
Wigfield, Sarah	Deed to	Young, Thomas	1806	P15	130	084
Wigfield, Sarah	Deed to	Wigfield, James J.	1807	S18	299	234
Wigfield, Sarah	Deed to	Kirby, John B.	1807	S18	012	011
Wigfield, Sarah	Deed fr	Wigfield, James J.	1807	S18	304	238
Wigfield, Sarah	D. of T. to	Wigfield, James	1810	Y24	170	155
Wigfield, Sarah	B. of S. fr	Davis, George S.	1810	Y24	337	306
Wigfield, Sarah	Deed fr	Davis, George Smith & Ann	1810	Y24	336	305
Wigfield, Sarah	Deed to	Richardson, Thomas R.H.	1812	AC28	297	216
Wigfield, Sarah	B. of S. fr	Davis, George S.	1813	AF31	335	239
Wigfield, Sarah	Deed fr	Davis, George & Ann	1814	AG32	210	147
Wight, John M. & George Moore	Assign fr	Connell, Catherine	1812	AD29	024	017
Wightt, John M.	Certificate	Deputy Marshall	1810	X23	379	304
Wightt, John M. & George Moore	Assign fr	Fitzgerald, William	1812	AC28	512	366
Wightt, John M.	Deed fr	Casanave, Ann	1815	AI34	015	016
Wightt, John Magruder	Manumis to	Posey, Richard (negro)	1810	Z25	037	028
Wikoff, Isaac, of Phila. PA	Deed fr	Carleton, Joseph, of G'tn.	1792	A1-1	115	169
Wilcox, Thomas	Deed fr	Kemp, James	1811	AC28	032	024
Wilcoxen, Lewis, Pend. Co. KY	Deed to	Peter, Robert	1804	L11	188	181
Wilcoxon, Lewis, of KY	Deed to	Peter, Robert	1802	H8	440	405
Wilder, William (C)	Manumis fr	Lattimer, Arthur	1817	AN38	176	128
Wiley, Abel	Deed fr	Diel, Ann Stacy	1802	H8	290	274
Wiley, Abel	Deed to	Kaldenbaugh, Andrew, of G'tn.	1802	H8	359	334
Wiley, Daniel	Deed fr	Ogle, Benjamin	1802	I9	339	558
Wiley, David	Deed fr	Orme, Thomas	1801	G7	043	055
Wiley, David	Deed fr	Beatty, Charles A., Dr.	1812	AD29	165	131

Party	What	Party	Year	Liber	Old	New
Wiley, David, of G'tn.	Deed to	Smith, Walter, of G'tn.	1812	AD29	166	132
Wiley, John	Qualify	First Lieutenant of cavalry	1813	AE30	425	313
Wiley, John et al	Deed fr	Beatty, Charles A.	1817	AO39	294	210
Wiliams, Elisha W., of G'tn. et al	Deed fr	Mulloy, John, of Montg. Co.	1807	Q16	394	303
Wilkerson, Maria Celesta Laveau	Deed fr	Trudeau, Maria Josepha Laveau	1815	AI34	288	324
Wilkins, William, of Annapolis	Deed to	Chandler, Walter Story	1795	B2A	184	249
Wilkinson, James, insolvent	D. of T. to	Williams, Eli & Elias B. Caldwell	1811	AC28	056	043
Wilkinson, James, insolvent	Deed to	Williams, Eli & Elias B. Caldwell	1811	AC28	057	044
Wilkinson, Joseph, Calvert Co.	Mortgage fr	Nicholson, John, of Phila. PA	1797	B2B	671	439
Wilkinson, Joseph, Calvert Co.	Mortgage fr	Nicholson, John, of Phila. PA	1797	B2B	670	438
Willcox, Thomas, of Phila. PA	Deed to	Lambert, Aaron, of Phila. PA	1813	AF31	374	269
Willett, Burgess, of Montg. Co.	Deed fr	Campbell, Alexander, s/o William	1816	AM37	135	105
Willett, Burgess, of Montg. Co.	Deed to	Bussard, Daniel, of G'tn.	1816	AM37	426	305
Willett, John, of Montg. Co.	Deed fr	West, Joseph D.	1816	AL36	296	293
Williams, A.J., collector	Report		1808	T19	399	
Williams, Benjamin, of Montg. Co.	Deed to	Peter, John, of G'tn.	1809	V21	369	271
Williams, Benjamin, of G'tn.	Deed fr	Davidson, Ann Maria, of G'tn.	1809	X23	203	153
Williams, Benjamin, of MD	Deed to	Smith, Clement	1810	Z25	283	222
Williams, Brooke	Deed to	Smith, Caroline, w/o John K.	1814	AG32	250	178
Williams, Brooke	Deed fr	Smith, John K.	1814	AG32	248	177
Williams, Brooke, of G'tn.	Deed fr	Smith, John K. & Caroline, G'tn.	1817	AO39	128	098
Williams, Brooke, of G'tn.	Deed to	St. John, Leonard, of G'tn.	1817	AO39	471	
Williams, Clementine Clement	Cert Free fr	Peter, John, mayor	1816	AL36	113	114
Williams, Edward O. & Betsey	Deed to	Luffborough, Nathan	1801	G7	282	391
Williams, Eilisha Owen, of G'tn.	Bond to	Steuart, William, of G'tn.	1804	K10	225	234
Williams, Eli & Elias B. Caldwell	Deed fr	Wilkinson, James, insolvent	1811	AC28	057	044
Williams, Eli & Elias B. Caldwell	D. of T. fr	Wilkinson, James, insolvent	1811	AC28	056	043
Williams, Elie	Mortgage fr	Williams, John S.	1817	AN38	054	045
Williams, Elie et al	Deed to	Ritchie, Abner	1801	G7	205	274
Williams, Elie et al	Deed fr	Patterson, Edgar, of G'tn.	1811	AC28	093	070
Williams, Elie, of Washington Co.	Deed to	Thomas, Philip	1792	A1-1	067	99
Williams, Elie, of G'tn.	Deed to	Key, Francis S. & William Brent	1817	AN38	205	149
Williams, Elie, plt.	Suit	Williams, John S., def.	1817	AN38	053	044
Williams, Elisha O.	Deed fr	Beall, Thomas, of George	1795	B2A	205	281
Williams, Elisha O.	Deed fr	Dorsey, William H.	1795	B2A	195	265
Williams, Elisha O. et al	Bond to	United States	1802	H8	520	479
Williams, Elisha O. et al	Deed fr	Beall, Upton & Lewis	1802	I9	576	933
Williams, Elisha O. & Harriet et al	Deed to	Beall, Lewis	1803	K10	089	95
Williams, Elisha O. & Harriot	Deed to	Stuart, William & Hellen	1804	K10	185	194
Williams, Elisha O. & Harriot	Deed fr	Steuart, William et al	1804	K10	190	199
Williams, Elisha O. & Harriet	Deed to	Mackall, Benjamin & Christiana	1804	K10	226	235
Williams, Elisha O.	Bond to	Corporation of Georgetown	1805	N13	094	086
Williams, Elisha, of G'tn.	Deed to	Bowie, Washington, of G'tn.	1810	Y24	100	091
Williams, Elisha Owen et al	Bond to	United States	1801	G7	013	016
Williams, Elisha Owen et al	Bond to	United States	1801	G7	013	016
Williams, Elisha W.	Deed fr	Murdock, Addison, Gent.	1806	P15	343	227
Williams, Elisha W., mer.	Deed fr	Beall, Thomas, of George, trustee	1806	P15	337	223
Williams, Elisha W., of G'tn.	B. of S. fr	Slye, Ann, of G'tn.	1807	R17	061	049
Williams, Elisha W., Gent.	Deed fr	Stains, Thomas	1809	V21	396	299
Williams, Elisha W., of G'tn.	Deed fr	Dixon, Thomas, of G'tn.	1809	W22	162	113
Williams, Elisha W.	Deed to	Kemp, Henry, of Frederick Co.	1809	W22	133	095
Williams, Elisha W.	Deed fr	Reintzel, Daniel	1809	W22	163	115
Williams, Elisha W., of G'tn.	Deed to	Kreager, John, of Frederick Co.	1809	W22	134	096
Williams, Elisha W., mer., G'tn.	Deed fr	Morsell, James S., of G'tn.	1809	X23	235	182
Williams, Elisha W.	Deed fr	Deakins, Leonard M. & John Hoye	1809	X23	206	156

Index to District of Columbia Land Records, 1792-1817

Party	What	Party	Year	Liber	Old	New
Williams, Elisha W.	Deed fr	Beatth, Charles, heirs of	1809	X23	234	181
Williams, Elisha W.	Slaves	From Frederick Co. VA	1810	X23	380	306
Williams, Elisha W., of G'tn.	Deed to	Hoye, John, of Montg. Co.	1810	Y24	086	077
Williams, Elisha W., of G'tn.	Deed to	Robertson, Thomas, of G'tn.	1810	Y24	347	315
Williams, Elisha W.	Slave	From VA	1810	Z25	262	205
Williams, Elisha W.	Deed to	Williams, Jeremiah	1810	X23	310	248
Williams, Elisha W., of G'tn.	Deed fr	Mountz, Jacob, collector, of G'tn.	1811	AA26	094	066
Williams, Elisha W., of G'tn.	Deed fr	Chandler, Walter S.	1811	AB27	035	031
Williams, Elisha W., of G'tn.	Plat	Fayette and Water streets	1811	AB27	038	033
Williams, Elisha W., of G'tn.	Deed fr	Williams, Jeremiah, of G'tn.	1811	AB27	038	033
Williams, Elisha W.	Manumis to	[ ], Anne (C), age about 40	1811	AB27	054	046
Williams, Elisha W., of G'tn.	Mortgage to	Johns, Leonard H., of G'tn.	1811	AB27	461	378
Williams, Elisha W., of G'tn.	Deed to	Bohrer, Jacob	1811	AC28	077	058
Williams, Elisha W., of G'tn.	Deed fr	Williams, Jeremiah, of G'tn.	1811	AC28	074	056
Williams, Elisha W. & Jeremiah	Deed to	Williams, Thomas Owen, P.G. Co.	1811	Z25	521	414
Williams, Elisha W., of G'tn.	Mortgage to	Berry, Zachariah, of P.G. Co.	1812	AB27	551	450
Williams, Elisha W.	D. of T. to	Johns, Leonard H.	1812	AC28	384	280
Williams, Elisha W., of G'tn.	Deed to	Johns, Leonard H., of G'tn.	1812	AC28	329	239
Williams, Elisha W., of G'tn.	Deed to	Hoye, John, of G'tn.	1812	AC28	361	261
Williams, Elisha W., of G'tn.	Deed fr	Mountz, Jacob, collector, G'tn.	1812	AC28	336	243
Williams, Elisha W., of G'tn.	Deed fr	Mountz, Jaocb, collector, G'tn.	1812	AC28	333	242
Williams, Elisha W., of G'tn.	Deed to	Berry, John W., of Balto. Co. MD	1812	AC28	135	101
Williams, Elisha W., of G'tn.	Deed to	Peyton, Thomas W., of Alexa.	1813	AE30	133	104
Williams, Elisha W., of G'tn.	Deed to	Bowie, Washington, of G'tn.	1814	AG32	024	019
Williams, Eveline	Cert Free fr	Peter, John, mayor	1816	AL36	113	114
Williams, Fanny & children	Cert Free fr	Peter, John, mayor	1816	AL36	113	114
Williams, Harriet	D. of T. to	Beall, Upton, of Montg. Co.	1810	X23	365	293
Williams, Harriet, w/o Capt. Elisha	Deed fr	Beall, Thomas, of George	1805	M12	398	411
Williams, Harriot	Deed to	Johns, Leonard Holliday	1813	AE30	365	271
Williams, Harriot, wid/o Elisha O.	Deed to	Morsell, James S.	1815	AI34	086	098
Williams, Henry & James	B. of S. fr	Williams, Prince	1815	AH33	559	478
Williams, James	Deed fr	Hanson, Alexander Contee	1799	D4	253	237
Williams, James	B. of S. to	Hicks, Lizzy	1812	AB27	537	438
Williams, James, of Annapolis	Deed fr	Harwood, Thomas, collector	1801	G7	085	110
Williams, James, of G'tn.	D. of T. to	Morgan, William, of G'tn.	1810	Y24	141	128
Williams, James, of G'tn.	B. of S. to	Hicks, Elizabeth, his mother	1812	AD29	200	163
Williams, Jeremiah	Deed fr	Stewart, John	1801	G7	297	414
Williams, Jeremiah	Qualify		1802	I9	466	768
Williams, Jeremiah	Slaves	From Fairfax Co. VA	1804	K10	155	
Williams, Jeremiah	Deed fr	Williams, Elisha W.	1810	X23	310	248
Williams, Jeremiah	D. of T. to	Johns, Leonard H.	1812	AC28	388	283
Williams, Jeremiah & Elisha W.	Deed fr	Templeman, John, of G'tn.	1804	L11	333	304
Williams, Jeremiah & Elisha W.	Deed fr	Templeman, John, of G'tn.	1805	M12	280	281
Williams, Jeremiah et al	Bond to	United States	1802	H8	519	478
Williams, Jeremiah, mer.	Deed fr	Dorsey, William Hammond, Esq.	1801	G7	424	559
Williams, Jeremiah, of G'tn.	Deed fr	Slater, Joseph	1800	E5	293	286
Williams, Jeremiah, of G'tn.	Deed to	Alexander, Robert	1805	M12	314	317
Williams, Jeremiah, of G'tn.	Deed fr	Johns, Richard et al	1805	M12	071	066
Williams, Jeremiah, of G'tn.	Deed to	Johns, Richard & Leonard H., G'tn.	1806	Q16	041	027
Williams, Jeremiah, of G'tn. et al	Deed fr	Mulloy, John, of Montg. Co.	1807	Q16	394	303
Williams, Jeremiah, of G'tn.	Deed to	Williams, Elisha W., of G'tn.	1811	AB27	038	033
Williams, Jeremiah, of G'tn.	Plat	Fayette and Water streets	1811	AB27	038	033
Williams, Jeremiah, of G'tn.	Deed to	Williams, Elisha W., of G'tn.	1811	AC28	074	056
Williams, John	Deed fr	Hollenback, William & Sarah	1816	AL36	301	298
Williams, John & Jacob Wagner	Deed fr	Southgate, John, of Norfolk	1814	AG32	136	098

Party	What	Party	Year	Liber	Old	New
Williams, John S. & J. Wagner	Deed fr	Thompson, John, of G'tn.	1813	AF31	493	359
Williams, John S., of G'tn.	Deed fr	Robertson, Thomas, of G'tn.	1813	AF31	040	028
Williams, John S.	Deed fr	Gantt, Fielder, of P.G. Co.	1813	AE30	360	267
Williams, John S., of G'tn.	Deed to	Wagner, Jacob, of G'tn.	1813	AF31	207	140
Williams, John S., of G'tn.	D. of T. fr	Hersey, John, of G'tn.	1814	AG32	339	246
Williams, John S., trustee	Bond fr	Hersey, John, of G'tn.	1814	AG32	344	249
Williams, John S., of G'tn.	Deed fr	Corcoran, Thomas, of G'tn.	1814	AG32	346	250
Williams, John S. & Jacob Wagner	Mortgage to	Thompson, John	1814	AH33	322	278
Williams, John S., of G'tn.	Deed to	Wagner, Jacob	1814	AH33	209	188
Williams, John S.	Deed fr	Wagner, Jacob	1814	AH33	355	307
Williams, John S., of G'tn.	Deed to	Pleasonton, Stephen	1814	AH33	126	119
Williams, John S., of G'tn.	Deed fr	Smoot, Samuel	1816	AL36	313	308
Williams, John S., of G'tn.	Deed fr	Murdock, John, of G'tn.	1816	AL36	316	311
Williams, John S., of G'tn.	Deed to	Owings, Isaac, of G'tn.	1816	AL36	462	436
Williams, John S., of G'tn.	Deed fr	Dorsey, William H., of Montg. Co.	1816	AL36	314	310
Williams, John S., of G'tn.	Deed to	Smith, Clement, of G'tn.	1816	AM37	085	068
Williams, John S. & John J. Stull	Ship List	Loockerman, John	1817	AN38	143	105
Williams, John S. & John J. Stull	D. of T. to	Loockerman, John	1817	AN38	130	096
Williams, John S.	Mortgage to	Williams, Elie	1817	AN38	054	045
Williams, John S., def.	Suit	Williams, Elie, plt.	1817	AN38	053	044
Williams, John Stull, of G'tn.	Deed fr	Southgate, John, of Norfolk	1814	AG32	065	050
Williams, John Stull	Deed to	Grayson, William, Dr., of G'tn.	1815	AH33	381	330
Williams, John Stull, of G'tn.	D. of T. to	Smith, Clement, of G'tn.	1815	AH33	383	332
Williams, Philip, of G'tn.	Mortgage to	Mayer & Wetzel	1809	W22	321	209
Williams, Prince	B. of S. to	Williams, Henry & James	1815	AH33	559	478
Williams, Richard John Albert	Cert Free fr	Peter, John, mayor	1816	AL36	113	114
Williams, Richard, Loudoun Co.	Manumis to	[ ], Evans (M)	1817	AN38	118	088
Williams, Robert, blacksmith, G'tn.	Deed to	Dawes, Isaac, farmer, Montg. Co.	1811	AA26	277	188
Williams, Robert, blacksmith, G'tn.	Deed fr	Dawes, Isaac, farmer, Montg. Co.	1811	AA26	286	194
Williams, Robert, insolvent	D. of T. to	Williams, Thomas, trustee	1811	AC28	031	023
Williams, Samuel, cooper	Deed fr	Beall, Thomas, of George	1795	B2A	206	283
Williams, Samuel et al	Deed fr	Holmead, Anthony	1800	E5	238	232
Williams, Sarah B.	Deed fr	Rutter, Thomas, of Balto.	1817	AO39	179	133
Williams, Steward	B. of S. fr	King, William, of G'tn.	1812	AD29	089	
Williams, Stuart, of P.G. Co.	Mortgage to	Beatty, Charles A., of G'tn.	1797	C3	053	44
Williams, Thomas	B. of S. to	Wier, Edward, Sr.	1802	H8	317	298
Williams, Thomas & Daniel Pearl	D. of T. to	Mahorney, Charles	1817	AN38	220	161
Williams, Thomas et al	Bond to	United States	1801	G7	013	016
Williams, Thomas O.	Deed fr	Davidson, John, of Annapolis	1799	D4	308	292
Williams, Thomas O.	Deed fr	Lingan, James M., of G'tn.	1801	G7	422	557
Williams, Thomas O.	Deed fr	Beatty, Charles, heirs of	1807	S18	158	129
Williams, Thomas, of P.G. Co.	Deed fr	Afflick, Thomas, of Montg. Co.	1796	B2B	426	100
Williams, Thomas, of P.G. Co.	Deed to	Johnson, Renaldo, of P.G. Co.	1796	B2B	432	110
Williams, Thomas, of P.G. Co.	Deed fr	Hodges, Thomas C., of G'tn.	1807	Q16	397	305
Williams, Thomas Owen	Deed fr	Stoddert, Benj. & Wm. Deakins	1793	A1-1	325	428
Williams, Thomas Owen	Deed to	Beall, Thomas & John M. Gantt	1793	A1-1	327	429
Williams, Thomas Owen	Deed fr	Stoddert, Benjamin	1802	H8	040	039
Williams, Thomas Owen, P.G. Co.	Deed fr	Clagett, Thomas John, Rt. Rev.	1805	N13	100	092
Williams, Thomas Owen, P.G. Co.	Deed fr	Williams, Elisha W. & Jeremiah	1811	Z25	521	414
Williams, Thomas Owen, of P.G.	Deed to	Burnett, Charles A., of G'tn.	1814	AG32	411	299
Williams, Thomas, trustee	D. of T. fr	Williams, Robert, insolvent	1811	AC28	031	023
Williams, Treasy	Cert Free fr	Fry, Thomas	1814	AF31	517	379
Williams, William, of G.B., s/o S.	Deed fr	Owings, Isaac	1805	N13	128	122
Williamson, Catherine	Deed fr	Stoddert, Benjamin	1802	I9	337	556
Williamson, Colin, of G'tn.	Cert fr	Commissioners of Washington	1792	B2A	289	405

Index to District of Columbia Land Records, 1792-1817

Party	What	Party	Year	Liber	Old	New
Williamson, Collin	Cert fr	Commissioners of Washington	1796	B2A	339	477
Williamson, David	Deed fr	Miller, George	1809	W22	046	034
Williamson, David	Assign fr	Broome, George	1809	W22	044	033
Williamson, David, of Balto.	Assign fr	Voss, Nicholas	1801	G7	082	106
Williamson, David, of Balto.	Deed fr	Commissioners of Washington	1801	G7	149	197
Williamson, David, of Balto.	Deed fr	Beatty, Charles, heirs of	1806	O14	230	151
Williamson, David, of Balto.	Deed fr	Edwards, John, of G'tn.	1807	S18	188	152
Williamson, David, of Balto.	Lease to	Ritchie, Abner, of G'tn.	1809	W22	064	048
Williamson, David, of Balto.	Lease to	Hurdle, Noble, of G'tn.	1813	AF31	348	248
Williamson, David, of Balto.	Deed to	Young, Patrick C., of G'tn.	1813	AF31	351	250
Williamson, David, of Balto. Co.	Lease to	Clements, Thomas, of Montg. Co.	1815	AK35	128	099
Williamson, John	Deed fr	Van Ness, John P. & Marcia	1805	O14	092	057
Williamson, John	Deed to	Van Ness, John P.	1806	O14	339	226
Williamson, John	Deed to	Watterston, David	1806	P15	020	012
Williamson, John	Mortgage to	Van Ness, John P.	1806	O14	338	225
Williamson, William et al	B. of S. fr	Yeamans, Royal	1817	AO39	147	111
Willing, Thomas et al	Deed to	Law, Thomas	1802	H8	351	327
Willing, Thomas et al	Release to	Nourse, Joseph	1813	AF31	011	008
Willing, Thomas Mayne et al	Deed to	Law, Thomas	1802	H8	351	327
Willing, Thomas, mer., of Phila. PA	Deed fr	Hellen, Walter	1801	G7	323	453
Willing, Thomas, of PA	Deed to	Bank of United States	1802	H8	214	204
Willing, Thomas, of Phila. et al	Deed to	Lenox, David	1811	AA26	333	223
Willing, Thomas, of Phila. et al	Deed fr	Bank of the United States	1811	AA26	344	230
Willings & Francis, of Phila. PA	Mortgage fr	Law, Thomas	1801	G7	172	229
Willink, Wilhem & Jan, Amsterdam	Deed fr	Walker, George	1796	B2B	435	113
Willis, Cornelius	B. of S. to	Willis, Hannah	1806	O14	275	182
Willis, Hannah	B. of S. fr	Willis, Cornelius	1806	O14	275	182
Willis, Hannah	Deed to	Willis, Joshua	1807	R17	210	157
Willis, John	Deed fr	Polock, Isaac	1802	H8	345	321
Willis, John	Deed fr	Burford, Henry	1802	H8	167	161
Willis, John	Mortgage fr	Beall, Thomas K.	1802	I9		188
Willis, John	Deed fr	Lovell, William	1802	H8	164	158
Willis, John	Deed fr	Gillis, Thomas Handy	1802	H8	584	548
Willis, John	Lease fr	Van Ness, John P. & Marcia	1804	K10	373	387
Willis, John, Dr.	Deed fr	Munroe, Thomas, Supt.	1802	H8	582	547
Willis, John, Dr.	Deed fr	Munroe, Thomas, Supt.	1804	L11	023	23
Willis, Joshua	Deed fr	Willis, Hannah	1807	R17	210	157
Willis, Perrin	B. of S. to	Van Ness, John P. et al	1816	AM37	366	265
Willmans, Frederick, Berks Co.	Deed to	Brent, William	1806	P15	124	079
Willock, William	Deed fr	Wheeler, Luke & John Cooper	1812	AC28	422	304
Willock, William, of Norfolk	Deed to	Barrie, Gaspard, of New Orleans	1817	AN38	174	126
Willson, David	Deed fr	Jones, Tristram F.	1802	H8	181	174
Willson, James	Deed to	Talbot, Bazil et al	1802	H8	495	455
Willson, James	Deed to	Breshears, Nathaniel et al	1802	H8	495	455
Willson, John A.	B. of S. to	Villard, Andrew J.	1809	X23	117	084
Willson, Joseph	Deed to	Shields, Easter	1802	H8	370	344
Willson, Richard	Deed to	Carpenter, Thomas	1802	I9	232	370
Willson, Robert	Deed to	Heron, William	1802	I9	026	033
Willson, Robert	Deed fr	Cloakey, Samuel	1802	I9	018	025
Willson, Robert	Deed to	Lyons, John	1802	H8	577	541
Willson, Samuel	Deed fr	Commissioners of Washington	1800	E5	226	220
Willson, Sarah	B. of S. to	Barney, John H.	1802	H8	201	193
Willson, Sarah	B. of S. to	Bridges, John	1804	K10	243	251
Willson, Sarah	B. of S. to	Dashiell, Thomas B.	1809	W22	211	145
Willson, William & Sarah	Deed to	Magruder, Charles	1793	A1-1	195	275

Party	What	Party	Year	Liber	Old	New
Wilmans, Frederick	Deed fr	Karrick, Joseph et al	1802	H8	080	074
Wilmans, Frederick	Deed fr	Percival, Joshua et ux, et al	1802	H8	080	074
Wilmington, John, of G'tn.	B. of S. fr	Beall, Samuel, of Montg. Co.	1816	AL36	309	305
Wilson, Alexander	Deed fr	Burnes, David	1797	C3	051	41
Wilson, Alexander	Deed to	Tolmie, Robert, of G'tn.	1800	E5	130	118
Wilson, Alexander	D. of T. fr	Wheeler, Luke & John Cowper	1817	AN38	062	049
Wilson, Ann	Deed fr	Hahn, Milly	1812	AC28	487	346
Wilson, Anne, of Balto.	Deed to	Milligan, Joseph, of G'tn.	1814	AH33	194	177
Wilson, Elizabeth, of Montg. Co.	Deed to	Mountz, John, of G'tn.	1815	AI34	350	381
Wilson, Henry	Deed fr	Norris, Isaac	1805	M12	354	361
Wilson, Henry	Deed to	Dawes, Isaac	1811	AA26	147	102
Wilson, Henry M.	Cert Free to	[ ], Harry (C), age 20	1816	AM37	142	110
Wilson, Henry M.	Cert Free to	[ ], Charlotte (C), age 14	1816	AM37	141	109
Wilson, Henry M.	Cert Free to	[ ], Nat (C), age 27	1816	AM37	141	109
Wilson, Henry M.	D. of T. fr	Burch, Samuel	1816	AL36	543	506
Wilson, Isaac & Levey G.	Deed to	Beall, Thomas Brook	1806	O14	291	193
Wilson, Isaac & Ignatius Newton	B. of S. fr	Jearvis, Henry	1817	AN38	339	249
Wilson, Isaac, of G'tn.	B. of S. to	Broadwell, James, of G'tn.	1814	AH33	230	201
Wilson, James	Deed to	Talbott, Basil	1802	I9	137	206
Wilson, Jane	B. of S. fr	Wilson, Joseph	1807	S18	112	092
Wilson, John	B. of S. fr	Evans, Charles	1802	G7	513	654
Wilson, John	Deed fr	Evans, Charles	1804	L11	141	142
Wilson, John A.	B. of S. fr	Butler, Edward M.	1805	O14	152	099
Wilson, John A.	Mortgage fr	Edwards, John, of G'tn.	1805	N13	318	256
Wilson, John A.	Deed fr	Bloor, John	1806	P15	283	186
Wilson, John A.	B. of S. fr	Fenwick, Richard	1809	V21	396	300
Wilson, John A.	Deed fr	Thorpe, Thomas	1810	Z25	035	026
Wilson, John A.	Agreement	Maupin, Catharine	1810	Y24	043	038
Wilson, John A.	Deed fr	Law, Edmund, atty. of Thomas	1810	Z25	264	207
Wilson, John A.	Mortgage fr	Slye, Thomas G.	1813	AE30	388	286
Wilson, John A., of G'tn.	Deed fr	Lee, Thomas Sim, of Fredk. Co.	1815	AI34	033	038
Wilson, John A.	Deed fr	Presbyterian Congregation of G'tn.	1815	AI34	277	312
Wilson, John A.	Deed fr	Craig, Henrietta, of G'tn., wid/o R.	1815	AI34	083	095
Wilson, John A.	Deed fr	Boyd, Washington	1815	AI34	218	249
Wilson, John A.	Deed fr	Murdock, John, of G'tn.	1815	AK35	183	142
Wilson, John A.	Deed fr	McDonald, John G.	1815	AK35	234	185
Wilson, John A.	Deed fr	Dorsey, William H., of Montg. Co.	1815	AK35	182	141
Wilson, John A.	Deed fr	Caldwell, Elias B. & John Coyle	1816	AL36	399	384
Wilson, John A.	Assign fr	Pritchard, Benjamin, Montg. Co.	1817	AN38	494	357
Wilson, John A.	Deed fr	Ratcliffe, Joseph, of G'tn.	1817	AO39	520	358
Wilson, John A.	Deed fr	Fields, William	1817	AN38	181	131
Wilson, John C., of Princess Ann	Deed fr	Commissioners of Washington	1800	F6	066	041
Wilson, John C.	Receipt to	McMantz, Charles	1800	F6	068	042
Wilson, John Custis, Somerset Co.	Deed fr	Stoddert, Benjamin et al	1801	G7	119	153
Wilson, John, of MD	Deed fr	Beall, Thomas Brook, Capt.	1805	O14	005	005
Wilson, John, of Henry	Deed fr	Thorpe, Thomas	1808	U20	407	228
Wilson, John, of Henry	Release fr	Dodge, Allen & Francis	1808	V21	001	001
Wilson, John, of Hy., of P.G. Co.	Deed fr	Livers, Ignatius, of G'tn.	1812	AD29	121	093
Wilson, John, of Henry, P.G. Co.	Lease to	Heise, John C., of G'tn.	1814	AG32	255	182
Wilson, John, of Henry, P.G. Co.	Deed fr	Smoot, Samuel	1817	AO39	390	264
Wilson, Joseph	Deed fr	Magrath, William	1793	A1-2	412	21
Wilson, Joseph	Deed to	St. Clere, Georg	1802	I9	124	185
Wilson, Joseph	Convey to	Watson, Elizabeth et al	1805	N13	046	044
Wilson, Joseph	B. of S. to	Watson, Elizabeth	1805	N13	048	045
Wilson, Joseph	Deed fr	Morsell, James S., trustee	1810	X23	300	239

Party	What	Party	Year	Liber	Old	New
Wilson, Joseph	Deed to	Wilson, Richard	1811	AB27	292	239
Wilson, Joseph	Deed fr	Chandler, Walter Story	1812	AE30	047	036
Wilson, Joseph [Willson]	B. of S. to	Wilson, Jane	1807	S18	112	092
Wilson, Lancelot	Exchange	Beall, Thomas, of George	1805	M12	359	367
Wilson, Lancelot	B. of S. to	Beall, Thomas, of George	1805	M12	359	367
Wilson, Lancelot	B. of S. to	Beall, Thomas, of George	1805	M12	092	085
Wilson, Lancelot	Deed fr	Kile, Alexander, of G'tn.	1813	AF31	258	180
Wilson, Lancelot, of Henry	Deed fr	Beall, Thomas Brooke	1808	T19	391	277
Wilson, Lanclot, of Henry	Deed to	Kelly, John	1814	AH33	148	140
Wilson, Levi G.	Lease fr	Magruder, Ninian, Dr.	1812	AD29	369	311
Wilson, Levi G.	Deed fr	Ritchie, Abner	1812	AD29	224	185
Wilson, Levi G., of G'tn.	Deed to	Magruder, Ninian, Dr., of G'tn.	1813	AE30	467	348
Wilson, Levi G., of G'tn.	Deed to	Baltzer, Jacob, of G'tn.	1814	AH33	100	092
Wilson, Levi G.	Deed fr	Magruder, Ninian, Dr.	1814	AH33	099	091
Wilson, Levi G.	Deed to	Weeden, Henry	1815	AI34	127	146
Wilson, Levi G.	Deed to	Paul, Nicholas	1816	AM37	144	111
Wilson, Offa	Deed to	Lewis, Winslow, of Boston MA	1812	AB27	360	299
Wilson, Offa	B. of S. to	Lewis, Winslow, of Boston MA	1815	AH33	455	390
Wilson, Offa, of P.G. Co.	Deed fr	Burch, Samuel	1817	AN38	416	311
Wilson, Richard	B. of S. to	Stewart, William, of G'tn.	1801	G7	219	293
Wilson, Richard	Deed fr	Wilson, Joseph	1811	AB27	292	239
Wilson, Robert	Deed fr	Cloakey, Samuel	1800	E5	331	319
Wilson, Samuel	Deed fr	O'Neale, William	1798	C3	285	231
Wilson, Samuel	Deed fr	Key, Philip Barton, of Annapolis	1800	E5	320	309
Wilson, Samuel	Deed to	Davidson, James, Jr., trustee	1805	M12	080	074
Wilson, Samuel & John Dennis	Deed fr	Stoddert, Benjamin et al	1801	G7	117	150
Wilson, Samuel, def.	Suit	Granger, Gideon, plt.	1808	T19	252	185
Wilson, Samuel et al	Deed fr	Lingan, John McCubbin	1801	G7	118	152
Wilson, Samuel [Willson]	Deed to	Granger, Gideon	1808	T19	252	185
Wilson, Sarah et al	B. of S. fr	Finigan, Rosannah	1816	AM37	145	112
Wilson, William	Deed to	Weightman, Roger Chew et al	1813	AE30	194	156
Wilson, William	Deed to	Wallach, Richard	1814	AH33	343	297
Wilson, William	Mortgage to	Kleiber, George	1814	AH33	333	288
Wilson, William, clerk	Cert Free to	Spellman, Abram	1817	AO39	467	321
Wilson, William, clerk	Cert Free to	Spellman, George	1817	AO39	467	321
Wilson, Zadock	Deed fr	Brent, Robert, trustee	1817	AO39	488	335
Wilson, Zadock	Deed fr	Carroll, John, Rev. & Robt. Brent	1817	AO39	483	332
Wilson, Zadock, of Montg. Co.	Deed fr	Beall, Thomas B., trustee	1804	K10	352	365
Wimsett, John & father James	Apprentice to	Smith, Job, as baker	1805	M12	233	235
Winder, Levin, Somerset Co. MD	Deed fr	Commissioners of Washington	1801	G7	317	444
Windle, Isaac	Deed fr	Kale, John	1802	H8	005	005
Wineberg, Jacob, of G'tn.	Deed to	Ott, John	1815	AI34	155	178
Wineberger, George	Deed fr	Beall, Thomas B.	1808	T19	286	209
Wineberger, George	Deed to	Wineberger, Jacob	1809	W22	075	056
Wineberger, George	Deed fr	Parrott, Richard	1810	Z25	266	208
Wineberger, George	Deed to	Pickrell, John	1811	Z25	402	316
Wineberger, George, of G'tn.	Assign to	Wineberger, Jacob, his son	1815	AK35	072	055
Wineberger, Jacob	Deed fr	Wineberger, George	1809	W22	075	056
Wineberger, Jacob	Deed fr	Hyde, Thomas	1810	Y24	545	479
Wineberger, Jacob	Deed fr	Newton, Ignatius, of G'tn.	1812	AC28	301	219
Wineberger, Jacob	Deed to	Holtzman, Jacob	1812	AC28	459	327
Wineberger, Jacob	Deed fr	Newton, Ignatius	1816	AL36	294	291
Wineberger, Jacob, of G'tn.	Deed fr	Brookes, William Henry, of G'tn.	1810	X23	287	228
Wineberger, Jacob, of G'tn.	Deed to	Bussard, Daniel	1812	AD29	523	441
Wineberger, Jacob, s/o George	Assign fr	Wineberger, George, of G'tn.	1815	AK35	072	055

Party	What	Party	Year	Liber	Old	New
Winebergh, Jacob	Deed fr	Ott, John, Dr.	1808	U20	285	152
Winebergh, Jacob	Deed fr	Ritchie, Abher	1808	U20	287	153
Wingard, Abraham	Deed fr	Love, Charles I.	1801	G7	198	264
Wingard, Abraham	Deed to	Bohrer, Mary	1801	G7	201	268
Wingard, Abraham	Deed to	McClan, Robert	1802	I9	511	837
Wingard, Abraham	Deed fr	Beatty, Charles	1802	I9	161	243
Wingard, Abraham	Deed to	Ritchie, Abner	1802	I9	434	718
Wingard, Abraham	Deed fr	Magruder, Edward	1804	K10	121	130
Wingard, Abraham	Deed fr	Beatty, Charles, heirs of	1805	N13	285	235
Wingard, Abraham	Deed fr	Ritchie, Abner	1808	U20	045	025
Wingard, Abraham	Deed fr	Schultze, J.L. Henry	1808	U20	048	027
Wingard, Abraham	Deed fr	Beall, Thomas, of Geo.	1814	AH33	085	077
Wingard, Abraham & W.H. Smith	B. of S. fr	Miller, Daniel, of G'tn.	1812	AD29	217	177
Wingard, Abraham, of G'tn.	Mortgage fr	Gailor, Thomas, of G'tn.	1804	K10	124	134
Wingard, Abraham, of G'tn.	Deed fr	Chapline, Joseph	1812	AD29	218	179
Wingard, Abraham, of G'tn.	Deed fr	Wood, Basil, constable, of G'tn.	1817	AO39	434	296
Wingard, Adam, of G'tn.	Deed fr	King, Adam & Grace, of G'tn.	1809	X23	212	162
Wingard, John, of VA	Deed fr	Hillsimer, Elizabeth, a.k.a. Brown	1797	C3	066	54
Wingart, Abraham	Deed to	Smith, Richard	1811	Z25	493	392
Wingart, John, of Harrisburg PA	Deed to	Magruder, Ninian, of G'tn.	1816	AL36	081	083
Winger, John, of Shepperds Town	Deed fr	Hitzimer, Elizabeth, of G'tn.	1813	AE30	130	100
Wingerd, Abraham	Deed to	Schultze, J.L. Henry	1808	U20	046	026
Wingerd, Abraham	Deed to	Ritchie, Abner	1808	U20	049	028
Wingerd, Abraham, of G'tn.	Deed fr	Laird, John, of G'tn.	1814	AH33	359	311
Wingert, Charles	P. of Atty. fr	Barnet, Thomas & Margaret	1814	AH33	107	100
Wingert, Charles, Harrisburg PA	Deed to	Magruder, Ninian, of G'tn.	1814	AH33	109	102
Winn, Timothy	Deed fr	Forrest, Joseph, trustee	1813	AF31	067	046
Winn, Timothy	Slaves	From Fairfax Co., VA	1813	AE30	164	130
Winn, Timothy	Deed fr	King, Benjamin	1815	AI34	131	150
Winn, Timothy	Mortgage to	Tingey, Thomas	1815	AK35	123	095
Winn, Timothy	Deed fr	Tingey, Thomas	1815	AI34	183	210
Winn, Timothy	Manumis to	Johnston, Jacob (C), age 35	1816	AM37	191	142
Winn, Timothy & Silas Butler	Deed fr	Bentley, John H., of Balto. MD	1813	AE30	161	128
Winn, Timothy & Silas Butler	Deed fr	Yeaton, William, of Alexa.	1813	AF31	103	070
Winn, Timothy & Silas Butler	Deed fr	Wadsworth, Elizabeth	1814	AH33	120	113
Winn, Timothy, purser in Navy	Deed fr	Davis, Thomas, ship carpenter	1813	AF31	405	291
Winsatt, Margaret	Assign to	Booth, Jeremiah	1805	O14	079	049
Winsatt, Margaret et al	Assign fr	Adams, William	1805	O14	077	047
Winsett, Kezia N.	Cert Free to	Salmon, Margaret (negro)	1807	R17	292	
Winters, William	B. of S. fr	Washington, Susanna, w/o Lund	1812	AD29	491	415
Winters, William	Manumis to	[ ], Elsey (C)	1812	AD29	492	416
Winters, William (C), age 42	Cert Free fr	Washington, Lund	1816	AM37	023	019
Wirt, Henry, of Ontario Co. NY	Deed to	Ferguson, David, Ontario Co. NY	1805	N13	336	270
Wirt, John	Deed to	Pickerill, Benjamin	1808	T19	238	175
Wirt, John	Deed to	Waters, Thomas Gibbons	1811	AB27	506	414
Wirt, John	Deed fr	Ober, Robert	1811	AB27	091	075
Wirt, John	D. of T. to	Kurtz, Daniel	1813	AE30	459	341
Wirt, John	Deed to	Garey, Ann	1815	AI34	030	035
Wirt, John et al	Lease fr	Reintzel, Anthony	1811	Z25	490	389
Wirt, John et al	Deed to	Joncherez, Alexander L.	1812	AD29	383	323
Wirt, John, joiner	Deed fr	Beall, Thomas, of George	1806	O14	240	157
Wirt, John, of G'tn.	Deed to	Linkins, James, of G'tn.	1808	U20	074	041
Wirt, John, of G'tn.	Agreement	Yerby, John, of G'tn.	1811	AB27	088	073
Wirt, John, of G'tn.	Deed fr	Holmead, John	1811	AB27	324	266
Wirt, John, of G'tn.	Lease fr	Peter, John, of G'tn.	1811	AB27	089	073

Index to District of Columbia Land Records, 1792-1817

Party	What	Party	Year	Liber	Old	New
Wirt, John, of G'tn.	Deed to	Duvall, William N., of G'tn.	1812	AC28	131	099
Wirt, John, of G'tn.	B. of S. fr	Wirt, Philip, of G'tn.	1812	AD29	506	426
Wirt, John, of G'tn.	Deed fr	Peter, John, of G'tn.	1813	AF31	096	064
Wirt, John, of G'tn.	Deed to	Pickerill, John, of G'tn.	1813	AE30	185	148
Wirt, John, of G'tn.	Deed to	Morgan, William	1813	AE30	209	170
Wirt, John, of G'tn.	Deed to	Kurtz, Daniel, of G'tn.	1815	AK35	316	252
Wirt, Philip, of G'tn.	B. of S. to	Wirt, John, of G'tn.	1812	AD29	506	426
Wise, John	Deed to	Magruder, Ninian	1802	I9	308	505
Wise, Samuel	B. of S. to	Jones, Charles	1810	Y24	422	379
Wiseman, Thomas S. (M), age 23	Cert Free fr	Proctor, Ann & Susannah Collins	1817	AO39	092	073
Wisenall, Bernard, Jefferson Co.	Deed to	Stoner, Stephen, Frederick Co.	1811	AA26	174	120
Wishair, Appetonia, wid/o George	Deed to	Beall, Thomas & John M. Gantt	1792	A1-1	092	134
Wishair, Christian, s/o George	Deed to	Beall, Thomas & John M. Gantt	1792	A1-1	092	134
Wistar, William, mer., of Phila.	Deed to	Magruder, Ninian, Dr. of G'tn.	1800	E5	176	166
Wite, Thomas	Deed fr	Keithley, Thomas & Thos. Young	1813	AF31	494	360
Wolcott, Oliver	Assign fr	Shannon, William	1800	E5	172	163
Wolcott, Oliver et al	Release to	Nourse, Joseph	1813	AF31	011	008
Wolgamoth, John	Deed to	Beall, Thomas & John M. Gantt	1793	A1-1	366	473
Woltz, Susanna, of G'tn.	B. of S. fr	Nixdorf, Samuel, of Fredk. Co.	1813	AF31	234	161
Wood, Basil	Deed to	Lane, William	1801	G7	147	194
Wood, Basil, constable, of G'tn.	Deed to	Wingard, Abraham, of G'tn.	1817	AO39	434	296
Wood, Eleanor	B. of S. fr	Wood, Hezekiah, her husband	1813	AF31	547	405
Wood, Hezekiah	B. of S. to	Brackenridge, John, of Montg. Co.	1810	Y24	078	069
Wood, Hezekiah	B. of S. to	Wood, Eleanor, his wife	1813	AF31	547	405
Wood, William	Lease fr	Prout, William	1809	V21	351	254
Wood, William	Assign to	Bentley, John Hunter, of Balto.	1810	X23	377	303
Wood, William	Qualify	Lieutenant in Militia	1812	AC28	381	278
Wood, William, trustee	Deed fr	Palmer, Jesse C., insolvent	1811	AA26	268	182
Woods, David	B. of S. to	Delphy, Richard	1808	U20	025	015
Woodward, Aug. B.	Qualify		1802	I9	314	516
Woodward, Augustine, of VA	Deed to	Prout, William	1797	B2B	661	425
Woodward, Augustine, of VA	Deed fr	Prout, William	1797	B2B	659	423
Woodward, Augustus	Deed to	Munroe, Thomas et al	1804	L11	244	225
Woodward, Augustus B., of MI	Deed to	Duvall, Gabriel	1806	Q16	240	166
Woodward, Augustus B., of MI	Deed fr	Duvall, Gabriel	1813	AE30	414	305
Woodward, Augustus Boost	Deed fr	Prout, William	1804	L11	087	89
Woodward, Augustus Brevoost	Deed to	Prout, William	1804	L11	085	87
Woodward, Augustus Brevoost	Deed fr	Prout, William	1804	L11	084	86
Woodward, Clement	Deed to	Beall, Thomas & John M. Gantt	1792	A1-1	015	23
Woodward, Frances, wid/o C.	Deed to	Prout, William	1798	C3	284	230
Woodward, Francis, Shen. Co. VA	Deed to	Ennis, Ezekiel, Shen. Co. VA	1804	K10	331	342
Woodward, J., A., C., H. & F. et al	Deed to	Prout, William	1798	D4	129	112
Woodward, John	Deed fr	Gamble, Thomas	1800	E5	147	136
Woodward, John, yellow, age 30	Cert Free fr	Venable, William	1813	AF31	360	257
Woodward, Salem	B. of S. fr	Swett, Samuel	1817	AN38	451	324
Woodward, Thomas & G. Cooke	Deed to	Yerby, John, of G'tn.	1815	AI34	079	090
Woodward, Thomas & G. Cooke	D. of T. to	Corcoran, Thomas, of G'tn.	1815	AH33	490	419
Woodward, Thomas & G. Cooke	Deed fr	Morgan, William, of G'tn.	1815	AK35	415	325
Woodward, Thomas & G. Cooke	D. of T. to	Corcoran, Thomas, of G'tn.	1816	AL36	077	079
Woodward, Thomas & G. Cooke	Deed to	Yerby, John, of G'tn.	1816	AL36	200	208
Woodward, Thomas & G. Cooke	Deed to	Foxall, Henry, of G'tn.	1816	AL36	131	132
Woodward, Thomas, of G'tn.	Deed to	Cooke, George, of G'tn.	1816	AL36	495	466
Woodward, William	Deed fr	Joy, Absalom	1801	G7	009	011
Woodward, William	Deed fr	Dorsey, William H.	1802	I9	335	552
Woodward, William	Lease fr	Dorsey, William H.	1802	I9	481	790

Party	What	Party	Year	Liber	Old	New
Woodward, William	Deed to	Nourse, Michael	1802	I9	311	510
Woodward, William	Deed fr	Dorsey, William H.	1802	H8	157	151
Woodward, William	Deed to	Tingey, Thomas	1803	K10	060	65
Woodward, William	Deed fr	Tingey, Thomas	1803	K10	092	99
Woodward, William	Agreement	Underwood, Robert	1806	O14	404	270
Woodward, William	Deed to	Walker, Archibald, Rev., Kent Co.	1806	P15	210	140
Woodward, William	Deed to	Underwood, Robert	1806	O14	396	264
Woodward, William & Anne	Deed to	Duane, William, of Phila.	1804	K10	300	303
Woodworth, Joseph	Release fr	Hughes, Thomas	1812	AD29	346	289
Woodworth, Joseph	D. of T. to	Hughes, Thomas	1812	AC28	356	258
Woodworth, Joseph	Deed fr	Van Ness, John P. & Marcia	1812	AC28	358	260
Woodworth, Joseph	Deed to	Moore, George	1813	AE30	108	083
Woodworth, Joseph	Deed to	Scoville, Hope	1814	AH33	236	206
Woodworth, Joseph	Deed fr	Moore, George	1815	AI34	081	092
Woodworth, Joseph	Deed to	Wagler, Frederick A.	1815	AI34	005	005
Woolls, George	Deed fr	Bells, James	1802	I9	252	406
Wools, George, of G'tn.	Deed to	Polkinhorn, Henry, of G'tn. et al	1804	K10	287	289
Wooten, Richard, of Montg. Co.	Deed to	Turner, Samuel, Jr., of G'tn.	1816	AL36	206	213
Wootten, Richard	Deed to	Davidson, John, of Annapolis	1799	D4	315	299
Wootton, Richard, planter	Deed fr	Burrell, John, s/o Alexander	1793	A1-2	439	47
Wootton, Turner, et al	Deed to	Beall, Thomas & John M. Gantt	1792	A1-1	052	77
Wootton, Turner, P.G. Co., planter	Deed to	Casanave, Peter, Montgomery Co.	1795	B2B	367	018
Wordworth, Joseph [Ann]	Deed to	Scovell, Hope	1814	AG32	240	172
Worman, George, of Balto.	Deed fr	Worman, Henry, of Frederick Co.	1800	F6	099	061
Worman, George, of Balto. Co.	Deed to	Stockwell, Mark	1801	G7	315	441
Worman, George, of Balto.	Deed fr	Worman, Henry, of Frederick Co.	1801	G7	303	422
Worman, Henry, of Frederick Co.	Deed to	Beall, Thomas & John M. Gantt	1793	A1-2	440	49
Worman, Henry, of Frederick Co.	Deed to	Warman, George, of Balto.	1800	F6	099	061
Worman, Henry, of Frederick Co.	Deed to	Worman, George, of Balto.	1801	G7	303	422
Wormley, James, of Britain	Deed fr	Fairfax, Ferdinando et ux, of VA	1802	I9	033	043
Worsley, John	B. of S. fr	Turner, Nanny	1802	I9	001	002
Worthan, Charles, carpenter	B. of S. to	Bradley, Phineas	1817	AN38	213	155
Worthen, Charles [Wathen]	B. of S. to	Threlkeld, John	1817	AO39	411	270
Worthington, Charles	Deed to	Beall, Thomas & John M. Gantt	1793	A1-1	371	478
Worthington, Charles	Deed fr	Templeman, John et al	1802	H8	533	492
Worthington, Charles	Deed to	Templeman, John	1802	H8	536	496
Worthington, Charles	Deed fr	Templeman, John et al	1802	H8	533	492
Worthington, Charles	Deed fr	Marbury, William	1804	L11	044	44
Worthington, Charles	Deed fr	Osburn, Archibald	1807	S18	380	302
Worthington, Charles	Deed fr	Ferguson, James	1807	R17	111	087
Worthington, Charles	Deed fr	Lingan, James M., of Montg. Co.	1810	Y24	164	149
Worthington, Charles, Dr., of G'tn.	Deed fr	Forrest, Uriah	1793	A1-2	447	55
Worthington, Charles, Dr., of G'tn.	Deed fr	Teackle, John, of G'tn.	1810	Z25	356	278
Worthington, Charles, Dr.	Deed fr	Mason, John T.	1812	AE30	051	038
Worthington, Charles et al	Deed fr	Beatty, Charles, of G'tn.	1803	K10	062	67
Worthington, Charles, of G'tn.	Deed fr	Lanham, Jeremiah	1793	A1-2	448	57
Worthington, Charles, of G'tn.	Deed fr	Tayloe, John, Richmond Co. VA	1808	U20	120	069
Worthington, William	Deed fr	Jackson, Agnes & William	1806	O14	258	170
Worthington, William	Deed fr	Lingan, James M., of Montg. Co.	1809	X23	082	061
Worthington, William	B. of S. fr	Hammond, Hezekiah	1810	Y24	346	313
Worthington, William	Deed fr	Stewart, William	1810	Z25	129	101
Worthington, William	Deed to	Briscoe, Richard Sothoron	1810	Y24	189	174
Worthington, William	Deed to	Moore, James	1812	AC28	226	167
Worthington, William	Deed to	Moore, James	1812	AC28	226	168
Worthington, William	Deed fr	Clarke, Joseph	1812	AC28	110	083

Party	What	Party	Year	Liber	Old	New
Worthington, William	Assign fr	Moore, James	1812	AC28	108	081
Worthington, William	Deed fr	Brown, Joel, of G'tn.	1815	AK35	276	219
Worthington, William	Deed fr	Hodgson, Rebecca, wid/o Joseph	1816	AL36	177	177
Worthington, William	Deed fr	Boyd, Washington	1816	AM37	024	019
Worthington, William et al	Suit ads	Potomac Company	1812	AG32	258	183
Worthington, William, Jr.	Deed fr	Deakins, Francis	1800	F6	109	067
Worthington, William, Jr.	Manumis to	[ ], Charlotte (negro)	1809	W22	242	163
Worthington, William, Jr.	Deed fr	Barber, Luke White, St. Mary's Co.	1815	AK35	279	222
Worthington, William, Jr.	Deed to	Thaw, Joseph	1815	AK35	229	180
Worthington, William, Jr.	Deed fr	Heugh, John, of G'tn., trustee	1815	AH33	547	468
Worthington, William, Jr.	Deed to	Tayloe, John, Col.	1816	AM37	188	141
Worthington, William, Jr.	Deed fr	Tayloe, John, Col.	1816	AM37	329	239
Worthington, William, the younger	Deed fr	Caldwell, Timothy	1806	O14	260	171
Wortz, Lucy	B. of S. fr	Black, Samuel	1814	AG32	097	073
Wothington, Charles	Deed fr	Osborn, Archibald	1810	Z25	358	280
Wright, Barzeller, of NJ	Lease fr	Vallet, Peter	1817	AN38	106	079
Wright, John M.	Deed to	Cheshire, Archibald	1817	AO39	159	119
Wright, John, of G'tn.	Deed to	Peck, Joseph, of Alexa.	1797	C3	233	193
Wright, John, of NY	Deed fr	Peters, Samuel, of NY	1817	AN38	466	336
Wright, John, oif Montg. Co.	Deed fr	Dorsey, William H., of Montg. Co.	1797	C3	230	192
Wright, Mary, wid., of NY	Deed fr	Peters, Samuel, of NY	1817	AN38	473	341
Wright, Mathew	Release to	Charlton, Ralph	1806	P15	079	048
Wright, Matthew	Deed fr	Charlton, Ralph	1804	L11	355	321
Wright, Matthew	Deed fr	Provott, Peter	1808	T19	360	259
Wright, Matthew	Deed fr	Brown, Robert	1808	T19	377	269
Wright, Matthew	Deed fr	Tuckfield, William H.P.	1808	T19	363	260
Wright, Matthew	B. of S. fr	Brown, Robert	1809	X23	062	046
Wright, Matthew	Deed fr	Dunlap, James, of G'tn. et al	1809	W22	301	197
Wright, Matthew	Release fr	Stoddert, Benjamin, Bladensburg	1811	AB27	370	306
Wright, Matthew	Deed fr	Nevitt, William, of G'tn.	1811	AB27	372	307
Wright, Matthew	Deed fr	Voss, Nicholas & wife, of VA	1811	AB27	374	310
Wright, Matthew	Deed fr	Tingey, Thomas & S.N. Smallwood	1811	AB27	377	312
Wright, Matthew	Deed fr	Chandler, Walter S.	1811	AB27	373	309
Wright, Matthew	Deed fr	Clephan, Lewis & A. McDonald	1812	AD29	275	227
Wright, Matthew	Deed fr	Clephan, Lewis & A. McDonald	1812	AC28	150	112
Wright, Mercy, wid., of NY	Deed fr	Peters, Samuel, of NY	1817	AN38	476	344
Wright, Reuben, of NY	Deed fr	Peters, Samuel, of NY	1817	AN38	480	346
Wright, Solomon, of NY	Deed fr	Peters, Samuel, of NY	1817	AN38	470	339
Wright, Stephen	Deed fr	Wheeler, Luke & John Cowper	1814	AG32	459	332
Wright, Thomas C., of G'tn.	Assign fr	Clarke, Joseph	1804	L11	312	286
Wright, Thomas C. et al	Release fr	Thornton, William	1805	M12	207	208
Wright, Thomas C., of G'tn. et al	Release to	Peacock, Robert Ware et al	1805	M12	209	
Wright, Thomas C., of G'tn. et al	Deed fr	Davidson, John	1805	M12	203	205
Wright, Thomas C.	Deed fr	Crow, John, of Frederick Co. VA	1806	P15	301	198
Wright, Thomas C., of G'tn.	Deed fr	Deakins, Leonard M., of G'tn. et al	1807	S18	316	248
Wright, Thomas C.	Deed fr	King, Nicholas et al	1807	Q16	358	275
Wright, Thomas C., of G'tn.	Deed fr	Jones, Raphael	1807	R17	147	113
Wright, Thomas C.	B. of S. fr	Dinmore, Richard	1808	U20	187	104
Wright, Thomas C., of G'tn.	Deed to	Cocking, William, of G'tn.	1808	V21	073	058
Wright, Thomas C., of G'tn.	Deed to	Morgan, William, mer., of G'tn.	1808	U20	177	099
Wright, Thomas C.	Deed to	Mauro, Philip	1809	V21	152	111
Wright, Thomas C.	Deed fr	Kilty, John & Josias Wilson King	1809	W22	055	041
Wright, Thomas C.	Deed fr	Vint, John	1809	X23	231	178
Wright, Thomas C.	Deed fr	Davis, Benjamin	1809	X23	237	184
Wright, Thomas C.	Deed fr	Vint, John	1809	X23	233	180

Party	What	Party	Year	Liber	Old	New
Wright, Thomas C.	Deed to	Renner, Daniel & Daniel Bussard	1809	X23	256	200
Wright, Thomas C.	Deed fr	Vint, John	1809	X23	229	177
Wright, Thomas C., of G'tn.	Deed to	Ott, John, Dr.	1810	Z25	139	110
Wright, Thomas C.	Mortgage to	Magruder, Ninian	1810	Z25	325	254
Wright, Thomas C., of G'tn.	Deed fr	Davidson, Ann Maria, exrx.	1810	Z25	304	238
Wright, Thomas C.	Deed fr	Vint, Thomas	1810	X23	227	175
Wright, Thomas C.	Deed fr	Eno, Richard	1810	Y24	371	336
Wright, Thomas C.	Deed to	Cocking, William	1811	AA26	224	154
Wright, Thomas C.	Deed to	Cocking, William	1811	AA26	227	155
Wright, Thomas C.	Deed to	Cocking, William	1811	AA26	230	158
Wright, Thomas C. & John Ott	Mortgage fr	Pic, Francis	1812	AD29	258	214
Wright, Thomas C.	Deed to	Cooper, William	1812	AD29	179	144
Wright, Thomas C.	Deed fr	Ober, Robert	1813	AE30	174	139
Wright, Thomas C.	Deed fr	Ott, John, of G'tn., trustee	1813	AE30	177	141
Wright, Thomas C.	Deed fr	Ober, Robert	1813	AE30	172	137
Wright, Thomas C., of G'tn.	Mortgage fr	Pic, Francis	1813	AE30	169	135
Wright, Thomas C., of G'tn.	Deed to	Westcott, James D., of NJ	1813	AF31	211	144
Wright, Thomas C.	B. of S. fr	Homans, Benjamin	1813	AF31	099	067
Wright, Thomas C.	Deed to	Ober, Robert	1813	AF31	042	029
Wright, Thomas C., of G'tn.	Deed to	Cozens, William R.	1813	AF31	410	295
Wright, Thomas C.	Mortgage fr	Homans, Benjamin	1813	AF31	099	067
Wright, Thomas C., of G'tn.	Assign to	English, David, of G'tn.	1814	AG32	429	311
Wright, Thomas C., of G'tn.	D. of T. to	Ott, John, of G'tn.	1814	AH33	310	268
Wright, Thomas C., of G'tn.	Deed to	Dinmore, Bridget	1814	AH33	244	212
Wright, Thomas C., of G'tn.	D. of T. to	English, David, of G'tn.	1814	AG32	433	313
Wright, Thomas C., of G'tn.	Deed to	Scott, Jesse, of G'tn.	1815	AH33	485	414
Wright, Thomas C.	Deed to	Cocking, William	1816	AL36	139	139
Wright, Thomas C. & R. Davis	D. of T. fr	Bixby, Nathaniel P., of G'tn.	1817	AO39	144	109
Wright, Thomas C., of G'tn.	Deed fr	Dinmore, Bridget	1817	AN38	539	392
Wright, Thomas Crafts, of G'tn.	Deed fr	Thomson, William, of G'tn.	1806	O14	320	212
Wright, Thomas, trustee	Assign fr	Jones, Raphael, insolvent	1809	V21	414	316
Wright, William B.	B. of S. to	Smothers, Henry	1809	V21	316	232
Wright, William, of KY	B. of S. to	Magruder, James A., of G'tn.	1817	AO39	247	178
Wuthank, William et al	Deed fr	Templeman, John	1802	I9	226	359
Wykoff, Isaac, of Phila. PA	Deed to	Deakins, William, Jr., of G'tn.	1796	B2B	556	287

Index to District of Columbia Land Records, 1792-1817

Party	What	Party	Year	Liber	Old	New
Y						
Yarro, Acquilla	Deed fr	[ ], Yarro (Negro), of G'tn. et al	1803	K10	071	77
Yates, John, of Balto.	Deed fr	Magruder, William B., of Balto.	1798	D4	122	105
Yates, John, of Balto.	Deed to	Amat, Thomas, of Phila.	1799	D4	242	224
Yates, William, of Alexa.	Deed fr	Tingey, Thomas	1805	M12	349	355
Yeamans, Royal	B. of S. to	Mechlin, Joseph et al	1817	AO39	147	111
Yeamans, Royal [Yeomans]	B. of S. to	Reeder, Charles, of Balto.	1817	AN38	375	278
Yeates, William	Deed to	Tingey, Thomas	1802	H8	184	177
Yeates, William	Deed to	Miller, John, Jr. et al	1802	H8	056	053
Yeates, William	Deed fr	Pratt, Henry et al	1802	H8	056	053
Yeates, William	Deed to	Skam, John	1809	W22	016	012
Yeates, William	Deed fr	Porter, Sarah & children, Alexa.	1816	AM37	406	292
Yeates, William, Jr.	Deed fr	Yeates, William, Sr., of Alexa.	1814	AG32	260	185
Yeates, William, Sr., of Alexa.	Deed to	Yeates, William, Jr.	1814	AG32	260	185
Yeaton, William	Deed fr	Forrest, Uriah et al	1802	H8	204	195
Yeaton, William	Deed fr	Hanson, Samuel, of Samuel et al	1802	H8	204	195
Yeaton, William & Lucia, of Alexa.	Deed to	Kalkman, Charles Frederick, Balto.	1810	Z25	368	289
Yeaton, William, of Alexa.	Deed to	Winn, Timothy & Silas Butler	1813	AF31	103	070
Yerby, David, of G'tn.	Deed fr	Peter, George, of G'tn.	1815	AI34	085	097
Yerby, John	Deed fr	Magruder, James A., of G'tn.	1816	AL36	089	090
Yerby, John, of G'tn.	Deed fr	Peter, John, of G'tn.	1811	AB27	033	029
Yerby, John, of G'tn.	Agreement	Wirt, John, of G'tn.	1811	AB27	088	073
Yerby, John, of G'tn.	Deed fr	Peter, John, of G'tn.	1812	AD29	551	463
Yerby, John, of G'tn.	Deed fr	Peter, John, of G'tn.	1812	AD29	413	
Yerby, John, of G'tn.	Deed fr	Woodward, Thomas & G. Cooke	1815	AI34	079	090
Yerby, John, of G'tn.	Manumis to	[ ], Milley (C), age 17	1816	AM37	304	222
Yerby, John, of G'tn.	Deed fr	Thompson, James	1816	AM37	507	373
Yerby, John, of G'tn.	Deed fr	Woodward, Thomas & G. Cooke	1816	AL36	200	208
Yerby, John, of G'tn.	Deed fr	Peter, John, of G'tn.	1817	AO39	378	255
Yost, Henry, of Bladensburgh	Deed to	Magruder, George Beall, of G'tn.	1808	T19	041	032
Yost, John et al, defs.	Suit	Scholfield, Andrew, plt.	1809	V21	326	240
Young, Abraham	Deed to	Beall, Thomas & John M. Gantt	1792	A1-1	029	45
Young, Abraham, planter	Deed to	King, William, of Montgomery Co.	1795	B2A	274	383
Young, Alexander	Deed to	Fairfax, Ferdinand, Berkeley Co.	1802	G7	556	704
Young, Anna (C), age 26	Cert Free fr	Butler, Chloe	1813	AE30	549	408
Young, Benjamin et al	Deed to	Brent, Eleanor & Robert Young	1802	H8	499	458
Young, Benjamin et al	Deed to	Young, Eleanor et al	1802	I9	022	029
Young, Benjamin et al	Deed to	Casanave, Ann et al	1802	I9	022	029
Young, Benjamin et al	Deed to	Young, Notley	1802	I9	021	028
Young, Benjamin et al	Deed fr	Webb, Thomas	1802	I9	190	295
Young, Benjamin et al	Deed fr	Lee, Thomas S.	1802	I9	261	422
Young, Benjamin, of MD	Deed to	Young, Nicholas, of MD	1802	I9	020	027
Young, Charles, of Montg. Co.	B. of S. fr	Powell, Adam	1811	Z25	525	416
Young, Eleanor et al	Deed fr	Young, Benjamin et al	1802	I9	022	029
Young, Eleanor et al	Deed to	Young, Notley	1802	I9	021	028
Young, Jacob, of Frederick Co.	Deed to	Barber, Luke, exr. of G. Goldie	1796	B2B	448	133
Young, James	Assign fr	Collard, George	1811	AA26	237	162
Young, James	Mortgage to	May, Frederick	1812	AB27	525	428
Young, James	Qualify	Captain in Militia	1812	AC28	493	351
Young, James	Deed fr	May, Frederick, Dr.	1812	AB27	189	155
Young, James	D. of T. to	McCormick, Alexander	1813	AF31	487	355
Young, James	Deed fr	Law, Thomas	1813	AF31	169	114
Young, James	D. of T. fr	McCauley, George	1815	AI34	464	476
Young, James	Agreement	Law, Thomas & Griffith Coombe	1816	AL36	278	277
Young, James	Deed fr	Law, Thomas	1816	AL36	277	276

Party	What	Party	Year	Liber	Old	New
Young, James	Release to	McCauley, George	1816	AL36	153	153
Young, James, trustee	Deed fr	Long, Robert, tavern keeper, et al	1813	AE30	094	072
Young, John	Deed to	Wheeler, Elizabeth	1799	D4	197	180
Young, Josiah	Manumis to	[ ], Lawrie (C)	1812	AC28	323	235
Young, Ludwick	Deed fr	Rentch, Jacob, exr. of John	1809	W22	145	103
Young, Manduit et al	Deed fr	Walker, George	1802	H8	070	065
Young, Mary	B. of S. to	Latrobe, Benjamin H.	1814	AG32	310	226
Young, Mary et al	Deed fr	Walker, George	1802	H8	070	065
Young, Mauduit	Deed to	Jenkins, Thomas	1807	R17	314	238
Young, Mauduit	Deed to	Jenkins, Francis	1808	T19	197	141
Young, Moses	Deed fr	Munroe, Thomas, Supt.	1809	X23	213	163
Young, Moses	Cert fr	Monroe, Thomas, Supt.	1809	X23	033	023
Young, Moses	Deed fr	McElwee, John	1809	X23	122	088
Young, Moses	Deed fr	May, Frederick	1809	X23	133	096
Young, Moses	Partition	Morris, Thomas, devisees of	1810	X23	216	165
Young, Moses	Mortgage fr	Clarke, Francis	1810	Y24	421	378
Young, Moses	Deed fr	McCormick, James, Jr.	1810	Y24	112	102
Young, Moses	Deed fr	McElwee, John	1810	Y24	111	101
Young, Moses	Deed fr	White, Patrick, painter	1811	AA26	087	062
Young, Moses	B. of S. fr	Coolidge, Samuel J.	1811	AB27	117	096
Young, Moses	Release fr	McElwee, Rebecca, of Phila. PA	1812	AD29	187	151
Young, Moses	Deed fr	Oden, Benjamin, of P.G. Co.	1812	AD29	133	103
Young, Moses	Deed fr	Forrest, Richard & Chas. Glover	1813	AF31	380	273
Young, Moses	Deed to	Tippett, Cartwright	1813	AF31	291	206
Young, Moses	B. of S. fr	Elzey, Arnold	1813	AF31	528	389
Young, Moses	D. of T. fr	Shuck, Frederick	1814	AH33	145	138
Young, Moses	Deed fr	Brent, William & Philip B. Key	1814	AG32	217	152
Young, Moses	Deed to	Curran, Morgan	1814	AG32	108	081
Young, Moses	Deed fr	Corporation of Washington	1815	AI34	161	185
Young, Moses	Deed fr	Peltz, John	1815	AK35	195	152
Young, Moses	Deed to	Walker, Zachariah	1815	AK35	185	144
Young, Moses	Deed fr	Van Ness, John P. & Marcia	1816	AK35	514	405
Young, Moses et al	Bond fr	Shuck, Frederick, of Alexa. Co.	1813	AE30	436	322
Young, Moses et al	Deed fr	Jackson, John G., fr. Harrison Co.	1814	AG32	295	215
Young, Moses, Gent.	Deed to	McCormick, Alexander, mer.	1810	Z25	361	283
Young, Nancy et al	Deed fr	Walker, George	1802	H8	070	065
Young, Nicholas	Deed to	Brent, Robert	1809	X23	196	148
Young, Nicholas	Deed to	Georgetown College, President of	1810	Y24	009	008
Young, Nicholas	Lease to	Moore, William	1814	AG32	119	088
Young, Nicholas et al	Deed to	Casanave, Ann et al	1802	I9	022	029
Young, Nicholas et al	Deed fr	Lee, Thomas S.	1802	I9	261	422
Young, Nicholas et al	Deed to	Young, Notley	1802	I9	021	028
Young, Nicholas et al	Deed fr	Webb, Thomas	1802	I9	190	295
Young, Nicholas, of MD	Deed fr	Young, Benjamin, of MD	1802	I9	020	027
Young, Nicholas, of MD	Deed to	Fenwick, James, of MD	1806	Q16	086	055
Young, Notley	Deed to	Beall, Thomas & John M. Gantt	1792	A1-1	010	16
Young, Notley	Deed fr	Addison, Anthony, s/o Rev. Henry	1792	A1-1	171	244
Young, Notley	Deed to	Queen, Richard	1793	A1-1	236	324
Young, Notley	Cert fr	Commissioners of Washington	1794	B2A	109	145
Young, Notley	Deed to	Mersen, Jacobus, of Holland	1794	B2A	119	159
Young, Notley	Deed to	Greenleaf, James, New York NY	1794	B2A	117	156
Young, Notley	Deed fr	Greenleaf, James, New York NY	1795	B2A	348	492
Young, Notley	Deed to	Brent, Robert	1795	B2A	228	317
Young, Notley	Deed to	Barry, James, of Balto.	1795	B2A	203	278
Young, Notley	Agreement	Commissioners of Washington	1797	B2B	463	153

Index to District of Columbia Land Records, 1792-1817

Party	What	Party	Year	Liber	Old	New
Young, Notley	Plat	Square 296	1802	I9	123	181
Young, Notley	Deed fr	Young, Nicholas et al	1802	I9	021	028
Young, Notley	Deed to	Giberson, William	1810	Y24	446	396
Young, Notley & George Digges	Deed to	Beall, Thomas & John M. Gantt	1792	A1-1	042	63
Young, Notley & Mary Carroll	Deed to	Carroll, Elizabeth	1799	D4	317	301
Young, Notley & Clement Hill	Deed fr	Bayly, William	1800	E5	315	305
Young, Notley & Clement Hill	Deed to	Reintzel, Anthony, of G'tn.	1800	E5	317	307
Young, Notley, devisees of	Cert Surv	*St. Elisabeth*	1806	O14	187	112
Young, Notley et al	Deed to	Carroll, Henry Hill, of Balto. Co.	1793	A1-1	353	459
Young, Notley et al	Deed to	Davidson, Samuel	1793	A1-1	356	463
Young, Notley et al	Deed to	Hill, Henry, Jr.	1793	A1-1	360	466
Young, Notley, exr. of	Receipt to	Docker, Gilbert	1805	N13	219	188
Young, Notley, exrs. of	Division	Brent, Robert et al	1808	T19	318	232
Young, Notley, heirs of	Deed to	Brent, Eleanor & Robert Young	1802	H8	499	458
Young, Notley, heirs of	Plat	Youngsburrough	1802	I9	025	032
Young, Notley, heirs of	Deed to	Barry, James	1806	O14	284	188
Young, Notley, heirs of	Division	Square 673	1809	V21	240	
Young, Notley, P.G. Co. et al	Deed to	Hall, Benjamin, of Q.A. Co.	1795	B2B	366	017
Young, Notley, Sr.	Deed fr	Addison, John, Jr.	1796	B2B	427	102
Young, Patrick C., of G'tn.	Deed fr	Williamson, David, of Balto.	1813	AF31	351	250
Young, Patrick C.	Assign to	Renner, Daniel	1816	AK35	501	394
Young, Richard	B. of S. to	Gales, Joseph, Jr.	1816	AM37	496	363
Young, Richard & Matilda et al	Deed to	Clarke, Joseph S.	1816	AL36	256	258
Young, Samuel W., s/o Abraham	Deed to	Moscrop, Henry, Anne Arundel	1801	G7	298	415
Young, Samuel W., Loudoun Co.	Assign fr	Cocking, William	1813	AF31	360	257
Young, Samuel W., Loudoun Co.	Lease fr	Cocking, William	1813	AF31	362	259
Young, Samuel Wade, of VA	Deed to	Fairfax, Ferdinand, Berkeley Co.	1801	G7	108	139
Young, Sarah H., of North. Co. PA	Deed fr	Lloyd, William A., of Fredk. Town	1814	AH33	249	216
Young, Thomas	Deed fr	Simm, Patrick, Jr.	1802	I9	448	740
Young, Thomas	Deed fr	Wigfield, Mathew	1806	P15	132	085
Young, Thomas	Deed fr	Wigfield, Sarah	1806	P15	130	084
Young, Thomas	Deed fr	Bates, David, constable	1808	U20	405	226
Young, Thomas	Deed fr	Potts, James Bowman et al	1808	T19	031	024
Young, Thomas	Assign fr	Tuckfield, William H.P.	1809	W22	202	140
Young, Thomas	Deed fr	Kilty, John & Josias Wilson King	1809	X23	014	009
Young, Thomas	Lease to	Bates, David	1809	W22	074	055
Young, Thomas	Deed fr	Summers, Thomas	1810	Z25	081	061
Young, Thomas	Agreement	Varnum, James M.	1811	Z25	484	384
Young, Thomas	Mortgage fr	Keithley, Thomas	1812	AD29	395	333
Young, Thomas	Deed to	Keithley, Thomas	1812	AD29	389	328
Young, Thomas	Deed fr	White, Thomas	1813	AF31	497	362
Young, Thomas	B. of S. to	Hodge, George	1815	AH33	413	356
Young, Thomas	Deed to	Heath, William	1815	AI34	349	380
Young, Thomas	Deed fr	Varnum, James M.	1815	AI34	374	401
Young, Thomas	Deed fr	Roach, Mahlon & Elizabeth, of VA	1816	AL36	401	385
Young, Thomas	Deed fr	Minitree, John, of G'tn.	1816	AK35	257	204
Young, Thomas & Thomas Taylor	Deed fr	Vidler, Edward	1807	R17	311	236
Young, Thomas & John Arnott	Deed fr	Sim, Patrick	1808	U20	114	065
Young, Thomas & Samuel	Deed fr	Chandler, Walter Story	1809	X23	152	110
Young, Thomas & Thomas Foyles	Deed to	Brown, Elizabeth	1813	AE30	167	132
Young, Thomas & Thos. Keithley	Deed to	White, Thomas	1813	AF31	494	360
Young, Thomas & Thomas Foyles	Deed to	Greenleaf, James, Allen Town PA	1814	AH33	299	253
Young, Thomas et al	Deed fr	Bloor, John	1802	I9	447	739
Young, Thomas et al	Mortgage fr	Sim, Patrick, Sr.	1806	P15	147	096
Young, Thomas et al	Lease fr	Prout, William	1806	P15	139	090

Index to District of Columbia Land Records, 1792-1817

Party	What	Party	Year	Liber	Old	New
Young, Thomas et al	Mortgage fr	Sim, Patrick, Sr.	1806	P15	147	096
Young, Thomas et al	Deed fr	Wigfield, Matthew	1808	U20	208	113
Young, William	Deed to	Beall, Thomas & John M. Gantt	1792	A1-1	003	5
Young, William & Alexander	Deed fr	Walker, George	1802	H8	070	065
Young, William et al	Deed to	Walker, George	1802	H8	030	002
Young, William, guardian	Deed to	Lorman, William, of Balto.	1817	AO39	117	090

Party	What	Party	Year	Liber	Old	New
Z						
Zantziner, William P.	Deed fr	Caldwell, Elias B.	1817	AN38	134	098
Zantzinger, William P.	Deed to	Caldwell, Elias B.	1816	AM37	235	173
Zantzinger, William P.	Deed to	Law, Edmund	1817	AN38	496	358
Zantzinger, William P.	Agreement	Fagan, Daniel	1817	AN38	504	364
Zantzinger, William P.	Agreement	Homans, Daniel	1817	AN38	502	363
Zeller, Jacob [Zoller]	Deed to	Beall, Thomas & John M. Gantt	1793	A1-2	413	22
Zimmerman, Michael et al	Deed to	Beall, Thomas & John M. Gantt	1792	A1-1	108	157
Zimmerman, Michael, Fredk. Co.	Deed to	Deakins, William, Jr., of G'tn.	1792	A1-1	124	181
Zoller, Jacob [Zeller]	Deed to	Beall, Thomas & John M. Gantt	1793	A1-2	413	22

Party	What	Party	Year	Liber	Old	New
No Surname						
[ ], Abraham (negro)	Manumis fr	Tingey, Thomas	1809	W22	213	193
[ ], Adam (C)	Manumis fr	Varnum, Joseph B., of MA	1813	AF31	103	069
[ ], Agey (negro)	Manumis fr	Peter, Robert	1802	H8	443	407
[ ], Airy (C), d/o Cassandra, age 5	Manumis fr	Ross, Richard	1814	AH33	127	121
[ ], Alfred (C)	Manumis fr	Grayson, Mary E., reps. of	1811	AB27	298	244
[ ], Alley & Charles	Manumis fr	Mahorney, Charles & Barney	1817	AO39	438	299
[ ], Amelia (C)	Manumis fr	Dorsey, Edward	1817	AN38	381	282
[ ], Amy, and son Peter	Manumis fr	Wayman, Henry	1806	Q16	301	229
[ ], Andrew (C)	Manumis fr	Washington, Sarah, w/o Aug.	1813	AE30	351	262
[ ], Ann [Short] (negro)	Manumis fr	Stone, Mathew, of Charles Co.	1806	P15	266	175
[ ], Ann (C), age 12	Manumis fr	Sprigg, Osborn, of P.G. Co.	1813	AE30	221	178
[ ], Ann (C), est. of A. Dow	Cert Free fr	Hunter, George W., exr.	1815	AK35	250	198
[ ], Anna (C)	Manumis fr	Beans, Colmore	1815	AG32	347	251
[ ], Anne (C), age about 40	Manumis fr	Williams, Elisha W.	1811	AB27	054	046
[ ], Anthony (negro)	Purchase by	Munroe, Thomas	1809	V21	318	234
[ ], Ara (negro)	Manumis fr	Henderson, Sarah	1804	L11	260	239
[ ], Arianna (negress)	Manumis fr	Middleton, Electus	1806	Q16	236	162
[ ], Austin	Cert Free fr	Miller, William	1808	T19	318	232
[ ], Austin (C)	Manumis fr	Hazle, Henry	1812	AC28	381	277
[ ], Barney (C), age 1	Manumis fr	Sprigg, Osborn, of P.G. Co.	1813	AE30	221	178
[ ], Baxter (C)	Manumis fr	Dulany, Daniel	1816	AK35	356	281
[ ], Beck (C)	Manumis fr	Baker, Ann H.	1812	AC28	351	254
[ ], Benjamin (negro)	Manumis fr	McCleland, John	1810	Y24	419	376
[ ], Benjamin (C), est. of A. Dow	Cert Free fr	Hunter, George W., exr.	1815	AK35	250	198
[ ], Bernard (C)	Manumis fr	Horsey, Outerbridge, of DE	1812	AC28	167	124
[ ], Bet (negro) et al	Manumis fr	Jackson, Joseph	1808	T19	374	267
[ ], Betsey (negro)	Manumis fr	Hutchinson, Samuel	1804	K10	334	345
[ ], Betsey (C)	Manumis fr	Washington, Sarah, w/o Aug.	1813	AE30	351	262
[ ], Betsey (C)	Manumis fr	Walker, Joseph	1816	AM37	210	156
[ ], Betty (negro)	Manumis fr	Fox, Josiah	1809	X23	280	222
[ ], Bill (C)	Manumis fr	Lipscomb, John, of G'tn.	1817	AN38	402	300
[ ], Blackston (C), age 28	Manumis fr	Hartman, Charles	1817	AN38	515	373
[ ], Bobadil (C)	Manumis fr	Carr, Overton, exrs. of	1812	AD29	131	101
[ ], Caroline (C), age 12	Manumis fr	Hanson, Samuel, of Samuel	1811	AA26	016	013
[ ], Caroline (C), age 10	Manumis fr	Sprigg, Osborn, of P.G. Co.	1813	AE30	221	178
[ ], Cassandra (C), age 43	Manumis fr	Ross, Richard	1814	AH33	127	121
[ ], Catherine (negro)	Manumis fr	Hutton, John, of Montg. Co.	1810	Y24	078	070
[ ], Cecilia (negro)	Manumis fr	Hutton, John, of Montg. Co.	1810	Y24	078	070
[ ], Chaney (N), alias Lucy	Cert Slave	Freeman, Constant	1816	AL36	431	411
[ ], Charity (negroe)	Cert Free fr	Merrill, Jeremiah	1808	T19	141	100
[ ], Charity (C) and others	Manumis fr	Beall, Aquila, of Montg. Co.	1814	AH33	077	069
[ ], Charles (negro)	Manumis fr	Lambert, Morris	1807	S18	025	021
[ ], Charlotte (negro)	Manumis fr	Worthington, William, Jr.	1809	W22	242	163
[ ], Charlotte (C), age 14	Cert Free fr	Wilson, Henry M.	1816	AM37	141	109
[ ], Chloe (C), age 28	Cert Slave fr	Gustine, J.T. et al	1814	AH33	203	184
[ ], Cloe (negro) and 4 children	Manumis fr	Beall, George	1807	R17	352	268
[ ], Daniel (C), age 4	Manumis fr	Sprigg, Osborn, of P.G. Co.	1813	AE30	221	178
[ ], Daniel (C), est. of A. Dow	Cert Free fr	Hunter, George W., exr.	1815	AK35	250	198
[ ], David (negro)	Manumis fr	Stone, Mathew, of Charles Co.	1806	P15	266	175
[ ], David (C), age 18	Cert Slave fr	Gustine, J.T. et al	1814	AH33	203	184
[ ], Delaware (C)	Manumis fr	Mackall, Leonard	1812	AC28	486	345
[ ], Dianna (negro)	Manumis fr	Pairo, Thomas W. & Loveday	1806	P15	388	259
[ ], Dick & Polly (negroes)	Deed fr	Lingan, Nicholas	1802	H8	581	546
[ ], Dick & Polly (negro)	Manumis fr	Lingan, Nicholas	1807	R17	174	133

Index to District of Columbia Land Records, 1792-1817   463

Party	What	Party	Year	Liber	Old	New
[ ], Dick (C)	Cert Free fr	Thomas, William	1816	AL36	293	291
[ ], Dinah (negro)	Manumis fr	Holmead, John	1806	O14	317	210
[ ], Dole (negro) and others	Manumis fr	Hiat, Henry, attorney	1807	S18	076	062
[ ], Dorah (negroe)	Manumis fr	King, George	1808	T19	129	091
[ ], Edward (M) and others	Manumis fr	Beall, Aquila, of Montg. Co.	1814	AH33	077	069
[ ], Edwin (negro)	Manumis fr	Fox, Josiah	1809	X23	279	221
[ ], Eliza (C), and other	Manumis fr	Pumphrey, James	1813	AE30	091	070
[ ], Eliza (C)	Manumis fr	Horsey, Outerbridge	1813	AF31	291	206
[ ], Elsey (C)	Manumis fr	Winters, William	1812	AD29	492	416
[ ], Emanuel (C)	Manumis fr	Hambleton, Samuel, of G'tn.	1815	AI34	395	419
[ ], Emily (C)	Manumis fr	Horsey, Outerbridge, of DE	1815	AG32	299	218
[ ], Esther, and her son William	Manumis fr	Caffrey, Daniel	1812	AD29	428	360
[ ], Evans (M)	Manumis fr	Williams, Richard, Loudoun Co.	1817	AN38	118	088
[ ], Fannie (negro)	Manumis fr	Adams, Thomas G.	1805	O14	117	074
[ ], Fanny (C), age 40	Manumis fr	Ewell, Thomas, Dr.	1813	AE30	240	190
[ ], Fender (negro)	Manumis fr	Elzey, Arnold	1807	S18	128	104
[ ], Flora (C), d/o Monica	Manumis fr	Beans, Colmore	1811	AB27	163	135
[ ], Forrester (negro)	Manumis fr	Lovell, William	1805	M12	048	046
[ ], Fortune (M)	Cert Slave	Freeman, Constant	1816	AL36	431	411
[ ], Frambo (negro)	Manumis fr	Dempsie, John & Elizabeth	1809	W22	338	236
[ ], Frank (C), age 25	Manumis fr	Ratcliff, Joseph	1811	AA26	072	052
[ ], Frederick (C)	Manumis fr	Foxall, Henry	1816	AL36	355	345
[ ], Frederick (C)	Manumis fr	Foxall, Henry	1816	AL36	354	344
[ ], George (mulatto)	Deed fr	Stoddert, Benjamin	1795	B2A	204	279
[ ], George (C)	Manumis fr	Digge, Robert F., of Alexa. Co.	1814	AG32	043	034
[ ], George (C), est. of A. Dow	Cert Free fr	Hunter, George W., exr.	1815	AK35	252	198
[ ], Hannah (C)	Manumis fr	Dick, Elizabeth	1812	AB27	503	411
[ ], Hanson (negro)	Manumis fr	Boyd, Washington et al	1808	T19	126	089
[ ], Harriott (C)	Manumis fr	Glover, Richard, now of G'tn.	1812	AD29	040	029
[ ], Harriott (C), est. of A. Dow	Cert Free fr	Hunter, George W., exr.	1815	AK35	250	198
[ ], Harry (negro)	Manumis fr	Forrest, Richard	1802	H8	276	261
[ ], Harry (C)	Manumis fr	Gaines, Richard	1813	AE30	171	136
[ ], Harry (C), age 20	Cert Free fr	Wilson, Henry M.	1816	AM37	142	110
[ ], Henny (negro)	Manumis fr	Chandler, Walter S.	1807	S18	091	074
[ ], Henny (C)	Manumis fr	Lingan, Nicholas et al	1812	AB27	481	394
[ ], Henny (C)	Manumis fr	Horsey, Outerbridge, of DE	1812	AC28	167	124
[ ], Henny (C)	Manumis fr	Brown, Joel, of G'tn.	1813	AF31	217	148
[ ], Henny (C)	Manumis fr	King, Josias W.	1816	AM37	054	044
[ ], Henrietta (negro)	Manumis fr	Foxall, Henry	1805	M12	144	140
[ ], Henrietta (M) & child Maria	Manumis fr	Canby, Israel T., of KY	1815	AH33	558	478
[ ], Hezekiah (negro)	Manumis fr	Heugh, John	1805	O14	113	071
[ ], Isaac (C), age 36	Manumis fr	Ball, James V.	1817	AN38	393	292
[ ], Jacob (negro), age 26y5m	Manumis fr	Boyd, Washington	1804	K10	143	155
[ ], Jacob (C)	Manumis fr	Brent, Daniel	1816	AK35	255	202
[ ], James (negro)	Manumis fr	Addison, Anthony, of P.G. Co.	1806	P15	262	173
[ ], James (C), age 2	Manumis fr	Key, Francis S.	1811	AC28	083	062
[ ], Jane (negro)	Manumis fr	Thompson, John	1810	Z25	317	248
[ ], Jenny (negro)	Manumis fr	Law, Thomas	1802	H8	412	381
[ ], Jenny (negress), and son	Manumis fr	Elzey, Arnold	1806	Q16	174	115
[ ], Jenny (C) and children	Manumis fr	Foxall, Henry	1811	AB27	116	095
[ ], Jerry (C)	Manumis fr	Cooper, George	1817	AO39	174	129
[ ], Jesse (negro)	Manumis fr	Poston, Bartholomew	1808	T19	384	273
[ ], Jesse (C)	Manumis fr	Grayson, Mary E., reps. of	1811	AB27	298	244
[ ], Jim (negro)	Manumis fr	Stewart, David R.	1802	I9		064
[ ], Joe (C), age 6m	Manumis fr	Key, Francis S.	1811	AC28	083	062

Party	What	Party	Year	Liber	Old	New
[ ], Joe (C)	Manumis fr	Addison, Anthony, of P.G. Co.	1812	AD29	141	110
[ ], Joe (C), age 38	Manumis fr	Clarke, Joseph S.	1812	AE30	005	004
[ ], John (negro)	Manumis fr	Thomas, Elizabeth	1809	X23	153	112
[ ], John (C), est. of A. Dow	Cert Free fr	Hunter, George W., exr.	1815	AK35	252	198
[ ], Kate (negress)	Manumis fr	Newton, John	1807	R17	336	256
[ ], Kate (C)	Manumis fr	Bowie, Walter, of P.G. Co. et al	1815	AI34	004	004
[ ], Katy (negro)	Receipt to	Cunningham, John	1801	G7		122
[ ], Kitt (C)	Slave	Pumphrey, James	1811	AA26	356	238
[ ], Kitty (negro)	Manumis fr	Pleasonton, Stephen	1807	R17	234	176
[ ], Kitty (negro)	Apprentice	Crawford, William	1809	W22	105	076
[ ], Kitty (negro)	Manumis fr	Addison, Walter D.	1810	Z25	194	152
[ ], Kitty (C), age 6, d/o Henny	Manumis fr	McCormick, A. & F.S. Key	1811	AC28	083	063
[ ], Lawrie (C)	Manumis fr	Young, Josiah	1812	AC28	323	235
[ ], Leonard (negro), age 36	Manumis fr	Harrison, Richard	1811	Z25	173	137
[ ], Letty (C), & dau. Patsey	Manumis fr	Carr, Overton	1813	AF31	158	106
[ ], Linda (C), age 40	Manumis fr	Sprigg, Osborn, of P.G. Co.	1813	AE30	221	178
[ ], Lizza (M), age 12, d/o Phillis	Freedom fr	Stoddert, Benjamin	1795	B2A	204	279
[ ], Lotty (C)	Manumis fr	Foxall, Henry	1811	AB27	115	094
[ ], Louisa (C)	Manumis fr	Horsey, Outerbridge	1813	AF31	291	206
[ ], Lucy (negro)	Manumis fr	Threlkeld, John	1804	L11	037	37
[ ], Lucy (C), w/o Gerard, children	Manumis fr	Horsey, Outerbridge	1813	AF31	291	206
[ ], Luke (negro)	Manumis fr	Mackall, Leonard, of G'tn.	1807	Q16	310	236
[ ], Malinda (negro)	Manumis fr	Carr, Samuel, Albemarle Co. VA	1809	V21	301	219
[ ], Margaret (negro) and children	Cert Free fr	Stewart, William	1807	S18	254	200
[ ], Margery (C)	Manumis fr	Dick, Elizabeth	1812	AB27	503	411
[ ], Maria (negro)	Manumis fr	Fleet, Henry	1809	V21	177	127
[ ], Maria (C)	Manumis fr	Wagner, Jacob & Alexander Kerr	1812	AD29	289	238
[ ], Maria (C)	Manumis fr	Beck, Dorcas	1814	AH33	092	084
[ ], Maria (C)	Manumis fr	Brumley, Mary	1816	AL36	127	128
[ ], Mary (negro)	Manumis fr	Addison, John	1802	G7		710
[ ], Mary (negro)	Manumis fr	Hutton, John, of Montg. Co.	1810	Y24	078	070
[ ], Mary (C), age 9	Manumis fr	Sprigg, Osborn, of P.G. Co.	1813	AE30	221	178
[ ], Mary (C)	Manumis fr	Brent, Daniel	1816	AK35	255	202
[ ], Mason	Manumis fr	Morris, Henry B., of Charles Co.	1816	AK35	300	240
[ ], Matilda (C)	Manumis fr	Peter, Thomas & Mary Bromley	1812	AC28	159	119
[ ], Milley (C), age 17	Manumis fr	Yerby, John, of G'tn.	1816	AM37	304	222
[ ], Milley (C)	Cert Free fr	Traverse, Mary, w/o Capt. Geo.	1816	AL36	143	143
[ ], Milly (negro)	Manumis fr	Gloyd, George H.	1811	Z25	457	361
[ ], Milly (M)	Cert Free fr	Hall, Edward, of West River	1816	AK35	499	393
[ ], Minty (C)	Manumis fr	Hughes, Thomas & W.A. Bradley	1816	AM37	076	062
[ ], Mordecai (negro)	Manumis fr	Fenwick, Richard	1808	U20	323	173
[ ], Motly (C), age 35	Cert Slave fr	Gustine, J.T. et al	1814	AH33	203	184
[ ], Nace (C), age 42	Manumis fr	Baker, Samuel et al	1813	AE30	229	183
[ ], Nan & children	Manumis fr	Fleet, Henry	1804	K10	243	250
[ ], Nan (negro)	Manumis to	Carroll, Elizabeth	1808	V21	112	083
[ ], Nancy (C), w/o Chas., children	Manumis fr	Brooks, Brooks	1812	AD29	100	076
[ ], Nanny (negress), two children	Manumis fr	Elzey, Arnold	1806	Q16	175	116
[ ], Nat (C)	Manumis fr	Anderson, Samuel T., of NY	1811	AB27	437	360
[ ], Nat (C), age 27	Cert Free fr	Wilson, Henry M.	1816	AM37	141	109
[ ], Nathaniel (C)	Manumis fr	Botelar, Alexander H.	1816	AL36	012	013
[ ], Ned (negro) et al	Manumis fr	Jackson, Joseph	1808	T19	374	267
[ ], Nice (negro)	Manumis fr	Coombs, Griffith, mer., Phila.	1806	P15	389	260
[ ], Nick (negro)	Manumis fr	Chandler, Walter Story	1802	H8	074	068
[ ], Pat (C)	Manumis fr	Horsey, Outerbridge, of DE	1815	AG32	299	218
[ ], Patsey (C), age 20	Manumis fr	Sprigg, Osborn, of P.G. Co.	1813	AE30	221	178

Party	What	Party	Year	Liber	Old	New
[ ], Patty & children Kitty & Henry	Manumis fr	Lowe, Nicholas	1802	H8	555	517
[ ], Patty (negro)	Manumis fr	Thomas, Augustus	1806	Q16	019	012
[ ], Paul (negro)	Manumis fr	Law, Thomas	1802	H8	412	381
[ ], Peggy (C), and children	Manumis fr	Barnes, John	1811	AB27	072	061
[ ], Peter (negro)	Manumis fr	Corcoran, Thomas, of G'tn.	1801	G7	326	457
[ ], Peter (negro)	Manumis fr	King, James C.	1804	L11	045	46
[ ], Peter (negro)	Manumis fr	Stone, Mathew, of Charles Co.	1806	P15	266	175
[ ], Peter (negro)	Manumis fr	Goulding, John	1806	O14	071	043
[ ], Peter [Big Peter] (negro)	Manumis fr	Fenwick, Richard	1808	U20	322	172
[ ], Phil (C), age 8	Manumis fr	Wallach, Richard	1813	AF31	364	260
[ ], Phillis (negro)	Manumis fr	Stoddert, Benjamin	1802	H8	318	299
[ ], Phillis (negro)	Manumis fr	Smith, Job, baker	1804	L11	167	164
[ ], Phillis (negro)	Manumis fr	Foxall, Henry	1805	M12	377	387
[ ], Phillis (C)	Manumis fr	Fisk, James, of Barre VA	1813	AF31	490	357
[ ], Phoebe (M)	Manumis fr	Middleton, Joseph, of Norfolk	1816	AL36	005	005
[ ], Polly (negro)	Manumis fr	Mackall, Leonard, of G'tn.	1807	S18	170	138
[ ], Polly (C)	Manumis fr	Clarke, Samuel	1812	AD29	085	063
[ ], Priscilla (negro)	Manumis fr	Chub, Robert	1806	P15	285	188
[ ], Priscilla (negro)	Manumis fr	Mackall, Leonard, of G'tn.	1807	R17	134	104
[ ], Rachael (C)	Manumis fr	Foxall, Henry	1816	AL36	356	347
[ ], Rachel (negro)	Manumis fr	McLaughlin, Charles	1805	O14	033	021
[ ], Rachel (negro)	Manumis fr	Wagman, Henry	1806	O14	207	137
[ ], Rachel (negro)	Manumis fr	Owens, Isaac, of G'tn.	1808	T19	295	216
[ ], Rachel (negro)	B. of S. fr	Whann, William, of G'tn. et al	1809	W22	115	083
[ ], Rachel (C)	Manumis fr	Watterston, David	1812	AC28	203	154
[ ], Rachel (C)	Manumis fr	Heronimus, Pendleton	1816	AL36	103	103
[ ], Rebecca (C), est. of A. Dow	Cert Free fr	Hunter, George W., exr.	1815	AK35	251	198
[ ], Rezin (negro)	Manumis fr	Pairo, Thomas W.	1810	X23	408	329
[ ], Rhodam (negro)	Manumis fr	Sanford, Hector	1802	I9		135
[ ], Richard (negro)	Manumis fr	Dunlap, Alexander	1805	N13	394	314
[ ], Richard (C)	Manumis fr	Bronaugh, William J.	1817	AN38	172	125
[ ], Robert, Eleanor & others	Manumis fr	Horsey, Outerbridge, of DE	1812	AD29	399	336
[ ], Robert (C)	Manumis fr	Horsey, Outerbridge	1813	AF31	291	206
[ ], Robin (negro)	Deed	King, Adam	1802	H8	206	196
[ ], Robin (negro)	Manumis fr	King, Adam	1802	H8	208	198
[ ], Sall (negro)	Manumis fr	Beall, Aquila, of P.G. Co.	1806	Q16	305	232
[ ], Sall (C)	Manumis fr	Cross, Rachel & Eli	1812	AB27	283	232
[ ], Sally (negro)	Manumis fr	King, Adam	1802	H8	208	198
[ ], Sally (negro)	Deed	King, Adam	1802	H8	206	196
[ ], Sam (C), age 7	Slave Cert.	Gardner, Isaac S.	1811	AA26	007	005
[ ], Samuel, shoemaker	Cert Free fr	Boarman, Charles, of G'tn.	1814	AG32	457	330
[ ], Sandy (C)	Manumis fr	Hunter, Andrew	1813	AE30	183	146
[ ], Sarah (negress)	Manumis fr	Cranch, William	1806	Q16	096	062
[ ], Sarah (C), est. of A. Dow	Cert Free fr	Hunter, George W., exr.	1815	AK35	250	198
[ ], Scipio	Manumis fr	Beans, Colmore	1815	AG32	457	331
[ ], Sciss (negro)	Manumis fr	Mackall, Leonard, of G'tn.	1804	L11	280	258
[ ], Sephania	Cert Free fr	Fairfax, Ferdinand	1816	AL36	509	478
[ ], Serena (M)	Manumis fr	Morsell, James S., of G'tn.	1816	AL36	433	412
[ ], Simon (M), age 22	Manumis fr	Roane, John, of King William Co.	1815	AH33	504	433
[ ], Suck (negro)	Manumis fr	Patterson, James	1807	R17	125	097
[ ], Suckey (mulatto)	Manumis fr	Matthews, William	1808	T19	224	164
[ ], Sukey (C) & daughters	Cert Free fr	Tiffin, Edward	1817	AO39	182	134
[ ], Susan (C), age 6	Manumis fr	Sprigg, Osborn, of P.G. Co.	1813	AE30	221	178
[ ], Susannah (negress) & child	Manumis fr	Waters, William	1808	U20	167	094
[ ], Terry (C)	Manumis fr	Boone, John	1811	AA26	094	066

Party	What	Party	Year	Liber	Old	New
[ ], Thamer (C), and others	Manumis fr	Pumphrey, James, of P.G. Co.	1813	AE30	091	070
[ ], Thomas [Rustin] (negro)	Manumis fr	Stone, Mathew, of Charles Co.	1806	P15	266	175
[ ], Tobias (negro)	Manumis fr	Simpson, William	1808	U20	384	151
[ ], Toby (negro)	Manumis fr	Mackall, Leonard, of G'tn.	1807	S18	170	139
[ ], Toby, age 45	Manumis fr	Morgan, Benjamin, New Orleans	1817	AN38	361	265
[ ], Tom (negro)	Manumis fr	Mackall, Leonard	1809	V21	253	180
[ ], Treacy (negro)	Manumis fr	Brashears, John W.	1807	R17	351	267
[ ], Wesley (negro)	Manumis fr	Richmond, Braddock	1810	Z25	041	031
[ ], Will (negro)	Manumis fr	Bastian, Charles	1805	N13	084	077
[ ], William (negro)	Manumis fr	Law, Thomas	1802	H8	411	380
[ ], William (negro)	Manumis fr	Fox, Josiah	1809	X23	281	222
[ ], William (M) and others	Manumis fr	Beall, Aquila, of Montg. Co.	1814	AH33	077	069
[ ], Yarro (negro), of G'tn. et al	Deed to	Yarro, Acquilla	1803	K10	071	77
[ ], Yarrow (negro)	Deed fr	Deakins, Francis, of G'tn.	1800	E5	080	067
[ ], Yarrow (negro)	Manumis fr	Beall, Upton, of Montg. Co.	1807	R17	264	201
[ ], Yorrick (negro)	Manumis fr	Addison, Thomas G.	1805	N13	405	322

Other Heritage Books by Wesley E. Pippenger:

Alexandria (Arlington) County, Virginia Death Records, 1853-1896

Alexandria City and Arlington County, Virginia Records Index: Vol. 1

Alexandria City and Arlington County, Virginia Records Index: Vol. 2

Alexandria County, Virginia Marriage Records, 1853-1895

Alexandria Virginia Marriage Index, January 10, 1893 to August 31, 1905

Alexandria, Virginia Marriages, 1870-1892

Alexandria, Virginia Town Lots, 1749-1801 Together with the Proceedings of the Board of Trustees, 1749-1780

Alexandria, Virginia Wills, Administrations and Guardianships, 1786-1800

Alexandria, Virginia 1808 Census (Wards 1, 2, 3, and 4)

Alexandria, Virginia Death Records, 1863-1896

Alexandria, Virginia Hustings Court Orders, Volume 1, 1780-1787

Connections and Separations: Divorce, Name Change and Other Genealogical Tidbits from the Acts of the Virginia General Assembly

Daily National Intelligencer *Index to Deaths, 1855-1870*

Daily National Intelligencer, *Washington, District of Columbia Marriages and Deaths Notices (January 1, 1851 to December 30, 1854)*

Dead People on the Move: Reconstruction of the Georgetown Presbyterian Burying Ground, Holmead's (Western) Burying Ground, and Other Removals in the District of Columbia

Death Notices from Richmond, Virginia Newspapers, 1841-1853

District of Columbia Ancestors, A Guide to Records of the District of Columbia

District of Columbia Death Records: August 1, 1874-July 31, 1879

District of Columbia Foreign Deaths, 1888-1923

District of Columbia Guardianship Index, 1802-1928

District of Columbia Interments (Index to Deaths) January 1, 1855 to July 31, 1874

District of Columbia Marriage Licenses, Register 1: 1811-1858

District of Columbia Marriage Licenses, Register 2: 1858-1870

District of Columbia Marriage Records Index June 28, 1877 to October 19, 1885: Marriage Record Books 11 to 20
Wesley E. Pippenger and Dorothy S. Provine

District of Columbia Marriage Records Index October 20, 1885 to January 20, 1892: Marriage Record Books 21 to 30

District of Columbia Marriage Records Index January 20, 1892 to August 30, 1896: Marriage Record Books 31 to 40

District of Columbia Marriage Records Index August 31, 1896 to December 17, 1900: Marriage Record Books 41 to 65

District of Columbia Probate Records, 1801-1852

District of Columbia: Original Land Owners, 1791-1800

Early Church Records of Alexandria City and Fairfax County, Virginia

Georgetown, District of Columbia 1850 Federal Population Census (Schedule I) and 1853 Directory of Residents of Georgetown

Georgetown, District of Columbia Marriage and Death Notices, 1801-1838

Husbands and Wives Associated with Early Alexandria, Virginia (and the Surrounding Area), 3rd Edition, Revised

Index to District of Columbia Estates, 1801-1929

Index to District of Columbia Land Records, 1792-1817

Index to Virginia Estates, 1800-1865
Volumes 4, 5 and 6

John Alexander, a Northern Neck Proprietor, His Family, Friends and Kin

Legislative Petitions of Alexandria, 1778-1861

Pippenger and Pittenger Families

Proceedings of the Orphan's Court, Washington County, District of Columbia, 1801-1808

The Georgetown Courier Marriage and Death Notices:
Georgetown, District of Columbia, November 18, 1865 to May 6, 1876

The Georgetown Directory for the Year 1830: to which is appended, a Short Description of the Churches, Public Institutions, and the Original Charter of Georgetown, and Extracts of the Laws Pertaining to the Chesapeake and Ohio Canal Company

The Virginia Gazette and Alexandria Advertiser:
Volume 1, September 3, 1789 to November 11, 1790

The Virginia Journal and Alexandria Advertiser:
Volume I (February 5, 1784 to January 27, 1785)

Volume II (February 3, 1785 to January 26, 1786)

Volume III (March 2, 1786 to January 25, 1787)

Volume IV (February 8, 1787 to May 21, 1789)

The Washington and Georgetown Directory of 1853

Tombstone Inscriptions of Alexandria, Volumes 1-4

www.ingramcontent.com/pod-product-compliance
Lightning Source LLC
Chambersburg PA
CBHW080404300426
44113CB00015B/2399